LITERARY OPINION
IN AMERICA

LITERARY OPINION
IN AMERICA

Essays Illustrating the Status, Methods,
and Problems of Criticism in the
United States in the Twentieth Century

EDITED BY
MORTON DAUWEN ZABEL

REVISED EDITION

HARPER & BROTHERS
New York

CONTENTS

FOREWORD xi
ACKNOWLEDGMENTS xix

MORTON DAUWEN ZABEL
Introduction: Criticism in America 1

PART I. SITUATION AND PROSPECTUS

HENRY JAMES
Criticism 47
The Question of the Opportunities 51
The Great Form 56

WILLIAM DEAN HOWELLS
The Question of a Criterion 58

JOHN JAY CHAPMAN
The Aesthetic 64

RANDOLPH BOURNE
Our Cultural Humility 68

JAMES GIBBONS HUNEKER
The Great American Novel 73

VAN WYCK BROOKS
The Critical Movement in America 80

PART II. VERSIONS OF TRADITION
AND RESPONSIBILITY

T. S. ELIOT
Tradition and the Individual Talent 91
Poetry and Propaganda 97

v

GEORGE SANTAYANA
    Penitent Art 108
    Tragic Philosophy 113

J. E. SPINGARN
    The American Critic 123

IRVING BABBITT
    The Critic and American Life 133

PAUL ELMER MORE
    How To Read "Lycidas" 146

H. L. MENCKEN
    The American Novel 157

EZRA POUND
    Date Line 165
    A Stray Document 168
    How To Read (Part II: Or What May be an Introduction to Method) 172

Part III. The Individual Talent

EDMUND WILSON
    James Joyce 183
    T. S. Eliot 207

ALLEN TATE
    Hart Crane 228
    Ezra Pound 237

KENNETH BURKE
    Thomas Mann and André Gide 243

W. H. AUDEN
    Makers of Modern Poetry
        I. *A Knight of the Infinite* (Gerard Manley Hopkins) . . 253
        II. *Heretics* (Rimbaud and Lawrence) 256
        III. *The Poet of the Encirclement* (Rudyard Kipling) . . 259
        IV. *The Public vs. the Late Mr. William Butler Yeats* . . 264

THEODORE SPENCER
    The Later Poetry of W. B. Yeats 270

CONTENTS

F. O. MATTHIESSEN
T. S. Eliot: The Four Quartets 282

R. P. BLACKMUR
Notes on E. E. Cummings' Language 296

PHILIP BLAIR RICE
Paul Valéry 315

WILLIAM TROY
Virginia Woolf: The Novel of Sensibility 324

KATHERINE ANNE PORTER
Gertrude Stein: A Self-Portrait 338

LOUISE BOGAN
James on a Revolutionary Theme 351

ERIC BENTLEY
Shaw at Ninety 357

HORACE GREGORY
D. H. Lawrence: The Posthumous Reputation 370

AUSTIN WARREN
Franz Kafka 376

MORTON DAUWEN ZABEL
A Literalist of the Imagination (Marianne Moore) 385

PART IV. THE WRITER AND CRITIC IN AMERICA

MARIANNE MOORE
Henry James as a Characteristic American 395
The Poetry of Wallace Stevens 401

LIONEL TRILLING
Reality in America 404

YVOR WINTERS
Robert Frost: or, The Spiritual Drifter as Poet 417
Robinson Jeffers 439

ROBERT PENN WARREN
Hemingway 444
William Faulkner 464

ROBERT MORSS LOVETT
Sherwood Anderson, American 478

MALCOLM COWLEY
John Dos Passos: The Poet and the World 485

ROBERT CANTWELL
Sinclair Lewis 494

E. K. BROWN
Willa Cather 502

FRANCIS FERGUSSON
√ Eugene O'Neill 513

STARK YOUNG
American Drama in Production
    I. Mourning Becomes Electra, by Eugene O'Neill . . . 522
    II. Street Scene, by Elmer Rice 529
    III. Winterset, by Maxwell Anderson 532

JOSEPH WOOD KRUTCH
Two American Playwrights
    I. The Austerity of George Kelly 535
    II. The Dramatic Variety of Sidney Howard 539

NEWTON ARVIN
Individualism and the American Writer 544

PHILIP RAHV
The Cult of Experience in American Writing 550

F. W. DUPEE
The Americanism of Van Wyck Brooks 561

DELMORE SCHWARTZ
The Literary Dictatorship of T. S. Eliot 573

RICHARD CHASE
An Approach to Melville 588

ALFRED KAZIN
William James and Henry James: "Our Passion is Our Task" . . 597

CONTENTS

Part V. Modern Criticism: Its Problems, Methods, and Prospects

T. S. ELIOT
Experiment in Criticism 607
Religion and Literature 617
From Poe to Valéry 626

JOHN CROWE RANSOM
Criticism as Pure Speculation 639

HARRY LEVIN
Literature as an Institution 655

KENNETH BURKE
Psychology and Form 667

LIONEL TRILLING
Freud and Literature 677

EDMUND WILSON
Marxism and Literature 693

WILLIAM PHILLIPS and PHILIP RAHV
Private Experience and Public Philosophy 706

R. S. CRANE
I. A. Richards on the Art of Interpretation 711

CLEANTH BROOKS
Irony as a Principle of Structure 729

RANDALL JARRELL
The End of the Line 742

WILLIAM BARRETT
The End of Modern Literature: Existentialism and Crisis . . . 749

STANLEY EDGAR HYMAN
Attempts at an Integration 757

R. P. BLACKMUR
A Critic's Job of Work 770

APPENDICES

I. *Recent Works of American Criticism* 793
II. *Collections of Contemporary American Criticism* . . . 805
III. *American Magazines Publishing Criticism* 812
IV. *Notes on Contributors* 822
V. *A Supplementary List of Essays in Criticism: 1900–1950* . 840
VI. *A Note on Contemporary English Criticism* 880

FOREWORD

THIS book, the second and revised edition of a volume of the same title that first appeared in 1937, offers a selection of seventy-seven essays by some fifty American critics of the past fifty years. The contents of the first edition were dated from 1918 to 1937. They have now been amplified both in range and in quantity, in order to show the full scope and development of American criticism in the first half of the Twentieth Century.

Essays that appeared in the first edition—which means the greater part of them—have been retained whenever they represent the characteristic work of their writers, or when they deal with subjects that have retained their value in illustrating the representative talents and literary issues of the past thirty years. These have now been prefaced by a group of essays by critics—Henry James, William Dean Howells, John Jay Chapman, James Gibbons Huneker, Randolph Bourne—who defined the prospects and problems of American literature in the earlier years of the century. There has also been added a considerable number of essays by younger men who show developments in criticism since 1937, as well as new essays by critics who appeared in the 1937 edition. The papers now collected range in date from 1889 to 1950—a period of sixty years. An effort has been made to show, by selection and within necessary limits of space, the conditions under which critics have worked in the United States, the problems they have met, the methods and standards they have defined, during a time of exceptional activity, dispute, and decision in American literature.

When the 1937 edition of *Literary Opinion in America* appeared it was one of the first exhibitions of what has come to be known during the past fifteen years as "the new criticism." That was not, however, its sole intention. The "new" criticism of the past two decades issued from earlier activities which were also "new" in their day. The work of T. S. Eliot, Edmund Wilson, Yvor Winters, Allen Tate, and the critics of the 1920's was thus rated a quarter-century ago; so were the writings and manifestoes of Randolph Bourne, Van Wyck Brooks, J. E. Spingarn, Ezra Pound, H. L. Mencken, and the men who argued for the "coming-of-age" of American literature between

1910 and 1920; so also were the cultural or aesthetic programs put forward by George Santayana, Paul Elmer More, Irving Babbitt, William Crary Brownell, Lewis Gates, and John Jay Chapman before 1910; so again was the work of the pioneers of contemporary criticism—Henry James, William Dean Howells, James Gibbons Huneker—as early as the 1880's and 1890's. These successive generations of critics all came on the literary scene as in some sense new. Their work was concerned with a renovation of values, the definition of criteria, the appraisal of original talents, and also with a problem that became between 1890 and 1910 freshly urgent in the native literature—the special character such values, criteria, and talents assume when they appear or demand attention in America.

Emphasis in the present volume has again been divided among these concerns and kinds of criticism. While a considerable part of the contents still shows the stress on formal, stylistic, and moral qualities in contemporary writing that has become paramount in our latest "new criticism," another and important part of it deals with the specific situation and problems of writing in America, with the conditions that have shaped characteristic American talents, with European writers who have come to dominate or influence the modern imagination, or with the American writer in his relation to a larger and international cultural development which, after his reassertion of his local and native bearings, he has from the time of Henry James down to the present day discovered himself to share. Thus the essays in this book which show a preoccupation with specifically or exclusively aesthetic issues are necessarily balanced—if only to show the varieties of modern American criticism with any degree of faithfulness—by discussions of what his age, his society, his traditions, his distraction by rival claims and responsibilities, have meant to the American writer since, following the earlier claims of Poe, Cooper, Emerson, Hawthorne, Melville, and Whitman, he has reëmerged in his conscious American character.

A book of American criticism must inevitably be a book about American literature, even if both the criticism and the literature hope to become valid as something more than American. The nationalism of our criticism and our literature has been a primary issue throughout the period here represented. But a serious criticism, like a serious literature, looks beyond nationalism. If it was the concern of James, Howells, Huneker, Bourne, Mencken, Babbitt, and Van Wyck Brooks to define the issue of "Americanism" in criticism and art, they also took it as their duty—like most of their serious followers—to redress this emphasis by rescuing American writing from provincialism and a suspicious estrangement from the larger claims and responsibilities of art. Thus, while the writers discussed by critics in this book are representatively American, ranging from Melville and James to Eliot, Pound, Crane, Hemingway, Faulkner, Cummings, and other talents of the present moment, they are also the modern talents—Yeats, Mann, Joyce, Valéry, Sartre—who show the force and meaning of modern literature to be unconfined by local or national loyalties. And these topics have been supplemented by discussions of ideas or influences—social, psychological, religious, experimental, Freudian, Marxist—which have worked in contemporary thought and writing regardless of locality or nation. The critics here included are all American by birth or residence. Their subjects are both American and international. Those who discuss the larger issues of modern art and thought—aesthetic, moral, social; Marxist, Humanist, Freudian, Existentialist—show particularly that the work of men like James, Santayana, Eliot, Pound, and Wilson has not gone for nothing; that the American critic or artist, whatever his local attachments and loyalties, today knows himself to be a member of a larger community where creation and craftsmanship are neither eased nor simplified in the interests of a privileged nationalism.

The editor's problem of representing these developments fairly has been much greater than it was in 1937. For one thing, critical activity in America has enormously increased. The 1937 edition was already much more difficult to assemble from the large body of available material than a 1927 or a 1917 edition would have been. This 1951 edition has had to cope with a correspondingly greater mass of critical writing that has appeared in books and journals in the past thirteen years. Full justice has not, inevitably, been arrived at. The appendices to the book will show the range and variety of publications in criticism that no single volume could hope to contain, and it is their purpose to suggest further reading in critics for whom space could not be found. The reader is referred to those bibliographies if he wishes to carry out a more complete program of study.

It will immediately be apparent that there is as little community of method and belief among the critics in this book as among the talents they discuss. But perhaps they have at least found some common ground of seriousness or workmanship in their efforts to discover the quality and significance of their subjects, either in terms of the conditions under which writers have worked or through their integrity and originality as craftsmen.

Four divisions may be made among the essays. One portion of them describes the situation and prospects of American literature in the earlier years of this century. Another states, from contrasting positions, principles of critical intelligence and responsibility, in reference both to past traditions and to present or impending creative problems. A third is made up of demonstrations in critical technique, analyses of literary form and style—these having been allowed a greater share of the pages in order to avoid the emphasis on abstract theory which often prevents the critic or his reader from understanding how the ideal qualities of art actually get into the work of fiction, drama, or poetry. Lastly, the final section of the book is given over to the particular problems the American writer and critic face today, and to certain issues of wider scope which the world situation of recent years has emphasized.

This book is not a collaborative project. Its entries support neither a common point of view nor the beliefs and prejudices of the editor. It finds whatever unity it possesses chiefly in a general recognition among its contributors of what literary quality and sincerity are, and in an approach to these from recognized requirements of sympathy, sensitiveness, and taste. These standards have been strongly challenged during the past two or three decades by the demands laid on literature by political, propagandist, and public interests. Conversely, the period has seen the reappearance of aesthetic, formalist, and autonomous "approaches" to literature. But critical activity in the United States has not, as in some modern countries, lost its right to difference, freedom, and disputation. The debate among schools and principles may still be trusted to correct the excesses of specialized and limiting attitudes, even where it has also stressed the importance of responsibility of judgment and belief in artists and critics. That debate is present in these pages. The tracing of its progress during fifty years is one of the most serious opportunities such a book as this has to offer.

The essays have been chosen from American books and magazines, and in selecting material from the latter it has been the intention to show the importance of independent and experimental journals in the United States during the past few decades. While their work has often been short-lived in the item, it has been continuous in effect. Between 1912 and the present day they have formed a channel of expression and opinion not previously available in America on a like scale. Their styles and personalities have been of all kinds. Some have lived out their short careers as purely personal or group organs. But they have had the advantage of their independence from commercial influence. Some of these periodicals—*The Seven Arts, The Dial, Poetry, The Little Review, The Hound and Horn, The Symposium, The Southern Review, Partisan Review, The Kenyon Review, The Sewanee Review, Accent, The Western Review, The Hudson Review*—had no predecessors in the particular work they have done for American literature. It has been an aim of this book to show the results of their work, to print specimens of the best of it, and to show how they have refreshed and stimulated critical thinking at a time when commercial exploitation and the confusions of politics and parties have tended to cancel the gains in critical awareness gradually achieved since men like Henry James and Howells were active.

There are two kinds of anthology which escape the more obvious forms of critical rebuke. One offers an impersonal survey of a field or period, as objective as scholarship and common acceptance can make it. The other develops an editorial argument, a "criticism by selection," from a specific or emphatically personal position. The present collection claims neither of these advantages, though it has taken hints from both of them. It covers a period still too recent and unresolved in its decisions to allow for historical detachment or impersonal agreement. And it has not been the purpose of the editor to illustrate a special or personal thesis. Such specialization has been the merit—and the limitation—of a number of recent collections of American criticism illustrating the Impressionist, the Humanist, or the Communist arguments. Their value lies in their singleness and certainty of purpose. Their handicap usually appears when they show what the reader need have no hope of finding, for the narrower an argument or doctrine becomes, the more likely it is that what will be missing is criticism itself, and the free intelligence. Such books often end by convincing us that while (as one distinguished modern critic has said) "the 'greatness' of literature cannot be determined solely by literary standards, we must remember that whether it is literature or not can be determined only by literary standards."

In choosing and arranging these essays, it has been hoped to show what such standards count for in America today, how they emerge from the past or develop in the present, and how the recognition of them comes through the responsibility of criticism as a craft—a craft open to suggestion from many different quarters, social, scientific, psychological, moral, political, but as far as possible unconfused by such influences. One of the first claims of the modern critic to seriousness comes from his awareness of what these appeals are, what they rise from in the social and moral adjustments of the age, what legitimate role they may play in aesthetic evaluation, and what part they may claim in deciding the values of literature *after* its existence and quality as literature are determined. Some of the present essays are on writers rather than on writing. Some deal with external ideas or conditions that have shaped contemporary talents. A few are written from obvious doctrinal positions. These are a necessary part of the history the book records, the scene it observes, the latitude it respects. They show the role played by literary criticism in what James, Howells, Bourne, and Van Wyck Brooks early defined as a general critical movement in our national life. It is chiefly through their intelligent sense of that tendency that the serious critics of the United States at any time, but especially in the last thirty years, have done their most effective work.

Two activities often considered hostile to an active critical tradition in America have been slighted, though intentionally. One is popular book-reviewing; the other is academic scholarship. The services of both, at their best, are not denied. Their omission has deprived the book of several distinguished and influential names. But each is provided for elsewhere too generously to require representation here. The absence of historical and philosophic scholarship is doubtless regrettable. The genuine part of it, in any age or country, is an achievement without which the labor of critics is easily misspent. But it is often by nature unconcerned with the existing conditions of an original literature, and its formulations or findings are seldom tested by the active problems and practices of writers. The absence of popular journalism is less a privation. A number of literary journalists have done useful propaganda for modern books and writers. A few, Huneker and Mencken first among them, prepared the day for remarkable gains in original writing. But generally this activity has little to do with criticism. It is an adjunct of the book trade, of literary promotion, or of nationalist interests that soon prove inimical to serious literary purpose. The work of the responsible critic is something else. It must take a stand, in Henry James's words, for "Criticism, for Discrimination, for Appreciation on other than infantile lines—as against the so almost universal Anglo-Saxon absence of these things; which tends, in our general trade, it seems to me, to break the heart."

Literary criticism in the United States has not, even in our advanced day, wholly outgrown the fear of a chronic immaturity which Poe and Lowell felt in theirs. (There is no cause to feel on this score a special affliction in American culture. Coleridge, Hazlitt, Arnold, I. A. Richards, and F. R. Leavis have felt a like distress in their country during the past century and a half.) But it will be agreed that if there has been a conscious effort toward serious critical standards in the United States, it has been made during the past fifty years, and that what the critic of literature has achieved in that time has been prompted by a wider scrutiny and conscience in the fields of social, political, and moral thought. Such conscience has grown at a time when writing itself has enjoyed a phenomenal revival, a huge public enthusiasm, a popular following outdistancing anything of its kind in our earlier history. These two tendencies may seem to operate at odds. Actually they do not, or at least not entirely. The fervor of the one stimulates the skepticism of the other. While writers produce something to think about, dissect, and evaluate, critics, freed from the provincial habits and complacency of less disturbed periods, may sharpen their wits and tools on the material thus supplied them. Political argument, no less than aesthetic and moral, has played its part in this zest. Rivalry and contention have spurred argument. But the age has been too serious in its problems and ominous in its evils to permit these to remain a game of cliques and factions.

The impulse of honest critics toward a community of responsibility and function is urgent as never before. A community of this kind is apparent today even where immediate aims and methods are least agreed. The threat of authoritarian tyranny touches the literary life as much as the political, and critics have been compelled to reassess their rights as liberals, disputants, and free agents in the common cause of the freedom of art and of the mind. America is still a place in which those rights exist, and where their perpetuity is arguable. The critic remains, perhaps, their chief custodian. The writers who here defend them have been included less for their eloquence on behalf of moral or human truths than because they show some signs of realizing the force of these truths in terms of the one valid evidence permitted the critic— that of the literary craft and of the insight and intelligence it embodies.

Omissions always irk an anthologist, however space limits impose them and even when he has no ambition toward impartiality. The reader is therefore referred again to the appendices where critics and essays are listed which might have been included had this book been two or three times its size. Difficulties of copyright or permission have sometimes proved prohibitive. Essays showing on a fuller scale the different controversies that have engaged critics, as well as the specialized programs of various critical schools, appear especially in Appendix II ("Collections of Contemporary American Criticism") and Appendix III ("American Magazines Publishing Criticism"). These, like Appendix I ("Books of Recent American Criticism") are selective, but their range is wide and their suggestions for further investigation unlimited. Appendix V ("A Supplementary List of Essays in Criticism: 1900–1950") has been designed as a guide to a more complete program of critical reading, both in critics whose work could not be represented in the book and in those who have been included. Appendix IV ("Notes on Contributors") gives bibliographies of the published works of the latter.

The reader or student will, in fact, find this book profitable to the degree in which it encourages him to become a critic himself, to disagree with the critics who speak here, to compare their findings, and to decide how far the effort at reading and writing seriously that has brought them into the same company can be achieved, perhaps improved upon, by studying the problems of modern literature.

M. D. Z.

January, 1951

ACKNOWLEDGMENTS

THE EDITOR acknowledges with gratitude the courtesy of the contributors to this volume whose permission to have their work included has made the collection possible. Full bibliographical details as to the serial and book publication of the essays are given at the end of each entry. In several cases the critics have written new essays or made extensive revisions of earlier ones. For this special thanks are due to Miss Marianne Moore, Horace Gregory, Philip Blair Rice, the late Theodore Spencer, William Troy, and Stark Young for essays carried over from the first edition, and to Cleanth Brooks, Randall Jarrell, Alfred Kazin, and Delmore Schwartz for essays which now appear in this second edition. The editor is also indebted to T. S. Eliot for permission to include two essays, "Poetry and Propaganda" and "Experiment in Criticism," which have not been included in his books of prose and which are reprinted here from *The Bookman* and from the 1937 edition of this book, as likewise for his permission to include the essay "From Poe to Valéry," which has thus far been published only in private form by Harcourt, Brace and Company of New York in 1948. Thanks are also due to the Librarian of Congress for the appearance of this last-named essay here, it having originally been given as a lecture at the Library of Congress in 1948.

For permission to use material from copyrighted volumes, acknowledgment is made to the following publishers:

Arrow Editions, New York, and Miss Florence Codman for "Notes on E. E. Cummings' Language" and "The Critic's Job of Work" from *The Double Agent: Essays in Craft and Elucidation,* by R. P. Blackmur, copyright 1935 by Richard P. Blackmur.

E. P. Dutton & Co. of New York for "The Critical Movement in America" from *Sketches in Criticism,* by Van Wyck Brooks, copyright 1932 by E. P. Dutton & Co.

Harcourt, Brace and Company, Inc. for "Thomas Mann and André Gide" and "Psychology and Form" from *Counter-Statement,* by Kenneth Burke, copyright 1931 by Harcourt, Brace and Company, Inc.; for "The American Critic" from *Creative Criticism and Other Essays* by J. E. Spingarn, copyright

1931 by J. E. Spingarn; for "Tradition and the Individual Talent" from *Selected Essays: 1917–1932*, by T. S. Eliot, copyright 1932 by Harcourt, Brace and Company, Inc.; for "Religion and Literature" from *Essays Ancient and Modern*, by T. S. Eliot, copyright 1933, 1936 by Harcourt, Brace and Company, Inc., now also included in *Selected Essays*, by T. S. Eliot, copyright 1950; and for "From Poe to Valéry," copyright 1948 by T. S. Eliot.

Harper & Brothers for selections from *Criticism and Fiction*, by William Dean Howells, copyright 1891 by Harper & Brothers, and for "Criticism" from *Essays in London and Elsewhere*, by Henry James, copyright 1893 by Harper and Bros.

Houghton Mifflin Company for "The Critic and American Life" from *On Being Creative and Other Essays*, by Irving Babbitt, copyright 1932 by Houghton Mifflin Company.

B. W. Huebsch of the Viking Press, New York, for "Our Cultural Humility" from *The History of a Literary Radical and Other Essays*, by Randolph Bourne, copyright 1920 by B. W. Huebsch, Inc.

Alfred A. Knopf, Inc., for "The American Novel" from *Prejudices: Fourth Series*, by H. L. Mencken, copyright 1924 by Alfred A. Knopf, Inc., and for "Attempts at an Integration" from *The Armed Vision*, by Stanley Edgar Hyman, copyright 1948 by Alfred A. Knopf, Inc.

Moffat, Yard and Company of New York for "The Aesthetic" from *Learning and Other Essays*, by John Jay Chapman, copyright 1910 by Moffat, Yard and Co.

New Directions for "How to Read: Part II" from *Polite Essays*, by Ezra Pound, copyright 1938 by Ezra Pound.

Oxford University Press for "T. S. Eliot: The *Four Quartets*" from *The Achievement of T. S. Eliot*, by F. O. Matthiessen, second edition, copyright 1947 by Oxford University Press; and for "Marxism and Literature" from *The Triple Thinkers*, by Edmund Wilson, revised and enlarged edition, copyright 1938, 1948 by Edmund Wilson.

Princeton University Press for "How to Read 'Lycidas'" from *On Being Human*, by Paul Elmer More, copyright 1936 by Princeton University Press; and for "Criticism as Pure Speculation" by John Crowe Ransom from *The Intent of the Critic*, edited by Donald A. Stauffer, copyright 1941 by Princeton University Press.

Paul Reynolds and Son, agents of the estate of Henry James, for permission to reprint "The Question of the Opportunities" and "The Great Form" by Henry James.

Charles Scribner's Sons for "The Great American Novel" from *Unicorns*, by J. G. Huneker, copyright 1917 by Charles Scribner's Sons; for "James Joyce" and "T. S. Eliot" from *Axel's Castle: A Study in the Imaginative Literature of 1870–1930*, by Edmund Wilson, copyright 1931 by Charles Scribner's

Sons; for "Penitent Art" from *Obiter Scripta*, by George Santayana, copyright 1936 by Charles Scribner's Sons, and "Tragic Philosophy" from *The Works of George Santayana*, Triton Edition, Volume II, copyright 1936 by Charles Scribner's Sons; for "Hart Crane" and "Ezra Pound" from *Reactionary Essays on Poetry and Ideas*, by Allen Tate, copyright 1936 by Charles Scribner's Sons; and for "Hemingway" by Robert Penn Warren which appears as a preface to a new edition of *A Farewell to Arms* by Ernest Hemingway, copyright 1949 by Charles Scribner's Sons.

University of Chicago Press for "Franz Kafka" from *Rage for Order*, by Austin Warren, copyright 1948 by University of Chicago Press.

The Viking Press for "Reality in America" and "Freud and Literature" from *The Liberal Imagination: Essays on Literature and Society*, by Lionel Trilling, copyright 1950 by Lionel Trilling.

Yale University Press for "Date Line: 1934" and "A Stray Document" from *Make It New*, by Ezra Pound, copyright 1935 by Ezra Pound.

The following magazines and their editors are likewise thanked for material that has appeared in their pages:

Accent, for "Literature as an Institution" by Harry Levin, VI, 159–165, Spring 1946.

The Atlantic Monthly, for "Shaw at Ninety" by Eric Bentley, CLXXVIII, 109–115, July 1946.

The Bookman, for "Experiment in Criticism" by T. S. Eliot, LXX, 225–233, November 1929, and "Poetry and Propaganda" by T. S. Eliot, LXX, 595–602, February 1930.

College English, for an earlier version of several portions of Cleanth Brooks's essay, "Irony as a Principle of Structure," which were adapted from his essay "Irony and 'Ironic' Poetry" in *College English*, IX, No. 5, 231–237, February 1948.

Ethics, for "I. A. Richards on the Art of Interpretation" by R. S. Crane, LIX, No. 2, Part I, 112–126, January 1949 (copyright 1949 by the University of Chicago Press).

Harper's Magazine, for "Gertrude Stein: A Self-Portrait" by Katherine Anne Porter, CXCV, 519–528, December 1947.

The Hound and Horn, for "Eugene O'Neill" by Francis Fergusson, III, 145–160, January 1930; for "The Later Poetry of W. B. Yeats" by Theodore Spencer, VII, 164–175, October 1933; and for "Henry James as a Characteristic American" by Marianne More, VII, 363–372, April 1934.

The Hudson Review, for "From Poe to Valéry" by T. S. Eliot, II, 327–342, Autumn 1949.

The Kenyon Review, for "Hemingway" by Robert Penn Warren, IX, 1–28, Winter 1947.

The Nation, for "Individualism and the American Writer" by Newton Arvin, CXXXIII, 391–393, October 14, 1931; for "The Austerity of George Kelly," CXXXVII, 240–242, August 30, 1933, and "The Dramatic Variety of Sidney Howard," CXXXVII, 294–295, September 13, 1933, both by Joseph Wood Krutch; for "James on a Revolutionary Theme" by Louise Bogan, CXLVI, 471–474, April 23, 1938; and for "The End of the Line" by Randall Jarrell, CLIV, 222–228, February 21, 1942.

The New Republic, for "Street Scene by Elmer Rice," LVII, 296–298, January 30, 1929, "*Mourning Becomes Electra* by Eugene O'Neill," LXVIII, 352–355, November 11, 1931, and "*Winterset* by Maxwell Anderson," LXXXIV, 365, November 6, 1935, all by Stark Young; for "John Dos Passos: The Poet and the World" by Malcolm Cowley, LXX, 303–305, April 27, 1932, and LXXXVIII, 34, September 9, 1936; for part of "A Literalist of the Imagination" by Morton Dauwen Zabel, LXXXIII, 370, August 7, 1935; for "Sinclair Lewis" by Robert Cantwell, LXXXVIII, 296–301, October 21, 1936; for "William Faulkner" by Robert Penn Warren, CXV, 176–180, 234–237, August 12 and 26, 1946; for three essays by W. H. Auden entitled "Heretics," C, 373–374, November 1, 1939, "The Poet of the Encirclement," CIX, 579–581, October 25, 1943, and "A Knight of the Infinite," CXI, 223–224, October 21, 1944; and for "William James and Henry James: 'Our Passion is our Task'" by Alfred Kazin, CVIII, 216–218, February 15, 1943.

Partisan Review, for "The Public vs. the Late Mr. William Butler Yeats" by W. H. Auden, VI, 46–51, Spring 1939; for "The Americanism of Van Wyck Brooks" by F. W. Dupee, VI, 69–85, Summer 1939; for "The Cult of Experience in American Writing" by Philip Rahv, VII, 412–424, November–December 1940; for "An Approach to Melville" by Richard Chase, XIV, 285–294, May–June 1947; for "The Literary Dictatorship of T. S. Eliot" by Delmore Schwartz, XVI, 119–137, February 1949; and for "The End of Modern Literature: Existentialism and Crisis" by William Barrett, XVI, 942–950, September 1949.

Poetry: A Magazine of Verse, for "Robinson Jeffers" by Yvor Winters, XXXV, 279–286, February 1930; for "A Literalist of the Imagination" by Morton Dauwen Zabel, XLVII, 326–336, March 1936; for "Private Experience and Public Philosophy" by William Phillips and Philip Rahv, XLVIII, 98–105, May 1936; and for "The Poetry of Wallace Stevens" by Marianne Moore, XLIX, 268–273, February 1937.

The Sewanee Review, for "Robert Frost: or, The Spiritual Drifter as Poet" by Yvor Winters, LVI, 564–596, Autumn 1948.

The Symposium, for "Paul Valéry" by Philip Blair Rice, I, 206–220, April 1930; and for "Virginia Woolf: The Novel of Sensibility" by William Troy, III, 53–63, 153–166, January and April, 1932.

The Virginia Quarterly Review, for "Sherwood Anderson, American" by Robert Morss Lovett, XVII, 379–388, Summer 1941.

The Yale Review, for "Willa Cather" by E. K. Brown, XXXVI (new series), 77–92, September 1946.

Besides the above essays reprinted directly from magazines, certain essays in this book, later incorporated in their original or in a revised form in books by their authors and here reprinted in that form, originally appeared in magazines, as follows: *The American Review,* New York ("How to Read 'Lycidas'" by Paul Elmer More); *The Atlantic Monthly* ("Our Cultural Humility" by Randolph Bourne, and "Marxism and Literature" by Edmund Wilson); *The Bookman* ("Thomas Mann and André Gide" by Kenneth Burke); *The Dial,* New York ("Penitent Art" by George Santayana, and "Psychology and Form" by Kenneth Burke); *The Egoist,* London ("Tradition and the Individual Talent" by T. S. Eliot); *The Forum,* New York ("The Critic and American Life" by Irving Babbitt); *The Freeman,* New York ("The Critical Movement in America" by Van Wyck Brooks); *Harper's Monthly,* New York ("The Question of a Criterion" in *Criticism and Fiction* by William Dean Howells); *The Hound and Horn* ("Notes on E. E. Cummings' Language" by R. P. Blackmur, and "Hart Crane" by Allen Tate); *The Kenyon Review* ("T. S. Eliot: The *Four Quartets*" by F. O. Matthiessen, and part of "Freud and Literature" by Lionel Trilling, the expanded form of this essay having later appeared in *Horizon,* London); *Literature,* London and New York ("The Question of the Opportunities" by Henry James); *The Nation* ("Ezra Pound" by Allen Tate, and part of "Reality in America" by Lionel Trilling); *The New Republic* ("James Joyce" and "T. S. Eliot" by Edmund Wilson); *The New Review,* London ("Criticism" by Henry James); *The New York Herald-Tribune: Books* ("How to Read" by Ezra Pound); *The New York Tribune* ("The Great Form" by Henry James, later republished in the *Times Literary Supplement,* London); *Partisan Review* (part of "Reality in America" by Lionel Trilling); *Poetry,* Chicago (part of "A Stray Document" by Ezra Pound); *Scrutiny,* Cambridge, England ("Tragic Philosophy" by George Santayana); *The Southern Review,* Baton Rouge, Louisiana ("Franz Kafka" by Austin Warren).

Certain essays that appeared in the 1937 edition of this book and are also in the present edition subsequently appeared in published volumes or were later reprinted in new books by their authors: thus Allen Tate's "Hart Crane" and "Ezra Pound," here taken from his *Reactionary Essays on Poetry and Ideas* as published by Charles Scribner's Sons in 1936, have recently been included in his *On the Limits of Poetry,* published by Swallow Press & William Morrow & Co., New York, 1948; Horace Gregory's "D. H. Lawrence: The Posthumous Reputation," first printed in *Literary Opinion in America* in 1937, has now been included in his *The Shield of Achilles,* published by Harcourt, Brace and Company, Inc. in 1944; Robert Cantwell's "Sinclair Lewis," here reprinted from *The New Republic,* reappeared in *After the Genteel Tradition,* edited by Malcolm Cowley and published by W. W. Norton and Company of New York, 1937; Stark Young's three essays, here reprinted from *The New Republic,* were included in his *Immortal Shadows,* published by Charles Scribner's Sons, New York, in 1948.

The material in some of the essays in this new edition of *Literary Opinion in America,* here reprinted from magazines, has been adapted or reworked in books by their authors: Eric Bentley's "Shaw at Ninety," here reprinted from *The Atlantic Monthly,* was reworked in his book *Bernard Shaw* (New Directions, 1947); the material in Richard Chase's "An Approach to Melville," here reprinted from *Partisan Review,* was incorporated in a different form in his book *Herman Melville* (New York: The Macmillan Company, 1949); that in Philip Rahv's "The Cult of Experience in American Writing," here reprinted from *Partisan Review,* was revised and expanded in his book *Image and Idea* (New Directions, 1949). The substance of Harry Levin's "Literature as an Institution," here reprinted from *Accent,* will be incorporated in his book *The Gates of Horn,* to be published by the Oxford University Press.

For special favors in the making of the book in its two editions I am indebted to R. P. Blackmur, Cleanth Brooks, Van Wyck Brooks, Kenneth Burke, T. S. Eliot, Horace Gregory, Harry Levin, H. L. Mencken, Marianne Moore, Paul Elmer More, Katherine Anne Porter, Philip Rahv, John Crowe Ransom, George Santayana, Lionel Trilling, Robert Penn Warren, and Edmund Wilson; as also to Professor Benedict Einarson, and to Miss Rosalind Lohrfinck, secretary to Mr. Mencken.

A NOTE ON THE TEXTS: In view of the liberal and unstable conditions of English orthography, a rigorous uniformity has not been imposed on the texts reproduced in this volume. Practices of capitalization and punctuation, which are largely a privilege of style, have usually been left unchanged. Spellings (except in the case of obvious errors or misprints which have been silently corrected) have been permitted to stand in the variant forms allowed by the dictionary, though consistency within individual essays has been attempted. Thus such variants as *criticize—criticise, enquiry—inquiry, defense—defence,* etc., have been allowed. It should be noted that one important word appears in its two permitted spellings: *aesthetic* and *esthetic* (so also *aesthetics— esthetics; aesthete—esthete,* etc.). The frequent employment of both these usages in the essays, sometimes even in their titles or in titles quoted within essays, has made insistence on a uniform spelling seem inadvisable. It is trusted that the reader will not be confused by this, and will recognize the word under either spelling. Forms of possessives have also been allowed to stand: thus *James's* and *James'*, *Yeats's* and *Yeats'*, etc. Standard practice has been applied to titles, however: titles of books and whole works have been set in italics; those of short, partial, or subordinate works have been set inside quotation marks and in Roman type.

The dates printed below the titles of the essays show as closely as possible when they were first written or published. Several of the authors have brought their discussions more nearly up to date by revision, or have added notes by way of observing recent aspects of their topics. Where essays have been otherwise or extensively revised, the fact is noted in the credit-lines at the end of the essays. The editor's footnotes (except for a few supplying dates or bibliographical details) are marked as such; footnotes not thus marked are by the authors of the essays. The value of these discussions lies partly in what they show of developments in literature and criticism during the sixty years covered by the book, and it has not been considered advisable consistently to alter essays that do this to advantage.

LITERARY OPINION
IN AMERICA

Introduction: Criticism in America

Ours, we are told, is an age of criticism. The fact, so far as it is one, has been disputed by some as illusory, by others as unfortunate, by still others as inimical to the prosperity of literature. But there can be no question that the age itself is critical—critical in its conditions and critical in the kind of intelligence they exact and stimulate. The Socratic principle that the life that remains uncriticized is not worth living has become an axiom of the times, a proverb among moralists, a necessity enforced by public events, a cardinal motive in the serious forms of literature, a habit of the contemporary mind. Even those who question the claims of criticism, or hold that it is "based upon the decay of the art criticized," or take refuge in simpler kinds of virtue or idealism, are obliged to recognize its necessity in the responsibilities of the modern intelligence. A condition once seen by Johnson as a distant prospect, by Coleridge as a remote possibility, by Poe and Lowell as a cognate to serious creation in the arts, by Henry James as an obligation of a mature culture, has become a prevalent feature of creative activity, education, and political society alike. It has, indeed, made so prominent what one recent critic has called "one of the most aggressive, hardest-working, and portentous critical movements the history of literature has known" that we may be encouraged to believe that criticism has become what one of its least expected defenders—Whitman —once called it: "a majestic office, perhaps an art, perhaps even a church."

Whatever the case, the critic of literature today occupies a position of remarkable advantages, of a kind almost unknown to his ancestors. He finds himself in an office of wide influence and in command of almost unlimited opportunities and public attention. No special conditions of locality or intellectual climate are needed to make his rank in the community an important one, or his work difficult. He deals with ideas in a state of unrest and with causes at crucial odds with one another, all of which pass through his hands in the form of books. His energies are spurred by every possible stimulus from other fields of activity—by the experiments of history and philosophy and by the researches of social and psychological science—but when these aids arrive they are likely to prove more confusing than helpful. He is expected to be everything but himself: patriot, moralist, and humanitarian; reformer, revolutionist, and prophet. Where once he was accused of "not knowing enough," he is now likely to know too much for his own good about everything but his craft, or about everything that makes his craft a baffling one to master. He is a recognized arbiter of opinion, but he serves a public whose needs are as difficult to determine as his own means of satisfying them are difficult to reduce to to an exact method or science. His office is so easily and commonly reduced to the cruder uses of journalism and propaganda that it is easy to forget that it can also be one of the most important in the well-being of society, and one of the few trustworthy indexes we have to the prosperity of intelligence and culture.

This is true in any country, but there are reasons for claiming a special importance for American criticism during the past half century. It forms the record of a nation's education, of its arrival at a point of moral maturity and at the responsibility of justifying its claims to a cultural and spiritual destiny of its own. This function would give dramatic force to any body of writing, and American criticism has become, in the hundred years since the day of Poe and Emerson, as dramatic in its local and political circumstances, in its pride of duty and purpose, as any activity of the age. It has found itself divided between the claims of tradition and those of an emancipation whose first promise was to simplify those claims or dismiss them altogether. When Emerson wrote *The American Scholar* and Whitman his preface to *Leaves of Grass* and *Democratic Vistas* it was possible to announce that hope confidently; it has been periodically renewed; but the day for an easy confidence is over. Art, for one thing, has refused to be simplified. For another, criticism has not been allowed to acquire much complacency. Its tools and methods, whatever their firmness or refinement, repeatedly prove inadequate to the strain laid upon them. No sooner is a royal road to critical wisdom charted than its progress becomes impeded by disputes and conflicts. In the United States this problem is thrown into a relief more difficult to visualize in European countries. For at the same moment that the creative energies of the nation have appeared at their height, the need of a critical discipline has announced itself with vigorous emphasis. The resulting conflict has made American criticism a battleground of ideals and purposes, as crowded with faction and argument as any to be seen in the countries of the West.

American criticism has seldom been primarily literary, and only a small part of it is so today. It has been ethical and moral, social and regional, political and religious. The special claims of art have, in fact, been obliged to put up a struggle for recognition. This condition existed in the past as an accepted fact, in spite of the protests of men like Poe, Lowell, and Henry James. But it has been equally present during the past quarter century, whatever gains in taste and sophistication may be boasted. When there appeared, toward the end of the Nineteenth Century, a "critical movement in American life," literature played a part in it with manners, morals, and social institutions, but usually a subordinate part. The nation, arriving at a sufficient political isolation and economic independence, began to loosen its protective armor of suspicion and self-esteem, and relaxed its vigilance over the contempt of foreigners and the irreverence of its own satirists. It allowed its "giddy minds" to turn from foreign quarrels and defensives to a healthy doubt about native life and its productions in manners and art. But this change did not come easily or without meeting resistance.

Once such irreverence was frankly considered sacrilegious. The hardpan of American complacency dulled the pick of anyone who tried to break it up. Poe was one of these. His attacks on the crusted dogmatism of his literary overlords and contemporaries crop up everywhere in his essays and reviews: "It is folly to assert, as some at present are fond of asserting, that the Literature of any nation or age was ever injured by plain speaking on the part of critics. As for American Letters, plain speaking about *them* is, simply, the one thing needed. They are in a condition of absolute quagmire." He fired his concentrated anger at the immediate tyrants in the field, the "Literati of New York," whose flourishing descendants have testified for the ensuing nine decades to the small effect of his demolitions. Lowell was more decorous in his sense of the same shortcomings; Emerson admitted them to Carlyle; and Hawthorne offered one of his earliest biographers, the young Henry James, a special case of the American author who, though acutely conscious of aesthetic standards, was doomed to labor on their behalf in an atmosphere from which serious aesthetic curiosity was almost totally banished, either by the philosophic ambitions of Boston and Concord or by a fatuous veneration of "the gentleman or the lady who has written a book." In his day an adulation of almost Renaissance-like fervor was accompanied by an artistic stolidity of equal proportions. "If the tone of the American world is in some respects provincial, it is in none more so than in this matter of the exaggerated homage rendered authorship. The gentleman or the lady who has written a book is in many circles the object of an admiration too indiscriminating to operate as an encouragement to good writing." James was writing in 1879 about conditions half a century earlier, but his remarks are open to more recent application:

The Age
Poe and
Emerson

There is no reason to suppose that this was less the case fifty years ago; but fifty years ago, greatly more than now, the literary man must have lacked the comfort and inspiration of belonging to a class. The best things come, as a general thing, from the talents that are members of a group; every man works better when he has companions working in the same line, and yielding the stimulus of suggestion, comparison, emulation. Great things of course have been done by solitary workers; but they have usually been done with double the pains they would have cost if they had been produced in more genial circumstances. The solitary worker loses the profit of example and discussion; he is apt to make awkward experiments; he is in the nature of the case more or less of an empiric. The empiric may, as I say, be treated by the world as an expert; but the drawbacks and discomforts of empiricism remain to him, and are in fact increased by the suspicion that is mingled with his gratitude, of a want in the public taste of a sense of the proportion of things.

If this isolation afflicted the American artist it was equally the lot of the honest critic, who lacked even the consolations of hero worship. He was likely to spend his thrift in wrangling with patriotic citizens and the regimented high priests of popular journalism, the Griswolds and Bryants of the hour. Melville said "I feel an exile here," and escaped into the created world of his imagination; Thoreau had the protection of Walden and his resolute individualism; Hawthorne himself was not prevented from writing his books by the critical poverty around him; and Emily Dickinson had her own way of keeping the "admiring bog" of the inept at a distance. But the critic, with his more practical business to perform, found himself shut out of the inner circles of literary influence. Poe's complaints come to mind again, a modern version of Ben Jonson's in *Timber*:

In a criticism of Bryant I was at some pains in pointing out the distinction between popular "opinion" of the merits of contemporary authors, and that held and expressed of them in private literary society. The former species of "opinion" can be called "opinion" only by courtesy. It is the public's own, just as we consider a book our own when we have bought it. In general, this opinion is adopted from the journals of the day, and I have endeavored to show that the cases are rare indeed in which these journals express any other sentiment about books than such as may be attributed directly or indirectly to the authors of the books. The most "popular," the most "successful" writers among us (for a brief period, at least) are, ninety-nine times out of a hundred, persons of mere address, perseverance, effrontery—in a word, busy-bodies, toadies, quacks. These people easily succeed in *boring* editors (whose attention is too often entirely engrossed by politics or other "business" matter) into the admission of favorable notices written or caused to be written by interested parties—or, at least, into the admission of *some* notice *where,* under ordinary circumstances, *no* notice would be given at all. In this way ephemeral "reputations" are manufactured which, for the most part, serve all the purposes designated—that is to say, the putting of money into the purse of the quack and the quack's publisher; for there never was a quack who could be brought to comprehend the value of mere fame. Now, men of genius will not resort to these manoeuvres, because genius involves in its very essence a scorn of chicanery; and thus for a time the quacks always get the advantage of them, both in respect to pecuniary profit and what *appears* to be public esteem.

This paradox, of homage for authors serving to cripple authorship, has always been the invention of journalism, commercial interest, and social coteries. It was never so depressing as in the middle of the Nineteenth Century, when it offered a special kind of critical confusion to the writers who formed what present-day historians have honored as our literary "golden day." It was a day whose true luminaries were likely to show, either by private seclusion or the sectarianism of groups and farms, the artist's instinctive withdrawal from the indignities of the public literary market or such disgusts as taxed Poe's intelligence in New York. It did the further damage of making critical discrimination appear incompatible with creative achievement at the very moment when such collaboration was necessary to the health of American literature. The visionary imagination of Whitman repelled Henry James, and the prophetic passion of Melville appalled the more aesthetic poets of his generation. The same division came to exist within the temperaments of individual writers, notably in such ambivalent and contradictory talents as Henry Adams. It created in other writers so open a contempt for American standards in art that they saved themselves by going abroad. The exile from American society had already, in Hawthorne, Thoreau, and Emily Dickinson, taken the form of the recluse. He now became an expatriate. The migrations of Whistler, James, and Lafcadio Hearn provided a model of escape from the practical responsibilities of American literature that remained feasible down to the years of mass exodus to Paris after the First World War.

The real task of criticism, however, does not fall on the conscience of the creative writer, even in an age like the present one when the artist and critic often appear in the same person. For a wider reform of the critical intelligence there was required a more thoroughgoing education in literary standards than an artist usually has the patience to give. The success of such a program in America depended on the appearance of men who were willing to make criticism their lifework. Until the last two decades of the Nineteenth Century no such body of writers came into view. By 1880 and 1890, however, a general sense of this deficiency was apparent. An important labor was waiting to be performed. The skeptical spirit abroad in the land was stimulating and healthy, but it needed translation into positive criteria of value and taste. The hour had arrived for setting up an American school of criticism that would face the duty of reconciling intelligent artists to their native birthright, and yet of developing in both them and the public sounder principles of appreciation and judgment. When that moment was recognized the contemporary movement in American criticism had its beginnings.

II

The sponsors of an American criticism had several models of purpose to remember from the past. Poe argued equally for a "poetic principle" in art and for a more complete aesthetic education in critics. Emerson examined literature in the empirical spirit of his English contemporaries, Macaulay, Carlyle, and Arnold, for evidences of that "peculiar fruit which each man was created to bear" and which ripens out of his personal hopes and struggles. Lowell had turned toward past masterpieces to find the qualities of moral character and idealism by which the writers around him might be invigorated. Whitman threw on poets his prophecy of the supreme humanitarian destiny of the American nation, and called on critics to instruct and defend the poet blessed with this mission. But these leaders had succeeded neither in founding schools nor in winning followers, and they were too much at odds to arouse concerted action among critics. What was needed was just such action, to coördinate dissenting views, instruct a new generation in the traditions of literature, and agree on the means by which the best talents should translate them into timely and active form. There was still missing a vital contact between the abstract standards of culture and the living experience and craftsmanship to which they were now to be applied.

It was one thing to see this program of action. It was another thing to act by it. The critical intelligence was faced not only with the duty of harmonizing tradition with the complexities of modern life, but with the need of an education in aesthetic principles that would apply less to the tested achievements of the past than to the books of a new generation. It had to grasp such matters as taste and style in better terms than the outworn usages of academic convention, and it had to acquire enough realism and sophistication to know what they mean in contemporary terms. Critics, seeing this responsibility, would inevitably turn toward European countries and learn many of their best lessons from older standards, but it was equally important that they should avoid the fallacy of thinking that the mere importation of a foreign example would bring such standards to the United States.

Henry James

Henry James was the first critic to undertake this task, and he saw its difficulties more clearly than any other man of his generation. The fact that he did not remain in America to complete his work is one of the tragedies of our literature—not by any failure of his in greatness, but by ours in sharing his intelligence more fully. As early as the 'sixties, when he had barely come of age, he was a diligent reviewer of books for *The Nation, The North American Review,* and other New York journals. He canvassed the taste and sentiments of the Victorian Age—the lady novelists and sentimental poets as soberly as Goethe, Sainte-Beuve, and Arnold. In another ten years his ground had shifted. He was looking for his bases in art and criticism. He studied Balzac and the realists, Eliot and the moral problem in fiction, George Sand for her imaginative and atmospheric methods, the new French naturalists for their inventories of contemporary society. In ten years more his European education was fairly complete. He had examined the contrasting purposes of the schools of Paris—romantic, symbolist, and realist. He listened to the counsels of Flaubert, Turgenev, Daudet, and Zola. He wrote his book on Hawthorne and the essays in *French Poets and Novelists* and *Partial Portraits*. He formed his friendship with Stevenson and arrived at his own creative maturity. He was perhaps the first American man of letters to follow a complete course of literary and critical education, to compare European writers and doctrines, to impose on his own craft and conscience an unprejudiced critical detachment.

He saw the modern creative problem in its two essential aspects: its oppression by social conflict and theories of scientific and moral determinism, and its acute subtilization by the defenses which the aesthetic techniques of the modern sensibility had set up against these oppressions. He saw modern criticism confronting the task of reconciling the real and the aesthetic, human life in "its unprejudiced identity" with the form and laws of art. That task was nowhere more urgent than in America, and during the 'eighties, when James still had the ambition of becoming an "American Balzac," he formulated his working principles as a critic. His critical doctrine had three clauses. He argued for subtlety and plasticity in the critic's sympathy as a first condition. As a second he demanded a tireless study of the vital experience upon which all art is based and its use as a test of material validity, since for him all art was "in basis moral." And he required finally a knowledge of how the intelligence of the artist stamps this material with its unmistakable impression of form and language, since that imprint constituted for James the "quality of mind" he looked for in any valid work of art.

He held to the mean in both art and criticism. He had an American's natural suspicion of cults and doctrine. He looked upon Gautier's "art for art" as an absurdity and upon naturalism as a "treacherous ideal." To him aesthetic quality was as indispensable as realistic documentation, but to insist on one without the other, or on either without the harmonizing presence of a moral conception, was futile. Criticism must being where a work of imagination begins: with experience tangibly perceived.

To lend himself, to project himself and steep himself, to feel and feel till he understands, and to understand so well that he can say, to have perception at the pitch of passion and expression as embracing as the air, to be infinitely curious and incorrigibly patient, and yet plastic and inflammable and determinable, stooping to conquer and yet serving to direct—these are fine chances for an active mind, chances to add the idea of independent beauty to the conception of success. Just in proportion as he is **sentient** and restless, just in proportion as he reacts and reciprocates and penetrates, **is** the critic a valuable instrument.

He thus pleaded for training in critical sensibility. It alone leads the critic directly into contact with the work of art and with art's own sources. But one must not make the mistake of confusing what James said with what Pater taught in the conclusion of *The Renaissance*. Impressionism was at that time almost as unknown in America as it had been exaggerated in Europe, and it had a service to perform in bringing critics back to an intimate sense of art; but neither James nor his American friends—Lowell, Norton, Howells—had any intention of subscribing to its methods. They were too thoroughly bred in ethical seriousness. When James declared in *Partial Portraits* that "the deepest quality of a work of art will always be the quality of the mind of the producer," he meant that for both art and criticism "the moral sense and the artistic sense lie very close together." Only their combination will supply the intellect's abstract operations with the vitality of a union that makes such "quality" possible. "The critic's judgment," he repeated, "being in the last analysis an estimate of the artist's quality of mind, is at once moral and aesthetic." The persistent linking of these terms runs like a motive through James's essays. To separate the moral from the aesthetic is to rob either of its vital complement. Genuine "unity of the mind" exists in such "fusions and interrelations," with "every part of the stuff encircled in every other." That is the secret of aesthetic form, a writer's ultimate achievement—just as its elucidation is the secret of the critic's success, his highest responsibility. These precepts stayed with James from his critical coming-of-age until he finally assayed his own achievement by their light when writing, a quarter century later, the prefaces for the New York edition of his works.

illiam
an
owells

American literature itself did not long remain, however, the subject matter of James's critical books. His removal from America after the disillusioning failure of his excursion into social realism in the 'eighties left the task in the hands of William Dean Howells and William Crary Brownell. In the new program of action Howells took the part of facts, Brownell that of ideals. Howells undertook to explain the foundations of American realism, Brownell the basis of taste and prudence necessary for the existence of cultural and literary achievement. Howells combined a frontier childhood with New England schooling, a study of past masters under the guidance of Lowell, Norton, and Aldrich with his own zest for art and history during European travels and consulships. But he found his roots in the ambition and vigor of the average American life, and he made the rationalization of its values the task of both his criticism and his novels.

He found two instruments at his service: the aesthetics of French naturalism (from whose rawer examples he recoiled, preferring the tempered version of Jane Austen or Tolstoy) and the scientific humanitarianism of the modern sociologists (which he studied not only in Mill, Comte, Spencer, Morris, and Bellamy, but in the social unrest of his middle years, the Pennsylvania coal strikes and Haymarket riots, "the slavery implicated in our liberty"). He defined the principles of this moral realism for critics in his essay in 1891, *Criticism and Fiction*. "Realism is nothing more and nothing less than the truthful treatment of material." He repudiated the aristocratic element in romanticism which "seeks to withdraw itself, to stand aloof, to be distinguished and not to be identified." Realism is the particular duty of the artist in the democratic society, for it enables him to feel "in every nerve the equality of things and the unity of men . . . to front the everyday world and catch the charm of its work-worn, careworn, brave, kindly face." To these doctrines Howells added two riders which locate him infallibly in his generation and define his critical limitations unmistakably. That realism is best which studies the "large cheerful average of health and success and happy life," since "the more smiling aspects of life" are "the more American." And that realism is most successful which rejects the deterministic science of the naturalists in favor of ethical judgment, since "morality penetrates all things, it is the soul of all things." Here Howells admitted his patriotic and ethical prejudices as frankly as his followers a quarter century later. He lacked their basis of special social doctrine, but he stuck to the conviction that unless a critic assumes such prejudices and makes them the source of his judgments, he fails in moral responsibility.

Brownell differed from Howells in many circumstances of temperament and training, but he agreed with him in one fundamental belief: the relation of art to life can be grasped only in terms of a realistic and practical dependence. His manner of demonstrating this principle was as different from Howells' as his sense of the spiritual deficiencies of the American people was different from Howells' firm confidence in their tough integrity. Brownell found his model in Arnold. He too became a priest of the cultural ideal, and he shared Arnold's combination of hope and pessimism in the face of the democratic future. He too believed that literature is a "criticism of life," and that criticism in turn "determines the relation of the two, and thus needs as close touch with life as with arts and letters." Yet the critic can do his work effectively only by a knowledge of ideal ends and standards. Standards, indeed, were Brownell's fetish, his touchstone to all worth. "To an intelligence fully and acutely alive, its own time must, I think, be more interesting than any other," he said; but the critic must go on "to discern and characterize the abstract qualities informing the concrete expression of the artist." "It is the *qualities* of the writer, painter, sculptor, and not the *properties* of their production that are his essential concern." Among his *American Prose Masters* he found only Cooper and James free of poverty in these qualities of experience and perception. Hawthorne "neglected imagination"; Emerson's "nature was flooded with light, but it lacked heat"; of Poe it was "impossible to make a great writer . . . because his writings lack the elements not only of great, but real literature. They lack substance." But the critic can also fail if he lacks emotional and aesthetic energy. Lowell for all his scholarship "was reflectively indolent." There is, in fact, only one cure for the imaginative poverty and degrading materialism of the times, and that is a cultural ideal. It alone saves the artist from the enervating antagonism of his physical and aesthetic faculties.

William
Crary
Brownell

This solvent Brownell looked for in the sustaining and renewing influence of a firmly ethical civilization. His models for it he found in the "culture" defined by Arnold and in the aesthetic achievements of France. He studied *French Traits* with the patient but always half-ironical hope of importing them to the United States. No one but James had his skill in the judicious inspection of such a model, and no one but James had the greater powers of imagination that could show how ineffectual Brownell's fastidious discretion would turn out to be. For forty years he taught his moderate and urbane gospel of discipline, decorum, and intellectual tact. The heresies of "self-expression," naturalism, and impressionism he considered aberrations from a desired norm. He insisted so austerely on this norm, this admirable but ultimately abstract principle, that he lost his hold on the very "substance" he demanded in his prose masters. When he faced the literary productions of the new age around him, or when he attempted to understand tradition as a reality that is valid only by its success in surviving in the present, he proved almost abjectly incompetent. His urgent counsels on taste and sophistication impressed themselves on a few respectful followers but on almost none of the artists and craftsmen he wished to enlighten. Today his precisely phrased and austerely bound books are unread. But excepting only those of James, they provided the most serious formulation of the responsibility that must be exchanged between artist, critic, and public that America had yet seen, and some of their views have never been restated to better effect. They may be recalled some day when another effort at integrating social and aesthetic thought comes due. By comparison with the puerilities of academic convention around him (Henry Van Dyke, or Hamilton Wright Mabie with his "White List of Books") he survives with the distinction of sensitive tastes which these prudish culturists never thought it worth their while to envy.

Taste, in those bewildered years of the late Nineteenth Century, was a faculty so threatened by anemia when refined and so exhausted by garish and unprincipled crudity when robust, that it is small wonder the word came to be the trademark of ludicrous elegance and snobbery among satirists like Mark Twain. James Huneker made something else of it. He was perhaps the first sybarite of the arts in America. His appetite and energy made him a valuable agent in combating the dead weight of genteel and Puritanic intolerance, the smug cant of "propriety" that acted as a customs barrier to aesthetic importations of any kind. Like George Moore and Arthur Symons in England, he was an ambassador of the aesthetic movement. He lavished his admiration on anything new, exotic, or rebellious, and his cascades of fervent publicity swept before the American public the novelties of modern music, drama, painting, fiction, and ballet, not to mention the gastronomic luxuries of every café and hostelry on the Continent. He wrote about the arts as he wrote about foods and menus, and before their rich fare professed

nothing but an unlimited epicurean capacity. His writings were the cosmopo-
lite's text books and involved few critical subtleties. They offered a plain man's
version of Pater's appetitive ideal and Anatole France's doctrine of aesthetic
exposure. The critic must aim "to spill his soul," and "humbly to follow and
register his emotions aroused by a masterpiece." He spared nothing in the way
of epithets, enigmas, and paradoxes when he spilled his soul, and upon the
ensuing flood his readers were buffeted by the complete carnival of modern
insurgence in the arts. The sheer gastronomic pleasure of this feast was
crowned by a kind of moral satisfaction in knowing that it was an affront to
all the inhibitions and hostilities of the Puritan tradition. There was no need
to discriminate special qualities in the items: they had the common quality of
scorning the pure and the prurient.

For the sophisticated children of the Gilded Age and for a few more serious
apprentices, Huneker was revered as a bringer of gifts. On the popular level
his influence was rapid and enormous. On the critical value of his work little
need be added. His foremost disciple has said that for him art was no longer
"even by implication a device for improving the mind. It is wholly a magnificent adventure. The notion of it is what Huneker brought into American
criticism, and it is for that bringing that he will be remembered." This, spoken
in tribute by Mencken, speaks for itself. In any serious sense Huneker did not
pretend to write criticism, even in his books on Liszt and Chopin. He wrote
aesthetic publicity. He brought the fleshpots of modern art into a genteel society, startled the literary conventions out of their frozen molds, shocked the
high priests of the Lyceum circuit, inducted a new generation of journalists
into a colorful style and extravagant zest for the arts, and introduced an easy
brand of impressionism into literary appreciation. He shaped the adolescent
phase of a new critical attitude, and as such his labors are preserved in the
shelf of books in which his enormous avidity and honest share of sensitive
enthusiasm for music, literature, and painting are preserved. He is the child
of his period, and to return to his books now, after the sobering events of the
last thirty years, is to realize how much of a child he remains. But he may
claim a tonic quality: he made American readers more keenly aware of international activities than Henry James managed to do. He probably ruined taste
more expertly than James improved it, but he also created an appetite for the
arts that had its due effect on the physical health and public prestige of the
American artist.

Around the work of James and Brownell, Howells and Huneker, a sizeable
critical activity went on between the 'nineties and 1912, but from it few lasting
services may be isolated. Much of this writing came from academic quarters,
another share was composed of newspaper reviews, most of which risked little
in the way of dispute or defense of new talent, and another part struck out
along independent lines which either ended at the impasse of theoretical

Woodberry
and
Matthews

vagueness or led back to conventional quarters. George Edward Woodberry was one critic who felt dissatisfaction in the stolid confines of the academic world and began to work toward freer purposes. He produced a series of volumes in which various critical positions were carefully scanned, the work of new critics plotted, and impending problems suggested. He also said much about the need of a new humanistic and realistic attitude toward values, and in such books as *America in Literature* (1903), *The Torch* (1905), *The Appreciation of Literature* (1910), and *Two Phases of Criticism* (1914) he provided the best surveys of the situation and of critical methods that existed in those years. But theory took him too far afield, and a lax belletristic idealism removed him from the irrepressible forces that were demanding expression. Brander Matthews had less of this. By combining a shrewd study of European dramatic criticism with a lively attention to the New York stage he lifted the criticism of drama over from the pontifical conservatism of William Winter's era to the brisk journalism soon to come from younger men.

eorge
antayana
By far the keenest refreshment of aesthetic interest to come from academic quarters, however, was supplied by George Santayana. His *Sense of Beauty* in 1896 claimed to be nothing but a new arrangement of "the scattered commonplaces of criticism into a system, under the inspiration of a naturalistic psychology." The last phrase of this apology explains the great influence the book and its sequels were to have on the study and appreciation of art in the United States. It was the first textbook to refurbish the classical routine of philosophical discourse and add the stimulation of a realistic motive. Santayana set aside the didactic and historical approach to art, and offered the psychological. He presented "aesthetic judgments as phenomena of mind and products of mental evolution." He combined his exposition with a vivid sense of his personal appreciation of the arts, and stepped gracefully over the barrier that separated the philosophical idealist of the American college from an active grasp of the work of art itself. When he distinguished the three orders of beauty as residing in material, in form, and in expression, he took these criteria out of the dark chamber of theory and made them applicable to existing masterpieces. And fourteen years later, in *Three Philosophical Poets,* he showed that figures like Lucretius, Dante, and Goethe could be used as opportunities for the collaboration between philosophical and literary criticism which was needed to rescue aesthetic teaching from endless and enfeebling conventionality. But the "inspiration of a naturalistic psychology" remained basic to Santayana's activity in this line. It gave him his popularity among realists and psychologists, and it provided a clue to a new line of reaction which was presently to put in an appearance and prepare a heated repudiation of his influence and affiliations. That reaction proceeded cautiously, built its attack conservatively, and took almost a quarter century before it faced the enemy of naturalism in open battle. In 1904 Paul Elmer More issued the first

volume of his *Shelburne Essays,* and in 1908 Irving Babbitt began his campaign against romanticism with *Literature and the American College.*

III

The work of the critics who attempted to bridge the distance between Nineteenth Century habits and the experimental conditions of modern literature now appears, especially when we recall the difficulties of prejudice and conventionality they faced, to gain in courage and distinction. More's phrase in his 1904 volume—"Before we can have an American literature, we must have an American criticism"—is a sufficient warrant of this. But when a new revival of literary activity arrived around 1912 it took, like most cases of insurgence, the immediately preceding generation as its first object of attack. It announced two purposes: the demolition of the genteel tradition and a rediscovery of the American spirit. These served to indict as academic, unrealistic, or corruptive the labors of most of the elder critics still on the scene. Henry James then appeared as a deserter from a sacred trust, a shirker of his duty as an American, tainted by the effete and artificial influences of English society and French theory. Brownell and Woodberry became supreme examples of academic dry rot and polite formulation. Paul Elmer More fell under contempt as a dogged apologist for ethical dogma. Huneker, in spite of his more attractive personality and acceptable epicureanism of taste, was lamed by vulgar aestheticism and exhausting garrulity, incapable of getting a close view of the serious duties of the artist, and rendered helpless as a judge of either life or art by his welter of gross and indiscriminate enthusiasms. The young critics who now took the field were of an equally heady breed, but they professed very different purposes. Reality was to provide their basic standard, and the existing life of the United States their chief test of values. In one of his essays Van Wyck Brooks suggested the new attitude toward history: "On Creating a Usable Past." The title of one of his most successful books gave the new criticism its label: *America's Coming-of-Age.* He and his colleagues corrected More's dictum. They believed that before there could be either an American literature or an American criticism there must appear a fresh and realistic understanding of what America itself meant. What they produced was not criticism in any pure or technical sense. It was Americanization.

That it was to be a critical and practical kind of Americanization, escaping the weakness of earlier prophecies and panegyrics, was made clear in another of Brooks's volumes, *Letters and Leadership.* There he took up a clue furnished by John Macy in his *Spirit of American Literature* (1913) and gave it as his conclusion that "our life is, on all its levels, in a state of arrested development, that it has lost, if indeed it has ever possessed, the principle of growth." He credited this adolescence to the commercial and materialistic obsessions of the nation. "We are," he said, "the victims of a systematic process

"America' Coming-o Age"

of inverse selection so far as the civilizing elements in the American nature are concerned. Our ancestral faith in the individual and what he is able to accomplish (or in modern parlance, to 'put over') as the measure of all things, has despoiled us of that science, art, philosophy, the self-subordinating service of which is almost the measure of the highest happiness. In consequence of this our natural capacities have been dissipated, they have become egocentric and socially centrifugal and they have hardened and become fixed in the most anomalous form." He sketched a program for the correction of this state of affairs, if only to keep alive "the hope of a 'national culture' to come . . . in order that America may be able in the future to give something to the rest of the world that is better than what the world too generally means by 'Americanism.' " The elder critics whom he condemned as "unpractical" had done little toward this end, chiefly because while "they say that we are emotional . . . what they really object to is that we are emotional at all, the strength of their own case resting wholly on the assumption that literature ought to spring not from the emotions but from the intellect." They had fostered a "fear of experience."

Such, in fact, is the deficiency of personal impulse, of the creative will, in America, so overwhelming is the demand laid upon Americans to serve ulterior and impersonal ends, that it is as if the springs of spiritual action had altogether evaporated. Launched in a society where individuals and their faculties appear only to pass away, almost wholly apart from and without acting upon one another, our writers find themselves enveloped in an impalpable atmosphere that acts as a perpetual dissolvent to the whole field of reality both within and without themselves, an atmosphere that invades every sphere of life and takes its discount from everything that they can do, an atmosphere that prevents the formation of oases of reality in the universal chaos.

In Brooks's program for critics, the new critical realism joined hands with this corrected view of the American ideal. It was immediately taken as a call to action both by the young critical talents of the prewar years and by a new group of "journals of opinion" which appeared on the scene—*The New Republic, The Masses, The Liberator,* the renovated *Nation,* the more aesthetic *Seven Arts,* and later *The Freeman.* These found an almost ideal condition for their activities: the unrest and dislocation of the prewar years, the excite-ment and controversy that followed our entry into the conflict, and a flourish-ing literary revival that brought the work of insurgent poets and novelists to reinforce what the critics hoped to achieve. Dreiser, Sandburg, Masters, Frost, Lindsay, Willa Cather, and Robinson supplied object lessons for the new critical text. The moment was alive with creative energy and rebellion, with the hope of casting out the venerable American superstitions. These critical journalists were able to boast that they saw the creative problem from the inside. They felt its motives and difficulties with the artist, instead of holding off in suspicion and condescending scorn.

"The older critics," said Randolph Bourne in his *History of a Literary Radical*, "long since disavowed the intention of discriminating among current writers. These men, who had to have an Academy to protect them, lumped the younger writers of verse and prose together as 'anarchic' and 'naturalistic,' and had become, in these latter days, merely peevish and querulous, protesting in favor of standards that no longer represented our best values. Everyone . . . bemoaned the lack of critics, but the older critics seemed to have lost all sense of hospitality and to have become tired and a little spitefully disconsolate, while the newer ones were too intent on their crusades against puritanism and philistinism to have time for a constructive pointing of the way." Bourne had nothing but contempt for academic standardizers or importers of foreign fashions, but he saw the unorthodox belligerents threatened by another danger. He saw, "on the one hand, Mr. Mencken and Mr. Dreiser and their friends, going heavily forth to battle with the Philistines, glorying in pachydermous vulgarisms that hurt the polite and cultivated young men of the old school." He saw "these violent critics, in their rage against Puritanism, becoming themselves moralists, with the same bigotry and tastelessness as their enemies." And he continued:

> The older American critic was mostly interested in getting the proper rank and reverence for what he borrowed. The new critic will take what suits his community of sentiment. He will want to link up not with the foreign canon but with that group which is nearest in spirit to the effort he and his friends are making. The American has to work to interpret and portray the life he knows. He cannot be international in the sense that anything but the life in which he is soaked, with its questions and its colors, can be the material for his art. But he can be international—and must be—in the sense that he works with a certain hopeful vision of a "young world," and with certain ideal values upon which the younger men, stained and revolted by war, in all countries are agreeing.

The "international" element in this program was chiefly an attack on provincialism. It had its earlier sponsors in Henry James and Brownell, its immediate godfather in Huneker, its practical workers in exiles like Ezra Pound and T. S. Eliot. Critics like Spingarn and Santayana had also, for different reasons, advised a familiarity with the critical ideas that were circulating in Europe. For the realists and liberals, however, this plea for an international point of view was incidental, a supplementary means of fighting down the conservatives and "professors." Against such foes any weapon was useful, and European radicalism offered ripe experience in the tactics of battle. Ludwig Lewisohn told the young critics to look toward France, where "their battle was fought and won thirty years ago," or toward Germany, "where the heritage of Goethe's supreme vision made the battle needless." Spingarn pointed toward the books of Croce. France was, as always, held up as a model of un-shackled liberalism in art and thought. But the defenders of the "authentic American" had work to do at home which no amount of internationalism and foreign example would make easier.

A great deal of it was negative in character. They attacked prudery, deco-rum, politeness, and every other evil that might be safely ascribed to the Puritans. But they also wanted to give American writers a genuine confidence in their native materials, a pragmatic and disillusioned approach to the life around them, a standard of honesty, and if possible a critical understanding of their problems. With so many prejudices to correct, it is little wonder that a critical basis for the new realism was never satisfactorily arrived at. The gusto of the "debunking" movement had little patience for that. Brooks and Bourne laid out a program, to which their colleagues, Robert Morss Lovett, Robert Littell, Harriet Monroe, Francis Hackett, Max Eastman, Alfred Kreymborg, Harold E. Stearns, and Lewis Mumford contributed their ener-gies. Among them a dominating voice was heard; the cause found its most entertaining spokesman in H. L. Mencken.

It is easy now, in rereading Mencken's books, to limit his performance to low-comedy journalism. The pages teem with the follies of twenty-five of the oddest years in American history and form a hilarious *Dunciad* of an age. Mencken delivered his barrage against them with the energy of a Swift or Voltaire. War-time jingoism, the Prohibition era, the "Monkey Trial" in Tennessee, the pieties of the Bible Belt, the orgies of Coolidge prosperity, and the endless prodigalities of the jazz age, the "alfalfa *Gelehrten*," and the *Booboisie* now almost bury the high reputation he once held as a literary influence who made *The Smart Set* and *The American Mercury* serious forces in the lives of important writers. But one fact must be remembered: he aimed less to be a critic than a commissary of literary materials. He ransacked Ameri-can life to justify writers like Dreiser, Masters, Sandburg, Lardner, and Lewis, and to show younger writers what the realistic and critical spirit had to work on. He was an evangelist of the vulgar, as much of an artist in his display of its phenomena as many of the novelists he praised. What Edmund Wilson has pointed out must be recalled: that while

Brooks exposed the negative aspects of our literary tradition and urged us to get away from our governesses, Mencken showed the positive value of our vulgar heritage; and he did more than anyone else in his field to bring about that "coming-of-age" for which Brooks sounded the hour. The publication of Mencken's *Book of Prefaces* in 1917, with its remarkable essay on Dreiser and its assault on "Puritanism as a Literary Force," was a cardinal event for the new American litera-ture. Mencken did not precisely discover Dreiser, but he was able to focus him clearly for the first time as a figure of dignity and distinction, because he appreciated and made us taste the Americanism of Dreiser as Americanism, without attempting to write him down for not being something other than American. This *positive* treatment of Dreiser—so different from the negative attitude with which even sympathetic critics had in the past approached American writers like Mark Twain,—was really a weight that tipped the scales.

His test of a book was rough and pragmatic. He mingled his burly prejudices with an uninhibited impressionism derived from Huneker. It is not hard to imagine what this procedure amounted to when he tackled an author beyond his depth or taste—Henry James, Herman Melville, or any poet of subtle originality. But at another level he brought an enormous stimulation to the literary scene, and he took that to be his function as a critic. "The function of a genuine critic of the arts is to provoke the reaction between the work of art and the spectator. The spectator, untutored, stands unmoved; he sees the work of art, but it fails to make any intelligible impression on him; if he were spontaneously sensitive to it, there would be no need for criticism." The common assumption, that a critic "writes because he is possessed by a passion to advance the enlightenment, to put down error and wrong, to disseminate some specific doctrine: psychological, epistemological, historical, or aesthetic" is true "only of bad critics, and its degree of truth increases in direct ratio to their badness. Criticism at bottom is indistinguishable from skepticism." Mencken rejected the arguments for "constructive criticism" as based "upon the same false assumption, that immutable truths exist in the arts, and that the artist will be improved by being made aware of them. . . . Truth is something that is believed in completely only by persons who have never tried personally to pursue it to its fastnesses and grab it by the tail. . . . The true aim of a critic is certainly not to make converts. He must know that very few of the persons who are susceptible to conversion are worth converting."

These remarks, scattered throughout his essays, indicate the elements in his literary outlook: a contempt of popular taste, a suspicion of intellectual and a skepticism of dogmatic attitudes toward art, and an ambition to demolish any tradition that had fostered the delusions of ethical and ideal theory in literature. Most of that tradition he labeled Puritan, and he translated his contempt of its moral absolutes into a scorn of aesthetic absolutes. "The American, save in moments of conscious and swiftly lamented deviltry, casts up all ponderable values, including even the values of beauty, in terms of right and wrong," and the only cure for this habit was to demolish the entire basis of rational and authoritarian judgment. Under tenets like these, it was hardly to be expected that Mencken would bring his literary preferences to the test of analysis or exact discrimination. His usefulness was of a more elementary character. He wrote a history of American manners, howled into perdition the genteel superstitions of culture and dignity, and provided a basis for evaluating the realistic principle in fiction for what it was worth. His own criticism will probably be remembered chiefly for the humor that accompanied its purgative effects.

n Wyck
ooks

In Van Wyck Brooks another form of the patriotic motive appeared. It combined affection and skepticism as Mencken's did, but it was tempered to a soberer employment. His early books on the revision of American society— *The Wine of the Puritans* (1909), *America's Coming-of-Age* (1915), and *Letters and Leadership* (1918)—were intended as manifestoes and were accepted as such. Brooks never intended an assault on genuine American loyalties; his reverence for these was instinctive and sincere, and he did not consider cosmopolitanism a cure-all for cultural ingrowth and provincialism. He proposed first to indict the traitors within the gates, the defilers of the pioneer idealism and all who had nursed along the enfeebling conformism of the academic life. After that he would take his "usable past" and apply its lessons to the unrealized present. In two of his books these purposes were first demonstrated in practical terms—*The Ordeal of Mark Twain* (1920) and *The Pilgrimage of Henry James* (1925). Both these inheritors of the American tradition were depicted as unworthy of its promise—Twain through pessimism and a failure of personal integrity, James through temperamental restlessness and aesthetic over-refinement. Brooks had set up in his mind the standard of American honesty and fortitude which he was later to apply in *The Flowering of New England* and the histories that followed it. In it he found his prescription for the authentic American artist, the source of his usable past and his productive present. Any betrayal of its promise spelled for him the secret failure of the artist.

It is in his book on James that the defects of Brooks's argument appear most strikingly. Starting with his thesis, he broke the body of James to fit it. James's qualities of irony and self-criticism, his subtle pessimism on the condition of English society and French literature, his sense of catastrophe in the European moral order, his skeptical detachment and unforgotten American loyalties, are all simplified or neglected in order to push to its logical conclusion the argument that they were ultimately stultified by James's refusal to return to his native shores to live and write. The words and speeches of James's fictions are used to convey his own personal attitude, ostensibly to give an "effect of immediacy" but actually with the result of reading into his personal career a coherent fiction which an exact reading of his letters, the autobiographical books, or the major novels themselves would have rendered impossible. Yet the desired effect was achieved. *The Pilgrimage of Henry James* becomes a parable of the American artist's betrayal of his birthright. The patriotic motive inhibits the critical. A valuable project of revision and reclamation falters in the individual test. In the end Brooks was to prove more adept as a pictorial and anecdotal historian of the past than as a student of the present. His *Opinions of Oliver Allston* in 1941 showed clearly his alienation from all but the most traditional and conservative of contemporary talents. His labors finally settled down to the writing of a literary chronicle of the United States which began with *The Flowering of New England* in 1936, and to the winning of a greater popular recognition, if a less serious achievement, than his early challenges ever hoped to arrive at.

Among Brooks's followers Lewis Mumford became a versatile leader. He wanted not merely to recover a usable past but to apply it as speedily as possible to the existing distractions and doubts of literature. He looked for it in the same quarter as Brooks did—in the *Golden Day* of New England culture, from whose high moment he saw modern American wealth and materialism as a decline. He studied the Utopian symbol as a means of combining its philosophic vitality with the mystic or humanitarian vision of Emerson, Whitman, and Melville. He took "Whitman with his cosmic faith" and "Melville in his cosmic defiance" as his prophets, and believed that "they will guide us to a splendid future" where the techniques of civilization will cease to tyrannize over man and provide a richer opportunity for his self-fulfillment. Like many of his contemporaries, Mumford was stronger on the side of indictments than of affirmations. In *Sticks and Stones* (1924) and *The Brown Decades* (1931) he produced two of the best accounts of American art and architecture that have yet been written, and in these books he shows that the practical arts furnish him with safer examples for speculation than the literary. He has fallen too glibly into the prophet's role to be anything but restive and generalizing in his treatment of literary style and craftsmanship. "The social sciences will lie beneath the foundations of the New Jerusalem precisely in the fashion that the physical sciences now underlie the stony exterior of New York" is one of Mumford's observations; and another: "The future of our civilization depends upon our ability to select and control our heritage from the past, to alter our present attitudes and habits, and to project fresh forms into which our energies may be freely poured." The glow here is messianic, the accent Whitman's, the skepticism as facile as the self-assurance is quick, and instead of producing the focus of scrutiny and discrimination where critical values come to a point, Mumford's energies have radiated and explored. He has contributed to the background of aesthetic thought more than he has given that thought principles and a discipline to work by.

Under the guidance of these men several things were accomplished. The past was revived in colorful and intimate terms, even though the uses to which it was put were not very intelligently defined, or free of a great deal of the cant about progress, patriotism, and disillusionment that circulated so recklessly in the postwar years. The term "American" was stripped of dogmatic and academic accretions. Large areas of subject matter formerly considered

Lewis
Mumford

The Gain
of Realisr
1910–192

out of polite artistic bounds were thrown open to conquest by writers. A necessary leaven of plain sense and active speech was added to the fare in which
novelists dealt and critics dealt. Literature was brought to closer terms with
experience and fortified by candor and audacity. It was reduced to those
simpler necessities and practices which correct the laxities of academic idealism or aesthetic refinement, but which may also put up the deluding appearance of being self-sufficient and in no need of the intellectual benefits of
aesthetic or philosophic discipline. In fact, this entire activity was so attractive
to journalists that it became vulgarized beyond its own intentions. It made
the writing of books seem as easy as talking about them. Under its influence
American literature was strengthened, but as often reduced to facile and
rapid-fire journalism, criticism meanwhile becoming equally loose in its language, haphazard in its terminology, indifferent in analysis, and complacently
hostile to anything in the way of intellectual attitudes or aesthetic experimentation. The realists and Americanizers nagged pure art and ridiculed its
defenders; they encouraged the flight of experimentalists to Paris; they scoffed
at originality by calling it "cerebralism"; and they did their part in keeping
the literary activity of the twenties on a fairly confused level.

However, they flourished in their day. *The Saturday Review of Literature*
became one of their strongholds, *The American Mercury* another, and independent or creative journalism was kept at the distance of Greenwich Village
(in *The Dial, Others,* and *The Little Review*), Chicago (in *Poetry*), or
Europe (in *Secession, Broom,* and *Transition*). Occasionally this vein of
American revivalism took on the colors of prophecy, as in Ludwig Lewisohn's
The Creative Life and *Expression in America* or in Waldo Frank's *The Re-
Discovery of America,* where the "great tradition" became a spectre of mystic
and international proliferations. Nothing showed better than these heavy-
handed conjurings how severely the realistic revival stood in need of critical
direction from both social and artistic authorities if it was to be saved from
bombast and rhetoric, or from a debasement of the American principle fully
as debilitating as the genteel conventions which it had opposed. Such correction began to appear some years after the First World War. One of the most
important manifestations of it came in the form of a regional principle in the
study of tradition and art, shown particularly among the group of Southern
critics—John Crowe Ransom, Donald Davidson, and Allen Tate—who combined literary study with cultural investigations and who had their first organ
in *The Fugitive* of Nashville. Another, from a different quarter, appeared in
the form of social criticism of the radical type, of which such writers as Upton
Sinclair and V. F. Calverton were pioneer professors, but which was ultimately to develop a method much more formal and extreme (particularly
under the tenets of Marxism) than these men had exhibited. In any case, the

arrogance and visionary gusto of the realistic movement were its weakest features. They exposed it most readily to critical attack and soon brought it under contempt from several quarters of the literary scene.

IV

One of these was occupied by the students of modern aesthetics who first found their ideas or centered their activities abroad. Paris and London were already before the War of 1914 the accepted capitals of artistic experimentation, and a revision of aesthetic ideas was in progress there far removed from the academic influences and public indifference that made such activity out of place at home. The departure from American shores of Ezra Pound and T. S. Eliot was taken as a hint that their talents were indifferent to the revival of an American ideal or the promotion of new standards of social realism. Their loadstone was neither the real nor the humanitarian, it was art; and they turned toward the schools of Italy, Paris, and prewar London to learn their lessons and ultimately to become recognized as leaders of the experimental groups that flourished there.

The deficiencies of American criticism in aesthetic and technical understanding had long been a byword. Poe had issued the first indictments on this score, and in the 1840's John Lothrop Motley had published in *The North American Review* a series of essays presenting the man of letters as an artist and pleading, especially in an essay on Balzac, that fiction be respected as an art before it is tested for its ethical and social respectability. These arguments later formed the chief responsibility of Henry James, but before 1900 the instructions of aesthetic critics in France, Germany, and England found scant hospitality in the United States, Huneker's defense of their doctrines being held a matter of highly questionable taste. Impressionism was as little known to American critics as to American writers. The Harvard professor, Lewis E. Gates, was probably its only sympathetic interpreter among the elect. In his essay on "Impressionism and Appreciation," published in *Studies and Appreciations* in 1900, he introduced his readers to the special conditions and mysteries of the aesthetic experience. There he argued that

> The history of literary criticism from Addison's day to our own is, if viewed in one way, the history of the ever-increasing refinement of the critic's sensorium; it is a growing tendency on the part of the critic to value, above all else, his own intimate personal relation to this or that piece of literature—a tendency that more and more takes the form of prizing the fleeting mood, the passing poignant moment of enjoyment in the presence of art, until at last certain modern critics refuse, on principle, to feel twice alike about the same poem.

"Impressionism," he said, "justifies itself historically. But more than this, it justifies itself psychologically; for it recognizes with peculiar completeness

The
Aesthetic
Principle

the vitalizing power of literature—its fashion of putting into play the whole nature of each reader it addresses and its consequent, unlimited, creative energy." Santayana had also aimed to combine the philosophical rationalization of art with modern principles of inductive psychology in determining the character of aesthetic experience, and in counteracting the academic and philosophical influence with a more practical training in sensibility. In 1910 these influences were challenged even more defiantly by J. E. Spingarn in a celebrated lecture on "The New Criticism." This was a manifesto for a completely new program among critics. Under the guidance of Croce he attempted to import into America an unsparing revision of the critical motive, described by his term "creative criticism," in which the appreciative faculties of the critic's trained sensibility would serve as a basis for testing and rationalizing the intuition of the work of art. "The New Criticism" made a clean sweep of existing conventions:

> We have done with all the old Rules. . . . We have done with the *genres,* or literary kinds. . . . We have done with the comic, the tragic, the sublime, and an army of vague abstractions of their kind. . . . We have done with theory of style, with metaphor, simile, and all the paraphernalia of Graeco-Roman rhetoric. . . . We have done with all moral judgment of art as art. . . . We have done with the confusion between the drama and the theatre which has permeated dramatic criticism for over half a century. . . . We have done with technique as separate from art. . . . We have done with the history and criticism of poetic themes. . . . We have done with the race, the time, the environment of a poet's work as an element in Criticism. . . . We have done with the "evolution" of literature. . . . We have done with the old rupture between genius and taste.

This provided a much-needed ventilation of the critical classrooms and it served for a time its purpose in affronting the conservative forces. Unfortunately Spingarn never demonstrated by inspection and analysis the technique he desiderated, and his usefulness was confined to stirring up controversy. It was the general limitation of these men that they had little talent for specific analysis. They taught, corrected, and debated, but they gave their readers little practical training in literary methods and craftsmanship.

zra
ound

"Active criticism" of this sort was what Ezra Pound went abroad to learn when he left America in 1907 and began his forty-year career in Italy, England, and France. In the early days of his apprenticeship he stood for a militantly aesthetic standard in literary experimentation, a rescue of art from formulae and discreet abstraction. He was drawn toward critics and editors like Henry James, Remy de Gourmont, W. B. Yeats, T. E. Hulme, and Ford Madox Hueffer, who made less pretense of organizing a philosophic system out of their tastes and appreciations than of refreshing and extending these by constant study of the problems of form and style. He put himself to school, as poet and critic, among the experimental masters of the past and the nonconformist teachers of the present. On an eclectic principle he studied the Latin lyrists, the balladists of Provence and medieval Italy, the Elizabethan translators and classicists, and the Chinese manuscripts he inherited from Ernest Fenollosa, all with the same zest as he gave to the ideas of Gourmont in Paris and Hulme in London. His enthusiasm was so contagious that he himself was soon a recognized leader in innovation and critical pedagogy.

From Gourmont he heard the conversations on style and aesthetic form which were epitomized in an aphorism that gives focal expression to the liaison now set up between the impressionistic principle and the new aesthetic formalism: *"Ériger en lois ses impressions personnelles, c'est le grand effort d'un homme s'il est sincère."* From Hulme he took up a protest against the romantic, the sentimental, the formally vague and subjective, the relative and the abstract, which the author of the fragmentary *Speculations* offered as his prophecy of a revival of classic formalism in modern literature. This principle of form, however, had little to do with the revival of the Aristotelian laws. It gained its chief stimulation from a contemptuous opposition to the degenerate romanticism of late Victorian and contemporary writers. For that reason it made a necessity of experiment, and Pound's career became a continuous participation in unconventionality—in Imagism, in Vorticism, in the aesthetic laboratories of Paris, in Objectivism, in any activity that satisfied his demand for novelty, exploration, and invention. These labors he never gave the appearance of a system—and purposely so, since "systems become tyrannies overnight"; and although he later, and disastrously, worked toward arguments of social, political, and economic reform, his purpose was never primarily moral, except in the sense that aesthetic discipline demands an integrity beyond the formality of practical ethics. His book titles indicate his motives: *Instigations, Irritations, How to Read, The A. B. C. of Reading, Make It New.* All of these were written less to persuade than to irritate and thus to *apply* the authority of creative literature itself. When he defined his "categories" of criticism he opposed the ineffectuality of abstract dogma with the dynamic value of the actual literary text. For him there were five categories of criticism:

(1) Criticism by discussion, extending from mere yatter, logic-chopping, and description of tendencies up to the clearly defined record of procedures and an attempt to formulate more or less general principles. . . . (2) Criticism by translation. . . . (3) Criticism by exercise in the style of a given period. . . . (4) Criticism by music, meaning definitely the setting of a poet's words. . . . This is the most intense form of criticism save: (5) Criticism in new composition.

And "Criticism so far as I have discovered has two functions:"

(1) Theoretically it tries to forerun composition, to serve as gunsight, though there is, I believe, no recorded instance of this foresight having *ever* been of the

slightest use save to actual composers. I mean the man who formulates any forward reach of co-ordinating principle is the man who produces the demonstration. . . . (2) Excernment. The general ordering and weeding out of what has actually been performed. The elimination of repetitions. The work analogous to that which a good hanging committee or curator would perform in a National Gallery or in a biological museum; the ordering of knowledge so that the next man (or generation) can most readily find the live part of it, and waste the least possible time among obsolete issues.

Pound brought criticism back to an active study of texts more directly and unequivocally than impressionism ever aimed to do, and with none of the obstruction by scientific methods that I. A. Richards and his disciples have brought about. His arguments have suffered as much as his style from their explosive purposes; so much so, in fact, that where his later books do not sin by endless reiteration of the familiar clichés of his much-boasted iconoclasm, they become an indistinguishable clutter of classifications that do not classify and distinctions that confuse discrimination. But Pound's work, for all its violence, haphazardness, and shock tactics, or its tragic political consequences, has had the virtues that go with these deliberate offenses: it has been direct, energetic, experimental, and seminal. It has also had a virtue to which academic criticism can rarely pretend: it has been useful to writers. It is in his role as a teacher of writers that Pound's service has been greatest and his importance in the aesthetic thought of our times most decided.

T. S. Eliot shares this distinction, but for very different reasons of temperament and method. In him contemporary criticism again finds an influence reinforced at every point by poetic practice. It is in his ability to suggest a principle by pointing out an example that his short essays show their vitality. In *The Sacred Wood* of 1920 Eliot began his work by defining the defects in modern critical methods—the historical and deterministic leanings of Sainte-Beuve and Taine, the ethical bias of the American schools (especially in More and Babbitt), the facile suggestibility of the impressionists, the rhetorical taste of romanticists like Swinburne and Wyndham, the exaggerated common sense of journalists like Charles Whibley. He found instead his first lessons in the books of Gourmont, whom he called "the critical consciousness of a generation." He set out to bridge the gap between impressionism and reason in critical thought, and his critical program was an attempt to educate the exact and conscientious sensibility (which is as basic to genuine criticism as it is to poetic creation) through discipline in the ideal conditions and formal principles of art, and only then in the ulterior purposes which art may serve. Eliot was temperamentally as much an antiromantic as Hulme, and yet he knew that the classic discipline cannot be obtained in modern art or thought through academic exhumation. "One must be firmly distrustful of accepting Aristotle in a canonical spirit; this is to lose the whole living force

. S.
iot

of him." It was for this reason that he took Gourmont as a model: "He combined to a remarkable degree sensitiveness, erudition, sense of fact and sense of history, and generalizing power," and this combination of assets served Eliot in his definition of "the perfect critic."

He himself found comparison and the exactly discriminating epithet his two most useful tools in determining the quality of a piece of writing. Though his essays are notable for their aphoristic generalizations, he resisted assuming a doctrine or principle without subjecting it to the empirical proof of his text. With this stress on the necessity of exact textual scrutiny he reproved, especially in his earlier essays where he was still more closely concerned with aesthetic and less with metaphysical problems, the tendencies in modern criticism toward historical explanation, biographical irrelevancies, and the deterministic effects of scientific method or sociological theory. The authors around whom he wrote his best criticism—the Elizabethan dramatists, the metaphysical poets, Dante, Donne, Blake, Baudelaire, Valéry, and Pound— gave those essays on style and form a practical virtue which begins to dissipate as Eliot's criticism has become more philosophically ambitious. His belief in the "isolated superiority" of the artist to practical justification has been modified by his desire to bring the literary object into closer relation with its historical tradition, its moral environment, and its wider human conditions: by his wish, in other words, to explain *The Use of Poetry and the Use of Criticism.* But he remains one of the most fructifying elements in contemporary literary thought, as anxious as ever to keep criticism close to its specific duties. In one of his essays, on "Experiment in Criticism," he defined the need of a dialectic discipline which will establish the terminology and analytical methods of literary study and thus correct a deficiency in means which still cripples the work of literary students; and in "Religion and Literature," he makes a statement that should be as corrective of existing critical confusions as it serves to indicate the line his own critical career has followed: "The 'greatness' of literature cannot be determined solely by literary standards; though we must remember that whether it is literature or not can be determined only by literary standards."

It was on a basis of the disciplines proposed by Pound and Eliot that aesthetic criticism was rescued from vague and static generalization and stimulated by contact with the processes of the modern sensibility. That contact was lacking in men like Brownell and More, and its absence produced in their minds and tempers an inflexible decorum that did an even greater injustice to their own refinement of taste than it did to the books that fell under their inspection. It was the maintenance of precisely such a contact that now engaged a younger generation of critics. In 1920 *The Dial* was transformed from its senile condition of reactionary conservatism in Chicago to a new life of literary experimentation in New York, and for a decade it was the chief organ of aesthetic critics in America. With *The Criterion* of London it provided a standard for the careers of *The Hound and Horn, The Symposium, The Kenyon Review, The Sewanee Review,* and *The Hudson Review* that followed. Some of its contributors, like Conrad Aiken, Charles Trueblood, and Cuthbert Wright, adhered to the impressionist manner but keyed it to new effects by their verbal and imaginative skill in poetic analysis. The most brilliant descriptive talent of this kind appeared in Marianne Moore, who showed in her essays the same wit in selecting, discriminating, and combining the effects of an aesthetic object that she manifested in her poems.

Two other members of *The Dial's* circle carried their study of modern texts to a point of masterly exposition: Kenneth Burke by situating a book in its setting of ideas and moral influences—the "quality of mind" reduced to the basic structure and complexity of the writer's imagination; and Edmund Wilson by producing from the book in hand an illumination of the specific experience and environment that produced it. Burke, in fact, has been distinguished among contemporary American critics by the persistence and alertness of his training in ideas. It has made him less effective than many of his colleagues in the handling of the literary item. His practical grasp of stylistic and imaginative properties—in books like *Counter-Statement* (1931), *Permanence and Change* (1935), *Attitudes Toward History* (1937), *The Philosophy of Literary Form* (1941), *A Grammar of Motives* (1945), and *A Rhetoric of Motives* (1950)—is diverted by his larger effort to synthesize the aesthetic with the moral, psychological, political, and "strategic" functions of literature. But he has examined and corrected the method, tactics, and terminology of modern criticism to better effect than any other American writer. His use of scientific and psychological resources has led him to become predominantly a kind of literary phenomenologist, but no one has assessed and indicated the relevance of such resources better than he has, or more systematically.

Edmund Wilson took another direction. He fell heir to the historical method of the Nineteenth Century French critics of the line of Sainte-Beuve, Taine, and Renan. Like these he looked to literature for evidences of the social and moral forces that produced it—for the materials of, as he said, "what literary criticism ought to be—a history of man's ideas and imaginings in the setting of the conditions which have shaped them." Where this procedure has led most modern critics to a deterministic view of art, or to the cruder mechanization of art through sociological and political theory, Wilson kept it critically vigorous by his sensitive reading of the text before him, by a brilliant talent for narrative summary and exposition, and by seeing aesthetic and imaginative developments as something subtler than the social conditions which surround and at times coerce them. Wilson brought the realistic and the aesthetic attitudes into a working alliance. At one point his shift (though a strongly unorthodox one) to social and political sympathies, and his study of Marxist theory and action (*To the Finland Station,* 1940), removed him from his earlier alliance with French and aesthetic influences. But he kept the Marxist principle under alert suspicion. His study of the symbolist tradition in *Axel's Castle* (1931), one of the most valuable books in American criticism in this century, was followed by further volumes of studies—*The Triple Thinkers* (1938), *The Wound and the Bow* (1941)—in which psychological enquiry joined with his earlier aesthetic and social analysis. The result has been a long series of enquiries in which historical, Marxist, Freudian, and personal motives have been defined in a wide range of subjects, and some of the most suggestive essays of our time. This is neither an aesthetic nor an analytical criticism, but a study of literature in its human and cultural values —sometimes boldly conjectural, often inviting strenuous resistance, but always vivid, dramatically presented, focal, and stimulating, one of the most vigorous records of the experience of literature that the period has produced.

A different approach to poetic and literary problems appeared in Yvor Winters. He carried into his criticism the same severe scrutiny of verbal and formal structures that made his verse notable as an indication of changing motives and disciplines in poetry. His effort to analyze the form of modern poetry, to define its processes and find a terminology for them, to rescue both poetry and prose from the disorder of aimless experimentation, led him toward principles of a formal and conservative type. He was influenced at one point by the neoclassical arguments of Irving Babbitt; at another by classical and French models; at another by a vigorous interest of his own in the moral elements that have shaped or confused the European and American traditions in literature—thus his trenchant assessments of American individualism, "obscurantism," and modernism in such books as *Maule's Curse* (1938) and *The Anatomy of Nonsense* (1943). In *Primitivism and Decadence* (1936), as again in his collected papers in *In Defense of Reason* (1947), he provided one of the most austere and fruitful statements of the classical position, with its emphasis on intellectual and moral relevances in art, that has been written in the present century, or that has appeared in the recent criticism of any country. His work joins tradition with an intensely reverent personal conception of art in an argument that is seminal, corrective, assertively personal, yet formally and ethically ordered.

Yvor Winters

A similar sense of traditional disciplines, deliberately called "reactionary," has worked in the criticism of Allen Tate; but in him these disciplines took on wider cultural and historical reference, with specific application to the situation in modern society and morality as measured by the classic standard in Southern life. Here again the obligation of poetic analysis and formal method preceded the use of historical or moral arguments. By combining these issues he made his volume of *Reactionary Essays* (1936) an important demonstra-

Allen Tate

tion of the problems a critic faces when he attempts to harmonize modern innovation or experiment with the formal order implicit in tradition; and the same joining of standards reappeared in his *Reason in Madness* (1941) and *On the Limits of Poetry* (1948). The principle at work is a principle of wholeness and integration, and while it has sometimes emphasized special phenomena in art—the idea of "tension," for instance—it has also animated a larger view of literature and culture which has yielded some of the liveliest attacks on utilitarian, deterministic, and philosophic irrelevances in the critical controversy of the past two decades. Again this is a criticism basically moral, philosophic, in its findings, but it has kept these findings relevant to literature through the vigor of a poetic sensibility and an acute intellectual energy.

. P.
ackmur

The special distinction of R. P. Blackmur's criticism, on the other hand, lies in its elucidation of verbal and stylistic properties as clues to the quality of thought and imagination. No one except William Empson in England has carried this method to greater lengths of meticulous discrimination, and no one has shown greater patience or curiosity in linguistic, structural, and imaginative analysis. It is a method difficult to raise from the descriptive to the synthetic or judicial level, and Blackmur has not always arrived at this coördination. But the effort, whatever its success, would be worthless without the exacting scrutiny of technique that he has made in *The Double Agent* (1935), *The Expense of Greatness* (1940), and many succeeding essays. If his criticism remains indecisive at many points it is largely because he has realized so fully the complexity of the problems which an exact analysis of the text can impose on a critic.

It is in fact the thoroughness of their stylistic investigations, their rigorous study of the words, patterns, and structures of the literary object, that has not only removed the best of these aesthetic students from the irresponsible conjurings of the impressionists, but has made them far too conscious of all that is implied and involved in the creative process to bring it into easy alignment with social or moral formulae. In them the impressionist procedure is at once rationalized and corrected, and more utilitarian critical methods are revealed in their routine of inflexible prejudice and ineptitude.

V

The apparent hostility among the new critical schools after 1918 was to some extent deceptive. Beneath it there existed a secret treaty between realists and aesthetes, a recognition of the common enemy of reaction, and an implicit alliance of the kind that may be detected beneath the conflicting appearances of naturalism, impressionism, and symbolism in the French schools of the late Nineteenth Century. They joined in accepting the heritage of romanticism, however they may have varied in their use of it. They assumed the unity of man and nature on a monistic principle, and the common belief that this unity is to be realized initially through sensory and intuitive agencies. They differed chiefly in their notions of the means—the instruments of aesthetic experience and expression—by which the work of art conveys this unity. They were divided as craftsmen and temperaments, but not as believers, and the same may be said of the critics who adhered to them as prophets or defenders.

There was also a general agreement among them concerning the subject matter of art—its freedom from, its value in, moral purpose; and when a sudden reaction struck from another quarter, it threw them into an alliance more strenuous than their two decades of public debate and divergence had prepared them for. The enemy was held in check for a number of years, but he was not inactive. Books like *Democracy and Leadership, Rousseau and Romanticism,* and the eleven volumes of *Shelburne Essays* had been appearing for twenty years. Mencken had fulminated against the "gloomy humors" of Paul Elmer More for several decades, and Babbitt had raised the dust of controversy in both academic and public circles. But critics as a whole had relegated such vexations to the dustbins of the Victorian Age. They were as certain of their emancipation as they were that the day was over for reviving beliefs about the dualism of man and nature, of good and evil, of reason and instinct, or convictions about the distance that lies between the purely natural order of experience and the art which results only when prudence selects, judgment shapes, and the moral will gives ethical value to that experience. Those beliefs were implicit in the American moral tradition and a fear of their eruption was implied by Lewisohn's anthology of 1918, *A Book of Modern Criticism,* which came as a warning against the slumbering dragon of reaction; by Spingarn's manifesto of a decade earlier; and by a critical symposium printed in *The New Republic* in 1921, which formed a fresh defense of impressionism and liberal rebellion for the younger critics of the hour.

Meanwhile the reaction was organizing its forces. Its name, "Humanism," had already been accepted from Babbitt's teachings. It had representatives all over the country, chiefly on college faculties: Prosser Hall Frye promoted the cause in Nebraska; Norman Foerster in North Carolina; Robert Shafer in Ohio; a considerable phalanx in the strongholds of New England; and Stuart Sherman in Illinois before he finally confessed himself a renegade from the ranks, became a literary editor in New York, turned liberal, and lost the wit and geniality he had contributed to his first allegiance. The acknowledged leaders of these men remained More and Babbitt, who wrote the program and creed by which all of them, with due allowance for personal errors and deviations, swore.

It was a creed which defined one central enemy, the Romantic Movement; one chief source of grievance, Rousseau; one main purpose, the integration of

The Humanist Movement

literary criticism with ethical; and one chief means of deciding the quality of
a work of literature, its validity in moral qualities. Inheriting the Puritan
austerity of the early American fathers, it had skirted the skepticism of Emerson and his generation in such a way as to remain aloof from commitment to
religious faith and dogma. It preferred the discipline not of theological beliefs
but of the human norm, and it looked for salvation not by sacrificing personal
energy to an acceptance of supernatural authority, but by enhancing its sense
of human values through restraint and self-control. Art thus became a means
of judging man's nature chiefly in the degree to which it expressed this discipline.

More published his first book of essays in 1904 and there, in an essay on
"Criticism," he lamented in Nineteenth Century critics like Arnold not "any
intrinsic want of efficiency in the critical spirit, not . . . any want of moral
earnestness," but the fact that "these men were lacking in another direction:
they missed a philosophy which could bind together their moral and their
aesthetic sense, a positive principle besides the negative force of ridicule and
irony; and missing this, they left criticism more easily subject to a one-sided
and dangerous development"—that which promoted the modern heresies of
"naturalism," impressionism, subjectivity, and moral anarchy. For him literary
criticism was "the specific exercise of a faculty which works in many directions. All scholars, whether they deal with history or sociology or philosophy
or language or, in the narrower use of the word, literature, are servants of the
critical spirit, in so far as they transmit and interpret and mold the sum of
experience from man to man and generation to generation."

The Humanist ethic gave More his binding principle. At first his sense of
art and the artist's personality was vivid and penetrating, but as the *Shelburne
Essays* mounted, his responsibility to "the sum of experience" subdued it
more and more, until finally he turned away from literature and explored the
historical background of modern humanism itself, attempting to integrate the
Christian idea with the humanistic principle of Plato and the Greeks.

What he brought to American philosophic and ethical thought was one
matter; what he contributed to criticism was another. He supplied a model of
erudition and high seriousness that admitted no suspicion of purely aesthetic
or vaguely cultural leanings. But unfortunately this model came to shed less
and less light on either the contemporary world around him or the literature
it produced; it stiffened his sensibilities as well as his integrity; and while he
never erred through the pedantry of his younger colleagues, his confinement
of acceptable art in the tight circle of his moral prejudice caused him to reject
the very art that would really have invigorated and humanized his doctrines.
He believed that "literature divorced from life is an empty pursuit," but his
conceptions of literature's dependence on experience became as arbitrary and
as remote from the moral struggles of his contemporaries as his sense of the

"meaning of life" stopped short of the understanding that kindles in imagination or language the fire of an overwhelming conviction. His belief that such conviction had failed to appear in modern literature may have been a reflection of its failure in his own thought.

Irving Babbitt

Irving Babbitt was always a keener controversialist than More, and to him fell the more polemical role in the Humanist revival that broke out late in the 'twenties. He was less a critic of books than of ideas, and the ideas he attacked inevitably led him back to the chief source of his vexations, Rousseau. He assayed creative works rarely, but made an exhaustive study of the influences and cultural circumstances that produce them—educational systems, political movements, religious bodies, academic standards, classical traditions, ethical beliefs. The modern condition of these he invariably deplored as anarchic and decadent. He accepted in his early years the classic ideal, and declared himself the enemy of all that opposed it under the romantic canon: democratic individualism, freedom of press and speech, free aesthetic experiment, any vestige of the eccentric or idiosyncratic in art or conduct. He formulated the tenets to which the younger Humanists subscribed—the ideals of wholeness, proportion, and the human norm; the constants of tradition as against the limiting "specialism" of the time-spirit; the discipline of reason, of imagination when controlled by reason, and of the virtues of restraint and humility which are the final evidence of the ethical dignity of man.

Babbitt's work had its aesthetic motive, and his prescription of virtues was intended to apply to criticism an instrument of discipline in the disordered world of modern culture. When he stated his rule for critics he made that much clear: the critic must "rate creation with reference to some standard set both above his own temperament and that of the creator. . . . He will begin to have taste only when he refers the creative expression and his impression of it to some standard that is set above both." This is a worthy precept for any kind of rational judgment, and Babbitt had the worthy intention of correcting by means of it the sterility and solipsism of critical license. But the validity of such a rule depends wholly on its grasp of the two terms it employs: the integrity of the "impression" gained from a literary investigation, and the authority of the "standard" to which it is referred. Babbitt's failure in sensibility was extreme: in his last book, *On Being Creative* (1931), he equated modern writers like Dreiser, Joyce, and Dos Passos with no effort at discriminating their qualities, and the standard he defined in Greek and Latin masterpieces proved so inert that he was incapable of sympathizing with, and therefore understanding, any but a few isolated or academic imitations of it in the past eight centuries. Babbitt's distinguished mind was a prey to this mechanistic and pharisaical inflexibility of doctrine; his critical limitations (as opposed to his scholarly and historical eminence) have been well pointed out by Yvor Winters: "His analysis of literary principles appears to me to be gravely vitiated by an almost complete ignorance of the manner in which the moral intelligence actually gets into poetry."

The battle over Humanism was unfortunately conducted in a mood too full of heat, rancor, and confusion to represent the issues involved fairly. Thus it appeared as a last stand of the Puritan tradition against the enemies that had multiplied around it. What it might have achieved in correcting the aimlessness and vulgarity of the more irresponsible talents around it was as much nullified by its own intolerance and imperviousness as by the violence of the forces it stirred to attack. There were looseness, irresponsibility, and crudity to reprove, and Humanism left certain good effects behind, even though they bore little resemblance to what Babbitt and More demanded. But it never attacked its problems squarely. It aimed to correct and guide the conflicts of the modern consciousness, but it succeeded chiefly in ignoring them. It reduced imaginative and creative processes to a mechanical routine. It missed the wider and profounder sympathy of a genuinely religious spirit and at the same time failed to grasp the struggles of the skeptical spirit in seeking a basis of values in experience. Thus it fell ambiguously between the rigor of realistic experience that has produced the valid thought of naturalist writers, and the genuine metaphysical convictions of Frenchmen like Gilson and Maritain, whose interpretations of Thomistic aesthetic doctrine were not for some time to encourage a similar activity in America. The controversy of 1929 and 1930 centered in serious issues, but these were reduced to the obtuse didacticism of the "genteel tradition," the pedantry and intolerance of an academic principle. When it died down it left the critical situation much as it found it, and another type of moral argument—that of the social critics and proletarian revolutionaries—took up the attack on such irresponsibility as was held to reside in realist and aesthetic liberalism. A new alignment of critics soon appeared, one closer to the specific conditions of modern writing and therefore more vigorous in its appeal to the public and in its grasp of the problems of imaginative literature.

VI

It was a more realistic attack that now rose against the free critical traffic of the 1920's. That decade ended under darker clouds than Humanism had conjured up. When the economic disaster of 1929 struck, it dropped its bolts on one of the most productive literary periods America had seen. The high hopes and privileges of the liberal generation were bent at a blow, and prophets of disaster—like Dreiser and Robinson—who had spoken in the hour of general illusion, found a new honor. From Paris the aesthetes returned with shorn incomes and roughly opened eyes, finding their historian in Malcolm Cowley, whose *Exile's Return* described their awakening from the "religion of art" to the realities of making a living in a jobless world. The confidences

iberalism
nder
ittack

of 1912 or 1918 sank as swiftly as the graphlines on stockbrokers' charts. The realist and aesthetic critics found their claims diminishing under harsh dispute, and deserters from their ranks began to take up the study and defense of economic arguments. Humanism had reacted chiefly against the claims of naturalism, but the awakened sense of social responsibility in reformers took aesthetic and liberal doctrines as its chief object of attack. It was by this alignment of creeds that the major critical issues of the 1930's were defined.

The necessity in criticism of a social principle was not a new argument. Whitman, Howells, and Adams were three of its early prophets, and the liberals of Bourne's generation made it a dominant tenet in their program of critical realism. These pioneers, however, submitted too easily to the malady of the humanitarian ideal to satisfy their inheritors. They accepted the grandeurs of the American future in too mystical a spirit, compromising too easily with the hopes of rugged individualism or democratic culture, and holding aloof from commitment to more positive beliefs. These required in their simplest essentials an attack on the capitalistic monopoly and competitive license which Howells, whatever sense he may have had of the ethical defects of American society, considered the proper complement of democratic enterprise. The Nineteenth Century reformers most acceptable to the American way of life had been acceptable because they left their revolutionary counsels at a mid-point of compromise, and stopped short of imposing the technical and forcible reforms of economic socialism. Some books were written, however, outside the literary field which forecast those reforms in highly trenchant language, and these in time were to influence critics of sociological sympathies more than the manuals of their own craft. The most important of these was Thorstein Veblen's *Theory of the Leisure Class*. More recently American criticism itself had turned toward economic premises: Upton Sinclair published *The Industrial Republic* as early as 1907 and *Mammonart* as late as 1925; and his angle of literary interpretation was turned to more aesthetic uses by V. F. Calverton in his "sociological criticism of literature," *The Newer Spirit* (1925), and in *The Liberation of American Literature* (1930). Both these men were urging a social principle while their recent rivals were still absorbed by now-repudiated liberal or aesthetic allegiances. But the shortcomings now commonly charged against them on dialectic grounds were fully as obvious on aesthetic grounds when their books were first published. They made literature a function of the social order without having arrived at a realistic articulation of the creative imagination with social necessities, and at the same time without a technique of rationalization which could cope successfully with the subtleties of aesthetic, as opposed to economic, experience. Calverton, though he was later to express a healthy dislike of the mechanistic routine of the average Marxist interpretation, accepted too smoothly the deterministic procedure of Taine. The result is that his *Liberation of American*

Literature is chiefly interesting for the lengths to which it pushed a prejudice and a method.

ocialist
nd
Marxist
Criticism

The social line of criticism since 1930 has profited by a situation much more conducive to serious discipline than existed before. For one thing, controversy is sufficiently active to offset the extravagances of party politics. For another, the defenders of the aesthetic approach to literature have stirred themselves to a more severe line of reasoning in order to match the subtleties of the materialist dialectic, and thus benefited their own cause while challenging the extremes of its opposite. Again, fresh growths of socially motivated literature have revealed the pitfalls of propaganda so obviously as to provide a caution to critics who have defended this function in art too glibly. And finally, the profound economic distress of the times has aroused a general agreement on the moral ends of literature, spurred a critical examination of them, and established much more forcefully than formerly the necessity of seeing what constitutes the truth and integrity of a work of literature before it can produce its desired effects in social or moral regeneration. Obviously these benefits have been accompanied by corresponding evils. Critical activity has been distracted by false simplifications and partisan bias. Its magazines have substituted personal abuse for sober thinking, and eloquence for logic. There has flourished a loose contempt for whatever is out of momentary fashion, and a consequent discarding of many literary works that might enlighten the dispute (or even support the cause of their condemners) to far greater advantage than the shoddy tracts that are often seized upon as profoundly significant. And there has risen so slovenly and uncritical a warfare of terms and premises —debates over the "function" of art, "utility," "ideology," "mass consciousness," "bourgeois" versus "proletarian," and "autonomy" versus "propaganda" —that the mere communication of intelligence about these causes, lacking as it does the very discipline of logic or dialectic that is the boasted advantage of their exponents, has lapsed into dilemma and confusion.

The implications of this problem are too complex to admit of easy statement. But the responsibilities of criticism remain at the same time too emphatic and unmistakable to allow the term to be applied to nine-tenths of what has passed by that title in the journals and newspapers of the past eighteen years. (This is equally true, however, of other kinds of apologetic; it would be unjust to make the reservation against the social critic any severer than against the common types of religious or political.) Yet the work of a number of writers in this field shows exceptional distinction, either in historical analysis or in a careful discrimination of issues. On the historical side the best statements appear in the last chapter of Wilson's *Axel's Castle,* where the divergence of art and life, pure poetry and social realism, in modern literature is described; in Cowley's *Exile's Return,* where the same division in the lives of present-day artists and critics is defined; and in such literary memoirs as

Granville Hicks's *John Reed* or Joseph Freeman's *An American Testament*, which form sequels to the sort of biographical study of literary problems that Bourne wrote in his *Literary Radical*. The most ambitious attempt to bring the literary history of America into alignment with the Marxist tenets was that of Granville Hicks's *Great Tradition* (1933), but its coherence of argument and graphic distinction are soon rendered suspect by the facility with which it accepts or dismisses the writers of American literature according to the degree to which they satisfy his highly simplified and crudely applied proposition on the interdependence of literature and economic law. It is their talent in a more closely reasoned, more broadly and soundly perceptive kind of interpretation that has made the essays of Phillip Rahv, William Phillips, Dwight Macdonald, and their contributors to *Partisan Review* and *Politics* a notable improvement over those of Hicks, Michael Gold, Joshua Kunitz, and other onetime writers in *The New Masses, Mainstream,* and other official Marxist (meaning, eventually, official Stalinist) organs. Though Hicks and a number of other spokesmen resigned from official Marxism around 1939 or 1940, their successors have continued in the prescribed line of Marxist literary doctrine; but it remained for journals like *Partisan Review* and *Politics* to correct the abuses of "leftist" and socialist interpretation and to produce the keenest radical journalism that has yet appeared in the United States.

Kenneth Burke's interest in social relevances in literature reinforced that distinction. So did the contributions to political-literary controversy that came from the novelist James T. Farrell in *A Note on Literary Criticism* (1936), *The League of Frightened Philistines* (1945), *The Fate of Writing in America* (1946), and *Literature and Morality* (1947). These essays were prompted by the flagrant lapses in valid reasoning among social critics, but equally by the regressive nationalism, commercialism, and sentimental special pleading that succeeded to Marxist polemic in the 1940's. They formed a challenging reproof to offenders and a sketch of necessary corrections for extremists of both types. They served further to remind the serious public that an escape from the mechanical routine of the average social criticism has come from men who have known, by their own creative practice, the creative task too intimately to permit it to be humbled by propagandist or official assignments. Thus is the value of the poetic criticism of Robert Penn Warren, Austin Warren, Louise Bogan, Horace Gregory, Delmore Schwartz, John Berryman, Randall Jarrell, Cleanth Brooks, Rolfe Humphries, and (now that he has become an American) W. H. Auden; or the criticism of fiction by Robert Penn Warren, Katherine Anne Porter, William Troy, Lionel Trilling, Diana Trilling, Alfred Kazin, Richard Chase, Mark Schorer, Albert Guérard, Jr., Irving Howe, Robert Gorham Davis, and Isaac Rosenfeld.

The firmer activity in force among these critics has been motivated by such purposes as were announced fifteen years ago by Phillips and Rahv:

Unfortunately many misguided enthusiasts of revolution, effacing their own experience, take for their subject-matter the public philosophy as such, or attempt to adorn with rhetorical language conventionalized patterns of feeling and action. What they don't see is that these patterns are, in the final analysis, just as impersonal as the philosophy itself. . . . If there is to be an ever-fresh balance between the accent of the poet and the attitude he shares with other people, he must understand the connection between what is *real* to him as an individual and what is *real* to him as a partisan of some given philosophy.

A warning from official quarters came from Joseph Freeman in 1935, in his introduction to the anthology *Proletarian Literature in the United States*. Admitting the immaturity of a great share of the writing and criticism of his colleagues, he indicated how much caution and discipline is required there:

No party resolution, no government decree, can produce art, or transform an agitator into a poet. A party card does not automatically endow a communist with artistic genius. Whatever it is that makes an artist, as distinguished from a scientist or man of action, it is something beyond the power of anyone to produce deliberately. But once the artist is there, once there is the man with the specific sensibility, the mind, the emotions, the images, the gift of language which make the creative writer, he is not a creature in a vacuum.

And Newton Arvin, who during a quarter century has remained one of the steadiest and most mature inspectors of the social standard in literature, gave in 1931 an early hint toward the correction of abuses at both extremes of aesthetic autonomy and political doctrine:

The case for a proletarian literature is not always cogently stated or wisely defended—any more than the case against it. One must insist that to adopt the proletarian point of view does not mean, for a novelist, to deal solely with economic conflicts, or, for a poet, to be a voice only for protest, momentous as both these things are and *implicit* as they are bound to be. That a truly proletarian literature, for us in America at least, would mean a break with the mood of self-pity, with the cult of romantic separatism, with sickly subjectivism and melodramatic misanthropy —this much is almost too clear to deserve stating. But the duty of the critic is certainly not to file an order for a particular sort of fiction or poetry before the event; his duty is to clarify, as best he can, the circumstances in which fiction and poetry must take shape, and to rationalize their manifestations when they arrive. For the moment, the important thing is that American criticism should define its position: in the midst of so much confusion, so much wasted effort, so much hesitation, this will itself be an advance.

These statements, while perhaps embarrassingly elementary, indicated the uneasy conscience that existed among the critics of the Left during the 1930's. By the time that decade came to an end, the high tide of Marxist and political influence in criticism had spent itself and begun to recede. Some critics of its excesses—Max Eastman, or Farrell, or the editors of *Partisan Review* and

Politics, or Edmund Wilson in his essay "Marxism and Literature," to name men of differing standards—had learned the dangers of that excess through their close participation in the radical political movement. They had found, all of them, a genuine schooling in political and social thought through their alliance, but they had also discovered the discomforts, didacticism, and strait-jacketing mentality under which both literature and criticism labor when subjected to party or political pressures. The outbreak of war in 1939 and the momentary alliance of Marxism with Nazism counted for a good deal in the recoil from official Marxist pressure which many partisans and sympathizers showed around 1940. The ensuing decade of the 1940's was by no means to make the critical problem simpler, but its political confinement was broken; the pressure of a revived nationalism, Americanism, or propagandist sentiment presented a new difficulty on the popular level of writing and journalism. But the war years also showed, unexpectedly, a revival of faith in aesthetic and moral standards. The revival and rediscovery of Henry James was one sign of it. So was the work done by a new series of critical journals—*The Kenyon Review* under John Crowe Ransom, the now independent and anti-Stalinist *Partisan Review,* the renovated *Sewanee* under Tate's editorship, or more independent ventures like *Accent* in Illinois, the surrealist *View* in New York, the classical-aesthetic *Hudson Review.* What survived of Marxist argument became more and more confined to the waning *New Masses,* to its affiliate *Mainstream,* to the scholarly quarterly *Science and Society,* and to the official Communist columns of *The Daily Worker.* The radical "red decade" of the thirties had recorded in its agitations and controversies a profound conflict in modern society and politics. Criticism played a part in this, but in the 'forties it was to reassert and reclaim its more specific and proper province. A revival of aesthetic, but also of moral and philosophic, claims appeared among both writers and critics, and a new decade of revision and critical discipline began.

VII

By the time the contemporary movement in American literature arrived at the fifth decade of the present century, criticism was able to take stock of a progress that had enriched its work and methods in a number of essential ways. The techniques of historical research had matured both through gains in scholarship and through philosophic enquiry. Aesthetic attitudes had outgrown their earlier preciosity or immaturity and become sharpened by analysis and a disciplined discrimination. The social, economic, and political elements of art had been redefined through the controversies and pressures of modern social thought. Certain kinds of scientific technique and theory—those of psychology, psychoanalysis, of philological and semantic research, of logical analysis, of biography, of the economic interpretation of history—had contributed both suggestion and new materials to critical method. The competition and interaction of these methods among critics had spurred literary students to an energy of controversy, a liveliness of dispute, that made the profession of criticism one of the most challenging in the entire field of literature.

There can be little question that the criticism of the past quarter century will be recorded in American literature as one of its liveliest chapters. The critic of literature has joined his forces with those of the creative writer himself. It is scarcely disputable that it has been the poets and novelists of our time who have shown the most vigorous *critical* sensibility, who have written the most forceful works of an imaginative order. A condition true of France, England, and Germany has become true also of the United States. The function of literary criticism has been defined as the analysis and evaluation of the forces already at work in a living literature, rather than to provide the impetus for new work; but this is a conception no longer as tenable as it used to be. A sound criticism does both these things. The existence of an active, virtually an organized, criticism during the past two or three decades—a criticism in working harmony with the best of contemporary creation—is possibly the most convincing evidence of the special character and importance of American literature at the present stage of its history.

While the writers of this criticism, like their fellow workers in fiction, poetry, and drama, have continued in several distinct lines of intention and method that had already declared themselves as long ago as 1925, they were aware, by 1950, of a change in their status and responsibility. They had not abandoned the idea of the "new"—of aesthetic innovation, of moral and intellectual revision, of social and political enquiry—so insistent in the earlier flush of literary radicalism or innovation; but a decade like the 1940's, however arresting or discouraging to original effort, was bound to impress its crisis upon the minds of both writers and critics and to impose that crisis in terms of the morality, the responsibility, the human and active values, of their craft. Their problem best defined itself in the fact that critics rediscovered that their business was that of a craft or an art; that only by maintaining its rights and existence as such could it hope to survive for higher or ulterior ends.

The pioneers of modern American criticism had by 1940 disappeared or turned to concerns other than those of literature. Babbitt and More died in the 1930's; Santayana turned to his later philosophical summations and personal records; Mencken to philological research and to reminiscence; Van Wyck Brooks to history and conservatism; Eliot himself, in spite of his continuing work in poetry and a persistent interest in craftsmanship, to an increasing program of religious and cultural enquiry—*The Idea of a Christian Society, The Classics and the Man of Letters, The Man of Letters and the*

Future of Europe, Notes towards the Definition of Culture. While a new generation of American scholars—F. O. Matthiessen, Alfred Kazin, Newton Arvin, Perry Miller, Lionel Trilling, Mark Van Doren, Allen Tate, Harry Levin, F. W. Dupee—inspected the bases of American experience and its bearing on cultural or literary achievement with a view to correcting or extending the arguments of their predecessors, Van Wyck Brooks, V. L. Parrington, Randolph Bourne, Constance Rourke, and Edmund Wilson, the specialist in criticism found himself facing the need for a new program of purpose and strategy. The result was not a single program, of course, but a series of programs whose radical divergences did not preclude a certain community of intention and effort.

The present situation in American criticism, at the mid-point of the Twentieth Century, may be described as falling into four or five fairly distinct lines of activity. (1) There is a continuing investigation of the social and cultural bases of literature, sequel to the critical realism that began around 1912 and continued through the political and economic controversies of the 'thirties, but which now attempts to bring such realism to terms with aesthetic and moral claims: thus the work of men like Lionel Trilling and F. O. Matthiessen, of Edmund Wilson in his later books, of Philip Rahv, William Phillips, William Barrett, Eliseo Vivas, Alfred Kazin. (2) There is likewise a continuation of the aesthetic line initiated by Pound and carried on by Eliot, now bent more systematically than ever toward integrating the study of craftsmanship with metaphysical or philosophic elements in literature: thus John Crowe Ransom with his demand for an "ontological" criticism, Allen Tate with his principle of "reaction" toward the unity of the moral tradition in art, Yvor Winters with his emphasis on an order based on the responsibility of moral integrity and reason, Austin Warren with another emphasis on the idea of "order," Cleanth Brooks with his studies of the interaction of tradition and irony in modern poetry. (3) The discipline of formal and textual analysis also continues, now rejecting the empirical methods of I. A. Richards or the scientific claims of logical, semantic, or pragmatic positivists in order to recover from classical doctrine, from Aristotle, or from formal philosophy an approach of wider range, eclectic choice, but aesthetic wholeness as a corrective to monistic emphasis and as a source of values: thus the work of Kenneth Burke, of Blackmur in certain of his recent undertakings, and of R. S. Crane and his Chicago colleagues. (4) This discipline has an ally in a renewed effort to apply criticism to the practical business of education by revising the teaching of poetry and prose through making the given text an organism of craft and values: thus Burke throughout his essays, Yvor Winters in his analysis of styles and poetic forms, the textbooks of Cleanth Brooks and Robert Penn Warren, the program of Ransom and his disciples, of Crane and his group, and of the conferences, seminars, and projects that have brought criticism

Programs
Criticism:
1940–195

more actively into the American college—Harvard, Chicago, Princeton, Stanford, Columbia, Yale, Iowa, Kenyon, Minnesota, Bennington—than was ever the case in its earlier history. (5) There is, further, the work of critics who are attempting to make viable in literary study the findings in related fields of enquiry—psychology, anthropology, semantics, history—with their disclosure of ethnic, mythic, and ritualistic elements that operate in art: thus the enquiries stimulated by scholars or theorists like Fraser, Freud, Rivers, Harrison, Jung, Spengler, and Malinowski, and carried into criticism by Americans like Burke, Wilson, Blackmur, W. H. Auden, Richard Chase, Stanley Edgar Hyman, Suzanne Langer, Joseph Campbell, Frederick Hoffman. And against these specialists in method there must be counted the students who aim to restore a broader program of human and realistic values to the examination of literature in order to correct the specialization of aesthetic, technical, and archetypal approaches: thus the defenders of a revived historical and humanistic view of literature—Harry Levin, Eric Bentley, Robert Gorham Davis, David Daiches, Alfred Kazin.

To name these phases of recent American criticism is, of course, to arrive at little more than rough approximations of the critical programs and positions now visible on the scene. To name exponents of them, as has been done above, is to suggest alliances of purpose where none may exist, or a simplicity of purpose and method which is unjustified. The critics named here are frequently at radical odds with one another in the specific intention and results of their work; a charting of their activity must allow for the injustice of suggesting a greater unity of motive, a simpler harmony of effort, than has actually been arrived at. Yet the programs here indicated are at work in American criticism today, and must account for the stimulating forces that compete in its advancement.

Also at work are certain fundamental problems that remain basic to the modern critic's task. The correction of the romantic and idealistic excesses of the native American tradition is one of them. Another is the correction of that "dissociation of sensibility" which Eliot defined thirty years ago as a radical liability of the modern intelligence as it expresses itself in art, and which, by his advocacy of the aesthetic and moral unity of literature, he followed Henry James in resisting. It remains today as essential a problem in the determination of values as it was when Eliot carried it forward out of the work of James, Gourmont, and Hulme, and gave it to his disciples as a basic responsibility of their task. A third concern of the critic is his resistance to the mechanistic and deterministic conceptions of art that descended to the Twentieth Century from the Nineteenth. Once such conceptions were historical or biological in origin; later they became economic, political, Marxist; later still they became psychological—Freudian, Jungian, Gestalt; more recently they have become anthropological, ethnic, and racial. Under whatever tenet, they have had the effect of forcing upon literature causal or conditioning references which tend ultimately to deny or reduce its aesthetic existence, and thus to impose on the critic the duty of recovering that existence in terms of its necessity, even its autonomy, as art. There can no longer be said to exist, as among earlier aesthetic or impressionist schools, any serious desire to make art or literature an isolated phenomenon, an absolute end in itself, a completely self-justifying or self-sustaining mode of experience; but there does persist, and now more seriously than ever, a passion to show art as possessing an integrity of its own, its own wholeness of existence and experience, a superiority to use and practical relevance. And this means that criticism today demands an aesthetic not arrived at by simplifying art through abstracting it from life but based on a relevance of art to life so continuous and inclusive as to make art the one valid means that remains to us of doing justice to the wholeness of experience and history. Thus the word *aesthetic* has come to imply a function, a responsibility, an inescapable commitment in the critic, that it never had in its earlier and more facile uses.

Perhaps no earlier space of fifty years has seen the conflict of so many critical schools as the half century which has been sketched here. America has felt the force and agitation of all of them, from those that have looked on art as no longer "even by implication a device for improving the mind" to those that recognize neither the artist nor the critic except in the role of moralist and reformer. This outline of developments has necessarily simplified the ideas of the critics it has discussed. It has barely suggested the problems in modern life and thought that have made their difficulties great. But it has attempted to trace a line of activity that brings us to the present moment, and even if it does little to solve the perplexities or answer the questions of those who go to criticism for guidance and advice, it may show why such perplexities exist; why, in fact, they exist in the critic himself and give his work, if he is faithful to the art and the age around him, its special importance in our time.

The title of critic is no longer allowed to the mere sampler of books, the enthusiast for art, the adventurer among masterpieces. Neither is it permitted to the custodian of academic convention, the official moralist, the protector of vested interests. A few men have written beautiful prose or forceful polemic in these roles, but real criticism comes much harder than that. It ranks next to art itself in the insight it commands into the intellectual and spiritual problems of an age and of humanity. It studies the most intense and subtle forms which those problems assume—the forms of literature. Unless the critic realizes that he is dealing with such problems in their fullest complexity, their most intense and vital focus of meaning, he is not likely to hold the respect of the serious reader or the serious artist, or to make a contribution to the intelligence of his contemporaries.

The difficulty with a great share of modern criticism is that it decides these problems long before it understands what literature makes of them. It looks for them in the shape of systematic argument, of practical statements of emotion and belief, of useful morality, applicable wisdom, or formulated conclusions. No definition of art was ever worth listening to that claimed for it no purpose but the rendering of the subtleties and conditions of human experience in such terms. That, however, is what many critics and readers continue to demand of it, and that is why they defeat their purposes as students of literature and do so little to advance the value of art, the intelligence of society, or even the causes they claim to defend.

The best contemporary critics, in America or elsewhere, have won their first distinction by refusing to be complacent, discreet, official, or easy to accept. Such virtues afflicted their calling when Poe, Whitman, and Henry James began to disturb the scene; whenever they regain prestige, criticism falls into pedantry, loses touch with art, lapses into abstract formulation or inert theory. Occasionally they threaten to return, but that danger is no longer so likely. Another has taken its place: the danger of making criticism, as well as art, the agent of propaganda, public morality, mass prejudice, or regimented opinion. When that kind of coercion succeeds, the critic falls into fully as great an impotence as when he submits to academic pedantry or polite discretion. However noble his cause, his claim to the title of critic is fully as spurious. He may express a rightful contempt of academic routine or the irresponsibilities of "impressionism" and "liberalism," but he may merely be shirking his own responsibility when he does so, and he is likely to have little of value to say about literature. Criticism has many obligations—to morality, to science, to philosophy, to society—but its one certain assurance of failure comes when it prefers these obligations to its first and primary duty—its contact with a living and active literature and with the forces in experience and the human personality that make such a literature possible.

We have had in our time a number of descriptions of the "perfect critic." If perfection is wanted or is to be kept in view as a possible goal, the simplest rule for it probably takes the form of requiring in the critic everything in the way of sensitiveness and perception, even of verbal skill, that the artist himself possesses. But the critic, instead of expressing his intelligence, explains it; instead of realizing it under the conditions of an art, he defines, examines, and justifies it by the laws of reason; instead of writing poetry or fiction, he decides why and how others have written them, and how successfully. It is only when he has made that decision to the fullest extent of his sensibility and intelligence that the critic can use his findings effectively and make his contribution to the living body of literature.

The American critic, arriving at the middle of the Twentieth Century, has as little right as ever to rest in pride or complacency, but he may at least take stock of an improvement in his status and office. He has succeeded in making criticism an active part of contemporary literature and culture. He may turn for support to a number of his fellow citizens—Henry James the first among them—who have not only assured him that his work is worth doing but have done a good deal to show him how it can be carried out. He lacks none of the conditions and challenges that are needed to keep his faculties alert, his equipment vigorous, and his purpose serious. He has made a tradition and defined a function for himself in the course of a hundred years which it has become his unmistakable duty to defend, to justify, and to keep alive. His work has not become easy. It has, however, become inescapable.

PART I

Situation and Prospectus

HENRY JAMES

Criticism

[1891]

IF LITERARY criticism may be said to flourish among us at all, it certainly flourishes immensely, for it flows through the periodical press like a river that has burst its dikes. The quantity of it is prodigious, and it is a commodity of which, however the demand may be estimated, the supply will be sure to be in any supposable extremity the last thing to fail us. What strikes the observer above all, in such an affluence, is the unexpected proportion the discourse uttered bears to the objects discoursed of—the paucity of examples, of illustrations and productions, and the deluge of doctrine suspended in the void; the profusion of talk and the contraction of experiment, of what one may call literary conduct. This, indeed, ceases to be an anomaly as soon as we look at the conditions of contemporary journalism. Then we see that these conditions have engendered the practice of "reviewing"—a practice that in general has nothing in common with the art of criticism. Periodical literature is a huge, open mouth which has to be fed—a vessel of immense capacity which has to be filled. It is like a regular train which starts at an advertised hour, but which is free to start only if every seat be occupied. The seats are many, the train is ponderously long, and hence the manufacture of dummies for the seasons when there are not passengers enough. A stuffed mannikin is thrust into the empty seat, where it makes a creditable figure till the end of the journey. It looks sufficiently like a passenger, and you know it is not one only when you perceive that it neither says anything nor gets out. The guard attends to it when the train is shunted, blows the cinders from its wooden face and gives a different crook to its elbow, so that it may serve for another run. In this way, in a well-conducted periodical, the blocks of *remplissage* are the dummies of criticism—the recurrent, regulated breakers in the tide of talk. They have a reason for being, and the situation is simpler when we perceive it. It helps to explain the disproportion I just mentioned, as well, in many a case, as the quality of the particular discourse. It helps us to understand that the "organs of public opinion" must be no less copious than punctual, that publicity must maintain its high standard, that ladies and gentlemen may turn an honest penny by the free expenditure of ink. It gives us a glimpse of the high figure

47

presumably reached by all the honest pennies accumulated in the cause, and throws us quite into a glow over the march of civilization and the way we have organized our conveniences. From this point of view it might indeed go far towards making us enthusiastic about our age. What is more calculated to inspire us with a just complacency than the sight of a new and flourishing industry, a fine economy of production? The great business of reviewing has, in its roaring routine, many of the signs of blooming health, many of the features which beguile one into rendering an involuntary homage to successful enterprise.

Yet it is not to be denied that certain captious persons are to be met who are not carried away by the spectacle, who look at it much askance, who see but dimly whither it tends, and who find no aid to vision even in the great light (about itself, its spirit, and its purposes, among other things) that it might have been expected to diffuse. "Is there any such great light at all?" we may imagine the most restless of the sceptics to inquire, "and isn't the effect rather one of a certain kind of pretentious and unprofitable gloom?" The vulgarity, the crudity, the stupidity which this cherished combination of the offhand review and of our wonderful system of publicity have put into circulation on so vast a scale may be represented, in such a mood, as an unprecedented invention for darkening counsel. The bewildered spirit may ask itself, without speedy answer, What is the function in the life of man of such a periodicity of platitude and irrelevance? Such a spirit will wonder how the life of man survives it, and, above all, what is much more important, how literature resists it; whether, indeed, literature does resist it and is not speedily going down beneath it. The signs of this catastrophe will not in the case we suppose be found too subtle to be pointed out—the failure of distinction, the failure of style, the failure of knowledge, the failure of thought. The case is therefore one for recognizing with dismay that we are paying a tremendous price for the diffusion of penmanship and opportunity; that the multiplication of endowments for chatter may be as fatal as an infectious disease; that literature lives essentially, in the sacred depths of its being, upon example, upon perfection wrought; that, like other sensitive organisms, it is highly susceptible of demoralization, and that nothing is better calculated than irresponsible pedagogy to make it close its ears and lips. To be puerile and untutored about it is to deprive it of air and light, and the consequence of its keeping bad company is that it loses all heart. We may, of course, continue to talk about it long after it has bored itself to death, and there is every appearance that this is mainly the way in which our descendants will hear of it. They will, however, acquiesce in its extinction.

This, I am aware, is a dismal conviction, and I do not pretend to state the case gayly. The most I can say is that there are times and places in which it strikes one as less desperate than at others. One of the places is Paris, and one of the times is some comfortable occasion of being there. The custom of rough-and-ready reviewing is, among the French, much less rooted than with us, and the dignity of criticism is, to my perception, in consequence much higher. The art is felt to be one of the most difficult, the most delicate, the most occasional; and the material on which it is exercised is subject to selection, to restriction. 'That is, whether or no the French are always right as to what they do notice, they strike me as infallible as to what they don't. They publish hundreds of books which are never noticed at all, and yet they are much neater bookmakers than we. It is recognized that such volumes have nothing to say to the critical sense, that they do not belong to literature, and that the possession of the critical sense is exactly what makes it impossible to read them and dreary to discuss them—places them, as a part of critical experience, out of the question. The critical sense, in France, *ne se dérange pas*, as the phrase is, for so little. No one would deny, on the other hand, that when it does set itself in motion it goes further than with us. It handles the subject in general with finer finger-tips. The bluntness of ours, as tactile implements addressed to an exquisite process, is still sometimes surprising, even after frequent exhibition. We blunder in and out of the affair as if it were a railway station—the easiest and most public of the arts. It is in reality the most complicated and the most particular. The critical sense is so far from frequent that it is absolutely rare, and the possession of the cluster of qualities that minister to it is one of the highest distinctions. It is a gift inestimably precious and beautiful; therefore, so far from thinking that it passes overmuch from hand to hand, one knows that one has only to stand by the counter an hour to see that business is done with baser coin. We have too many small schoolmasters; yet not only do I not question in literature the high utility of criticism, but I should be tempted to say that the part it plays may be the supremely beneficent one when it proceeds from deep sources, from the efficient combination of experience and perception. In this light one sees the critic as the real helper of the artist, a torch-bearing outrider, the interpreter, the brother. The more the tune is noted and the direction observed the more we shall enjoy the convenience of a critical literature. When one thinks of the outfit required for free work in this spirit, one is ready to pay almost any homage to the intelligence that has put it on; and when one considers the noble figure completely equipped—armed *cap-à-pie* in curiosity and sympathy—one falls in love with the apparition. It certainly represents the knight who has knelt through his long vigil and who has the piety of his office. For there is something sacrificial in his function, inasmuch as he offers himself as a general touchstone. To lend himself, to project himself and steep himself, to feel and feel till he understands, and to understand so well that he can say, to have perception at the pitch of passion and expression as embracing as the air, to be infinitely curious and incorrigibly patient, and yet plastic and inflammable and determinable, stooping to conquer and serving to direct —these are fine chances for an active mind, chances to add the idea of independent beauty to the conception of success. Just in proportion as he is sentient and restless, just in proportion as he reacts and reciprocates and penetrates, is the critic a valuable instrument; for in literature assuredly criticism *is* the critic, just as art is the artist; it being assuredly the artist who invented art and the critic who invented criticism, and not the other way round.

And it is with the kinds of criticism exactly as it is with the kinds of art— the best kind, the only kind worth speaking of, is the kind that springs from the liveliest experience. There are a hundred labels and tickets, in all this matter, that have been pasted on from the outside and appear to exist for the convenience of passers-by; but the critic who lives *in* the house, ranging through its innumerable chambers, knows nothing about the bills on the front. He only knows that the more impressions he has the more he is able to record, and that the more he is saturated, poor fellow, the more he can give out. His life, at this rate, is heroic, for it is immensely vicarious. He has to understand for others, to answer for them; he is always under arms. He knows that the whole honor of the matter, for him, besides the success in his own eyes, depends upon his being indefatigably supple, and that is a formidable order. Let me not speak, however, as if his work were a conscious grind, for the sense of effort is easily lost in the enthusiasm of curiosity. Any vocation has its hours of intensity that is so closely connected with life. That of the critic, in literature, is connected doubly, for he deals with life at second-hand as well as at first; that is, he deals with the experience of others, which he resolves into his own, and not of those invented and selected others with whom the novelist makes comfortable terms, but with the uncompromising swarm of authors, the clamorous children of history. He has to make them as vivid and as free as the novelist makes *his* puppets, and yet he has, as the phrase is, to take them as they come. We must be easy with him if the picture, even when the aim has really been to penetrate, is sometimes confused, for there are baffling and there are thankless subjects; and we make everything up to him by the peculiar purity of our esteem when the portrait is really, like the happy portraits of the other art, a text preserved by translation.

From *Essays in London and Elsewhere* by Henry James. Copyright, 1893, by Harper & Brothers. Copyright, 1921, by Mrs. Henry James. Reprinted by permission of Harper & Brothers. First published in *The New Review*, Vol. IV (May, 1891), pp. 398–401, under the title "The Science of Criticism."

The Question of the Opportunities
[1898]

ANY fresh start of speech today on American literature seems to me so in-evitably a more direct and even a slightly affrighted look at the mere num-bers of the huge, homogeneous and fast-growing population from which the flood of books issues and to which it returns that this particular impression admonishes the observer to pause long enough on the threshold to be sure he takes it well in. Whatever the "literature" already is, whatever it may be destined yet to be, the public to which it addresses itself is of proportions that no other single public has approached, least of all those of the periods and societies to which we owe the comparatively small library of books that we rank as the most precious thing in our heritage. This question of numbers is brought home to us again and again with force by the amazing fortune apparently open now, any year, to the individual book—usually the lucky novel—that happens to please; by the extraordinary career, for instance, yesterday, of *Trilby*, or, today (as I hear it reported), of an historical fiction translated from the Polish and entitled *Quo Vadis?* It is clear enough that such a public must be, for the observer, an immense part of the whole ques-tion of the concatenation and quality of books, must present it in conditions hitherto almost unobserved and of a nature probably to give an interest of a kind so new as to suggest for the critic—even the critic least sure of where the chase will bring him out—a delicious rest from the oppressive *a priori*. There can be no real sport for him—if I may use the term that fits best the critical energy—save in proportion as he gets rid of *that*; and he can hardly fail to get rid of it just in the degree in which the conditions are vivid to his mind. They are, of course, largely those of other publics as well, in an age in which, everywhere, more people than ever before buy and sell, and read and write, and run about; but their scale, in the great common-schooled and news-papered democracy, is the largest and their pressure the greatest we see; their characteristics are magnified and multiplied. From these characteristics no intelligent forecast of the part played in the community in question by the printed and circulated page will suffer its attention too widely to wander.

Homogeneous I call the huge American public, with a due sense of the variety of races and idioms that are more and more under contribution to build it up, for it is precisely in the great mill of the language, our predominant and triumphant English, taking so much, suffering perhaps even so much, in the process, but giving so much more, on the whole, than it has to "put up" with, that the elements are ground into unity. Into its vast motherly lap the supreme speech manages somehow or other—with a robust indifference to trifles and shades—to see these elements poured; and just in this unique situation of the tongue itself we may surely find, if we attend, the interest of the drama and the excitement of the question. It is a situation that strikes me as presenting to the critic some of the strain and stress—those of suspense, of life, movement, change, the multiplication of possibilities, surprises, disappointments (emotions, whatever they may be, of the truth-hunter)—that the critic likes most to encounter. What may be, from point to point, noted as charming, or even as alarming, consequences? What forms, what colours, what sounds may the language take on or throw off in accommodating itself to such a growth of experience; what life may it—and most of all may the literature that shall so copiously testify for it—reflect and embody? The answer to these inquiries is simply the march of the critic's drama and the bliss, when not the misery, of that spectator; but while the endless play goes on the spectator may at least so far anticipate deferred conclusions as to find a savour in the very fact that it has been reserved not for French, not for German, not for Italian to meet fate on such a scale. That consciousness is an emotion in itself and, for large views, which are the only amusing ones, a great portent; so that we can surely say to ourselves that we shall not have been called upon to supply the biggest public for nothing.

To overflow with the same confidence to others is indeed perhaps to expose ourselves to hearing it declared improbable that we have been called upon to supply it, at any rate, for literature—the moral mainly latent in literature for the million, or rather for the fast-arriving billion, finding here inevitably a tempting application. But is not our instant rejoinder to that, as inevitably, that such an application is precipitate and premature? Whether, in the conditions we consider, the supply shall achieve sufficient vitality and distinction really to be sure of itself as literature, and to communicate the certitude, is the very thing we watch and wait to discover. If the retort to that remark be in turn that all this depends on what we may take it into our heads to *call* literature, we work round to a ground of easy assent. It truly does much depend on that. But that, in its order, depends on new light—on the new light struck out by the material itself, the distinguishable symptoms of which are the justification for what I have called the critic's happy release from the cramped posture of foregone conclusions and narrow rules. There will be no real amusement if we are positively prepared to be stupid. It is assuredly true that literature for the billion will not be literature as we have hitherto known it at its best. But if the billion give the pitch of production and circulation, they do something else besides; they hang before us a wide picture of opportunities—opportunities that would be opportunities still even if, reduced to the *minimum,* they should be only those offered by the vastness of the implied habitat and the complexity of the implied history.

It is impossible not to entertain with patience and curiosity the presumption that life so colossal must break into expression at points of proportionate frequency. These places, these moments will be the chances.

The first chance that, in the longer run, expression avails herself of may, of course, very well be that of breaking up into pieces and showing thereby that—as has been hitherto and in other parts of the world but imperfectly indicated—the public we somewhat loosely talk of as for literature or for anything else is really as subdivided as a chess-board, with each little square confessing only to its own *kind* of accessibility. The comparison too much sharpens and equalizes; but there are certainly, as on a map of countries, divisions and boundaries; and if these varieties become, to assist individual genius or save individual life, accentuated in American letters, we shall immediately to that tune be rewarded for our faith. It is, in other words, just from the very force of the conditions making for reaction in spots and phases that the liveliest appeal of future American production may spring— reaction, I mean, against the grossness of any view, any taste or tone, in danger of becoming so extravagantly general as to efface the really interesting thing, the traceability of the individual. Then, for all we know, we may get individual publics positively more sifted and evolved than anywhere else, shoals of fish rising to more delicate bait. That is a possibility that makes meanwhile for good humour, though I must hasten to add that it by no means exhausts the favourable list. We know what the list actually shows or what, in the past, it has mainly shown—New England quite predominantly, almost exclusively, the literary voice and dealing with little else than material supplied by herself. I have just been reading two new books that mark strikingly how the Puritan culture both used and exhausted its opportunity, how its place knows it no longer with any approach to the same intensity. Mrs. Fields' *Life and Letters of Harriet Beecher Stowe* and Mr. John Jay Chapman's acute and admirable *Emerson and Other Essays* (the most penetrating study, as regards his main subject, to my sense, of which that subject has been made the occasion) appear to refer to a past already left long behind, and are each, moreover, on this ground and on others, well worth returning to. The American world of to-day is a world of combinations and proportions different from those amid which Emerson and Mrs. Stowe could reach right and left far enough to fill it.

The note of the difference—at least of some of it—is sharply enough struck in an equally recent volume from which I have gathered many suggestions and that exhibits a talent distinctly to come back to—Mr. Owen Wister's *Lin McLean* (episodes in the career of a young "cattle-puncher"), in which the manners of the remoter West are worked into the general context, the American air at large, by a hand of a singularly trained and modern lightness. I but glance in passing, not to lose my thread, at these things; but

Mr. Owen Wister's tales (an earlier strong cluster of which, *Red Men and White*, I a year or two ago also much appreciated) give me a pretext for saying that, not inexplicably perhaps, a novelist interested in the general outlook of his trade may find the sharpest appeal of all in the idea of the chances in reserve for the work of the imagination in particular—the vision of the distinguishable poetry of things, whether expressed in such verse or (rarer phenomenon) in such prose as really does arrive at expression. I cannot but think that the American novel has in a special, far-reaching direction to sail much closer to the wind. "Business" plays a part in the United States that other interests dispute much less showily than they sometimes dispute it in the life of European countries; in consequence of which the typical American figure is above all that "business man" whom the novelist and the dramatist have scarce yet seriously touched, whose song has still to be sung and his picture still to be painted. He is often an obscure, but not less often an epic, hero, seamed all over with the wounds of the market and the dangers of the field, launched into action and passion by the immensity and complexity of the general struggle, a boundless ferocity of battle—driven above all by the extraordinary, the unique relation in which he for the most part stands to the life of his lawful, his immitigable womankind, the wives and daughters who float, who splash on the surface and ride the waves, his terrific link with civilization, his social substitutes and representatives, while, like a diver for shipwrecked treasure, he gasps in the depths and breathes through an air-tube.

This relation, even taken alone, contains elements that strike me as only yearning for their interpreter—elements, moreover, that would present the further merit of melting into the huge neighbouring province of the special situation of women in an order of things where to be a woman at all—certainly to be a young one—constitutes in itself a social position. The difficulty, doubtless, is that the world of affairs, as affairs are understood in the panting cities, though around us all the while, before us, behind us, beside us, and under our feet, is as special and occult a one to the outsider as the world, say, of Arctic exploration—as impenetrable save as a result of special training. Those who know it are not the men to paint it; those who might attempt it are not the men who know it. The most energetic attempt at portrayal that we have anywhere had—*L'Argent*, of Emile Zola—is precisely a warning of the difference between false and true initiation. The subject there, though so richly imagined, is all too mechanically, if prodigiously, "got up." Meanwhile, accordingly, the American "business man" remains, thanks to the length and strength of the wires that move him, *the* magnificent theme *en disponibilité*. The romance of fact, indeed, has touched him in a way that quite puts to shame the romance of fiction. It gives his measure for purposes of art that it was he, essentially, who embarked in the great war of

1861–65, and who, carrying it on in the North to a triumphant conclusion, went back, since business was his standpoint, to his very "own" with an undimmed capacity to mind it. When, in imagination, you give the type, as it exists to-day, the benefit of its great double lustre—that of these recorded antecedents and that of its preoccupied, systematic and magnanimous abasement before the other sex—you will easily feel your sense of what may be done with its overflow.

To glance at that is, at the point to which the English-speaking world has brought the matter, to remember by the same stroke that if there be no virtue in any forecast of the prospect of letters, any sounding of their deeps and shallows that fails to take account of the almost predominant hand now exercised about them by women, the precaution is doubly needful in respect to the American situation. Whether the extraordinary dimensions of the public be a promise or a threat, nothing is more unmistakable than the sex of some of the largest masses. The longest lines are feminine—feminine, it may almost be said, the principal front. Both as readers and as writers on the other side of the Atlantic women have, in fine, "arrived" in numbers not equalled even in England, and they have succeeded in giving the pitch and marking the limits more completely than elsewhere. The public taste, as our fathers used to say, has become so largely *their* taste, their tone, their experiment, that nothing is at last more apparent than that the public cares little for anything that they cannot do. And what, after all, may the very finest opportunity of American literature be but just to show that they can do what the peoples will have ended by regarding as everything? The settlement of such a question, the ups and downs of such a process surely more than justify that sense of sport, in this direction, that I have spoken of as the privilege of the vigilant critic.

From *Literature*, published by *The Times* (London); American edition published by Harper & Brothers; Vol. II (March 26, 1898), pp. 356–358, where it appeared as an "American Letter" with the title as here printed. The essay was not reprinted by Henry James in his books.

The Great Form
[1889]

[In the summer of 1889 there was held, at Deerfield, Massachusetts, a summer school on "The Novel," to which Henry James, then in England, was invited to contribute, the appeal of the school's organizers having told him it was their object to discuss and resist "the materialism of our present tendencies" in this form of literature. Henry James, unable to attend the sessions, participated by letter, his message being then published in full in the *New York Tribune* of Sunday, August 4, 1889, and summarized in briefer form in the *Critic* (New York) of August 17, 1889. This letter was rediscovered by Mr. Leon Edel and published by him in the *Times Literary Supplement* (London) of July 29, 1939, with a note in which he remarks that the letter "is interesting, for it is a reiteration, in concise form, of the views set forth by James in his famous essay 'The Art of Fiction,' while being at the same time probably the most concrete advice he ever vouchsafed his countrymen on novel-writing."]

I AM afraid I can do little more than thank you for your courteous invitation to be present at the sittings of your delightfully sounding school of romance, which ought to inherit happiness and honour from such a name. I am so very far away from you that I am afraid I can't participate very intelligently in your discussions, but I can only give them the furtherance of a dimly discriminating sympathy. I am not sure that I apprehend very well your apparent premise "the materialism of our present tendencies," and I suspect that this would require some clearing up before I should be able (if even then) to contribute any suggestive or helpful word. To tell the truth, I can't help thinking that we already talk too much about the novel, about and around it, in proportion to the quantity of it having any importance that we produce. What I should say to the nymphs and swains who propose to converse about it under the great trees at Deerfield is: "Oh, do something from your point of view; an ounce of example is worth a ton of generalities; do something with the great art and the great form; do something with life. Any point of view is interesting that is a direct impression of life. You each have an impression coloured by your individual conditions; make that into a picture, a picture framed by your own personal wisdom, your glimpse of the American world. The field is vast for freedom, for study, for observation, for satire, for truth." I don't think I really do know what you mean by "materializing tendencies" any more than I should by "spiritualizing" or "etherealizing." There are no tendencies worth anything but to see the actual or the imaginative, which is just as visible, and to paint it. I have only two little words for the matter remotely approaching to rule or doctrine; one is life and the other freedom. Tell the ladies and gentlemen, the ingenious inquirers, to consider life directly and closely, and not to be put off with mean and puerile falsities, and be conscientious about it. It is infinitely large, various and comprehensive. Every sort of mind will find what it looks for in it, whereby the novel becomes truly multifarious and illustrative. That is what I mean by liberty; give it its head and let it range. If it is in a bad way, and the English novel is, I think, nothing but absolute freedom can refresh it and restore its self-respect. Hence these raw brevities and please convey to your companions, my dear sir, the cordial good wishes of yours and theirs,

HENRY JAMES

WILLIAM DEAN HOWELLS
The Question of a Criterion
[1891]

THE question of a final criterion for the appreciation of art is one that perpetually recurs to those interested in any sort of aesthetic endeavor. Mr. John Addington Symonds, in a chapter of *The Renaissance in Italy* treating of the Bolognese school of painting, which once had so great cry, and was vaunted the supreme exemplar of the grand style, but which he now believes fallen into lasting contempt for its emptiness and soullessness, seeks to determine whether there can be an enduring criterion or not; and his conclusion is applicable to literature as to the other arts. "Our hope," he says, "with regard to the unity of taste in the future then is, that all sentimental or academical seekings after the ideal having been abandoned, momentary theories founded upon idiosyncratic or temporary partialities exploded, and nothing accepted but what is solid and positive, the scientific spirit shall make men progressively more and more conscious of these *bleibende Verhältnisse,* more and more capable of living in the whole; also, that in proportion as we gain a firmer hold upon our own place in the world, we shall come to comprehend with more instinctive certitude what is simple, natural, and honest, welcoming with gladness all artistic products that exhibit these qualities. The perception of the enlightened man will then be the task of a healthy person who has made himself acquainted with the laws of evolution in art and in society, and is able to test the excellence of work in any stage from immaturity to decadence by discerning what there is of truth, sincerity, and natural vigor in it."

*　　*　　*　　*　　*

That is to say, as I understand, that moods and tastes and fashions change; people fancy now this and now that; but what is unpretentious and what is true is always beautiful and good, and nothing else is so. This is not saying that fantastic and monstrous and artificial things do not please; everybody knows that they do please immensely for a time, and then, after the lapse of a much longer time, they have the charm of the rococo. Nothing is more curious than the charm that fashion has. Fashion in women's dress, almost every fashion,

58

is somehow delightful, else it would never have been the fashion; but if any one will look through a collection of old-fashioned plates, he must own that most fashions have been ugly. A few, which could be readily instanced, have been very pretty, and even beautiful, but it is doubtful if these have pleased the greatest number of people. The ugly delights as well as the beautiful, and not merely because the ugly fashion is associated with the young loveliness of the women who wear the ugly fashions, and wins a grace from them, not because the vast majority of mankind are tasteless, but for some cause that is not perhaps ascertainable. It is quite as likely to return in the fashions of our clothes and houses and furniture, and poetry and fiction and painting, as the beautiful, and it may be from an instinctive or a reasoned sense of this that some of the extreme naturalists have refused to make the old discrimination against it or to regard the ugly as any less worthy of celebration in art than the beautiful; some of them, in fact, seem to regard it as rather more worthy, if anything. Possibly there is no absolutely ugly, no absolutely beautiful; or possibly the ugly contains always an element of the beautiful better adapted to the general appreciation than the more perfectly beautiful. This is a somewhat discouraging conjecture, but I offer it for no more than it is worth; and I do not pin my faith to the saying of one whom I heard denying, the other day, that a thing of beauty was a joy forever. He contended that Keats's line should have read, "Some things of beauty are sometimes joys forever," and that any assertion beyond this was too hazardous.

* * * * *

In the mean time the average of criticism is not wholly bad with us. To be sure, the critic sometimes appears in the panoply of the savages whom we have supplanted on this continent; and it is hard to believe that his use of the tomahawk and the scalping-knife is a form of conservative surgery. It is still his conception of his office that he should assail with obloquy those who differ with him in matters of taste or opinion; that he must be rude with those he does not like, and that he ought to do them violence as a proof of his superiority. It is too largely his superstition that because he likes a thing it is good, and because he dislikes a thing it is bad; the reverse is quite possibly the case, but he is yet indefinitely far from knowing that in affairs of taste his personal preference enters very little. Commonly he has no principles, but only an assortment of prepossessions for and against; and this otherwise very perfect character is sometimes uncandid to the verge of dishonesty. He seems not to mind misstating the position of any one he supposes himself to disagree with, and then attacking him for what he never said, or even implied; the critic thinks this is droll, and appears not to suspect that it is immoral. He is not tolerant; he thinks it a virtue to be intolerant; it is hard for him to understand that the same thing may be admirable at one time and deplorable at another; and that it is really his business to classify and analyze the fruits of the human mind very much as the naturalist classifies the objects of his study, rather than to praise or blame them; that there is a measure of the same absurdity in his trampling on a poem, a novel, or an essay that does not please him as in the botanist's grinding a plant underfoot because he does not find it pretty. He does not conceive that it is his business rather to identify the species and then explain how and where the specimen is imperfect and irregular. If he could once acquire this simple idea of his duty he would be much more agreeable company than he now is, and a more useful member of society; though I hope I am not yet saying that he is not extremely delightful as he is, and wholly indispensable. He is certainly more ignorant than malevolent; and considering the hard conditions under which he works, his necessity of writing hurriedly from an imperfect examination of far more books, on a greater variety of subjects, than he can even hope to read, the average American critic—the ordinary critic of commerce, so to speak—is very well indeed. Collectively he is more than this; for the joint effect of our criticism is the pretty thorough appreciation of any book submitted to it.

*   *   *   *   *

The misfortune rather than the fault of our individual critic is that he is the heir of the false theory and bad manners of the English school. The theory of that school has apparently been that almost any person of glib and lively expression is competent to write of almost any branch of polite literature; its manners are what we know. The American, whom it has largely formed, is by nature very glib and very lively, and commonly his criticism, viewed as imaginative work, is more agreeable than that of the Englishman; but it is, like the art of both countries, apt to be amateurish. In some degree our authors have freed themselves from English models; they have gained some notion of the more serious work of the Continent; but it is still the ambition of the American critic to write like the English critic, to show his wit if not his learning, to strive to eclipse the author under review rather than illustrate him. He has not yet caught on to the fact that it is really no part of his business to display himself, but that it is altogether his duty to place a book in such a light that the reader shall know its class, its function, its character. The vast good-nature of our people preserves us from the worst effects of this criticism without principles. Our critic, at his lowest, is rarely malignant; and when he is rude or untruthful, it is mostly without truculence; I suspect that he is often offensive without knowing that he is so. If he loves a shining mark because a fair shot with mud shows best on that kind of target, it is for the most part from a boyish mischievousness quite innocent of malice. Now and then he acts simply under instruction from higher authority, and denounces because it is the tradition of his publication to do so.

In other cases the critic is obliged to support his journal's repute for severity, or for wit, or for morality, though he may himself be entirely amiable, dull, and wicked; this necessity more or less warps his verdicts.

The worst is that he is personal, perhaps because it is so easy and so natural to be personal, and so instantly attractive. In this respect our criticism has not improved from the accession of numbers of ladies to its ranks, though we still hope so much from women in our politics when they shall come to vote. They have come to write, and with the effect to increase the amount of little-digging, which rather superabounded in our literary criticism before. They "know what they like"—that pernicious maxim of those who do not know what they ought to like—and they pass readily from censuring an author's performance to censuring him. They bring a lively stock of misapprehensions and prejudices to their work; they would rather have heard about than known about a book; and they take kindly to the public wish to be amused rather than edified. But neither have they so much harm in them: they, too, are more ignorant than malevolent.

* * * * *

Our criticism is disabled by the unwillingness of the critic to learn from an author, and his readiness to mistrust him. A writer passes his whole life in fitting himself for a certain kind of performance; the critic does not ask why, or whether the performance is good or bad, but if he does not like the kind, he instructs the writer to go off and do some other sort of thing—usually the sort that has been done already, and done sufficiently. If he could once understand that a man who has written the book he dislikes, probably knows infinitely more about its kind and his own fitness for doing it than any one else, the critic might learn something, and might help the reader to learn; but by putting himself in a false position, a position of superiority, he is of no use. He ought, in the first place, to cast prayerfully about for humility, and especially to beseech the powers to preserve him from the sterility of arrogance and the deadness of contempt, for out of these nothing can proceed. He is not to suppose that an author has committed an offence against him by writing the kind of book he does not like; he will be far more profitably employed on behalf of the reader in finding out whether they had better not both like it. Let him conceive of an author as not in any wise on trial before him, but as a reflection of this or that aspect of life, and he will not be tempted to browbeat him or bully him.

The critic need not be impolite even to the youngest and weakest author. A little courtesy, or a good deal, a constant perception of the fact that a book is not a misdemeanor, a decent self-respect that must forbid the civilized man the savage pleasure of wounding, are what I would ask for our criticism, as something which will add sensibly to its present lustre.

I would have my fellow-critics consider what they are really in the world for. It is not, apparently, for a great deal, because their only excuse for being is that somebody else has been. The critic exists because the author first existed. If books failed to appear, the critic must disappear, like the poor aphis or the lowly caterpillar in the absence of vegetation. These insects may both suppose that they have something to do with the creation of vegetation; and the critic may suppose that he has something to do with the creation of literature; but a very little reasoning ought to convince alike aphis, caterpillar, and critic that they are mistaken. The critic—to drop the others—must perceive, if he will question himself more carefully, that his office is mainly to ascertain facts and traits of literature, not to invent or denounce them; to discover principles, not to establish them; to report, not to create.

It is so much easier to say that you like this or dislike that, than to tell why one thing is, or where another thing comes from, that many flourishing critics will have to go out of business altogether if the scientific method comes in, for then the critic will have to know something beside his own mind, which is often but a narrow field. He will have to know something of the laws of that mind, and of its generic history.

The history of all literature shows that even with the youngest and weakest author criticism is quite powerless against his will to do his own work in his own way; and if this is the case in the green wood, how much more in the dry! It has been thought by the sentimentalist that criticism, if it cannot cure, can at least kill, and Keats was long alleged in proof of its efficacy in this sort. But criticism neither cured nor killed Keats, as we all now very well know. It wounded, it cruelly hurt him, no doubt; and it is always in the power of the critic to give pain to the author—the meanest critic to the greatest author—for no one can help feeling a rudeness. But every literary movement has been violently opposed at the start, and yet never stayed in the least, or arrested, by criticism; every author has been condemned for his virtues, but in no wise changed by it. In the beginning he reads the critics; but presently perceiving that he alone makes or mars himself, and that they have no instruction for him, he mostly leaves off reading them, though he is always glad of their kindness or grieved by their harshness when he chances upon it. This, I believe, is the general experience, modified, of course, by exceptions.

Then, are we critics of no use in the world? I should not like to think that, though I am not quite ready to define our use. More than one sober thinker is inclining at present to suspect that aesthetically or specifically we are of no use, and that we are only useful historically; that we may register laws, but not enact them. I am not quite prepared to admit that aesthetic criticism is useless, though in view of its futility in any given instance it is hard to deny that it is so. It certainly seems as useless against a book that strikes the popular fancy, and prospers on in spite of condemnation by the best critics, as it is against a book which does not generally please, and which no critical favor can make acceptable. This is so common a phenomenon that I wonder it has never hitherto suggested to criticism that its point of view was altogether mistaken, and that it was really necessary to judge books not as dead things, but as living things—things which have an influence and a power irrespective of beauty and wisdom, and merely as expressions of actuality in thought and feeling. Perhaps criticism has a cumulative and final effect; perhaps it does some good we do not know of. It apparently does not affect the author directly, but it may reach him through the reader. It may in some cases enlarge or diminish his audience for a while, until he has thoroughly measured and tested his own powers. If criticism is to affect literature at all, it must be through the writers who have newly left the starting-point, and are reasonably uncertain of the race, not with those who have won it again and again in their own way. I doubt if it can do more than that; but if it can do that I will admit that it may be the toad of adversity, ugly and venomous, from whose unpleasant brow he is to snatch the precious jewel of lasting fame.

I employ this figure in all humility, and I conjure our fraternity to ask themselves, without rancor or offence, whether I am right or not. In this quest let us get together all the modesty and candor and impartiality we can; for if we should happen to discover a good reason for continuing to exist, these qualities will be of more use to us than any others in examining the work of people who really produce something.

From *Criticism and Fiction* by William Dean Howells (being the "Introduction," and Chapters I, VI, VII, VIII, and IX). Copyright, 1891, by Harper & Brothers. Based on material that originally appeared in *Harper's Monthly* ("The Editor's Study"), Vols. LXXII–LXXXI (February, 1886–October, 1890). The present title has been supplied by the editor.

JOHN JAY CHAPMAN

The Aesthetic

[1910]

THERE are two distinct functions of the mind with regard to art: first, the creative function; second, the enjoying function. The first is the role of the artist, the second, the rôle of the public. The difference between these two rôles is that in the artist's rôle the active part—the part that counts, the part that makes the beholder have sensations—is unconscious. The artist should be wholly creator, and not at all spectator. If, while he works, there is anything in him that applauds and enjoys as a spectator might do, this part will leave a touch of virtuosity, of self-consciousness, of exaggeration, in his work. If the matter be humorous, this exaggeration will perhaps appear in the form of smartness; if the matter be serious, as sentimentality or melodrama.

The artist must not try to enjoy his own work by foretaste, or he will injure it. His aesthetic sense must not be active during the hours of creation; it must be consumed in the furnace of unconscious intellectual effort. The *reductio ad absurdum* of the view here suggested would be somewhat as follows:—The supremely great artist would be indifferent to the fate of his own works, because he would not know they were great. The whole creature would have become so unconscious during the act of creation that there would be nothing left over which should return to mankind and say, "See this great work!" This seems to have happened in the case of Shakespeare.

It must be confessed that there are very great artists in whose work we find a self-conscious, self-appreciatory note. There is, at times, such a note in Dante, and in Goethe. And it seems to me that even here the note a little deflects our attention from the matter in hand. Not by reason of this element, but in spite of it, does their work prevail.

The practical lesson for any artist to draw from such an analysis as the present is the lesson of detachment, almost of indifference. An artist must trust his material. The stuff in hand is serious, delicate, self-determined and non-emotional. The organic, inner logic of the thing done may reach points of complexity, points of climax, which—except in the outcome—are incomprehensible. They must not be appreciated in the interim, but only obeyed.

64

In the final review, and at a distance they are to justify themselves, but no the making.

The question of whether or not an artist has succeeded, whether or not has made something that speaks, is one which it is generally impossible for the artist himself to answer. He cares too much, and he stands too near the material. Sometimes a man having immense experience, and having acquired that sort of indifference which grows out of a supernal success, can make a just estimate of one of his own later works; but, in general, the artist must stand mum and bite his nails if he wishes to find out what there was in him. Let him be perfectly assured that the truth of the matter will get to him, if he will only do nothing except desire the truth. Someone will say something not intended for his ears, which will reveal the whole matter. This is the hard, heroic course which wisdom dictates to all artists, except, perhaps, to those very gifted persons who by their endowment are already among the elect. Most men are obliged to mine in their endowment and draw it to the surface through years of hard labor. The pretty good artist has need of the fortitude and self-effacement of a saint. *patience*

Thus much of the creative side of art. Our conceptions of the subject, however, are colored by the emotional view proper to the grand public. The receptive function, the enjoying function, the aesthetic sense, as it is often called, is very generally supposed to be art itself. Almost all writing on art has been done by men who knew only the aesthetic side of the matter. Now the enjoyment of art is a very common, very conscious, very intense experience; and yet it is not a very serious affair compared to the creation of art. It does not affect the recipient to any such depths of his nature, as one might expect it to do, from the vividness of his feelings during the experience. It leaves in him, as a general rule, no knowledge about the art itself, no understanding of the rod he has been lashed with, no suspicion of the intellectual nature of the vehicle.

Aesthetic appreciation gives a man the illusion that he is being spiritually made over and enlarged; and yet that appreciation is capable of an absolute divorcement from the intellect. It is—to take the extreme case—very strong in sleep. Dr. Holmes has recorded, in his own felicitous way, the experience, common to sensitive people, of writing down a dream-poem at midnight and discovering in its place at dawn a few lines of incomprehensible rubbish. The aesthetic sense is easily intensified by stimulants, by tea, coffee and tobacco. Anything that excites the heart or stimulates the emotions—praise, happiness, success, change of scene, any relief from mental tension—is apt to give a man new and sudden entry into unexplored worlds of art. He thinks himself a new man. And yet this man stands, perhaps, in as great danger of loss as he does in hope of gain. It is not through receptivity, but through activity, that men are really changed.

How trivial men become who live solely in the appreciation of the fine arts all of us know. The American who lives abroad is an intensely receptive being; but he has divorced himself from the struggles of a normal social existence, from communal life and duty. His love of the fine arts does not save him, but seems rather to enfeeble him the more. No European can effect a similar divorce in his own life; for the European is living at home: his social and political obligations make a man of him. Besides this, the fine arts are an old story to the European; and he does not go mad about them, as the American Indian goes mad about whiskey. The European is immune to the aesthetic; and neither a fine wainscot nor a beautiful doorknob can have the same power over him that it may have over that zealous, high-strung, new discoverer of the old world, the American who begins to realize what good decoration really means. Let anyone who thinks that this impoverishment is a purely American disease read the description of the Stanhope family in Trollope's *Barchester Towers*. Here is the beefiest kind of a British county family, reduced to anemia by residence in Italy. Prolonged exile and mere receptivity have withdrawn the energy from the organs of these people.

It will be noticed that in those cases where art is an enfeebling influence there is always a hiatus between the public and the artist. Let us consider the case of the folk-song as sung by the peasants of Suabia. Such songs are written by one peasant and sung by the next. The author and the singer and the hearer are all one. To the audience the song is life and emotion, social intercourse, love, friendship, the landscape, philosophy, prayer, natural happiness. You can hardly differentiate, in this case, between the artist and the public: both are unconscious. But if you take that song and sing it in a London drawing-room, or on a ranch in Colorado, it will perform a very different function in the audience. To these foreigners the song is a pleasing opiate. They hold it like a warm animal to their breast. The Oxford pundit who raves over a Greek coin, the cold-hearted business magnate in New York who enjoys the opera—these people live in so remote a relation to the human causes, impulses, and conditions behind the arts they love, that their enjoyment is exotic: it is more purely receptive, more remote from personal experience than the enjoyment of any living and native art could be.

A certain sickness follows the indulgence in art that is remote from the admirer's environment. This slightly morbid side of aestheticism has been caricatured to the heart's content. The dilettante and the critic are well-known types. To a superficial view these men seem like enemies of the living artist. They are always standing ready to eat up his works as soon as they shall be born. Goethe thought criticism and satire the two natural enemies to all liberty, and to all poetry proceeding from a spontaneous impulse. And surely the massive authority of learned critics who know everything, and are yet ignorant of the first principles of their subject, hangs like an avalanche above the head of every young creator. We cannot, however, to-day proceed as if we were early Greeks, stepping forward in roseate unconsciousness. The critics and their hurdy-gurdy are a part of our life, and have been so for centuries.

The brighter side of the matter is that the aesthetic person, even when morbid, is often engaged in introducing new and valuable arts to his countrymen. The dilettante who brings home china and violins and Japanese bronzes is the precursor of the domestic artist.

We must now return to the two functions of art, and endeavor to bring them into some sort of common focus. We cannot hope to understand or to reconcile them perfectly. We cannot hope to know what art is. Art is life, and any expression of art becomes a new form of life. A merchant in Boston in 1850 travels in Italy, and brings home a Murillo. Some years later a highly educated dilettante discovers the Murillo in Boston, and writes his dithyrambs about it. Some years later still, there arises a young painter, who perhaps does not paint very well, and yet he is nearer to the mystery than the other two. All these men are parts of the same movement, and are essential to each other; though the contempt they feel for each other might conceal this from us, as it does from themselves. All of them are held together by an invisible attraction and are servants of the same force. This force it is which, in the future, may weld together a few enthusiasts into a sort of secret society, or may even single out some one man, and see and speak through him. Then, as the force passes, it will leave itself reflected in pictures, which remain as the record of its flight.

From *Learning and Other Essays* by John Jay Chapman, pp. 235–242. Moffat, Yard and Company, 1910.

RANDOLPH BOURNE

Our Cultural Humility

[1914]

IT WAS Matthew Arnold, read and reverenced by the generation immediately preceding our own, who set to our eyes a definition and a goal of culture which has become the common property of all our world. To know the best that had been thought and said, to appreciate the master-works which the previous civilizations had produced, to put our minds and appreciations in contact with the great of all ages,—here was a clear ideal which dissolved the mists in which the vaguenesses of culture had been lost. And it was an ideal that appealed with peculiar force to Americans. For it was a democratic ideal; everyone who had the energy and perseverance could reasonably expect to acquire by taking thought that orientation of soul to which Arnold gave the magic name of culture. And it was a quantitative ideal; culture was a matter of acquisition—with appreciation and prayerfulness perhaps, but still a matter of adding little by little to one's store until one should have a vision of that radiant limit, when one knew all the best that had been thought and said and pictured in the world.

I do not know in just what way the British public responded to Arnold's eloquence; if the prophetic wrath of Ruskin failed to stir them, it is not probable that they were moved by the persuasiveness of Arnold. But I do know that, coming at a time when America was producing rapidly an enormous number of people who were "comfortably off," as the phrase goes, and who were sufficiently awake to feel their limitations, with the broader horizons of Europe just opening on the view, the new doctrine had the most decisive effect on our succeeding spiritual history. The "land-of-liberty" American of the era of Dickens still exists in the British weeklies and in observations of America by callow young journalists, but as a living species he has long been extinct. His place has been taken by a person whose pride is measured not by the greatness of the "land of the free," but by his own orientation in Europe.

Already in the nineties, our college professors and our artists were beginning to require the seal of a European training to justify their existence. We appropriated the German system of education. Our millionaires began the collecting of pictures and the endowment of museums with foreign works of art. We began the exportation of school-teachers for a summer tour of Europe. American art and music colonies sprang up in Paris and Berlin and Munich. The movement became a rush. That mystical premonition of Europe, which Henry James tells us he had from his earliest boyhood, became the common property of the talented young American, who felt a certain starvation in his own land, and longed for the fleshpots of European culture. But the bourgeoisie soon followed the artistic and the semi-artistic, and Europe became so much the fashion that it is now almost a test of respectability to have traveled at least once abroad.

Underlying all this vivacious emigration, there was of course a real if vague thirst for "culture," and, in strict accord with Arnold's definition, the idea that somehow culture could be imbibed, that from the contact with the treasures of Europe there would be rubbed off on us a little of that grace which had made the art. So for those who could not travel abroad, our millionaires transported, in almost terrifying bulk and at staggering cost, samples of everything that the foreign galleries had to show. We were to acquire culture at any cost, and we had no doubt that we had discovered the royal road to it. We followed it, at any rate, with eye single to the goal. The naturally sensitive, who really found in the European literature and arts some sort of spiritual nourishment, set the pace, and the crowd followed at their heels.

This cultural humility of ours astonished and still astonishes Europe. In England, where "culture" is taken very frivolously, the bated breath of the American, when he speaks of Shakespeare or Tennyson or Browning, is always cause for amusement. And the Frenchman is always a little puzzled at the crowds who attend lectures in Paris on "How to See Europe Intelligently," or are taken in vast parties through the Louvre. The European objects a little to being so constantly regarded as the keeper of a huge museum. If you speak to him of culture, you find him frankly more interested in contemporaneous literature and art and music than in his worthies of the olden time, more interested in discriminating the good of today than in accepting the classics. If he is a cultivated person, he is much more interested usually in quarreling about a living dog than in reverencing a dead lion. If he is a French *lettré*, for instance, he will be producing a book on the psychology of some living writer, while the Anglo-Saxon will be writing another on Shakespeare. His whole attitude towards the things of culture, be it noted, is one of daily appreciation and intimacy, not that attitude of reverence with which we Americans approach alien art, and which penalizes cultural heresy among us.

The European may be enthusiastic, polemic, radiant, concerning his culture; he is never humble. And he is, above all, never humble before the culture of another country. The Frenchman will hear nothing but French music, read nothing but French literature, and prefers his own art to that of any other nation. He can hardly understand our almost pathetic eagerness to learn of the culture of other nations, our humility of worship in the presence of art that in no sense represents the expression of any of our ideals and motivating forces.

To a genuinely patriotic American this cultural humility of ours is somewhat humiliating. In response to this eager inexhaustible interest in Europe, where is Europe's interest in us? Europe is to us the land of history, of mellow tradition, of the arts and graces of life, of the best that has been said and thought in the world. To Europe we are the land of crude racial chaos, of skyscrapers and bluff, of millionaires and "bosses." A French philosopher visits us, and we are all eagerness to get from him an orientation in all that is moving in the world of thought across the seas. But does he ask about our philosophy, does he seek an orientation in the American thought of the day? Not at all. Our humility has kept us from forcing it upon his attention, and it scarcely exists for him. Our advertising genius, so powerful and universal where soap and biscuits are concerned, wilts and languishes before the task of trumpeting our intellectual and spiritual products before the world. Yet there can be little doubt which is the more intrinsically worth advertising. But our humility causes us to be taken at our own face value, and for all this patient fixity of gaze upon Europe, we get little reward except to be ignored, or to have our interest somewhat contemptuously dismissed as parasitic.

And with justice! For our very goal and ideal of culture has made us parasites. Our method has been exactly wrong. For the truth is that the definition of culture, which we have accepted with such devastating enthusiasm, is a definition emanating from that very barbarism from which its author recoiled in such horror. If it were not that all our attitude showed that we had adopted a quite different standard, it would be the merest platitude to say that culture is not an acquired familiarity with things outside, but an inner and constantly operating taste, a fresh and responsive power of discrimination, and the insistent judging of everything that comes to our minds and senses. It is clear that such a sensitive taste cannot be acquired by torturing our appreciations into conformity with the judgments of others, no matter how "authoritative" those judgments may be. Such a method means a hypnotization of judgment, not a true development of soul.

At the back of Arnold's definition is, of course, the implication that if we have only learned to appreciate the "best," we shall have been trained thus to discriminate generally, that our appreciation of Shakespeare will somehow spill over into admiration of the incomparable art of Mr. G. Lowes Dickinson. This is, of course, exactly to reverse the psychological process. A true appreciation of the remote and the magnificent is acquired only after the judgment has learned to discriminate with accuracy and taste between the good and bad, the sincere and the false, of the familiar and contemporaneous art and writing of every day. To set up an alien standard of the classics is merely to give our lazy taste a resting point, and to prevent forever any genuine culture.

This virus of the "best" rages throughout all our Anglo-Saxon campaign for culture. Is it not a notorious fact that our professors of English literature make no attempt to judge the work produced since the death of the last consecrated saint of the literary canon,—Robert Louis Stevenson? In strict accordance with Arnold's doctrine, they are waiting for the judgment upon our contemporaries which they call the test of time, that is, an authoritative objective judgment, upon which they can unquestioningly rely. Surely it seems as if the principle of authority, having been ousted from religion and politics, had found a strong refuge in the sphere of culture. This tyranny of the "best" objectifies all our taste. It is a "best" that is always outside of our native reactions to the freshnesses and sincerities of life, a "best" to which our spontaneities must be disciplined. By fixing our eyes humbly on the ages that are past, and on foreign countries, we effectually protect ourselves from that inner taste which is the only sincere "culture."

Our cultural humility before the civilizations of Europe, then, is the chief obstacle which prevents us from producing any true indigenous culture of our own. I am far from saying, of course, that it is not necessary for our arts to be fertilized by the civilizations of other nations past and present. The culture of Europe has arisen only from such an extensive cross-fertilization in the past. But we have passed through that period of learning, and it is time for us now to set up our individual standards. We are already "heir of all the ages" through our English ancestry, and our last half-century of European idolatry has done for us all that can be expected. But, with our eyes fixed on Europe, we continue to strangle whatever native genius springs up. Is it not a tragedy that the American artist feels the imperative need of foreign approval before he can be assured of his attainment? Through our inability or unwillingness to judge him, through our cultural humility, through our insistence on the objective standard, we drive him to depend on a foreign clientele, to live even in foreign countries, where taste is more confident of itself and does not require the label, to be assured of the worth of what it appreciates.

The only remedy for this deplorable situation is the cultivation of a new American nationalism. We need that keen introspection into the beauties and vitalities and sincerities of our own life and ideals that characterizes the French. The French culture is animated by principles and tastes which are as old as art itself. There are "classics," not in the English and Arnoldian sense of a consecrated canon, dissent from which is heresy, but in the sense that each successive generation, putting them to the test, finds them redolent of those qualities which are characteristically French, and so preserves them as a precious heritage. This cultural chauvinism is the most harmless of patriotisms; indeed it is absolutely necessary for a true life of civilization. And it can hardly be too intense, or too exaggerated. Such an international art exhibition as was held recently in New York, with the frankly avowed purpose of showing American artists how bad they were in comparison with the modern

French, represents an appalling degradation of attitude which would be quite impossible in any other country. Such groveling humility can only have the effect of making us feeble imitators, instead of making us assert, with all the power at our command, the genius and individuality which we already possess in quantity, if we would only see it.

In the contemporary talent that Europe is exhibiting, or even in the genius of the last half-century, one will go far to find greater poets than our Walt Whitman, philosophers than William James, essayists than Emerson and Thoreau, composers than MacDowell, sculptors than Saint-Gaudens. In any other country such names would be focuses to which interest and enthusiasms would converge, symbols of a national spirit about which judgments and tastes would revolve. For none of them could have been born in another country than our own. If some of them had their training abroad, it was still the indigenous America that their works expressed,—the American ideals and qualities, our pulsating democracy, the vigor and daring of our pioneer spirit, our sense of *camaraderie*, our dynamism, the big-heartedness of our scenery, our hospitality to all the world. In the music of MacDowell, the poetry of Whitman, the philosophy of James, I recognize a national spirit, "l'esprit américain," as superbly clear and gripping as anything the culture of Europe has to offer us, and immensely more stimulating, because of the very body and soul of to-day's interests and aspirations.

To come to an intense self-consciousness of these qualities, to feel them in the work of these masters, and to search for them everywhere among the lesser artists and thinkers who are trying to express the soul of this hot chaos of America,—this will be the attainment of culture for us. Not to look on ravished while our marvelous millionaires fill our museums with "old masters," armor, and porcelains, but to turn our eyes upon our own art for a time, shut ourselves in with our own genius, and cultivate with an intense and partial pride what we have already achieved against the obstacles of our cultural humility. Only thus shall we conserve the American spirit and saturate the next generation with those qualities which are our strength. Only thus can we take our rightful place among the cultures of the world, to which we are entitled if we would but recognize it. We shall never be able to perpetuate our ideals except in the form of art and literature; the world will never understand our spirit except in terms of art. When shall we learn that "culture," like the kingdom of heaven, lies within us, in the heart of our national soul, and not in foreign galleries and books? When shall we learn to be proud? For only pride is creative.

From *The History of a Literary Radical, and Other Essays* by Randolph Bourne, edited, with an Introduction, by Van Wyck Brooks. B. W. Huebsch, 1920. Reprinted by permission of B. W. Huebsch. First published in *The Atlantic Monthly*, Vol. CXIV (October, 1914), pp. 503–507.

JAMES GIBBONS HUNEKER

The Great American Novel

[1917]

WHEN the supreme master of the historical novel modestly confessed that he could do the "big bow-wow strain," but to Jane Austen must be accorded the palm of exquisite craftsmanship, there was then no question upon the critical map of the so-called "great American novel." Sir Walter Scott—to whom such authors of historical novels as Châteaubriand and his Martyrs, the *Salammbô* of Flaubert, and that well-nigh perfect fiction, *The History of Henry Esmond,* by Thackeray, yield precedence—might have achieved the impossible: the writing of a library, epitomising the social history of "These States"—as Walt Whitman would say. After Scott no name but Balzac's occurs to the memory; Balzac, who laid all France under his microscope (and France is all of a piece, not the checker-board of nationalities we call America). Even the mighty Tolstoy would have balked the job. And if these giants would have failed, what may be said of their successors? The idea of a great American novel is an "absolute," and nature abhors an absolute, despite the belief of some metaphysicians to the contrary. Yet the notion still obtains and inquests are held from time to time, and the opinions of contemporary novelists are taken toll of; as if each man and woman could give aught else but their own side of the matter, that side which is rightfully enough personal and provincial. The question is, after all, an affair for critics, and the great American novel will be in the plural; thousands perhaps. America is a chord of many nations, and to find the key-note we must play much and varied music.

While a novelist may be cosmopolitan at his own risk, a critic should be ever so. (Consider the names of such widely contrasted critical temperaments as Sainte-Beuve, Taine, De Gourmont, Matthew Arnold, Brandes, Swinburne, Arthur Symons, Havelock Ellis, Henry James, Gosse, and W. C. Brownell; all cosmopolitan as well as national.) The sublime tenuities of Henry James, like the black music of Michael Artzibashef, are questions largely temperamental. But the Russian is all Slavic, and no one would maintain that Mr. James shows a like ingrained nationalism. Nevertheless, he is American, though dealing only with a certain side of American life, the cosmopolitan phase. At his peril an American novelist sails eastward to describe the history of his countrymen abroad. With the critic we come upon a different territory. He may go gadding after new mud-gods (the newest god invented by man is always the greatest), for the time being, and return to his native heath mentally refreshed and broadened by his foreign outing. Not so the maker of fiction. Once he cuts loose his balloon he is in danger of not getting home again.

Mr. James is a splendid case for us; he began in America and landed in England, there to stay. Our other felicitous example of cosmopolitanism is Henry Blake Fuller, the author of *The Chevalier of Pensieri-Vani* and *The Châtelaine of la Trinité,* who was so widely read in the nineties. After those charming excursions into a rapidly vanishing Europe Mr. Fuller reversed the proceeding of James; he returned to America and composed two novels of high artistic significance, *The Cliff Dwellers* and *With the Procession,* which, while they continued the realistic tradition of William Dean Howells, were also the forerunners of a new movement in America. It is not necessary to dwell now on *The Last Refuge,* or on that masterly book of spiritual parodies, *The Puppet-Booth.* But Mr. Fuller did not write the great American novel. Neither did Mr. Howells, nor Mr. James. Who has? No one. Is there such a thing? Without existing it might be described in Celtic fashion, this mythical work, as pure fiction. Let us admit for the sake of argument that if it were written by some unknown monster of genius, it would, like Lewis Carroll's Snark, turn into a Boojum.

Henry James has said that no one is compelled to admire any particular sort of writing; that the province of fiction is all life, and he has also wisely remarked that "when you have no taste you have no discretion, which is the conscience of taste," and may we add, when you have no discretion you perpetrate the shocking fiction with which America is deluged at this hour. We are told that the new writers have altered the old canons of bad taste, but *"plus ça change, plus c'est la même chose."* A liquorish sentimentality is the ever-threatening rock upon which the bark of young American novelists goes to pieces. (Pardon the mixed metaphor.) Be sentimental and you will succeed! We agree with Dostoievsky that in fiction, as well as in life, there are no general principles, only special cases. But these cases, could they not be typical? even if there are not types, only individuals. And are men and women so enthralled by the molasses of sentimentalism in life? Have the motion-pictures hopelessly deranged our critical values? I know that in America charity covers a multitude of mediocrities, nevertheless, I am loath to believe that all one reads in praise of wretched contemporary fiction is meant in earnest.

Well, *chacun à ses dégoûts!* The "thrilling" detective story, the romantic sonorities of the ice-cream-soda woman novelist?—with a triple-barrelled name, as Rudyard Kipling put it once upon a time—or that church of Heavenly Ennui, the historical novel—what a cemetery of ideas, all of them! An outsider must be puzzle-pated by this tumult of tasteless writing and worse observation. However, history in fiction may be a cavalcade of shining shadows, brilliant, lugubrious, dull, or joyful happenings; but where Thackeray succeeded multitudes have failed. Who shall bend the bow of that Ulysses? Native talent, subtle and robust, we possess in abundance; thus far it has cultivated with success in its own parochial garden—which is as it should be. The United States of Fiction. America is Cosmopolis.

II

As to the Puritanism of our present novels one may dare to say in the teeth of youthful protestants that it is non-existent. The pendulum has swung too far the other way. And as literary artists are rare, the result has not been reassuring. Zola seems prudish after some experiments of the younger crowd. How badly they pull off the trick. How coarse and hard and heavy their touch. Most of these productions read like stupid translations from a dull French original. They are not immoral, only vulgar. As old Flaubert used to say: such books are false, nature is not like that. How keenly he saw through the humbug of "free love"—a romantic tradition of George Sand's epoch—may be noted in his comment that Emma Bovary found in adultery all the platitudes of marriage. Ah! that much-despised, stupid, venerable institution, marriage! How it has been flouted since the days of Rousseau—the father of false romanticism and that stupefying legend, the "equality" of mankind. (O! the beautiful word, "equality," invented for the delectation of rudimentary minds.) A century and more fiction has played with the theme of concubinage. If the Nacquet divorce bill had been introduced a decade or so before it was in France, what would have become of the threatre of Dumas *fils,* or later, of the misunderstood woman in Ibsen's plays? All such tribal taboos make or unmake literature.

So, merely as a suggestion to ambitious youngsters, let the novelist of the future in search of a novelty describe a happy marriage, children, a husband who doesn't drink or gamble, a wife who votes, yet loves her home, her family, and knows how to cook. What a realistic bombshell he would hurl into the camp of sentimental socialists and them that believe a wedding certificate is like Balzac's *La Peau de Chagrin*—a document daily shrinking in happiness. Absurdities make martyrs, but of all the absurd and ineffectual martyrdoms that of running off with another's wife is usually the crowning one. "I don't call this very popular pie," said the little boy in Richard Grant White's story; and the man in the case is usually the first to complain of his bargain in pastry.

However, categories are virtually an avowal of mental impuissance, and all marriages are not made in heaven. In the kingdom of morality there are many mansions. When too late you may sport with the shade—not in the shade— of Amaryllis, and perhaps elbow epigrams as a lean consolation. That is your own affair. Paul Verlaine has told us that *"j'ai vécu énormement,"* though his living enormously did not prove that he was happy. Far from it. But he had at least the courage to relate his terrors. American novelists may agree with Dostoievsky that "everything in the world always ends in meanness"; or with Doctor Pangloss that all is for the best in the best of possible worlds. An affair of temperament. But don't mix the values. Don't confuse intellectual substances. Don't smear a fact with treacle and call it truth. Above all, don't preach. Impiety is an indiscretion, yet, don't be afraid to tell the truth. From Jane Austen and Walter Scott, the parents of the modern English novel, to many modern instances, fiction has thrived best on naked truth. All the rest is sawdust, tripe-selling, and sentimentalism. Didn't Mr. Roundabout declare in one of his famous papers that "Figs are sweet, but fictions are sweeter"? In our land we can't get the latter sweet enough. Altruism, Brotherhood of Man Uplifting. These are the shibboleths of the *"nouvelles couches sociales."* Prodigious!

III

J. K. Huysmans declared that in the land of books there are no schools; no idealism, realism, symbolism; only good writers and bad. Whistler said the same about painting and painters. Setting aside the technical viewpoint of such dicta, we fancy that our "best sellers" do not preoccupy themselves with the "mere writing" of their fictions, but they have developed a formidable faculty of preaching. Old-fashioned fiction that discloses personal charm, that delineates manners, or stirs the pulse of tragedy—not melodrama, is vanishing from publishers' lists. Are there not as many charming men and women perambulating the rind of the planet as there were in the days when Jane Austen, or Howells, or Turgenev wrote? We refuse to believe there are not; but there is little opportunity, in a word, no market, for the display of these qualities. The novel with a purpose, generally an unpleasant purpose, has usurped the rule of the novel of character and manners. Boanerges, not Balzac, now occupies the pasteboard pulpit of fiction.

I quoted Henry James to the effect that all life is the province of the novelist. Nevertheless, the still small garden wherein is reared the tender solitary flower does but ill represent the vaster, complicated forest of common humanity. The ivory tower of the cultivated egoist is not to be unduly admired; rather Zola's *La Terre* with its foul facts than a palace of morbid art. Withal, the didactic side of our fiction is overdone. I set it down to the humbug about the "masses" being opposed to the "classes." Truly a false antithesis. As if the French bourgeois were not a product of the revolution (poor bourgeois, always abused by the novelist). As if a poor man suddenly enriched didn't prove, as a rule, the hardest taskmaster to his own class. Consider the new-rich. What a study they afford the students of manners. A new generation has arisen. Its taste, intelligence, and culture; its canned manners, canned music—preferably pseudo-African—canned art, canned food, canned literature; its devotion to the mediocre—what a field for our aspiring young "secretaries to society."

Cheap prophylactics, political and religious—for religion is fast being butchered to make the sensational evangelists' holiday—are in vogue. They affect our fiction-mongers, who burn to avenge wrongs, write novels about the "downtrodden masses," and sermons on social evils—evils that have always existed, always will exist. Like the knife-grinder, story they have none to tell. Why write fiction, or what they are pleased to call fiction? Why not join the brave brigade of agitators and pamphleteers? The lay preachers are carrying off the sweepstakes. For them Mr. Howells is a superannuated writer. Would there were more like him in continence of speech, wholesomeness of judgment, nobility of ideals, and in the shrewd perception of character.

Fiction, too, is a fine art, though this patent fact has escaped the juvenile Paul Prys, who are mainly endeavouring to arouse class against mass. It's an old dodge, this equality theory, as old as Beelzebub, Lord of Flies. When all fruit fails, welcome envy and malicious slandering. When you have nothing else to write about, attack your neighbour, especially if he hath a much-coveted vineyard. Max Stirner, least understood of social philosophers, wrote, "Mind your own business," and he forged on the anvil of experience a mighty leading motive for the conduct of life. But our busy little penmen don't see in this golden motto a sufficient sentimental appeal. It doesn't flatter the "masses." Mr. Bryan a few years ago told us that we were all middle class. What is middle class? In Carlyle's day it was a "gigman"; in ours is it the owner of a "flivver"? But in the case of Snob vs. Mob, Snob always wins.

This twaddle about "democratic art" is the bane of our literature. There is only good art. Whether it deals with such "democratic" subjects as *L'Assommoir* or *Germinie Lacerteux,* or such "aristocratic" themes as those of D'Annunzio and Paul Bourget, it is the art thereof that determines the product. I hold no brief for the sterile fiction that is enrolled under the banner of "Art for Art." I go so far as to believe that a novelist with a beautiful style often allows that style to get in the way of human nature. Stained-glass windows have their use, but they falsify the daylight. A decorative style may suit pseudo-mediaeval romances, but for twentieth-century realism it is sadly amiss. Nor is the arterio-sclerotic school of psychological analysis to be altogether commended. It has been well-nigh done to death by Stendhal, Meredith, James, and Bourget; and it is as cold as a star. Flaubert urged as an objection to writing a novel, proving something that the other fellow can prove precisely the opposite. In either case selection plays the role.

The chief argument against the novel "with a purpose"—as the jargon goes —is its lack of validity either as a document or as art. A novel may be anything, but it must not be polemical. Zola has been, still is, the evil genius of many talented chaps who "sling ink," not to make a genuine book, but to create a sensation. Such writers lack patience, art, and direction. They always keep one eye on the box-office. Indeed, the young men and women of the day, who are squandering upon paper their golden genius, painfully resemble in their productions the dime novels once published by the lamented Beadle or the lucubrations in the Saturday weeklies of long ago. But in those publications there was more virility. The heroes then were not well-dressed namby-pambies; the villains were villainous; the detectives detected real crimes, and were not weavers of metaphysical abstractions like your latter-day miracle-workers of an impossible Scotland Yard; and the girls were girls, neither neurasthenic, nor did they outgolf all creation. The "new novelists still deal with the same raw material of melodrama. Their handling of love-episodes has much of the blaring-brass quality of old-fashioned Italian opera. They loudly twang the strings of sloppy sentiment, which evoke not music, but mush and moonshine. And these are our "motion-masters" to-day.

IV

There can be no objection to literature and life coming to grips. Letters should touch reality. Many a sturdy blow has been struck at abuses by penmen masquerading behind fiction. No need to summon examples. As for realism—I deny there are commonplace people. Only those writers are commonplace that believe in the phrase. It is one of the paradoxes of art that the commonplace folk of Thackeray, Flaubert, or Anthony Trollope who delight us between covers would in life greatly bore us. The ennui is artistically suggested, though not experienced by the reader. It is the magic of the novelist, his style and philosophy, that make his creations vital.

Dostoievsky says there are no old women—to be sure he puts the expression in the mouth of the sensualist Karamazov—and as a corollary I maintain that nothing is uninteresting if painted by a master hand, from carrots to Chopin. As for the historical novel, there is *Sentimental Education* as a model, if you desire something epical in scale and charged with the modern ironic spirit. A Flaubertian masterpiece, this book, with its daylight atmosphere; the inimitable sound, shape, gait, and varied prose rhythms of its sentences, its marvellous gallery of portraits executed in the Dutch manner of Hals and Vermeer, its nearness to its environment, and its fidelity to the pattern of life. It is a true "historical" novel, for it is real—to employ the admirable simile of Mr. Howells.

No need to transpose the tragic gloom of Artzibashef to America; we are an optimistic people, thanks to our air and sky, political conditions, and the immigration of sturdy peasant folk. Yet we, too, have our own peculiar gloom and misery and social problems to solve. We are far from being the "shadowland" of fiction, as a certain English critic said. When I praise the dissonantal art of Michael Artzibashef it is not with the idea that either his style or his pessimism should be aped. That way unoriginality lies. But I do contend that in the practice of his art, its sincerity, its profundity, he might be profitably patterned after by the younger generation. Art should elevate as well as amuse. Must fiction always be silly and shallow? It need be neither sordid nor didactic.

William James put the matter in a nutshell when he wrote that "the whole atmosphere of present-day Utopian literature tastes mawkish and dish-watery to people who still keep a sense of life's more bitter flavours." And on this fundamentally sound note I must end my little sermon—for I find that I have been practising the very preaching against which I warned embryo novelists. But, then, isn't every critic a lay preacher?

VAN WYCK BROOKS

The Critical Movement in America

[1921]

It was only the other day that America first came in for its effective share of self-criticism. The critical movement in America happened, as it were, overnight; and the critic in this country is still so new a type that we cannot be surprised if he is regarded as an undesirable alien, even a traitor. There is nothing else in all modern history like the unanimity of praise and confidence with which, by its passengers, the American Ship of State was launched and manned. In all our long nineteenth-century past, there was scarcely a breath of dissent, doubt, or censure: the semi-outlaw Whitman's *Democratic Vistas* was almost unique in this regard, for Emerson's and Lowell's strictures were lost in the flood of their social optimism. No wonder we became the most complacent of peoples. No wonder the tide of criticism rose at last.

One thinks of all this as one considers, for instance, such an alien point of reference as John Ruskin. To most of us, no doubt, Ruskin has always seemed a normal and familiar possession. Yet, as one reflects on his career, the thought comes to one's mind: How different this man was from anything the America of his day could have produced! Hear, for example, what Mr. Masefield recently said of him: "Ruskin, looking out upon his native land some eighty years ago, decided that he could not believe in it, that there was nothing spiritual there which he could trust, nor human work being done which he could share." Imagine a nineteenth-century American giving utterance to such a sentiment, the sentiment from which Ruskin's work sprang! Yet this was surely the animating sentiment of the greatest English literature of the century, even of Charles Dickens: who but Macaulay, of all the writers of England, was not filled, as regards the future of his people, with more or less fundamental doubts? And meanwhile the writers of America chanted a unanimous hymn to progress. They were happy, they were hopeful. They agreed, or seemed to agree, with the famous utterance of Edward Everett: "Our government is in its theory perfect, and in its operation it is perfect also. Thus we have solved the great problem in human affairs." Was this because the American life of their epoch was finer and more wholesome than English life? Because it contained a greater spiritual promise? Few in our generation would

80

affirm this. We know too well how fully justified were most of the European travelers' reflections on our old social life—which used to cause such resentment in American breasts: they were not malignant, those travelers' reflections, any more than the comments of the European critics and scholars—Ruskin himself, for instance—who looked upon "Americanism" as a poisonous growth that might well infect and destroy all civilization. And as we observe the complacency to which our national optimism gave birth, we ask ourselves whether this optimism was ever a symptom of health, whether it was not indeed the symptom of a great evil: the loss of a clear sense of the true values of life.

It is certain, in any case, that our criticism has suffered from the obvious necessity of making up for much lost time. We do not understand criticism, and this is because we have had so little of it. We have had no candid friends of our own race, no "national conscience," in short, such as every European people has had, for England is not unique in this respect: and, consequently, it was difficult a few years ago for most Americans to question the belief of Mr. Meredith Nicholson, for instance, that "if there is any manifestation on earth of a divine ordering of things, it is here in America." This is the sort of belief the Philistine majority in every country cherishes in its heart; it is the sort of belief that Matthew Arnold so well described as "vulgar, and not only vulgar but retarding," for retarding it surely is if, in order to go somewhere, to get somewhere, to advance, to develop, we must first have an inner conviction that we have not already arrived. If American life as we know it is indeed a manifestation of a divine ordering of things, there is nothing for us to do but to continue to manifest our divinity. But is our life divine? Is it so much better than the life of England, France, Germany, Russia that the comments of a Ruskin, a Renan, a Nietzsche would have been sheer impertinences on our side of the Atlantic? The prosperous middle class the world over looks upon itself and its own fatness with an overkindly eye; but America is the only modern country where, until recent years, the prosperous middle class has gone unchallenged, where the Philistines have never been aroused to a sense of their limitations. Heine never permitted the Germans to forget how much they had to learn; no one was ever more outspoken than Nietzsche in regard to "what the Germans lack." The French are complacent enough; but Renan never ceased to remind them of their "incurable religious mediocrity," of "the alternations of levity and dullness, of narrow timidity and foolish temerity" which are among the features of the French mind. Arnold, Ruskin, Carlyle, as we know, kept their guns steadily trained on the weaknesses of the English character; and while Ibsen lived how many illusions in regard to their peculiar superiority were the people of Norway suffered to cherish?

Merely to mention these names is to suggest how uniformly our American fur has been rubbed the right way. For while Emerson, Lowell, Whitman deplored the imperfections of our social life, their criticism was neither sustained nor drastic. Emerson was the incarnation of optimism and lived, besides, too much in a timeless world to concern himself with a single phase of history: this was not his rôle. Lowell was so conscious of that "certain condescension in foreigners" that he could not sufficiently draw the veil over the short-comings of his countrymen. And there was Howells, with his rosy vision of the American scene, all the more delusive because he professed an intransigent realism. There was even Henry James, whom nothing could have induced to live in America: did he not apologize in one of his prefaces for having spoken in terms of disrespect of a certain small city in Massachusetts, adding so much thereby to the ultimate obloquy of those who have since reproached our Gopher Prairies? These men, of course, were not primarily critics, and that is just the point; Thoreau was not primarily a critic; in fact, before the war we had no critics. Those who could not put up with our life in the East quietly went West, and those who could not put up with our life at all quietly went to Europe. No one stood still and spoke out; and after the Civil War, even the voices of the traveling foreigners who told the truth about many of our ways were cloaked and muffled. Everyone waited, waited, by common consent, to see how the great experiment of democracy was going to work out. We had sixty years of grace while the oracles were dumb.

We were, in a word, singularly unconscious. America "just growed"—in the manner of the British Empire perhaps, but certainly in a very different man-ner from England itself, or France or Germany. It grew by sheer activity, expansion, immigration, without forethought, afterthought, reflection of any kind. That is to say, since no population is ever aware of itself as a population, save perhaps in times of war, it had no governing and directing minority more conscious than the multitude, more conscious of human values, no class of thinkers who, while having no administrative authority, might yet have ex-ercised a real authority over popular opinion, interpreting the movements of society in the light of historical principles, and arousing in those who were intelligent and articulate a just sense of what was really happening. Who knew, for instance, that America was becoming an empire, apprehended this fact in all its implications? America never "meant" to become an empire, and few Americans know, even today, really know, I mean *apprehend*, that Amer-ica is an empire, with all the paraphernalia of imperialism. This change came automatically, as it were, because, contrary as it plainly was to the professed genius of the Republic, no strong, articulate minority showed the people what was taking place before their eyes. One has only to compare the feeble protests that arose throughout this country over the annexation of the Philippines with the outburst of resentment and remonstrance, of satire and impassioned poetry, evoked in England by the Boer War, to perceive the difference be-tween a conscious and an unconscious society; and the difference only widens when we remember that imperialism in the England of those days had been for generations a deliberate national policy.

So it was that after the Civil War our social history became an illustration of what might be called a policy of indifference. The individual stood aside and let things take their course. To a large extent, this has been true of our thought from the beginning: whether optimistic, as with Emerson and Whitman, or pessimistic, as with Henry Adams and Mark Twain, it has always tended to be fatalistic. It has assumed, or tended to assume, that things were "coming out all right," because Americans are Americans, or else that things were coming out all wrong, because nothing could stop them from doing so, because human life itself is a mistake, as Mark Twain thought, or because, as Henry Adams thought, evolution is merely a matter of thermodynamics. These attitudes are all fatalistic because they beg the question of human control or deny its possibility; and together they have formed the various strands of a national tradition in which the critical intellect has played scarcely any part whatever. That America must and will be perfect just by being itself, or that America is doomed and damned: these are the two poles between which, even to this day, our public opinion oscillates. The cultivated classes are too often convinced, although they keep their opinion to themselves, that the country is already doomed and damned. The rest are equally sure, not that the country will be, but that the country already is what Mr. Nicholson calls it; and they have plainly arrived at this opinion by lowering their human standards to a point where the great values of life do not exist. Mr. Nicholson, who speaks so complacently of the "divine ordering of things" in America, also says that a "town is better advertised by enlightened sanitary ordinances duly enforced than by the number of its citizens who are acquainted with the writings of Walter Pater. If Main Street knows," he adds, "what America is all about, and bathes itself and is kind and considerate of its neighbors, why not leave the rest on the knees of the gods?" Why, indeed, if we share Mr. Nicholson's indifference to the great human values? "We do not know," he says again, "we do not know but that in some far day a prowling New Zealander, turning up a banjo and a trap-drum amid the ruins of some American college, will account them nobler instruments than the lyre and lute." But why wait for the "ruins" of this American college? The ruins are with us already if we have lost a sense of the distinction between the trap-drum and the lyre and lute.

And the sense of this distinction has been lost, too largely lost, because criticism, in all these years, has failed to keep it alive. Mr. William Allen White has observed that he would like to collect the junior pessimists who are raking America with their criticism and duck them in the town-pump. One readily understands Mr. White's resentment, for he has himself gone through life without once being held up, without once being checked in his rampant career of self-congratulation over the virtues of Kansas. And Mr. White's resentment is widely shared; one constantly hears of apostles of good-Americanism who have "had about enough" of these junior pessimists. And it cannot be denied that for this resentment there exists a certain reason, for few indeed of the pessimists in question are not open to the retort that they are themselves no more essentially civilized than the civilization they attack. We are always well aware of what they hate; we are seldom aware at all of what they love, and only what they love can civilize us. This is true; yet, save for these same vipers, whose critical equipment is, one admits, defective, where else in America can we turn for criticism? The "best" magazines freely open their columns to Mr. Nicholson's and Mr. White's opinions; the "best" people, as we are led to suppose, delight in these opinions. At every adverse comment on our civilization the cry still goes up: But there is so much to be said on the other side! And no one questions this; what one asserts, and asserts, and asserts again, is that there is so much to be said on *this* side. If it were not for these vipers who have risen among us, we should all find ourselves intellectually on the level of the "man in the street" for whom Messrs. Nicholson and White are so proud to speak. The conservative reviews, as one might think, exist for the purpose of combating the radical reviews, giving aid and comfort to that false-Americanism, now dominant through the world, the rise and spread of which was the nightmare of those European critics of the nineteenth century whose standards they profess to uphold.

In short, before the emergence of our critical movement, the clear sense of the great values of life had long been submerged in America. For we are obliged to take Mr. White and Mr. Nicholson at their word and assume that they really do not know the difference between the trap-drum and the lyre and lute, or between the Valley of Democracy and the Kingdom of Heaven. We are even obliged to take at their word the defenders of some pseudo-American tradition who failed to challenge Edward Bok, for instance, when he adopted the word "Americanization" to describe a career that was throughout devoted, with whatever good intentions, to the vulgarization of American life. And we cannot expect that those who are color-blind to the great values of life, in the name of which criticism speaks, will see anything but animus in this criticism, or regard it as anything but insulting. This indeed would be true if our criticism were ten times more certain of its values than it is: we know that Mr. White would as readily duck a Ruskin as a Mencken. For Americans are not accustomed to plain speaking. We cherish a romantic view of our activities, and an American spade, to most of us, is not a spade at all: it is a sword, an implement of knighthood, and to call it a spade is to challenge our fondest prepossessions. The romantic soul dwells in the region of hyperbole, and its virtues are not the virtues of understatement. This fact explains the apparent censoriousness of much of our recent social criticism. Some of this criticism has really been censorious, it has been so by reaction; but much of it has only appeared censorious. If we had been accustomed to a realistic view of affairs, and a true historic sense of human values, we should have accepted this criticism and even rejoiced in it.

For we know how America appears in the eyes of the world. The Japanese poet, Mr. Yone Noguchi, is the spokesman of contemporary humanity when he describes our country as "floating comfortably on the ocean all by itself, as if a well-fed seal or lazy iceberg." And those who have an interest in America, its true life, its true historic rôle, are aware that such a posture is a perilous posture. No doubt, in the beginning, this uncritical attitude, this attitude of uncriticised faith and hope, contributed much to our dawning civilization. A new country is obliged to affirm its existence, to believe in itself against all comers. If the America of three generations ago had seen itself as Europeans saw it, as its own cultivated minds saw it in the privacy of their souls, it would have lost heart; for with nations as with individuals nothing is more paralyzing than a premature self-consciousness. Our old writers were surely aware of all that was imperfect in our society, but they were aware also that too much cannot be expected of a new country. They saw, moreover, that America was too deeply in the grip of unusual natural forces for criticism to have much effect upon it; for, as Frederick Turner pointed out in his study of *The Frontier in American History,* the development of American civilization in the nineteenth century exhibited a constant return to primitive conditions on a continually advancing frontier-line. Our social development was always beginning again *de novo* on the frontier, and this largely prevented Americans even in the settled areas from retaining a firm hold upon civilized values. And so our old writers, convinced of the futility of criticism, turned their reluctant energies in other directions. Meanwhile, with few exceptions, the immigrants from the Old World belonged to the inarticulate classes; and for them it was enough, or seemed enough, that the New World afforded them opportunities, of an economic sort, which they had not possessed in the Old. We know how these immigrants expressed themselves. Such works as *The Promised Land* and *The Making of an American* contributed immensely to our national self-esteem; and, what is more to the point, in the absence of native spokesmen who might have maintained the sense of human values, they served as the final proof in American eyes that our civilization was superior in all essentials to the civilization of Europe. In this realm, the realm of self-congratulation, it never rains but it pours.

Because of these peculiar circumstances, our social history differs from that of any of the European countries. We have never conceived it as possible to shape our social life. This social life has grown and changed so rapidly, so many racial strains have merged themselves in it, so many territories have opened before it, this life has indeed existed in such a flux that the idea of molding it has scarcely entered our calculations. It was this that prevented for so long the development of criticism in America. We know how quietistic Hawthorne was regarding every prospect of social change: we know his fear, embodied in the character of Hollingsworth, of tampering with "the natural order of things." A similar-diffidence inhibited Mark Twain, and surely this was one of the reasons that led Henry Adams to hide his life and restrained him from coming forward as the critic he plainly wished to be. They felt, these gifted men, that the only course for them was to stand aside and watch the American process—some in faith, others in despair, and more and more in despair, as they saw how little the process contemplated of what to them was important for civilization. For they felt that they could never shape the process, or control it in any way. Yet the longer the process continued, the more it became apparent that Americans, in so far as they were Americans who piqued themselves on their "Americanism," were ceasing to desire, were ceasing even to be able to desire, consciously and with their minds and wills, any goals in life except the goals that were placed before them by the world of trade. Yes, even to the point where their perceptions had come to rest on a purely physical plane.

But *autres temps, autres mœurs.* We have nourished ourselves on hope in America, where we should have nourished ourselves on desire. Many have hoped for America, few have desired for America. And desire is the mother of intention. And desire cannot come without criticism. "It is an *idea,*" as John Eglinton says, for which we wait. "Without an idea man is frivolous, dissatisfied, despicable. With an idea the long-hoarded initiatives of his nature are liberated, he strains forward to new consummations." Criticism, so silent in the past, is vocal now in America; and why should it be vocal if there were not within it a sudden faith in the ability of Americans to shape their destiny, to mold it and give it form, to ride things as things have ridden them? The division between the two great camps of modern American writers is a division between those who are still satisfied with a national state of adolescence and those who exact of America the traits and responsibilities of maturity; and if the latter appear a little rough and importunate, it is because they are obliged to shake out of a deep sleep a population that should have been kept awake by an unbroken succession of gentle proddings. The recent damming-up of our social energies, through the closing of the frontier at the West and the slackening of immigration at the East, enables us really for the first time to submit to a candid scrutiny our prepossessions in regard to property and every other fundamental issue, to desire a great and beautiful corporate life. How scattered our forces have been! We have taken pleasure, it seems, in making machines of men; and repudiating the vision of a good society, we have not discouraged our finest intellects from giving up society as a bad job and devoting to the material periphery the passion they might have devoted to human beings. Our thought has been centrifugal instead of centripetal; it has gone out to the frame, it has never fixed itself upon the picture.

The great social thinkers, the great critics have given us a sense of society as a whole, and of man as a social animal, capable of molding his environment towards a humane ideal. And Ruskin, as Lawrence Binyon says, might well have taken as his motto the lines of Blake:

> I will not cease from mental fight,
> Nor shall my sword sleep in my hand,
> Till we have built Jerusalem
> In England's green and pleasant land.

American criticism, too, is capable of such a vision. But this is certain, American criticism will never attain its object as long as it fails to conceive, as something ever-present in its purview, the "green and pleasant land" it contemplates. The great critics have always convinced the world in spite of the prepossessions of the world; it is their ability to do so that makes these critics great and worthy of attention, for unless they speak with reasonableness and human understanding they confess in their own words that they do not possess that in the name of which they pretend to speak. No doubt, for many years in this country the critics and the unconverted public are destined to wage the blindest kind of warfare; for the critical attitude in our general mind has perished from disuse. But as long as this continues let us remember that our work is only a kind of spadework, which antecedes the real task of criticism. To forget this is to have lost the battle. For Amiel expressed the just motto of critics in those memorable words: "Truth should not merely conquer, it should win."

From *Sketches in Criticism* by Van Wyck Brooks, pp. 11–25. Copyright, 1932, by E. P. Dutton & Co. Reprinted by permission of the author and publishers. An earlier form of this material appeared in *The Freeman* ("A Reviewer's Notebook"), Vol. IV (Oct. 12, 1921), pp. 118–119, and other issues of that year.

PART II
Versions of Tradition and Responsibility

T. S. ELIOT

Tradition and the Individual Talent

[1919]

In English writing we seldom speak of tradition, though we occasionally apply its name in deploring its absence. We cannot refer to "the tradition" or to "a tradition"; at most, we employ the adjective in saying that the poetry of So-and-so is "traditional," or even "too traditional." Seldom, perhaps, does the word appear except in a phrase of censure. If otherwise, it is vaguely approbative, with the implication, as to the work approved, of some pleasing archaeological reconstruction. You can hardly make the word agreeable to English ears without this comfortable reference to the reassuring science of archaeology.

Certainly the word is not likely to appear in our appreciations of living or dead writers. Every nation, every race, has not only its own creative, but its own critical turn of mind; and is even more oblivious of the shortcomings and limitations of its critical habits than of those of its creative genius. We know, or think we know, from the enormous mass of critical writing that has appeared in the French language the critical method or habit of the French; we only conclude (we are such unconscious people) that the French are "more critical" than we, and sometimes even plume ourselves a little with the fact, as if the French were the less spontaneous. Perhaps they are; but we might remind ourselves that criticism is as inevitable as breathing, and that we should be none the worse for articulating what passes in our minds when we read a book and feel an emotion about it, for criticising our own minds in their work of criticism. One of the facts that might come to light in this process is our tendency to insist, when we praise a poet, upon those aspects of his work in which he least resembles anyone else. In these aspects or parts of his work we pretend to find what is individual, what is the peculiar essence of the man. We dwell with satisfaction upon the poet's difference from his predecessors, especially his immediate predecessors; we endeavor to find something that can be isolated in order to be enjoyed. Whereas if we approach a poet without this prejudice we shall often find that not only the best, but the most individual parts of his work may be those in which the dead poets, his ancestors, assert their immortality most vigorously. And I do not mean the impressionable period of adolescence, but the period of full maturity.

Yet if the only form of tradition, of handing down, consisted in following the ways of the immediate generation before us in a blind or timid adherence to its successes, "tradition" should positively be discouraged. We have seen many such simple currents soon lost in the sand; and novelty is better than repetition. Tradition is a matter of much wider significance. It cannot be inherited, and if you want it you must obtain it by great labor. It involves, in the first place, the historical sense, which we may call nearly indispensable to anyone who would continue to be a poet beyond his twenty-fifth year; and the historical sense involves a perception, not only of the pastness of the past, but of its presence; the historical sense compels a man to write not merely with his own generation in his bones, but with a feeling that the whole of the literature of Europe from Homer and within it the whole of the literature of his own country has a simultaneous existence and composes a simultaneous order. This historical sense, which is a sense of the timeless as well as of the temporal and of the timeless and of the temporal together, is what makes a writer traditional. And it is at the same time what makes a writer most acutely conscious of his place in time, of his own contemporaneity.

No poet, no artist of any art, has his complete meaning alone. His significance, his appreciation is the appreciation of his relation to the dead poets and artists. You cannot value him alone; you must set him, for contrast and comparison, among the dead. I mean this as a principle of esthetic, not merely historical, criticism. The necessity that he shall conform, that he shall cohere, is not onesided; what happens when a new work of art is created is something that happens simultaneously to all the works of art which preceded it. The existing monuments form an ideal order among themselves, which is modified by the introduction of the new (the really new) work of art among them. The existing order is complete before the new work arrives; for order to persist after the supervention of novelty, the *whole* existing order must be, if ever so slightly, altered; and so the relations, proportions, values of each work of art toward the whole are readjusted; and this is conformity between the old and the new. Whoever has approved this idea of order, of the form of European, of English literature will not find it preposterous that the past should be altered by the present as much as the present is directed by the past. And the poet who is aware of this will be aware of great difficulties and responsibilities.

In a peculiar sense he will be aware also that he must inevitably be judged by the standards of the past. I say judged, not amputated, by them; not judged to be as good as, or worse or better than, the dead; and certainly not judged by the canons of dead critics. It is a judgment, a comparison, in which two things are measured by each other. To conform merely would be for the new work not really to conform at all; it would not be new, and would therefore not be a work of art. And we do not quite say that the new is more valuable because it fits in; but its fitting in is a test of its value—a test, it is true, which can only be slowly and cautiously applied, for we are none of us infallible judges of conformity. We say: it appears to conform, and is perhaps individual, or it appears individual, and may conform; but we are hardly likely to find that it is one, and not the other.

To proceed to a more intelligible exposition of the relation of the poet to the past: he can neither take the past as a lump, an indiscriminate bolus, nor can he form himself wholly on one or two private admirations, nor can he form himself wholly upon one preferred period. The first course is inadmissible, the second is an important experience of youth, and the third is a pleasant and highly desirable supplement. The poet must be very conscious of the main current, which does not at all flow invariably through the most distinguished reputations. He must be quite aware of the obvious fact that art never improves, but that the material of art is never quite the same. He must be aware that the mind of Europe—the mind of his own country—a mind which he learns in time to be much more important than his own private mind—is a mind which changes, and that this change is a development which abandons nothing *en route*, which does not superannuate either Shakespeare, or Homer, or the rock drawing of the Magdalenian draughtsman. That this development, refinement perhaps, complication certainly, is not, from the point of view of the artist, any improvement. Perhaps not even an improvement from the point of view of the psychologist or not to the extent which we imagine: perhaps only in the end based upon a complication in economics and machinery. But the difference between the present and the past is that the conscious present is an awareness of the past in a way and to an extent which the past's awareness of itself cannot show.

Someone said: "The dead writers are remote from us because we *know* so much more than they did." Precisely, and they are that which we know.

I am alive to a usual objection to what is clearly part of my programme for the *métier* of poetry. The objection is that the doctrine requires a ridiculous amount of erudition (pedantry), a claim which can be rejected by appeal to the lives of poets in any pantheon. It will even be affirmed that much learning deadens or perverts poetic sensibility. While, however, we persist in believing that a poet ought to know as much as will not encroach upon his necessary receptivity and necessary laziness, it is not desirable to confine knowledge to whatever can be put into a useful shape for examinations, drawing-rooms, or the still more pretentious modes of publicity. Some can absorb knowledge, the more tardy must sweat for it. Shakespeare acquired more essential history from Plutarch than most men could from the whole

British Museum. What is to be insisted upon is that the poet must develop or procure the consciousness of the past and that he should continue to develop this consciousness throughout his career.

What happens is a continual surrender of himself as he is at the moment to something which is more valuable. The progress of an artist is a continual self-sacrifice, a continual extinction of personality.

There remains to define this process of depersonalization, and its relation to the sense of tradition. It is in this depersonalization that art may be said to approach the condition of science. I, therefore, invite you to consider, as a suggestive analogy, the action which takes place when a bit of finely filiated platinum is introduced into a chamber containing oxygen and sulphur dioxide.

II

Honest criticism and sensitive appreciation are directed not upon the poet but upon the poetry. If we attend to the confused cries of the newspaper critics and the *susurrus* of popular repetition that follows, we shall hear the names of poets in great numbers; if we seek not Blue-book knowledge but the enjoyment of poetry, and ask for a poem, we shall seldom find it. I have tried to point out the importance of the relation of the poem to other poems by other authors, and suggested the conception of poetry as a living whole of all the poetry that has ever been written. The other aspect of this Impersonal theory of poetry is the relation of the poem to its author. And I hinted, by an analogy, that the mind of the mature poet differs from that of the immature one not precisely in any valuation of "personality," not being necessarily more interesting, or having "more to say," but rather by being a more finely perfected medium in which special, or very varied, feelings are at liberty to enter into new combinations.

The analogy was that of the catalyst. When the two gases previously mentioned are mixed in the presence of a filament of platinum, they form sulphurous acid. This combination takes place only if the platinum is present; nevertheless the newly formed acid contains no trace of platinum, and the platinum itself is apparently unaffected; has remained inert, neutral, and unchanged. The mind of the poet is the shred of platinum. It may partly or exclusively operate upon the experience of the man himself; but the more perfect the artist, the more completely separate in him will be the man who suffers and the mind which creates; the more perfectly will the mind digest and transmute the passions which are its material.

The experience, you will notice, the elements which enter the presence of the transforming catalyst, are of two kinds: emotions and feelings. The effect of a work of art upon the person who enjoys it is an experience different in kind from any experience not of art. It may be formed out of one emotion, or may be a combination of several; and various feelings, inhering for the writer in particular words or phrases or images, may be added to compose the final result. Or great poetry may be made without the direct use of any emotion whatever: composed out of feelings solely. Canto XV of the *Inferno* (Brunetto Latini) is a working up of the emotion evident in the situation; but the effect, though single as that of any work of art, is obtained by considerable complexity of detail. The last quatrain gives an image, a feeling attaching to an image which "came," which did not develop simply out of what precedes, but which was probably in suspension in the poet's mind until the proper combination arrived for it to add itself to. The poet's mind is, in fact, a receptacle for seizing and storing up numberless feelings, phrases, images, which remain there until all the particles which can unite to form a new compound are present together.

If you compare several representative passages of the greatest poetry you see how great is the variety of types of combination, and also how completely any semi-ethical criterion of "sublimity" misses the mark. For it is not the "greatness," the intensity, of the emotions, the components, but the intensity of the artistic process, the pressure, so to speak, under which the fusion takes place, that counts. The episode of Paolo and Francesca employs a definite emotion, but the intensity of the poetry is something quite different from whatever intensity in the supposed experience it may give the impression of. It is no more intense, furthermore, than Canto XXVI, the voyage of Ulysses, which has not the direct dependence upon an emotion. Great variety is possible in the process of transmutation of emotion: the murder of Agamemnon, or the agony of Othello, gives an artistic effect apparently closer to a possible original than the scenes from Dante. In the *Agamemnon,* the artistic emotion approximates to the emotion of an actual spectator; in *Othello* to the emotion of the protagonist himself. But the difference between art and the event is always absolute; the combination which is the murder of Agamemnon is probably as complex as that which is the voyage of Ulysses. In either case there has been a fusion of elements. The ode of Keats contains a number of feelings which have nothing particular to do with the nightingale, but which the nightingale, partly, perhaps, because of its attractive name, and partly because of its reputation, served to bring together.

The point of view which I am struggling to attack is perhaps related to the metaphysical theory of the substantial unity of the soul: for my meaning is, that the poet has, not a "personality" to express, but a particular medium, which is only a medium, and not a personality, in which impressions and experiences combine in peculiar and unexpected ways. Impressions and experiences which are important for the man may take no place in the poetry, and those which become important in the poetry may play quite a negligible part in the man, the personality.

I will quote a passage which is unfamiliar enough to be regarded with fresh attention in the light—or darkness—of these observations:

> And now methinks I could e'en chide myself
> For doating on her beauty, though her death
> Shall be revenged after no common action.
> Does the silkworm expend her yellow labours
> For thee? For thee does she undo herself?
> Are lordships sold to maintain ladyships
> For the poor benefit of a bewildering minute?
> Why does yon fellow falsify highways,
> And put his life between the judge's lips,
> To refine such a thing—keeps horse and men
> To beat their valours for her? . . .

In this passage (as is evident if it is taken in its context) there is a combination of positive and negative emotions: an intensely strong attraction toward beauty, and an equally intense fascination by the ugliness which is contrasted with it and which destroys it. This balance of contrasted emotion is in the dramatic situation to which the speech is pertinent, but that situation alone is inadequate to it. This is, so to speak, the structural emotion, provided by the drama. But the whole effect, the dominant tone, is due to the fact that a number of floating feelings, having an affinity to this emotion by no means superficially evident, have combined with it to give us a new art emotion.

It is not in his personal emotions, the emotions provoked by particular events in his life, that the poet is in any way remarkable or interesting. His particular emotions may be simple, or crude, or flat. The emotion in his poetry will be a very complex thing, but not with the complexity of the emotions of people who have very complex or unusual emotions in life. One error, in fact, of eccentricity in poetry is to seek for new human emotions to express; and in this search for novelty in the wrong place it discovers the perverse. The business of the poet is not to find new emotions, but to use the ordinary ones, and, in working them up into poetry, to express feelings which are not in actual emotions at all. And emotions which he has never experienced will serve his turn as well as those familiar to him. Consequently, we must believe that "emotion recollected in tranquillity" is an inexact formula. For it is neither emotion nor recollection, nor, without distortion of meaning, tranquillity. It is a concentration, and a new thing resulting from the concentration, of a very great number of experiences which to the practical and active person would not seem to be experiences at all; it is a concentration which does not happen consciously or of deliberation. These experiences are not "recollected," and they finally unite in an atmosphere which is "tranquil" only in that it is a passive attending upon the event. Of course, this is not quite the whole story. There is a great deal, in the writing of poetry, which must be conscious and deliberate. In fact, the bad poet is usually unconscious where he ought to be conscious, and conscious where he ought to be unconscious. Both errors tend to make him "personal." Poetry is not a turning loose of emotion, but an escape from emotion; it is not the expression of personality, but an escape from personality. But, of course, only those who have personality and emotions know what it means to want to escape from these things.

III

ὁ δὲ νοῦς ἴσως θειότερόν τι καὶ ἀπαθές ἐστιν.[1]

This essay proposes to halt at the frontier of metaphysics or mysticism, and confine itself to such practical conclusions as can be applied by the responsible person interested in poetry. To divert interest from the poet to the poetry is a laudable aim: for it would conduce to a juster estimation of actual poetry, good and bad. There are many people who appreciate the expression of sincere emotion in verse, and there is a smaller number of people who can appreciate technical excellence. But very few know when there is an expression of *significant* emotion, emotion which has its life in the poem, and not in the history of the poet. The emotion of art is impersonal. And the poet cannot reach this impersonality without surrendering himself wholly to the work to be done. And he is not likely to know what is to be done unless he lives in what is not merely the present, but the present moment of the past, unless he is conscious, not of what is dead, but of what is already living.

From *Selected Essays, 1917–32* by T. S. Eliot, pp. 3–11. Copyright, 1932. Reprinted by permission of Harcourt, Brace and Company, Inc. Reprinted from *The Sacred Wood* (1920). First published in *The Egoist* (London), Vol. VI (September–October, 1919), pp. 54–55, and (November–December, 1919), pp. 72–73.

Poetry and Propaganda

[1930]

THE text for this paper is taken from Whitehead's *Science and the Modern World*, page 127:

The literature of the nineteenth century, especially its English poetic literature, is a witness to the discord between the esthetic intuitions of mankind and the mechanism of science. Shelley brings vividly before us the elusiveness of the eternal ob-

[1] Aristotle, *De Anima*, I. 4, 408b29: "mind is, no doubt, something more divine and impassible" (J. A. Smith, Oxford translation). (Editor's note.)

jects of sense as they haunt the change which infects underlying organisms. Wordsworth is the poet of nature as being the field of enduring permanences carrying within themselves a message of tremendous significance. The eternal objects are also there for him,

<blockquote>The light that never was, on sea or land.</blockquote>

Both Shelley and Wordsworth emphatically bear witness that nature cannot be divorced from its esthetic values; and that these values arise from the cumulation, in some sense, of the brooding presence of the whole onto its various parts. Thus we gain from the poets the doctrine that a philosophy of nature must concern itself at least with these six notions: change, value, eternal objects, endurance, organism, interfusion.

So far Professor Whitehead. Now I must insist clearly at the beginning that what I have to say has nothing to do with this book as a whole, or with Mr. Whitehead's theory as a whole: I am not here judging or valuing his theory or his method or his results. I am concerned only with this one chapter, which is called "The Romantic Reaction," and only with this one passage in that chapter. And only, therefore, with two specific questions: can poetry be cited to *prove* anything? and to what extent can it even be cited to *illustrate* anything?

It appears to me that Mr. Whitehead is here summoning Shelley and Wordsworth to *prove* something in connection with what he calls a "philosophy of nature"; that is what his words *thus we gain from the poets the doctrine that,* seem to me to mean; even if the author did not mean that, it is at least what many of his readers must have taken it to mean.

When so distinguished a scientist and philosopher makes this use of poetry, a great many people will follow him, in the belief that anyone who can understand symbolic logic must certainly understand anything so simple as poetry. And indeed I must say that in the earlier part of his book Mr. Whitehead does prepare us to consent to any use of literature he may choose to make: his knowledge and appreciation of history and literature are so great, and his summaries and reviews of historical processes and periods so very skillful, his allusions so apt, that we are charmed into assent. Nevertheless, I believe that the passage I have just read is nonsense, and dangerous nonsense at that. Consider first how really remarkable it is that we should

. . . gain from the poets the doctrine that a philosophy of nature must concern itself at least with these six notions: change, value, eternal objects, endurance, organism, interfusion.

There are, to begin with, two steps in Whitehead's legerdemain. He has quoted, and discussed generally, two poets of one period, Shelley and Wordsworth. These two then become "the poets"; would any beginner in scientific inquiry ever exhibit such a perfect example of imperfect induction? And then the poets are said to demonstrate that a philosophy of nature must be concerned at least with the six concepts mentioned.

Let us take the first sentence:

The literature of the nineteenth century, especially its English poetic literature, is a witness to the discord between the esthetic intuitions of mankind and the mechanism of science.

To call the whole of English poetry of the nineteenth century to witness such a generality is certainly rash, and the meaning of the sentence is not clear. It might mean that the great English poets were all *aware* of this discord between intuitions and mechanism. In this form the statement might be true of the author of *In Memoriam*. But how far is it true of Browning or Swinburne, and as far as it may be true how significant is it in their respective views of life? But perhaps Mr. Whitehead means merely that poets, by affirming the reality of values, are denying by implication the sufficiency of a mechanistic philosophy. But in this form the statement is too comprehensive, for it applies to all artists at every time, as they all have affirmed the validity of esthetic intuitions. And in the proposition there are two terms to be examined, "esthetic intuitions," and "the mechanism of science"; and we must then consider in what way there can be any "discord" between terms so disparate.

That poor old creature, "mechanistic philosophy" or "materialism" has been in our time thoroughly repudiated by its old friends the scientists, and receives no kindness from anyone but a few liberal theologians. It is not of course quite the same thing as "the mechanism of science": the latter is strictly merely the corpus of pre Einstein and pre-Rutherford physical theory, which has been rejected more or less by physicists on the good ground that it does not account for all the facts—not on the doubtful ground that it offends poetic intuitions. The mechanism of science is not the same thing as a *philosophy* based on that science, which would assert that physical science would explain the whole universe, and that what would not be explained in this way was unworthy of notice. But in any case, I find myself in the curious position of having to defend the "mechanism of science," which is no friend of mine, against an eminent scientist.

Are we to suppose that a mechanistic philosophy is fundamentally antagonistic to the esthetic intuitions of mankind? That is certainly surprising, as some works of literary art seem to have been built upon it. The philosophy, such as it is, of Thomas Hardy's novels, seems to be based upon the mechanism of science. I think it is a very bad philosophy indeed, and I think that Hardy's work would be better for a better philosophy, or none at all; but there it is: has he not exploited determinism to extract his esthetic values from the contemplation of a world in which values do not count? There is a more important poet than Hardy, who is Lucretius. We cannot deny "esthetic intuitions" to Lucretius. His world was mechanical enough, in all conscience; and just because it was, Lucretius gets the particular emotional values that he does get. We may admit therefore a discord between the mechanism of science and *some* esthetic intuitions; but then we shall have to say that *every* philosophy is discordant with *some* intuitions. The new philosophy of Professor Eddington, for instance, is discordant with some of the intuitions of all Christians except members of the Society of Friends; the philosophy of Dante is not the ideal ground on which to reap the intuitions of Wordsworth.

So far I have not questioned the term "esthetic intuitions"; but this term is beset with ambiguity and vagueness. I suppose that Mr. Whitehead means such intuitions as are more or less common to mankind, but of which the artist is the most sensitive receiver, and without which he would not have the material for great art. But however we define the term, there is a gulf, and I think an impassable one, between the intuitions of poets *as such*, and any particular philosophy, or even any philosophical direction rather than any other. The existence of art certainly implies the reality of values, but that does not take us anywhere, and certainly points to no philosophic theory of value.

If I examined each of the sentences I should quickly grow tedious, so I will pass now to the last of them:

Thus we gain from the poets the doctrine that a philosophy of nature must concern itself at least with these six notions: change, value, eternal objects, endurance, organism, interfusion.

The first question is, if we get all this from the poets, where do the poets get it? Take *change* and *endurance*, for which Mr. Whitehead is so obliged to Shelley. Shelley, I suspect, got them where everybody else has got them in the end—that is, from Plato. The reality of eternal objects sounds to me much more like Plato than a discovery of Shelley, or all the romantic poets together. I do not deny the possibility that Shelley may have had a fresh intuition of these things, but Plato did get there first. And also it is very difficult to spot these intuitions: Shelley must have had an esthetic intuition that there is no God, and that the Christian religion is an odious lie; for he could hardly have reached such passionate conviction on the subject from mere reasoning. (Of course it is possible that he read Rousseau and Voltaire, or even Godwin.) Even if we gain the doctrine in question from *the poets*, we hardly needed to have gone to the poets for that. And in passing, I wonder whether the concept of *organism* is so fundamental to a philosophy of nature as Mr. Whitehead supposes. We may get a better term some day, or we may even return to Aristotle, who knew as much about what this term represents as anybody.

At the very best, Mr. Whitehead is, I think, confusing the *persuasive* power of poetry with evidence of truth. He is transferring to poetry, as a scientist, that credulity which previous generations, including some poets, are said to have bestowed upon science.

Professor Whitehead may serve as a warning that a man may be one of the greatest living exponents of formal logic, and yet be quite helpless in a field with which he is not familiar. I should not however have devoted this space merely to the churlish pleasure of attacking a famous man; but because I believe that the theory of poetry implicit in Whitehead's chapter is dangerous, because we could prove by it, choosing our examples judiciously, almost anything we like. I also believe, what is a related point which I cannot deal with here, that Mr. Whitehead errs by his ignorance of theology just as he errs by his not having thought seriously enough about poetry.

Now among those persons who have thought directly about poetry—and indeed some of them are greatly indebted to Mr. Whitehead and Mr. Russell for their logical training—there have arisen lately two interesting views. One is that of Mr. Montgomery Belgion, in one chapter of his recent book *Our Present Philosophy of Life*. His theory is that the *literary* artist—he is not concerned with the other arts—is what he calls an "irresponsible propagandist." That is to say, every writer adopts a view or theory of life; his choice may have been more or less justified or capricious, may be more or less right, may be true or false: it happens to be the view which suits *him;* he makes use of it as material for his literary art. The effect of the work of literary art is always to *persuade* the reader to accept that view or theory. This persuasion is always illicit. That is to say, that the reader is always led to believe something, and that assent is hypnotic—the art of the presentation seduces the reader: even if what he is led to believe is right to believe, the reader has been *mis*lead into believing it. This theory is, as you see, rather depressing, and is remotely similar to that of Plato, who ejected the poets from his ideal republic; but it is neither fantastic nor easy to overthrow.

The other theory is that of Mr. I. A. Richards, as expressed particularly in his recent book *Practical Criticism*. Mr. Richards holds that while it is probably necessary for the poet to believe something, in order to write his poetry—although he inclines to think that a further step will be made when the poet believes nothing—the ideal reader will appreciate the poetry in a state of mind which is not belief, but rather a temporary suspension of disbelief. The one critic would say, you see, that you will value Dante more highly if you are a Catholic; or alternatively, that if you are enchanted by the poetry of Dante you will probably become a Catholic. Mr. Richards would say, I think, that the more you know about what Dante believed or more exactly the more you know about the philosophy of life on which Dante's poem is based—leaving out of account the question of what and how Dante himself believed—the better: but that when you are enjoying Dante's poem to the full as poetry, you cannot be said either to believe, or to doubt, or to disbelieve, its scholastic philosophy. So you *ought* to be able to appreciate, as literature, *all* literature, of whatever place, race or time.

These two theories are not so antithetical as they at first seem. Mr. Belgion is more concerned with what actually does happen; he says that, whether you know it or not, you tend to believe, you are *influenced,* by any author whose form of expression you admire. Mr. Richards is less concerned with the actual than with the ideal reader: he says, in effect, this may happen, but in so far as it does happen your reaction is impure; you *ought not* to be affected in this way: it is possible and it is right to enjoy poetry as poetry, and you merely use in the reading the philosophy of the author; just as the author was using, unconsciously, that philosophy in order to write the poetry.

In a note to a recent essay which I have published on Dante, I made a first attempt to criticise both views, and to find some way of mediation between the truth of both. I am now making a fresh start.

First of all no art, and particularly and especially no literary art, can exist in a vacuum. We are, in practice, creatures of divers interests, and in many of our ordinary interests there is no obvious coherence. Read, for instance, the information given by those personages in *Who's Who* who condescend to fill in that space of the form marked *Recreations.* There is no apparent relation, to fabricate a specimen, between breeding prize Persian cats and racing toy yachts. This is one extreme of the scale. At the other end, we do tend, I am sure, to unify our interests. To suppose that anyone likes only the *best* poetry, and that he likes all of the best poetry equally, and that he likes all of the second-best poetry in a second-best liking, and so on until he detests all of the worst poetry equally, is to suppose a monster. I do not suppose that there ever has been, or ever will be, a critic of any art, whose appreciation was a separate faculty, quite judicious and wholly isolated from his other interests and his private passions: if there was, is or will be, he was, is or will be a bore with nothing at all to say. And yet, on the other hand, there is no worse bore, and no more futile critic, than the one who renounces all objective standards in order to recount his own reactions. "A voyage among masterpieces" is, I believe, the phrase that Anatole France used to describe his own criticism, implying that it was merely an account of his own feelings—yet the phrase itself admits that the masterpieces were there as masterpieces, before the voyage began.

But this apparent paradox—this need of aiming at one thing in order to do another—this apparent gospel of hypocrisy or self-deception, is right, because it is in the nature of the human soul and embodies its need and craving for perfection and unity. We do tend, I think, to organize our tastes in various arts into a whole; we aim in the end at a theory of life, or a view of life, and so far as we are conscious, to terminate our enjoyment of the arts in a philosophy, and our philosophy in a religion—in such a way that the personal to oneself is fused and completed in the impersonal and general, not extinguished, but enriched, expanded, developed, and more itself by becoming more something not itself.

There is, according to my view, not one, but a series, of appreciators of poetry. One of the errors, I think, of critical theory, is to conceive one hypothetical poet on the one hand, and one hypothetical reader on the other. It is perhaps a less dangerous error than to have no hypotheses at all. My point is that the legitimate motives of the poet, and also the legitimate responses of the reader, vary very widely, but that there is a possible order in the variations. In my series let us put Mr. Belgion at one end of the scale and Mr. Richards at the other. The one extreme is to like poetry merely for what it has to say: that is, to like it merely because it voices our own beliefs or prejudices—which is of course to be quite indifferent to the *poetry* of the poetry. The other extreme is to like the poetry because the poet has manipulated his material into perfect art, which is to be indifferent to the material, and to isolate our enjoyment of poetry from life. The one extreme is not enjoyment of poetry at all, the other is enjoyment of an abstraction which is merely *called* poetry. But between these extremes occurs a continuous range of appreciations, each of which has its limited validity.

The validity of this range of appreciations is confirmed by our examination of the impulses of different poets. We may for convenience contrast three different types. There is the philosophic poet like Lucretius and Dante, who accepts one philosophy of life, so to speak, in advance, and who constructs his poem on one idea. There is the poet like Shakespeare, or possibly Sophocles, who accepts current ideas and makes use of them, but in whose work the question of belief is much more baffling and evasive. There is finally another type, of which we might take Goethe as an example, who neither quite accepts a particular view of the whole, nor merely sees views of life to make poetry out of, but who in himself more or less combines the functions of philosopher and poet—or perhaps Blake; poets who have their own ideas and definitely believe them.

Some poets are of so mixed a type that it is impossible to say how far they write their poetry because of what they believe, and how far they believe a thing merely because they see that they can make poetry out of it. And if I am justified in allowing this range of possible motives to the true poet (and an analogous range to the true reader of poetry) then Mr. Belgion's and Mr. Richards' theories must be considerably modified. For the "irresponsible propaganda" is sometimes less irresponsible, and sometimes less propaganda. Lucretius and Dante, for instance, are what Mr. Belgion would call propagandists, certainly, but they are particularly conscious and responsible ones: you have only to read what Dante says in the *Convivio* and in his letter to Can-Grande to understand what his purpose was.

Milton was also a deliberate propagandist; but here we must allow for another difference. The philosophies of Lucretius and Dante, different as they are from each other, are still potent to influence mankind. I cannot imagine any reader today being affected in his theological views by Milton. The reason is, I think, that Lucretius and Dante are each summing up and restating in great poetry two views which are central to the history of the mind of western man; whereas Milton is merely restating in great poetry a view which was very largely his own invention, or his own concoction, and which represents an eccentric heresy revived in his own mind. In Milton it is much easier to separate the greatness of the poetry from the thought, serious as it is, behind that poetry. Milton, therefore, is much more apprehensible from the Richards point of view; because in reading Milton we are, I think, rapt by the splendid verse without being tempted to believe the philosophy or theology. In considering whether a literary artist is an irresponsible propagandist or not, we have therefore to take into account both varieties of intention, and varieties of effect in time. Milton may, I feel, have had this powerful influence at one time which I feel that Lucretius and Dante can have at any time; but I do not believe that he has it now. And in general, the element of propaganda in the actual effect of any piece of literature upon us will depend either upon the permanence of the doctrine, or upon its nearness to us in time. The effect of a book like *The Way of All Flesh* was, I am sure, for the generation immediately following Butler much what he intended; for the next generation it is not at all the same.

You will infer, perhaps, that we must come to the conclusion that it is impossible to enjoy (or judge) a work of art as such, until sufficient time has elapsed for its doctrines to be quite out of date: so that we merely inspect and accept them, as Mr. Richards would have us do: wait a few hundred years, and we shall know how good any piece of literature is. There are several reasons why this simple solution will not do. One is that when an author is so remote from us, in time or in race, that we know nothing of his material and cannot at all understand his beliefs, we cannot appreciate his work as poetry. To enjoy Homer as poetry, we need a good deal more than Greek vocabulary and Greek accidence and syntax; and the more we saturate ourselves in the life of the ancient Greeks, the more we attempt to recreate imaginatively their world, the better we understand and enjoy the poetry of that world. Another reason is that time, alas, does not necessarily bring detachment. It may merely substitute for a set of prejudices favorable to the poet, another set unfavorable to him. It is interesting to read the comments of Mr. Richards' students, as set forth in *Practical Criticism,* on Donne's great sonnet "At the round world's imagined corners. . . ." Some of the misunderstanding is due, I believe, not so much to ignorance of the theology of Donne's time, as to these students' more or less conscious acceptance of another set of beliefs current in our own time.

I have called Lucretius and Dante *responsible propagandists*. But there are some poets whom it is a strain to think of as propagandists at all. Take Shakespeare. He is never, like the former, expounding one definite philosophical system. I am aware that many attempts have been made, and will be made, to expound in clear prose the theory of life which Shakespeare is supposed to have held; and that any number of views of life have been extracted from Shakespeare. I do not say that such attempts are illegitimate or altogether futile; it is a natural tendency to philosophize on Shakespeare just as it is to philosophize on the world itself. Only, the philosophy of Shakespeare is quite a different thing from that of Dante; it really has more in common with, let us say, the philosophy of Beethoven. That is to say, those of us who love Beethoven find in his music something that we call its meaning, though we cannot confine it in words; but it is this meaning which fits it in, somehow, to our whole life; which makes it an emotional exercise and discipline, and not merely an appreciation of virtuosity. Shakespeare does certainly influence us; but as he influences each man according to his own education, temperament and sensibility, and as we have no clue to the relation of his influence upon any one mind with what Shakespeare actually meant, it is almost fantastic to call it propaganda.

When we come to Mr. Whitehead's mentors, Shelley and Wordsworth, the situation is again different. Judging from their effect upon Mr. Whitehead, we should certainly call them irresponsible propagandists. But I suspect that their influence upon such a mind as Mr. Whitehead's is in direct ratio to the vagueness of their ideas, or to the fact that they take certain things for granted, instead of expounding them. The orthodox Christian, for example, is hardly likely to take Dante as proving Christianity; the orthodox materialist is hardly likely to adduce Lucretius as evidence of materialism or atomism. What he will find in Dante or in Lucretius is the *esthetic* sanction: that is, the partial justification of these views of life by the art to which they give rise. And there is no doubt that we are all of us powerfully influenced by the esthetic sanction; and that any way or view of life which gives rise to great art is for us more plausible than one which gives rise to inferior art or to none. And on the other hand I do not believe that a Christian can fully appreciate Buddhist art, or vice versa.

But Mr. Whitehead was not, I suspect, making this use, which I consider legitimate, of the esthetic sanction. You do not get this by going to the poets for maxims or gnomic sayings, or by attributing to them some inspiration as of the Delphic oracle. You can only say: this or that poet had used these ideas to make poetry, and has accordingly shown that these ideas can and do give rise to certain values. These ideas consequently are valid not merely in a theory, but can be integrated into life through art. But in order to do this we are obliged to value first the art of a Shelley or a Wordsworth. How complete, how intelligent, how well understood, is the philosophy used by the poet, how completely does he realize it poetically; where does he get it from, how much of life does it cover? Such questions we must ask first. And what poetry proves about any philosophy is merely its possibility for being lived—for life includes both philosophy and art.

But, we may ask, is the greatness, the comprehensiveness of the philosophy in any actual or theoretical relation to the greatness of the poetry? Actually, we may find a poet giving greater validity to an inferior philosophy, by realizing it more fully and masterfully in literary art, and another employing a better philosophy and realizing it less satisfactorily. Yet we can hardly doubt that the "truest" philosophy is the best material for the greatest poet; so that the poet must be rated in the end both by the philosophy he realizes in poetry and by the fullness and adequacy of the realization. For poetry—here and so far I am in accord with Mr. Richards—is not the assertion that something is true, but the making that truth more fully real to us; it is the creation of a sensuous embodiment. It is the making the Word Flesh, if we remember that for poetry there are various qualities of Word and various qualities of Flesh. Of course, as I said above, for some kinds of poetry it is necessary that the poet himself should believe the philosophy of which he is making use. I do not wish however to overemphasize the importance of the philosophy, or to speak of it as if it was the exclusive material. What we find when we read Lucretius or Dante is that the poet has effected a fusion between that philosophy and his natural feelings, so that the philosophy becomes real, and the feelings become elevated, intensified and dignified.

And we must remember that part of the *use* of poetry for human beings is similar to their use for philosophy. When we study philosophy as a humane discipline we do not do so merely in order to pick out one which we shall adopt as "true," or either to confect a philosophy of our own out of all philosophies. We do so largely for the exercise in assumption or entertaining ideas; for the enlargement and exercise of mind we get by trying to penetrate a man's thought and think it after him, and then passing out of that experience to another. Only by the exercise of understanding without believing, so far as that is possible, can we come in full consciousness to some point where we believe *and* understand. Similarly with the experience of poetry. We aim ideally to come to rest in some poetry which shall realize poetically what we ourselves believe; but we have no contact with poetry unless we can pass in and out freely, among the various worlds of poetic creation. In practice, our literary judgment is always fallible, because we inevitably tend to overestimate a poetry which embodies a view of life which we can understand and which we accept; but we are not really entitled to prize such poetry so highly unless we also make the effort to enter those worlds of poetry in which we are alien. Poetry cannot prove that anything is *true;* it can only create a variety of wholes composed of intellectual and emotional constituents, justifying the emotion by the thought and the thought by the emotion: it proves successively, or fails to prove, that certain worlds of thought and feeling are *possible.* It provides intellectual sanction for feeling, and esthetic sanction for thought.

From *The Bookman, LXX* (February, 1930), pp. 595–602. Reprinted by permission of author and editor. The essay has not been reprinted by the author.

GEORGE SANTAYANA

Penitent Art

[1922]

ART is like a charming woman who once had her age of innocence in the nursery, when she was beautiful without knowing it, being wholly intent on what she was making or telling or imagining.

Then she has had a season of passion and vanity, when having discovered how beautiful she was, she decked herself out in all possible pomp and finery, invented fashion after fashion to keep admiration alive, and finally began to put on rouge and false hair and too much scent, in the hope of still being a belle at seventy.

But it sometimes happens, during her long decline, that she hears a call to repentance, and thinks of being converted. Naturally, such a fine lady cannot give up her carriage; she is obliged occasionally to entertain her old friends at dinner, and to be seen now and then at the opera. Habit and the commitments she has in the world, where no function is complete without her, are too strong for her to be converted suddenly, or altogether; but henceforth something in her, in her most sensitive and thoughtful hours, upbraids her for the hollowness of her old airs and graces. It is really a sorry business, this perpetual presence of being important and charming and charmed and beautiful.

Art seems to be passing at present through a lenten mood of this sort. Not all art, of course: somebody must still manufacture official statues and family portraits, somebody must design apartment houses, clubs, churches, skyscrapers, and stations. Visible through the academic framework of these inevitable objects, there is often much professional learning and judgment; there is even, sometimes, a glint of poetic life, or a suggestion of exotic beauty. In Mr. Sargent's painting, for instance, beneath the photographic standards of the studio, we often catch a satirical intention, or a philosophic idea, or love of the sensuous qualities in the model and in the accessories; a technical echo of Velasquez and Goya, though without plastic vitality or dramatic ease; a sort of Van Dyck, as it were, for the days of Edward VII; the dreadful lapse in refinement not being greater, perhaps, than is requisite for the documentary value of a true mirror of fashion in the later age. Taste of the old honest worldly sort is far from dead; it is found still in milliners and designers of fashionable garments, of furniture and ornaments. All this luxurious traditional art is as far as possible from repentance. Yet as the Magdalene was potentially a saint—perhaps always a saint really—so the most meretricious contrivances in the arts may sometimes include and betray the very principle of redemption, which is love; in this case the love of beauty. For example, here is the Russian ballet, doubling the dose of luxurious stimulation in every direction, erotic, tragic, historical, and decorative; yet see how it glides at times into simplicity, and in spite of all the paraphernalia of expert estheticism, issues in forms of unmistakably penitent art, like pure color and caricature.

I call pure color and caricature penitent art, because it is only disappointment in other directions that drives artists back to these primary effects. By an austere and deliberate abstinence from everything that naturally tempts them, they achieve in this way a certain peace; but they would far rather have found it by genuinely recovering their naïveté. Sensuous splendor and caricature would then have seemed to them not the acme of abstract art, but the obvious truth of things; they would have doted on puppets and pantomime as a child dotes on dolls, without ever noticing how remote they are from reality. In the nineteenth century some romantic artists, poets, and philosophers actually tried being rebaptized, hoping that a fresh dip in the Jordan might rejuvenate them; but it was of no use. The notion of *recovering innocence* is a contradiction in terms; conversion can only initiate a non-natural life of grace; death must intervene before corruption can put on incorruption. That age was accordingly an age of revivals, of antiquaries, nothing in art and religion but retrospective; it was progressive only in things material and in the knowledge of them. Even its philosophical idealism and psychology were meant to be historical and descriptive of facts, literary and egotistical as the view of the facts might be. Romanticism thought it was exquisitely sensitive to the spirit of remote things, but in reality it was sensitive only to material perspectives, to costume and stage-setting; it grew sentimental over legends and ruins, and being moonstruck, thought it was imbibing the spirit of the past. But the past had not been consciously romantic; what the ancients actually thought and felt was understood much better before the nineteenth century than since; for formerly they were regarded simply as men, essentially contemporary—which comes much nearer the truth. Of course, the passion that can drive people to such earnest affectations must be itself genuine. Keats or Ruskin or Oscar Wilde had abundant vitality and expressed, each in his studied archaism, the profound helplessness that beset him; but what was vital in them was some sensuous or moral or revolutionary instinct of their own, such as in Shelley had existed pure; only in them it was contorted by their terrible preoccupation with being early, or rich, or choice. They were hypnotized by dead beauty; and not having invention nor influence enough to remodel their own age, they fled from it to exotic delights, sometimes primitive, sometimes luxurious, sometimes religious, and sometimes all these things at once. Similarly the revivals in architecture and in the minor crafts expressed a genuine love of color, ornament, and beauty; they gave the snobbish middle classes a taste of cheap luxury; they could sip culture in a teacup. Yet the particular fashions revived were unstable; each successive affectation had hardly ceased to seem exquisite when it began to look foolish. Art at best is subject to fashion, because there is a margin of arbitrary variation in its forms, even when their chief lines are determined by their function; but in revived art fashion is all; it is a fancy dress, unsatisfying even in the glamour of the ballroom, which we are positively ashamed to be seen in in the morning.

Fortunately revivals now seem to be over. Ruins and museums are interesting to the antiquary; they stir the historical imagination, and dazzle us here and there with some ray of living beauty, like that of a jewel; but they cannot supply inspiration. In art, in poetry, unless you become as a little child you cannot enter the kingdom of heaven. Little children is what artists and poets are now striving hard to be; little children who instead of blowing a tin trumpet blow by chance through a whole orchestra, but with the same emotion as the child; or who, instead of daubing a geometrical skeleton with a piece of chalk, can daub a cross-eyed cross-section of the entire spectrum or a compound fracture of a nightmare. Such is Cubism: by no means an inexpert or meaningless thing. Before you can compose a chaos or paint the unnamable, you must train yourself to a severe abstention from all practical habits of perception; you must heroically suppress the understanding. The result, when the penance is genuinely performed, has a very deep and recondite charm; you revert to what the spinal column might feel if it had a separate consciousness, or to what the retina might see if it could be painlessly cut off from the brain; lights, patterns, dynamic suggestions, sights and memories fused together, hypnotic harmonies such as may visit a vegetative or even mineral sensibility; you become a thousand prisms and mirrors reflecting one another. This is one kind of esthetic repentance. Vain, vain, it says to itself, was the attempt to depict or beautify external objects; let material things be what they will; what are they to the artist? Nature has the urgency of life, which art cannot rival; it has the lure, the cruelty, of actual existence, where all is sin and confusion and vanity, a hideous strife of forms devouring one another, in which all are mutilated and doomed. What is that to the spirit? Let it confess its own impotence in that field, and abandon all attempts to observe or preserve what are called *things:* let it devote itself instead to cleansing the inside of the cup, to purifying its sensibility, which is after all what nature plays upon when she seems to us to be beautiful. Perhaps in that way spirit may abstract the gold of beauty and cast the dross away—all that alloy of preoccupation with material forms and external events and moral sentiments and vain animal adventures which has so long distracted the misguided artist, when he could paint the whole world and had lost his own soul. It is always the play of sensibility, and nothing else, that lends interest to external themes; and it was an evil obsession with alien things that dragged sensibility into a slavery to things which stifled and degraded it: *salvation lies in emancipating the medium.*

To renounce representation, or be representative only by accident, is accordingly one sort of penitent art; but there is another sort, more humble and humorous. This second sort makes no attempt to resist the impulse to observe and to express external things. It does not proudly imagine that the medium, which is the human contribution to representation, can be sufficient unto itself. On the contrary, in its sensuous orchestration it is content to be rudimentary, to work in clay or in wood, and to dress in homespun. It is all feeling, all childlike tenderness, all sense of life. Persons and animals fascinate it. At the same time, warned by the fate of explicit poets and realistic painters, it does not attempt, in its portraiture, to give more than a pregnant hint, some large graphic sign, some profound caricature. Don't be rhetorical, it says; don't try to be exhaustive; all that is worth saying can be said in words of one syllable. Look long, and be brief. It is not in their material entirety and detail that things penetrate to the soul, but in their simple large identity, as a child knows his mother, nurse, or dog. Fresh inchoate forms, voices draped in mantles, people the mind, and return to it in dreams. Monsters and dwarfs were the first gods; the half, said a Greek proverb, is better than the whole. The implicit is alone important where life is concerned: nothing is more eloquent than an abstract posture, an immovable single gesture. Let art abandon reproduction and become indication. If it threatens thereby to become caricature, know that profound art can never be anything else. If men, when seen truly, take on the aspect of animals or puppets, it is because they are animals and puppets at bottom. But all caricature need not be unkind; it may be tender, or even sublime. The distortion, the single emphasis, the extreme simplification may reveal a soul which rhetoric and self-love had hidden in a false rationality. The absurd is the naked truth, the pathetic appeal of sheer fact, attempting to come into existence, like a featherless chick peeping out of its eggshell. All this pompous drapery of convention was a disguise; strip it away. Do not make maps of your images; make companions of them, make idols. Be reticent, emphatic, moody, bold; *salvation lies in caricature.*

Accustomed as they are to revivals, some critics have called this form of esthetic penance a revival of savage art; but the mood is reversed. Savages were never rudimentary on purpose; they were not experimenting in the distortion or simplification of forms; much less, of course, did they voluntarily eliminate all representation of objects in order to deepen sensibility for the medium. They simply painted as well as they could. We have got far beyond that. Penitent art, childish as it may seem at times, is a refinement, perhaps an over-refinement; it is not so much crude or incompetent, as ascetic or morbid. It is also sometimes a little vulgar; because one of the forms of caricature and self-revelation is to be brutal, to flaunt what is out of place, what spoils the picture. Tragedy used to be noble; there is a new refinement in seeing how often it is ignoble; there is a second tragedy in that. Perhaps what we regard at first sight as a terrible decline in art may be sometimes the awakening of this sort of self-scorn. See how ugly I am, it cries, how brutish, common, and deformed! There are remains of sculpture and paintings of the late Roman Empire in some respects like our latest experiments. The decorative splendor (which was very marked) is lost; we miss the colored marbles, the gold, the embroideries, the barbaric armor and jewels; but the stunted pathetic human figures remain in crowds. It seems that the spirit had no joy in man any more; it hid him in hieratic garments or pityingly recorded his gregarious misery. He was a corpse laid out in pontifical vestments. We too are dying; but in nature the death of one thing is commonly the birth of another. Instead of decorating a Byzantine sanctuary, our artists do penance in a psychological desert, studying their own sensations, the mysteries of sheer light and sound; and as music was long ago divorced from poetry and instrumental music from singing, so a luxurious but strident art is detaching itself from everything but its own medium. This on the decorative side; in representation the same retrenchment stops at another level. Representation too has a psychological medium; fancy must create the images which the observer or reproducer of things conceives to be their forms. These images are not the forms of things at all; not only is their perspective created by the observer, but their character, when it is truly considered, is amazingly summary, variable, and fantastic—a mere wraith, a mere hint, a mere symbol. What we suppose we see, what we *say* things look like, is rather an inventory, collected in memory and language, of many successive observations; it is discursive study, registered perhaps in discursive painting. But as the total composition never was nor ever could be a living image, so its parts are not images any longer; in being arrested they have acquired new boundaries and lost half their primitive essence. We may paint the things we see, we cannot arrest the images by which we see them; all we can do—if the images and not the things are what interest us—is to paint something that, by some occult trick of optics, may revive the image in some particular; and then, although the picture when studied discursively may not resemble the thing at all, it may bring back to us, as it were by scent, the feeling which the thing originally gave us; and we may say that it has caught the *spirit* of the thing. It is the medium that in such a case animates the object, and seems to obscure it; and this medium which we call sense in so far as things affect us through it, we call spirit in so far as it modifies our view of the things. The more we transform things in seeing them, the more we seem to spiritualize them and turn them into forms of our own sensibility, regarding the living image in us as the dramatic essence of the object. It is the business of science to correct this illusion; but the penitent artist— who has taken refuge in the spirit and is not striving to stretch his apprehension into literal truth, since the effort to depict things discursively has proved a vain and arid ambition—the penitent artist is content with the rhythms, echoes, or rays which things awaken within him; and in proportion as these reverberations are actually renewed, the poem remains a cry, the story a dream, the building a glimpse, the portrait a caricature.

From *Obiter Scripta* by George Santayana, pp. 151–161. Copyright, 1936, by Charles Scribner's Sons. Reprinted by permission of the author and publishers. First published in *The Dial*, Vol. LXXIII (July, 1922), pp. 25–31.

Tragic Philosophy
[1936]

IN COMPARING a passage from *Macbeth* with one from the *Paradiso*, Mr. T. S. Eliot tells us that poetically the two are equally good, but that the philosophy in Shakespeare is inferior. By what standard, I am tempted to ask, may the poetic value of different types of poetry in different languages be declared equal? By the equal satisfaction, perhaps, that fills the critic's mind? But the total allegiance of a mature person, his total joy in anything, can hardly be independent of his developed conscience and his sense for ultimate realities. He cannot be utterly enchanted by what he feels to be trivial or false. And if he is not utterly enchanted, how should he recognize the presence of the supremely beautiful? Two passages could hardly be pronounced equal in poetic force if the ultimate suggestions of the one were felt to be inferior to those of the other.

Admitting, then, that poetry expressing an inferior philosophy would to that extent be inferior poetry, we may ask this further question: In what respect other than truth may philosophies be called inferior or superior? Perhaps in being more or less poetical or religious, more or less inspired? Sometimes a philosophy may spring up imaginatively, and in that sense may be inspired rather than strictly reasoned or observed, as the myths of Plato are inspired; but nobody would call such inspired philosophy *superior* unless he felt it to spring from the total needs and total wisdom of the heart; and in that case he would certainly believe, or at least hope, that this superior philosophy was true. How then should the poetic expression of this inspired philosophy not be conspicuously superior as poetry, and more utterly enchanting, than the expression of any other philosophy?

Let me postpone generalities, and turn to the passages in question.

Lady Macbeth is dead. Macbeth foresees his own end. All the prophecies flattering his ambition have been fulfilled, and after the mounting horror of his triumph he stands at the brink of ruin. Surveying the whole in a supreme moment, he consents to his destiny.

> Tomorrow, and tomorrow and tomorrow
> Creeps in this petty pace from day to day
> To the last syllable of recorded time;
> And all our yesterdays have lighted fools
> The way to dusty death. Out, out, brief candle!
> Life's but a walking shadow; a poor player
> That struts and frets his hour upon the stage,
> And then is heard no more. It is a tale
> Told by an idiot, full of sound and fury,
> Signifying nothing.

Mr. Eliot says that this philosophy is derived from Seneca; and it is certain that in Seneca's tragedies, if not in his treatises, there is a pomp of diction, a violence of pose, and a suicidal despair not unlike the tone of this passage. But would Seneca ever have said that life signified nothing? It signified for him the universal reign of law, of reason, of the will of God. Fate was inhuman, it was cruel, it excited and crushed every finite wish; yet there was something in man that shared that disdain for humanity, and triumphed in that ruthless march of order and necessity. Something superior, not inferior, Seneca would have said; something that not only raised the mind into sympathy with the truth of nature and the decrees of heaven, but that taught the blackest tragedy to sing in verse. The passions in foreseeing their defeat became prophets, in remembering it became poets; and they created the noblest beauties by defying and transcending death.

In Seneca this tragic philosophy, though magnificent, seems stilted and forced; it struts rhetorically like an army of hoplites treading down the green earth. He was the last of ancient tragedians, the most aged and withered in his titanic strength; but all his predecessors, from Homer down, had proclaimed the same tragic truths, softened but not concealed by their richer medium. Some of them, like Virgil, had rendered those truths even more poignant precisely by being more sensitive to the loveliness of perishable things. After all, the same inhuman power that crushes us, breeds us and feeds us; life and death are but two aspects of the same natural mutation, the same round of seed-time and harvest. And if all human passions must be fugitive, they need not all be unamiable: some are merry in their prime, and even smile at their own fading. An accident of ritual led the ancients to divide tragedy sharply from comedy; I think it has been a happy return to nature in modern dramatists and novelists to intermingle the two. Comic episodes abound in the most tragic experience, if only we have the wit to see them; and even the tragic parts are in reality relieved by all sorts of compensations that stimulate our sense of life and prompt us to high reflection. What greater pleasure than a tear that pays homage to something beautiful and deepens the sense of our own profundity?

Not every part of this classic philosophy re-echoes in the pessimism of Macbeth. Shakespeare was not expressing, like Seneca, a settled doctrine of his own or of his times. Like an honest miscellaneous dramatist, he was putting into the mouths of his different characters the sentiments that, for the moment, were suggested to him by their predicaments. Macbeth, who is superstitious and undecided, storms excessively when he storms; there is something feverish and wild in his starts of passion, as there is something delicate in his perceptions. Shakespeare could give rein in such a character to his own subtle fancy in diction and by-play, as well as in the main to the exaggerated rhetoric proper to a stage where everybody was expected to declaim, to argue, and to justify sophistically this or that extravagant impulse. So at this point in Macbeth, where Seneca would have unrolled the high maxims of orthodox Stoicism, Shakespeare gives us the humors of his distracted hero; a hero nonplussed, confounded, stultified in his own eyes, a dying gladiator, a blinded lion at bay. And yet intellectually—and this is the tragedy of it—Macbeth is divinely human, rational enough to pause and survey his own agony, and see how brutish, how insignificant, it is. He sees no escape, no alternative; he cannot rise morally above himself; his philosophy is that there is no philosophy, because, in fact, he is incapable of any.

Shakespeare was a professional actor, a professional dramatist; his greatness lay there, and in the gift of the gab; in that exuberance and joy in language which everybody had in that age, but he supremely. The Renaissance needed no mastering living religion, no mastering living philosophy. Life was gayer without them. Philosophy and religion were at best like travels and wars, matters for the adventurer to plunge into, or for the dramatist to describe; never in England or for Shakespeare central matters even in that capacity, but mere conventions or tricks of fancy or moods in individuals. Even in a Hamlet, a Prospero or a Jacques, in a Henry VI or an Isabella, the poet feels no inner loyalty to the convictions he rehearses; they are like the cap and bells of his fools; and possibly if he had been pressed by some tiresome friend to propound a personal philosophy, he might have found in his irritation nothing else to fall back upon than the animal despair of Macbeth. Fortunately we may presume that burgherly comfort and official orthodoxy saved him from being unreasonably pressed.

That which a mastering living philosophy or religion can be, we may see at once by turning to the passage from Dante. In the lowest circle of Paradise, that of the inconstant moon, dwells the spirit of Piccarda, a lady who, having once been a nun but having been carried off and married by force, when later she became a widow preferred to continue her life in the world rather than return to her convent. Dante asks her if those who dwell in this part of Heaven ever desire to go higher, so as to see more and to love more. And she replies, No: for the essence of religious love is union with the order of creation. Perfect happiness would be impossible, if we were not perfectly happy in what God has given us; and in his will is our peace.

> Frate, la nostra volontà quieta
>> Virtù di carità, che fa volerne
>> Sol quel ch'avemo, e d'altro non ci asseta
> Se disiassimo esser più superne,
>> Foran discordi gli nostri disiri
>> Dal voler di colui che qui ne cerne;
> Che vedrai non capere in questi giri,
>> S'essere in carità è qui necesse,
>> E se la sua natura ben rimiri.
> Anzi è formale ad esto beato esse
>> Tenersi, dentro a la divina voglia,
>> Per ch'una fansi nostre voglie stesse;
> Si che, come noi sem di soglia in soglia
>> Per questo regno, a tutto il regno piace
>> Com' a lo re ch'a suo voler ne invoglia.
> E'n la sua volontade è nostra pace:
>> Ell'è quel mare al qual tutto si move
>> Ciò ch'ella crea e che natura face.
> Chiaro mi fu allor come ogni dove
>> In cielo è paradiso, e sì la grazia
>> Del sommo ben d'un modo non vi piove.[1]

[1] "Brother, the quality of love stilleth our will,
and maketh us long only for what we have,
and giveth us no other thirst.
Did we desire to be more aloft, our longings
were discordant from his will who here
assorteth us,
and for that, thou wilt see, there is no room
within these circles, if of necessity we have
our being here in love, and if thou think again
what is love's nature.
Nay, it is the essence of this blessed being to
hold ourselves within the divine will, whereby
our own wills are themselves made one.
So that our being thus, from threshold unto
threshold throughout the realm, is a joy to all

I questioned at the beginning whether the poetic value of unlike things could be pronounced equal: and if now I compare this whole passage with the passage from Macbeth I find that to my sense they are incommensurable. Both are notable passages, if that is all that was meant; but they belong to different poetic worlds, appealing to and developing different sides of the mind. And there is more than disparity between these two worlds; there is contrariety and hostility between them, in as much as each professes to include and to subordinate the other, and in so doing to annul its tragic dignity and moral finality. For the mood of Macbeth, religion and philosophy are insane vapors; for the mood of Dante, Macbeth is possessed by the devil. There is no possible common ground, no common criterion of truth, and no common criterion even of taste or beauty. We might at best say that both poets succeed in conveying what they wish to convey, and that in that sense their skill is equal: but I hardly think this is true in fact, because in Shakespeare the medium is rich and thick and more important than the idea; whereas in Dante the medium is as unvarying and simple as possible, and meant to be transparent. Even in this choice passage, there are stretches of pure scholastic reasoning, not poetical at all to our sensuous and romantic apprehension; yet the studious and rapt poet feels himself carried on those wings of logic into a paradise of truth, where choir answers choir, and everything is beautiful. A clear and transparent medium is admirable, when we love what we have to say; but when what we have to say is nothing previously definite, expressiveness depends on stirring the waters deeply, suggesting a thousand half-thoughts, and letting the very unutterableness of our passion become manifest in our disjointed words. The medium then becomes dominant: but can this be called success in expression? It is rather success in making an impression, if the reader is impressed; and this effect seems essentially incomparable with that of pure lucidity and tireless exact versification in one chosen form. To our insecure, distracted, impatient minds, the latter hardly seems poetry.

Voltaire said that Dante's reputation was safe, because nobody read him. Nowadays that is hardly true; all superior persons read him a little or read a great deal about him. He sets tempting problems for professional critics and antiquarians, and he appeals to archaistic taste, that flies for refuge into the fourth dimension, to everything that seems pure and primitive. But as living poetry, as a mold and stimulus for honest feeling, is Dante for us at all com-

---

the realm as to the king, who draweth our
   wills to what he willeth;
and his will is our peace; it is that sea to
   which all moves that it createth and that nature maketh."
Clear was it then to me how everywhere in heaven
   is Paradise, even though the grace of the chief
Good doth not rain there after one only fashion.
            Paradiso, III, 70–90. (Wicksteed's translation)

parable to Shakespeare? Shakespeare, in passages such as this from *Macbeth*, is orchestrated. He trills away into fancy: what was daylight a moment ago, suddenly becomes a candle: we are not thinking or reasoning, we are dreaming. He needs but to say "all our yesterdays," and presently the tedium of childhood, the tedium of labor and illness, the vacancy of friendships lost, rise like vague ghosts before us, and fill us with a sense of the unreality of all that once seemed most real. When he mentions "a poor player" we think at once of the poet himself, because our minds are biographical and our sympathies novelesque; we feel the misery and the lurid contrasts of a comedian's life; and the existence that just now seemed merely vain, now seems also tempestuous and bitter. And the rhythms help; the verse struts and bangs, holds our attention suspended, obliges our thoughts to become rhetorical, and brings our declamation round handsomely to a grand finale. We should hardly have found courage in ourselves for so much passion and theatricality; but we bless Shakespeare for enabling us still to indulge in such emotions, and to relieve ourselves of a weight that we hardly knew we were carrying.

Nothing of the sort in the Italian: the simplest language, the humble vernacular, made pungent and to us often obscure only by an excess of concision and familiarity, or by allusions to events then on everybody's tongue. Dante allows his personal fortunes and hatreds to crop out in many places, perhaps quickening the interest of the modern gossip-loving reader. Yet these are incidental indiscretions, which the poet's own conscience might have regarded as blemishes. His work as a whole, and in intention, is that of a consecrated mind. A single thread of thought guides him; the eye is focused on pure truth, on human wills illustrating the divine laws against which they profess to rebel; hell in the heart of earth, and earth enveloped in celestial harmonies. No occasion, as in modern edifying works, to avoid mentioning things unpleasant or to explain them away. Every detail is noted, not bashfully or apologetically but with zest; when anything is wicked, its wickedness is exhibited and proved for our instruction. We learn the scientific complexity of the moral world, all plain facts, demonstrable truths, principles undoubted and certified. Mastered and chastened by this divine dispensation, what need should we feel of verbal opulence or lurid rhetoric? Not one rare epithet, not one poetic plum; instead, a childlike intellectual delight in everything being exact, limpid, and duly named, and dovetailed perfectly into everything else. Each word, each rhyme, files dutifully by in procession, white verses, three abreast, like choristers, holding each his taper and each singing in turn his appointed note. But what sweetness in this endless fugue, what simple exactitude, what devout assurance; and how unanimously these humble voices, often harsh and untutored if taken singly, rise together into a soaring canticle! The poetry, you might say, of industrious children, careful to make no mistake, but having nothing of their own to say, or not daring to say it. And indeed Dante's mind is busy, learned, and intense; exact even in allegory, as in a sort of heraldry; yet this very minuteness and pedantry are the work of love. Never was heart more tender or subtle or passionate; only that its intensity is all turned towards metaphysical joys, and transferred to an inward spiritual heaven.

I doubt whether either the beauty or the weakness of such poetry can be understood without understanding the nature of religion, as neither religious people nor irreligious people are likely to do; not the irreligious, because of insensibility, and not the religious because of delusion. Still, a disinterested student, say of the origins of Christianity, ought to understand. Religion is not essentially a supplement to common knowledge or natural affection on the same level as the latter: it is not essentially a part of rational life, adjusted however gropingly to cosmic or social influences, and expressing them and their effect. Religion is rather a second life, native to the soul, developed there independently of all evidence, like a waking dream: not like dreams coming in sleep and composed largely of distorted waking impressions, but an autonomous other life, such as we have also in music, in games, and in imaginative love. In religion the soul projects out of her own impulses, especially when these are thwarted, the conditions under which she will regard herself as living. If she need salvation, she will posit a savior; if the thought of death offends her, she will posit resurrection or even immortality; if she is troubled at the injustice of fortune, she will posit previous crimes or original sins of her own, to explain her misery. If in general she wishes to impose her will where she is impotent, she will utter that will in prayers or imprecations, and posit an invisible power inclined to listen, and able to help.

Now such an inner fountain of life and thought is evidently akin to poetic inspiration. As in poetry, so in religion, imagination evokes a more or less systematic invisible world in which the passions latent in the soul may work themselves out dramatically. Yet there are differences. The profane poet is by instinct a naturalist. He loves landscape, he loves love, he loves the humor and pathos of earthly existence. But the religious prophet loves none of these things. It is precisely because he does not love them that he cultivates in himself, and summons the world to cultivate, a second more satisfying life, more deeply rooted, as he imagines, in the nature of things. Earthly images therefore interest him only as symbols and metaphors, or as themes for denunciation. He is hardly a poet in the ordinary sense, except in so far as (like Milton, for instance) he may owe a double allegiance, and be a profane poet altogether when he is a poet at all. Religion is often professed and intellectually accepted without ever having flowered in the soul, or being suspected to have any kinship with poetry. It may have withered into a forced and angry metaphysics or semi-political party doctrine, poetically deplorable.

The opposite is the case in Dante, whose poetry is essentially religious, as his religion is essentially poetical. We are in the presence of an overpowering inspiration, become traditional, become also learned and quasi-scientific, but still kindled by moral passion and fertile in poetic ideas. The Hebrew prophets had begun by denouncing that which was and proclaiming that which should be; but that which should be could evidently never become actual without a miracle and a total revolution in the world; so that prophecy turned to eschatology and to expectation of a Messiah. At this point pagan streams of inspiration began to mingle with the Hebraic stream. Perhaps the Messiah had already come. Perhaps he was to be no conquering monarch, but a god in disguise. Perhaps he had been crucified, as the spirit is always crucified. Perhaps his kingdom was not of this world. Were there not reports that Jesus, who had been crucified, had been seen, risen from the dead? Would he not surely come again with glory in the clouds of heaven? Transfigured by this new spiritual faith, many current legends and maxims were ascribed to Jesus, and beautifully set down in the Gospels. The fathers worked out the theology. The saints repeated the miracles and explored all the phases of ascetic and mystical experience. Nothing remained but for Dante, with exquisite fidelity and minuteness, to paint a total picture of the Christian universe. The whole substance of that universe was poetry; only the details could threaten to become prosaic; but his danger was removed, in the more important places, by Dante's extraordinary sensitiveness. He had had a revelation of his own in childhood, interrupted later by the false glare of the world, but finally restored in the form of religious wisdom and consecration. The fresh dew of poetry and love trembled upon everything. Indeed, for our modern feeling the picture is too imaginative, too visionary, soaked too much in emotion. In spite of the stern historical details, when we rub our eyes and shake off the spell, the whole thing seems childishly unreal. We can understand why Mr. Eliot feels this to be a "superior" philosophy; but how can he fail to see that it is false?

Inspiration has a more intimate value than truth and one more unmistakably felt by a sensitive critic, since inspiration marks a sort of spring-tide in the life of some particular creature, whereas truth impassively maps the steady merciless stretches of creation at large. Inspiration has a kind of truth of its own, truth to the soul; and this sincerity in intuition, however private and special it might be, would never conflict with the truth of things, if inspiration were content to be innocently free and undogmatic, as in music or lyric poetry. The inmost vegetative impulses of life might then come to perfect flower, feeling and celebrating their own reality without pretending to describe or command reality beyond, or giving any hostages to fortune. But unfortunately animals cannot long imitate the lilies of the field. Where life is adventurous, combative and prophetic, inspiration must be so too. Ideas, however spontaneous, will then claim to be knowledge of ulterior facts, and will be in constant danger of being contradicted by the truth. Experience, from being lyrical, will become tragic; for what is tragedy but the conflict between inspiration and truth? From within or, as we may fancy, from above, some passionate hope takes shape in the mind. We fall in love or hear a voice from heaven; new energies seem to leap up within us; a new life begins crowding the old life out, or making it seem dreary or wicked. Even when inspiration is not moral, but merely poetical, it kindles a secret fire and an inner light that put vulgar sunshine to shame. Yet not for long, nor for ever; unless we passionately shut ourselves up in the *camera obscura* of our first inspiration, and fear the darkness of other lights. The more profound and voluminous that first inspiration was, the more complete at last will be our astonishment and despair. We shall cry with *Le Cid:*

> Percé jusque au fond du cœur
> D'une atteinte imprévue aussi bien que mortelle . . .
> Je demeure immobile, et mon âme abattue
> Cède au coup qui me tue.

Tragedy must end in death: for any immortality which the poet or his hero may otherwise believe in is irrelevant to the passion that has absorbed him. That passion, at least, dies, and all he cares for dies with it. The possibility of ulterior lives or alien interests destined in future to agitate the world makes no difference to this drama in this soul; and the mention of those irrelevant sequels to ruin, and to this ruin, and to this tragic acceptance of ruin, would tinkle with a ghastly mockery at this supreme moment, when a man is entering eternity, his measure taken, his heart revealed, and his pride entire.

These considerations may help us to understand why Shakespeare, although Christianity was at hand, and Seneca, although a Platonic philosophy was at hand, based like Christianity on moral inspiration, nevertheless stuck fast in a disillusioned philosophy which Mr. Eliot thinks inferior. They stuck fast in the facts of life. They had to do so, whatever may have been their private religious convictions, because they were dramatists addressing the secular mind and concerned with the earthly career of passionate individuals, of inspired individuals, whose inspirations contradicted the truth and were shattered by it. This defeat, together with a proud and grandiloquent acceptance of it, is final for the tragic poet. His philosophy can build only on such knowledge of the world as the world can give. Even in the seventeenth century, when Christian orthodoxy was most severe, most intellectual, and most dominant, also most courtly and presentable to the worldly mind, Christianity was nevertheless strictly banished from the stage, except in a few expressly religious plays written for young ladies. Both Christian and pagan personages talked and felt throughout like thoroughly unregenerate mortals. To have allowed religion to shift the scenes, override the natural passions of men, and reverse the moral of the story, would have seemed an intolerable anti-climax.

Nor does even Dante, who calls his vision a comedy, really escape this tragic reality. Existence is indeed a comedy, in that it is a series of episodes, each blind and inconclusive, though often merry enough, but all having their justification beyond themselves, in a cosmic music which they help to make without knowing it. Nonetheless, the individual souls in Dante's hell and heaven speak the language of tragedy, either in desperate pride or in devout self-surrender. In either case, in eternity, they have no further hopes, fears, or ambitions. Their lives *there* are simply the full knowledge of what their lives had been *here*. In the *Divine Comedy* had not had in it this sublime note of recollection, if it had attempted to describe new adventures and fanciful Utopias succeeding one another *ad infinitum*, it would not have been divine at all, but only a romantic medley like the second part of *Faust*. In Dante the hurly-burly is rounded out into a moral tale, into a joyful tragedy, with that sense of finality, of eternity, which Christian eschatology had always preserved.

I can think of only one tragedy in which religion might well play a leading part, and that is the tragedy of religion itself. The point would be to show that a second life of pure inspiration, freely bred in the soul out of moral impulses, must sooner or later confront the cold truth. The illusions then surrendered would not lose their poetic value, since their source would remain alive in the soul; and the element of deception involved might disappear insensibly, as it did in paganism, yielding with a good grace to an impartial philosophy. Such a philosophy need not be in the least hostile to inspiration. There is inspiration wherever there is mind. The sensuous images and categories of thought on which common knowledge relies are themselves poetic and wholly original in form, being products of a kind of inspiration in the animal organism. But they are controlled in their significance and application by experiment in the field of action. Higher fictions are more loosely controlled by the experience of the heart. They are less readily revived or communicated. They flare up into passionate prophecies, take themselves for revealed truths, and come more often to a tragic end.

From *The Works of George Santayana,* Triton Edition, Vol. II, pp. 275–288. Copyright, 1936, by Charles Scribner's Sons. Reprinted by permission of the author and publishers. First published in *Scrutiny* (Cambridge, England), Vol. IV (March, 1936), pp. 365–376.

J. E. SPINGARN
The American Critic
[1922]

WHEN I wrote the essays which were collected in a volume bearing the subtitle of "Essays on the Unity of Genius and Taste," the pedants and the professors were in the ascendant, and it seemed necessary to emphasize the side of criticism which was then in danger, the side that is closest to the art of the creator. But now the professors have been temporarily routed by the dilettanti, the amateurs, and the journalists, who treat a work of the imagination as if they were describing fireworks or a bullfight (to use a phrase of Zola's about Gautier); and so it is necessary now to insist on the discipline and illumination of knowledge and thought—in other words, to write an "Essay on the Divergence of Criticism and Creation."

American criticism, like that of England, but to an even greater extent, suffers from a want of philosophic insight and precision. It has neither inherited nor created a tradition of esthetic thought. Golden utterances there have been aplenty—utterances wise, or acute, or daring enough to confound those who refuse to recognize the American spirit except where they find a faded moralism—utterances that anticipate the most modern concepts of criticism throughout the world. To this American ancestry of my own thought I "point with pride." How can we forget Jefferson's literary Declaration of Independence, with its contempt for "the artificial canons of criticism" and its insistence that the only test of literary excellence is whether a work gives pleasure and is "animating, interesting, attaching"—even though the idea of pleasure no longer sums up for us the whole spiritual world of art? How can we forget Poe's conception of poetry as "the rhythmical creation of beauty" and of beauty as having "no concern whatever either with Duty or with Truth"; of Emerson's kindred idea that beauty, no less than truth, is "an ultimate end," and his definition of criticism, with its striking challenge, "Here was a new mind, and it was welcome to a new style"? Margaret Fuller believed like Goethe that the best critics "enter into the nature of another being and judge his work by its own law, but having done so, having ascertained his design and the degree of his success in fulfilling it, they do also know how to put this aim in its place and how to judge its relations," and said of Lowell as a poet that "his interest in the moral questions of the day has supplied the want of vitality in himself"; and yet even Lowell, as a critic, has clearly defined "the difference between what appeals to our esthetic or to our moral sense, between what is judged of by our taste or by our conscience." The author of our first formal treatise on esthetics, Moffat's *Introduction to the Study of Aesthetics*, published before the Civil War, and his successor, John Bascom, whose *Aesthetics* was contemporary with the battle of Antietam, write in the same spirit; for the former, "Art, in itself considered, is neither moral nor immoral; it belongs to an entirely separate class of things," while the latter insists that the processes of reasoning and judgment "have no power over Beauty," which is arrived at by the faculty of "internal intuition." Whether these ideas are false or true, one thing is clear: they are thoroughly American, and even though momentarily forgotten, are an integral part of the heritage of American criticism.

If we have forgotten these utterances, it is because they have remained more or less isolated, and their implications but half apprehended; they have never been consolidated into a body of thought or imposed themselves as a state of mind on American critics. For virtually all of us every critical problem is a separate problem, a problem in a philosophic vacuum, and so open for discussion to any astute mind with a taste for letters. Realism, classicism, romanticism, imagism, impressionism, expressionism, and other terms or movements as they spring up, seem ultimate realities instead of matters of very subordinate concern to any philosophy of art—mere practical programs which bear somewhat the same relation to esthetic truth that the platform of the Republican Party bears to Aristotle's *Politics* or Marx's *Capital*.

As a result, critics are constantly carrying on a guerrilla warfare of their own in favor of some vague literary shibboleth or sociological abstraction, and discovering anew the virtues or vices of individuality, modernity, Puritanism, the romantic spirit or the spirit of the Middle West, the traditions of the pioneer, and so on ad infinitum. This holds true of every school of American criticism, "conservative" or "radical"; for nearly all of them a disconnected body of literary theories takes the place of a real philosophy of art. "Find an idea and then write about it" sums up the average American writer's conception of criticism. There are even those who conceive this scattering of casual thoughts as the sole duty of a critic, on the extraordinary assumption that in this dispersion of thought and power the critic is "expressing himself" as an "artist." Now, while the critic must approach a work of literature without preconceived notion of what that individual work should attempt, he cannot criticize it without some understanding of what all literature attempts. The critic without an esthetic is a mariner without chart, compass, or knowledge of navigation; for the question is not where the ship should go or what cargo it should carry, but whether it is going to arrive at any port at all without sinking.

Criticism is essentially an expression of taste, or that faculty of imaginative sympathy by which the reader or spectator is able to relive the vision created by the artist. This is the soil without which it cannot flourish; but it attains its end and becomes criticism in the highest sense only when taste is guided by knowledge and rises to the level of thought, for then, and only then, does the critic give us something that the artist as artist cannot give. Of these three elements, implicit in all real criticism, the professors have made light of taste, and have made thought itself subservient to knowledge, while the dilettanti have considered it possible to dispense with both knowledge and thought. But even dilettante criticism is preferable to the dogmatic and intellectualist criticism of the professors, on the same grounds that Sainte-Beuve is superior to Brunetière, or Hazlitt to Francis Jeffrey; for the dilettante at least meets the mind of the artist on the plane of imagination and taste, while the intellectualist or moralist is precluded by his temperament and his theories from ever understanding the primal thrill and purpose of the creative act.

Back of any philosophy of art there must be a philosophy of life, and all esthetic formulae seem empty unless there is richness of content behind them. To define criticism without defining art, to define art without distinguishing it from philosophy and history, and to make this distinction without some understanding of the meaning of philosophy and history themselves, can only be compared with the mythical tasks of Tantalus. So that the critic, like the poet or the philosopher, has the whole world to range in, and the farther he ranges in it, the better his work will be. Yet this does not mean that criticism, in so far as it remains criticism of the arts of expression, should focus its attention on morals, history, life, instead of on the forms into which the artist transforms them. Art has something else to give us; and to seek moral or economic theories in it is to seek moral or economic theories, but not art. It is true that art is the product of human personality, and that personality has little meaning when divorced from moral personality, that is, from some actual or imaginative sense of moral values; but out of that moral personality must be created an aqueduct or an airplane, a treatise on logic or chemistry, a poem or a picture, and a host of other products whose excellence must be judged by their own standards, without reference to ethics. The personality behind the poem or the picture is merely, as it were, inchoate material and not the new and essential *form* that distinguishes the work of art. Even in the larger sense in which a poem may be said to be moral in so far as it aims at unity and order, at some relation with the whole of life, we may ask whether the esthetic order is identical with the moral order, or whether we have not here two commensurate but not identical planes or aspects of life.

But "to those who cannot understand the voice of Nature or Poetry, unless it speak in apothegms, and tag each story with a moral," as Margaret Fuller put it nearly eighty years ago, "I have nothing to say." A critic guilty of the incredible assertion that Goethe almost failed of being a great poet merely because he makes Mephistopheles say, "I am the spirit that denies," may be a distinguished moralist, but has completely failed to apprehend the meaning both of criticism and of poetry. The United States is the only civilized country where moral judgment takes precedence over esthetic judgment when face to face with a work of art; France, Germany, and Italy liberated themselves from this faded obsession long ago, except for a few unimportant reactionary cliques; even in England critics of authority hesitate to make moral standards the first and foremost tests of critical judgment. Yet this is precisely what divides the two chief schools of American criticism, the moralists and the anti-moralists, though even among the latter masquerade some whose only quarrel with the moralists is the nature of the moral standards employed. The seeds of a more fruitful tradition had been planted in our earlier criticism, as we have seen, but the seed had been left to wither and bore no ample fruit.

The main forces that have influenced the present clashes in the American attitude toward literature seem to be three. There is first of all the conception of literature as a moral influence, a conception which goes back to the Graeco-Roman rhetoricians and moralists, and after pervading English thought from Sidney to Johnson, finds its last stronghold today among the American descendants of the Puritans. There is, secondly, the Shavian conception of literature as the most effective instrument for the conversion of the world to a new Weltanschauung, to be judged by the novelty and freshness of its ideas, a conception particularly attractive to the school of young reformers, radicals, and intellectuals whose interest in the creative imagination is secondary, and whose training in esthetic thought has been negligible; this is merely an obverse of the Puritan moralism, and is tainted by the same fundamental misconception of the meaning of the creative imagination. And there is finally the conception of literature as an external thing, a complex of rhythms, charm, technical skill, beauty without inner content, or mere theatrical effectiveness, which goes back through the English Nineties to the French Seventies, when the idea of the spiritual autonomy of art—that "beauty is its own excuse for being"—was distorted into the merely mechanical theory of "art for art's sake"; the French have a special talent for narrowing esthetic truths into hard-and-fast formulae, devoid of their original nucleus of philosophic reality, but all the more effective on this account for universal conquest as practical programs.

All three of these conceptions have their element of truth, but all three are inadequate and incomplete. Works of literature, as mere documents, provide important material for history; the winged words of great poets have had a profound moral and social influence; the prophetic quality of the imagination gives its message an explosive force; and the technique of art is part of the material out of which the artist fashions his creations. All this the historian of culture may, indeed must, take into consideration; out of these elements the moralist or the esthete may draw material for his studies; yet to rest the case here is to ignore the essential problem of art. Pity the poor esthete, for whom art, in any of its single outer manifestations, is the whole life of the spirit; pity the poor moralist for whom the life of the spirit in one of its highest moments is cribbed and confined by a narrow theory of the meaning of art and life. It may be difficult to tell which of them misses the most; yet who can doubt that when we meet them in practical life the error of the moralist seems the nobler of the two? And how could it be otherwise—for it is precisely in the life of action that we seek for the guiding star of moral values, which the esthete attempts to evade in assuming that the ideal freedom of the artist as an artist is one with the practical duty of the artist as a man. But in the ideal world of art moralism must always find itself homeless and dispossessed. The very nature of poetry must forever be a bitter challenge to those who have only this narrow single standard; and there is no other way out except that of Plato, who because of the "immorality" of poetry banishes all poets forever from the ideal Republic. Of all the moralistic critics, Plato is one of the very few who are thoroughly consistent.

The apparent paradox which none of these critics face is that the Weltanschauung of the creative artist, his moral convictions, his views on intellectual, economic, and other subjects, furnish the content of his work and are at the same time the chief obstacles to his artistic achievement. Out of morals or philosophy he has to make, not morals or philosophy, but poetry; for morals and philosophy are only a part, and a small part, of the whole reality which his imagination has to encompass. The man who is overwhelmed with moral · theories and convictions would naturally find it easiest to become a moralist, and moralists are prosaic, not poetic. A man who has strong economic convictions would find it easiest to become an economist or economic reformer, and economic theory as well as practice is also the prose of life, not the poetry. A man with a strong philosophic bias would find it easiest to become a pure thinker, and the poet's visionary world topples when laid open to the cold scrutiny of logic. A poet is a human being, and therefore likely to have convictions, prejudices, preconceptions, like other men; but the deeper his interest in them is, the easier it is for him to become a moralist, economist, philosopher, or what not, and the harder (without the divine aid of the Muses) to transcend them and to become a poet.

But if the genius of the poet (and by poet I mean any writer of imaginative literature) is strong enough, it will transcend them, pass over them by the power of the imagination, which leaves them behind without knowing it. It has been well said that morals are one reality, a poem is another reality, and the illusion consists in thinking them one and the same. The poet's conscience as a man may be satisfied by the illusion, but woe to him if it is not an illusion, for that is what we tell him when we say, "He is a moralist, not a poet." Such a man has merely expressed his moral convictions, instead of *leaping over and beyond them* into that world of the imagination where moral ideas must be interpreted from the standpoint of poetry, or the artistic needs of the characters portrayed, and not by the logical or reality value of morals. When we say with Emerson that beauty, like truth, is "an ultimate end," the narrow moralist or the man of practical mind assumes that we are giving advice to the dilettante trifler in verse (who is not an artist at all) instead of attempting to define the essential secret of the art of Aeschylus and Dante, Shakespeare and Goethe, Milton and Racine, and all their high compeers, classic and romantic, in the ancient and modern world. But how can we solve that secret if we see no difference whatever between their art and the thought of a Plato or Spinoza, the moral illumination of an Emerson or Franklin, or the noble exaltation of the Gettysburg Address? The critic who has missed that difference has missed everything. By ignoring one of the vital elements necessary to form a synthesis, he has even missed the power of understanding their essential unity in the life of the spirit.

That is what we mean when we say that this "leaping over" is the test of all art, that it is inherent in the very nature of the creative imagination. It explains a myriad problems. It explains, for example, how Milton the moralist started out to make Satan a demon and how Milton the poet ended by making him a hero; and from this "hymning of the devil" we learn how our moralistic critics cannot understand even a Puritan poet. From another angle, it explains the blindness of the American critic who recently objected to the "loose thinking" of Carl Sandburg's poem, *Smoke and Steel,* in which steel is conceived as made of "smoke and blood," and who propounded this question to the Walrus and the Carpenter: "How can smoke, the lighter refuse of steel, be one of its constituents, and how can the smoke which drifts away from the chimney and the blood which flows in the steelmaker's veins be correlates in their relation to steel?"

Where shall we match this precious gem? Over two centuries ago, Othello's cry after the death of Desdemona,

> O heavy hour,
> Methinks it should now be a huge eclipse
> Of sun and moon!

provoked another intellectualistic critic to inquire whether "the sun and moon can bothe together be so hugely eclipsed in any one heavy hour whatsoever"; but Rymer has been called "the worst critic that ever lived" for applying tests like these to the poetry of Shakespeare. Over a century ago a certain Abbé

Morellet, unmoved by the music of Chateaubriand's description of the moon—

She pours forth in the woods this great secret of melancholy which she loves to recount to the old oaks and the ancient shores of the sea—

asked his readers: "How can the melancholy of night be called a secret; and if the moon recounts it, how is it still a secret; and how does she manage to recount it to the old oaks and the ancient shores of the sea rather than to the deep valleys, the mountains, and the rivers?" And so when Macbeth, stung by his agony into immortal eloquence—"tomorrow and tomorrow and tomorrow" —finds time but a petty pace that has lighted fools the way to dusty death, and life itself nothing but a tale

> Told by an idiot, full of sound and fury,
> Signifying nothing,

can we not imagine some of our own professors, for whom Art is but a pretty page serving King Virtue and Queen Truth, crying out in disdain: "And it is this passage, gentlemen, in which a false and immoral conception of life is expounded, that some of the so-called esthetic critics consider the highwater mark of poetry"? Or if we cannot imagine it, it is only because the passage is not by a modern poet without the prestige of Shakespeare's fame.

These are simply exaggerations of the inevitable consequence of subjecting the world of the imagination to the moods and tests of actual life. "Sense, sense, nothing but sense!" cried a great Austrian poet, "as if poetry in contrast with prose were not always a kind of divine nonsense. Every poetic image bears within itself its own certain demonstration that logic is not the arbitress of art." And Alfieri spoke for every poet in the world when he said of himself, "Reasoning and judging are for me only pure and generous forms of feeling." The trained economist, philosopher, or moralist, examining the ideas of a poet, is always likely to say: "These are not clearly thought out or logical ideas; they are just a poet's fancy or inspiration"; and the sneer of the expert may be the final praise of the poet. To give us a vision of reality, and not reality, imagination rather than thought or morals, is the eternal mission of the artist. To forego that vision is to miss one of the highest moments of the life of the spirit. No other experience can serve as a substitute; no life that has not known it can regard itself as completely fulfilled.

These are some of the elementary reasons why those who demand of the poet a definite code of morals or manners, the ready-made standards of any society, however great, that is bounded by space or time—"American ideals," or "Puritanism," or on the other side, "radical ideas"—seem to me to show their incompetence as critics. Life, teeming life, with all its ardors and agonies, is the only limit within which the poet's vision can be cabined and confined; and all we ask of him is that he create a new life in which the imagination can breathe and move as naturally as our practical selves can live in the world of reality. How can we expect illumination from critics who share the "typical American business man's" inherent inability to live in the world of fantasy which the poets have created, without the business man's ability to face the external facts of life and mould them to his will? These men are schoolmasters, pedants, moralists, policemen, but neither critics nor true lovers of the spiritual food that art provides. To the creative writers of America I should give a wholly different message from theirs. I should say to them: "Express what is in you, all that serene or turbulent vision of multitudinous life which is yours by right of imagination, trusting in your own power to achieve discipline and mastery, and leave the theoretical discussion of 'American ideals' to statesmen, historians, and philosophers, with the certainty that if you truly express the vision of your highest self, the statesmen, historians, and philosophers of the future will point to your work as a fine expression of the 'American ideals' you have helped to create. Do not wait for the flux of time to create a society that you can copy, but create your own society; and if you are a great writer it will be a Great Society, which the world will never cease to live in and to love. For you America must always be not old but new, something unrealised, something to be created and to be given as an incredible gift to a hundred million men. Courage is the birthright of the poet as much as of the soldier or statesman; and courage in trusting your imagination is to you the very breath of life. But mastery of the imagination, and not mere submission to it, must be your goal; for how can the true artist express himself in terms of slavery rather than power? By giving what is best in him to his art, the American artist serves America best."

A profound inner reform is needed in order that the critics of America may prepare themselves adequately to interpret this new literature, to separate the chaff from the wheat, and in so doing to purify and ennoble the taste and enlarge the imaginative sympathies of a whole people.

The first need of American criticism today is education in esthetic thinking. It needs above all the cleansing and stimulating power of an intellectual bath. Only the drenching discipline that comes from mastery of the problems of esthetic thought can train us for the duty of interpreting the American literature of the future. The anarchy of impressionism is a natural reaction against the mechanical theories and jejune text-books of the professors, but it is a temporary haven and not a home. The haphazard empiricism of English criticism and the faded moralism of some of our own will serve us no more. We must desert these muddy waters, and seek purer and deeper streams. For the conception of the critic as censor or as eulogist we must substitute the conception of the critic as esthetic thinker. In a country where philosophers urge men to cease thinking, it may be the task of the critic to revivify and reorganize thought.

The second need of American criticism can be summed up in the word scholarship—that discipline of knowledge which will give us at one and the same time a wider international outlook and a deeper national insight. One will spring from the other, for the timid colonial spirit finds no place in the heart of the citizen of the world; and respect for native talent, born of a surer knowledge, will prevent us alike from overrating its merits and from holding it too cheap. For the lifeless pedantry of the antiquarians, who think that tradition actually lives in monuments, heirlooms, dead ancestors, and printed books, we must substitute the illumination of a humane scholarship, which realizes that learning is but a quest for the larger self and that tradition is a state of the soul. Half-knowledge is either too timid or too cocksure; and only out of the spiritual discipline that is born of intellectual travail and adventure can come a true independence of judgment and taste.

For taste is after all both the point of departure and the goal; and the third and at this moment the greatest need of American criticism is a deeper sensibility, a more complete submission to the imaginative will of the artist, before attempting to rise above it into the realm of judgment. The critic is not a man seated on a block of ice watching a bright fire, or how could he realize the full force of its warmth and power? If there is anything that American life can be said to give least of all, it is training in taste. There is a deadness of artistic feeling, which is sometimes replaced or disguised by a fervor of sociological obsession, but this is no substitute for the faculty of imaginative sympathy which is at the heart of all criticism. By taste, I mean, of course, not the "good taste" of the dilettante or the amateur collector, or taste in its eighteenth-century sense, but that creative moment of the life of the spirit which the artist and the enjoyer of art share alike. For this the ardor of the reformer, the insight of the historian, even the moral passion of the saint is no substitute; for taste, or disciplined esthetic enjoyment, is the only gateway to the critic's judgment, and over it is a flaming signpost, "Critic, abandon all hope when this gate is shut."

This is your task, critics of America—to see that Plato's dream of banishing poets from the ideal Republic does not come true. It is your chief duty, against moralist and hedonist and utilitarian alike, to justify the ways of the artist to Americans. In a land where virtuous platitudes have so often been mistaken for poetry, it is your task to explain the real meaning of the esthetic moment for the higher lives of men. But no one knows better than I that you cannot rest satisfied even with this. For the modern critic has learnt to distinguish clearly between art, philosophy, history, religion, morals, not for the purpose of denying but of establishing their essential unity in the life of the spirit. Those who deny this unity and those who would substitute for it a muddle-headed if well-meaning confusion are alike the Enemy. Though you reject the criticism in which art is forever measured and tested by the moralist's rigid rules and justified by virtues that are not her own, still less can you be satisfied with the criticism in which "ideas" are struck out in random and irresponsible flashes like sparks from the anvil of a gnome. You cannot be satisfied with anything but truth—that whole truth which is life— even in the service of art and beauty.

From *Creative Criticism and Other Essays* by J. E. Spingarn, pp. 123–147. Copyright, 1931, by J. E. Spingarn. Reprinted by permission of Harcourt, Brace and Company, Inc. First published in *Civilization in the United States: An Enquiry by Thirty Americans,* edited by Harold E. Stearns. Harcourt, Brace and Company, Inc., 1922.

IRVING BABBITT

The Critic and American Life

[1928]

A FREQUENT remark of the French about Americans is: "They're children"; which, interpreted, means that from the French point of view Americans are childishly uncritical. The remark is relevant only in so far as it refers to general critical intelligence. In dealing with the special problems of a commercial and industrial society, Americans have shown that they can be abundantly critical. Certain Americans, for example, have developed a critical keenness in estimating the value of stocks and bonds that is nothing short of uncanny.[1] The very persons, however, who are thus keen in some particular field are, when confronted with questions that call for general critical intelligence, often puerile. Yet in an age like the present, which is being subjected to a constant stream of propaganda in everything from the choice of religion to its cigarettes, general critical intelligence would seem desirable.

As a matter of fact, most persons aspire nowadays to be not critical but creative. We have not merely creative poets and novelists, but creative readers and listeners and dancers. Lately a form of creativeness has appeared that may in time swallow up all the others—creative salesmanship. The critic himself has caught the contagion and also aspires to be creative. He is supposed to become so when he receives from the creation of another, conceived as pure temperamental overflow, so vivid an impression that, when passed through his temperament, it issues forth as a new creation. What is eliminated in both critic and creator is any standard that is set above temperament, and that therefore might interfere with their eagerness to get themselves expressed.

This notion of criticism as self-expression is important for our present subject, for it has been adopted by the writer who is, according to the

[1] This was written before the collapse of the great common stock bubble in the autumn of 1929. It then became evident that what the financial leaders of the "Boom" period lacked was not so much expertness in their own field as general critical intelligence—especially some working knowledge of the ways of Nemesis. There were, of course, honorable exceptions. The late Paul M. Warburg showed that he was one of them when he remarked, apropos of the so-called business cycle, that "it is a subject for psychologists rather than for economists." [What is involved] "is the answer to the question: How long—in industry, commerce and finance—does the memory of painful experiences prevent human greed and conceit from regaining control, etc."

Encyclopedia Britannica,[2] "The greatest critical force in America"—Mr. H. L. Mencken. Creative self-expression, as practiced by himself and others, has, according to Mr. Mencken, led to a salutary stirring up of the stagnant pool of American letters: "Today for the first time in years there is strife in American criticism. . . . Heretics lay on boldly and the professors are forced to make some defense. Often going further they attempt counterattacks. Ears are bitten off, noses are bloodied. There are wallops both above and below the belt."

But it may be that criticism is something more than Mr. Mencken would have us believe, more in short than a squabble between Bohemians, each eager to capture the attention of the public for his brand of self-expression. To reduce criticism indeed to the satisfaction of a temperamental urge, to the uttering of one's gustos and disgustos (in Mr. Mencken's case chiefly the latter) is to run counter to the very etymology of the word which implies discrimination and judgment. The best one would anticipate from a writer like Mr. Mencken, possessing an unusual verbal virtuosity and at the same time temperamentally irresponsible, is superior intellectual vaudeville. One must grant him, however, certain genuine critical virtues—for example, a power of shrewd observation within rather narrow limits. Yet the total effect of his writing is nearer to intellectual vaudeville than to serious criticism.

The serious critic is more concerned with achieving a correct scale of values and so seeing things proportionately than with self-expression. His essential virtue is poise. The specific benefit he confers is to act as a moderating influence on the opposite insanities between which mankind in the lump is constantly tending to oscillate—oscillations that Luther compares to the reelings of a drunken peasant on horseback. The critic's survey of any particular situation may very well seem satirical. The complaint that Mr. Mencken is too uniformly disgruntled in his survey of the American situation rather misses the point. Behind the pleas for more constructiveness it is usually easy to detect the voice of the booster. A critic who did not get beyond a correct diagnosis of existing evils might be very helpful. If Mr. Mencken has fallen short of being such a diagnostician, the failure is due not to his excess of severity but to his lack of discrimination.

The standards with reference to which men have discriminated in the past have been largely traditional. The outstanding fact of the present period, on the other hand, has been the weakening of traditional standards. An emergency has arisen not unlike that with which Socrates sought to cope in ancient Athens. Anyone who is untraditional and seeks at the same time to be discriminating must almost necessarily own Socrates as his master. As is well known, Socrates above all sought to be discriminating in his use of general

[2] Thirteenth edition. In the fourteenth edition we are informed that Mr. Mencken is a satirist rather than a critic.

terms. Before allowing one's imagination and finally one's conduct to be controlled by a general term, it would seem wise to submit it to a Socratic scrutiny.

It is, therefore, unfortunate that at a time like the present, which plainly calls for a Socrates, we should instead have got a Mencken. One may take as an example of Mr. Mencken's failure to discriminate adequately, his attitude towards the term that for several generations past has been governing the imagination of multitudes—democracy. His view of democracy is simply that of Rousseau turned upside down, and nothing, as has been remarked, resembles a hollow so much as a swelling. A distinction of which he has failed to recognize the importance is that between a direct or unlimited and a constitutional democracy. In the latter we probably have the best thing in the world. The former, on the other hand, as all thinkers of any penetration from Plato and Aristotle down have perceived, leads to the loss of liberty and finally to the rise of some form of despotism. The two conceptions of democracy involve not merely incompatible views of government but ultimately of human nature. The desire of the constitutional democrat for institutions that act as checks on the immediate will of the people implies a similar dualism in the individual—a higher self that acts restrictively on his ordinary and impulsive self. The partisan of unlimited democracy on the other hand is an idealist in the sense the term assumed in connection with the so-called romantic movement. His faith in the people is closely related to the doctrine of natural goodness proclaimed by the sentimentalist of the eighteenth century and itself marking an extreme recoil from the dogmas of total depravity. The doctrine of natural goodness favors the free temperamental expansion that I have already noticed in speaking of the creative critic.

It is of the utmost importance, however, if one is to understand Mr. Mencken, to discriminate between two types of temperamentalist—the soft and sentimental type, who cherishes various "ideals" and the hard, or Nietzschean type, who piques himself on being realistic. As a matter of fact, if one sees in the escape from traditional controls merely an opportunity to live temperamentally, it would seem advantageous to pass promptly from the idealistic to the Nietzschean phase, sparing oneself as many as possible of the intermediary disillusions. It is at all events undeniable that the rise of Menckenism has been marked by a certain collapse of romantic idealism in the political field and elsewhere. The numerous disillusions that have supervened upon the War have provided a favoring atmosphere.

The symptoms of Menckenism are familiar: a certain hardness and smartness and disposition to rail at everything that, rightly or wrongly, is established and respected; a tendency to identify the real with what Mr. Mencken terms "the cold and clammy facts" and to assume that the only alternative to facing these facts is to fade away into sheer romantic unreality. These and similar traits are becoming so widely diffused that, whatever one's opinion of Mr. Mencken as a writer and thinker, one must grant him representativeness. He is a chief prophet at present of those who deem themselves emancipated but who are, according to Mr. Brownell, merely unbuttoned.

The crucial point in any case is one's attitude towards the principle of control. Those who stand for this principle in any form or degree are dismissed by the emancipated as reactionaries or, still graver reproach, as Puritans. Mr. Mencken would have us believe that the historical Puritan was not even sincere in his moral rigorism, but was given to "lamentable transactions with loose women and fiery jugs." This may serve as a sample of the assertions, picturesquely indiscriminate, by which a writer wins immediate notoriety at the expense of his permanent reputation. The facts about the Puritan happen to be complex and need to be dealt with very Socratically. It has been affirmed that the point of view of the Puritan was stoical rather than truly Christian, and the affirmation is not wholly false. The present discussion of the relationship between Puritanism and the rise of capitalism with its glorification of the acquisitive life also has its justification. It is likewise a fact that the Puritan was from the outset unduly concerned with reforming others as well as himself, and this trait relates him to the humanitarian meddler or "wowser" of the present day, who is Mr. Mencken's pet aversion.

Yet it remains true that awe and reverence and humility are Christian virtues and that there was some survival of these virtues in the Puritan. For a representative Puritan like Jonathan Edwards they were inseparable from the illumination of grace, from what he terms a "divine and supernatural light." In the passage from the love and fear of God of an Edwards to the love and service of man professed by the humanitarian, something has plainly dropped out, something that is very near the center. What has tended to disappear is the inner life with the special type of control it imposes. With the decline of this inner control there has been an increasing resort to outer control. Instead of the genuine Puritan we then have the humanitarian legalist who passes innumerable laws for the control of people who refuse to control themselves. The activity of the uplifters is scarcely suggestive of any "divine and supernatural light." Here is a discrimination of the first importance that has been obscured by the muddy thinking of our half-baked intelligentsia. One is thus kept from perceiving the real problem, which is to retain the inner life, even though one refuse to accept the theological nightmare with which the Puritan associated it. More is involved in the failure to solve this problem than the Puritan tradition. It is the failure of our contemporary life in general. Yet, unless some relation is reached by a full and free exercise of the critical spirit, one remains a mere modernist and not a thoroughgoing and complete modern; for the modern spirit and the critical spirit are in their essence one.

What happens, when one sets out to deal with questions of this order without sufficient depth of reflection and critical maturity, may be seen in Mr. Sinclair Lewis's *Elmer Gantry*. He has been lured from art into the writing of a wild diatribe which, considered even as such, is largely beside the mark. If the Protestant Church is at present threatened with bankruptcy, it is not because it has produced an occasional Elmer Gantry. The true reproach it has incurred is that, in its drift toward modernism, it has lost its grip not merely on certain dogmas, but simultaneously on the facts of human nature. It has failed above all to carry over in some modern and critical form the truth of a dogma that unfortunately receives much support from these facts—the dogma of original sin. At first sight Mr. Mencken would appear to have a conviction of evil—when, for example, he reduces democracy in its essential aspect to a "combat between jackals and jackasses"—that establishes at least one bond between him and the austere Christian.

The appearance, however, is deceptive. The Christian is conscious above all of the "old Adam" in himself; hence his humility. The effect of Mr. Mencken's writing, on the other hand, is to produce pride rather than humility, a pride ultimately based on flattery. The reader, especially the young and callow reader, identifies himself imaginatively with Mr. Mencken, and conceives of himself as a sort of morose and sardonic divinity surveying from some superior altitude an immeasurable expanse of "boobs." This attitude will not seem especially novel to anyone who has traced the modern movement. One is reminded in particular of Flaubert, who showed a diligence in collecting bourgeois imbecilities comparable to that displayed by Mr. Mencken in his *Americana*. Flaubert's discovery that one does not add to one's happiness in this way would no doubt be dismissed by Mr. Mencken as irrelevant, for he has told us that he does not believe in happiness. Another discovery of Flaubert's may seem to him more worthy of consideration. "By dint of railing at idiots," Flaubert reports, "one runs the risk of becoming idiotic oneself."

It may be that the only way to escape from the unduly complacent cynicism of Mr. Mencken and his school, is to reaffirm once more the truths of the inner life. In that case it would seem desirable to disengage, so far as possible, the principle of control on which the inner life finally depends from mere creeds and traditions and assert it as a psychological fact; a fact, moreover, that is neither "cold" nor "clammy." The coldness and clamminess of much so-called realism arises from its failure to give this fact due recognition. A chief task, indeed, of the Socratic critic would be to rescue the noble term "realist" from its present degradation. A view of reality that overlooks the element in man that moves in an opposite direction from mere temperament, the specifically human factor, in short, may prove to be singularly one-sided. Is the Puritan, John Milton, when he declares that "he who reigns within himself and rules passions, desires, and fears is more than a king," less real than Mr. Theodore Dreiser when he discourses in his peculiar dialect of "those rearranging chemisms upon which all the morality and immorality of the world is based"?

As a matter of fact, according to the degree and nature of the exercise of the principle of control, one may distinguish two main types of realism which may be denominated respectively religious and humanistic: as the principle of control falls into abeyance, a third type tends to emerge, which may be termed naturalistic realism. That the decline of the traditional controls has been followed by a lapse to the naturalistic level is indubitable. The characteristic evils of the present age arise from unrestraint and violation of the law of measure and not, as our modernists would have us believe, from the tyranny of taboos and traditional inhibitions. The facts cry to heaven. The delicate adjustment that is required between the craving for emancipation and the need of control has been pointed out once for all by Goethe, speaking not as a Puritan, but as a clear-eyed man of the world. Everything, he says, that liberates the spirit without a corresponding growth in self-mastery is pernicious. This one sentence would seem to cover the case of our "flaming youth" rather completely.

The movement in the midst of which we are still living was from its inception unsound in its dealing with the principle of control. It is vain to expect from the dregs of this movement what its "first sprightly running failed to give." Mr. Carl Sandburg speaks of the "marvelous rebellion of man at all signs reading *Keep off.*" An objection to this purely insurrectional attitude is that, as a result of its endless iteration during the past century and more, it has come to savor too strongly of what has been called the "humdrum of revolt." A more serious objection to the attitude is that it encourages an unrestricted and merely temperamental liberty which, paradoxically enough, at first sight affords the modern man no avenue of escape from the web that is being woven about him by the scientific determinist.

Realists of the current type are in point of fact intimately allied with the psychologists—glandular, behavioristic, and psychoanalytical—who, whatever their divergences among themselves, unite in their deterministic trend and therefore class fundamentally with both religious and humanistic realists. The proper method of procedure in defending the freedom of the will would seem to insist upon it as a fact of experience, a fact so primary that the position of the determinist involves an evasion of one of the immediate data of consciousness in favor of a metaphysical dream. What is genuinely experimental in naturalistic psychology should of course be received with respect; but the facts of which it takes account in its experiments are unimportant compared with the facts it either neglects or denies. Practically it is running into grotesque extremes of pseudo-science that make it a shining mark for the Socratic critic.

Here at all events is the issue on which all other issues finally hinge; for until the question of moral freedom—the question of whether man is a responsible agent or only the plaything of his impulses and impressions—is decided, nothing is decided; and to decide the question under existing circumstances calls for the keenest critical discrimination. Creation that is not sufficiently supported by such discrimination is likely to prove premature.

One may illustrate from Mr. Dreiser's *American Tragedy,* hailed in certain quarters as the "Mount Everest" of recent fiction. He has succeeded in producing in this work something genuinely harrowing; but one is harrowed to no purpose. One has in more than full measure the tragic qualm but without the final relief and enlargement of spirit that true tragedy succeeds somehow in giving, and that without recourse to explicit moralizing. It is hardly worth while to struggle through eight hundred and more very pedestrian pages to be left at the end with a feeling of sheer oppression. The explanation of this oppression is that Mr. Dreiser does not rise sufficiently above the level of "rearranging chemisms," in other words, of animal behavior. Tragedy may admit fate—Greek tragedy admits it—but not of the naturalistic variety. Confusion on this point may compromise in the long run the reputations of writers more eminent that Mr. Dreiser—for example, of Thomas Hardy. Fatalism of the naturalistic type is responsible in large measure for the atmosphere of futility and frustration that hangs heavily over so much contemporary writing. One finally comes to feel with a recent poet that "dust" is the common source from which

> . . . . stream
> The cricket's cry and Dante's dream.

Anyone who admits reality only in what derives from the dust, whether in a cricket or Dante, must, from the point of view of the religious or the humanistic realist, be prepared to make substantial sacrifices. In the first place, he must sacrifice the depth and subtlety that arise from the recognition in some form of the duality in man's nature. For the interest that may rise from the portrayal of the conflict between a law of the spirit and a law of the members, the inordinate interest in sex for its own sake promoted by most of the so-called realists is a rather shabby substitute. A merely naturalistic realism also involves the sacrifice of beauty in almost any sense of that elusive term. Closely related to this sacrifice is the sacrifice of delicacy, elevation, and distinction. The very word realism has come to connote the opposite of these qualities. When we learn, for example, that someone has written a realistic study of a great man, we are sure in advance that he has devoted his main effort to proving that "Plutarch lied." The more the great man is reduced to the level of commonplace or worse, the more we feel he has been "humanized."

Mr. Sherwood Anderson has argued ingeniously that, inasmuch as we ourselves are crude, our literature, if it is not to be unreal and fictitious, should be crude likewise. But the writer who hopes to achieve work of importance cannot afford to be too deeply immersed in the atmosphere of the special place and passing moment. Still less can he afford to make us feel, as writers like Mr. Anderson and Mr. Dreiser and Mr. Sinclair Lewis do, that, if there were any lack of vulgarity in what they are depicting, they would be capable of supplying the defect from their own abundance. More is involved here than the mere loss of distinction. We have come, indeed, to the supreme sacrifice that every writer must make who does not transcend a naturalistic realism. He must forego the hope of the enduring appeal—the hope that every writer worthy of his salt cherishes in some degree. In the absence of humanistic or religious standards, he is prone to confound the real with the welter of the actual, and so to miss the "grandeur of generality."

Certain books in the current mode are so taken up with the evanescent surfaces of life that they will survive, if at all, not as literature but as sociological documents. The very language in which they are written will, in a generation or two, require a glossary. So far from imposing an orderly pattern on the raw material of experience, they rather emphasize the lack of pattern. The resulting effect, to borrow a phrase from the late Stephen Crane, who has had a marked influence on the recent movement, is that of a "cluttered incoherency." As an extreme example of this tendency one may cite *Manhattan Transfer*, by John Dos Passos. In the name of reality Mr. Dos Passos has perpetrated a literary nightmare. Such a work would seem to have slight value even as a sociological document; unless, indeed, one is prepared to admit that contemporary Manhattan is inhabited chiefly by epileptic Bohemians.

"It is as much a trade," says La Bruyère, "to make a book as it is to make a clock"; in short, literature is largely a matter of technique. The technique of *Manhattan Transfer* is as dubious as its underlying philosophy. Neither can be justified save on the assumption that the aim of art is to exaggerate the clutter and incoherency of the mundane spectacle instead of eliciting its deeper meaning. Technique counts for even more in poetry than in prose. It would be possible to base on technical grounds alone a valid protest against the present preposterous overestimate of Walt Whitman. Fundamental questions need, in these very untraditional days, to be critically elucidated with a view to right definition if the poet is not to lack technique or still worse, if he is not, like certain recent practitioners of free verse, to be hagridden by a false technique. It evidently concerns both the form and substance of poetry, whether one define it with Aristotle as the portrayal of representative human action, or whether one define it with Mr. Carl Sandburg as a "mystic, sensuous mathematics of fire, smokestacks, waffles, pansies, people, and purple sunsets."

There is no doubt much in America of today that suggests a jazzy impressionism. Still our naturalistic deliquescence has probably not gone so far as one might infer from poetry like that of Mr. Sandburg or fiction like that of Mr. Dos Passos. The public response to some of the realistic novels has been considerable: allowance must be made however for the *succès de scandale,* also for the skill attained by the modern publisher in the art of merchandising. The reputation of certain books one might mention may be regarded as a triumph of "creative" advertising. What has been created is a mirage of masterpieces where no masterpieces are. It is well also to remember in regard to some of the works that have been most discussed that, so far from being an authentic reflection of the American scene, they are rather a belated echo of certain European movements. For it is as certain that in our literary and artistic modes we follow Europe—usually at an interval of from five to forty years—as it is that we lead Europe in our bathtubs and sanitary plumbing. Anyone who resided in Paris in the nineties and later in America, will, as I can testify from personal experience, have the sense of having lived through the same literary fads twice. Mr. Dreiser reminds one of Zola and his school. The technique of Mr. Dos Passos recalls that of the Goncourts. Our experimenters in free verse have followed in the wake not merely of Walt Whitman but of the French symbolists, and so on.

We shall presently begin to hear of certain new developments in French literature and critical thought that point, though indecisively as yet, to a radical departure from what has been the main current since the eighteenth century and in some respects since the Renaissance. It is well that we should become familiar with the writers who reveal in different ways this latest trend —notably with Maritain, Maurras, Lasserre, Seillière, and Benda; for they give evidence of a quality of cerebration that is rare in our own literati. At the same time we should not adopt with our usual docility the total outlook of any of these writers: for no one of them has worked out a point of view exactly adapted to our requirements. In general, it is not fitting that a great nation at the very height of its power should go on indefinitely trailing after Europe. It is time for us to initiate something of our own. This does not mean that we should proceed forthwith to inbreed our own "originality." It means almost the exact opposite. The most original thing one could do nowadays would be to question the whole theory of originality as mere temperamental overflow and self-expression that has prevailed from the "geniuses" of the eighteenth century down to one of our youthful and very minor bards who aspires to "spill his bright illimitable soul."

A genuinely critical survey would make manifest that the unsatisfactoriness of our creative effort is due to a lack of the standards that culture alone can supply. Our cultural crudity and insignificance can be traced in turn to the inadequacy of our education, especially our higher education. Mr. Mencken's attack on the "professors" is therefore largely justified; for if the professors were performing their function properly Mr. Mencken himself would not be possible. One must add in common justice that the professors themselves, or at least some of them, are becoming aware that all is not well with existing conditions. One could not ask anything more perspicacious than the following paragraph from a recent report of Committee G to the American Association of University Professors:

American education has suffered from the domination, conscious or unconscious, direct or indirect, of political and sentimental, as well as educational, theories that are demonstrably false. If the views of some men are to prevail the intellectual life of the country is doomed; everybody except the sheer idiot is to go to college and pursue chiefly sociology, nature study, child study, and community service—and we shall have a society unique only in its mediocrity, ignorance, and vulgarity. It will not do to dismiss lightly even so extreme a view as this; it is too indicative. Such influences are very strong, their pressure is constant; and if education has largely failed in America, it has been due primarily to them.

In short, as a result of the encroachments of an equalitarian democracy, the standards of our higher education have suffered in two distinct particulars: first, as regards the quality of students; second, as regards the quality of the studies these students pursue. The first of these two evils is generally recognized. There is even some prospect of remedial measures. Certain institutions, Harvard, for example, without being as yet severely selective, are becoming more critical of the incompetent student. On the other hand, there seems to be less hope than ever of any righting of the second and more serious evil—the failure to distinguish qualitatively between studies. The main drift is still towards what one may term a blanket degree. (Dartmouth, for example, has just merged its bachelor of arts and bachelor of science.) Yet rather than blur certain distinctions it would have been better, one might suppose, to use up all the letters of the alphabet devising new degrees to meet the real or supposed educational needs of the modern man. To bestow the A.B. degree indiscriminately on a student for whom education has meant primarily a specialization in chemistry and one for whom it has meant primarily an assimilation of the masterpieces of Greek literature is to empty it of any effective meaning. At the present rate, indeed, the time may come when the A.B. degree will not throw much more light on the cultural quality of its recipient than it would if, as has been suggested, it were bestowed on every American child at birth.

It goes without saying that those who have been lowering and confusing educational standards have been profuse in their professions of "service." A critical examination, not merely of American education, but of American life at the present time, will almost necessarily hinge on this term. The attitude of the Socratic critic toward it is not to be confounded with that of Mr. Mencken and the "hardboiled" contingent. "When a gang of real estate agents," says Mr. Mencken, "bond salesmen, and automobile dealers get together to sob for Service, it takes no Freudian to surmise that someone is about to be swindled." But if one entertains doubts about this current American gospel, why waste one's ammunition on any such small fry? Other and more exalted personages than the members of the Rotary Club at Zenith have, in Mr. Mencken's elegant phrase, been "yipping for Service." If one is to deal with this idea of service Socratically, one needs to consider it in relation to the two figures who have rightly been taken to be most representative in our cultural background—Benjamin Franklin and Jonathan Edwards. Franklin's idea of service is already humanitarian. Edwards' idea is still traditionally Christian—service not of man but of God. What Franklin stood for is flourishing prodigiously at the present moment, so much so that he may perhaps be defined in his chief line of influence as the great superrotarian. What Edwards stood for is, on the other hand, largely obsolete or survives only in the form of habits, which, lacking doctrinal support, are steadily declining along with the whole Puritan culture.

Intermediary types are possible. One may in one's character reflect the Puritan background and at the same time in one's idea of service derive rather from Franklin. Precisely that combination is found in the most influential of our recent educational leaders—the late President Eliot. A legitimate admiration for his personal qualities should not interfere with the keenest critical scrutiny of his views about education, for the two things stand in no necessary connection. Practically this means to scrutinize the humanitarian ideal that he probably did more than any other man of his generation to promote. In this respect most of the heads of our institutions of learning have been and still are understudies of President Eliot.

In an address on the occasion of his ninetieth birthday President Eliot warned his hearers against introspection, lest it divert them from a whole-hearted devotion to service. Between this attitude and a religious or humanistic attitude there is a clash of first principles. Both humanism and religion require introspection as a prerequisite of the inner life and its appropriate activity. With the disappearance of this activity what is left is the outer activity of the utilitarian, and this leads straight to the one-sided cult of material efficiency and finally to the standardization that is, according to nearly all foreign critics and many of our own, a chief American danger. We cannot return to the introspection of the Puritan. We shudder at the theology an Edwards would impose as the condition of his "divine and supernatural light." Yet it does not follow, as I have already suggested, that we should reject the inner life along with this theology. One may recognize innumerable advantages in the gospel of service and yet harbor an uneasy suspicion withal that in the passage from the old religion to the modern humanitarian dispensation something vital has disappeared, something from which neither the outer working of the utilitarian nor again the expansive sympathy of the sentimentalist can offer an equivalent.

The problem of the inner life is very much bound up with two other problems that are now pressing for solution in our higher education and have as yet found none: the problem of the specialist and the problem of leisure. The man of leisure is engaged in an inner and specifically human form of activity, a form that is, according to Aristotle, needful if he is to compass the end of ends—his own happiness. The question is whether one should consent like the specialist to forego this activity and to live partially and as a mere instrument for the attainment of some outer end—even though this end be the progress of humanity. We are beginning to hear a great deal nowadays about the "menace" of leisure. It has been estimated that with the prefecting of mechanical devices the man of the future will be able to satisfy his material wants by working not more than four hours a day. It is vain to anticipate that the rank and file will use this release from outer activity intelligently unless the leaders, notably those in high academic station, show the way. The notion of true leisure is the ultimate source of the standards of any education that deserves to be called liberal. When even a few of our college and university presidents show that they are thinking to some purpose on the nature of leisure it will be time enough to talk of "America's coming of age."

As it is, our institutions of learning seem to be becoming more and more hotbeds of "idealism." Their failure, on the whole, to achieve standards as something quite distinct from ideals, on the one hand, and standardization, on the other, may prove a fact of sinister import for the future of American civilization. The warfare that is being waged at the present time by Mr. Sinclair Lewis and others against a standardized Philistinism continues in the main the protest that has been made for several generations past by the temperamentalists, hard or soft, against the mechanizing of life by the utilitarian. This protest has been, and is likely to continue to be, ineffectual. The fruitful opposite of the standardized Philistine is not the Bohemian, nor again the hard temperamentalist or superman, as Mr. Mencken conceives him, but the man of leisure. Leisure involves an inner effort with reference to standards that is opposed to the sheer expansion of temperament, as it is to every other form of sheer expansion.

Perhaps a reason why the standards of the humanist are less popular in this country than the ideals of the humanitarian is that these standards set bounds to the acquisitive life; whereas it seems possible to combine a perfect idealism with an orgy of unrestricted commercialism. It is well for us to try to realize how we appear to others in this matter. Our growing unpopularity abroad is due no doubt in part to envy of our material success, but it also arises from the proneness of the rest of the world to judge us, not by the way we feel about ourselves, but by our actual performance. If we are in our own eyes a nation of idealists, we are, according to a recent French critic, M. André Siegfried,[3] a "nation of Pharisees." The European, M. Siegfried would have us believe,

---

[3] See his volume *Les États-Unis d'aujourd'hui* (1927), translated under the title *America Comes of Age.*

still has a concern for the higher values of civilization, whereas the American is prepared to sacrifice these values ruthlessly to mass production and material efficiency.

It is easy to detect under this assumption the latest form of a "certain condescension in foreigners." The breakdown of cultural standards is European as well as American. It is not clear that M. Siegfried himself has an adequate notion of the form of effort that can alone serve as a counterpoise to the one-sided activity of the utilitarian. At the same time his anatomy of our favorite ideal of service is not without interest. This ideal opposes no effective barrier to our expansiveness. An unchecked expansiveness on the national scale is always imperialistic. Among the ingredients of a possible American imperialism M. Siegfried enumerates the American's "great self-satisfaction, his rather brutal sense of his own interests, and *the consciousness, still more dangerous, of his 'duties' towards humanity.*" M. Siegfried admits however that our imperialism is likely to be of a new and subtle essence, not concerned primarily with territorial aggrandizement.

A proper discussion of M. Siegfried's position as well as of other issues I have been raising would transcend the limits of an essay. My end has been accomplished if I have justified in some measure the statement with which I started as to the importance of cultivating a general critical intelligence. James Russell Lowell's dictum that before having an American literature we must have an American criticism was never truer than it is today. The obvious reply to those who call for more creation and less criticism is that one needs to be critical above all in examining what now passes for creation. A scrutiny of this kind would, I have tried to show, extend beyond the bounds of literature to various aspects of our national life and would converge finally on our higher education.

We cannot afford to accept as substitute for this true criticism the self-expression of Mr. Mencken and his school, unless indeed we are to merit the comment that is, I am told, made on us by the South Americans: "They are not a very serious people!" To be sure, the reader may reflect that I am myself a critic, or a would-be critic. I can only express the hope that, in my magnifying of the critical function, I do not offer too close a parallel to the dancing-master of Molière who averred, it will be remembered, that "all the mistakes of men, the fatal reverses that fill the world's annals, the shortcomings of statesmen, and the blunders of great captains arise from not knowing how to dance."

From *On Being Creative* by Irving Babbitt, pp. 201–234. Houghton Mifflin Company, 1932. Reprinted by permission. First published in *The Forum*, Vol. LXXIX (February, 1928), pp. 161–176.

PAUL ELMER MORE

How to Read "Lycidas"

[1936]

AFTER passing, as I might say, through the valley of the shadow of death, after months of physical prostration so abject that reading of any sort was beyond the strength of a depleted brain, the poet to whom I turned instinctively with the first renewal of health was Milton. And so I have been reading Milton again and books about him, with the old zest I had as a boy, and with an added joy of almost tremulous excitement such as a miser might feel at the rediscovery of a treasure of gold stolen from him and long buried out of sight. But with this delight have been mingled certain scruples which had troubled me in the old days and for which I had never found quite a satisfactory answer. Again, as many times before, on laying down one of the poems the familiar words of Tennyson would come unbidden to my mind:

> O mighty-mouth'd inventor of harmonies,
> O skill'd to sing of Time or Eternity,
> God-gifted organ-voice of England,
> Milton, a name to resound for ages.

Of the mighty harmonies there would be no doubt; God-gifted voice certainly; organ-voice certainly, for those who have ears to hear. If anyone in English, Milton had the divine craft of words, the mastery of sonorous speech. His is not Shakespeare's incalculable gift; it lacks the element of magic that captures us in Shakespeare; it is, or soon after his earliest experiments it was, an art that came by reflection, and as we read him we imagine that we might by equal deliberation attain the same perfection—only we never do attain it. And something of this distinction Milton himself seems to have felt when he wrote of Shakespeare:

> For whil'st to th' shame of slow-endeavoring Art
> Thy easie numbers flow.

The same distinction, I think, was present to Irving Babbitt when he spoke, as I have heard him do more than once, of his experience in quoting. It was Babbitt's custom in the first draught of his essays to cite from memory, and then, before printing, to verify the quotation by reference to the text. He would find occasionally that even his retentive memory had slipped and that he had substituted a word of his own for the poet's. And sometimes, he would say, he could not see that the substitution was inferior to the original— except in the case of Shakespeare. He never made a change in Shakespeare's language but some force or charm was lost. That was not so even with Milton. Such a difference exists between the seemingly careless spontaneity and the elaborated art of our two supreme masters of poetical diction; and he would be a rash judge who should say that the advantage was all on one side or the other.

But to return to the question that vexed my mood of acquiescent joy. God-gifted organ-voice Milton possessed in full measure—but "voice of England"? Does he speak for the whole of England, or, that being scarcely possible, does he speak for the heart of England, giving articulate expression to that central quality which has made England what we know and love? And by his influence did he maintain that balance and moderation, that sense of law enveloping the individual, which made a Falkland a true type of the Englishman that was to be? Here the question begins with style, but extends beyond mere style to psychology and to principles of government and life.

Now, if there be any hesitation with me to accept Milton's style as the norm of good English, it is certainly not on the ground of that "dissociation of sensibility" which draws a school of modern critics and poets to repudiate what may be called the Miltonic line of development and to seek their parentage in Shakespeare and Donne and the "Metaphysicals." If I understand what the leader of that Choir means by this rather obscure phrase, it is that Milton by conscious choice and judgment dissociated his mind from one whole range of perceptions, refusing to respond to them emotionally as unrelated to a fixed theory of values, and by the same deliberate act of selection created a more or less artificial language, whereas the poets proceeding from Donne held their sensibility open to any and every perception and employed words to convey the sharp immediate impression of each fact of sense and experience without discrimination. The distinction is valid, and it is interesting; for the "modernist" in poetry it is of vital significance. But I am not sure that the "dissociation of sensibility," so taken, has been the source of dead monotony and of verbal unreality in our literature; and I am sure that if Milton failed in national leadership it was not for this reason. Rather I should say that his influence in this respect has made for sanity and form and for limitations which are characteristically English. Rather I should maintain that Milton's failure, so far as he failed, was owing to something essentially un-English, or only partially English, to something belonging to his individual temperament, which passed into his philosophy of life and diverted the love of liberty, which was the central driving force of all his being, into a morbid and isolating passion. Here too Milton was clear-headed in his application of the law to others, but curiously perverse when his own interests were affected. In the second of the sonnets on the book called *Tetrachordon,* he berates his fellow countrymen as "Owles and Cuckoos, Asses, Apes and Doggs" for the very reason that they have lost the true meaning of liberty, while they

> . . . bawle for freedom in this senceless mood,
> And still revolt when truth would set them free.
> License they mean when they cry libertie;
> For who loves that, must first be wise and good;
> But from that mark, how far they roave we see
> For all this wast of wealth, and loss of blood.

That is sound doctrine, but—alas to say it!—Milton did not see how apt would be the retort, *de te fabula;* how easy the reply: License he meant when he cried liberty.

This book called *Tetrachordon,* written by Milton himself, was the second of his treatises on divorce, and is a bitter invective against those who, by opposing the facile freedom of marital separation, enslave the soul under man-made laws, forgetting that which "makes us holiest and likest to God's immortal image," and, for the law of liberty, setting up "that which makes us most conformable and captive to civil and subordinate precepts: . . . although indeed no ordinance, human or from heaven, can bind against the good of man." By "the good of man," as Mr. Tillyard observes in his comment on the passage, Milton means what elsewhere he calls "nature"—damnable word, I add, into which have been distilled all the fallacies of human wit through thousands of years. If you track the word down through its many ambiguities, you will discover that in the end it signifies that which a man temperamentally and personally desires as distinguished from that which is prescribed for him by human rule or divine precept. So it was that Milton, fretted and humiliated because his wife, finding existence with him intolerable, left him and ran away home—so it was that incontinently he rebelled against the human divine laws of marriage and wrote his pleas for freedom of divorce as complying with natural law and the good of man. If ever there was a case of liberty becoming license, it was here. However they may have differed in other respects, in this quality Milton resembled Shelley: they both identified what they desired at any moment with the natural good of man; they both made self-righteousness the law of right.

That was the beginning of Milton's public career and of his prose writings, and it was typical of what ensued. If the bishops in any way interfered with his personal idea of worship, then down with episcopacy and away with the Church; if the monarchical form of government hampered his political independence, then down with monarchy and away with the Constitution.

There is no more painful reading in English literature than these apologies for free divorce and regicide which occupied the greatest genius of the age between "Lycidas" and *Paradise Lost,* and the style in which they are written is as heavy and un-English as their spirit is perverse. There are purple patches scattered through these treatises, which are all that most readers know of Milton's prose and which would give the impression that he is as magnificent here as in his verse; but if these passages are examined it will be found that, taken apart from their context, they are expressions of a personal ambition, legitimate in itself and magnificent in its devotion to the aim of a poet, while all about them floats and rages a sea of rebellious discontent. I will not endorse Hilaire Belloc's sweeping condemnation of the prose in his study of *Milton,* but as a whole it must be admitted to form a repellent body of reading. Following the ideas of the tractates through the surging verbiage, one is reminded of the monsters in the account of creation, "wallowing unweildie" in

> . . . the vast immeasurable Abyss
> Outrageous as a Sea, dark, wasteful, wilde,
> Up from the bottom turn'd by furious windes.

There is something disconcerting in the spectacle of a supreme artist, as Milton was in his verse, so losing his craftsmanship in another medium; what I would insist on is that the very style of his prose has a close relation to the fact that when he passes from imagination to theory his voice is not that of his people but of an exasperated individual. The seventeenth century, with all its greatness, is an age of frustration, filled with fine promises that, except in the field of science, came to no fruition, replete with noble utterance that somehow failed to convince. In the Church, in the State, in society, the one thing needed and not found was a commanding genius that should have indeed the voice of England. It is the tragedy of the time that he who had the genius so to speak should have wasted his energies in querulous complaints against what was, and in the future was to show itself, the true spirit of the land. In a word that spirit may be decribed precisely as liberty, not license, as centrality, not dissent.

But I am not concerned to pass judgment on Milton's character and its effect upon his work as a whole; that is a longer theme than I care now to discuss. What I started out to do was to consider one small piece of his output, the "Lycidas," and to ask myself how it should be read. To this question, at least in its acuter form, I was moved by chancing to take up at the same time Mr. Tillyard's estimation of the poem and Dr. Johnson's. As a whole I should regard Mr. Tillyard's *Milton* as about the best book we have on the man and the poet, a study admirable for its scholarship and discrimination, and particularly notable for its treatment of the philosophical problems raised by *Paradise Lost,* such as Milton's conception of the nature of evil and the cause of man's fall.

Now to Mr. Tillyard " 'Lycidas' is the last and greatest English poem of Milton's youth; though shorter, it is greater than *Comus,* written with newly won but complete mastery and expressing a mental experience both valuable and profound." That is a sentiment with which my own reaction is in perfect accord; indeed, I should go further and hold it to be the greatest short poem of any author in English, the very criterion and touchstone of poetical taste.

Yet with that opinion I have felt bound to remember the sweeping condemnation of Johnson, to whom "the diction" of the poem "is harsh, the rhymes uncertain, and the numbers unpleasing." It is without passion and without art. In part no doubt Johnson's lack of appreciation can be set down to his known deficiency in the higher faculty of imagination. His comment on the diction and rhythm does nothing more than indicate a certain insensitiveness to the finer and more delicate effects of poetry in general. But one cannot read the whole essay without perceiving that his hostile criticism of the art of "Lycidas" sprang not so much from his miscomprehension and esthetic obtuseness as from hostility to the poet and to all that Milton as a man stood for. Touching Milton's plea for looser laws of divorce, the neglect of which by the ruling Presbyterians turned him against that sect, Johnson observes, and justly: "He that changes his party by his humor is not more virtuous than he that changes it by his interest; he loves himself rather than truth." As for the political tirades, Johnson in his attack ran true to form: "Milton's republicanism was . . . founded in an envious hatred of greatness, and a sullen desire of independence. . . . He hated monarchs in the State, and prelates in the Church; for he hated all whom he was required to obey. . . . He felt not so much the love of liberty as repugnance to authority." Now for myself I do not like Belloc's summary and contemptuous characterization of Milton as "a man rotten with the worst vices: falsehood and pride"; for somehow one shrinks from using such language of a very great poet. To Johnson's charge, on the contrary, I can subscribe without reservation (indeed I have already said much the same thing in weaker language), and I do not see how the charge, in substance, can be countered by any impartial student of Milton's life. But to Johnson the faults of the man were ruinous to the earlier work of the poet, and he denounced "Lycidas" because he read into it the author's ecclesiastical and political heresies; whereas I must reject the maker whilst admiring what he has made. And there the difficulty lies—or has lain for me: how can one so combine detestation and love? how can one make so complete a separation between Milton the destroyer of Church and State, and Milton the creative artist? how is one to read "Lycidas"?

That particular difficulty, it will be observed, opens up into one of the major problems of criticism in general: the relation between the content of a poem and the art of a poem independent of its content. In the beginning, when that distinction first presented itself to the Greek mind, it took a very simple form and indeed scarcely provoked any doubt: the *Iliad* and the *Odyssey* were valued theoretically, not for their charm and interest, but because in them the statesman, the soldier, the athlete, the man who desired to live honorably, could find the wisest precepts and the best models. For later times, and for us of the West, the principle involved was formulated by Horace in his famous saying that the most successful poet was he who knew how to mix the *utile* and the *dulce*. What Horace meant by the *dulce* is clear enough; it is just that in a poem which gives pleasure to a reader. And what he meant by the *utile* is equally clear; it is that in a poem from which we draw instruction. So in one of the *Epistles* he tells a friend, held in Rome by the practice of declaiming, no doubt about the schools of philosophy, that he is in the country reading Homer, who is a better teacher than all the philosophers:

> Qui, quid sit pulchrum, quid turpe, quid utile, quid non,
> Plenius ac melius Chrysippo et Crantore dicit.

In exactly that form the question reached the Renaissance critics, with the emphasis still heavily on the *utile*. So Puttenham, to cite a single example, thinks it necessary to preface his treatise on *The Arte of English Poesie* with a long apology, wherein is shown how "poets were the first priests, the first prophets, the first Legislators and politicians in the world," as seen in Homer, Orpheus, Amphion, and the rest. You are back a thousand years and more, and might be reading one of the ancient Greek commentators. But a change came with the advent of the romantic movement. The *utile* and the *dulce* took on a new significance, and the old division was sharpened to something like an absolute contrast between two irreconcilable criteria of excellence. The *utile* was broadened so as to embrace the whole substance of a poem whether instructive or not, its sense or meaning. The *dulce* on the other hand was refined to a conception of pure poetry, the quintessence of art, as a sort of abstract entity which could be felt and judged somehow apart from any articulate thought or story conveyed; indeed the ideal poem would be a succession of beautiful words with no meaning at all.

Such a thesis, baldly stated, is manifestly bare nonsense; but practically the early romantics applied it to criticism by taking "Kubla Khan" as the ideal poem, because, while the content was no more than the shimmering matter of a dream, it reeked of that mysterious entity called pure poetry. And it was not so long ago that the theory flared up again in France under the impulse of the Abbé Brémond's monograph on *La Poésie pure*. The discussion that ensued was confused by the Abbé's association of esthetic rapture with a mystical view of the function of prayer. More illuminating, to me at least, is T. S. Eliot's pursuit and final rejection of the same ideal of absolute poetry. In his earlier essays, particularly those on Seneca, Shakespeare, and Dante, you will see him tentatively using this *ignis fatuus* as the ultimate standard of value.

In the first of those studies he ranks Shakespeare and Dante together as the supreme poets of the world, and the two are equally great though the Italian has taken up into the *Commedia* the profoundest wisdom of human experience as expounded in the Thomistic theology, whereas the Englishman has no interpretation of life's riddle beyond the stale platitudes of Seneca. "Perhaps it was Shakespeare's special rôle in history to have effected this peculiar union—perhaps it is a part of his special eminence to have expressed an inferior philosophy in the greatest poetry." It is true that Mr. Eliot has his reservations in supporting this romantic dream of pure poetry, which came to him from certain, as I think unfortunate, associations in the period before he had fully found himself, and which has haunted him all through his years of self-development. It is more important to note that in his latest enunciation he has worked himself quite clear of the disturbing inheritance. There lies before me now his recently published volume of *Essays Ancient and Modern,* and in the opening paragraph of one of the "modern" (that is, hitherto unprinted) essays I am held by this sentence: "The 'greatness' of literature cannot be determined solely by literary standards; though we must remember that whether it is literature or not can be determined only by literary standards." That I take to be a complete truth perfectly formulated; and the whole essay on "Religion and Literature" is a masterly application of this sentence to modern currents in verse and fiction. It is the critic come to full maturity after years of probation.

And so, to apply this canon of taste to "Lycidas," it may be possible for a young man, enamored of the sheer beauty of words and untroubled as yet by the graver issues of life, to enjoy the marvelous art of the poem with no thought of what the poem means if connected with the poet's place in the world of ideas and action. But such a rupture between the form and the substance of literature cannot long be maintained with the ripening of experience. Sooner or later we are bound to make up our account with that law of taste so ably formulated: "The 'greatness' of literature cannot be determined solely by literary standards; though we must remember that whether it is literature or not can be determined only by literary standards." That "Lycidas" is literature, poetry and not mere verse, depends on the language, the images, the form, on that mysterious working of the imagination which we can feel but cannot ultimately analyze or adequately describe; that it is great literature must depend on the junction of such qualities with nobility of content. And such nobility is there, in full measure.

The poem is an elegy prompted by the drowning of a college friend of the author. It has been the complaint of more than one critic that the expression of grief has little of that warmth which might be expected from such a subject. Dr. Johnson can find no "effusion of real passion, for passion runs not after remote allusions and obscure opinions." Against this charge of frigidity

Mr. Tillyard contends with great acumen that the true theme of the poem is not the death of Edward King at all, but the possible death of the poet himself. Milton was writing just before he set out on his voyage to Italy, when such an adventure was more or less perilous, and the possibility of shipwreck and drowning might very well have occupied his mind. So taken, the charge of coldness towards a friend might be changed to one of cowardice or egotism. But Milton was no coward and, however he may have shown himself elsewhere, the note of egotism is relieved by the artful, though doubtless unconscious transference of anxiety for himself to sorrow for another. And it was not the mere termination of life that made him anxious, but the fear that his one all-absorbing ambition might so be left unfulfilled. To understand his state of mind and the emotion that was impelling him to write, the elegy should be read in the light of those passages of self-dedication scattered through his prose works. These purple patches laid upon the coarse cloth of controversy are too well-known to need repeating here. The keynote is given by the words inserted in the gross *Apology for Smectymnuus:*

He who would not be frustrate of his hope to write well hereafter in laudable things, ought himself to be a true poem; that is, a composition and pattern of the best and honourablest things; not presuming to sing high praises of heroic men, or famous cities, unless he have in himself the experience and the practice of all that which is praiseworthy.

And joined with this personal ambition was the conviction that no loftier or purer service could be rendered to one's country and to the world than such a work as he was preparing himself to produce. Under the spell of a great heroic poem the mind of the people would respond in efforts towards great and heroic living. That was Milton's faith. It was the spirit of the reformer engrafted upon the temperament of the artist. In such a profession, wherein personal glory is identified with public welfare, pride with humility, there lurks, let us admit, a subtle danger; to fall short of brilliant success must leave the professor a monument of ridicule, like the mountains in labor that brought forth only a mouse. But, on the other hand, such a purpose, if carried through valiantly to a successful issue, makes the ordinary ambition of the artist and poet to appear in comparison no more than a cheap parade of vanity. And Milton had the courage of conviction and the genius to succeed. In the history of English letters there is nothing like this determination carried through from youth to age except the solemn dedication of Wordsworth to a similar purpose. All this must be read into "Lycidas." Under the pretext of grief for the loss of a comrade in hope the poem is in reality as it were the quintessence of those prose passages through which there speaks a self-confidence as sublime as it was justified.

It is in the light of this life-long ambition that we should read the savage attack on the abuses in Church and State which raises the note of elegy to the "higher mood" of righteous indignation:

> Last came and last did go,
> The Pilot of the *Galilean* lake . . .
> He shook his Miter'd locks, and stern bespake,
> How well could I have spar'd for thee, young swain,
> Anow of such as for their bellies sake,
> Creep and intrude, and climb into the fold? . . .
> But that two-handed engine at the door,
> Stands ready to smite once, and smite no more.

And apart from any theory of episcopacy and royalty the abuses were there and cried out for remedy. Laud knew them as well as did Baxter, Charles as well as Cromwell; but none but Milton possessed the "dread voice" which—alas, but for defects of temper!—might have done so much to set them right.

In this light also we should interpret the allegorical symbolism of the poem:

> The hungry Sheep look up, and are not fed.

To Dr. Johnson all this masquerade of sheep and shepherds is "easy, vulgar, and therefore disgusting," a cheap device of images without passion and without art. Johnson had good reason to be suspicious of a *genre* that has invited so many weak poets to indulge in flim-flam. But he should not have forgotten how all through the Old Testament, from the call that came to Amos, "who was among the herdmen of Tekoa," and all through the New Testament, from the angelic vision that broke upon the shepherds who were "abiding in the field" about Bethlehem to the parable that Jesus spake to his disciples, "I am the good shepherd and know my sheep,"—how all through the Bible this pastoral allegory of the Church runs like the very music of religion.

These were the thoughts that haunted the memory of the poet when he linked himself with his friend as shepherds:

> Together both, ere the high Lawns appear'd
> Under the opening eye-lids of the morn,
> We drove a field.

Together they were practicing their "rural ditties" in preparation for the louder chant that was to stir the nation from its ignoble lethargy, when one of the twain was washed away by the sounding sea, and his voice forever silenced. And what if a like fate awaited the other, who also was about to start on a voyage? "What boots it with incessant care . . . to meditate the thankless Muse," of what avail to "live laborious dayes," when, just as we

> . . . think to burst out into sudden blaze,
> Comes the blind *Fury* with th' abhorred shears,
> And slits the thin spun life?

"But not the praise," he exclaims; the reward and the outcome are not confined to this world nor are they measured by success "on mortal soil," but in heaven before the "witness of all judging *Jove*." I do not know how others are affected, but I can never peruse the climax of the poem without a thrill such as scarcely any other verses of the language excite.

> Weep no more, woful Shepherds weep no more,
> For *Lycidas* your sorrow is not dead,
> Sunk though he be beneath the watry floor,
> So sinks the day-star in the Ocean bed,
> And yet anon repairs his drooping head,
> And tricks his beams, and with new spangled Ore,
> Flames in the forehead of the morning sky:
> So *Lycidas* sunk low, but mounted high,
> Through the dear might of him that walk'd the waves
> Where other groves, and other streams along,
> With *Nectar* pure his oozy Lock's he laves,
> And hears the unexpressive Nuptiall Song,
> In the blest Kingdoms meek of joy and love.
> There entertain him all the Saints above,
> In solemn troops, and sweet Societies
> That sing, and singing in their glory move,
> And wipe the tears for ever from his eyes.

Milton always rang true when he wrote of the world to come, but never before nor after did he attain quite this elevation, or achieve so realistic an expression of the invisible mysteries wrapt in the future. A few of his contemporaries possessed this power of giving substance to the hopes of eternity —notably Vaughan—but none of them approach the master. And in later times the art was simply lost. Choose the best of the moderns, Newman for instance in *The Dream of Gerontius,* and they will appear cold and unconvincing beside Milton. Nor did any of the great poets of the earlier ages of faith quite equal him in this field. I would not compare the few lines of an elegy with the mighty structure of Dante's *Paradiso,* but for myself at least there is no single incident in Dante's voyage through the celestial spheres that touches me with the shock of actuality like that which I feel when I read "Lycidas." I am not competent to explain by what devices, by what choice of words, Milton obtains his sublime effect. It would be easy of course, if it seemed worth while, to point to the rich manipulation of vowel sounds in this or that verse, to note the startling obviousness of the allusion to the might of him that walked the waves, but the final alchemy of art escapes such an analysis; indeed I question whether any skill of criticism can penetrate to the heart of that mystery of the word which we call inspiration, and leave at that. But one phase of Milton's method impresses me: the fact that his images are borrowed from the simplest commonplaces of faith—the return of dawn after the sinking of the sun in the ocean stream, the tears wiped away, the heavenly choiring of the blest. A comparison of Newman's attempt to translate the subtler speculations of theology into a poetic account of the soul's awakening after death shows how inevitably right was Milton's choice. There are regions of spiritual experience where the untutored imagination of the people goes deeper into reality than all the groping wisdom of philosophy.

One thing in the end is certain, the "greatness" of "Lycidas" is determined by an intimate marriage of form and matter, expression and substance. He who would read the poem worthily must see this, and must be equally sensitive to the delicacy of its art and to the sublimity of its ideas. This does not mean that he will forget or slur over the disagreeable traits of the poet's character or the repulsiveness of his ecclesiastical and political theories. But for our good fortune what repels us in the man and roused Johnson to a fury of protest is reserved for his prose and is excluded from his poetry—not completely indeed, for, not to mention the more outrageous sonnets, occasionally the bitterness of his disappointed soul breaks out in his later works, yet to such an extent that it is not impossible to keep the poet and the controversialist apart as two almost separate powers. That divorce has its unhappy aspect; for one thing it debars Milton, in his total effect, from being accepted as the voice of England. But it leaves to him the high credit of having raised in *Paradise Lost,* to the honor of his native land, the one monumentally successful product of that humanistic culture of the Renaissance in which originality of genius and faithfulness to the classical tradition are combined in perfect union. And for "Lycidas" there is this further apology, that the elegy was composed before Milton's splendid spirit of liberty was exacerbated by opposition into petulant license, when his personal pride flamed with a yet undiverted zeal to make of his own life a true poem and so to train himself for creating such a work of art as would lift his people from the ugly slough of faction and greed, where they were grovelling, into the finer atmosphere where pure religion and the love of beauty might flourish together.

From *On Being Human* by Paul Elmer More, pp. 184–202. Princeton University Press. Copyright, 1936. Reprinted by permission. First published in *The American Review,* Vol. VII (May, 1936), pp. 140–158.

H. L. MENCKEN

The American Novel

[1924]

It is an ancient platitude of historical criticism that great wars and their sequelae are inimical to the fine arts, and particularly to the arts of letters. The kernel of truth in it lies in the obvious fact that a people engaged in a bitter struggle for existence have no time for such concerns, which demand not only leisure but also a certain assured feeling of security, well-being and self-sufficiency—in brief, the thing often called aristocratic (or sometimes intellectual) detachment. No man ever wrote good poetry with his wife in parturition in the next room, or the police preparing to raid his house, or his shirt-tail afire. He needs to be comfortable to do it, and if not actually comfortable, then at all events safe. Wars tend to make life uncomfortable and unsafe—but not, it must be observed, inevitably and necessarily, not always and invariably. A bitter and demoralizing struggle goes with wars that are lost, and the same struggle goes with wars that are won only by dint of stupendous and ruinous effort, but it certainly does not go with wars that are won easily. These last do not palsy and asphyxiate the artist, as he is palsied and asphyxiated by cholera morbus, suits for damages or marriage. On the contrary, they pump him full of ozone, and he is never more alive and lively than following them.

I point to a few familiar examples. The Civil War, as everyone knows, bankrupted the South and made life a harsh and bitter struggle for its people, and especially for the gentler and more civilized minority of its people. In consequence, the South became as sterile artistically, after Lee's surrender, as Mexico or Portugal, and even today it lags far behind the North in beautiful letters, and even further behind in music, painting and architecture. But the war, though it went on for four years, strained the resources of the North very little, either in men or in money, and so its conclusion found the Northerners very rich and cocky, and full of a yearning to astonish the world, and that yearning, in a few decades, set up a new and extremely vigorous American literature, created an American architecture of a revolutionary character, and even laid the first courses of American schools of music and painting.

Reprinted from *Prejudices: Fourth Series* by H. L. Mencken, pp. 278–293, by permission of Alfred A. Knopf, Inc. Copyright, 1924, by Alfred A. Knopf, Inc.

Mark Twain, Walt Whitman, Henry James, and William Dean Howells, all of them draft dodgers in the war itself, were in a very real sense products of the war, for they emerged as phenomena of the great outburst of creative energy that followed it, and all of them, including even James, were as thoroughly American as Jay Gould, P. T. Barnum, or Jim Fisk. The stars of the national letters in the years before the war had been Americans only by geographical accident. About Emerson there hung a smell of Königsberg and Weimar; Irving was simply a New York Englishman; Poe was a citizen of No Man's Land; even Hawthorne and Cooper, despite their concern with American themes, showed not the slightest evidence of an American point of view. But Mark Twain, Howells and Whitman belonged to the Republic as palpably as Niagara Falls or Tammany Hall belonged to it, and so did James, though the thought horrified him and we must look at him through his brother William to get the proof. Turn now to Europe. France, harshly used in the war of 1870–71, was sterile for a decade, but the wounds were not deep, and recovery was in full swing by 1880. Germany, injured scarcely at all, produced Nietzsche almost before the troops got home, and was presently offering an asylum and an inspiration to Ibsen, preparing the way for the reform and modernization of the theatre, and making contributions of the utmost value to practically all of the arts and sciences. Spain, after the Armada, gave the world Cervantes and then expired; England produced Shakespeare and founded a literature that is not surpassed in history.

What has thus happened over and over again in the past—and I might pile up examples for pages—may be in process of repetition today, and under our very noses. All Europe, plainly enough, is in a state of exhaustion and depression, and in no department of human activity is the fact more visible than in that of the arts. Not only are the defeated nations, Russia, Germany, and Austria, producing nothing save a few extravagant eccentricities; there is also a great lowness of spirit in the so-called victorious nations, for their victory was almost as ruinous as defeat. France, as after 1870, is running to a pretentious and artificial morbidity in letters, and marking time in music and painting; Italy is producing little save psychopathological absurdities by such mountebanks as D'Annunzio and Papini; even England shows all the signs of profound fatigue. The great English writers of the age before the war are passing. Meredith is gone; Hardy has put up his shutters; Kipling went to wreck in the war itself; Conrad is dead; Shaw, once so agile and diverting, becomes a seer and prophet. Nor is there any sign of sound progress among the younger men. Arnold Bennett, a star of brilliant promise in 1913, is today a smoking smudge. Wells has ceased to be an artist and become a prophet in the Sunday supplements. Masefield has got no further than he was on August 2, 1914. The rest of the novelists are simply chasing their own tails. The Georgian poets, having emerged gloriously during the war, now disappear behind their manners. Only a few women, led by May Sinclair, and a few iconoclastic young men, led by Aldous Huxley, are still indubitably alive.

It seems to me that, in the face of this dark depression across the water, the literary spectacle on this side takes on an aspect that is extremely reassuring, and even a bit exhilarating. For the first time in history, there begins to show itself the faint shadow of a hope that, if all goes well, leadership in the arts, and especially in all the art of letters, may eventually transfer itself from the eastern shore of the Atlantic to the western shore. Our literature, as I have more than once pointed out in the past, is still oppressed by various heavy handicaps, chiefly resident in the failure of the new aristocracy of money to function as an aristocracy of taste. The artist among us is still a sort of pariah, beset by public contempt on the one hand and by academic enmity on the other; he still lacks the public position that his brothers enjoy in older and more civilized countries. Nevertheless, it must be obvious to everyone that his condition tends to improve materially—that, in our own time, it has improved materially—that though his rewards remain meager, save in mere money, his freedom grows steadily greater. And it must be obvious, too, that he begins to show that that increasing freedom is not wholly wasted upon him—that he knows how to use it, and is disposed to do so with some gusto. What all the younger American writers have in common is a sort of new-found elasticity or goatishness, a somewhat exaggerated sense of aliveness, a glowing delight in the spectacle before them, a vigorous and naïve self-consciousness. The schoolmaster critics belabor them for it, and call it a disrespect for tradition, and try to put it down by denouncing it as due to corrupt foreign influences. But it is really a proof of the rise of nationalism—perhaps of the first dawn of a genuine sense of nationality. No longer imitative and timorous, as most of their predecessors were, these youngsters are attempting a first-hand examination of the national scene, and making an effort to represent it in terms that are wholly American. They are the pioneers of a literature that, whatever its defects in the abstract, will at least be a faithful reflection of the national life, that will be more faithful, indeed, in its defects than in its merits. In England the novel subsides into formulae, the drama is submerged in artificialities, and even poetry, despite occasional revolts, moves toward scholarliness and emptiness. But in America, since the war, all three show the artless and superabundant energy of little children. They lack, only too often, manner and urbanity; it is no wonder that they are often shocking to pedants. But there is the breath of life in them, and that life is far nearer its beginning than its end.

The causes of all this are not far to seek. The American Legion is right: we won the war. It cost us nothing in men; it brought us a huge profit in money; as Europe has gone down, we have gone up. Moreover, it produced a vast discharge of spiritual electricity, otherwise and more injuriously dissipated in the countries more harshly beset. The war was fought ignobly; its first and most obvious effect was to raise up a horde of cads, and set them in authority as spokesmen of the nation. But out of that swinishness there was bound to come reaction, and out of the reaction there was bound to flow a desire to re-examine the whole national pretension—to turn on the light, to reject old formulae, to think things out anew and in terms of reality. Suddenly the old houses of cards came tumbling down, and the professors inhabiting them ran about in their nightshirts, bawling for the police. The war, first and last, produced a great deal more than John Dos Passos' *Three Soldiers*. It also produced Lewis' *Babbitt*, and Cabell's *Jurgen*, and Fergusson's *Capitol Hill* and O'Neill's *The Emperor Jones*. And, producing them, it ended an epoch of sweetness and light.

II

The young American literatus of today, with publishers ready and eager to give him a hearing, can scarcely imagine the difficulties which beset his predecessor of twenty years ago; he is, indeed, far too little appreciative of the freedom he has, and far too prone to flee from hard work to the solace of the martyr's shroud. When I first began practice as a critic, in 1908, there was yet plenty of excuse for putting it on. It was a time of almost inconceivable complacency and conformity. Hamilton Wright Mabie was still alive and still taken seriously, and all the young pedagogues who aspired to the critical gown imitated him in his watchful stupidity. This camorra had delivered a violent wallop to Theodore Dreiser eight years before, and he was yet suffering from his bruises; it was not until 1911 that he printed *Jennie Gerhardt*. Miss Harriet Monroe and her gang of new poets were still dispersed and inarticulate; Miss Amy Lowell, as yet unaware of Imagism, was writing polite doggerel in the manner of a New England schoolmarm; the reigning dramatists of the nation were Augustus Thomas, David Belasco, and Clyde Fitch; Miss Cather was imitating Mrs. Wharton; Hergesheimer had six years to go before he'd come to *The Lay Anthony*; Cabell was known only as one who provided the text for illustrated gift-books; the American novelists most admired by most publishers, by most readers and by all practicing critics were Richard Harding Davis, Robert W. Chambers, and James Lane Allen. It is hard indeed, in retrospect, to picture those remote days just as they were. They seem almost fabulous. The chief critical organ of the Republic was actually the Literary Supplement of the *New York Times*. *The Dial* was down with diabetes in Chicago; *The Nation* was made dreadful by the gloomy humors of Paul Elmer More; *The Bookman* was even more saccharine and sophomoric than it is today. When the mild and pianissimo revolt of the middle 90's—a feeble echo of the English revolt—had spent itself, the Presbyterians marched in and took possession of the works. Most of the erstwhile revoltés boldly took the veil— notably Hamlin Garland. No novel that told the truth about life as Americans were living it, no poem that departed from the old patterns, no play that had the merest ghost of an idea in it had a chance. When, in 1908, Mrs. Mary Roberts Rinehart printed a conventional mystery story which yet managed to have a trace of sense in it, it caused a sensation. And when, two years later, Dr. William Lyon Phelps printed a book of criticism in which he actually ranked Mark Twain alongside Emerson and Hawthorne, there was as great a stirring beneath the college elms as if a naked fancy woman had run across the campus. If Hergesheimer had come into New York in 1908 with *Cytherea* under his arm, he would have worn out his pantaloons on publishers' benches without getting so much as a polite kick. If Eugene O'Neill had come to Broadway with *The Hairy Ape,* he would have been sent to Edward E. Rose to learn the elements of his trade. The devilish and advanced thing, in those days, was for the fat lady star to give a couple of matinées of Ibsen's *A Doll's House.*

A great many men and a few women addressed themselves to the dispersal of this fog. Some of them were imaginative writers who found it simply impossible to bring themselves within the prevailing rules; some were critics; others were young publishers. As I look back, I can't find any sign of concerted effort; it was, in the main, a case of each on his own. The more contumacious of the younger critics, true enough, tended to rally 'round Huneker, who, as a matter of fact, was very little interested in American letters, and the young novelists had a leader in Dreiser, who, I suspect, was quite unaware of most of them. However, it was probably Dreiser who chiefly gave form to the movement, despite the fact that for eleven long years he was silent. Not only was there a useful rallying-point in the idiotic suppression of *Sister Carrie;* there was also the encouraging fact of the man's massive immovability. Physically and mentally he loomed up like a sort of headland—a great crag of basalt that no conceivable assault seemed able to touch. His predecessor, Frank Norris, was of much softer stuff. Norris, had he lived longer, would have been wooed and ruined, I fear, by the Mabies, Boyntons, and other such Christian critics, as Garland had been wooed and ruined before him. Dreiser, fortunately for American letters, never had to face any such seduction. The critical schoolmarms, young and old, fell upon him with violence the moment he appeared above the horizon of his native steppe, and soon he was the storm center of a battle-royal that lasted nearly twenty years. The man himself was solid, granitic, without nerves. Very little cunning was in him and not much bellicose enterprise, but he showed a truly appalling tenacity. The pedagogues tried to scare him to death, they tried to stampede his partisans and they tried to put him into Coventry and get him forgotten, but they failed every time. The more he was reviled, sneered at, neglected, the more resolutely he stuck to his formula. That formula is now every serious American novelist's formula. They all try to write better than Dreiser, and not a few of them succeed, but they all follow him in his fundamental purpose—to make the novel true. Dreiser added something, and here following him is harder: he tried to make the novel poignant—to add sympathy, feeling, imagination to understanding. It will be a long while before that enterprise is better managed than he managed it in *Jennie Gerhardt*.

Today, it seems to me, the American imaginative writer, whether he be novelist, poet or dramatist, is quite as free as he deserves to be. He is free to depict the life about him precisely as he sees it, and to interpret it in any manner he pleases. The publishers of the land, once so fearful of novelty, are now so hospitable to it that they constantly fail to distinguish the novelty that has hard thought behind it from that which has only some Village mountebank's desire to stagger the wives of Rotarians. Our stage is perhaps the freest in the world—not only to sensations, but also to ideas. Our poets get into print regularly with stuff so bizarre and unearthly that only Christian Scientists can understand it. The extent of this new freedom, indeed, is so great that large numbers of persons appear to be unable to believe in it; they are constantly getting into sweats about the taboos and inhibitions that remain, for example, those nourished by comstockery. But the importance and puissance of comstockery, I believe, is quite as much over-estimated as the importance and puissance of the objurgations still hurled at sense and honesty by the provincial professors of American Idealism, the Genius of America, and other such phantasms. The Comstocks, true enough, still raid an occasional book, particularly when their funds are running low and there is need to inflame Christian men, but that their monkeyshines ever actually suppress a book of any consequence I very much doubt. The flood is too vast for them. Chasing a minnow with desperate passion, they let a whole school of whales go by. In any case, they confine their operations to the single field of sex, and it must be plain that it is not in the field of sex that the hottest battles against the old American manner have been fought and won. *Three Soldiers* was far more subversive of that manner than all the stories of sex ever written in America— and yet *Three Soldiers* came out with the imprint of one of the most respectable American publishers, and was scarcely challenged. *Babbitt* scored a victory that was still easier, and yet more significant, for its target was the double one of American business and American Christianity; it set the whole world to laughing at two things that are far more venerated in the United States than the bodily chastity of women. Nevertheless, *Babbitt* went down so easily that even the alfalfa *Gelehrten* joined in whooping for it, apparently on the theory that praising Lewis would make the young of the national species forget Dreiser. Victimized by their own craft, the *Gelehrten* thus made a foul attack upon their own principles, for if their principles did not stand against just such anarchistic and sacrilegious books, then they were without any sense whatever, as was and is, indeed, the case.

I shall not rehearse the steps in the advance from *Sister Carrie,* suppressed and proscribed, to *Babbitt,* swallowed and hailed. The important thing is that, despite the caterwauling of the Comstocks and the pedagogues, a reasonable freedom for the serious artist now prevails—that publishers stand ready to print him, that critics exist who are competent to recognize him and willing to do battle for him, and that there is a large public eager to read him. What use is he making of his opportunity? Certainly not the worst use possible, but also certainly not the best. He is free, but he is not yet, perhaps, worthy of freedom. He lets the popular magazine, the movie and the cheap-John publisher pull him too hard in one direction; he lets the vagaries of his politics pull him too hard in another. Back in 1908 I predicted the destruction of Upton Sinclair the artist by Upton Sinclair the visionary and reformer. Sinclair's bones now bleach upon the beach. Beside them repose those of many another man and woman of great promise—for example, Winston Churchill. Floyd Dell is on his way—one novel and two doses of Greenwich Village psychology. Hergesheimer writes novelettes for the *Saturday Evening Post.* Willa Cather has won the Pulitzer Prize—a transaction comparable to the election of Charles W. Eliot to the Elks. Masters turns to prose that somehow fails to come off. Dreiser, forgetting his trilogy, experiments rather futilely with the drama, the essay, free verse. Fuller renounces the novel for book reviewing. Tarkington is another Pulitzer prizeman, always on the verge of first-rate work but always falling short by an inch. Many of the White Hopes of ten or fifteen years ago perished in the war, as surely victims of its slaughter as Rupert Brooke or Otto Braun; it is, indeed, curious to note that practically every American author who moaned and sobbed for democracy between the years 1914 and 1919 is now extinct. The rest have gone down the chute of the movies.

But all this, after all, may signify little. The shock troops have been piled up in great masses, but the ground is cleared for those that follow. Well, then, what of the youngsters? Do they show any sign of seizing their chance? The answer is yes and no. On the one hand there is a group which, revolving 'round *The Bookman,* talks a great deal and accomplishes nothing. On the other hand there is a group which, revolving 'round *The Dial* and *The Little Review,* talks even more and does even less. But on the third hand, as it were, there is a group which says little and saws wood. There seems to be little in common between its members, no sign of a formal movement, with its blague and its bombast, but all of them have this in common: that they owe both their opportunity and their method to the revolution that followed *Sister Carrie.* Most of them are from the Middle West, but they are distinct from the Chicago crowd, now degenerated to posturing and worse. They are sophisticated, disillusioned, free from cant, and yet they have imagination. The raucous protests of the evangelists of American Idealism seem to have no more effect upon them than the advances of the Expressionists, Dadaists, and other such café-table prophets. Out of this dispersed and ill-defined group, I believe, something will come. Its members are those who are free from the two great delusions which, from the beginning, have always cursed American letters: the delusion that a work of art is primarily a moral document, that its purpose is to make men better Christians and more docile cannon-fodder, and the delusion that it is an exercise in logic, that its purpose is to prove something. These delusions, lingering beyond their time, are responsible for most of the disasters visible in the national literature today—the disasters of the radicals as well as those of the 100 per cent. dunderheads. The writers of the future, I hope and believe, will carefully avoid both of them.

Reprinted from *Prejudices: Fourth Series* by H. L. Mencken, pp. 278–293, by permission of Alfred A. Knopf, Inc. Copyright, 1924, by Alfred A. Knopf, Inc.

EZRA POUND

Date Line

[1934]

CRITICISM has at least the following categories, differing greatly in the volume of their verbal manifestation, and not equally zoned.

1. Criticism by discussion, extending from mere yatter, logic-chopping, and description of tendencies up to the clearly defined record of procedures and an attempt to formulate more or less general principles.

Aristotle being neither poet nor complete imbecile contented himself with trying to formulate some of the general interior and exterior relations of work already extant.

He has presumably the largest bastard family of any philosopher. Ninkus, Pinkus and Swinky all try to say what the next writer must do.

Dante who was capable of executing the work and of holding general ideas, set down a partial record of procedures.

2. Criticism by translation.

3. Criticism by exercise in the style of a given period.

As you would not seriously consider a man's knowledge of tennis until he either could make or had made some sort of show in a tournament, so we can assume that until a man can actually control a given set of procedures there must be many elements in them of which he has but an imperfect knowledge.

This introduces almost a personal note, or at least a long-delayed reply to carpers who objected to my spending three days in translating Fontenelle on the grounds that I should have been "doing original work and not wasting my energies in translation." They took the *Divagation* as a proof that I was merely gathering daisies.

4. Criticism via music, meaning definitely the setting of a poet's words; e.g. in *Le Testament*, Villon's words, and in *Cavalcanti*, I have set Guido's and Sordello's. In the famous caricature of Edward and Alfonso, seated on a bench in the Bois, the elder monarch remarks to the younger: "A votre âge j'étais

seulement Prince de Galles, c'est le seul moyen de bien connaître Paris."
This is the most intense form of criticism save:

5. Criticism in new composition.
For example the criticism of Seneca in Mr. Eliot's *Agon* is infinitely more
alive than in his essay on Seneca.

Years ago I made the mistake of publishing a volume (*Instigations*) without blatantly telling the reader that the book had a design. Coming after an
era of gross confusion and irrelevance, wherein malicious camouflage is infinitely more general than any sort of coherence whatsoever, such violent
rupture with the general public habit is perfectly useless, and may, for all I
know, be unfair to those readers who inhabit a middle zone between effulgent
intellect and *les cuistres*.

There would have been no point in asking indulgence as long as the appearances were so greatly against one, I mean so long as the appearance of
mere haphazard gave ground for argument, and the reader of ill-will had
ample basis for hostile demonstration.

II

Criticism so far as I have discovered has two functions:

1. Theoretically it tries to forerun composition, to serve as gun-sight, though
there is, I believe, no recorded instance of this foresight having EVER been of
the slightest use save to actual composers. I mean the man who formulates any
forward reach of co-ordinating principle is the man who produces the demonstration.

The others who use the principle learn usually from the example, and in
most cases merely dim and dilute it.

I think it will usually be found that the work outruns the formulated or at
any rate the published equation, or at most they proceed as two feet of one
biped.

2. Excernment. The general ordering and weeding out of what has actually
been performed. The elimination of repetitions. The work analogous to that
which a good hanging committee or a curator would perform in a National
Gallery or in a biological museum;

The ordering of knowledge so that the next man (or generation) can most
readily find the live part of it, and waste the least possible time among obsolete issues.

"Admitted that it had nothing to do with life but said that it couldn't be
changed, therefore I did not take the course." (Letter from Cambridge student,
Nov. 1933. The letter referred to economics and not to literature, but it is too

good an example of the academic, of the, alas, "university" spirit to leave un-
used.)

It is impossible to deal with the whole question of education, "culture,"
paideuma, in one volume of literary criticism. What Mr. Eliot calls "Para
something or other" need not for a few hundred pages concern us, save to say
that University education during my time failed from lack of attention to its
circle of reference:

(a) Society in general.

(b) The general intellectual life of the nation.

I take it this was equally true of England, the U.S.A. and several other
nations with which I have had less painful experience.

We have passed from the time wherein it was possible to illude oneself by
a "glittering" or other generality. The contemporary philosopher on the Greek
model with one profound (? if any) central (more or less) intuition and a
lot of unverified hypotheses, analogies, uninspected detail, no longer inveigles
serious attention. Philosophy since Leibnitz (at least since Leibnitz) has been
a weak trailer after material science, engaging men of tertiary importance.

It is not to be expected that the knowledge of the human consciousness, or
its most efficient registering material, language, can dispense with progress in
method at least par with that of the particular sciences, nor that any one individual can escape all the limitations of his confrères. No biologist expects
to formulate a WHOLE new biology. At best he expects to explore a limited
field, to improve the knowledge of certain details, and, if lucky, to clarify the
relations of that field, both in regard to the field itself, and to its exterior
reference.

You don't necessarily expect the bacilli in one test tube to "lead to" those
in another by a mere logical or syllogistic line. The good scientist now and
then discovers similarities, he discovers family groups, similar behaviour in
presence of like reagents, etc. Mark Carleton "the great" improved American
wheat by a series of searches. I see no reason why a similar seriousness should
be alien to the critic of letters.

Language is not a mere cabinet curio or museum exhibit. It does definitely
function in all human life from the tribal state onward. You cannot govern
without it, you cannot make laws without it. That is you make laws, and they
become mere mare's nests for graft and discussion. "The meaning has to be
determined," etc.

There are other means of direct human communication but they are all
narrowly zoned to their *specific* departments, plastic directness, mathematical
relations (in music, or engineering), and in borderline territory where a little
very clear language has to be used along with the "technical" expression.
(Even if it be only to label the photograph or the slide.) However much you
accept of Frobenius' theory of *paideuma* as general and overreaching, over-

stretching the single man, whether you take this as literal fact, or as convenient modus of correlation, the spoken idiom is not only a prime factor, but certainly one of the most potent, progressively so as any modality of civilization ages. Printed word or drum telegraph are neither without bearing on the aggregate life of the folk. As language becomes the most powerful instrument of perfidy, so language alone can riddle and cut through the meshes. Used to conceal meaning, used to blur meaning, to produce the complete and utter inferno of the past century . . . discussion of which would lead me out of the bounds of this volume . . . against which, SOLELY a care for language, for accurate registration by language avails. And if men too long neglect it their children will find themselves begging and their offspring betrayed. Summaries of my conclusions after thirty years' search are now available (*How to Read, ABC of Reading*).

From *Make It New,* by Ezra Pound, pp. 3–7.
Yale University Press, 1935. Copyright, 1935.
By permission of the publishers and the author.

A Stray Document
[1913; 1934]

THE "Don'ts" in the following reprint had a plain utilitarian purpose in that they were intended as a rejection slip to be used by a trade paper. They are aimed at the faults most prevalent of poetry as we found it 1905–1912.

Naturally the second clause in the Imagist triad was the first to be avoided. That really did require a little thought and consciousness, and was promptly followed by various more wordy formulae designed to avoid the trouble.

It is not to be expected that a great number of people in any age will be able to maintain an interesting tenseness in verbal manifestation, any more than we are likely to be beset by a large herd of great draughtsmen or an overwhelming swarm of composers capable of great melodic invention.

A RETROSPECT

In the spring or early summer of 1912, "H. D.," Richard Aldington and myself decided that we were agreed upon the three principles following:

1. Direct treatment of the "thing" whether subjective or objective.

2. To use absolutely no word that does not contribute to the presentation.

3. As regarding rhythm: to compose in the sequence of the musical phrase, not in sequence of a metronome.

Upon many points of taste and of predilection we differed, but agreeing upon these three positions we thought we had as much right to a group name as a number of French "schools" proclaimed by Mr. Flint in the August number of Harold Munro's magazine for 1911.

This school was later "joined" or "followed" by numerous people who, whatever their merits, do not show any signs of agreeing with the second specification. *Vers libre* has become as prolix and as verbose as any of the flaccid varieties of verse that preceded it. It has brought in faults of its own. The actual language and phrasing in it is often as bad as that of our elders, without having even the excuse that the words are shoveled in to fill a metrical pattern or to complete the noise of a rhyme-sound. Whether or no the phrases followed by the followers are musical must be left to the reader's decision. At times I can find a marked metre in *"vers libres,"* as stale and hackneyed as any pseudo-Swinburnian, at times the writers seem to follow no musical structure whatever. But it is, on the whole, good that the field should be ploughed. A few excellent poems have come from the new method, thereby is it justified.

Criticism is not a circumscription or a set of prohibitions. It offers fixed points of departure. It may startle a dull reader into alertness. That little of it which is good is to be found mostly in stray phrases; an older artist helping a younger in great measure by rules of thumb or cautions gained by experience.

A FEW DON'TS

An "Image" is that which presents an intellectual and emotional complex in an instant of time. I use the term "complex" rather in the technical sense employed by the newer psychologist, such as Hart, though we might not agree absolutely in our application.

It is the presentation of such a "complex" instantaneously which gives that sense of sudden liberation; that sense of freedom from time limits and space limits; that sense of sudden growth, which we experience in the presence of the greatest works of art.

It is better to present one Image in a lifetime than to produce voluminous works.

All this, however, some may consider open to debate. The immediate necessity is to tabulate A LIST OF DON'TS for those beginning to write verses. I can not put all of them into Mosaic negative.

To begin with, consider the three propositions (demanding direct treatment, economy of words, and the sequence of the musical phrase), not as dogma—never consider anything as dogma—but as the result of long contemplation, which, even if it is someone else's contemplation, may be worth consideration.

Pay no attention to the criticism of men who have never themselves written a notable work. Consider the discrepancies between the actual writing of the Greek poets and dramatists, and the theories of the Graeco-Roman grammarians, concocted to explain their metres.

LANGUAGE

Use no superfluous word, no adjective, which does not reveal something.

Don't use such an expression as "dim lands *of peace.*" It dulls the image. It mixes an abstraction with the concrete. It comes from the writer's not realizing that the natural object is always the *adequate* symbol.

Go in fear of abstractions. Do not re-tell in mediocre verse what has already been done in good prose. Don't think any intelligent person is going to be deceived when you try to shirk all the difficulties of the unspeakably difficult art of good prose by chopping your composition into line lengths.

What the expert is tired of to-day the public will be tired of tomorrow.

Don't imagine that the art of poetry is any simpler than the art of music, or that you can please the expert before you have spent at least as much effort on the art of verse as the average piano teacher spends on the art of music.

Be influenced by as many great artists as you can, but have the decency either to acknowledge the debt outright, or to try to conceal it.

Don't allow "influence" to mean merely that you mop up the particular decorative vocabulary of some one or two poets whom you happen to admire. A Turkish war correspondent was recently caught red-handed babbling in his dispatches of "dove-gray" hills, or else it was "pearl-pale." I can not remember.

Use either no ornament or good ornament.

RHYTHM AND RHYME

Let the candidate fill his mind with the finest cadences he can discover, preferably in a foreign language[1] so that the meaning of the words may be less likely to divert his attention from the movement; e.g., Saxon charms, Hebridean Folk Songs, the verse of Dante, and the lyrics of Shakespeare—if he can dissociate the vocabulary from the cadence. Let him dissect the lyrics of Goethe coldly into their component sound values, syllables long and short, stressed and unstressed, into vowels and consonants.

It is not necessary that a poem should rely on its music, but if it does rely on its music that music must be such as will delight the expert.

Let the neophyte know assonance and alliteration, rhyme immediate and rhyme delayed, simple and polyphonic, as a musician would expect to know harmony and counterpoint and all the minutiae of his craft. No time is too great to give to these matters or to any one of them, even if the artist seldom have need of them.

[1] This is for rhythm; his vocabulary must of course be found in his native tongue.

Don't imagine that a thing will "go" in verse just because it's too dull to go in prose.

Don't be "viewy"—leave that to the writers of pretty little philosophic essays. Don't be descriptive; remember that the painter can describe a landscape much better than you can, and that he has to know a deal more about it.

When Shakespeare talks of the "Dawn in russet mantle clad" he presents something which the painter does not present. There is in this line of his nothing that one can call description; he presents.

Consider the way of the scientists rather than the way of an advertising agent for a new soap.

The scientist does not expect to be acclaimed as a great scientist until he has *discovered* something. He begins by learning what has been discovered already. He goes from that point onward. He does not bank on being a charming fellow personally. He does not expect his friends to applaud the results of his freshman class work. Freshmen in poetry are unfortunately not confined to a definite and recognizable class room. They are "all over the shop." Is it any wonder "the public is indifferent to poetry"?

Don't chop your stuff into separate *iambs*. Don't make each line stop dead at the end, and then begin every next line with a heave. Let the beginning of the next line catch the rise of the rhythm wave, unless you want a definite longish pause.

In short, behave as a musician, a good musician, when dealing with that phase of your art which has exact parallels in music. The same laws govern, and you are bound by no others.

Naturally, your rhythmic structure should not destroy the shape of your words, or their natural sound, or their meaning. It is improbable that, at the start, you will be able to get a rhythm-structure strong enough to affect them very much, though you may fall a victim to all sorts of false stopping due to line ends and caesurae.

The musician can rely on pitch and the volume of the orchestra. You can not. The term harmony is misapplied to poetry; it refers to simultaneous sounds of different pitch. There is, however, in the best verse a sort of residue of sound which remains in the ear of the hearer and acts more or less as an organ-base.

A rhyme must have in it some slight element of surprise if it is to give pleasure; it need not be bizarre or curious, but it must be well used if used at all.

Vide further Vildrac and Duhamel's notes on rhyme in *Technique Poétique*.

That part of your poetry which strikes upon the imaginative *eye* of the reader will lose nothing by translation into a foreign tongue; that which appeals to the ear can reach only those who take it in the original.

Consider the definiteness of Dante's presentation as compared with Milton's rhetoric. Read as much of Wordsworth as does not seem too unutterably dull.

If you want the gist of the matter go to Sappho, Catullus, Villon, Heine when he is in the vein, Gautier when he is not too frigid; or, if you have not the tongues, seek out the leisurely Chaucer. Good prose will do you no harm, and there is good discipline to be had by trying to write it.

Translation is likewise good training, if you find that your original matter "wobbles" when you try to rewrite it. The meaning of the poem to be translated can not "wobble."

If you are using a symmetrical form, don't put in what you want to say and then fill up the remaining vacuums with slush.

Don't mess up the perception of one sense by trying to define it in terms of another. This is usually only the result of being too lazy to find the exact word. To this clause there are possibly exceptions.

The first three simple proscriptions will throw out nine tenths of all the bad poetry now accepted as standard and classic; and will prevent you from many a crime of production.

". . . *Mais d'abord il faut être un poète*," as MM. Duhamel and Vildrac have said at the end of their little book, *Notes sur la Technique Poétique*.

Since March, 1913, Ford Madox Hueffer has pointed out that Wordsworth was so intent on the ordinary or plain word that he never thought of hunting for *le mot juste*.

John Butler Yeats has handled or man-handled Wordsworth and the Victorians, and the criticism, contained in letters to his son, is now printed and available.

From *Make It New: Essays* by Ezra Pound, pp. 335–341. Yale University Press, 1935. Reprinted by permission. "A Few Don'ts" first appeared as "A Few Don'ts by an Imagist" in *Poetry: A Magazine of Verse*, Vol. I (March, 1913), pp. 200–206.

How to Read

(PART II: OR WHAT MAY BE AN INTRODUCTION TO METHOD)

[1929]

It is as important for the purpose of thought to keep language efficient as it is in surgery to keep tetanus bacilli out of one's bandages.

In introducing a person to literature one would do well to have him examine works where language is efficiently used; to devise a system for getting directly and expeditiously at such works, despite the smoke-screens erected by half-knowing and half-thinking critics. To get at them, despite the mass of dead matter that these people have heaped up and conserved round about them in the proportion: one barrel of sawdust to each half-bunch of grapes.

Great literature is simply language charged with meaning to the utmost possible degree.

When we set about examining it we find that this charging has been done by several clearly definable sorts of people, and by a periphery of less determinate sorts.

(a) *The inventors,* discoverers of a particular process or of more than one mode and process. Sometimes these people are known, or discoverable; for example, we know, with reasonable certitude, that Arnaut Daniel introduced certain methods of rhyming, and we know that certain finenesses of perception appeared first in such a troubadour or in G. Cavalcanti. We do not know, and are not likely to know, anything definite about the precursors of Homer.

(b) *The masters.* This is a very small class, and there are very few real ones. The term is properly applied to inventors who, apart from their own inventions, are able to assimilate and co-ordinate a large number of preceding inventions. I mean to say they either start with a core of their own and accumulate adjuncts, or they digest a vast mass of subject-matter, apply a number of known modes of expression, and succeed in pervading the whole with some special quality or some special character of their own, and bring the whole to a state of homogeneous fulness.

(c) *The diluters,* those who follow either the inventors or the "great writers," and who produce something of lower intensity, some flabbier variant, some diffuseness or tumidity in the wake of the valid.

(d) (And this class produces the great bulk of all writing.) The men who do more or less good work in the more or less good style of a period. Of these the delightful anthologies, the song books, are full, and choice among them is the matter of taste, for you prefer Wyatt to Donne, Donne to Herrick, Drummond of Hawthornden to Browne, in response to some purely personal sympathy, these people add but some slight personal flavour, some minor variant of a mode, without affecting the main course of the story.

At their faintest *"Ils n'existent pas, leur ambiance leur confert une existence."* They do not exist: their ambience confers existence upon them. When they are most prolific they produce dubious cases like Virgil and Petrarch, who probably pass, among the less exigent, for colossi.

(e) *Belles Lettres.* Longus, Prévost, Benjamin Constant, who are not exactly "great masters," who can hardly be said to have originated a form, but who have nevertheless brought some mode to a very high development.

(f) And there is a supplementary or sixth class of writers, the starters of crazes, the Ossianic Macphersons, the Gongoras whose wave of fashion flows over writing for a few centuries or a few decades, and then subsides, leaving things as they were.

It will be seen that the first two classes are the more sharply defined: that the difficulty of classification for particular lesser authors increases as one descends through the list, save for the last class, which is again fairly clear.

The point is, that if a man know the facts about the first two categories, he can evaluate almost any unfamiliar book at first sight. I mean he can form a just estimate of its worth, and see how and where it belongs in this schema.

As to crazes, the number of possible diseases in literature is perhaps not very great, the same afflictions crop up in widely separated countries without any previous communication. The good physician will recognize a known malady, even if the manifestation be superficially different.

The fact that six different critics will each have a different view concerning what author belongs in which of the categories here given, does not in the least invalidate the categories. When a man knows the facts about the first two categories, the reading of work in the other categories will not greatly change his opinion about those in the first two.

LANGUAGE

Obviously this knowledge cannot be acquired without knowledge of various tongues. The same discoveries have served a number of races. If a man have not time to learn different languages he can at least, and with very little delay, be told what the discoveries were. If he wish to be a good critic he will have to look for himself.

Bad critics have prolonged the use of demoded terminology, usually a terminology originally invented to describe what had been done before 300 B.C., and to describe it in a rather exterior fashion. Writers of second order have often tried to produce works to fit some category or term not yet occupied in their own local literature. If we chuck out the classifications which apply to the outer shape of the work, or to its occasion, and if we look at what actually happens, in, let us say, poetry, we will find that the language is charged or energized in various manners.

That is to say, there are three "kinds of poetry":

MELOPOEIA, wherein the words are charged, over and above their plain meaning, with some musical property which directs the bearing or trend of that meaning.

PHANOPOEIA, which is a casting of images upon the visual imagination.

LOGOPOEIA, "the dance of the intellect among words," that is to say, it employs words not only for their direct meaning, but it takes count in a special way of habits of usage, of the context we *expect* to find with the word, its usual concomitants, of its known acceptances, and of ironical play. It holds the aesthetic content which is peculiarly the domain of verbal manifestation, and cannot possibly be contained in plastic or in music. It is the latest come, and perhaps most tricky and undependable mode.

The *melopoeia* can be appreciated by a foreigner with a sensitive ear, even though he be ignorant of the language in which the poem is written. It is practcially impossible to transfer or translate it from one language to another, save perhaps by divine accident, and for half a line at a time.

Phanopoeia can, on the other hand, be translated almost, or wholly, intact. When it is good enough, it is practically impossible for the translator to destroy it save by very crass bungling, and the neglect of perfectly well-known and formulatable rules.

Logopoeia does not translate; though the attitude of mind it expresses may pass through a paraphrase. Or one might say, you can *not* translate it "locally," but having determined the original author's state of mind, you may or may not be able to find a derivative or an equivalent.

PROSE

The language of prose is much less highly charged, that is perhaps the only availing distinction between prose and poesy. Prose permits greater factual presentation, explicitness, but a much greater amount of language is needed. During the last century or century and a half, prose has, perhaps for the first time, perhaps for the second or third time, arisen to challenge the poetic pre-eminence. That is to say, *Un Coeur Simple*, by Flaubert, is probably more important than Théophile Gautier's *Carmen*, etc.

The total charge in certain nineteenth-century prose works possible surpasses the total charge found in individual poems of that period; but that merely indicates that the author has been able to get his effect cumulatively, by a greater heaping up of factual data; imagined fact, if you will, but nevertheless expressed in factual manner.

By using several hundred pages of prose, Flaubert, by force of architectonics, manages to attain an intensity comparable to that in Villon's *Heaulmière*, or his prayer for his mother. This does not invalidate my dissociation of the two terms: poetry, prose.

In *phanopoeia* we find the greatest drive toward utter precision of word; this art exists almost exclusively by it.

In *melopoeia* we find a contrary current, a force tending often to lull, or to distract the reader from the exact sense of the language. It is poetry on the borders of music, and music is perhaps the bridge between consciousness and the unthinking sentient or even insentient universe.

All writing is built up of these three elements, plus "architectonics" or "the form of the whole," and to know anything about the relative efficiency of various works one must have some knowledge of the maximum already attained by various authors, irrespective of where and when.

It is not enough to know that the Greeks attained to the greatest skill in *melopoeia,* or even that the Provençaux added certain diverse developments and that some quite minor, nineteenth-century Frenchmen achieved certain elaborations.

It is not quite enough to have the general idea that the Chinese (more particularly Rihaku and Omakitsu) attained the known maximum of *phanopoeia,* due perhaps to the nature of their written ideograph, or to wonder whether Rimbaud is, at rare moments, their equal. One wants one's knowledge in more definite terms.

It is an error to think that vast reading will automatically produce any such knowledge or understanding. Neither Chaucer with his forty books, nor Shakespeare with perhaps half a dozen, in folio, can be considered illiterate. A man can learn more music by working on a Bach fugue until he can take it apart and put it together, than by playing through ten dozen heterogeneous albums.

You may say that for twenty-seven years I have thought consciously about this particular matter, and read or read at a great many books, and that with the subject never really out of my mind, I don't yet know half there is to know about *melopoeia.*

There are, on the other hand, a few books that I still keep on my desk, and a great number that I shall never open again. But the books that a man needs to know in order to "get his bearings," in order to have a sound judgment of any bit of writing that may come before him, are very few. The list is so short, indeed, that one wonders that people, professional writers in particular, are willing to leave them ignored and to continue dangling in mid-chaos emitting the most imbecile estimates, and often vitiating their whole lifetime's production.

Limiting ourselves to the authors who actually invented something, or who are the "first known examples" of the process in working order, we find:

OF THE GREEKS: Homer, Sappho. (The "great dramatists" decline from Homer and depend immensely on him for their effects; their "charge," at its highest potential, depends so often, and so greatly on their being able to count on their audience's knowledge of the *Iliad.* Even Aeschylus is rhetorical.)

OF THE ROMANS: As we have lost Philetas, and most of Callimachus, we may suppose that the Romans added a certain sophistication; at any rate, Catullus, Ovid, Propertius, all give us something we cannot find now in Greek authors.

A specialist may read Horace if he is interested in learning the precise demarcation between what can be learned about writing, and what cannot. I mean that Horace is the perfect example of a man who acquired all that is acquirable, without having the root. I beg the reader to observe that I am being exceedingly iconoclastic, that I am omitting thirty established names for every two I include. I am chucking out Pindar, and Virgil, without the slightest compunction. I do not suggest a "course" in Greek or Latin literature, I name a few isolated writers; five or six pages of Sappho. One can throw out at least one-third of Ovid. That is to say, I am omitting the authors who can teach us no new or no more effective method of "charging" words.

OF THE MIDDLE AGES: The Anglo-Saxon *Seafarer,* and some more cursory notice of some medieval narrative, it does not so greatly matter what narrative, possibly the *Beowulf,* the *Poema del Cid,* and the sagas of *Grettir* and *Burnt Nial.* And then, in contrast, troubadours, perhaps thirty poems in Provençal, and for comparison with them a few songs by Von Morungen, or Wolfram von Essenbach, and von der Vogelweide; and then Bion's *Death of Adonis.*

From which mixture, taken in this order, the reader will get his bearings on the art of poetry made to be sung; for there are three kinds of *melopoeia:* (1) that made to be sung to a tune; (2) that made to be intoned or sung to a sort of chant; and (3) that made to be spoken; and the art of joining words in each of these kinds is different, and cannot be clearly understood until the reader knows that there are three different objectives.

OF THE ITALIANS: Guido Cavalcanti and Dante; perhaps a dozen and a half poems of Guido's, and a dozen poems by his contemporaries, and the *Divina Commedia.*

In Italy, around the year 1300, there were new values established, things said that had not been said in Greece, or in Rome or elsewhere.

VILLON: After Villon and for several centuries, poetry can be considered as *fioritura,* as an efflorescence, almost an effervescence, and without any new roots. Chaucer is an enrichment, one might say a more creamy version of the "matter of France," and he in some measure preceded the verbal richness of the classic revival, but beginning with the Italians after Dante, coming through the Latin writers of the Renaissance, French, Spanish, English, Tasso, Ariosto, etc., the Italians always a little in the lead, the whole is elaboration, medieval basis, and wash after wash of Roman or Hellenic influence. I mean one need not read any particular part of it for purpose of learning one's comparative values.

If one were studying history and not poetry, one might discover the medieval mind more directly in the opening of Mussato's *Ecerinus* than even in Dante. The culture of Chaucer is the same which went contemporaneously into Ferrara, with the tongue called *"francoveneto."*

One must emphasize one's contrasts in the quattrocento. One can take Villon as pivot for understanding them. After Villon, and having begun before his time, we find this *fioritura,* and for centuries we find little else. Even in Marlowe and Shakespeare there is this embroidery of language, this talk about the matter, rather than presentation. I doubt if anyone ever acquired discrimination in studying "The Elizabethans." You have grace, richness of language, abundance, but you have probably nothing that isn't replaceable by something else, no ornament that wouldn't have done just as well in some other connection, or for which some other figure of rhetoric couldn't have served, or which couldn't have been distilled from literary antecedents.

The "language" had not been heard on the London stage, but it had been heard in the Italian law courts, etc.; there were local attempts, all over Europe, to teach the public (in Spain, Italy, England) Latin diction. "Poetry" was considered to be (as it still is considered by a great number of drivelling imbeciles) synonymous with "lofty and flowery language."

One Elizabethan specialist has suggested that Shakespeare, disgusted with his efforts, or at least despairing of success, as a poet, took to the stage. The drama is a mixed art; it does not rely on the charge that can be put into the word, but calls on gesture and mimicry and "impersonation" for assistance. The actor must do a good half of the work. One does no favour to drama by muddling the two sets of problems.

Apologists for the drama are continually telling us in one way or another that drama either cannot use at all, or can make but a very limited use of words charged to their highest potential. This is perfectly true. Let us try to keep our minds on the problem we started with, i.e., the art of writing, the art of "charging" language with meaning.

After 1450 we have the age of *fioritura;* after Marlowe and Shakespeare came what was called a "classic" movement, a movement that restrained without inventing. Anything that happens to mind in England has usually happened somewhere else first. Someone invents something, then someone develops, or some dozens develop a frothy or at any rate creamy enthusiasm or over-abundance, then someone tries to tidy things up. For example, the estimable Pleiad emasculating the French tongue, and the French classicists, and the English classicists, etc., all of which things should be relegated to the subsidiary zone: period interest, historical interest, bric-à-brac for museums.

At this point someone says: "O, but the ballads." All right, I will allow the voracious peruser a half-hour for ballads (English and Spanish, or Scotch, Border, and Spanish). There is nothing easier than to be distracted from one's point, or from the main drive of one's subject by a desire for utterly flawless equity and omniscience.

Let us say, but strictly in parenthesis, that there was a very limited sort of *logopoeia* in seventeenth- and eighteenth-century satire. And that Rochester and Dorset may have introduced a new note, or more probably re-introduced an old one, that reappears later in Heine.

Let us also cut loose from minor details and minor exceptions: the main fact is that we "have come" or that "humanity came" to a point where verse-writing can or could no longer be clearly understood without the study of prose-writing.

Say, for the sake of argument, that after the slump of the Middle Ages, prose "came to" again in Machiavelli; admit that various sorts of prose had existed, in fact nearly all sorts had existed. Herodotus wrote history that is literature, Thucydides was a journalist. (It is a modern folly to suppose that vulgarity and cheapness have the merit of novelty; they have always existed, and are of no interest in themselves.)

There had been bombast, oratory, legal speech, balanced sentences, Ciceronian impressiveness; Petronius had written a satiric novel, Longus had written a delicate nouvelle. The prose of the Renaissance leaves us Rabelais, Brantôme, Montaigne. A determined specialist can dig interesting passages, or sumptuous passages, or even subtle passages out of Pico, the medieval mystics, scholastics, Platonists, none of which will be the least use to a man trying to learn the art of "charging language."

I mean to say that from the beginning of literature up to 1750 A.D., poetry was the superior art, and was so considered to be, and if we read books written before that date we find the number of interesting books in verse at least equal to the number of prose books still readable; and the poetry contains the quintessence. When we want to know what people were like before 1750, when we want to know that they had blood and bones like ourselves, we go to the poetry of the period.

But, as I have said, this *"fioritura* business" set in. And one morning Monsieur Stendhal, not thinking of Homer, or Villon, or Catullus, but having a very keen sense of actuality, noticed that "poetry," *la poésie,* as the term was then understood, the stuff written by his French contemporaries, or sonorously rolled at him from the French stage, was a damn nuisance. And he remarked that poetry, with its bagwigs and its bobwigs, and its padded calves and its periwigs, its "fustian à la Louis XIV," was greatly inferior to prose for conveying a clear idea of the diverse states of our consciousness (*"les mouvements du coeur"*).

And at that moment the serious art of writing "went over to prose," and for some time the important developments of language as means of expression were the developments of prose. And a man cannot clearly understand or justly judge the value of verse, modern verse, any verse, unless he have grasped this.

From *Polite Essays* by Ezra Pound, pp. 166–179. New Directions, 1938. Reprinted by permission. *How to Read* first appeared serially in *The New York Herald-Tribune* (*Books*) for January 13, 20, and 27, 1929, and in book form as here printed, from Desmond Harmsworth, London, in 1931.

PART III

The Individual Talent

EDMUND WILSON

James Joyce

[1931]

JAMES JOYCE'S first work of fiction, the volume of short stories called *Dubliners*, was finished in 1904 and was to have been brought out by a Dublin publisher; but for a combination of reasons, including the supposed impropriety of certain of the stories, the introduction by name of the Dublin shops, restaurants and pubs, and some disrespectful references to Queen Victoria and Edward VII on the part of one of the characters, the Irish publishers could never bring themselves to publish the book until it had first been brought out in England in 1914, ten years after it had been written. *A Portrait of the Artist as a Young Man* was published first in New York in 1916. Neither of these books had much in common with the English fiction then being written: the typical novelists of that time were H. G. Wells and Arnold Bennett, and Joyce was not in the least like either. In their recent literary renaissance the Irish had been closer to the Continent than to London; and James Joyce, like George Moore, was working in the tradition, not of English, but of French fiction. *Dubliners* was French in its objectivity, its sobriety and its irony, at the same time that its paragraphs ran with a music and a grace quite distinct from the taut metallic quality of Maupassant and Flaubert. And *A Portrait of the Artist as a Young Man*, coming at a time when the public was already surfeited with the early histories of sensitive young men—the Edward Ponderevos, the Clayhangers, the Jacob Stahls, the Michael Fanes—not only was able to attract attention, but had the effect of making most of these books look psychologically superficial and artistically shoddy.

Ulysses was published in Paris in 1922. It had originally been conceived as a short story for *Dubliners*, and was to have been called "Mr. Bloom's Day in Dublin" or something of the sort. But this idea was afterwards combined with the further history of Stephen Dedalus, the hero of the autobiographical *Portrait of the Artist as a Young Man*. *Ulysses*, however, in its final form as a volume of seven hundred-odd large pages, took shape as something entirely different from either of Joyce's earlier books, and it must be approached from a different point of view than as if it were merely, like the others, a straight work of Naturalistic fiction.

183

The key to *Ulysses* is in the title—and this key is indispensable if we are to appreciate the book's real depth and scope. Ulysses, as he figures in the *Odyssey,* is a sort of type of the average intelligent Greek: among the heroes, he is distinguished for cunning rather than for exalted wisdom, and for common sense, quickness and nerve rather than for, say, the passionate bravery of an Achilles or the steadfastness and stoutness of a Hector. The *Odyssey* exhibits such a man in practically every situation and relation of an ordinary human life—Ulysses, in the course of his wanderings, runs the whole gauntlet of temptations and ordeals and through his wits he survives them all to return at last to his home and family and to reassert himself there as master. The *Odyssey* thus provides a classical model for a writer attempting a modern epic of the ordinary man—and a model particularly attractive to a modern writer by reason of the apparently calculated effectiveness, the apparent sophistication, of its form. By a device suggestive of some of the novels of Conrad, Homer has framed the wanderings of Ulysses between an introductory group of books in which our interest is aroused in the hero before we meet him by Telemachus' search for his lost father, and a culminating group of books which present dramatically and on a larger scale the wanderer's return home.

Now the *Ulysses* of Joyce is a modern *Odyssey,* which follows closely the classical *Odyssey* in both subject and form; and the significance of the characters and incidents of its ostensibly Naturalistic narrative cannot properly be understood without reference to the Homeric original. Joyce's Telemachus of the opening books is Stephen Dedalus—that is, Joyce himself. The Dedaluses, as we have already learned from *A Portrait of the Artist as a Young Man,* are a shabby-genteel family of Dubliners. Stephen's father, Simon Dedalus, has run through a great variety of employments to end up as nothing in particular, a drinker, a decayed sport, an amateur tenor, a well-known character of the bars. But Stephen has been given a good education at a Jesuit college, and we have seen him, at the end of the earlier novel, on the point of leaving for France to study and write. At the beginning of *Ulysses,* he has been back in Dublin a year: he had been summoned home from Paris by a telegram that his mother was dying. And now, a year after her death, the Dedalus family, already reduced to poverty, has become completely demoralized and disintegrated. While Stephen's young sisters and brothers have hardly enough to eat, Simon Dedalus makes the rounds of the pubs. Stephen, who has always resented his father, feels now that in effect he has none. He is more isolated in Dublin than ever. He is Telemachus in search of a Ulysses. His friend, the medical student, Buck Mulligan, with whom he is living in an old tower on the coast and who believes himself to share Stephen's artistic tastes and intellectual interests, really humiliates him by patronizing him and turns to ridicule his abilities and ambitions. He is Antinous, the boldest of Penelope's suitors, who, while Ulysses is away, tries to make himself master of his house and mocks at Telemachus. Stephen has announced at the end of the earlier book that he is going forth "to forge in the smithy of my soul the uncreated conscience of my race"; and now he has returned to Dublin baffled and disinherited—his life with Mulligan is dissolute and unproductive. Yet as Telemachus finds friends and helpers, so Stephen is reminded by the old woman who brings the milk for breakfast in the tower of that Ireland whose uncreated conscience it is still his destiny to forge: "Old and secret . . . maybe a messenger." She is Athene in the guise of Mentor who provides Telemachus with his ship; and the memory of Kevin Egan, an Irish exile in Paris, is the Menelaus who speeds him on his way.

The scene now shifts, as it does in the *Odyssey,* to the lost Ulysses himself. Joyce's Ulysses is a Dublin Jew, an advertisement canvasser named Bloom. Like Stephen, he dwells among aliens: a Jew and the son of a Hungarian father, he is still more or less of a foreigner among the Irish; and a man of something less than mediocre abilities, but of real sensibility and intelligence, he has little in common with the other inhabitants of the lower middle-class world in which he lives. He has been married for sixteen years to the buxom daughter of an Irish army officer, a professional singer, of prodigious sexual appetite, who has been continually and indiscriminately unfaithful to him. They have had one daughter, who is already growing up and apparently going the way of her mother; and one son, of whom Bloom had hoped that he might resemble, that he might refine upon, himself, but who died eleven days after he was born. Things have never been the same between the Blooms since the death of this son; it is now more than ten years since Bloom has attempted complete intercourse with his wife—it is as if the birth of the sickly Rudy had discouraged him and made him doubt his virility. He is aware that his wife has lovers; but he does not complain or try to interfere—he is even resigned to her accepting money from them. He is a Ulysses with no Telemachus and cut off from his Penelope.

We now follow Bloom's adventures on the day of June 16, 1904 (the whole of *Ulysses* takes place within less than twenty-four hours). Lotus-eaters allure him; he is affrighted by Laestrygonians. He assists at the burial of an Elpenor and descends with him in imagination to the underworld; he suffers from the varying favor of an Aeolus. He escapes by ruse from the ferocity of a Cyclops and he disengages himself through prudence from the maiden charms of a Nausicaa. And he emerges finally a man again from the brothel of a Circe who had transformed him into a swine.

The comings and goings of Stephen during the day are woven in and out among the wanderings of Bloom: the two encounter each other twice but do not recognize each other. Both men, we become aware, are constantly accompanied and oppressed by ideas which they have tried to dismiss from their minds: the family situation of each really lies back of and explains all that he does that day. In Stephen's case, it is only a few days from the anniversary of his mother's death, and he is haunted by the memory of it: she had begged him on her deathbed to kneel down and pray for her soul and, in rebellion against the Catholic education which had disciplined and maimed his spirit, jealous of the independence he had won and in fear of the past to which he had returned, he had cruelly refused and had allowed her to die without the comfort of believing that he had repented of his apostasy. But now that she is dead, this incident tortures him. He has in the early morning reproached Mulligan—accusing really himself—for something the latter had said about Stephen's mother at the time of her death which Stephen had overheard and resented; and, as he has looked out upon the bright morning sea, the pathos and horror of her life have become suddenly vivid to him—he has been dragged back to relive all that she had suffered. Then, "No, mother!" he has cried out within himself as he thrust her memory down out of his mind, "let me be and let me live!" But through his whole bitter and baffled day, it is his helpless feeling of guilt toward his mother, his hopeless discouragement and disgust with his father, which govern all his thoughts and movements. When he teaches school, he brings the class to a close by a hysterical joke about "the fox burying his grandmother under a hollybush," and in a stupid boy who cannot do his sums he can see now only his own graceless youth which his mother had shielded from the world. After school, he has gone to walk on the beach and has contemplated paying a visit to the family of a maternal uncle whom he despises, as if he could do penance in this fashion for his hardness to his mother and somehow make it up to her now by kindness to her wretched relatives; but again the counter-impulse which had proved too strong on the former occasion comes into play to block his intention: his mind drifts off to other things and he walks beyond where he should have turned. The artist still conflicts with the son—the two are irreconcilable: he sets out to compose a poem, but the poem itself breaks down and he is left gazing at a silent homing ship.—Visiting the library later in the day, he improvises a long, pretentious lecture on the relation of Shakespeare to his father—a lecture which has little to do with Shakespeare, but a good deal to do with Stephen himself.

And as Stephen is ridden by thoughts of his parents, so Bloom is ridden by thoughts of his wife. He has seen Molly at breakfast get a letter which he suspects—and suspects rightly—to be from Blazes Boylan, a flashy buck about town who is managing a concert tour for her and with whom she is having a love affair. All day he has to change the subject when Boylan's name is mentioned—all day he avoids meeting him in the street. In the afternoon, while Bloom is eating at the Ormond Hotel, Boylan comes into the bar, gets a drink and sets off to call on Mrs. Bloom, and when he has gone, Bloom hears the men in the bar talking and laughing about Molly's easy favors. And the conversation, later on in the pub, about Boylan's having won money in a boxing-match—in spite of Bloom's gently insistent efforts to induce the company to talk about tennis—is one of the incidents which give rise to an antagonism between Bloom and the rest of the company and eventually to the quarrel between the Cyclops-Citizen and Bloom. At the end of the Nausicaa episode, the voice of the cuckoo-clock from the priest's house tells Bloom that he is now a cuckold.

In the evening, Bloom goes to a maternity hospital to inquire after the wife of a friend who has been having a hard delivery: there he meets and recognizes Stephen, who is drinking with the medical students. In the *Odyssey*, the final shipwreck of Ulysses and his subsequent misfortunes are the result of the impiety of his companions, who in defiance of all his warnings have killed and eaten the Oxen of the Sun. So Bloom is pained by the impiety of the medical students as they joke obscenely about childbirth and maternity. On the part of Stephen, whose mother died only a year ago, this levity seems especially shocking, but Stephen's very feeling of guilt about her makes him particularly blasphemous and brutal. Yet Bloom has himself in his own way offended against the principle of fertility by his recent prolonged neglect of Molly: the Calypso who has detained him since his shipwreck is the nymph who hangs in his bedroom and whom he makes the object of amorous fantasies. It is this sin against fertility which—at the hour when Mrs. Bloom is entertaining Boylan—has landed Bloom on the Phaeacian strand indulging in further erotic daydreams in connection with little Gerty MacDowell, the Nausicaa of the Dublin beach.

When Mrs. Purefoy's child has finally been born, the party rushes out to a public house; and, later on—after a drunken altercation between Dedalus and Buck Mulligan at the tram station, in which Antinous and Telemachus apparently dispute over the key to the tower and Telemachus goes away homeless—Stephen, with one of his companions and with Bloom following some distance behind, proceeds to a brothel. Both, by this time, are pretty drunk—though Bloom, with his invincible prudence, is not so drunk as Stephen. And in their drunkenness, in the sordid gaslight and to the tune of the mechanical piano of the brothel, their respective preoccupations emerge fully for the first time since the morning into their conscious minds: Bloom beholds himself, in a hideous vision, looking on at Blazes Boylan and Molly, an abject cuckold, the laughing-stock of the world; and there rises suddenly in Stephen's imagination the figure of his dead mother come back from the grave to remind him of her bleak disheartened love and to implore him to pray for her soul. But again he will not, cannot, acquiesce; in a desperate drunken gesture, intolerably torn by his conflict of impulses, by his emotions which deadlock each other, he lifts his stick and smashes the chandelier—then rushes out into the street, where he gets embroiled with two English Tommies and knocked down. Bloom has followed and, as he bends over Stephen, beholds an appari-

tion of his own dead son, little Rudy, as Bloom would have had him live to be
—learned, cultivated, sensitive, refined: such a youth, in short, as Stephen
Dedalus. Ulysses and Telemachus are united.

Bloom picks Stephen up and takes him first to a coffee-stand, then home
to his own house. He tries to talk to him of the arts and sciences, of the general
ideas which interest him; but Stephen is morose and exhausted and makes
little response. Bloom begs him to spend the night—to come and live with
them, but Stephen declines and presently takes his leave. Bloom goes up, goes
to bed with Molly, describes to her his adventures of the day, and soon drops
off to sleep.

But Bloom's encounter with Stephen is to affect both Stephen's life and
the relations between the Blooms. To have rescued and talked with Stephen
has somehow restored Bloom's self-confidence. He has gotten into the habit
in the past of cooking breakfast for Molly in the morning and bringing it to
her in bed—it is the first thing we have seen him doing at the beginning of the
day; but tonight, before he goes to sleep, he gives her to understand that he
expects her to get breakfast next morning herself and to bring it up to him.
This amazes and disconcerts Mrs. Bloom, and the rest of the book is the record
of her meditations as she lies awake thinking over Bloom's homecoming. She
has been mystified by his recent behavior, and her attitude toward him now
is at first a mixture of jealousy and resentment. She congratulates herself upon
the fact that, if Bloom neglects her nowadays, her needs are ably supplied by
Blazes Boylan. But as she begins to ruminate on the possibility of Stephen
Dedalus's coming to live with them, the idea of Blazes Boylan's coarseness becomes intolerable to her: the thought of Stephen has made her fastidious,
and, rapidly becoming very tender about him, she prefigures a relation between them of an ambiguous but intimate character, half-amorous, half-
maternal. Yet it is Bloom himself who has primarily been the cause of this
revolution in Molly's mind: in telling her about Stephen, he has imposed
upon her again his own values; in staying away from the house all day and
coming back very late at night, and in asking for his breakfast in bed, he has
reasserted his own will. And she goes back in her mind over her experience
of Bloom—their courtship, their married life. She remembers how, when she
had promised to marry him, it had been his intelligence and his sympathetic
nature, that touch of imagination which distinguished him from other men,
which had influenced her in his favor—"because he understood or felt what
a woman is and I knew I could always get around him"; and on the day when
he had first kissed her, he had called her "a flower of the mountain." It is in
the mind of his Penelope that this Ulysses has slain the suitors who have been
disputing his place.

As for Stephen, unresponsive as he has seemed to Bloom's interest and cor-
diality, he has at last, none the less, found in Dublin someone sufficiently

sympathetic to himself to give him the clew, to supply him with the subject, which will enable him to enter imaginatively—as an artist—into the common life of his race. It is possible that Molly and Bloom, as a result of Bloom's meeting with Stephen, will resume normal marital relations; but it is certain that Stephen, as a result of this meeting, will go away and write *Ulysses*. Buck Mulligan has told us that the young poet says he is going "to write something in ten years": that was in 1904—*Ulysses* is dated at the end as having been begun in 1914.

II

This is the story of *Ulysses* in the light of its Homeric parallel; but to describe the book in such a way gives no idea of what it is really like—of its psychological and technical discoveries or of its magnificent poetry.

Ulysses is, I suppose, the most completely "written" novel since Flaubert. The example of the great prose poet of Naturalism has profoundly influenced Joyce—in his attitude toward the modern bourgeois world and in the contrast implied by the Homeric parallel of *Ulysses* between our own and the ancient world, as well as in an ideal of rigorous objectivity and of adaptation of style to subject—as the influence of that other great Naturalistic poet, Ibsen, is obvious in Joyce's single play, *Exiles*. But Flaubert had, in general, confined himself to fitting the cadence and the phrase precisely to the mood or object described; and even then it was the phrase rather than the cadence, and the object rather than the mood, with which he was occupied—for mood and cadence in Flaubert do not really vary much: he never embodies himself in his characters nor identifies his voice with theirs, and as a result, Flaubert's own characteristic tone of the somber-pompous-ironic becomes, in the long run, a little monotonous. But Joyce has undertaken in *Ulysses* not merely to render, with the last accuracy and beauty, the actual sights and sounds among which his people move, but, showing us the world as his characters perceive it, to find the unique vocabulary and rhythm which will represent the thoughts of each. If Flaubert taught Maupassant to look for the definitive adjectives which would distinguish a given cab-driver from every other cab-driver at the Rouen station, so Joyce has set himself the task of finding the precise dialect which will distinguish the thoughts of a given Dubliner from those of every other Dubliner. Thus the mind of Stephen Dedalus is represented by a weaving of bright poetic images and fragmentary abstractions, of things remembered from books, on a rhythm sober, melancholy and proud; that of Bloom by a rapid staccato notation, prosaic but vivid and alert, jetting out in all directions in little ideas growing out of ideas; the thoughts of Father Conmee, the Rector of the Jesuit college, by a precise prose, perfectly colorless and orderly; those of Gerty-Nausicaa by a combination of school-girl colloquialisms with the jargon of cheap romance; and the ruminations of Mrs.

Bloom by a long, unbroken rhythm of brogue, like the swell of some profound sea.

Joyce takes us thus directly into the consciousness of his characters, and
in order to do so, he has availed himself of methods of which Flaubert never
dreamed—of the methods of Symbolism. He has, in *Ulysses*, exploited together, as no writer had thought to do before, the resources both of Symbolism
and of Naturalism. Proust's novel, masterly as it is, does perhaps represent a
falling over into decadence of psychological fiction: the subjective element is
finally allowed to invade and to deteriorate even those aspects of the story
which really ought to be kept strictly objective if one is to believe that it is
actually happening. But Joyce's grasp on his objective world never slips: his
work is unshakably established on Naturalistic foundations. Where *A la
Recherche du Temps Perdu* leaves many things vague—the ages of the characters and sometimes the actual circumstances of their lives, and—what is
worse—whether they may not be merely bad dreams that the hero has had;
Ulysses has been logically thought out and accurately documented to the last
detail: everything that happens is perfectly consistent, and we know precisely
what the characters wore, how much they paid for things, where they were
at different times of the day, what popular songs they sang and what events
they read of in the papers, on June 16, 1904. Yet when we are admitted to
the mind of any one of them, we are in a world as complex and special, a
world sometimes as fantastic or obscure, as that of a Symbolist poet—and a
world rendered by similar devices of language. We are more at home
in the minds of Joyce's characters than we are likely to be, except after some
study, in the mind of a Mallarmé or an Eliot, because we know more about
the circumstances in which they find themselves; but we are confronted with
the same sort of confusion between emotions, perceptions and reasonings,
and we are likely to be disconcerted by the same sort of hiatuses of thought,
when certain links in the association of ideas are dropped down into the unconscious mind so that we are obliged to divine them for ourselves.

But Joyce has carried the methods of Symbolism further than merely to set
a Naturalistic scene and then, in that frame, to represent directly the minds
of his different characters in Symbolistic monologues like *Prufrock* or *L'Après-
midi d'un Faune*. And it is the fact that he has not always stopped here which
makes parts of *Ulysses* so puzzling when we read them for the first time. So
long as we are dealing with internal monologues in realistic settings, we are
dealing with familiar elements merely combined in a novel way—that is, instead of reading, "Bloom said to himself, 'I might manage to write a story to
illustrate some proverb or other. I could sign it, Mr. and Mrs. L. M. Bloom,'"
we read, "Might manage a sketch. By Mr. and Mrs. L. M. Bloom. Invent a
story for some proverb which?" But as we get further along in *Ulysses*, we
find the realistic setting oddly distorting itself and deliquescing, and we are

astonished at the introduction of voices which seem to belong neither to the characters nor to the author.

The point is that of each of his episodes Joyce has tried to make an independent unit which shall blend the different sets of elements of each—the minds of the characters, the place where they are, the atmosphere about them, the feeling of the time of day. Joyce had already, in *A Portrait of the Artist,* experimented, as Proust had done, in varying the form and style of the different sections to fit the different ages and phases of his hero—from the infantile fragments of childhood impressions, through the ecstatic revelations and the terrifying nightmares of adolescence, to the self-possessed notations of young manhood. But in *A Portrait of the Artist,* Joyce was presenting everything from the point of view of a single particular character, Dedalus; whereas in *Ulysses* he is occupied with a number of different personalities, of whom Dedalus is no longer the center, and his method, furthermore, of enabling us to live in their world is not always merely a matter of making us shift from the point of view of one to the point of view of another. In order to understand what Joyce is doing here, one must conceive a set of Symbolistic poems, themselves involving characters whose minds are represented Symbolistically, depending not from the sensibility of the poet speaking in his own person, but from the poet's imagination playing a rôle absolutely impersonal and always imposing upon itself all the Naturalistic restrictions in regard to the story it is telling at the same time that it allows itself to exercise all the Symbolistic privileges in regard to the way it tells it. We are not likely to be prepared for this by the early episodes of *Ulysses:* they are as sober and as clear as the morning light of the Irish coast in which they take place: the characters' perceptions of the external world are usually distinct from their thoughts and feelings about them. But in the newspaper office, for the first time, a general atmosphere begins to be created, beyond the specific minds of the characters, by a punctuation of the text with newspaper heads which announce the incidents in the narrative. And in the library scene, which takes place in the early afternoon, the setting and people external to Stephen begin to dissolve in his apprehension of them, heightened and blurred by some drinks at lunchtime and by the intellectual excitement of the conversation amid the dimness and tameness of the library—"Eglintoneyes, quick with pleasure, looked up shybrightly. Gladly glancing, a merry puritan, through the twisted eglantine." Here, however, we still see all through Stephen's eyes—through the eyes of a single character; but in the scene in the Ormond Hotel, which takes place a couple of hours later—our reveries absorb the world about us progressively as daylight fades and as the impressions of the day accumulate—the sights and sounds and the emotional vibrations and the appetites for food and drink of the late afternoon, the laughter, the gold-and-bronze hair of the barmaids, the jingling of Blazes Boylan's car on his way to visit Molly Bloom, the ringing of the hoofs of the horses of the viceregal cavalcade clanging in through the open window, the ballad sung by Simon Dedalus, the sound of the piano accompaniment and the comfortable supper of Bloom—though they are not all, from beginning to end, perceived by Bloom himself—all mingle quite un-Naturalistically in a harmony of bright sound, ringing color, poignant indistinct feeling and declining light. The scene in the brothel, where it is night and where Dedalus and Bloom are drunk, is like a slowed-up moving-picture, in which the intensified vision of reality is continually lapsing into phantasmagoric visions; and the let-down after the excitement of this, the lassitude and staleness of the cabman's shelter where Bloom takes Stephen to get him some coffee, is rendered by a prose as flavorless, as weary and as banal as the incidents which it reports. Joyce has achieved here, by different methods, a relativism like that of Proust: he is reproducing in literature the different aspects, the different proportions and textures, which things and people take on at different times and under different circumstances.

III

I do not think that Joyce has been equally successful with all these technical devices in *Ulysses;* but before it will be possible to discuss them further, we must approach the book from another point of view.

It has always been characteristic of Joyce to neglect action, narrative, drama, of the usual kind, even the direct impact on one another of the characters as we get it in the ordinary novel, for a sort of psychological portraiture. There is tremendous vitality in Joyce, but very little movement. Like Proust, he is symphonic rather than narrative. His fiction has its progressions, its developments, but they are musical rather than dramatic. The most elaborate and interesting piece in *Dubliners*—the story called "The Dead"—is simply a record of the modification brought about during a single evening in the relations of a husband and wife by the man's becoming aware, from the effect produced on the woman by a song which she has heard at a family party, that she has once been loved by another man; *A Portrait of the Artist as a Young Man* is simply a series of pictures of the author at successive stages of his development; the theme of *Exiles* is, like that of "The Dead," the modification in the relations of a husband and wife which follows the reappearance of a man who has been the wife's lover. And *Ulysses* again, for all its vast scale, is simply the story of another small but significant change in the relations of yet another married couple as a result of the impingement on their household of the personality of an only slightly known young man. Most of these stories cover a period of only a few hours, and they are never carried any further. When Joyce has explored one of these situations, when he has established the small gradual readjustment, he has done all that interests him.

All, that is, from the point of view of ordinary incident. But though Joyce almost entirely lacks appetite for violent conflict or vigorous action, his work is prodigiously rich and alive. His force, instead of following a line, expands itself in every dimension (including that of Time) about a single point. The world of *Ulysses* is animated by a complex inexhaustible life: we revisit it as we do a city, where we come more and more to recognize faces, to understand personalities, to grasp relations, currents and interests. Joyce has exercised considerable technical ingenuity in introducing us to the elements of his story in an order which will enable us to find our bearings: yet I doubt whether any human memory is capable, on a first reading, of meeting the demands of *Ulysses*. And when we reread it, we start in at any point, as if it were indeed something solid like a city which actually existed in space and which could be entered from any direction—as Joyce is said, in composing his books, to work on the different parts simultaneously. More than any other work of fiction, unless perhaps the *Comédie Humaine, Ulysses* creates the illusion of a living social organism. We see it only for twenty hours, yet we know its past as well as its present. We possess Dublin, seen, heard, smelt and felt, brooded over, imagined, remembered.

Joyce's handling of this immense material, his method of giving his book a shape, resembles nothing else in modern fiction. The first critics of *Ulysses* mistook the novel for a "slice of life" and objected that it was too fluid or too chaotic. They did not recognize a plot because they could not recognize a progression; and the title told them nothing. They could not even discover a pattern. It is now apparent, however, that *Ulysses* suffers from an excess of design rather than from a lack of it. Joyce has drawn up an outline of his novel, of which he has allowed certain of his commentators to avail themselves, but which he has not allowed them to publish in its entirety (though it is to be presumed that the book on *Ulysses* which Mr. Stuart Gilbert has announced will include all the information contained in it);[1] and from this outline it appears that Joyce has set himself the task of fulfilling the requirements of a most complicated scheme—a scheme which we could scarcely have divined except in its more obvious features. For even if we had known about the Homeric parallel and had identified certain of the correspondences—if we had had no difficulty in recognizing the Cyclops in the ferocious professional Fenian or Circe in the brothel-keeper or Hades in the cemetery—we should never have suspected how closely and how subtly the parallel had been followed—we should never have guessed, for example, that when Bloom passes through the National Library while Stephen is having his discussion with the literary men, he is escaping, on the one hand, a Scylla—that is, Aristotle, the rock of Dogma; and, on the other, a Charybdis—Plato, the whirlpool of Mysticism; nor that, when Stephen walks on the seashore, he is re enacting the com-

[1] Stuart Gilbert's book *James Joyce's Ulysses* appeared in 1930 (London: Faber & Faber; New York: Alfred A. Knopf).

bat with Proteus—in this case, primal matter, of whose continual transforma-
tions Stephen is reminded by the objects absorbed or washed up by the sea,
but whose forms he is able to hold and fix, as the Homeric Proteus was held
and vanquished, by power of the words which give him images for them. Nor
should we have known that the series of phrases and onomatopoetic syllables
placed at the beginning of the Sirens episode—the singing in the Ormond
Hotel—and selected from the narrative which follows, are supposed to be
musical themes and that the episode itself is a fugue; and though we may have
felt the ironic effect of the specimens of inflated Irish journalism introduced
at regular intervals in the conversation with the patriot in the pub—we should
hardly have understood that these had been produced by a deliberate technique of "gigantism"—for, since the Citizen represents the Cyclops, and since
the Cyclops was a giant, he must be rendered formidable by a parade of all
the banalities of his patriotic claptrap swollen to gigantic proportions. We
should probably never have guessed all this, and we should certainly never
have guessed at the ingenuity which Joyce has expended in other ways. Not
only, we learn from the outline, is there an elaborate Homeric parallel in
Ulysses, but there is also an organ of the human body and a human science
or art featured in every episode. We look these up, a little incredulously, but
there, we find, they all actually are—buried and disguised beneath the realistic
surface, but carefully planted, unmistakably dwelt upon. And if we are tipped
off, we are able further to discover all sorts of concealed ornaments and emblems: in the chapter of the Lotus-Eaters, for example, countless references to
flowers; in the Laestrygonians, to eating; in the Sirens, puns on musical terms;
and in Aeolus, the newspaper office, not merely many references to wind but,
according to Mr. Gilbert—the art featured in this episode being Rhetoric—
some hundred different figures of speech.

Now the Homeric parallel in *Ulysses* is in general pointedly and charm-
ingly carried out and justifies itself: it does help to give the story a universal
significance and it enables Joyce to show us in the actions and the relations of
his characters meanings which he perhaps could not easily have indicated in
any other way—since the characters themselves must be largely unaware of
these meanings and since Joyce has adopted the strict objective method, in
which the author must not comment on the action. And we may even accept
the arts and sciences and the organs of the human body as making the book
complete and comprehensive, if a little laboriously systematic—the whole of
man's experience in a day. But when we get all these things together and
further complicated by the virtuosity of the technical devices, the result is
sometimes baffling or confusing. We become aware, as we examine the outline, that when we went through *Ulysses* for the first time, it was these organs
and arts and sciences and Homeric correspondences which sometimes so discouraged our interest. We had been climbing over these obstacles without

knowing it, in our attempts to follow Dedalus and Bloom. The trouble was that, beyond the ostensible subject and, as it were, beneath the surface of the narrative, too many other subjects and too many different orders of subjects were being proposed to our attention.

It seems to me difficult, then, not to conclude that Joyce elaborated *Ulysses* too much—that he tried to put too many things into it. What is the value of all the references to flowers in the Lotus-Eaters chapter, for example? They do not create in the Dublin streets an atmosphere of lotus-eating—we are merely puzzled, if we have not been told to look for them, as to why Joyce has chosen to have Bloom think and see certain things, of which the final explanation is that they are pretexts for mentioning flowers. And do not the gigantic interpolations of the Cyclops episode defeat their object by making it impossible for us to follow the narrative? The interpolations are funny in themselves, the incident related is a masterpiece of language and humor, the idea of combining them seems happy, yet the effect is mechanical and annoying: in the end we have to read the whole thing through, skipping the interpolations, in order to find out what has happened. The worst example of the capacities for failure of this too synthetic, too systematic, method seems to me the scene in the maternity hospital. I have described above what actually takes place there as I have worked it out, after several readings and in the light of Joyce's outline. The Oxen of the Sun are "Fertility"—the crime committed against them is "Fraud." But, not content with this, Joyce has been at pains to fill the episode with references to real cattle and to include a long conversation about bulls. As for the special technique, it seems to me in this case not to have any real appropriateness to the situation, but to have been dictated by sheer fantastic pedantry: Joyce describes his method here as "embryonic," in conformity to the subject, maternity, and the chapter is written as a series of parodies of English literary styles from the bad Latin of the early chronicles up through Huxley and Carlyle, the development of the language corresponding to the growth of the child in the womb. Now something important takes place in this episode—the meeting between Dedalus and Bloom—and an important point is being made about it. But we miss the point because it is all we can do to follow what is happening at the drinking-party, itself rather a confused affair, through the medium of the language of the *Morte d'Arthur,* the seventeenth-century diaries, the eighteenth-century novels, and a great many other kinds of literature in which we are not prepared at the moment to be interested. If we pay attention to the parodies, we miss the story; and if we try to follow the story, we are unable to appreciate the parodies. The parodies have spoiled the story; and the necessity of telling the story through them has taken most of the life out of the parodies.

Joyce has as little respect as Proust for the capacities of the reader's attention; and one feels, in Joyce's case as in Proust's, that the *longueurs* which

break our backs, the mechanical combinations of elements which fail to coalesce, are partly a result of the effort of a supernormally energetic mind to
compensate by piling things up for an inability to make them move.

We have now arrived, in the maternity hospital, at the climactic scenes of
the story, and Joyce has bogged us as he has never bogged us before. We shall
forget the Oxen of the Sun in the wonderful night-town scene which follows
it—but we shall be bogged afterwards worse than ever in the interminable
let-down of the cabman's shelter and in the scientific question-and-answer
chapter which undertakes to communicate to us through the most opaque and
uninviting medium possible Dedalus's conversation with Bloom. The night-
town episode itself and Mrs. Bloom's soliloquy, which closes the book, are,
of course, among the best things in it—but the relative proportions of the other
three latter chapters and the jarring effect of the pastiche style sandwiched
in with the straight Naturalistic seem to me artistically absolutely inde-
fensible. One can understand that Joyce may have intended the colorless and
tiresome episodes to set off the rich and vivid ones, and also that it is of the
essence of his point of view to represent the profoundest changes of our lives
as beginning naturally between night and morning without the parties' appreciating their importance at the time; but a hundred and sixty-one more or
less deliberately tedious pages are too heavy a dead weight for even the brilliant flights of the other hundred and ninety-nine pages to carry. Furthermore,
Joyce has here half-buried his story under the virtuosity of his technical devices. It is almost as if he had elaborated it so much and worked over it so long
that he had forgotten, in the amusement of writing parodies, the drama which
he had originally intended to stage; or as if he were trying to divert and over-
whelm us by irrelevant entertainments and feats in order that we might not
be dissatisfied with the flatness—except for the drunken scene—of Dedalus's
final meeting with Bloom; or even perhaps as if he did not, after all, quite
want us to understand his story, as if he had, not quite conscious of what he
was doing, ended by throwing up between us and it a fortification of solemn
burlesque prose—as if he were shy and solicitous about it, and wanted to
protect it from us.

IV

Yet even these episodes to which I have objected contribute something valuable to *Ulysses*. In the chapter of parodies, for example, Joyce seems to be
saying to us: "Here are specimens of the sort of thing that man has written
about himself in the past—how naïve or pretentious they seem! I have broken
through these assumptions and pretences and shown you how he must recognize himself today." And in the question-and-answer chapter, which is written
entirely from the conventional point of view of science and where we are
supplied with every possible physical, statistical, biographical and astronom-

ical fact about Stephen's visit to Bloom: "This is all that the twentieth-century man thinks he knows about himself and his universe. Yet how mechanical and rigid this reasoning seems when we apply it to Molly and Bloom—how inadequate to explain them!"

For one of the most remarkable features of *Ulysses* is its interest as an investigation into the nature of human consciousness and behavior. Its importance from the point of view of psychology has never, it seems to me, been properly appreciated—though its influence on other books and, in consequence, upon our ideas about ourselves, has already been profound. Joyce has attempted in *Ulysses* to render as exhaustively, as precisely and as directly as it is possible in words to do, what our participation in life is like—or rather, what it seems to us like as from moment to moment we live. In order to make this record complete, he has been obliged to disregard a number of conventions of taste which, especially in English-speaking countries, have in modern times been pretty strictly observed, even by the writers who have aimed to be most scrupulously truthful. Joyce has studied what we are accustomed to consider the dirty, the trivial and the base elements in our lives with the relentlessness of a modern psychologist; and he has also—what the contemporary Naturalist has seldom been poet enough for—done justice to all those elements in our lives which we have been in the habit of describing by such names as love, nobility, truth and beauty. It is curious to reflect that a number of critics—including, curiously enough, Arnold Bennett—should have found Joyce misanthropic. Flaubert is misanthropic, if you like—and in reproducing his technique, Joyce sometimes suggests his acrid tone. But Stephen, Bloom and Mrs. Bloom are certainly not either unamiable or unattractive—and for all their misfortunes and short-comings, they inspire us with considerable respect. Stephen and Bloom are played off a little against the duller and meaner people about them; but even these people can scarcely be said to be treated with bitterness, even when, as in the case of Buck Mulligan or the elder Dedalus, Stephen's feeling about them is bitter. Joyce is remarkable, rather, for equanimity: in spite of the nervous intensity of *Ulysses*, there is a real serenity and detachment behind it—we are in the presence of a mind which has much in common with that of a certain type of philosopher, who in his effort to understand the causes of things, to interrelate the different elements of the universe, has reached a point where the ordinary values of good and bad, beautiful and ugly, have been lost in the excellence and beauty of transcendent understanding itself.

I believe that the first readers of *Ulysses* were shocked, not merely by Joyce's use of certain words ordinarily excluded today from English literature, but by his way of representing those aspects of human nature which we tend to consider incongruous as intimately, inextricably mingled. Yet the more we read *Ulysses*, the more we are convinced of its psychological truth, and the more we are amazed at Joyce's genius in mastering and in presenting, not through analysis or generalization, but by the complete recreation of life in the process of being lived, the relations of human beings to their environment and to each other; the nature of their perception of what goes on about them and of what goes on within themselves; and the interdependence of their intellectual, their physical, their professional and their emotional lives. To have traced all these interdependences, to have given each of these elements its value, yet never to have lost sight of the moral through preoccupation with the physical, nor to have forgotten the general in the particular; to have exhibited ordinary humanity without either satirizing it or sentimentalizing it—this would already have been sufficiently remarkable; but to have subdued all this material to the uses of a supremely finished and disciplined work of art is a feat which has hardly been equaled in the literature of our time.

In Stephen's diary in *A Portrait of the Artist,* we find this significant entry apropos of a poem by Yeats: "Michael Robartes remembers forgotten beauty and, when his arms wrap her round, he presses in his arms the loveliness which has long faded from the world. Not this. Not at all. I desire to press in my arms the loveliness which has not yet come into the world."

And with *Ulysses,* Joyce has brought into literature a new and unknown beauty. Some readers have regretted the extinction in the later Joyce of the charming lyric poet of his two little books of poems and the *fin de siècle* prose writer of the *fin de siècle* phases of *A Portrait of the Artist as a Young Man* (both the prose and verse of the early Joyce showed the influence of Yeats). This poet is still present in *Ulysses:* "Kind air defined the coigns of houses in Kildare Street. No birds. Frail from the housetops two plumes of smoke ascended, pluming, and in a flaw of softness softly were blown." But the conventions of the romantic lyric, of "esthetic" *fin de siècle* prose, even of the esthetic Naturalism of Flaubert, can no longer, for Joyce, be made to accommodate the reality of experience. The diverse elements of experience are perceived in different relations and they must be differently represented. Joyce has found for this new vision a new language, but a language which, instead of diluting or doing violence to his poetic genius, enables it to assimilate more materials, to readjust itself more completely and successfully than that of perhaps any other poet of our age to the new self-consciousness of the modern world. But in achieving this, Joyce has ceased to write verse. I have suggested, in connection with Valéry and Eliot, that verse itself as a literary medium is coming to be used for fewer and fewer and for more and more special purposes, and that it may be destined to fall into disuse. And it seems to me that Joyce's literary development is a striking corroboration of this view. His prose works have an artistic intensity, a definitive beauty of surface and of form, which make him comparable to the great poets rather than to most of the great novelists.

Joyce is indeed really the great poet of a new phase of the human conscious-ness. Like Proust's or Whitehead's or Einstein's world, Joyce's world is always changing as it is perceived by different observers and by them at different times. It is an organism made up of "events," which may be taken as infinitely inclusive or infinitely small and each of which involves all the others; and each of these events is unique. Such a world cannot be presented in terms of such artificial abstractions as have been conventional in the past: solid insti-tutions, groups, individuals, which play the parts of distinct durable entities —or even of solid psychological factors: dualisms of good and evil, mind and matter, flesh and spirit, instinct and reason; clear conflicts between passion and duty, between conscience and interest. Not that these conceptions are left out of Joyce's world: they are all there in the minds of the characters; and the realities they represent are there, too. But everything is reduced to terms of "events" like those of modern physics and philosophy—events which make up a "continuum," but which may be taken as infinitely small. Joyce has built out of these events a picture, amazingly lifelike and living, of the everyday world we know—and a picture which seems to allow us to see into it, to fol-low its variations and intricacies, as we have never been able to do before.

Nor are Joyce's characters merely the sum of the particles into which their experience has been dissociated: we come to imagine them as solidly, to feel their personalities as unmistakably, as we do with any characters in fiction; and we realize finally that they are also symbols. Bloom himself is in one of his aspects the typical modern man: Joyce has made him a Jew, one supposes, partly in order that he may be conceived equally well as an inhabitant of any provincial city of the European or Europeanized world. He makes a living by petty business, he leads the ordinary middle-class life—and he holds the con-ventional enlightened opinions of the time: he believes in science, social re-form and internationalism. But Bloom is surpassed and illuminated from above by Stephen, who represents the intellect, the creative imagination; and he is upheld by Mrs. Bloom, who represents the body, the earth. Bloom leaves with us in the long run the impression that he is something both better and worse than either of them; for Stephen sins through pride, the sin of the intellect; and Molly is at the mercy of the flesh; but Bloom, though a less powerful personality than either, has the strength of humility. It is difficult to describe the character of Bloom as Joyce finally makes us feel it: it takes precisely the whole of *Ulysses* to put him before us. It is not merely that Bloom is mediocre, that he is clever, that he is commonplace—that he is comic, that he is pathetic—that he is, as Rebecca West says, a figure of abject "squatting" vulgarity, that he is at moments, as Foster Damon says, the Christ—he is all of these, he is all the possibilities of that ordinary humanity which is somehow not so ordinary after all; and it is the proof of Joyce's greatness that, though we recognize Bloom's perfect truth and typical character, we cannot pigeonhole him in any familiar category, racial, social, moral, literary or even—because he does really have, after all, a good deal in common with the Greek Ulysses—historical.

Both Stephen and Molly are more easily describable because they represent extremes. Both are capable of rising to heights which Bloom can never reach. In Stephen's rhapsody on the seashore, when he first realizes his artist's vocation, in *A Portrait of the Artist as a Young Man*, we have had the ecstasy of the creative mind. In the soliloquy of Mrs. Bloom, Joyce has given us another ecstasy of creation, the rhapsody of the flesh. Stephen's dream was conceived in loneliness, by a drawing apart from his fellows. But Mrs. Bloom is like the earth, which gives the same life to all: she feels a maternal kinship with all living creatures. She pities the "poor donkeys slipping half asleep" in the street of Gibraltar, as she does "the sentry in front of the governor's house . . . half roasted" in the sun; and she gives herself to the bootblack at the General Post Office as readily as to Professor Goodwin. But, none the less, she will tend to breed from the highest type of life she knows: she turns to Bloom, and, beyond him, toward Stephen. This gross body, the body of humanity, upon which the whole structure of *Ulysses* rests—still throbbing with so strong a rhythm amid obscenity, commonness and squalor—is laboring to throw up some knowledge and beauty by which it may transcend itself.

These two great flights of the mind carry off all the ignominies and trivialities through which Joyce has made us pass: they seem to me—the soaring silver prose of the one, the deep embedded pulse of the other—among the supreme expressions in literature of the creative powers of humanity: they are, respectively, the justifications of the woman and the man.

V

Since finishing *Ulysses*, Joyce has been engaged upon another work, about half of which has been published in the transatlantic monthly, *Transition*.[2] It is not possible to judge this book properly in the imperfect form in which it has appeared. It is intended as a sort of complement to *Ulysses*; Joyce has explained that, as *Ulysses* deals with the day and with the conscious mind, so his new work is to deal with the night and with the subconscious. The whole book is apparently to occupy itself with the single night's sleep of a single character. Joyce has already exhibited in *Ulysses* a unique genius for

[2] In 1931. This then unfinished work of Joyce's was known as *Work in Progress* until it was published in its completed form as *Finnegans Wake* in 1939. Mr. Wilson's essay on the whole book appears as "The Dream of H. C. Earwicker" in his volume *The Wound and the Bow*, pages 243–271 (Boston, 1941; new edition, New York, 1947). Among other discussions of *Finnegans Wake*, the following may be mentioned here: *An Exagmination . . . of "Work in Progress,"* by various writers (Paris, 1929; Norfolk, Conn., 1937); *James Joyce*, by Harry Levin (Norfolk, Conn., 1941); and *A Skeleton Key to Finnegans Wake*, by Joseph Campbell and Henry Morton Robinson (New York, 1944). (Editor's note, 1950.)

the representation of special psychological states: I know of nothing else in literature, for example, like the drunken night-town scene, with its astounding recreation of all the deliriums, dazes, gibberings, exaltations and hallucinations of drunkenness. And Joyce's method of rendering the phases of sleep is similar to his methods in the Circe episode. But he is here attempting something even more difficult, and his way of doing it raises an important question in regard to all Joyce's later work. Joyce, as I have said, always nowadays represents the consciousness of his characters directly: but his method of representing consciousness is to let you overhear his characters talking to themselves. Joyce's people think and feel exclusively in terms of words, for Joyce himself thinks in terms of words. This is partly due, no doubt, to his defective eyesight, which of late years has become so serious as to make it difficult for him to work. There is an interesting passage in *A Portrait of the Artist* in which Joyce himself discusses this aspect of his writing:

He drew forth a phrase from his treasure and spoke it softly to himself:
—A day of dappled seaborne clouds.—
The phrase and the day and the scene harmonized in a chord. Words. Was it their colors? He allowed them to glow and fade, hue after hue: sunrise gold, the russet and green of apple orchards, azure of waves, the greyfringed fleece of clouds. No, it was not their colors: it was the poise and balance of the period itself. Did he then love the rhythmic rise and fall of words better than their associations of legend and color? Or was it that, being as weak of sight as he was shy of mind, he drew less pleasure from the reflection of the glowing sensible world through the prism of a language many colored and richly storied than from the contemplation of an inner world of individual emotions mirrored perfectly in a lucid supple periodic prose?

And in *Ulysses* we hear the characters far more plainly than we see them: Joyce supplies us with descriptions of them in sparse, scrupulous phrases, one trait here, another there. But the Dublin of *Ulysses* is a city of voices. Who has a clear idea of how Bloom or Molly Bloom looks?—and should we have a clear idea of Stephen if we had never seen photographs of Joyce? But their eternally soliloquizing voices become our intimate companions and haunt us long afterwards.

Joyce already seems sometimes, in *Ulysses,* to go a little beyond the probabilities in the vocabulary which he allows Bloom to command. When Bloom, in the drunken scene, for example, imagines himself giving birth to "eight male yellow and white children," all "with valuable metallic faces" and each with "his name printed in legible letters on his shirt-front: Nasodoro, Goldfinger, Chrysostomos, Maindorée, Silversmile, Silberselber, Vifargent, Panargyros" —we have difficulty in believing that he would have been learned enough for this. Yet I do not suppose that Joyce means us to think of Bloom as actually formulating these words in his mind: it is the author's way of conveying in words a vision which on the part of Bloom must have been a good deal less distinct, or at least a good deal less literary, than this. Now, in his new book, Joyce has tried to make his hero express directly in words, again, states of mind which do not usually in reality make use of words at all—for the subconscious has no language—the dreaming mind does not usually speak—and when it does, it is more likely to express itself in the looking-glass language of "Jabberwocky" than in anything resembling ordinary speech. Joyce's attempts to write the language of dreams have a good deal in common with those of Lewis Carroll; but the difference between his new novel and the Alice books is that, whereas in the Alice books it is the author who is supposed to be telling in straight English the adventures which his heroine thinks she is having and the literary language peculiar to dreams appears only in a poem which she reads, in Joyce's book he is plunging us directly into the consciousness of the dreamer itself, which is presented, without explanations by the author, entirely in the Jabberwocky language. The book is thus more easily comprehensible to literary people than to people who are not "word-minded," whose minds do not habitually breed words in response to sensations, emotions and thoughts. Yet it is worth making the effort to understand, because what Joyce is trying to do is both artistically and psychologically extremely interesting, and it may be that he will turn out to have written the most remarkable piece of dream-literature in existence.

The best way to understand Joyce's method is to note what goes on in one's own mind when one is just dropping off to sleep. Images—or words, if one thinks in words like Joyce—which were already in the conscious mind will suddenly acquire an ominous significance which has nothing to do with their ordinary functions; some vivid incident which may have taken place just before one went to bed will begin to swell with a meaning, an emotion, which at first we do not recognize because it has come up from the submerged part of the mind and is attempting to pass itself off in the clothes of an immediate experience—because it is dissociated from the situation out of which it originally arose. Or conversely, one may rid oneself of a troublesome abstract idea with which one has been preoccupied by allowing it to transform itself into some innocuous concrete image more easily dismissed from the attention: the page of a philosophical book, for example, where one had been continually stumbling over phrases and terms may vanish on the threshold of sleep in the guise of a spotted man, the spots having substituted themselves for the impenetrable words and phrases. And so the images which our waking mind would keep distinct from one another incongruously mix in our sleep with an effect of perfect congruity. A single one of Joyce's sentences, therefore, will combine two or three different meanings—two or three different sets of symbols; a single word may combine two or three. Joyce has profited, in inventing his dream-language, by Freud's researches into the principles which govern the language actually spoken in dreams: certain people, it appears, do make up "portmanteau-words" in their sleep; but we are not, I take it, to suppose that Joyce's hero necessarily frames all these sentences to himself. Except when he dreams he is reading something or carrying on a conversation, the language is merely a literary equivalent for sleeping states not even articulate in fancy. Nor are we to assume that Joyce's sleeper is actually master of all the languages or understands all the allusions of which Joyce makes him avail himself in his dream. We are now at a level below particularized languages—we are in the region whence all languages arise and where the impulses to all acts have their origin.

The hero of the night's sleep in question is, we gather, a man named H. C. Earwicker, a Norwegian or descendant of Norwegians, living in Dublin. He seems to have attempted a number of occupations—to have been a postman, to have worked in Guiness's Brewery, to have kept a hotel and a shop. He is married and has children, but has apparently been carrying on a flirtation with a girl named Anna Livia. This, along with other lapses from respectability associated with it in his mind, troubles his conscience and his repose. We are introduced, at the very beginning, into Earwicker's drowsing consciousness, and we have to make what we can of the names, the shapes, and above all, of the voices, which fill that dim and shifting world—they combine and recombine, they are always changing into one another—but as we go on, we find the same themes recurring and we begin to be able to understand them in relation to one another—we become familiar with the character of Earwicker—we begin to guess at his condition and history. We identify Maggie and the children, the house in which they live, the four old men with the donkey, Earwicker's drunken misdemeanors and his fear of being caught by the police, the washerwomen gathering up their washing, Anna Livia on the bank of the Liffey, the Hill of Howth, the tree and the stone. But none of these elements is seen clearly or objectively—they are all aspects, the dramatic projection of aspects, of Earwicker himself: men and women, old and young, stronger and weaker, river and mountain, tree and stone—it is the dreamer who speaks or is spoken to, who sees or is seen, in all of them. The old men come to admire him as he is sleeping on the mountainside, but in a moment it is Earwicker himself who is talking about himself; or he splits up into two personalities, one of whom bullies or accuses the other. He is coming out of a pub into the street with a party of drunken companions, many people are standing about but the revelers do not care how much attention they attract: they egg on one of their number to sing but the song turns out to be a recital of all Earwicker's failures and sins—he has proved himself a fool and a swindler to the derision of all Dublin, his wife is going to read him the Riot Act. Or he sets out very sweetly to explain something by a fable of "the Mookse and the Gripes": the Mookse comes swaggering up to the Gripes, who is hanging on a tree—a sort of altercation takes place, and it turns into rather a painful re-enactment of one of Earwicker's encounters with the police —but dusk falls and the washerwomen come out and carry off the Mookse and the Gripes, who are now merely two pieces of laundry.

One of the most remarkable parts which have so far appeared is the *allegro* conclusion to the first of the four long sections which are to make up the completed work. (Joyce has allowed it to be published separately in a little book called *Anna Livia Plurabelle*.) Here the washerwomen have become identified with the stone and elm on the river bank—we hear them gossiping about Anna Livia, who is both the girl with whom the hero is in love and the river Liffey; and their gossip is the voice of the river itself, light, rapid, incessant, almost metrical, now monotonously running on one note, now impeded and synocopated, but vivaciously, interminably babbling its indistinct rigmarole story, half-unearthly, half-vulgarly human, of a heroine half-legendary, half-real:

Oh tell me all about Anna Livia! I want to hear all about Anna Livia. Well, you know Anna Livia? Yes, of course, we all know Anna Livia. Tell me all. Tell me now. You'll die when you hear. . . . Tell me, tell me, how cam she camlin through all her fellows, the neckar she was, the diveline? Linking one and knocking the next, tapting a flank and tipting a jutty and palling in and pietaring out and clyding by on her eastway. Waiwhou was the first thurever burst? . . . She says herself she hardly knows whuon the annals her graveller was, a dynast of Leinster, a wolf of the sea, or what he did or how blyth she played or how, when, why, where and who offon he jumnpad her. She was just a young thin pale soft shy slim slip of a thing then, sauntering, by silvamoonlake, and he was a heavy trudging lurching lieabroad of a Curraghman, making his hay for whose sun to shine on, as tough as the oaktrees (peats be with them!) used to rustle that time down by the dykes of killing Kildare, that forstfellfoss with a plash across her. She thought she's sankh neathe the ground with nymphant shame when he gave her the tigris eye!

As darkness falls between stone and elm, the voices grow husky and vague:

And ho! Hey? What all men. Hot? His tittering daughters of Whawk?

Can't hear with the waters of. The chittering waters of. Flittering bats, field-mice, bawk talk. Ho! Are you not gone ahome? What Tom Malone? Can't hear with bawk of bats, all the liffeying waters of. Ho, talk save us. My foos won't moos. I feel as old as yonder elm. A tale told of Shaun or Shem? All Livia's daughtersons. Dark hawks hear us. Night! Night! My ho head halls. I feel as heavy as yonder stone. Tell me of John or Shaun? Who were Shem and Shaun the living sons or daughters of? Night now! Tell me, tell me, tell me, elm! Night night! Tell me tale of stem or stone. Beside the rivering waters of, hitherandthithering waters of. Night!

Night is just falling in this first section of the book, and the shadow of the past, the memory presumably of the day before, darkens the hero's sleep—the vulgarities of his waking life oppress him and pursue him; but after midnight, as dawn approaches, as he becomes dimly aware of the first light, the dream begins to brighten and to rise unencumbered. If I am not mistaken, the middle-aged Earwicker reverts to the period of his youth, once again he is carefree, attractive, well-liked—his spirit turns refreshed to the new day. Are we to leave him on the verge of waking or are we finally to see the fantasies of the dream closed down into the commonplace fate which we have already been able to divine?

This new production of Joyce's exaggerates the qualities we have noted in *Ulysses*. There is even less action than in *Ulysses*. Joyce has set out with certain definite themes and the themes are evidently all to have their developments, but these developments take a long time. We make progress—we pass from night to morning—and no doubt, when the whole book is before us, we shall see that some sort of psychological drama has been played out in Earwicker's mind—but, as we progress, we go round and round. And whereas in *Ulysses* there is only one parallel, in this new book there are a whole set: Adam and Eve, Tristan and Isolde, Swift and Vanessa, Cain and Abel, Michael and Lucifer, Wellington and Napoleon. The multiplication of references does, to be sure, deepen and extend the significance of Earwicker: he and Anna Livia are the eternal woman and the eternal man, and during the early hours of heaviness and horror of Earwicker's dream, he is an Adam fallen from grace —to be redeemed, Joyce is said to have announced, with the renewal of the morning light. And it would seem that Joyce has provided plausible reasons for the appearance of all these personages in his hero's dream: Napoleon and Wellington have gotten in by way of the Wellington monument in the Phoenix Park, near which one of Earwicker's misdemeanors has been committed; and Michael and Lucifer—it appears from the last installment published, in which Earwicker is partly waked up toward morning by the crying of one of his children—by a picture on the bedroom wall. Yet the effect of the superposition, one upon the other, of such a variety of parallels seems sometimes less to enrich the book than to give it a mere synthetic complication. Joyce is again, we come to the conclusion, trying to do too many things at once. The style he has invented for his purpose works on the principle of a palimpsest: one meaning, one set of images, is written over another. Now we can grasp a certain number of such suggestions simultaneously, but Joyce, with his characteristic disregard for the reader, apparently works over and over his pages, packing in allusions and puns. This appears clearly from the different versions which have been published in various places of the Anna Livia Pluribelle section. (I have given in an appendix three stages of the same passage from this.) Joyce has improved it in making the texture denser, but this enrichment also obscures the main outlines and somewhat over-solidifies and impedes the dim ambiguous fluidity of the dream—especially when it takes the form of introducing in the final version puns on the names of some five hundred rivers. And so soon as we are aware of Joyce himself systematically embroidering on his text, deliberately inventing puzzles, the illusion of the dream is lost.

Yet, on the whole, this illusion is created and kept up with extraordinary success. There is a curious fascination about becoming gradually acquainted with a character whom we know only from the inside and from his dreams. And without the complications of his vocabulary, Joyce would no doubt never be able to paint for us with so sensitive and sure a hand the turbid life of that mental half-world where the unconscious is merged with the conscious—as without his machinery of history and myth, he would not be able to give his subject any poetic freedom of significance beyond the realistic framework which holds it firm. We are to see in H. C. Earwicker Everyman (he imagines his initials standing for Here Comes Everybody). We are to find in his dream all human possibilities—for out of that human nature, that psychological plasm, which swims dark and deep beneath the surface of the meager words, the limited acts, the special mask, of one man's actual daytime career, all history and myth have arisen—victim and conqueror, lover and beloved, childhood and old age—all the forms of human experience. And what humor, what imagination, what poetry, what psychological wisdom, Joyce has put into Earwicker's dream! I have offered the criticisms above only tentatively and without assurance: when we come to think about what we take at first to be the defects in Joyce's work, we find them so closely involved with the depth of his thought and the originality of his conception that we are obliged to grant them a certain necessity. And whatever difficulties we may have with this book in its present fragmentary and incomplete state, I feel confident that, when we read it as a whole, we shall find, not only that it is not unworthy—as the snappers at the heels of genius have been so eager and prompt to assert—of the great master of letters who wrote it, but that he is still at the height of his power.

From *Axel's Castle* by Edmund Wilson, pp. 191–236. Charles Scribner's Sons. Copyright, 1931. Reprinted by permission of the author and publishers. An earlier version of this essay appeared in *The New Republic*, Vol. LXI (December 18, 1929), pp. 84–93.

T. S. Eliot

[1931]

I HAVE noted the similarity between the English seventeenth-century poets and the French nineteenth-century Symbolists. The poetry of T. S. Eliot has, in our own time, brought together these two traditions, as it is Eliot who, so far as I know, has for the first time called attention to their resemblance. "The form," he says, "in which I began to write, in 1908 or 1909, was directly drawn from the study of Laforgue together with the later Elizabethan drama; and I do not know anyone who started from exactly that point."

I have so far, in discussing the early Symbolists, spoken chiefly of Mallarmé. But T. S. Eliot derived, as he indicates, from a different branch of the Symbolist tradition. In 1873 there had appeared in Paris a book of poems called *Les Amours Jaunes,* by a writer who signed himself Tristan Corbière. *Les Amours Jaunes* was received with complete indifference, and scarcely more than a year after it appeared, the author died of consumption. Only thirty at the time of his death, Tristan Corbière had been an eccentric and very maladjusted man: he was the son of a sea captain who had also written sea stories and he had had an excellent education, but he chose for himself the life of an outlaw. In Paris, he slept all day and spent the nights in the cafés or at his verses, greeting at dawn the Paris harlots as they emerged from the station house or the hotel with the same half-harsh, half-tender fellow-feeling for the exile from conventional society which, when he was at home in his native Brittany, caused him to flee the house of his family and seek the company of the customs-men and sailors—living skeleton and invalid as he was, performing prodigies of courage and endurance in the navigation of a little cutter which he sailed by preference in the worst possible weather. He made a pose of his unsociability and of what he considered his physical ugliness, at the same time that he undoubtedly suffered over them. Melancholy, with a feverishly active mind, full of groanings and vulgar jokes, he used to amuse himself by going about in convict's clothes and by firing guns and revolvers out the window in protest against the singing of the village choir; and on one occasion, on a visit to Rome, he appeared in the streets in evening dress, with a mitre on his head and two eyes painted on his forehead, leading a pig decorated with ribbons. And Corbière's poetry was a poetry of the outcast: often colloquial and homely, yet with a rhetoric of fantastic slang; often with the manner of slapdash doggerel, yet sure of its own morose artistic effects; full of the parade of romantic personality, yet incessantly humiliating itself with a self-mockery scurrilous and savage, out of which, as Huysmans said, would sometimes rise without warning "a cry of sharp pain like the breaking of a 'cello string"—Corbière's verse brought back into French poetry qualities which had been alien to its spirit since François Villon's day.

So outlandish did Corbière appear even from the point of view of the Romantics that he was dismissed, when he was noticed at all, as not merely unseemly but insane—till Paul Verlaine, in 1883, did him honor in a series of articles *Les Poètes Maudits,* which was one of the important critical events in the development of Symbolism. Verlaine himself, a more accomplished artist, but a less original and interesting personality, had been strongly influenced by *Les Amours Jaunes*—he seems, indeed, to have caught over from Corbière, not only certain artistic effects, but even something of his own poetic personality, his peculiar accent of wistful naïveté: compare Corbière's "Rondels pour Après" with Verlaine's sonnet which begins, "L'espoir luit comme un brin de paille dans l'étable"; or "Paria" with "Casper Hauser."

But another French poet, Jules Laforgue, nineteen years younger than Corbière, had independently developed a tone and technique—poignant-ironic, grandiose-slangy, scurrilous-naïve—which had much in common with Corbière's. Laforgue was the son of a schoolmaster and, for all his nonchalance in handling rudely the conventions of French poetry, much more a professional man of letters than Corbière. Laforgue even errs through preciosity in his fashion; what with Corbière seems a personal and inevitable, if eccentric, manner of speech, in Laforgue sounds self-conscious and deliberate, almost sometimes a literary exercise. He was tubercular, as Corbière was also, and dead at twenty-seven—and his gentleness and sadness are still those of a sick well-cared-for child; his asperities, his surprising images, his coquetries, his cynicism, and his impudence, are still those of a clever schoolboy. Laforgue's friends procured him a post as reader to the Empress Augusta of Germany; and, falling under the spell of German philosophy, he brought its jargon into his verse, contributing thereby to Symbolism perhaps the one element of obscurity which it had lacked.

Yet Laforgue is a very fine poet and one of the most remarkable of the Symbolists. He and Corbière had introduced a new variety of vocabulary and a new flexibility of feeling. With Mallarmé, it may be said that, on the whole, it is the imagery, not the feeling, which is variable: though sometimes playful, he is classical in the sense (as Yeats and Valéry are) that he sustains a certain grandeur of tone. But it is from the conversational-ironic, rather than from the serious-esthetic, tradition of Symbolism that T. S. Eliot derives. Corbière and Laforgue are almost everywhere in his early work. The emphatic witty quatrains of Corbière, with their sudden lapses into tenderness or pathos, are heard again in the satiric verse of Eliot: a poem like "Mr. Eliot's Sunday Morning Service" would hardly, one imagines, have been written without Corbière's "Rapsodie Foraine." And as "Conversation Galante" derives clearly from certain poems in Laforgue's "Complaintes" and "Imitation de Notre-Dame la Lune," so the more elaborate "Portrait of a Lady" and "The Love Song of J. Alfred Prufrock" follow closely the longer poems of Laforgue. Compare the conclusion of "Prufrock" with the conclusion of the early version of Laforgue's poem "Légende":

> I grow old . . . I grow old . . .
> I shall wear the bottoms of my trousers rolled.

Shall I part my hair behind? Do I dare to eat a peach!
I shall wear white flannel trousers, and walk upon the beach,
I have heard the mermaids singing, each to each.

I do not think that they will sing to me.

I have seen them riding seaward on the waves
Combing the white hair of the waves blown back
When the wind blows the water white and black.

We have lingered in the chambers of the sea
By sea-girls wreathed with seaweed red and brown
Till human voices wake us, and we drown.

      *   *   *   *   *

      Hier l'orchestre attaqua
      Sa dernière polka

      Oh! L'automne, l'automne!
        Les casinos
        Qu'on abandonne
      Remisent leurs pianos! . . .

    Phrases, verroteries,
    Caillots de souvenirs.
    Oh! comme elle est maigrie!
    Que vais-je devenir? . . .

    Adieu! Les filles d'ifs dans les grisailles
    Ont l'air de pleureuses de funerailles
    Sous l'autan noir qui veut que tout s'en aille.

        Assez, assez,
      C'est toi qui as commencé.

    Va, ce n'est plus l'odeur de tes fourrures.
    Va, vos moindres clins d'yeux sont des parjures.
    Tais-toi, avec vous autres rien ne dure.

        Tais-toi, tais-toi,
      On n'aime qu'une fois . . .

Here it will be seen that Eliot has reproduced Laforgue's irregular metrical
scheme almost line for line. Furthermore, the subject of Laforgue's poem—the
hesitations and constraints of a man either too timid or too disillusioned to

make love to a woman who provokes his ironic pity at the same time that she stirs gusts of stifled emotion—has a strong resemblance to the subjects of "Prufrock" and the "Portrait of a Lady." And in another poem, "La Figlia Che Piange," Eliot has adapted a line of Laforgue's: "Simple et sans foi comme un bonjour"—"Simple and faithless as a smile and shake of the hand." He has even brought over into English some of the unstressed effect of French verse: how different, for example, is the alexandrine of Eliot's just quoted from the classical English alexandrine "which like a wounded snake drags its slow length along" or "with sparkless ashes loads an unlamented urn." (In his exhaustive *Influence du Symbolisme Français sur la Poésie Américaine de 1910 à 1920,* M. René Taupin has shown the influence of Gautier also in Eliot's satiric poems: "The Hippopotamus," it appears, is almost a transcript of a hippopotamus by Gautier, and the "Grishkin is nice" passage in "Whispers of Immortality" repeats a "Carmen est maigre" of Gautier.)

It must not be supposed, however, that Eliot is not original or that he is not the equal of either of his masters. Those longer and more elaborate poems —"Derniers Vers" in the collected edition—which Laforgue was constructing at the time of his death out of more fragmentary and less mature work are certainly his most important performances: through his masterly flexibility of vocabulary and metric, he has here achieved one of the definitive expressions of the pathetic-ironic, worldly-esthetic moods of the *fin de siècle* temperament. Yet, though Eliot has, in certain obvious respects, applied Laforgue's formula so faithfully, he cannot properly be described as an imitator because he is in some ways a superior artist. He is more mature than Laforgue ever was, and his workmanship is perfect in a way that Corbière's and Laforgue's were rarely. T. S. Eliot's peculiar distinction lies, as Clive Bell has said, in his "phrasing." Laforgue's images are often far-fetched and inappropriately grotesque: his sins in this respect are really very closely akin to those of the English metaphysical poets; but Eliot's taste is absolutely sure—his images always precisely right. And the impression that Eliot leaves, even in these earliest poems, is clear, vivid and unforgettable: we do not subordinate him to his Symbolist predecessors any more than, when we find him, as in "Gerontion," writing in the rhythms of late Elizabethan blank verse, we associate him with Middleton or Webster.

When we come to examine Eliot's themes, we recognize something which we have found already in Laforgue, but which appears in Eliot in a more intense form. One of the principal preoccupations of Flaubert—a great hero of Eliot's, as of Eliot's fellow-poet, Ezra Pound's—had been the inferiority of the present to the past: the Romantics had discovered the possibilities of the historical imagination; with their thirst for boldness, grandeur, and magnificence, they had located these qualities in past epochs—especially the Middle Ages and the Renaissance. And Flaubert, who shared with the Romantics this appetite for the gorgeous and the untamed, but who constrained himself, also, to confront the actual nineteenth-century world, pursued two parallel lines of fiction which lent significance and relief to each other. On the one hand, he reconstructed, in *Salammbô* and in *La Tentation de Saint-Antoine,* the splendid barbarities of the pagan world and the heroic piety of the early Christian; and on the other, he caricatured, in *Madame Bovary,* in *L'Education Sentimentale* and in *Bouvard et Pécuchet,* the pusillanimity and mediocrity of contemporary bourgeois France. This whole point of view of Flaubert's —summed up, as it were, in *Trois Contes,* where the three periods are contrasted in one book—was profoundly to affect modern literature. We shall find it later on in Joyce; but in the meantime we must note its reappearance in the poetry of Eliot. Eliot, like Flaubert, feels at every turn that human life is now ignoble, sordid or tame, and he is haunted and tormented by intimations that it has once been otherwise. In "Burbank with a Baedeker: Bleistein with a Cigar," the young American tourist in Venice, superseded in his affair with the Princess Volupine by a vulgar Austrian Jew, meditates on the clipped wings and pared claws of the Lion of St. Mark's, the symbol of the old arrogant Venice and of the world where such a city was possible. In "A Cooking Egg," the poet demands, after a call upon a very mild, dull spinster: "Where are the eagles and the trumpets?" and himself returns the saddened answer: "Buried beneath some snow-deep Alps." In "Lune de Miel," the Middle Western American travelers, stifled with the summer heat and devoured by the bedbugs of Ravenna, are contrasted with the noble crumbling beauty of the old Byzantine church less than a league away, of which they are totally unaware and to which they have apparently no relation; and in "Mr. Eliot's Sunday Morning Service," the combined grossness and aridity of the modern clergymen is contrasted with the pure and fresh religious feeling of a picture of the baptism of Christ by "a painter of the Umbrian school." In the best and most effective of these poems, "Sweeney Among the Nightingales," the poet, during a drowsy, idiotic and mildly sinister scene in some low dive, where two of the girls are supposed to be plotting against one of the men, remembers, at the sound of nightingales singing, the murder of Agamemnon in Aeschylus:

> The host with someone indistinct
> Converses at the door apart,
> The nightingales are singing near
> The Convent of the Sacred Heart,
>
> And sang within the bloody wood
> When Agamemnon cried aloud,
> And let their liquid siftings fall
> To stain the stiff dishonoured shroud.

The present is more timid than the past: the bourgeois are afraid to let themselves go. The French had been preoccupied with this idea ever since the first days of Romanticism; but Eliot was to deal with the theme from a somewhat different point of view, a point of view characteristically American. For T. S. Eliot, though born in St. Louis, comes from a New England family and was educated at Harvard; and he is in some ways a typical product of our New England civilization. He is distinguished by that combination of practical prudence with moral idealism which shows itself in its later developments as an excessive fastidiousness and scrupulousness. One of the principal subjects of Eliot's poetry is really that regret at situations unexplored, that dark rankling of passions inhibited, which has figured so conspicuously in the work of the American writers of New England and New York from Hawthorne to Edith Wharton. T. S. Eliot, in this respect, has much in common with Henry James. Mr. Prufrock and the poet of the "Portrait of a Lady," with their helpless consciousness of having dared too little, correspond exactly to the middle-aged heroes of *The Ambassadors* and "The Beast in the Jungle," realizing sadly too late in life that they have been living too cautiously and too poorly. The fear of life, in Henry James, is closely bound up with the fear of vulgarity. And Eliot, too, fears vulgarity—which he embodies in the symbolic figure of "Apeneck Sweeney"—at the same time that he is fascinated by it. Yet he chafes at the limitations and pretenses of the culture represented by Boston—a society "quite uncivilized," as he says, "but refined beyond the point of civilization." He has some amusing satiric poems about old New England ladies—in one of which he reflects on his way to the house of his Cousin Harriet, how

> . . . evening quickens faintly in the street,
>   Wakening the appetites of life in some
>   And to others bringing the *Boston Evening Transcript*.

And the "Portrait of a Lady," whether the scene be laid in Boston or in London, is essentially a poem of that New England society "refined beyond the point of civilization": from the Lady, who serves tea among lighted candles—"an atmosphere of Juliet's tomb"—with her dampening efforts at flattery and flirtation through the medium of cultured conversation—her slightly stale and faded gush about Chopin and her memories of Paris in the spring—the poet is seized with an impulse to flee:

> I take my hat: how can I make a cowardly amends
> For what she has said to me?
> You will see me any morning in the park
> Reading the comics and the sporting page.
> Particularly I remark
> An English countess goes upon the stage,

> A Greek was murdered at a Polish dance,
> Another bank defaulter has confessed.
> I keep my countenance,
> I remain self-possessed
> Except when a street piano, mechanical and tired,
> Reiterates some worn-out common song
> With the smell of hyacinths across the garden
> Recalling things that other people have desired.

But he is always debating things with his conscience: his incurable moral solicitude makes him wonder:

> Are these ideas right or wrong?

So Mr. Prufrock in the room where

> . . . women come and go
> Talking of Michelangelo,

wistfully asks himself:

> Shall I say, I have gone at dusk through narrow streets
> And watched the smoke that rises from the pipes
> Of lonely men in shirt-sleeves, leaning out of windows? . . .

And Mr. Prufrock wonders also whether he should not put a question to his lady—but he never gets to the point of putting it.

II

But Eliot's most complete expression of this theme of emotional starvation is to be found in the later and longer poem called *The Waste Land* (1922). The Waste Land of the poem is a symbol borrowed from the myth of the Holy Grail: it is a desolate and sterile country ruled by an impotent king, in which not only have the crops ceased to grow and the animals to reproduce, but the very human inhabitants have become incapable of having children. But this sterility we soon identify as the sterility of the Puritan temperament. On the first pages we find again the theme of the girl with the hyacinths (themselves a symbol for the rearisen god of the fertility rites who will save the rainless country from drouth) which has already figured in "La Figlia Che Piange" and "Dans le Restaurant"—a memory which apparently represents for the poet some fulfillment foregone in youth and now agonizingly desired; and in the last pages it is repeated. We recognize throughout *The Waste Land* the peculiar conflicts of the Puritan turned artist: the horror of vulgarity and the shy sympathy with the common life, the ascetic shrinking from sexual experience and the distress at the drying up of the springs of sexual emotion, with the straining after a religious emotion which may be made to take its place.

Yet though Eliot's spiritual and intellectual roots are still more firmly fixed in New England than is, I believe, ordinarily understood, there is in *The Waste Land* a good deal more than the mere gloomy moods of a New Englander regretting an emotionally undernourished youth. The colonization by the Puritans of New England was merely an incident in that rise of the middle class which has brought a commercial-industrial civilization to the European cities as well as to the American ones. T. S. Eliot now lives in London and has become an English citizen; but the desolation, the esthetic and spiritual drouth, of Anglo-Saxon middle-class society oppresses London as well as Boston. The terrible dreariness of the great modern cities is the atmosphere in which *The Waste Land* takes place—amidst this dreariness, brief, vivid images emerge, brief pure moments of feeling are distilled; but all about us we are aware of nameless millions performing barren office routines, wearing down their souls in interminable labors of which the products never bring them profit—people whose pleasures are so sordid and so feeble that they seem almost sadder than their pains. And this Waste Land has another aspect: it is a place not merely of desolation, but of anarchy and doubt. In our post-war world of shattered institutions, strained nerves and bankrupt ideals, life no longer seems serious or coherent—we have no belief in the things we do and consequently we have no heart for them.

The poet of *The Waste Land* is living half the time in the real world of contemporary London and half the time in the haunted wilderness of the medieval legend. The water for which he longs in the twilight desert of his dream is to quench the spiritual thirst which torments him in the London dusk; and as Gerontion, "an old man in a dry month," thought of the young men who had fought in the rain, as Prufrock fancied riding the waves with mermaids and lingering in the chambers of the sea, as Mr. Apollinax has been imagined drawing strength from the deep sea-caves of coral islands—so the poet of *The Waste Land*, making water the symbol of all freedom, all fecundity and flowering of the soul, invokes in desperate need the memory of an April shower of his youth, the song of the hermit thrush with its sound of water dripping and the vision of a drowned Phoenician sailor, sunk beyond "the cry of gulls and the deep sea swell," who has at least died by water, not thirst. The poet, who seems now to be traveling in a country cracked by drouth, can only feverishly dream of these things. One's head may be well stored with literature, but the heroic prelude of the Elizabethans has ironic echoes in modern London streets and modern London drawing-rooms: lines remembered from Shakespeare turn to jazz or refer themselves to the sound of phonographs. And now it is one's personal regrets again—the girl in the hyacinth garden—"the awful daring of a moment's surrender which an age of prudence can never retract"—the key which turned once, and once only, in the prison of inhibition and isolation. Now he stands on the arid plain again, and the dry-rotted world of London seems to be crumbling about him —the poem ends in a medley of quotations from a medley of literatures—like Gérard de Nerval's "Desdichado," the poet is disinherited; like the author of the *Pervigilium Veneris,* he laments that his song is mute and asks when the spring will come which will set it free like the swallow's; like Arnaut Daniel, in Dante, as he disappears in the refining fire, he begs the world to raise a prayer for his torment. "These fragments I have shored against my ruins."

The Waste Land, in method as well as in mood, has left Laforgue far behind. Eliot has developed a new technique, at once laconic, quick, and precise, for representing the transmutations of thought, the interplay of perception and reflection. Dealing with subjects complex in the same way as those of Yeats' poem "Among School-Children" and Valéry's "Cimetière Marin," Eliot has found for them a different language. As May Sinclair has said of Eliot, his "trick of cutting his corners and his curves makes him seem obscure when he is clear as daylight. His thoughts move very rapidly and by astounding cuts. They move not by logical stages and majestic roundings of the full literary curve, but as live thoughts move in live brains." Let us examine, as an illustration, the lovely nightingale passage from *The Waste Land*. Eliot is describing a room in London:

> Above the antique mantel was displayed
> As though a window gave upon the sylvan scene
> The change of Philomel, by the barbarous king
> So rudely forced; yet there the nightingale
> Filled all the desert with inviolable voice
> And still she cried, and still the world pursues,
> "Jug Jug" to dirty ears.

That is, the poet sees, above the mantel, a picture of Philomela changed to a nightingale, and it gives his mind a moment's swift release. The picture is like a window opening upon Milton's earthly paradise—the "sylvan scene," as Eliot explains in a note, is a phrase from "Paradise Lost"—and the poet associates his own plight in the modern city, in which some "infinitely gentle, infinitely suffering thing," to quote one of Eliot's earlier poems, is somehow being done to death, with Philomela, raped and mutilated by Tereus. But in the earthly paradise, there had been a nightingale singing: Philomela had wept her woes in song, though the barbarous king had cut out her tongue— her sweet voice had remained inviolable. And with a sudden change of tense, the poet flashes back from the myth to his present situation:

> And still she *cried,* and still the world *pursues,*
> "Jug Jug" to dirty ears.

The song of birds was represented in old English popular poetry by such outlandish syllables as "Jug Jug"—so Philomela's cry sounds to the vulgar. Eliot has here, in seven lines of extraordinary liquidity and beauty, fused the picture, the passage from Milton and the legend from Ovid, into a single moment of vague poignant longing.

The Waste Land is dedicated to Ezra Pound, to whom Eliot elsewhere acknowledges a debt; and he has here evidently been influenced by Pound's *Cantos*. *The Waste Land,* like the *Cantos,* is fragmentary in form and packed with literary quotation and allusion. In fact, the passage just discussed above has a resemblance to a passage on the same subject—the Philomela-Procne myth—at the beginning of Pound's Fourth Canto. Eliot and Pound have, in fact, founded a school of poetry which depends on literary quotation and reference to an unprecedented degree. Jules Laforgue had sometimes parodied, in his poems, the great lines of other poets—

> O Nature, donne-moi la force et le courage
> De me croire en âge . . .

And Eliot had, in his early poetry, introduced phrases from Shakespeare and Blake for purposes of ironic effect. He has always, furthermore, been addicted to prefacing his poems with quotations and echoing passages from other poets. But now, in *The Waste Land,* he carries this tendency to what one must suppose its extreme possible limit: here, in a poem of only four hundred and three lines (to which are added, however, seven pages of notes), he manages to include quotations from, allusions to, or imitations of, at least thirty-five different writers (some of them, such as Shakespeare and Dante, laid under contribution several times)—as well as several popular songs; and to introduce passages in six foreign languages, including Sanskrit. And we must also take into consideration that the idea of the literary medley itself seems to have been borrowed from still another writer, Pound. We are always being dismayed, in our general reading, to discover that lines among those which we had believed to represent Eliot's residuum of original invention had been taken over or adapted from other writers (sometimes very unexpected ones: thus, it appears now, from Eliot's essay on Bishop Andrewes, that the first five lines of "The Journey of the Magi," as well as the "word within a word, unable to speak a word" of "Gerontion," had been salvaged from Andrewes's sermons; and the "stiff dishonoured shroud" of "Sweeney Among the Nightingales" seems to be an echo of the "dim dishonoured brow" of Whittier's poem about Daniel Webster). One would be inclined *a priori* to assume that all this load of erudition and literature would be enough to sink any writer, and that such a production as *The Waste Land* must be a work of second-hand inspiration. And it is true that, in reading Eliot and Pound, we are sometimes visited by uneasy recollections of Ausonius, in the fourth century, composing Greek-and-Latin macaronics and piecing together poetic mosaics out of verses from Virgil. Yet Eliot manages to be most effective precisely—in *The Waste Land*—where he might be expected to be least original—he succeeds in conveying his meaning, in communicating his emotion, in spite of all his learned or mysterious allusions, and whether we understand them or not.

In this respect, there is a curious contrast between Eliot and Ezra Pound. Pound's work *has* been partially sunk by its cargo of erudition, whereas Eliot, in ten years' time, has left upon English poetry a mark more unmistakable than that of any other poet writing English. It is, in fact, probably true at the present time that Eliot is being praised too extravagantly and Pound, though he has deeply influenced a few, on the whole unfairly neglected. I should explain Eliot's greater popularity by the fact that, for all his fragmentary method, he possesses a complete literary personality in a way that Pound, for all his integrity, does not. Ezra Pound, fine poet though he is, does not dominate us like a master imagination—he rather delights us like a miscellaneous collection of admirably chosen works of art. It is true that Pound, in spite of his inveterate translating, is a man of genuine originality—but his heterogeneous shorter poems, and the heterogeneous passages which go to make his longer ones, never seem to come together in a whole—as his general prose writing gives scrappy expression to a variety of ideas, a variety of enthusiasms and prejudices, some ridiculous and some valid, some learned and some half-baked, which, though valuable to his generation as polemic, as propaganda and as illuminating casual criticism, do not establish and develop a distinct reasoned point of view as Eliot's prose-writings do. T. S. Eliot has thought persistently and coherently about the relations between the different phases of human experience, and his passion for proportion and order is reflected in his poems. He is, in his way, a complete man, and if it is true, as I believe, that he has accomplished what he has credited Ezra Pound with accomplishing—if he has brought a new personal rhythm into the language— so that he has been able to lend even to the borrowed rhythms, the quoted words, of his great predecessors a new music and a new meaning—it is this intellectual completeness and soundness which has given his rhythm its special prestige.

Another factor which has probably contributed to Eliot's extraordinary success is the essentially dramatic character of his imagination. We may be puzzled by his continual preoccupation with the possibilities of a modern poetic drama—that is to say, of modern drama in verse. Why, we wonder, should he worry about drama in verse—why, after Ibsen, Hauptmann, Shaw and Chekhov, should he be dissatisfied with plays in prose? We may put it down to an academic assumption that English drama ended when the blank verse of the Elizabethans ran into the sands, until it occurs to us that Eliot himself is really a dramatic poet. Mr. Prufrock and Sweeney are characters as none of the personages of Pound, Valéry or Yeats is—they have become a part of our modern mythology. And most of the best of Eliot's poems are based on unexpected dramatic contrasts: *The Waste Land* especially, I am sure, owes a large part of its power to its dramatic quality, which makes it peculiarly effective read aloud. Eliot has even tried his hand at writing a play,[1] and the two episodes from "Wanna Go Home, Baby" which he has published in *The Criterion* seem rather promising. They are written in a sort of jazz dramatic meter which suggests certain scenes of John Howard Lawson's *Processional*; and there can be no question that the future of drama in verse, if it has any future, lies in some such direction. "We cannot reinstate," Eliot has written, "either blank verse or the heroic couplet. The next form of drama will have to be a verse drama, but in new verse forms. Perhaps the conditions of modern life (think how large a part is now played in our sensory life by the internal combustion engine!) have altered our perception of rhythms. At any rate, the recognized forms of speech-verse are not as efficient as they should be; probably a new form will be devised out of colloquial speech."

In any case, that first handful of Eliot's poems, brought out in the middle of the War (1917) and generally read, if at all, at the time, as some sort of modern *vers de société*, was soon found, as Wyndham Lewis has said, to have had the effect of a little musk that scents up a whole room. And as for *The Waste Land*, it enchanted and devastated a whole generation. Attempts have been made to reproduce it—by Aldington, Nancy Cunard, etc.—at least a dozen times. And as Eliot, lately out of Harvard, assumed the rôle of the middle-aged Prufrock and today, at forty, in one of his latest poems, "The Song of Simeon," speaks in the character of an old man "with eighty years and no tomorrow"—so "Gerontion" and *The Waste Land* have made the young poets old before their time. In London, as in New York, and in the universities both here and in England, they for a time took to inhabiting exclusively barren beaches, cactus-grown deserts, and dusty attics overrun with rats—the only properties they allowed themselves to work with were a few fragments of old shattered glass or a sparse sprinkling of broken bones. They had purged themselves of Masefield as of Shelley for dry tongues and rheumatic joints. The dry breath of the Waste Land now blighted the most amiable country landscapes; and the sound of jazz, which had formerly seemed jolly, now inspired only horror and despair. But in this case, we may forgive the young for growing prematurely decrepit: where some of even the finest intelligences of the elder generation read *The Waste Land* with blankness or laughter, the young had recognized a poet.

III

As a critic, Eliot occupies today a position of distinction and influence equal in importance to his position as a poet. His writings have been comparatively

[1] Eliot's further work in drama has since appeared: *The Rock* in 1934, *Murder in the Cathedral* in 1935, *The Family Reunion* in 1939. A fourth play in poetic form, *The Cocktail Party*, was produced at the Edinburgh Festival in the summer of 1949 and was published in book form in 1950. (Editor's note, 1950.)

brief and rare—he has published only four small books of criticism[2]—yet he has probably affected literary opinion, during the period since the War, more profoundly than any other critic writing English. Eliot's prose style has a kind of felicity different from that of his poetic style; it is almost primly precise and sober, yet with a sort of sensitive charm in its austerity—closely reasoned and making its points with the fewest possible words, yet always even, effortless and lucid. In a reaction against the impressionistic criticism which flourished at the end of the century and which had survived into our own time—the sort of criticism which, in dealing with poetry, attempts to reproduce its effect by having recourse to poetic prose—T. S. Eliot has undertaken a kind of scientific study of esthetic values: avoiding impressionistic rhetoric and *a priori* esthetic theories alike, he compares works of literature coolly and tries to distinguish between different orders of artistic effects and the different degrees of satisfaction to be derived from them.

And by this method, Eliot has done more than perhaps any other modern critic to effect a revaluation of English literature. We sometimes follow his literary criticism with the same sort of eagerness and excitement with which we follow a philosophical inquiry. Professor Saintsbury has played in literature much the same sort of rôle that he has played as a connoisseur of wines, that of an agreeable and entertaining guide of excellent taste and enormous experience; Edmund Gosse, often intelligent and courageous in dealing with French or Scandinavian writers, could never quite, when it came to English literature, bring himself to drop his official character of Librarian of the House of Lords—his attitude was always a little that of the Beef Eater in the Tower of London, who assumes the transcendent value of the Crown Jewels which he has been set to guard and does not presume to form a personal opinion as to their taste or their respective merits; and the moral passion of Paul Elmer More has ended by paralyzing his esthetic appreciation. But T. S. Eliot, with an infinitely sensitive apparatus for esthetic appreciation, approaching English literature as an American, with an American's peculiar combination of avidity and detachment and with more than the ordinary English critic's reading in the literatures, ancient and modern, of the Continent, has been able to succeed as few writers have done in the excessively delicate task of estimating English, Irish and American writers in relation to one another, and writers in English in relation to writers on the Continent. The extent of Eliot's influence is amazing: these short essays, sent out without publicity as mere scat-

---

[2] In 1931. Eliot has since issued four further volumes: *The Use of Poetry and the Use of Criticism* (1933), *After Strange Gods* (1934), *Elizabethan Essays* (1934), and *Essays Ancient and Modern* (1936). He has also published two books of speculative prose: *The Idea of a Christian Society* (1939) and *Notes towards the Definition of Culture* (1948). Certain later critical papers and lectures have likewise appeared, usually in pamphlet form: *The Music of Poetry* (1942), *The Classics and the Man of Letters* (1942), *What is a Classic?* (1945), *The Man of Letters and the Future of Europe* (1945), *Milton* (1947), *From Poe to Valéry* (1948). See Appendix IV. (Editor's note, 1950.)

tered notes on literature, yet sped with so intense a seriousness and weighted with so wide a learning, have not only had the effect of discrediting the academic clichés of the text-books, but are even by way of establishing in the minds of the generation now in college a new set of literary clichés. With the ascendancy of T. S. Eliot, the Elizabethan dramatists have come back into fashion, and the nineteenth-century poets gone out. Milton's poetic reputation has sunk, and Dryden's and Pope's have risen. It is as much as one's life is worth nowadays, among young people, to say an approving word for Shelley or a dubious one about Donne. And as for the enthusiasm for Dante—to paraphrase the man in Hemingway's novel, there's been nothing like it since the Fratellinis!

Eliot's rôle as a literary critic has been very similar to Valéry's in France: indeed, the ideas of the two men and their ways of stating them have corresponded so closely that one guesses they must influence each other a good deal. Like Valéry, Eliot believes that a work of art is not an oracular outpouring, but an object which has been constructed deliberately with the aim of producing a certain effect. He has brought back to English criticism something of that trenchant rationalism which he admires in the eighteenth century, but with a much more catholic appreciation of different styles and points of view than the eighteenth century allowed. The Romantics, of course, fare badly before this criticism. Vague sentiment vaguely expressed, rhetorical effusion disguising bad art—these Eliot's laconic scorn has nipped. For him, Byron is "a disorderly mind, and an uninteresting one": Keats and Shelley "not nearly such great poets as they are supposed to be"; whereas the powers of Dryden are "wider, but no greater than those of Milton." Just as Valéry lately protested in a lecture that he was unable to understand the well-known lines of Alfred de Musset:

> Les plus désespérés sont les chants les plus beaux,
> Et j'en sais d'immortels qui sont de purs sanglots,

so Eliot, in an essay on Crashaw, has confessed, with a certain superciliousness, his inability to understand the following stanza from Shelley's "Skylark":

> Keen as are the arrows
> Of that silver sphere
> Whose intense lamp narrows
> In the white dawn clear,
> Until we hardly see—we feel that it is there.

"For the first time, perhaps," says Eliot, "in verse of such eminence, sound exists without sense."

It will be seen that Eliot differs from Valéry in believing that poetry should make "sense." And he elsewhere, in his essay on Dante in The Sacred Wood, remonstrates with Valéry for asserting that philosophy has no place in poetry. Yet Eliot's point of view, though more intelligently reasoned and expressed, comes down finally to the same sort of thing as Valéry's and seems to me open to the same sort of objection. Eliot's conclusion in respect to the relation of philosophy to poetry is that, though philosophy *has* its place in poetry, it is only as something which we "see" among the other things with which the poet presents us, a set of ideas which penetrate his world, as in the case of the *Divina Commedia*: in the case of such a poet as Lucretius, the philosophy sometimes seems antagonistic to the poetry only because it happens to be a philosophy "not rich enough in feeling . . . incapable of complete expansion into pure vision." Furthermore, "the original form of philosophy cannot be poetic": the poet must use a philosophy already invented by somebody else. Now, though we may admire the justice of Eliot's judgments on the various degrees of artistic success achieved by Dante, Lucretius and others, it becomes plainer and plainer, as time goes on, that the real effect of Eliot's, as of Valéry's, literary criticism, is to impose upon us a conception of poetry as some sort of pure and rare esthetic essence with no relation to any of the practical human uses for which, for some reason never explained, only the technique of prose is appropriate.

Now this point of view, as I have already suggested in writing about Paul Valéry, seems to me absolutely unhistorical—an impossible attempt to make esthetic values independent of all the other values. Who will agree with Eliot, for example, that a poet cannot be an original thinker and that it is not possible for a poet to be a completely successful artist and yet persuade us to accept his ideas at the same time? There is a good deal in Dante's morality which he never got out of the Scholastics, as, for all we know, there may be a good deal in Lucretius which he never got out of Epicurus. When we read Lucretius and Dante, we are affected by them just as we are by prose writers of eloquence and imagination—we are compelled to take their opinions seriously. And as soon as we admit that prose writing may be considered on the same basis with verse, it becomes evident that we cannot, in the case of Plato, discriminate so finely as to the capacity of his philosophy for being "expanded into pure vision" that we are able to put our finger on the point where the novelist or poet stops and the scientist or metaphysician begins; nor, with Blake any more than with Nietzsche and Emerson, distinguish the poet from the aphorist. The truth is, of course, that, in Lucretius' time, verse was used for all sorts of didactic purposes for which we no longer consider it appropriate—they had agricultural poems, astronomical poems, poems of literary criticism. How can the *Georgics*, the *Ars Poetica* and Manilius be dealt with from the point of view of the capacity of their material for being "expanded into pure vision"? To modern readers, the subjects of the *Georgics*—bee-keeping, stock-raising, and so forth—seem unsuitable and sometimes annoying in verse;

yet for Virgil's contemporaries, the poem must have been completely successful
—as, indeed, granted the subject, it is. Nor does it follow that, because we are
coming to use poetry for fewer and fewer literary purposes, our critical taste is
becoming more and more refined, so that we are beginning to perceive for the
first time the true, pure and exalted function of poetry: that is, simply, as
Valéry says, to produce a "state"—as Eliot says, to afford a "superior amusement." It is much more likely that for some reason or other, verse as a technique of literary expression is being abandoned by humanity altogether—perhaps because it is a more primitive, and hence a more barbarous technique
than prose. Is it possible to believe, for example, that Eliot's hope of having
verse reinstated on the stage—even verse of the new kind which he proposes—
is likely ever to be realized?

The tendency to keep verse isolated from prose and to confine it to certain
highly specialized functions dates in English at least from the time of Coleridge, when, in spite of the long narrative poems which were fashionable,
verse was already beginning to fall into disuse. Coleridge defined a poem as
"that species of composition which is opposed to works of science by proposing
for its *immediate* object pleasure, not truth; and from all other species (having
this object in common with it), it is discriminated by proposing to itself such
delight from the *whole,* as is compatible with a distinct gratification from each
component part." Poe, who had doubtless read Coleridge on the subject, wrote
thirty years later that there was no such thing as a long poem, that "no very
long poem would ever be popular again," etc. Eliot and Valéry follow Coleridge and Poe in their theory as well as in their verse, and they seem to me to
confuse certain questions by talking as if the whole of literature existed simultaneously in a vacuum, as if Homer's and Shakespeare's situations had
been the same as Mallarmé's and Laforgue's, as if the latter had been attempting to play the same sort of rôles as the former and could be judged on the
same basis. It is inevitable, of course, that we should try to arrive at absolute
values through the comparison of the work of different periods—I have just
praised Eliot for his success at this—but it seems to me that in this particular
matter a good many difficulties would be cleared up if certain literary discussions could be removed from the artificially restricted field of verse—in which
it is assumed that nothing is possible or desirable but a quintessential distillation called "poetry," and that that distillation has nothing in common with
anything possible to obtain through prose—to the field of literature in general.
Has not such a great modern novel as *Madame Bovary,* for example, at least
as much in common with Virgil and Dante as with Balzac and Dickens? Is it
not comparable from the point of view of intensity, music and perfection of
the parts, with the best verse of any period? And we shall consider Joyce in
this connection later.

With all gratitude, therefore, for the salutary effect of Eliot's earlier criticism in curbing the carelessness and gush of the aftermath of Romanticism, it seems plain that the anti-Romantic reaction is leading finally into pedantry and into a futile estheticism. "Poetry," Eliot wrote in *The Sacred Wood*, "is not a turning loose of emotion, but an escape from emotion; it is not the expression of personality, but an escape from personality. But, of course, only those who have personality and emotion know what it means to want to escape from them." This was valid, and even noble in 1920 when *The Sacred Wood* was published; but today, after ten years of depersonalized and over-intellectualized verse, so much of it written in imitation of Eliot, the same sort of thing in the mouths of Eliot's disciples sounds like an excuse for *not* possessing emotion and personality.

Yet, in spite of the weaknesses of Eliot's position as he has sometimes been driven to state it dogmatically, he has himself largely succeeded in escaping the vices which it seems to encourage. The old nineteenth-century criticism of Ruskin, Renan, Taine, Sainte-Beuve, was closely allied to history and novel writing, and was also the vehicle for all sorts of ideas about the purpose and destiny of human life in general. The criticism of our own day examines literature, art, ideas and specimens of human society in the past with a detached scientific interest or a detached esthetic appreciation which seems in either case to lead nowhere. A critic like Herbert Read makes dull discriminations between different kinds of literature; a critic like Albert Thibaudet discovers dull resemblances between the ideas of philosophers and poets; a critic like I. A. Richards writes about poetry from the point of view of a scientist studying the psychological reactions of readers; and such a critic as Clive Bell writes about painting so exclusively and cloyingly from the point of view of the varying degrees of pleasure to be derived from the pictures of different painters that we would willingly have Ruskin and all his sermonizing back. And even Virginia Woolf and Lytton Strachey have this in common with Clive Bell that they seem to feel they have done enough when they have distinguished the kind of pleasure to be derived from one kind of book, the kind of interest to be felt in one kind of personality, from the kind to be found in another. One is supposed to have read everything and enjoyed everything and to understand exactly the reasons for one's enjoyment, but not to enjoy anything excessively nor to raise an issue of one kind of thing against another. Each of the essays of Strachey or Mrs. Woolf, so compact yet so beautifully rounded out, is completely self-contained and does not lead to anything beyond itself; and finally, for all their brilliance, we begin to find them tiresome.

Now there is a good deal in T. S. Eliot of this pedantry and sterility of his age. He is very much given, for example, to becoming involved in literary Houses-that-Jack-Built: "We find this quality occasionally in Wordsworth," he will write, "but it is a quality which Wordsworth shares with Shenstone rather than with Collins and Gray. And for the right sort of enjoyment of

Shenstone, we must read his prose as well as his verse. The 'Essays on Men and Manners' are in the tradition of the great French aphorists of the seventeenth century, and should be read with the full sense of their relation to Vauvenargues, La Rochefoucauld and (with his wider range) La Bruyère. We shall do well to read enough of Theophrastus to understand the kind of effect at which La Bruyère aimed. (Professor Somebody-or-other's book on 'Theophrastus and the Peripatetics' gives us the clew to the intellectual atmosphere in which Theophrastus wrote and enables us to gauge the influences on his work—very different from each other—of Plato and Aristotle.)" At this rate (though I have parodied Eliot), we should have to read the whole of literature in order to appreciate a single book, and Eliot fails to supply us with a reason why we should go to the trouble of doing so. Yet against the background of the criticism of his time, Eliot has stood out unmistakably as a man passionately interested in literature. The real intensity of his enthusiasm makes us forget the primness of his tone; and his occasional dogmatism is redeemed by his ability to see beyond his own ideas, his willingness to admit the relative character of his conclusions.

IV

But if Eliot, in spite of the meagreness of his production, has become for his generation a leader, it is also because his career has been a progress, because he has evidently been on his way somewhere, when many of his contemporaries, more prolfic and equally gifted, have been fixed in their hedonism or despair. The poet of *The Waste Land* was too serious to continue with the same complacence as some of his contemporaries inhabiting that godforsaken desert. It was certain he would not stick at that point, and one watched him to see what he would do.

This destination has now, however, become plain. In the preface to the new 1928 edition of *The Sacred Wood,* poetry is still regarded as a "superior amusement," but Eliot reports on his part "an expansion or development of interests." Poetry is now perceived to have "something to do with morals, and with religion, and even with politics perhaps, though we cannot say what." In *For Lancelot Andrewes,* published in the same year, Eliot declares himself a classicist in literature, an Anglo-Catholic in religion and a royalist in politics, and announces that he has in preparation "three small books" treating to these subjects and to be called respectively "The School of Donne," "The Principles of Modern Heresy," and "The Outline of Royalism." There follows a slender selection of essays, which hint quietly at what may be expected.

We must await the further exposition of Eliot's new body of doctrine before it will be possible to discuss it properly. In the meantime, we can only applaud his desire to formulate a consistent central position, at the same time that we may regret the unpromising character of the ideals and institutions which he invokes. One cannot but recognize in Eliot's recent writings a kind of reactionary point of view which had already been becoming fashionable among certain sorts of literary people—a point of view which has much in common with that of the neo-Thomists in France and that of the Humanists in America. "Unless by civilizations," writes Eliot, "you mean material progress, cleanliness, etc. . . . if you mean a spiritual coördination on a high level, then it is doubtful whether civilization can endure without religion, and religion without a church." Yet you can hardly have an effective church without a cult of Christ as the son of God; and you cannot have such a cult without more willingness to accept the supernatural than most of us today are able to muster. We feel in contemporary writers like Eliot a desire to believe in religious revelation, a belief that it would be a good thing to believe, rather than a genuine belief. The faith of the modern convert seems to burn only with a low blue flame. "Our literature," Eliot has himself recently made a character in a dialogue say, "is a substitute for religion, and so is our religion." From such a faith, uninspired by hope, unequipped with zeal or force, what guidance for the future can we expect?

One cannot, however, doubt the reality of the experience to which Eliot testifies in his recent writings—though it seems to us less an Anglo-Catholic conversion than a reawakening of the New Englander's conscience, of the never quite exorcised conviction of the ineradicable sinfulness of man. Eliot admires Machiavelli because Machiavelli assumes the baseness of human nature as an unalterable fact; and he looks for light to the theologians who offer salvation, not through economic readjustment, political reform, education or biological and psychological study, but solely through "grace." Eliot apparently today regards "Evil" as some sort of ultimate reality, which it is impossible either to correct or to analyze. His moral principles seem to me stronger and more authentic than his religious mysticism—and his relation to the Anglo-Catholic Church appears largely artificial. The English seventeenth-century divines whose poetry and sermons he admires so much, upon whom he seems so much to depend for nourishment, exist in a richer, a more mysterious, a more heavily saturated atmosphere, in which even monumental outlines are blurred; Eliot himself is stiffer and cooler, more intent, more relentless, more clear. He has his own sort of graciousness, but he seems, as the phrase is, a little thin-lipped. His religious tradition has reached him by way of Boston.

In any case, Eliot's new phase of piety has brought with it a new humility. He apologizes in his 1928 preface for the "assumption of pontifical solemnity" which he now detects in *The Sacred Wood,* and his recent little book on Dante (a most admirable introduction) not merely surprises but almost embarrasses us by the modesty with which Eliot professes to desire nothing but to be of use to beginners and to tell us of a few of the beautiful things which

he has found in the great poet. I will not say that this humility has enfeebled
his poetry. The three devout little poems which he has published as Christmas
cards since "The Hollow Men" announced the nadir of the phase of sterility
and despair given such effective expression in *The Waste Land*, seem comparatively uninspired; but the long poem or group of poems, *Ash-Wednesday*
(1930), which follows a scheme somewhat similar to that of *The Waste Land*,
is a not unworthy successor to it.

  The poet begins with the confession of his bankruptcy:

> Because I do not hope to turn again
> Because I do not hope
> Because I do not hope to turn
> Desiring this man's gift and that man's scope
> I no longer strive to strive towards such things
> (Why should the agèd eagle stretch its wings?)
> Why should I mourn
> The vanished power of the usual reign? . . .
>
> Because these wings are no longer wings to fly
> But merely vans to beat the air
> The air which is now thoroughly small and dry
> Smaller and dryer than the will
> Teach us to care and not to care
> Teach us to sit still.
>
> Pray for us sinners now and at the hour of our death
> Pray for us now and at the hour of our death.

There follow passages in which the prayer is apparently answered: the poet's
contrition and pious resignation are rewarded by a series of visions which first
console then lighten his heart. We find an imagery new for Eliot, a symbolism
semi-ecclesiastical and not without a Pre-Raphaelite flavor: white leopards, a
Lady gowned in white, junipers and yews, "The Rose" and "The Garden,"
and jeweled unicorns drawing a gilded hearse: these are varied by an interlude which returns to the imagery and mood of *The Waste Land*, and a swirl-
ing churning anguished passage which suggests certain things of Gertrude
Stein's. At last the themes of the first section recur: the impotent wings of
the agèd eagle seem to revive, as,

> From the wide window toward the granite shore
> The white sails still fly seaward, seaward flying
> Unbroken wings.
> And the lost heart stiffens and rejoices
> In the lost lilac and the lost sea voices
> And the weak spirit quickens to rebel
> For the bent golden-rod and the lost sea smell
> Quickens to recover
> The cry of quail and the whirling plover

And the blind eye creates
The empty forms between the ivory gates
And smell renews the salt savour of the sandy earth . . .

The broken prayer, at once childlike and mystically subtle, with which the poem ends seems to imply that the poet has come closer to the strength and revelation he craves: grace is about to descend.

> Blessèd sister, holy mother, spirit of the fountain,
>   spirit of the garden,
> Suffer us not to mock ourselves with falsehood
> Teach us to care and not to care
> Teach us to sit still
> Even among these rocks,
> Our peace in His will
> And even among these rocks
> Sister, mother
> And spirit of the river, spirit of the sea,
> Suffer me not to be separated
>
> And let my cry come unto Thee.

The literary and conventional imagery upon which *Ash-Wednesday* so largely relies and which is less vivid because more artificial than that of Eliot's earlier poems, seems to me a definite feature of inferiority; the "devil of the stairs" and the "shape twisted on the banister," which are in Eliot's familiar and unmistakable personal vein, somehow come off better than the jeweled unicorn, which incongruously suggests Yeats. And I am made a little tired at hearing Eliot, only in his early forties, present himself as an "agèd eagle" who asks why he should make the effort to stretch his wings. Yet *Ash-Wednesday*, though less brilliant and intense than Eliot at his very best, is distinguished by most of the qualities which made his other poems remarkable: the exquisite phrasing in which we feel that every word is in its place and that there is not a word too much; the metrical mastery which catches so naturally, yet with so true a modulation, the faltering accents of the supplicant, blending the cadences of the liturgy with those of perplexed brooding thought; and, above all, that "peculiar honesty" in "exhibiting the essential sickness or strength of the human soul" of which Eliot has written in connection with Blake and which, in his own case, even at the moment when his psychological plight seems most depressing and his ways of rescuing himself from it least sympathetic, still gives him a place among those upon whose words we reflect with most interest and whose tones we remember longest.

From *Axel's Castle* by Edmund Wilson, pp. 93–131. Charles Scribner's Sons. Copyright, 1931. Reprinted by permission of the author and publishers. An earlier and shorter version of this essay appeared in *The New Republic*, Vol. LX (November 13, 1929), pp. 341–349.

ALLEN TATE

Hart Crane

[1932]

THE career of Hart Crane will be written by future critics as a chapter in the neo-symbolist movement. A historical view of his poetry at this time would be misleading and incomplete. Like most poets of his age in America, Crane discovered Rimbaud through Eliot and the Imagists; it is certain that long before he had done any of his best work he had come to believe himself the spiritual heir of the French poet. While it is true that he mastered the symbolist use of fused metaphor, it is also true that this is a feature of all poetic language. Whether Crane's style is symbolistic, or should, in many instances like the first six or seven stanzas of "The River," be called Elizabethan, is a question that need not concern us now.

Between *The Bridge* and *Une Saison d'Enfer* there is little essential affinity. Rimbaud achieved "disorder" out of implicit order, after a deliberate cultivation of "derangement," but in our time the disintegration of our intellectual systems is accomplished. With Crane the disorder is original and fundamental. That is the special quality of his mind that belongs peculiarly to our own time. His esthetic problem, however, was more general; it was the historic problem of romanticism.

Harold Hart Crane, one the great masters of the romantic movement, was born in Garrettsville, Ohio, on July 21, 1899. His birthplace is a small town near Cleveland, in the old Western Reserve, a region which, as distinguished from the lower portions of the state, where people from the southern up-country settled, was populated largely by New England stock. He seems to have known little of his ancestry, but he frequently said that his maternal forebears had given Hartford, Connecticut, its name, and that they went "back to Stratford-on-Avon"—a fiction surely, but one that gave him distinct pleasure. His formal education was slight. After the third year at high school, when he was fifteen, it ended, and he worked in his father's candy factory in Cleveland, where the family had removed in his childhood. He repeatedly told me that money had been set aside for his education at college, but that it had been used for other purposes. With the instinct of genius he read the great poets, but he never acquired an objective mastery of any literature, or even of the history of his country—a defect of considerable interest in a poet whose most ambitious work is an American epic.

In any ordinary sense Crane was not an educated man; in many respects he was an ignorant man. There is already a Crane legend, like the Poe legend— it should be fostered because it will help to make his poetry generally known —and the scholars will decide that it was a pity that so great a talent lacked early advantages. It is probable that he was incapable of the discipline of a formal classical education, and probable too that the eclectic education of his time would have scattered and killed his talent.

His poetry not only has defects of the surface, it has a defect of vision; but its great and peculiar value cannot be separated from its limitations. Its qualities are bound up with a special focus of the intellect and sensibility, and it would be foolish to wish that his mind had been better trained or differently organized.

The story of his suicide is well known. The information that I have seems authentic, but it is incomplete and subject to excessive interpretation. Toward the end of April, 1932, he embarked on the S.S. *Orizaba* bound from Vera Cruz to New York. On the night of April 26 he got into a brawl with some sailors; he was severely beaten and robbed. At noon the next day, the ship being in the Caribbean a few hours out of Havana, he rushed from his stateroom clad in pajamas and overcoat, walked through the smoking-room out onto the deck, and then the length of the ship to the stern. There without hesitation he made a perfect dive into the sea. It is said that a life-preserver was thrown to him; he either did not see it or did not want it. By the time the ship had turned back he had disappeared. Whether he forced himself down— for a moment he was seen swimming—or was seized by a shark, as the captain believed, cannot be known. After a search of thirty-five minutes his body was not found, and the *Orizaba* put back into her course.

In the summer of 1930 he had written to me that he feared his most ambitious work, *The Bridge*, was not quite perfectly "realized," that probably his soundest work was in the shorter pieces of *White Buildings*, but that his mind, being once committed to the larger undertaking, could never return to the lyrical and more limited form. He had an extraordinary insight into the foundations of his work, and I think this judgment of it will not be refuted.

From 1922 to 1928—after that year I saw him and heard from him irregularly until his death—I could observe the development of his style from poem to poem; and his letters—written always in a pure and lucid prose— provide a valuable commentary on his career. This is not the place to bring all this material together for judgment. As I look back upon his work and its relation to the life he lived, a general statement about it comes to my mind that may throw some light on the dissatisfaction that he felt with his career.

It will be a judgment on the life and works of a man whom I knew for ten years as a friend.

Suicide was the sole act of will left to him short of a profound alteration of his character. I think the evidence of this is the locked-in sensibility, the insulated egoism, of his poetry—a subject I shall return to. The background of his death was dramatically perfect: a large portion of his finest imagery was of the sea, chiefly the Caribbean:

> O minstrel galleons of Carib fire,
> Bequeath us to no earthly shore until
> Is answered in the vortex of our grave
> The seal's wide spindrift gaze toward paradise.

His verse is full of splendid images of this order, a rich symbolism for an implicit pantheism that, whatever may be its intrinsic merit, he had the courage to vindicate with death in the end.

His pantheism was not passive and contemplative, it arose out of the collision between his own locked-in sensibility and the ordinary forms of experience. Every poem is a thrust of that sensibility into the world: his defect lay in his inability to face out the moral criticism implied in the failure to impose his will upon experience.

The Bridge is presumably an epic. How early he had conceived the idea of this poem and the leading symbolism, it is difficult to know: certainly as early as February, 1923. Up to that time, with the exception of "For the Marriage of Faustus and Helen" (1922), he had written only short poems, but most of them, "Praise for an Urn," "Black Tambourine," "Paraphrase," and "Emblems of Conduct," are among his finest work. It is a mistake then to suppose that all of *White Buildings* is early experimental writing; a large portion of that volume, and perhaps the least successful part of it, is made up of poems written after *The Bridge* was begun. "Praise for an Urn" was written in the spring of 1922—one of the finest elegies by an American poet—and although his later development gave us a poetry that the period would be much the less rich for not having, he never again had such perfect mastery of his subject—because he never again knew precisely what his subject was.

Readers familiar with "For the Marriage of Faustus and Helen" admire it by passages, but the form of the poem, in its framework of symbol, is an abstraction empty of any knowable experience. It is a conventional revival of the kind of diction that a young poet picks up in his first reading. Crane, I believe, felt that this was so; and he became so dissatisfied not only with the style of the poem, which is heavily influenced by Eliot and Laforgue, but with the "literary" character of the symbolism, that he set about the greater task of writing *The Bridge*. He had looked upon his "Faustus and Helen" as an answer to the cultural pessimism of the school of Eliot, and *The Bridge* was to be an even more complete answer.

There was a fundamental mistake in Crane's diagnosis of Eliot's problem. Eliot's "pessimism" grows out of an awareness of the decay of the individual consciousness and its fixed relations to the world; but Crane thought that it was due to something like pure "orneryness," the unwillingness to "share with us the breath released," the breath being a new kind of freedom that he identified emotionally with the age of the machine. This vagueness of purpose, in spite of the apparently concrete character of the Brooklyn Bridge, which became the symbol of his epic, he never succeeded in correcting. The "bridge" stands for no well-defined experience; it differs from the Helen and Faust symbols only in its unliterary origin. I think Crane was deceived by this difference, and by the fact that Brooklyn Bridge is "modern," and a fine piece of "mechanic." His more ambitious later project permitted him no greater degree of formal structure than the more literary symbolism of his youth.

The fifteen parts of *The Bridge* taken as one poem suffer from the lack of a coherent structure, whether symbolistic or narrative: the coherence of the work consists in the personal quality of the writing—in mood, feeling, and tone. In the best passages Crane has a perfect mastery over the qualities of his style; but it lacks an objective pattern of ideas elaborate enough to carry it through an epic or heroic work. The single symbolistic image, in which the whole poem centers, is at one moment the actual Brooklyn Bridge; at another, it is any bridge or "connection"; at still another, it is a philosophical pun, and becomes the basis of a series of analogies.

In "Cape Hatteras," the aeroplane and Walt Whitman are analogous "bridges" to some transcendental truth. Because the idea is variously metaphor, symbol, and analogy, it tends to make the poem static. The poet takes it up, only to be forced to put it down again *when the poetic image of the moment is exhausted.* The idea does not, in short, fill the poet's mind; it is the starting point for a series of short flights, or inventions connected only in analogy—which explains the merely personal passages, which are obscure, and the lapses into sentimentality. For poetic sentimentality is emotion undisciplined by the structure of events or ideas of which it is ostensibly a part. The idea is not objective and articulate in itself; it lags after the poet's vision; it appears and disappears; and in the intervals Crane improvises, often beautifully, as in the flight of the aeroplane, sometimes badly, as in the passage on Whitman in the same poem.

In the great epic and philosophical works of our tradition, notably the *Divine Comedy,* the intellectual groundwork is not only simple philosophically; we not only know that the subject is personal salvation, just as we know that Crane's is the greatness of America; we are also given the complete articulation of the idea down to the slightest detail, and we are given it objectively apart from anything that the poet is going to say about it. When the poet extends his perception, there is a further extention of the groundwork ready to meet and discipline it, and compel the sensibility of the poet to stick to the subject. It is a game of chess; neither side can move without consulting the other. Crane's difficulty is that of modern poets generally: they play the game with half of the men, the men of sensibility, and because sensibility can make any move, the significance of all moves is obscure.

If we subtract from Crane's idea its periphery of sensation, we have left only the dead abstraction, the Greatness of America, which is capable of elucidation neither on the logical plane nor in the generally accepted idea of America.

The theme of *The Bridge* is, in fact, an emotional simplification of a subject-matter that Crane did not, on the plane of narrative and idea, simplify at all. The poem is emotionally homogeneous and simple—it contains a single purpose; but because it is not structurally clarified it is emotionally confused. America stands for a passage into new truths. Is this the meaning of American history? The poet has every right to answer yes, and this he has done. But just what in America or about America stands for this? Which American history? The historical plot of the poem, which is the groundwork on which the symbolic bridge stands, is arbitrary and broken, where the poet would have gained an overwhelming advantage by choosing a single period or episode, a concrete event with all its dramatic causes, and by following it up minutely, and being bound to it. In short, he would have gained an advantage could he have found a subject to stick to.

Does American culture afford such a subject? It probably does not. After the seventeenth century the sophisticated history of the scholars came into fashion; our popular, legendary chronicles come down to us only from the remoter European past. It was a sound impulse on Crane's part to look for an American myth, some simple version of our past that lies near the center of the American consciousness; a heroic tale with just enough symbolism to give his mind both direction and play. The soundness of his purpose is witnessed also by the kind of history in the poem: it is inaccurate, and will not at all satisfy the sticklers for historical fact. It is the history of the motion picture, of naïve patriotism. This is sound; for it ignores the scientific ideal of historical truth-in-itself, and looks for a cultural truth which might win the spontaneous allegiance of the people. It is on such simple integers of truth, not of fact but of religious necessity, that men unite. The American mind was formed by the eighteenth-century Enlightenment, which broke down the European truths, and gave us a temper deeply hostile to the making of new religious truths of our own.

The impulse in *The Bridge* is religious, but the soundness of an impulse is no warrant that it will create a sound art form. The form depends on too many factors beyond the control of the poet. The age is scientific and pseudo-scientific, and our philosophy is John Dewey's instrumentalism. And it is possibly this circumstance that has driven the religious attitude into a corner where it lacks the right instruments for its defense and growth, and where it is in a vast muddle about just what these instruments are. Perhaps this disunity of the intellect is responsible for Crane's unphilosophical belief that the poet, unaided and isolated from the people, can create a myth.

If anthropology has helped to destroy the credibility of the myths, it has shown us how they rise; their growth is mysterious from the people as a whole. It is probable that no one man ever put myth into history. It is still a nice problem among higher critics whether the authors of the Gospels were deliberate myth-makers, or whether their minds were simply constructed that way; but the evidence favors the latter. Crane was a myth-maker, and in an age favorable to myths he would have written a mythical poem in the act of writing an historical one.

It is difficult to agree with those critics who find his epic a single poem, and as such an artistic success. It is a collection of lyrics, the best of which are not surpassed by anything in American literature. The writing is most distinguished when Crane is least philosophical, *when he writes from sensation.* "The River" has some blemishes toward the end, but by and large it is a masterpiece of order and style; it alone is enough to place Crane in the front rank of American poets, living or dead. Equally good, but less ambitious are the "Proem: to Brooklyn Bridge," and "Harbor Dawn," and "The Dance" from the section called "Powhatan's Daughter."

These poems bear only the loosest relation to the symbolic demands of the theme; they contain allusions to the historical pattern or extend the slender structure of analogy running through the poem. They are primarily lyrical, and each has its complete form. The poem "Indiana," written presumably to complete the pattern of "Powhatan's Daughter," does not stand alone, and is one of the most astonishing performances ever made by a poet of Crane's genius. "The Dance" gives us the American background for the coming white man, and "Indiana" carries the stream of history to the pioneer West. It is a nightmare of sentimentality. Crane is at his most "philosophical" in a theme in which he feels no poetic interest whatever.

The structural defect of *The Bridge* is due to this functional contradiction of purpose. In one of his best earlier poems, "The Wine Menagerie," he exclaims: "New Thresholds, new Anatomies!"—new sensation, but he could not subdue the new sensation to a symbolic form.

His pantheism is necessarily a philosophy of sensation without point of view. An epic is a judgment of human action, an implied evaluation of a civilization, a way of life. In *The Bridge* the civilization that contains the subway hell of the section called "The Tunnel" is the same civilization that contains the aeroplane that the poet apostrophizes in "Cape Hatteras": there is no reason why the subway should be a fitter symbol of damnation than the aeroplane: both were produced by the same mentality on the same moral plane. There is a concealed, meaningless analogy between, on the one hand, the height of the plane and the depth of the subway, and, on the other, "higher" and "lower" in the religious sense. At one moment Crane faces his predicament of blindness to any rational order of value, and knows that he is damned; but he cannot face it long, and he tries to rest secure upon the intensity of sensation.

To the vision of the abyss in "The Tunnel," a vision that Dante passed through midway of this mortal life, Crane had no alternative: when it became too harrowing he cried to his Pocahontas, a typically romantic and sentimental symbol:

> Lie to us—dance us back our tribal morn!

It is probably the most perfect word of romanticism in this century. When Crane saw that his leading symbol, the bridge, would not hold all the material of his poem, he could not sustain it ironically, in the classical manner, by probing its defects; nor in the personal sections, like "Quaker Hill," does he include himself in his Leopardian denunciation of life. He is the blameless victim of a world whose impurity violates the moment of intensity, which would otherwise be enduring and perfect. He is betrayed, not by a defect of his own nature, but by the external world; he asks of nature, perfection—requiring only of himself, intensity. The persistent, and persistently defeated pursuit of a natural absolute places Crane at the center of his age.

Alternately he asserts the symbol of the bridge and abandons it, because fundamentally he does not understand it. The idea of bridgeship is an elaborate blur leaving the inner structure of the poem confused.

Yet some of the best poetry of our times is in *The Bridge*. Its inner confusion is a phase of the inner cross-purposes of the time. Crane was one of those men whom every age seems to select as the spokesmen of its spiritual life; they give the age away. The accidental features of their lives, their place in life, their very heredity, seem to fit them for the rôle: even their vices contribute to their preparation. Crane's biographer will have to study the early influences that confirmed him in narcissism, and thus made him typical of the rootless spiritual life of our time. The character formed by those influences represents an immense concentration, and becomes almost a symbol, of American life in this age.

Crane's poetry has incalculable moral value: it reveals our defects in their extremity. I have said that he knew little of the history of his country. It was not a mere defect in education, but a defect, in the spiritual sense, of the modern mind. Professor Charles A. Beard has immense information about American history, but understands almost none of it: Crane lacked the sort of indisputable understanding of his country that a New England farmer has who has never been out of his township. *The Bridge* attempts to include all American life, but it covers the ground with seven-league boots, and like a sightseer, sees nothing. With reference to its leading symbol, it has no subject matter. The poem is the effort of a solipsistic sensibility to locate itself in the external world, to establish points of reference.

It seems to me that by testing out his capacity to construct a great objective piece of work, in which his definition of himself should have been perfectly articulated, he brought his work to an end. I think he knew that the structure of *The Bridge* was finally incoherent, and for that reason—as I have said— he could no longer believe in even his lyrical powers; he could not return to the early work and take it up where he had left off. Far from "refuting" Eliot, his whole career is a vindication of Eliot's major premise—that the integrity of the individual consciousness has broken down. Crane had, in his later work, no individual consciousness: the hard firm style of "Praise for an Urn," which is based upon a clear-cut perception of moral relations, and upon their ultimate inviolability, begins to disappear when the poet goes out into the world and finds that the simplicity of a child's world has no universal sanction. From then on, instead of the effort to define himself in the midst of almost overwhelming complications—a situation that might have produced a tragic poet—he falls back upon the intensity of consciousness, rather than clarity, for his center of vision. And that is romanticism.

His world had no center, and the compensatory action that he took is responsible for the fragmentary quality of his most ambitious work. This action took two forms, the blind assertion of the will, and the blind desire for self-destruction. The poet did not face his first problem, which is to define the limits of his personality and to objectify its moral implications in an appropriate symbolism. Crane could only assert a quality of will against the world, and at each successive failure of the will he turned upon himself. In the failure of understanding—and understanding, for Dante, was a way of love— the romantic modern poet of the age of science attempts to impose his will upon experience and to possess the world.

It is this impulse of the modern period that has given us the greatest romantic poetry: Crane instinctively continued the conception of the will that was the deliberate discovery of Rimbaud. A poetry of the will is a poetry of sensation, for the poet surrenders to his sensations of the object in his effort to identify himself with it, and to own it. Some of Crane's finest lyrics—those written in the period of *The Bridge*—carry the modern impulse as far as you will find it anywhere in the French romantics. "Lachrymae Christi" and "Passage," though on the surface made up of pure images without philosophical meaning of the sort explicit in *The Bridge,* are the lyrical equivalents of the epic: the same kind of sensibility is at work. The implicit grasp of his material that we find in "Praise for an Urn" the poet exchanged for an external, random symbol of which there is no possibility of realization. *The Bridge* is an irrational symbol of the will, of conquest, of blind achievement in space; its obverse is "Passage," whose lack of external symbolism exhibits the poetry of the will on the plane of sensation; and this is the self-destructive return of the will upon itself.

Criticism may well set about isolating the principle upon which Crane's poetry is organized. Powerful verse overwhelms its admirers, and betrays them into more than technical imitation. That is one of the arguments of Platonism against literature; it is the immediate quality of an art rather than its whole significance that sets up schools and traditions. Crane not only ends the romantic era in his own person; he ends it logically and morally. Beyond Crane no future poet can go. (This does not mean that the romantic impulse may not rise and flourish again.) The finest passages in his work are single moments in the stream of sensation; beyond the moment he goes at peril; for outside it there lies the discrepancy between the sensuous fact, the perception, and its organizing symbol—a discrepancy that plunges him into chaos and sentimentality. A true symbol has in it, within the terms of its properties, all the qualities that the artist is able to attribute to it. But the "bridge" is empty and static, it has no inherent content, and the poet's attribution to it of the qualities of his own moral predicament is arbitrary. That explains the fragmentary and often unintelligible framework of the poem. There was neither complete action nor ordered symbolism in terms of which the distinct moments of perception could be clarified.

This was partly the problem of Rimbaud. But Crane's problem was nearer to the problem of Keats, and *The Bridge* is a failure in the sense that *Hyperion* is a failure, and with comparable magnificence. Crane's problem, being farther removed from the epic tradition, was actually more difficult than Keats', and his treatment of it was doubtless the most satisfactory possible in our time. Beyond the quest of pure sensation and its ordering symbolism lies the total destruction of art. By attempting an extreme solution of the romantic problem, Crane proved that it cannot be solved.

From *Reactionary Essays on Poetry and Ideas* by Allen Tate, pp. 26–42. Charles Scribner's Sons. Copyright, 1936. Reprinted by permission of the author and publishers. First published, in part, in *The Hound and Horn,* Vol. V (July–September, 1932), pp. 612–619. Recently included in *On the Limits of Poetry* by Allen Tate (New York: Swallow Press & William Morrow & Co., 1948).

Ezra Pound
[1931]

and as for text we have taken it
from that of Messire Laurentius
and from a codex once of the Lords Malatesta . . .

ONE is not certain who Messire Laurentius was; one is not very certain that it makes no difference. Yet one takes comfort in the vast range of Mr. Pound's obscure learning, which no one man could be expected to know much about. In this great work[1] one is continually uncertain, as to space, time, history. The codex of the Lords Malatesta would be less disconcerting than Laurentius— if we were sure it existed—for more than half of the thirty cantos contain long paraphrases or garbled quotations from the correspondence, public and private, of the Renaissance Italians, chiefly Florentine and Venetian. About a third of the lines are versified documents. Another third are classical allusions, esoteric quotations from the ancients, fragments of the Greek poets with bits of the Romans thrown in; all magnificently written into Mr. Pound's own text. The rest is contemporary—anecdotes, satirical pictures of vulgar Americans, obscene stories, evenings in low Mediterranean dives, and gossip about amazing rogues behind the scenes of European power. The three kinds of material in the cantos are antiquity, the Renaissance, and the modern world. They are combined on no principle that seems in the least consistent to a first glance. They appear to be mixed in an incoherent jumble, or to stand up in puzzling contrasts.

This is the poetry which, in early and incomplete editions, has had more influence on us than any other of our times; it has had an immense "underground" reputation. And deservedly. For even the early reader of Mr. Pound could not fail to detect the presence of a new poetic form in the individual cantos, though the full value and intention of this form appears for the first time in the complete work. It is not that there is any explicit feature of the whole design that is not contained in each canto; it is simply that Mr. Pound must be read in bulk; it is only then that the great variety of his style and the apparent incoherence turn into order and form. There is no other poetry like the Cantos in English. And there is none quite so simple in form. The form is, in fact, so simple that almost no one has guessed it, and I suppose it will

[1] A Draft of XXX Cantos, by Ezra Pound. Paris: The Hours Press, 1930; New York: Farrar and Rinehart, 1933. Further installments of the Cantos appeared in the following years: A Draft of Cantos XXXI–XLI, The Fifth Decad of Cantos, etc., the latest being The Pisan Cantos (1948) and a complete collection of all the Cantos to date (also in 1948). (Editor's note, 1950.)

continue to puzzle, perhaps to enrage, our more academic critics for a generation to come. But this form by virtue of its simplicity remains inviolable to critical terms: even now it cannot be technically described.

I begin to talk like Mr. Pound, or rather like the way in which most readers think Mr. Pound writes. The secret of his form is this: conversation. The cantos are talk, talk, talk; not by anyone in particular to anyone else in particular; they are just rambling talk. At least each canto is a cunningly devised imitation of a polite conversation, in which no one presses any subject very far. The length of breath, the span of conversational energy, is the length of canto. The conversationalist pauses; there is just enough left hanging in the air to give him a new start; so that the transitions between the cantos are natural and easy.

Each canto has the broken flow and the somewhat elusive climax of a good monologue: because there is no single speaker, it is a many-voiced monologue. That is the method of the poems—though there is another quality of the form that I must postpone for a moment—and *that is what the poems are about.*

There are, as I have said, three subjects of conversation—ancient times, Renaissance Italy, and the present—but these are not what the cantos are about. They are not about Italy, nor about Greece, nor are they about us. They are not about anything. But they are distinguished poetry. Mr. Pound himself tells us:

> And they want to know what we talked about?
> > *"de litteris et de armis, praestantibus ingeniis,*
> Both of ancient times and our own; books, arms,
> And men of unusual genius
> Both of ancient times and our own, in short the usual subjects
> Of conversation between intelligent men."

II

There is nothing in the cantos more difficult than that. There is nothing inherently obscure; nothing too profound for any reader who has enough information to get to the background of all the allusions in a learned conversation. But there is something that no reader, short of some years of hard textual study, will understand. This is the very heart of the cantos, the secret of Mr. Pound's poetic character, which will only gradually emerge from a detailed analysis of every passage. And this is no more than our friends are constantly demanding of us; we hear them talk, and we return to hear them talk, and we return to hear them again, but we never know what they talk about; we return for that mysterious quality of charm that has no rational meaning that we can define. It is only after a long time that the order, the direction, the rhythm of the talker's mind, the logic of his character as distinguished from anything logical he may say—it is a long time before this begins to take on form for us. So with Mr. Pound's cantos. It is doubtless easier for us (who are trained in the more historic brands of poetry) when the poems are about God, Freedom, and Immortality, but there is no reason why poetry should not be so perplexingly simple as Mr. Pound's, and be about nothing at all.

The ostensible subjects of the cantos—ancient, middle, and modern times—are only the materials round which Mr. Pound's mind plays constantly; they are the screen upon which he throws a beautiful, flowing quality of poetic thought. Now in conversation the memorable quality is a sheer accident of character, and is not designed; but in the cantos the effect is deliberate, and from the first canto to the thirtieth the set tone is maintained without a single lapse.

It is this tone, it is this quality quite simply, which is the meaning of the cantos, and although, as I have said, it is simple and direct, it is just as hard to pin down, it is as hidden in its shifting details, as a running, ever-changing conversation. It cannot be taken out of the text; and yet the special way that Mr. Pound has of weaving his three materials together, of emphasizing them, of comparing and contrasting them, gives us a clue to the leading intention of the poems. I come to that quality of the form which I postponed.

The easiest interpretation of all poetry is the symbolic method: there are few poems that cannot be paraphrased into a kind of symbolism, which is usually false, being by no means the chief intention of the poet. It is very probable, therefore, that I am about to falsify the true simplicity of the cantos into a simplicity that is merely convenient and spurious. The reader must bear this in mind, and view the slender symbolism that I am going to read into the cantos as a critical shorthand, useful perhaps, but which when used must be dropped.

One of the finest cantos is properly the first. It describes a voyage:

> And then went down to the ship,
> Set keel to breakers, forth on the godly sea, and
> We set up mast and sail on that swart ship,
> Bore sheep aboard her, and our bodies also
> Heavy with weeping, and winds from sternward
> Bore us out onward with bellying canvas,
> Circe's this craft, the trim-coifed goddess.

They land, having come "to the place aforesaid by Circe"—whatever place it may be—and Tiresias appears, who says:

> "Odysseus
> Shalt return through spiteful Neptune, over dark seas,
> Lose all companions." And then Anticlea came.
> Lie quiet Divus. I mean, that is, Andreas Divus,
> In officina Wecheli, 1538, out of Homer.
> And he sailed, by Sirens and thence outward and away
> And unto Circe.

Mr. Pound's world is the scene of a great Odyssey, and everywhere he lands it is the shore of Circe, where men "lose all companions" and are turned into swine. It would not do at all to push this hint too far, but I will risk one further point: Mr. Pound is a typically modern, rootless, and internationalized intelligence. In the place of the traditional supernaturalism of the older and local cultures, he has a cosmopolitan curiosity which seeks out marvels, which are all equally marvelous, whether it be a Greek myth or the antics in Europe of a lady from Kansas. He has the bright, cosmopolitan *savoir faire* which refuses to be "taken in": he will not believe, being a traditionalist at bottom, that the "perverts, who have set money-lust before the pleasures of the senses," are better than swine. And ironically, being modern and a hater of modernity, he sees all history as deformed by the trim-coifed goddess.

The cantos are a book of marvels—marvels that he has read about, or heard of, or seen; there are Greek myths, tales of Italian feuds, meetings with strange people, rumors of intrigues of state, memories of remarkable dead friends like T. E. Hulme, comments on philosophical problems, harangues on abuses of the age; the "usual subjects of conversation between intelligent men."

It is all fragmentary. Now nearly every canto begins with a bit of heroic antiquity, some myth, or classical quotation, or a lovely piece of lyrical description in a grand style. It invariably breaks down. It trails off into a piece of contemporary satire, or a flat narrative of the rascality of some Italian prince. This is the special quality of Mr. Pound's form, the essence of his talk, the direction of these magnificent conversations.

For not once does Mr. Pound give himself up to any single story or myth. The thin symbolism from the Circe myth is hardly more than a leading tone, an unconscious prejudice about men which he is not willing to indicate beyond the barest outline. He cannot believe in any of them, not even in his own power of imagining them out to a conclusion. None of his myths is compelling enough to draw out his total intellectual resources; none goes far enough to become a belief or even a momentary faith. They remain marvels to be looked at, but they are meaningless, the wrecks of civilization. His powerful juxtapositions of the ancient, the Renaissance, and the modern worlds reduce all three elements to an unhistorical miscellany, timeless and without origin, and no longer a force in the lives of men.

III

And that is the peculiarly modern quality of Mr. Pound. There is a certain likeness in this to another book of marvels, those stories of late antiquity known to us as *The Golden Ass*. The cantos are a sort of *Golden Ass*. There is a likeness, but there is no parallel beyond the mere historical one: both books are the production of worlds without convictions and given over to a hard secular program. Here the similarity ends. For Mr. Pound is a powerful reactionary, a faithful mind devoted to those ages when the myths were not merely pretty, but true. And there is a cloud of melancholy irony hanging over the cantos. He is persuaded that the myths are only beautiful, and he drops them after a glimpse, but he is not reconciled to this estheticism: he ironically puts the myths against the ugly specimens of modern life that have defeated them. But neither are the specimens of modernity worthy of the dignity of belief:

> She held that a sonnet was a sonnet
> And ought never to be destroyed
> And had taken a number of courses
> And continued with hope of degrees and
> Ended in a Baptist learnery
> Somewhere near the Rio Grande.

I am not certain that Mr. Pound will agree with me that he is a traditionalist; nor am I convinced that Mr. Pound, for his part, is certain of anything under heaven but his genius for poetry. He is probably one of two or three living Americans who will be remembered as poets of the first order. Yet there is no reason to infer from that that Mr. Pound, outside his craft, or outside his conversation, knows in the least what he is doing or saying. He is and always has been in a muddle of revolution; and for some appalling reason he identifies his crusade with liberty—liberty of speech, liberty of press, liberty of conduct—in short, liberty. I do not mean to say that either Mr. Pound or his critic knows what liberty is. Nevertheless, Mr. Pound identifies it with civilization and intelligence, of the modern and scientific variety. And yet the ancient cultures, which he so much admires, were, from any modern viewpoint, hatched in barbarism and superstition. One is entitled to the suspicion that Mr. Pound prefers barbarism, and that by taking up the rôle of revolution against it he has bitten off his nose to spite his face. He is the confirmed enemy of provincialism, never suspecting that his favorite, Lorenzo the Magnificent, for example, was provincial to the roots of his hair.

This confusion runs through the cantos, and it makes the irony that I have spoken of to a certain extent unconscious. For as the apostle of humane culture, he constantly discredits it by crying up a rationalistic enlightenment. It would appear from this that his philosophical tact is somewhat feminine, and that, as intelligence, it does not exist. His poetic intelligence is of the finest: and if he doesn't know what liberty is, he understands poetry, and how to write it. This is enough for one man to know. And the thirty *Cantos* are enough to occupy a loving and ceaseless study—say a canto a year for thirty years, all thirty to be read every few weeks just for the tone.

From *Reactionary Essays on Poetry and Ideas* by Allen Tate, pp. 43–51. Charles Scribner's Sons. Copyright, 1936. Reprinted by permission of the author and publishers. First published as "Ezra Pound's Golden Ass" in *The Nation*, Vol. CXXXII (June 10, 1931), pp. 632–634. Recently included in *On the Limits of Poetry* by Allen Tate (New York: Swallow Press & William Morrow & Co., 1948).

KENNETH BURKE
Thomas Mann and André Gide
[1930]

WHEN Gustav von Aschenbach, the hero of Thomas Mann's *Death in Venice*, was about thirty-five years of age, he was taken ill in Vienna. During the course of a conversation, one keen observer said of him: "You see, Aschenbach has always lived like this," and the speaker contracted the fingers of his left hand into a fist; "never like this," and he let his hand droop comfortably from the arm of a chair. It is with such opening and closing of the hand that this essay is to deal.

In the early writings of both Mann and Gide the characters are exceptional, though always in keeping with our metaphor. Mann's concern is with serious and lonely fellows, deviations from type, who are over-burdened with a feeling of divergency from their neighbors. In stories like "Der Bajazzo" the deformations are more mental, but generally the subject is simplified by his imagining characters who are physically extravagant. There is Tobias Mindernickel, whose ill-dressed, gaunt, ungainly figure excites the persecution of all healthy children. He buys a little puppy, and names it Esau. They become inseparable, but one day Esau leaps for food, is accidentally wounded by a knife which Tobias is holding, whereupon Tobias nurses his puppy with great tenderness. After some days it is cured, it no longer lies gazing at him with bewildered, suffering eyes, it leaps down from its sick-bed, goes racing about with full delight in its puppyhood, with no thought that it is showing how it no longer needs Tobias's morbid tenderness. It is a cheerful little mutt—and maddened at his loss, Tobias plunges his knife into it again, then forlornly gathers its dying body in his arms. Similarly, there is the little Herr Friedemann, who, humble as he is, can by the course of his story be still further humiliated and, in the very act of taking his life, grovels. Mann also writes of an abnormally fat man, who worships his adulterous wife abjectly, and falls dead of apoplexy at a particularly comical moment, topples like a collapsing building, when he feels the full weight of the indignities which have been heaped upon him. And Piepsam, Herr Gottlob Piepsam, a decayed alcoholic, a victim of life if there ever was one, is insulted as he goes to visit the grave of his wife. On the path to the cemetery he is passed by a boy on a bicycle, the merest child who is too happy to be anything but well-meaning, yet Piepsam resents him and works himself into a fatal rage—the story being told fancifully, even cheerfully. After Piepsam has been bundled off in an ambulance, one feels how brightly the sun is shining.

These outsiders (Mann later took over the word "outsider" from the English) appear under many guises. They watch, they compare themselves with others to their own detriment, they are earnest to the point of self-disgust, and they are weighted with vague responsibilities. In "Tonio Kröger" the concept has matured. Tonio's divergencies are subtler. As a writer, he observes the unliterary with nostalgia. Vacillating by temperament, one might almost say vacillating by profession, he seeks simple people, who form for him a kind of retrogressive ideal. He does not fraternize with them, he spies upon them. A Bohemian, he distrusts Bohemianism. He watches these others, awed by the healthiness, or the ease, of their satisfaction. It is a kind of inverted praising, since he envies them for qualities which he himself has outgrown. And it is melancholy.

Against this earnestness, this non-conforming mind's constant preoccupation with conformity, we find in the early writings of Gide much the same rotten elegance as characterizes Wilde's *The Picture of Dorian Gray*. Religious thinking is perverted to produce an atmosphere of decay and sinfulness. There is the Baudelairean tendency to invoke Satan as redeemer. Even in a work as late as *Les Nourritures terrestres*, we find a crooked evangelism, calling us to vague and unnatural revelations. These artificial prophecies, with a rhetorical, homiletic accent which Gide has since abandoned, suggest a kind of morbid Whitmanism. In place of expansion across an unpeopled continent, we have a pilgrimage through old, decaying cities, erotic excitations at the thought of anonymity and freedom among the ruins of other cultures. The hero who cries out to Nathaniel is seeking, not the vigor of health, but the intensity of corruption. The mood, if I understand it correctly, has by now lost much of its immediacy, but in his later works Gide has shown it capable of great readaptation; what we find earlier, in an archaistic terminology, is subsequently transformed into something wholly contemporary.

The most thorough contrast between these writers probably arises from the juxtaposition of Mann's *Death in Venice* and Gide's *The Immoralist*. Gustav von Aschenbach is nationally respected as a master of his calling. Parts of his works are even among the prescribed reading of school children. His austerity, his "morality of production," is emphasized. Aschenbach has clearly erected a structure of external dignity in keeping with the sobriety, the earnestness, which he has brought to the business of writing. But he is now undergoing a period of enervation. He finds that he cannot tackle his page with the necessary zest. As a purely therapeutic measure, he permits himself a trip to Venice, and here becomes fascinated by a young Polish boy, Tadzio, who is living at the same hotel. In his shy and troubled contemplation of this boy he finds an absorption which is painful, but imperious. Von Aschenbach remains outwardly the man of dignity honored by his nation—he does not, as I recall, ever exchange a word with this Tadzio, whose freshness, liquidity, immaturity, are the sinister counterpart of the desiccation of Aschenbach's declining years. But inwardly he is *notwendig liederlich und Abenteurer des Gefühls.* Necessarily dissolute—an adventurer of the emotions—the words are Mann's, when discussing this book in his *Betrachtungen eines Unpolitischen* years afterwards. We thus find again the notion that the artist faces *by profession* alternatives which are contrary to society. The theme of Aschenbach's gloomy infatuation coexists with the theme of the plague—and we observe the elderly man's erotic fevers metamorphose gradually into the fevers of incipient cholera. A poignant and inventive passage describing his cosmetic treatment at the hands of a barber is followed by Aschenbach's delirious remembrance of lines from the *Phaedrus,* wherein Socrates is speaking words of courtship and metaphysics indiscriminately, a merging which Aschenbach makes more pronounced by his own diseased reworking of the Platonic dialogue. A few pages later "a respectably shocked world" receives the news of his death.

The same themes, sickness and sexual vagary, underlie Gide's *The Immoralist.* Michel, after being at the verge of death and being nursed by his bride into vigorous health, subtly drives her to her own grave. Throughout the novel he is profuse in his tenderness, he is almost hysterically attentive to her, but at the same time he is steadily destroying her—and during the final march of her illness he takes her on that savage pilgrimage from city to city which inevitably results in her death. There has been a young Arab on the fringes of this plot, an insolent fellow who first charmed Michel by stealing from his wife. The reader places him unmistakably as a motive in this unpunishable murder. Despite the parallelism between *Death in Venice* and *The Immoralist,* the emphasis is very different. Whereas in Mann we feel most the sense of resistance, of resignation to the point of distress, and Aschenbach's dissolution is matched by a constant straining after self-discipline, in Gide we hear a narrator who relates with more than pride, with something akin to positive advocacy, the unclean details of his life. *"Je vais vous parler longuement de mon corps,"* he opens one chapter in a tone which I sometimes regret he has seen fit to drop from his later work; there is no mistaking its connotations; it is the accent of evangelism, of pleading.

Buddenbrooks and *Lafcadio's Adventure* do not fall in corresponding stages of their author's developments. *Buddenbrooks,* a remarkably comprehensive realistic novel of life in North Germany, comes much earlier. But the same contrast in attitude is apparent. We might interpret *Buddenbrooks* as having the theme of "Tonio Kröger" greatly subtilized and ramified. This "fall of a family" through four generations is also the "growth of an artist" through four generations. What is lost in health and moral certitude is gained in questioning and conscientiousness, in social and esthetic sensitiveness, until we arrive at little Hanno the musician, who, like Aschenbach, finally mingles inspiration with disease, as we watch his improvisations become the first symptoms of the typhoid fever that is to result in his death. In *Lafcadio's Adventure*, however, we meet with a brilliant type of villainy, an "esthetic criminal" who commits crimes for pure love of the art. The character of Lafcadio is perhaps Gide's most remarkable discovery. It suggests a merging of Stendhal's Julien Sorel with those criminals of Dostoevsky whose transgressions are inexplicable from the standpoint of utilitarian purpose.

In *Lafcadio's Adventure* Gide makes a notable change in nomenclature, recasting his "corruption" in more characteristically contemporary molds of thought. The transgressions have become "secular," advancing from sin to crime. If theology remains, it is relegated to a more superficial function; it becomes background, the story being built about a swindle whereby certain picturesque crooks fleece Catholic pietists. Lafcadio, who remembers five uncles but no father, has placed villainy on a distinguished and difficult plane. The author endows him with accomplishments somewhat lavishly, perhaps even a bit credulously; he seems eager that our sympathies be with this experimenter in crime, who can look upon kindly and vicious acts as almost interchangeable:

The old woman with the little white cloud above her head, who pointed to it and said: "It won't rain today!" that poor shrivelled old woman whose sack I carried on my shoulders (he had followed his fancy of travelling on foot for four days across the Apennines, between Bologna and Florence, and had slept a night at Covigliajo) and whom I kissed when we got to the top of the hill . . . one of what the *curé* of Covigliajo would have called my "good actions." I could just as easily have throttled her—my hand would have been as steady—when I felt her dirty wrinkled skin beneath my fingers . . . Ah! how caressingly she stroked and dusted my coat collar and said *"figlio mio! carino!"* . . . I wonder what made my joy so intense when afterwards—I was still in a sweat—I lay down on the moss—not smoking though—in the shade of that big chestnut-tree. I felt as though I could have clasped the whole of mankind to my heart in my single embrace—or strangled it, for that matter.

We shall not reconstruct here that gratuitous murder which recommends the hero particularly to our attention when poor Fleurissoire, attracted by this pleasant-seeming lad, chooses to seat himself in the same compartment with him and unknowingly excites Lafcadio to homicidal criticism. Gide exacts a very complex reception on the part of the reader. He asks us to observe a moral outrage committed by a charming scoundrel to whose well-being we are considerably pledged. Fleurissoire is the butt of much injustice in this book but it is Lafcadio, insolent, despotic, with his mercurial slogan "what would happen if . . ." who earns our suffrage.

The war ends, the mythical post-war period begins, and Thomas Mann issues *The Magic Mountain,* Gide *The Counterfeiters.* Our contrast is by no means imperiled. Mann shows how for seven years, during his illness in the mountains, Hans Castorp has lain exposed to moral questionings. While each day observing his temperature and eating five enormous meals to combat the wastage of his phthisis, he is privileged to hear the grave problems of our culture aired by sparring critics, themselves diseased, who speak with much rhetorical and dialectic finish. In particular, a humanist and a Jesuit altercate for his benefit, until Mynheer Peeperkorn enters (a much grander version of Herr Klöterjahn in the story "Tristan") and routs them both by his inarticulate vitality. He is life, himself ailing, to be sure, but magnificent and overwhelming while he lasts—and Castorp's melancholy respect for him is, in a matured and complex form, Tonio Kröger's respect for the burghers whom he watched with aloof humility. Castorp has the attitude of a student. Under ordinary circumstances he would probably have been unthinking, but he is made sensitive by his illness and his seven years' elevation above the century. He amasses greater understanding chapter by chapter, or at least learns to play one statement against another—until once more we come to that bewildered fever which marks the close of both *Buddenbrooks* and *Death in Venice.* At the last, as we see him on the battlefield, advancing to the aimless business of slaughter, simplified, regimented, unquestioning, we comprehend his evasion. For years he has been uncertain—he now embraces the arbitrary certainty of war. "Moralism, pessimism, humor"—these three qualities, whose interrelation Mann himself has stressed, are the dominant traits of this momentous novel, a summarization book, a comprehensive and symbolic work to be included in the world's literature of last wills and testaments.

To turn from *The Magic Mountain* to *The Counterfeiters* is to turn from brooding to shrewdness. Cruelty, malice, sensuality, intrigue—such elements are assiduously welded into an entertaining volume, of much subtle literary satisfaction. The reader of *The Magic Mountain* may have to deal with the fruits of complexity on the part of the author, but he receives them simply. The reader of *The Counterfeiters* finds complexity unresolved—he is not even at liberty to differentiate between the absurd and the beautiful. He is left fluctuant, in great tenuousness of moral values. The book contains Gide's development from sin to crime, and reaffirms his sympathy with deviations from the average ethical stock.

Returning to Aschenbach, ill at the age of thirty-five in Vienna, we find ourselves with correspondences for the closed and opened hand. It seems that Mann, who himself has situated the mainspring of his work in conscientiousness, is like his protagonist Aschenbach, with the hand contracted. And Gide, whose works could readily be taken by the immature or the trivial as invitations to the most unscrupulous kinds of living, who masters an air of suave corruption beyond any possible corrupt act, Gide can be the hand relaxed. *Gewissenhaftigkeit, Einsamkeit*—loneliness, the sense of responsibility—are Mann's words; but as the most distinctive device for Gide, I would quote from his Journal the triptych: *"nouveauté, vice, art."*

Our primary purpose, however, in establishing this distinction between the conscientious and the corrupt is to destroy it. One need not read far in the writings of Gide to discover the strong ethical trait which dominates his thinking. Perhaps no other modern writer has quoted the New Testament so frequently, or shown such readiness to settle secular issues by formulas drawn from religion. His critical work on Dostoevsky, with its theological distinction between the psychology of humility and the psychology of humiliation, is throughout an exercise in moral sensitiveness. And his Lafcadio is a mass of categorical imperatives. We learn from entries in his diary how, with the athleticism of an anchorite, he plunges a knife into his side for penance, one thrust "for having beaten Protos at chess," another thrust "for having answered before Protos," four thrusts "for having cried at hearing of Faby's death." Faby was one of his "uncles." Protos was his master in adventure, his accomplished rival, and Lafcadio punished himself, it seems, for not having been disdainful enough to let Protos win. Lafcadio's lamentable conduct might even be derived from an excess of scruples, though these scruples are peculiar to himself.

"I began to feel," Gide has written on this subject in his autobiography, *Si le Grain ne meurt,* "that perhaps all men's obligations were not the same, and that God himself might well abhor the uniformity which nature protests but towards which the Christian ideal seems to lead us in aiming to bring nature under control. I could concede none but an individual morality, its imperatives sometimes in conflict with those of other moralities. I was persuaded that each person, or at least each one of the elect, had to play a rôle on earth, which was wholly his own and did not resemble any other. And every attempt to submit to a general rule became treason in my eyes, yes, treason which I likened to that great unpardonable sin against the Holy Ghost, since the individual lost his precise, irreplaceable significance, his 'savor.' "

We should also consider Gide's *Strait is the Gate,* which constructs a sympathetic idyll out of the perverse rigors of chastity. As Alissa is courted by Jerome, the two progress into a difficult relationship, obscuring their sensual attraction in a state of pietistic exaltation. Jerome seeks her patiently and unerringly—and with the vocabulary of nobility she beckons to him while continually delaying the time of their union. At first she can offer logical pretexts for this delay, but as they are one by one removed she retreats behind the subterfuges of her faith, and with the assistance of Biblical quotations, morbidly chosen, she remains to the end difficult, pure, intact, a treasure, while loving Jerome with hysterical effusiveness. From the standpoint of its genesis the book is doubtless a companion piece to *The Immoralist*. Both are perverse studies in the frustration of heterosexual union, the one with the connotations of corruption, the other with connotations of great conscientiousness. When bringing them together, we see that Alissa's moral sensitiveness was no greater than that of Michel. Similarly we should recall in *The Counterfeiters* the brutal letter which the bastard Bernard Profitendieu writes to his nominal father, a dutifully vicious letter, and the first step, we might say, in the growth of Bernard's affection.

Has not Mann, on the other hand, spoken with fervor of a "sympathy with the abyss," an admitting of the morally chaotic, which he considers not merely the prerogative, but the duty, of the artist? Aschenbach is committed to conflict: whatever policy he decides upon for his conduct, he must continue to entertain disintegrating factors in contemplation. That practical "virtuous" procedure which silences the contrary is not allowed him. He must contain dissolution. In "the repellent, the diseased, the degenerate," Mann situates the ethical. Distinguishing between the moral and the virtuous, he finds that the moralist is "exposed to danger" and "resists no evil." As essential components of art he names "the forbidden, the adventurous, scrutiny, and self-abandonment." Defining sin as doubt, he pleads for sinfulness. His work might be called an epistemology of dignity, for he never relinquishes the love of dignity, and never ceases to make the possession of it difficult.

Mann has defined the problematical as the proper sphere of art ("art is the problematical sphere of the human"). In any event, the problematical is the sphere of his own art. Implicit in his work there is a cult of conflict, a deliberate entertaining of moral vacillation, which could not permit a rigid standard of judgments. He has said that the artist must contain his critic, must recognize the validity of contraries. This attitude could make such simple certainty as moral indignation impossible. It would imply exposure to mutually exclusive codes of conduct, diverse modes of behavior. Esthetically, as he himself has said, he finds the unification of this attitude in irony, which merges the sympathetic and antipathetic aspects of any subject. Unlike the satirist, the standpoint of the ironist is shifting—he cannot maintain a steady attack—by the standards of military morale he is treacherous; he belittles the things he lives for, and with melancholy praises what he abandons. He is equally tentative towards *Leben*, life, nature, and *Geist*, spirit, the intellectual order erected above life. The vigor of the pamphleteer is denied him. To the Rooseveltian mind he is corrosive—wherefore that "sympathy with the abyss" which anyone of rigid criteria, of sure distinctions between the admirable and the reprehensible, must feel as corrupting, and which Mann himself, ap-

proaching from the attitude of alien criticism, chose to designate as "dissolute."
The ironist is essentially impure, even in the chemical sense of purity, since
he is divided. He must deprecate his own enthusiasms, and distrust his own
resentments. He will unite waveringly, as the components of his attitude,
"dignity, repugnance, the problematical art."

To the slogan-minded, the ralliers about a flag, the marchers who convert
a simple idea into a simple action, he is an "outsider." Yet he must observe
them with nostalgia, he must feel a kind of awe for their fertile assurance,
even while remaining on the alert to stifle it with irony each time he discovers
it growing in unsuspected quarters within himself. It will continue to rise
anew, for man has a tremendous fund of certainty—and one will find only
too little of Mann's best ironic manner in his essays written during the war,
or will find it without its counterpart of melancholy. Yet I grant that the
slogans of his opponents were enough to infuriate any subtle man in his position; the temporary disorientation which turned him away from the ironist
and towards the pamphleteer is readily understandable. In *The Magic Mountain*, however, the author has recovered from his citizenship to become again
the artist. Castorp descends, not to a specific European war, but to regimenta-
tion, to the relief, even the suicidal relief, of the slogan-minded. He, the hero,
represents the ultimate betrayal of his author's own most serious message.
After years of vacillation he seeks the evasion of a monastery, though in these
secular days, when the power of theology has dwindled, the dogmatic certainties for which people are burned will more often be those of patriotism,
and the equivalent of churchly penance becomes the advance in numbers
under arms.

What Mann does with irony, Gide parallels with experimentalism, with
curiosity. He views any set code of values with distrust, because it implies
the exclusion of other codes. He speculates as to "what would happen if . . ."
He is on guard lest the possible be obscured by the real. In his autobiography
we find him, characteristically, considering a whole civilization gratuitously
different from our own:

"I thought of writing the imaginary history of a people, a nation, with wars,
revolutions, changes of administration, typical happenings. . . . I wanted
to invent heroes, sovereigns, statesmen, artists, an artistic tradition, an apocryphal literature, explaining and criticising movements, recounting the evolution of forms, quoting fragments of masterpieces. . . . And all to what purpose? To prove that the history of man could have been different—our
habits, morals, customs, tastes, judgments, standards of beauty could have all
been different—and yet the humanity of mankind would remain the same."

By recalling *Gulliver's Travels*, we see again how far removed we are from
satire. Perhaps, in a much simpler and more lyrical form, Gide did write this
book. I refer to *La Symphonie pastorale*, where he speculates upon a world

foreign to him, an arbitrary world so far as this author is concerned, the world of blindness. He even contrives to forget his own knowledge, as when his blind heroine, trying to meditate her way into the world of sight, surmises that sunlight must be like the humming of a kettle.

Perhaps one may interpret Gide's "corruption" too literally. I do not believe that his work can be evaluated properly unless we go beyond the subject-matter to the underlying principles. His choice of material even implies a certain obscurantism, assuming a sophistication on the part of the reader whereby the reader would not attempt too slavishly to become the acting disciple of his author's speculations. Surely Gide would be the first to admit that we could not build a very convenient society out of Lafcadios, however admirable they are. I should take the specific events in Gide as hardly more than symbols: their parallel in life would not be the enacting of similar events, but the exercising of the complex state of mind which arises from the contemplation of such events with sympathy. To live a life like the life in Gide's books would be to commit under another form the very kind of exclusion which he abhors—Lafcadio is for the pious, he is not for poisoners and forgers. Nor must one, in placing this author's malice, forget his *Travels in the Congo,* with its protests against the systematic injustice meted out to the Negroes at the hands of the concessionaires.[1]

Irony, novelty, experimentalism, vacillation, the cult of conflict—are not these men trying to make us at home in indecision, are they not trying to humanize the state of doubt? A philosopher has recently written of this new wilderness we now face, a wilderness not of nature, but of social forces. Perhaps there is an evasion, a shirking of responsibility, in becoming certain too quickly, particularly when our certainties involve reversions to an ideology which has the deceptive allurement of tradition. To seek the backing of the past may be as cowardly as to seek the backing of the many, and as flattering to our more trivial needs of conformity. Need people be in haste to rebel against the state of doubt, when doubt has not yet permeated the organs of our body, the processes of our metabolism, the desire for food and companion-ship, the gratification with sun and water? There is a large reserve of physical unquestioning, and until we find this reserve itself endangered by the humiliation of tentative living and unauthoritative thinking, are we compelled to reach out impetuously for set criteria? Since the body is dogmatic, a generator

---

[1] It is doubtful, I grant, whether Gide arrived at his useful position through wholly untrammelled motives. The Olympian result shows traces of troubled, Orphic beginnings. It seems likely that his concern with homosexuality, and his struggle for its "recognition," early gave him a sense of divergence from the social norms among which he lived, and in time this sense of divergence was trained upon other issues. In seeking, let us say, to defend a practice which society generally considered reprehensible, he came to defend practices which society considered more reprehensible—as a child who resented a cruel father might end by slaying the king.

of belief, society might well be benefited by the corrective of a disintegrating art, which converts each simplicity into a complexity, which ruins the possibility of ready hierarchies, which concerns itself with the problematical, the experimental, and thus by implication works corrosively upon those expansionistic certainties preparing the way for our social cataclysms. An art may be of value purely through preventing a society from becoming too assertively, too hopelessly, itself.

From *Counter-Statement* by Kenneth Burke, pp. 116–135. Harcourt, Brace and Company, Inc. Copyright, 1931. Reprinted by permission of Harcourt, Brace and Company, Inc. First published in *The Bookman,* Vol. LXXI (June, 1930), pp. 257–264.

W. H. AUDEN
Makers of Modern Poetry

A KNIGHT OF THE INFINITE
(Gerard Manley Hopkins)
[1944]

BIOGRAPHIES of the great masters are unnecessary. Living in humdrum domestic bliss with their gifts, their huge families are their whole story. Resembling each other more than they resemble anyone else, their lives seem too atypical to illuminate either their age or the human heart. The artists whom we want to know personally, and Hopkins is one, are those whose relation to their art is romantically difficult, full of rows, infidelities, miscarriages, strain, and Miss Ruggles deserves our thanks for a neat, competent job.[1] Both as an eccentric poet and as a Jesuit, Hopkins invites an all-or-none response, but she manages remarkably well to keep her balance. Apart from a few careless phrases out of the Poetry Appreciation Class, e.g., "the stanzas seem to rock and rend themselves in a long ecstatic intolerable shudder, an all but physical movement," her comments on his poems are sensible and suggestive, and in her treatment of his faith, she has so far succeeded in concealing her own beliefs that this reader may be quite wrong in suspecting that she finds Jowett more congenial than Pusey.

There are two eternal classes of men, the Knight and the Bourgeois, Don Quixote and Sancho Panza, Holmes and Watson, Pascal and Montaigne, the man who is capable of excess, and the man who is not. Each needs the other: the Knight needs the Bourgeois to nurse him and laugh at him, the Bourgeois needs the Knight as a subject for absolute devotion. Alone, since the former can never remember the finite and the latter can never perceive the infinite, each becomes a killer, the Knight by violence because he begins to despise life, the Bourgeois by sneers because he begins to fear death.

The pure types, the ideal comradeship, are, of course, to be found only in books, but in fuzzy, faint forms they occur quite often in real life, and the friendship of Hopkins and Bridges is one example.

[1] *Gerard Manley Hopkins: A Life,* by Eleanor Ruggles. New York: W. W. Norton · & Company, 1944.

Bridges was a poet and if it has always been difficult for a poet not to think of himself as a Knight—since the Romantic movement it has become almost impossible—how could a refined esthete, educated at Eton and Oxford, be, nevertheless, a Sancho Panza? Bridges' devotion, therefore, to a man whose heroic rejection of the esthetic he could not understand, his preservation and publication of greater poems than his own which it lay completely in his power to suppress, is extraordinary and enormously to his credit. Hopkins' other friend, Dixon, was a minor Knight, so that their relationship is less surprising but more touching. "Can I do anything? I have said something of the institution of your society in my next volume of Church history, which is not yet published. I could very well give an abrupt footnote about your poems, if you thought good. You may think it odd for me to propose to introduce you into the year 1540, but I know how to do it." The lance is only an umbrella, but the voice is Don Quixote's.

The affectionate exasperation of the Bourgeois is one form in which the Knight finds the necessary corrective for his excess; another is the impersonal discipline of an order, military or monastic, and among such, the most uncompromising is the Society of Jesus. It is unequivocally Catholic, yet prefers as recruits those who by nature are protestant, not conformist; hence its double insistence that the will shall be surrendered, but that the surrender shall be a free choice. It demands the monastic virtues of chastity and poverty, and then demands as well the military virtues of an active life in the world; hence its exercises in the *use* of images, in contrast to the conventional contemplative training in their rejection.

Compared with his fellow-novice Kerr, a cheerful old bruiser and Crimean veteran, Hopkins, unbusinesslike, rather sissy, must have seemed to his superiors unpromising material, and very probably they shook their heads over him to the end. It cannot, after all, have been easy for the officials of an order founded to preach and teach, to be enthusiastic over one who from the pulpit compared the seven sacraments of Mother Church to the seven teats of a milch-cow, and in the classroom, "from a quixotic sense of justice towards members who failed to attend, refused to allow his examination questions to refer to his lectures, so that students only came to find out what would not be set."

What the Society of Jesus did for Hopkins is clearer: it did not make him happy—only Wales could do that—it prevented him from writing much and from finishing even the little he did get written, but it turned an esthete, no better or worse than half a dozen bright young men of the sixties and seventies, into a serious and unique artist.

In the child who wailed when shut up with his sick brother, "Cyril has become so ugly," one hears the voice of Wilde; in the undergraduate's journal, "She had made a call, she had met the Miss Finlayson, she had

done some shopping, she had been round half the place and seen the naked-
ness of the land, and now it struck her how hateful was Clapham. Especially
she abominated the Berlin woolshop," the voice of Firbank; and there are
lines in his weaker poems like "The Bugler's First Communion," which show
how constantly he had to struggle against that confusion of the religious
with the erotic to which Whitman succumbed. Again, there was in Hopkins,
as in most people whose senses are abnormally acute, an impulse towards
their *dereglement*. To a skinny boy who, to compare his endurance with a
shipwrecked sailor's can go without water for a week (some say three), the
road that Masoch and Sade took is always open. It is precisely to such natures
that Loyola's exercises are designed to give meaning and purpose, and "The
Wreck of the Deutschland" is Hopkins' witness to their success.

Miss Ruggles points out how directly much of that poem derives from his
experiences as a novice in his Long Retreat. The objective wreck of the ship
is counterpointed with the subjective breaking of the self-loving will. (Someone could make a comparative study of "The Deutschland" with other poems
dealing with disastrous sea-trips, like "Un Voyage à Cythère," or "Le Voyage"
of Baudelaire, and with the death of the self, like Rimbaud's *Une Saison en
Enfer*.)

Miss Ruggles also draws attention to the intellectual support that the neglected philosophy of Duns Scotus gave to Hopkins' feeling for esthetic
uniqueness. Here, as in so much else, Hopkins was ahead of fashion, and
translators from the German *Existenz* school might, for instance, find a worse
equivalent than *inscape* for that stumper *Dasein*.

He didn't matter: he had a silly face; he was a martyr to piles; he bored
his congregations and was a joke to his students; he fiddled around with
Egyptian and with Welsh and with Gregorian music; he wrote a few poems
which his best friends couldn't understand and which would never be published; after forty-four years he died. Yes, like Don Quixote. His poems gloss
over none of the suffering and defeat, yet when we read them, as when we
read Cervantes, the final note is not the groan of a spiritual Tobacco Road,
but the cry of gratitude which Hopkins once heard a cricketer give for a
good stroke, "Arrah, sweet myself!"

From *The New Republic,* Vol. CXI (August 21,
1944), pp. 223–224. Reprinted by permission
of the author and editors.

HERETICS

(Rimbaud and Lawrence)

[1939]

A COMPARISON of these two books proves very clearly the impossibility of writing about someone you dislike.[1] Miss Starkie is just as critical of her subject as Mr. Tindall is of his—she whitewashes nothing—but she loves Rimbaud and he does not love Lawrence. Pascal regarded Montaigne as an enemy, but he recognized his greatness; whereas when one has finished reading Mr. Tindall, one feels: "If that is all that Lawrence was, why bother to write a whole book about him?"

It is not that Mr. Tindall's remarks are unjust or untrue; they are acute as far as they go, but nowhere does he give any sign of recognizing that Lawrence was not only, like thousands of others, a neurotic, but also a uniquely gifted writer who owes his influence for good or evil to his gift. It is significant that Mr. Tindall concentrates on the novels and philosophical works, pays a grudging tribute to the travel books but does not discuss them, and ignores completely the poems and short stories, which are Lawrence's best work. Lawrence thought of himself primarily as a poet, and said that he wrote the novels mainly for money. One may reasonably argue that, gifted or not, he was a heretic whose pernicious influence must be destroyed, but any study of heresy requires a definition of orthodoxy, and on that subject Mr. Tindall is reticent; the most that emerges is a sort of nineteenth-century liberal rationalism, which is by now a very vulnerable position.

Miss Starkie's interest in Rimbaud as a poet makes such a statement on her part less necessary, but as a matter of fact it emerges far more clearly. Her general thesis, though elaborated with all the detailed scholarship which her study of Baudelaire has led one to expect from her, is simple: Rimbaud conceived of the poet as a pure *voyant,* and of poetry as a mystical exercise through which he could become God. When he realized that, however far one may push the disorganization of the senses, the self cannot be eliminated from the creative act, he abandoned writing and attempted self-annihilation by leading what he imagined to be the "ordinary" life, but his idea of this was as extravagant as his previous overvaluation of poetry. Miss Starkie brings out very clearly the pathetic inefficiency of his later years; as a man of action he was a self-tortured failure, for no one can live by will alone.

Mr. Tindall sees Lawrence as a romantic irrationalist intent on the founding of a private religion, and condemns him for not separating his art from his

[1] *Arthur Rimbaud,* by Enid Starkie. New York: W. W. Norton & Company, 1939, and *D. H. Lawrence and Susan His Cow,* by William York Tindall. New York: Columbia University Press, 1939.

beliefs. If we must have religion, he would rather it were kept in church where it can do no harm. I do not believe such a separation is possible. Lawrence's beliefs were certainly heretical, but so were the beliefs of the mechanistic science from which they were a reaction. Lawrence is artistically successful where they fail, and vice versa. No writer has been more illuminating about birds, beasts and flowers; few have been sillier about those areas of human life where conscious planning is necessary.

At any moment in history there always is an orthodoxy, i.e., the sum of human knowledge forms an interdependent whole, but today the specialization of function inseparable from an industrialized society makes its conscious formulation extremely difficult. One method of approach is through a study of eccentric deviations, of their differences and resemblances: to such an approach Mr. Tindall will be useful but Miss Starkie indispensable.

Rimbaud and Lawrence have much in common. Both their mothers married beneath them, both had mother-fixations, both combined a personal messianic arrogance with attacking Christian individualism, both were attracted by Eastern mysticism and primitive peoples, both were inveterate wanderers. But there are significant differences. Rimbaud was born a Catholic in an anti-clerical country at a time when dogmatic scientific materialism was still unchallenged; Lawrence was born a non-conformist, and, by the time he reached maturity, science had abandoned all claim to give an objective picture of reality. While Rimbaud went from extreme individualism, a belief in poetry and a mystic technique, to an extreme collectivism and a belief in engineering and textbooks, from the Cabala to Comte, Lawrence changed essentially little during his life. To understand either, one must see them as sensitive individuals in an atomized industrial society, seeking an orthodoxy, a universally valid faith. Their protest against the atomization is linked to a belief that science was responsible.

When the Catholic world picture was replaced by the Protestant, science took over the public worlds of neutral matter, and art and religion the individual private worlds of value and emotion. However much they might grumble, the early romantics were really content enough; they had their worlds to themselves. But by Rimbaud's time both worlds were already overpopulated and demanding *Lebensraum*. Science, biology in particular, was invading art and religion, and the rhetorical romanticism of de Musset was no longer possible. Poetry was being pushed closer and closer toward the dark corner of the unconscious where, since expression is a conscious activity, it would be impossible to write. Unless an *Anschluss* of the two worlds took place which would enable men to "enjoy truth in one body and soul," art must perish. Rimbaud saw this and gave up art for activism; Verlaine did not, and I think that this was the basic reason which made their marriage impossible.

But just when its complete victory seemed assured, science voluntarily re-treated. Hitherto it had confidently affirmed that its truth was objectively real and independent of all considerations of human value and feeling. Now it came more and more to regard its statements not as eternal truths but as "as if" conveniences for organizing its experience. In his extremely important Harvard lectures, recently published under the title, *The Place of Value in a World of Fact,* Professor Köhler has a dream encounter with a modern physicist:

"What is an electron?" he asks.

"A volume of space that resists the approach of more electrons and attracts protons."

"What is a proton?"

"A volume of space that resists the approach of more protons and attracts electrons."

"But what is in these volumes?"

"I could not tell you. Nobody knows."

This is worse than Henry James dialogue. And on every part the attack on objectivity has been carried on, by the Marxists, by the psychoanalysts, by the anthropologists.

Encouraged by this, the poets recovered their nerve. In a curious way the relative positions of poetry and science became reversed; now it was the scientists who showed the caution and self-criticism of Mathew Arnold, while the poets displayed all the dogmatic self-confidence, the *concupiscence d'esprit* of T. H. Huxley. Lawrence, striking his solar plexus as someone tried to ex-plain to him the Copernican theory, and crying, "But I don't feel it here," is typical of the new attitude. So is modern political propaganda. Works like *A Fantasia of the Unconscious* or Yeats's *A Vision* are not humble attempts at private myths, but are designed as the new and only science. Seeing the abuses of our civilization and ascribing them, quite wrongly, to science, they imagine at the same time that science has rejected itself and given its blessing to a nihilistic subjectivism. This is untrue. Modern science is be-coming more and more isomorphic: it sees the subject-object relation as an indissoluble unity. If the nature of the subject determines its perception of the object, the nature of the subject is equally determined by the existence of the object. The formulation of truth can never be absolute, but neither is truth nonexistent nor anything we like to make it.

In his essays on Wagner and Freud, Thomas Mann points out that a backward looking toward the night, the folk-soul, death, can be not only reactionary but also an indispensable preparation for a new step forward. The effect of this attraction depends upon whether or not it is harnessed to a will to serve enlightenment. Artists are always vulnerable to reaction be-cause, unlike science, art has no objective practical end to control its excesses.

The only corrective for the artist lies within himself, not in his gift, which is neutral to reaction or progress, but in his self-knowledge of his weaknesses and the abdication of the desire to avenge them. Goethe was the last individual to attempt to formulate an orthodoxy, to effect a synthesis of human knowledge. Today such a thing is impossible: it is idle to suppose that the dialects of the various specialists will ever coalesce into a common tongue, but we shall not despair if we realize that they are all only different angles of approach to the same single field, and that among these techniques art has a responsible and not unimportant place.

From The New Republic, Vol. C (November 1, 1939), pp. 373–374. Reprinted by permission of the author and editors.

THE POET OF THE ENCIRCLEMENT

(Rudyard Kipling)

[1943]

ART, as the late Professor R. G. Collingwood pointed out, is not Magic, i.e., a means by which the artist communicates or arouses his feelings in others, but a mirror in which they may become conscious of what their own feelings really are: its proper effect, in fact, is disenchanting.

By significant details it shows us that our present state is neither as virtuous nor as secure as we thought, and by the lucid pattern into which it unifies these details, its assertion that order is *possible,* it faces us with the command to make it *actual.* In so far as he is an artist, no one, not even Kipling,[1] is intentionally a magician. On the other hand, no artist, not even Eliot, can prevent his work being used as magic, for that is what all of us, highbrow and lowbrow alike, secretly want Art to be. Between the schoolmaster who quoted "If," and the undergraduate who quoted "The Waste Land," there was not so much difference. Had the former really read his poem, he would have had to say, "Yes, *if.* Unfortunately, I do not keep my head . . . etc. I realize now that I am not a man." Instead, of course, he said, "Admirably put. That's exactly what the boys need to realize." Similarly, had the undergraduate really read his poem, he would have had to say: "Now I realize I am not the clever young man I thought, but a senile hermaphrodite. Either I must recover or put my head in the gas-stove." Instead, of course, he said, "That's wonderful. If only they would read this, Mother would understand why I

---

[1] *A Choice of Kipling's Verse.* Made by T. S. Eliot with an Essay on Rudyard Kipling. New York: Charles Scribner's Sons, 1943.

can't stay home nights, and Father would understand why I can't hold a job."

If today the war makes people discover that Kipling is good, it will be an excellent thing, but if at the same time they start saying that Eliot is "defeatist," it will prove that they have not discovered a poet, but only changed their drug to suit the new climate.

In his essay, Mr. Eliot draws a distinction between poetry and verse:

For other poets—at least, for some other poets—the poem may begin to shape itself in fragments of musical rhythm, and its structure will first appear in terms of something analogous to musical form. . . . What fundamentally distinguishes his (Kipling's) "verse" from "poetry" is the subordination of musical interest. . . . There is a harmonics of poetry which is not merely beyond the range of the poems —it would interfere with the intention.

This distinction is real and neatly describes the difference between the kind of poetry written by Eliot and the kind written by Kipling, but, so defined, there are more verse or ballad writers and fewer poets, I think, than Mr. Eliot seems to imply. Ben Jonson, for instance, who wrote out a prose draft which he then versified, Dunbar, Butler's *Hudibras,* most of Burns, Byron's *Don Juan,* etc.

I mention this only because I agree with Mr. Eliot that Kipling is an odd fish, but doubt if his capacity to write great verse is a sign of this.

What is it then, that makes Kipling so extraordinary? Is it not that while virtually every other European writer since the fall of the Roman empire has felt that the dangers threatening civilization came from *inside* that civilization (or from inside the individual consciousness), Kipling is obsessed by a sense of dangers threatening from *outside?*

Others have been concerned with the corruptions of the big city, the *ennui* of the cultured mind; some sought a remedy in a return to Nature, to childhood, to Classical Antiquity; others looked forward to a brighter future of liberty, equality and fraternity: they called on the powers of the subconscious, or prayed for the grace of God to inrupt and save their souls; they called on the oppressed to arise and save the world. In Kipling there is none of this, no nostalgia for a Golden Age, no belief in Progress. For him civilization (and consciousness) is a little citadel of light surrounded by a great darkness full of malignant forces and only maintained through the centuries by everlasting vigilance, will-power and self-sacrifice. The philosophers of the Enlightenment shared his civilization-barbarism antithesis, but their weapon was reason, i.e., coming to consciousness, whereas for Kipling too much thinking is highly dangerous, an opening of the gates to the barbarians of melancholia and doubt. For him the gates are guarded by the conscious Will (not unlike the Inner Check of Irving Babbitt).

Poem after poem, under different symbolic disguises, presents this same situation of the danger without, the anxiety of encirclement—by inanimate forces, the Picts beyond the Roman Wall:

> No indeed! We are not strong
>   But we know Peoples that are.
> Yes, and we'll guide them along
>   To smash and destroy you in War.
> We shall be slaves just the same,
>   Yes, we have always been slaves,
> But you—you will die of the shame,
>   And then we shall dance on your graves.

The Danes, the Dutch, the Huns, the "new-caught sullen peoples, half devil and half child," even the Female of the Species—by inanimate forces, Karela, the club-footed vine, the sea:

> Coming, like stallions they paw with their hooves,
>   going, they snatch with their teeth,

the ice

> Once and again as the Ice came South
> The glaciers ground over Lossiemouth

and by Spiritual Powers:

> They builded a tower to shiver the sky and wrench
>   the stars apart,
> Till the Devil grunted behind the bricks: "It's
>   striking, but is it Art?"

> Very softly down the glade runs a waiting watching shade
> And the whisper spreads and widens far and near,
> And the sweat is on thy brow, for he passes even now—
> He is Fear, O little Hunter, he is Fear.

It is noteworthy that the *interested* spirits are all demonic; the Divine Law is aloof.

Given such a situation, the important figure in society is, of course, the man on guard, and it is he who, in one form or another, from the sentry on the Afghanistan frontier to the gardener

> Grubbing weeds from gravel paths with broken dinner knives

is the Kipling hero. Unlike the epic hero, he is always on the *defensive.* Thus Kipling is interested in engineering, in the weapons which protect man against the chaotic violence of nature, but not in physics, in the intellectual *discovery* that made the weapons possible.

His ethics and his politics are those of a critical emergency, which is why it is impossible to classify them under conventional party labels, for they presuppose a state where differences of opinion are as irrelevant as they are to a soldier in a foxhole, and, in so far as they apply at all, apply to everyone, Democrat, Nazi or Communist.

Of the guardians, Kipling has profound understanding. He knows that most of them are prodigal sons, given to drink and fornication, acquainted with post-dated checks, now cruel, now sentimental, and he does not try to present them as nice people. But when he turns from them to the Sons of Mary whom they are paid to guard (the shift from religious to social meaning is significant), his vision becomes dim and his touch uncertain, for his interest is not really in them, but only in their relation to the sons of Martha, so that what he sees is either too soft, the exile's nostalgic daydream of Mom and the roses round the door, or too hard, the sentry's resentful nightmare of the sleek and slack stay-at-homes dining and wining while he and his sufferings are forgotten.

Kipling has been rightly praised for his historical imagination, but it is questionable if historical is the right word. If by history we mean *irreversible* temporal changes as contrasted with the cyclical and reversible changes of Nature, then Kipling's imaginative treatment of the past is an affirmation of Nature and a denial of History, for his whole concern is to show that the moment of special emergency is everlasting:

> As it will be in the future, it was at the birth of Man—
> There are only four things certain since Social Progress began.
> That the Dog returns to his Vomit and the Sow returns to her Mire,
> And the Burnt Fool's bandaged finger goes wabbling back to the Fire.

But if Nature and History are the same, how can Nature and Man, the Jungle and the City, be opposed to each other, as Kipling is clearly certain that they are? If one asks him "What is civilization?" he answers, "The People living under the Law, who were taught by their fathers to discipline their natural impulses and will teach their children to do the same":

> This we learned from famous men,
>   Knowing not its uses,
> When they showed, in daily work
> Man must finish off his work—
> Right or wrong his daily work
> And without excuses

in contrast to the barbarian who is at the mercy of his selfish appetites. But if one asks him "What is this Law and where does it come from?" he refers one back to Nature, to the Darwinian law of the Jungle, "Be Fit," or to the Newtonian law of the Machine:

> We are not built to comprehend a lie
> We can neither love nor pity nor forgive.
> If you make a slip in handling us, you die.

One might almost say that Kipling had to concentrate his attention and ours upon the special emergency in order to avoid the embarrassment of this paradox, for it is precisely when We are threatened by Them that we can naturally think of the ethical relation between Me and You as one of self-sacrifice, and the ethical relation between Us and Them as one of self-interest. It is precisely when civilization is in mortal danger that the immediate necessity to defend it has a right to override the question of just what it is we are defending.

It may not be too fanciful, either, to see in the kind of poetry Kipling wrote, the esthetic corollary of his conception of life. His virtuosity with language is not unlike that of one of his sergeants with an awkward squad:

> Said England unto Pharaoh: "You've had miracles before
>   When Aaron struck your rivers into blood,
> But if you watch the sergeant he can show you something more
>   He's a charm making riflemen from mud."
> It was neither Hindustani, French or Coptics,
>   It was odds and ends and leavings of the same
> Translated by a stick (which is really half the trick)
>   And Pharaoh hearkened to Sergeant Whatsisname.

Under his will, the vulgarest words learn to wash behind their ears and to execute complicated movements at the word of command, but they can hardly be said to learn to think for themselves. His poetry is arid; personally, I prefer this to the damp poetry of self-expression, but both are excesses.

His poems in their quantity, their limitation to one feeling at a time, have the air of brilliant tactical improvisations to overcome sudden unforeseen obstacles, as if, for Kipling, experience were not a seed to cultivate patiently and lovingly, but an unending stream of dangerous feelings to be immediately mastered as they appear.

No doubt his early experiences of India gave him a sense of the danger of Nature which it is hard for a European to realize (though easier perhaps for an American), but these are not sufficient to explain the terror of demons, visible and invisible, which gives his work its peculiar excitement, any more than the English Civil War expresses Hobbes's terror of political disorder. Nor does it matter particularly what the real cause may have been. The "mirror" that Kipling holds out to us is one in which, if we see anything, we see vague, menacing shapes which can be kept away by incessant action but can never be finally overcome:

> Heart may Fail, and Strength outwear, and Purpose turn
>   to Loathing

But the everyday affair of business, meals and clothing
Builds a bulkhead 'twixt Despair and the Edge of Nothing.

> I get it as well as you—oo—oo
> If I haven't enough to do—oo—oo
> We all get hump,
> Camelions hump,
> Kiddies and grown-ups too.

From *The New Republic*, Vol. CIX (October 25, 1943), pp. 579–581. Reprinted by permission of the author and editors.

THE PUBLIC VS. THE LATE MR. WILLIAM BUTLER YEATS

[1939]

THE PUBLIC PROSECUTOR:

Gentlemen of the Jury. Let us be quite clear in our minds as to the nature of this case. We are here to judge, not a man, but his work. Upon the character of the deceased, therefore, his affectations of dress and manner, his inordinate personal vanity, traits which caused a fellow countryman and former friend to refer to him as the greatest literary fop in history, I do not intend to dwell. I must only remind you that there is usually a close connection between the personal character of a poet and his work, and that the deceased was no exception.

Again I must draw your attention to the exact nature of the charge. That the deceased had talent is not for a moment in dispute; so much is freely admitted by the prosecution. What the defense are asking you to believe, however, is that he was a great poet, the greatest of this century writing in English. That is their case, and it is that which the prosecution feels bound most emphatically to deny.

A great poet. To deserve such an epithet, a poet is commonly required to convince us of these things: firstly a gift of a very high order for memorable language, secondly a profound understanding of the age in which he lived, and thirdly a working knowledge of and sympathetic attitude towards the most progressive thought of his time.

Did the deceased possess these? I am afraid, gentlemen, that the answer is, no.

On the first point I shall be brief. My learned friend, the counsel for the defense, will, I have no doubt, do his best to convince you that I am wrong. And he has a case, gentlemen. O yes, a very fine case. I shall only ask you to apply to the work of the deceased a very simple test. How many of his lines can you remember?

Further, it is not unreasonable to suppose that a poet who has a gift for language will recognize that gift in others. I have here a copy of an Anthology edited by the deceased entitled *The Oxford Book of Modern Verse*. I challenge anyone in this court to deny that it is the most deplorable volume ever issued under the imprint of that highly respected firm which has done so much for the cause of poetry in this country, The Clarendon Press.

But in any case you and I are educated modern men. Our fathers imagined that poetry existed in some private garden of its own, totally unrelated to the workaday world, and to be judged by pure aesthetic standards alone. We know that now to be an illusion. Let me pass, then, to my second point. Did the deceased understand his age?

What did he admire? What did he condemn? Well, he extolled the virtues of the peasant. Excellent. But should that peasant learn to read and write, should he save enough money to buy a shop, attempt by honest trading to raise himself above the level of the beasts, and O, what a sorry change is there. Now he is the enemy, the hateful huxter whose blood, according to the unseemly boast of the deceased, never flowed through *his* loins. Had the poet chosen to live in a mud cabin in Galway among swine and superstition, we might think him mistaken, but we should admire his integrity. But did he do this? O dear no. For there was another world which seemed to him not only equally admirable, but a deal more agreeable to live in, the world of noble houses, of large drawing rooms inhabited by the rich and the decorative, most of them of the female sex. We do not have to think very hard or very long, before we shall see a connection between these facts. The deceased had the feudal mentality. He was prepared to admire the poor just as long as they remained poor and deferential, accepting without protest the burden of maintaining a little Athenian band of literary landowners, who without their toil could not have existed for five minutes.

For the great struggle of our time to create a juster social order, he felt nothing but the hatred which is born of fear. It is true that he played a certain part in the movement for Irish Independence, but I hardly think my learned friend will draw your attention to that. Of all the modes of self-evasion open to the well-to-do, Nationalism is the easiest and most dishonest. It allows to the unjust all the luxury of righteous indignation against injustice. Still, it has often inspired men and women to acts of heroism and self-sacrifice. For the sake of a free Ireland the poet Pearse and the countess Markiewicz gave their all. But if the deceased did give himself to this movement, he did so with singular moderation. After the rebellion of Easter Sunday 1916, he wrote a poem on the subject which has been called a masterpiece. It is. To succeed at such a time in writing a poem which could offend neither the Irish Republicans nor the British army was indeed a masterly achievement.

And so we come to our third and last point. The most superficial glance at the last fifty years is enough to tell us that the social struggle towards greater equality has been accompanied by a growing intellectual acceptance of the scientific method and the steady conquest of irrational superstition. What was the attitude of the deceased towards this? Gentlemen, words fail me. What are we to say of a man whose earliest writings attempted to revive a belief in fairies and whose favorite themes were legends of barbaric heroes with unpronounceable names, work which has been aptly and wittily described as Chaff about Bran!

But you may say, he was young; youth is always romantic; its silliness is part of its charm. Perhaps it is. Let us forgive the youth, then, and consider the mature man, from whom we have a right to expect wisdom and common sense. Gentlemen, it is hard to be charitable when we find that the deceased, far from outgrowing his folly, has plunged even deeper. In 1900 he believed in fairies; that was bad enough; but in 1930 we are confronted with the pitiful, the deplorable spectacle of a grown man occupied with the mumbo-jumbo of magic and the nonsense of India. Whether he seriously believed such stuff to be true, or merely thought it petty, or imagined it would impress the public, is immaterial. The plain fact remains that he made it the centre of his work. Gentlemen, I need say no more. In the last poem he wrote, the deceased rejected social justice and reason, and prayed for war. Am I mistaken in imagining that somewhat similar sentiments are expressed by a certain foreign political movement which every lover of literature and liberty acknowledges to be the enemy of mankind?

THE COUNSEL FOR THE DEFENSE:

Gentlemen of the Jury. I am sure you have listened with as much enjoyment as I to the eloquence of the prosecution. I say enjoyment because the spectacle of anything well-done, whether it be a feat of engineering, a poem, or even an outburst of impassioned oratory, must always give pleasure.

We have been treated to an analysis of the character of the deceased which for all I know, may be as true as it is destructive. Whether it proves anything about the value of his poetry is another matter. If I may be allowed to quote my learned friend. "We are here to judge, not a man but his work." We have been told that the deceased was conceited, that he was a snob, that he was a physical coward, that his taste in contemporary poetry was uncertain, that he could not understand physics and chemistry. If this is not an invitation to judge the man I do not know what is. Does it not bear an extraordinary resemblance to the belief of an earlier age that a great artist must be chaste? Take away the frills, and the argument of the prosecution is reduced to this:

"A great poet must give the right answers to the problems which perplex his generation. The deceased gave the wrong answers. Therefore the deceased was not a great poet." Poetry in such a view is the filling up of a social quiz; to pass with honours the poet must score not less than 75%. With all due respect to my learned friend, this is nonsense. We are tempted so to judge contemporary poets because we really do have problems which we really do want solved, so that we are inclined to expect everyone, politicians, scientists, poets, clergymen, to give us the answer, and to blame them indiscriminately when they do not. But who reads the poetry of the past in this way? In an age of rising nationalism, Dante looked back with envy to the Roman Empire. Was this socially progressive? Will only a Catholic admit that Dryden's "The Hind and the Panther" is a good poem? Do we condemn Blake because he rejected Newton's theory of light, or rank Wordsworth lower than Baker, because the latter had a deeper appreciation of the steam engine?

Can such a view explain why

> Mock Emmet, Mock Parnell
> All the renown that fell

is good; and bad, such a line as

> Somehow I think that you are rather like a tree

In pointing out that this is absurd, I am not trying to suggest that art exists independently of society. The relation between the two is just as intimate and important as the prosecution asserts.

Every individual is from time to time excited emotionally and intellectually by his social and material environment. In certain individuals this excitement produces verbal structures which we call poems; if such a verbal structure creates an excitement in the reader, we call it a good poem. Poetic talent, in fact, is the power to make personal excitement socially available. Poets, i.e., persons with poetic talent, stop writing good poetry when they stop reacting to the world they live in. The nature of that reaction, whether it be positive or negative, morally admirable or morally disgraceful, matters very little; what is essential is that the reaction should genuinely exist. The later Wordsworth is not inferior to the earlier because the poet had altered his political opinions, but because he had ceased to feel and think so strongly, a change which happens, alas, to most of us as we grow older. Now, when we turn to the deceased, we are confronted by the amazing spectacle of a man of great poetic talent, whose capacity for excitement not only remained with him to the end, but actually increased. In two hundred years when our children have made a different and, I hope, better social order, and when our science has developed out of all recognition, who but a historian will care a button whether the deceased was right about the Irish Question or wrong about the transmigration of souls? But because the excitement out of which his poems arose was genuine, they will still, unless I am very much mistaken, be capable of exciting others, different though their circumstances and beliefs may be from his.

However, since we are not living two hundred years hence, let us play the schoolteacher a moment, and examine the poetry of the deceased with reference to the history of our time.

The most obvious social fact of the last forty years is the failure of liberal capitalist democracy, based on the premises that every individual is born free and equal, each an absolute entity independent of all others. And that a formal political equality, the right to vote, the right to a fair trial, the right of free speech, is enough to guarantee his freedom of action in his relations with his fellow men. The results are only too familiar to us all. By denying the social nature of personality, and by ignoring the social power of money, it has created the most impersonal, the most mechanical and the most unequal civilization the world has ever seen, a civilization in which the only emotion common to all classes is a feeling of individual isolation from everyone else, a civilization torn apart by the opposing emotions born of economic injustice, the just envy of the poor and the selfish terror of the rich.

If these latter emotions meant little to the deceased, it was partly because Ireland compared with the rest of western Europe was economically backward, and the class struggle was less conscious there. My learned friend has sneered at Irish Nationalism, but he knows as well as I that Nationalism is a necessary stage towards socialism. He has sneered at the deceased for not taking arms, as if shooting were the only honorable and useful form of social action. Has the Abbey Theatre done nothing for Ireland?

But to return to the poems. From first to last they express a sustained protest against the social atomisation caused by industrialism, and both in their ideas and their language a constant struggle to overcome it. The fairies and heroes of the early work were an attempt to find through folk tradition a binding force for society; and the doctrine of Anima Mundi found in the later poems is the same thing, in a more developed form, which has left purely local peculiarities behind, in favor of something that the deceased hoped was universal; in other words, he was working for a world religion. A purely religious solution may be unworkable, but the search for it is, at least, the result of a true perception of a social evil. Again, the virtues that the deceased praised in the peasantry and aristocracy, and the vices he blamed in the commercial classes were real virtues and vices. To create a united and just society where the former are fostered and the latter cured is the task of the politician, not the poet.

For art is a product of history, not a cause. Unlike some other products, technical inventions for example, it does not re-enter history as an effective agent, so that the question whether art should or should not be propaganda is unreal. The case for the prosecution rests on the fallacious belief that art ever makes anything happen, whereas the honest truth, gentlemen, is that, if not a poem had been written, not a picture painted, not a bar of music composed, the history of man would be materially unchanged.

But there is one field in which the poet is a man of action, the field of language, and it is precisely in this that the greatness of the deceased is most obviously shown. However false or undemocratic his ideas, his diction shows a continuous evolution towards what one might call the true democratic style. The social virtues of a real democracy are brotherhood and intelligence, and the parallel linguistic virtues are strength and clarity, virtues which appear even more clearly through successive volumes by the deceased.

The diction of *The Winding Stair* is the diction of a just man, and it is for this reason that just men will always recognize the author as a master.

From *The Partisan Review,* Vol. VI (Spring, 1939), pp. 46–51. Reprinted by the permission of the author and editors.

THEODORE SPENCER

The Later Poetry of W. B. Yeats

[1933]

A DISTINGUISHED critic, Mr. Yvor Winters, has recently compared the poetry of W. B. Yeats with the poetry of T. Sturge Moore.[1] His remarks are challenging and need to be discussed. In his opinion, Moore is a greater poet than Yeats; he says that Yeats, at crucial moments, suffers from the "fundamental post-Romantic defect, the abandonment of logic," that Yeats achieves a "factitious coherence," is guilty of intellectual confusion, and is an "unregenerate Romantic." These adverse criticisms sum up very well the case against Yeats as an important poet, and the reason they need to be discussed by anyone concerned with Yeats' poetry is that they have a plausibility which may make them a serious obstacle to a satisfactory judgment of Yeats' position.

There is not much to be said about the first of them. To say that Moore is a better poet than Yeats seems to me meaningless, and I cannot imagine any standards of criticism by which such a statement can be defended. In subtlety of rhythm, in intensity, in richness of verbal association, in force, in everything which implies an original and individual style, the later poems of Yeats are superior to anything by Moore. Compare, for example, the opening lines of Moore's sonnet, "Apuleius Meditates," which Mr. Winters praises very highly, with the opening of Yeats' sonnet on Leda and the Swan. This is Moore:

> An old tale tells how Gorgo's gaze distilled
> Horror to petrify men's mobile limbs:
> Endymion's moonlit beauty never dims,
> Hard-frozen as the fond chaste goddess willed.

And Yeats:

> A sudden blow: the great wings beating still
> Above the staggering girl, her thighs caressed
> By the dark webs, her nape caught in his bill,
> He holds her helpless breast upon his breast.

[1] "T. Sturge Moore," by Yvor Winters. *The Hound and Horn,* Vol. VI, No. 3 (April–June, 1933), pages 534–545.

There is an important distinction illustrated here, a distinction which applies to other poetry than that of Moore and Yeats. It is the distinction between the poetry of revery and the poetry of immediacy. I do not, of course, mean by the poetry of revery poetry which is written necessarily about past events; what I am describing, to put it loosely, is the associative climate into which we feel the poet has moved when he got himself ready for writing, and in which he has remained during the composition of the poem. Even without the revealing phrase "An old tale tells," which begins Moore's sonnet, we know from the rhythm, the fairly obvious and hence unregenerated adjectives, that the subject is being viewed from a distance, that it is not apprehended immediately. The poet and his material have not passed through a period of "intimate welding"; they have been contiguous, not fused. But, "A sudden blow: the great wings beating still": here the poet has put the reader in the midst of the action; the subject is not considered and contemplated from outside; we are convinced that the matter has been so vividly an essential part of the poet's experience, that it becomes, if we are reading with the proper attention, an equally vivid part of the reader's experience too.

The distinction between these two ways of regarding the subject matter of a poem becomes obvious if we think of Wordsworth's famous definition of the origin of poetry. "It takes its origin," he says, "from emotion recollected in tranquillity; the action is contemplated till, by a species of reaction, the tranquillity gradually disappears, and an emotion, kindred to that which was before the subject of contemplation, is gradually produced, and does itself actually exist in the mind." It is the last part of this sentence, the part usually left unquoted, which is important. Without the disappearance of tranquillity no good poem can be written, and the trouble with the kind of poetry I have called the poetry of revery is that when we are reading it we feel the tranquillity is still there; the "emotion which was before the subject of contemplation" has not turned up. It is because we never feel like this about Shakespeare that we consider Shakespeare so great a poet, and it is because we often feel like this about Tennyson, that Tennyson's reputation is dubious.

The difference between immediate poetry and the poetry of revery is a reflection of a difference in poetic temperament, and like all differences in temperament it shows itself in a number of ways. One does not expect that a temperament addicted to revery will seek for startling words or for arrangements of images and thoughts that will surprise the mind. Revery in any form not being a function of the human personality as a whole, its aim, when expressed in poetry, will be to lull rather than excite, to describe, or even lament, as beautifully as possible, rather than to assert or protest. Not that poetry of this kind is without intensity; one has only to think of sections *liv* to *lvi* of *In Memoriam;* but it is not the intensity of immediacy, of anger, or of satire, because it is not an intensity which fully includes the intellect.

Of course the contrast between these two kinds of poetic temperament may be carried too far, and one can waste one's time in putting various poets into the various categories they imply, which is foolish because in many cases it is impossible to draw a satisfactory line between them. The reason I mention the matter at all is that it throws an interesting light on the poetry of Yeats. He is a striking example of a man whose poetic development has been from the one way of writing to the other, of a man who has tried to move from a partial to a complete way of looking at the experience he is putting into words. This change, and the success with which he has brought it about, is one of the reasons why his later poetry is so interesting, and is one of the facts which justify the assertion that Yeats is the greatest of living English poets.

The point can be made clearer if we compare one of his earlier poems, "The Sad Shepherd," with one written about forty years later, the poem, "Coole Park, 1929," in *Words for Music Perhaps*.[2] "The Sad Shepherd" begins:

> There was a man whom Sorrow named his friend,
> And he, of his high comrade Sorrow dreaming,
> Went walking with slow steps along the gleaming
> And humming sands, where windy surges wend.

There is little, except its rhythm, to recommend that. It is typical writing of an "unregenerate Romantic." The weak personification of Sorrow, the phrase "high comrade" (this emotive use of the adjective "high" is usually suspicious), the inaccuracy and looseness of the rhyme word "wend"—all these make bad writing, for they are the result of soft feeling and of practically no thinking at all. And the poem, with the exception of the closing lines, gets worse as it goes on. It is an excellent example of the poetry of revery at its weakest; of poetry written not with the object imaginatively vivid and sharp before the mind's eye, but written, so to speak, from memory, with the object wrapped in the falsifying haze of illusion, the kind of illusion that flourishes, like algae in a stagnant pool, when the mind is not stirring.

Bad poetry like this can be found in any age, and the kind of mistiness that makes it bad depends on the particular literary conventions of the time. The minor poets of the eighteenth century had a chilly poetic diction which hampered clarity, and the minor poets of the '90's had little clarity because they used a poetic diction which, one is tempted to say, was too warm. Closely connected with this, and in fact inseparable from it, they had a languorous and evasive habit of feeling, which is as dangerous to good writing as it is difficult to get rid of. What makes Yeats so worthy of admiration is that he did get rid of it. He tells us, in his *Autobiographies*, how, by sleeping upon a board (or at least by thinking of sleeping upon a board), by making his

---

[2] *Words for Music Perhaps and Other Poems,* by W. B. Yeats. Dublin: Cuala Press, 1932. (In *Collected Poems.* New York: Macmillan Co. 1933.)

rhythms "faint and nervous," by contemplating the Dantesque image, by changing his subject matter and his vocabulary, he struggled to make his poems bare and clear, and expressive of the whole man. That he has succeeded is one reason why Mr. Winters' comparison of his verse to Sturge Moore's seems to me so imperceptive. His "quarrel with himself," to use his own phrase, has made Yeats a great poet, with a style of communicating his experience which is authentic and individual, whereas the style of Sturge Moore, careful craftsman though he be, never rises above the commonplace.

It is, of course, an over-simplification of the truth to say that Yeats has entirely turned from one way of writing to the other. He has not lost, he has enriched and perfected, the sensitive rhythms which were at the beginning the best thing about his style. What has happened is that Yeats has taught himself to give the exactly right, and hence unsentimentalized, emotional tone to what he wants to say. "I tried," he says in his preface (1925) to the collected edition of his early poems, "after the publication of the *Wanderings of Oisin* to write of nothing but emotion, and in the simplest language, and now I have had to go through it all, cutting out or altering passages that are sentimental from lack of thought." Few poets have had more difficulties to escape from, more veils of unreality to break through—or, to change the metaphor, more intangible vapors to condense into solids—than Yeats. The late Romanticism of the '90's, Irish super-nationalism, the use of occult symbols, reliance upon a private metaphysical system; any one of these might have been the ruin of a lesser talent. But Yeats, in spite of what at times seemed unavoidable disaster, has triumphantly survived. Perhaps a life of action, and the anger it has sometimes generated—anger is an excellent emotion, if aimed at the right things, for a poet to cultivate—has helped to put iron into his style. At any rate, even when writing about the past, Yeats is no longer a poet of revery, in the sense that I have defined. That is the point I want to make by referring to his poem "Coole Park, 1929."

> I meditate upon a swallow's flight,
> Upon an aged woman and her house:
> A sycamore and lime tree lost in night
> Although that western cloud is luminous,
> Great works constructed there in nature's spite
> For scholars and for poets after us,
> Thoughts long knitted into a single thought,
> A dance-like glory that those walls begot.

At first sight this stanza would seem to be an excellent example of revery. The poet is looking back upon the past, the tone is not "active," the rhythm is appropriate for retrospection. But on a more careful reading, it will be seen that every image is at once individually specific and symbolically general in

its reference, that no word can be changed except for the worse, and that the
climax of the last line is prepared for by the contrasting images and symbols
that have gone before. And how admirably the poem continues:

> There Hyde before he had beaten into prose
> That noble blade the Muses buckled on,
> There one that ruffled in a manly pose
> For all his timid heart, there that slow man,
> That meditative man John Synge and those
> Impetuous men Shawe-Taylor and Hugh Lane,
> Found pride established in humility,
> A scene well set and excellent company.
>
> They came like swallows and like swallows went,
> And yet a woman's powerful character
> Could keep a swallow to its first intent;
> And half a dozen in formation there
> That seemed to whirl upon a compass point
> Found certainly upon the dreaming air. . . .

It is tempting to quote the whole poem, but I will leave the last stanza unquoted—though with its swelling rhythm and superb rhetoric it is the finest
of all—in hopes that what I have already quoted will send the reader to the
book itself.

There are other poems of this kind in *Words for Music Perhaps,* and I
should like to call attention particularly to "The Burning Tree" and to "Coole
Park and Ballylee, 1932," both written, like "Coole Park, 1929," in ottava
rima, and both containing that reverberative haunting quality which Yeats,
in such a masterly way, can give to his rhythms. Equally striking, and equally
masterly, is the way Yeats uses, in these latest poems, the individual word to
its fullest effect. He has always been able, as the result of his control over
rhythm, to emphasize any word he pleased, but the word itself has not always
been the final word for its context. Now, with his more recent intensity of
vision, his control of focus, the individual word has that combination of immediate exactness with potential expansion which is the mark of great poetry.
Yeats is particularly successful with adjectives; I can think of few poets who
in this respect are his equals. Consider, for example, his use of the word
"resinous" in the last line of the following stanza; it is the end of the final
chorus to his play "Resurrection":

> Everything that man esteems
> Endures a moment or a day;
> Love's pleasure drives his love away,
> The painter's brush consumes his dreams;
> The herald's cry, the soldier's tread

> Exhaust his glory and his might:
> Whatever flames upon the night
> Man's own resinous heart has fed.

We have only to compare with this an earlier expression of a similar idea to see how far Yeats has progressed. I quote from "The Happy Shepherd (1889)."

> Nor seeks; for this is also sooth;
> To hunger fiercely after truth,
> Lest all thy toiling only breed
> New dreams, new dreams; there is not truth
> Saving in thine own heart . . .

That is rhythmically effective, but little more; there are too many unnecessary words ("nor," "also," "only," etc.), and nowhere is there the concreteness and inevitability of the later poem.

II

The second part of the present volume consists of a number of short poems and songs, many of them built around a figure whom Yeats at first called Cracked Mary, but who now appears as Crazy Jane; an old woman who sings of the wild ineradicable love she had in her youth. I can best give the the quality of these poems by quotation.

> I know, although when looks meet
> I tremble to the bone,
> The more I leave the door unlatched
> The sooner love is gone,
> For love is but a skein unwound
> Between the dark and dawn.
>
> A lonely ghost the ghost is
> That to God shall come;
> I—love's skein upon the ground,
> My body in the tomb—
> Shall leap into the light lost
> In my mother's womb.
>
> But were I left to lie alone
> In an empty bed,
> The skein so bound us ghost to ghost
> When you turned your head
> Passing on the road that night,
> Mine would walk, being dead.

The technique of this is very interesting. The spondee at the end of the first lines of the first and second stanzas (why does it not occur in the third as well?), the interlocking rhymes, by which the third line of one stanza rhymes with the fifth line of the stanza preceding, the cumulative effect of the triple rhyme, all these form a technical triumph which widens the limits of English poetry.

A further technical device, used very often in these poems, is the refrain, and I should like to examine for a moment the way Yeats handles it, for with its help, he gives a remarkable muscle and pungency to his verse form, and there is much to be learned, by a practicing versifier, from the success of his experiments.

There are, generally speaking, three chief ways in which the refrain has been used by English poets. The first is that found in popular ballads, and to a less extent in Elizabethan songs. Here the effect achieved is rhythmical poignancy and contrast; the repetition of a meaningless phrase, unrelated to the subject of the poem, and balanced in a different rhythm, can first create a kind of rhythmical suspense, and then resolve it:

> There were twa sisters in a bower,
> *Edinburgh, Edinburgh,*
> There were twa sisters in a bower,
> *Sterling for aye;*
> There were twa sisters in a bower,
> There cam a knight to be their wooer,
> *Bonnie St. Johnston stands upon Tay.*

Or it can produce rhythmical variety alone, as in Elizabethan songs:

> Ho ho, ho ho, this world doth pass
> Right merrily, I'll be sworn,
> When many an honest Indian ass
> Goes for a unicorn.
> *Tara-diddle-deino; this is idle feino.*

> Tee-hee, tee-hee, O sweet delight,
> He tickles this age who can
> Call Tullia's ape a marmosite,
> And Leda's goose a swan.
> *Tara-diddle-deino; this is idle feino.*

The second use of the refrain is to bind together and intensify the chief subject-matter of the poem. In the earliest English example, the Anglo-Saxon "Deor's Lament," the repeated words, "That passed over, so may this," by which the poet refers to past calamities in relation to his own, connect the various incidents under one emotional roof, and give unity to what would otherwise be an unrelated series of incidents. Milton, imitating Virgil, uses this device with great success in his "Epitaphium Damonis," where the repetition, at irregular intervals, of the words, "Ite domum impasti, domino iam non vacat, agni," has a singularly haunting effect.

And there is a third, more sophisticated way of using the refrain to be found in the marriage songs of Spenser. Keeping the standard rhythm of the poem, it supplies a background of natural description, and it places the action in a definite environment: "Sweete Themmes! runne softlie, till I end my song." A notable use of this method has been made by Hardy, in a poem called "The Sacrilege," where the refrain descriptive of Nature, "And Dunkery frowned on Exon Moor," changes from gloomy to gay, or rather (characteristically) from gay to gloomy, according to the events in the story.

I make these somewhat pedantic classifications because they throw light on what Yeats has done. He has used the refrain in all three ways, and with each use has broadened its possibilities. We can find the first in "Crazy Jane Reproved," the second in "Crazy Jane on God," and the third in "Three Things." But even more interesting are the poems in which he has used the refrain in two or three ways at the same time.

> Bring me to the blasted oak
> That I, midnight upon the stroke,
> *All find safety in the tomb,*
> May call down curses on his head
> Because of my dear Jack that's dead
> "Cockscomb" was the least he said
> *The solid man and the cockscomb.*

Here we have a combination of the first and second methods: the indirect allusion, *All find safety in the tomb,* grows into a necessary reference; by binding the poem together and giving it rhythmical variety—*The solid man and the cockscomb*—the refrain adds intensity, and the result is that we have, not a single note, as we should have if the refrain were missing, but a chord.

Frequently, as here, Yeats chooses for a refrain some general statement upon which the poem itself is a specific comment. An admirable example is the poem "Crazy Jane Grown Old Looks at the Dancers," where the line, *Love is like the lion's tooth,* repeated at the end of each stanza, is both a statement of a general truth and a representation of the fierceness of the old woman's remembered passion. In fact there is no better example of Yeats' genius than the way in which he chooses his refrains to give this double effect; it was essential to find the right words, and in nearly every poem, Yeats has found them. In his use of this device, as in everything else, we find the later Yeats making his poems a reflection of a complete experience, not of a discrete layer of experience only. Comparison with the earlier poems is again illuminating, and it is interesting to compare a poem called "Running to Paradise" (1914), where the refrain gives merely a rhythmical variety, though it is very effective and surprising, with either of the poems I have just mentioned, where the refrain gives emotional vividness and tautness as well.

In my opinion the finest of all these poems is the one called "I am of Ireland," where the refrain is used more elaborately, with a more subtle rhythmical sway, than anywhere else. In fact it is difficult to tell which is the refrain and which is the chief part of the poem; the refrain is at once a voice and an echo, a question and a reply, and the fusion between the two takes place in that deep part of consciousness, or perhaps unconsciousness, which only true poetry can spring from or can reach. I quote the poem in full, for only by doing so can I hope to explain why I find it so moving.

> "I am of Ireland,
> And the Holy Land of Ireland,
> And time runs on" cried she,
> "Come out of charity
> Come dance with me in Ireland."
>
> One man, one man alone
> In that outlandish gear,
> One solitary man
> Of all that rambled there
> Had turned his stately head,
> "That is a long way off,
> And time runs on," he said
> "And the night grows rough."
>
> "I am of Ireland
> And the Holy Land of Ireland
> And time runs on," cried she.
> "Come out of charity
> And dance with me in Ireland."
>
> "The fiddlers are all thumbs,
> Or the fiddle string accursed,
> The drums and the kettle drums
> And the trumpets all are burst
> And the trombone," cried he,
> "The trumpet and trombone,"
> And cocked a malicious eye
> "But time runs on, runs on."
>
> "I am of Ireland
> And the Holy Land of Ireland

And time runs on," cried she.
"Come out of charity
And dance with me in Ireland."

III

I have written at some length about the technique of Yeats' poetry because a deep respect for Yeats as a craftsman is necessary to a proper understanding of his work. But his craftsmanship would hardly be worth mentioning if it were an end in itself; what is significant about these later poems is that the substitution, to use Yeats' own description, of "sound for sense and ornament for thought," which was the fault of his early style, has given place to vigor and toughness, to a style where thought is substance and not accident, and which is able to communicate, in an entirely individual way, important emotions. It remains to enquire what these are.

About ten years ago, it appeared likely that Yeats was in danger of losing himself in a tangle of occult metaphysics; he published a book on the subject called A Vision, "which book," to use Chaucer's words,

Spak muchel of the operaciouns
Touchynge the eighte and twenty mansiouns
That longen to the moone, and swich folye
As in oure dayes is nat worth a flye,

and he wrote several poems which depended, if they were to be understood, on a fable connected with the philosophy described in this volume. And though Yeats has since remarked (1929) that nearly all of A Vision "fills me with shame," he also attributes to the experience behind it the fact that his poetry has gained in "self-possession and power."

This is doubtless true, and it is therefore unfair to apply Chaucer's words too literally to A Vision. At the present time a poet must take what external aid he can find to plan the structure and symbolism of his poetry; but if he is a good poet the mechanics will obviously be more helpful to him than to the reader, and most of the time they will be out of sight. This is what occurs in Yeats' later poems; specific references to the philosophy of A Vision are very scarce, only an occasional metaphor is derived from it, and the subject matter of the poems is not a private world of dreams, as the most acute of contemporary English critics once feared it would be, but the subject matter of all great poetry.

That, to be sure, is a very loose statement, for the subject matter of great poetry is a difficult and complex thing to define. But if one were pressed for a definition, the reply would be, I believe, that at the bottom of all great poetry, as at the bottom of all human experience, lies the problem of the relation between the transient and the permanent, expressed in innumerable ways, and regarded from innumerable angles. In mystical poetry, such as Dante's, the permanent is found and described as the center of experience, for it is the object of both emotion and thought; in Shelley's poetry it is sought for by the mind, but found only temporarily, for it is discovered by the emotions alone; while in Shakespeare, though the sense of permanence is nearly always somewhere in the background, it is change, not permanence, the Many, not the One, that is emphasized, and the passion, as in *Lear,* can play itself out in the dark. Today, as has been frequently said ("What are all those fish that lie gasping on the strand?"), the flux itself seems the only thing that does not change, and to seek a pattern of permanence elsewhere appears an impossible task. *A Vision* is such an attempt, and the apparent intractability of its philosophy for poetry is significant. Yet without such an attempt Yeats' later poetry would lose its richness and its "power." The philosophy may not be acceptable to others, but to Yeats it represents a sense of values which recognizes the importance of the permanent, and without such recognition all statements about life, whether in poetry or prose, are shallow.

The chief subject matter of these poems is the passing of youth into age, of passion into death.

> Earth in beauty dressed
> Awaits returning spring.
> All true love must die,
> Alter at the best
> Into some lesser thing.
> Prove that I lie.

> Such bodies lovers have,
> Such exacting breath
> That they touch or sigh.
> Every touch they give
> Love is nearer death.
> Prove that I lie.

It is a poetry of change, striving for stability, for transmutation into "monuments of unaging intellect." And though both the ephemeral and the lasting are continually brought to our attention, it is the passing of the ephemeral that remains most vivid to us. One might expect, as a result, that the prevailing tone would be one of pathos, but this is not true; the emotions here expressed go deeper than pathos, and slight as these poems are, they leave in the mind an impression of tragedy.

I trust that I have said enough to show that I consider Yeats' poetry to have more than a contemporary value. It does not, as Mr. Winters says it does, abandon logic; it springs from a deeper well than mere logic ever swam in, and its coherence is far from "factitious." Even if we may sometimes feel that an individual poem is not entirely successful, the great majority of these poems do not grow commonplace with familiarity, nor are they easily forgotten. On the contrary they sing into the memory, and we feel, after contemplating them, that Yeats did himself no more than justice when he once wrote:

> There is not a fool can call me friend,
> And I may dine at journey's end
> With Landor and with Donne.

From *The Hound and Horn*, Vol. VII (October–December, 1933), pp. 164–175. Reprinted by permission.

F. O. MATTHIESSEN
T. S. Eliot: The Four Quartets
[1943]

IN THE course of an artist's development certain phases may detach themselves and challenge comprehension as completed wholes. Eliot has rounded out such a cycle with *Little Gidding,* and we are now able to see the full significance of the experiments with structure which he inaugurated in *Burnt Norton* eight years previously.[1] He speaks of the four poems which form this cycle as "quartets," and has evolved for them all the same kind of sequence of five parts with which he composed *Burnt Norton. The Waste Land* was also composed in this fashion, but the contrast is instructive. In his earlier desire for intense concentration the poet so eliminated connectives that *The Waste Land* might be called an anthology of the high points of a drama. It was as though its author had determined to make his poem of nothing but Arnold's "touchstones," or had subscribed to Poe's dictum that no longer poem could exist than one to be read at a sitting. In the intervening years Eliot has given further thought to the problem, and he has recently concluded that "in a poem of any length there must be transitions between passages of greater and lesser intensity, to give rhythm of fluctuating emotion essential to the musical structure of the whole." He has also enunciated "a complementary doctrine" to that of Arnold's "touchstones": the test of a poet's greatness by "the way he writes his less intense but structurally vital matter."

None of the four quartets is much more than half as long as *The Waste Land,* but he has included in them all transitional passages that he would previously have dismissed as "prosaic." His fundamentally altered intention is at the root of the matter. The dramatic monologues of Prufrock or Gerontion or of the various *personae* of *The Waste Land* have yielded to gravely modulated meditations of the poet's own. The vivid situations of his *Inferno* have been followed by the philosophic debates of his *Purgatorio.* He has made quite explicit the factors conditioning his new structures in the essay from which I

[1] Before appearing in collected form in 1943, Eliot's *Four Quartets* appeared as separate booklets, as follows: "Burnt Norton" in 1941, "East Coker" in 1940, "The Dry Salvages" in 1941, "Little Gidding" in 1942. Thus these titles are printed here in italics. Similarly, "Triumphal March" appeared in separate book form in 1931, "Journey of the Magi" in 1927, and the essay "The Music of Poetry" in 1942. (Editor's note, 1950.)

have just quoted, *The Music of Poetry*. As is always the case with Eliot, this essay throws the most relevant light upon his poetic intentions, and is thus a further piece of refutation to those who persist in the fallacy that there is no harmony beween his "revolutionary" creative work and his "traditionalist" criticism.

Looking back now over the past generation, he finds the poetry of our period to be best characterized by its "search for a proper modern colloquial idiom." He develops the same theme near the close of *Little Gidding* where he envisages the right equilibrium between "the common word" and "the formal word." Only through their union of opposites do we get

The complete consort dancing together.

Eliot, no less than the later Yeats, has helped to restore to poetry the conversational tones which had been muffled by the ornamental forms and diction of the end of the century. But now Eliot is thinking of the other partner to the union, and remarks that "when we reach a point at which the poetic idiom can be stabilized, then a period of musical elaboration can follow." Just as Donne, in his later work, returned to the formal pattern of the sonnet which he had mocked in the broken rhythms of his early lyrics, so Eliot now believes that there is such a "tendency to return to set, and even elaborate patterns" after any period when they have been laid aside.

The present phase of his own return seems to have started with *New Hampshire* and *Virginia,* the short musical evocations which grew out of his renewed impressions of America in the early nineteen thirties. The impulse to write a series of such place-name poems led on in turn to the more ambitious *Burnt Norton,* which borrows its title from a Gloucestershire manor near which Eliot has stayed. The titles of the other three quartets indicate more intimate relationships: East Coker, in Somerset, is where the Eliot family lived until its emigration in the mid-seventeenth Century to the New England coast; the Dry Salvages, a group of rocks off Cape Ann, mark the part of that coast which the poet knew best as a boy; Little Gidding, the seat of the religious community which Nicholas Ferrar established and with which the names of George Herbert and Crashaw are associated, is a shrine for the devout Anglican, but can remind the poet also that

History is now and England.[1]

[1] By including in *Little Gidding* a refrain from Juliana of Norwich—

Sin is Behovely, but
All shall be well, and
All manner of thing shall be well—

Eliot also aimed, as he has said, "to escape any suggestion of historical sentimentality about the seventeenth century by this reiterated reference to the fourteenth century and therefore to get more bearing on the present than would be possible if the relation was merely between the present and one particular period of the past."

The rhythmical pattern of *Burnt Norton* is elaborated far beyond the delicate melodies of the brief "Landscapes." Eliot seems to have found in the interrelation of its five parts a type of structure which satisfied him beyond his previous experiments. For he has adhered to it with such remarkably close parallels in the three succeeding quartets that a description of the structure of one of them involves that of all, and can reveal the deliberateness of his intentions. In each case the first part or movement might be thought of as a series of statements and counterstatements of a theme in lines of an even greater irregularity than those of the late Jacobean dramatists. In each of these first movements a "landscape" or presented scene gives a concrete base around which the poet's thoughts gather.

The second movement opens with a highly formal lyric: in *The Dry Salvages* this is a variant of a sestina, rising from the clang of the bell buoy; in *Little Gidding* each of the three eight-line stanzas ends with a refrain—and thus does Eliot signalize his own renewal of forms that would have seemed played out to the author of *Prufrock*. In the other two poems he has also illustrated a remark which he has been repeating in his recent essays, that "a poem, or a passage of a poem, may tend to realize itself first as a particular rhythm before it reaches expression in words." The lyric in *Burnt Norton*—which is echoed perhaps too closely in *East Coker*—is as pure musical incantation as any Eliot has written. Not only does its opening image, "Garlic and sapphires in the mud," take its inception from Mallarmé's line "Tonnerre et rubis aux moyeux"; but the rhythm of the poem in which that line occurs, *M'introduire dans ton histoire*, seems also to have haunted Eliot's ear until it gave rise to a content which, with the exception of its opening line, is wholly different from Mallarmé's.

Following the lyric in the second movement, Eliot has relaxed his rhythms for a sudden contrast; and in *The Dry Salvages*, and especially in *East Coker*, has carried his experiment with the prosaic virtually over the border into prose:

> That was a way of putting it—not very satisfactory:
> A periphrastic study in a worn-out poetical fashion,
> Leaving one still with the intolerable wrestle
> With words and meanings. The poetry does not matter.
> It was not (to start again) what one had expected.

The sharp drop from incantation is designed to have the virtue of surprise; but it would seem here to have gone much too far, and to have risked the temporary collapse of his form into the flatness of a too personal statement. The variant in *Little Gidding* substitutes for such a sequence a modified terza rima, where the poet uses instead of rhyme a sustained alternation of masculine and feminine endings, in a passage that makes the strongest testimony for the value of formal congruence.

What the third parts have in common is that each is an account of movement. In *Burnt Norton* it is a descent into the London underground, which becomes also a descent into the dark night of the soul. In *East Coker* the allusion to Saint John of the Cross is even more explicit. The poet's command to his soul to

> be still and wait without hope,
> For hope would be hope of the wrong thing,

borrows its sequence of paradoxes directly from tht text of the 16th Century Spanish mystic. In *The Dry Salvages* where the concluding charge is

> Not fare well
> But fare forward, voyagers,

the doctrine of action beyond thought of self-seeking is, again explicitly, what Krishna urged to Arjuna on the field of battle; and we recall Eliot's remarking, in his essay on Dante, that "the next greatest philosophical poem" to *The Divine Comedy* within his experience was the *Bhagavad-Gita*. In *Little Gidding* the passage of movement is the terza rima passage at the close of the second part, and the deliberately prosaic lines open the third section. The movement described is the "dead patrol" of two air raid wardens.

The versification in these third parts is the staple for the poems as a whole, a very irregular iambic line with many substitutions, of predominantly four or five beats, but with syllables ranging from six to eighteen. The fourth movement, in every case, is a short lyric, as it was in *The Waste Land*. The fifth movement is a resumption and resolution of themes, and becomes progressively more intricate in the last two poems, since the themes are cumulative and are all brought together at the close of *Little Gidding*.

It seems doubtful whether at the time of writing *Burnt Norton*, just after *Murder in the Cathedral*, Eliot had already projected the series. His creative energies for the next three years were to be largely taken up with *The Family Reunion*, which, to judge from the endless revisions in the manuscript, caused him about as much trouble as anything he has done. With *East Coker* in the spring of 1940 he made his first experiment in a part for part parallel with an earlier work of his own. Again Donne's practice is suggestive: when he had evolved a particularly intricate and irregular stanza, he invariably set himself the challenge of following it unchanged to the end of his poem. But in assigning himself a similar problem for a poem two hundred lines long, Eliot has tried something far more exacting, where failure could be caused by the parallels becoming merely mechanical, and by the themes and rhythms becoming not subtle variations but flat repetitions. *East Coker* does indeed have something of the effect of a set piece. Just as its high proportion of prosaic lines seems to spring from partial exhaustion, so its resumption of themes from *Burnt Norton* can occasionally sound as though the poet was merely imitating himself. But on the whole he had solved his problem. He had made a renewal of form that was to carry him successively in the next two years through *The Dry Salvages* and *Little Gidding*. The discrimination between repetition and variation lies primarily in the rhythm; and these last two poems reverberate with an increasing musical richness.

A double question that keeps insisting itself through any discussion of these structures is the poet's consciousness of analogies with music, and whether such analogies are a confusion of arts. One remembers Eliot's comment on Lawrence's definition of "the essence of poetry" for our age "of stark and unlovely actualities" as a "stark, bare, rocky directness of statement." "This speaks to me," Eliot remarked a decade ago, "of that at which I have long aimed in writing poetry"; and he drew an analogy with the later quartets of Beethoven. This does not mean that he has ever tried to copy literally the effects of a different medium. But he knows that poetry is like music in being a temporal rather than a spatial art; and he has by now thought much about the subject, as the concluding paragraph of *The Music of Poetry* shows:

I think that a poet may gain much from the study of music: how much technical knowledge of musical form is desirable I do not know, for I have not that technical knowledge myself. But I believe that the properties in which music concerns the poet most nearly, are the sense of rhythm and the sense of structure. I think that it might be possible for a poet to work too closely to musical analogies: the result might be an effect of artificiality.

But he insists—and this has immediate bearing on his own intentions—that "the use of recurrent themes is as natural to poetry as to music." He has worked on that assumption throughout his quartets, and whether he has proved that "there are possibilities of transitions in a poem comparable to the different movements of a symphony or a quartet," or that "there are possibilities of contrapuntal arrangement of subject-matter," can be known only through repeated experience of the whole series. All I wish to suggest here is the pattern made by some of the dominant themes in their interrelation and progression.

Burnt Norton opens as a meditation on time. Many comparable and contrasting views are introduced. The lines are drenched with reminiscences of Heraclitus' fragments on flux and movement. Some of the passages on duration remind us that Eliot listened to Bergson's lectures at the Sorbonne in the winter of 1911 and wrote an essay then criticizing his *durée réelle* as "simply not final." Other lines on the recapture of time through consciousness suggest the aspect of Bergson that most stimulated Proust. But the chief contrast around which Eliot constructs this poem is that between the view of time as a mere continuum, and the difficult paradoxical Christian view of how man lives both "in and out of time," how he is immersed in the flux and yet can penetrate to the eternal by apprehending timeless existence within time and above it. But even for the Christian the moments of release from the pressures of the flux are rare, though they alone redeem the sad wastage of otherwise unillumined existence. Eliot recalls one such moment of peculiar poignance, a childhood moment in the rose garden—a symbol he has previously used, in many variants, for the birth of desire. Its implications are intricate and even ambiguous, since they raise the whole problem of how to discriminate between supernatural vision and mere illusion. Other variations here on the theme of how time is conquered are more directly apprehensible. In dwelling on the extension of time into movement, Eliot takes up an image he had used in *Triumphal March*: "at the still point of the turning world." This notion of "a mathematically pure point" (as Philip Wheelwright has called it) seems to be Eliot's poetic equivalent in our cosmology for Dante's "unmoved Mover," another way of symbolising a timeless release from the "outer compulsions" of the world. Still another variation is the passage on the Chinese jar in the final section. Here Eliot, in a conception comparable to Wallace Stevens' "Anecdote of the Jar," had suggested how art conquers time:

> Only by the form, the pattern,
> Can words or music reach
> The stillness, as a Chinese jar still
> Moves perpetually in its stillness.

Burnt Norton is the most philosophically dense of the series, and any adequate account of Eliot's development of his themes would demand detailed analysis. With the opening phase of *East Coker*, "In my beginning is my end," he has extended his meditation on time into history. In such a phrase, which is close to Heraclitus' "The beginning and the end are common," the poet has also indicated the recurrent attraction he feels to the reconciliation of opposites which characterizes that pre-Socratic philosopher. Eliot is using these words in a double sense. He is thinking historically—as the first section goes on to make clear, he is thinking back to the conception of order and harmony as propounded by a 16th Century Thomas Elyot in his *Booke named the Governour*. And near the close of the poem, the overtones of history and of family are blended in the phrase, "Home is where one starts from." But the continuity with which he is concerned is not simply that of race. He is also thinking in religious terms—in my beginning, in my birth, is implied my end, death; yet, in the Christian reversal of terms, that death can mean rebirth, and the culminating phrase of *East Coker* is "In my end is my beginning."

As his thought becomes involved with the multiple meanings of history, with how the moments of significance and illumination bisect "the world of time," he dwells also on the course of the individual history, and his reflections become deeply personal as he confronts the disappointments of old age. He weighs the "limited value" of what can be learned from experience, since its accustomed pattern may restrict and blind us to what comes with the "new and shocking" moment. When the soul is sick, it can learn only through humility, only if it accepts the paradox which is developed both by St. John of the Cross and by Marvell in his *Dialogue Between the Soul and Body,* that "Our only health is the disease." Man may come to the end of his night of dark vacancy only if he learns that he "must go by the way of dispossession."

The three middle sections of *East Coker* are as somber as anything Eliot has written, and culminate in his pronouncing his career which has fallen between two wars as "twenty years largely wasted." The danger of such a declaration is that it risks false humility, and the inertness of these lines contrasts unsatisfactorily with the comparable passage in *Burnt Norton* on what is gained through form. But the contrast is structurally deliberate, and with the phrase, "Home is where one starts from," there comes the quickening reflection that old men should be explorers "into another intensity/ For a further union." What they must pass through is such "empty desolation" at the sea's, and in developing that image in the concluding lines of *East Coker,* the poet prepares the most thrilling transition of the whole series. For *The Dry Salvages* opens with a contrast between the river and the sea, between the two forces that have most conditioned Eliot's sense of rhythm. For nationalist critics of the Van Wyck Brooks school who declare that Eliot has broken away from his roots since he has not included in his poems realistic details from the Middle West, it could be profitable to note that the river is "the big river,"—at first the frontier, then the "useful, untrustworthy" conveyor of shipping, then a problem to be solved by the bridge builder, and at last "almost forgotten" by the city dwellers. This passage gives an insight into the sources of a poet's rhythm; and into how he penetrates for his material beneath all surface details, in order to repossess his essential experience. The significance of the river for Eliot shows in what he wrote to a St. Louis paper in 1930:

I feel that there is something in having passed one's childhood beside the big river, which is incommunicable to those who have not. Of course my people were Northerners and New Englanders, and of course I have spent many years out of America altogether; but Missouri and the Mississippi have made a deeper impression on me than any other part of the world.

The contrapuntal balance of sea and river reinforces, throughout *The Dry Salvages,* the themes of time and movement. And yet the underlying changelessness of the sea beneath its tides, with its tolling bells measuring "time not our time," underscores also the contrasting theme of the timeless. History is again dwelt on, and is now discerned as not just the blind corridor it seemed

to Gerontion, since "Time the destroyer is time the preserver." This perception
gives foundation for Krishna's counsel of disinterested action. Then, after the
bell buoy's "perpetual angelus" has resounded through the lyrical fourth movement, as it had in the sestina at the opening of the second, Eliot makes his
most complete articulation of what can be involved in "the intersection of the
timeless with time." By allusions to the rose garden and to the other moments
of illumination that he has symbolized in the three poems so far, he suggests
the common basis of such moments in their "hints" of grace. He goes farther,
and states that such "hints" lead also to the central truth in his religious convictions:

> But to apprehend
> The point of intersection of the timeless
> With time, is an occupation for the saint—
> No occupation either, but something given
> And taken, in a lifetime's death in love,
> Ardour and selflessness and self-surrender.
> For most of us, there is only the unattended
> Moment, the moment in and out of time,
> The distraction fit, lost in a shaft of sunlight,
> The wild thyme unseen, or the winter lightning,
> Or the waterfall, or music heard so deeply
> That it is not heard at all, but you are the music
> While the music lasts. These are only hints and guesses,
> Hints followed by guesses; and the rest
> Is prayer, observance, discipline, thought and action.
> The hint half guessed, the gift half understood, is Incarnation.
> Here the impossible union
> Of spheres of existence is actual,
> Here the past and future
> Are conquered and reconciled. . . .

The doctrine of Incarnation is the pivotal point on which Eliot's thought
has swung well away from the 19th Century's romantic heresies of Deification. The distinction between thinking of God become Man through the
Saviour, or of Man becoming God through his own divine potentialities, can
be at the root of political as well as of religious belief. Eliot has long affirmed
that Deification, the reckless doctrine of every great man as a Messiah, has led
ineluctably to Dictatorship. What he has urged in his *Idea of a Christian Society*, is a reestablished social order in which both governors and governed
find their completion in their common humility before God. The above passage, therefore, compresses, at the climax of *The Dry Salvages*, the core of
Eliot's thought on time, on history, and on the destiny of man.

The content of *Little Gidding* is most apparently under the shadow of the war. But it underlines what Eliot declared in a recent essay on "Poetry in War-time," that the more permanently valuable war poetry of 1914–18 was "more of sadness and pity than of military glory." The secluded chapel enforces thoughts of pilgrimage and prayer, but a further reflection on history carries the poet to the realization that

> We cannot restore old policies
> Or follow an antique drum.

If "history may be servitude, history may be freedom," and

> Here the intersection of the timeless moment
> Is England and nowhere. Never and always.

In the final movement he resumes successively all his major themes, opening with "The end is where we start from." This leads into another passage on words and form, since "every sentence is an end and a beginning," "every poem an epitaph." Comparably, every action is a step towards death, but may likewise be a step towards redemption. Once again we have a recognition of the potentialities of history far more resolute than what was seen in the tired backward look in *East Coker*. For now the poet affirms that

> We shall not cease from exploration
> And the end of all our exploring
> Will be to arrive where we started
> And know the place for the first time.

What we will know is adumbrated through allusions that take us back through the series, back to "the source of the longest river," back, indeed, to the moment of release that he evoked in "New Hampshire," to "the children in the apple tree." But the completion of that glimpsed vision, as was the case with Dante's childhood love for Beatrice, must be sought through full matur-ity, through

> A condition of complete simplicity
> (Costing not less than everything).

The value of Eliot's device of incremental repetition hinges most on this final section of *Little Gidding*, since there is hardly a phrase that does not recall an earlier passage in the series. Some readers may object that this makes too much for a circular movement, with insufficient resolution at the close. In one sense this is true, but only in as much as the questions on which the poet is meditating are endless in their recurrent urgency. And such structural recurrence of themes, as Proust also found, is the chief device by which the writer can convey the recapture of time. The concluding lines mount to final-ity in their enunciation that all

> shall be well
> When the tongues of flame are in-folded
> Into the crowned knot of fire
> And the fire and the rose are one.

Out of their context these lines may seem to be merely a decorative allusion to Dante's paradise. But once you have observed the central rôle that fire plays, intermittently through the series and dominantly in *Little Gidding,* the potential reconciliation of the flames of destruction with the rose of light is weighted with significance. A glance at Eliot's varied symbolic use of fire can also give us an opportunity to examine more closely than we have so far the texture of the poetry he has developed through the structures of his quartets.

The lyric at the opening of the second part of *Little Gidding* recounts the successive death of the elements. It versifies, with amplification, a sentence of Heraclitus that dwells both on the ceaseless flux and on the reconciliation of opposites, "Fire lives in the death of air, and air in the death of fire; water lives in the death of earth, and earth in the death of water." We can observe again the lasting impression made on the poet's consciousness by this philosopher, concerning whom he recorded in his student's notebook of thirty years ago: "By God he meant fire." But the fire in this lyric, and in the terza rima lines which follow it, is not the fire of creation:

> In the uncertain hour before the morning
> Near the ending of interminable night
> At the recurrent end of the unending
> After the dark dove with the flickering tongue
> Had passed below the horizon of his homing. . . .

The "dark dove" is the bird that haunts now all our skies; its "flickering tongue" is the airman's fire of destruction. The figures who meet "between three districts when the smoke arose" and who tread "the pavement in a dead patrol" need no annotation of their function. But Eliot is occupied here with other meetings as well. It is no usual fellow warden whom he encounters but "a familiar compound ghost." This "ghost" is akin, as some phrases show, to Brunetto Latini, whose meeting with Dante in Hell is one of the passages which has impressed Eliot most. A characteristic of Eliot's poetic thought ever since *Ash Wednesday* has been to make free transitions from the *Inferno* to the *Purgatorio;* and the last words spoken in this "disfigured street" as the day is breaking, are advice to the poet that he cannot escape from the "exasperated spirit" of old age,

> unless restored by that refining fire
> Where you must move in measure, like a dancer.

And here, in the image of the dance—as Theodore Spencer has remarked to me—one also moves in anticipation beyond the searing flames of purgatory to the radiant spheres of paradise.

The other chief passage on fire in *Little Gidding* is the fourth movement, as impressive a lyric as any Eliot has produced:

> The dove descending breaks the air
> With flame of incandescent terror
> Of which the tongues declare
> The one discharge from sin and error.
> The only hope or else despair
>   Lies in the choice of pyre or pyre—
>   To be redeemed from fire by fire.
>
> Who then devised the torment? Love.
> Love is the unfamiliar Name
> Behind the hands that wove
> The intolerable shirt of flame
> Which human power cannot remove.
>   We only live, only suspire
>   Consumed by either fire or fire.

The control of the range of meanings here is masterly. On one level, the choice in the first stanza is between destruction and destruction, for as "the tongues" on both sides declare it is either "we" or "they," the "incandescent terror" must blot out either London or Berlin. But the descending dove is, more profoundly, that of annunciation, and "the tongues" of prophecy declare the terms of our possible redemption. The poem reaches the heart of its meaning in the heavily stressed end-word of the opening line of the second stanza. That most familiar word is yet unfamiliar to mankind, which "cannot bear very much reality." We can hardly face the fact that love is essentially not release but suffering; and that the intolerable burden of our desires—our Nessus shirt—can be removed by nothing within our power, but solely through grace. All we have is the terms of our choice, the fire of our destructive lusts or the inscrutable terrible fire of divine Love.

The poetry of purgation, as Eliot has observed, is ordinarily less exciting than that of either damnation or beatitude, but this lyric transcends such limitation through its fervor. The encounter between the air raid wardens is the other most dramatic passage in the poem. Since it marks Eliot's first experiment with terza rima, it carries further the long series of his debts to Dante. But its method follows more particularly the lesson of another master. The "forgotten, half-recalled" figure is evoked by the device of multiple reference which Henry James used in his "ghost" stories. The figure, "too strange . . .

for misunderstandings," suggests not only Brunetto Latini or Arnaut Daniel. When he reminds Eliot how their common concern with speech impelled them "to purify the dialect of the tribe," he virtually translates from Mallarmé's *Le Tombeau d'Edgar Poe* ("donner un sens plus pur aux mots de la tribu"), and indicates that he may be thought of as any of Eliot's dead masters. When he proceeds to disclose "the gifts reserved for age," it is interesting to recall that Eliot's bitter "Lines for an Old Man" contain in the manuscript the epigraph, "to Stéphane Mallarmé."

It may be objected that such a range of suggestion detracts from dramatic singleness. It is more certainly true that Eliot, from the time of his earliest poems, has been more successful in posing a dramatic moment than in developing a sustained action. It may also be charged that he betrays a limitation of content in comparison with some of the other strange meetings that he recalls. Whereas the lines spoken by Brunetto Latini are, as Eliot himself has said, Dante's "testimony of a loved master of arts"; and Wilfred Owen's hallucinated pitiful encounter was with no less than the enemy he had killed; the main burden that Eliot's "ghost" has to convey is the impotent lacerations of growing old.

It has been charged against Eliot ever since his conversion that his content has been tenuous; but the range of reflection and feeling in the quartets alone should serve to give a persuasive refutation. The trouble has been that whereas Eliot's earlier poetry was difficult in form, his later work is difficult in thought. The reader of *Gerontion* had to learn how to supply the missing connectives. The reader of the quartets finds a sufficiently straightforward logic, but is confronted with realms of discourse largely unfamiliar to a secular age. Sustained knowledge of the dark night of the soul is a rare phase of mystical experience in any age; and it is at that point that agnostic and atheist readers have been most severe in demanding whether Eliot's lines express anything more than mere literary allusions. The severity is desirable, but it should not be forgotten that authentic poetry often takes us into experiences equally remote from our ordinary hours, as in Oedipus' vision at Colonnos, in Rilke's *Duino Elegies,* or in almost the whole *Paradiso.* Misconceptions of Eliot's content may be avoided if we remain aware, at least, of what he is aiming to do. As our examination of the structures of his quartets has borne out, the greatest change from his earlier poems is that his intentions now are only intermittently dramatic. Or rather, he has tried to concentrate his desire for drama into his two plays; and what he has produced in his quartets is what in the 17th Century would have been called meditations. Yet the most striking change in the texture of his verse is his abandonment of the devices that he learned from Donne and the other metaphysicals. The qualities for which he now aspires are those of a less popular 17th Century master, Lancelot Andrewes, whose "spiritual discipline" he has contrasted with Donne's broken intensity. The three attributes of Andrewes' style that Eliot singled out for praise can belong to poetry as well as to prose: "ordonnance, or arrangement and structure, precision in the use of words, and relevant intensity." Those attributes seemed very far from the poetical aims of "The Hollow Men" which he had written the year before in his essay on Andrewes; but something comparable to the "purely contemplative" emotion he found in Andrewes is what he now wants most to express.

The measure of an author's attraction for Eliot can always be read in what that author has taught him about the development of his medium; and it is notable that the passage which Eliot cited to show how Andrewes' spiritual reflections can yet force "a concrete presence upon us," provided him with the starting point of his own *Journey of the Magi.* Another sentence ("Let us then make this so accepted a time in itself twice acceptable by our accepting . . ."), which illustrated how Andrewes did "not hesitate to hammer, to inflect, even to play upon a word for the sake of driving home its meaning," gave Eliot a similar word-play in *Burnt Norton* ("There they were as our guests, accepted and accepting"), and stimulated him to such an independent development as the startling

Distracted from distraction by distraction.

Those who demand that a poet's content should be immediately useful will take no satisfaction in Eliot's belief that the poet in wartime should as a man "be no less devoted to his country than other men," but that "his first duty as a poet is towards his native language, to preserve and to develop that language." To the nationalist critics that will seem to beg the question of content altogether. But the cheapness of Van Wyck Brooks's opinion that Eliot is a poet of little hope, less faith, and no charity, should be substantially refuted by the lyric on the kinds of love alone. But such a lyric does not exist alone; it rises organically as the summation of one of Eliot's profoundest themes. And those who are suspicious of the inertness of the passages which urge the soul to wait in the dark without hope, should remember that the final declaration, even in *East Coker,* is that

We must be still and still moving.

The reconciliation of opposites is as fundamental to Eliot as it was to Heraclitus. Only thus can he envisage a resolution of man's whole being. The "heart of light" that he glimpsed in the opening movement of *Burnt Norton* is at the opposite pole from the "Heart of Darkness," from which he took the epigraph for "The Hollow Men." Essential evil still constitutes more of Eliot's subject-matter than essential good, but the magnificent orchestration of his themes has prepared for that paradisal glimpse at the close, and thereby makes it no decorative allusion, but an integrated climax to the content no less than to the form. Such spiritual release and reconciliation are the chief reality for which he strives in a world that has seemed to him increasingly threatened with new dark ages.

From *The Achievement of T. S. Eliot* by F. O. Matthiessen, pp. 177–195. Copyright, 1947, by Oxford University Press, Inc. Reprinted by permission of the author and publishers. First published in *The Kenyon Review* as "Eliot's Quartets," Vol. V (Spring, 1943), pp. 161–178.

R. P. BLACKMUR

Notes on E. E. Cummings' Language

[1930]

In his four books of verse, his play, and the autobiographical *Enormous Room*,[1] Mr. Cummings has amassed a special vocabulary and has developed from it a special use of language which these notes are intended to analyze and make explicit. Critics have commonly said, when they understood Mr. Cummings' vocabulary at all, that he has enriched the language with a new idiom; had they been further interested in the uses of language, they would no doubt have said that he had added to the general sensibility of his time. Certainly his work has had many imitators. Young poets have found it easy to adopt the attitudes from which Mr. Cummings has written, just as they often adopt the superficial attitudes of Swinburne and Keats. The curious thing about Mr. Cummings' influence is that his imitators have been able to emulate as well as ape him; which is not so frequently the case with the influence of Swinburne and Keats. Mr. Cummings is a school of writing in himself; so that it is necessary to state the underlying assumptions of his mind, and of the school which he teaches, before dealing with the specific results in poetry of those assumptions.

It is possible to say that Mr. Cummings belongs to the anticulture group; what has been called at various times vorticism, futurism, dadaism, surrealism, and so on.[2] Part of the general dogma of this group is a sentimental denial of the intelligence and the deliberate assertion that the unintelligible is the only object of significant experience. These dogmas have been defended with considerable dialectical skill, in the very practical premise that only by presenting the unintelligible as viable and actual *per se* can the culture of the *dead intelligence* (Brattle Street, the Colleges, and the Reviews) be shocked into sentience. It is argued that only by denying to the intelligence its function of discerning quality and order, can the failures of the intelligence be overcome; that if we take things as they come without remembering what has gone before or guessing what may come next, and if we accept these

[1] As of 1930. There would seem little modification of these notes necessary because of *Eimi* or the subsequent volumes of verse.

[2] The reader is referred to the late numbers *Transition* for a serial and collaborative expression of the latest form which this group has assumed: the Battle of the Word.

things at their face value, we shall know life, at least in the arts, as it really is. Nothing could be more arrogant, and more deceptively persuasive to the childish spirit, than such an attitude when held as fundamental. It appeals to the intellect which wishes to work swiftly and is in love with immediate certainty. A mind based on it accepts every fragment of experience as final and every notion as definite, yet never suffers from the delusion that it has learned anything. By an astonishing accident, enough unanimity exists among these people to permit them to agree among themselves; to permit them, even, to seem spiritually indistinguishable as they appear in public.

The central attitude of this group has developed, in its sectaries, a logical and thoroughgoing set of principles and habits. In America, for example, the cause of the lively arts has been advanced against the ancient seven; because the lively arts are necessarily immediate in appeal and utterly transitory. Thus we find in Mr. Cummings' recent verse and in his play *Him* the side show and the cabaret set up as "inevitable" frames for experience. Jazz effects, tough dialects, tough guys, slim hot queens, barkers, fairies, and so on, are made into the media and symbols of poetry. Which is proper enough in Shakespeare where such effects are used ornamentally or for pure play. But in Cummings such effects are employed as substance, as the very mainstay of the poetry. There is a continuous effort to escape the realism of the intelligence in favor of the realism of the obvious. What might be stodgy or dull because not properly worked up into poetry is replaced by the tawdry and by the fiction of the immediate.

It is no great advantage to get rid of one set of flabby generalities if the result is merely the immersion of the sensibility in another set only superficially less flabby. The hardness of the tough guy is mostly in the novelty of the language. There is no hardness in the emotion. The poet is as far from the concrete as before. By denying the dead intelligence and putting on the heresy of unintelligence, the poet only succeeds in substituting one set of unnourished conventions for another. What survives, with a deceptive air of reality, is a surface. That the deception is often intentional hardly excuses it. The surface is meant to clothe and illuminate a real substance, but in fact it is impenetrable. We are left, after experiencing this sort of art, with the certainty that there was nothing to penetrate. The surface was perfect; the deceit was childish; and the conception was incorrigibly sentimental: all because of the dogma which made them possible.

If Mr. Cummings' tough-guy poems are excellent examples of this sentimentality, it is only natural that his other poems—those clothed in the more familiar language of the lyric—should betray even more obviously, even more perfectly, the same fault. There, in the lyric, there is no pretense at hardness of surface. We are admitted at once to the bare emotion. What is most striking, in every instance, about this emotion is the fact that, in so far as it exists at all, it is Mr. Cummings' emotion, so that our best knowledge of it must be, finally, our best guess. It is not an emotion resulting from the poem; it existed before the poem began and is a result of the poet's private life. Besides its inspiration, every element in the poem, and its final meaning as well, must be taken at face value or not at all. This is the extreme form, in poetry, of romantic egoism: whatever I experience is real and final, and whatever I say represents what I experience. Such a dogma is the natural counterpart of the denial of the intelligence.

Our interest is not in the abstract principle, but in the results of its application in poetry. Assuming that a poem should in some sense be understood, should have a meaning apart from the poet's private life, either one of two things will be true about any poem written from such an attitude as we have ascribed to Mr. Cummings. Either the poem will appear in terms so conventional that everybody will understand it—when it will be flat and no poem at all; or it will appear in language so far distorted from convention as to be inapprehensible except by lucky guess. In neither instance will the poem be genuinely complete. It will be the notes for a poem, from which might flow an infinite number of possible poems, but from which no particular poem can be certainly deduced. It is the purpose of this paper to examine a few of the more obvious types of distortion which Mr. Cummings has practiced upon language.

The question central to such a discussion will be what kind of meaning does Mr. Cummings' poetry have; what is the kind of equivalence between the language and its object? The pursuit of such a question involves us immediately in the relations between words and feelings, and the relations between the intelligence and its field in experience—all relations which are precise only in terms themselves essentially poetic—in the feeling for an image, the sense of an idiom. Such relations may only be asserted, may be judged only tentatively, only instinctively, by what seems to be the disciplined experience, but what amounts, perhaps, only to the formed taste. Here criticism is appreciation. But appreciation, even, can take measures to be certain of its grounds, and to be full should betray the constant apprehension of an end which is the necessary consequence, the proper rounding off, of just those grounds. In the examination of Mr. Cummings' writings the grounds will be the facts about the words he uses, and the end will be apprehended in the quality of the meaning his use of these words permits.

There is one attitude towards Mr. Cummings' language which has deceived those who hold it. The typographical peculiarities of his verse have caught and irritated public attention. Excessive hyphenation of single words, the use of lower case "i," the breaking of lines, the insertion of punctuation between the letters of a word, and so on, will have a possible critical importance to the textual scholarship of the future; but extensive consideration of these peculiarities today has very little importance, carries almost no reference to the meaning of the poems. Mr. Cummings' experiments in typography merely extend the theory of notation by adding to the number, *not* to the *kind,* of conventions the reader must bear in mind, and are danger- ous only because since their uses cannot readily be defined, they often obscure rather than clarify the exact meaning. No doubt the continued practice of such notation would produce a set of well-ordered conventions susceptible of general use. At present the practice can only be "allowed for," recognized in the particular instance, felt, and forgotten: as the diacritical marks in the dictionary are forgotten once the sound of the word has been learned. The poem, after all, only takes wing on the page. It persists in the ear.[3]

Considering typographical peculiarities for our present purposes as either irrelevant or unaccountable, there remain the much more important pecu- liarities of Mr. Cummings' vocabulary itself; of the poem *after* it has been read, as it is in the mind's ear, as it is on the page only for reassurance and correction.

If a reader, sufficiently familiar with these poems not to be caught on the snag of novelty, inspects carefully any score of them no matter how widely scattered, he will especially be struck by a sameness among them. This sameness will be in two sorts—a vagueness of image and a constant re- currence of words. Since the one depends considerably upon the other, a short list of some of Mr. Cummings' favorite words will be a good preliminary to the examination of his images. In *Tulips and Chimneys* words such as these occur frequently: thrilling, flowers, serious, absolute, sweet, unspeaking, utter, gradual, ultimate, final, serene, frail, grave, tremendous, slender, fragile, skillful, carefully, musical, intent, young, gay, untimid, incorrigible, groping, dim, slow, certain, deliberate, strong, chiselled, subtle, tremulous, perpetual, crisp, perfect, sudden, faint, strenuous, minute, superlative, keen, ecstatic, fleet, delicious stars, enthusiastic, capable, dull, bright. In listing these as favorite words, it is meant that these words do the greater part of the work in the poems where they occur; these are the words which qualify the subject-matter of the poems, and are sometimes even the subjects themselves. Observe that none of them, taken alone, are very concrete words; and ob- serve that many of them are the rather abstract, which is to say typical, names for precise qualities, but are not, and cannot be, as orginally important words

---

[3] It is not meant to disparage Mr. Cummings' inventions, which are often excellent, but to minimize an exaggerated contemporary interest. *A Survey of Modernist Poetry* by Laura Riding and Robert Graves, is a study in original punctuation and spelling. Their point is made by printing sonnet 129 in its original notation beside a modern ver- sion; the point being that Shakespeare knew what he was doing and that his editors did not.

in a poem, very precise or very concrete or very abstract: they are middling words, not in themselves very much one thing or the other and should be useful only with respect to something concrete in itself.

If we take Mr. Cummings' most favored word "flower" and inspect the uses to which he puts it, we should have some sort of key to the kind of poetry he writes. In *Tulips and Chimneys* the word "flower" turns up, to a casual count, forty-eight times, and in *&*, a much smaller volume, twenty-one times. We have among others the following: smile like a flower; riverly as a flower; steeped in burning flowers; last flower; lipping flowers; more silently than a flower; snow flower; world flower; softer than flowers; forehead a flight of flowers; feet are flowers in vases; air is deep with flowers; slow supple flower of beauty; flower-terrible; flower of thy mouth; stars and flowers; mouth a new flower; flower of silence; god's flowers; flowers of reminding; dissonant flowers; flower-stricken air; Sunday flower; tremendous flower; speaking flower; flowers of kiss; futile flowers, etc., etc. Besides the general term there is a quantity of lilies and roses, and a good assortment of daisies, pansies, buttercups, violets and chrysanthemums. There are also many examples of such associated words as "petals" and "blooms" and "blossoms," which, since they are similarly used, may be taken as alternative to flowers.

Now it is evident that this word must attract Mr. Cummings' mind very much; it must contain for him an almost unlimited variety and extent of meaning; as the mystic says God, or at least as the incomplete mystic repeats the name of God to every occasion of his soul, Mr. Cummings in some of his poems says flower. The question is, whether or not the reader can possibly have shared the experience which Mr. Cummings has had of the word; whether or not it is possible to discern, after any amount of effort, the precise impact which Mr. Cummings undoubtedly feels upon his whole experience when he uses the word. "Flower" like every other word not specifically the expression of a logical relation, began life as a metaphor, as a leap from feeling to feeling, as a bridge in the imagination to give meaning to both those feelings. Presumably, the amount of meaning possible to the word is increased with each use, but only the meaning *possible*. Actually, in practice, a very different process goes on. Since people are occupied mostly with communication and argument and conversation, with the erection of discursive relationships, words are commonly spoken and written with the least possible meaning preserved, instead of the most. History is taken for granted, ignored or denied. Only the outsides of words, so to speak, are used; and doubtless the outsides of words are all that the discursive intellect needs. But when a word is used in a poem it should be the sum of all its appropriate history made concrete and particular in the individual context; and in poetry all words act *as if* they were so used, because the only kind of meaning poetry can have requires that all its words resume their full life: the full life being modified and made unique by the *qualifications* the words perform one upon the other in the poem. Thus even a very bad poem may seem good to its author, when the author is not an acute critic and believes that there is life in his words merely because there was life (and a very different sort of life, truly) in the feelings which they represent. An author should remember, with the Indians, that the reality of a word is anterior to, and greater than, his use of it can ever be; that there is a perfection to the feelings in words to which his cannot hope to attain, but that his chief labor will be toward the approximation of that perfection.

We sometimes speak of a poet as a master of his words, and we sometimes say that a man's poetry has been run away with by words—meaning that he has not mastered his words but has been overpowered by his peculiar experience of certain among them. Both these notions are commonly improper, because they represent misconceptions of the nature of poetry in so far as they lay any stress upon originality, or lack of it, in the poet's use of words. The only mastery possible to the poet consists in that entire submission to his words which is perfect knowledge. The only originality of which the poet is properly capable will be in the choice of order, and even this choice is largely a process of discovery rather than of origination. As for words running away with a poet or poem, it would be more accurate to say that the poet's *ideas* had run away with him than his words.

This is precisely what has occurred to Mr. Cummings in his use of the word "flower" as a maid of all work. The word has become an idea, and in the process has been deprived of its history, its qualities, and its meaning. An idea, the intellectual pin upon which a thought is hung, is not transmissible in poetry as an important element in the poem and ought only to be employed to pass over, with the greatest possible velocity, the area of the uninteresting (what the poet was not interested in). That is, a poem whose chief intent was the notation of character and yet required a descriptive setting might well use for the description such vague words as space and time, but could not use such words as goodness or nobleness without the risk of flatness. In Mr. Cummings' poetry we find the contrary; the word "flower," because of the originality with which he conceives it, becomes an idea and is used to represent the most interesting and most important aspect of his poem. Hence the center of the poem is permanently abstract and unknowable for the reader, and remains altogether without qualifications and concreteness. It is not the mere frequency of use that deadens the word flower into an idea; it is the kind of thought which each use illustrates in common. By seldom saying *what* flower, by seldom relating immitigably the abstract word to the specific experience, the content of the word vanishes; it has no inner mystery, only an impenetrable surface.

This is the defect, the essential deceit, we were trying to define. Without questioning Mr. Cummings, or any poet, as to sincerity (which is a personal attitude, irrelevant to the poetry considered) it is possible to say that when in any poem the important words are forced by their use to remain impenetrable, when they can be made to surrender nothing actually to the senses—then the poem is defective and the poet's words have so far deceived him as to become ideas merely.[4] Mr. Cummings is not so much writing poetry, as he is dreaming, idly ringing the changes of his reveries.

Perhaps a small divagation may make clearer the relation of these remarks to Mr. Cummings' poems. Any poetry which does not consider itself as much of an art and having the same responsibilities to the consumer as the arts of silversmithing or cobbling shoes—any such poetry is likely to do little more than rehearse a waking dream. Dreams are everywhere ominous and full of meaning; and why should they not be? They hold the images of the secret self, and to the initiate dreamer betray the nerve of life at every turn, not through any effort to do so, or because of any inherited regimen, but simply because they cannot help it. Dreams are like that—to the dreamer the maximal limit of experience. As it happens, dreams employ words and pictorial images to fill out their flux with a veil of substance. Pictures are natural to everyone, and words, because they are prevalent, seem common and inherently sensible. Hence, both picture and word, and then with a little stretching of the fancy the substance of the dream itself, seem expressible just as they occur—as things created, as the very flux of life. Mr. Cummings' poems are often nothing more than the report of just such dreams. He believes he knows what he knows, and no doubt he does. But he also believes, apparently, that the words which he encourages most vividly to mind are those most precisely fitted to put his poem on paper. He transfers the indubitable magic of his private musings from the cell of his mind, where it is honest incantation, to the realm of poetry. Here he forgets that poetry, so far as it takes a permanent form, is written and is meant to be read, and that it cannot be a mere private musing. Merely because his private fancy furnishes his liveliest images, is the worst reason for assuming that this private fancy will be approximately experienced by the reader or even indicated on the printed page.

But it is unfair to limit this description to Mr. Cummings; indeed, so limited, it is not even a description of Mr. Cummings. Take the *Oxford Book of English Verse,* or any anthology of poems equally well known, and turn

---

[4] It should be confessed that for all those persons who regard poetry only as a medium of communication, these remarks are quite vitiated. What is communicated had best remain as abstract as possible, dealing with the concrete as typical only; then "meaning" will be found to reside most clearly in the realm of ideas, and everything will be given as of equal import. But here poetry is regarded not at all as communication but as expression, as statement, as presentation of experience, and the emphasis will be on what is made known concretely. The question is not what one shares with the poet, but what one knows in the poem.

from the poems printed therein of such widely separated poets as Surrey, Crashaw, Marvell, Burns, Wordsworth, Shelley, and Swinburne, to the collected works of these poets respectively. Does not the description of Mr. Cummings' mind at work given above apply nearly as well to the bulk of this poetry as to that of Mr. Cummings, at least on the senses' first immersion? The anthology poems being well known are conceived to be understood, to be definitely intelligible, and to have, without inspection, a precise meaning. The descent upon the collected poems of all or of any one of these authors is by and large a descent into tenuity. Most of their work, most of any poet's work, with half a dozen exceptions, is tenuous and vague, private exercises or public playthings of a soul in verse. So far as he is able, the reader struggles to reach the concrete, the solid, the definite; he must have these qualities, or their counterparts among the realm of the spirit, before he can understand what he reads. To translate such qualities from the realm of his private experience to the conventional forms of poetry is the problem of the poet; and the problem of the reader, likewise, is to come well equipped with the talent and the taste for discerning the meaning of those conventions as they particularly occur. Neither the poet's casual language nor the reader's casual interlocution is likely to be much help. There must be a ground common but exterior to each: that is the poem. The best poems take the best but not always the hardest reading; and no doubt it is so with the writing. Certainly, in neither case are dreams or simple reveries enough. Dreams are natural and are minatory or portentous; but except when by accident they fall into forms that fit the intelligence, they never negotiate the miracle of meaning between the poet and the poem, the poem and the reader.

Most poetry fails of this negotiation, and it is sometimes assumed that the negotiation was never meant, by the poet, to be made. For the poet, private expression is said to be enough; for the reader, the agitation of the senses, the perception of verbal beauty, the mere sense of stirring life in the words, are supposed sufficient. If this defense had a true premise—if the poet did express himself to his private satisfaction—it would be unanswerable; and to many it is so. But I think the case is different, and this is the real charge against Mr. Cummings: the poet does not ever express himself privately. The mind cannot understand, cannot properly know its own musings until those musings take some sort of conventional form. Properly speaking, a poet, or any man, cannot be adequate to himself in terms of himself. True consciousness and true expression of consciousness must be external to the blind seat of consciousness—man as sensorium. Even a simple image must be fitted among other images, and conned with them, before it is understood. That is, it must take a form in language which is highly traditional and conventional. The genius of the poet is to make the convention apparently disappear into the use to which he puts it.

Mr. Cummings and the group with which he is here roughly associated, the anti-culture or anti-intelligence group, persists to the contrary. Because experience is fragmentary as it strikes the consciousness it is thought to be essentially discontinuous and therefore essentially unintelligible except in the fragmentary form in which it occurred. They credit the words they use with immaculate conception and there hold them unquestionable. A poem, because it happens, must mean something and mean it without relation to anything but the private experience which inspired it. Certainly it means something, but not a poem; it means that something exciting happened to the writer and that a mystery is happening to the reader. The fallacy is double: they believe in the inexorable significance of the unique experience; and they have discarded the only method of making the unique experience into a poem —the conventions of the intelligence. As a matter of fact they do not write without conventions, but being ignorant of what they use, they resort most commonly to their own inefficient or superficial conventions—such as Mr. Cummings' flower and doll. The effect is convention without substance; the unique experience becomes a rhetorical assurance.

If we examine next, for the sake of the greatest possible contrast, one of the "tough" poems in *Is 5*, we will find a similar breach with the concrete. The use of vague words like "flower" in the lyrical poems as unexpanded similes, is no more an example of sentimental egoism than the use of vague conventions about villains. The distortion differs in terms but is essentially identical.

Sometimes the surface of the poem is so well constructed that the distortion is hard to discover. Intensity of process occasionally triumphs over the subject. Less frequently the subject itself is conceived directly and takes naturally the terms which the language supplies. The poem numbered "One-XII" in *Is 5* is an example in so far as the sentimental frame does not obscure the process.

> now dis "daughter" uv eve (who aint precisely slim) sim
> ply don't know duh meanin uv duh woid sin in
> not disagreeable contras tuh dat not exactly fat
> "father" (adjustin his robe) who now puts on his flat hat.

It is to be noted in this epigram, that there is no inexorable reason for either the dialect or the lapses from it into straight English. No one in particular is speaking, unless it be Mr. Cummings slumming in morals along with he-men and lady social workers, and taking it for granted that the dialect and the really refined language which the dialect exercises together give a setting. There are many other poems in *Is 5*, more sentimental and less successful, where the realism is of a more obvious sort; not having reference to an ideal so much as to a kind of scientific reality. That is, there is an effort to ground an emotion, or the facts which make the emotion, in the style of the character to whom the emotion happens. It is the reporter, the man with the good ear for spoken rhythms, who writes out of memory. The war poems and the poem about Bill and his chip ("One-XVI") are examples. Style in this sense (something laid on) is only an attribute; is not the man; is not the character. And when it is substituted for character, it is likely to be sentimental and melodramatic. That is, the emotion which is named in the poem (by one of its attributes) is in excess of its established source (that same attribute). There is a certain immediate protection afforded to this insufficiency by the surface toughness, by the convention of burlesque; as if by mocking oneself one made sure there was something to mock. It is a kind of trickery resulting from eager but lazy senses; where the sensation itself is an excess, and appears to have done all the work of intuition and intelligence; where sensation seems expert without incorporation into experience. As if sensation could be anything more than the idea of sensation, so far as poetry goes, without being attached to some central body of experience, genuinely understood and *formed* in the mind.

The intrusion of science into art always results in a sentimental realism and always obfuscates form when that science is not kept subordinate to the qualitative experience of the senses—as witness the run of sociological novels. The analogues of science, where conventions are made to do the work of feeling instead of crowning it, are even more dangerous. Mr. Cummings' tough guy and his hard-boiled dialects are such analogues.

Mr. Cummings has a fine talent for using familiar, even almost dead words, in such a context as to make them suddenly impervious to every ordinary sense; they become unable to speak, but with a great air of being bursting with something very important and precise to say. "The bigness of cannon is *skilful* . . . enormous rhythm of *absurdity* . . . *slimness* of *evenslicing* eyes are chisels . . . electric Distinct face haughtily vital *clinched* in a swoon of *synopsis* . . . my friend's being continually whittles *keen* careful futile *flowers*," etc. With the possible exception of the compound *evenslicing* the italicized words are all ordinary words; all in normal contexts have a variety of meaning both connotative and denotative; the particular context being such as to indicate a particular meaning, to establish precisely a feeling, a sensation or a relation.

Mr. Cummings' contexts are employed to an opposite purpose in so far as they wipe out altogether the history of the word, its past associations and general character. To seize Mr. Cummings' meaning there is only the free and *uninstructed* intuition. Something precise is no doubt intended; the warrant for the belief is in the almost violent isolation into which the words are thrown; but that precision can seldom, by this method, become any more than just that "something precise." The reality, the event, the feeling, which we will allow Mr. Cummings has in mind, is not sensibly in the word. It is one thing for meaning to be difficult, or abstruse—hidden in its heart, that is. "Absent thee from *felicity* a while," Blake's "Time is the mercy of eternity" are reasonable examples; there the mystery is inside the words. In Mr. Cummings' words the mystery flies in the face, is on the surface; because there is no inside, no realm of possibility, of essence.

The general movement of Mr. Cummings' language is away from communicable precision. If it be argued that the particular use of one of the italicized words above merely makes the word unique, the retort is that such uniqueness is too perfect, is sterile. If by removing the general sense of a word the special sense is apotheosized, it is only so at the expense of the general sense itself. The destruction of the general sense of a word results in the loss of that word's individuality; for in practice the character of a word (which is its sense) is manifest only in good society, and meaning is distinguished only by conventional association. Mr. Cummings' use of words results in a large number of conventions, but these conventions do not permeate the words themselves, do not modify their souls or change their fates; they cannot be adopted by the reader because they cannot be essentially understood. They should rather be called inventions.

If we take a paragraph from the poem beginning on page thirty in *Is 5*, we will discover another terminus of the emotional habit of mind which produced the emphasis on the word "flower" in *Tulips and Chimneys*.

the Bar. tinking luscious jugs dint of ripe silver with warmlyish wetflat splurging smells waltz the glush of squirting taps plus slush of foam knocked off and a faint piddle-of-drops she says I ploc spittle what the lands thaz me kin in no sir hopping sawdust you kiddo he's a palping wreaths of badly Yep cigars who jim hin why gluey grins topple together eyes pout gestures stickily point made glints squinting who's a wink bum-nothing and money fuzzily mouths take big wobbly foot-steps every goggle cent of it get out ears dribbles sofe right old feller belch the chap hic summore eh chuckles skulch.

Now the point is that the effect of this whole paragraph has much in common with the effect of the word "flower." It is a flower disintegrated, and the parts are not component; so that by presenting an analysis of his image Mr. Cummings has not let us into its secret; the analysis is not a true analysis, because it exhibits, finally, what are still only the results, not the grounds, of his private conventions, his personal emotions. It is indubitable that the words are alive; they jostle, even overturn, the reader in the assurance of their vitality; but the notion of what their true vitality is remains Mr. Cummings' very own. The words remain emotive. They have a gusty air of being something, but they defeat themselves in the effort to say what, and come at last to a bad end, all fallen in a heap.

The easiest *explanation* of the passage would be to say that each separate little collection of words in it is a note for an image; an abstraction, very keen and lively in Mr. Cummings' mind, of something very precise and concrete. Some of the words seem like a painter's notes, some a philologist's. But they are all, as they are presented, notes, abstractions, ideas—with their concrete objects unknown—except to the most arbitrary guess. The guess must be arbitrary because of the quantity, not the quality, of the words employed. Mr. Cummings is not here overworking the individual words, but by heaping so many of them together he destroys their individuality. Meaning really residual in the word is not exhausted, is not even touched; it must remain abstract and only an emotional substitute for it can be caught. The interesting fact about emotional substitutes in poetry, as elsewhere, is their thinness, and the in- adequacy resulting from the thinness. The thinness is compulsory because they can, so far as the poem is concerned, exist only as a surface; they cannot possess tentacular roots reaching into, and feeding on, feelings, because the feelings do not exist, are only present by legerdemain. Genuine emotion in poetry perhaps does not *exist* at all; though it is none the less real for that, because a genuine emotion does not need the warrant of existence: it is the necessary result, in the mind, of a convention of feelings: like the notion of divine grace.

In *Tulips and Chimneys* (p. 109) there is a poem whose first and last lines supply an excellent opposition of proper and improper distortion of language.

> the Cambridge ladies who live in furnished souls . . .
> the
> moon rattles like a fragment of angry candy.

In the context the word "soul" has the element of surprise which is surprise at *justness*; at *aptness*; it fits in and finishes off the notion of the line. "Fur- nished souls" is a good, if slight, conceit; and there is no trouble for the reader who wishes to know what the line means: he has merely to *extend* his knowl- edge slightly, just as Mr. Cummings merely extended the sense of his lan- guage slightly by releasing his particular words in this particular order. The whole work that the poet here demands of his reader is pretty well defined. The reader does not have to *guess*; he is enabled to *know*. The reader is not collecting data, he is aware of a meaning.

It would be unfair not to quote the context of the second line.

> . . . the Cambridge ladies do not care, above
> Cambridge if sometimes in its box of
> sky lavender and cornerless, the
> moon rattles like a fragment of angry candy.

We can say that Mr. Cummings is putting beauty next to the tawdry; juxta- posing the dead with the live; or that he is being sentimentally philosophical in verse—that is, releasing from inadequate sources something intended to be an emotion.[5]

We can go on illustrating Mr. Cummings' probable intentions almost infinitely. What Mr. Cummings likes or admires, what he holds dear in life, he very commonly calls flowers, or dolls, or candy—terms with which he is astonishingly generous; as if he thought by making his terms general enough their vagueness could not matter, and never noticed that the words so used enervate themselves in a kind of hardened instinct. We can understand what Mr. Cummings intended by "moon" and "candy" but in the process of understanding, the meaning of the words themselves disappears. The thrill of the association of "rattles" with "moon" and "angry" with "candy" becomes useless as a guide. "Rattles" and "angry" can only be continued in the meaning of the line if the reader supplies them with a force, a definiteness of suggestion, with which Mr. Cummings has not endowed them.

The distortion is here not a release of observation so keen that commonplace language would not hold it; it is not the presentation of a vision so complete that words must lose their normal meanings in order to suggest it. It is, on the contrary, the distortion of the commonplace itself; and the difficulty about a commonplace is that it cannot be known, it has no character, no fate, and no essence. It is a substitute for these.

True meaning (which is here to say knowledge) can only exist where some contact, however remote, is preserved between the language, forms, or symbols in which it is given and something concrete, individual, or sensual which inspired it; and the degree in which the meaning is seized will depend on the degree in which the particular concreteness is realized. Thus the technique of "meaning" will employ distortion only in so far as the sense of this concreteness is promoted by it. When contrast and contradiction disturb the ultimate precision of the senses the distortion involved is inappropriate and destructive. Mr. Cummings' line about the moon and candy does not weld a contradiction, does not identify a substance by a thrill of novel association. It leaves the reader at a loss: where it is impossible to *know*, after any amount of effort and good will, what the words mean. If it be argued that Mr. Cummings was not interested in meaning then Mr. Cummings is not a serious poet, is a mere collector of sensations, and can be of very little value to us. And to defend Mr. Cummings on the ground that he is in the pretty good company of Swinburne, Crashaw, and Victor Hugo, is partly to ignore the fact that by the same argument all four also enjoy the companionship of Edgar Guest. Such defense would show a very poor knowledge of the verses of Mr. Cummings, who is nothing if not serious in the attempt to exhibit precise knowledge. His in-

[5] That is, as the most common form of sentimentality is the use of emotion in *excess* of its impetus in the feelings, here we have an example of emotion which fails by a great deal to *come up* to its impetus. It is a very different thing from understatement, where the implications are always definite and where successful disarming.

terest in words and in their real meanings is probably greater than that of most poets of similar dimensions. He has consciously stretched syntax, word order, and meaning in just the effort to expand knowledge in poetry; and his failure is because he has gone too far, has lost sight of meaning altogether—and because, perhaps, the experience which he attempts to translate into poetry remained always personal to him and was never known objectively as itself. By his eagerness Mr. Cummings' relation to language has become confused; he has put down what has meant much to him and can mean little to us, because for us it is not put down—is only indicated, only possibly there. The freshness and depth of his private experience is not denied; but it is certain that, so far as its meaning goes, in the poetry into which he translated it, sentimentality, empty convention, and commonplace rule. In short, Mr. Cummings' poetry ends in ideas *about* things.

When Mr. Cummings resorts of language for the *thrill* that words may be made to give, when he allows his thrill to appear as an equivalent for concrete meaning, he is often more successful than when he is engaged more ambitiously. This is true of poets like Swinburne and Poe, Shelley and the early Marlowe: where the first pair depended almost as much upon *thrill* as Mr. Cummings in those poems where they made use of it at all, and where the second pair, particularly Marlowe, used their thrills more appropriately as ornament: where all four were most successful in their less ambitious works, though perhaps not as interesting. Likewise, today, there is the example of Archibald MacLeish, whose best lines are those that thrill and do nothing more. So that at least in general opinion Mr. Cummings is in this respect not in bad company. But if an examination of thrill be made, whether in Mr. Cummings' verse or in that of others, it will be shown that the use of thrill has at heart the same sentimental impenetrability that defeats the possibility of meaning elsewhere. Only here, in the realm of thrill, the practice is comparatively less illegitimate. Thrill, by itself, or in its proper place, is an exceedingly important element in any poem: it is the circulation of its blood, the *quickness* of life, by which we know it, when there is anything in it to know, most intimately. To use a word for its thrill is to resurrect it from the dead; it is the incarnation of life in consciousness; it is movement.[6]

[6] Cf. Owen Barfield's *Poetic Diction* (London, Faber and Gwyer, 1928), page 202. "For what is absolutely necessary to the present existence of poetry? Movement. The wisdom which she has imparted may remain for a time at rest, but she herself will always be found to have gone forward to where there is life, and therefore movement, *now*. And we have seen that the experience of aesthetic pleasure betrays the real presence of movement. . . . But without the continued existence of poetry, without a steady influx of new meaning into language, even the knowledge and wisdom which poetry herself has given in the past must wither away into a species of mechanical calculation. Great poetry is the progressive incarnation of life in consciousness." That is, we must know what thrills us; else being merely thrilled we are left gasping and aghast, like the little girl on the roller-coaster.

But what Mr. Cummings does, when he is using language as thrill, is not to resurrect a word from the dead: he more often produces an apparition, in itself startling and even ominious, but still only a ghost: it is all a thrill, and what it is that thrilled us cannot be determined. For example, in *XLI Poems,* the following phrases depend considerably for their effect upon the thrill that is in them: "Prisms of sharp *mind;* where strange birds *purr;* into the *smiling* sky *tense* with *blending;* ways cloaked with *renewal;* sinuous riot; *steeped* with burning flowers; little kittens who are called *spring;* electric Distinct face haughtily vital clinched in a *swoon* of synopsis; unreal *precise* intrinsic fragment of actuality; an orchid whose *velocity* is *sculptural;* scythe takes *crisply* the *whim* of thy *smoothness;* perpendicular taste; wet stars, etc., etc." (The italics are mine.)

Take especially the phrase, "scythe takes *crisply* the *whim* of thy *smoothness.*" We know in the poem that it is the scythe of death and that it is youth and beauty (in connection with love) that is to be cut off. So much is familiar, is very conventional; and so the conventional or dead emotion is placed before us; the educated reader receives it and reacts to it without a whimper. But Mr. Cummings must not have been content with presenting the conventional emotion in its conventional form; he felt bound to enliven it with metaphor, with overtones of the senses and the spirit: so that he substituted for the direct statement a rather indirect image combining three usually sensed words for the sake of the *thrill* the special combination might afford. As the phrase stands there is no precision in it. There is a great suggestion of precision about it—like men going off to war; but precisely *what* is left for the reader to guess, to supply from his own heart. By themselves *whim* and *smoothness* are abstract quality words; and in order for them to escape the tensity, the firm disposition, of concrete meaning, they should demand a particular reference.

Smoothness is probably the smoothness of the body and is used here as a kind of metonymy; but it may be pure metaphor and represent what is really to die—the spirit—taken in its physical terms; or it may be that all that is to be understood is a pure tautology. And so on. Even with this possible variety of reference, *smoothness* would not be very objectionable, were it the only. word in the phrase used in this way, or were the other words used to clarify the *smoothness.* But we have also the noun *whim* bearing directly on *smoothness* and the adverb *crisply* which while it directly modifies *takes,* really controls the entire phrase. Taken seriously, *whim,* with reference to the smoothness of either the body or the spirit or the love it inspires, is to say the least a light word; one might almost say a "metrical" word, introduced to stretch the measure, or because the author liked the sound of it, or enjoyed whimsy. It diminishes without limiting the possibilities of *smoothness.* Because it is here, in the phrase, it is inseparable from the phrase's notion of smoothness; yet instead of assisting, tends to prevent what that notion of smoothness is from being divulged.

Crisply is even more difficult to account for; associated with a scythe it perhaps brings to mind the sound of a scythe in a hayfield, which is surely not the reference here intended; it would be very difficult for such a crispness to associate itself with death, which the scythe represents, or *whim,* or *smoothness* in either the spiritual or fleshly sense. If it implies merely a cleanness, a swiftness of motion in the apparition of death, some other word would have seemed better chosen. If this analysis be correct, the three words are unalterably combined by the force of *crisply* in such a way as to defeat the only possible sense their *thrilling* use would have had. They are, so to speak, only the notions of themselves and those selves must remain forever unknown. All we are left with in such a phrase as this is the strangeness which struck us on our first encounter; and the only difference is that the strangeness is the more intensified the more we prolong the examination. This is another test of poetry: whether we understand the *strangeness* of a poem or not.[7]

As it happens there is an exquisite example of the proper use of this strangeness, this thrill, in another poem of Mr. Cummings'; where he speaks of a cathedral before whose face "the streets turn *young* with rain." While there might be some question as to whether the use of *young* presents the only adequate image, there is certainly no question at all that the phrase is entirely successful: that is, the suggestive feeling in *young* makes the juncture, the emotional conjugation, of streets and rain transparent and perfect. This may be so because there is no element of essential contradiction, in the terms of feeling, between the emotional word *young* and the factual word *streets* and *rain;* or because, positively, what happens to the context by the insertion of *young* is, by a necessary leap of the imagination, something qualified. *Young* may be as abstract a word by itself, as purely relative and notional a word, as any other; but here it is brought into the concrete, is fixed there in a proper habitation. Just because reference is not commonly made either to young streets or young rain, the combination here effected is the more appropriate. The surprise, the contrast, which lend force to the phrase, do not exist in the poem; but exist, if at all, rather in the mind of the reader who did not foresee the slight stretch of his sensibility that the phrase requires—which the phrase

---

[7] *Poetic Diction, op. cit.,* pp. 197–8: "It (strangeness) is not synonymous with wonder; for wonder is our reaction to things which we are conscious of not quite understanding, or at any rate of understanding less than we had thought. The element of strangeness in beauty has the contrary effect. It arises from contact with a different kind of *consciousness* from our own, different, yet not so remote that we cannot partly share it, as indeed, in such a connexion, the mere word 'contact' implies. Strangeness, in fact, arouses wonder when we do not understand; aesthetic imagination when we do."

not only requires but necessitates. This then is a *strangeness* understood by its own viableness. No preliminary agreement of taste, or contract of symbols, was necessary.

The point is that Mr. Cummings did not here attempt the impossible, he merely stretched the probable. The business of the poet who deals largely with tactual and visual images, as Mr. Cummings does, for the meat of his work, is to escape the prison of his private mind; to use in his poem as little as possible of the experience that happened to him personally, and on the other hand to employ as much as possible of that experience as it is data.

It is idle for a critic to make the familiar statement that the mind of the writer is his work, or that "the style is the man," when by mind and man is meant the private experience of the author. So far as, in this sense, the mind *is* the work, or the style *is* the man, we can understand the work or the style only through an accidental unanimity; and what we understand is likely to be very thin—perhaps only the terms of understanding. For the author himself, in such circumstances, can have understood very little more. He has been pursuing the impossible, when the probable was right at hand; he has been transcending his experience instead of submitting to it. And this is just what Mr. Cummings does in the phrases quoted above.

It would be ungracious to suppose that as a poet "a swoon of synopsis" did not represent to Mr. Cummings a very definite and very suggestive image. But to assent to that image would be a kind of *tour de force;* the application of such assent would imply that because the words appear, and being words contain notions, they must in this particular instance exhibit the undeniable sign of interior feeling. The proper process of poetry designs exactly what the reader will perceive; that is what is meant when a word is said to be inevitable or *juste.* But this exactness of perception can only come about when there is an extreme fidelity on the part of the poet to his words as living things; which he can discover and control—which he must learn, and nourish, and stretch; but which he cannot invent. The unanimity in our possible experience of words implies that the only unanimity which the reader can feel in what the poet represents must be likewise exterior to the poet; must be somehow both anterior and posterior to the poet's own experience. The poet's mind, perhaps, is what he is outside himself with; is what he has learned; is what he knows; it is also what the reader knows. So long as he is content to remain in his private mind, he is unknowable, impenetrable, and sentimental. All his words perhaps must thrill us, because we cannot know them in the very degree that we sympathize with them. But the best thrills are those we have without knowing it.

This essay has proceeded so far on the explicit assumption that the poems of Mr. Cummings are unintelligible, and that no amount of effort on the part of the reader can make them less so. We began by connecting Mr. Cummings to two schools, or groups, which are much the same essentially—the anti-culture group which denies the intelligence, and the group, not limited to writers, of which the essential attitude is most easily defined as sentimental egoism or romantic idealism. Where these schools are most obviously identical is in the poetry they nourish; the avowed interest is the relentless pursuit of the actual in terms of the immediate as the immediate is given, without overt criticism, to the ego. Unintelligibility is a necessary consequence of such a pursuit, if by the intelligible we mean something concrete, qualified, permanent, and public. Poetry, if we understand it, is not in immediacy at all. It is not given to the senses or to the free intuition. Thus, when poetry is written as if its substance were immediate and given, we have as a result a distorted sensibility and a violent inner confusion. We have, if the poet follows his principles, something abstract, vague, impermanent, and essentially private. When every sensation and every word is taken as final and perfect, the substance which sensations report and for which words must stand remains inexplicable. We can understand only by accident.

Of course there is another side to the matter. In a sense anyone can understand Mr. Cummings and his kind by the mere assertion that he does understand. Nothing else is needed but a little natural sympathy and a certain aptness for the resumption of a childish sensibility. In much the same way we understand a stranger's grief—by setting up a private and less painful simulacrum. If we take the most sentimental and romantic writers as they come, there will be always about their works an excited freshness, the rush of sensation and intuition, all the ominous glow of immediacy. They will be eagerly at home in the mystery of life. Adroitness, expertness, readiness for any experience, will enlighten their activities even where they most miserably fail. They are all actors, ready to take any part, for they put themselves, and nothing else, into every part they play. Commonly their real success will depend on the familiarity of the moments into which they sink themselves; they will depend on convention more than others, because they have nothing else to depend on.

So with the poetry of Mr. Cummings we might be altogether contented and pleased, were he himself content with the measure of his actual performance. But no poetry is so pretentious. No poetry ever claimed to mean more; and in making this claim it cannot avoid submitting itself, disastrously, to the criticism of the intelligence. So soon as we take it seriously, trying to discover what it really says about human destiny and the terms of love and death, we see how little material there is in this poetry except the assurance, made with continuous gusto, that the material exists. We look at the poetry. Sometimes one word, in itself vague and cloudy, is made to take on the work of an entire philosophy—like flower. Sometimes words pile themselves up blindly, each defeating the purport of the others. No feeling is ever defined. No emotion betrays a structure. Experience is its own phantoms, and flows willy-nilly. With the reality of experience the reality of language is lost. No metaphor crosses the bridge of tautology, and every simile is unexpanded. All the *thought* is metonymy, yet the substance is never assigned; so in the end we have only the thrill of substance.

Such an art when it pretends to measure life is essentially vicarious; it is a substitute for something that never was—like a tin soldier, or Peter Pan. It has all the flourish of life and every sentimental sincerity. Taken for what it is, it is charming and even instructive. Taken solemnly, as it is meant to be, the distortion by which it exists is too much for it, and it seems a kind of baby-talk.

From *The Double Agent. Essays in Craft and Elucidation* by R. P. Blackmur, pp. 1–29. Arrow Editions. Copyright, 1935, by R. P. Blackmur. Reprinted by permission of the author. First published in *The Hound and Horn*, Vol. IV (January–March, 1931), pp. 163–192.

PHILIP BLAIR RICE

Paul Valéry •

[1930]

M. PAUL VALÉRY has declared from time to time that his poetry is only an exercise. Perhaps this is but mock humility: in any case, his readers refuse to believe that verse so lovely as much of his can fail to be worth while for itself alone. Certainly no other poet enjoys an equal esteem in France today, and it was as a practitioner of *poésie pure* that he was elected to the French Academy, through the able publicity work of the Abbé Brémond. M. Valéry, furthermore, is one of the few poets of his nation who have been widely read abroad; floods of essays on his poetic technique have appeared in many languages.

But for once let us take the man at his word. He has versified only intermittently. He does not seem to care whether anyone reads his poetry or not: his volumes are issued in limited editions, which sell at four times their marked price as soon as they appear. This may be, as M. Souday suggests, merely "une espèce de coquetterie, de manège habile pour se faire désirer." Nevertheless it is difficult to read Valéry's works or to hear him speak without believing in his sincerity. Both his verse and his prose have centered around certain problems which for long periods of time have become so absorbing that he has given up poetical composition entirely. If his poetry is only an exercise, an exercise for what?

Before he was twenty, under Mallarmé's influence the poet began to write Symbolist verse, which appeared in the reviews of the cult. Then in 1894, at the age of twenty-three, Valéry was asked to do an essay on Leonardo. Ever since, he has been in quest of something, and the germs of that quest are to be found in the early *Introduction à la Méthode de Léonard de Vinci*. Valéry saw in Leonardo, so he later wrote, the "principal character of that *Comédie Intellectuelle* which has not hitherto found its poet, and which would be, to my taste, still more precious than the *Comédie Humaine,* and even than the *Divine Comedy*." The object of this study he stated as follows: "I felt that this master of his means, this possessor of design, of images, of calculation, had found the central attitude starting from which the undertakings of knowledge and the operations of art are equally possible, and a happy reciprocity between analysis and acts is singularly probable."

315

With Leonardo, then, the accepted example of the universal man, did Valéry's search begin. The universal man, he indicates, is not necessarily a jack-of-all-trades. In the first place, he is universal not in the sense of one who is able to do a little of everything but of one who attains to a balance of his faculties. This mental proportion enabled Leonardo, in both his art and his science, to discover universal laws. The secret of this man of the Renaissance lay in his ability to find relations between "things whose law of continuity escapes us." His method was what Valéry calls "construction," a word used "to designate more emphatically the problem of human intervention in the things of the world and to direct the reader's mind toward the logic of the subject, a material suggestion."

Valéry takes up Leonardo's paintings and his architectural and engineering works, showing that his hero sought objective standards for their construction. These standards are found in the geometrical aspects of composition, in the dictates of perspective and in Leonardo's fancy that "the air is filled with an infinite number of straight and radiating lines, intersecting and interweaving without ever borrowing each other's paths, and they represent for each object the true form of its explanation (or its essence)."

As the fine arts go farther from architecture, the more intractable "human element" becomes of increasing importance, and it is necessary to find a non-mathematical objectivity in valuing the work of art. For literature this is difficult and Valéry does little but adduce Poe's theory that the poem must be made not for the poet's own good pleasure, but according to psychological laws by which it will realise a common state in those who read it, even if the readers be taken as a choice few with a similar foundation of culture. "The function of the poet is not to be inspired himself, but to create inspiration in his readers," as M. Valéry later phrased it.

Universality, or objectivity, therefore, requires a discounting of the artist's personal eccentricities. Here Valéry breaks with the main Romantic tradition, which coddled the artist with the notion that all he had to do was to develop his individuality and let it drip over on paper or canvas. Valéry is struggling to escape from the subjectivism which infected the art and thought of the nineteenth century: "Our personality is only a *thing*, mutable and accidental. . . . All criticism is dominated by the superannuated principle that the man is the *cause* of the work—as the criminal in the eyes of the law is the cause of the crime. They are rather the effect!" Or again: "An artist pays for every genuine discovery with a decrease in the importance of his 'ego.' A *person* loses something of himself for everything beautiful he has created." The superior man, he reminds us, is never an "original," and the history of his life is wholly inadequate to explain his works.

If the works are so important, why did Leonardo leave so much unfinished? Valéry implies that even works are incidental to the great artist. "To live, and even to live well, is only a means for him. . . . To act is only an exercise. To love—I don't know if he can." All are subsidiary to the attainment of true universality, which is at the same time to achieve consciousness of self. What self is it that Valéry is trying to know? Not the individual self, the personality, certainly. The superior man, he believes, moves toward a state of pure consciousness, or the pure ego (*le moi pur*), which is identical with the knowledge of universal laws and relations. Rather than Hegelian, it is Spinozistic: Valéry arrives at something very like Spinoza's Intellectual Love of God. This conclusion, it should be remarked, was at most only implicit in the early *Introduction,* for it is first given full statement in the "Note and Digression" which he wrote as a preface to that essay in 1919.

We may, then, find it fruitful to approach Valéry's life work by taking it as the quest for universality. His success may be judged accordingly. From the beginning we find him torn by two seductions which perhaps are irreconcilable. He is lured by action—by the fulfillment and human balance achieved in shaping matter into some concrete embodiment of universal laws which have been discovered by the artist. On the other hand, the discovery of these laws itself seems at times to be the ultimate fulfillment. After long and vigorous travail, "pure consciousness"—this clear flash of a universal law from the hidden bosom of reality—brings an exaltation to which the making of any individual thing, however splendid, seems an anticlimax.

Which then, if either, is the universal man: the builder or the pure spirit? Our author vacillates.

II

In *Monsieur Teste,* which followed soon after the *Introduction,* Valéry swung toward asceticism. M. Teste, this extraordinary bourgeois, this impeccably precise talker, who does not even read, who merely observes and reflects, has attained a perfect working of the intellect. Everything about him—his voice, his bearing, his manner of eating, his absence of gesture—shows the complete abnegation of individuality. His room is the Platonic idea of a room: it contains nothing which bears the stamp of a personality; the chairs, the bed, the table, are as "general" as could be imagined. He spends his hours in contemplating such subjects as the nature of time and consciousness, and in finding the exact word to express his observations. That M. Teste left a deep impression on Valéry is obvious when one hears him speak: the lecture, no matter what the subject, flows with the lucidity and the seeming inevitability of a geometrical theorem.

M. Teste has achieved the "obstinate rigor," the *netteté désespérée* of Leonardo. But he is not the universal man in the sense of the builder. He does not act at all! Furthermore—but this is to raise another point—emotion and certain kinds of sensibility in him are starved by the intellect, the faculty of concepts, as they would not be in a mind that used all its functions. As a counterpoise to M. Teste, who has been called the *animus,* Valéry creates Mme. Teste, the *anima.* She says of her husband: "Quand il me revient de la profondeur! . . . Il retombe sur moi comme si j'étais la terre même!"

Yet the attractiveness of M. Teste for Valéry proved irresistible. For twenty years he gave himself to the exact disciplines. He studied the foundations of geometry, the nature of time, attention, formal logic, physiology. A few of the notes that Valéry took during his long reclusion have lately trickled into the magazines. More in the fashion of Pascal than of a systematic philosopher, they are inflections upon the personality, its metamorphoses, and its self-abnegating labor of creation.

At the end of this period Valéry, like André Gide, wished to pay "a last debt to the past." He planned to write *La Jeune Parque* in his earlier Symbolist manner. But his prepossession grew upon him. The poem is a long paean of the young Fate awakening to self-consciousness. Then came a scattering of essays and eventually another book of poems, *Charmes.* Among the most important of these works are the charming dialogues, *L'Âme et la Danse,* and *Eupalinos ou l'Architecte.* In the former, Socrates and his companions watch a ballet, giving the most exquisite description of it, and philosophizing upon its significance. Socrates finally decides that the dance does not represent a story, or an emotion such as love, but "the pure act of metamorphosis," "love as well as the sea, and life itself and thoughts." The dancer escapes entirely from her personality to become this pure act. When she comes out of her trance she says:

Asile, asile, ô mon asile, ô Tourbillon!—J'étais en toi, ô mouvement, en dehors de toutes choses.

After twenty years of silence the poet has proceeded from analysis to act, and he celebrates in this song of triumph. But further reflection, in *Eupalinos,* somewhat dampens his joy. The shades of Socrates and Phaedrus are discoursing in the dim Elysian fields. Their talk gradually shifts to the nature of beauty. Phaedrus quotes his friend, Eupalinos the architect, as saying that there are "buildings which sing"; these are the temples which are built for sheer beauty of form. A factory, on the other hand, talks; it is constructed for utility only. Music and architecture are held to be the supreme arts because of their "purity." Painting, for example, can never escape altogether into a world of its own. It must cover a given surface, and it cannot wholly avoid representing objects or persons. But a melody or a temple feigns to be nothing but itself; it expresses pure relations which have no necessary reference to any other created thing. Thus it attains a sort of universality, in that it is not bound to take any of the individual conformations in which the Demiurge left the world.

Architecture and music, then, have pure beauty. But another advantage is imputed to architecture which makes it superior to music—its "solidity or duration." Duration is inappropriate here, in one meaning of the word: Many of Socrates' sayings, for example, have endured, while the temples of Eupalinos are in ruins. And it is probable that Bach's music will be played long after the Mestrovic chapel in Cavtat will have been destroyed by shells. A temple, like a statue or a painting, can have more duration than a piece of music only by the fact that it exists continuously through time, while the music—though it may "subsist," or float in the realm of essence forever—is embodied but intermittently, that is, when it is played. Why one type of duration should be more sublime than the other is a question. Valéry's rather curious preference for architecture might be taken as a gesture of courtesy—he wrote *Eupalinos* for an architectural magazine—but the psychological explanation would perhaps be more just. After his long period of inactivity . .

tant d'étrange
Oisivité; mais pleine de pouvoir . . .

Valéry had come to glorify action in its most materialistic sense, the shaping of good solid earth and stone. At the end of the dialogue, Socrates, the mere talker, concluding that his life in the other world was misspent, evokes and praises anti-Socrates, the builder.

In the same way, doubtless, Valéry has found even his versifying unsatisfactory. A poet has something of the pure spirit's pitiful ineptitude. He performs overt actions, indeed, but to one enamored of "pure beauty," how unsatisfying are these scrawls and scratchings with a pencil! Affairs are even worse if the poet's handwriting is bad; he has not even the minor satisfaction of seeing his thoughts embodied in beautiful curves and flourishes. He yearns for the sculptor's chisel, test-tubes, the piano, brush, and canvas; any apparatus by which he could manipulate matter would give him release. And the ultimate product, a book, is but a receptacle for symbols, which as such are nothing to the senses: they speak to the mind in its terrible remoteness and isolation.

Yet the poet, and even the philosopher, is by Valéry's definition somewhat of a builder: "The builder whom I now conjure up finds before him, as chaos and primitive matter, precisely the order of the world that the Demiurge drew from the disorder of the beginning. Nature is formed and its elements are separated; but something compels him to consider this work as incomplete, and needing to be reworked and again put in motion, in order that it may be satisfying more specifically to mankind. Man begins his activity precisely at the point where the god left off." Valéry brought together images and ideas to combine them in a form which the Demiurge—Nature and mankind before him, that is—had never created; Socrates found universal laws about the human mind, the State, and logical reality, which until then had dwelt in limbo. And if the Athenians had only listened to him, perhaps his ideas, too, would have been embodied—not, it is true, in temples, but in human beings living beautifully and intelligently. The architect has no exclusive claim to be the Demiurge's successor.

III

The other question raised in the dialogue, that of the "purity" of the arts, is more important to the subject of the universal man. It was put rather well by Kant in the *Critique of Judgment,* when he made his distinction between free or pure beauty, and dependent beauty. Enjoyment of a flower or an arabesque, he says, presupposes no concept of what the object ought to be, whereas enjoyment of dependent beauty, such as that of a man or a horse (Kant even includes buildings—"be it church, palace, arsenal, or summer-house") "presupposes a concept of what the thing is to be, and consequently a concept of its perfection." Even Valéry's favorites, music and architecture, are not simon-pure arts. Music, for example, is not a mere pattern of sounds. It produces what may be called an emotional tone in the listener, or, more accurately, a developed emotional experience. To state the matter simply, and rather crudely, in Bach this emotional experience may be one of grandeur; in Mozart, of dignified joy or sadness; in Berlioz or Liszt, of fake heroism or bar-baric disorder. The quality of the emotion communicated—to take the emo-tion alone—is one criterion for judging the worth of the music; and this emo-tion is akin to the emotions which enter into the rest of life. Likewise, it would be a very limited view of architecture that did not take into account its function, which in the case of the Greek temple involves the congruity of its meaning with that of the Olympian religion.

Valéry applied his esthetic ideas to his own art in the doctrine of *poésie pure,* which he derived, or thought he derived, from Poe through Baudelaire. What Poe was getting at in *The Poetic Principle,* the essay to which Valéry refers, and which Baudelaire plagiarized, may be summed up as follows: First, he tried to find the psychological laws governing the effect of the poem on the reader. In this he did not go much farther than to insist that a poem should not be too long to be read in a half-hour or an hour, because the poetic exaltation cannot be maintained for more than that span of time, and the unity of the effect is destroyed if the poem cannot be finished in one reading. Second, he objected to the didacticism of such moralists as Longfellow, on the basis of the old division of mental faculties into pure intellect, taste, and moral sense. Poetry should aim to satisfy "taste," and not to instruct or exhort. Its object is the attainment of "Supernal Loveliness." Poe says further (in his essay on Longfellow) that the test for specious poetry is to ask the question: "Might not this matter be as well or better handled in prose?" He does not object to narrative or drama as such, and he adds that "it does not follow that the incitements of Passion, the precepts of Duty, or even the lessons of Truth, may not be introduced into a poem, and with advantage; for they may subserve, incidentally, in various ways the general purposes of the work."

In spite of a dash of estheticism, Poe's concern was to keep the ethical and intellectual elements of a poem in their due proportion, and to ensure that the poem be primarily a poem, and not a scientific treatise or a tract. The doctrine of *poésie pure* would go still further. According to it, poetry aspires to the "pure state," in which science, morality, and history (including story-telling?) should be ruled out altogether, and poetry becomes sheer word-music. Valéry, indeed, has only dallied with this notion; he has never, as many of his encomiasts would have us believe, held to it strictly. Such absolute poetry, as Valéry realizes, is at best an ideal limit: "Rien de si pur ne peut coexister avec les conditions de la vie." Consequently, he decided to admit an element of thought, and to allow his verse to please the intellect as well as the ear. He had long cherished, in any event, the hope of writing the Comedy of Intellect. Poetic immaculateness would receive fewer stains in the high altitude of metaphyics than in the smoky region of conflicts between man and man. He treated such abstruse subjects as time and change (*Le Cimetière Marin, Palme*). In *Ébauche d'un Serpent,* he sang the strange emergence of life, desire, existence—all symbolized by the snake—from the infinite nothingness of the realm of essence, where

> L'univers n'est qu'un défaut
> Dans le pureté du Non-Être.

But his principal theme was the old one of the mind awakening to self-consciousness (*La Jeune Parque, Air de Sémiramis, Narcisse, La Pythie, La Fausse Morte,* etc.). This preoccupation led to the charge of Narcissism, although, of course, Valéry is far from making an idol of his own personality. His is rather an impersonal Narcissism of the intellect looking at its own conditions and workings. And the Narcissus of the poem died the moment he kissed the image of his own lips in the water. To a large extent, the poet has been concerned with the form of the mind's action—or rather, with the *fact* of its acting, and he has neglected its content.

IV

Just as Lucretius was the epic poet of Intellect, Valéry is the lyric. And this is no mean distinction. Criticism of a poet who has done well what he set out to do must always seem carping. Yet the critic in the long run has to ask: Why is this poet not the perfect poet? Although M. Valéry is, of course, much too modest ever to have claimed that he was trying to be the universal man, in his case the critic's question takes the form: What progress has he made toward that elusive ideal of his youth, universality?

His poetry has a wealth of music, a plenitude of ideas, poetically expressed. It has the rigor necessary to a true universality. Yet there is something lacking. As E. R. Curtius says: "Valéry's poetry oscillates between the icy region of a thought that is pure play with forms, and the dry fire of a sensibility that is pure impulsion and is directed toward no goal. It is the poetry of sensuous intellectuality. . . . The mean between intellect and sensation—the region of the soul and her beauty, in which we are accustomed to see the home of poetry and her beauty—is missing from Valéry. Here is, if you like, a void."[1] Those who would not use the word "soul" with the connotations that it has in the German language might prefer to rephrase Herr Curtius' criticism as follows: Is the universal poet to be a pure spirit or a rational animal? The pure spirit may spend his days intellectualizing his sensations; the rational animal, and the poet who is truly universal, would also take his themes from the wisdom of life. His model would be, not Leonardo, but another geometer-painter of the Renaissance, Piero della Francesca. With even greater purity of form than Leonardo's, Piero seized that moment of delicate equilibrium when human life was in the flower of a pagan fullness which had not yet lost the restraint of the Middle Ages. And so skillful was the artist that his humanism does not detract from the formal beauty of the work but fuses with it and gives it meaning. But a humanist Valéry is not: he does not live in a world of men.

Before a final judgment can be hazarded as to Valéry's success thus far in his arduous undertaking, it is necessary to consider *La Crise de l'Esprit* and the extract from the lecture given at Zürich in 1922, both of which are included in the *Variété*. Shaken from his delvings into psychology and esthetics, our author looks at some of the questions that confront civilization after the World War. He sets out to discover why the Europe of the past has been more than its geographical position alone would have made it—a mere cape on the mainland of Asia. Its pre-eminence he finds to have been due to the characteristics of the European man: "eager activity, ardent and disinterested curiosity, a happy blend of imagination and logical rigor, a certain scepticism which is yet not pessimistic, a mysticism without resignation."

But whatever unity there was in the mind of Europe has dissolved. Valéry shows us that European Hamlet looking down on the mental disorder of a continent, which is attributed to "the free coexistence in all cultivated minds of the most dissimilar ideas and the most opposed principles of life and knowledge. That is what characterizes the modern epoch." T. S. Eliot has spoken of the need for the construction of a new spiritual unity of the Occident, which would consist in a unified view of the world such as the Thomistic

[1] *Französischer Geist im Neuen Europa*, pp. 158–159.

system supplied for the Middle Ages. In this, what Valéry calls "principles of life" are probably more fundamental than the problems disputed at Geneva. Within his necessary limits, and in his concrete fashion, the poet too can contribute to this synthesis—perhaps a poet will be the first to sketch its outlines and to create its ritual and mythology. And thereby he may attain the sort of universality that is possible in our day.

V

For the last decade M. Valéry has relapsed into a poetic silence almost as complete as that which followed *Monsieur Teste*. He seems to have put his mind into some kind of order, and it may be that he is seeking an object worthy of its employment.

In his later poems the hymn of joy sung by the mind awakening becomes ever more triumphant. From the impure body of the Pythoness, writhing, panting, drunk, exhaling fumes from nostrils toughened by incense—

A la fumée, à la fureur! . . .

. . . comes at last the voice of the god bringing with it

Illumination, largesse!

We wait, expectantly, to learn if M. Valéry is addressing himself when the Dawn speaks to Semiramis:

EXISTE! . . . Sois enfin toi-même! dit l'Aurore,
O grande âme, il est temps que tu formes un corps!
Hâte-toi de choisir un jour digne d'éclore,
Parmi tant d'autres feux, tes immortels trésors!

From *The Symposium*, Vol. I (April, 1930), pp. 206–220. Reprinted by permission.

Note—Although my opinion of M. Valéry's success in his intellectual quest has not been modified greatly in the years since this essay was published, subsequent developments call for these comments: 1. Immediately after the publication of this essay, M. Valéry became prolific, and his works were issued in popular editions. 2. His new writings were not such as to fulfill the sanguine expectations suggested in the conclusion of the essay. 3. Although T. S. Eliot's dream of a new synthesis still seems to me a worthy ideal, I should not like to be taken as seconding anything Mr. Eliot has said since then about the content of that synthesis, its social and economic foundation, or the method of its attainment.—P. B. R., 1937.

(Valéry died in 1945. He continued to publish during the last years of his life: a new edition of *Regards sur le monde actuel*, his essays on contemporary history; several *discours* before the Académie Française; *Mélange; Mauvaises pensées et autres;* the final volumes of his five series of essays titled *Variété;* two volumes of another series titled *Tel quel;* a collected edition of his *Oeuvres complètes* in twelve volumes; etc., as well as the posthumous *Mon Faust* of 1946. Mr. Rice's essay stands here as it first appeared in 1930. [Editor's note, 1950.])

WILLIAM TROY

Virginia Woolf: The Novel of Sensibility

[1932]

Life is not a series of gig-lamps symmetrically arranged; but *a luminous halo, a semi-transparent envelope* surrounding us from the beginning of consciousness to the end.

NOT only in rhythm and tone but also in the imponderable vagueness of its diction this statement has a familiar ring to the modern ear. The phrases in italics alone are sufficient to suggest its proper order and place in contemporary thought. For if this is not the exact voice of Henri Bergson, it is at least a very successful imitation. Dropped so casually by Mrs. Woolf in the course of a dissertation on the art of fiction, such a statement really implies an acceptance of a whole theory of metaphysics. Behind it lies all that resistance to the naturalistic formula, all that enthusiastic surrender to the world of flux and individual intuition, which has constituted the influence of Bergson on the art and literature of the past thirty years. Whether Mrs. Woolf was affected by this influence directly, or through the medium of Proust or some other secondary source, is not very important. The evidence is clear enough in her work that the fundamental view of reality on which it is based derives from what was the most popular ideology of her generation. What is so often regarded as unique in her fiction is actually less the result of an individual attitude than of the dominant metaphysical bias of a whole generation.

For members of that generation concerned with fiction the philosophy of flux and intuition offered a relief from the cumbersome technique and mechanical pattern of naturalism. (Against even such mild adherents to the doctrine as Wells and Bennett Mrs. Woolf raised the attack in *Mr. Bennett and Mrs. Brown*.) Moreover, the new philosophy opened up sources of interest for the novel which allowed it to dispense with whatever values such writers as George Eliot and Henry James had depended on in a still remoter period. Like naturalism, it brought with it its own version of an esthetic; it supplied a medium which involved no values other than the primary one of self-expression. Of course one cannot wholly ignore the helpful co-operation of psychoanalysis. But to distinguish between the metaphysical and the psychological origins of the new techniques is not a profitable task. It is not difficult to understand how the subjective novel could have derived its assumptions from the one field, its method from the other. And the fusion between them had been completed by the time Mrs. Woolf published her little pamphlet. Everybody, in Rebecca West's phrase, was "doing" a novel in the period immediately following the World War. Everybody, that is to say, was writing a quasi-poetic rendition of his sensibility in a form which it was agreed should be called the novel.

Possessing a mind schooled in abstract theory, especially alert to the intellectual novelties of her own time, Mrs. Woolf was naturally attracted by a method which in addition to being contemporary offered so much to the speculative mind. But the deeper causes of the attraction, it is now evident, were embedded in Mrs. Woolf's own temperament of sensibility. The subjective mode is the only mode especially designed for temperaments immersed in their own sensibility, obsessed with its movements and vacillations, fascinated by its instability. It was the only mode possible for someone like Proust; it was alone capable of projecting the sensibility which because it has remained so uniform throughout her work we may be permitted to call Mrs. Woolf's own. Here it happens to be Bernard, in *The Waves,* speaking:

A space was cleared in my mind. I saw through the thick leaves of habit. Leaning over the gate I regretted so much litter, so much unaccomplishment and separation, for one cannot cross London to see a friend, life being so full of engagements; nor take ship to India and see a naked man spearing fish in blue water. I said life had been imperfect, an unfinished phrase. It had been impossible for me, taking snuff as I do from any bagman met in a train, to keep coherency—that sense of the generations, of women carrying red pitchers to the Nile, of the nightingale who sings among conquests and migrations. . . .

But this might be almost any one of Mrs. Woolf's characters; and from such a passage we can appreciate how perfectly the subjective or "confessional" method is adapted to the particular sensibility reflected throughout her work.

And if we require in turn some explanation for this hieratic cultivation of the sensibility, we need only examine for a moment the nature and quality of the experience represented by most of her characters. From *The Voyage Out* to *The Waves* Mrs. Woolf has written almost exclusively about one class of people, almost one might say one type of individual, and that a class or type whose experience is largely vicarious, whose contacts with actuality have been for one or another reason incomplete, unsatisfactory, or inhibited. Made up of poets, metaphysicians, botanists, water-colorists, the world of Mrs. Woolf is a kind of superior Bohemia, as acutely refined and aristocratic in its way as the world of Henry James, except that its inhabitants concentrate on their sensations and impressions rather than on their problems of conduct.

(Such problems, of course, do not even exist for them since they rarely allow themselves even the possibility of action.) Life for these people, therefore, is painful less for what it has done to them than for what their excessive sensitivity causes them to make of it. Almost every one of them is the victim of some vast and inarticulate fixation: Mrs. Dalloway on Peter Walsh, Lily Briscoe in *To the Lighthouse* on Mrs. Ramsay, everyone in *The Waves* on Percival. All of them, like Neville in the last-named book, are listening for "that wild hunting-song, Percival's music." For all of them what Percival represents is something lost or denied, something which must remain forever outside the intense circle of their own renunciation. No consolation is left them but solitude, a timeless solitude in which to descend to a kind of self-induced Nirvana. "Heaven be praised for solitude!" cries Bernard toward the close of *The Waves*. "Heaven be praised for solitude that has removed the pressure of the eye, the solicitation of the body, and all need of lies and phrases." Through solitude these people are able to relieve themselves with finality from the responsibilities of living, they are able to complete their divorce from reality even to the extent of escaping the burden of personality. Nothing in Mrs. Woolf's work serves as a better revelation of her characters as a whole than these ruminations of Mrs. Ramsay in *To the Lighthouse*:

To be silent; to be alone. All the being and the doing, expansive, glittering, vocal, evaporated; and one shrunk, with a sense of solemnity, to being oneself, a wedge-shaped core of darkness. . . . When life sank down for a moment, *the range of experience seemed limitless*. . . . Losing personality, one lost the fret, the hurry, the stir; and there rose to her lips always some exclamation of triumph over life when things came together in this peace, this rest, this eternity. . . .

What Mrs. Ramsay really means to say is that when life sinks down in this manner the range of *implicit* experience is limitless. Once one has abandoned the effort to act upon reality, either with the will or the intellect, the mind is permitted to wander in freedom through the stored treasures of its memories and impressions, following no course but that of fancy or simple association, murmuring Pillicock sat on Pillicock's Hill or Come away, come away, Death, "mingling poetry and nonsense, floating in the stream." But experience in this sense is something quite different from experience in the sense in which it is ordinarily understood in referring to people in life or in books. It does not involve that active impact of character upon reality which provides the objective materials of experience in both literature and life. And if it leads to its own peculiar triumphs, it does so only through a dread of being and doing, an abdication of personality and a shrinking into the solitary darkness.

Because of this self-imposed limitation of their experience, therefore, the characters of Mrs. Woolf are unable to *function* anywhere but on the single plane of the sensibility. On this plane alone is enacted whatever movement, drama, or tragedy occurs in her works. The movement of course is centrifugal, the drama unrealized, the tragedy hushed. The only truly dramatic moments in these novels are significantly enough precisely those in which the characters seem now and again to catch a single brief glimpse of that imposing world of fact which they have forsworn. The scenes we remember best are those like the one in *Mrs. Dalloway* in which the heroine, bright, excited and happy among the guests at her party, is brought suddenly face to face with the fact of death. Or like the extremely moving one at the end of *To the Lighthouse* in which Lily Briscoe at last breaks into tears and cries aloud the hallowed name of Mrs. Ramsay. In such scenes Mrs. Woolf is excellent; no living novelist can translate these nuances of perception in quite the same way; and their effect in her work is of an occasional transitory rift in that diaphanous "envelope" with which she surrounds her characters from beginning to end.

II

For the novelist of sensibility the most embarrassing of all problems, of course, has been the problem of form. From Richardson to Mrs. Woolf it has been the problem of how to reconcile something that is immeasurable, which is what experience as *feeling* very soon becomes, with something that is measured and defined, which has remained perhaps our most elementary conception of art. In the eighteenth century the impulse toward reconciliation was undoubtedly less acute than it has become today: Richardson and Sterne were working in a medium which did not yet make serious pretensions to being opposed to poetry and drama as a distinct art form. There was not yet a Flaubert or a Tolstoy, a Turgenev or a Henry James. Feeling was enough; and feeling was allowed to expand in volumes whose uncontrollable bulk was an eloquent demonstration of its immeasurability. But when at the turn of the present century, under distinguished philosophical auspices, feeling was restored to the novel, when the sensibility finally triumphed over the floundering nineteenth-century Reason, no such artistic insouciance was possible for anyone at all conscious of the literary tradition. In Proust we see the attempt to achieve form on a large scale through the substitution of a purely metaphysical system for the various collapsing frameworks of values—religious, ethical, and scientific—on which the fiction of the nineteenth century had depended. In Joyce it is through a substitution of quite a different kind, that of a particular myth from the remote literary past, that the effort is made to endow the treasures of the sensibility with something like the *integritas* of the classical estheticians. And in the case of Mrs. Woolf, who is in this respect representative of most of the followers of these two great contemporary exemplars, the pursuit of an adequate form has been a strenuous one from first to last.

In her earliest two books, to be sure, this strain is not too clearly apparent. But *The Voyage Out,* although an interesting novel in many respects, is notably deficient in what we usually designate as narrative appeal. In retrospect the excellence of the dialogue, the skill with social comedy, the objective portraiture of character—all traditional elements which Mrs. Woolf has since chosen to discard—seem remarkable. But already one can observe a failure or reluctance to project character through a progressive representation of motives, which provides the structure in such a novelist as Jane Austen, for example, whom Mrs. Woolf happens to resemble most in this novel. For an ordered pattern of action unfolding in time Mrs. Woolf substitutes a kind of spatial unity (the setting is a yacht at sea and later a Portuguese hotel), a *cadre,* so to speak, within which everything—characters, scenes and ideas—tends to remain fixed and self-contained. This would be an altogether true description if it were not for the promise of some larger development in the love affair that emerges at the end. But even here, in Mrs. Woolf's first novel, no fulfillment is allowed; death is invoked; death supplies a termination which might not otherwise be reached since none is inherent in the plan. *Night and Day* is an effort to write a novel on a thoroughly conventional model, and the result is so uncertain that we can understand the rather sudden turning to a newer method. It is as if Mrs. Woolf had persuaded herself by these experiments (how consciously we may judge from her essay *Mr. Bennett and Mrs. Brown)* that her view of personality did not at all coincide with the formal requirements of the conventional novel. Of course she was not alone in this discovery for there already existed the rudiments of a new tradition, whose main tendency was to dispense with form for the sake of an intensive exploitation of method.

Despite the number of artists in every field who assume that an innovation in method entails a corresponding achievement in form, method cannot be regarded as quite the same thing as form. For the novelist all that we can mean by method is embraced in the familiar phrase "the point of view." As his object is character his only method can be that by which he endeavors to attain to a complete grasp and understanding of that object. "Method" in fiction narrows down to nothing more or less than the selection of a point of view from which character may be studied and presented. The drastic shift in the point of view for which Henry James prepared English fiction has undeniably resulted in many noticeable effects in its form or structure. But it is not yet possible to declare that it has resulted in any *new* form. Dorothy Richardson, in the opening volume of *Pilgrimage,* was among the first to apply this new method but in none of the volumes which followed has she allied it to anything like a consistent form. What Mrs. Woolf absorbed from Miss Richardson, from May Sinclair and from James Joyce, all of whom had advanced its use before 1918, was therefore only method, and not form.

In the collection of sketches called *Monday or Tuesday* Mrs. Woolf definitely announced her affiliation with the new tradition. But such pieces as "Kew Gardens" and "The Mark on the Wall" were so slight in scope that they could make their appeal (like the essays of Lamb, for example) without the aid of any formal order or plan. Not until *Jacob's Room* does Mrs. Woolf attempt to use the method at any length, and in this book, with which her larger reputation began, we can first perceive the nature of the problem suggested by her work.

In one sense, the structure of *Jacob's Room* is that of the simplest form known to story-telling—the chronicle. From its intense pages one is able to detach a bare continuity of events: Jacob goes to the seashore, to Cambridge, to Greece, to the War. But what his creator is manifestly concerned with is not the relation of these events to his character, but their relation to his sensibility. The latter is projected through a poetic rendering of the dreams, desires, fantasies and enthusiasms which pass through his brain. The rendering is poetic because it is managed entirely by images, certain of which are recurrent throughout—the sheep's jaw with yellow teeth, "the moors and Byron," Greece. The theme also would seem to be a kind of poetic contrast between the outward passage of events and the permanence of a certain set of images in the mind. It happens that there is enough progression of outward events to give the book about as much movement as any other biographical (or autobiographical) chronicle. But one cannot point to any similar movement, any principle of progressive unity in the revelation of all that implicit life of the hero which makes up the substance of the book. As a sensibility Jacob remains the same throughout; he reacts in an identical fashion to the successive phenomena of his experience. Since he reacts only through his sensibility, since he does not act directly upon experience, he fails to "develop," in the sense in which characters in fiction usually develop. Instead of acting, he responds, and when death puts an end to his response, the book also comes to an end. "What am I to do with these?" his mother asks at the close, holding up an old pair of shoes, and this bit of romantic pathos is all the significance which his rich accumulation of dreams and suffering is made to assume in our minds.

In *Mrs. Dalloway* there is a much more deliberate use of recurrent images to identify the consciousness of each of the characters. The effort is not toward an integration of these images, for that would amount to something which is opposed to Mrs. Woolf's whole view of personality. It is toward no more than the emphasis of a certain rhythm in consciousness, which is obviously intended to supply a corresponding rhythm to the book as a whole. Moreover, in this work use is made for the first time of an enlarged image, a symbol that is fixed, constant and wholly outside the time-world of the characters. The symbol of Big Ben, since it sets the contrast between physical time and the measureless duration of the characters' inner life, serves as a sort of standard or center of reference. But neither of these devices, it should be realized, has anything directly to do with the organization of character: rhythm, the rhythm of images in the consciousness, is not the same thing as an order of the personality; the symbol of Big Ben is no real center because it exists outside the characters, is set up in contrast with them. By means of these devices carried over from lyric poetry, a kind of unity is achieved which is merely superficial or decorative, corresponding to no fundamental organization of the experience.

In her next book, however, Mrs. Woolf goes much further toward a fusion of character and design. *To the Lighthouse,* which is probably her finest performance in every respect, owes its success not least to the completeness with which the symbol chosen is identified with the will of every one of the characters. The lighthouse is the common point toward which all their desires are oriented; it is an object of attainment or fulfillment which gives direction to the movements of their thought and sensibility; and since it is thus associated with them it gives a valid unity to the whole work. Moreover, alone among Mrs. Woolf's works, *To the Lighthouse* has for its subject an action, a single definite action, *"going* to the lighthouse," which places it clearly in the realm of narrative. In fact, as narrative, it may be even more precisely classified as an *incident.* The sole objection that might be raised on esthetic grounds is whether Mrs. Woolf's method has not perhaps caused her to extend her development beyond the inherent potentialities of this form. The question is whether such a narrow structure can support the weight of the material and the stress of its treatment. More relevant to the present question, however, is the consideration that so much of the success of the book rests on the unusually happy choice of symbol, one that is very specially adapted to the theme, and not likely to be used soon again. Not many more such symbols occur to the imagination.

Certainly Mrs. Woolf does not make use of the same kind of symbol in her next novel; for in *The Waves* she returns to the devices of rhythm and symbolical contrast on which she depended in her earlier books. (*Orlando* is not a novel, but a "biography," and has only to follow a simple chronological order. Whatever hilarious variations its author plays on the traditional concept of time do not affect her adherence to this simple order.) In *The Waves* Mrs. Woolf again presents her characters through the rhythm of images in the brain, again bases her structure on a contrast between these and a permanent symbol of the objective world. There is, first of all, the image or set of images which serves as a *motif* for each of the characters: for Louis, a chained beast stamping on the shore, for Bernard, the willow tree by the river; for Neville, "that wild hunting-song, Percival's music." And also there is the cumulative image of each of their lives taken as a whole set in a parallel relationship to the movements of the sea.

Such a parallel, of course, is not an unfamiliar one. "Dwellers by the sea cannot fail to be impressed by the sight of its ceaseless ebb and flow," remarks Frazer in *The Golden Bough,* "and are apt . . . to trace a subtle relation, a secret harmony, between its tides and the life of man." What is unique is Mrs. Woolf's effort to expand what is usually no more than an intuition, a single association, a lyrical utterance to the dimensions of a novel. In one sense this is accomplished by a kind of multiplication: we are given six lyric poets instead of the usual one. For what Mrs. Woolf offers is a rendering of the subjective response to reality of six different people at successive stages in their lives. We are presented to them in childhood, adolescence, youth, early and late middle-age. *"The waves broke on the shore"* is the last line in the book, and from this we are probably to assume that at the close they are all dead. Such a scheme has the order of a chronicle, of a group of parallel biographies, but Mrs. Woolf is much more ambitious. Each period in her characters' lives corresponds to a particular movement of the sea; the current of their lives at the end is likened to its "incessant rise and fall and rise and fall again." In addition, the different periods correspond to the changing position of the sun in the sky on a single day, suggesting a vision of human lives *sub specie aeternitatis.* (The ancillary images of birds, flowers and wind intensify the same effect.) The theme is best summed up by one of the characters in a long monologue at the end: "Let us again pretend that life is a solid substance, shaped like a globe, which we turn about in our fingers. Let us pretend that we can make out a plain and logical story, so that when one matter is despatched —love for instance—we go on, in an orderly manner to the next. I was saying there was a willow tree. Its shower of falling branches, its creased and crooked bark had the effect of what remains outside our illusions yet cannot stay them, is changed by them for the moment, yet shows through stable, still, with a sternness that our lives lack. Hence the comment it makes; the standard it supplies, the reason why, as we flow and change, it seems to measure." In conception and form, in method and style, this book is the most poetic which Mrs. Woolf has yet written. It represents the extreme culmination of the method to which she has applied herself exclusively since *Monday or Tuesday.* It is significant because it forces the question whether the form in which for her that method has resulted is not essentially opposed to the conditions of narrative art.

For this form is unmistakably that of the extended or elaborated lyric; and criticism of these novels gets down ultimately to the question with what impunity one can confuse the traditional means of one literary form with the traditional means of another. This is no place to undertake another discussion of the difference between poetry and prose—or, more particularly, the difference between the lyrical and the narrative. It is a difference which we immediately recognize, and which criticism has always rightly recognized, even when it has not been altogether certain of its explanations. The least sensible of these explanations has undoubtedly been that which would make us believe that the difference between them is *qualitative*—that poetry deals with different things from prose, with the implication that the things of poetry are of higher order than those of prose. This is a snobbery which, fortunately in one sense, has been pretty well removed in our time, although unfortunately in another it has led to a different kind of confusion. And this is the confusion which consists in removing any *formal* distinctions between the two modes.

The objection to the lyrical method in narrative is that it renders impossible the peculiar kind of interest which the latter is designed to supply. By the lyrical method is meant the substitution of a group of symbols for the orderly working-out of a motive or a set of motives which has constituted the immemorial pattern of narrative art. Perhaps the simplest definition of symbols is that they are things used to stand for other things; and undoubtedly the most part of such a definition is the word "stand." Whatever operations of the imagination have gone on to produce them, symbols themselves become fixed, constant, and static. They may be considered as the end-results of the effort of the imagination to fix itself somewhere in space. The symbol may be considered as something *spatial*. Symbols are thus ordinarily used in lyric poetry, where the effort is to fix ideas, sentiments, or emotions. By themselves, of course, symbols in poetry are no more than so many detached, isolated and unrelated points in space. When projected separately, as in the poetry of the Imagist school, or in too great confusion, as in much contemporary poetry, they do not possess any necessary meaning or value to the intelligence: the worlds that they indicate are either too small or too large to live in. Moreover, whether separate or integrated into a total vision symbols are capable of being grasped, like any other objects of space, by a single and instantaneous effort of perception. The interval of time between their presentation and our response to them is ideally no longer than the time required for our reading of a poem. Even when their presentation is like a gradual exfoliation, as in certain poems by Donne and Baudelaire, for example, that time is never allowed to be too greatly prolonged. We do not require Poe's axiom that all lyrics must be brief to understand why they must be so. The symbols on which they are constructed can be perceived in a moment of time.

When narrative based itself on a simple chronological record of action, it was assured of a certain degree of interest. When, later, it based itself on an arrangement of action which corresponded to an orderly view of life or reality, it attained to the very high interest of a work of art. As long as it based itself firmly on action according to one pattern or another, it was certain of some degree of interest. To understand the nature of the satisfaction which we seem to take in the representation of reality in a temporal order we should have to know more about certain primitive elements of our psychology than science has yet been able to discover. It is enough to recognize that whatever the reasons this satisfaction is rooted in our sense of *time*. It is enough to realize that this is the basis of the appeal which narrative has made through the whole history of fiction, from the earliest fables of the race to the most complex "constructions" of Henry James. For this reason, for example, description has always occupied a most uncertain place in fiction. Description, which deals with things rather than events, interposes a space-world in the march of that time-world which is the subject of fiction. For this reason the use of poetic symbols in fiction, as in all Mrs. Woolf's work since *Monday or Tuesday*, seems to be in direct contradiction to the foundations of our response to that form.

III

Because it is in an almost continuous state of moral and intellectual relaxation that Mrs. Woolf's characters draw out their existence, they can be projected only through a more or less direct transcription of their consciousness. Such a qualification is necessary, however, for the method here is rarely if ever as direct as that of Joyce or his followers. Between the consciousness and the rendition of it there is nearly always interposed a highly artificial literary style. This style remains practically uniform for all the characters; it is at once individual and traditional. The effect of its elegant diction and elaborately turned periods is to make one feel at times as if these sad and lonely people were partly compensated for the vacuity of their lives by the gift of casting even their most random thoughts in the best literary tradition. For some of them, like Bernard in *The Waves* (or is it the author herself speaking?), language is more than a compensation; it has an absolute value in itself: "A good phrase, however, seems to me to have an independent existence." Others may go to religion, to art, to friendship, but Mrs. Woolf's people more often than not go "to seek among phrases and fragments something unbroken." It is as if they seek to net the world of time and change with a phrase, to retrieve the chaos with words. For this reason the presentation of character by Mrs. Woolf gets down finally to a problem of style, to the most beautiful arrangement of beautiful words and phrases.

Here also Mrs. Woolf is pre-eminently the poet; for as an unwillingness to use motives and actions led to her substitution of poetic symbols in their stead so is she also compelled to use a metaphorical rather than a narrative style. In this practice of course she is not without precedent; other novelists have relied on metaphor to secure their finest effects of communication. But while such effects are ordinarily used to heighten the narrative, they are never extended to the point where they assume an independent interest. In Mrs. Woolf's books metaphorical writing is not occasional but predominate; from the beginning it has subordinated every other kind; and it was inevitable that it should one day be segmented into the purely descriptive prose-poems of *The Waves*.

No sooner is the essentially poetic character of this writing admitted than one is confronted with the whole host of problems associated with the general problem of imagery in poetry. It happens, however, that the peculiar use of imagery in Mrs. Woolf's prose suggests among other things a particular distinction, and one which has not been often enough made, although it was recognized by both Coleridge and Baudelaire, a distinction between two kinds of sensibility.

Of the two kinds of sensibility that we can identify in examining works of poetry the first would seem to be incapable of receiving impressions except through the prism of an already acquired set of language symbols. It is as if poets with this type of sensibility are uncontrollably *determined* in the kind of response they can make to reality. And because they are so determined in their initial response they are determind also in their manner of expression. The original language-symbols, acquired through culture, training, or unconscious immersion in some tradition, are infinitely perpetuated in their writing. At its worst such writing is anemic and invertebrate, like the minor verse of any period or like the earlier work of many excellent poets. In such verse the language gives the effect of having occasioned the feeling more often than the feeling the language. At its most sophisticated, however, this verse is capable of achieving a certain superficial quality of distinction all its own. It is a quality of distinction undoubtedly made possible by the reduced effort to discover precise images to convey very definite and particular sensations or emotions. It may consist in the pure musicalization of language through the draining of all specific content from the imagery that we find in Mallarmé or (on a lower plane) in Swinburne. Or it may consist in that plastic manipulation of surfaces which is another department of the interesting verse of any period. The effect in either case is the same, that of a resuscitation rather than a re-creation of language.

The other type of sensibility, of course, is in the habit of receiving direct impressions, of forming images which possess the freshness, uniqueness, and body of the original object. It has the faculty of creating new language-symbols to convey what it has perceived or, as sometimes happens, of re-creating traditional symbols with enough force to make them serve again. (For used symbols are capable of being recharged, so to speak, under the pressure of the new emotion they are called upon to convey.) Only when the original perception is solid and clear is it able to crystallize into images capable of transmitting emotion; and only when the emotion is adequate are these images capable of creating or re-creating language. The difference is between language which is made its own object and language which is made to realize emotion by evoking particular objects of concrete experience. It is the difference between writing which secures a certain effectiveness through being recognizable in a particular tradition and writing which is an exact verbal equivalent for a precise emotion or set of emotions. It is the difference, among the writers of our time, between Conrad Aiken and T. S. Eliot, or between Thornton Wilder and Ernest Hemingway. And in the most characteristic lines of the best writers of any time it is this latter kind of sensibility that we can see at work. We see it in Antony's rebuke to Cleopatra:

> I found you as a morsel, cold upon
> Dead Caesar's trencher

or in Baudelaire's

> J'ai cherché dans l'amour un sommeil oublieux;
> Mais l'amour n'est pour moi qu'un matelas d'aiguilles

or in Yeats'

> I pace upon the battlements and stare
> On the foundations of a house, or where
> Tree, like a sooty finger, starts from the earth.

In prose fiction, when the language approaches the precision and density of poetry, it is a result of the same necessity on the part of author or character, under stress of exceptional feeling, to seize upon his experience for the particular image or images necessary to express his state. The only difference is that the images of fiction are likely to be less remote, less "difficult" perhaps, than those of poetry. And the reason of course is that the images are likely to arise out of the immediate background of the novel. No better example of this can be offered than in the speech in *Wuthering Heights* in which Catherine, in her delirium, shakes the feathers out of her pillow:

That's a turkey's . . . and this is a wild duck's; and this is a pigeon's. Ah, they put pigeons' feathers in the pillows—no wonder I couldn't die! . . . And here is a moor-cock's; and this—I should know it among a thousand—it's a lapwing's. Bonny bird; wheeling over our heads in the middle of the moor. It wanted to get to its nest, for the clouds had touched the swells, and it felt rain coming.

In Mrs. Woolf's novels, as replete with imagery as they are, the effect is never quite the same as in this passage from Emily Brontë. The images that pass through in her characters' minds are rarely seized from any *particular* background of concrete experience. There are few of them which we have not encountered somewhere before. They belong not so much to the particular character as to the general tradition of literature. The effect is of an insidious infiltration of tradition into the sensibility. And this effect is the same whether it is a straight description by the author, as in *To the Lighthouse:*

The autumn trees, ravaged as they are, take on the flash of tattered flags kindling in the gloom of cool cathedral caves where gold letters on marble pages describe death in battle and how bones bleach and burn far away on Indian sands. The autumn trees gleam in the yellow moonlight, in the light of harvest moons, the light which mellows the energy of labour, and smooths the stubble, and brings the wave lapping blue to the shore.

or a presentation of mood, as in *Mrs Dalloway:*

Fear no more, says the heart. Fear no more, says the heart, committing its burden to some sea, which sighs collectively for all sorrows, and renews, begins, collects, lets fall. And the body alone listens to the passing bee; the wave breaking; the dog barking, far away barking and barking.

or a translation of ecstasy, as in *The Waves:*

Now tonight, my body rises tier upon tier like some cool temple whose floor is strewn with carpets and murmurs rise and the altars stand smoking; but up above, here in my serene head, come only fine gusts of melody, waves of incense, while the lost dove wails, and the banners tremble above tombs, and the dark airs of midnight shake trees outside the open windows.

From such examples it should be apparent to what extent the sensibility here is haunted by the word-symbols of the past. The consciousness of each of these characters is a Sargasso Sea of words, phrases, broken relics of poetry and song. The phrases which rise to the surface are like bright shells resonant with the accumulated echoes of their past histories. Some of them have the familiar charm of cherished heirlooms; only a few retain completely whatever power to stir the imagination they may once have had. Almost all of them depend for their effect on their associations to the cultivated mind rather than on their ability to evoke the fullness and immediacy of concrete experience. And the reason of course is that there is insufficient experience of this sort anywhere reflected in the course of Mrs. Woolf's work.

It is also clear in such passages how Mrs. Woolf has come more and more to cultivate language for its own sake, to seek in phrases some "independent existence" which will give them an absolute beauty in themselves. But detached from experience as they are they attain to no more substantial beauty than that of a charming virtuosity of style. It is not the beauty but the cleverness of Mrs. Woolf's writing which is responsible for the final effect on the reader. "No woman before Virginia Woolf has used our language with such easy authority," wrote the late Sara Teasdale. Indeed few writers of either sex have written English with the same mastery of traditional resources, the same calculated effectiveness, the same facility. And when this facile traditionalism is allied with an appropriate subject, as in a frank burlesque like *Orlando*, the result is truly brilliant. It is only when it is used as the vehicle for significant serious thoughts and emotions, as in the larger portion of Mrs. Woolf's work, that its charm seems false, its authority invalid, and its beauty sterile.

It is only fair to point out what would seem to be a sincere self-questioning in the long monologue at the end of *The Waves*. Bernard, the inveterate phrasemonger, recalling the scene in which he and his friends first heard of Percival's death, remembers that they had compared him to a lily. "So the sincerity of the moment passed," Bernard cries, "so it had become symbolical; and that I could not stand. Let us commit any blasphemy of laughter and criticism rather than exude this lily-sweet glue; and cover him over with phrases." Perhaps it is too much to read into this lapse into sincerity on the part of a single character a confession of dissatisfaction by the author with the kind of language that she has been using all along in her work. But while such an interpretation may be too eager there is at least the implication that she is aware that reality when it is encountered is something far too important to be covered over with beautiful phrases. The vague hope is thrown out that in her later work she may finally be tempted to give us Percival himself, that she may spare him from death and allow him a more solid existence than he ever enjoyed in the minds and memories of his friends.

But no sooner is this idea expressed than one is reminded of the profound changes that would have to happen in Mrs. Woolf's whole metaphysical outlook before any such hope could be realized. For every element of her work that we have considered—her form, her method of characterization, her style even—is affected by the same fundamental view of personality at its root. These elements of form and of style can hardly be expected to change as long as the view which determines them remains unchanged. And nothing in Mrs. Woolf's recent work, it must be admitted, justifies the belief that this view is likely to be changed in the near future.

From *The Symposium*, Vol. III (January–March, 1932), pp. 53–63; and (April–June, 1932), pp. 153–166. Reprinted in this revision by permission of the author and editors.

KATHERINE ANNE PORTER

Gertrude Stein: A Self-Portrait

[1947]

. . . I want to say that just today I met Miss Hennessy and she was carrying, she did not have it with her, but she usually carried a wooden umbrella. This wooden umbrella is carved out of wood and looks like a real one even to the little button and the rubber string that holds it together. It is all right except when it rains. When it rains it does not open and Miss Hennessy looks a little foolish but she does not mind because it is after all the only wooden umbrella in Paris. And even if there were lots of others it would not make any difference.

Gertrude Stein: *Everybody's Autobiography*

WHEN Kahnweiler the picture dealer told Miss Stein that Picasso had stopped painting and had taken to writing poetry, she confessed that she had "a funny feeling" because "things belonged to you and writing belonged to me. I know writing belongs to me, I am quite certain," but still it was a blow. ". . . No matter how certain you are about anything belonging to you if you hear that somebody says it belongs to them it gives you a funny feeling."

Later she buttonholed Picasso at Kahnweiler's gallery, shook him, kissed him, lectured him, told him that his poetry was worse than bad, it was offensive as a Cocteau drawing and in much the same way, it was unbecoming. He defended himself by reminding her that she had said he was an extraordinary person, and he believed an extraordinary person should be able to do anything. She said that to her it was repellent sight when a person who could do one thing well dropped it for something else he could not do at all. Convinced, or defeated, he promised to give back writing to its natural owner.

Writing was no doubt the dearest of Miss Stein's possessions, but it was not the only one. The pavilion atelier in rue de Fleurus was a catchall of beings and created objects, and everything she looked upon was hers in more than the usual sense. Her weighty numerous divans and armchairs covered with dark, new-looking horsehair; her dogs, Basket and Pépé, conspicuous, special, afflicted as neurotic children; her clutter of small tables each with its own clutter of perhaps valuable but certainly treasured objects; her Alice B. Toklas; her visitors; and finally, ranging the walls from floor to ceiling, giving the impres-

338

sion that they were hung three deep, elbowing each other, canceling each other's effects in the jealous way of pictures, was her celebrated collection of paintings by her collection of celebrated painters. These were everybody of her time whom Miss Stein elected for her own, from her idol Picasso (kidnapped bodily from brother Leo, who saw him first) to miniscule Sir Francis Rose, who seems to have appealed to the pixy in her.

Yet the vaguely lighted room where things accumulated, where they appeared to have moved in under a compulsion to be possessed once for all by someone who knew how to take hold firmly, gave no impression of disorder. On the contrary, an air of solid comfort, of inordinate sobriety and permanence, of unadventurous middle-class domesticity—respectability is the word, at last—settled around the shoulders of the guest like a Paisley shawl, a borrowed shawl of course, something to be worn and admired for a moment and handed back to the owner. Miss Stein herself sat there in full possession of herself, the scene, the spectators, wearing thick no-colored shapeless woolen clothes and honest woolen stockings knitted for her by Miss Toklas, looking extremely like a handsome old Jewish patriarch who had backslid and shaved off his beard.

Surrounded by her listners, she talked in a slow circle in her fine deep voice, the word "perception" occurring again and again and yet again like the brass ring the children snatch for as their hobby horses whirl by. She was in fact at one period surrounded by snatching children, the literary young, a good many of them American, between two wars in a falling world. Roughly they were divided into two parties: those who were full of an active, pragmatic unbelief, and those who searched their own vitals and fished up strange horrors in the style of *transition*. The first had discovered that honor is only a word, and an embarrassing one, because it was supposed to mean something wonderful and was now exposed as meaning nothing at all. For them, nothing worked except sex and alcohol and pulling apart their lamentable midwestern upbringings and scattering the pieces. Some of these announced that they wished their writings to be as free from literature as if they had never read a book, as indeed too many of them had not up to the time. The *transition* tone was even more sinister, for though it was supposed to be the vanguard of international experimental thought, its real voice was hoarse, anxious, corrupted mysticism speaking in a thick German accent. The editor, Eugene Jolas, had been born in the eternally disputed land of Alsace, bilingual in irreconcilable tongues, French and German, and he spoke both and English besides with a foreign accent. He had no mother tongue, nor even a country, and so he fought the idea of both, but his deepest self was German: he issued frantic manifestoes demanding that language be reduced to something he could master, crying aloud in "defense of the hallucinative forces," the exploding of the verb, the "occult hypnosis of language," "chthonian grammar"; reason he hated, and defended the voice of the blood, the disintegration of syntax—with a special grudge against English—preaching like an American Methodist evangelist in the wilderness for "the use of a language which is a mantic instrument, and which does not hesitate to adopt a revolutionary attitude toward word syntax, going even so far as to invent a hermetic language, if necessary." The final aim was "the illumination of a collective reality and a totalistic universe." Meanwhile Joyce, a man with a mother tongue if ever there was one, and a master of languages, was mixing them in strange new forms to the delight and enrichment of language for good and all.

Miss Stein had no problems: she simply exploded a verb as if it were a soap bubble, used chthonian grammar long before she heard it named (and she would have scorned to name it), was a born adept in occult hypnosis of language without even trying. Serious young men who were having a hard time learning to write realized with relief that there was nothing at all to it if you just relaxed and put down the first thing that came into your head. She gave them a romantic name, the Lost Generation, and a remarkable number of them tried earnestly if unsuccessfully to live up to it. A few of them were really lost, and disappeared, but others had just painted themselves into a very crowded corner. She laid a cooling hand upon their agitated brows and asked with variations, What did it matter? There were only a few geniuses, after all, among which she was one, only the things a genius said made any difference, the rest was "just there," and so she disposed of all the dark questions of life, art, human relations, and death, even eternity, even God, with perfect Stein logic, bringing the scene again into its proper focus, upon herself.

Some of the young men went away, read a book, began thinking things over, and became the best writers of their time. Humanly, shamefacedly, they then jeered at their former admiration, and a few even made the tactical error of quarreling with her. She enjoyed their discipleship while it lasted, and dismissed them from existence when it ended. It is easy to see what tremendous vitality and direction there was in the arts all over the world; for not everything was happening only in France, for life was generated in many a noisy seething confusion in many countries. Little by little the legitimate line of succession appeared, the survivors emerged each with his own shape and meaning, the young vanguard became the Old Masters and even old hat.

In the meantime our heroine went on talking, vocally or on paper, and in that slow swarm of words, out of the long drone and mutter and stammer of her lifetime monologue, often there emerged a phrase of ancient native independent wisdom, for she had a shrewd deep knowledge of the commoner human motives. Her judgments were neither moral nor intellectual, and least of all aesthetic, indeed they were not even judgments, but simply her description from observation of acts, words, appearances giving her view; limited, personal in the extreme, prejudiced without qualification, based on assumptions founded in the void of pure unreason. For example, French notaries' sons have always something strange about them—look at Jean Cocteau. The Spaniard has a natural center of ignorance, all except Juan Gris. On the other hand, Dali had not only the natural Spanish center of ignorance, but still another variety, quite maligant, of his own. Preachers' sons do not turn out like other people—E. E. Cummings, just for one. Painters are always little short round men—Picasso and a crowd of them. And then she puts her finger lightly on an American peculiarity of our time: ". . . so perhaps they are right the Americans in being more interested in you than in the work you have done, although they would not be interested in you if you had not done the work you had done." And she remarked once to her publisher that she was famous in America not for her work that people understood but for that which they did not understand. That was the kind of thing she could see through at a glance.

It was not that she was opposed to ideas, but that she was not interested in anybody's ideas but her own, except as material to put down on her endless flood of pages. Like writing, opinion also belonged to Miss Stein, and nothing annoyed her more—she was easily angered about all sorts of things—than for anyone not a genius or who had no reputation that she respected, to appear to be thinking in her presence. Of all those GI's who swarmed about her in her last days, if any one showed any fight at all, any tendency to question her pronouncements, she smacked him down like a careful grandmother, for his own good. Her GI heroes Brewsie and Willie are surely as near to talking zombies as anything ever seen in a book, and she loved, not them, but their essential zombiness.

Like all talkers, she thought other people talked too much, and there is recorded only one instance of someone getting the drop on her—who else but Alfred Stieglitz? She sat through a whole session at their first meeting without uttering one word, a feat which he mentioned with surprised approval. If we knew nothing more of Stieglitz than this we would know he was a great talker. She thought that the most distressing sound was that of the human voice, other peoples' voices, "as the hoot owl is almost the best sound," but in spite of this she listened quite a lot. When she was out walking the dogs, if workmen were tearing up the streets she would ask them what they were doing and what they would be doing next. She only stopped to break the monotony of walking, but she remembered their answers. When a man passed making up a bitter little song against her dog and his conduct vis-á-vis lamp posts and house walls, she put it all down, and it is wonderfully good reporting. Wise or silly or nothing at all, down everything goes on the page with the air of everything being equal, unimportant in itself, important because it happened to her and she was writing about it.

II

She had not always been exactly there, exactly that. There had been many phases, all in consistent character, each giving way in turn for the next, of her portentous being. Ford Madox Ford described her, in earlier Paris days, as trundling through the streets in her high-wheeled American car, being a spectacle and being herself at the same time. And this may have been near the time of Man Ray's photograph of her, wearing a kind of monk's robe, her poll clipped, her granite front and fine eyes displayed at their best period.

Before that, she was a youngish stout woman, not ever really young, with a heavy shrewd face between a hard round pompadour and a round lace collar, looking more or less like Picasso's earliest portrait of her. What saved her then from a good honest husband, probably a stockbroker, and a houseful of children? The answer must be that her envelope was a tricky disguise of Nature, that she was of the company of Amazons which nineteenth-century America produced among its many prodigies: not-men, not-women, answerable to no function in either sex, whose careers were carried on, and how successfully, in whatever field they chose: they were educators, writers, editors, politicians, artists, world travelers, and international hostesses, who lived in public and by the public and played out their self-assumed, self-created roles in such masterly freedom as only a few early medieval queens had equaled. Freedom to them meant precisely freedom from men and their stuffy rules for women. They usurped with a high hand the traditional masculine privileges of movement, choice, and the use of direct, personal power. They were few in number and they were not only to be found in America, and Miss Stein belonged with them, no doubt of it, in spite of a certain temperamental passivity which was Oriental, not feminine. With the top of her brain she was a modern girl, a New Woman, interested in scientific experiment, historical research, the rational view; for a time she was even a medical student, but she could not deceive herself for long. Even during her four years at Radcliffe, where the crisp theories of higher education battled with the womb-shaped female mind (and they always afterward seemed foolish to her at Radcliffe) she worried and worried, for worrying and thinking were synonyms to her, about the meaning of the universe, the riddle of human life, about time and its terrible habit of passing, God, death, eternity, and she felt very lonely in the awful singularity of her confusions. Added to this, history taught her that whole civilizations die and disappear utterly, "and now it happens again," and it gave her a great fright. She was sometimes frightened afterward, "but now well being frightened is something less frightening than it was," but her ambiguous mind faced away from speculation. Having discovered with relief that all knowledge was not her province, she accepted rightly, she said, every superstition. To be in the hands of fate, of magic, of the daemonic forces, what freedom it gave her not to decide, not to act, not to accept any responsibility for anything—one held the pen and let the mind wander. One sat down and somebody did everything for one.

Still earlier she was a plump solemn little girl abundantly upholstered in good clothes, who spent her allowance on the work of Shelley, Thackeray, and George Eliot in fancy bindings, for she loved reading and *Clarissa Harlowe* was once her favorite novel. These early passions exhausted her; in later life she swam in the relaxing bath of detective and murder mysteries, because she liked somebody being dead in a story, and of them all Dashiell Hammett killed them off most to her taste. Her first experience of the real death of somebody had taught her that it could be pleasant for her too. "One morning we could not wake our father." This was in East Oakland, California. "Leo climbed in by the window and called out that he was dead in his bed and he was." It seems to have been the first thing he ever did of which his children, all five of them, approved. Miss Stein declared plainly they none of them liked him at all: "As I say, fathers are depressing but our family had·one," she confessed, and conveys the notion that he was a bore of the nagging, petty sort, the kind that worries himself and others into the grave.

Considering her tepid, sluggish nature, really sluggish like something eating its way through a leaf, Miss Stein could grow quite animated on the subject of her early family life, and some of her stories are as pretty and innocent as lizards running over tombstones on a hot day in Maryland. It was a solid, getting-on sort of middle-class Jewish family of Austrian origin, Keyser on one side, Stein on the other: and the Keysers came to Baltimore about 1820. All branches of the family produced their individual eccentrics—there was even an uncle who believed in the Single Tax—but they were united in their solid understanding of the value of money as the basis of a firm stance in this world. There were incomes, governesses, spending money, guardians appointed when parents died, and Miss Stein was fascinated from childhood with stories about how people earned their first dollar. When, rather late, she actually earned some dollars herself by writing, it changed her entire viewpoint about the value of her work and of her own personality. It came to her as revelation that the only difference between men and four-footed animals is that men can count, and when they count, they like best to count money. In her first satisfaction at finding she had a commercial value, she went on a brief binge of spending money just for the fun of it. But she really knew better. Among the five or six of the seven deadly sins which she practiced with increasing facility and advocated as virtues, avarice became her favorite. Americans in general she found to be rather childish about money: they spent it or gave it away and enjoyed wastefully with no sense of its fierce latent power. "It is hard to be a miser, a real miser, they are as rare as geniuses it takes the same kind of thing to make one, that is time must not exist for them. . . . There must be a reality that has nothing to do with the passing of time. I have it and so had Hetty Green. . . ." and she found only one of the younger generation in America, a young man named Jay Laughlin, who had, she wrote, praising him, avarice to that point of genius which makes the true miser. She made a very true distinction between avarice, the love of getting and keeping, and love of money, the love of making and spending. There is a third love, the love of turning a penny by ruse, and this was illustrated by brother Michael, who once grew a beard to make himself look old enough to pass for a G. A. R. veteran, and so disguised he got a cut-rate railway fare for a visit home during a G. A. R. rally, though all the men of this family fought on the Confederate side.

The question of money and of genius rose simultaneously with the cheerful state of complete orphanhood. Her mother disappeared early after a long illness, leaving her little nest of vipers probably without regret, for vipers Miss Stein shows them to have been in the most Biblical sense. They missed their mother chiefly because she had acted as a buffer between them and their father, and also served to keep them out of each other's hair. Sister Bertha and Brother Simon were simple-minded by family standards, whatever they were, Brother Leo had already started being a genius without any regard for the true situation, and after the death of their father, Brother Michael was quite simply elected to be the Goat. He had inherited the family hatred of responsibility—from their mother, Miss Stein believed, but not quite enough to save him. He became guardian, caretaker, business manager, handy-man, who finally wangled incomes for all of them, and set them free from money and from each other. It is pleasant to know he was a very thorny martyr who did a great deal of resentful lecturing about economy, stamping and shouting around the house with threats to throw the whole business over and let them fend for themselves if they could not treat him with more consideration. With flattery and persuasion they would cluster around and get him back on the rails, for his destiny was to be useful to genius, that is, to Miss Stein.

She had been much attached to her brother Leo, in childhood they were twin souls. He was two years older and a boy, and she had learned from Clarissa Harlowe's uncle's letter that older brothers are superior to younger sisters, or any boy to any girl in fact. Though she bowed to this doctrine as long as it was convenient, she never allowed it to get in her way. She followed her brother's advice more or less, and in turn he waited on her and humored and defended her when she was a selfish lazy little girl. Later he made a charming traveling companion who naturally, being older and a man, looked after all the boring details of life and smoothed his sister's path everywhere. Still, she could not remember his face when he was absent, and once was very nervous when she went to meet him on a journey, for fear she might not recognize him. The one thing wrong all this time was their recurring quarrel about who was the genius of the two, for each had assumed the title and neither believed for a moment there was room for more than one in the family. By way of proving himself, brother Leo took the pavilion and atelier in the rue de Fleurus, installed himself well, and began trying hard to paint. Miss Stein, seeing all so cozy, moved in on him and sat down and began to write— no question of trying. "To try is to die," became one of her several hundred rhyming aphorisms designed to settle all conceivable arguments; after a time, no doubt overwhelmed by the solid negative force of that massive will and presence, her brother moved out and took the atelier next door, and went on being useful to his sister, and trying to paint.

But he also went on insisting tactlessly that he, and not she, was the born genius; and this was one of the real differences between them, that he attacked on the subject and was uneasy, and could not rest, while his sister reasoned with him patiently at first defending her title, regretting she could not share it. Insist, argue, upset himself and her as much as he liked, she simply, quietly knew with a Messianic revelation that she was not only a genius, but *the* genius, and sometimes, she was certain, one of not more than half a dozen real ones in the world. During all her life, whenever Miss Stein got low in her mind about anything, she could always find consolation in this beautiful knowledge of being a born genius, and her brother's contentiousness finally began to look like treason to her. She could not forgive him for disputing her indivisible right to her natural property, genius, on which all her other rights of possession were founded. It shook her—she worried about her work. She had begun her long career of describing "how every one who ever lived eats and drinks and loves and sleeps and talks and walks and wakes and forgets and quarrels and likes and dislikes and works and sits,"—everybody's autobiography, in fact, for she had taken upon herself the immense task of explaining everybody to himself, of telling him all he needed to know about life, and she simply could not have brother Leo hanging around the edges of this grandiose scheme pinching off bits and holding them up to the light. By and by, too, she had Alice B. Toklas to do everything for her. So she and her brother drifted apart, but gradually, like one of Miss Stein's paragraphs. The separation became so complete that once, on meeting her brother unexpectedly, she was so taken by surprise she bowed to him, and afterward wrote a long poem about it in which her total confusion of mind and feeling were expressed with total incoherence: for once, form, matter and style stuttering and stammering and wallowing along together with the agitated harmony of roiling entrails.

III

There are the tones of sloth, of that boredom which is a low-pressure despair, of monotony, of obsession, in this portrait; she went walking out of boredom, she could drive a car, talk, write, but anything else made her nervous. People who were doing anything annoyed her: to be doing nothing, she thought, was more interesting than to be doing something. The air of deathly solitude surrounded her; yet the parade of names in her book would easily fill several printed pages, all with faces attached which she could see were quite different from each other, all talking, each taking his own name and person for granted—a thing she could never understand. Yet she could see what they were doing and could remember what they said. She only listened attentively to Picasso—for whose sake she would crack almost any head in sight—so she half-agreed when he said Picabia was the worst painter of all; but still, found herself drawn to Picabia because his name was Francis. She had discovered that men named Francis were always elegant, and though they might not know anything else, they always knew about themselves. This would remind her that she had never found out who she was. Again and again she would doubt her own identity, and that of everyone else. When she worried about this aloud to Alice B. Toklas, saying she believed it impossible for anyone ever to be certain who he was, Alice B. Toklas made, in context, the most inspired remark in the whole book. "It depends on who you are," she said, and you might think that would have ended the business. Not at all.

These deep-set, chronic fears led her to a good deal of quarreling, for when she quarreled she seems to have felt more real. She mentions quarrels with Max Jacob, Francis Rose, with Dali, with Picabia, with Picasso, with Virgil Thomson, with Braque, with Bréton, and how many others, though she rarely says just why they quarreled or how they made it up. Almost nobody went away and stayed, and the awful inertia of habit in friendships oppressed her. She was sometimes discouraged at the prospect of having to go on seeing certain persons to the end, merely because she had once seen them. The world seemed smaller every day, swarming with people perpetually in movement, full of restless notions which, once examined by her, were inevitably proved to be fallacious, or at least entirely useless. She found that she could best get rid of them by putting them in a book. "That is very funny if you write about any one they do not exist any more, for you, so why see them again. Anyway, that is the way I am."

But as she wrote a book and disposed of one horde, another came on, and worried her afresh, discussing their ludicrous solemn topics, trying to understand things, and being unhappy about it. When Picasso was fretful because she argued with Dali and not with him, she explained that "one discusses things with stupid people but not with sensible ones." Her true grudge against intelligent people was that they talked "as if they were getting ready to change something." Change belonged to Miss Stein, and the duty of the world was to stand still so that she could move about in it comfortably. Her top flight of reasoning on the subject of intelligence ran as follows: "The most actively war-like nations could always convince the pacifists to become pro-German.

That is because pacifists were such intelligent beings they could follow what any one is saying. If you follow what any one is saying then you are a pacifist you are a pro-German . . . therefore understanding is a very dull occupation."

Intellectuals, she said, always wanted to change things because they had an unhappy childhood. "Well, I never had an unhappy childhood, what is the use of having an unhappy anything?" Léon Blum, then Premier of France, had had an unhappy childhood, and she inclined to the theory that the political uneasiness of France could be traced to this fact.

There was not, of course, going to be another war (this was in 1937!), but if there was, there *would* be, naturally; and she never tired of repeating that dancing and war are the same thing "because both are forward and back," while revolution, on the contrary, is up and down, which is why it gets nowhere. Sovietism was even then going rapidly out of fashion in her circles, because they had discovered that it is very conservative, even if the Communists do not think so. Anarchists, being rarities, did not go out of fashion so easily. The most interesting thing that ever happened to America was the Civil War; but General Lee was severely to be blamed for leading his country into that war, just the same, because he must have known they could not win; and to her, it was absurd that any one should join battle in defense of a principle in face of certain defeat. For practical purposes, honor was not even a word. Still it was an exciting war and gave an interest to America which that country would never have had without it. "If you win you do not lose and if you lose you do not win." Even as she was writing these winged words, the Spanish Civil War, the Republicans against the Franco-Fascists, kept obtruding itself. And why? "Not because it is a revolution, but because I know so well the places they are mentioning and the things there they are destroying." When she was little in Oakland, California, she loved the big, nice American fires that had "so many horses and firemen to attend them," and when she was older, she found that floods, for one thing, always read worse in the papers than they really are; besides how can you care much about what is going on if you don't see it or know the people? For this reason she had Santa Teresa being indifferent to far-away Chinese while she was founding convents in Spain. William Seabrook came to see her to find out if she was as interesting as her books. She told him she was, and he discovered black magic in the paintings of Sir Francis Rose. And when she asked Dashiell Hammett why so many young men authors were writing novels about tender young male heroines instead of the traditional female ones, he explained that it was because as women grew more and more self-confident, men lost confidence in themselves, and turned to each other, or became their own subjects for fiction. This, or something else, reminded her several times that she could not write a novel, therefore no one could any more, and no one should waste time trying.

Somehow by such roundabouts we arrive at the important, the critical event in all this eventful history. Success. Success in this world, here and now, was what Miss Stein wanted. She knew just what it was, how it should look and feel, how much it should weigh and what it was worth over the counter. It was not enough to be a genius if you had to go on supporting your art on a private income. To be the center of a recondite literary cult, to be surrounded by listeners and imitators and seekers, to be mentioned in the same breath with James Joyce, and to have turned out bales of titles by merely writing a half-hour each day: she had all that, and what did it amount to? There was a great deal more and she must have it. As to her history of the human race, she confessed: "I have always been bothered . . . but mostly . . . because after all I do as simply as it can, as commonplacely as it can say, what everybody can and does do; I never know what they can do, I really do not know what they are, I do not think that any one can think because if they do, then who is who?"

It was high time for a change, and yet it occurred at hazard. If there had not been a beautiful season in October and part of November 1932, permitting Miss Stein to spend that season quietly in her country house, the *Autobiography of Alice B. Toklas* might never have been written. But it was written, and Miss Stein became a best seller in America; she made real money. With Miss Toklas, she had a thrilling tour of the United States and found crowds of people eager to see her and listen to her. And at last she got what she had really wanted all along: to be published in the *Atlantic Monthly* and the *Saturday Evening Post*.

Now she had everything, or nearly. For a while she was afraid to write any more, for fear her latest efforts would not please her public. She had never learned who she was, and yet suddenly she had become somebody else. "You are you because your little dog knows you, but when your public knows you and does not want to pay you, and when your public knows you and does want to pay you, you are not the same you."

This would be of course the proper moment to take leave, as our heroine adds at last a golden flick of light to her self-portrait. "Anyway, I was a celebrity." The practical result was that she could no longer live on her income. But she and Alice B. Toklas moved into an apartment once occupied by Queen Christina of Sweden, and they began going out more, and seeing even more people, and talking, and Miss Stein settled every question as it came up, more and more. But who wants to read about success? It is the early struggle which makes a good story.

IV

She and Alice B. Toklas enjoyed both the wars. The first one especially being a lark with almost no one getting killed where you could see, and it ended so nicely too, without changing anything. The second was rather more serious. She lived safely enough in Bilignin throughout the German occupation, and there is a pretty story that the whole village conspired to keep her presence secret. She had been a citizen of the world in the best European tradition; for though America was her native land, she had to live in Europe because she felt at home there. In the old days people paid little attention to wars, fought as they were out of sight by professional soldiers. She had always liked the notion, too, of the gradual Orientalization of the West, the peaceful penetration of the East into European culture. It had been going on a great while, and all Western geniuses worth mentioning were Orientals: look at Picasso, look at Einstein. Russians are Tartars, Spaniards are Saracens—had not all great twentieth-century painting been Spanish? And her cheerful conclusion was, that "Einstein was the creative philosophic mind of the century, and I have been the creative literary mind of the century also, with the Oriental mixing with the European." She added, as a casual afterthought, "Perhaps Europe is finished."

That was in 1938, and she could not be expected to know that war was near. They had only been sounding practice *alertes* in Paris against expected German bombers since 1935. She spoke out of her natural frivolity and did not mean it. She liked to prophesy, but warned her hearers that her prophecies never came out right, usually the very opposite, and no matter what happened, she was always surprised. She was surprised again: as the nations of Europe fell, and the Germans came again over the frontiers of France for the third time in three generations, the earth shook under her own feet, and not somebody else's. It made an astonishing difference. Something mysterious touched her in her old age. She got a fright, and this time not for ancient vanished civilizations, but for this civilization, this moment; and she was quite thrilled with relief and gay when the American Army finally came in, and the Germans were gone. She did not in the least know why the Germans had come, but they were gone, and so far as she could see, the American Army had chased them out. She remembered with positive spread-eagle patriotism that America was her native land. At last America itself belonged to Miss Stein, and she claimed it, in a formal published address to other Americans. Anxiously she urged them to stay rich, to be powerful and learn how to use power, not to waste themselves; for the first time she used the word "spiritual." Ours was a spiritual as well as a material fight; Lincoln's great lucid words about government of the people by the people for the people suddenly sounded like a trumpet through her stammering confession of faith; she wanted nothing now to stand between her and her newly discovered country. By great good luck she was born on the winning side and she was going to stay there. And we were not to forget about money as the source of power; "Remember the depression, don't be afraid to look it in the face and find out the reason why, if you don't find out the reason why you'll go poor and my God, how I would hate to have my native land go poor."

The mind so long shapeless and undisciplined could not now express any knowledge out of its long willful ignorance. But the heart spoke its crude urgent language. She had liked the doughboys in the other war well enough, but this time she fell in love with the whole American Army below the rank of lieutenant. She "breathed, ate, drank, lived GI's," she told them, and inscribed numberless photographs for them, and asked them all to come back again. After her flight over Germany in an American bomber, she wrote about how, so often, she would stand staring into the sky watching American war planes going over, longing to be up there again with her new loves, in the safe, solid air. She murmured, "Bless them, bless them."

It was the strangest thing, as if the wooden umbrella feeling the rain had tried to forsake its substance and take on the nature of its form; and was struggling slowly, slowly, much too late, to unfold.

From *Harper's Magazine,* Vol. CXCV (December, 1947), pp. 519–528. Reprinted by permission of the author and editors.

LOUISE BOGAN

James on a Revolutionary Theme

[1938]

FOR all the varied critical attention given, in the last twenty years, to the novels of Henry James, those of his middle period are seldom read. When they are read, their real intention is often missed or is interpreted in some peculiar, special way. F. R. Leavis has recently pointed out several flagrant misinterpretations of James (including the classic mistake made by the critic who thought Isabel Archer divorced her husband and married an American business man at the end of *The Portrait of a Lady*) and has explained the neglect of the early and middle James by the fact that readers, steered toward the works of the late, "difficult" period, and baffled by these, make no further investigation. The three books which, appearing in the center of James's career, fully exemplify the virtues of his early manner—*The Bostonians, The Princess Casamassima* and *The Tragic Muse*—are those most completely ignored.

The Princess Casamassima, it is true, has recently come in for some attention, since critics interested in novels concerned with revoluntionary activities have discovered that in this book James deals with revolutionaries in the financially depressed London of the '80's. Although I cannot claim to have unearthed every scrap of material written about this book, I have read a fair amount and can say that not one commentator has shown signs of understanding the design James has so clearly presented in it. Usually *The Princess* has been put down as a melodramatic and rather fumbling attempt at a novel dealing with a revolutionary theme.[1]

[1] In 1938. Since the present essay was written *The Princess Casamassima* has been discussed in other studies of Henry James: by F. O. Matthiessen in *Henry James: The Major Phase* (1944), by Osborn Andreas in *Henry James and the Expanding Horizon* (1948), by Elizabeth Stevenson in *The Crooked Corridor* (1949), etc., but particularly by Lionel Trilling in his Introduction to a new edition of the novel published by The Macmillan Company, New York, 1948, and now included in Mr. Trilling's book *The Liberal Imagination* (New York: The Viking Press, 1950), pp. 58–92. The earlier discussions of the novel to which Miss Bogan refers here are those in *The Pilgrimage of Henry James* by Van Wyck Brooks (1925), in *The Three Jameses: A Family of Minds* by C. Hartley Grattan (1932), and in "The School of Experience in the Early Novels" by Stephen Spender, *The Hound and Horn*, Vol. VII (April–June, 1934), pp. 417–433, this later incorporated in Spender's book *The Destructive Element* (1935). (Editor's note, 1950.)

Several good reasons exist for these critical misconceptions, but before we deal with them, it would be well to get clear in our minds, since one of the charges against the book is that its material has not been thoroughly grasped, exactly what degree of mastery over his material, of insight into his characters, James had reached when he wrote it. *The Princess* was probably written concurrently with *The Bostonians*. Both novels were complete failures when they appeared (in 1886). James believed in both books, although for reasons that remain obscure he did not include *The Bostonians* in the definitive New York edition. But *The Princess* was included, with a preface which delicately but firmly pointed up the book's intention.

During the '70's James had produced no completely successful long work. And certainly *Watch and Ward* (1878) and *Confidence* (1880) are not only the most clumsy novels ever signed by James but the most clumsy pieces of fiction ever signed by a man of genius. They display the unsure approach of the writer who is doing it all from the outside—from the notebook, the stiff plan, the bad guess. Through some spurt of development James, in 1881, wrote the finely balanced, deeply observed *Washington Square* and *The Portrait of a Lady*. He was now able to base his books upon his characters, as opposed to supporting the action with some artificial diagram of conduct. Each character now casts light and shadow and is in turn accented or illuminated by the darkness or brilliance of the others. James had not finished profiting from Balzac, but he was now Turgenev's intelligent pupil as well. The realistic method was becoming more effortless at the same time that the technique of suggestion took in more territory with greater ease. So that the chance of James's fumbling, at this period, any problem he put his hand to is small.

The Princess Casamassima, it is true, opens with a block of Balzacian realism mixed with Dickensian melodrama that is extremely hard for modern readers to accept. In the later chapters of the book detail and suspense are to be brought in with sureness and ease; every part of the situation is to be elucidated by that sure technical skill so characteristic of the pre-theater James. The first three chapters, however, are thick with underlining and filled with a kind of cardboard darkness. The characters are so overloaded with reasons that they closely approach the line dividing drama from burlesque. The delicate little boy called Hyacinth, the son of a French working girl, who is also a murderess, and an earl, her victim; Miss Pynsent, the tender old maid who has raised the child; Mr. Vetch, the battered fiddler with leanings toward anarchism—at first glance these appear cut out of whole cloth. And in spite of a few flashes of insight, the scene in which Hyacinth witnesses his mother's death in prison is dated and overcharged. Thus balked at the outset, it is little wonder that the reader expects to find a measure of falseness everywhere in the story.

Given the remarkable figure of Hyacinth and the remarkable fact of his sharply divided inheritance, what use does James make of them? It may be best to give the story in bare outline. Hyacinth, grown to young manhood, is apprenticed to M. Poupin, an exiled veteran both of '48 and the Commune. (Hyacinth's own maternal grandfather, James tells us at an early point, died on the Paris barricades.) Poupin teaches him revolutionary principles along with the trade (James considers it a minor art) of book-binding. The youth then meets the two people who are to bring about the crisis in his life. The Princess Casamassima, separated from her husband and footloose in London on her husband's money, first dazzles Hyacinth with her interest in revolutionary plots and then with her interest in himself. And Paul Muniment, son of a north-country miner, an active, realistic, and inscrutable worker deep in revolutionary activities, attracts the ardent boy. Hyacinth actually gives over his life to Muniment, promising in a moment of enthusiasm that he will be the instrument for an act of violence whenever the need arises. Muniment accepts his pledge and binds Hyacinth fully, by a vow taken before witnesses. Hyacinth tells the Princess, after she has given him some minor glimpses of the great world, of his origin and dedication. Miss Pynsent dies; her small legacy enables Hyacinth to go to the Continent. He comes back changed. What he has seen has convinced him that certain objects, of which he had no former notion, should be preserved, not destroyed. The Princess has meanwhile met Muniment. She brings her charm to bear on him, with the secondary purpose of extricating Hyacinth from his vow; but primarily to get herself deeper into true conspiratorial circles. Hyacinth, whose determination to do what he can to further the cause of the people remains unchanged in spite of his secret change of heart, thinks that the pair have cast him off. Then the call comes: a duke is to be assassinated and Hyacinth is picked by the mysterious instigator of these affairs to be the assassin. The revolutionary group, at this news, splits into two factions: those who wish to save Hyacinth and those who are willing to let matters take their course. Muniment, although he professes sympathy for Hyacinth and says that he is free to choose, does nothing. The Princess rushes to save the boy and to offer herself in his stead. She and a kind, methodical German conspirator meet at Hyacinth's lodgings. But the boy has already shot himself, with the revolver meant for the assassination.

Critics have construed this story according to the set of their own convictions. Van Wyck Brooks, for example, although appreciative of James's success with Poupin, Vetch, Miss Pynsent, and others, considers Hyacinth an insufferable little snob. And Hyacinth is, according to Brooks, an embodiment of James's own yearning after the glories of the British upper classes.

This unfortunate but remarkably organized youth . . . is conscious of nothing but the paradise of which he has been dispossessed. . . . In real life the last thing that would have occurred to a young man of Hyacinth's position would have been to "roam and wander and yearn" about the gates of that lost paradise: he would have gone to Australia, or vanished into the slums, or continued *with the utmost indifference* at his *trade* of binding books. But this attitude represents the feeling of Hyacinth's creator. [Italics mine.]

C. Hartley Grattan believes that Hyacinth's "sense of deprivation" vitiates the worth of his radical impulses:

The conviction that it is senseless to do anything, no matter how small the act, to destroy the upper classes leads to the climax of the novel in [Hyacinth's] suicide.

But Grattan admits James's insight into his material.

When the social-minded young English disinterred the book some years ago because of its theme, Stephen Spender wrote in *The Destructive Element*:

The observation of political types in this book is really remarkable and curiously undated . . . Paul Muniment . . . is a true revolutionary type. He has the egoism, the sense of self-preservation, the cynicism of a person who identifies himself so completely with a cause that he goes through life objectively guarding himself from all approach, as one might preserve for the supreme eventuality a very intricate and valuable torpedo.

Spender's evaluation of Hyacinth is this:

Hyacinth, with his strong leaning toward the upper classes and yet his feeling that he is somehow committed to the cause of the workers, might today have become a Socialist Prime Minister: a Ramsay MacDonald who . . . would dismay his followers by going over to the other side and becoming the most frequent visitor at large country houses and of dinners at Buckingham Palace.

Now Hyacinth, in the very essence of his character as James with great care and at considerable length presents it, could never become what Spender thinks he could become, any more than what Brooks thinks James should have made him become. Before turning to Hyacinth, let us examine the character of the Princess. Who is she? What is she? What has she been, and what is she likely to be? The development of her character must have meant a good deal to James since she is the only figure he ever "revived" and carried from one book to another.

She was Christina Light in *Roderick Hudson*, the character in that early work who evokes the mixed feelings of admiration and exasperation that James was later to call up through many of his women. She is the daughter of an Anglo-American shrew and adventuress who forces her, by a threat of scandal, into a marriage with the highest bidder. James managed to bring out, even at a time when his art was still imperfect, Christina's marred idealism and ignorant, rather than innocent, pride, so that they freshen every page on which she appears. The coarser and weaker people, in contrast with her straightforwardness, show up in a sorry way. Roderick Hudson, with whom she falls in love and whom she tries to galvanize into some kind of manhood, crumbles, after losing her, in much the same way, James makes us feel, as he would have crumbled had he won her. Brought up to deadening shifts, she has one flaw. She is not truly courageous. She marries the prince at once after receiving the shock of her mother's revelations.

In the later book she is the single person who is continuously presented from the outside. James never "goes behind" her. We are never told what she thinks or how she feels; we merely see her act. James clearly presupposes a knowledge in the reader of her early tragedy. To watch her casting her charm and enthusiasm about; to see her reacting more and more violently against her money and position; to see her—after Muniment has told her that it is her money alone which interests his circle, and has prophesied her certain return to her husband now that the Prince has stopped the flow of that money— rushing in desperation to offer herself as a substitute in the affair of the duke's assassination—all this can puzzle us if we know nothing of the beautiful girl who moved through the scenes of *Roderick Hudson*.

Now "the cleverest woman in Europe," she bears a grudge against society strong enough to force her into repudiation of everything her trained taste fully values. When Hyacinth bares his own tragedy to her, the relation of the two is lifted out of a stupid contrast between a revolutionary-minded woman of the world and a talented pauper. For what the Princess knows, as she listens to him, and what the reader should also know, is that she is herself a bastard. James, far from being taken in by it, deeply realizes that the life she represents is as undermined by the results of cruelty and passion, for all its beautiful veneer, as Hyacinth's own. Having failed in her youth to face a crisis and see it through, she knows in her heart that when she thinks of herself as "one of the numerous class who could be put on a tolerable footing only by a revolution," she is thinking dishonestly. It is her despair and her defects which push her toward extreme revolutionary enthusiasm, as much as her generosity of spirit. But in Hyacinth she recognizes—after she has emerged from her first sentimental ideas concerning him—complete devotion, consistency, and fineness. This boy "never makes mistakes," and is incapable of going back on a given promise. She shows him specimens of English county families, toward whom her own reaction is: "You know, people oughtn't to be both corrupt and dreary." But what Hyacinth tenders them, as he tenders her, beneath his devotion, is a kind of gentle pity.

For this son of a criminal and an aristocrat is not, as he has been made out to be, a little snob, an affected artisan with a divided nature and ambitions beyond his station. James, with every subtle device of his mature art, from the first sentence describing him to the last, shows the boy as an artist, a clear, sensitive intelligence, filled with the imagination "which will always give him the clue about everything." James has endowed him, indeed, with the finest qualities of his own talent; and this is what is meant when James says that Hyacinth had watched London "very much as I had watched it." Hyacinth is, like James, "a person on whom nothing is lost." If the character has a fault, it is that James has distilled too purely into his creature the sharp insight, the capacity for selfless devotion, the sense of proportion, the talent for self-mockery and gentle irony which seldom exist in genius without an admixture of cruder ingredients. But James wanted a cool and undistorting mirror to shine between the dark and violent world of the disinherited on the one hand and the preposterous world of privilege on the other. Such a clear lens (Maisie, Nanda) James was later to place in the center of psychological situations. He was never again to place it, and with the final polish of genius added, between social classes. For that matter it has never been placed there, up to the present, by anyone else, although Conrad, in *Under Western Eyes,* a book almost certainly modeled on *The Princess,* examined the revolutionary side of the picture through the intense spirit of Razumov. We are used, in fiction dealing with social problems, to the spectacle of the artist absorbed or deflected into one class or another. James kept Hyacinth detached to the end. And though the solution for the artist, in the insoluble situation James has constructed, is death, as the symbols of the two extremes he has instinctively rejected (after he knows that his own life must exist independently, apart from either) stand by his deathbed, we feel that what they both have been left to is not exactly life.

The book is full of wonderful moments. Short mention should be made of the ultimate opacity and brutality of Muniment, as he is shown in contrast not only to Hyacinth but to the more humane members of the revolutionary circle; of James's masterly analysis of Hyacinth's spiritual coming of age, resulting, on his return from abroad, in increased self-sufficiency and a more complete grasp of his art; of the complex rendering of Hyacinth's rejection of the thought of violence when his mother's murderous hands come before him; of the superb portraits of the solidly disillusioned Madame Grandoni, the morbidly jealous Prince, and those true fools and snobs—Captain Sholto and Muniment's horrible invalid sister. The scenes of submerged London have been praised. What is even more astonishing than these is James's knowledge of the relentless mechanisms of poverty—poverty's minutiae.

It is interesting to trace down the source of James's understanding of Muniment. We remember that the elder James was surrounded by socialists of the Fourier school, and that he "agreed with Fourier that vice and crime were the consequences of our present social order, and it would not survive them." The younger James had, no doubt, seen Muniment's counterpart multiplied about him, in Fourier's more fanatical followers, in his childhood.

"Very likely . . . all my buried prose will kick off its tombstones at once," James wrote to Howells in 1888. After, it would seem, Stendhal's hundred years.

From *The Nation,* Vol. CXLVI (April 23, 1938), pp. 471–474. Reprinted by permission of the author and editors.

ERIC BENTLEY

Shaw at Ninety

[1946]

ON THE twenty-sixth of July, Bernard Shaw will be ninety years old.[1] How should we—or he—feel about it? The ninetieth birthday of the man who once wrote, "Every man over forty is a scoundrel," is an ambiguous occasion. Ambiguous because he does not believe in celebrating any birthdays, let alone ninetieth birthdays. Ambiguous because, in the opinion of so many, Mr. Shaw has outlived his genius and even his usefulness. Ambiguous because, it is thought, the politics of the twentieth century has traveled far beyond the ken of Fabianism. Ambiguous because twentieth-century literature has taken quite a different turn since the days when Shavian drama was the latest thing. And yet, despite Mr. Shaw's indifference to celebrations, despite the indifference of my contemporaries to Mr. Shaw, I propose to celebrate the ninety-year span of this man's life by asking the Shavian question: What use has it been? To what end has Bernard Shaw lived?

Seventy years ago a young Irishman went to live in London. Another twenty years had to pass before London was fully aware of the fact that it possessed a new critic, a new novelist, a new thinker, a new wit, and—rarest of all—a new dramatist. In the first decade of the twentieth century Shaw's reputation swept across America and Central Europe. On the death of Anatole France in 1924 he was declared the leading Great Man of European letters. A new play by Shaw was a world event. Between 1923 and 1925 the part of Saint Joan was enacted by Winifred Lenihan in America, Sybil Thorndike in England, Ludmilla Pitoëff in Paris, Elisabeth Bergner in Berlin. On the occasion of his seventieth birthday a *New York Times* editorial declared Shaw "probably the most famous of living writers."

Soon the fame won by plays and books was doubled by the fame won by his films. Shaw's opinions on everything were reported in the press almost weekly. Has any other author ever been so famous during his lifetime? (Since 1905 many articles on Shaw have been published every year. Some forty whole books have been written about him.) True, none of his books has sold like *Gone With the Wind*, none of his plays has run as long as *Tobacco Road*.

[1] Written in 1946, on the occasion of Shaw's ninetieth birthday. (Editor's note.)

But even by the economic criterion, Shaw's career was "sounder" than any merely popular author's, for his books went on selling indefinitely and his plays returned to the stage again and again. True, as a "best-selling classic" Shaw does not rival Shakespeare or the Bible. But then it takes the death of its author to put the final seal of respectability upon a classic. And Shaw refuses to die.

If, as Freud says, the life of the artist is a quest for honor, riches, fame, love, and power, Shaw must be one of the most successful men who ever lived. Then why is he, rather obviously, a sad old man? Because he is sorry to leave a world which he has so brilliantly adorned? That is too shallow an explanation. Honor, riches, fame, the love of women, these he has been granted in abundance. Yet the striking thing about Shaw is his relative aloofness from all these worldly advantages. He talks about them all as if they belonged to somebody else.

But Freud mentioned a fifth goal: power. And this Shaw has only had to the same extent as any other rich writer, and that is to a very small extent indeed. Not that Shaw wanted to be Prime Minister or anything of that sort. The only time Shaw stood as candidate in a large-scale election his abstention from demagogy amounted to a Coriolanus-like repudiation of his electors. When the electors turned him down, they were returning a compliment.

This was not the kind of power Shaw wanted. Crude personal ambition is something he scarcely understands. What he did feel was the consciousness of great spiritual resources within him, the consciousness of a message—of, as he put it, being used by something larger than himself. When, therefore, people paid attention to the ego of Shaw and not to the message of Shaw, when they paid attention to the small and not to the large thing, that was for Shaw the ultimate catastrophe. More plainly put, Shaw's aim has been to change our minds and save civilization; but we are still in the old ruts and civilization has gone from bad to worse. For Shaw this must be the cardinal fact of his career. "I have produced no permanent impression because nobody has ever believed me."

Anyone who knows Shaw's aims and attitudes knows that this is as complete a confession of failure as old Carlyle's famous sentence: "They call me a great man now, but not one believes what I have told them." Three years after Carlyle's death Shaw wrote on behalf of the peaceful Fabians that "we had rather face a Civil War than such another century of suffering as this has been." And then came, of all things, the twentieth century, the age of Wilhelm II, Tojo, and Hitler! In 1932 Shaw was again addressing the Fabians. He said: "For forty-eight years I have been addressing speeches to the Fabian Society and to other assemblies in this country. So far as I can make out, those speeches have not produced any effect whatsoever."

"So what?" some will be content to say, reconciling themselves with cynical ease to the ways of the world. Why should Shaw think he can change civilization by thinking, writing, and talking? This, says one of his Marxist critics, is the "bourgeois illusion." Winston Churchill does not use the Marxist vocabulary, but his essay on Shaw, in *Great Contemporaries*, conveys the same contempt. He will accept Shaw only on condition that he does not ask to be taken seriously. He ignored Shaw's repeated assertion: "The real joke is that I am in earnest."

II

The fact that Shaw has been easy to brush off can be explained by the method which he has used to spread his fame, a method he expounded forty years ago with characteristic frankness:

> In order to gain a hearing it was necessary for me to attain the footing of a privileged lunatic with the license of a jester. My method has therefore been to take the utmost trouble to find the right thing to say and then say it with the utmost levity.

The lunatic jester was named "G. B. S.," a personage who from the start was known to many more people than Bernard Shaw could ever hope to be, a Very Funny Man, whose perversities were so outrageous that they could be forgiven only under the assumption that they were not intended, whose views and artistic techniques seemed to be arrived at by the simple expedient of inverting the customary. Unfortunately Bernard Shaw proved a sorcerer's apprentice: he could not get rid of "G. B. S." The very method by which Shaw made himself known prevented him from being understood. The paradox of his career is that he should have had so much fame and so little influence.

So little influence? Is the phrase disparaging? After all, Shaw had an appreciable influence at least on the generation of 1910. And yet even this is hardly something that Shaw would congratulate himself upon, for it was mainly negative. It represented only the superficial part of his teaching, his anti-Victorianism. It was often the kind of influence he had positively to disown—as in the case of the young criminal whose plea of being a disciple of Shaw was later embodied in *The Doctor's Dilemma*. The attention Shaw attracts must not be confused with influence.

During the first decades "G. B. S." was a Dangerous Spirit, distinctly Mephistophelian, red-bearded, young, and aggressive. No kind of philosopher can more easily be dismissed. Eugene O'Neill's play *Ah, Wilderness* portrays this early Shavian "influence" as a sort of measles which the more literary high school boy must have and then forget. After the First World War, the great dividing line in Shaw's career, "G. B. S." was regarded as rather cute, a Santa Claus if not a Simple Simon. William Archer crowned his long series of attempts to discredit Shaw with a final blow: Shaw was a Grand Old Man.

"Not taking me seriously," said Shaw, "is the Englishman's way of refusing to face facts." And by "the Englishman" Shaw has always meant Monsieur Tout-le-monde. "What is wrong with the prosaic Englishman is what is wrong with the prosaic men of all countries: stupidity."

Before the First World War, Shaw was the leader of the *avant-garde*. After it he was the Grand Old Man—which meant that he had lost the support of the rebellious young. In 1898 Shaw had written: "I may dodder and dote; I may potboil and platitudinize; I may become the butt and chopping-block of all the bright original spirits of the rising generation; but my reputation shall not suffer; it is built up fast and solid, like Shakespeare's, on an impregnable basis of dogmatic reiteration." Like Shakespeare's! What an irony, for the man who wished to have, not literary prestige "like Shakespeare's," but *influence* like Voltaire's or Luther's. "I see there is a tendency," Shaw said in 1921, "to begin treating me like an archbishop. I fear in that case that I must be becoming a hopeless old twaddler."

The new "G. B. S." proved another spirit that could not be exorcised. And the new "G. B. S." was worse than the old, for fogies have even less influence than iconoclasts. The old critics had at least feared and scorned Shaw. An admirer of the new sort wrote: "But I do not believe that we will thus scorn him or forget him when the irritation of his strictures on events that are close to our hearts or to our pride is removed." Unfortunately, for Shaw's purposes, irritation to our hearts and our pride was desirable, while praise for the irritator was neither here nor there. If the undirected rebelliousness of Mencken —whose first book of criticism (1905) was also the first book ever written about Shaw—was only a negative and distorted Shavianism, that is the only sort of Shavianism that has as yet had any currency at all.

The people who have revered Shaw in his later years—revered him as patriarch, as senile prodigy—have not bothered to imbibe any of his teaching. This is best illustrated by the fact that Broadway, though always reluctant to stage anything but a new play, has revived old Shaw plays and made money with them, while his new plays were either left alone or played to half-empty houses. It was not that Shaw's new plays were so obviously inferior to his old plays. They were in any case much better plays than most of those on Broadway. It was that Shaw was no longer welcome as a living force. He was a Classic—that is, the author of plays old and awesome enough to be innocuous.

When Shaw won popular fame he lost his serious reputation. "The bright and original spirits of the rising generation" repudiated him and passed on. A *Nation* editorial of October, 1909, already reflects new departures: "The time has come . . . when the insolent Shavian advertising no longer fills us with astonishment or discovery, or disables our judgment from a cool inspection of the wares advertised. The youthful Athenians who darted most impetuously after his novelties are already hankering after some new thing. The deep young souls who looked to him as an evangelist are beginning to see through him and despair." The occasion of these patronizing remarks was the publication of Chesterton's brilliant book (still the best) on Shaw, which, despite Chesterton's avowed dislike of "time snobbery," was an attempt to make Shaw sound dated.

In 1913, D. H. Lawrence wrote that there ought to be a revolt against the generation of Shaw and Wells. In the same year a young English critic, Dixon Scott, who was soon after to be killed at Gallipoli, interpreted Shaw, in one of the best critical essays of that generation, as essentially a child of London in the 'eighties. Shortly after the First World War the leading poet of the new generation, T. S. Eliot, was careful to put Shaw in his place as "an Edwardian," a quaint survivor from before the flood. Several of the clever critics of this clever decade wrote essays to prove Shaw an old fool. Theatrical criticism followed the general trend. The gist of George Jean Nathan's notices in the 'twenties and 'thirties is that Shaw is played out.

When William Archer conferred the title of Grand Old Man, Shaw was not yet seventy. The wheel turned, and lo! an ancient of seventy-five, eighty, eighty-five. Diamond jubilees followed jubilees as the figure rose and rose. This year, when Shaw is ninety, some will laugh with him and some will laugh at him, some will laugh sentimentally and some will laugh superciliously. Few will laugh in the true Shavian fashion—seriously.

I hope some of the main features of Shaw's career are now clear. To gain an audience he invented a pose. The pose gained him his audience but prevented him from having any influence. The mask of clowning in Shaw's career has as its counterpoint the mask of clowning, of farce and melodrama, of *Kitsch* and sheer entertainment, in his plays. Of this second mask a great theatrical critic, Egon Friedell, remarked that it was clever of Shaw so to sugar his pill but that it was even cleverer of the public to lick off the sugar and leave the pill alone. In that battle with his audience which is the main conflict in Shavian drama, in that battle with the public which is the main conflict in everything that Shaw writes or says, the audience, the public, has won. "I have solved practically all the pressing questions of our time," Shaw says, "but . . . they keep on being propounded as insoluble just as if I had never existed."

Up to this point Shaw's secret is an open one. Shaw's famous method, his "Shavianism," by which people mean his pose of arrogance, was a deliberate strategy in an altruistic struggle. As I have suggested, it was precisely because Shaw was so unusually immune from the common frailties of ambition and egoism that he could adopt the manner of the literary exhibitionist without risk to his integrity. His campaign of self-promotion was not the campaign of a clever careerist who decides to secure at once by cunning what he will never secure later by genius. Shaw had artistic genius enough, and knew it, but he was not primarily interested in artistic genius and artistic reputation. He wanted his pen to be his sword in a struggle that was more ethical than aesthetic.

Wishing to change the world, Shaw wished to speak to the public at large, not merely to his literary confreres. So he put his genius at the service of his moral passion. He knew that he risked sacrificing altogether a high literary reputation (like, say, Henry James's); and the fact that his name is so often linked with the publicist Wells indicates that, for a time at least, Shaw has forgone that kind of reputation. The arrogant pose was an act of self-sacrifice. Shaw's modesty was offered up on the altar of a higher purpose. In order to be influential he consented to be notorious.

His failure was double. Willingly he forwent his literary reputation. Unwillingly he had to admit his lack of influence as a thinker. The term Artist-Philosopher which Shaw coined for himself is perhaps a concealed admission that both as artist and as philosopher he had failed to make his mark.

III

If this were the whole story, Shaw would be no more important than a hundred other men who have abandoned art for "action" or propaganda without making any noticeable dent in the world's armor. Shaw's is a more complicated case. If he is today a sad old man it is not himself that he has found disappointing. His unhappiness is not that of a Citizen Kane finding that success does not bring contentment. It is in *us* that he is disappointed. It is modern civilization he grieves over. To the man who now proceeds to ask: but is not Shaw one of us? is he not an integral part of modern civilization? one would have to reply: his ideas are indeed typically modern, a synthesis of all our romanticism and realism, our traditionalism and our revolutionism, yet he himself is not one of us. He is further apart from his contemporaries than any other thinker since Nietzsche.

Shaw was born and bred a Protestant in the most fanatically Catholic city in the world. That indeed is his situation in a nutshell. His home, far from being one of puritanic pressures like Samuel Butler's, was one of abnormally tepid relationships. From the beginning Shaw was encouraged to be independent. Practically the only thing his education taught him was how to stand alone. His keenest pleasures were those which the imagination could feast on without intrusion from people around him; when he speaks of his voluptuous youth he means he read novels, wandered round an art gallery, reveled in opera and melodrama. Since his schooling was as untyrannical as his home, he was largely unaffected by it. The first time he felt the pressure of society was when he became a clerk. It was too much for him. He broke with his whole environment by going to seek his fortune in London. If he lived with his mother there, it was only to save money. Mother and son continued to see little of each other.

Shaw entered British society by the Bohemian gate. He never tried to become an established member of the upper, middle, or lower class. He remained "unassimilated." His first circle of acquaintance consisted largely of musicians, his later circle of writers and actors. Even his journalistic experience did not bring Shaw overmuch into contact with the general run of men. As book reviewer, art, drama, and music critic, he worked at home, at the gallery, the theater, and the concert hall, not at the office. A brief connection with the telephone business convinced Shaw for a second time that he must never try to "earn an honest living."

From 1882 on, Shaw was a socialist, addressed mass audiences, served on committees, was elected borough councillor, stood as candidate for the London County Council. But how far all this work was from any mingling with the working class, the middle class, or any class except that of intellectuals is clear to anyone who studies the life of Shaw in particular or the history of the Fabian Socialists in general. The Fabian Society should be thought of less as one of the several branches of the British Labor movement than as one of the many societies for intellectuals which abounded in Victorian, and especially Late Victorian, England.

One might almost say that the Fabians were nearer to the Aesthetes than to the trade-unions. Theirs was but another form of Bohemianism. "Instead of velvet jackets and a slap-dash joviality," as Dixon Scott put it, the young writers of the 'eighties "took to *saeva indignatio* and sandals," to "Jaeger and Ibsen and Esoteric Buddhism." "They became infidels," he added, "atheists, anarchists, cosmogonists, vegetarians, anti-vivisectionists, anti-vaccinationists." Far from involving Shaw personally in ordinary British society, socialism helped to keep him out of it. And for good. For he married a wealthy Fabian in 1898, and in the twentieth century has barely pretended to be a part of our world at all. At best he descends upon us from his country house at Ayot St. Lawrence like a prophet descending from mountain solitude.

If this version of Shaw's career seems fanciful, turn to the last page of the preface to *Immaturity*, the long essay which is the nearest approach to an autobiography that Shaw will ever write. Calling himself "a sojourner on this planet rather than a native of it," Shaw continues:

Whether it be that I was born mad or a little too sane, my kingdom was not of this world: I was at home only in the realm of my imagination, and at my ease only with the mighty dead. Therefore I had to become an actor, and create for myself a fantastic personality fit and apt for dealing with men, and adaptable to the various parts I had to play as author-journalist, orator, politician, committeeman, man of the world and so forth. In this I succeeded later on only too well. In my boyhood I saw Charles Mathews act in a farce called Cool as a Cucumber. The hero was a young man just returned from a tour of the world, upon which he had been set to cure him of an apparently hopeless bashfulness; and the fun lay in the cure having overshot the mark and transformed him into a monster of outrageous impudence. I am not sure that something of the kind did not happen to me; for when my imposture was at last accomplished, and I daily pulled the threads of the puppet who represented me in the public press, the applause that greeted it was not unlike that which Mathews drew in Cool as a Cucumber. . . . At the time of which I am writing, however, I had not yet learned to act, nor come to understand that my natural character was impossible on the great London stage. When I had to come out of the realm of imagination into that of actuality I was still uncomfortable. I was outside society, outside politics, outside sport, outside the church. If the term had been invented then I should have been called the Complete Outsider.

Shaw was certainly an outsider. And, as we have seen, the ruse by which he sought to get Inside was by no means successful.

IV

At this point Shaw's career is revealed to us as something more than a picturesque misadventure, and Shaw as something more than a frustrated propagandist or a frustrated man of action. Of course he *is* a frustrated propagandist to some extent—all preachers are. But he is not a man of action at all. He is an artist, and therefore, whatever his didactic urge, whatever the naturalistic ardor with which he seeks to portray the outer world, he gives expression to his own nature and tells the story of himself. In the art of persuasion one Hitler or one Hearst is worth a thousand Shaws. The fact that Shaw did not descend to the methods of the politician, let alone of the demagogue, would indicate that—in spite of himself—he was not fundamentally a propagandist.

When remarking that the good advice of the Gospels, Dickens, Plato, has never been heeded, Shaw says in the foreword to his *Prefaces:* "You may well ask me why, with such examples before me, I took the trouble to write them. I can only reply that I do not know. There was no why about it: I had to: that was all." A cryptic solution? To those who know their Shaw it is suggestive of other Shavian tenets. Most basic of them is the statement in *The Sanity of Art:* "We are afraid to look life in the face and see in it, not the fulfilment of a moral law or of the deductions of reason, but the satisfaction of a passion in us of which we can give no account whatever." To satisfy passions we do many things because we "have to"—there is "no why about it." If the passion is a sufficiently high one—according to Shaw, chastity is passion, thought is passion—the action is justified.

Shaw's passions are high. In the preface to *Immaturity,* which I have already cited, Shaw refers to himself as an Insider. "The moment music, painting, literature, or science came into question the positions were reversed: it was I who was the Insider. I had the intellectual habit; and my natural combination of critical faculty with literary resource needed only a clear comprehension of life in the light of an intelligible theory: in short, a religion, to set it in triumphant operation." One of the most interesting portraits of Shaw is his own John Tanner, the man of ideas who in this world of ours is rightly regarded as even more a gasbag than an iconoclast, but who in the realm of the spirit, as Don Juan Tenorio, is a true master.

Whatever his duties to us, Shaw had his duty to himself. Whatever his function as a deliberate preacher, Shaw also knew himself to be a *force* that had to act according to the inscrutable laws of its own nature. He was being used—for an unknown purpose—through the agency of a passion "of which we can give no account whatever." This passion led the man who thought of himself as a propagandist to what looks like the weakest and most unpromising of all propagandist media—the theater. Nor are the plays the most propagandist of plays. As far as the presentation of opinions is concerned, Shaw's forte is for presenting both sides of a question with equal conviction, an art he brought to such a pitch that some thought his *Saint Joan* a defense of the Inquisition, while others thought his later political plays a defense of fascism. From beginning to end Shaw's drama expresses his nature—his apprehension of many-faceted reality—much more than it champions particular doctrines. It even mirrors Shaw's life rather closely in a series of self-portraits.

V

It is not of course true, despite Mr. Wells, that *all* Shaw's characters are Shaw—at least not in any obvious or important way. Nor can one, as Mr. Laski hints, simply look for a character who talks a lot, who believes in socialism, or creative evolution, and stamp him as Shaw. In *Candida*, for example, there is actually more of Shaw's philosophy, more of Shaw's plight too, in the Pre-Raphaelite poet Marchbanks than in the platform-speaking socialist Morell. These two characters might perhaps be taken as two halves of Shaw's nature: his outer, glib, and confident half, at once socialist and social, and his spiritual, lonely, and artistic half, the half that puts him beyond the pale of society. Certainly the secret in the poet's heart is the secret of Shaw the Outsider who is the real Insider, the man who is strong enough to leave the homestead and live with himself and his vision.

In the later plays the two most interesting self-portraits are Captain Shotover in *Heartbreak House* and King Magnus in *The Apple Cart*. Both portray Shaw's role in modern civilization and in England in particular. In *Heartbreak House*, England is represented as a ship, with no captain, heading for the rocks. In a ship within this ship—a house in which the only room we see is got up like a ship's cabin—lives Shotover, half lunatic, half sage, an ex-sailor

who sold himself to the devil at Zanzibar. He is conducting researches with
the aim of discovering a death ray ostensibly "to blow up the human race if it
goes too far."

Actually Shaw borrowed the death ray from a novel by Bulwer Lytton in
order to repeat a fancy he had aired long before in an essay: either we must
learn to respect justice as such or acquire the power to kill each other instantaneously by merely thinking. *Responsibility* (our supreme desideratum according to Shaw) must be attained by whatever method—if not by a passion
for justice, then by the passion of fear. It is significant that Shaw does not
present Shotover as a noble character but as a senile eccentric. As poignantly
as Nietzsche, Shaw recognized his own limitation. Although Shotover marries
a young woman, in sadly ironic recognition of the Shavian union of Artist
Man and Creator Woman, he does not discover the death ray any more than
England learns to respect justice. The end is chaos and misunderstanding.

The Apple Cart was discussed flat-footedly at the time of its first productions as a play advocating monarchy. This is a misunderstanding. The situation of the play—a king confronting his Labor cabinet—is actually a fantasy
which, like all Shavian fantasies, has very concrete implications. The king is
a philosopher-king. In fact he is Shaw (even to his love life, which includes a
humdrum wife whom he prefers to a romantic mistress). The problem of the
play is not King George versus Ramsay MacDonald but the question: Who
knows better what is going on and who is better fitted to cope with it—
Bernard Shaw the artist-philosopher or Ramsay MacDonald the prime minister? Their common enemy is Breakages Limited—that is, capitalism, the sinister power, thriving on destruction, which the critics took no notice of because
it is not personified on the stage. It lurks in the background. Now just as in
Shotover Shaw does not make himself patriarchal, so in Magnus he does not
make himself majestic. It is not clear that Magnus could really have won if he
had gone to the polls, as he threatened, against the politicians. It is not clear
that the philosopher can replace the prime minister. No basic problems are
cleared up at the end. We are left with the not very encouraging title of
the play.

But perhaps the most complete picture of what I have called "Shaw's role in
modern civilization" was long ago provided in *John Bull's Other Island*. As
in *Man and Superman* Shaw represents himself by two characters and, as in
Candida, the two Shaws are brought up against a more masterful person, one
who really assumes that he—in *Candida*, it is *she*—has inherited the earth. In
Candida the emphasis is chiefly psychological. In *John Bull's Other Island* it
is chiefly philosophic, a matter of rival outlooks. The Antagonist is not a
charming lady but the Shavian Englishman, the Shavian professional man,
the Shavian politician, Broadbent, the two syllables of whose name tell us
nearly all we need to know of him. Shaw himself, I think, is part Larry Doyle,

part Father Keegan; that is, partly the worldly Irishman whose realism drives him to have his revenge on England by "succeeding" as an Englishman, partly the divinely mad priest who believes (Shaw has been quoting the line ever since) that "every jest is an earnest in the womb of time."

There is no passage in Shaw that more clearly shows what he is for and what he is against; there is no passage that more openly reveals his estrangement from our world, than this brief encounter between Keegan and Broadbent:

BROADBENT: I find the world quite good enough for me: rather a jolly place in fact.

KEEGAN: You are satisfied?

BROADBENT: As a reasonable man, yes. I see no evils in the world—except of course, natural evils—that cannot be remedied by freedom, self-government, and English institutions. I think so, not because I am an Englishman, but as a matter of commonsense.

KEEGAN: You feel at home in the world then?

BROADBENT: Of course. Don't you?

KEEGAN (*from the very depths of his nature*): No.

BROADBENT: Try phosphorus pills. I always take them when my brain is overworked. I'll give you the address in Oxford Street.

At the end of the play, when Larry Doyle again expresses his contempt for dreaming—it is Shaw's own contempt for illusions, for idealism—and Broadbent tells us he has dreamt of heaven as a dreadful place, "a sort of pale blue satin," Keegan gives us *his* dream. It is Shaw's own ideal, which he hopes is no illusion:

In my dreams it is a country where the State is the Church and the Church the people: three in one and one in three. It is a commonwealth in which work is play and play is life: three in one and one in three. It is a temple in which the priest is the worshipper and the worshipper the worshipped: three in one and one in three. It is a godhead in which all life is human and all humanity divine: three in one and one in three.

But Father Keegan is obviously even madder than Captain Shotover. He summarizes his own vision: "It is in short the dream of a madman." To which Shaw's Englishman retorts: "What a regular old Church and State Tory he is! He's a character: he'll be an attraction here. Really almost equal to Ruskin and Carlyle." To which Shaw's other half, Larry Doyle, adds: "Yes: and much good *they* did with all their talk!"

Shaw's dream of a better world, his impatience with dreams of a better world, his idealism and his anti-idealism, his knowledge of the world of "Englishmen" and his alienation from this world—all these are implicit in the last pages of *John Bull's Other Island*. These are not pages of the Bernard Shaw the public knows. They are pages of the man who once wrote haughtily: "My heart knows only its own bitterness." They are pages of one whom the poet A. E. called a "suffering sensitive soul."

VI

We are now in a position to see what Shaw's career means over and above the well-attested fact that he wanted to be taken seriously and was not taken seriously. We can see that Shaw is a clear case of misunderstood genius. But, lest the story sound too much like that of the perennial "clown with a broken heart," we must see also that Shaw never relaxed into self-pity; that his celebrated gayety is precisely a prophylactic against such relaxation; that, alienated as he was, Shaw made a very special and subtle adjustment. He turned his alienation to artistic and moral profit. He is one of the very few great modern artists who have not been dismayed by their own estrangement.

Our times suffer from sick conscience, and our geniuses suffer with the times. Modern artists are mainly of two types. The first, to use Flaubert's figure, wants to vomit at the thought of the horror of our epoch, which it nevertheless looks straight in the eyes. The second looks in the other direction and calls loudly for literary Uplift, Patriotism, and something Wholesome. Shaw belonged to the first group. He vomited, but eventually emerged from the *vomitorium* with an incredibly optimistic smile on his face. Had he decided to join the second group? No, but he had decided that vomiting did no good, that the facts had to be faced but that they had also to be changed, and that if one is alienated from one's environment one can recognize the fact and work out a plan of campaign.

Shaw's older contemporary, Nietzsche, had come to a similar conclusion but had followed up his affirmations of health by losing his reason. Shaw found a happier though in some ways a no less desperate solution: he pretended to have no reason to lose. If modern life was as unreasonable as *King Lear,* Shaw would cast himself as the Fool. Trace the word *mad* through his plays and you will find that the finest characters and the finest actions usually have it applied to them.

Accordingly I do not think Shaw can find a place in the paradise of the middle-brows despite his cheerful and moralistic manner. To be sure, there are subterraneous realms which Shaw never enters, and we cannot find in him what we go to Dostoevsky, Proust, or Kafka for. Yet, like Ibsen, Shaw has had "a strange, fairy-tale fate," strange because in some ways so close to his age and in others so remote from it, strange because it was so hard for him to *communicate.* The problem of communication in the arts is never simple; the artist is one who tries to communicate the incommunicable. For the *modern* artist the problem, I think, is especially acute, and Shaw resorted to some very bizarre shifts. Living in this queer age, he found he had to give the impression that his highest quality—a sort of delicate spirituality, purity, or holiness—was fooling when what he meant was that his fooling was holy. The devil's advocate was a saint. The clown was a superman.

Unlike Nietzsche, who finished few of his major works, Shaw has been able to give his very remarkable mind full expression. Although the ninety-year campaign of his life has not abolished war or even capitalism, it has at least made us the beneficiaries of some of the best pamphlets and plays in the language. And in them is recorded for all time a great spirit.

I have reiterated the fact that, on his own confession, Shaw has been a failure as a propagandist. I would not say he is a failure as a teacher. (The teacher not only *need* not be a propagandist; I would say he *cannot* be a propagandist—defining a teacher as one who helps people to learn, learning being something a man has to do for himself.) *John Bull's Other Island* does not solve the Irish problem. It does not, as Mr. Odets's *Waiting for Lefty* tried to do, send the audience rushing out to take action. Nor does it present a situation with the merely external truth ("objectivity") of naturalists like Galsworthy. When Shaw feels the importance of a human situation, he presents it truthfully—that is to say, in all its many-sidedness—and with a passionate accuracy that betokens commitment without prejudice. This is teaching. Shaw's plays are not, though they seem to be, entertainments with propaganda awkwardly added. Their "propaganda" is itself a high art, their art is itself didactic. When they are faulty it is the "entertainment" that is awkwardly added—added to the art, added to the didacticism, added as a sheer redundancy.

The fact that Shaw really wrote his plays because he "had to" (and not to change the world) was in the end the saving of Shavian drama both as art and as teaching. Writing merely what he *had* to write, Shaw will leave us a rich legacy. He has obeyed the Life Force, lived out his Destiny, worn the mask of the madman "G. B. S." without really knowing why. We may learn in time not to despise even the mask, much less Bernard Shaw, as we have learned (I hope) not to despise the Bohemian mask of Oscar Wilde and the Diabolical mask of Nietzsche, two other lonely, estranged teachers of our times. The influence of a propagandist may be prodigious, as we learned from the case of Josef Goebbels. But that was not all we learned from the case of Josef Goebbels. The influence of teachers is lamentably small—or the world would not be in its present state. Yet to the extent that we believe that influence negligible we are cynics. To the extent that we find in that influence a solace and a hope we are men.

From *The Atlantic Monthly,* Vol. CLXXVIII (July, 1946), pp. 109–115. Reprinted by permission of the author and editor. The material of this essay was adapted by Mr. Bentley in a different form in his book *Bernard Shaw* (New Directions, 1947).

HORACE GREGORY

D. H. Lawrence: The Posthumous Reputation

[1937]

I SHALL live just as blithely, unbought and unsold," wrote D. H. Lawrence in 1925. And in this remark there is a note of warning that describes the curious nature of his survival during the half dozen years following his death. Perhaps none of the earlier objections to his work has been removed since 1930, yet his influence has endured in the kind of fame that Matthew Arnold perceived in Shelley's reputation which was both legend and literature and both "ideal" and "ridiculous." Much of his ardent pamphleteering which gave his latter years the semblance of vivid, inexhaustible energy is now outmoded. And nothing seems to have grown so clearly out of fashion in a few short years as Lawrence's specific lectures on sex and obscenity. Today they seem to have gone to the same place reserved in memory for the events of early post-war Europe and America. Yet even in Lawrence's most perishable writing the character of his influence remains.

However, where Lawrence is reread, whether in scattered posthumous papers, or in the poems, short stories, or in the novels, it is the speaking voice that is heard clearest and remembered. We then recall Lawrence's letters, which seem always to renew at each date line a briefly interrupted conversation and with them we remember Mr. David Garnett's little sketches of how he worked: writing as he cooked his meals or sat in one corner of a room while others talked, writing as he unpacked boxes and suitcases, writing almost as he moved and breathed, as though the traveling of his hand across paper were the very reflex of his being. Surely this prodigality was "art for my sake" and was the visible power of the thing he called his "demon," which is to say that much of it was scarcely art at all. Artfulness was sometimes deftly concealed within the larger rhythm of conversation; and sometimes his "demon" was called upon to gratify an urgently explicit demand of form: these moments are identified with the writing of Sons and Lovers as well as the writing of a half dozen poems and three or four short stories, but in the rest of everything he wrote the more flexible rule of "art for my sake" was applied and satisfied.

Lawrence, of course, was by no means unaware of what was happening; he had read his critics and matched his wit with theirs:

For me, give me a little splendour, and I'll leave perfection to the small fry . . . Ugh, Mr. Muir, think how horrible for us all, if I were perfect! or even if I had "perfect" gifts! Isn't splendour enough for you, Mr. Muir? Or do you find the peacock more "perfect" when he is moulting and has lost his tail, and therefore isn't so exaggerated, but is more "down to normal"?——For "perfection" is only one of "the normal" and the "average" in modern thought.

How well he knew that the image of the peacock's tail would fill the reader's eye; and there in the image itself, he had uncovered a fragment of the "splendor" he had sought, and with an eloquent gesture, passed it over to the reader. It was as though he had been saying: Mr. Muir has given me bread and I give you cake. My transformation of Mr. Muir's gift, dear reader, is your reward for reading me. This answer was always Lawrence's reply to authority, whether the authority was the Evangelist, preaching from a Nottinghamshire pulpit, or Roman law concealed within the new laws of the Fascisti, whether it was the British censor or Mr. Muir. But he was always least fortunate whenever he attempted to answer that authority directly: his ingenuity lay in the art of improvised distraction. And in distracted argument he was never more successful than in his reply to Mr. Muir.

With Lawrence's rejection of the average man came his distrust of the society around him: "Only the people we don't meet are the 'real' people," he wrote in "Jimmy and the Desperate Woman"—and his "real" people were "the simple, genuine, direct, spontaneous, unspoilt souls," which, of course, were not to be found among the people Lawrence saw on city streets, not in "London, New York, Paris," for "in the bursten cities, the dead tread heavily through the muddy air," and in each face he saw the same stigmata Blake had witnessed, "marks of weakness, marks of woe." These were his average, "normal" people, branded by service in the World War like Captain Herbertson in *Aaron's Rod*, mutilated by war and sanctified by bourgeois wealth like Chatterley, malformed by ignorance and poverty like the Nottinghamshire miner, or tricked and defeated like the American Indian, "Born with a caul, a black membrane over the face." And as Lawrence traveled he saw the same disease spread over half the earth and he was not to be identified with any of that kind, the meek or humble or the dead. Though the physical resemblance to Lawrence's speaking voice may be traced throughout his novels, through Paul Morel, Lilly of *Aaron's Rod* or Mellors of *Lady Chatterley's Lover*, he was happiest in another kind of personality; the image of the bird was best: the mythical phoenix, the peacock, or the Tuscan nightingale. To defend the nightingale (as well as himself) against the "plaintive anthem" of John Keats' ode, he wrote:

How astonished the nightingale would be if he could be made to realize with what sort of answer the poet was answering his song. He would fall off the bough with amazement.

Because a nightingale, when you answer him back, only shouts and sings louder. Suppose a few other nightingales pipe up in the neighboring bushes—as they always do. Then the blue-white sparks of sound go dazzling up to heaven. And suppose you, mere mortal, happen to be sitting on the shady bank having an altercation with the mistress of your heart, hammer and tongs, then the chief nightingale swells and goes at it like Caruso in the Third Act—simply a brilliant, bursting frenzy of music, singing you down, till you simply can't hear yourself speak to quarrel.

Of course the nightingale was the very thing Lawrence wished himself to be, the thing apart from the quarreling couple on the shady bank and his "art for my sake" had for its model the work of a creature who

. . . sings with a ringing, pinching vividness and a pristine assertiveness that makes a mere man stand still. A kind of brilliant calling and interweaving of glittering exclamation such as must have been heard on the first day of creation.

This was the splendor that was Lawrence's great concern, the "bursting frenzy of music" that emanated from a source within the body, and was itself the body, the physical being of a living creature. The lack of that physical force was his definition of modern tragedy, and it was the same emptiness he had witnessed in the lives of the civilized people who surrounded him. In that self-pitying, sad, silent company he had seen the image of Paul Morel, his early self of *Sons and Lovers*.

. . . left in the end naked of everything, with the drift toward death. . . . It's the tragedy of thousands of young men in England.

But Lawrence's instructions to live the splendid life always had the tendency to oversimplify the cure for complex (and human) silences and fears. They were all too much like telling friends and neighbors to be natural, to go be a *man*. His work had all the skill and all the confident lack of knowledge of a man who had carefully trained himself to conduct an orchestra by ear. Throughout Lawrence's verse and prose a dominant rhythm persists above loose phrasing and verbal monotony; his ear had been trained to catch the idiomatic inflection of English speech, avoiding always the outmoded rhythms of literary usage. In this respect his work shares the vitality of Whitman's verse and Melville's prose, and like them it contains the same self-taught art that controlled its imagery.

Even the most casual reader of Lawrence will soon become aware of how deliberately he avoided the urban image and how through prose and verse there is a literal predominance of "birds, beasts and flowers." And as their number increases, how tropical they seem, and we remember that his need for physical well-being followed the hot course of the sun. But it is characteristic of Lawrence's imagery that its action remains suspended in utter darkness or in the full flood light of noon; and though it is frequently breathing and alive, it seldom extends its force to an actual climax. How many of his images start bravely and end in helplessness, as though they could not carry the burden of their swelling heat and color to move elsewhere. And this same helplessness enters the majority of his many poems, all incomplete, all lacking in the distinction of a verb to give them motion and finality. How many of his novels end with the promise of a life beyond them yet to be fulfilled in the next novel, perhaps, but for the moment still unwritten. Only in *Sons and Lovers,* and in a few of the short stories do we find a definite space of time and action brought to an ultimate conclusion—only in these and in three or four of the *Last Poems.* The rest of his work leans heavily into the future, as though the next page to be written would complete the large design of which his fragments were pencil sketches from the living model.

I suspect that this very characteristic of incompleted action is responsible for the air of expectancy which welcomed the publication of each posthumous volume of letters, stories, poems, essays or incidental papers. Lawrence in death seemed still in flight around the globe and it has been difficult to think of him as a middle-aged writer dying nerveless and exhausted in a sun-lit room in Southern France. The biographies of Lawrence, his self-imposed exile from England, the disorder among camp-followers of the Lawrence household may be used as sources for a facile parallel to Shelley's death and the legends which grew out of it. But how eagerly Lawrence would have hated Shelley and would have cheerfully denied all he had written, and did in fact answer his "Skylark" in the same language in which he replied to Keats' nightingale: ·

"Hail to thee, blithe Spirit!—bird thou never wert." Why should he insist on the bodilessness of beauty when we cannot know of any save embodied beauty? Who would wish that the skylark were not a bird, but a spirit? If the whistling skylark were a spirit, then we should all wish to be spirits. Which were impious and flippant.

We need not stop to consider the flaws in Lawrence's heavy-footed questioning, but in this reply there is implied an entire century's increased distrust of Platonic reasoning. Between Shelley and Lawrence arose the shadow of Nietzsche's Zarathustra, who said as he descended from the mountain:

To blaspheme the earth is now the dreadfulest sin. . . . Man is a rope stretched between the animal and the Superman. . . . Aye, for the game of creating, my brethren, there is needed a holy Yea unto Life. . . .

Lawrence's great error, of course, was to echo the sound of Zarathustra's warning without clear knowledge of the myth from which Nietzsche's hero sprang, and lacking this knowledge he could not stride into another world that lay beyond good and evil. The literary heritage of the early nineteenth century had come down to him by way of Herman Melville and Walt Whitman. As he entered the latter phases of his career, traces of Whitman's eloquence spread throughout his writing, yet he was always to reject Whitman's democracy with uneasy violence. Whatever was to remain revolutionary in Lawrence's thinking was something that resembled philosophic anarchy. In a recently discovered paper, "Democracy" in the posthumous volume *Phoenix*, written in 1923, he used Whitman as text, in praise and blame, to reiterate his distrust of a bourgeois democracy and its possession of property. His rejection of authority included a consistent denial of Marx as well as Plato, of Aquinas as well as Judaism and all law of church and state.

Yet in this wide negation of authority lies one secret of his influence with a younger generation of post-war writers. To deny bourgeois authority and to leave England was to break down the barriers of class and national prejudice that had seemed impassable before 1918, or rather, had remained unbroken for nearly a hundred years. He had survived many forms of British bourgeois hostility which brought with them the lack of a large reading public, persecution from the War office, and the action of the British censor as well as charges of religious heresy. And there was ample evidence to convict him on any or all of these charges of public disfavor. His reply was that he alone remained alive in a dead world, a world in which the memory of its millions killed in a World War had spread the shadow of mass murder as well as lonely suicide over the furthest reaches of Anglo-Saxon civilization. And when his own death came, he made his own choice in preparation for it, convincing himself and those who read him that he had chosen the path of stilled and dark waters into oblivion.

Almost with his last breath he was to write, "For man the vast marvel is to be alive. For man, as for flower, and beast and bird . . ." and this reassurance in the goodness of physical being from someone whose self-taught and imperfect gifts alone sustained his eloquence, created a hero for a generation that feared the stillness of its own despair. It is not without perception that T. S. Eliot as well as others have read the warning of disease in Lawrence's heresies of behavior and craftsmanship. We know only too well his many failures, and among them we learn his refusal to abide by the truth of his observation in writing a brilliant analysis of Baron Corvo's *Hadrian the Seventh*: "A man must keep his earnestness nimble to escape ridicule." Yet his insight was never more profound or more direct than when he associated Whitman with his own name, for it is through the work of Lawrence that the younger men in the present generation of British writers have learned the actual significance of Whitman's enduring reputation. Like Whitman, Lawrence left behind him no model of technique that would serve to crystallize the style of prose or poetry in those who followed him; like Whitman's, Lawrence's influence as a teacher was irrevocably bad; surely his literal imitators, like Horace Traubel's discipleship of Whitman, illustrate the master's flaws until their burlesque becomes so clear that pity or contempt deflects all criticism. Such imitation is the pathetic attempt to reproduce the absence of form, as though the devoted student had amputated his arm to stimulate the sensation of his master's missing hand. Lawrence's real strength, like his invisible presence living "blithely, unbought and unsold," is explicit only in the combined force of his legend with a small selection from his prolific work of less than twenty years, and from these fragments we learn again how vividly he revived the memory of the maker in English literature, restoring the moment of vision and insight as a mark of genius in English prose and poetry.

First published in the first edition of the present book, *Literary Opinion in America,* in 1937. Later included by the author in his collection of critical essays, *The Shield of Achilles,* published by Harcourt, Brace and Company, Inc., 1944.

AUSTIN WARREN

Franz Kafka

[1941]

KAFKA's novels evoke a world as self-coherent and characteristic as that of Dickens, of Dostoevski, of Proust, of Poe, of Hawthorne. Like Hawthorne's and Poe's, Kafka's is a limited, a lyric, world. Kafka is a metaphysical poet in symbolist narrative.

His is a city world. Like Dickens' London, it flourishes in grotesques. But they have not the vigor, the delight in their own salt being, of Quilp and Miss Mowcher; and they are chiefly unnamed and seen but momentarily. Old women look out of inquisitive windows; in the gutters sit leering irreverent mocking children; a young lad, his nose half eaten away, scrutinizes arrivals; the warden wears a gross body, ill-adjusted to his "dry bony face, with a great nose twisted to one side."

It is an overcrowded, airless world, within which it is difficult to sustain faith in the weight and worth of the individual. In Georg Salter's illustration to *The Trial,* most persons except the hero are but shapes of shadow. Kafka's solipsism is intelligible, is defensible, as necessary to sustaining, in a city of the anonymous, the belief that the soul and its choices matter.

Even Kafka's imagined America is not a land of broad cornfields shining in the sun but a chiefly metropolitan affair, already stratified, weary, and hopeless—a land of hotels and of slums. "Karl thought of the east end of New York which his uncle had promised to show him where it was said that several families lived in one little room and the house of a whole family consisted of one corner where many children clustered around their parents." Kafka read Franklin's *Autobiography,* we are told, and admired Walt Whitman, and liked the Americans because he believed them to be "healthy and optimistic." But his imagination does not so present them. A sort of W. P. A. theater opens hospitably at the end, to be sure; yet the novel follows Dickens, not Alger. Karl is the young Copperfield, the young Oliver Twist, the sensitive boy ejected from home on charges which puzzle him. He finds America gleaming but hard. Before landing, he encounters social injustice in the case of "The Stoker"; his uncle, who suddenly appears and assumes his support, as suddenly and less plausibly renounces responsibility; he is deceived and maltreated by his chance traveling companions; for no fault of his own, he is discharged from the hotel; he comes near to ending as a slavey in a delirious apartment. America is a world in which elevators whiz up and down, phonographs play incessantly without anyone's listening, political candidates get lost in the crowds which are to elect them. It offers the image of the ascent to Brunelda's apartment: long stairs moving up into squalid darkness; beside the stair-railing, a little girl weeps, then rushes up the steps gasping for breath.

Kafka's is a world known in nightmares—a rational, unnatural world in which unnatural situations are rationally worked out—in which everyone is able, like Lewis Carroll's creatures, to argue long, ingeniously, and convincingly. It is a nightmare world in which the "I," all innocent and eager to submit, all desirous to propitiate, is pushed about, pursued, regimented by potencies veiled of visage—in which one is forever being orally examined by dignitaries who forever flunk one. The self and the world are juxtaposed in opposition. If one is not being pursued by the world or carried off by the world, one is running after it. There is the image of the old father trying to catch the ear of the Castle dignitaries—trying in vain, for the officials go at a gallop, their carriages "race like mad." It is the world of a Mack Sennett comedy—one of chase and pursuit, of intense movement, horizontal and vertical: of running and climbing. It is a world of uncertainty and insecurity, of fear and trembling.

It is a world of hierarchy, created by Kafka in the parodic imitation of the Austrian bureaucracies under which he lived, within which, as underofficial, he worked. In its chief traits it could be a feudal estate or it could be an American department store or a chain of restaurants or a metropolitan public library. Hierarchy provides, negatively, for deferment of responsibility or infinite regress. One's complaint always reaches the wrong office; one is passed on from office to office, in general moving up the scale of delegated authority, only to find that the proper official to handle the complaint is out of town, or the necessary documents are lost, or by delay one's claim is outlawed. Wonderful is the efficiency of an order so complexly gradated that every expert is inexpert at satisfying the simple need for justice.

There are other difficulties. Hierarchic order is necessary in a universe densely populated, whether with atoms or souls; yet, in an order so intricate, instrumentalities must, almost unavoidably, turn into ends: readers exist in order that librarians may make card catalogues, pupils in order that educationalists may publish books on Methods of Teaching, worshipers in order that janitors may sweep and lock churches. Underofficials, those who administer the rules to the public, can scarcely be expected to understand the spirit of the rules or what, as formulated by unseen and doubtless long dead "higher-ups," the rules aimed at. A teeming universe must, of course, be a "planned," even if an ill planned, or a too fussily planned, society. The easy improvization which fits the New England village cannot be transported to the city. Indeed, by one of his most brilliant audacities, Kafka imagines that even the Village cannot really be a village, for if its multiple needs are adequately to be taken care of, there will be business enough to require busy attention from a whole caste of officials.

Kafka's novels can be taken as burlesques of bureaucracy. Satiric of course they are. Yet they lack satiric norm, a contrasting model of elegance and humanity. The hero is too uncertain of himself to sit in judgment on duly constituted authorities and too intent upon learning their ways to have leisure for criticizing them. As for bureaucracy, it is even at its worst a corruption of order; and order is a state so blessed, so indispensable, that even its parodies deserve respect. As for bureaucrats, the common charge against them is that they are too insistent upon the importance of their work, too narrow in their conception of it; but surely it is the duty of officials to be officious, and narrowness and even scrupulosity are marks of their being dedicated to their profession. The work of the world is carried on by experts, not by gentlemen; and if we want to deepen the sense of "work" and "world," we must add, "strait is the gate and narrow the way"; the price of salvation is the forced sale of all that one has.

Hierarchy is pyramidal. Is there, for Kafka, any Reason, any Supreme Will, at the top and the end? Or is hierarchy a staircase which ends not in a dome or a tower but in a fall into darkness? The answer is uncertain. Of a chief justice we never hear or of a head-manager of a hotel. In *The Castle,* we hear for a preliminary moment of the "Count West-West," but soon he and any direct view of the Castle itself are lost or forgotten. Doubtless there is an ultimate authority, but we never reach it except through its intermediaries: there is no direct vision. In "Before the Law," the lowest doorkeeper can see a few doors ahead of him into what he believes to be a vast series of ascents: "From hall to hall keepers stand at every door, one more powerful than the other. Even the third of these has an aspect that even I cannot bear to look at." Of the ascending series we can say that there is no point at which we observe it to stop. Olga explains to K.: "Who is it that Barnabas speaks to there in the Castle I have no idea—perhaps the clerk is lowest in the whole staff; but even if he is lowest he can put one in touch with the next man above him, and if he can't even do that he can refer to somebody who can give the name." They are men set under authority; and "Does not the least degree of authority contain the whole?"

In both *The Trial* and *The Castle,* under-officials, advocates, and villagers spend much time in speculating upon the ways of the "higher-ups." In the latter we hear Amalia ask, "Is it Castle gossip you're at? . . . There are people in the village who live on it; they stick their heads together just like you two and entertain each other by the hour"; to which K. replies that he is just such a person, "and moreover people who don't care for such gossip and leave it all to others don't interest me particularly." So the talk goes on. We "gossip" or speculate about Klamm, attempting to adjust to coherence the glimpses we catch. A man like Klamm "who is so much sought after and rarely seen is apt to take different shapes in people's imaginations"—to give rise to theophanies very diverse each from the other.

Yet Kafka's officials, however otherwise various, have in common a certain obtrusive perversity, their lack of elegance. So, too, the rooms in which the courts sit have none of the grandeur or even decent neatness we might anticipate, and the Castle is unimpressive, disappointing to strangers. Instead of being better balanced and more humanistic than the villagers, the officials are officious, pompous, and pedantic. But the "virtues of the pagans are splendid vices"; "officious, pompous, and pedantic" are dyslogistic terms to be transvaluated as "conscientious, dignified, and properly accurate."

These paper-reading officials are scholars, intellectuals; and their scholarly life bears no discernible relation to their biological and affective lives: they have their mistresses; and they have their papers.

"Papers," we see, both bless and curse. They are not only the records of law and the ledgers of business but the annals of history and the memory of the race, the possibility of preserving and interpreting our past experience. They represent the effort of the intellect to understand by dissection, arrangement, systemization. "Papers" constitute civilization; without them we remain barbarians. Yet they clutter up the world and menace our freedom. They may be "busy work" to amuse old children, to keep scholars from thinking and the timid from knowing themselves afraid. The academic vice is the substitution of "research" for existential thinking; to preserve records without selection, to multiply discriminations until one is incapable of singleness of mind and simplicity of action. Papers assemble, by the most laudable of intentions, into libraries; yet for every man who, like Arnold, fears he may know more than he feels, a great library must be an object of terror—a monument to the futility of past speculation, a deterrent to future action.

There are some rich, fantastic scenes in which Kafka's papers become objects in themselves, figures in a Disney cartoon: in *The Castle* the search through the superintendent's bedroom for a missing document—in the process of which papers half cover the floor and go on mounting—or the description of Sordini's office, every wall of which is covered with columns of documents tied together, piled on top of one another; "Those are only the documents that Sordini is working on at the time, and as bundles of papers are continually being taken away and brought in, and all in great haste, those columns are always falling on the floor, and it's just those perpetual crashes, following fast on one another, that have come to distinguish Sordini's workroom."

The copiousness of the papers has an approximate correspondence in the volubility of official speech. Ready argument characterizes almost all Kafka's people—not merely his lawyers and secretaries. In these novels all are dialecticians: all are conscious of *pro et contra*, fertile in "various lections." Unlike Mann's controversialists, Naphtha and Settembrini, who argue in abstract terms, Kafka's are existential thinkers and deploy their subtlety on the obscure and difficult matter of how to live aright.

The Trial and *The Castle* are composed very largely of dialogues, and dialogues dialectic. Indeed, the characteristic excitement of these later novels, written by a student of Plato and Kierkegaard, lies in the wit and intellectual suspense of the dialogue. No more than the papers in Sordini's office do the thoughts stand still; like the action in a murder mystery, they move by sudden shifts of direction, convincing evasions of the foregone conclusion.

What does Kafka intend us to make of his argumentation? Is it ridiculously specious, or—so far as it goes—true: "Both" would have to be the answer. It is absurd to speculate about the nature of the highest, for of course we cannot know; we cannot even know how near we come to knowing. Yet it is man's true nature and highest function to engage himself upon these speculative questions concerning the nature of reality; and there can be no delegation of this duty to others.

Kafka's world is one of mystery. In stories like "The Country Doctor" and "Metamorphosis," the unnatural thrusts itself into the orderly sequence of nature. The redaction of a young clerk into a bug neither allows of allegorical sterilization, nor is presented as a dream. It is the chief horror of the story, perhaps, that no one within it sees what happens as "impossible"; it is horrible, to be sure, but in various ways these people, obviously sane and simple, adjust themselves to a painful situation. There are occasional bits of near or even sheer magic in Kafka: in *The Castle*, Barnabas disappears with the rapidity of an elf or a thought; the first day passes and it grows night, within an hour or two after morning; after a few days of living with K., Frieda, formerly "unnaturally seductive," is withering in his arms. But it is not Kafka's ordinary or best practice thus to deal in legerdemain. He secures his sense of mystery chiefly through his device of multiple interpretation.

His method offers a superficial analogy with that of Hawthorne. But Hawthorne offers alternatives—usually supernaturalism and some form of naturalism. Thus, at the elaborate ending of *The Scarlet Letter*, we are tendered the preliminary option of supposing that there was, or was not, a scarlet letter imprinted upon the breast of the minister, and then a choice of three methods for the possible production of the stigmata: by the natural means of penance; by means of magic and drugs; or by the outgoing operation of the spirit. "The reader," says Hawthorne, "may choose among these theories."

It is not Kafka's method thus to contrast a supernatural with a natural reading. It is, for him, in and through the natural that the supernatural operates and, with whatever intermittence and illusion, is revealed.

Kafka's world is neither the world of the average sensual man nor yet fantasy. It is the world seen slightly askew, as one looks through his legs or stands on his head, or sees it in a distorting mirror. Nor does his adjustment take, like Swift's in *Gulliver,* the method of segregation. With Swift, the fantastic is safely corralled and tucked away in the initial assumption; with Kafka, realism and fantasy move in more close and sensitive relation. In *The Trial* and *The Castle* the whole sequence is so improbable as to suggest some kind of pervasive allegory, but at no point (or almost no point) does one encounter downright impossibility. It is improbable that any law courts of a wealthy city should be lodged high up in dingy tenement houses or that a village should require the service of a vast staff of busy, hurrying officials, or that, upon looking into a lumber-room in one's own office building, one should discover two court-wardens being flogged. Yet these things "could be"; they are not like centaurs, oceans flowing with lemonade, and trees growing greenbacks. And Kafka's multiple interpretations are all possible options within one world. They represent the same fact or situation read from successive views, as the operations of a mind which keeps correcting itself.

Kafka offers a convincing interpretation; then, with rapidity, substitutes another, yet more convincing. A scene in *Amerika* shows Robinson, his face and arms swathed in manifold bandages. "It was horrible to see him lift his arms to his eyes to wipe away his tears with the bandages—tears of pain or grief or perhaps even of joy at seeing Karl again." Then we see the horror dissolve. "The trivial nature of his wounds could be seen from the old rags of bandages with which the lift-boys, obviously in jest, had swathed him round."

The Castle abounds in more subtle shifts. A woman sits in a chair in a kitchen. The pale light gives a "gleam of silk" to her dress; she seems to be an aristocrat, "although of course illness and weariness give even peasants a look of refinement." To a question from K., the woman replies disdainfully, but "whether contemptuous of K. or of her own answer was not clear." If one is self-conscious or otherwise fearful, it is necessary and difficult to interpret the looks of others. Thus K. sees the peasants gazing fixedly at him; he thinks it done out of malice—yet perhaps they really wanted something from him but could not express it, or, perhaps, on the other hand, they were simply childish. But if the first view of the peasants and their attitude was mistaken, what about the first view of Barnabas? One doubt, one disillusionment, infects the judge with a general mistrust of his judgment. "Perhaps K. was as mistaken in Barnabas' goodness as in the malice of the peasants." Frieda's hands "were certainly small and delicate, but they could quite as well have been called weak and characterless." After Olga's account of Amalia's defiance of Sordini, K. says, "Amalia's act was remarkable enough, but the more you say about it

the less clearly can it be decided whether it was noble or petty, clever or foolish, heroic or cowardly." Longer, more structural examples are the discussion
between K. and the Superintendent concerning the meaning of Klamm's letter, and K.'s talk with Frieda about the landlady, and Olga's discussion with
K. regarding the nature of Barnabas' relation to the Castle.

Kafka's "mystery" is, then, the apparent sign of how elusive is the truth.
What happens is tolerably easy to ascertain, but what it means is precarious
as well as important.

Such scrupulosity of interpretation recalls a characteristic feature of hierarchy everywhere prominent in Kafka's novels—the connection between promotion, pleasing, and propitiation. Kafka's worlds are patriarchies or theoc-
racies. One's success or failure depends on one's skill in divining the wishes of
the great man; and among underlings there develops a necessary skill in calculating his mood by his complexion, step, tone of voice. Cases there naturally
are in which the signs allow of differing interpretation between experts.

The interpretative complexity recalls also the elaborations of rabbinic and
patristic commentary. John Mason Neale's commentary on the Song of Songs
offers, out of innumerable Fathers, Doctors, and Saints, all manner of conflicting yet severally edifying glosses: on the text, "his left hand is under my
head, and his right hand doth embrace me," for example. What is the distinction between the hands, and why their positions? According to some, the
hands distinguish temporal from spiritual goods; according to another view,
the left hand equates the law, the right hand the gospel; according to another,
the left hand indicates punishment, the right, blessings and rewards. Other
comments differentiate mystical states—the left being the Illuminative as the
right is the Unitive Way. And "the loveliest interpretation of all," says Neale,
is that which sees in the left the Manhood of Christ, and in the right his
Godhead.

Not until late in his life did Kafka begin to study the *Talmud;* but already, in the priest's discourse at the Cathedral (*The Trial*), Kafka shows
his ingenuity and depth as the exegete of a given fable. The priest cites the
studies of innumerable rabbis who had already concerned themselves with
the story. "I am only showing you different opinions about it," he says.
"You mustn't have too much regard for opinions. The text is unchangeable
and opinions are often only an expression of doubt about it." Like Kierkegaard, whose *Fear and Trembling* starts from and repeatedly returns to the
story of Abraham and Isaac, so Kafka, delighting in speculation, yet offers
his story as a mythic fable the meaning of which is anterior to and un-
exhausted by any included commentary.

Myth is not allegory; and Kafka is not an allegorist. An allegory is a series
of concepts provided with a narrative or a narrative accompanied by a conceptual parallel. Strictly, it is a philosophical sequence which systematically

works itself out in images. But allegory is rarely as pure as *Pilgrim's Progress* or *The Romance of the Rose:* it deviates from purity in two directions—by losing its systematic character, becoming a series of intermittent symbolisms; or by keeping its system but abstaining from offering a conceptual key to its parable.

The novels of Kafka are not, in any exact sense, allegorical. From his diaries and aphorisms and his friend Brod's commentaries, we know that he intended the novels to give creative expression to the mysteries of Justice and Grace; that they are "metaphysical" novels we should surely have discerned without aid. But Kafka provided them with no conceptual chart; they require none; and it is their special richness that they have much particularity untranslatable into generality. We need not systematically recall that the Castle is Heaven or that K.'s disappointments show the mysterious ways in which God moves. The ways of men are, for men who seek to understand them, baffling enough.

Kafka's symbols are, indeed, capable of more than the religious interpretation. According to Brod, K. symbolizes the Jew, in his exclusion from society and his eagerness for inclusion, as well as the seeker after the Kingdom of Heaven. But K. is also the bachelor in search of marriage and companionship; and K. is also every man in respect to his final aloneness.

The novels all, significantly, remained unfinished. Of them Kafka wrote: "What sense would there be in reviving such . . . bungled pieces of work? Only if one hoped to create a whole out of such fragments, some complete work to which one could make a final appeal. . . .". We have for each novel, however, a notion of the ending. *Amerika* was to conclude with the young hero's finding, within the Nature Theatre of Oklahoma, his freedom, "even his old house and his parents." *The Trial* is of Brod's assembling, and a chapter like "The Whipper" could only vaguely be placed. Parts of the novels—for example, "The Stoker" and "Before the Law"—were published separately.

With some plausibility, one might call these books novels of the spiritual picaresque. Yet they are not completely episodic: even in the loosest, *Amerika,* the two rascals, Delamarcke and Robinson, reappear after we suppose ourselves to have seen the last of them; and in *The Castle* there is a very considerable integration of the materials: one notes in particular the fashion in which the matter of chapter I (the teacher, the Lasemann family, Hans Brunswick and his mother) is subsequently developed. Each novel begins in substantially the same way: the hero breaks with his past. In two of them he has left his home, and we meet him as he enters a new world; in a third his thirtieth birthday and his summons collaborate to start a new life.

The question of method is: Can there be a logic of composition when one's theme is the irruption of the irrational? There might, of course, be a psychological unwinding; the episodes might grow more complex, deeper, or more wry. In the unfinished state of the novels, no such progress is obvious. If one compares these novels with the mystical documents of SS. Teresa and John of the Cross, he finds no such obvious symmetry and development as that of *The Interior Mansions*. Such systematic structure was too rational for Kafka.

It is Kafka's narrative method (with occasional lapses) to write from within the mind of the hero. The introspective hero, through whose eyes we have glimpses of other persons, static figures, is man alone, man hunted, man confronted with powers which elude him and with women with whom he is never at ease, man prosecuted and persecuted. He is the man eager to do right but perpetually baffled and thwarted and confused as to what it is to do right—the man for whom the sense of duty, of responsibility, the irreducibility of "ought," has survived the positive and particular codes of religions and moral systems—the man in search of salvation.

A narrow, moving writer, Kafka is both an artist and a symbol. The appeal of this symbol has been extraordinarily wide to Europeans and Americans in the past decade. One secular hope after another has failed. Kafka can be the symbol for what is left. He is illiberal, unrelenting, unsentimental; as Spender has said, he combines the power of the visionary with the self-criticism of the skeptic, so that he communicates the sense of there being something to believe without the claim of being able to define what it is. It is difficult today to believe in the reality of a world of comfort, good sense, and progress; we doubt that we shall ever see such a world again; we think it wise to prepare ourselves spiritually for worlds more exacting and metaphysical; and of such worlds Kafka is initiate.

From *Rage for Order: Essays in Criticism* by Austin Warren, pp. 104–118. University of Chicago Press, 1948. Reprinted by permission of the author and publishers. First published as "Kosmos Kafka" in *The Southern Review*, Vol. VII (Autumn, 1941), pp. 350–365.

MORTON DAUWEN ZABEL

A Literalist of the Imagination

[1935]

MARIANNE MOORE's poetry demands gratitude, but to express it by referring to the qualities for which her work has usually been ignored or disputed may seem more a matter of convenience than of good grace. She is a poet about whom praise and blame are not wholly at odds; her detractors and admirers see fairly eye to eye. What irritates the hostile reader exhilarates the admiring, and in the case of a poet so prominent among "difficult" writers, it is pleasant to have no doubt about what is up for reference. Miss Moore's meanings may be mistaken, but not her character. Compared with her, many of her contemporaries become chameleons of evasive and convenient color. She stays fixed under scrutiny and refuses to pose as an illusionist. From the beginning she has protected herself by working out her poetic problems before allowing her poems to be printed; she has had no need to practice the subterfuges of less vigilant writers—the changes of face, manner, and other sleights of hand demanded by public success or moral insecurity. The external traits of her latest poems are those of her earliest: a dispassionate accuracy of detail, literalness of manner, indifference to the standardized feelings and forms of verse, and an admission that virtually any subject-matter or reference is fully as appropriate to poetry as to prose. It would not require the addition of eccentric titling, typography, and rhyming to give the suspicious their argument or the irritated a voice.

Her *Observations* of 1924 were rightly named. Among modern poets she is exceptional for a detachment that lifts personal enthusiasm above private uses. She observes, but her eye shows neither the innocence nor the wile of showmanship that obstructs the vision of her contemporaries. It is a vision as complex as it is candid, and as easily mistaken. She would not have survived the decade of post-war innovations if her stylistic novelty rested on nothing but the strained intellection, the forced sophistication, for which it is commonly dismissed. She is a complicated poet, but one suspects that her finished poem is far simpler than the experience from which it sprang. The process that complicates it is not one of artificial refraction. It is Miss Moore's way of piercing—with the aid of humor, obliquity, and an instinctive compassion—

385

through the pretense, erudition, and false emotion that encrust the essential meaning in the life around her.

She may be writing about marriage and poetry with the evasive casuistry of "culture"; or about art and statecraft in the polysyllabic rhetoric of senators and undergraduates; or about animals with the passionless accuracy of a treatise or text-book. Her style combines the frigid objectivity of the laboratory with the zeal of naïve discovery; it mixes the statistics of newspapers with the casual hints and cross-references of a mind constructed like a card catalogue. This is not a perversity of erudition, or of ironic parody. It is a picture of the problem of the modern intelligence. Irony and curiosity are means towards Miss Moore's intense discriminations, but her purpose is essentially plain and carries the pathos of a passionate sincerity. When asked, in a recent questionnaire, what distinguishes her, she answered: "Nothing; unless it is an exaggerated tendency to visualize; and on encountering manifestations of life— insects, lower animals, or human beings—to wonder if they are happy, and what will become of them."

But her problem is not simple, and grants her neither the charm nor the success of conventional poetry. Hers is no book of neat lyric masterpieces. She is not satisfied to search out the law or purpose beneath the swarming phenomena around her; she feels it in the words she uses. Her language reveals, beneath its calculated technicalities and pastiche, the shock of concealed rhymes and harmonies. Her sentences, whether colloquial or rhetorical, move with a rhythm nerved by humor and "elegance." Her care for meaning makes her break a phrase, or even a word, to bring to the surface a suppressed quality—an embedded assonance, cadence, or tone of thought. Hers is a poetry of superimposed meanings, and her object is to lift the layers of convention, habit, prejudice, and jargon that mask the essential and irreducible truth. She is neither facile nor insincere enough to pretend that these impediments do not exist. In facing them she has not only defined, with the minuteness of an exorbitant sensitiveness, the ordeal of the contemporary conscience; she has energized, by the agility of her imagination, the language in which she works.

In the *Selected Poems* Miss Moore has omitted several short poems which a discussion might conveniently use as "beginnings." Simple aphorisms like "To an Intra-mural Rat" and "To a Prize Bird," and examples of imagism like "To a Chameleon" and "A Talisman," are not reprinted, although Mr. Eliot has fitly quoted the last-named in his preface. These slighter works served their purpose in *Observations,* in 1924, but they would not be out of place here also. Even a brief epigram on Shaw like "To a Prize Bird" escaped the risk of cleverness; it contained three metaphors of exact wit; and one is inclined to guess that it has now been omitted as much because Miss Moore has modified her opinion of Shaw during the past fifteen years as because she finds the style of the poem less than wholly her own. Similarly "A Talisman" departed from the conventional symbolism of the Imagists by not allowing its image to act beyond its powers: the figure of the seagull is developed through a severely spare stanzaic form, it is brought to terms with the formal attitude described by such a structure, and it still retains the impersonality required of true imagism. Of her new poems only one shows Miss Moore working in this simplified manner—"No Swan So Fine." The others exhibit a method much more elaborate than in any of the individual items of *Observations* with the possible exception of "An Octopus" and "Marriage," the second of which still remains her one extended venture in the field of human phenomena where obliquity of treatment is offset by the authority and convention of practical judgment. Only "The Hero" re-enters that province, but it does so with a stricter detachment, and with less assistance from the irony and erudition of quoted texts.

Her special world reappears: the world of lesser life—plant, animal, and mineral—which she scrutinizes unsparingly and translates into a major reality through a sympathy that surpasses mere pathos in becoming intellectual; but it is now far more extensive. This comes not merely by selecting from nature objects of a more formidable character—formidable in their complexity like the Plumet Basilisk or the Frigate Pelican, their wiry delicacy like the Jerboa, their massive subtlety like the Buffalo, or in their sumptuous elegance like *Camellia Sabina* and the porcelain nectarines. All these suggest a greater complexity of attention; they have encouraged a corresponding elaboration of form which marks the one notable advance made by the *Selected Poems* over Miss Moore's two previous books. Her idea of the stanza was already established there, but it had not reached such massive effects of verbal interplay and structure as in seven of the later poems. Along with this there has developed a greater luxuriance of detail, austere annotation having given way to a freer imaginative fascination. The cat, fish, and snake have been supplanted by creatures of a subtler and more exotic existence, and from this one may infer a similar elaboration in the mind that has observed and conferred on them, with unfaltering deftness, the form and scale of its ideas. Where Miss Moore once defined the fish's life of fluid and evasive grace, the cat's imperturbable self-sufficiency, and unity made absolute in the snake, she now analyzes the life of miraculous co-ordination ("The Frigate Pelican"), of impenetrable purposes ("The Plumet Basilisk"), of exquisite nervous vitality ("The Jerboa"), of masked and submissive wit ("The Buffalo"). Her animals have grown in meaning as well as in size and mechanism; they may be considered enlargements of the original vision; but they show the same rigor in definition and sympathy, the same scruple in activity and feature. The swan moves with its "gondoliering legs"; the jerboa with its "three-cornered smooth-working Chippendale claws . . . makes fern-seed foot-prints with Kangaroo speed";

the lizard "smites the water, and runs on it—a thing difficult for fingered feet"; the Pelican "rapidly cruising or lying on the air . . . realizes Rasselas' friend's project of wings uniting levity with strength"; the Indian buffalo wields "those two horns which, when a tiger coughs, are lowered fiercely and convert the fur to harmless rubbish."

Attributes like these are found among the animals and human beings of literature only when the physical reality of the creature has become so passionately accepted and comprehended that its external appearance, noted with the laconic felicity of science, is indistinguishable from its spirit, and all the banalities of allegory can be discarded. At that level the imagination seizes attributes and makes them act in place of the false sentimental values upon which man's observation of nature usually thrives. In her poem on "Poetry" Miss Moore improves Yeats' characterization of Blake by insisting that poets must be "literalists of the imagination"; they must see the visible at the focus of intelligence where sight and concept coincide, and where it becomes transformed into the pure and total realism of ideas. By this realism, the imagination permits ideas to claim energy from what is usually denied them—the vital nature that exists and suffers, and which alone can give poetic validity to the abstract or permit the abstract intelligence to enhance experience. Blake had such a notion of poetry in mind when he stated his theory of vision: "I question not my corporeal or vegetative eye any more than I would question a window concerning a sight; I look through it and not with it." And he reminds us especially of Miss Moore's rapt gaze at birds:

> How do you know but every bird that cuts the airy way
> Is an immense world of delight, closed by your senses five?

Miss Moore means this when she holds that poetry stands "above insolence and triviality and can present for inspection, imaginary gardens with real toads in them"; that it combines "the raw material . . . in all its rawness and that which is on the other hand genuine." Her literalness of manner should not remain a source of confusion after one has read the works in which her poetics is made fairly explicit—"Poetry," "When I Buy Pictures," "Critics and Connoisseurs," and "Picking and Choosing." If that manner seems ambiguous, it is because she considers poetic truth in opposite terms from those commonly accepted by lovers of the lyric. For her the spirit gives light, but not until the letter gives it first. If the letter is lifeless until the spirit enters it, without it the spirit is equally wasted: it has no body to animate and no clay in which to breathe. She stands poles removed from the poets of disembodied emotion, of Love, Honor, Hope, Desire, and Passion in capitalized abstraction. She does not write in the large and easy generality of sentiment or sensation. She has written about animals without dramatizing her pity, about wedlock without mentioning love, about America with none of the usages of patriotism, and about death without parading awe or reverence. But it would be difficult to name four poems more poignant in their sense of these emotions, or more accurate in justifying them, than "The Buffalo," "Marriage," "England," and "A Grave."

It is not the intention of any of these poems to free the reader from effort, but it is remarkable that difficulty diminishes statement by statement if the poems are read in that order. It is only when read through the translating medium of the whole poetic attitude and form (as they must be ultimately, since they are poems), or under the inhibition of prejudices and conventions about these, that Miss Moore's meaning itself can be, in the initial stages of one's appreciation, an obstruction. Her poems are complex both in origin and in process, and they will remain so finally, thus resembling all poetry of considerable weight; but their first complexity lies in the way they have avoided using the simplifications of the lyric tradition—its language, form, and rhythms. When they present a thought, they do so in terms of all the accidents, analogies, and inhibitory influences that went into its formulation; thus they preserve, along with the clarifying idea, a critical sense of how these accidents and impurities condition the use of the contemporary intelligence. It is, in fact, her recognition and use of such impediments to direct lyric clairvoyance that enables Miss Moore to combine the functions of critic and poet in one performance, and to preserve, along with the passion and penetration of her emotions, her modernity of appeal. One aspect of this is her use of the erudite style—the tone of wordy decorum and learnedness which probably wins her the harshest reproach. This has become her natural manner, but one is never left without hints of its sources; the rhetorical decorum of the past (Bacon, Burke, Richard Baxter) and the literary casuistry of the present (James, Yeats, Pound) combine with ironic overtones derived from the naïveté, pretentiousness, or candor of scientific treatises, orations, "business documents and school books," and intimate conversation. The interpenetration of these tones is not left entirely to the reader's guess-work. Miss Moore's "Notes" at the back of her volumes are a consolation and a stimulus. It is because they give just enough hint of the clues she has used in tracing out a conception or a truth that they spur the reader to analysis, without drugging him by explanation. In this they exceed the notes to *The Waste Land*. It is both amusing and provoking to know that the poem "New York" was given substance through an article on albino deer in *Field and Stream*, that "Novices" drew hints from Gordon's *Poets of the Old Testament*, Forsyth's *Christ on Parnassus*, Landor, and the *Illustrated London News*, that the biological subjects are reinforced by the treatises of R. L. Ditmars, W. P. Pycraft, and Alphonse de Candolle, that "No Swan So Fine" combines a remark from the *New York Times* with "a pair of Louis XV candelabra with

Dresden figures of swans belonging to Lord Balfour," and that Peter is a
"cat owned by Miss Magdalen Hueber and Miss Maria Weniger." Beyond
or below this information and the tentacular curiosity it sets growing, lies a
basis of moral and intellectual absolutes—the truth; but Miss Moore has no intention of reducing her sense of this truth to impotence by abstracting it from
the details and confusion with which experience happened to surround it.
To do so would not only be an act of unscrupulous evasion; it would not be
poetry.

It is profitable to make an attempt at separating in such verse the simpler
components that make it up—its basic information, the inference made from
it, and the conviction or judgment finally established; and to see in these a
possible correspondence with the three stylistic elements that immediately arrest the reader—imagery, syntax (with its diction and rhetorical tone), and
the final form (stanzaic or otherwise) of the complete poem. These pages are
particularly safe against studious demolition of this kind. "The Fish" is one
of Miss Moore's most brilliant and condensed achievements. The poem is first
a matter of acute observation: "the crow-blue mussel-shells," one of which
"keeps opening and shutting itself like an injured fan," "ink-bespattered jelly-
fish," "crabs like green lilies." These reach a second existence—become mobile
without ceasing to be objects of exact and literal statement—when arranged
into sentences; and anyone who finds the poem obscure as a whole will be
shocked to find how straightforward it becomes (at least through its first five
stanzas) when considered in its normal syntax:

> The fish wade through black jade. Of the crow-blue mussel-shells, one keeps ad-
> justing the ash-heaps; opening and shutting itself like an injured fan. . . . The
> water drives a wedge of iron through the iron edge of the cliff; whereupon the stars,
> pink rice-grains, ink-bespattered jelly-fish, crabs like green lilies, and submarine
> toadstools, slide each on the other. . . .

But one immediately sees what this sequence of statements has produced
in the details: a sense of impersonal scrutiny that minimizes the exotic character of the original images, and at the same time an austere alignment that
heightens and perfects it. Then, imposed on these statements, comes the shaping poetic form of the stanzas, with their regularly varying line-lengths and
suddenly discovered rhymes; the physical and emotional impact of the whole
experience is confessed; observation and statement have abruptly advanced
into the brilliance and intensity of a poetic vision.

THE FISH

wade
   through black jade
      Of the crow-blue mussel-shells, one keeps

             adjusting the ash-heaps;
                  opening and shutting itself like

   an
   injured fan.
             The barnacles which encrust the side
                  of the wave, cannot hide
                       there for the submerged shafts of the ·

   sun
   split like spun
             glass, move themselves with spotlight swiftness
                  into the crevices
                       in and out, illuminating

   the
   turquoise sea
        of bodies. . . .

Whether this process was gradual in the poet, or immediate and involuntary, is beside the point; the reader has, if he is serious, a reverence in his
destruction, and a duty in his analysis. He sees the three simplest elements in
the work; he notices its double structure, syntactical and stanzaic; and by
realizing the interdependence of the two he approaches Miss Moore's method.
He begins to see that ambiguity has not only advanced from imagery and
syntax to the form of the stanzas themselves, but that it is deliberate and
functional. It continues to be so in other poems. In "England" there is an intended duplicity of meaning both in the formal organization of the thought
and in the contrasts by which it is developed. In "Those Various Scalpels" a
criticism of feminine vanity is made by means of romantic comparisons, and
by exaggerating the intended effect of jewels, clothes, and cosmetics until
they react upon themselves and become their own criticism. In "A Grave"
"the disturbing vastness of ocean" is made fatal and sublime by the calm and
contradictory lucidity with which its casual incidents are observed:

men lower nets, unconscious of the fact that they are desecrating a grave,
and row quickly away—the blades of the oars
moving together like the feet of water-spiders as if there were no such thing as
   death.
The wrinkles progress upon themselves in a phalanx—beautiful under networks of
   foam,
and fade breathlessly while the sea rustles in and out of the seaweed. . . .

Confronting Miss Moore's poems, in other words, calls for a renovation not
only of the attention, but of one's habits, definitions, and prejudices; and of
what these have done to one's understanding of the words, rhythms, and
sentences of poetry. Here, as Mr. Eliot says, "an original sensibility and alert

intelligence and deep feeling have been engaged in maintaining the life of the English language," but to any self-improving reader it is also valuable to discover that such external discouragements as novelty, eccentricity, and intellectual irony can be justified by a scrupulous poetic purpose; they cease to appear as irritants or as abuses of originality, and become agents of a new vitality in the reader himself. If there is presumption in these poems, it is the presumption of a sincere and ruthless insight; if there are limitations—and there obviously and deliberately are—they are those of a contented but passionate humility. I think these virtues must be admitted by anyone; only then will qualifying criticisms be in order. When Miss Moore instructs herself on art she also instructs her reader:

Too stern an intellectual emphasis upon this quality or that detracts from one's enjoyment.
It must not wish to disarm anything; nor may the approved triumph easily be honored—
that which is great because something else is small.
It comes to this: of whatever sort it is,
it must be "lit with piercing glances into the life of things";
it must acknowledge the spiritual forces which have made it.

From *The New Republic*, Vol. LXXXIII (August 7, 1935), p. 370; and *Poetry: A Magazine of Verse*, Vol. XLVII (March, 1936), pp. 326–336. Reprinted by permission.

PART IV

The Writer and Critic in America

MARIANNE MOORE
Henry James as a Characteristic American
[1934]

To SAY that "the superlative American" and the characteristic American are not the same thing perhaps defrauds anticipation, yet one must admit that it is not in the accepted sense that Henry James was a big man and did things in a big way. But he possessed the instinct to amass and reiterate, and is the rediscerned Small Boy who had from the first seen Europe as a verification of what in its native surroundings his "supersensitive nostril" fitfully detected and liked. Often he is those elements in American life—as locality and as character—which he recurrently studied and to which he never tired of assigning a meaning.

Underlying any variant of Americanism in Henry James' work, is the doctrine, embodied as advice to Christopher Newman, "Don't try to be anyone else"; if you triumph, "let it then be all you." The native Madame de Mauves says to Euphemia, "You seem to me so all of a piece that I am afraid that if I advise you, I shall spoil you," and Hawthorne was dear to Henry James because he "proved to what a use American matter could be put by an American hand. . . . An American could be an artist, one of the finest, without 'going outside' about it . . . quite, in fact, as if Hawthorne had become one just by being American enough."

An air of rurality as of Moses Primrose at the fair struck Henry James in his compatriots, and a garment worn in his childhood revealed "that we were somehow queer." Thackeray, he says, "though he laid on my shoulder the hand of benevolence, bent on my native costume the spectacles of wonder." On his return from Europe he marveled at the hats men wore, but it is hard to be certain that the knowledge-seeking American in Europe is quite so unconsciously a bumpkin as Henry James depicts him. When Newman has said, "I began to earn my living when I was almost a baby," and Madame de Bellegarde says, "You began to earn your living in the cradle?" the retort, "Well, madam, I'm not absolutely convinced I had a cradle," savors of the connoisseur. Since, however, it is over-difficult for Henry James in portrayals of us, not to be portraying himself, there is even in the rendering of the callow

395

American, a sharpness and tightening of the consciousness that threaten the integrity of the immaturity.

" I am not a scoffer," the fellow-countryman says to Theobald, the American painter, and if with Henry James it were a question of being either guarded or ridiculous, he would prefer to seem ridiculous. His respectful humility toward emotion is socially brave, and in diffidence, reserve, and strong feeling, he reminds one of Whittier, another literary bachelor whom the most ardent sadist has not been able to soil. We remember his sense of responsibility for the United States during the World War and that in *Notes of a Son and Brother* he says of the Civil War, "The drama of the War . . . had become a habit for us without ceasing to be a strain. I am sure I thought more things under that head . . . than I thought in all other connections together." What is said in the same book of the death of Mary Temple, the cousin who so greatly "had a sense for verity of character and play of life in others," is an instance of reverent, and almost reverend, feeling that would defend him against the charge of lightness in anything, if ever one were inclined to make it. It is not the artist, but the responsibility for living and for family, that wonders here about death and has about "those we have seen beaten, this sense that it was not for nothing they missed the ampler experience . . . since dire as their defeat may have been, we don't see them . . . at peace with victory." Things for Henry James glow, flush, glimmer, vibrate, shine, hum, bristle, reverberate. Joy, bliss, ecstasies, intoxication, a sense of trembling in every limb, the heart-shaking first glimpse, a hanging on the prolonged silence of an editor; and as a child at Mr. Burton's small theatre in Chambers Street, his wondering not if the curtain would rise but "if one could exist till then"; the bonfires of his imagination, his pleasure in "the tender sea-green" or "rustling rose-color" of a seriously best dress, are too live to countenance his fear that he was giving us "an inch of canvas and an acre of embroidery."

Idealism which was willing to make sacrifices for its self-preservation, is always an element in the conjuring-wand of Henry James. The fear of profanation is apparent in a remark in connection with the later America, that he felt "like one who has seen a ghost in his safe old house." Of "Independence Hall . . . and its dignity not to be uttered . . . halls and spreading staircase and long-drawn upper gallery . . . one of those rare precincts of the past against which the present has kept beating in vain," he says, "nothing . . . would induce me to revisit . . . the object I so fondly evoke." He would not risk disturbing his recollection of *The Wonder-Book* and *Tanglewood Tales* by reading them over, and Dickens "always remained better than the taste of over-hauling him." The value of the thing is more than the thing. New Hampshire in September was "so delicately Arcadian, like . . . an old legend, an old love-story in fifteen volumes," and "Newport . . . the dainty isle of Aquidneck" and "its perpetually embayed promontories of mossy rock,"

had "ingenuous old-time distinction . . . too latent and too modest for notation." Exasperated by the later superficiality of New York's determination
"to blight the superstition of rest," he terms the Public Libraries "mast-heads
on which spent birds sometimes alight in the expanses of ocean" and thought
Washington Irving's Sunnyside with its "deep, long lane, winding, embanked,
over-arched, such an old-world lane as one scarce ever meets in America . . .
easy for everything but rushing about and being rushed at." The "fatal and
sacred" enjoyment of England "buried in the soil of our primary culture"
leads him to regard London as "the great distributing heart of our traditional
life"; to say of Oxford, "no other spot in Europe extorts from our barbarous
hearts so passionate an admiration"; and for the two Americans in "hedgy
Worcestershire" beneath an "English sky bursting into a storm of light or
melting into a drizzle of silver . . . nothing was wanting; the shaggy, mouse-
colored donkey, nosing the turf . . . the towering ploughman with his white
smock-frock, puckered on chest and back." "We greeted these things," says
the narrator, "as children greet the loved pictures in a story-book, lost and
mourned and found again . . . a gray, gray tower, a huge black yew, a cluster of village graves, with crooked headstones. . . . My companion was overcome. . . . How it makes a Sunday where it stands!"

Henry James' warmth is clearly of our doting native variety. "Europe had
been romantic years before, because she was different from America," he says;
"wherefore America would now be romantic because she was different from
Europe." His imagination had always included Europe; he had not been alienated by travel nor changed by any "love-philtre or fear-philtre" intenser
than those he had received in New York, Newport, or our American Cambridge. "Culture, as I hold, is a matter of attitude quite as much as of opportunity," he says in *Notes of a Son and Brother,* and "one's supreme relation,
as one had always put it, was one's relation to one's country." In alluding to
"our barbarous hearts" he had, of course, no thought of being taken at his
word—any more than Mrs. Cleve did when abusing America, and he is de-
lineating grossness in Baron de Mauves who "seemed to regard the New
World as a colossal *plaisanterie.*" It entertained James to describe Mrs. Gereth
as aristocratically British and clannishly dowdy when she went to Church;—
as it pleased him to recall "a contemporary cousin" who "was with her stature
and shape the finest possible person to carry clothes," and even in the disillusions attendant upon return to this country, he betrays a parentally local satisfaction in the American girl's fitness of costume.

Nationally and internationally "the sensitive citizen," he felt that patriotism
was a matter of knowing a country by perceiving the clue. Our understanding
of human relations has grown—more perhaps than we realize in the last
twenty years; and when Henry James disappoints us, by retaining the North-
erner's feeling about the Confederate, we must not make him directly con-

temporary, any more than we dispute his spelling peanut with a hyphen. He had had no proximity with the South and all that the bother-taking Henry James needed for doing justice to feeling, was opportunity to feel. "Great things . . . have been done by solitary workers," he says, "but with double the pains they would have cost if they had been produced in more genial circumstances." Education for him, in a large sense, was conversation. Speaking of Cambridge, he says,

When the Norton woods, nearby, massed themselves in scarlet and orange, and when to penetrate and mount a stair and knock at a door, and enjoying response, then sink into a window-bench and inhale at once the vague golden November and the thick suggestion of the room where nascent "thought" had again and again piped or wailed, was to taste as I had never done before, the poetry of the prime initiation and of associated growth.

We observe in the memoirs treasured American types: "silent Vanderpool . . . incorruptibly and exquisitely dumb" who "looked so as if he came from 'good people' . . . the very finest flower of shyness . . . a true welter of modesty, not a grain of it anything stiffer—"; "the ardent and delicate and firm John May"—student at Harvard; and there was Robert Temple—a cousin "with a mind almost elegantly impudent . . . as if we had owed him to Thackeray"; and Mary Temple, " 'natural' to an effect of perfect felicity . . . all straightness and charming tossed head, with long light and yet almost sliding steps and a large light postponing laugh." There was "a widowed grandmother who dispensed an hospitality seemingly as joyless as it was certainly boundless" and Uncle Albert, a kinsman who was " 'Mr.' to his own wife— . . . his hair bristling up almost in short-horn fashion at the sides," with "long, slightly equine countenance, his eyebrows ever elevated as in the curiosity of alarm."

To say that a child was a student of "history and custom . . . manners and types" would be saying too much, but to say that Henry James as a child was "a-throb" with the instinct for meanings, barely suggests that formidable paraphernalia which he was even then gathering. It is in "the waste of time, of passion, of curiosity, of contact—that true initiation resides," he said later; and no scene, strange accent, no adventure—experienced or vicarious—was irrelevant. The elder Henry James alludes to "the maidenly letters" of Emerson but Emerson in New York was strange and wonderful to Henry James, the child invited "to draw near to him, off the hearth-rug." He was "an apparition sinuously and elegantly slim . . . commanding a tone alien to any we heard around about"; and the school-master Louis De Coppet, in "his French treatment of certain of our native local names, Ohio and Iowa for instance, which he rendered . . . O-ee-oh and Ee-o-wah . . . opened vistas." "There hung about the Wards, to my sense, that atmosphere of apples and nuts . . .

and jack-knives and 'squrruls,' of domestic Bible-reading and attendance at 'evening lecture,' of the fear of parental discipline and the cultivated art of dodging it, combined with great personal toughness and hardihood"; and there was " 'Stiffy' Norcom . . . whom we supposed gorgeous . . . (Divided I was, I recall, between the dread and the glory of being so greeted, 'Well, Stiffy—!' as a penalty for the least attempt at personal adornment.)"

"You cannot make a man feel low," his Christopher Newman says, "unless you can make him feel base," and "a good conscience" is a pebble with which Henry James is extremely fond of arming his Davids. Longmore's "truthtelling eyes" are that in him which puzzled and tormented the Baron. "They judged him, they mocked him, they eluded him, they threatened him, they triumphed over him, they treated him as no pair of eyes had ever treated him." In every photograph of Henry James that we have, the thing that arrests one is a kind of terrible truthfulness. We feel also, in the letters and memoirs, that "almost indescribable naturalness" which seemed to him as behavior, expressive of his Albany relatives; a naturalness which disappears in the fancy writing of his imitators. If good-nature and reciprocity are American traits, Henry James was a characteristic American—too much one when he patiently suffered unsuitable persons to write to him, call on him, and give him their "work." Politeness in him was "more than a form of luxurious egotism" and is in keeping with the self-effacement of his determination to remain a devotee of devotees to George Eliot "for his own wanton joy" though unwittingly requested to "take away please, away, away!" two books he had written. Mrs. Greville had lent the books as introductory, previous to her calling with Henry James on the Leweses, but no connection had been noticed between books and visitor. The same characteristic appears in the account of his meeting with Dickens. He speaks of "the extremely handsome face . . . which met my dumb homage with a straight inscrutability. . . . It hadn't been the least important that we should have shaken hands or exchanged platitudes. . . . It was as if I had carried off my strange treasure just exactly from under the merciless military eye—placed there on guard of the secret. All of which I recount for illustration of the force of action, unless I call it passion, that may reside in a single pulse of time."

Henry James belonged to "the race which has the credit of knowing best, at home and abroad, how to make itself comfortable" but there was in him an ascetic strain which causes him to make Longmore think with disgust of the Baron's friend who "filled the air with the odor of heliotrope"; and Eugene Pickering's American friend found "something painful in the spectacle of absolute inthralment, even to an excellent cause." Freedom; yes. The confidant, in comparing himself compassionately with the Eugene of their schooldays says, "I could go out to play alone, I could button my jacket myself, and sit up till I was sleepy." Yet the I of the original had not "been exposed on breezy uplands under the she-wolf of competition" and there was not about him "the impertinent odor of trade." Some persons have grudged Henry James his freedom and have called it leisure; but as Theobald, the American painter, said of art, "If we work for ourselves, of course we must hurry. If we work for her, we must often pause." James says of *The Tragic Muse* in a letter, "I took long and patient and careful trouble which no creature will recognize"; and we may declare of him as he did of John La Farge, "one was . . . never to have seen a subtler mind or a more generously wasteful passion, in other words a sincerer one." Reverting to the past of his own life, he is over-powered by "the personal image unextinct" and says, "It presents itself, I feel, beyond reason and yet if I turn from it the ease is less."

There was in him "the rapture of observation" but more unequivocally even than that, affection for family and country. "I was to live to go back with wonder and admiration," he says, "to the quantity of secreted thought in our daily medium, the quality of intellectual passion, the force of cogitation and aspiration, as to the explanation both of a thousand surface incoherences and a thousand felt felicities." Family was the setting for his country and the town was all but synonymous with family; as would appear in what is said of "the family-party smallness of old New York, those happy limits that could make us all care . . . for the same thing at once." It "is always a matter of winter twilight, fire-light, lamplight." "We were surely all gentle and generous together, floating in such a clean light social order, sweetly proof against ennui." "The social scheme, as we knew it, was, in its careless charity, worthy of the golden age— . . . the fruits dropped right upon the board to which we flocked together, the least of us and the greatest"; "our parents . . . never caring much for things we couldn't care for and generally holding that what was good to them would be also good for their children." A father is a safe symbol of patriotism when one can remember him as "genially alert and expert"—when " 'human fellowship' " is "the expression that was perhaps oftenest on his lips and his pen." "We need never fear not to be good enough," Henry James says, "if only we were social enough . . ." and he recalls his mother as so participatingly unremote that he can say, "I think we almost contested her being separate enough to be proud of us—it was too like our being proud of ourselves." Love is the thing more written about than anything else, and in the mistaken sense of greed. Henry James seems to have been haunted by awareness that rapacity destroys what it is successful in securing. He feels a need "to see the other side as well as his own, to feel what his adversary feels"; to be an American is not for him "just to glow belligerently with one's country." Some complain of his transferred citizenship as a loss; but when we consider the trend of his fiction and his uncomplacent denouements, we have no tremor about proving him to have been an American. What we scarcely dare ask is, how many Americans are there who can be included with him in his Americanism? Family affection is the fire that burned within him and America was the hearth on which it burned. He thinks of the American as "intrinsically and actively ample, . . . reaching westward, southward, any-where, everywhere," with a mind "incapable of the shut door in any direction."

From *The Hound and Horn*, Vol. VII (April–June, 1934), pp. 363–372. Reprinted by permission.

The Poetry of Wallace Stevens
[1937]

FOR some of us, Wallace Stevens[1] is America's chief conjuror—as bold a virtuoso and one with as cunning a rhetoric as we have produced. He has, naturally, in some quarters been rebuked for his skill; writers cannot excel at their work without being, like the dogs in *Coriolanus*, "as often beat for barking As therefore kept to do so." But for healthy seductiveness, like the patterned correspondences in Handel's Sonata No. 1, he has not been rivaled:

> The body dies; the body's beauty lives.
> So evenings die in their green going,
> A wave, interminably flowing.

His repercussive harmonics, set off by the small compass of the poem, "prove" mathematically to admiration, and suggest a linguist creating several languages within a single language. The plaster temporariness of subterfuge is, he says,

> Like a word in the mind that sticks at artichoke
> And remains inarticulate.

And besides the multiplying of *h*'s, a characteristically ironic use of scale should be noted, in "Bantams in Pine Woods":

> Chief Iffucan of Azcan in caftan
> Of tan with henna hackles, halt!

The playfulness, that is to say humor, of such rhymings as *egress* and *negress*, *Scaramouche* and *barouche*, is just right, and by no means a joke; one's sense of humor being a clue to the most serious part of one's nature. But best of all, the bravura. Upon the general marine volume of statement is set a parachute-spinnaker of verbiage which looms out like half a cantaloupe and gives the body of the theme the air of a fabled argosy advancing.

[1] *Harmonium*, by Wallace Stevens. New York: Alfred A. Knopf, 1931. *Ideas of Order*, by Wallace Stevens. New York: Alfred A. Knopf, 1936. *Owl's Clover*, by Wallace Stevens. Alcestis Press, 1936.

A harmonist need not be proud of dominating us illusorily, by causing a flower in bloom to appear where a moment before there was none; and not infrequently Wallace Stevens' "noble accents and lucid, inescapable rhythms" point to the universal parent, Shakespeare. A novice of verse, required in an examination to attribute to author or century the line, "These choirs of welcome choir for me farewell," might pay Wallace Stevens a high compliment.

> Remember how the crickets came
> Out of their mother grass, like little kin,

has perfectly Shakespeare's miniature effect of innocent sadness, and the consciously pertinaciously following of a word through several lines, as where we see the leaves

> Turning in the wind,
> Turning as the flames
> Turned in the fire,

are cousin to the pun of Elizabethan drama. We feel, in the tentatively detached method of implication, the influence of Plato; and an awareness of if not the influence of T. S. Eliot. Better say that each has influenced the other; with "Sunday Morning" and the Prufrock-like lines in "Le Monocle de Mon Oncle" in mind,

> Shall I uncrumple this much crumpled thing?
> .   .   .   .   .   .
> For it has come that thus I greet the spring

and the Peter Quince-like rhythmic contour of T. S. Eliot's "La Figlia Que Piange." As if it were Antipholus of Ephesus and Antipholus of Syracuse, each has an almost too acute concept of "the revenge of music"; a realization that the seducer is the seduced; and a smiling, strict, Voltaire-like, straight-seeing, self-directed humor which triumphs in its pain. Each is engaged in a similar though differently expressed search for that which will endure.

We are able here to see the salutary effect of insisting that a piece of writing please the writer himself before it pleases anyone else; and how a poet may be a wall of incorruptibleness against any concessive violating of the essential aura of contributory vagueness. Such tense heights of the romantic are intimated by mere titles, that one might hesitate to make trial of the content lest it seem bathos, but Wallace Stevens is a delicate apothecary of savors and precipitates, and no hauteurs are violated. His method of hints and disguises should have Mercury as their patron divinity, for in the guise of "a dark rabbi," an ogre, a traveler, a comedian, an old woman, he deceives us as the god misled the aged couple in the myth.

Again, and moreover, to manner and harmonics is added a fine and exultant grasp of beauty—a veritable refuge of "blessed mornings, meet for the eye of the young alligator"; an equivalence for jungle beauty, arctic beauty, marine beauty, meridian, hothouse, consciously urban or unconsciously natural beauty—which might be alarming were it not for the persistent foil of dissatisfaction with matter. This frugally unified opulence, epitomized by the "green vine angering for life"—in *Owl's Clover* by the thought of plundered harassed Africa, "the Greenest Continent" where "memory moves on leopard's feet"—has been perfected stroke by stroke, since the period of "the magenta Judas-tree," "the indigo glass in the grass," "oceans in obsidian," the white of "frogs," of "clays," and in "withered reeds"; until now, tropic pinks and yellows, avocado and Kuniyoshi cabouchon emerald-greens, the blent but violent excellence of ailanthus silk-moths and metallic breast-feathers—as open and unpretending as Rousseau's Snake-Charmer and Sleeping Gipsy—combine in an impression of incandescence like that of the night-blooming cereus.

Despite this awareness of the world of sense—which at some points, to a prudish asceticism approximates wickedness—one notices the frequent recurrence of the word heaven. In each clime which the author visits and under each disguise, it is the dilemma of tested hope which confronts him. In *Owl's Clover* "the search for a tranquil belief," and the protest against the actualities of experience, become a protest against the death of world hope; against the unorder and chaos of this "age of concentric mobs." Those who dare to forget that "As the man the state, not as the state the man," who divert "the dream of heaven from heaven to the future, as a god," are indeed the carnivorous owl with African greenness for its repast. The land of "ploughmen, peacocks, doves," of "Leonardo," has been "Combating bushmen for a patch of gourds, Loosing black slaves to make black infantry"; "the widow of Madrid Weeps in Segovia"; in Moscow, in all Europe, "Always everything That is is dead except what ought to be"; aeroplanes which counterfeit "the bee's drone" and have the powers of "the scorpion" are our "seraphim." Mr. Stevens' book is the sable requiem for all this. But requiem is not the word when anyone hates lust for power and ignorance of power, as the author of this book does. So long as we are ashamed of the ironic feast, and of our marble victories—horses or men—which will break unless they are first broken by us, there is hope for the world. As R. P. Blackmur has said, "the poems rise in the mind like a tide." They embody hope, that in being frustrated becomes fortitude; and they prove to us that the testament to emotion ·is not volubility. It is remarkable that a refusal to speak should result in such eloquence and that an implied heaven could be made so definite. Unanimity of word and rhythm has been attained, and we have the seldom exhilaration of knowing that America has in Wallace Stevens at least one artist whom professionalism will never demolish.

From *Poetry: A Magazine of Verse*, Vol. XLIX (February, 1937), pp. 268–273. Reprinted by permission.

LIONEL TRILLING

Reality in America

[1950]

IT IS possible to say of V. L. Parrington that with his *Main Currents in American Thought* he has had an influence on our conception of American culture which is not equaled by that of any other writer of the last two decades. His ideas are now the accepted ones wherever the college course in American literature is given by a teacher who conceives himself to be opposed to the genteel and the academic and in alliance with the vigorous and the actual. And whenever the liberal historian of America finds occasion to take account of the national literature, as nowadays he feels it proper to do, it is Parrington who is his standard and guide. Parrington's ideas are the more firmly established because they do not have to be imposed—the teacher or the critic who presents them is likely to find that his task is merely to make articulate for his audience what it has always believed, for Parrington formulated in a classic way the suppositions about our culture which are held by the American middle class so far as that class is at all liberal in its social thought and so far as it begins to understand that literature has anything to do with society.

Parrington was not a great mind; he was not a precise thinker or, except when measured by the low eminences that were about him, an impressive one. Separate Parrington from his informing idea of the economic and social determination of thought and what is left is a simple intelligence, notable for its generosity and enthusiasm but certainly not for its accuracy or originality. Take him even with his idea and he is, once its direction is established, rather too predictable to be continuously interesting; and, indeed, what we dignify with the name of economic and social determinism amounts in his use of it to not much more than the demonstration that most writers incline to stick to their own social class. But his best virtue was real and important—he had what we like to think of as the saving salt of the American mind, the lively sense of the practical, workaday world, of the welter of ordinary undistinguished things and people, of the tangible, quirky, unrefined elements of life. He knew what so many literary historians do not know, that emotions and ideas are the sparks that fly when the mind meets difficulties.

Yet he had after all but a limited sense of what constitutes a difficulty.

Whenever he was confronted with a work of art that was complex, personal and not literal, that was not, as it were, a public document, Parrington was at a loss. Difficulties that were complicated by personality or that were expressed in the language of successful art did not seem quite real to him and he was inclined to treat them as aberrations, which is one way of saying what everybody admits, that the weakest part of Parrington's talent was his aesthetic judgment. His admirers and disciples like to imply that his errors of aesthetic judgment are merely lapses of taste, but this is not so. Despite such mistakes as his notorious praise of Cabell, to whom in a remarkable passage he compares Melville, Parrington's taste was by no means bad. His errors are the errors of understanding which arise from his assumptions about the nature of reality.

Parrington does not often deal with abstract philosophical ideas, but whenever he approaches a work of art we are made aware of the metaphysics on which his aesthetics is based. There exists, he believes, a thing called *reality*; it is one and immutable, it is wholly external, it is irreducible. Men's minds may waver, but reality is always reliable, always the same, always easily to be known. And the artist's relation to reality he conceives as a simple one. Reality being fixed and given, the artist has but to let it pass through him, he is the lens in the first diagram of an elementary book on optics: Fig. 1, Reality; Fig. 2, Artist; Fig. 1′, Work of Art. Figs. 1 and 1′ are normally in virtual correspondence with each other. Sometimes the artist spoils this ideal relation by "turning away from" reality. This results in certain fantastic works, unreal and ultimately useless. It does not occur to Parrington that there is any other relation possible between the artist and reality than this passage of reality through the transparent artist; he meets evidence of imagination and creativeness with a settled hostility the expression of which suggests that he regards them as the natural enemies of democracy.

In this view of things, reality, although it is always reliable, is always rather sober-sided, even grim. Parrington, a genial and enthusiastic man, can understand how the generosity of man's hopes and desires may leap beyond reality; he admires will in the degree that he suspects mind. To an excess of desire and energy which blinds a man to the limitations of reality he can indeed be very tender. This is one of the many meanings he gives to *romance* or *romanticism*, and in spite of himself it appeals to something in his own nature. The praise of Cabell is Parrington's response not only to Cabell's elegance—for Parrington loved elegance—but also to Cabell's insistence on the part which a beneficent self-deception may and even should play in the disappointing fact-bound life of man, particularly in the private and erotic part of his life.[1]

---

[1] See, for example, how Parrington accounts for the "idealizing mind"—Melville's—by the discrepancy between "a wife in her morning kimono" and "the Helen of his dreams." Vol. II, p. 259.

The second volume of *Main Currents* is called *The Romantic Revolution in America* and it is natural to expect that the word romantic should appear in it frequently. So it does, more frequently than one can count, and seldom with the same meaning, seldom with the sense that the word, although scandalously vague as it has been used by the literary historians, is still full of complicated but not wholly pointless ideas, that it involves many contrary but definable things; all too often Parrington uses the word romantic with the word romance close at hand, meaning *a* romance, in the sense that *Graustark* or *Treasure Island* is a romance, as though it signified chiefly a gay disregard of the limitations of everyday fact. Romance is refusing to heed the counsels of experience (p. iii); it is ebullience (p. iv); it is utopianism (p. iv); it is individualism (p. vi); it is self-deception (p. 59)—"romantic faith . . . in the beneficent processes of trade and industry" (as held, we inevitably ask, by the romantic Adam Smith?); it is the love of the picturesque (p. 49); it is the dislike of innovation (p. 50) but also the love of change (p. iv); it is the sentimental (p. 192); it is patriotism, and then it is cheap (p. 235). It may be used to denote what is not classical, but chiefly it means that which ignores reality (pp. ix, 136, 143, 147, and *passim*); it is not critical (pp. 225, 235), although in speaking of Cooper and Melville, Parrington admits that criticism can sometimes spring from romanticism.

Whenever a man with whose ideas he disagrees wins from Parrington a reluctant measure of respect, the word romantic is likely to appear. He does not admire Henry Clay, yet something in Clay is not to be despised—his romanticism, although Clay's romanticism is made equivalent with his inability to "come to grips with reality." Romanticism is thus, in most of its significations, the venial sin of *Main Currents;* like carnal passion in the *Inferno,* it evokes not blame but tender sorrow. But it can also be the great and saving virtue which Parrington recognizes. It is ascribed to the transcendental reformers he so much admires; it is said to mark two of his most cherished heroes, Jefferson and Emerson: "they were both romantics and their idealism was only a different expression of a common spirit." Parrington held, we may say, at least two different views of romanticism which suggest two different views of reality. Sometimes he speaks of reality in an honorific way, meaning the substantial stuff of life, the ineluctable facts with which the mind must cope, but sometimes he speaks of it pejoratively and means the world of established social forms; and he speaks of realism in two ways: sometimes as the power of dealing intelligently with fact, sometimes as a cold and conservative resistance to idealism.

Just as for Parrington there is a saving grace and a venial sin, there is also a deadly sin, and this is turning away from reality, not in the excess of generous feeling, but in what he believes to be a deficiency of feeling, as with Hawthorne, or out of what amounts to sinful pride, as with Henry James. He tells us that there was too much realism in Hawthorne to allow him to give his faith to the transcendental reformers: "he was too much of a realist to change fashions in creeds"; "he remained cold to the revolutionary criticism that was eager to pull down the old temples to make room for nobler." It is this cold realism, keeping Hawthorne apart from his enthusiastic contemporaries, that alienates Parrington's sympathy—"Eager souls, mystics and revolutionaries, may propose to refashion the world in accordance with their dreams; but evil remains, and so long as it lurks in the secret places of the heart, utopia is only the shadow of a dream. And so while the Concord thinkers were proclaiming man to be the indubitable child of God, Hawthorne was critically examining the question of evil as it appeared in the light of his own experience. It was the central fascinating problem of his intellectual life, and in pursuit of a solution he probed curiously into the hidden, furtive recesses of the soul." Parrington's disapproval of the enterprise is unmistakable.

Now we might wonder whether Hawthorne's questioning of the naïve and often eccentric faiths of the transcendental reformers was not, on the face of it, a public service. But Parrington implies that it contributes nothing to democracy, and even that it stands in the way of the realization of democracy. If democracy depends wholly on a fighting faith, I suppose he is right. Yet society is after all something that exists at the moment as well as in the future, and if one man wants to probe curiously into the hidden furtive recesses of the contemporary soul, a broad democracy and especially one devoted to reality should allow him to do so without despising him. If what Hawthorne did was certainly nothing to build a party on, we ought perhaps to forgive him when we remember that he was only one man and that the future of mankind did not depend upon him alone. But this very fact serves only to irritate Parrington; he is put out by Hawthorne's loneliness and believes that part of Hawthorne's insufficiency as a writer comes from his failure to get around and meet people. Hawthorne could not, he tells us, establish contact with the "Yankee reality," and was scarcely aware of the "substantial world of Puritan reality that Samuel Sewall knew."

To turn from reality might mean to turn to romance, but Parrington tells us that Hawthorne was romantic "only in a narrow and very special sense." He was not interested in the world of, as it were, practical romance, in the Salem of the clipper ships; from this he turned away to create "a romance of ethics." This is not an illuminating phrase but it is a catching one, and it might be taken to mean that Hawthorne was in the tradition of, say, Shakespeare; but we quickly learn that, no, Hawthorne had entered a barren field, for although he himself lived in the present and had all the future to mold, he preferred to find many of his subjects in the past. We learn too that his romance of ethics is not admirable because it requires the hard, fine pressing of ideas, and we are told that "a romantic uninterested in adventure and afraid of sex is likely to become somewhat graveled for matter." In short, Hawthorne's mind was a thin one, and Parrington puts in evidence his use of allegory and symbol and the very severity and precision of his art to prove that he suffered from a sadly limited intellect, for so much fancy and so much art could scarcely be needed unless the writer were trying to exploit to the utmost the few poor ideas that he had.

Hawthorne, then, was "forever dealing with shadows, and he knew that he was dealing with shadows." Perhaps so, but shadows are also part of reality and one would not want a world without shadows, it would not even be a "real" world. But we must get beyond Parrington's metaphor. The fact is that Hawthorne was dealing beautifully with realities, with substantial things. The man who could raise those brilliant and serious doubts about the nature and possibility of moral perfection, the man who could keep himself aloof from the "Yankee reality" and who could dissent from the orthodoxies of dissent and tell us so much about the nature of moral zeal, is of course dealing exactly with reality.

Parrington's characteristic weakness as a historian is suggested by his title, for the culture of a nation is not truly figured in the image of the current. A culture is not a flow, nor even a confluence; the form of its existence is struggle, or at least debate—it is nothing if not a dialectic. And in any culture there are likely to be certain artists who contain a large part of the dialectic within themselves, their meaning and power lying in their contradictions; they contain within themselves, it may be said, the very essence of the culture, and the sign of this is that they do not submit to serve the ends of any one ideological group or tendency. It is a significant circumstance of American culture, and one which is susceptible of explanation, that an unusually large proportion of its notable writers of the nineteenth century were such repositories of the dialectic of their times—they contained both the yes and the no of their culture, and by that token they were prophetic of the future. Parrington said that he had not set up shop as a literary critic; but if a literary critic is simply a reader who has the ability to understand literature and to convey to others what he understands, it is not exactly a matter of free choice whether or not a cultural historian shall be a literary critic, nor is it open to him to let his virtuous political and social opinions do duty for percipience. To throw out Poe because he cannot be conveniently fitted into a theory of American culture, to speak of him as a biological sport and as a mind apart from the main current, to find his gloom to be merely personal and eccentric, "only the atrabilious wretchedness of a dipsomaniac," as Hawthorne's was "no more than the skeptical questioning of life by a nature that knew no fierce storms," to judge Melville's response to American life to be less noble than that of Bryant or of Greeley, to speak of Henry James as an escapist, as an artist similar to Whistler, a man characteristically afraid of stress—this is not merely to be mistaken in aesthetic judgment; rather it is to examine without attention and from the point of view of a limited and essentially arrogant conception of reality the documents which are in some respects the most suggestive testimony to what America was and is, and of course to get no answer from them.

Parrington lies twenty years behind us, and in the intervening time there has developed a body of opinion which is aware of his inadequacies and of the inadequacies of his coadjutors and disciples, who make up what might be called the literary academicism of liberalism. Yet Parrington still stands at the center of American thought about American culture because, as I say, he expresses the chronic American belief that there exists an opposition between reality and mind and that one must enlist oneself in the party of reality.

II

This belief in the incompatibility of mind and reality is exemplified by the doctrinaire indulgence which liberal intellectuals have always displayed toward Theodore Dreiser, an indulgence which becomes the worthier of remark when it is contrasted with the liberal severity toward Henry James. Dreiser and James: with that juxtaposition we are immediately at the dark and bloody crossroads where literature and politics meet. One does not go there gladly, but nowadays it is not exactly a matter of free choice whether one does or does not go. As for the particular juxtaposition itself, it is inevitable and it has at the present moment far more significance than the juxtaposition which once used to be made between James and Whitman. It is not hard to contrive factitious oppositions between James and Whitman, but the real difference between them is the difference between the moral mind, with its awareness of tragedy, irony, and multitudinous distinctions, and the transcendental mind, with its passionate sense of the oneness of multiplictiy. James and Whitman are unlike not in quality but in kind, and in their very opposition they serve to complement each other. But the difference between James and Dreiser is not of kind, for both men addressed themselves to virtually the same social and moral fact. The difference here is one of quality, and perhaps nothing is more typical of American liberalism than the way it has responded to the respective qualities of the two men.

Few critics, I suppose, no matter what their political disposition, have ever been wholly blind to James's great gifts, or even to the grandiose moral intention of these gifts. And few critics have ever been wholly blind to Dreiser's great faults. But by liberal critics James is traditionally put to the ultimate question: of what use, of what actual political use, are his gifts and their intention? Granted that James was devoted to an extraordinary moral perceptiveness, granted too that moral perceptiveness has something to do with politics and the social life, of what possible practical value in our world of impending disaster can James's work be? And James's style, his characters, his subjects, and even his own social origin and the manner of his personal life are adduced to show that his work cannot endure the question. To James no quarter is given by American criticism in its political and liberal aspect. But in the same degree that liberal criticism is moved by political considerations to treat James with severity, it treats Dreiser with the most sympathetic indulgence. Dreiser's literary faults, it gives us to understand, are essentially social and political virtues. It was Parrington who established the formula for the liberal criticism of Dreiser by calling him a "peasant": when Dreiser thinks stupidly, it is because he has the slow stubbornness of a peasant; when he writes badly, it is because he is impatient of the sterile literary gentility of the bourgeoisie. It is as if wit, and flexibility of mind, and perception, and knowledge were to be equated with aristocracy and political reaction, while dullness and stupidity must naturally suggest a virtuous democracy, as in the old plays.

The liberal judgment of Dreiser and James goes back of politics, goes back to the cultural assumptions that make politics. We are still haunted by a kind of political fear of the intellect which Tocqueville observed in us more than a century ago. American intellectuals, when they are being consciously American or political, are remarkably quick to suggest that an art which is marked by perception and knowledge, although all very well in its way, can never get us through gross dangers and difficulties. And their misgivings become the more intense when intellect works in art as it ideally should, when its processes are vivacious and interesting and brilliant. It is then that we like to confront it with the gross dangers and difficulties and to challenge it to save us at once from disaster. When intellect in art is awkward or dull we do not put it to the test of ultimate or immediate practicality. No liberal critic asks the question of Dreiser whether *his* moral preoccupations are going to be useful in confronting the disasters that threaten us. And it is a judgment on the proper nature of mind, rather than any actual political meaning that might be drawn from the works of the two men, which accounts for the unequal justice they have received from the progressive critics. If it could be conclusively demonstrated —by, say, documents in James's handwriting—that James explicitly intended his books to be understood as pleas for co-operatives, labor unions, better housing, and more equitable taxation, the American critic in his liberal and progressive character would still be worried by James because his work shows so many of the electric qualities of mind. And if something like the opposite were proved of Dreiser, it would be brushed aside—as his doctrinaire anti-Semitism has in fact been brushed aside—because his books have the awkwardness, the chaos, the heaviness which we associate with "reality." In the American metaphysic, reality is always material reality, hard, resistant, unformed, impenetrable, and unpleasant. And that mind is alone felt to be trustworthy which most resembles this reality by most nearly reproducing the sensations it affords.

In *The Rise of American Civilization,* Professor Beard uses a significant phrase when, in the course of an ironic account of James's career, he implies that we have the clue to the irrelevance of that career when we know that James was "a whole generation removed from the odors of the shop." Of a piece with this, and in itself even more significant, is the comment which Granville Hicks makes in *The Great Tradition* when he deals with James's stories about artists and remarks that such artists as James portrays, so concerned for their art and their integrity in art, do not really exist: "After all, who has ever known such artists? Where are the Hugh Verekers, the Mark Ambients, the Neil Paradays, the Overts, Limberts, Dencombes, Delavoys?" This question, as Mr. Hicks admits, had occurred to James himself, but what answer had James given to it? "If the life about us for the last thirty years refused warrant for these examples," he said in the preface to volume XII of the New York Edition, "then so much the worse for that life. . . . There are decencies that in the name of the general self-respect we must take for granted, there's a rudimentary intellectual honor to which we must, in the interest of civilization, at least pretend." And to this Mr. Hicks, shocked beyond argument, makes this reply, which would be astonishing had we not heard it before: "But this is the purest romanticism, this writing about what ought to be rather than what is!"

The "odors of the shop" are real, and to those who breathe them they guarantee a sense of vitality from which James is debarred. The idea of intellectual honor is not real, and to that chimera James was devoted. He betrayed the reality of what is in the interests of what ought to be. Dare we trust him? The question, we remember, is asked by men who themselves have elaborate transactions with what ought to be. Professor Beard spoke in the name of a growing, developing, and improving America. Mr. Hicks, when he wrote *The Great Tradition,* was in general sympathy with a nominally radical movement. But James's own transaction with what ought to be is suspect because it is carried on through what I have called the electrical qualities of mind, through a complex and rapid imagination and with a kind of authoritative immediacy. Mr. Hicks knows that Dreiser is "clumsy" and "stupid" and "bewildered" and "crude in his statement of materialistic monism"; he knows that Dreiser in his personal life—which is in point because James's personal life is always supposed to be so much in point—was not quite emancipated from "his boyhood longing for crass material success," showing "again and again a desire for the ostentatious luxury of the successful business man." But Dreiser is to be accepted and forgiven because his faults are the sad, lovable, honorable faults of reality itself, or of America itself—huge, inchoate, struggling toward expression, caught between the dream of raw power and the dream of morality.

"The liability in what Santayana called the genteel tradition was due to its being the product of mind apart from experience. Dreiser gave us the stuff of our common experience, not as it was hoped to be by any idealizing theorist, but as it actually was in its crudity." The author of this statement certainly cannot be accused of any lack of feeling for mind as Henry James represents it; nor can Mr. Matthiessen be thought of as a follower of Parrington—indeed, in the preface to *American Renaissance* he has framed one of the sharpest and most cogent criticisms of Parrington's method. Yet Mr. Matthiessen, writing in the *New York Times Book Review* about Dreiser's posthumous novel, *The Bulwark,* accepts the liberal cliché which opposes crude experience to mind and establishes Dreiser's value by implying that the mind which Dreiser's crude experience is presumed to confront and refute is the mind of gentility.

This implied amalgamation of mind with gentility is the rationale of the long indulgence of Dreiser, which is extended even to the style of his prose. Everyone is aware that Dreiser's prose style is full of roughness and ungainliness, and the critics who admire Dreiser tell us it does not matter. Of course it does not matter. No reader with a right sense of style would suppose that it does matter, and he might even find it a virtue. But it has been taken for granted that the ungainliness of Dreiser's style is the only possible objection to be made to it, and that whoever finds in it any fault at all wants a prettified genteel style (and is objecting to the ungainliness of reality itself). For instance, Edwin Berry Burgum, in a leaflet on Dreiser put out by the Book Find Club, tells us that Dreiser was one of those who used—or, as Mr. Burgum says, utilized—"the diction of the Middle West, pretty much as it was spoken, rich in colloquialism and frank in the simplicity and directness of the pioneer tradition," and that this diction took the place of "the literary English, formal and bookish, of New England provincialism that was closer to the aristocratic spirit of the mother country than to the tang of everyday life in the new West." This is mere fantasy. Hawthorne, Thoreau, and Emerson were for the most part remarkably colloquial—they wrote, that is, much as they spoke; their prose was specifically American in quality, and, except for occasional lapses, quite direct and simple. It is Dreiser who lacks the sense of colloquial diction—that of the Middle West or any other. If we are to talk of bookishness, it is Dreiser who is bookish; he is precisely literary in the bad sense; he is full of flowers of rhetoric and shines with paste gems; at hundreds of points his diction is not only genteel but fancy. It is he who speaks of "a scene more distingué than this," or of a woman "artistic in form and feature," or of a man who, although "strong, reserved, aggressive, with an air of wealth and experience, was *soi-disant* and not particularly eager to stay at home." Colloquialism held no real charm for him and his natural tendency is always toward the "fine:"

Moralists come and go; religionists fulminate and declare the pronouncements of God as to this; but Aphrodite still reigns. Embowered in the festal depths of the spring, set above her altars of porphyry, chalcedony, ivory and gold, see her smile the smile that is at once the texture and essence of delight, the glory and despair of the world! Dream on, oh Buddha, asleep on your lotus leaf, of an undisturbed Nirvana! Sweat, oh Jesus, your last agonizing drops over an unregenerate world! In the forests of Pan still ring the cries of the worshippers of Aphrodite! From her altars the incense of adoration ever rises! And see, the new red grapes dripping where votive hands new-press them!

Charles Jackson, the novelist, telling us in the same leaflet that Dreiser's style does not matter, remarks on how much still comes to us when we have lost by translation the stylistic brilliance of Thomas Mann or the Russians or Balzac. He is in part right. And he is right too when he says that a certain kind of conscious, supervised artistry is not appropriate to the novel of large dimensions. Yet the fact is that the great novelists have usually written very good prose, and what comes through even a bad translation is exactly the power of mind that made the well-hung sentence of the original text. In literature style is so little the mere clothing of thought—need it be insisted on at this date?—that we may say that from the earth of the novelist's prose spring his characters, his ideas, and even his story itself.[2]

To the extent that Dreiser's style is defensible, his thought is also defensible. That is, when he thinks like a novelist, he is worth following—when by means of his rough and ungainly but no doubt cumulatively effective style he creates rough, ungainly, but effective characters and events. But when he thinks like, as we say, a philosopher, he is likely to be not only foolish but vulgar. He thinks as the modern crowd thinks when it decides to think: religion and morality are nonsense, "religionists" and moralists are fakes, tradition is a fraud, what is man but matter and impulses, mysterious "chemisms," what value has life anyway? "What, cooking, eating, coition, job holding, growing,

[2] The latest defense of Dreiser's style, that in the chapter on Dreiser in the *Literary History of the United States,* is worth noting: "Forgetful of the integrity and power of Dreiser's whole work, many critics have been distracted into a condemnation of his style. He was like Twain and Whitman, an organic artist; he wrote what he knew—what he was. His many colloquialisms were part of the coinage of his time, and his sentimental and romantic passages were written in the language of the educational system and the popular literature of his formative years. In his style, as in his material, he was a child of his time, of his class. Self-educated, a type or model of the artist of plebeian origin in America, his language, like his subject matter, is not marked by internal inconsistencies." No doubt Dreiser was an organic artist in the sense that he wrote what he knew and what he was, but so, I suppose, is every artist; the question for criticism comes down to *what* he knew and *what* he was. That he was a child of his time and class is also true, but this can be said of everyone without exception; the question for criticism is how he transcended the imposed limitations of his time and class. As for the defense made on the ground of his particular class, it can only be said that liberal thought has come to a strange pass when it assumes that a plebeian origin is accountable for a writer's faults through all his intellectual life.

aging, losing, winning, in so changeful and passing a scene as this, important? Bunk! It is some form of titillating illusion with about as much import to the superior forces that bring it all about as the functions and gyrations of a fly. No more. And maybe less." Thus Dreiser at sixty. And yet there is for him always the vulgarly saving suspicion that maybe, when all is said and done, there is Something Behind It All. It is much to the point of his intellectual vulgarity that Dreiser's anti-Semitism was not merely a social prejudice but an idea, a way of dealing with difficulties.

No one, I suppose, has ever represented Dreiser as a masterly intellect. It is even commonplace to say that his ideas are inconsistent or inadequate. But once that admission has been made, his ideas are hustled out of sight while his "reality" and great brooding pity are spoken of. (His pity is to be questioned: pity is to be judged by kind, not amount, and Dreiser's pity—*Jennie Gerhardt* provides the only exception—is either destructive of its object or it is self-pity.) Why has no liberal critic ever brought Dreiser's ideas to the bar of political practicality, asking what use is to be made of Dreiser's dim, awkward speculation, of his self-justification, of his lust for "beauty" and "sex" and "living" and "life itself," and of the showy nihilism which always seems to him so grand a gesture in the direction of profundity? We live, understandably enough, with the sense of urgency; our clock, like Baudelaire's, has had the hands removed and bears the legend, "It is later than you think." But with us it is always a little too late for mind, yet never too late for honest stupidity; always a little too late for understanding, never too late for righteous, bewildered wrath; always too late for thought, never too late for naïve moralizing. We seem to like to condemn our finest but not our worst qualities by pitting them against the exigency of time.

But sometimes time is not quite so exigent as to justify all our own exigency, and in the case of Dreiser time has allowed his deficiencies to reach their logical, and fatal, conclusion. In *The Bulwark* Dreiser's characteristic ideas come full circle, and the simple, didactic life history of Solon Barnes, a Quaker business man, affirms a simple Christian faith, and a kind of practical mysticism, and the virtues of self-abnegation and self-restraint, and the belief in and submission to the hidden purposes of higher powers, those "superior forces that bring it all about"—once, in Dreiser's opinion, so brutally indifferent, now somehow benign. This is not the first occasion on which Dreiser has shown a tenderness toward religion and a responsiveness to mysticism. *Jennie Gerhardt* and the figure of the Reverend Duncan McMillan in *An American Tragedy* are forecasts of the avowals of *The Bulwark,* and Dreiser's lively interest in power of any sort led him to take account of the power implicit in the cruder forms of mystical performance. Yet these rifts in his nearly monolithic materialism cannot quite prepare us for the blank pietism of *The Bulwark,* not after we have remembered how salient in Dreiser's work has been the long surly rage against the "religionists" and the "moralists," the men who have presumed to believe that life can be given any law at all and who have dared to suppose that will or mind or faith can shape the savage and beautiful entity that Dreiser liked to call "life itself." Now for Dreiser the law may indeed be given, and it is wholly simple—the safe conduct of the personal life requires only that we follow the Inner Light according to the regimen of the Society of Friends, or according to some other godly rule. And now the smiling Aphrodite set above her altars of porphyry, chalcedony, ivory, and gold is quite forgotten, and we are told that the sad joy of cosmic acceptance goes hand in hand with sexual abstinence.

Dreiser's mood of "acceptance" in the last years of his life is not, as a personal experience, to be submitted to the tests of intellectual validity. It consists of a sensation of cosmic understanding, of an overarching sense of unity with the world in its apparent evil as well as in its obvious good. It is no more to be quarreled with, or reasoned with, than love itself—indeed, it is a kind of love, not so much of the world as of oneself in the world. Perhaps it is either the cessation of desire or the perfect balance of desires. It is what used often to be meant by "peace," and up through the nineteenth century a good many people understood its meaning. If it was Dreiser's own emotion at the end of his life, who would not be happy that he had achieved it? I am not even sure that our civilization would not be the better for more of us knowing and desiring this emotion of grave felicity. Yet granting the personal validity of the emotion, Dreiser's exposition of it fails, and is, moreover, offensive. Mr. Matthiessen has warned us of the attack that will be made on the doctrine of *The Bulwark* by "those who believe that any renewal of Christianity marks a new 'failure of nerve.' " But Dreiser's religious avowal is not a failure of nerve—it is a failure of mind and heart. We have only to set his book beside any work in which mind and heart are made to serve religion to know this at once. Ivan Karamazov's giving back his ticket of admission to the "harmony" of the universe suggests that *The Bulwark* is not morally adequate, for we dare not, as its hero does, blandly "accept" the suffering of others; and the Book of Job tells us that it does not include enough in its exploration of the problems of evil, and is not stern enough. I have said that Dreiser's religious affirmation was offensive; the offense lies in the vulgar ease of its formulation, as well as in the comfortable untroubled way in which Dreiser moved from nihilism to pietism.[3]

[3] This ease and comfortableness seem to mark contemporary religious conversions. Religion nowadays has the appearance of what the ideal modern house has been called, "a machine for living," and seemingly one makes up one's mind to acquire and use it not with spiritual struggle but only with a growing sense of its practicability and convenience. Compare *The Seven Storey Mountain,* which Monsignor Sheen calls "a twentieth-century form of the *Confessions* of St. Augustine," with the old, the as it were original, *Confessions* of St. Augustine.

The Bulwark is the fruit of Dreiser's old age, but if we speak of it as a failure of thought and feeling, we cannot suppose that with age Dreiser weakened in mind and heart. The weakness was always there. And in a sense it is not Dreiser who failed but a whole way of dealing with ideas, a way in which we have all been in some degree involved. Our liberal, progressive culture tolerated Dreiser's vulgar materialism with its huge negation, its simple cry of "Bunk!," feeling that perhaps it was not quite intellectually adequate but certainly very *strong*, certainly very *real*. And now, almost as a natural consequence, it has been given, and is not unwilling to take, Dreiser's pietistic religion in all its inadequacy.

Dreiser, of course, was firmer than the intellectual culture that accepted him. He *meant* his ideas, at least so far as a man can mean ideas who is incapable of following them to their consequences. But we, when it came to his ideas, talked about his great brooding pity and shrugged the ideas off. We are still doing it. Robert Elias, the biographer of Dreiser, tells us that "it is part of the logic of [Dreiser's] life that he should have completed *The Bulwark* at the same time that he joined the Communists." Just what kind of logic this is we learn from Mr. Elias's further statement. "When he supported left-wing movements and finally, last year, joined the Communist Party, he did so not because he had examined the details of the party line and found them satisfactory, but because he agreed with a general program that represented a means for establishing his cherished goal of greater equality among men." Whether or not Dreiser was following the logic of his own life, he was certainly following the logic of the liberal criticism that accepted him so undiscriminatingly as one of the great, significant expressions of its spirit. This is the liberal criticism, in the direct line of Parrington, which establishes the social responsibility of the writer and then goes on to say that, apart from his duty of resembling reality as much as possible, he is not really responsible for anything, not even for his ideas. The scope of reality being what it is, ideas are held to be mere "details," and, what is more, to be details which, if attended to, have the effect of diminishing reality. But ideals are different from ideas; in the liberal criticism which descends from Parrington ideals consort happily with reality and they urge us to deal impatiently with ideas—a "cherished goal" forbids that we stop to consider how we reach it, or if we may not destroy it in trying to reach it the wrong way.

From *The Liberal Imagination*, by Lionel Trilling. The Viking Press. Copyright, 1940, 1946, by Lionel Trilling. Reprinted by permission of the author and publishers. Based in part on "Parrington, Mr. Smith, and Reality" in *The Partisan Review*, Vol. VII (January–February, 1940), pp. 24–40; and on "Dreiser and the Liberal Mind" in *The Nation*, Vol. CLXII (April 20, 1946), pp. 466–472.

YVOR WINTERS

Robert Frost: or, The Spiritual Drifter as Poet

[1948]

I

ROBERT FROST is one of the most talented poets of our time, but I believe that his work is both overestimated and misunderstood; and it seems to me of the utmost importance that we should understand him with some accuracy. If we can arrive at a reasonably sound understanding of him, we can profit by his virtues without risk of acquiring his defects; and we may incidentally arrive at a better understanding of our present culture.

A popular poet is always a spectacle of some interest, for poetry in general is not popular; and when the popular poet is also within limits a distinguished poet, the spectacle is even more curious, for commonly it is bad poetry which is popular. When we encounter such a spectacle, we may be reasonably sure of finding certain social and historical reasons for the popularity. Frost is similar in his ways and attitudes and perceptions to a very large number of the more intelligent, if not the most intelligent, of his contemporaries: to the school teachers, the English professors, the more or less literate undergraduates, the journalists, and the casual readers of every class. These people are numerous and are in a position to perpetuate their ways and attitudes; this similarity, therefore, is worth examining.

Frost has been praised as a classical poet, but he is not classical in any sense which I can understand. Like many of his contemporaries, he is an Emersonian Romantic, although with certain mutings and modifications which I shall mention presently, and he has labeled himself as such with a good deal of care. He is a poet of the minor theme, the casual approach, and the discreetly eccentric attitude. When a reader calls Frost a classical poet, he probably means that Frost strikes him as a "natural" poet, a poet who somehow resembles himself and his neighbors; but this is merely another way of saying that the reader feels a kinship to him and likes him easily. Classical literature is said to judge human experience with respect to the norm; but it does so with respect to the norm of what humanity ought to be, not with respect to the norm of what it happens to be in a particular place and time. The human average has never been admirable, and in certain cultures it has departed very far from the admirable; that is why in the great classical periods of literature we are likely to observe great works in tragedy and satire, the works of a Racine and a Molière, of a Shakespeare and a Jonson, works which deal in their respective ways with sharp deviations from the ideal norm; and that is why literature which glorifies the average is sentimental rather than classical.

Frost writes of rural subjects, and the American reader of our time has an affection for rural subjects which is partly the product of the Romantic sentimentalization of "nature," but which is partly also a nostalgic looking back to the rural life which predominated in this nation a generation or two ago; the rural life is somehow regarded as the truly American life. I have no objection to the poet's employing rural settings; but we should remember that it is the poet's business to evaluate human experience, and the rural setting is no more valuable for this purpose than any other or than no particular setting, and one could argue with some plausibility that an exclusive concentration on it may be limiting.

Frost early began his endeavor to make his style approximate as closely as possible the style of conversation, and this endeavor has added to his reputation: it has helped to make him seem "natural." But poetry is not conversation, and I see no reason why poetry should be called upon to imitate conversation. Conversation is the most careless and formless of human utterance; it is spontaneous and unrevised, and its vocabulary is commonly limited. Poetry is the most difficult form of human utterance; we revise poems carefully in order to make them more nearly perfect. The two forms of expression are extremes, they are not close to each other. We do not praise a violinist for playing as if he were improvising; we praise him for playing well. And when a man plays well or writes well, his audience must have intelligence, training, and patience in order to appreciate him. We do not understand difficult matters "naturally."

The business of the poet can be stated simply. The poet deals with human experience in words. Words are symbols of concepts, which have acquired connotation of feeling in addition to their denotation of concept. The poet, then, as a result of the very nature of his medium, must make a rational statement about an experience, and as rationality is a part of the medium, the ultimate value of the poem will depend in a fair measure on the soundness of the rationality: it is possible, of course, to reason badly, just as it is possible to reason well. But the poet is deliberately employing the connotative content of language as well as the denotative: so that what he must do is make a rational statement about an experience, at the same time employing his language in such a manner as to communicate the emotion which ought to be communicated by that rational understanding of the particular subject. In so far as he is able to do this, the poem will be good; in so far as the subject itself is important, the poem will be great. That is, a poem which merely describes a stone may be excellent but will certainly be minor; whereas a poem which deals with man's contemplation of death and eternity, or with a formative decision of some kind, may be great. It is possible, of course, that the stone may be treated in such a way that it symbolizes something greater than itself; but if this occurs, the poem is about something greater than the stone. The poet is valuable, therefore, in proportion to his ability to apprehend certain kinds of objective truth; in proportion as he is great, he will not resemble ourselves but will resemble what we ought to be. It becomes our business, then, to endeavor to resemble him, and this endeavor is not easy and for this reason few persons make it. Country conversation and colloquial charm are irrelevant to the real issue. The great poets, men like Ben Jonson, Fulke Greville, and Richard Crashaw, have few readers; though some of them, like Milton, are widely admired from a distance. But they offer us, in their best efforts, the finest understanding of human experience to which we have access; some people are able and willing to understand them; and the human intelligence, however precariously, is thus kept alive. If we set up false ideals of human nature, and our best poets judge experience in terms of them and so beguile us into doing likewise, the human intelligence is to that extent diminished.

Frost has said that Emerson is his favorite American poet, and he himself appears to be something of an Emersonian. Emerson was a Romantic pantheist: he identified God with the universe; he taught that impulse comes directly from God and should be obeyed, that through surrender to impulse we become one with God; he taught that reason is man-made and bungling and should be suppressed. In moral and aesthetic doctrine, Emerson was a relativist; his most thorough-going disciples in American literature were Walt Whitman and Hart Crane. In Frost, on the other hand, we find a disciple without Emerson's religious conviction: Frost believes in the rightness of impulse, but does not discuss the pantheistic doctrine which would give authority to impulse; as a result of his belief in impulse, he is of necessity a relativist, but his relativism, apparently since it derives from no intense religious conviction, has resulted mainly in ill-natured eccentricity and in increasing melancholy. He is an Emersonian who has become sceptical and uncertain without having reformed; and the scepticism and uncertainty do not appear to have been so much the result of thought as the result of the impact upon his sensibility of conflicting notions of his own era—they appear to be the result of his having taken the easy way and having drifted with the various currents of his time.

II

I should like first of all to describe a few poems which deal with what in the hands of a more serious writer one could describe as the theme of moral choice. These poems throw more light on Frost as a whole, perhaps, than do any others, and they may serve as an introduction to his work. I have in mind especially three poems from *Mountain Interval*: the introductory piece entitled "The Road Not Taken," the post-scriptive piece entitled "The Sound of the Trees," and the lyrical narrative called "The Hill Wife"; and one poem from *A Further Range*: the poem entitled "The Bearer of Evil Tidings." These poems all have a single theme: the whimsical, accidental, and incomprehensible nature of the formative decision; and I should like to point out that if one takes this view of the formative decision, one has cut oneself off from understanding most of human experience, for in these terms there is nothing to be understood—one can write of human experience with sentimental approval or with sentimental melancholy, but with little else.

"The Road Not Taken," for example, is the poem of a man whom one might fairly call a spiritual drifter; and a spiritual drifter is unlikely to have either the intelligence or the energy to become a major poet. Yet the poem has definite virtues, and these should not be overlooked. In the first place, spiritual drifters exist, they are real; and although their decisions may not be comprehensible, their predicament is comprehensible. The poem renders the experience of such a person, and renders the uncertain melancholy of his plight. Had Frost been a more intelligent man, he might have seen that the plight of the spiritual drifter was not inevitable, he might have judged it in the light of a more comprehensive wisdom. Had he done this, he might have written a greater poem. But his poem is good as far as it goes; the trouble is that it does not go far enough, it is incomplete, and it puts on the reader a burden of critical intelligence which ought to be borne by the poet. We are confronted with a similar critical problem when the Earl of Rochester writes remarkably beautiful poems to invite us to share in the pleasures of drunkenness. The pleasures of drunkenness are real—let no one delude himself on that score—and the Earl of Rochester is one of the most brillian: masters of English verse. But if the pleasures of drunkenness are regarded in what the sentimental critics are wont to term a true perspective, they are seen to be obstacles to other experiences of far greater value, and then they take on the appearance of temptations to sin. Dante would have dealt with these pleasures truly, placing them where they belong in the hierarchy of values; Rochester was not equal to the task, but Rochester gave us a good evaluation of the experience of a man in his predicament as he himself sees it. He is like the demon defined by Aquinas: good in so far as he may be said to exist, but a demon is so far as his existence is incomplete. And like the demon he is also enticing, for he has more than usual powers of persuasion. We are protected against his incompleteness and against his enticements if we understand his limitations, and we can then profit by what he possesses; but without understanding, we may be drawn to emulate him, to form ourselves upon him—we may, in a sense, become possessed by an evil power which is great enough to control us and diminish our own being.

The comparison of Rochester to Frost is unjust in one respect, for Rochester was a consciously vicious man; whereas Robert Frost would not willingly injure anyone. Yet the comparison in other ways is just, for Frost, as I shall show, has willfully refrained from careful thinking and so is largely responsible for his own condition; and his condition is less dramatic and more easily shared by large numbers of his contemporaries than was the condition of Rochester, so that he is probably a greater menace to the general intelligence. Rochester knew himself to be a sinner, and he knew that he would be regarded as one. Frost by a process of devious evasions has convinced himself that he is a wise and virtuous man, and he is regarded as a kind of embodiment of human wisdom by hundreds of thousands of Americans from high school age to the brink of senility. He embodies a common delusion regarding human nature, and he is strongly reinforcing that delusion in the minds of his contemporaries.

"The Sound of the Trees" deals with a longing to depart which has never quite been realized. The trees

> are that which talks of going
> But never gets away.

The poem ends as follows:

> I shall make the reckless choice
> Some day when they are in voice
> And tossing so as to scare
> The white clouds over them on.
> I shall have less to say,
> But I shall be gone.

The poem has the same quality of uncertainty and incomprehension as "The Road Not Taken"; it is written with about the same degree of success, with about the same charm, and with about the same quality of vague melancholy. In considering either of these poems, especially if one compares them even to minor works by sixteenth- and seventeenth-century masters, one will observe not only the limitations of intelligence which I have mentioned, but a quality, slight though it may be, of imprecision in the rendering of the detail and of the total attitude, which is the result of the limitations. Such a poem as Robert Herrick's "Night-Piece to Julia" is as sharp as a knife in comparison. Herrick knew exactly what he was saying and exactly what it was worth. Frost, on the other hand, is mistaking whimsical impulse for moral choice, and the blunder obscures his understanding and even leaves his mood uncertain with regard to the value of the whole business. He is vaguely afraid that he may be neither wrong nor right.

"The Hill Wife" is a less happy specimen than the poems just mentioned. It deals, not with a personal experience of the author, but with a dramatic situation seen from without; and the dramatic crisis is offered as something incomprehensible. The wife leaves her husband because she is lonely on their back-country farm, but there is no clear understanding of her motive; we are told that she is disturbed when the birds leave in the fall, and frightened by a casual tramp, and that a pine near the window obsesses her thoughts. The last section, characteristically entitled "The Impulse," describes her final act as a sudden and unpremeditated one. The poem has an eerie quality, like that of dream or of neurosis, but it has little else. As a study in human relationships, it amounts to nothing, and one has only to compare it to "Eros Turannos" by Robinson to discern its triviality. "The Bearer of Evil Tidings" deals with a similarly casual and sudden decision, although it is a more interesting poem. And one might mention also the poem from *A Witness Tree* entitled "A Serious Step Lightly Taken": the serious step in question is merely the buying of a farm; but the title is characteristic, and the title implies approval and not disapproval—it implies that serious steps ought to be lightly taken. But if serious steps are to be lightly taken, then poetry, at least, is impoverished, and the poet can have very little to say. Most of the world's great poetry has had to do with serious steps seriously taken, and when the seriousness goes from life, it goes from the poetry.

III

I shall consider next some of the more clearly didactic poems, which will reinforce what I have been saying. I should perhaps mention briefly as one of these, a short lyric in *West-Running Brook,* a lyric called "Sand Dunes," of which the clearly stated theme is the Emersonian notion that man can think better if he frees himself wholly from the past. The last poem in the same volume, at least as the volume originally appeared, is called "The Bear." The poem compares the wild bear to the bear in a cage; the uncaged bear is a creature of free impulse and is compared by implication to man as he would be were he guided by impulse; and the caged bear is compared to rational man as he is. The poem is amusing on first reading, but it wears thin with time. The difficulty is this, that satirical poetry is a branch of didactic poetry, for whereas purely didactic poetry endeavors to convince directly, satirical poetry endeavors to convince indirectly by ridiculing what the poet takes to be a deviation from wisdom; and both forms depend rather obviously upon the soundness of the ideas which they expound or assume. Frost tells us in this poem that reasoning man is ridiculous because he appears to labor and to change his mind; and he implies that impulsive man would be a wiser and a nobler creature. The fact of the matter is, however, that impulsive man, if he is restrained, like Frost, by conventions and habits the nature and origins of which he does not understand, is likely to be merely confused, uncertain, and melancholy; and if he is not so restrained may degenerate to madness or to criminality. Within relatively recent years, we have had two tragic examples, in Hart Crane and in Ezra Pound, of what a man of genius can do to himself and to his work by energetically living the life of impulse. It is not foolish to change one's mind; one learns by changing one's mind. Life is a process of revision in the interests of greater understanding, and it is by means of this process that men came down from the trees and out of the caves; and although civilization is very far from what it should be, nevertheless mankind has shown a marked improvement over the past ten thousand years. This improvement is the result of the fact that man is a rational animal, as I believe that a certain Greek once remarked. The uncaged bear, or the reflective caveman, is inferior to Thomas Aquinas and to Richard Hooker, to Dante and to Ben Jonson, and to assert the contrary is merely irresponsible foolishness. Frost then is satirizing the intelligent man from the point of view of the unintelligent; and the more often one reads the poem, the more obvious this fact becomes, and the more trivial the poem appears.

Frost expounds the same ideas more directly still in his poem "To a Thinker," in *A Further Range*. The idea in this poem is the same as that in "The Bear," but is even more plainly stated; we have the commonplace Romantic distrust of reason and trust in instinct. The poem ends as follows:

> So if you find you must repent
> From side to side in argument,
> At least don't use your mind too hard,
> But trust my instinct—I'm a bard.

The poem is badly written, but one couplet is momentarily amusing:

> I own I never really warmed
> To the reformer or reformed.

Yet when we examine it more carefully, there is something almost contemptible about it. There are, of course, reformers and reformers, and many of them have been ludicrous or worse. Frost is invoking the image of the soap-box politician or the street-corner preacher in order to discredit reason. But the word *reform* can be best evaluated if one separates the syllables for a moment. To reform means to re-form. And the progress of civilization has been a process of re-forming human nature. Socrates re-formed the human mind; Jesus re-formed man's moral and religious nature; Aquinas re-formed philosophical method and content; and William the Silent re-formed the idea of the state. Frost endeavors to gain his point by sleight-of-hand; he endeavors to obscure the difference between St. Thomas Aquinas and Pussyfoot Johnson.

Even Frost, with his instinct to guide him, is not proof against wavering, however. In the same volume with the poem just described is a poem called "The White-Tailed Hornet," in which Frost describes the activities of a hornet and the errors it commits under the guidance of instinct, and he reprehends mankind for having engaged in "downward comparisons":

> As long on earth
> As our comparisons were stoutly upward
> With gods and angels, we were men at least,
> But little lower than the gods and angels.
> But once comparisons were yielded downward,
> Once we began to see our images
> Reflected in the mud and even dust,
> 'Twas disillusion upon disillusion.
> We were lost piecemeal to the animals
> Like people thrown out to delay the wolves.

Yet we have seen Frost himself engaging in downward comparisons, and we shall see him doing it again. This is the only poem in Frost's works which seems to represent a conscious rejection of his usual ideas, and this poem, as I have said, even occurs in the same volume with the poem which I quoted previously, "To a Thinker." It is possible that Frost shares the contempt felt by Emerson and by Whitman for consistency, or he may be so inexperienced a thinker as to be unaware of his inconsistency; the point is of little importance, for he nowhere else takes up this argument.

Frost has something to say of the relationship of the individual to society. His most extensive poem on this subject is called "Build Soil—A Political Pastoral," and was delivered at Columbia University, May 31, 1932, before the national party conventions of that year. It will be remembered that these were the conventions which led to the first election of Franklin D. Roosevelt, and that the time was one of the darkest periods in the history of the nation. The poem is Frost's most ambitious effort to deal with his social, political, and economic views. As to his economic views, he says that if he were dictator of the country:

> I'd let things take their course
> And then I'd claim the credit for the outcome.

This statement, if it means anything at all, is a statement of belief in an unrestrained laissez-faire system, of the sort that Emerson would have approved; a belief that if things are left alone they must come right. It represents a doctrine of political drifting which corresponds to the doctrine of personal drifting which we have already seen; in practice, it could lead only to the withdrawal from public affairs of the citizen not concerned primarily with personal aggrandizement, and to the surrender of the nation to the unscrupulous go-getter, who, though he may not be a drifter, is not governed by admirable aims. It is similarly an obscurantist doctrine: it implies that this realm of human activity, like others, cannot be dealt with rationally and is better if not understood. As to the behavior of the private citizen, Frost says:

> I bid you to a one-man revolution—
> The only revolution that is coming.
> We're too unseparate out among each other—
> With goods to sell and notions to impart . . .
> We congregate embracing from distrust
> As much as love, and too close in to strike
> And so be very striking. Steal away
> The song says. Steal away and stay away.
> Don't join too many gangs. Join few if any.
> Join the United States and join the family—
> But not much in between unless a college. . . .

The individual is thus advised against any kind of political activity in a time of national collapse. The difficulties of effective political action are obvious; the English-speaking peoples have been struggling with the problems of constitutional government for centuries. But if the reality of the difficulties results in our stealing away from them, society will be taken over, as I have said, by the efficient scoundrels who are always ready to take over when everyone else abdicates. In a dictatorship by scoundrels, the Frosts and the Thoreaus, the amateur anarchists and village eccentrics, would find life somewhat more difficult than they have found it to date. Frost objects in the last passage to the commerce of minds, and he objects to it earlier in the poem:

> Suppose someone comes near me who in rate
> Of speech and thinking is so much my better
> I am imposed on, silenced and discouraged.
> Do I submit to being supplied by him
> As the more economical producer?
> No, I unostentatiously move off
> Far enough for my thought-flow to resume.

It does not occur to Frost that he might learn from his betters and improve himself; he can see only two possibilities in his relationship with them—he can be silenced by them or he can ignore them and proceed as before. There is the implication in this passage that his personal "thought-flow" is valuable merely because it is his own, that it should remain uncontaminated. He believes that the man and the nation equally will reach their fullest development through a kind of retreat to passivity, through letting things happen as they may with a minimum of influence from without.

The same sentimental dislike for society, for community of interest, can be found in the poem called "The Egg and the Machine," a poem appended in the *Collected Poems* to the group called *West-Running Brook*. The poem tells of a Thoreau-like adventurer who is exasperated to encounter a railroad running through his favorite marsh. After a locomotive passes him, he proceeds to find a nestful of turtle eggs, and Frost writes:

> If there was one egg in it there were nine,
> Torpedo-like, with shell of gritty leather
> All packed in sand to wait the trump together.
> 'You'd better not disturb me any more,'
> He told the distance, 'I am armed for war.
> The next machine that has the power to pass
> Will get this plasm in its goggle-glass.'

Here are several familiar Romantic attitudes: resentment at being unable to achieve the absolute privacy which Frost names as a primary desideratum in "Build Soil," the sentimental regard for the untouched wilderness (the untouched wilderness would provide absolute privacy for the unique Romantic), and the sentimental hatred for the machine. I am willing to admit, in connection with the last matter, that machinery is sometimes far from beautiful, both in itself and in some of its effects; but its benefits have been overwhelmingly great, and the literary farmer in Vermont could scarcely hope to subsist either as farmer or as writer without its help, any more than he could hope to subsist unless a good many people faced moral and political realities; and it is curiously unjust that the locomotive, that patient and innocuous draft horse of civilization, should be selected to symbolize the viciousness of machinery. Frost's real objection to the machine, I suspect, is its social nature; it requires and facilitates cooperation, and Frost is unwilling to recognize its respectability mainly for this reason.

There have been other literary works dealing with resentment at the machine and the changes it has introduced; the resentment I believe to be foolish, but in certain settings it may have a tragic if barbarous dignity. Bret Harte wrote a story called "Maruja," which tells of the first railroad to proceed through the San Antonio Ranch in what is now Los Altos, California, and of the resentment of the old Indian overseer at this destruction of the old order. The Indian, Pereo, whose resentment against the incoming Anglo-Americans had developed to the point of paranoia, and who had murdered one of the newcomers by roping him about the neck from horseback and dragging him to death, rode out against the first locomotive, roped it, and tried to drag it from the tracks, and was himself dragged and killed. The negro ballad of John Henry tells of a "steel-driving man" who broke his back in the attempt to out-hammer a steam-drill. These actions are naïve and primitive, but they are heroic in a fashion, they at least have the seriousness of honest violence. Frost's protagonist, however, expresses his feelings by threatening to throw

a turtle-egg into the headlight of a locomotive. The turtle-egg, of course, may
be intended as something more than a simple missile: it is "plasm," raw life,
and hence capable of confounding (although only symbolically) the mechanical product of human reason. The trouble is again that the symbols will not
stand inspection: the locomotive cannot be equated with human reason, for
it is merely something created by human reason to facilitate higher activities;
there is nothing either of wisdom or of greatness in the egg of a turtle; and the
locomotive and human reason about equally would be quite unperturbed by
the egg of a turtle. As we pursue the symbolism, we are left where we began,
with a petulant and self-righteous gesture, a feeble joke.

There is a kind of half dramatic, half didactic poem occasionally, of which
I shall mention two examples: "West-Running Brook" and *A Masque of
Reason*. The first of these is a brief affair in the form of a dialogue between a
young husband and wife who apparently have just established themselves on
a farm next to a brook which runs west instead of east; they observe a ripple
in the brook, in which the water is thrown upward and apparently backward
against the current. The husband, in certain lines which are the chief part of
the poem, comments upon the ripple:

> Speaking of contraries, see how the brook
> In that white wave runs counter to itself.
> It is from that in water we were from
> Long, long before we were from any creature.
> Here we, in our impatience of the steps,
> Get back to the beginning of beginnings,
> The stream of everything that runs away . . .
> It has this throwing backward on itself
> So that the fall of most of it is always
> Raising a little, sending up a little.
> Our life runs down in sending up the clock.
> The brook runs down in sending up our life.
> The sun runs down in sending up the brook.
> And there is something sending up the sun.
> It is this backward motion toward the source
> Against the stream that most we see ourselves in,
> The tribute of the current to the source.
> It is from this in nature we are from.

The theology of this passage, if we may call it theology, is tenuous and incomplete; it is what a certain kind of critic would call suggestive, rather than
definitive; there is, in brief, very little to it. Frost seems to have suspected this,
for he did not let his meditation on the ripple stand alone on its merits; he
framed it in the dialogue I have mentioned and made his young people
responsible for it. Yet the people are not depicted as characters, and their

remarks lead to no dramatic action; the meditation gives the momentary illusion that the characters are more important than they are; the conversational
framework gives the momentary illusion that the meditation is more important than it is. Thus the structure of the poem is actually a piece of deception,
and the substance of the poem is negligible.

A Masque of Reason is the same kind of poem on a larger scale. The characters are God, the Devil, Job, and Job's wife. The scene is "A fair oasis in the
purest desert"; the time is the Day of Judgment. Job and his wife suddenly
discover the presence of the Burning Bush. She says:

> There's a strange light on everything today.

> Job: The myrrh tree gives it. Smell the rosin burning?
> The ornaments the Greek artificers
> Made for the Emperor Alexius,
> The Star of Bethlehem, the pomegranates,
> The birds, seem all on fire with Paradise.
> And hark, the gold enameled nightingales
> Are singing. Yes, and look, the Tree is troubled.
> Someone's caught in the branches.

> Wife: So there is.
> He can't get out.

> Job: He's loose! He's out!

> Wife: It's God.
> I'd know him by Blake's picture anywhere.
> Now what's he doing?
> Job: Pitching throne, I guess.
> Here by our atoll.

> Wife: Something Byzantine.

> (The throne's a ply-wood flat, prefabricated,
> That God pulls lightly upright on its hinges
> And stands beside, supporting it in place.)

This brief passage gives a clue to the nature of the whole poem. Job's first
speech above is a piece of remarkable rhetoric: there is nothing else in the
poem to equal it. It reminds one of Yeats, especially of Yeats's brilliant but
whimsical poem called "Sailing to Byzantium." From that passage onward,
through the references to Blake and to the plywood throne, we have details
which are offered merely for the shock of cleverness; the details are irrelevant
to any theme discernible in the poem. Frost, the rustic realist of North of
Boston, appears in his old age as a standard exemplar of irresponsible Roman-

tic irony, of the kind of irony that has degenerated steadily from the moderately low level of Laforgue, through Pound, Eliot, Cummings, and their younger imitators. The method is employed throughout the poem.

The poem falls roughly into three parts. The first of these deals with God's first explanation to Job of the treatment Job had been accorded in life. God tells him:

> You helped me
> Establish once for all the principle
> There's no connection man can reason out
> Between his just deserts and what he gets.
> Virtue may fail and wickedness succeed. . . .
> You realize by now the part you played
> To stultify the Deuteronomist
> And change the tenor of religious thought.
> My thanks are to you for releasing me
> From moral bondage to the human race.
> The only free will there at first was man's,
> Who could do good or evil as he chose.
> I had no choice but I must follow him
> With forfeits and rewards he understood—
> Unless I liked to suffer loss of worship.
> I had to prosper good and punish evil.
> You changed all that. You set me free to reign.

So far as the ideas in this passage are concerned, the passage belongs to the fideistic tradition of New England Calvinism; the ideas can be found in more than one passage in Jonathan Edwards, as well as elsewhere. The carefully flippant tone, however, is something else; it belongs to the tradition of Romantic irony which I have already mentioned, and is used to make the ideas seem trivial. The ideas and the tone together express the Romantic ennui or disillusionment which is born of spiritual laziness, the laziness which is justified by the Romantic doctrine that one can best apprehend the truth by intuition and without labor. One can find the same ennui, expressed in various ways, in Henry Adams, in Laforgue, in Eliot, and in scores of others.

The second passage of chief importance is the one in which God revises his explanation. Job insists that God's explanation is not the true one, that God is concealing something, and God makes the following admission:

> I'm going to tell Job why I tortured him
> And trust it won't be adding to the torture.
> I was just showing off to the Devil, Job,
> As is set forth in chapters One and Two.
> (*Job takes a few steps pacing.*) Do you mind?
> (*God eyes him anxiously.*)

Job: No. No, I mustn't.
'Twas human of You. I expected more
Than I could understand and what I get
Is almost less than I can understand.
But I don't mind. Let's leave it as it stood.
The point was it was none of my concern.
I stick to that. But talk about confusion . . .

The general idea is the same as in the preceding passage, but the debasement
of the attitude toward the idea becomes now a matter of explicit statement as
well as of stylistic tone. There is no understanding of good and evil in themselves, of the metaphysical questions involved. Good is submission to an
anthropomorphic and undignified God and is made to seem preposterous.
Evil is made equally preposterous, and for similar reasons. The poem resembles
"The Bear," but is on a larger scale. If these concepts of good and evil were
the only concepts available, or if they were the best concepts available, then
Frost's satire would be justified. But they are not, and in reading the poem one
can only be appalled at Frost's willful ignorance, at his smug stupidity.

In spite of the close relationship between the two passages which I have
quoted, however, the poem is far from unified. These two passages are separated by various outbursts of indignation on the part of Job's wife at the way
female witches are treated, in spite of the fact that male prophets have always
been received with honor; and there are other minor excursions. The concluding pages are devoted to the appearance of the Devil, who is called up by
God, so that Job's wife may photograph the three main actors in the old drama
as a memento. This passage is in itself an excursion from the main theme, but
it is employed to permit subsidiary excursions:

God: Don't *you* twit. He's unhappy. Church neglect
And figurative use have pretty well
Reduced him to a shadow of himself.

Job's Wife: *That* explains why he's so diaphanous
And easy to see through. But where's he off to?
I thought there were to be festivities
Of some kind. We could have charades.

God: He has his business he must be about.
Job mentioned him and so I brought him in
More to give his reality its due
Than anything.

Job's Wife: He's very real to me
And always will be. Please don't go. Stay, stay
But to the evensong and having played
Together we will go with you along.

There are who won't have had enough of you
If you go now. Look how he takes no steps!
He isn't really going, yet he's leaving.

Job: (*Who has been standing dazed with new ideas*)
He's on that tendency that like the Gulf Stream,
Only of sand, not water, runs through here.
It has a rate distinctly different
From the surrounding desert; just today
I stumbled over it and got tripped up.

Job's Wife: Oh, yes, that tendency! Oh, do come off it.
Don't let it carry you away. I hate
A tendency. The minute you get on one
It seems to start right off accelerating. . . .

In this passage, the satire is aimed at the word *tendency*, but the exact meaning of the word is not clear: it may mean a trivial fashion; it may mean an
intellectual movement; it may indicate that Frost is unable to distinguish between a trivial fashion and an intellectual movement, just as he is unable to
differentiate among reformers. The mutilated fragment from Herrick serves
no purpose, but is merely an aimless effort to be funny. The poem as a whole
is at loose ends; no single part of it is intelligent or even tries to be intelligent.
It is a curious performance to signalize the seventieth birthday of a poet of so
great a reputation. It is matched in triviality and general ineptitude by the
collection of short poems entitled *Steeple Bush* and published more recently.

The best of the didactic poems is the one called "The Lesson for Today."
The poem is for the most part a suavely satirical comment upon that school of
contemporary criticism which holds that the modern poet is condemned to
mediocrity because of the degeneracy of the age, and to this extent the poem
is one with which it is hard not to sympathize. Frost addresses his hypothetical
poet of the court of Charles the Great as follows:

I can just hear you call your Palace class:
Come learn the Latin Eheu for alas.
You may not want to use it and you may.
O paladins, the lesson for today
Is how to be unhappy yet polite.
And at the summons Roland, Olivier,
And every sheepish paladin and peer,
Being already more than proved in fight,
Sits down in school to try if he can write
Like Horace in the true Horatian vein,
Yet like a Christian disciplined to bend
His mind to thinking always of the end.
Memento mori and obey the Lord.

Art and religion love the sombre chord.
Earth's a hard place in which to save the soul,
And could it be brought under state control,
So automatically we all were saved,
Its separateness from Heaven could be waived;
It might as well at once be kingdom-come.
(Perhaps it will be next millenium.)

From this subject, however, the poem wanders into a brief discussion of mortality in general and the poet's concern with the subject; and after that topic the poem closes on the poet's epitaph for himself:

I hold your doctrine of Memento Mori.
And were an epitaph to be my story
I'd have a short one ready for my own.
I would have written of me on my stone:
I had a lover's quarrel with the world.

These two transitions are casual rather than structural, and the poem falls badly apart. The last lines, moreover, are extremely bad. There is a weak sentimentality about them which one perceives easily, but the reason for which deserves mention. There are good reasons for quarreling with the world, or at least with large segments of it; much of the world is evil, and the evil had better be recognized and taken seriously. If the quarrel can be reduced to a lover's quarrel, it is not serious. It is as if one said to a murderer: "After all, you are human, and you have a perfect right to your own opinions, attitudes, and behavior; we are all human and should respect and admire each other." The principle back of the final line is vicious and corrupts the line. And the intellectual vagueness which is responsible for this weak ending is responsible likewise for the fragmentary structure of the poem and for the weakness of the other poems which I have been considering.

Frost, as far as we have examined him, then, is a poet who holds the following views: he believes that impulse is trustworthy and reason contemptible, that formative decisions should be made casually and passively, that the individual should retreat from cooperative action with his kind, should retreat not to engage in intellectual activity but in order to protect himself from the contamination of outside influence, that affairs manage themselves for the best if left alone, that ideas of good and evil need not be taken very seriously. These views are sure to be a hindrance to self-development, and they effectually cut Frost off from any really profound understanding of human experience, whether political, moral, metaphysical, or religious. The result in the didactic poems is the perversity and incoherence of thought; the result in the narrative poems is either slightness of subject or a flat and uninteresting apprehension of the subject; the result in the symbolic lyrics is a disturbing dislocation between the descriptive surface, which is frequently lovely, and the ultimate meaning, which is usually sentimental and unacceptable. The result in nearly all the poems is a measure of carelessness in the style, sometimes small and sometimes great, but usually evident: the conversational manner will naturally suit a poet who takes all experience so casually, and it is only natural that the conversational manner should often become very conversational indeed.

It is worth while to mention one other poem in connection with Frost's retreat from the serious subject. The poem I have in mind is called "The Times Table." The poem deals with a farmer who is given to commenting on death and who is reproved by Frost: Frost remarks that such comments should not be made

> Unless our purpose is doing harm,
> And then I know of no better way
> To close a road, abandon a farm,
> Reduce the births of the human race,
> And bring back nature in people's place.

We should remember that Frost is a poet and normally speaks with full consciousness of his role as poet; it is reasonable to assume that this poem applies to the poet as well as to other persons. The poet, then, should not deal with death or with comparably disturbing topics, because these topics distress and discourage people. Yet I wish to point out that all people die, that human life is filled with tragedy, and that commonly the tragedies accumulate all but overwhelmingly toward the end. To ignore the tragic subject is to leave oneself unprepared for the tragic experience; it is likely to lead to disaster and collapse. It is the business of the poet, let me repeat, to understand his subjects, and as far as may be the most difficult and important subjects, in rational terms, and at the same time to communicate the feeling which ought to be communicated by that rational understanding. The great poet judges the tragic subject completely, that is, rationally and emotionally; the nature of the human mind is such that we can enter the poet's mind by way of his poem, if we are willing to make the effort, and share his judgment. In this way we may gain both understanding and strength, for the human mind is so made that it is capable of growth and of growth in part through its own self-directed effort. This is the virtue of poetry; in so far as it is good, and we understand both its goodness and its limitations, it enables us to achieve a more nearly perfect and comprehensive being, to reduce that margin of spiritual privation which is evil. But Frost advises us to turn away from serious topics, and for the greater part he confines himself to minor topics. The major topics impinge upon his personal experience, however, for after all they are unavoidable; but his treatment of them is usually whimsical, sentimental, and evasive; and in his later years his poetry is more and more pervaded by an obscure melancholy which he can neither control nor understand.

IV

Yet Frost has a genuine gift for writing, as I have pointed out, and this gift emerges more clearly in his later work than in his earlier, though still hesitantly and momentarily. The view of human nature which we have seen Frost to hold is one that must lead of necessity to a feeling that the individual man is small, lost, and unimportant in the midst of a vast and changing universe. This feeling is expressed in the well-known poem entitled "On Going Unnoticed." The nostalgic love for the chaotic and the dream-like, which Frost inherits from the Romantic tradition, along with an habitual but unreasoned hesitancy or fear, which is the heritage of the earlier New England, keeps Frost looking two ways, unable to move decisively in either direction. He is neither a truly vigorous Romantic, such as Hart Crane, nor a truly reactionary Classicist, such as E. A. Robinson. He cannot decide whether to go or to stay, and the result is uncertainty and increasing melancholy. One may see the same difficulty in "Tree at My Window." Frost sees his own mind as similar to the vague dream-head of the tree, the thing next most diffuse to cloud, and the feeling of the poem is one of a melancholy longing to share the dream-like experience more fully. One can trace the manner in which Frost has arrived at this state of mind, and to that extent the poem is comprehensible. The feeling appears to be rendered more or less truly; that is, it seems to be an acceptable version of the feelings of a man in this predicament. But the poet does not understand the nature or the limitations of the predicament; and to that extent the poem is incomplete and not quite sure of itself. Like "The Road Not Taken" it puts on the reader a burden of critical intelligence which ought to have been borne more fully by the poet; and if the reader is not capable of the necessary intelligence, the poem is likely to draw him into a similar state of mind.

"The Last Mowing" deals with the same subject, and even more beguilingly. It describes a meadow which is being abandoned and is about to be taken over by the wild flowers before the more massive wilderness moves in:

> The place for the moment is ours,
> For you, oh tumultuous flowers
> To go to waste and go wild in,
> All shapes and colors of flowers,
> I needn't call you by name.

The next to the last line of this poem—"All shapes and colors of flowers"— is a curious triumph of rhetoric. Shape and color are named as pure abstractions; no particular shape or color is given; and what we get is an image of the shapeless and the shadowy, of haunting confusion, of longing for something unrealizable, of the fields of asphodel. This poem in its subdued and melancholy, yet somehow violent, abandonment to chaos, is one of the most explicit statements of Frost's predicament, and one of the most moving of them. "Spring Pools," from the same volume, appears to treat the same subject, but less explicitly. In paraphrase, it is a warning to the summer woods not to drink up the pools of snow water and the flowers that grow from them—these flowery waters and these watery flowers—and organize them into something greater. It is a poem on the love for the small, the fleeting, and the elusive experience of the late Romantic; in this respect, and in respect to the extraordinary sensitivity of its execution, it reminds me strongly of a poem by Paul Verlaine: *"Le Piano que baise une main frêle."* Superficially considered, the poem by Verlaine deals with a subject which is very different and more obviously decadent; but decadence is a state of mind, not a matter of the landscape which happens to provide the symbols, and in spiritual quality the two poems are remarkably similar.

The symbolic lyrics which I have been discussing are all to be found in the volume called *West-Running Brook,* the fifth collection. There is one poem in the volume, the sonnet entitled "Acquainted with the Night," which surpasses any poem thus far mentioned and which seems to me one of the two or three best poems that Frost has written. Superficially, the poem deals with the feeling of loneliness which one has when walking late at night in a strange city; but symbolically it deals with the poet's loneliness in a strange and obscure world, and the clock which tells him that the time is neither wrong nor right is a symbol of the relativism which causes his melancholy. The understanding of his predicament appears to be greater in this poem than in most of the others; he knows, at least, that it is a predicament and realizes the state of mind to which it has brought him. In the seventh volume, *A Witness Tree,* there is an even more impressive piece entitled "The Most of It." This poem represents a momentary insight into the vast and brute indifference of nature, the nature toward which Frost has cherished so sentimental a feeling through so many poems. For a moment the poet appears to be appalled. The poem deals with a protagonist who seems to have cultivated solitude, like Frost, and who heard only the echo of his own voice in the wilderness but who longed for a personal reply from nature. The reply, when it came, was not the one he had wanted. One morning he saw a splash on the far side of the lake, and something swimming toward him, and then:

> Instead of proving human when it neared
> And some one else additional to him,
> As a great buck it powerfully appeared,
> Pushing the crumpled water up ahead,
> And landed pouring like a waterfall,

> And stumbled through the rocks with horny tread,
> And forced the underbrush—and that was all.

Frost's buck has much the same kind of symbolic grandeur as the apocryphal beast in "The Second Coming," by Yeats, and he has the advantage of greater reality; the style combines descriptive precision with great concentration of meaning and at the same time is wholly free from decoration, ineptitude, and other irrelevancy. The poem gives one some idea of how great a poet Frost might conceivably have been, had he been willing to use his mind instead of letting it wither. In this poem especially, and to some extent in "Acquainted with the Night," the poet confronts his condition fairly and sees it for what it is, but the insight is momentary: he neither proceeds from this point to further understanding nor even manages to retain the realization that he has achieved. Much else in *A Witness Tree* is similar to the earlier work, and the next and last two books, *A Masque of Reason* (which I have described in some detail) and *Steeple Bush*, are his feeblest and least serious efforts.

There are a few other poems in the later books, however, which are impressive, and they ought to be mentioned in justice to their author, although little would be gained from a detailed account of them. In *A Further Range* there is a moderately long lyric entitled "The Vindictives," which deals with the looting of the Inca empire by the Spaniards, and with the way in which the Incas in return sacked their own country and buried the gold.

> One Inca prince on the rack,
> And late in his last hour alive,
> Told them in what lake to dive
> To seek what they seemed so to want.
> They dived and nothing was found.
> He told them to dive till they drowned.
> The whole fierce conquering pack
> Hunted and tortured and raged.
> There were suns of story and vaunt
> They searched for into Brazil
> Their tongues hanging out unassuaged.

This is probably the only poem in Frost in which one can find anything resembling heroic action; the poem is motivated by a simple and honest hatred of brutality and injustice so obvious that they cannot be overlooked. The hatred in question, however, can be justified only by certain ideas, the ideas of Christian and classical philosophy, which, although they are a part of Frost's background and influence him to this extent, he has during all of his career neglected or explicitly maligned. The poem is a little loose in construction and is occasionally careless in style; but it has an honesty and a controlled violence which make it very impressive. In *A Witness Tree* there are several other fine but minor lyrics which stay in one's mind, especially "The Rabbit Hunter," "Never Again Would Birds' Song Be the Same," and "I Could Give All to Time." "Come In" is a memorable lyric, but perhaps it contains too much of Frost's professional and somewhat sentimental charm.

In *A Witness Tree* there is a narrative of considerable interest, "The Discovery of the Madeiras." It retells a story from Hakluyt about a pair of lovers who elope from England; the captain of their vessel, who had been a slaver, tells the man a singularly brutal story about the murder of a pair of Negroes who were lovers; the man repeats it to his lady, and she withdraws to her cabin, becomes ill, and eventually dies. In style the poem resembles "The Vindictives," but it has less force at its best and is often undistinguished. It is written in eight-syllable lines rhyming in couplets and has something of the effect of a modern and sophisticated ballad. But the best of the old border ballads differ in one important respect: they deal, commonly, with an important decision consciously made, and with the resultant action, which is frequently violent but which is also important, either for good or for evil; Frost's poem deals with the accidental impingement of a brutal fact upon a morbid sensibility and the collapse of the sensibility. Frost's poem to this extent is the product of a decadent state of mind. Frost runs up against another difficulty in this poem which he encounters in all his narratives: the virtual impossibility of writing a short and purely realistic narrative which shall attain great power. The narrative, if it is to be short, must be symbolical or allegorical, it must be packed with the power of generalization; if it is to be purely realistic, it must be developed and explored fully in its capacity as a particular history. The short story writer in prose meets the same difficulty, but the short story is a longer and freer form and so has a better chance of success; and furthermore it makes a more modest claim upon our expectations, so that we are less likely to trouble ourselves about its limits.

V

These remarks have been unfair to Frost in certain respects. I have quoted most extensively from his didactic poems, and especially from those in blank verse. Frost is at his worst in didactic writing, in spite of his fondness for it: his ideas are impossible and his style is exceptionally shoddy. Furthermore, although Frost is frequently very skillful in the handling of short rhymed forms, he is extremely inept in managing blank verse; in blank verse his theory of conversational style shows itself at its worst—the rhythms are undistinguished and are repetitious to the point of deadly monotony. But it is in these poems that Frost states his ideas most unmistakably, and it is necessary to understand the ideas to form an estimate of him at all. He is at his best, as regards style, in the short rhymed lyric, but his short lyrics are less explicit in stating their themes, and unless one comes to them with a clear concept of

Frost's principal themes one may overlook the themes or mistake them. Frost is at his best in such poems as "The Most of It" and "Acquainted with the Night," in which he seems to be more or less aware of the untenability of his own position and to face his difficulty, or as "The Vindictives," in which as the result of a fortunate accident of some kind he is able simply to ignore his usual themes and write as if he had never heard of them. The bulk of his really memorable work, however, is to be found among the symbolic lyrics, of which "The Last Mowing" and "Spring Pools" are excellent examples, lyrics in which the descriptive element is beautifully handled, in which the feeling is communicated with a sufficient degree of success to make them unforgettable but with so great a degree of imprecision as to make them curiously unsatisfactory. For the feeling does not arise merely from the contemplation of the natural objects described: if it did so, it would be too strong and too mysteriously elusive for its origins; the feeling arises mainly from the concepts of which the natural objects are the symbolic vehicles, and those concepts, as I have shown, are unacceptable, and when one tries to project them clearly into terms of human action are unimaginable. Frost's instinctualism, his nostalgia for dream and chaos, are merely the symptoms of sentimental obscurantism when, as in Frost's work, they are dealt with lightly and whimsically, but if taken seriously, as in the work of Crane and Pound, they may lead to more serious difficulties. They do not lead toward intelligence, no matter how far the individual devotee may travel in their company; they lead away from intelligence. They lead away from the true comprehension of human experience which makes for great, or even for successful, poetry. The element of the unimaginable, and hence of the imprecise, which lurks in the theme of "The Last Mowing" will make it forever, and in spite of its real and extraordinary virtues, a very imperfectly successful poem; this poem simply will not stand comparison with such pieces, for example, as "Low Barometer," by Robert Bridges, as Howard Baker's poem on Psyche, or as J. V. Cunningham's epigrams on Swift and on the calculus. "The Last Mowing" will for some years be a more popular poem than these, however, for, as I have said, Frost's confusion is similar to that of the public, and most readers of poetry still regard poetry as a vague emotional indulgence: they do not take poetry seriously and they dislike serious poetry.

Frost, then, may be described as a good poet in so far as he may be said to exist, but a dangerous influence in so far as his existence is incomplete. He is in no sense a great poet, but he is at times a distinguished and valuable poet. In order to evaluate his work and profit by it, however, we must understand him far better than he understands himself, and this fact indicates a very serious weakness in his talent. If we do not so understand him, his poetry is bound to reinforce some of the most dangerous tendencies of our time; his weakness is commonly mistaken for wisdom, his vague and sentimental feel-

ing for profound emotion, as his reputation and the public honors accorded
him plainly testify. He is the nearest thing we have to a poet laureate, a national poet; and this fact is evidence of the community of thought and feeling
between Frost and a very large part of the American literary public. The principles which have saved some part of Frost's talent, the principles of Greek
and Christian thought, are principles which are seldom openly defended and
of which the implications and ramifications are understood by relatively few
of our contemporaries, by Frost least of all; they operate upon Frost at a distance, through social inheritance, and he has done his best to adopt principles
which are opposed to them. The principles which have hampered Frost's development, the principles of Emersonian and Thoreauistic Romanticism, are
the principles which he has openly espoused, and they are widespread in our
culture. Until we understand these last and the dangers inherent in them and
so abandon them in favor of better, we are unlikely to produce many poets
greater than Frost, although a few poets may have intelligence enough to work
clear of such influences; and we are likely to deteriorate more or less rapidly
both as individuals and as a nation.

From *The Sewanee Review,* Vol. LVI (Autumn,
1948), pp. 564–596. Reprinted by permission of
the author and editor.

Robinson Jeffers
[1930]

It is difficult to write of Mr. Jeffers' latest book[1] without discussing his former
volumes; after his first collection he deals chiefly with one theme in all of his
poems; and all of his works illustrate a single problem, a spiritual malady of
considerable significance. Mr. Jeffers is theologically a kind of monist; he envisages, as did Wordsworth, Nature as Deity; but his Nature is the Nature of
the physics textbook and not of the rambling botanist—Mr. Jeffers seems to
have taken the terminology of modern physics more literally than it is meant
by its creators. Nature, or God, is thus a kind of self-sufficient mechanism, of
which man is an offshoot, but from which man is cut off by his humanity (just
what gave rise to this humanity, which is absolutely severed from all connection with God, is left for others to decide): there is consequently no mode of
communication between the consciousness of man and the mode of existence
of God; God is praised adequately only by the screaming demons that make
up the atom. Man, if he accepts this dilemma as necessary, is able to choose

[1] *Dear Judas,* by Robinson Jeffers. New York: Horace Liveright, 1929.

between two modes of action: he may renounce God and rely on his humanity, or he may renounce his humanity and rely on God.

Mr. Jeffers preaches the second choice: union with God, oblivion, the complete extinction of one's humanity, is the only good he is able to discover; and life, as such, is "incest," an insidious and destructive evil. So much, says Mr. Jeffers by implication, for Greek and Christian ethics. Now the mysticism of, say, San Juan de la Cruz offers at least the semblance of a spiritual, a human, discipline as a preliminary to union with Divinity; but for Mr. Jeffers a simple and mechanical device lies always ready; namely, suicide, a device to which he has not resorted.

In refusing to take this logical step, however, Mr. Jeffers illustrates one of a very interesting series of romantic compromises. The romantic of the ecstatic-pantheist type denies life, yet goes on living; nearly all romantics decry the intellect and philosophy, yet they offer justifications (necessarily foggy and fragmentary) of their attitude; they deride literary "technique" (the mastery of, and development of the sensitivity to, relationships between words, so that these relationships may extend almost illimitably the vocabulary) yet they write (of necessity, carelessly, with small efficiency). Not all romantics are guilty of all of these confusions, nor, doubtless, is Mr. Jeffers; but all of these confusions are essentially romantic—they are very natural developments of moral monism. And Mr. Jeffers, having decried human life as such, and having denied the worth of the rules of the game, endeavors to write narrative and dramatic poems—poems, in other words, dealing with people who are playing the game. Jesus, the hero of *Dear Judas*, speaking apparently for Mr. Jeffers, says that the secret reason for the doctrine of forgiveness is that all men are driven by the mechanism-God to act as they do, that they are entirely helpless; yet he adds in the next breath that this secret must be guarded, for if it were given out, men would run amuck, would get out of hand—*they would begin acting differently.*

The Women at Point Sur is a perfect laboratory of Mr. Jeffers' philosophy. Barclay, an insane divine, preaches Mr. Jeffers' religion, and his disciples, acting upon it, become emotional mechanisms, lewd and twitching conglomerations of plexi, their humanity annulled. Human experience, in these circumstances, having necessarily and according to the doctrine no meaning, there can be and is no necessary sequence of events: every act is equivalent to every other; every act is at the peak of hysteria; most of the incidents could be shuffled around into varying sequences without violating anything save, perhaps, Mr. Jeffers' private sense of their relative intensity. Since the poem is his, of course, such a private sense is legitimate enough; the point is that this is not a narrative, nor a dramatic, but a lyrical criterion. A successful lyrical poem of one hundred and seventy-five pages is unlikely, for the essence of lyrical expression is concentration; but it is at least theoretically possible. The difficulty is that the lyric achieves its effect by the generalization of emotion (that is, by the separation of the emotion from the personal history that gives rise to it in actual concrete experience) and by the concentration of expression. Narrative can survive in a measure without concentration, or intensity of detail, provided the narrative logic is detailed and compelling, as in the case of Balzac, though it is only wise to add that this occurs most often in prose. Now Mr. Jeffers, as I have pointed out, has abandoned narrative logic with the theory of ethics, and he has never achieved, in addition, a close and masterly style. His writing is loose, turgid, and careless; like most anti-intellectualists, he relies on his feelings alone and has no standard of criticism for them outside of themselves. There are occasional good flashes in his poems, and to these I shall return later, but they are very few, are very limited in their range of feeling and in their subject matter, and they are very far between. Mr. Jeffers has no remaining method of sustaining his lyric, then, other than the employment of an accidental (i.e., non-narrative) chain of anecdotes (i.e., details that are lyrically impure); his philosophical doctrine and his artistic dilemma alike decree that these shall be anecdotes of hysteria. By this method Mr. Jeffers continually *lays claim* to a high pitch of emotion which has no narrative support (that is, support of the inevitable accumulation of experience), nor lyrical support (that is, support of the intense perception of pure, or transferable, emotion), which has, in short, no support at all, and which is therefore simply unmastered and self-inflicted hysteria.

Cawdor alone of Mr. Jeffers' poems contains a plot that in its rough outlines might be sound, and *Cawdor* likewise contains his best poetry; the poem as a whole, and in spite of the confused treatment of the woman, is moving, and the lines describing the seals at dawn are fine, as are the two or three last lines of the apotheosis of the eagle. Most of the preceding material in the latter passage, however, like most of the material in the sections that give Mr. Jeffers' notions of the post-mortem experience of man, are turgid, repetitious, arbitrary, and unconvincing. The plot itself is blurred for lack of stylistic finish (that is, for lack of ability on the part of the poet to see every detail of sense and movement incisively down to the last preposition, the last comma, as every detail *is* seen in Racine or Shakespeare); and it remains again a fair question whether a moral monist *can* arrive at any clear conclusions about the values of a course of action, since he denies the existence of any conceivable standard of values within the strict limits of human life as such. In *The Tower Beyond Tragedy* Mr. Jeffers takes a ready-made plot, the Clytemnestra-Orestes situation, which is particularly strong dramatically, because Orestes is forced to choose between two sins, the murder of his mother and the refusal to avenge his father. But at the very last moment, in Mr. Jeffers' version, Orestes is converted to Mr. Jeffers' religion and goes off explaining (to Electra, who has just tried to seduce him) that though men may think he is

fleeing before the furies he is really just drifting up to the mountains to meditate on the stars; and the preceding action is, of course, rendered morally and
emotionally meaningless.

In the present volume, the title poem, *Dear Judas,* is a kind of dilution of
The Women at Point Sur, with Jesus as Barclay, and with a less detailed
background. Mr. Jeffers' mouthpiece and hero, Jesus, is little short of revolt-
ing as he whips reflexively from didactic passion to malice, self-justification,
and vengeance. The poem shares the structural principles, or lack of them, of
The Women at Point Sur; and it has no quotable lines, save, possibly, the last
three, which are, however, heavy with dross. "The Loving Shepherdess," the
other long poem of the present volume, deals with a girl who knows herself
doomed to die at a certain time in childbirth, and who wanders over the countryside caring for a small and diminishing flock of sheep in an anguish of devotion. The events here again are anecdotal and reversible, and the emotion
is lyrical or nothing. The theme had two possibilities: the poet could have immersed the girl in a dream of approaching death, or he could have immersed
her in the sentimental pathos of the immediate situation. There are moments
when he seems to be trying for the former effect, but his perceptions are not
fine enough and the mass of anecdotal detail is too heavy; the poem succeeds
in being no more than a very Wordsworthian embodiment of a kind of maud-
lin humanitarianism—which is a curious but not an unexpected outcome of
Mr. Jeffers' sentimental misanthropy. The heroine is turned cruelly from door
to door, and the sheep fall one by one before the reader's eyes, the doors and
the sheep constituting the bulk of the anecdotal material; till finally the girl
dies in a ditch in an impossible effort to give birth to her child.

The short poems in the book deal with themes that Mr. Jeffers has handled
better before. He has written here and there impressive lines descriptive of
the sea and its rocks, and of dying birds of prey. "Hurt Hawks II," in the
Cawdor volume, is the most perfect short poem and is quite fine; there are
excellent lines scattered through other pieces. These poems are, however, limited both in paraphrasable content and in experiential implication: they glorify brute nature and annihilation and are numb to the intricacies of human
feeling; they share in the latter respect the limitations of all mystical poetry.
Mr. Jeffers' insistence on another of his favorite lyrical themes, his own aloofness, is becoming, by dint of repetition, almost embarrassing; one has the constant feeling that he is trying to bully the reader into accepting him at his own
evaluation.

Self-repetition has been the inevitable effect of anti-intellectualist doctrine
on all of its supporters. If life is valued, explored, subdivided, and defined,
poetic themes are infinite in number; if life is denied, the only theme is the
rather sterile and monotonous one of the denial. Similarly, those poets who
flee from form, which is infinitely variable, since every form is a definite and

an individual thing, can achieve only the uniformity of chaos; and those individuals who endeavor to escape morality, which is personal form and controlled direction, can, in the very nature of things, achieve nothing, save the uniformity of mechanism. One might classify Mr. Jeffers as a "great failure" if one meant by the phrase that he had wasted unusual talents; but not if one meant that he had failed in a major effort, for his aims are badly thought-out and are essentially trivial.

From *Poetry: A Magazine of Verse*, Vol. XXXV (February, 1930), pp. 279–286. Reprinted by permission.

ROBERT PENN WARREN

Hemingway

[1947]

THE situations and characters of Hemingway's world are usually violent. There is the hard-drinking and sexually promiscuous world of *The Sun Also Rises;* the chaotic and brutal world of war as in *A Farewell to Arms, For Whom the Bell Tolls,* many of the inserted sketches of *In Our Time,* the play *The Fifth Column,* and some of the stories; the world of sport, as in "Fifty Grand," "My Old Man," "The Undefeated," "The Snows of Kilimanjaro"; the world of crime as in "The Killers," "The Gambler, the Nun, and the Radio," and *To Have and Have Not.* Even when the situation of a story does not fall into one of these categories, it usually involves a desperate risk, and behind it is the shadow of ruin, physical or spiritual. As for the typical characters, they are usually tough men, experienced in the hard worlds they inhabit, and not obviously given to emotional display or sensitive shrinking, men like Rinaldi or Frederick Henry of *A Farewell to Arms,* Robert Jordan of *For Whom the Bell Tolls,* Harry Morgan of *To Have and Have Not,* the big-game hunter of "The Snows of Kilimanjaro," the old bullfighter of "The Undefeated," or the pugilist of "Fifty Grand." Or if the typical character is not of this seasoned order, he is a very young man, or boy, first entering the violent world and learning his first adjustment to it.

We have said that the shadow of ruin is behind the typical Hemingway situation. The typical character faces defeat or death. But out of defeat or death the character usually manages to salvage something. And here we discover Hemingway's special interest in such situations and such characters. His heroes are not defeated except upon their own terms. They are not squealers, welchers, compromisers, or cowards, and when they confront defeat they realize that the stance they take, the stoic endurance, the stiff upper lip mean a kind of victory. Defeated upon their own terms, some of them have even courted their defeat; and certainly they have maintained, even in the practical defeat, an ideal of themselves, some definition of how a man should behave, formulated or unformulated, by which they have lived. They represent some notion of a code, some notion of honor, which makes a man a man, and

444

which distinguishes him from people who merely follow their random impulses and who are, by consequence, "messy."

In case after case, we can illustrate this "principle of sportsmanship," as one critic has called it, at the center of a story or novel. For instance, Brett, the heroine of *The Sun Also Rises,* gives up Romero, the young bullfighter with whom she is in love, because she knows she will ruin him, and her tight-lipped remark to Jake, the newspaper man who is the narrator of the novel, might almost serve as the motto of Hemingway's work: "You know it makes one feel rather good deciding not to be a bitch."

It is the discipline of the code which makes man human, a sense of style or good form. This applies not only in isolated, dramatic cases such as those listed above, but in a more pervasive way which can give meaning, partially at least, to the confusions of living. The discipline of the soldier, the form of the athlete, the gameness of the sportsman, the technique of an artist can give some sense of the human order, and can achieve a moral significance. And here we see how Hemingway's concern with war and sport crosses his concern with literary style. If a writer can get the kind of style at which Hemingway professed, in *Green Hills of Africa,* to aim, then "nothing else matters. It is more important than anything else he can do." It is more important because, ultimately, it is a moral achievement. And no doubt for this reason, as well as for the reason of Henry James's concern with cruxes of a moral code, he is, as he says in *Green Hills of Africa,* an admirer of the work of James, the devoted stylist.

But to return to the subject of Hemingway's world: the code and the discipline are important because they can give meaning to life which otherwise seems to have no meaning or justification. In other words, in a world without supernatural sanctions, in the God-abandoned world of modernity, man can realize an ideal meaning only in so far as he can define and maintain the code. The effort to define and maintain the code, however limited and imperfect it may be, is the characteristically human effort and provides the tragic or pitiful human story. Hemingway's attitude on this point is much like that of Robert Louis Stevenson as Stevenson states it in one of his essays, "Pulvis et Umbra":

—everywhere some virtue cherished or affected, everywhere some decency of thought or carriage, everywhere the ensign of man's ineffectual goodness . . . under every circumstance of failure, without hope, without help, without thanks, still obscurely fighting the lost fight of virtue, still clinging, in the brothel or on the scaffold, to some rag of honor, the poor jewel of their souls! They may seek to escape, and yet they cannot; it is not alone their privilege and glory, but their doom; they are condemned to some nobility. . . .

Hemingway's code is more rigorous than Stevenson's and perhaps he finds fewer devoted to it, but like Stevenson he can find his characteristic hero and characteristic story among the discards of society, and like Stevenson is aware of the touching irony of that fact. But for the moment the important thing in the parallel is that, for Stevenson, the world in which this drama of pitiful aspiration and stoic endurance is played out is, objectively considered, a violent and meaningless world—"our rotary island loaded with predatory life and more drenched with blood than ever mutinied ship . . . scuds through space." Neither Hemingway nor Stevenson invented this world. It had already appeared in literature before their time, and that is a way of saying that this cheerless vision had already begun to trouble men. It is the world we find pictured (and denied) in Tennyson's "In Memoriam"—the world in which human conduct is a product of "dying Nature's earth and lime." It is the world pictured (and not denied) in Hardy and Housman, a world which seems to be presided over by blind Doomsters (if by anybody), as Hardy put it in his poem "Hap," or made by some brute and blackguard (if by anybody), as Housman put it in his poem "The Chestnut Casts Its Flambeaux." It is the world of Zola or Dreiser or Conrad or Faulkner. It is the world of, to use Bertrand Russell's phrase, "secular hurryings through space." It is the God-abandoned world, the world of Nature-as-all. We know where the literary men got this picture. They got it from the scientists of the 19th Century. This is Hemingway's world, too, the world with nothing at center.

Over against this naturalistic view of the world, there was, of course, an argument for Divine Intelligence and a Divine purpose, an argument which based itself on the beautiful system of nature, on natural law. The closely knit order of the natural world, so the argument ran, implies a Divine Intelligence. But if one calls Hemingway's attention to the fact that the natural world is a world of order, his reply is on record in a story called "A Natural History of the Dead." There he quotes from the traveller Mungo Park, who, naked and starving in an African desert, observed a beautiful little moss-flower and meditated thus:

Can the Being who planted, watered, and brought to perfection, in this obscure part of the world, a thing which appears of so small importance, look with unconcern upon the situation and suffering of creatures formed after his own image? Surely not. Reflections like these would not allow me to despair: I started up and, disregarding both hunger and fatigue, travelled forward, assured that relief was at hand; and I was not disappointed.

And Hemingway continues:

With a disposition to wonder and adore in like manner, as Bishop Stanley says [the author of A Familiar History of Birds], can any branch of Natural History be studied without increasing that faith, love and hope which we also, every one of us, need in our journey through the wilderness of life? Let us therefore see what inspiration we may derive from the dead.

Then Hemingway presents the picture of a modern battlefield, where the bloated and decaying bodies give a perfect example of the natural order of chemistry—but scarcely an argument for faith, hope, and love. That picture is his answer to the argument that the order of nature implies meaning in the world.

In one of the stories, "A Clean, Well-Lighted Place," we find the best description of this world which underlies Hemingway's world of violent action. Early in the story we see an old man sitting late in a Spanish café. Two waiters are speaking of him.

"Last week he tried to commit suicide," one waiter said.

"Why?"

"He was in despair."

"What about?"

"Nothing."

"How do you know it was nothing?"

"He has plenty of money."

The despair beyond plenty of money—or beyond all the other gifts of the world: its nature becomes a little clearer at the end of the story when the older of the two waiters is left alone, reluctant too to leave the clean, well-lighted place.

Turning off the electric light he continued the conversation with himself. It is the light of course but it is necessary that the place be clean and pleasant. You do not want music. Certainly you do not want music. Nor can you stand before a bar with dignity although that is all that is provided for these hours. What did he fear? It was not fear or dread. It was a nothing that he knew too well. It was all a nothing and a man was nothing too. It was only that and light was all it needed and a certain cleanness and order. Some lived in it and never felt it but he knew it all was nada y pues nada y nada y pues nada.[1] Our nada who art in nada, nada be thy name thy kingdom nada thy will be nada in nada as it is in nada. Give us this nada our daily nada and nada us our nada as we nada our nadas and nada us not into nada but deliver us from nada; pues nada. Hail nothing full of nothing, nothing is with thee. He smiled and stood before a bar with a shining steam pressure coffee machine.

"What's yours?" asked the barman.

"Nada."

At the end the old waiter is ready to go home:

Now, without thinking further, he would go home to his room. He would lie in bed and finally, with daylight, he would go to sleep. After all, he said to himself, it's probably only insomnia. Many must have it.

And the sleepless man—the man obsessed by death, by the meaningless of the world, by nothingness, by nada—is one of the recurring symbols in the

[1] *nada y pues nada,* etc.: nothing and after that nothing, etc.

works of Hemingway. In this phase Hemingway is a religious writer. The despair beyond plenty of money, the despair which makes a sleeplessness beyond insomnia, is the despair felt by a man who hungers for the certainties and meaningfulness of a religious faith but who cannot find in his world a ground for that faith.

Another recurring symbol, we have said, is the violent man. But the sleepless man and the violent man are not contradictory but complementary symbols. They represent phases of the same question, the same hungering for meaning in the world. The sleepless man is the man brooding upon nada, upon chaos, upon Nature-as-all. (For Nature-as-all equals moral chaos; even its bulls and lions and kudu are not admired by Hemingway as creatures of conscious self-discipline; their courage is meaningful only in so far as it symbolizes human courage.) The violent man is the man taking an action appropriate to the realization of the fact of nada. He is, in other words, engaged in the effort to discover human values in a naturalistic world.

Before we proceed with this line of discussion, it might be asked, "Why does Hemingway feel that the quest necessarily involves violence?" Now, at one level, the answer to this question would involve the whole matter of the bias toward violence in modern literature. But let us take it in its more immediate reference. The typical Hemingway hero is the man aware, or in the process of becoming aware, of nada. Death is the great nada. Therefore whatever solution the hero gets must, to be good, stick even against the fact of death. It has to be good in the bullring or on the battle field and not merely in the study or lecture room. In fact, Hemingway is anti-intellectual, and has a great contempt for any type of solution arrived at without the testings of immediate experience. One of his more uningratiating passages—again from "A Natural History of the Dead"—makes the point amply clear:

The only natural death I've ever seen, outside of the loss of blood, which isn't bad, was death from Spanish influenza. In this you drown in mucus, choking, and how you know the patient's dead is: at the end he turns to be a little child again, though with his manly force, and fills the sheets as full as any diaper with one vast, final yellow cataract that flows and dribbles on after he is gone. So now I want to see the death of any self-styled Humanist because a persevering traveller like Mungo Park or me lives on and maybe yet will see the actual death of members of this literary sect and watch the noble exits they make. In my musings as a naturalist it has occurred to me that while decorum is an excellent thing, some must be indecorous if the race is to be carried on since the position described for procreation is indecorous, highly indecorous, and it occurred to me that perhaps that is what these people are, or were: the children of decorous cohabitation. But regardless of how they started I hope to see the finish of a few, and speculate how worms will try that long preserved sterility; with their quaint pamphlets gone to bust and into foot-notes all their lust.

So aside from the question of a dramatic sense which would favor violence, and aside from the mere matter of personal temperament (for Hemingway describes himself on more than one occasion as obsessed by death), the presentation of violence is appropriate in his work because death is the great nada. In taking violent risks man confronts in dramatic terms the issue of nada which is implicit in all of Hemingway's world.

But to return to our general line of discussion. There are two aspects to this violence which is involved in the quest of the Hemingway hero, two aspects which seem to represent an ambivalent attitude toward nature.

First, there is the conscious sinking into nature, shall we call it. On this line of reasoning we would find something like this: if there is at center only nada, then the only sure compensation in life, the only reality, is gratification of appetite, the relish of sensation. Continually in the stories and novels one finds such sentences as this from *Green Hills of Africa*: ". . . drinking this, the first one of the day, the finest one there is, and looking at the thick bush we passed in the dark, feeling the cool wind of the night and smelling the good smell of Africa, I was altogether happy." What is constantly interesting in such sentences is the fact that happiness, a notion which we traditionally connect with a complicated state of being, with notions of virtue, of achievement, etc., is here equated with a set of merely agreeable sensations. The careful relish of sensation—that is what counts, always.

This intense awareness of the world of the senses is, of course, one of the things which made the early work of Hemingway seem, upon its first impact, so fresh and pure. Physical nature is nowhere rendered with greater vividness than in his work, and probably his only competitors in this department of literature are William Faulkner, among the modern, and Henry David Thoreau, among the older American writers. The meadows, forests, lakes, and trout streams of America, and the arid, sculpturesque mountains of Spain, appear with astonishing immediacy, an immediacy not dependent upon descriptive flourishes. But not only the appearance of landscape is important; a great deal of the freshness comes from the discrimination of sensation, the coldness of water in the "squlchy" shoes after wading, the tangy smell of dry sage brush, the "cleanly" smell of grease and oil on a field piece. Hemingway's appreciation and rendering of the aesthetic quality of the physical world is important, but a peculiar poignancy is implicit in the rendering of those qualities; the beauty of the physical world is a background for the human predicament, and the very relishing of the beauty is merely a kind of desperate and momentary compensation possible in the midst of the predicament.

This careful relishing of the world of the senses comes to a climax in drinking and sex. Drink is the "giant-killer," the weapon against man's thought of nada. And so is sex, for that matter, though when sexual attraction achieves the status of love, the process is one which attempts to achieve a meaning rather than to forget meaninglessness in the world. In terms of drinking and sex, the typical Hemingway hero is a man of monel-metal stomach and Homeric prowess in the arts of love. And the typical situation is love, with some drinking, against the background of nada—of civilization gone to pot, or war, or death—as we get it in all of the novels in one form or another, and in many of the stories.

It is important to remember, however, that the sinking into nature, even at the level of drinking and mere sexuality, is a self-conscious act. It is not the random gratification of appetite. We see this quite clearly in *The Sun Also Rises* in the contrast between Cohn, who is merely a random dabbler in the world of sensation, who is merely trying to amuse himself, and the initiates like Jake and Brett, who are aware of the nada at the center of things and whose dissipations, therefore, have a philosophical significance. The initiate in Hemingway's world raises the gratification of appetite to the level of a cult and a discipline.

The cult of sensation, as we have already indicated, passes over very readily into the cult of true love, for the typical love story is presented primarily in terms of the cult of sensation. (*A Farewell to Arms*, as we shall see when we come to a detailed study of that novel, is closely concerned with that transition.) Even in the cult of true love it is the moment which counts, and the individual. There is never any past or future to the love stories and the lovers are always isolated, not moving in an ordinary human society within its framework of obligations. The notion of the cult—a secret cult composed of those who have been initiated into the secret of nada—is constantly played up. In *A Farewell to Arms*, for instance, Catherine and Frederick are, quite consciously, two against the world, a world which is, literally as well as figuratively, an alien world. The peculiar relationship between Frederick and the priest takes on a new significance if viewed in terms of the secret cult. We shall come to this topic later, but for the moment we can say that the priest is a priest of Divine Love, the subject about which he and Frederick converse in the hospital, and that Frederick himself is a kind of priest, one of the initiate in the end, of the cult of profane love. This same pattern of two against the world, with an understanding confidante or interpreter, reappears in *For Whom the Bell Tolls*—with Pilar, the gipsy woman who understands "love," substituting for the priest of *A Farewell to Arms*.

The initiates of the cult of love are those who are aware of nada, but their effort, as members of the cult, is to find a meaning to put in place of the nada. That is, there is an attempt to make the relationship of love take on a religious significance in so far as it can give meaning to life. This general topic is not new with the work of Hemingway. It is one of the literary themes of the 19th Century—and has, as a matter of fact, a much longer history than that. But we find it fully stated in the last century in many instances. To take one, there is "Dover Beach" by Matthew Arnold. In a world from which religious faith has been removed the lovers can only turn to each other to find significance in life:

> Ah, love, let us be true
> To one another! for the world, which seems
> To lie before us like a land of dreams,
> So various, so beautiful, so new,
> Hath really neither joy, nor love, nor light,
> Nor certitude, nor peace, nor help for pain;
> And we are here as on a darkling plain
> Swept with confused alarms of struggle and flight,
> Where ignorant armies clash by night.

If the cult of love arises from and states itself in the language of the cult of sensation, it is an extension of the sinking-into-nature aspect of the typical Hemingway violence; but in so far as it involves a discipline and a search for a "faith," it leads us to the second aspect of the typical violence.

The violence, although in its first aspect it represents a sinking into nature, at the same time, in its second aspect, represents a conquest of nature, and of nada in man. It represents such a conquest, not because of the fact of violence, but because the violence appears in terms of discipline, a style, and a code. It is, as we have already seen, in terms of a self-imposed discipline that the heroes make one gallant, though limited, effort to redeem the incoherence of the world: they attempt to impose some form upon the disorder of their lives, the technique of the bullfighter or sportsman, the discipline of the soldier, the fidelity of the lover, or even the code of the gangster, which, though brutal and apparently dehumanizing, has its own ethic.

The discipline, the form, is never quite capable of subduing the world, but fidelity to it is part of the gallantry of defeat. By fidelity to it the hero manages to keep one small place "clean" and "well-lighted," and manages to retain, or achieve for one last moment, his dignity. As the old Spanish waiter muses, there should be a "clean, well-lighted place" where one could keep one's dignity at the late hour.

We have said earlier that the typical Hemingway character is tough and, apparently, insensitive. But only apparently, for the fidelity to a code, to the discipline, may be the index to a sensitivity which allows the characters to see, at moments, their true plight. At times, and usually at times of stress, it is the tough man in the Hemingway world, the disciplined man, who is actually aware of pathos or tragedy. The individual toughness (which may be taken to be the private discipline demanded by the world) may find itself in conflict with the natural human reaction; but the Hemingway hero, though he may be aware of the claims of the natural reaction, the spontaneous human emotion, cannot surrender to it because he knows that the only way to hold on to the definition of himself, to "honor" or "dignity," is to maintain the discipline, the code. For example, when pity appears in the Hemingway world—as in "The Pursuit Race"—it does not appear in its maximum but in its minimum manifestation.

What this means in terms of style and method is the use of understatement. This understatement, stemming from the contrast between the sensitivity and the superimposed discipline, is a constant aspect of the work, an aspect which was caught in a cartoon in the *New Yorker*. The cartoon showed a brawny, muscle-knotted forearm and a hairy hand which clutched a rose. It was entitled "The Soul of Ernest Hemingway." Just as there is a margin of victory in the defeat of the Hemingway characters, so there is a little margin of sensitivity in their brutal and apparently insensitive world. Hence we have the ironical circumstance—a central circumstance in creating the pervasive irony of Hemingway's work—that the revelation of the values characteristic of his work arises from the most unpromising people and the most unpromising situations—the little streak of poetry or pathos in "The Pursuit Race," "The Killers," "My Old Man," "A Clean, Well-Lighted Place," or "The Undefeated." We have a perfect example of it in the last named story. After the defeat of the old bullfighter, who is lying wounded on an operating table, Zurito, the picador, is about to cut off his pigtail, the mark of his profession. But when the wounded man starts up, despite his pain, and says, "You couldn't do a thing like that," Zurito says, "I was joking." Zurito becomes aware that, after all, the old bullfighter is, in a way, undefeated, and deserves to die with his coleta on.

This locating of the poetic, the pathetic, or the tragic in the unpromising person or situation is not unique with Hemingway. It is something with which we are acquainted in a great deal of our literature since the Romantic Movement. The sensibility is played down, and an anti-romantic surface sheathes the work; the point is in the contrast. The impulse which led Hemingway to the simple character is akin to that which drew Wordsworth to the same choice. Wordsworth felt that his unsophisticated peasants were more honest in their responses than the cultivated man, and were therefore more poetic. Instead of Wordsworth's peasant we have in Hemingway's work the bullfighter, the soldier, the revolutionist, the sportsman, and the gangster; instead of Wordsworth's children we have the young men like Nick, the person just on the verge of being initiated into the world. There are, of course, differences between the approach of Wordsworth and that of Hemingway, but there is little difference on the point of marginal sensibility. In one sense, both are anti-intellectual, and in such poems as "Resolution and Independence" or "Michael" one finds even closer ties.

I have just indicated a similarity between Wordsworth and Hemingway on the grounds of a romantic anti-intellectualism. But with Hemingway it is far more profound and radical than with Wordsworth. All we have to do to see the difference is to put Wordsworth's Preface to the *Lyrical Ballads* over against any number of passages from Hemingway. The intellectualism of the 18th Century had merely put a veil of stereotyped language over all the world and a veil of snobbism over a large area of human experience. That is Wordsworth's indictment. But Hemingway's indictment of the intellectualism of the past is that it wound up in the mire and blood of 1914 to 1918; that it was a pack of lies leading to death. We can put over against the Preface of Wordsworth, a passage from *A Farewell to Arms*:

I was always embarrassed by the words sacred, glorious, and sacrifice and the expression in vain. We had heard them, sometimes standing in the rain almost out of earshot, so that only the shouted words came through, and had read them, on proclamations that were slapped up by billposters over other proclamations, now for a long time, and I had seen nothing sacred, and the things that were glorious had no glory and the sacrifices were like the stockyards at Chicago if nothing was done with the meat except to bury it. There were many words that you could not stand to hear and finally only the names of places had dignity. . . . Abstract words such as glory, honor, courage, or hallow were obscene beside the concrete names of villages, the numbers of roads, the names of rivers, the numbers of regiments and the dates.

I do not mean to say that the general revolution in style, and the revolt against the particular intellectualism of the 19th Century was a result of the World War, 1914–18. As a matter of fact, that revolt was going on long before the war, but for Hemingway, and for many others, the war gave the situation a peculiar depth and urgency.

Perhaps we might scale the matter thus: Wordsworth was a revolutionist— he truly had a new view of the world—but his revolutionary view left great tracts of the world untouched; the Church of England, for instance. Arnold and Tennyson, a generation or so later, though not revolutionists themselves, are much more profoundly stirred by the revolutionary situation than ever Wordsworth was; that is, the area of the world involved in the debate was for them greater. Institutions are called into question in a more fundamental way. But they managed to hang on to their English God and their English institutions. With Hardy, the area of disturbance has grown greater, and what can be salvaged is much less. He, like the earlier Victorians, had a strong sense of community to sustain him in the face of the universe which was for him, as not finally for Arnold and Tennyson, unfriendly, or at least neutral and Godless. But his community underlay institutions, a human communion which as a matter of fact was constantly being violated by institutions; and this violation is, in fact, a constant source of subject matter and a constant spring of irony. Nevertheless Hardy could refer to himself as a meliorist.

But with Hemingway, though there is a secret community, it has greatly shrunk, and its definition has become much more specialized. Its members are those who know the code. They recognize each other, they know the password and the secret grip, but they are few in number, and each is set off against the world like a wounded lion ringed round by waiting hyenas. (*Green Hills of Africa* gives us the hyena symbol—the animal whose death is comic because it is all hideously "appetite"; wounded, it eats its own intestines.) Furthermore, this secret community is not constructive; Hemingway is no meliorist. In fact, there are hints that somewhere in the back of his mind, and in behind his work, there is a kind of Spenglerian view of history: our civilization is running down. We get this most explicitly in *Green Hills of Africa*:

A continent ages quickly once we come. The natives live in harmony with it. But the foreigner destroys, cuts down the trees, drains the water, so that the water supply is altered and in a short time the soil, once the sod is turned under, is cropped out and, next, it starts to blow away as it has blown away in every old country and as I had seen it start to blow in Canada. The earth gets tired of being exploited. A country wears out quickly unless man puts back in it all his residue and that of all his beasts. When he quits using beasts and uses machines, the earth defeats him quickly. The machine can't reproduce, nor does it fertilize the soil, and it eats what he cannot raise. A country was made to be as we found it. We are the intruders and after we are dead we may have ruined it but it will still be there and we don't know what the next changes are. I suppose they all end up like Mongolia.

I would come back to Africa but not to make a living from it. . . . But I would come back to where it pleased me to live; to really live. Not just let my life pass. Our people went to America because that was the place for them to go then. It had been a good country and we had made a bloody mess of it and I would go, now, somewhere else as we had always had the right to go somewhere else and as we had always gone. You could always come back. Let the others come to America who did not know that they had come too late. Our people had seen it at its best and fought for it when it was well worth fighting for. Now I would go somewhere else.

This is the most explicit statement, but the view is implicit in case after case. The general human community, the general human project, has gone to pot. There is only the little secret community of, paradoxically enough, individualists who have resigned from the general community, and who are strong enough to live without any illusions, lies, and big words of the herd. At least, this is the case up to the novel *To Have and Have Not*. In that novel and in *For Whom the Bell Tolls* Hemingway attempts to return, as it were, his individualistic hero to society, to give him a common stake with the fate of other men.

But to come back to the matter of Wordsworth and Hemingway. What in Wordsworth is merely simple or innocent is in Hemingway violent: the gangster or bullfighter replaces the leech-gatherer or the child. Hemingway's world

is a more disordered world, and the sensibility of his characters is more ironically in contrast with their world. The most immediate consideration here is
the playing down of the sensibility as such, the sheathing of it in the code of
toughness. Gertrude Stein's tribute is here relevant: "Hemingway is the shy-
est and proudest and sweetest-smelling story-teller of my reading." But this
shyness manifests itself in the irony. In this, of course, Hemingway's irony
corresponds to the Byronic irony. But the relation to Byron is even more fundamental. The pity is only valid when it is wrung from the man who has been
seasoned by experience. Therefore a premium is placed on the fact of violent
experience. The "dumb ox" character, commented on by Wyndham Lewis,
represents the Wordsworthian peasant; the character with the code of the
tough guy, the initiate, the man cultivating honor, gallantry, and recklessness,
represents the Byronic aristocrat.

The failures of Hemingway, like his successes, are also rooted in this situation. The successes occur in those instances where Hemingway accepts the
essential limitations of his premises, that is, when there is an equilibrium between the dramatization and the characteristic Hemingway "point," when the
system of ironies and understatements is coherent. On the other hand, the
failures occur when we feel that Hemingway has not respected the limitations
of his premises; that is, when the dramatization seems to be "rigged" and the
violence, therefore, merely theatrical. The characteristic irony, or understatement, in such cases, seems to be too self-conscious. For example, let us glance
at Hemingway's most spectacular failure, *To Have and Have Not*. The
point of the novel is based on the contrast between the smuggler and the rich
owners of the yachts along the quay. But the irony is essentially an irony
without center or reference. It is superficial, for, as a critic in the *Partisan
Review* indicated, the only difference between the smuggler and the rich is
that the rich were successful in their buccaneering. The revelation which
comes to the smuggler dying in his launch—"a man alone ain't got no . . .
chance"—is a meaningless revelation, for it has no reference to the actual
dramatization. It is, finally, a failure in intellectual analysis of the situation.
In the same way, the much advertised "The Snows of Kilimanjaro" is a
failure.

Much has been said to the effect that *To Have and Have Not* and *For
Whom the Bell Tolls* represent a basic change of point of view, an enlargement of what I have called the secret community. Now no doubt that is the
intention behind both books, but the temper of both books is the old temper,
the cast of characters is the old cast, and the assumptions lying far below the
explicit intention are the old assumptions.

The monotony and self-imitation into which Hemingway's work sometimes
falls is again an effect of a failure in dramatization. Hemingway, apparently,
can dramatize his "point" in only one basic situation and with only one set of

characters. As we have seen, he has only two key characters, with certain variations from them in terms of contrast or counterpoint. His best women characters, by the way, are those which most nearly approximate the men; that is, they embody the masculine virtues and point of view characteristic of Hemingway's work.

But the monotony is not merely a monotony deriving from the characters as types; it derives, rather from the limitations of the author's sensibility, which can find interest only in one issue. A more flexible sensibility, one capable of making nicer discriminations, might discover great variety in such key characters and situations. But Hemingway's successes are due, in part at least, to the close coordination which he sometimes achieves between the character and situation on the one hand, and the sensibility as it reflects itself in the style, on the other hand.

The style characteristically is simple, even to the point of monotony. The characteristic sentence is simple, or compound; and if compound, there is no implied subtlety in the coordination of the clauses. The paragraph structure is, characteristically, based on simple sequence. There is an obvious relation between this style and the characters and situations with which the author is concerned—a question of dramatic decorum. (There are, on the other hand, examples, especially in the novels, of other more fluent, lyrical effects, but even here this fluency is founded on the conjunction *and*; it is a rhythmical and not a logical fluency. And the lyrical quality is simply a manifestation of that marginal sensibility, as can be demonstrated by an analysis of the occasions on which it appears.) But there is a more fundamental aspect of the question, an aspect which involves not the sensibility of the characters but the sensibility of the author. The short simple rhythms, the succession of coordinate clauses, the general lack of subordination——all suggest a dislocated and ununified world. The figures which live in this world live a sort of hand-to-mouth existence perceptually, and conceptually, they hardly live at all.

II

A Farewell to Arms is a love story. It is a compelling story at the merely personal level, but is much more compelling and significant when we see the figures of the lovers silhouetted against the flame-streaked blackness of war, of a collapsing world, of nada. For there is a story behind the love story. That story is the quest for meaning and certitude in a world which seems to offer nothing of the sort. It is, in a sense, a religious book; if it does not offer a religious solution it is nevertheless conditioned by the religious problem.

The very first scene of the book, though seemingly casual, is important if we are to understand the deeper motivations of the story. It is the scene at the officers' mess where the captain baits the priest. "Priest every night five against one," the captain explains to Frederick. But Frederick, we see in this and later scenes, takes no part in the baiting. There is a bond between him and the priest, a bond which they both recognize. This becomes clear when, after the officers have advised Frederick where he should go on his leave to find the best girls, the priest turns to him and says that he would like for him to go to Abruzzi, his own province:

"There is good hunting. You would like the people and though it is cold it is clear and dry. You could stay with my family. My father is a famous hunter."
"Come on," said the captain. "We go whorehouse before it shuts."
"Goodnight," I said to the priest.
"Goodnight," he said.

In the preliminary contrast between the officers, who invite the hero to go to the brothels, and the priest, who invites him to go to the cold, clear, dry country, we have in its simplest form the issue of the novel.

Frederick does go with the officers that night, and on his leave he does go to the cities, "to the smoke of cafes and nights when the room whirled and you needed to look at the wall to make it stop, nights in bed, drunk, when you knew that that was all there was, and the strange excitement of waking and not knowing who it was with you, and the world all unreal in the dark and so exciting that you must resume again unknowing and not caring in the night, sure that this was all and all and all and not caring." Frederick at the opening of the novel lives in the world of random and meaningless appetite, knowing that it is all and all and all, or thinking that he knows that. But behind that there is a dissatisfaction and disgust. Upon his return from his leave, sitting in the officers' mess, he tries to tell the priest how he is sorry that he had not gone to the clear, cold, dry country—the priest's home, which takes on the shadowy symbolic significance of another kind of life, another view of the world. The priest had always known that other country.

He had always known what I did not know and what, when I learned it, I was always able to forget. But I did not know that then, although I learned it later.

What Frederick learns later is the story behind the love story of the book.

But this theme is not merely stated at the opening of the novel and then absorbed into the action. It appears later, at crucial points, to define the line of meaning in the action. When, for example, Frederick is wounded, the priest visits him in the hospital. Their conversation makes even plainer the religious background of the novel. The priest has said that he would like to go back after the war to the Abruzzi. He continues:

"It does not matter. But there in my country it is understood that a man may love God. It is not a dirty joke."
"I understand."
He looked at me and smiled.

"You understand but you do not love God."

"No."

"You do not love him at all?" he asked.

"I am afraid of him in the night sometimes."

"You should love Him."

"I don't love much."

"Yes," he said. "You do. What you tell me about in the nights. That is not love. That is only passion and lust. When you love you wish to do things for. You wish to sacrifice for. You wish to serve."

"I don't love."

"You will. I know you will. Then you will be happy."

We have here two items of importance. First, there is the definition of Frederick as the sleepless man, the man haunted by nada. Second, at this stage in the novel, the end of Book I, the true meaning of the love story with Catherine has not yet been defined. It is still at the level of appetite. The priest's role is to indicate the next stage of the story, the discovery of the true nature of love, the "wish to do things for." And he accomplishes this by indicating a parallel between secular love and Divine love, a parallel which implies Frederick's quest for meaning and certitude. And to emphasize further this idea, Frederick, after the priest leaves, muses on the high, clean country of the Abruzzi, the priest's home which has already been endowed with the symbolic significance of the religious view of the world.

In the middle of Book II (Chapter xviii), in which the love story begins to take on the significance which the priest had predicted, the point is indicated by a bit of dialogue between the lovers.

"Couldn't we be married privately some way? Then if anything happened to me or if you had a child."

"There's no way to be married except by church or state. We are married privately. You see, darling, it would mean everything to me if I had any religion. But I haven't any religion."

"You gave me the Saint Anthony."

"That was for luck. Some one gave it to me."

"Then nothing worries you?"

"Only being sent away from you. You're my religion. You're all I've got."

Again, toward the end of Book IV (Chapter xxxv), just before Frederick and Catherine make their escape into Switzerland, Frederick is talking with a friend, the old Count Greffi, who has just said that he thought H. G. Wells's novel *Mr. Britling Sees It Through* a very good study of the English middle-class soul. But Frederick twists the word *soul* into another meaning.

"I don't know about the soul."

"Poor boy. We none of us know about the soul. Are you Croyant?"

"At night."

Later in the same conversation the Count returns to the topic:

"And if you ever become devout pray for me if I am dead. I am asking several of my friends to do that. I had expected to become devout myself but it has not come." I thought he smiled sadly but I could not tell. He was so old and his face was very wrinkled, so that a smile used so many lines that all graduations were lost.

"I might become very devout," I said. "Anyway, I will pray for you."

"I had always expected to become devout. All my family died very devout. But somehow it does not come."

"It's too early."

"Maybe it is too late. Perhaps I have outlived my religious feeling."

"My own comes only at night."

"Then too you are in love. Do not forget that is a religious feeling."

So here, again, we find Frederick defined as the sleepless man, and the relation established between secular love and Divine love.

In the end, with the death of Catherine, Frederick discovers that the attempt to find a substitute for universal meaning in the limited meaning of the personal relationship is doomed to failure. It is doomed because it is liable to all the accidents of a world in which human beings are like the ants running back and forth on a log burning in a campfire and in which death is, as Catherine says immediately before her own death, "just a dirty trick." But this is not to deny the value of the effort, or to deny the value of the discipline, the code, the stoic endurance, the things which make it true—or half true—that "nothing ever happens to the brave."

This question of the characteristic discipline takes us back to the beginning of the book, and to the context from which Frederick's effort arises. We have already mentioned the contrast between the officers of the mess and the priest. It is a contrast based on the man who is aware of the issue of meaning in life and those who are unaware of it, who give themselves over to the mere flow of accident, the contrast between the disciplined and the undisciplined. But the contrast is not merely between the priest and the officers. Frederick's friend, the surgeon Rinaldi, is another who is on the same "side" of the contrast as the priest. He may go to the brothel with his brother officers, he may even bait the priest a little, but his personal relationship with Frederick indicates his affiliations; he is one of the initiate. Furthermore, he has the discipline of his profession, and as we have seen, in the Hemingway world, the discipline which seems to be merely technical, the style of the artist or the form of the athlete or bullfighter, may be an index to a moral value. "Already," he says, "I am only happy when I am working." (Already because the seeking of pleasure in sensation is inadequate for Rinaldi.) This point appears more sharply in the remarks about the doctor who first attends to Frederick's wounded leg. He is incompetent and does not wish to take the responsibility for a decision.

Before he came back three doctors came into the room. I have noticed that doctors who fail in the practice of medicine have a tendency to seek one another's company and aid in consultation. A doctor who cannot take out your appendix properly will recommend to you a doctor who will be unable to remove your tonsils with success. These were three such doctors.

In contrast with them there is Dr. Valentini, who is competent, who is willing to take responsibility, and who, as a kind of mark of his role, speaks the same lingo, with the same bantering, ironical tone, as Rinaldi—the tone which is the mark of the initiate.

So we have the world of the novel divided into two groups, the initiate and the uninitiate, the aware and the unaware, the disciplined and the undisciplined. In the first group are Frederick, Catherine, Rinaldi, Valentini, Count Greffi, the old man who cut the paper silhouettes "for pleasure," and Passini, Manera, and the other ambulance men in Frederick's command. In the second group are the officers of the mess, the incompetent doctors, the "legitimate hero" Ettore, and the "patriots"—all the people who do not know what is really at stake, who are decided by the big words, who do not have the discipline. They are the messy people, the people who surrender to the flow and illusion of things. It is this second group who provide the context of the novel, and more especially the context from which Frederick moves toward his final complete awareness.

The final awareness means, as we have said, that the individual is thrown back upon his private discipline and his private capacity to endure. The hero cuts himself off from the herd, the confused world, which symbolically appears as the routed army at Caporetto. And, as Malcolm Cowley has pointed out, the plunge into the flooded Tagliamento, when Frederick escapes from the battle police, has the significance of a rite. By this "baptism" Frederick is reborn into another world; he comes out into the world of the man alone, no longer supported by and involved in society.

Anger was washed away in the river along with my obligation. Although that ceased when the carabiniere put his hands on my collar. I would like to have had the uniform off although I did not care much about the outward forms. I had taken off the stars, but that was for convenience. It was no point of honor. I was not against them. I was through. I wished them all the luck. There were the good ones, and the brave ones, and the calm ones and the sensible ones, and they deserved it. But it was not my show any more and I wished this bloody train would get to Mestre and I would eat and stop thinking.

So Frederick, by a decision, does what the boy Nick, in *In Our Time*, does as the result of the accident of a wound. He makes a "separate peace." And from the waters of the flooded Tagliamento arises the Hemingway hero in his purest form, with human history and obligation washed away, ready to enact the last phase of his appropriate drama, and learn from his inevitable defeat the lesson of lonely fortitude.

III

This is not the time to attempt to give a final evaluation of Hemingway's work as a whole or even of this particular novel—if there is ever a time for a "final" evaluation. But we may touch on some of the objections which have been brought against his work.

First, there is the objection that his work is immoral or dirty or disgusting. This objection appeared in various quarters against *A Farewell to Arms* at the time of its first publication. For instance, Robert Herrick, himself a respected novelist, wrote that if suppression were to be justified at all it would be justified in this case. He said that the book had no significance, was merely a "lustful indulgence," and smelled of the "boudoir," and summarized his view by calling it "garbage." That objection has for the most part died out, but its echoes can still be occasionally heard, and now and then, at rare intervals, some bigot or highminded but uninstructed moralist will object to the inclusion of *A Farewell to Arms* in a college course.

The answer to such an objection is fundamentally an answer to the charge that the book has no meaning. The answerer must seek to establish the fact that the book does deal seriously with a moral and philosophical issue, which, for better or worse, does exist in the modern world in substantially the terms presented by Hemingway. This means that the book, even if it does not end with a solution which is generally acceptable, still embodies a moral effort and is another document of the human will to achieve ideal values. As for the bad effect it may have on some readers, the best answer is perhaps to be found in a quotation from Thomas Hardy, who is now sanctified but whose most famous novels, *Tess of the D'Urbervilles* and *Jude the Obscure*, once suffered the attacks of the dogmatic moralists, and one of whose books was burned by a bishop:

Of the effects of such sincere presentation on weak minds, when the courses of the characters are not exemplary and the rewards and punishments ill adjusted to deserts, it is not our duty to consider too closely. A novel which does mortal injury to a dozen imbeciles, and has bracing results upon intellects of normal vigor, can justify its existence; and probably a novel was never written by the purest-minded author for which there could not be found some moral invalid or other whom it was capable of harming.

Second, there is the objection that Hemingway's work, especially of the period before *To Have and Have Not*, has no social relevance, that it is off the main stream of modern life, and that it has no concern with the economic structure of society. Critics who hold this general view regard Heming-

way, like Joseph Conrad and perhaps like Henry James, as an exotic. There
are several possible lines of retort to this objection. One line is well stated in
the following passage if we substitute the name of Hemingway for Conrad:

Thus it is no reproach to Conrad that he does not concern himself at all with the
economic and social background underlying human relationships in modern civilization, for he never sets out to study those relationships. The Marxists cannot accuse him of cowardice or falsification, because in this case the charge is not relevant
[though it might be relevant to *To Have and Have Not* or to *For Whom the
Bell Tolls*]. That, from the point of view of the man with a theory, there are accidents in history, no one can deny. And if a writer chooses to discuss those accidents
rather than the events which follow the main stream of historical causation, the
economic or other determinist can only shrug his shoulder and maintain that these
events are less instructive to the students than are the major events which he
chooses to study; but he cannot accuse the writer of falsehood or distortion.[2]

That much is granted by one of the ablest critics of the group who would
find Hemingway an exotic. But a second line of retort would fix on the word
instructive in the foregoing passage, and would ask what kind of instruction,
if any, is to be expected of fiction, as fiction. Is the kind of instruction expected of fiction in direct competition, at the same level, with the kind of
instruction offered in Political Science I or Economics II? If that is the case,
then out with Shakespeare and Keats and in with Upton Sinclair.

Perhaps *instruction* is not a relevant word, after all, for this case. This is a
very thorny and debatable question, but it can be ventured that what good
fiction gives us is the stimulation of a powerful image of human nature trying
to fulfill itself and not instruction in an abstract sense. The economic and the
political man are important aspects of human nature and may well constitute
part of the materials of fiction. But the economic or political man is not the
complete man and other concerns may still be important enough to engage
worthily the attention of a writer—such concerns as love, death, courage, the
point of honor, and the moral scruple. A man does not only have to live with
other men in terms of economic and political arrangements; he has to live with
them in terms of moral arrangements, and he has to live with himself, he has
to define himself. It can truly be said that these concerns are all inter-related
in fact, but it might be dangerously dogmatic to insist that a writer should
not bring one aspect into sharp, dramatic focus.

And it might be dangerously dogmatic to insist that Hemingway's ideas are
not relevant to modern life. The mere fact that they exist and have stirred a
great many people is a testimony to their relevance. Or to introduce a variation on that theme, it might be dogmatic to object to his work on the ground
that he has few basic ideas. The history of literature seems to show that good
artists may have very few *basic* ideas. They may have many ideas, but the ideas

[2] David Daiches: *Fiction in the Modern World*.

do not lead a life of democratic give-and-take, of genial camaraderie. No, there are usually one or two basic, obsessive ones. Like the religious reformer Savonarola, the artist may say: "Le mie cose erano poche e grandi"—my ideas were few and grand. And the ideas of the artist are grand because they are intensely felt, intensely realized—not because, by objective standards, by public, statistical standards, "important." No, that kind of public, statistical importance may be a *condition* of their being grand but is not of the special essence of their grandeur. (Perhaps not even the condition—perhaps the grandeur inheres in the fact that the artistic work shows us a parable of meaning—how idea is felt and how passion becomes idea through order.)

An artist may need few *basic* ideas, but in assessing his work we must introduce another criterion in addition to that of intensity. We must introduce the criterion of area. In other words, his basic ideas do not operate in splendid isolation; to a greater or lesser degree, they operate in terms of their conquest of other ideas. Or again differently, the focus is a focus of experience, and the area of experience involved gives us another criterion of condition, the criterion of area. Perhaps an example would be helpful here. We have said that Hemingway is concerned with the scruple of honor, that this is a basic idea in his work. But we find that he applies this idea to a relatively small area of experience. In fact, we never see a story in which the issue involves the problem of definition of the scruple, or we never see a story in which honor calls for a slow, grinding, day-to-day conquest of nagging difficulties. In other words, the idea is submitted to the test of a relatively small area of experience, to experience of a hand-picked sort, and to characters of a limited range.

But within that range, within the area in which he finds the congenial material and in which competing ideas do not intrude themselves too strongly, Hemingway's expressive capacity is very powerful and the degree of intensity is very great. He is concerned not to report variety of human nature or human situation, or to analyze the forces operating in society, but to communicate a certain feeling about, a certain attitude toward, a special issue. That is, he is essentially a lyric rather than a dramatic writer, and for the lyric writer virtue depends upon the intensity with which the personal vision is rendered rather than upon the creation of a variety of characters whose visions are in conflict among themselves. And though Hemingway has not furnished—and never intended to furnish—document and diagnosis of our age, he has given us one of its most compelling symbols.

Used as "Introduction" to *A Farewell to Arms* by Ernest Hemingway. Copyright, 1949, by Charles Scribner's Sons. Reprinted by permission of the author and publisher. First published in *The Kenyon Review*, Vol. IX (Winter, 1947), pp. 1–28.

William Faulkner

[1946]

MALCOLM COWLEY's editing of *The Portable Faulkner*[1] is remarkable on two counts. First, the selection from Faulkner's work is made not merely to give a cross section or a group of good examples but to demonstrate one of the principles of integration in the work. Second, the introductory essay is one of the few things ever written on Faulkner which is not hagridden by prejudice or preconception and which really sheds some light on the subject.

The selections here are made to describe the place, Yoknapatawpha County, Mississippi, which is, as Cowley puts it, "Faulkner's mythical kingdom," and to give the history of that kingdom. The place is the locale of most of Faulkner's work. Its 2400 square miles lie between the hills of north Mississippi and the rich, black bottom lands. It has a population of 15,611 persons, composing a society with characters as different as the Bundrens, the Snopeses, Ike McCaslin, Percy Grimm, Temple Drake, the Compsons, Christmas, Dilsey, and the tall convict of *The Wild Palms*. No land in all fiction lives more vividly in its physical presence than this mythical county—the "pine-winey" afternoons, the nights with "a thin sickle of moon like the heel print of a boot in wet sand," the tremendous reach of the big river in flood, "yellow and sleepy in the afternoon," and the "little piddling creeks, that run backward one day and forward the next and come busting down on a man full of dead mules and hen houses," the ruined plantation which was Popeye's hangout, the swamps and fields and hot, dusty roads of the Frenchman's Bend section, and the remnants of the great original forests, "green with gloom" in summer, "if anything actually dimmer than they had been in November's gray dissolution, where even at noon the sun fell only in windless dappling upon the earth which never completely dried."

And no land in all fiction is more painstakingly analyzed from the sociological standpoint. The descendants of the old families, the descendants of bushwhackers and carpetbaggers, the swamp rats, the Negro cooks and farm hands, bootleggers and gangsters, peddlers, college boys, tenant farmers, country store-keepers, county-seat lawyers are all here. The marks of class, occupation, and history are fully rendered and we know completely their speech, dress, food, houses, manners, and attitudes. Nature and sociology, geography and human geography, are scrupulously though effortlessly presented in Faulkner's work, and their significance for his work is very great; but the significance is of a conditioning order. They are, as it were, aspects

[1] *The Portable Faulkner,* edited by Malcolm Cowley. New York: Viking Press.

of man's "doom"—a word of which Faulkner is very fond—but his manhood in the face of that doom is what is important.

Cowley's selections are made to give the description of the mythical kingdom, but more important, they are made to give its history. Most critics, even those who have most naïvely or deliberately misread the meaning of the fact, have been aware that the sense of the past is crucial in Faulkner's work. Cowley has here set up selections running in date of action from 1820 to 1940. The first, "A Justice," is a story about Ikkemotubbe, the nephew of a Chickasaw chief who went to New Orleans, where he received the name of *du Homme,* which became Doom; who came back to the tribe to poison his way to the Man-ship; and who, in the end (in Faulkner's "history" though not in "A Justice" itself), swaps a mile square of "virgin north Mississippi dirt" for a racing mare owned by Jason Lycurgus Compson, the founder of the Compson family in Mississippi. The last selection, "Delta Autumn," shows us Isaac McCaslin, the man who brings the best of the old order, philosopher, aristocrat, woodsman, into the modern world and who gives the silver-mounted horn which General Compson had left him to a mulatto woman for her bastard son by a relative of McCaslin's. In between "A Justice" and "Delta Autumn" fall such pieces as the magnificent "Red Leaves," the profoundly symbolic story called "The Bear," the Civil War and Reconstruction stories, "Rain" (from *The Unvanquished*) and "Wash," "Old Man" (the story of the tall convict from *The Wild Palms*), and the often anthologized "That Evening Sun" and "A Rose for Emily," and the brilliant episode of "Percy Grimm" (from *Light in August*). There are other pieces included, but these are the best, and the best for showing the high points in the history of Yoknapatawpha County.

Cowley's introduction undertakes to define the significance of place and history in Faulkner's work, that "labor of imagination that has not been equaled in our time." That labor is, as he points out, a double labor: "first, to invent a Mississippi county that was like a mythical kingdom, but was complete and living in all its details; second, to make his story of Yoknapatawpha County stand as a parable or legend of all the Deep South." The legend—called a legend "because it is obviously no more intended as a historical account of the country south of the Ohio than *The Scarlet Letter* was intended as a history of Massachusetts"—is, as Cowley defines it, this:

The South was settled by Sartorises (aristocrats) and Sutpens (nameless, ambitious men) who, seizing the land from the Indians, were determined to found an enduring and stable order. But despite their strength and integrity their project was, to use Faulkner's word, "accursed" by slavery, which, with the Civil War as instrument, frustrated their design. Their attempt to rebuild according to the old plan and old values was defeated by a combination of forces—the carpetbaggers and Snopeses ("a new exploiting class descended from the landless whites"). Most of the descendants of the old order are in various ways incompetent: They are prevented by their code from competing with the codeless Snopeses, they cling to the letter and forget the spirit of their tradition, they lose contact with the realities of the present and escape into a dream world of alcohol or rhetoric or gentility or madness, they fall in love with defeat or death, they lose nerve and become cowards, or they, like the last Jason in *The Sound and the Fury*, adopt Snopesism and became worse than any Snopes. Figures like Popeye (eyes like "rubber knobs," a creature having "that vicious depthless quality of stamped tin," the man "who made money and had nothing he could do with it, spend it for, since he knew that alcohol would kill him like poison, who had no friends and had never known a woman") are in their dehumanized quality symbols of modernism, for the society of finance capitalism. The violence of some of Faulkner's work is, according to Cowley, "an example of the Freudian method turned backward, being full of sexual nightmares that are in reality social symbols. It is somehow connected in the author's mind with what he regards as the rape and corruption of the South."

This is, in brief, Cowley's interpretation of the legend, and it provides an excellent way into Faulkner; it exactly serves the purpose which an introduction should serve. The interpretation is indebted, no doubt, to that of George Marion O'Donnell (the first and still an indispensable study of Faulkner's theme), but it modifies O'Donnell's tendency to read Faulkner with an allegorical rigidity and with a kind of doctrinal single-mindedness.

It is possible that the present view, however, should be somewhat modified, at least in emphasis. Although no writer is more deeply committed to a locality than Faulkner, the emphasis on the Southern elements may blind us to other elements, or at least other applications, of deep significance. And this is especially true in so far as the work is interpreted merely as Southern apologetics or, as it is by Maxwell Geismar, as the "extreme hallucinations" of a "cultural psychosis."

It is important, I think, that Faulkner's work be regarded not in terms of the South against the North, but in terms of issues which are common to our modern world. The legend is not merely a legend of the South, but is also a legend of our general plight and problem. The modern world is in moral confusion. It does suffer from a lack of discipline, of sanctions, of community of values, of a sense of a mission. It is a world in which self-interest, workableness, success, provide the standards. It is a world which is the victim of abstraction and of mechanism, or at least, at moments, feels itself to be. It can look back nostalgically upon the old world of traditional values and feel loss and perhaps despair—upon the world in which, as one of Faulkner's characters puts it, men "had the gift of living once or dying once instead of being diffused and scattered creatures drawn blindly from a grab bag and assembled"

—a world in which men were, "integer for integer," more simple and complete.

If it be objected that Faulkner's view is unrealistic, that had the old order satisfied human needs it would have survived, and that it is sentimental to hold that it was killed from the outside, the answer is clear in the work: the old order did not satisfy human needs—the Southern old order or any other —for it, not being founded on justice, was "accursed" and held the seeds of its own ruin in itself. But even in terms of the curse the old order, as opposed to the new order (in so far as the new is to be equated with Snopesism), allowed the traditional man to define himself as human by setting up codes, concepts of virtue, obligations, and by accepting the risks of his humanity. Within the traditional order was a notion of truth, even if man in the flow of things did not succeed in realizing that truth. Take, for instance, the passage from "The Bear":

"All right," he said. "Listen," and read again, but only one stanza this time and closed the book and laid it on the table. "She cannot fade, though thou has not thy bliss," McCaslin said: "Forever wilt thou love, she be fair."

"He's talking about a girl," he said.

"He had to talk about something," McCaslin said. Then he said, "He was talking about truth. Truth is one. It doesn't change. It covers all things which touch the heart—honor and pride and pity and justice and courage and love. Do you see now?"

The human effort is what is important, the capacity to make the effort to rise above the mechanical process of life, the pride to endure, for in endurance there is a kind of self-conquest.

When it is said, as it is often said, that Faulkner's work is "backward-looking," the answer is that the constant ethical center is to be found in the glorification of the human effort and of human endurance, which are not in time, even though in modernity they seem to persist most surely among the despised and rejected. It is true that Faulkner's work contains a savage attack on modernity, but it is to be remembered that Elizabethan tragedy, for instance, contained just such an attack on its own special "modernity." (Ambition is the most constant tragic crime, and ambition is the attitude special to an opening society; all villains are rationalists and appeal to "nature" beyond traditional morality for justification, and rationalism is, in the sense implied here, the attitude special to the rise of a secular and scientific order before a new morality can be formulated.)

It is not ultimately important whether the traditional order (Southern or other) as depicted by Faulkner fits exactly the picture which critical historical method provides. Let it be granted, for the sake of discussion, that Faulkner does oversimplify the matter. What is ultimately important, both ethically and artistically, is the symbolic function of that order in relation to the world which is set in opposition to it. The opposition between the old order and the new does not, however, exhaust the picture. What of the order to come? "We will have to wait," old Ike McCaslin says to the mulatto girl who is in love with a white man. A curse may work itself out in time; and in such glimpses, which occur now and then, we get the notion of a grudging meliorism, a practical supplement to the idealism, like Ike McCaslin's, which finds compensation in the human effort and the contemplation of "truth."

The discussion, even at a larger scope and with more satisfactory analysis, of the central theme of Faulkner would not exhaust the interest of his work. In fact, the discussion of this question always runs the risk of making his work appear too schematic, too dry and too complacent when in actual fact it is full of rich detail, of shadings and complexities of attitude, of ironies and ambivalences. Cowley's introduction cautions the reader on this point and suggests various fruitful topics for investigation and thought. But I shall make bold—and in the general barrenness of criticism on Faulkner it does not require excessive boldness—to list and comment on certain topics which seem to me to demand further critical study.

Nature. The vividness of the natural background is one of the impressive features of Faulkner's work. It is accurately observed, but observation only provides the stuff from which the characteristic effects are gained. It is the atmosphere which counts, the poetry, the infusion of feeling, the symbolic weight. Nature provides a backdrop—of lyric beauty (the meadow in the cow episode of *The Hamlet*), of homely charm (the trial scene of the "Spotted Horses" story from the same book), of sinster, brooding force (the river in "Old Man" from *The Wild Palms*), of massive dignity (the forest in "The Bear")—for the human action and passion. The indestructible beauty is there: "God created man," Ike McCaslin says in "Delta Autumn," "and He created the world for him to live in and I reckon He created the kind of world He would have wanted to live in if He had been a man."

Ideally, if man were like God, as Ike McCaslin puts it, man's attitude toward nature would be one of pure contemplation, pure participation in its great forms and appearances; the appropriate attitude is love, for with Ike McCaslin the moment of love is equated with godhood. But since man "wasn't quite God himself," since he lives in the world of flesh, he must be a hunter, user, and violator. To return to McCaslin: God "puts them both here: man and the game he would follow and kill, foreknowing it. I believe He said, 'So be it.' I reckon He even foreknew the end. But He said 'I will give him his chance. I will give him warning and foreknowledge too, along with the desire to follow and the power to slay. The woods and the fields he ravages and the game he devastates will be the consequence and signature of his crime and guilt, and his punishment.' "

There is, then, a contamination implicit in the human condition—a kind of Original Sin, as it were—but it is possible, even in the contaminating act, the violation, for man to achieve some measure of redemption, a redemption through love. For instance, in "The Bear," the great legendary beast which is pursued for years to the death is also an object of love and veneration, and the symbol of virtue, and the deer hunt of "Delta Autumn" is for Ike Mc-Caslin a ritual of renewal. Those who have learned the right relationship to nature—"the pride and humility" which young Ike McCaslin learns from the half-Negro, half-Indian Sam Fathers—are set over against those who have not. In "The Bear," General Compson speaks up to Cass McCaslin to defend the wish of the boy Ike McCaslin to stay an extra week in the woods: "You got one foot straddled into a farm and the other foot straddled into a bank; you ain't even got a good hand-hold where this boy was already an old man long before you damned Sartorises and Edmondses invented farms and banks to keep yourselves from having to find out what this boy was born knowing and fearing too maybe, but without being afraid, that could go ten miles on a compass because he wanted to look at a bear none of us had ever got near enough to put a bullet in and looked at the bear and came the ten miles back on the compass in the dark; maybe by God that's the why and the wherefore of farms and banks."

Those who have the wrong attitude toward nature are the pure exploiters, the apostles of abstractionism, the truly evil men. For instance, the very open-ing of *Sanctuary* presents a distinction on this ground between Benbow and Popeye. While the threat of Popeye keeps Benbow crouching by the spring, he hears a Carolina wren sing, and even under these circumstances tries to recall the local name for it. And he says to Popeye: "And of course you don't know the name of it. I don't suppose you'd know a bird at all, without it was singing in a cage in a hotel lounge or cost four dollars on a plate." Popeye, as we may remember, spits in the spring (he hates nature and must foul it), is afraid to go through the woods ("Through all them trees?" he demands when Benbow points out the short cut), and when an owl whisks past them in the twilight, claws at Benbow's coat with almost hysterical fear ("It's just an owl," Benbow says. "It's nothing but an owl.").

The pure exploiters, though they may gain ownership and use of a thing, never really have it; like Popeye, they are impotent. For instance, Flem Snopes, the central character and villain of *The Hamlet,* who brings the exploiter's mentality to Frenchman's Bend, finally marries Eula Varner, a kind of fertility goddess or earth goddess; but his ownership is meaningless, for she always refers to him as "that man" (she does not even have a name for him), and he has only got her after she has given herself willingly to one of the bold, hot-blooded boys of the neighborhood. In fact, nature can't, in one sense, be "owned." Ike McCaslin, in "The Bear," says of the land which has come down to him: "It was never Father's and Uncle Buddy's to bequeath me to repudiate, because it was never Grandfather's to bequeath them to bequeath me to repudiate, because it was never old Ikkemotubbe's to sell to Grandfather for bequeathment and repudiation. Because it was never Ikkemotubbe's father's father's to bequeath Ikkemotubbe to sell to Grandfather or any man because on the instant when Ikkemotubbe discovered, realized, that he could sell it for money, on that instant it ceased ever to have been his forever, father to father, to father, and the man who bought it bought nothing."

The right attitude toward nature is, as a matter of fact, associated with the right attitude toward man, and the mere lust for power over nature is associated with the lust for power over other men, for God gave the earth to man, we read in "The Bear," not "to hold for himself and his descendants inviolable title forever, generation after generation, to the oblongs and squares of the earth, but to hold the earth mutual and intact in the communal anonymity of brotherhood, and all the fee He asked was pity and humility and sufferance and endurance and the sweat of his face for bread." It is the failure of this pity which curses the earth (the land in Faulkner's particular country is "accursed" by chattel slavery, but slavery is simply one of the possible forms of the failure). But the rape of nature and the crime against man are always avenged. The rape of nature, the mere exploitation of it without love, is always avenged because the attitude which commits that crime also commits the crime against men which in turn exacts vengeance, so that man finally punishes himself. It is only by this line of reasoning that one can, I think, read the last page of "Delta Autumn":

This land which man has deswamped and denuded and deriverded in two generations so that white men can own plantations and commute every night to Memphis and black men own plantations and ride in Jim Crow cars to Chicago to live in millionaires' mansions on Lake Shore Drive; where white men rent farms and live like niggers and niggers crop on shares and live like animals; where cotton is planted and grows man-tall in the very cracks of the sidewalks, and usury and mortgage and bankruptcy and measureless wealth, Chinese and African and Aryan and Jew, all breed and spawn together until no man has time to say which one is which nor cares. . . . No wonder the ruined woods I used to know don't cry for retribution! he thought: The people who have destroyed it will accomplish its revenge.

The attitude toward nature in Faulkner's work, however, does not involve a sinking into nature. In Faulkner's mythology man has "suzerainty over the earth," he is not of the earth, and it is the human virtues which count —"pity and humility and sufferance and endurance." If we take even the extreme case of the idiot Snopes and his fixation on the cow in *The Hamlet* (a scene whose function in the total order of the book is to show that even the idiot pervert is superior to Flem), a scene which shows the human being as close as possible to the "natural" level, we find that the scene is the most lyrical in Faulkner's work: even the idiot is human and not animal, for only human desires, not animal, clothe themselves in poetry. I think that George Marion O'Donnell is right in pointing to the humanism-naturalism opposition in Faulkner's work, and over and over again we find that the point of some novel or story has to do with the human effort to find or create values in the mechanical round of experience—"not just to eat and evacuate and sleep warm," as Charlotte Rittenmeyer says in *The Wild Palms,* "So we can get up and eat and evacuate in order to sleep warm again," or not just to raise cotton to buy niggers to raise cotton to buy niggers, as it is put in another place. Even when a character seems to be caught in the iron ring of some compulsion, of some mechanical process (the hunted Negro of "Red Leaves," the tall convict of *The Wild Palms,* Christmas of *Light in August*), the effort may be discernible. And in Quentin's attempt, in *The Sound and the Fury,* to persuade his sister Caddy, who is pregnant by one of the boys of Jefferson, to confess that she has committed incest with him, we find among other things the idea that "the horror" and "the clean flame" would be preferable to the meaninglessness of the "loud world."

Humor. One of the most important remarks in Cowley's introduction is that concerning humor. There is, especially in the later books, "a sort of homely and sober-sided frontier humor that is seldom achieved in contemporary writing." Cowley continues: "In a curious way, Faulkner combines two of the principal traditions in American letters: the tradition of psychological horror, often close to symbolism, that begins with Charles Brockden Brown, our first professional novelist, and extends through Poe, Melville, Henry James (in his later stories), Stephen Crane and Hemingway; and the other tradition of frontier humor and realism, beginning with Augustus Longstreet's *Georgia Scenes* and having Mark Twain as its best example." The observation is an acute one, for the distortions of humor and the distortions of horror in Faulkner's work are closely akin and frequently, in a given instance, can scarcely be disentangled.

It is true that the most important strain of humor in Faulkner's work is derived from the tradition of frontier humor (though it is probable that he got it from the porches of country stores and the courthouse yards of county-seat towns and not from any book), and it is true that the most spectacular displays of Faulkner's humor are of this order—for example, the "Spotted Horses" episode from *The Hamlet* or the story "Was." But there are other strains which might be distinguished and investigated. For example, there is a kind of Dickensian humor; the scene in the Memphis brothel from *Sanctuary,* which is reprinted here under the title "Uncle Bud and the Three Madams," is certainly more Dickensian than frontier. There is a subdued humor, sometimes shading into pathos, in the treatment of some of the Negro characters and in their dialogue. And there is an irony ranging from that in the scene in *Sanctuary* where Miss Reba, the madam, in offended decency keeps telling Temple, "Lie down and cover up your nekkidness," while the girl talks with Benbow, to that in the magnificently sustained monologue of Jason at the end of *The Sound and the Fury*.

In any case, humor in Faulkner's work is never exploited for its own sake. It is regularly used as an index, as a lead, to other effects. The humor in itself may be striking, but Faulkner is not a humorist in the sense, say, that Mark Twain is. His humor is but one perspective on the material and it is never a final perspective, as we can see from such an example as the episode of "Spotted Horses." Nothing could be more wide of the point than the remark in Maxwell Geismar's essay on Faulkner to the effect that Faulkner in *The Hamlet* "seems now to accept the antics of his provincial morons, to enjoy the chronicle of their low-grade behavior; he submerges himself in their clownish degradation." All the critic seems to find in Mink Snopes' victim with his life-long devotion to the memory of his dead wife, and Ratliff with his good heart and ironical mind and quiet wisdom, is comic "descendants of the gangling and giggling Wash Jones."

The Poor White. The above remark leads us to the not uncommon misconception about the role of the poor white in Faulkner's work. It is true that the Snopeses are poor whites, descendants of bushwhackers (and therefore outside society, as the bushwhacker was outside society, had no "side" in the Civil War but tried to make a good thing of it), and it is true that Snopesism represents a special kind of villainy and degradation, the form that the pure doctrine of exploitation and degradation takes in the society of which Faulkner writes, but any careful reader realizes that a Snopes is not to be equated with a poor white. For instance, the book most fully about the poor white, *As I Lay Dying*, is full of sympathy and poetry. There are a hundred touches like that in Cash's soliloquy about the phonograph: "I reckon it's a good thing we aint got ere a one of them. I reckon I wouldn't never get no work done a-tall for listening to it. I dont know if a little music aint about the nicest thing a fellow can have. Seems like when he comes in tired of a night, it aint nothing could rest him like having a little music played and him resting." Or like the long section toward the middle of the book devoted to Addie Bundren, a section which is full of eloquence like that of this paragraph: "And then he died. He did not know he was dead. I would lie by him in the dark, hearing the dark land talking of God's love and His beauty and His sin; hearing the dark voicelessness in which the words are the deeds, and the other words that are not deeds, that are just the gaps in peoples' lacks, coming down like the cries of geese out of the wild darkness in the old terrible nights, fumbling at the deeds like orphans to whom are pointed out in a crowd two faces and told,

That is your father, your mother." Do these passages indicate a relish in the "antics of his provincial morons"?

The whole of *As I Lay Dying* is based on the heroic effort of the Bundren family to fulfill the promise to the dead mother, to take her body to Jefferson; and the fact that Anse Bundren, after the heroic effort has been completed, immediately gets him a new wife, the "duck-shaped woman" with the "hard-looking pop-eyes," does not negate the heroism of the effort nor the poetry and feeling which give flesh to the book. We are told by one critic that "what should have been the drama of the Bundrens thus becomes in the end a sort of brutal farce," and that we are "unable to feel the tragedy because the author has refused to accept the Bundrens, as he did accept the Compsons, as tragic." Rather, I should say, the Bundrens may come off a little better than the latter-day Compsons, the whining mother, the promiscuous Caddy, the ineffectual Quentin, and the rest. The Bundrens, at least, are capable of the heroic effort, and the promise is fulfilled. What the conclusion indicates is that even such a fellow as Anse Bundren (who is not typical of his family, by the way), in the grip of an idea, in terms of promise or code, is capable of rising out of his ordinary level; Anse falls back at the end, but only after the prop of the idea and obligation have been removed. And we may recall that even the "gangling and giggling Wash Jones" has always been capable of some kind of obscure dream and aspiration (his very attachment to Sutpen indicates that), and that in the end he achieves dignity and manhood.

The final and incontrovertible evidence that Snopes is not to be equated with poor whites comes in *The Hamlet* (though actually most of the characters in the book, though they may be poor, are not strictly speaking, "poor whites" at all, but rather what uninstructed reviewers choose to call by that label). The point of the book is the assault made on a solid community of plain, hard-working small farmers by Snopeses and Snopesism. Ratliff is not rich, but he is not Flem Snopes. And if the corruption of Snopesism does penetrate into the community, there is not one here who can be compared in degradation and vileness to Jason of *The Sound and the Fury*, the Compson who has embraced Snopesism. In fact, Popeye and Flem, Faulkner's best advertised villains, cannot, for vileness and ultimate meanness, touch Jason.

The Negro. In one of Faulkner's books it is said that every white child is born crucified on a black cross. Remarks like this have led to a gross misconception of the place of the Negro in Faulkner's work, to the notion that Faulkner "hates" Negroes. For instance, we find Maxwell Geismar exclaiming what a "strange inversion" it is to take the Negro, who is the "tragic consequence," and to exhibit him as the "evil cause" of the failure of the old order in the South.

This is a misreading of the text. It is slavery, not the Negro, which is defined, quite flatly, as the curse, over and over again, and the Negro is the black cross in so far as he is the embodiment of the curse, the reminder of the guilt, the incarnation of the problem. That is the basic point. But now and then, as a kind of tangential irony, we have the notion, not of the burden of the white on the black, but of the burden of the black on the white, the weight of obligation, inefficiency, and so on, as well as the weight of guilt (the notion we find in the old story of the plantation mistress who, after the Civil War, said: "Mr. Lincoln thought he was emancipating those slaves, but he was really emancipating me.").

For instance, we get hints of this notion in "Red Leaves"; one of the Indians, sweating in the chase of the runaway Negro who is to be killed for the Man's funeral, says, "Damn that Negro," and the other Indian replies, "Yao. When have they ever been anything but a trial and a care to us?" But the black cross is, fundamentally, the weight of the white man's guilt, the white man who now sells salves and potions "to bleach the pigment and straighten the hair of Negroes that they might resemble the very race which for two hundred years had held them in bondage and from which for another hundred years not even a bloody civil war would have set them completely free." The curse is still operative, as the crime is still compounded.

The actual role of the Negro in Faulkner's fiction is consistently one of pathos or heroism. It is not merely, as has been suggested more than once, that Faulkner condescends to the good and faithful servant, the "white folks' nigger." There are figures like Dilsey, but they are not as impressive as the Negro in "Red Leaves" or Sam Fathers, who, with the bear, is the hero of "The Bear." The fugitive, who gains in the course of the former story a shadowy symbolic significance, is told in the end by one of the Indians who overtake him, "You ran well. Do not be ashamed," and when he walks among the Indians, he is "the tallest there, his high, close, mud-caked head looming above them all." And Sam Fathers is the fountainhead of the wisdom which Ike McCaslin finally gains, and the repository of the virtues which are central for Faulkner—"an old man, son of a Negro slave and an Indian king, inheritor on the one hand of the long chronicle of a people who had learned humility through suffering and learned pride through the endurance which survived suffering, and on the other side the chronicle of a people even longer in the land than the first, yet who now existed there only in the solitary brotherhood of an old and childless Negro's alien blood and the wild and invincible spirit of an old bear."

Even Christmas, in *Light in August*, though he is sometimes spoken of as a villain, is a mixture of heroism and pathos. He is the lost, suffering, enduring creature (the figure like Sam Fathers, the tall convict of *The Wild Palms*, or Dilsey in *The Sound and the Fury*), and even the murder he commits at the end is a fumbling attempt to define his manhood, is an attempt to break out of the iron ring of mechanism, to lift himself out of "nature," for the woman whom he kills has become a figure of the horror of the human which has surrendered the human attributes. (We may compare Christmas to Mink Snopes in *The Hamlet* in this respect: Mink, mean and vicious as he is, kills out of a kind of warped and confused pride, and by this affirmation is set off against his kinsman Flem, whose only values are those of pure Snopesism.)

Even such a brief comment on the Negro in Faulkner's work cannot close without this passage from "The Bear":

"Because they will endure. They are better than we are. Stronger than we are. Their vices are vices aped from white men or that white men and bondage have taught them: improvidence and intemperance and evasion—not laziness: evasion: of what white men had set them to, not for their aggrandizement or even comfort but his own—" and McCaslin

"All right. Go on: Promiscuity. Violence. Instability and lack of control. Inability to distinguish between mine and thine—" and he

"How distinguish when for two hundred years mine did not even exist for them?" and McCaslin

"All right. Go on. And their virtues—" and he

"Yes. Their own. Endurance—" and McCaslin

"So have mules:" and he

"—and pity and tolerance and forbearance and fidelity and love of children—" and McCaslin

"So have dogs:" and he

"—whether their own or not or black or not. And more: what they got not only from white people but not even despite white people because they had it already from the old free fathers a longer time free than us because we have never been free—"

And there is the single comment under Dilsey's name in the annotated genealogy of the Compsons which Faulkner has prepared for the present volume: "They endured."

Technique. There are excellent comments on this subject by Cowley, Conrad Aiken, Warren Beck, Joseph Warren Beach, and Alfred Kazin, but the subject has not been fully explored. One difficulty is that Faulkner is an incorrigible and restless experimenter, is peculiarly sensitive to the expressive possibilities of shifts in technique and has not developed (like Hemingway or Katherine Anne Porter—lyric rather than dramatic writers, artists with a great deal of self-certainty) in a straight line.

Provisionally, we may distinguish in Faulkner's work three basic methods of handling a narrative. One is best typified in *Sanctuary,* where there is a tightly organized plot, a crisp, laconic style, an objective presentation of character—an impersonal method. Another is best typified by *As I Lay Dying* or *The Sound and the Fury,* where each character unfolds in his own language or flow of being before us—a dramatic method in that the author does not obtrude, but a method which makes the subjective reference of character the medium of presentation. Another is best typified by "Was," "The Bear," or the story of the tall convict in *The Wild Palms,* where the organization of the narrative is episodic and the sense of a voice, a narrator's presence (though not necessarily a narrator in the formal sense), is almost constantly felt—a method in which the medium is ultimately a "voice" as index to sensibility. The assumptions underlying these methods, and the relations among them, would provide a study.

Cowley's emphasis on the unity of Faulkner's work, the fact that all the novels and stories are to be taken as aspects of a single, large design, is very important. It is important, for one thing, in regard to the handling of character. A character, Sutpen, for instance, may appear in various perspectives, so that from book to book we move toward a final definition much as in actual life we move toward the definition of a person. The same principle applies to event, as Conrad Aiken has pointed out, the principle of the spiral method which takes the reader over and over the same event from a different altitude, as it were, and a different angle. In relation to both character and event this method, once it is understood by the reader, makes for a kind of realism and a kind of suspense (in the formal not the factual sense) not common in fiction.

The emphasis on the unity of Faulkner's work may, however, lead to an underrating of the degree of organization within individual works. Cowley is right in pointing out the structural defect in *Light in August,* but he may be putting too much emphasis on the over-all unity and not enough on the organization of the individual work when he says that *The Hamlet* tends to resolve into a "series of episodes resembling beads on a string." I think that in that novel we have a type of organization in which the thematic rather than the narrative emphasis is the basic principle, and once we grasp that fact the unity of the individual work may come clear. In fact, the whole subject of the principle of thematic organization in the novels and long stories, "The Bear," for instance, needs investigation. In pieces which seem disjointed, or which seem to have the mere tale-teller's improvisations, we may sometimes discover the true unity if we think of the line of meaning, the symbolic ordering, and surrender ourselves to the tale-teller's "voice." And it may be useful at times to recall the distinction between the formal, forensic realism of Ibsen as opposed to the fluid, suggestive realism of Chekhov.

Symbol and Image. Cowley and O'Donnell have given acute readings of the main symbolic outline of Faulkner's fiction, but no one has yet devoted himself to the study of symbolic motifs which, though not major, are nevertheless extremely instructive. For instance, the images of the hunt, the flight, the pursuit, such as we have in "Red Leaves," *The Wild Palms,* the episode of Peter Grimm in *Light in August*, "The Bear," "Delta Autumn," "Was," and (especially in the hordes of moving Negroes) in *The Unvanquished*. Or there is the important symbolic relationship between man and earth. Or there is the contrast between images of compulsion and images of will or freedom. Or there is the device of what we might call the frozen moment, the arrested action which becomes symbolic, as in the moment when, in "An Odor of Verbena" (from *The Unvanquished*), Drusilla offers the pistols to the hero.

Polarity. To what extent does Faulkner work in terms of polarities, oppositions, paradoxes, inversions of roles? How much does he employ a line of concealed (or open) dialectic progression as a principle for his fiction? The study of these questions may lead to the discovery of principles of organization in his work not yet defined by criticism.

The study of Faulkner is the most challenging single task in contemporary American literature for criticism to undertake. Here is a novelist who, in mass of work, in scope of material, in range of effect, in reportorial accuracy and symbolic subtlety, in philosophical weight, can be put beside the masters of our own past literature. Yet this accomplishment has been effected in what almost amounts to critical isolation and silence, and when the silence has been broken it has usually been broken by someone (sometimes one of our better critics) whose reading has been hasty, whose analysis unscholarly and whose judgments superficial. The picture of Faulkner presented to the public by such criticism is a combination of Thomas Nelson Page, a fascist and a psychopath, gnawing his nails. Of course, this picture is usually accompanied by a grudging remark about genius.

Cowley's book, for its intelligence, sensitivity, and sobriety in the introduction, and for the ingenuity and judgment exhibited in the selections, would be valuable at any time. But it is especially valuable at this time. Perhaps it can mark a turning point in Faulkner's reputation. That will be of slight service to Faulkner, who, as much as any writer of our place and time, can rest in confidence. He can afford to wait. But can we?

From *The New Republic*, Vol. CXV (August 12, 1946), pp. 176–180; and (August 26, 1946), pp. 234–237. Reprinted by permission of the author and editors.

ROBERT MORSS LOVETT

Sherwood Anderson, American

[1941]

I FIRST met Sherwood Anderson in the summer of 1913 at one of the little shops converted into studios, relics of the World's Fair of 1893, which stand on the edge of Jackson Park in Chicago. He was in his workman's clothes (he was then a house Painter) but dangled a manuscript instead of a paint pail. He was then nearly forty, but seemed younger, though there was something a little grim and repressed in his manner, unlike the buoyant and genial disposition which later was so habitual. Perhaps he realized that this was a somewhat momentous occasion. The opening chapter of the novel which he proceeded to read was a piece of stark realism in the manner of Dreiser, who that year was living in Chicago. I do not know whether Sherwood met Dreiser at that time, but he did meet Floyd Dell, who recommended to John Lane in London the publication of *Windy McPherson's Son* as a piece of Americana.

Anderson thus began his writing career under the influence and patronage of the realists at the time when realism was being modified by symbolism. In 1919 his next book, *Winesburg, Ohio,* showed clearly the quality which was to become his characteristic, the extension of the realistic method by a groping sense of the significance behind the trivial human phenomena which he recorded so accurately. Individually the sketches of persons and episodes which make up the volume seem to reflect a suggestion from the *Spoon River Anthology.* Together they add up to a unit, and *Winesburg, Ohio* is a character sketch of a town. This construction marked less emphatically two later volumes of short stories, *The Triumph of the Egg* and *Horses and Men,* which consolidated his reputation in this field. A novel published in 1920, *Poor White,* opens like *Windy McPherson's Son,* with superb realism, but falls off into rather feeble romance. In 1925, however, with *Dark Laughter,* Sherwood Anderson achieved a genuine triumph, and took his place among our leading novelists.

Hitherto his career has been of a highly indeterminate character, of which we gain elusive glimpses through his two autobiographies, *Tar* and *A Story Teller's Story.* The latter is by no means an organized narrative, but rather a

478

post-impressionist picture of a life, with planes and cubes thrown together to catch the light. His father kept a harness shop in the small Ohio town where Sherwood spent his boyhood as related in *Tar*. He left home early, it would seem, and spent many years in learning and practicing life—sporting life at race tracks, farming life in field work, industrial life in a bicycle factory, military life in the Spanish War, business life as a writer of advertising copy. One event stands out because of his frequent reference to it. After having become the proprietor of a clothespin factory, which bade fair to make him a prosperous bourgeois, he walked out on that prospect and took to the open road, doubtless in the mood ascribed to young Tom Edwards in *An Ohio Pagan*: ". . . as he walked in the dusty roads under the moon, he thought of American towns and cities as places for beautifully satisfying adventures for all such fellows as himself."

In these years he supplemented his own experience by vast areas of conversation, in which he gathered the reports of life by others, first of all his father, who was a natural story teller, then Judge Turner and Alonzo Berners. When he had a run of luck in gambling or had saved a little money he took a few weeks off to haunt libraries. His pages thus offer a profusion of tramping, fighting, talking, toiling, seeing, reading, thinking; but it is all life, felt with extraordinary sensitiveness and rendered with verve and color. One of the books which impressed him was *The Education of Henry Adams*. His own story might be called *The Education of Sherwood Anderson*, and put forth as an account of the curriculum of life as opposed to that of the schools.

This education was directed, at first instinctively, later with increasing intelligence, to the making of an American artist. Very early he realized the sterility of the divorce between the formal culture of his time, personally directed from New England, and the natural cultural inheritance of the country gained through its absorption of a hundred racial strains. "I was to see," he cries, "the grip of the old New England, the Puritan culture, begin to loosen. The physical coming of the Celts, Latins, Slavs, men of the Far East, the blood of the dreaming nations of the world gradually flowing thicker and thicker in this body of the American, and the shrewd shop-keeping money-saving blood of the Northern men getting thinner and thinner—."

It was this sense of abundance which characterized Anderson as a writer of the Middle West. The economy of New England had no appeal to him, nor did the safety-first philosophy of worldly success. He took life and all of it with gusto, and he reveled in its richness and color. "I have never for a moment," he wrote, "subscribed to the philosophy of life as set forth by *The Saturday Evening Post, The Alantic Monthly*, Yale, 'Upward and Onward,' 'The White Man's Burden,' etc. There was always within me a notion of another aspect of life—at least faintly felt—a life that dreamed a little of more colorful and gaudy things—cruelty and tragedy creeping in the night, laughter, splashing sunlight, the pomp and splendor of the old tyrants, the simple devotion of old devotees."

One cannot fail to be reminded in these passages of his contemporary, Vachel Lindsay, who had so much in common, by temperament, attitude toward life, and experience, with Sherwood Anderson. They were both prophets and priests of democracy in the years of its last glory.

A rough generalization in regard to writers of fiction divides them into two classes, those who start from a theme or a plot, and whose problem it is to find material with which to give it flesh and blood, and those who find their inspiration in the stuff of life itself, and whose problem is to discover in that substance a significance or a pattern which will justify its treatment as a unit. Sherwood Anderson was unmistakably of the second type. He was overwhelmed by the abundance of the material pressing on him for expression. He saw it as tales, stories wandering among the realities about him, naked, waiting to be clothed, while he sat, to use his own figure, like a tailor fashioning clothes for them from his imagination. His lyrical preface to *The Triumph of the Egg* pleads for them:

> Tales are people who sit on the doorstep of the house of
>   my mind.
> It is cold outside, and they sit waiting.
> I look out at a window.
>   The tales have cold hands
>   Their hands are freezing.
> A short thickly-built tale arises and threshes his arms about.
> His nose is red and he has two gold teeth.
>
> I am a helpless man—my hands tremble.
> I should be sitting on a bench like a tailor.
> I should be weaving warm cloth out of the threads of
>   thought.
> The tales should be clothed.
> They are freezing on the doorstep of the house of my mind.

Sherwood Anderson felt the supreme joy of creation as he moved in his world, giving life to the creatures of his imagination. His characters are the children of his body, as well as of his mind—Wing Biddlebaum, Hugh McVey, Elizabeth Willard, Kate Swift, Jesse Bentley, Tom Means. "They had lived within me, and I had given a kind of life to them. They had lived for a passing moment anyway in the consciousness of others besides myself." One is reminded of Wordsworth's rapture over inanimate nature by Anderson's intoxication with the spectacle of even the most humble life going on about him. An example of the power of trivial circumstance to stir him to imaginative activity is given in *A Story Teller's Story*. He was looking out of his window one day upon his neighbor's garden where he saw a man picking potato bugs off the vine while his wife was scolding him for having forgotten to bring home some sugar. "I was unconscious," he writes, "of a dinner being put on a table downstairs in my house, unconscious of any need of food I would ever feel again, unconscious of the regime of my household, of the affairs of my factory. A man and a woman in a garden had become the center of a universe about which it seemed to me I might think and feel in joy and wonder forever."

This rapture in the face of the teeming reality of the world is the source of the almost uncanny excitement which we feel in Anderson's most noteworthy stories, especially those in which he extends by intuition the mental experience of men and women who in physical form pass across his vision. In his direct perception of them he resembles Chekhov, and like Chekhov he allows no pattern or structure to interfere with the immediate appeal of fact. Western art of fiction or of the stage tends to be centripetal; it draws attention to a group of characters whose interrelations develop into a plot. In Russian stories and plays, such as *The Cherry Orchard*, the action is centrifugal; it diffuses attention and carries it beyond the immediate action to more remote implications of life that is unrevealed but none the less significant. This is an essential quality of Anderson's stories. They reach outward into the unknown, and this sense of something beyond to which humanity vainly aspires brings him near to Maeterlinck. His characters are indubitably real in the things they do and say; and yet this reality is but jetsam and flotsam on the sea of the unconscious. And as with Maeterlinck his absorption in reality passes over into mysticism. The Man in the Brown Coat says: "I'll tell you what—sometimes the whole life of this world floats in a human face in my mind. The unconscious face of this world stops and stands still before me."

Many of Anderson's stories are concerned with the frustration of human life that comes from isolation, the inability of one being to come near, to enter into understanding with another. One might infer from the repetition of this theme that it was a reflection of his own suffering, but in fact he seemed to be the least inhibited of beings in his intercourse with others. This constant reaching out for human relations on his part, which revealed itself in such genial and sympathetic companionship, was, however, in essence a defense against a loneliness in which he saw the deepest of human tragedies. There is the story "Unlighted Lamps," in which father and daughter remain strangers. The Man in the Brown Coat symbolizes by that garment his isolation from his wife. "We sit together in the evening but I do not know her. I wear a brown coat and I cannot come out of my coat. I cannot come out of myself. My wife is very gentle and she speaks softly, but she cannot come out of herself."

Sherwood Anderson found in the short story of varying length a form admirably fitted to his hand. Sometimes it is a mere sketch, as in "Milk Bottles," or it may be a novelette, which in *Out of Nowhere into Nothing* is exactly proportioned to its function. Within the dimensions of the short story he could rely entirely on the experience of his characters, which came to him by observation or valid intuition. In his novels he was driven to extend that experience by imagination. In *Windy McPherson's Son* and *Poor White* it is plainly to be seen where truthful fiction gives way to badly imagined romance.

Poor White opens with a hauntingly real picture of Hugh McVey, an overgrown lout of a boy, living with his father on the mud bank of a river town, asleep much of the time, infested by flies, earning a few cents by cleaning saloons and outhouses. A New England woman takes hold of him, arouses his ambition, teaches him to control his awkward body and fix his wandering mind. With his great physical strength he becomes a terrific worker and an inventor of machines to multiply his work. All of this may be read as an allegory of the uncouth, powerful masculine West, disciplined by the feminine hand of New England; but when the hero passes into the hands of his enemies, prosperity and marriage, he passes likewise out of the real world.

Dark Laughter is the story of John Stockton, a reporter with a flair for facts, whose wife Bernice wrote stories for the magazines. Naturally she looked down on her husband. He did not resent this but it bored him. So one day he walked out of the apartment, made for oldtown, where he had been brought up, and as Bruce Dudley found a job in Fred Grey's carriage factory. There he worked beside Sponge Martin, who taught him to paint carriage wheels. Grey's wife Aline looked at Bruce, who reminded her of a man she had once wanted, and engaged him as a gardener. Fred Grey, one of Anderson's best understood characters, found the only course compatible with his dignity in ignoring the triangle which was forming, and from which two characters eventually stepped out on the road to freedom.

This pattern of life guided by frail intelligence and wavering will shades off into a background of humanity, a chorus of primitive men and women strong in instinct. One of Bruce Dudley's memories is of a steamboat excursion:

From the throats of ragged black men as they trotted up and down the landing-stage, strange haunting notes. Words were caught up, tossed about, held in the throat. Word-lovers, sound-lovers—the blacks seemed to hold a tone in some warm place, under their red tongues perhaps. Their thick lips were walls under which the tone hid. Unconscious love of inanimate things lost to the whites—skies, the river, a moving boat—black mysticism—never expressed except in song or in the movement of bodies.

Later the drama played by Bruce and Aline is surrounded by a cloud of witnesses. "The two Negro women in the house watched and waited. Often they looked at each other and giggled. The air on the hilltop was filled with laughter—dark laughter."

Dark Laughter contains all the distinguishing notes of Anderson's fiction. What marks it as an advance on his earlier novels is that here he has achieved an artistic unity through a clearer view and a stronger, more persistent grasp of his material and its meaning. That material is, as always, experience, and its meaning is in the contrast between the logic of events, of an actual situation, and that of intellectual discrimination and classification. Fred Grey relies on a classification, a conventional simplification of life known as marriage, within which such things as Bruce and Aline meditate. Bruce and Aline are thrown back on a primitive situation. At first they are among the characters of whom Anderson has give us so many, who are "all mussed up." It is the desire for stability and meaning that causes Bruce and Aline to integrate themselves with one another.

Throughout *Dark Laughter* runs another principle which Anderson has always exemplified: it is the importance of art as a means of mastering the crude material fact of the world. He is repelled by the notion of art as something external, decorative. It is this conception on the part of Bernice which disgusts Bruce with the meretricious life in which she would entangle him, symbolized by "that story Bernice was writing about the man who saw the wax figure in a shop window and thought it was a woman." What attracts him to Sponge Martin is the latter's closeness to reality and his power of manipulating it to a perfect result. "Sponge could fill his brush very full, and yet handle it in such a way that the varnish did not drip down, and he left no ugly thick places on the wheels. The stroke of the brush was like a caress." So Bruce comes to hold the pragmatist's view of art as a process of making the world a different place in which to live:

Perhaps if you got the thoughts and fancies organized a little, made them work through your body, made thoughts and fancies a part of yourself—they might be used then—perhaps as Sponge Martin could lay varnish on. Suppose about one man in a million got things organized a little. What would that mean? What would such a man be? Would he be a Napoleon, a Caesar?

It is evidence of Anderson's unconscious absorption of the spirit of the age in which he so completely lived that his fiction offers so many points of contact with the characteristic philosophy of the time.

When Sherwood Anderson felt the urge to write his masterpiece he settled for a winter in Marion, in the southwest corner of Virginia. There he bought a newspaper, and later a second—one Democratic, the other Republican, for the news was the same and the editorial column only needed reversing. He peopled his staff with a number of appropriate characters, the sports writer, the society editor, the man about town, who became so real to his rural readers that when they came to town they asked for them at the newspaper office. He wrote *Dark Laughter;* with the proceeds he bought a farm twenty miles out of town, and built a house largely with his own hand and brain. There he lived a modest life of a country squire, interrupted by many journeys. He was an indefatigable rolling stone. As a sage he sat in council for the young at writers' conferences; he lectured at colleges and literary clubs on literature and small town journalism; he met friends everywhere and expanded in his talk. He very nearly abandoned fiction for direct reporting of life as he found it in conversation. When I asked him once about making a trip to Mexico he refused because he feared that language would stand in the way of his daily diet of human stuff.

With his neighbors at Marion his relations were delightful. They accepted him as one of them. On a visit I made to him an episode occurred which might have been one of the unclothed tales sitting on his doorstep. Sherwood was driving us to Marion and took a side road which speedily showed itself as the wrong road. Woods enclosed it like a tunnel. The ruts were too deep for the wheels, and the car balanced precariously on the raised center and one side bank. The road was muddy and slippery. It was raining. Finally the car slipped off its perch and sank into the ruts from which the efforts of three men could not lift it. There was nothing to do but push forward on foot. Soon there appeared a clearing with a saw mill, which was apparently a front for something less legal. A half-dozen men came to our help with great cheerfulness, lifted the car out of the ruts, turned it around, and blew up a flat tire, when there appeared a big truck, completely filling the tunnel, and confirming our uncomfortable feeling that we were where we had no business to be. The truck stopped, a man got out and advanced menacingly. Sherwood moved toward him with a little uncertainty in his steps. Suddenly a bright look came to his face. "Thank God," he said, "I went to that man's wife's funeral last Sunday." The bond so established held. The truck was driven crashing into the trees to make room for us to pass. And as we drove cautiously back to the highroad Sherwood discoursed of the life and character of our benefactor. A day or two later, on the way to the Tennessee Valley, we learned of the death of Thomas Wolfe, and Sherwood fell into reminiscence of his dead friend, with racy anecdote and subtle characterization, full of affection and insight. These two occasions remain among my last memories of Sherwood Anderson—with his appreciation of the distorted and incongruous elements of life, at once humorous and sympathetic. What a friend he was! And as a writer a friend to all humanity, simple, unpretentious, sincere; modest in his claims on his public, generous to his contemporaries in the field. His contribution to American literature was of definite importance; his influence on a younger generation remains, and more than this, his example.

From *The Virginia Quarterly Review*, Vol. XVII (Summer, 1941), pp. 379–388. Reprinted by permission of the author and editors.

MALCOLM COWLEY
John Dos Passos: The Poet and the World
[1932-1936]

JOHN DOS PASSOS[1] is in reality two novelists. One of them is a late-Romantic, an individualist, an esthete moving about the world in a portable ivory tower; the other is a collectivist, a radical historian of the class struggle. These two authors have collaborated in all his books, but the first had the larger share in *Three Soldiers* and *Manhattan Transfer*. The second, in his more convincing fashion, has written most of *The 42nd Parallel* and almost all of *1919*. The difference between the late-Romantic and the radical Dos Passos is important not only in his own career: it also helps to explain the recent course of American fiction.

The late-Romantic tendency in his novels goes back to his years in college. After graduating from a good preparatory school, Dos Passos entered Harvard in 1912, at the beginning of a period which was later known as that of the Harvard esthetes. I have described this period elsewhere, in reviewing the poems of E. E. Cummings, but I did not discuss the ideas which underlay its picturesque manifestations, its mixture of incense, patchouli and gin, its erudition displayed before barroom mirrors, its dreams in the Cambridge subway of laurel-crowned Thessalian dancers. The esthetes themselves were not philosophers; they did not seek to define their attitude; but most of them would have subscribed to the following propositions:

That the cultivation and expression of his own sensibility are the only justifiable ends for a poet.

That originality is his principal virtue.

That society is hostile, stupid and unmanageable: it is the world of the philistines, from which it is the poet's duty and privilege to remain aloof.

That the poet is always misunderstood by the world. He should, in fact, deliberately make himself misunderstandable, for the greater glory of art.

That he triumphs over the world, at moments, by mystically including it

[1] *1919*, by John Dos Passos. *The Big Money*, by John Dos Passos. New York: Harcourt, Brace & Company, 1932, 1936. (The complete trilogy by John Dos Passos, made up of *The 42nd Parallel*, *1919*, and *The Big Money*, was later published under the collective title, *U. S. A.*, in 1937. [Editor's note.])

within himself: these are his moments of *ecstasy,* to be provoked by any means in his power—alcohol, drugs, madness or saintliness, venery, suicide.

That art, the undying expression of such moments, exists apart from the world; it is the poet's revenge on society.

That the past has more dignity than the present.

There are a dozen other propositions which might be added to this unwritten manifesto, but the ideas I have listed were those most generally held, and they are sufficient to explain the intellectual atmosphere of the young men who read *The Hill of Dreams,* and argued about St. Thomas in Boston bars, and contributed to *The Harvard Monthly.* The attitude was not confined to one college and one magazine. It was often embodied in *The Dial,* which for some years was almost a postgraduate edition of *The Monthly;* it existed in earlier publications like *The Yellow Book* and *La Revue Blanche;* it has a history, in fact, almost as long as that of the upper middle class under capitalism. For the last half-century it has furnished the intellectual background of poems and essays without number. It would seem to preclude, in its adherents, the objectivity that is generally associated with good fiction; yet the esthetes themselves sometimes wrote novels, as did their predecessors all over the world. Such novels, in fact, are still being published, and favorably criticised: "Mr. Zed has written the absorbing story of a talented musician tortured by the petty atmosphere of the society in which he is forced to live. His wife, whom the author portrays with witty malice, prevents him from breaking away. After an unhappy love affair and the failure of his artistic hopes, he commits suicide. . . ."

Such is the plot forever embroidered in the type of fiction that ought to be known as the art novel. There are two essential characters, two antagonists, the Poet and the World. The Poet—who may also be a painter, a violinist, an inventor, an architect or a Centaur—is generally to be identified with the author of the novel, or at least with the novelist's ideal picture of himself. He tries to assert his individuality in despite of the World, which is stupid, unmanageable and usually victorious. Sometimes the Poet triumphs, but the art novelists seem to realize, as a class, that the sort of hero they describe is likely to be defeated in the sort of society which he must face. This society is rarely presented in accurate terms. So little is it endowed with reality, so great is the author's solicitude for the Poet, that we are surprised to see him vanquished by such a shadowy opponent. It is as if we were watching motion pictures in the darkhouse of his mind. There are dream pictures, nightmare pictures; at last the walls crash in and the Poet disappears without ever knowing what it was all about; he dies by his own hand, leaving behind him the memory of his ecstatic moments and the bitter story of his failure, now published as a revenge on the world of the philistines.

The art novel has many variations. Often the World is embodied in the

Poet's wife, whose social ambitions are the immediate cause of his defeat. Or the wife may be painted in attractive colors: she is married to a mediocre Poet who finally and reluctantly accepts her guidance, abandons his vain struggle for self-expression, and finds that mediocrity has its own consolations, its country clubs and business triumphs—this is the form in which the art novel is offered to readers of *The Saturday Evening Post*. Or again the Poet may be a woman who fights for the same ambitions, under the same difficulties, as her male prototypes. The scene of the struggle may be a town on the Minnesota prairies, an English rectory, an apartment on Washington Square or Beacon Hill; but always the characters are the same; the Poet and the World continue their fatal conflict; the Poet has all our sympathies. And the novelists who use this plot for the thousandth time are precisely those who believe that originality is a writer's chief virtue.

Many are unconscious of this dilemma. The story rises so immediately out of their lives, bursts upon them with such freshness, that they never recognize it as a family tale. Others deliberately face the problem and try to compensate for the staleness of the plot by the originality of their treatment. They experiment with new methods of story-telling—one of which, the stream of consciousness, seems peculiarly fitted to novels of this type. Perhaps they invest their characters with new significance, and rob them of any real significance, by making them symbolic. They adopt new manners, poetic, mystical, learned, witty, allusive or obfuscatory; and often, in token of their original talent, they invent new words and new ways of punctuating simple declarative sentences. Not all their ingenuity is wasted. Sometimes they make valuable discoveries; a few of the art novels, like *The Hill of Dreams*, are among the minor masterpieces of late-Romantic literature; and a very few, like *A Portrait of the Artist as a Young Man*, are masterpieces pure and simple.

Dos Passos' early books are neither masterpieces nor are they pure examples of the art novel. The world was always real to him, painfully real; it was never veiled with mysticism and his characters were rarely symbolic. Yet consider the plot of a novel like *Three Soldiers*. A talented young musician, during the War, finds that his sensibilities are being outraged, his aspirations crushed, by society as embodied in the American army. He deserts after the Armistice and begins to write a great orchestral poem. When the military police come to arrest him, the sheets of music flutter one by one into the spring breeze; and we are made to feel that the destruction of this symphony, this ecstatic song choked off and dispersed on the wind, is the real tragedy of the War. Some years later, in writing *Manhattan Transfer*, Don Passos seemed to be undertaking a novel of a different type, one which tried to render the color and movement of a whole city; but the book, as it proceeds, becomes the story of Jimmy Herf (the Poet) and Ellen Thatcher (the Poet's wife), and the Poet is once again frustrated by the World: he leaves a Greenwich Village party after a last drink of gin and walks out alone, bareheaded, into the dawn. It is obvious, however, that a new conflict has been superimposed on the old one: the social ideas of the novelist are now at war with his personal emotions, which remain those of *The Dial* and *The Harvard Monthly*. Even in *1919*, this second conflict persists, but less acutely; the emotional values themselves are changing, to accord with the ideas; and the book as a whole belongs to a new category.

1919 is distinguished, first of all, by the very size of the project its author has undertaken. A long book in itself, containing 473 pages, it is merely the second chapter, as it were, of a novel which will compare in length with *Ulysses*, perhaps even with *Remembrance of Things Past*. Like the latter, it is a historical novel dealing with the yesterday that still exists in the author's memory. It might almost be called a news novel, since it uses newspaper headlines to suggest the flow of events, and tells the story of its characters in reportorial fashion. But its chief distinction lies in the author's emphasis. He is not recounting the tragedy of bewildered John Smith, the rise of ambitious Mary Jones, the efforts of sensitive Richard Robinson to maintain his ideals against the blundering malice of society. Such episodes recur in this novel, but they are seen in perspective. The real hero of *The 42nd Parallel* and *1919* is society itself, American society as embodied in forty or fifty representative characters who drift along with it, struggle to change its course, or merely to find a secure footing—perhaps they build a raft of wreckage, grow fat on the refuse floating about them; perhaps they go under in some obscure eddy— while always the current sweeps them onward toward new social horizons. In this sense, Dos Passos has written the first American collective novel.

The principal characters are brought forward one at a time; the story of each is told in bare, straightforward prose. Thus, J. Ward Moorehouse, born in Wilmington, Delaware, begins his business career in a real-estate office. He writes songs, marries and divorces a rich woman, works for a newspaper in Pittsburgh—at the end of fifty-seven pages he is a successful public-relations counselor embarked on a campaign to reconcile labor and capital at the expense of labor. Joe and Janey Williams are the children of a tugboat captain from Washington, D. C.; Janey studies shorthand; Joe plays baseball, enlists in the navy, deserts after a brawl and becomes a merchant seaman. Eleanor Stoddard is a poor Chicago girl who works at Marshall Field's; she learns how to speak French to her customers and order waiters about "with a crisp little refined moneyed voice." All these characters, first introduced in *The 42nd Parallel,* reappear in *1919,* where they are joined by others: Richard Ellsworth Savage, a Kent School boy who goes to Harvard and writes poetry; Daughter, a warm-hearted flapper from Dallas, Texas; Ben Compton, a spectacled Jew from Brooklyn who becomes a Wobbly. Gradually their careers draw closer together, till finally all of them are caught up in the War.

"This whole goddam war's a gold brick," says Joe Williams. "It ain't on the level, it's crooked from A to Z. No matter how it comes out, fellows like us get the s——y end of the stick, see? Well, what I say is all bets is off . . . every man go to hell in his own way . . . and three strikes is out, see?" Three strikes is out for Joe, when his skull is cracked in a saloon brawl at St. Nazaire, on Armistice night. Daughter is killed in an airplane accident; she provoked it herself in a fit of hysteria after being jilted by Dick Savage—who for his part survives as the shell of a man, all the best of him having died when he decided to join the army and make a career for himself and let his pacifist sentiments go hang. Benny Compton gets ten years in Atlanta prison as a conscientious objector. Everybody in the novel suffers from the War and finds his own way of going to hell—everybody except the people without bowels, the empty people like Eleanor Stoddard and J. Ward Moorehouse, who stuff themselves with the proper sentiments and make the right contacts.

The great events that preceded and followed the Armistice are reflected in the lives of all these people; but Dos Passos has other methods, too, for rendering the sweep of history. In particular he has three technical devices which he uses both to broaden the scope of the novel and to give it a formal unity. The first of these consists of what he calls "Newsreels," a combination of newspaper headlines, stock-market reports, official communiqués and words from popular songs. The Newsreels effectively perform their function in the book, that of giving dates and atmospheres, but in themselves, judged as writing, they are not successful. The second device is a series of nine biographies interspersed through the text. Here are the lives, briefly told, of three middle-class rebels, Jack Reed, Randolph Bourne and Paxton Hibben; of three men of power, Roosevelt, Wilson and J. P. Morgan; and of three proletarian heroes. All these are successful both in themselves and in relation to the novel as a whole; and the passage dealing with the Wobbly martyr, Wesley Everest, is as powerful as anything Dos Passos has ever written.

The "Camera Eye," which is the third device, introduces more complicated standards of judgment. It consists in the memories of another character, presumably the author, who has adventures similar to those of his characters, but describes them in a different style, one which suggests Dos Passos' earlier books. The "Camera Eye" gives us photographs rich in emotional detail:

Ponte Decimo   in Ponte Decimo ambulances were parked in a moonlit square of bleak stone working-people's houses   hoarfrost covered everything   in the little bar the Successful Story Writer taught us to drink cognac and maraschino half and half

havanuzzerone

it turned out he was not writing what he felt he wanted to be writing   What can you tell them at home about the war?   it turned out he was not wanting what he wrote he wanted to be feeling cognac and maraschino   was no longer young

(It made us damn sore we greedy for what we felt we wanted tell 'em all they lied
see new towns go to Genoa)   havanuzzerone?   it turned out that he wished he
was a naked brown shepherd boy sitting on a hillside playing a flute in the sunlight

Exactly the same episode, so it happens, is described in Dos Passos' other
manner, his prose manner, during the course of a chapter dealing with Dick
Savage:

That night they parked the convoy in the main square of a godforsaken little
burg on the outskirts of Genoa. They went with Sheldrake to have a drink in a bar
and found themselves drinking with the Saturday Evening Post correspondent,
who soon began to get tight and to say how he envied them their good looks and
their sanguine youth and idealism. Steve picked him up about everything and argued bitterly that youth was the lousiest time in your life, and that he ought to be
goddam glad he was forty years old and able to write about the war instead of
fighting in it.

The relative merit of these two passages, as writing, is not an important
question. The first is a good enough piece of impressionism, with undertones
of E. E. Cummings and Gertrude Stein. The style of the second passage, except for a certain conversational quality, is almost colorless; it happens to be
the most effective way of recording a particular series of words and actions;
it aspires to no other virtue. The first passage might add something to a book
in which, the plot being hackneyed or inconsequential, the emphasis had to
be placed on the writing, but *1919* is not a novel of that sort. Again, the Camera Eye may justify itself in the next volume of this trilogy—or tetralogy—by
assuming a closer relation to the story and binding together the different
groups of characters; but in that case, I hope the style of it will change. So far
it has been an element of disunity, a survival of the art novel in the midst of
a different type of writing, and one in which Dos Passos excels.

He is, indeed, one of the few writers in whose case an equation can accurately and easily be drawn between social beliefs and artistic accomplishments.
When he writes individualistically, with backward glances toward Imagism,
Vorticism and the Insurrection of the Word, his prose is sentimental and
without real distinction. When he writes as a social rebel, he writes not flaw-
lessly by any means, but with conviction, power and a sense of depth, of striking through surfaces to the real forces beneath them. This last book, in which
his political ideas have given shape to his emotions, and only the Camera Eye
remains as a vestige of his earlier attitude, is not only the best of all his novels;
it is, I believe, a landmark in American fiction.

II

Four years ago in reviewing *1919*, the second volume of John Dos Passos'
trilogy, I tried to define two types of fiction that have been especially promi-

nent since the War. An *art novel*, I said, was one that dealt with the opposition between a creatively gifted individual and the community surrounding him—in brief, between the Poet and the World. Usually in books of this type the Poet gets all the attention; he is described admiringly, tenderly, and yet we learn that he is nagged and broken and often, in the end, driven to suicide by an implacably stupid World. Dos Passos' earlier novels had applied this formula, but *The 42nd Parallel* and *1919* belonged to a second category: they were *collective novels*, whose real hero was American society at large, and this fact helped to explain their greater breadth and vigor. I added, however, that certain elements in these later books—and notably the autobiographical passages called the "Camera Eye"—suggested the art novel and therefore seemed out of place.

But after reviewing *The Big Money* and rereading the trilogy as a whole, it seems to me that this judgment has to be partly revised. I no longer believe that the art novel is a "bad" type of fiction (though the philosophy behind it is a bad philosophy for our times), nor do I believe that the collective novel is necessarily a "good" type (though it has advantages for writers trying to present our period of crisis). With more and more collective novels published every year, it is beginning to be obvious that the form in itself does not solve the writer's problems. Indeed, it raises new problems and creates new disadvantages. The collective novelist is tempted to overemphasize the blindness and impotence of individuals caught in the rip tides of history. He is obliged to devote less space to each of his characters, to relate their adventures more hastily, with the result that he always seems to be approaching them from the outside. I can see now that the Camera Eye is a device adopted by Dos Passos in order to supply the "inwardness" that is lacking in his general narrative.

I can see too that although the device is borrowed from the art novel—and indeed is a series of interior monologues resembling parts of Joyce's *Ulysses*—it is not in the least alien to the general plan of the trilogy. For the truth is that the art novel and the collective novel as conceived by Dos Passos are not in fundamental opposition: they are like the two sides of a coin. In the art novel, the emphasis is on the individual, in the collective novel it is on society as a whole; but in both we get the impression that society is stupid and all-powerful and fundamentally evil. Individuals ought to oppose it, but if they do so they are doomed. If, on the other hand, they reconcile themselves with society and try to get ahead in it, then they are damned foerver, damned to be empty, shrill, destructive insects like Dick Savage and Eleanor Stoddard and J. Ward Moorehouse.

In an earlier novel, *Manhattan Transfer*, there is a paragraph that states one of Dos Passos' basic perceptions. Ellen Herf, having divorced the hero, decides to marry a rich politician whom she does not love:

Through dinner she felt a gradual icy coldness stealing through her like novocaine. She had made up her mind. It seemed as if she had set the photograph of herself in her own place, forever frozen into a single gesture. . . . Everything about her seemed to be growing hard and enameled, the air bluestreaked with cigarette smoke was turning to glass.

She had made up her mind. . . . Sometimes in reading Dos Passos it seems that not the nature of the decision but the mere fact of having reached it is the unforgivable offense. Dick Savage the ambulance driver decided not to be a pacifist, not to escape into neutral Spain, and from that moment he is forever frozen into a single gesture of selfishness and dissipation. Don Stevens the radical newspaper correspondent decides to be a good Communist, to obey party orders, and immediately he is stricken with the same paralysis of the heart. We have come a long way from the strong-willed heroes of the early nineteenth century—the English heroes, sons of Dick Whittington, who admired the world of their day and climbed to the top of it implacably; the French heroes like Julien Sorel and Rastignac and Monte Cristo who despised their world and yet learned how to press its buttons and pull its levers. To Dos Passos the world seems so vicious that any compromise with its standards turns a hero into a villain. The only characters he seems to like instinctively are those who know they are beaten, but still grit their teeth and try to hold on. That is the story of Jimmy Herf in *Manhattan Transfer;* to some extent it is also the story of Mary French and her father and Joe Askew, almost the only admirable characters in *The Big Money*. And the same lesson of dogged, courageous impotence is pointed by the Camera Eye, especially in the admirable passage where the author remembers the execution of Sacco and Vanzetti:

America our nation has been beaten by strangers who have turned our language inside out who have taken the clean words our fathers spoke and made them slimy and foul
    their hired men sit on the judge's bench they sit back with their feet on the tables under the dome of the State House they are ignorant of our beliefs they have the dollars the guns the armed forces the power-plants . . .
    all right we are two nations

"The hired men with guns stand ready to shoot," he says in another passage, this one dealing with his visit to the striking miners in Kentucky. "We have only words against POWER SUPERPOWER." And these words that serve as our only weapons against the machine guns and tear gas of the invaders, these words of the vanquished nation are only that America in developing from pioneer democracy into monopoly capitalism has followed a road that leads toward sterility and slavery. Our world is evil, and yet we are powerless to change or direct it. The sensitive individual should cling to his own standards, and yet he is certain to go under. Thus, the final message of Dos Passos' three collective novels is similar to that of his earlier novels dealing with maladjusted artists. Thus, for all the vigor of *1919* and *The Big Money*, they leave us wondering whether the author hasn't overstated his case. For all their scope and richness, they fail to express one side of contemporary life—the will to struggle ahead, the comradeship in struggle, the consciousness of new men and new forces continually rising. Although we may be for the moment a beaten nation, the fight is not over.

From *The New Republic,* Vol. LXX (April 27, 1932), pp. 303–305; and Vol. LXXXVIII (September 9, 1936), p. 34. Reprinted by permission.

ROBERT CANTWELL

Sinclair Lewis

[1936]

WITH some fifteen novels to his credit at the age of fifty, together with enough short stories to fill several more volumes, Sinclair Lewis stands out as the most prolific author of his generation, with the mournful exception of Upton Sinclair. It is almost the worst thing you can say about him. For although Lewis has written at least two first-rate novels, and created a dozen powerful characters, and produced half-a-hundred masterly satirical sketches scattered throughout these books—as well as added new words to the language and popularized, more than anybody else, a new and skeptical slant on American life—he has also turned out as much journalistic rubbish as any good novelist has signed his name to, and he has written novels so shallow and dull they would have wrecked any reputation except his own.

He has, in fact, been one of the most plunging and erratic writers in our literary history; unpredictability, waywardness, unevenness are his distinguishing characteristics, as a brooding inconclusiveness is the mark of Sherwood Anderson. He has written the best novel of American business in *Babbitt*, only to make up for it by writing the worst in *Work of Art* and adding half-a-dozen wretched *Saturday Evening Post* stories on the same subject to the bargain. He has written the sharpest parodies of the lush, rococo, euphemistic sales-talk of American business life that we have, but he has also weighed down his novels with a heavy burden of unreal and exaggerated jargon, palmed off as common speech, with unfunny topical jokes, passed on as native humor, and the weight of that dated mockery grows heavier every year.

But Lewis has not only been the most uneven of American novelists; he has also been one of the most ambitious. There is an architectural symmetry in the order of the books that followed *Main Street*. Unlike his contemporaries, who seem always to have been improvising in the sequence of their work, Lewis apparently recognized a conscious program for his writing simultaneously with his recognition of his power, and seems to have driven toward its realization with something of the high-pressure intensity he has satirized so often. Where Dreiser gives the impression of having brooded, with a sort of ponderous aimlessness, over whatever lay close at hand, forever turning aside,

494

distracted by every incidental issue, and where Anderson and Vachel Lindsay, more than any of the others, were blown about in the cross-currents of American life until they were saturated with its apparently patternless variety, Lewis visualized on the strength of *Main Street* a cycle of novels comparable at least in scope to those of Zola and Balzac.

It was a spacious and inclusive project, bolder than anything an American novelist had tried to do, signalizing a final break with that narrowness of outlook which, exemplified in a thousand old swimming-hole sentimentalities, pathetic regionalisms and phony family dilemmas, had become almost the sole driving force of American fiction. And even now, when the limitations and shortcomings of that imaginative exploration are more apparent than its freshness and originality, it is still a little breath-taking to consider the broad outlines of the work that Lewis laid out for himself, to see that he planned nothing less than a catalogue of the interwoven worlds of American society, the small towns and cities, the worlds of business, of science, of religion, of education, and eventually the worlds of labor and professional politics, working it out at a time when the shabby, optimistic, patriotic smugness of the American literary tradition—the tradition of Henry Van Dyke that, significantly, he attacked in his Nobel Prize address—still imprisoned the imaginations of so many of his contemporaries.

Lewis had a line on American society, and tenacity, if not much flexibility and resourcefulness, in following it. But more than that he had a sense of the physical variety and the cultural monotony of the country, an easy familiarity with the small towns and square cities, the real-estate developments and restricted residential areas, the small business men, the country doctors, the religious fakers, the clubwomen, the county officeholders, the village atheists and single-taxers, the schoolteachers, librarians, the windbags of the lower income groups, the crazy professors and the maddened, hyperthyroid, high-pressure salesmen—the main types of middle-class and lower-middle-class provincial society, conspicuous now because he has identified them so thoroughly. He had a grasp of these people and their environments, together with a sense of the country as a whole, where so many of his generation had nothing but an oppressed conviction of its emptiness or a dread of its rawness.

Only Vachel Lindsay and Upton Sinclair had seen so much of the country, in the elementary geographical sense of the term. Lewis had never taken any of the wild and pathetic zigzag journeys of Lindsay, dropping in on miners and hill-billies and reading poems for his supper, nor had he spent a season in the hell of the stockyards, as did Upton Sinclair, his first guide, at the beginning of a career no less extraordinary. But he had knocked around at an impressive variety of jobs after he left Yale in 1904—he had been a janitor in Upton Sinclair's Helicon Hall, a soda jerk, a reporter on *The San Francisco Bulletin*—which was probably, under Fremont Older in the days before his

capitulation, the best paper in the country to be a reporter on—a ghost writer
for Jack London and an editor, in Washington, of a magazine for the deaf;
he had taken the grand cruise of his generation on a cattle boat to England
and had hitchhiked through the Middle West. He had traveled over the face
of the country and, although within pretty narrow limits, up and down
through its social strata. And although his first four books were hack jobs, the
native experiences he had packed away were too powerful to be satisfied with
evocations of the joys of a stenographer's work, or of the wisdom of picturesque and homely old folks, or of an aristocratic Eastern girl made wholesome by contact with the great West—the substance of *The Job, The Innocents* and *Free Air*. Even as hack work those books are bad. They seem to
tremble with some internal explosive disgust; in a way they are like the bad
jokes and stale opinions that Babbitt and his friends take refuge in at their
parties, when they dare not express even a little of what is going on in their
minds, lest they betray their hatred of their environments, their boredom,
their thwarted desire for change.

Apparently Lewis thought at the beginning of his career that the muse
could be embraced and laid aside at will, and that she would not take her revenge by addling the wits of her ravisher—at least his first books prove nothing except that he did not believe the writing of fiction demanded a writer's
full energy and his deepest understanding. That implicit irresponsibility has
been his greatest limitation as a novelist and the source of much of the unevenness of his work. Even the broad project mentioned above—the cycle of
novels following *Main Street*—is a vision of an imaginative survey of American life such as a glorified and super-competent hack writer might conceive: a
writer, that is, who thought of his writing, not in terms of its momentary inspirations and the pressure of living that played through him and upon him, but
in terms of the accomplishment of a foreknown task; who thought of a novel of
business, of religion, of science, as if he believed he could turn his art to any
subject, regardless of how much it meant to him and how close to his heart it
lay; who felt that it lay within his power to "collect material" without becoming emotionally entangled in it or acting in response to what it implied. T. K.
Whipple, who has written the only searching study of Lewis that we have,
has compared his attitude in studying American society with that of a Red
Indian stalking through the land of his enemies—it is a good description, for
it suggests his wariness and vigilance, the surface accuracy of his observation,
what can be called the heartlessness of his approach, and above all his enforced detachment from the scene he viewed and the solitary and personal
basis of his satire.

Now that the scandals that attended the publications of Lewis' books
have been forgotten, the outlines of the world he created are clearer. On re-

examination that world seems in a more advanced state of decay and disintegration than Lewis' first critics were willing to admit—it is, as Whipple has
said, a city of the dead, in which the dead are above all determined that no
one shall live. After *Main Street* his characters were still the long-winded,
provincial, narrow-visioned old folks, the dreamy and timid job-holders, the
clerks and salesmen and doctors—with here and there a workman from the
semi-independent crafts—who figured in his first books and were all dominated by those strange, self-satisfied, self-possessed, jovially witless bankers
and business men who loom so large in Lewis' world. But where such characters had been harmless and happy in the early novels, they were now vindictive, spiteful, vaguely threatening in their inertia and immobility. Before the
War Lewis had written of their provincialism as if it were a source of serenity,
however its expression might rasp on the sensibilities of the cultivated; for the
provincials and the innocents themselves, it was an insulation against the
cares of the world and not without its own homely poetry and wisdom.

But with *Main Street* that provincialism was identified as an evil force, destructive not only to the Carol Kennicotts and Eric Valborgs, to Martin Arrowsmith and Paul Reisling—it was also poisoning the lives of those who
clung to it and triumphed and, when their guards were down for a moment,
were seen to be bewildered, distressed, clinging desperately to their appearance of smugness because they had nothing else to cling to. The problem of
Main Street might have been "how much of Gopher Prairie's eleven miles of
cement walk" was "made out of the tombstones of John Keatses"—but the
message of *Babbitt, Arrowsmith, Elmer Gantry*, however Lewis might deny
that it was his intention to preach it, was simply that American society was
death to any disinterested effort, to any human tolerance, almost to any human
sympathy; that it was regimented within an inch of its intellectual life; that
any deviation from its norm of self-seeking, money-grubbing, career-making,
throat-cutting, treachery, slander, blackmailing, was instantly punished with
exile and disgrace; that spontaneity or generous emotions or a freedom from
calculation, among the calculating wolves of business, amounted to suicide of
a long-drawn-out and painful kind. Lewis drew a revolutionary picture of
American middle-class life without coming to revolutionary conclusions about
it, unlike Upton Sinclair, who leaped to revolutionary conclusions and then
filled in the picture; he recognized the mechanics of capitalist control, and
satirized them, without challenging the ends to which they were applied or
visualizing any alternative except an escape—for those sensitive souls enlightened enough to be aware of their horror—into reverie and day-dreaming.

The moral atmosphere, with exceptions that will be noted, grew thicker
and more poisonous with each succeeding book. Carol Kennicott's sensibilities
were outraged by Gopher Prairie, and she was revolted by the hypocrisy and
narrowness she found there, but the enemies she faced were largely passive—

inertia, sluggishness and sullenness, the dominance of petrified prejudice. In comparison with *Babbitt* and the books that followed it, this is an almost pastoral view of life. The difference is not only in the greater violence of the later books, the general strike that interrupts *Babbitt* midway, the flare of melodrama in Reisling's attempt to murder his wife, the corruption and blackmail that accompany Babbitt's business career. It is rather in the cagey watchfulness with which Babbitt's friends of the service clubs bear down on each other for every deviation from their class line, and it is nowhere better dramatized than in the sequence that follows Reisling's tragedy—when Babbitt, shaken by it, develops an intermittent sort of tolerance, the others, particularly the sinister Virgil Gunch, get their knives ready for him at once, and the high point of the book, perhaps the highest point of Lewis' writing, is the realization that they are ready to spring, like the stronger wolves on a crippled member of the pack, at the first sign of Babbitt's confusion and dismay.

Yet even Babbitt's sacrifices for the good opinion of such prosperous thugs is nothing compared with the desperation of Angus Duer, in *Arrowsmith*, who tries to cut the throat of a watchman who has inadvertently threatened his career, and the indifference that Carol Kennicott faced in Gopher Prairie is nothing compared with the sustained enmity and malice that Arrowsmith faces in Wheatsylvania. The enemy—the provincial, conforming, suspicious enemy—is no longer merely passive and mocking; it has become aggressive, strident, criminal; it turns to blackmail and violence; it is ready to frame and destroy anyone who even raises questions that it cannot answer. And by the time *It Can't Happen Here* was written, Lewis' picture of the world was such that the violence with which the book is filled had become obsessive and perverse, divorced from any purpose and uncontrolled by any aim, an eruption of cruelty and horror and little more.

Spaced unevenly between the works in which this panorama of social damnation is drawn are those books of Lewis' that even his acquiescent critics usually overlook: *Mantrap, The Trail of the Hawk, Work of Art, Ann Vickers, Dodsworth,* the grotesque short stories that he wrote for *The Saturday Evening Post* and that seem particularly bad because there is so much evidence that Lewis knew so much better when he wrote them. He has never been a fastidious writer—he has a gift for slogans, a talent for mimicry, a kind of tormented delight in some of the cruder commonplaces of American speech, but he has always manipulated his people awkwardly to make them demonstrate what he wanted them to reveal about society, and his works have always been weakened, even in their moments of gravity, by a tumultuous and slapstick humor that seems less an expression of emotion than of a desire to escape it. As his career has developed he has relied more and more on his ability to capture the perishable local color of American life, the blaring and raucous Babbittry that surrounds his people, the pep-talks, the idiot drooling of advertisers and go-getters, instead of the indefinite but still sustained and consequential conflicts of Carol and her husband, of Babbitt and his friends—but this material, which was used in *Main Street* to show what a character who could not stomach it was up against, began to be used in the novels that followed almost for its own sake, until with *The Man Who Knew Coolidge* there was scarcely anything else in the book.

But precisely because Lewis has attached so little fundamental importance to such outpourings as Dr. Pickerbaugh's health sermons, or Chum Frinkley's poems, his increasing insistence on material of this sort is all the more clearly a sign of imaginative indecision and doubt. And how, after having so clearly shown the mechanics of American business control in *Babbitt,* and the psychological ravages of it, could he have drawn so unrealistic a figure of a millionaire as Dodsworth, or so romantic a business man as the Ora Weagle of *Work of Art?* In his best books Lewis had told us that the pursuit of wealth— or even a career in a business-dominated society—was a fierce and scrambling affair that killed its victims and crippled its victors; now he presented an industrialist whose unaccountable naïveté persisted (although he collected secret reports on the dissipations of his employees), and a starry-eyed, well-meaning hotel manager whose poetic dreams revolved around the creation of more elaborate comforts for the exhausted Babbitts who could afford them— presented without art, without irony, at best with a kind of curdled romanticism that gave an impression of spleen and exasperation on the part of their author. With these books Lewis' explorations into American society stopped. His characters had become idealizations of the Babbitts he had previously condemned; his satire had degenerated to a kind of stylized mockery, closer in spirit to George Ade's *Fables in Slang* or to some of Mencken's less purposeful buffoonery than to the realities of American life—or it had become so broad and farcical that it had lost its point, just as, in his antifascist novel, his fascists were presented as so weird and unearthly that no practicing strike-breakers, vigilantes, lynchers, anti-Semites, jingoes or acquiescent journalists need feel an instant's identification with them.

But with all this acknowledged, the positive contribution of Lewis' novels remains—and, in one sense, if books like *Dodsworth, Work of Art,* or *Ann Vickers* seem so shallow, it is in large part because Lewis himself has made us conscious in his best work of the native realities that are absent in them. In his best books he has caught, better than anybody else, the desultory, inhibited, half-sad and half-contented middle-class life of the Middle West, a life of spiritless conflicts and drives in the country, of social gatherings as nerve-racking and exhausting as final examinations, of interminable business plots and fears of ruin, of frightened infidelities, limitless ambitions, of forced enthusiasms and false simplicities—a life hedged in behind social barriers set by

the least enlightened members of the community and existing under a dictatorship that is no less powerful for being masked and unadmitted by those
who bow to it. And even in his worst books Lewis has always been able to
summon up some neglected, recognizable corner of the country—the run-
down, red-leather hotel lobbies of *Work of Art,* the formaldehyde, oiled-floor,
civil-service stench of public buildings in *Ann Vickers*—with such graphic
power that he has always seemed to be setting the stage for some more momentous drama than he has ever shown taking place.

That effect may be the result of his inability clearly to imagine any antagonist capable of sustained struggle with the rulers of his city of the dead. He is
more aware of the monstrous extent of the stables that must be cleaned than
he is of the possibility of any Hercules ever cleaning them; and when he pictures people who are pitted against their environments he usually shows them
struggling without much hope of victory, without allies, and often with in-
grown doubts as to whether or not they are on the right side. And most often,
when their feeble feints establish the strength of the enemy, they merely sub-
side into that outward acquiescence and inward rebellion that is the death of
drama—so Carol Kennicott, defeated in Gopher Prairie, dreams of a grass hut
over some tropical river bank; Babbitt hungers for some wild woodland spirit
as he awakens into the steel world of Zenith; Ora Weagle plans gigantic and
flawless super-hotels as he fires the help of a run-down Florida boarding house,
and these vague aspirations to escape their own environments are presented
by Lewis as conferring some secret distinction on the people who hold them.

In denying that he is a satirist Lewis has said that he is a romantic, in much
the same sense that these characters of his are romantics, and that he has rebelled against American society because it has none of the picturesque feudal
remains that he associated with a rich and stable culture. But his characters
are not romantic rebels committed to struggle. They are self-dramatists whose
imaginations flower from their evasions of conflict—they are always posing
before themselves and others, not in order to fulfill a consistent Byronic rôle,
and to take the responsibility for it, but in order to conceal their true reactions
and to hide the concerns that oppress them. They are always in the camp of
their enemies; they cannot forget themselves for a moment, lest they reveal
the depths of their revulsion. They dramatize themselves in order to endure
the demands of a society that they have no hope of bettering and whose reality they cannot face, and they imagine themselves in all kinds of rôles—except the ones they actually occupy—because they cannot get through their
days without the help of such fantasy.

So the final testimony of Lewis' novels always seems a little grimmer than
he apparently intended it to be, and never so grim as when he envisions the
rebels and aspiring spirits who front the resolute conformists. He never comes
so close to giving a clinical description of psychic breakdown as when he

shows his characters making their peace with the world. It was a mistake of his critics to see in these novels evidence of that intellectual awakening and skeptical self-criticism which has become known as America's coming-of-age. For Lewis is the historian of America's catastrophic going-to-pieces—or at least of the going-to-pieces of her middle class—with no remedy to offer for the decline that he records; and he has dramatized the process of disintegration, as well as his own dilemma, in the outlines of his novels, in the progress of his characters, and sometimes, and most painfully, in the lapses of taste and precision that periodically weaken the structure of his prose.

From *The New Republic,* Vol. LXXXVIII (October 21, 1936), pp. 298–301. Reprinted by permission.

E. K. BROWN

Willa Cather

[1946]

BEFORE the year ends, Willa Cather will be seventy.[1] Lately her fiction has been of less concern to critics than it was ten years ago, and even then was of less concern than in the second and third decades of the century. It is among the gross abuses of much recent American criticism—I mean, of the criticism which mirrors the time, has influence, is widely quoted, and passes into anthologies—to discuss books primarily as illustrations or turning points of social and aesthetic tendencies, rather than as entities delightful and significant in themselves, made so by a beauty of craftsmanship and depth of vision. A well-read critic will find it very easy, even if he has little or no perception of depth and beauty, to discuss a book in the current fashion; he has no need to find his way into the core of the book, to discover its inmost principle, the source of its unity, warmth, and color; instead he may pontificate upon qualities he has known in a hundred other books, and about whose worth he has long ago made up his mind and closed it.

It is by no means easy to relate Miss Cather's fiction to the vogue of technical stunts and of psychoanalytical explorations which distinguished the Nineteen-twenties, and it is scarcely easier to relate it to the ill-digested massive sociological inquiries which bloated so much of the fiction of the Nineteen-thirties. There are relations. It was amid the technical enthusiasms of the Twenties that Miss Cather developed a new method of narration and a new use of setting, shaking off all the heavinesses and dulnesses of the traditional novel as she had formerly conceived it and as most of her contemporaries continued to practise it. Her fiction, too, has its sociology: she broke off her history of the decay of the small Mid-Western town just where Sinclair Lewis began his. Between *A Lost Lady* and *Main Street* there are many threads of relationship, and there are almost as many between *One of Ours* and *Babbitt*. No novelist has seen with a more discerning eye the role the railroad plays in the social and ethical life of the Western town. Still, the fullest understanding of such relationships would carry one but a very small distance towards the rare essence of Miss Cather's fiction. This may be apprehended not by the

[1] Written in 1946. Willa Cather died on April 24, 1947. (Editor's note.)

critic who is forever remembering what her contemporaries have been thinking and devising, but only if one will forget the characteristics of the historical moment in which she happened to write and look long and directly at
what she actually has written. Before the historical moment is wholly left behind there is, however, one fact to be noted—her strong, conscious, and rapidly increasing aversion from it.

Ten years ago, in the prefatory note to *Not Under Forty,* Miss Cather remarked that "the world broke in two in 1922 or thereabouts," confessed that
she was among those who had remained on the far side of the chasm, and
warned all under forty that the expressions of her mind could scarcely interest
them. 1922 is the year of *Ulysses* and *The Waste Land,* and in method and
temper these works are a world apart from the serenity and lucidity of her
fiction. But her estrangement from the modern world, particularly the modern American world, is much more than literary. When she spoke of 1922 I
doubt that she was primarily remembering Joyce or T. S. Eliot; indeed, I
should not be surprised to hear that she was not thinking of them at all. She
was certainly thinking much more painfully of changes closer to the actual
fabric of living in America. In her memorial portrait of Mrs. James T. Fields,
the widow of the great Boston publisher, she evokes the old house in Charles
Street, where she had so often sat at tea with the tireless hostess and Sarah
Orne Jewett, amid so many relics of what was most distinguished in English
and American arts and letters and song in the last century, and where conversation continued to have that fusion of fragrance with substance which
was a mark of the older time when people could still linger like Dr. Johnson
and have their talk out, and when into that talk they distilled suggestions of
their deepest thoughts and most considered feelings. That house in Charles
Street has, she says, given way to a garage. "Perhaps," she suggests, "the garage and all it stands for represent the only real development and have altogether taken the place of things formerly cherished on that spot." The garage is her real enemy, not *Ulysses.* In "Coming, Aphrodite!" a short story
written not long before 1922, and expressing with delicate truth what Greenwich Village was like when it was the true home of poetry and art, there is a
deeply felt picture of Washington Square in the spring, the grass "blindingly
green," the fountain alive again after its winter arrest, and through the Arch
a vista of "the young poplars with their bright sticky leaves, and the Brevoort
glistening in its spring coat of paint, and shining horses and carriages," and
marring all, the portent of "an automobile, misshapen and sullen, like an ugly
threat in a stream of things that were bright and beautiful and alive."

In 1922 Miss Cather must have been at work upon *A Lost Lady,* which
came out in the following year. In it and in *One of Ours,* which actually appeared in 1922, the ruling mood is one new to her fiction. She had always
been critical of that aspect of American life for which the garage was to be so

bountiful a fulfilment, although it was not until she wrote these novels that she went in fear of it. Standardized, money-minded, complacently respectable folk, devoted to mechanical things, or spiritual things mechanically apprehended, had always fared ill in her fiction. In one of the most biting of her short stories, "A Gold Slipper," she had exhibited lightly but firmly the core of emptiness in a pillar of Pittsburgh (a city she knew well from her years of reporting and teaching), a coal-dealer, member of the Presbytery of the First Church, and despiser of all living things. In his premature old age he goes to his office every week-end because there is no other place in the whole round of his life that interests him, and turns over his will and his insurance policies. He had laid his finger upon reality only once, when a great singer, out of devilment, left a gold slipper in his Pullman when she withdrew after a futile conversation to her drawing room. He had made nothing of her at the time except that she was a nuisance and that he was glad to have told her some brief home truths about herself and her art, but after a while he was pleased that he had not thrown the slipper away, and could turn it over in his hands between readings of the will and the policies. "The Black Hawk boys," Miss Cather wrote in *My Antonia,* "looked forward to marrying the Black Hawk girls, and living in a brand-new little house, with best chairs that must not be sat upon and hand-painted china that must not be used." But this contemptible half-dead world of the prairie town was no real danger to heroic or distinguished character; the vigorous, beautiful, dynamic Scandinavian and Slavic girls from the surrounding farms had the future in their keeping; if they had a rough time so long as they served in the town, one made a fortune in the Klondike, another as the leading *couturière* in San Francisco; and Antonia herself, the finest of all, had a dozen magnificent children, and ruled over a vast and fertile farm. The townsfolk of Black Hawk were impotent creatures, and in the end they did not matter. In *The Song of the Lark,* the same confidence appeared. Thea Kronborg appreciated that the characteristic townsfolk of Moonstone were her natural enemies; she accepted, while she was still young, as the inevitable lot of great talent, that she should find disapproval and envy among even her own brothers and sisters. But Moonstone could not delay her in her course; it could irritate and grieve her, but that was all. Toward 1922, Miss Cather came to feel that such confidence was misplaced. Black Hawk and Moonstone and pillars of the Presbytery of the First Church in Pittsburgh were much more powerful than she had supposed; it was they who determined the future. In *One of Ours* she fights the new and appalling conviction, and there is a roughness in the texture of the novel. In *A Lost Lady* she has the perception under control: the shaping idea which imparts so admirable a unity to the book, and allows it to be written with such a tension of restrained resentment and regret, is the contrast between a dying way of life which is spacious and noble and a new way which is petty and crude. The figure that primarily represents the old way has a grandeur that had not been within her reach before, a poetic beauty. In old Captain Forrester Archbishop Latour is already implicit.

A Lost Lady is one of the books on which Miss Cather's survival will depend, by which it will be assured. For all their vigor and truth, the earlier novels suffer from what Henry James criticised in Arnold Bennett and the other realistic novelists of the first decade of the century, an excess of saturation in material detail, a failure to make the figure in the carpet the true centre. In her essay on "The Novel Démeublé" Miss Cather is as critical of saturation as James had been. The novelist, she says, is to suggest rather than to state, is to aim primarily at that kind of effect which is given by a bare stage and a handful of characters coming into impacts which disclose nothing but their essential selves. *A Lost Lady* is the first of her novels to be wholly uncluttered. In *My Antonia* she had adopted the relaxed form of the memoir, and in introducing it had emphasized how casually the memoir grew, how capriciously it took its dimensions. The memoir is supposed to be Jim Burden's; he is a busy New York lawyer, but still a Nebraskan in spirit, who has occupied himself at long intervals over many years during long trips by train in evoking Antonia and his own youth, now one aspect, now another. "I didn't take time to arrange it," he says in the introductory note, "I simply wrote down pretty much all that her name recalls to me. I suppose that is hasn't any form." *My Antonia* is not at all the insufferably garrulous book to which these warnings point; but material details do heap together in it, and for whole chapters the figure in the carpet is partly obscured and by the reader forgotten. The structure of *The Song of the Lark* is perfectly conventional; in this respect, even in its radically revised form, it does not differ from a Dreiser novel. Thea Kronborg's states of mind, the slow and difficult development of her great voice along with her growth, harsh and rough, as a great personality, are at the centre of the book; but they do not strictly govern the choice of material, and they do not always mesh with the incidents in the narrative. It is a massive work, and it communicates an impression of perfect truth, but it is somewhat cluttered; it lags, especially in the urban chapters; the controlling idea does not always control. With *O Pioneers!* the case is not very different.

In comparison with these novels, so massive, so firmly stamped with material truth, *A Lost Lady* seems very slight, even attenuated. But in essential substance, it is richer than any of Miss Cather's books that preceded and, in force of feeling as well as in the exhibition of the figure in its particular carpet, vastly their superior. It was Antonia's greatness that she could "leave images in the mind that did not fade—that grew stronger with time." It is a large part of her creator's greatness to do the same. *Shadows on the Rock* was to be a sequence of such memorable images; they are already beautifully strong and frequent in *A Lost Lady*. When I took up the novel recently it was ten years since I had read it, but I could turn at once to a number of the images which had kept all their original strength during that time and had also gathered a depth of increasing meaning. The chief of these images is in the second part of the seventh chapter. Young Niel Herbert goes through the fields near Sweet Water in the summer dawn to pick a bouquet of roses and lay it outside the shuttered French windows of Mrs. Forrester's bedroom. "As he bent to place the flowers on the sill, he heard from within a woman's soft laughter; impatient, indulgent, teasing, eager. Then another laugh, very different, a man's. And it was fat and lazy,—ended in something like a yawn." In an instant, the gleaming candor of the dawn and of the boy's innocent idealism is blotted out. The style has not yet acquired the full beauty of surface which makes every page of the historical novels a radiant thing; it has not yet the glow or the firmness of contour; but only the shortcoming in style—a merely relative shortcoming, for Miss Cather was already writing as well as any contemporary novelist—prevents one from saying that this half-chapter could go unchanged into *Madame Bovary,* which is one of her principal admirations as it must be with anyone who cherishes the art of fiction without being the victim of sectarian prejudice. *A Lost Lady* is full of symbolic images abounding with suggestion and with beauty. In place of the elaborate descriptions of the earlier novels—one could find his way in the dark from the depot at Moonstone to the Kronborg parsonage, and then out by the sandhills and by the grove of the Kohlers—stand such golden moments arrested forever in their force and beauty.

Yet *A Lost Lady* is not of Miss Cather's very best. It has a grave intellectual weakness, a weakness of vision. Her pioneers will not quite bear the weight she assigns to them. The tone in which she always refers to Captain Forrester's powerful friends who travel back and forth on the Burlington in their private cars and break the trip at Sweet Water—railroad-builders, financiers, founders of great department stores like Marshall Field—arouses some uneasiness. It is a simple thing to grant that men in the habit of great affairs, men for whom the breaking of new ground is the breath of life, "great-hearted adventurers," are of another and higher kind than small-town shysters, vulgarians, and gossips. But Miss Cather presses us to do much more than grant this; she asks us to believe that as a group, by definition, her builders and founders have a spiritual breadth, a heroic wisdom, for which it is difficult indeed to extort our assent. One cannot long escape the feeling that she has built them up somewhat artificially out of a need to annihilate the petty present. In *One of Ours* the hero, Claude Wheeler, remarks that "no battlefield or shattered country was ever as ugly as this world would be if men like his brother Bayliss controlled it altogether." It is easy to agree, and Bayliss is of the same gross stuff as Ivy Peters, the shyster and gossip who rules the last phase of *A Lost Lady.* Still, the countervailing characters in these novels—those who represent the splendors of the Western past, and must do so for there is no other past except the almost unknown aboriginal for the area these novels picture—are not grand enough for their role. Even Captain Forrester, impressive as he is by his silences, his fixities, his genial calm, is not quite grand enough.

The hunger for a glorious past in the West appeared early in Miss Cather's writing, and is its deepest emotional motive. There is a curiously moving chapter in *My Antonia* where the Scandinavian and Slavic girls ask to hear the tale of Coronado and his search for the Seven Golden Cities, and find in the thought that the Spanish adventurers have been in Nebraska the source of a new radiance in the wheat fields and the sunset. This is a reworking of a beautiful sketch, "The Enchanted Bluff," still uncollected. In *The Song of the Lark* the most formative of all Thea Kronborg's experiences, far more significant than any contact she ever had with a person—the experience which lent wings to her spirit and so to her voice—was a summer in Arizona when she lay every day at the mouth of one of the caves in a village of the "ancient people," the Cliff-Dwellers. To be from the West would no longer mean to her being from Moonstone; it would mean being from the region of the builders of those caves. "The Cliff-Dwellers had lengthened her past. She had older and higher obligations." She grew to meet them. In *The Professor's House,* the small Mid-Western college town with its petty professorial rivalries and the bright superficialities of academic families suddenly vanishes. In the most melodramatic strangeness of structure in all Miss Cather's fiction, the long narrative from Tom Outland's notebook breaks in upon the pace of life in the town, with its tale of the mesas. Tom Outland had taken from the Indians of the Southwest just what Thea Kronborg had taken: "I had read of filial piety in the Latin poets," he wrote, "and I knew that was what I felt for this place." The old Indian civilization turns to ridicule the new house which has been built, with its elaborate bathrooms and, of course, its garage, from the prize money the professor received for the many-volumed work on the Spanish adventurers, which was the best part of his life. He finds that he does not care to move into his new house: the bleak old house, with the creaking stairs leading to the uncomfortable attic where the great feat of imaginative reconstruction had taken place, is far more akin to his spirit. It is not so absurdly unlike what the Cliff-Dwellers had made.

The old Southwest had ruled in Miss Cather's imagination since the time of her earliest novels; but she had shied away from it in the conviction that it was eminently a subject for a Catholic to realize. In the end, she could not be content with using it merely as a background. In *Death Comes for the Archbishop* it is the core of the work. Here Indian villages, the exploits of the Spanish adventurers and missionaries, the coming of a new layer of high civilization with the French priests, and the small but true contribution of the best of the great-hearted adventurers of Anglo-Saxon blood, men like Kit

Carson, are set before us as on a frieze. *Death Comes for the Archbishop* is her great book, the most beautiful achievement of her imagination; in it at last her craftsmanship and her vision are in relation, and that relation is complete. The length of her unconscious preparation to write it had served her well indeed.

Miss Cather had always understood that a person's relation to a place might be as valuable to him, and as decisive in his growth or retardation, as any relation he might have with other persons. What happens in one place could not have taken from Moonstone or from Chicago what the villages of the Cliff-Dwellers gave her. But in the earlier novels the landscape did not impinge upon the reader with the vitality that distinguishes it in *Death Comes for the Archbishop*. Much to his own surprise, Archbishop Latour decides against returning to his native Auvergne to pass the years of his retirement and preparation for death. The ties of his family, the promise of fine architecture on every side, and of the scholarly associations of which through his long years in Santa Fe he had been deprived, were, he found, less powerful than the atmosphere of New Mexico. When he wakens in the early morning at Santa Fe, the southwestern air communicates to him a conviction of eternal youth, of energy, of ever-possible spiritual growth. A response of this kind might have been a part of *My Antonia* or of *The Song of the Lark,* but at the time when she wrote these novels Miss Cather could not have found such language as she uses in conveying the quality of the atmosphere at Santa Fe. "His first consciousness was a sense of the light dry wind blowing in through the windows, with the fragrance of hot sun and sage-brush and sweet clover. . . . Something soft and wild and free that whispered to the ear on the pillow, lightened the heart, softly, softly picked the lock, slid the bolts, and released the spirit of man into the wind, into the blue and gold, into the morning, into the morning!" Her craftsmanship in language, her sense of a true economy, her command of rhythms individual without being eccentric, had never before reached such a delicate sureness. It is the language which makes the impressions of the New Mexico landscape superior to any presentation of setting in the earlier books. She had borne the memories of this landscape in her mind for a long time, and at last she had the words to convey them in simple, perfect strength.

The same sure delicacy marks her manipulation of character and incident, a richer material than she had ever before worked in, more varied, more intense, and at times more heroic. The deliberate and often ponderous movement in the earlier narratives is now replaced by a movement wonderfully quick and light, beautifully appropriate to the atmosphere. In the structure what might easily have become solid masses, comparable with long reaches in the earlier novels, is broken up by brief tales inset with an apparent casualness which recalls the ingenuous narrative manner of Cervantes or Smollett.

Everything in *Death Comes for the Archbishop* is from the past, but it is not all from the same past, and in this lies much of the great formal beauty and almost as much of the great emotional effect of the novel. The framework belongs to the mid-nineteenth century when two priests from a quiet town in Auvergne who had worked not too happily along the Ohio, set out to revive the Catholic faith and discipline in the Southwest. In their missionary travels throughout the immense diocese they made fragmentary acquaintance with a far older past—the sixteenth century when the Spanish Franciscans first entered the region coming up from the see of Durango, and the slightly later time when their successors, isolated and often degenerate, gave individual twists to the gospel and the priestly estate. It is in the tales of this older past, picked up by the French priests in their wanderings, that Miss Cather's narrative art is most remarkable. She was always an admirable writer of short stories, and shortly after the appearance of *Death Comes for the Archbishop* her mastery of shorter media came to its height in the *nouvelles* of *Obscure Destinies*, particularly in the moving "Old Mrs. Harris." Her manner in the tales inset in *Death Comes for the Archbishop* is even more accomplished. It is the manner appropriate to the older and better kind of hagiography, simple, concrete, unemphatic, concentrated. The tale of the bold and evil friar who ruled on the crag at Acoma is among the perfect short narratives, suggestive, swimming in the atmosphere of the time and the place, without a touch of false exaggeration or falser complexity. At every turn in the story, the setting is alive, almost overpoweringly sensible. The friar and his clerical guests at dinner and the servant whom he kills say next to nothing, but we catch them in their characterizing attitudes and know them as human beings. The height of Miss Cather's success is in the pages which follow the death and evoke a silence and immobility as thick and ominous as Conrad with his more lavish methods could suggest. With the simplest of means, which are also the most difficult, she has accomplished a triumph.

The method of *Death Comes for the Archbishop* was used again, with minor changes, in *Shadows on the Rock*. In a letter to Wilbur L. Cross, Miss Cather defined with a preciseness unusual for her in speaking of her own work the subtle effect at which she aimed in her novel of French Canada at the end of the seventeenth century. "I . . . tried to develop it into a prose composition not too conclusive, not too definite: a series of pictures remembered rather than experienced; a kind of thinking, a mental complexion inherited, left over from the past, lacking in robustness, and full of pious resignation." The Indians and Spaniards who had given such vigorous color to *Death Comes for the Archbishop* have no equivalent in the later novel. Nor has it the peculiar depth given to *Death Comes for the Archbishop* by the inset tales of a remoter past.

Shadows on the Rock is a novel of the north. The great rock of Quebec in all its grayness is the eternal antagonist supported by the endless Canadian winter and the untouched wastes. But on the rock, stronger than its strength, the spirit of European civilization preserves its precarious life: this is a novel of survivals, a series of pictures illustrating the will of a highly civilized people to preserve its civilization. To maintain French cookery through the six or seven frozen months—not to subsist on frozen meat or coarse fare, but to have vegetables growing in the cellar and fowls laid away in lard—becomes not only significant but in its way heroic. On uncommonly cold nights little Cécile Auclair, taking her dead mother's place as head of the household before she was in her teens, would throw off the covers and stir her chilly legs to cover the parsley. Her father would call out: *"Qu'est-ce que tu fais, petite?"* The sleepy voice would reply: *"Papa, j'ai peur pour le persil."* It had not frozen in her mother's time, it should not freeze in hers. Euclide Auclair's household, a particle of Louis XIV's Paris accidentally transported to Quebec, is cherished by not only those who live in it but all sorts of people, even by Monseigneur Laval, because they find in the food and the furniture and in the spirit of the critical enlightened apothecary something that appeals to their nostalgia and promises the continuance in the colony of what they admired in the distant and at times incredible capital. The light cheerful quality of the Auclairs, father and daughter, is beautifully balanced by such grim figures as Laval with his terrifying features, his formidable language, and his immense disappointments, and Jeanne Le Ber, recluse of Montreal, won for a religious life by no less a person than the Venerable Marguerite Bourgeoys. Laval comes before us ringing the cathedral bell at every hour all through the long night before All Souls', a punctual reminder to all on the rock of the force by which it is ruled and linked with Europe. The recluse, living in her bare rooms inset in the cathedral, worn to nothing by her devotions, is an evidence that in French Canada God is already served as He had been in the deserts of Egypt in the early centuries of Christianity, that the great cold of the Montreal winter cannot alter in one iota the creed the French had planted with the lilies. Light and dark shadows are so juxtaposed that in the novel as a whole there is an image of life in its variety and promise.

It is far too little to say of *Shadows on the Rock* that it is the best novel drawn from the rich material of Canadian history. Beside it William Kirby's *Golden Dog* is clumsy and external, Charles G. D. Roberts's *Forge in the Forest* conventional, and Gilbert Parker's *Seats of the Mighty* merely facile. Nor would any historical novels written by French Canadians sustain a comparison with Miss Cather's craftsmanship and vision. Still, if *Shadows on the Rock* is perfect in the beauty of structure and style, if the author's sense of relevance is unfailing, if the mood of nostalgic charm is perfectly conveyed, it is a novel with but little dramatic incident, and the personages are figures in a legend rather than living characters. These are indeed but shadows! The shortcomings in drama and in vitality of character are quite deliberate, the coloring in the sequence of pictures is intentionally faint, for the book was to be an equivalent in prose of a fresco by Puvis de Chavannes. No more graceful book has been accomplished in our time.

Shadows on the Rock was followed by a collection of three *nouvelles, Obscure Destinies.* From the appearance of *One of Ours,* Miss Cather had avoided the massiveness of the full-length novel; in everything she has written since the crucial year 1922 the literal dimensions have been relatively brief, and the method has been that of the tale or *nouvelle,* or of the short novel with shorter works inset. Nowhere does her discrimination show more finely than in *Obscure Destinies* or in *My Mortal Enemy,* that somewhat earlier work in which the same method was tried out. In the *nouvelle* she finds sufficient space to work in the symbols and pictures on which she has come more and more to depend, and to allow an occasional incident to flow into a dramatic scene, and yet has no need to make of a character a complex personality. In "Old Mrs. Harris," she exhibits in their essence the powers that in her later years she has most wished to exercise, the power of picture, the power of symbol, the power of structure, the power of style. In it also her vision of the aged, defeated, lonely, and unhappy comes to its clearest and most moving expression.

What Miss Cather has published since the appearance of *Obscure Destinies* in 1932—it has been remarkably little—has revealed no new kinds of power or charm, nor has it ever quite matched the work of the preceding decade, which will more and more be recognized as the time in which her craftsmanship and her vision attained their height. *Lucy Gayheart,* in which she returned to her own Middle West, is slight, not as *A Lost Lady* is slight but with the slightness of minor work, although the last part is, for feeling and form, comparable with almost anything in *A Lost Lady. Sapphira and the Slave Girl,* more nearly a successor to the historical novels, evokes Virginia before the Civil War, the Virginia of which she heard tales when she was growing up near Winchester, in a series of quiet pictures which have the charm but not the depth of those in *Death Comes for the Archbishop* or *Shadows on the Rock.* It came out six years ago, and since then Miss Cather has been silent.

While she is still among us, although her work must be nearly over, if the time for a formal and considered estimate has perhaps not yet arrived, we may yet see her fiction in sufficient perspective to tell her on the occasion of her seventieth anniversary something of what her craftsmanship and vision mean to us. What we have gained by her craftsmanship is, above all, a beautiful lightening of the novel form. From George Eliot's time down to ours, the load upon the novel form has been steadily increasing until in works such as *The Financier* and *The World of William Clissold*—to choose examples from novelists who have recently died—the form broke beneath the stress. I suppose that for popular fiction of a semi-serious sort, and for fiction which aspires to distinction without fully attaining it, the characteristic formula during the past fifteen years or so has been the memoir of a crowded life, abounding in rather crude sexual experience and with somewhat hasty reflections on education, industry, and the social system, and coming to a climax in a melodramatic ethical regeneration or else in an equally melodramatic recognition of life's futility. Examples of such fiction, written for the day, or at best for the decade, will be in everyone's mind. In most of them, character and story are mere props and are handled with an almost unbelievable clumsiness; structure and tone are scarcely considered; and in style the model appears to be the manner of the more lively foreign correspondents. Against such a degradation of the art of fiction to mere journalism, Miss Cather's craftsmanship stands out with an alien definiteness and firmness of beauty.

Her vision is of essences. In her earlier novels the essential subject, a state of mind or of feeling, was enveloped in the massiveness of the conventional modern realist novel. It was there, but it was muffled. Then Miss Cather saw that if she abandoned the devices of massive realism, if she depended upon picture and symbol and style, she could disengage her essential subject, and make it tell upon the reader with a greater directness and power, help it to remain uncluttered in his mind. The things that pass, the things that merely adhere to states of mind and feeling, she began to use with a severe economy. Her fiction became a kind of symbolism, with the depths and suggestions that belong to symbolist art, and with the devotion to a music of style and structure for which the great literary symbolists strove, Pater and Moore and the later James. Over their work hers has the advantage that her vision was never eccentric, disproportioned, or perverse. What she cares for in humanity and in nature many sensitive and cultivated people have cared for in every time. There could be not better assurance that her fiction will endure and that some of the novels and tales will interpret us to a later day. At seventy, it may be a satisfaction to her that she has written not for the day or the decade but for the long future, and that in a time when most of those works which usurp the leading places in our book reviews will have nothing to say, *My Antonia* (despite its passages of excessive detail), *A Lost Lady, Death Comes for the Archbishop, Shadows on the Rock,* and *Obscure Destinies* will be the sources of pleasure and the subjects of thought.

Meanwhile her contemporaries may ask, like little Oliver, for more—more of that firm and radiant prose, of the pictures and the symbols, of the light quick movement, of the essences which are central to all civilization and will outlast even the garage.

From *The Yale Review,* copyright Yale University Press, Vol. XXXVI (September, 1946), pp. 77–92. Reprinted by permission of the author and editors.

FRANCIS FERGUSSON
Eugene O'Neill
[1930]

AFTER Eugene O'Neill had spent several years traveling about the country with his father, James O'Neill, who was playing in *The Count of Monte Cristo,* and a few more bumming all over the world, he fell ill; and while recovering in a sanatorium, decided he wanted to write plays. His first plays, written while he was studying under Professor Baker at Harvard, and working with the young Provincetown Playhouse, are the product of his romantic youth and a desire to write for the stage. They are not complicated by the anxiety about his own soul which gets in his way later, and, more clearly than his later work, they show the real nature of his vocation to the stage. The first published volume, *Thirst,* is now repudiated. Mr. Barrett Clark, whose book on O'Neill contains all the available information about his life and the origins of his plays, says that the plays collected under this title are similar to those in the earliest preserved collection, *The Moon of the Caribbees,* though cruder.

The first thing that strikes one on reading the latter collection is the over-emphatic language. The characters, usually the crew of a tramp steamer, communicate almost entirely in profanity. Mr. Clark, who once made the crossing on a cattle-boat, testifies that the dialogue is not inaccurate; but the more educated people in the later plays, while not so profane, also seem to be laboring to express the inexpressible, and achieving a similar flatness. I conclude that the fault is with the dramatist rather than with his material. This conclusion is borne out by the fact that, except in the "atmospheric" play, *The Moon of the Caribbees,* the author remains on a level with his characters. We are required to accept people with ineffable sorrows or longings as carrying the main burden of the play. And the plots and situations are built on a similar assumption of a vast emotion which cannot be put into words.

I understand that O'Neill has never liked *In the Zone;* but it seems to differ from the other plays in the volume we are discussing, chiefly in having a neater and more self-conscious technique. It may be that O'Neill thinks that this interferes with its sincerity; or it may be that I do him an injustice. The crew of a tramp steamer crossing the submarine-infested zone, is nervously on the watch for spies. What a spy would be doing there is never satisfactorily explained. This does not prevent the men, in search of a scapegoat, from suspecting Smitty. This character is a recurrent figure in the early plays: a melancholy and solitary hobo "of the higher type." Someone discovers him reading a batch of letters one night; they tie him up in spite of his screams, and investigate. But instead of the telegrams from the Kaiser which they expected, they find letters from Smitty's lady-love, who rejected him years ago because he drank. One dried rose falls to the floor. At this sudden revelation of hidden sorrow the rough sailors, whose hearts are really of gold, are abashed and conscience-stricken.

This plot, which, however absurd it may sound in the telling never fails to move an audience, is really as helplessly bombastic as the language; a language of childish superlatives which are always trying to imply more than they succeed in stating. I take it that the essence of melodrama is to accept emotions uncritically; which, in the writing, amounts to assuming or suggesting emotions that are never realized either in language or action. Melodrama in this sense is a constant quality in O'Neill's work. It disfigures his middle period, when his feeling for a character is out of all proportion to that character's importance to the play, as well as his later period, when his attempt to deal with his own unattached emotion takes the unhappy form of a passion for some large idea. In fact it seems that O'Neill typically resorts to the stage, not to represent emotions through which he has already passed; which have been criticised and digested, and so may be arranged in patterns to form works of art: he resorts to the stage to convey a protest, the *first* cry of the wounded human being. His fundamental feeling for the stage, so clearly shown in these first plays, is not that of the artist, but of the melodramatist: the seeker after sensational effect.

Nevertheless, his naïve belief in emotion is related to a priceless quality, which one may call histrionic sincerity, the essence of mummery. Every dramatist as well as every actor depends for his power over his audience on his own belief in what he is trying to put on the stage, whether it be an emotion, a character, or a situation. An audience is extremely malleable. It may be swayed by suggestion, hypnotized by the concentration of the stage figure. This complete concentration, which would be wrecked by a wakeful critical faculty or a touch of humor at the wrong time, O'Neill possesses in a very high degree. It is the secret of his success; and when it is joined to an interest in a character, it produces his best scenes.

II

After O'Neill had exhausted the vein of mood and atmosphere derived from his early experiences of bumming, he ceased to write melodrama for its own sake, and developed an interest in people he had known or heard about. His next plays begin with an interest in a character or characters. O'Neill thus explains the origin of *Beyond the Horizon,* the earliest play of this type to be preserved: "I think the real life experience from which the idea of *Beyond the Horizon* sprang was this: On the British tramp steamer on which I made a voyage as ordinary seaman, Buenos Aires to New York, there was a Norwegian A. B. and we became quite good friends. The great sorrow and mistake of his life, he used to grumble, was that as a boy he had left the small paternal farm to run away to sea. He had been at sea twenty years, and had never gone home once in that time. . . . Yet he cursed the sea and the life it had led him—affectionately. . . . I thought, 'What if he had stayed on the farm, with his instincts? What would have happened?' . . . And from that point I started to think of a more intellectual, civilized type . . . a man who would have my Norwegian's inborn craving for the sea's unrest, only in him it would be diluted into a vague, intangible wanderlust. . . . He would throw away his instinctive dream and accept the thraldom of the farm for— why, for almost any nice, little poetical craving—the romance of sex, say." Though we do not have O'Neill's account of the origins of most of his plays, I should say, from internal evidences, that *Gold, Anna Christie, Diff'rent, All God's Chillun Got Wings,* and perhaps *Desire Under the Elms,* started from a similar interest in a character, which was sometimes real, sometimes partly or entirely imaginary. I shall look at *All God's Chillun* as typical of this group. It shows his most characteristic failings as well as some of his very best results.

The first scene shows Ella, a white girl, and Jim, a sensitive little negro boy, having a childish love affair in their native slum. This scene, unnecessary for the main theme of the play, is typical of O'Neill. Its only possible relevance is as psychological and sociological background, for the important information is duplicated later. I shall have more to say later about O'Neill's use of this type of realism. Meanwhile observe that the realism of the dialogue and the natural history of the stage full of children (which, I may say, is extremely difficult to do practically), are complicated by a kind of symbolism or super-realism of the set. The scene is a street-corner, one street being full of black faces and negro tunes, the other street full of white faces and their tunes. Aside from the sloppiness of leaving so much to the carpenter and the régisseur (which I shall also mention later), it may be doubted whether realism with a superimposed symbolism of this kind is ever a success. Even Ibsen, with his Wild Ducks and his sea-ladies, has the greatest difficulty in making it seem anything but artificial, and Mr. O'Neill hasn't a tenth of his skill.

Ella falls in with tough companions and gradually degenerates, while Jim painfully acquires education and starts to study Law. Ella, disillusioned with her own kind, marries Jim in a moment of depression, as the only "white" man she knows. There is a good "symbolistic" scene showing the newly married couple emerging from the church between rows of hostile faces, white on one side and black on the other. And then the real drama begins: the struggle in Jim between his love for Ella and his ambition to succeed in the world; the struggle in Ella between her love for Jim and her hatred of him as the cause of her exile from her own people. The point of conflict is Jim's career: for his self-respect he needs to become a lawyer, while Ella, who has never really accepted Jim as her husband, needs to preserve her spiritual ascendancy by preventing him from passing his examinations. Tied together by their love and by their solitude, they alternately take refuge in each other's arms and fight for mastery or vengeance. The scenes throughout this middle part of the play, in spite of their inadequate language, are deeply convincing. But at the end they both give up: Jim agrees to play a little boy to Ella's little girl. In effect, they cease to strive for an adult relation of husband and wife and accept a childish one.

Now if the previous scenes mean anything, this conclusion marks a degeneration on both their parts. But O'Neill, under the necessity of ending his play, asks us to accept it as a hard won *Verklärung*:

Jim—Forgive me, God—and make me worthy! . . . Let this fire of burning suffering purify me of selfishness and make me worthy of the child you send me for the woman you take away!
Ella—Honey, Honey, I'll play right up to the gates of heaven with you!

What is the reason for this extraordinary failure of O'Neill's to master his material? Between the untidy and unnecessary first scene and the bathetic and evasive finale, there are several scenes of really tragic significance. Beginning with a person, and proceeding with that complete concentration on the stage figure which I described above, O'Neill sometimes sees his people so deeply that they acquire overtones of universal import. One may sometimes feel Jim and Ella, through their excellent concreteness, as every pair of exiles in love, and their story as realizing certain profound truths about the relation between a man, his work, and his wife. But these jewels are so rare, and are embedded in such a disheartening matrix of psychology, bathos, and cheap symbolism that they seem not only accidental but misunderstood when they appear. And the end finally persuades one that the author wrought better than he knew. He turns away from his tragic vision, and all is lost.

But did he ever have a tragic vision? The finale, so wrong for the middle scenes, is not inconsistent with the characters. The reason it jars is that it belies the point of view from which their struggles were seen as having a dignity and a significance beyond themselves. It might be appropriate in some terrible comedy, but the characters are not seen as in any sense comic figures. In fact, they are not seen "as" anything: if they at times reveal heights and depths, that is an accident, for O'Neill's relation to them is personal. They are for him friends and enemies, other individuals in an anarchical universe, not parts of any larger vision. He is prepared to echo their cry, "Can such things be?" It is all very well for a character in a play to demonstrate this emotion, but when an author shows it it means that he has not digested his material to the point where it becomes suitable for a work of art. Interested in his people's psychology, yes: hence the filling in of naturalistic background in scene 1; but interested in the esthetic value of their dignity, no: and hence no possible ending for their story. O'Neill is right when he says, "Life doesn't end, one experience is but the birth of another. Violent death is seldom the solution of anything, in life or in fiction. It is too often a makeshift device. . . ." Life doesn't end, but a work of art does; a work of art is a bounded whole, and O'Neill's unsatisfying endings are a proof that his interest in his people is not the disinterested and final one of the artist, but the developing and tentative one of a man among men.

But O'Neill's power of convincing an audience is vastly aided by the fact that his belief in his characters is so purely naturalistic. Where there is no publicly established convention, the only way to make a character acceptable is to establish him naturalistically. An audience will believe in a character who used to play on a certain street-corner in Harlem, and whose father was in the coal business, but it will not believe in one who can only be identified by the qualities of his soul, and toward whom it is invited to adopt no personal attitude. The limitations of this type of realism have been admirably studied by Virginia Woolf, in her essay, *Mr. Bennett and Mrs. Brown*. It has this inestimable advantage of being publicly understood, but the most that can be said for it as an art form is that it may, as in this play of O'Neill's, lead to the accidental discovery of a few muddy diamonds. O'Neill himself has never been satisfied with it; he has never called himself a realist: we have seen that even in these plays of his middle period he resorts to symbolism. And finally he abandons his interest in character altogether and attempts to enunciate general ideas.

III

Beginning perhaps with *The Hairy Ape*, and continuing through *The Fountain, The Great God Brown, Marco Millions, Lazarus Laughed,* and *Dynamo*, Mr. O'Neill's character studies are interspersed with, and finally superseded by, plays in which the author shows no interest in the concrete, and assumes the rôle of prophet. It is as though he had ceased to interrogate his acquaintainces about which course he is to expect of "Life," and had begun to interrogate Nietzsche and other nineteenth-century philosophers. About the prophecies themselves Mr. Clark says the last word: "If O'Neill were a genuinely original thinker, or even a brilliant spokesman for the ideas of a brilliant thinker, we might argue as to whether we should be the losers if he were to give up writing plays altogether, but his ideas as contributions to contemporary thought are negligible; they are at best slightly varied forms of what we have all been reading during the past decade or so." Lazarus' Nietzschean exclamation is typical: "Men are also unimportant! . . . Man remains! Man slowly arises from the past of the race of men that was his tomb of death! For Man death is not! Man, Son of God's Laughter, is!" O'Neill is not a thinker, and we need not attempt to investigate his thought any further. It is true that Lazarus sounds a little like O'Neill's own fundamental cry, that "life goes on"—implying, perhaps, some confusion between pessimism and the unhappy ending, which would affect his ability to write plays; moreover, it is doubtful whether Lazarus' generalized and rather hysterical optimism could ever be realized in live characters; but the question which concerns us more nearly, in our attempt to understand O'Neill as a playwright, is not so much the quality of the thought as the relation between the thought, the author, and the play.

O'Neill, we find, is more interested in affirming his ideas than in representing the experience in which they are implied. The example of Elizabethan drama seems to prove that an unsatisfying philosophy may underlie a great play. But there the play is the thing, and the philosophy may at most be deduced from it as from a direct experience of life. In *Lazarus Laughed*, on the other hand, there is little or no play at all, for Caligula, the anti-Lazarus, is no more credible than Lazarus himself, and their conflicts fail entirely to move us. The burden of the play is carried by two elements: by Lazarus' philosophical arias, and by spectacular effects of crowd movements and colored lights. About the first of these, enough has been said. With regard to the element of spectacle, Reinhardt has shown us what can be achieved in this line, especially in his production of Büchner's *Danton*. Gordon Craig has hailed these departures as first steps toward a new form, his hypothetical "pure art of the theatre." As a form, it is related to the seventeenth-century masque, and the modern revue. It seems to mean a dissolution of the classic partnership of actor and author, to which we owe most great drama, in favor of a third figure, the régisseur. A good régisseur may of course get artistically satisfying effects with well-trained crowds and carefully calculated light and sound effects—too often at the author's expense. When an author resorts to it, it usually means that he has ceased to be interested in mastering the medium of the stage. This is certainly true in *Lazarus Laughed*: the stage becomes O'Neill's lifeless megaphone. Nothing stands between the audience and O'Neill, shouting his views. For his relation to his ideas, in these prophetic plays, is the same as his relation to his characters in his middle period: they are emotionally significant to him, they play a part in his equilibrium as a man. Attaining no vision outside himself, his plays remain attached to him by his eternal immaturity.

We are not surprised to find, therefore, that his audience is often more interested in the author than in his play: "It is salvation the agnostic play-wright is seeking. One might trace his life like one of those dry southwestern roads where the Penitente Brothers have laid down the dead man they are are carrying." O'Neill's plays are crosses. Follow the road he travels and you will often hear the sound of flagellation. Look and you will often see that the whip is brought down by a tormented soul on his own back. But flowers grow on this desert track, and the mountains and the sunset lie *Beyond the Horizon*. The very imperfection which connects the author with his play also connects the author with his audience. The one quality which his admir-ers agree in stressing is his sincerity. We have seen that he believes in his own mood in his early plays, and in the personal reality of his characters in his middle period, while in his latest plays he is in earnest in asserting some Nietzschean war-cry. As a person, he is sincerely interested in figuring out his life, and perhaps in attaining a stable point of view—though unconsciously. He has in fact never attained it. He has managed to recognize his emotional demands, but he has not reached the further heroism of accepting what be-comes of them: of describing them with reference to some independent reality. He has a sense of human needs, but none of human destiny. He offers us the act of seeking, but no disinterested contemplation; himself, therefore, rather than his work. Only the dead cease to change; but by discipline it is some-times possible to produce a work complete and independent of the suffering individual. O'Neill's failings may all be ascribed to the fact that he has never found any such discipline.

IV

I do not intend, in this essay, to enquire directly to what extent O'Neill's failure to find a discipline through which to realize his talent is due to his own shortcomings, and to what extent to "conditions" beyond his control. A slight acquaintance with modern drama since Ibsen shows one how difficult it is to write plays of artistic as distinguished from sentimental or sociological interest. But to tackle the general question of O'Neill as a modern dramatist —and an American—would involve questions which I am not competent to treat. It seems more profitable to compare briefly O'Neill's career with those of two other American playwrights, George Kelly and E. E. Cummings, who followed very different paths to the stage, in the hope that some sense of O'Neill's place in the contemporary scene may emerge by implication.

O'Neill began to work about the time of the 1912 Renaissance. He belongs with Mencken, Sherwood Anderson, and Theodore Dreiser (who was in advance of his time). This was the generation that raised the hue and cry about Puritanism. They were, as a group, impatient of tradition and con-vention, and their great discovery was their emotional needs. They were more interested in man's emotions than in a map of them; therefore, more interested in the man than his work. Most of them wrote fiction—a genre which is much better suited to this temperament than the stage; but they also gave birth to the Little Theatre, and O'Neill, whose first plays were produced by the Provincetown, is in many ways a Little Theatre product. This movement seems never to have had anything more positive than a dissatisfaction with Broadway, and an ambition. It was a revolt against narrow commercialism; it asserted that the theatre was an art; but, having no standards and no technique, it remained somewhat ineffectual in its new freedom.

George Kelly on the other hand is a product of the commercial, which is also the professional stage. He began as a vaudeville actor and presently he was writing his own skits. He stood behind the scenes with a stop-watch, and if the audience did not laugh soon enough, he rewrote the act. From vaudeville he graduated to the three-act comedy, and finally to the drama. His experience proves that a certain sense of craftsmanship is not incompatible with Broadway, rare though it is there: having set himself the comparatively modest problem of making the *honnête* Babbitts laugh, he was rewarded by the natural discipline which an actual audience and a particular stage can give. Assuming the viewpoint of "common sense" where O'Neill urges some large idea; accepting the realistic set and the realistic dialogue which he found publicly established, where O'Neill was always making strange demands on the carpenter and the electrician, Kelly's work was that of the artist: to master and refine a given medium to the point where it can be made to realize his vision. While O'Neill's freedom has resulted in a complete loss of bearings, so that he has of late almost ceased to be a dramatist, Kelly has bequeathed us several comedies which are complete, and refer to nothing outside themselves. If they are rather trivial, and if there are signs that his home-folks, having moved to more expensive suburbs and learned to drink gin, are no longer to be satisfied with his neat little interiors, the fault is not with his method, which was after all the method of Shakespeare and Molière. Kelly seems to have encountered the limitations of the theatre as it exists with us here and now. It is doubtful whether a method, which depends upon an acceptance of the existing theatre, would ever prove the solution for a man of O'Neill's potential dimensions.

If the Little Theatre, in its revolt against commercialism, forfeited incidentally the discipline of the craftsman which a Kelly could work out for himself on Broadway, it never showed the slightest tendency to develop its own standards and its own conventions. A play with a "kick" has remained its ideal. We have seen that the personality of the author or the agony of some unassimilated "character" can satisfy its cravings for drama better than a formal and autonomous play.

E. E. Cummings, however, was a poet before he tried to write for the stage. That is to say, he had trained himself—with what success I shall not attempt to say: his method rather than his results concern us here—to see his material as an artist. His play, *Him*, is evidently more "autobiographical" than any of O'Neill's and yet the characters at least of Him and Me are acceptable as parts of the pattern of the play without reference to the author. Without trying to judge the merit of the play as a whole, I should say that the scenes between Him and Me have all the qualities we have failed to find in O'Neill's work. The characters, the rhythm, and the sense of the stage are all of a piece, whereas in O'Neill's plays we find realistic dialogue, symbolistic settings, and characters which are unamenable to any pattern or underlying rhythm. In a real writer for the stage, language, character, and the sound and movement of the stage, spring from the same root conception. A Molière dialogue implies the stage empty save for a few spectators, a little furniture, and the actors; it implies a rhythm derived from the pantomime of the "Commedia dell'Arte," and a certain relation between actor and audience. A Cummings dialogue implies a brief light interval between "blackouts," a certain rhythm derived from the vaudeville act, and an audience which good-humoredly challenges the performer to "put his stuff across." Cummings' work, in fact, has style. His solitary discipline has enabled him to work in stage terms, disinterestedly, and with a mastery which O'Neill, for all his experience, has never attained.

But Cummings, unlike Kelly, is an artist of the theatre without either theatre or audience. I have said that his style was derived from vaudeville, but no vaudeville actor could manage a speech of Him's and no vaudeville audience could understand his play. In spite of his very authentic feeling for the stage, and in spite of his ingenious and courageous effort to dramatize his very lack of connection with a live stage and audience (so neatly of a piece with the "stunt" feeling of his vaudeville style), Cummings' first play remains mere closet drama. It was in fact produced at O'Neill's native theatre; but the Provincetown's crowd of Greenwich Villagers, just the thing to relish a revival of *In the Zone* and *Moon of the Caribbees*, were at a loss to deal with *Him*. Cummings does not belong at the Provincetown. So far he does not seem to belong anywhere. But O'Neill indubitably belongs at the Provincetown, at the Guild, in the suburbs of London, in Berlin, and in Little Theatres all over the English-speaking world. The man O'Neill is very close to a vast audience.

From *The Hound and Horn*, Vol. III (January–March, 1930), pp. 145–160. Reprinted by permission.

STARK YOUNG

American Drama in Production

MOURNING BECOMES ELECTRA
Eugene O'Neill[1]

[1931]

To HEAR the bare story, shortly told, of this new O'Neill play, with all its crimes and murders, may easily bring a flouting smile or recall Mrs. Malaprop's announcement of Sir Lucius' and Bob Acres' duel: "So, so, here's fine work, here's fine suicide, parricide, and simulation going on in the fields!" The same thing could be said of *Hamlet* or *King Lear* or *Oedipus King,* of course, but this is sure to be the line the jibes will take from such of the play's critics as are unfriendly or impatient or incapable. As to the length of the event, the actual performance at the Guild could be considerably shortened by going faster in many places; the length of the play itself is for the most part organic with both its meaning and its effect. As to the depressing effects of the play, we will come to that later.

The title, as we see, intends to dispose at the start of the relation of *Mourning Becomes Electra* to the Greek drama. The story of the house of Atreus was set down by Homer, Pindar, Aeschylus, Sophocles, Euripides and diverse Greek writers whose works are not extant. From this house shadowed by an ancient curse, Agamemnon, brother of Menelaus, goes forth to the war at Troy. His wife Clytaemnestra, the sister of Helen, during her husband's absence takes for her paramour Aegisthos and shares the government of Argos with him. In due time Agamemnon, having at the god's behest sacrificed his daughter Iphigenia and bringing with him Cassandra, Priam's daughter, returns, and is murdered by Clytaemnestra and her lover. Electra, his daughter, is shamed and degraded and prays for the return of her brother Orestes, long ago sent out of the country by his mother and now become a man. Orestes returns, kills Clytaemnestra and Aegisthos. He is pursued by the Erinyes, and only after wandering and agony and a vindication of himself before the tribunal of Athena's Areopagos is he cleansed of his sin.

[1] *Mourning Becomes Electra,* a trilogy: *Homecoming, The Hunted, The Haunted,* by Eugene O'Neill. Guild Theatre, New York City. October 26, 1931.

Mourning Becomes Electra begins with the mother and daughter, Christine and Lavinia, waiting, there in this house of the Mannons, the return of Ezra Mannon from the war, which with Lee's surrender is almost over. A thread of romance is introduced between, on the one side, Hazel and Peter, a brother and sister, and, on the other, the son, Orin, and Lavinia. Meanwhile Captain Brant comes to call; he pays a certain court to Lavinia, and she, acting on a cue from the hired man, who has been on the place these sixty years, traps him into admitting that he is the son of one of the Mannons who had seduced a Canadian maid-servant and been driven from home by his father, Lavinia's grandfather. She has all her data straight now. She has suspected her mother, followed her to New York, where Christine has pretended to go because of her own father's illness but has in fact been meeting Adam Brant. Lavinia has written her father and her brother, hinting at the town gossip about her mother. We learn that Captain Brant had returned to avenge his mother but instead had fallen passionately in love with Christine, who loves him as passionately as she hates her husband. From this point the play moves on, with the father's hatred of the son, who returns it, the son's adoration of his mother, the daughter's and the mother's antagonism, the daughter's and the father's devotion, to Christine's murder of her husband with the poison sent by Brant and substituted for the medicine prescribed against his heart trouble. Part One of the plays ends here. Orin returns, after an illness from a wound in the head. Christine tries to protect herself in her son's mind against the plots of Lavinia. Lavinia, in the room where her father's body lies, convinces Orin with the facts; they trail Christine to Brant's ship, where she has gone to warn him against Orin. Orin shoots Brant. Christine next day kills herself. Brother and sister take a long voyage to China, stop at the southern isles, come home again. Substitutions have taken place, Lavinia has grown like her mother, Orin more like his father. Meanwhile his old affair with Hazel, encouraged at last by Lavinia, who now wants to marry Peter, is canceled; he finds himself making an incestuous proposal to Lavinia and is repulsed by her. He shoots himself. In the end Lavinia, speaking words of love to Peter, finds Adam's name on her lips. She breaks with Peter, orders the blinds of her house nailed shut, and goes into the house, to live there till her death. Justice has been done, the Mannon dead will be there and she will be there.

So bare an account serves the plot a little, but can give scant indication of the direct speeches and actions heavily charged with the burden and meaning of the scenes; nor does it convey the power and direct arrangement of some of them, that, for example, of the brother and sister at Brant's cabin, where the mere visual elements convey as much as the words. The chanty with which this scene opens, the song and the singer's drunkenness, the lonely ship in the dusk, establishing as it does the mood of longing, futility, land chains and the sea's invitation and memory, is a fine idea and greatly enriches the scene's texture, though the performance did not fully establish the current or motive.

It will be obvious that the American dramatist, as the Greek did, used a well-known outline which he could fill in to his purpose. Obviously, too, Ezra Mannon is Agamemnon, Captain Brant Aegisthos, Christine Clytaemnestra, Lavinia Electra, and Orin Orestes. But to dismiss the matter by saying that Mr. O'Neill has merely repeated the classic story in modern terms is off the track. Let it go at that and you will miss even the really classic elements in the play and get only the Greek side of it that is self-evident and that would be easy for any dramatist.

The story itself follows the Greek plays up to the middle of the third division of the play, and here the incest motive, the death of Orin and the transference of the whole situation and dramatic conclusion to the sister depart from Aeschylus, Sophocles and Euripides. The blood motive in the lover, Adam Brant's relation to the family, is an addition. The old hired man, the confidant, parallels to some extent a Greek device, familiar to us, however, in countless plays. The townspeople and workmen are now and again a kind of chorus. Many of the shadings and themes are from the older plays; for an example, the servant's line in Aeschylus,

I see the dead are killing one who lives

which underlies one of the new play's main themes. The death of the lover, as in Aeschylus and Euripides, not as in Sophocles, comes before that of the mother, which throws the stress where the O'Neill play needs it. The division of the play into three parts is of course like the trilogy of the Greek dramatists. On the other hand, the dividing line is much less distinct in *Mourning Becomes Electra*; the final curtain of the first part, for example, falls, it is true, on Mannon's death, as in Aeschylus it does on Agamemnon's, but there is not the same effect of totality because of the stress put on Lavinia; in *Agamemnon* Electra does not even appear.

The magnificent theme that there is something in the dead that we cannot placate falsely is in the Greek plays and in the O'Neill play. The end of the play is by imaginative insight Greek in spirit: Lavinia goes into the house, the blinds are closed forever, the stage is silent, the door shut, the exaltation is there, the completion, the tragic certainty. Finally, the peculiar kind of suspense employed in the play is Greek. The playwright has learned the adult suspense of the classics as compared with the adolescent sense of it, hit off happily enough at times, that reigns in the romantic drama of the North. Classic suspense does not depend on a mere crude strain, wondering how things will turn out, however entertaining and often dramatic that effect may be. The classic suspense has even a biological defense: you know that in life you will come to death, but just how the course of all your living will shade and fulfill itself you do not know, and you are borne up by an animal will to survive, a passionate participation, an absorbed contemplation of the course, till the last moment completes itself. In the classic form where the outcome is already known, lies the highest order of suspense. Knowing how things will end, you are left free to watch what qualities and what light will appear in their progression toward their due and necessary finish. You hang on what development, what procession exactly of logic, ecstasy or fate, will ensue with them, what threads of beautiful or dark will come into their human fabric.

It is interesting in our confused and feministic epoch that this new employment of the theme gives the play to Electra. Nowhere in Greek does this happen. From Sophocles there survives what must be only a section of a trilogy, the *Electra;* and though so much of the torment and waiting has been hers, Electra is at the end let off with a betrothal to Orestes' faithful Horatio, Pylades, and the forebodings and remorse rise in Orestes only, who has struck the death blow on his mother. In Euripides' *Electra* the conclusion is the forebodings of Orestes and the marriage of Electra to Pylades; in his *Orestes* Electra cleaves to her brother, who is in a violent neurotic sickness, quite modernly indicated; they are both in danger from the State for their action, and the whole situation is solved with a trivial and silly dénouement, gods from the machine, killings and abductions, wholly undramatic and redeemed, in so far as it is redeemed, only by Euripides' dialectic and poetic glamor. In Aeschylus, Electra appears only in the middle of the trilogy; the central hero is the royal line, Agamemnon and Orestes.

Along with these more accessible and manifest likes and dislikes, there are numerous points about Mr. O'Neill's play that so far at least as the Greek original goes, are variations or additions. The most brilliant of these is the incest motive, coming toward the last of the play. (We must recall Shelley's remark that of all tragic motives incest is the most powerful, since it brings the passions most violently into play.) For Orestes the gray forms at the back, invisible at first to all but himself, are the Erinyes, the Furies who will avenge the crime he has committed within his own blood. They are the daughters of night, and when they have been appeased, their other selves, the Eumenides, the Gentle Ones, will pass by and leave him peace. For Orin Mannon there comes the sudden form of his desire: incest: the realization and admission of what it has all been about all along, his feelings toward his father, toward his mother, toward Brant, toward Lavinia. This recognition of his obsession is his avenging Erinyes. The mother in *Mourning Becomes Electra* is not killed by her son but takes her own life; his essential murder of his mother turns in his mind with a terror more modern but no less destroying; his mind storms with the Furies—"thoughts that accuse each other," as Cicero, writing in the sophistication of four centuries later, defined them. In such details alone might rest the argument that Eugene O'Neill, placing a Greek theme in the middle of the last century, has written the most modern of all his plays.

It is not wholly the Guild's fault if there is no overwhelming performance in *Mourning Becomes Electra*. The casting of such a play is very difficult, and doubly so in the absence of any training in our theatre that would prepare actors for the requirements of such parts. The best performances came in the scenes between the mother and son, where Mme. Nazimova's sense of theatre and her fluid response combined with Mr. Earle Larimore's simple and right attack on his part, were truly convincing, and in the scene between husband and wife, where Mr. Lee Baker gave a wholly right impersonation and the exact dramatic value for the play. Mr. Erskine Sanford turns out admirably in two character parts, the village doctor and the old workman who takes a bet on braving the ghost in the house. Miss Alice Brady had the rôle of all rôles in the play most difficult. Her performance of this modern Electra was sincere, and was sustained at times not only by a sort of tour-de-force achievement, but with real physical power, voice and all. In a few scenes she was pathetic as well, clear and moving, and her beauty most impressive. No doubt there was some instruction from the author himself as to keeping the face like a mask, rigid and motionless, as if fate itself were living there in this passionate and resolute being. As for the Greek of that intention, we must recall that in the Attic theatre the mask for Electra was very likely one of tortured lines, that the Greek theatre changed masks if need be from one scene to another, and that the Greek actor in the part could avail himself of gesture, dance movement, and a thorough training in voice, meter, speech, and singing. Realistically—that is to say in life—such rigidity never occurs except as a sign of disease. Esthetically it belongs only in the midst of a general stylistic whole, as in the Greek drama or the Chinese theatre that Mei Lan-fang brought to us. Technically it is immensely difficult, and derives not from an actual rigidity at all. Rigidity, masklike to the utmost, if you will, is a form of rhythm, as silence exists with a rhythm, when perceptible. It is unfair to bring so great an artist as Mei Lan-fang into the argument, but he gave us the whole model for such a problem in acting—the eyes constantly moving, the head imperceptibly in motion, supported by a complete and often almost invisible rhythm of the body, the emotions precise and compelling because of their very abstraction. Miss Brady's performance had several unforgetable moments. On the whole it moved gravely and in a manner remarkably well sustained just below the surface of the motives set for her by the dramatist; but her performance by failing both the darkness and the exaltation of the part often made only oppressive and unvaried what should have been burning and unconquerably alive and dominating. When we come right down to it, however, the best acting in the play is Mr. Earle Larimore's. In all his scenes up to the very last part, where he mouths too much and makes faces instead of a more intense concentration on his effects, he comes off first. In the scenes with his mother especially, he surpassed everybody else in the company; he conveyed to us the dramatist's meanings completely, without implying that the character himself was conscious of them; and by a certain emotional humility before the moment in which he shared, he came out securely right.

Out of Mr. Robert Edmond Jones' curtain and four settings, the rooms and the ship seem to me adequate without any haunting of the imagination, the front of the house dramatically right save for the lighting toward the rear, unnecessarily cruel to the actors. Mr. Philip Moeller's directing was admirable all through for its taste and evenness, its clear movement and fine placing of the scene. Its one fault was its tempo. There can be no doubt that Mr. O'Neill's play suffers greatly and will be accused of pretentiousness where it is wholly sincere and direct, in the first section especially, by the slowness with which the speeches are taken. Very often the effect is only that of a bourgeois respect for something to be taken as important. If it is the Greek spirit that is sought, the answer is that the Greek reading of lines was certainly formal but not necessarily slow; the chances are, in fact, that in the Greek theatre the cues were taken closely in order to keep the music going. And the Greeks had the advantage of music, dancing, and a great declamatory style, the lack of which will have to be balanced by anything rather than this obvious spacing and pausing and trend toward monotone, a great deal of which anyway proceeds only from a theoretical stage New England.

The two gifts that Eugene O'Neill up to now has displayed are for feeling and for dramatic image. His plays have often conveyed a poignancy that is unique in the modern drama, you felt that whatever was put down was at the dramatist's own expense, he paid out of himself as he went. His great theatre gift has been in the creation of images that speak for themselves, such for instance as the tittering of the Great Khan's ladies-in-waiting at the western Marco Polo, the dynamo in the play by the same name, and another, images so vivid that their mere repetition in people's talk makes the play sound better and more complete than it ever was. Sometimes this dramatic image spreads to the scope of a dramatic pattern that is the whole sum of the play. This happened not in more recent and elaborate plays, such as *Strange Interlude,* but in at least two of the earlier, *The Emperor Jones* and *The Hairy Ape,* where the whole plot was like an expanded sentence. In *Mourning Becomes Electra* Mr. O'Neill comes now into the full stretch of clear narrative design. He discovers that in expressive pattern lies the possibility of all that parallels life, a form on which fall infinite shadings and details, as the light with its inexhaustible nuances and elements appears on a wall. He has come to what is so rare in Northern art, an understanding of repetition and variation on the same design, as contrasted with matter that is less deep or subtle, though expressed with lively surprise, variety or novelty. It is a new and definite state in his development.

None of the old tagging appears in this play, no scientific terms that can be mistaken for psychological finalities. The feeling of Orin toward his father, for example, or of the daughter toward him, is not labeled. They are motives contrived to speak for themselves, and no specious explanation appears to be offered. The lapses in taste, as regards the writing itself, the trite jargon or the pushing of a situation to an obvious extreme, have vanished. The interest in shocking the bourgeois, not always lacking hitherto, has matured into the desire only to put in the truth. On the other hand the feeling remains. If not always as lyric as before, it has spread out into a more impersonal and distributed but no less passionate element in the play. The novelties and causes, masks, labor, sex, and asides, devices, are not in evidence, or rather have moved inward whatever there was in them beyond sheer theatrical effectiveness. Through most of its length the play moves steadily. The uncertainty in progression, comparative only, appears in the final scenes. This is a modern difficulty, due to the fact that the matter turns inward, where the Greeks, in contrast, had the advantage of robust and sure outward symbols, tribunals, ceremonial processions, and the forms of music and dance.

As to the depressing element of *Mourning Becomes Electra,* I have only to say that this play seems to me above anything else exhilarating. I trust I will not be thought pedantic when I say that what depresses me in the theatre is when the author dabbles in what is deep, enters where he has no right to be, and is glib about what he does not even taste the savor of. I need take no example, the stage is full of such. In *Mourning Becomes Electra* the end is fulfilled; Lavinia follows her direction, the completion of herself and her own inevitable satisfaction are seen. It may be that here life, as the Greek proverb said, wails as to a tomb. There may be other ways to manage, Rotarian healthy thoughts, exercise, good sense, saving the situation, leaving us more cheerful, marching on; but what of that? It is another situation that would be saved. There is a line of Leopardi's where he speaks of "my delight and my Erinyes"; and once, thinking of the eternal silence, he hears the wind among the trees and goes comparing the infinite silence to that voice, and remembers the eternal, and the dead seasons, and the present and living, and the sound of it, *e il suon di lei.* In this immensity his thought drowns, and shipwreck is sweet to him in such a sea. When the play ended, and the last Mannon was gone into the house, the door shut, I felt in a full, lovely sense that the

Erinyes were appeased, and that the Eumenides, the Gentle Ones, passed over the stage.

From *The New Republic,* Vol. LXVIII (November 11, 1931), pp. 352–355. Reprinted by permission. Later included in Mr. Young's volume of dramatic essays and reviews, *Immortal Shadows* (Charles Scribner's Sons, 1948).

STREET SCENE

Elmer Rice[1]

[1929]

IN A dry season, when so many theatres are closed and not a few managers have given up the game for the nonce and gone off to sunny beaches and Hollywood, Mr. Elmer Rice's *Street Scene* has come to many people as a treat, an excellent play, a worthy entertainment; and there is no need to throw any blight over the flower of their enthusiasm. In the realm of the blind, following the Spanish proverb, let the one-eyed be king; we may cheer *Street Scene* and wish it well.

In a setting by Mr. Jo Mielziner, cleverly realistic without being foolishly so and photographic without idle intrusions of dusty neighborhood detail from Ninth Avenue, where the play is laid, we see the story unwind itself entertainingly, with an amiable pace and plenty of time for the talk of the apartment house people as they go in and out, with engaging colors drawn from the contact of diverse nationalities, Jews, Germans, Irish, Italians and 100 per cent Americans, and with a due complaisance and tidy willingness to please. There is a genuinely expert economy in the way in which the life of the Maurrant family is conveyed to us, and an economy of means that is even finer in the portrait of the wife's career, this doomed Anna Maurrant, whose husband is brutal and indifferent in his treatment of her, is given to drink, is full of principles and ideas of what a family should be and what his own has got to be, he'll see to that.

The inmates of the apartment house, then, go in and out, linger about the doorstep in the stifling summer heat, sit at their windows, gossip of their children and each other, of the little husband on the third floor who acts as if he were having the baby instead of his thin little wife, of the Hildebrand family whose head has disappeared and who are about to be dispossessed. And through the whole texture of conversation they weave the thread of this pale woman's tragedy on the second floor, the visits of the milk collector

[1] *Street Scene,* by Elmer Rice. The Playhouse Theater, New York City. January 10, 1929.

that they have all observed, the spreading scandal about Mrs. Maurrant. Idly and emptily they are doing her to death, but it is all a part of the day's chatter and the neighborhood news. We see Rose, her daughter, and the married suitor, who wants to take her from the job in his office and set her up in an apartment and a place on the stage; we see Maurrant himself, a member of the stage-hands' union, a drinker, sullen and bullying. Meanwhile, Mrs. Jones has something to say about everything, takes her husband, George, to task, and her dog, Queenie, to walk, and professes complete ease of mind about her children, one of whom is a hulking thug and the other almost a tart.

From that on, the play takes its course, clearly foreseen. The baby is born upstairs, Mrs. Maurrant tends the mother all night, she is even more brutally treated by her suspicious husband; he says he is going out of town with a show, her daughter is at the funeral of a member of the firm she works for, and Mrs. Maurrant asks the milk collector—cleverly portrayed by the author as by no means attractive and so more indicative of the woman's despair—to come up to her rooms. The husband returns, kills the lover, and mortally wounds the wife, and after a long search is caught by the police. Rose, his daughter, refuses the attentions of the married suitor, and at the last does not accept the love of the Jewish student; she goes away for her own life, with her own ideas about one's dependence on something within oneself and reflections on the history of her father and mother in the light of that theory.

All this time, as a kind of matrix for the story, people have been passing, an ingenious assemblage of types and interests, curiosities of the town, vignettes of Manhattan, incidents of a day, and so on and so on, rendered with an amiable and accurate diversity that carries matters pleasantly along. And in the apartment house itself the well-edited sayings of the different persons and races accompany this drab pageantry and sweet genre.

Mr. Rice's directing is good. Among the many players necessary for this *monde* of the West Side, Miss Mary Servoss, as the tragic central figure of the woman who is killed, gives a performance that is always convincing, and that, while she is on the stage, lifts the scenes to something like pathos and point. Miss Erin O'Brien Moore, as her daughter, Rose, has to surmount many platitudinous approaches to the character, and speeches that are without imagination or reality, but plays well; she presents a young image that our eyes easily believe in, and a sincere and simple rendering of the character, so far as is possible with the lines. She illustrates, however, one melancholy point that may as well be aired now as any other time, and this is in the matter of clothes. In play after play on Broadway, where there is a young creature whose muted life is in some factory, slum or dingy, tragic neighborhood, we see these young ladies whose rôles are leading ones—the other players may be as mussy as you like and as photographic as the actor or the author chooses

—walking about in their trim little frocks and perfect shoes, simple but smartly turned out, and, however modest, taking no chances at lessening the drawing power of their pretty looks. American girls, however poor, may have, if you like, a trick of looking smart, what with the sales and all, but there is a *chic* higher up and more costly that fools nobody with pretenses of humility, and it is the pale cast of this thought that makes so absurd the picture of these leading young ladies in drab plays; and makes us ponder the problem of sincerity in art. Miss Beulah Bondi's Mrs. Jones is excellent playing.

So much for *Street Scene,* then, which on one plane of consideration is pleasantly entertaining. On another plane, where you take the play seriously and where you ask yourself whether for an instant you have believed in any single bit of it, either as art, with its sting of surprise and creation, or as life, with its reality, *Street Scene* is only rubbish, or very close to rubbish. For me, who was not bored with it as an evening's theatre, it is something less than rubbish, theatrical rubbish, in that curious, baffling way that the stage provides. The presence of living beings in the rôles engages us, and gives a certain plausibility to whatever takes place, and a certain actuality to any character whatever. But is it possible that anyone who could understand the values of the first act of *Anna Christie,* for example, or a play of Chekhov's, could fail to see that the last act in *Street Scene*—to take the most evident letdown—is empty and made up? The girl has found her mother shot, seen blood, at the hospital she has seen her mother die without speaking, she has seen her father caught and torn and bleeding, the Jewish boy, who loves her so much, offers to leave everything and go away with her, and she stands there making a little speech about dependence on one's self, and so on and so on, while nurses with perambulators have appeared and various persons come prowling around at the scene of a murder, and the obvious life goes on, amusing remarks from odd characters, and the rest of it—obliging journalism in sum. It must be a very elementary principle that the essential idea of a work of art goes through it, and that the themes and conceptions to be expressed must lie inherently in the substance of it, and that they are to be expressed in creation, not in superimposed sentiments.

Must we gloomily conclude that what most human beings like in the theatre is a farrago of living matter with the sting taken out of it? If this Anna Maurrant's life and death really bit into us, cost us something, instead of providing a mere thrill and the comfort of pseudo-thought afterward, would we not wreck the stage for rage when we see how little this matter has stung the dramatist? One of the ways we know a work of art is by the cost of its unity in kind, in the same way that the soul within him, determining his form as he comes into the world, prevents a man's having the bulk, strength and peace of an elephant. One of the ways we can tell an artist is by the extent to which reality puts the fear of God into him; a painter of no worth will paint you anything from Napoleon crossing the Alps to an old mill in Vermont, but a real painter trembles before the mere character of human hands and the problem of their conversion into the unity that is his style. Is it any wonder that Ingres, in his despair at the success of the second-rate, threatened to paint an Allegory of Mediocrities?

On a milder level of discourse, we may say that the acting in *Street Scene* furnishes a good instance of one of the problems in the art. For the most part the company at the Playhouse is made up of people who fit the characters ready-made. An Italian plays an Italian, a Jewess a Jewess, and so on, though the roster of names is mostly shining Anglo-Saxon—but that is nothing new in the theatre. In the hurry and pressure of things there is little time to discover or train actors, perhaps, and perhaps the need for actuality in this particular piece led the casting toward these ready-made types. The result is that there is a good deal of entertainment in *Street Scene* that comes from watching these actual people as we might see them on Ninth Avenue, but very little interest in watching them as actors. They are mostly neither bad nor good. Their looks are better than their acting, and they seem better than what they say. As a minor by-product of the perplexity induced by such a situation, I have no idea whether the player written down as Mr. James M. Qualen, whose janitor, Olsen, seems to me the best performance of the evening, is only a Nordic of that ilk, chosen for his type, or a capital actor.

From *The New Republic*, Vol. LVII (January 30, 1929), pp. 296–298. Reprinted by permission.

WINTERSET

Maxwell Anderson[1]

[1935]

I HAD intended from the start to see Mr. Maxwell Anderson's *Winterset* again; and a second visit, as was always manifest, merely enlarges the first impression. The purpose of a work of art is to arouse our response to its content; the ideal means employed will be that which will bring forth the fullest of responses. In the case of *Winterset* the means is, of course, a poetic medium of expression. But there is also a list of characters unusually clear and firm in their outline, and raised far beyond the limits of our familiar stage. These varieties of character are further intensified, each in itself, so that they strike one against another at a high level, or on an intense plane. All

[1] *Winterset*, by Maxwell Anderson. Martin Beck Theatre, New York City. September 25, 1935.

these people are seen in a tremendous—and genuinely created—perspective: the judge haunted by a sentence he passed, the son of the victim haunted by his father's innocence, and divers others driven forward by forces within the years. This uncommonly strong element of perspective in the play relates it further, in some elusive sense, to the poetic medium. The alternating resistance and advance of metrical form appears doubly right in the conveyance of this check and impulse, memory and passion, fateful past and power of life, that the characters' lives proceed upon.

Discussion of the use of poetry in drama will always be likely to end in confusion. To some persons the mere term implies the great and deep, to others the soft and pretty. To some—this notion is more nearly ineradicable—great intellectual conceptions appear in prose; we go to poetry for a beautiful and moving expression of concepts already known to us. This is but partially true. The successful poetic expression of a concept is likely to be the first complete expression of it, since in such a case the concept in full is expressed in terms of the complete human being and the human being in terms of the concept. One of the great descriptions of poetry is Dante's saying that poetry is the loving use of wisdom. In praising the poetic style we must not say that our present American drama may be too austere or stark. The proper word is barren (or arid, or merely journalistic).

It gets nowhere to say, as Mr. Richard Watts, Jr., did in the *Herald Tribune* of a fortnight back, that "the state of dramatic poetry being what it is, the playwright who relies on the quality of his conception rather than on the turn of his phrases is most likely to qualify as a master of a great lyric mood." Conception is inseparable from expression. The playwright who relies on the turn of a phrase, except in so far as that phrase is organic and necessary to the conception, writes not only bad drama, he writes bad poetry. The defects in *Winterset*, in the last act especially, are not due to the fact that the poetic form is being employed, but rather to the fact that the poetry is bad, bad either *per se* or bad in relation to the scene—it comes to the same thing.

Mr. Watts says also that "recognized lyric forms are clearly no more adapted to the use of drama these days than they are to other types of current narrative and, since they were originally devised for other days, it is not easy to employ their archaic mannerisms in the service of authentic and convincing dramatic speech." You may almost as well say recognized human forms are with difficulty suited to acting. A poet-playwright will, naturally, in so far as he is successful, use only such poetic forms as express his content. But much of any content belongs to centuries, not decades. And recognized lyric forms do not necessarily imply archaic mannerisms.

"The last fifteen minutes of the play strike me as dull and unfortunate, chiefly because Mr. Anderson appears to be presenting a defeatist argument on behalf of the beauties of compromise in modern life, and although that message of his may have its practical virtues it does not exactly express a poetic subject." For my part, I thought merely that Mr. Anderson got himself rather far afield with some handsome semi-Irish-poetical, often extraneous and willful, lines and cadences, and thus crippled the effect. At any rate, it is true that there is no such thing as a non-poetic subject. The possibilities, near and far, of any subject will depend on the artist undertaking it. "I fear," says Mr. Watts, of the last quarter-hour, "that the slightly muddy confusion of the play's ideas may hurt the poetic drama in so far as it suggests that lyricism and hard-headed contemplation have difficulty in getting along together in the theatre." Suggesting difficulty in art hurts nothing; it intimidates fools; it raises the level of the enterprise.

Whatever confusion there may be does not arise from lyricism and contemplation finding it hard to get along together in the theatre; the confusion arises from the writing not having absorbed or expressed the thought with completeness sufficient to include the writer's full self, brain, emotions, and so on. As a matter of fact, all theatrical expression of thought includes immediately a certain lyricism. Contemplation in itself—if there be such a thing —will not project itself into the audience. Nor will the audience contemplate what it can acquire no feeling for.

Speaking practically, on our American theatre's behalf, the greatest compliment we could pay a poetic play is to say it does no harm to poetic drama's chances. In spite of its defects, and in spite of the threats in the last act to do so, *Winterset* does not harm the cause of poetic drama. In its best moments we are aware of the poetic medium only as a matter of heightened respiration on our part. The lines hint of intensified feeling and thought, and of words with all the emphasis of passionate life repeated. At its worst we have only verses that are sucking a sugar-teat in the Muses' nursery. In such of Mr. Anderson's verse the images appear to be a hangover of the period when Stephen Phillips' cadences were petals of blown roses on the grass. In such cases, Mr. Anderson, both as poet and playwright, needs to get away, not so much from traditional forms in poetry as from a merely traditional use of them regardless of their content.

It is true, of course, that on Broadway one must be completely successful, tossing off with facility what the greatest artists might retreat from in despair. *Winterset* is fair enough melodrama at bottom, which is saying a good deal. Why should we expect, also, that a playwright should, almost single-handed, produce a completely successful poetic drama? I should rather say that *Winterset* is not only and easily the most important play of this season, but also the most notable effort in the poetic dramatic medium that up to now we have had in the American theatre.

From *The New Republic*, Vol. LXXXIV (November 6, 1935), p. 365. Reprinted by permission.

JOSEPH WOOD KRUTCH

Two American Playwrights

THE AUSTERITY OF GEORGE KELLY

[1933]

GEORGE KELLY is something of an anomaly in the contemporary theatre. Two of his plays have enjoyed phenomenal runs on Broadway and one of the two won the Pulitzer prize besides. Yet neither of these is as characteristic of the author as others less successful, and it would not be rash to wager that neither is as close to Mr. Kelly's own heart as one or two which the public has classed as failures. Both of his "hits"—*The Show-Off* and *Craig's Wife*— richly deserved their popularity. Both were soundly constructed and both were based upon shrewd and honest observation, but each had, in addition, the advantage of belonging to a familiar and popular genre. The first, with a blustering Babbitt for a hero, was a recognizable addition to the growing literature of native satire. The second, which drew at full length the portrait of a hard woman in whom the virtue of being a good housekeeper had become a vice, was typically "modern" in a slightly different way. It illustrated admirably that tendency to "transvaluate values" which Ibsen had introduced into the theatre and which, in a somewhat popularized form, one will discover in such typical plays of the recent past as *The Silver Cord* and *Rain*. No wonder that Mr. Kelly was set down as a dramatist working in a current tradition and sufficiently of Broadway to find ready acceptance. No wonder, also, that his public was somewhat *froissé* by the increasing bitterness of *Daisy Mayme* or that it should have been frankly bewildered by the almost mystical tone of *Behold the Bridegroom*. Mr. Kelly refused to stay put and was determined to accentuate those aspects of his attitude which were the least familiar and the least acceptable to his audience. He was saying with a calm and cold emphasis: "Make no mistake. I am not of Broadway."

With his latest work in mind it is easy to look back over the earlier plays and to catch in their text ominous hints of this more stern and acrid tone. Even in *The Show-Off* there are moments when a certain unexpected bitterness rises momentarily to the surface, as when, for example, the harassed mother hears the remark that her daughter must lie on the bed she has made and replies quite simply: "It's often not the people who make the beds who have to lie on them. It's someone else." A few moments later the observation has been forgotten in the flow of pure fun, but for an instant there has found expression something in the author which would be cynicism if it were not too sternly moralistic to be quite that. Indeed, the whole character of this mother adds to the play an element quite foreign to its dominant tone, for she is a sort of chorus supplying disillusioned comment, prophesying woe, and refusing to enter fully into the easy joy of the rest when good fortune solves all their difficulties.

Even more significant is the one-act play, *Smarty's Party*, written long before, during the five years when Mr. Kelly was appearing in vaudeville in playlets of his own composition. Here the story is that of a vulgar adventuress who entangles a young man supposed to be very wealthy, who comes to his supposed mother to enjoy her moment of triumph, and who then is crushed with the information that her victim is not really that woman's son at all. Here Mr. Kelly first delineates with cruel expertness the vulgarity of the adventuress and then, with a kind of savage delight, destroys her utterly. Thus the pattern of the play is exactly the same as the pattern of *Craig's Wife*, where another evil woman is analyzed at full length before the author, with an almost sadistic fury, plunges her into a special circle of hell so arranged that her vice will constitute the means by which she is tortured. The heroine of *Smarty's Party* wanted money and got poverty; Craig's wife loved her home so much that she found herself homeless at last.

One cannot help observing that Mr. Kelly's three most bitterly excoriated characters—namely, the two just mentioned and one to be discussed later— are all women. There is in him, therefore, a strain of what one is tempted to call misogyny, but it is not certain that the term would be exactly accurate. He does not seem to be saying that women as a sex are worse than men. He is only saying instead, "Lilies that fester smell far worse than weeds," and the key to his temperament is a particular kind of austerity which goes commonly under the name of puritanism. Vulgarity offends him, not only esthetically but morally as well, and the kind of meanness which he sees most commonly in men and women strikes him always as a sort of vulgarity of the soul. He despises it with a certain cold fury, and his desire is the puritanical desire to see a crushing justice meted out to it. Others may feel that to understand all is to pardon all, but to the puritan that saying is incomprehensible nonsense. To understand all is to hate all—if that "all" be hateful. Each of his most striking heroine-victims is understood with a cruel clarity, but none is pardoned and none, be it noted also, is reformed and then rewarded. All three are cast out instead into outer—and utter—darkness.

It was *Craig's Wife* produced in October, 1925, which won the Pulitzer prize. The next year Kelly produced without great success another acrid study of family life called *Daisy Mayme,* but it is *Behold the Bridegroom* (1928) which represents Mr. Kelly's most determined and most nearly successful effort to break completely away from the themes and methods of the contemporary stage in order to give full expression to his underlying attitude.

All of Mr. Kelly's other plays are richly overlaid with local color. The immediate effectiveness of all depends in large part upon skillful mimicry and upon the literal realism with which he pictures middle-class American life. Here, however, he departs from his accustomed milieu. Manners are more elegant, characters more self-consciously analytic, and the whole style is more formally literary. But the effect is only to disengage more completely the essential moral problem and to make the discussion of it quite clearly the only *raison d'être* of the play. Again the hero—if she can be called that—is a woman, but this time her sin is that vulgarity which results from the indulgence of a too facile and too shallow emotional nature. She is smart, sophisticated, and charming. She has moved gracefully from one love affair to another and thinks that she has demonstrated by her success how completely the intelligence may dispense with those simple rules of puritan morality which are never far from Mr. Kelly's mind. But the moment comes when she realizes that she really loves for the first time in her life. And her creator seizes the opportunity to destroy her as he had destroyed Craig's wife. She looks into the bridegroom's eyes, reads there his contempt, and then dies, not so much because of that contempt as because she has realized at last her own emptiness.

Probably most persons were made a little uncomfortable by the mercilessness with which justice was visited upon Mr. Kelly's earlier heroines. Some have even suggested that a more knowing playwright would not have pushed retribution so far as to swing the sympathy of the audience round in the direction of its victim. But it is no mere dramaturgic mistake which is responsible for Mr. Kelly's relentlessness either in the case of *Craig's Wife* or in the case of *Behold the Bridegroom*. He must have known very well that the public would not judge the heroine of the latter play so harshly as he did, that there is, as a matter of fact, no sin which this public is more ready to forgive—in fiction at least—than the sin of light love. Indeed, the romantic-sentimental tradition makes it almost the necessary prelude to a grand passion. But Mr. Kelly would not compromise here with his puritan conscience or make any effort to hide his contempt for contemporary morality. His heroine had wasted her capacities on cheap loves, she was not ready when the bridegroom came, and she had forfeited all right to the thing whose value she had come to understand only when it was too late. Hence she awakes, not to be saved, but only in order that she may realize what she has lost. Only thus can the puritan sense of justice be served, for the damned must be given one glimpse of paradise before they are plunged into hell forever.

No other play by Mr. Kelly—indeed, few contemporary plays by any author whatsoever—has, in certain respects, a finer literary quality than this one has. There is a passionate sincerity in the conception and a beautiful clarity in the dialogue which raise it far above the level of merely successful dramatic writing. The author seems to be struggling to free himself from the limitations of mere naturalism, and very nearly succeeds, by his passion and his coherence, in raising it to the level of quasi-poetic tragedy. Yet the fact remains that the play was commercially a failure and, what is more important, that all the respect which one feels for it does not prevent certain objections from arising in the mind of either the spectator or the reader.

One is, to put it briefly, neither quite convinced nor quite sure that one ought to be. "Men have died from time to time and worms have eaten them, but not for love." This we have upon the authority of one of Shakespeare's heroines, and it may be urged against the conclusion which Mr. Kelly has given to his play, but the most serious of my doubts are not of this naturalistic kind. I can accept the physical features of his conclusion and I can respect the moral sincerity which has enabled him to develop an almost pietistic thesis without falling into mere priggishness on the one hand or into rant on the other, but I honestly doubt that nature is constructed upon any plan so in accord with a puritan sense of moral fitness. Perhaps a spoiled and empty woman should die of self-contempt when she sees herself; perhaps she should feel herself forever unworthy of love if she chances at last to meet it; but I doubt that she would actually feel so or that there is anything to be gained by trying to make her. We forgive ourselves more easily and it is as well that we should. Artists and moralists both love to contemplate the irreparable—it helps the one to be dramatic and it helps the other to satisfy his sense of justice. But nature is more compliant. Time cannot be called back, and what has been physically destroyed cannot be found again, but nothing else is irretrievably lost and there are no sins that ought not and cannot be forgiven.

Mr. Kelly has been silent since he produced *Maggie the Magnificent* in November, 1929.[1] In this latest of his plays he returned to the middle-class milieu and the more realistic manner. But here again he is concerned with integrity of character as it is brought out in the contrast between the disorderly soul of an uncultivated mother and the efficient determination of a daughter who lifts herself by her own efforts above the vulgarity amidst

[1] A new play, *Reflected Glory*, was produced in 1936; another, *The Deep Mrs. Sykes*, in 1945; a third, *The Fatal Weakness*, in 1946. George Kelly's principal earlier plays were produced as follows: *The Torchbearers* in 1921, *The Show-Off* in 1923, *Craig's Wife* in 1925, *Daisy Mayme* in 1926, *Behold the Bridegroom* in 1927, *Maggie the Magnificent* in 1929, *Philip Goes Forth* in 1931. (Editor's note, 1950.)

which she grew up. But Mr. Kelly seems incapable of making either men or women as likable as they ought to be. There is in the characters whom he admires something stiff and prim and priggish which chills the beholder and seems to suggest that the author hates what is cheap and common with such an all-absorbing fury that he has become incapable of exercising his critical judgment upon anyone who escapes the one vice he cannot forgive. The "bridegroom" in the previous play was not intended to be repellently self-righteous, but there was a suggestion of repellent self-righteousness in him. Similarly, the Maggie of this piece is actually a good deal less than magnificent. She is neat, orderly, assured, decent, and correct, but only Mr. Kelly would admire her with warmth. We are expected to feel in her an austere nobility, but we actually feel a kind of spinsterish frigidity, and we cannot rejoice as we should in her triumph because we cannot sympathize warmly enough with her essentially negative aspirations.

This suggests, I think, the key to the mystery surrounding the fact that Mr. Kelly's most characteristic and most seriously meant plays do not quite achieve the success that they seem at times about to reach. There is a touch of coldness in his nature, a certain stubborn negativeness in his moral attitude, which lays a blight upon his plays. Essentially they are rather dour and frost-bitten, rather bleak at the very moments when a grave beauty ought to emerge. He wants, like Milton, to express the grandeur of puritanism, but he is somehow earthbound and cannot entirely escape from a certain unlovely rigidity. There is too much realism, too much prose, where a kind of ecstasy is called for. When a puritan is also a poet, the result can be magnificent, but Mr. Kelly is not quite poet enough. He commands respect but he cannot quite inspire a genuine enthusiasm.

From *The Nation*, Vol. CXXXVII (August 30, 1933), pp. 240–242. Reprinted by permission of the author.

THE DRAMATIC VARIETY OF SIDNEY HOWARD

[1933]

THE theatrical season which began in the fall of 1924 was made remarkable by the appearance of two very original plays from the pens of little-known playwrights. The first was *What Price Glory?* by the Messrs. Anderson and Stallings, the other *They Knew What They Wanted,* by Sidney Howard. In many respects the two were different enough, but they were commonly mentioned together for the very good reason that they were the first thoroughly successful efforts to express in dramatic form a realistic attitude marked by certain novel features. All three of the authors were fresh from their experiences in the Great War, and the fact may very well have had something to do with the tone of the plays, but the best way to describe them would be, perhaps, to say that both were essentially serious without being in the slightest degree "high-brow."

This in itself was a kind of novelty. The "new American drama" written by the "experimental playwrights" who had grown up around the Provincetown Playhouse and the Washington Square Company had been very self-conscious and very much under foreign influences. Sometimes it tended to be a kind of neo-Ibsen problem play, sometimes it was "arty" in much less substantial ways, but it was very much inclined to think of itself as a thing apart, as the product of a "movement" if not actually of a cult. Mr. Howard, on the other hand, had somehow managed to escape from all that. The Theatre Guild produced his play for a general public which found it highly acceptable, and one way to define the fact that he was a new kind of "new playwright" would be to say that he was writing for the commercial theatre. But to say that is to imply something much more important than the fact itself. It is to imply that he had thoroughly assimilated the attitude of the generation which had been busy rebelling against the long lingering Victorianism of our theatre, and that, without arguing or explaining, he could assume it as the point of view from which men and women were to be presented. The "new drama" had lost its self-conscious newness. It was taking itself and asking that it be taken as a matter of course.

Underlying the play was a moral attitude which a Victorian would certainly have found incomprehensible and which an anti-Victorian would certainly have made it his chief business to expound. The heroine is the mother of an illegitimate child conceived on the eve of her marriage to a kindly old man whom she does not love; the hero is this kindly old man, who discovers the wrong which has been done him but who ends by accepting the child because a child was what he really wanted. What an opportunity—entirely neglected by Mr. Howard—to expound a paradoxical morality, to define Love, to explain the Case for the Unmarried Mother, and, in general, *épater les bourgeois!* But the explanation supplied by Mr. Howard for these events is not intellectual at all. They become understandable and acceptable purely in terms of the characters; convincing and satisfactory as a series of concrete situations which work themselves out in that way. The play, in other words, is not a play about ideas but a play about men and women, and the same may be said of all its author's best work. Behind that work may of necessity lie a point of view and a philosophy; but the concrete situation and the concrete persons who find themselves in it always come first. They are not invented to illustrate a thesis. The thesis, if any, is discovered by the audience—and I suspect by the author as well—by contemplating them.

They Knew What They Wanted was Mr. Howard's third play. He had come from California and the University of California to spend one year in Professor Baker's class. After that he had served in the ambulance corps on the western front during the early days of the war and as a captain in the flying service after the United States became involved. He had also collaborated on a book of reporting, *The Labor Spy,* and produced *Swords* (1922) and *Bewitched* (1924)—the latter in collaboration with Edward Sheldon. The first of these plays was a romantic melodrama with more than a suggestion of pastiche; the second a romance rather poetic than realistic. Both achieved a certain *succès d'estime* without attracting any large audience, and both were apprentice work for a man who found himself as a dramatist in *They Knew What They Wanted.*

Since the latter was produced—and won the Pulitzer prize—Mr. Howard has had nine plays on Broadway. The themes of the nine show a variety which would probably be impossible for a playwright who did not, like him, find his inspiration in the concrete situation, and they have met a variety of fates—ranging all the way from flat failure like that which attended *Half Gods* to the triumphant success won by *Ned McCobb's Daughter* (1926), *The Silver Cord* (1926), and *The Late Christopher Bean* (1932). In the meanwhile he has also found time for a very successful career as a writer in Hollywood, and, as an active member of the Willard Straight Post of the American Legion, to help that post be a thorn in the side of the national organization.[1]

All this suggests the energy and vigor which are so characteristic of his work. Being enthusiastic and impulsive rather than primarily reflective, he is both prolific and not the best judge of his own work. Indeed, the public has been more right than he, and his finest plays since his first success have been the other successes, *Ned McCobb's Daughter, The Silver Cord,* and *The Late Christopher Bean.* Moreover, each is, despite the variety of moods and materials, like *They Knew What They Wanted* in that the author has devoted himself in each to the task of presenting concrete situations and concrete characters. He has, to be sure, a conspicuous gift for achieving a clear, straightforward dramatic construction; he has also been lucky in having a series of excellent actors—Pauline Lord, Richard Bennett, Alfred Lunt, Laura Hope Crewes, and Walter Connolly—for his best pieces. But essentially their effectiveness has been due to the fact that they were less comments on contemporary life than presentations of it. One never knows what Mr. How-

[1] Sidney Howard died on August 23, 1939. His principal plays were: *Swords* (1921), *They Knew What They Wanted* (1925), *Lucky Sam McCarver* (1926), *Ned McCobb's Daughter* (1926), *The Silver Cord* (1927), *Half Gods* (1930), *Alien Corn* (1933), *The Late Christopher Bean* (after René Fauchois, 1933), *Dodsworth* (after Sinclair Lewis, 1934), *Yellow Jack* (with Paul de Kruif, 1934), *Paths of Glory* (after Humphrey Cobb, 1935), *The Ghost of Yankee Doodle* (1938). (Editor's note, 1950.)

ard is going to say. With him, one sometimes feels, a conviction is an enthusiasm and, like any other enthusiasm, likely to disappear as soon as it has emerged. But one is always sure that the situations will be dramatic, the characters vivid, and the motives understandable.

The Silver Cord is the only one of his plays which develops in accordance with a rationalistic formula. It deals quite explicitly with a mother complex, and the most dogmatic Freudian would find nothing to disagree with. Yet Mr. Howard is known to have quarreled violently with the Theatre Guild because its directors insisted upon discussing it in Freudian terms, and the fact is significant of his temperamental antipathy to intellectual formulas, of his impatience with anybody's ideas even though they happen to be also his own. Last year he was one of those writers who signed the manifesto in favor of William Z. Foster. Put that fact alongside the further facts that he rushed into the war as soon as possible and then, once it was over, helped organize the obstreperous Willard Straight Post of the American Legion. Together they give you the picture of a man who loves a row, or, rather, who loves a joyous participation in dramatic events. That also is the man who writes the plays. In them the clash of creeds and temperaments interests him for his own sake. He can take sides enthusiastically but he can also change them. He is, whether he knows it or not, pretty certain to be on the side most likely to precipitate a dramatic crisis and pretty likely, in his plays, to see to it that one takes place. Being also a man of intelligence, his attitude is usually intelligible and his crisis significant. But it is the happening which interests him and the happening which interests his audience.

Under the circumstances it would obviously be useless to inquire what his leading ideas are. He is not, like Mr. Kelly, primarily a moralist. Neither is he, like Mr. O'Neill, a writer of tragedy, nor, like Mr. Behrman, a consistent writer of comedy. He can expound Freudianism in *The Silver Cord*, approach tragedy in *They Knew What They Wanted,* declaim rather intemperately in *Half Gods,* and achieve a serene comedy in *The Late Christopher Bean.* But none is more characteristic of him than the rest. Neither is there anything common to them all except the vigor of the characterization plus a certain robust delight in the conflict for its own sake. Their unity, therefore, is only the unity of a temperament, and the only way to describe what kind of plays Mr. Howard writes is to describe what sort of man he reveals himself to be.

To witness one of his plays is to experience the same sort of exhilarating pleasure that one gets from the society of an active man with quick and vigorous perceptions. One is plunged at once into a series of happenings and made to share the wholehearted interest of a writer who throws himself into everything with an unreserved enthusiasm. The characters are observed with extraordinary intentness and set down in sharp bold strokes. Something of the author's own decisiveness is communicated to them, and the dialogue has something of the crisp clarity of his own speech. Subtlety of a kind is by no means absent and poetry of a kind is also present. But the subtlety does not exhibit itself as hair-splitting and the poetry is neither rhapsodical nor dreamy. The men and women are plain people with their feet on the ground; the scene, some very definite corner of our particular America. Obviously Mr. Howard hates any sort of artistic pretentiousness as much as he hates intellectual dogmas. He is determined to exercise his subtlety in the accurate observation of familiar things, to find his poetry in the loves and hates of people who may be distinguished by the strength and the clarity of their passions but who remain, nevertheless, essentially familiar types.

His is, therefore, a daylight world, in which common sense is still the standard by which everything is judged. An epigram may flash forth here and there, but in no other way does he ever permit himself to approach a conventionally literary style. There are no Orphic utterances, no purple patches, no evocation of what the more esoteric devotees of the drama call "moods." Nothing ever eludes the spectator, nothing ever seems vaguely to mean more than it says. But what it does unmistakably say is enough for anyone capable of sharing Mr. Howard's very active pleasure in straightforward passions and straightforward events. His plays are not highbrow plays because their author is not a highbrow, and they teach no doctrine because he is not a doctrinaire. Essentially tough-minded, he is interested in facts and out of them he builds his plays. It is for that reason, no doubt, that the captain of aviation never wrote a patriotic play nor the supporter of Mr. Foster a communistic one. He took part in a war and some day he may, conceivably, help along a revolution. But it would be safe to wager that he will never either preach loyalty to the flag or write a treatise on dialectic materialism.

Writers who are intelligent without being "intellectual," and artistic without being in any sense "arty," frequently get from critics somewhat less consideration than they deserve. They are too clear to require explaining and too popular to need defense. Your critic, accordingly, all too frequently prefers to discourse at more length upon the merits of those persons whose excellences are less evident. But the fact remains that Mr. Howard's plays are among the best ever written in America. They have, in addition, probably had more influence upon dramatic writing than can ever be directly measured. Mr. Howard stands very near to the head of the list of those who rescued the popular drama from that sentimentality which for some reason continued to be considered indispensable there long after it had disappeared from most serious writing in other forms.

From *The Nation*, Vol. CXXXVII (September 13, 1933), pp. 294–295. Reprinted by permission of the author.

NEWTON ARVIN

Individualism and the American Writer

[1931]

THE artist, it cannot be too clearly understood," says Arthur Symons in his book on the symbolist movement, "has no more part in society than a monk in domestic life." The dogma of literary individualism has never been phrased more simply or more grotesquely; and, as Mr. Symons belongs to a generation now pretty completely superseded, it is no longer fashionable to say the thing in just these terms, or to appeal to such authority as his for support. But the spirit behind his epigram is a spirit that still operates not only in British but in American letters. Even sentimental estheticism, though the cut of its clothes is no longer in the mode of the nineties, has by no means disappeared; and, on a less fatuous level, the doctrine of irresponsibility—in more forms than one, of course—is virtually the prevailing gospel. The breach between our writers and our society could hardly be wider: one gets a measure of it by trying to imagine a contemporary poet or novelist of distinction occupying the kind of official post—an ambassadorship, a professorship, the editorship of a prosperous magazine or newspaper—which, fifty and sixty years ago, was one of the natural rewards of literary celebrity. This sort of thing is now a joke, and a stale joke at that. Yet there is intrinsically nothing funny in the conception of a writer's rôle in society as responsible to the point of officialdom; and many things are more unlikely than that we shall return to it in the course of events. Meanwhile, and for excellent reasons, the literary life in America is the scene of a sweeping separatism: the typical American writer is as tightly shut up in his own domain, and as jealous of his prerogatives, as one of the Free Cities of the late Middle Ages. Is this in the very nature of things, or is it a passing circumstance?

To ask such a question is to go, at once, below or beyond the purely literary terrain. It is to pose the whole problem of individuality and its life history. But it is to pose the problem in a form to which writers neither *as* writers nor as human beings can afford to be indifferent. There is really no more acute, no more concrete, no more pressingly personal a problem, at the moment, than this. Is our familiar individualism, our conception of ourselves as "simple, separate persons," equivalent any longer to the achievement of a sound individuality? "Trust thyself": does every heart still vibrate to that "iron

544

string"? Specifically, can American writers hope to develop fully as individuals while divorcing themselves not only from society as a whole but from any class or group within society? With what group or class, indeed, *can* they ally themselves? Is the alternative to literary individualism the surrender to a merely political movement, or, worse still, to some form of repressive standardization? Are there now no supra-personal purposes with which a writer can affiliate himself?

Our answers to such questions will be really satisfactory only if, in giving them, we are able to look back upon the road we have come on. For the story of American letters is the story of the blossoming, the fruition, and the corruption of exactly the individualism that is now on trial. It is far from being a new thing: it is a many times more than twice-told tale. In its origins it was a fruitful principle because it corresponded to a historical reality, to a historical reality that is now part of our past. In short, American writers have always belonged to the middle class, and not only in the literal sense of being born in it: they have belonged to the middle class spiritually, and their self-reliance, their self-expression, their self-consciousness have expressed the sociological individualism of their class heritage. It is no accident that, emblematically at least, at the very gateway of American literature should stand two autobiographies: no accident that Jonathan Edwards should have written his "Personal Narrative" or Franklin the story of his life. Nothing was more natural than that Edwards and Franklin should have taken themselves as subjects; between them, they span the whole reach, upward and downward, of the individualist principle; they are the sacred and profane extremes of one spirit— Edwards, with his Calvinistic particularism, his intense introspectiveness, his spiritual egoism; Franklin, with his complete system of self-help, his enlightened careerism, his pragmatic worship of frugality and diligence. Neither man can be imagined in a precapitalist order. Only one essential note in our national chorus remained to be struck, and that was the secessionist note of the frontier; when Fenimore Cooper created the character of Leatherstocking, the embodiment of backwoods resourcefulness, independence, and idiosyncracy, the ensemble was complete.

Complete, that is, psychologically. In a literary sense, American individualism was not to reach its apogee until the generation which filled in the twenty or thirty years before the Civil War. These years witnessed, from a cultural point of view, the historic culmination of the principle of self-reliance: during these years that principle, because it rationalized the true needs of society, had a genuine spiritual authority. It was a period, in short, when our special form of individualism could really be reconciled with the deeper-lying claims of individuality; when a man could achieve distinction as a person without going much beyond the limits of self-reliance. This is, of course, what accounts for the literary pre-eminence, in the age, of Emerson ("Accept your genius and say what you think"), of Thoreau ("I would rather sit on a pumpkin and have it all to myself than be crowded on a velvet cushion"), and of Whitman ("I will effuse egotism"). In these three men our individualism, on its brighter side, attained its classic meridian. There was of course, even then, a darker side; there were men for whom the gospel of self-help—or the habit of estrangement, which is a form it may always take—proved to be the path toward confusion, morbidity, and a kind of impotence; and Poe, Hawthorne, and Melville, men of the richest endowments, paid a tragic price for sitting on pumpkins and effusing egotism. Their careers suggest that the principle, from the artist's point of view, is at best a precarious one; and that its spiritual fruitfulness is exhausted almost before it is realized.

The sequel of the Civil War demonstrated the exhaustion at least of its youthful energies. The triumph of economic irresponsibility, in the feverish burgeoning of big business after the war, coincided with the corruption of individualism as a cultural motive. Two things happened: on the one hand, the writers of secondary talents watered down and deodorized the old contumacy until it became reconcilable with the mildest heresies and even with a conformity in which neither self-reliance nor self-expression had breathing-space; on the other hand, the writers of genius, incapable of such surrender, went still farther along the path taken by Poe, Hawthorne, and Melville. To turn from Emerson to G. W. Curtis, from Thoreau to John Muir, from Whitman to Burroughs, is to turn, as if in a single life-span, from Moses to Zedekiah. The contrast is instructive enough, yet it is less eloquent than the spectacle offered by the higher careers of Henry James, Mark Twain, and Henry Adams. Hawthorne's theme of estrangement, the Ishmaelite theme that obsessed Melville, were driven by Henry James to a formulation still more extreme; and expatriation, the frankest form of desertion, became both his literary munition and his personal fate. With Mark Twain the Fenimore Cooper wheel came full circle: the old, heroic anarchism of the backwoods is travestied, in its decay, by Mark Twain's vacillation between a servile conformity and the puerile philosophy of self-interest outlined in "What Is Man?" ("From his cradle to his grave a man never does a single thing which has any *first and foremost* object but one—to secure peace of mind, spiritual comfort *for himself*.") For Mark Twain the outcome was, not Emerson's and Whitman's "fatalistic optimism," but an equally fatalistic pessimism; and Henry Adams, who had a truer sense of the limits of self-interest, but whose social impotence and personal isolation were still more thoroughgoing, stands very close to Mark Twain as our first consistent preacher of futility.

II

By the turn of the century the old class basis of American literature was rapidly entering upon the cycle of erosion, subsidence, and re-emergence. It was still true that American writers belonged personally to the middle classes, but the old bond between literary expression and the middle-class philosophy had been broken once for all; and henceforth there seemed to be only the choice between a loyalism that was the negation of individuality and a repudiation that too generally left its heresiarchs high and dry. For a fresh alignment of a positive sort the time was not yet ripe; and by the second decade of the century we found ourselves in the midst of an individualistic revolt which superficially seemed to appeal to the authority of Emerson, Thoreau, and Whitman, but which, unlike theirs, was radically personal and anti-social. It had been anticipated, a few years before, by the Nietzschean egoism of Jack London and the antinomianism of Dreiser; and it was to mingle the elements of misanthropy, transcendentalism, anarchism, and high aspiration in bewildering proportions. The new individualism ran the whole gamut from the Menckenian-Cabellian praise of aristocracy to Anderson's primitivism and O'Neill's romantic affirmations, from Lewis' exposure of the standardized bourgeois to Van Wyck Brooks' subtle studies in frustration. In the perspective of history, the high colors in which this generation dealt will doubtless show like the hues in the clouds that surround a setting sun. It was the last chapter of one volume, not the first of a new one; and of this essential belatedness the patriarchal gravity, the chilly sagacity of such poets as Robinson and Frost are but convenient measures.

The vitality of that movement was naturally still shorter-lived than the "Emersonian June" itself had been. The hopeless sterility of a pure individualism at this moment in history could hardly be more dramatically demonstrated than by the collapse of the Menckenian boom in our own "reconstruction" after the war. The men who led it, of course, still survive, but they have subsided either into silence or into a bewilderment that masks itself variously; and their juniors, for the most part, have drawn the moral from their experience in either one of two disastrous but natural ways. One group, the heirs of Poe, Hawthorne, and Melville, have retreated, in their despair of finding solid ground on which to build a personal life, to an explicit philosophy of negation; and pitched here and there on the sands of the Waste Land one descries the tents, black as Tamburlaine's on the third day of a siege, of Jeffers and MacLeish, of Krutch and Aiken, of Hemingway and Faulkner. The other group, less honest emotionally, but intellectually more impressive, has taken refuge from the high winds of individualism in the shelter of some archaic code, religious, authoritarian, or sociological: humanism, neo-Thomism, Alexandrianism, royalism, or agrarianism. Both the negativists and the authoritarians betray all the symptoms of corruption: both shine with the phosphorescence of decay; but the latter have at least the logic that goes with positive loyalties.

For the necessary answers to the questions we began with are becoming clearer and clearer to middle-class intellectuals; they have long been clear to our handful of working-class writers. That it is not possible for a writer to develop a rich individuality and remain loyal to an individualist society in its later stages—this was the discovery of the Menckenian generation. All questions of humanitarian sentiment aside, that generation discovered that to cooperate with an inhumane system is to be personally corrupted and demoralized. The experience of the last decade has shown, though the proof was hardly needed, that mere nonconformity leads nowhere but to barrenness. If individuality means anything, as distinguished from individualism, it means the achievement, personally, of a many-sided unity, a rich and complicated integration; and in an individualistic economy it is not possible for anyone, certainly not for a writer, either to develop freely on all sides or to unify his personal life in the only fruitful way—that is, by organizing it with reference to a significant purpose. It is the paradox of individuality that it is meaningless without its social pole: neither the variety nor the centrality that go to make it up can be described except with constant (though of course not exclusive) reference to a group. Now that American writers, consciously or unconsciously, have made their final break with the middle class, it should be obvious that, unless they prefer a bleak or an elegant futility, they can turn in but one direction, to the proletariat. By identifying their interests with the life and needs of that class they can at once enrich and unify their own lives in the one way now historically open to them. Far from being a merely political or sociological affiliation, this joining of forces with the working class is chiefly important, even now, and certainly in the long run, on psychological and cultural grounds. It is a question, for the writer, not of sentiment or quixotism, but of self-preservation. Our literary history is the true argument, and this it would be idle to labor further.

How many things this may mean as time goes on, there is no space to say here; and indeed it would be both presumptuous and irrelevant, in this connection, to undertake to say them. One must grant that the case for a proletarian literature is not always cogently stated or wisely defended—any more than the case against it. One must insist that to adopt the proletarian point of view does not mean, for a novelist, to deal solely with economic conflicts, or, for a poet, to be a voice only for protest, momentous as both things are and *implicit* as they are bound to be. That a truly proletarian literature, for us in America at least, would mean a break with the mood of self-pity, with the cult of romantic separatism, with sickly subjectivism and melodramatic misanthropy— this much is almost too clear to deserve stating. But the duty of the critic is certainly not to file an order for a particular sort of fiction or poetry before the event; his duty is to clarify, as best he can, the circumstances in which fiction and poetry must take shape, and to rationalize their manifestations when they arrive. For the moment the important thing is that American criticism should define its position: in the midst of so much confusion, so much wasted effort, so much hesitation, this will itself be an advance.

From *The Nation,* Vol. CXXXIII (October 14, 1931), pp. 391–393. Reprinted by permission of the author and editors.

PHILIP RAHV

The Cult of Experience in American Writing

[1940]

EVERY attentive reader of Henry James remembers that highly dramatic scene in *The Ambassadors*—a scene singled out by its author as giving away the "whole case" of his novel—in which Lambert Strether, the elderly New England gentleman who had come to Paris on a mission of business and duty, proclaims his conversion to the doctrine of experience. Caught in the spell of Paris, the discovery of whose grace and form is marked for him by a kind of meaning and intensity that can be likened only to the raptures of a mystic vision, Strether feels moved to renounce publicly the morality of abstention he had brought with him from Woollett, Mass. And that mellow Sunday afternoon, as he mingles with the charming guests assembled in the garden of the sculptor Gloriani, the spell of the world capital of civilization is so strong upon the sensitive old man that he trembles with happiness and zeal. It is then that he communicates to little Bilham his newly acquired piety towards life and the fruits thereof. The worst mistake one can make, he admonishes his youthful interlocutor, is not to live all one can.—"It doesn't so much matter what you do in particular so long as you have your life. If you haven't had that what *have* you had? . . . Live, live!"

To an imaginative European, who is unfamiliar with the prohibitive American past and with the long-standing American habit of playing hide and seek with experience, Strether's pronouncement in favor of sheer life may well seem so commonplace as hardly to be worth the loving concentration of a major novelist. While the idea that one should "live" one's life came to James as a revelation, to the contemporary European novelists this idea had long been a completely assimilated and natural assumption; experience to them was the medium in which they tested and created values, whereas to him it represented something more than that—romance, reality, civilization, a self-propelling, autonomous value inexhaustibly alluring in its own right. This attitude to experience in James is often overlooked by readers who are excessively impressed (or depressed?) by his oblique methods and effects of remoteness and ambiguity. Actually, from the standpoint of the history of the national letters, the lesson taught by James in *The Ambassadors,* as in many of his other books, must be understood as no less than a revolutionary appeal. It is a veritable declaration of the rights of man—not, to be sure, of the rights of the public, of the political man, but of the rights of the private man, of the rights of personality, whose openness to experience provides the sole effective guaranty of its development.

Strether's appeal, in curiously elaborated, varied, as well as ambivalent forms, pervades all of James's work; and for purposes of critical symbolisation it might well be regarded as the compositional key to the whole modern movement in American writing. No literature, it might be said, takes on the qualities of a truly national body of expression unless it is possessed by a basic theme and unifying principle of its own. Thus the German creative mind has in the main been actuated by philosophical interests, the French by the highest ambitions of the intelligence unrestrained by system or dogma, the Russian by the passionately candid questioning and shaping of values. And since Whitman and James the American creative mind, seizing at last upon what had long been denied to it, has found the terms and objects of its activity in the urge toward and immersion in experience. It is this search for experience, conducted on diverse and often conflicting levels of consciousness, which has been the dominant, quintessential theme of the characteristic American literary productions—from *Leaves of Grass* to *Winesburg, Ohio* and beyond; and the more typically American the writer—a figure like Thomas Wolfe is a patent example—the more deeply does it engulf him.

More adequately, I believe, than any other factor that could be cited, it is this preoccupation that accounts for some of the striking peculiarities of modern American writing: its unique indifference, for instance, to the larger cultural aims implicit in the esthetic rendering of experience—to theories of value, to the wit of the speculative and problematical, and to ideas generally. In his own peculiar way even an artist as supremely aware as James—who was the analyst of fine consciences but scarcely of fine minds—shared this indifference. The intellectual is the only character missing in the American novel, which contains everything except ideas. But what are ideas? At best judgments of reality and at worst substitutes for it. The American novelist's conversion to reality, however, has been so belated that he cannot but be baffled by judgments and vexed by substitutes.

The American novel exhibits a singular pattern consisting, on the one hand, of a disinclination to thought and, on the other, of an intense predilection for the real: and the real it conceives as a vast phenomenology swept by waves of sensation and feeling. In this welter there is little room for the intellect, which in the unconscious belief of many imaginative Americans is naturally impervious, if not actually inimical, to reality. Consider the literary qualities of Ernest Hemingway, for example. There is nothing Hemingway despises more than experience of a make-believe, vague, or frigid nature, but in order to safeguard himself against the counterfeit he consistently avoids drawing upon the more abstract resources of the mind, he snubs the thinking man and mostly confines himself to the depiction of life on its physical levels. Of course, his extraordinary mastery of the sensuous element amply compensates for whatever losses he may sustain in other spheres. But Hemingway is only a particular instance. Other writers, less gifted and not so self-sufficiently and incisively one-sided as he is, have through this same creative psychology come to grief. Under its conditioning some of them have produced work so limited to the recording of the immediately apparent and unmistakably and recurrently real that it can truly be said of them that their art ends exactly where it should begin.

"How can one make the best of one's life?" André Malraux asks in one of his novels. "By converting as wide a range of experience as possible into conscious thought." It is precisely this reply which is alien to the typical American artist, who is so utterly absorbed in experience that he is often satisfied to let it "write its own ticket"—to carry him to its own chance or casual destination.

II

The disunity of American literature, its polar division into above and below or highbrow and lowbrow writing, has been noted more than once. Whitman and James, who form a kind of fatal antipodes, have repeatedly served as the standard examples of this dissociation. There is one sense, however, in which the contrast between these two arch-typical Americans might be said to have been overdrawn. There is, after all, a common ground on which they finally, though perhaps briefly, meet—an essential Americanism subsuming them both that is best defined by their mutual affirmation of experience. True, what one affirmed the other was apt to negate; still it is not in their attitude to experience as such that the difference between them becomes crucial but rather in their contradictory conceptions of what constitutes experience. One sought its ideal manifestations in America, the other in Europe. Whitman, plunging with characteristic heedlessness into the turbulent, formless life of the frontier and of the big cities, accepted experience in its total ungraded state, whereas James, insisting on a precise scrutiny of its origins and conditions, was endlessly discriminatory, thus carrying forward his ascetic inheritance into the very act of reaching out for the charms and felicities of the great European world. But the important thing to keep in mind here is that this plebeian and patrician are historically associated in the radical enterprise of subverting, each from his own end, the puritan code of stark utility in the conduct of life and in releasing the long compressed springs of experience in the national letters. In this sense, Whitman and James are the true initiators of the American line of modernity.

If a positive approach to experience is the touchstone of the modern, a negative approach is the touchstone of the classic in American writing. The literature of early America is a sacred rather than a profane literature. Immaculately spiritual at the top and local and anecdotal at the bottom, it is essentially, as the genteel literary historian Barrett Wendell accurately noted, a "record of the national inexperience" marked by "an instinctive disregard of actual fact." For this reason it largely left untouched the two chief experiential media—the novel and the drama. Brockden Brown, Cooper, Hawthorne, and Melville were "romancers" rather than novelists. They were incapable of apprehending the vitally new principle of realism by virtue of which the art of fiction in Europe was in their time rapidly evolving toward an hitherto inconceivable condition of objectivity and familiarity with existence. Not until James did a fiction-writer appear in America who was able to sympathize with and hence to take advantage of the methods of Thackeray, Balzac, and Turgenev. Since the principle of realism presupposes a thoroughly secularized relationship between the ego and experience, Hawthorne and Melville could not possibly have apprehended it. Though not religious men themselves, they were nevertheless held in bondage by ancestral conscience and dogma, they were still living in the afterglow of a religious faith that drove the ego, on its external side, to aggrandize itself by accumulating practical sanctions while scourging and inhibiting its intimate side. In Hawthorne the absent or suppressed experience reappears in the shape of spectral beings whose function is to warn, repel, and fascinate. And the unutterable confusion that reigns in some of Melville's narratives (*Pierre, Mardi*), and which no amount of critical labor has succeeded in clearing up, is primarily due to his inability either to come to terms with experience or else wholly and finally to reject it.

Despite the featureless innocence and moral-enthusiastic air of the old American books, there is in some of them a peculiar virulence, a feeling of discord that does not easily fit in with the general tone of the classic age. In such worthies as Irving, Cooper, Bryant, Longfellow, Whittier, and Lowell there is scarcely anything more than meets the eye, but in Poe, Hawthorne, and Melville there is an incandescent symbolism, a meaning within meaning, the vitality of which is perhaps only now being rightly appreciated. D. H. Lawrence was close to the truth when he spoke of what serpents they were, of the "inner diabolism of their underconsciousness." Hawthorne, "that blue-eyed darling," as well as Poe and Melville, insisted on a subversive vision of human nature at the same time as cultivated Americans were everywhere relishing the orations of Emerson who, as James put it, was helping them "to take a picturesque view of one's internal possibilities and to find in the landscape of the soul all sorts of fine sunrise and moonlight effects." Each of these three creative men displays a healthy resistance to the sentimentality and vague idealism of his contemporaries; and along with this resistance they display morbid qualities that, aside from any specific biographical factors, might perhaps be accounted for by the contradiction between the poverty of the experience provided by the society they lived in and the high development of their moral, intellectual, and affective natures—though in Poe's case there is no need to put any stress on his moral character. And the curious thing is that whatever faults their work shows are reversed in later American literature, the weaknesses of which are not to be traced to poverty of experience but to an inability to encompass it on a significant level.

The dilemma that confronted these early writers chiefly manifests itself in their frequent failure to integrate the inner and outer elements of their world so that they might stand witness for each other by way of the organic linkage of object and symbol, act and meaning. For that is the linkage of art without which its structure cannot stand. Lawrence thought that *Moby Dick* is profound *beyond* human feeling—which in a sense says as much against the book as for it. Its further defects are dispersion, a divided mind: its real and transcendental elements do not fully interpenetrate, the creative tension between them is more fortuitous than organic. In *The Scarlet Letter* as in a few of his shorter fictions, and to a degree in *The Blithedale Romance*, Hawthorne was able to achieve an imaginative order that otherwise eluded him. A good deal of his writing, despite his gift for precise observation, consists of phantasy unsupported by the conviction of reality.

Many changes had to take place in America before its spiritual and material levels could fuse in a work of art in a more or less satisfactory manner. Whitman was already in the position to vivify his democratic ethos by an appeal to the physical features of the country, such as the grandeur and variety of its geography, and to the infinite detail of common lives and occupations. And James, too, though sometimes forced to resort to makeshift situations, was on the whole successful in setting up a lively and significant exchange between the moral and empiric elements of his subject-matter. Though he was, in a sense, implicitly bound all his life by the morality of Hawthorne, James none the less perceived what the guilt-tossed psyche of the author of *The Marble Faun* prevented him from seeing—that it is not the man trusting himself to experience but the one fleeing from it who suffers the "beast in the jungle" to rend him.

The Transcendentalist movement is peculiar in that it expresses the native tradition of inexperience in its particulars and the revolutionary urge to experience in its generalities. (Perhaps that is what Van Wyck Brooks meant when, long before prostrating himself at his shrine, he wrote that Emerson was habitually abstract where he should be concrete, and vice versa.) On a purely theoretical plane, in ways curiously inverted and idealistic, the cult of experience is patently prefigured in Emerson's doctrine of the uniqueness and infinitude, as well as in Thoreau's equally steep estimate, of the private man.

American culture was then unprepared for anything more drastic than an affirmation of experience in theory alone, and even the theory was modulated in a semi-clerical fashion so as not to set it in too open an opposition to the dogmatic faith that, despite the decay of its theology, still prevailed in the ethical sphere. No wonder, then, that Transcendentalism declared itself most clearly and dramatically in the form of the essay—a form in which one can preach without practicing.

Isolation was the price Whitman and James were compelled to pay for their break with the tradition of inexperience. James was protected somewhat by his social tone and expatriate interests, but Whitman suffered the full penalty of his iconoclasm. W. D. Howells survived by assuming the role of mediator between the old and the new. But it was not until the twentieth century that the urge to experience at last overwhelmed and decisively transformed literary art.

III

Personal liberation from social taboos and conventions was the war-cry of the group of writers that came to the fore in the second decade of the century. They employed a variety of means to formulate and press home this program. Dreiser's tough-minded though somewhat arid naturalism, Anderson's softer and spottier method of articulating the protest of shut-in people, Lewis' satires of Main Street, Cabell's florid celebrations of pleasure, Edna Millay's emotional expansiveness, Mencken's worldly wisdom and assaults on the provincial pieties, the early Van Wyck Brooks's high-minded though bitter evocations of the inhibited past, his ideal of creative self-fulfilment—all these were weapons brought to bear by the party of rebellion in the struggle to gain free access to experience. And the secret of energy in that struggle seems to have been the longing for what was then called "sexual freedom"; for at the time Americans seeking emancipation were engaged in a truly elemental discovery of sex whose literary expression on some levels, as Randolph Bourne remarked, easily turned into "caricatures of desire." The novel, the poem, the play—all contributed to the development of a complete symptomatology of sexual frustration and release. In retrospect much of this literature seems but a naïve inversion of the dear old American innocence, a turning inside out of inbred fear and reticence, but the qualities one likes about it are its positiveness of statement, its zeal, and its pathos of the limited view.

The concept of experience was then still an undifferentiated whole. But as the desire for personal liberation, even if only from the less compulsive social pressures, was partly gratified and the tone of the literary revival changed from eagerness to disdain, the sense of totality gradually wore itself out. Since the 1920's a process of atomization of experience has forced each of its spokesmen into a separate groove from which he can step out only at the risk of ut-

terly disorienting himself. Thus, to cite some random examples, poetic technique became the special experience of Ezra Pound, language that of Gertrude
Stein, the concrete object was appropriated by W. C. Williams, super-Ameri-
can phenomena by Sandburg and related nationalists, Kenneth Burke experienced ideas (which is by no means the same as thinking them), Archibald
MacLeish experienced public attitudes, F. Scott Fitzgerald the glamor of the
very rich, Hemingway death and virile sports, and so on and so forth. Finally
Thomas Wolfe plunged into a chaotic recapitulation of the cult of experience
as a whole, traversing it in all directions and ending nowhere.

   Though the crisis of the 1930's arrested somewhat the progress of the experiential mode, it nevertheless managed to put its stamp on the entire social-
revolutionary literature of the decade. A comparison of European and American left-wing writing of the same period will at once show that whereas
Europeans like Malraux and Silone enter deeply into the meaning of political
ideas and beliefs, Americans touch only superficially on such matters, as
actually their interest is fixed almost exclusively on the class war as an experience which, to them at least, is new and exciting. They succeed in representing incidents of oppression and revolt, as well as sentimental conversions,
but conversions of the heart and mind they merely sketch in on the surface
or imply in a gratuitous fashion. (What does a radical novel like *The Grapes
of Wrath* contain, from an ideological point of view, that agitational journalism cannot communicate with equal heat and facility? Surely its vogue cannot be explained by its radicalism. Its real attraction for the millions who read
it lies elsewhere—perhaps in its vivid recreation of a "slice of life" so hor-
rendously unfamiliar that it can be made to yield an exotic interest.) The
sympathy of these presumably political writers with the revolutionary cause
is often genuine, yet their understanding of its inner movement, intricate
problems, and doctrinal and strategic motives is so deficient as to call into
question their competence to deal with political material. In the complete
works of the so-called proletarian school you will not find a single viable portrait of the Marxist intellectual or of any character in the revolutionary drama
who, conscious of his historical role, is not a mere automaton of spontaneous
class force or impulse. What really happened in the 1930's is that due to certain events the public aspects of experience appeared more meaningful than
its private aspects, and literature responded accordingly. But the subject of
political art is *history,* which stands in the same relation to experience as
fiction to biography: and just as surely as failure to generalize the biographical
element thwarts the aspirant to fiction, so the ambition of the literary Left to
create a political art was thwarted by its failure to lift experience to the level
of history.[1]

   [1] For the benefit of those people who habitually pause to insist on what they call
"strictly literary values," I might add that by "history" in this connection I do not mean

Experience is the main but by no means the total substance of literature. The part experience plays in the esthetic sphere might well be compared to the part that the materialist conception of history assigns to economy. Experience, in the sense of this analogy, is the substructure of literature above which there rises a superstructure of values, ideas, and judgments—in a word, of the multiple forms of consciousness. But this base and summit are not stationary: they continually act and react upon each other.

It is precisely this superstructural level which is seldom reached by the typical American writer of the modern era. Most of the well-known reputations will bear out my point. Whether you approach a poet like Ezra Pound or novelists like Steinbeck and Faulkner, what is at once noticeable is the uneven, and at times quite distorted, development of the various elements that constitute literary talent. What is so exasperating about Pound's poetry, for example, is its peculiar combination of a finished technique (his special share in the distribution of experience) with amateurish and irresponsible ideas. It could be maintained that for sheer creative power Faulkner is hardly excelled by any living novelist, yet who would seriously compare him to Mann or Joyce? The diversity and intensity of the experience represented in his narratives cannot make up for their lack of order, of a self-illuminating structure, and for their irksome obscurity of value and meaning.[2] One might naturally counter this criticism by stating that though Faulkner rarely or never sets forth values directly, they none the less exist in his work by implication. Yes, but implications incoherently expressed are no better than mystifications, and nowadays it is values that we can least afford to take on faith. Moreover, in a more startling manner perhaps than any of his contemporaries, Faulkner illustrates the tendency of the experiential mode, if pursued to its utmost extreme, to turn into its opposite through unconscious self-parody. In Faulkner the excess, the systematic inflation of the horrible is such a parody of experience. In Thomas Wolfe the same effect is produced by his swollen rhetoric and by his compulsion to repeat himself—and repetition is an obvious form of parody. This repetition-compulsion has plagued a good many American writers. Its first and most conspicuous victim, of course, was Whitman, who also occasionally slipped into unintentional parodies of himself.

Yet there is a positive side to the primacy of experience in late American literature. For this primacy has conferred certain benefits upon it, of which none is more bracing than its relative immunity from abstraction and other-

---

"history-books" or anything resembling what is known as the "historical novel" or drama. A political art would succeed in lifting experience to the level of history if its perception of life—any life—were organised around a perspective relating the artist's sense of the *society* of the dead to his sense of the *society* of the living and the yet unborn.

  [2] His recent novel, *The Hamlet*, includes so many imaginative marvels that one is appalled by the ease with which it nevertheless runs aground.

worldliness. The stream of life, unimpeded by the rocks and sands of ideology, flows through it freely. If inept in coping with the general, it particularizes not at all badly; and the assumptions of sanctity that so many European artists seem to require as a kind of guaranty of their professional standing are not readily conceded in the lighter and clearer American atmosphere. "Whatever may have been the case in years gone by," Whitman wrote in 1888, "the true use for the imaginative faculty of modern times is to give ultimate vivification to facts, to science, and to common lives, endowing them with glows and glories and final illustriousness which belong to every real thing, and to real things only." As this statement was intended as a prophecy, it is worth noting that while the radiant endowments that Whitman speaks of—the "glows and glories and final illustriousness"—have not been granted, the desired and predicted vivification of facts, science, and common lives has in a measure been realized, though in the process Whitman's democratic faith has as often been belied as confirmed.

IV

It is not the mere recoil from the inhibitions of puritan and neo-puritan times that instigated the American search for experience. Behind it is the extreme individualism of a country without a long past to brood on, whose bourgeois spirit had not worn itself out and been debased in a severe struggle against an old culture so tenacious as to retain the power on occasion to fascinate and render impotent even its predestined enemies. Moreover, in contrast to the derangements that have continually shaken Europe, life in the United States has been relatively fortunate and prosperous. It is possible to speak of American history as a "successful" history. Within the limits of the capitalist order—and until the present period the objective basis for a different social order simply did not exist here—the American people have been able to find definitive solutions for the great historical problems that faced them. Thus both the Revolutionary and Civil War were complete actions that once and for all abolished the antagonisms which had initially caused the breakdowns of national equilibrium. In Europe similar actions have usually led to festering compromises that in the end reproduced the same conflicts in other forms.

It is plain that in America there has really been no urgent need for high intellectual productivity. Indeed, the American intelligentsia developed very slowly as a semi-independent grouping; and what is equally important, for more than a century now and especially since 1865, it has been kept at a distance from the machinery of social and political power.[3] What this means is that insofar as it has been deprived of certain opportunities, it has also been

[3] The situation in this respect has changed considerably during the last decade. The New Deal government is the first administration since the early days of the Republic that has shown any disposition to avail itself of the particular gifts of the intelligentsia.

sheltered and pampered. There was no occasion or necessity for the intervention of the intellectuals—it was not mentality that society needed most in order to keep its affairs in order. On the whole the intellectuals were left free to cultivate private interests, and, once the moral and esthetic ban on certain types of exertion had been removed, uninterruptedly to solicit individual experience. It is this lack of a sense of extremity and many-sided involvement which explains the peculiar shallowness of a good deal of American literary expression. If some conditions of insecurity have been known to retard and disarm the mind, so have some conditions of security. The question is not whether Americans have suffered less than Europeans, but of the quality of whatever suffering and happiness have fallen to their lot.

The consequence of all this has been that American literature has tended to make too much of private life, to impose on it, to scour it for meanings that it cannot always legitimately yield. Henry James was the first to make a cause, if not a fetish, of personal relations; and the justice of his case, despite his vaunted divergence from the pioneer type, is that of a pioneer too, for while Americans generally were still engaged in "gathering in the preparations and necessities" he resolved to seek out the "amenities and consummations." Furthermore, by exploiting in a fashion altogether his own the contingencies of private life that fell within his scope, he was able to dramatize the relation of the new world to the old, thus driving the wedge of historical consciousness into the very heart of the theme of experience. Later not a few attempts were made to combine experience with consciousness, to achieve the balance of thought and being characteristic of the great traditions of European art. But except for certain narratives of James, I know of very little American fiction which can unqualifiedly be said to have attained this end.

Since the decline of the regime of gentility many admirable works have been produced, but in the main it is the quantity of felt life comprised in them that satisfies, not their quality of belief or interpretative range. In poetry there is evidence of more distinct gains, perhaps because the medium has reached that late stage in its evolution when its chance of survival depends on its capacity to absorb ideas. The modern poetic styles—metaphysical and symbolist—depend on a conjunction of feeling and idea. But, generally speaking, bare experience is still the *Leitmotif* of the American writer, though the literary depression of recent years tends to show that this theme is virtually exhausted. At bottom it was the theme of the individual transplanted from an old culture taking inventory of himself and of his new surroundings. This inventory, this initial recognition and experiencing of oneself and one's surroundings, is all but complete now, and those who persist in going on with it are doing so out of mere routine and inertia.

The creative power of the cult of experience is almost spent, but what lies beyond it is still unclear. One thing, however, is certain: whereas in the past, throughout the nineteenth and well into the twentieth century, the nature of American literary life was largely determined by national forces, now it is international forces that have begun to exert a dominant influence. And in the long run it is in the terms of this historic change that the future course of American writing will define itself.

From *The Partisan Review*, Vol. VII (November–December, 1940), pp. 412–424. Reprinted by permission of the author and editors. This essay, in an expanded form, has been included in the author's volume of critical essays, *Image and Idea* (New Directions, 1949).

F. W. DUPEE
The Americanism of Van Wyck Brooks
[1939]

NEW ENGLAND has given to the United States its most literate body of native tradition, and educated Americans, regardless of their particular backgrounds, are always tending to become spiritual New Englanders. If the Yankee tradition is no longer very much alive, so much the worse for educated Americans.

Of this type of native mind Van Wyck Brooks is an excellent example. It is true that years ago, as the spokesman of an American city culture which was then just emerging in its strength, Brooks made a great effort to master the spiritual New Englander in himself. He did not quite carry it off; his Yankee alter ego has since taken entire possession of him. It is now clear that he has always owed to the older tradition a great many of his qualities—the restraint and conscience that have marked all his work; the taste for arduous scholarship; the rather elaborate prose which is the conscious register of his highly-organized individuality; but above all the air of unworldliness, of consecration, which comes perhaps from his allegiance to the New England principle of intensive cultivation. "The great thing is to be saturated with something," Henry James, another spiritual New Englander, used to maintain. Brooks has saturated himself with the problems of art and society in the United States. And it was another tendency of the rhapsodic Yankee strain to turn everybody—novelists, philosophers, critics, historians, naturalists—into poets; Brooks, too, admirable though he has been as a scholar and social critic, has always at bottom worked and thought in the manner commonly ascribed to poets. Like them he tends to see all experience in the light of a single overmastering situation. In his case the great situation, the *donnée,* is associated with the vicissitudes of creative inspiration in the United States, with the difficulty of realizing oneself, not only as an artist in America, but as an American artist. The effort to reconcile art and society in terms of our national experience has dominated all his work, both the early and the late, and has given an otherwise episodic career an urgent inner consistency.

II

By working very hard a single important piece of territory a writer may earn, at the very least, the reputation of being a "phenomenon." This has been the case with Brooks, yet it has always been hard to say just what kind of phenomenon he is. During the years when aestheticism was the prevailing literary creed, he used to be called, rather invidiously, a sociologist. But as sociology came to seem to us less alien, less of a mystery, it was decided that Brooks's social insights were the by-products of a temperament primarily ethical. People pointed to his *Freeman* essays, which showed that when hard-pressed by disappointments, as he appears to have been during the post-war years, he was capable of taking up a position of reproachful righteousness barely distinguishable from that of the New Humanists, whom he had always assailed. Let us see to what extent these various distinctions were justified. Morality, it is true, is the socialism of the individualist, who seeks to extend to society at large the codes that have come to govern people in their individual relationships. Brooks has been as consistently an individualist as he has been consistently preoccupied with the larger questions of society. But in deriving his ethical ideas from the new psychology of the Unconscious, he broke in part with the philosophy of traditional moral individualists. Like them he continued to conceive society by analogy with the structure of the human personality, but instead of picturing personality as a complex of higher and lower selves, as a Plato or an Arnold—moralists even in their psychology—normally pictured it, Brooks saw in it the Freudian pattern of repression and sublimation. This pattern, modified as much by vestiges in him of the old ethical severity as by elements of modern materialism, he extended to social experience. Thus, the United States was to him a case of "atrophied personality," a "prodigious welter of unconscious life" which it was the task of the new intelligentsia to bring to consciousness.

In America where the middle class, filling the whole picture, had made life as precarious for specialized types of individuality as it had made it safe for the more standard varieties, it was natural that a critic like Brooks should seize upon the new psychology, apply its insights to American writers of the past, and preach its ethic of self-fulfillment to the writers of the present. His criticism had therefore its intimate connection with his time and place, a connection that we shall presently consider in detail. But let us first look at Brooks's criticism in its more technical aspects. His generation was making a great point of the importance of being "creative," a slogan which Brooks translated into his own medium, developing a criticism that had many of the qualities of imaginative literature. In form it was eloquent, concentrated, boldly thematic; and it carried the biographical method to a higher point of development than it had yet reached in America. In a sense Brooks's approach is merely a variant of methods employed by Sainte-Beuve and Taine, but it has acquired a special character through the intensity both of his individualism and of his preoccupation with psychology. The questions of culture at large he approaches in terms of leading individuals; the work of single writers he considers in the light of their biography. Thus *The Ordeal of Mark Twain*, *The Pilgrimage of Henry James* and *The Life of Emerson* are all attempts to characterize entire cultural periods through the experience of leading individuals; and even *The Flowering of New England*, as someone has said, is not so much a history as a composite biography. The biographical method is commonly used to cast light on the work of literature. With Brooks, this procedure is usually reversed. When he appeals to the work it is in order to confirm some theory about the man. Literature gets dissolved into biography in such a way that the work itself with its four walls and established furniture as given by its author is often quite lost to view. And this is true concerning his treatment of the intellectual as well as the structural properties of literature. For all his vital interest in the New England tradition, he has never made it very clear just what transcendentalism, considered as a philosophy, really was. And surely it is a paradox of his career that he should have been so warm in his championship of the artist, yet so cold to the work of art, so ready to proclaim America's intellectual poverty, yet in practice so indifferent to ideas.

There have been many instances where Brooks's critical methods involved no particular difficulties. The literary portraits in "Our Poets" were certainly not lacking in a vivid aesthetic concreteness, nor were they demonstrably inconsistent with the actual work of the authors concerned. But other books, notably the *Pilgrimage* and the *Ordeal*, have been deplored because the accomplishment of James and Mark Twain was so largely ignored or distorted. Let us consider these objections, taking up first *The Pilgrimage of Henry James*. This book testifies to Brooks's ability to say things of value and to raise important issues even when in his main argument he appears most mistaken. For the picture of James that emerges from the *Pilgrimage* is a deduction rather from Brooks's general theory of literary nationalism than from the novels themselves, the latter having a complex irony which Brooks fails to take into account and which in the end seriously undermines his thesis. Yet it is curious that in this case Brooks *did* examine the novels, and one concludes, not that his method is necessarily faulty in itself, but that he possesses in any case a strongly metaphysical cast of mind. To the sober scholar in him there is yoked a visionary and the two have some trouble pulling together in harmony. A myth-maker on one side of his nature, he sometimes strikes us as being himself that very poet-prophet, that reincarnated Whitman, which he once had the habit of invoking; but on the other side he is a sceptic, a critic, and an historian. Of the effects of this ambivalence there is further evidence in *The Ordeal of Mark Twain*. The general thesis here is much sounder than that of the *Pilgrimage;* and in addition to having been a pioneer in the attempt to fuse the historical and Freudian perspectives, the *Ordeal* was a splendid example of closely-textured argument, analytical wit and the restrained use of local color. It would be hard indeed to forget its picture of Mark Twain,

"that shorn Samson, led about by a little child, who in the profound som-
nolence of her spirit, was simply going through the motions of an inherited
domestic piety." Nevertheless the *Ordeal* is full of difficulties. It is one thing
to muckrake a period, as Brooks here so effectively muckrakes the genteel era,
pointing out its stultifying effects on a writer of genius; but it is another thing
again to assume that in happier conditions your writer would have been a
Tolstoy. That is more or less what Brooks does assume, with the result that the
historical Mark Twain is everywhere dogged by the shadow of an ideal or
potential or Unconscious Mark Twain, a kind of spectral elder brother whose
brooding presence is an eternal reproof to the mere author of *Huckleberry
Finn*. In addition to being highly speculative, Brooks's approach has the disadvantage of diverting him from what Mark Twain really achieved through
the cultivation, however fragmentary, of his richly plebeian sensibility. This
achievement it was left to Ernest Hemingway and other practicing artists to
discover for themselves.

III

Brooks's habit of using the materials of history and biography to construct
didactic myths, literary lessons in the shape of parables, was probably the
effect of the period in which he came to maturity and of what he was trying to
accomplish in that period. Throughout the years of industrial revolution following the Civil War, writers in America had been consigned, some of them
to a limbo of servility, others to virtual oblivion, depending on whether they
accepted or embraced the prevailing standards of that iron age. But when
Brooks's first volume appeared, in 1909, the old exploitative phalanx of American society had been for some years breaking up. There was a great increase
of radical consciousness on the part of the working classes, and intellectuals
had taken advantage of the general ferment to assert once more the claims of
the individual. For the first time since the 1850's, there came into existence a
body of professionals sufficiently independent, militant and cohesive to be
called an intelligentsia. It had in a sense been the creation of the radical movement; it therefore applied itself to politics, in turn, and evolved a special type
in the shape of the muckraker. But this was only the first phase in the career
of the new intelligentsia. Later on, in Brooks's generation, a reaction set in
against social reformism, which had so plainly missed its mark, and writers
turned from politics to literature. The "artist" supplanted the muckraker as the
standard intellectual type; consciousness of self was cultivated in place of
class consciousness; and writers set out to express and assert and fulfill themselves. Thus the old subjective ethos of romanticism, freshly implemented by
modern psychology, was reborn in America some sixty years after the decline
of Emersonianism.

Nothing was more remarkable in Brooks than the flair for assimilation and synthesis which permitted him to bring to focus in his criticism all the chief tendencies of those decades. For Brooks, in the long run, art and politics were to seem two separate universes; but his early criticism embodied a notable attempt to bring the two into a better relation and so to combine the ideals of the muckrakers with those of his own primarily aesthetic generation. The actual political content of his criticism was vague and shifting; yet whenever he attempted a definite formulation it became clear that he regarded socialism as a pre-condition of the "creative life" in America. In many respects his early writings provided the United States with its closest parallel to the social-democratic literatures then flourishing in Europe.

Nevertheless Brooks was at heart a psychologist and he was to keep the morality of self-fulfillment squarely in the center of his work. Nor did his socialist convictions in the long run prevent him from conceiving art as a process essentially self-contained, commanding an area of experience to all purposes special and separate. He seems to have taken over from Carlyle and Ruskin the "organic" view of society while rejecting the faith in authoritarian institutions that usually goes with it. The mysticism inherent in this view conflicted all along the line with the scientific perspectives of socialism, forcing upon him a kind of unsystematic dualism. Concerning the relation of politics to literature he tended to conceive the first as a function of a material world, the second as an enterprise connected with a world of the spirit. But Brooks did not exploit the music of antinomies to the extent that it has been exploited by a Thomas Mann, and in practice his dualism merely meant that in his opinion intellectuals ought to keep out of politics. They had, he assured them, a special mission, which was to "articulate the whole life of the people" by supplying the United States with new myths and new values. To this role he advised them to apply themselves with the fervor of a consecrated minority, a priesthood, as he said, or a hierarchy. It was an age that made much of seers and cosmic vocations. Writers were looking for prophets—particularly among themselves. Every nation, every social group, considered itself to have a "special mission." If Brooks was akin to Ruskin and Arnold, he was a Ruskin or an Arnold brought up to date: the *culture* which they had advocated as social medicine, he endeavored to implement in terms of an *organized intelligentsia*. For it was an age, too, of heightened crisis and organized struggle in the field of social relations.

In his preoccupation with the intelligentsia there was a considerable value. More than anyone else, unless it was Randolph Bourne, he grasped the importance to America of the emergence of such a body. He understood what it could mean to the labor movement, and he knew, too, that its absence had for half a century inflicted great hardship on American artists, leaving them solitary and exposed in the arena of a hostile society. It was on the new intelligentsia, then, that Brooks set his hopes for the country's future, to them that he addressed his case histories in literary frustration, his essays in diagnosis and prescription, in short the whole of that prodigious anatomy of the creative life which took shape in his early writings. When, eventually, he ceased to exhort the intellectuals, he lost at the same time a good share of his intellectual vitality.

In view of his socialist professions it is curious that Brooks came to concentrate so exclusively on conditions in a single country. He appears to have felt that in Europe the abuses of capitalism had been somewhat mitigated by the social-democratic movement, a movement whose success he was inclined to attribute to the efforts of literary critics. The United States, on the other hand, was a full-blown capitalist nation which possessed only the weak beginnings of a critical culture. We must develop such a culture if we were ever to experience a genuine social transformation. It was by some such reasoning as this that Brooks tended to justify his exclusive concern with the United States, his tendency to idealize Europe, his habit of ascribing to literary culture the decisive role in reformist politics.

Proceeding always by the rule of opposites, he thought of the United States as the antithesis of Europe in respect to the quality, the unity and the social use-value of its culture. French culture, he pretended, had at the touch of Montaigne fallen together like a single organism. But America had lacked such a master-spirit. Here there had always existed, between literature and experience, theory and practice, a profound cleavage which had affected for the worse both our intellectual and our daily life, condemning the first to impotent idealism and the second to stark materialism. From the beginning the Highbrow and the Lowbrow had divided things between them. An effective middle tradition had failed to appear. In default of the spiritual checks which such a tradition might have exercised, Big Business had got firmly into the saddle and the Acquisitive Life had prevailed over the Creative Life. And with the optimism of a latter-day Whitman—the optimism of a generation pioneering in social aesthetics (they used indeed to declare that social reform constituted the new American "frontier") as their fathers had pioneered in industry—Brooks foresaw a culture which should replace the obsolete hegemony of New England, and represent the country in all its racial, class and sectional complexity.

IV

It is true that on the programmatic side Brooks's early writings were infected with the extravagance that is common to the "organic" conception of society. French critics, we have reason to believe, would be the first to disclaim any super-unity in the culture supposedly begotten by Montaigne. As for America: its intractable minorities and far-flung regions have offered to the literary nationalist a problem so stubborn that it refuses to be solved short of a social reconstruction more profound than any envisaged by Brooks. But on the critical side his work, attracting to it all the severity of a mind divided between poles of scepticism and faith, was of a trenchancy and cleverness rare in American writing. Our culture did actually suffer, as he maintained, from a split personality which expressed itself in various idealistic chivalries on the one hand, and on the other in a plebeian vigor, unlighted by consciousness. Surely, considering the provocation, Brooks was justified in preaching a bold scepticism. "It is of no use," he told the patriots of his day, "to go off in a corner with American literature . . . in a sulky, private sort of way, taking it for granted that if we give up world values we are entitled to our own little domestic rights and wrongs, criticism being out of place by the fireside." Not that Brooks was the only cosmopolitan critic of American letters; but where the New Humanists, for example, took as their standard of comparison the achievements of some remote Periclean or Racinian age, Brooks looked to the European literature of his time. Moreover, in his account of the Genteel Tradition as "the culture of an age of pioneering, the reflex of the spirit of material enterprise," as in a whole range of similar insights, he went far towards situating the country's cultural problems in a concrete atmosphere of social and economic forces. In the long run, however, the value of his early work seems mainly to lie in the skill and courage with which he isolated the data of intellectual maturity in America. In his hands the Highbrow-Lowbrow antithesis served rather as a descriptive than as an analytical tool. And what he really produced was a kind of symptomology sprinkled with clues and half-clues, with partial explanations, with portents adduced as causes and causes in the guise of portents. The materialist in him was always coming into conflict with the "organic" visionary, the social historian with the psychologist. Accustomed to conceiving matter and spirit in the shape of an antithesis, he never attained a stable view of cultural phenomena; and his lack of clarity on this point caused his criticism to veer back and forth between extremes of free will and determinism, so that while it seemed to him at times that the single writer might change the world unaided, at other times it appeared that one was very much at history's mercy. And psychology came to dominate his thought to the extent that he ended by giving the impression that he wanted to fasten upon American writers a cultural inferiority complex. It was probably this impression rather than simply the severity of his critiques that would help to bring him into partial eclipse in later years. His work would presently appear to belong neither to literary criticism nor to realistic social analysis. When he had finished trying to reconcile politics and literature, mysticism and science, he would be left with an ideology as diffuse as that of an Emerson or a Whitman; and he would seem, like them, to belong to some more primitive stage of American society, the intellectual disorder of whose prophets signified a lack of urgent pressures in the age itself. Even Gide and Mann, accomplished dialecticians and great writers, have not really achieved "universality" in our time: they have merely undergone a series of significant conversions. And Brooks, endeavoring to embrace the Whole, ended by losing touch with its parts; his sensibility acquired a certain abstractness; and in time he was to seem almost the type of that Liberal critic whom Eliot from one angle, and Mencken from another, were to assail with so much effectiveness.

V

The fate of Brooks's ideas was to receive a kind of summing-up, concentrated and dramatic, in the brief career of the *Seven Arts* review. Appearing in the fall of 1916, *The Seven Arts* had Brooks as its chief spokesman; his theme was the necessity of a national literature for an America made acutely conscious of its individuality by the war in Europe. But a year later, America having entered the war, *The Seven Arts* showed a growing distaste for the struggle and was obliged to cease publication. Meanwhile Randolph Bourne had all but replaced Brooks as spokesman, and Bourne's theme was, more and more, the social revolution. What had happened to push *The Seven Arts,* in a single year, from literary nationalism to literary revolutionism? Had we come of age in a world already too far advanced in decay? Had the United States, in attaining to the level of the great powers, likewise fallen heir to a crisis common to the entire capitalist world? This was more or less what had happened, as we can see in retrospect. Nationalism, having simply turned into a sordid imperialism, could no longer inspire a literature. Nor could the idea of the organic society survive the violent manifestations of a period of general revolution. *The Seven Arts,* in its rapid transition, was a fair register of the fact that ideas could appear viable at one moment, only to be swept the next into obsolescence.

The war had witnessed America's maturing as a world power: would we by the same token "catch up" with the elder nations in a cultural sense? To Brooks, at least, it began very shortly to appear that we would not. In America as elsewhere literature's response to war and crisis was both violent and immediate. And the centrifugal tendencies which it developed were the reverse of what Brooks had preached and anticipated. Writers who, like Bourne and Reed, shared his social idealism, were steered by its logic towards socialist theory and politics. There remained the literary majority which, in the main hostile to all politics, was split between two groups. The expatriate generation, addressing themselves to poetry and tradition, pretty much ignored America. The "Titans," who were presently to found *The American Mercury,* stayed in this country, as Mencken boldly confessed, solely to make merry at the spectacle of its foolishness. In the United States itself the aftermath of the war witnessed the definitive triumph of Bohemia over the universities and other centers of genteel culture. Instead of merging with the Highbrow to produce a middle tradition, the Lowbrow staged a *coup d'état*. Debunking replaced the respectable profession of muckraking. The common man, whom Brooks had respected as an element in his proposed national synthesis, was now to be widely scorned as a simple moron. And if Brooks had taken issue with Dreiser on the grounds that his determinism prevented his fiction from qualifying as healthy social realism, he was now to be faced with a whole generation of Dreisers. In America, in short, there was none of the philosophical scepticism which Brooks had advocated but only the "fashionable pessimism" (as he said) of parvenu plebeians, the coarse laughter of irresponsible satirists. And among the exiles there was an atmosphere of "fashionable pedantry," reactionary metaphysics, symbolist mystification—and Brooks had never cared much for symbolism. The age of prophets and special missions had largely passed. The present age demanded of its artists and critics above all a concrete literary consciousness. Brooks was in no position either to sympathize with its aims or to fulfill its demands. The papers he wrote for the *Freeman* in the early Twenties, and indirectly the biographies of Mark Twain and Henry James, were an index to his opinion of the times. As for the opinion that came generally to be held of him: it was not long before people began to complain that "for all his apparent enthusiasm for the artist, he does not seem vitally interested in art when it appears." He fails to criticize, they said, he merely exhorts. And "the development of young artists is not achieved through exhortation." These strictures were made by Paul Rosenfeld in the mid-Twenties. They reveal the strongly experimental cast of the decade on which Brooks, with his *a priori* temper, had had the misfortune to fall.

VI

In *The Pilgrimage of Henry James* he remarked that to the expatriated author of *The Ambassadors* Europe had remained "a fairy tale to the end." This was scarcely just to James but it showed the high value which Brooks himself, in 1925, still placed on the critical spirit. The years that followed were to witness his rapid retreat from this position.

In 1920 he had published *The Ordeal of Mark Twain*, which was followed some years later by the *Pilgrimage*, and then after a long interval by *The Life of Emerson*. These books, which, together with the *Freeman* papers, constitute a transition between the earlier and later works, show Brooks in the process of trying to thrash his way out of the isolation in which he has landed. Someone has compared the three biographies to the phases of the Hegelian dialectic, that of Mark Twain being the "thesis," that of Henry James the "antithesis" and that of Emerson the "synthesis." But note that this is a dialectic that opens out towards the past. Brooks is intent not only upon making studies in literary frustration, not only upon furnishing the Twenties with didactic parables (there is reason to think that the *Ordeal*, with its stress upon

Mark Twain's immature pessimism, was aimed at the Menckenites, as the *Pilgrimage,* elaborating on the expatriate sensibility, is directed at Eliot's gen-. eration), but he is also intent upon discovering the ideal American writer. He finds him at last in the man of old Concord, the "barbaric sage" as W. C. Brownell had called him. And from the rediscovery of Emerson there follows a transfiguration of Emerson's entire society. Brooks has found the key to American literature; he begins to write a cultural history in several volumes, the first of which turns out to be a chronicle, charming as literature, largely fabulous as history, of the creative life in New England. The present has failed us, it is evil; doesn't the past, then, by the law of contraries become good? The modern world has proven to be sadly incoherent; let us seek the organic virtues in the little pre-metropolitan half-agrarian universe of Concord and Boston. It was a Springtime culture and Spring is always virtuous. And if anyone feels disposed to remind us of "world values," let us reply that "we are entitled to our own little domestic rights and wrongs, criticism being out of place by the fireside."

Prefigured in the closing chapters of the *Pilgrimage* (it was Brooks, one feels, much more than it was James who longed to take passage for America), his nostalgia begins to affect his style and the very structure of his work. The pointed, argumentative, and analytical manner gives way to a prose of anecdote and local color, a blur of sensuous matter, a dreamlike pastiche of remembered quotations. And one sees that Brooks has affixed to his camera a soft-focus filter.

A comparison of the early and later work reveals, then, an astonishing reversal of opinion in respect to the achievement of New England. "An age of rude, vague, boisterous, dyspeptic causes" was the way he had formerly characterized that time. Its puritanism he had described as "a noble chivalry to which provinciality was almost a condition." Its Ripleys and Danas and Alcotts had seemed "a queer miasmatical group of lunar phenomena." Longfellow had been "an expurgated German student," whom it was foolish to approach critically. And Hawthorne for all his charm had felt life "rather as a phantom than as a man." But already in *The Life of Emerson* Hawthorne has become "a reminder as it were of some vast Cimmerian universe . . . a real Sphinx, with a subterranean self buried fathoms deep in the desert sand." What has happened is that Hawthorne has altered not so much in kind as in scale; he has been blown up to enormous stature in order that he may play the Prince of Darkness to Emerson's Son of Light in a kind of veiled cosmological allegory that runs all through the *Life.* And if Hawthorne, once a little less than a man, is capable of becoming something only short of a god, we can imagine how it will be with Emerson. As New England's chief intelligence Emerson had always figured to Brooks as the personification of a tradition shot through with false sublimities and seriously deficient in experience of life. For

Emerson were reserved the most caustic phrases in *America's Coming-of-Age*. "A strange fine ventriloquism . . . a continual falsetto . . . abstract at the wrong times and concrete at the wrong times . . . he could write page after page about a poet or painter without one intelligibly apt utterance . . . he was not interested in human life; he cared nothing for emotion, possessing so little himself . . . all the qualities of the typical baccalaureate sermon." And so on. But compare this portrait with the estimate of Emerson's virtues implied (for, as in the case of Hawthorne, it is only implied) in the *Life* and *The Flowering of New England*. Here the author of *Representative Men* has become a veritable embodiment of the creative spirit, a Yankee Balder. His prose evokes images of mountain streams, his passage through the New England world is accompanied by the springing up of greenery and flowers.

A few reservations are necessary if we are to see Brooks's two periods in a proper light. Needless to say he was never a debunker, even in his most militant phase, and the severity of his judgments on the New England school was plentifully sweetened with qualification. Indeed he was the writer of his generation who strove hardest to play the mediator between past and present. If he stressed the shortcomings of the Yankee tradition it was because that tradition seemed at best a sectional phenomenon and because it had come to block the growth of a larger intellectual consciousness in America. Nor can we ignore the very considerable merits of Brooks's latest work. The *Life* may seem a rather flimsy performance, but surely the *Flowering* has notable qualities. The opening chapters, dealing with the birth of the artistic spirit in a young nation, and the closing pages, describing Lowell and Holmes as characters of the Yankee twilight, cause the book to be enclosed in a frame of excellent criticism. But in the absence of any such criticism in the case of Emerson, Thoreau, Hawthorne and the rest, the frame only serves to set off a certain sponginess in the picture itself. Here, then, is a New England crowded with creative spirits but virtually bare of masterpieces, for Brooks has given up almost entirely the practice of correlating biography with literature. Here, above all, is a New England purged of conflict and contradiction, presented as an idyll of single-hearted effort; for Brooks had likewise given up the habit of correlating literary enterprise with social history. His perspective as a man of the twentieth century, his values as a socialist and an historian, have all gone by the board in the interests of an impressionistic *immediacy*. We are invited to survey the New England renaissance as if through the eyes of some actual participant, some breathless Lyceum ticket-holder of the period.

So the *Flowering* represents not so much a frank revision of Brooks's earlier judgments as a shift to a sphere where critical judgment operates only by implication. The Yankee culture has been lifted from the plane of "world values," where it shows as very small and incomplete, into an historical void where it becomes as great as you please. Indeed it is symptomatic of Brooks's present tendency that he nowhere tries to come to terms with his earlier work or to offer a reasonable explanation of the apparent disjunction between his two periods. The most he has done along these lines has been to remark, in the preface to a reissue of three early essays, that the judgments of his first period were the indiscretions of a youth bent on following an iconoclastic fashion. A fashion! So much then for the ardors, the sincerities, the hopes that went into *America's Coming-of-Age*. In dispensing with a rational view of American history it seems that he has lost the desire to make sense of his own history.

And the once-powerful critic of American life has become the chief curator of its antiquities; the oracle of the intellectuals has turned into the oracle of the book-clubs. He has accomplished his lifelong purpose of reconciling the native artist with the native society—but he has accomplished it in terms of a distant past, an imaginary past. If Europe was a fairy tale to Henry James, what has the United States become to Van Wyck Brooks?

From *The Partisan Review*, Vol. VI (Summer, 1939), pp. 69–85. Reprinted in this revised version by permission of the author and editors.

DELMORE SCHWARTZ
The Literary Dictatorship of T. S. Eliot
[1949]

WHEN we think of the character of literary dictators in the past, it is easy to see that since 1922 Eliot has occupied a position in the English-speaking world analogous to that occupied by Ben Jonson, Dryden, Pope, Samuel Johnson, Coleridge, and Matthew Arnold. It is significant that each of these dictators has been a critic as well as a poet, and we may infer from this the fact that it is necessary for them to practice both poetry and criticism.

Another characteristic is that each of these literary dictators has in some way reversed the judgments of his immediate predecessor. For example, Arnold denied that Pope and Dryden were really poets, declaring that they were merely "wit-writers." Eliot in the same way has declared that Pope and Dryden were truly poets and that Keats and Shelley, two of Arnold's favorites, were really insufficient and inadequate as poets.

One can hardly use such a term as dictatorship without suggesting unfortunate political associations. A literary dictatorship, however, is quite unlike a political one because you cannot force people to like poets or poetry, although you can persuade them. The remarkable thing about most literary dictators is that they succeeded in persuading at least one generation of readers to accept their literary taste.

When we come to Eliot's reign, we find that something has really been added: we have virtually two dictatorships from one literary dictator. Between 1922 and 1933 Eliot, in a series of unprecedented essays which were initially disguised as book reviews, evaluated the history of English poetry in one set of terms; between 1933 and 1946 he gradually reversed his whole evaluation, so that, for example, Tennyson, whom he scorned in 1922, was the object of serious and elevated commendation in 1936. In the same way Yeats, who in 1922 was said to be outside of the tradition of English poetry merely because he was Irish, was praised in the highest terms in 1933 as someone who "by a great triumph of development began to write and is still writing some of the most beautiful poetry in the language, some of the clearest, simplest, most direct." Some of the poems that Eliot refers to were written long before 1922. Thus it is almost possible to say of Eliot, "The

573

dictator has abdicated. Long live the dictator!" This is the only instance I know where anyone has abdicated and immediately succeeded to his own throne.

We can take 1922 as the approximate beginning of the first period, for in that year Eliot began to edit *The Criterion,* and *The Waste Land* was published in the first number. It was in 1921 that Eliot published the reviews in the London *Times Literary Supplement* which were later collected as three essays in *Homage to John Dryden.* In the most famous of these essays, "The Metaphysical Poets," Eliot declared that English poetry had not been the same since the death of John Donne. Dryden was a good poet, and Milton was a good poet, but their very virtues brought about a dissociation of sensibility in their successors. Since the time of Donne, according to this essay, there have been no poets in English who really enjoyed a unity of sensibility. What Eliot means by "unity of sensibility," a dubious psychological phrase, is difficult to make clear, but can perhaps best be stated by paraphrasing Eliot's remark that Donne felt his thoughts at the tips of his senses. All poets since Donne, with a few exceptional moments of unity, have permitted their thoughts and their emotions to be separated. "In the seventeenth century," says Eliot, "a dissociation of sensibility set in from which we have never recovered; this dissociation was not natural and was aggravated by the two most powerful poets of the century, Milton and Dryden. . . . The sentimental age began early in the eighteenth century and continued. Poets revolted against the ratiocinative; they thought and felt by fits unbalanced. . . . In one or two passages of Shelley's 'Triumph of Life' and Keats' second 'Hyperion' there are traces of struggle toward unification of sensibility. But Keats and Shelley died, and Tennyson and Browning ruminated." The poets prior to Dryden and Milton, however, "are more mature . . . and were better than later poets of certainly not less literary ability."

By 1934 Eliot had fruitfully contradicted, modified or qualified practically all the literary and critical judgments implicit in this essay. He had praised not only Tennyson and Yeats, but also Wordsworth and Coleridge, who were more or less rejected in 1921. In 1937, when questioned during a radio interview on the British Broadcasting Company about what he regarded as great poetry, he replied that Wordsworth's "Independence and Resolution" and Coleridge's "Ode on Dejection" were probably "touchstones of greatness." This is a far cry from what Eliot said in 1922 and what has been echoed a countless number of times by critics who have been influenced by Eliot.

And yet I do not mean to imply in the least that Eliot is merely contradictory. It is true that no one could have guessed, by reading his essay on "The Metaphysical Poets" in 1922, that by 1937 he would admire Wordsworth and Coleridge very much and cite them, rather than Donne, as "touchstones of greatness." Nor could anyone have guessed or suspected that he would praise Byron and Kipling, among other unlikely possibilities. But on the other hand, there is a real unity in back of all of these seemingly contradictory judgments. One basis of this unity is the admiration for Dante which obviously began when Eliot was still an undergraduate. If we understand Eliot's gradual and profound re-reading of Dante, then we can see how at one point, fascinated by one aspect of Dante, he would be likely to salute Donne, while at a later stage it would be natural for him to admire the characteristic directness and clarity of the poems by Wordsworth and Coleridge which he cited as touchstones of what is great in poetry. If we examine these poems carefully, we can see that in the most direct way they resemble the very beginning of *The Divine Comedy*.

And here, too, we can find at least one explanation of the distaste Eliot has expressed at various times for the poetry of Milton. It was in 1933 at Columbia that Eliot, by using what we may call the method of invidious comparison, compared Milton to Dante, although the two poets are not really comparable. Since Milton was a dedicated, self-conscious literary artist who decided to write an epic poem which would be like other epic poems and which would be a national epic, it seems clear to me that the true comparison would be to Virgil. How, then, are we to explain Eliot's dispraise of Milton?

We have as possibilities all sorts of unconvincing explanations: for example, it is said that Eliot depreciates Milton because Milton was anti-authoritarian in religious matters, while Eliot himself is nothing if not authoritarian,—an explanation which might be based upon Eliot's remark that "Milton's celestial and infernal regions are large but insufficiently furnished apartments, filled by heavy conversation; and one remarks about the Puritan mythology its thinness." But this is clearly not a sufficient explanation, since we know that Ezra Pound expressed an equal dislike of Milton, and no one can suppose that Ezra Pound's literary opinions were influenced by Anglo-Catholicism.

Another possible explanation is that Milton is not the kind of poet that Eliot himself desired to be, and there is, as everyone knows, a natural tendency upon the part of a poet who writes criticism to try to justify and praise in his criticism what he attempts to accomplish in his poetry. Thus Eliot criticizes Milton and reduces his importance by saying that "the very greatest poets set you before real men talking, carry you on in real events, moving." In the same essay in which Eliot makes this remark he says, "There is a large class of persons, including some who appear in print as critics, who regard any censure upon a great poet as a breach of the peace, as an act of wanton iconoclasm, or even hoodlumism. The kind of derogatory criticism that I have to make upon Milton is not intended for such persons, who cannot understand that it is more important, in some vital respects, to be a good poet than to be a great poet." This sounds to me as if Mr. Eliot were protesting far too much.

Milton is a crucial instance, because Milton is the one poet for whom Eliot expresses a distaste in both his revaluations of English poetry. Let us take the sentence I have just quoted. In the same essay Eliot says, "It must be admitted that Milton is a very 'great' poet indeed." We have then to determine, if we can, the difference between being a "very great poet" and being "one of the very greatest," and since Eliot puts the term "great" in quotation marks as if it were a dubious one, it would not be strange if a man from Mars decided that some infinitesimal hair-splitting were involved, or that Eliot, like Milton, had found darkness visible, for surely there is a kind of darkness in distinguishing between "very great" and "the very greatest."

II

What standards were involved in Eliot's initial evaluation of the history of English poetry and his subsequent revaluation?

They can be named in a summary and incomplete way as follows: first, actuality; second, honesty (closely connected with actuality); third, the purification and maintenance of the English language; fourth, the dramatic sense, which I shall try to define in a moment; fifth, the quality of the versification.

Needless to say, this list is not by any means exhaustive and obviously each of these sought-for qualities overlaps and interconnects with the others. For example, the sense of the actual is necessary to a poet's being dramatic; a sensitivity to the manifold possibilities of versification cannot really be separated from a desire to purify, maintain and sustain the English language.

Let me now try briefly to define and illustrate each of these qualities as they manifest themselves in Eliot's criticism of English poetry. First, the sense of the actual, which is perhaps the most difficult of all to define, since whenever we attempt to define anything, we must do so by referring to the actual and perhaps by merely pointing to it.

An illustration, not from Eliot himself, but from James Joyce, who in so many ways is profoundly close to Eliot as an author, may be useful. A would-be novelist came to Joyce with the manuscript of a novel she had just finished, telling Joyce that she would like his opinion of the novel and saying that only one other person had read the book, the porter of the hotel in which she was living. "What did the porter say?" Joyce inquired. "He objected to only one episode," replied the female novelist. "The episode in which the lover finds the locket of his beloved while walking in the woods, picks it up, and kisses it passionately." "What was the porter's objection?" said Joyce. "He said," she replied, "that before kissing the locket passionately, the lover should have rubbed it against his coat to get the dirt off it." "Go back," said Joyce, "to that porter. There is nothing I can tell you that he does not already know." This too is not as complete a pointing to the actual as one might wish, since the actual might be misunderstood to mean only that which is sordid, only that which the muckraker concerns himself with, while Eliot has in mind the actuality of human emotion and human nobility as well.

Moreover, Eliot makes it clear that a sense of the actual is really incomplete and warped without a sense of the past, that sense of the past which, he says, is indispensable to "anyone who wants to continue to be a poet after his twenty-fifth year." But we must be careful not to misunderstand Eliot's con· cern with a sense of the past as mere nostalgia for the days when knighthood was in flower. It is the past as actual, as an actual part of the present, which concerns Eliot. And one must have a strong sense of actuality in order to know just what of the past is alive in the present and what is merely a monument or a souvenir. Without a sense of the past, one's sense of the actual is likely to be confused with an obsessive pursuit of what is degraded, or idiosyncratic, or transitory, or brand-new. This is the dead-end of the naturalistic novelist who supposes that the slum is somehow more real than the library. Conversely, a sense of the actual enables one to understand the past itself as something which was not by any means Arcadian. Perhaps one can go so far as to say that one cannot have much of a sense of the past without a sense of the actual or much of a sense of the actual without a sense of the past. Thus, to use an example which can stand for much that is characteristic of Eliot, if one looks at a church, one does not really see very much of what one is looking at if one does not have both a sense of the actual, a sense of the past, and a sense of the past *as* actual in the present.

Let me turn now to a few instances of how Eliot uses the criterion of actuality in his criticism. Blake is praised because one of his poems expresses "the naked observation" and another "the naked insight":

> But most through midnight streets I hear
> How the youthful harlot's curse
> Blasts the newborn infant's ear
> And blights with plagues the marriage hearse.

In the same essay, which was written in 1920, Blake is praised because he possesses the peculiar honesty which, according to Eliot, is peculiar to all great poetry, an honesty which is to be found, Eliot says, in Homer, Aeschylus, and Dante, and an honesty which is, he adds, in a world too frightened to be honest, curiously terrifying, an honesty against which the whole world con-spires because it is unpleasant. Here we can see how closely connected in Eliot's mind are the sense of the actual and the ability of a poet to be honest.

Now let us take a negative instance, that of Swinburne. Swinburne for

Eliot is a poet whose real virtue was his verbalism, his use of words for their own sake. "In the verse of Swinburne the object (or we might say the actual) has ceased to exist. . . ." Swinburne, says Eliot, dwelt exclusively and consistently among words divorced from any reference to objects and actualities, and this kind of poetry is compared not only with that of Campion, which has both a beauty of language and a reference to actuality, but also with "the language which is more important to us . . . that which is struggling to digest new objects . . . new feelings, new aspects, as, for instance, the prose of James Joyce or the earlier Conrad."

There is another important negative instance. Eliot speaks of the images in the plays of Beaumont and Fletcher as "cut and slightly withered flowers stuck in the sand" in comparison with the images of Shakespeare, Donne, Webster, and Middleton, which have, he says, "tentacular roots" which reach down to "the deepest terrors and desires." In the same way, Tennyson is praised for his great technical skill but the quotations which Eliot cites, in 1936 when he reverses his judgment of Tennyson, are praised partly because they are descriptions of a particular time and place.

Now, to return for a moment to my general subject, we can see here the underlying unity which is involved in Eliot's revision of his first evaluation of English poetry. For in praising Blake as one who was unpleasantly honest and full of naked observations and insights, Eliot said that such honesty could not exist apart from great technical skill. In his first evaluation Eliot had praised Tennyson for his technical skill but dismissed him as one who merely ruminated. When Eliot came to revise his judgment of Tennyson in 1936, his revision was consequent upon a study of Tennyson's versification, which led him to see how that poet's great technical skill did in fact, at times, enable him to render the actual and not merely ruminate upon it. Thus, in a sense, Eliot is consistent throughout; the reason that a revision has been necessary is that Eliot was burdened by preconceptions which belonged to the period in which he was writing, and perhaps he had simply not read sufficiently in some of the poets he dismissed.

So too with the poetry of Milton, although I do not think that here it is a question of insufficient reading. When Eliot says in depreciation of some of Milton's poems that they are conventional, artificial, and enamelled, he is objecting to the absence of the actual, as we see further in the same essay when he says that "the greatest poets set you before real men talking, carry you on in real events, moving." It seems to me likely enough that by now Eliot has perceived beneath the perhaps artificial and certainly grandiloquent surface of Milton's language precisely that peculiar honesty about the essential strength or sickness of the human soul which he found in Dante, Shakespeare, Blake, and other of the very greatest poets. I should think that this desirable revision of opinion may also have come about as a result of the development of Eliot's own writing during recent years. When Eliot spoke of Milton at Columbia in 1933, he said that "Samson Agonistes" is not really a dramatic poem but rather an extended lyric. In the *Four Quartets*, there are many indications that the kind of experience Milton deals with in "Samson Agonistes"—Samson, shorn, blind and chained to the wheel, and Milton himself blind and chained to old age—will be more understandable to the poet and critic who writes:

> The poetry does not matter.
> It was not (to start again) what one had expected.
> What was to be the value of the long looked forward to,
> Long hoped for calm, the autumnal serenity
> And the wisdom of age?

And who writes later in the same group of poems:

> Since our concern was speech, and speech impelled us
>   To purify the dialect of the tribe
>   And urge the mind to aftersight and foresight,
> Let me disclose the gifts reserved for age
>   To set a crown upon your lifetime's effort.
>   First, the cold friction of expiring sense
> Without enchantment, offering no promise,
>   But bitter tastelessness of shadow fruit
>   As body and soul begin to fall asunder.
> Second, the conscious impotence of rage
>   At human folly, and the laceration
>   Of laughter at what ceases to amuse.
> And last, the rending pain of re-enactment
>   Of all that you have done, and been; the shame
>   Of motives late revealed, and the awareness
> Of things ill done and done to others' harm
>   Which once we took for exercise of virtue.
>   Then fools' approval stings, and honor stains.

It seems to me that the poet who wrote these lines cannot fail to recognize at last both the spiritual grandeur of "Samson Agonistes" and also the concern with speech, the effort to purify the dialect of the tribe, and urge the mind to aftersight and foresight, which is characteristic of that great poem.

In thus supposing that Eliot's experience of the last decade will lead him to a new recognition and admiration of Milton, it seems to me that I am illustrating another aspect of the sense of the actual.[1] It is actuality itself, the

---

[1] Mr. Eliot's later revaluation of Milton appeared in his lecture before the British Academy in 1947 and was published in the *Proceedings of the British Academy* in that year; reprinted in *The Sewanee Review*, Vol. LVI (April–June, 1948), pp. 185–209. (Editor's note, 1950.)

actuality of middle age approaching old age, which leads to a deeper understanding of Milton's major poetry, most of which, after all, was written in middle or old age.

III

Let us return now to the other touchstones, or criteria, of poetic genuineness.

Honesty is perhaps a shorthand term for a willingness to face the reality of one's emotions. Thomas Middleton is given what seems to me virtually fabulous praise by being said to have created in *The Changeling*, "an eternal tragedy, as permanent as *Oedipus* or *Antony and Cleopatra* . . . the tragedy of the unmoral nature suddenly trapped in the inexorable toils of morality. . . . A play which has a profound and permanent moral value and horror." Thus we can see how a poet's honesty is, in fact, very often a concern with morality, with the actuality of morality. Yet this moralism must be distinguished carefully from that overt didacticism which has spoiled the work of many great artists such as Tolstoy and resulted in the censorship of more than one masterpiece. Notice I have said the actuality of morality rather than simply morality as such. A further elucidation is to be found in Eliot's discussion of Hamlet, a character who suffered, says Eliot, from "the intense feeling, ecstatic or terrible, without an object or exceeding its object, which every person of sensibility has known. . . . The ordinary person puts such feelings to sleep, or trims down his feelings to fit the business world. The artist keeps them alive. . . ." In *Hamlet* Shakespeare "tackled a problem that proved too much for him. Why he attempted it at all, is an insoluble puzzle; under the compulsion of what experience he attempted to express the inexpressibly horrible, we cannot ever know." To conclude that *Hamlet* is a failure, as Eliot does, though it is the most read, performed, and studied of all plays, seems to me to have a curious notion of success. To enquire as to why Shakespeare wrote the play at all is strange in view of what Eliot says about the artist's effort to deal with emotions which are ecstatic, terrible, and inexpressibly horrifying. But I am not concerned so much with the wrongness of Eliot's judgment, in an essay written as early as 1919, as with the relation of these remarks to the honesty of the poet and the actuality of moral existence, to which these remarks point. The poet's honesty, and thus his morality, consists in his ability to face the ecstasy and the terror of his emotions, his desires, his fears, his aspirations, and his failure to realize his and other human beings' moral allegiances. Thus the morality of the poet consists not in teaching other human beings how to behave, but in facing the deepest emotional and moral realities in his poems, and in this way making it possible for his readers to confront the total reality of their existence, physical, emotional, moral and religious.

As Eliot says in one of his poems, "Mankind cannot bear very much reality," and Eliot looks always for those qualities in a poem which are likely to help the reader to see reality, if not to bear it.

IV

Eliot's theory of the nature and history of English poetry as stated in 1921 can be summarized as follows: "The metaphysical poets possessed a mind and sensibility which could devour *any* kind of experience." (Here, in passing, we may question whether any poet can devour any or all kinds of experience, and further whether such a poet as Wordsworth was not capable of taking hold of certain kinds of experience which the metaphysical poets know little or nothing about.)

Eliot continues by saying that Milton and Dryden were so powerful— "performed certain poetic functions so magnificently that the magnitude of the effect conceals the absence of others." The language of poetry improved from that time forward, says Eliot, but "the feeling became more crude." In the metaphysical poets and their predecessors, "there is a direct sensuous apprehension of thought, or a recreation of thought into feeling," and there is also a kind of intellectual wit, as Eliot observes in his companion essay on Andrew Marvell. But in Collins, Gray, Wordsworth, Shelley, Tennyson, Browning, Hardy, Yeats, and practically every poet since the time of Donne, there is missing that capacity of the mind, that wholeness of sensibility which makes it possible to say of Donne that "a thought was to him an experience," while Tennyson and Browning "merely ruminated"—"they are poets and they think; but they do not feel their thought as immediately as the odor of a rose." When Eliot adds Hardy to this list because he was a modern English-man and Yeats because he was Irish, it seems to me that we may justifiably say that seldom have so many poets been depreciated or dismissed in so few pages. Yet, exterme and sectarian as this view is, it depends nonetheless upon a profound sense of the nature of poetry. We can see what this sense comes to when Eliot says that "those critics who tell poets to look into their hearts and write do not tell them to look deep enough. . . . Racine and Donne looked into a great deal more than the heart. One must look into the cerebral cortex, the nervous system, and the digestive tracts."

V

The third of the standards with which Eliot has criticized poetry is language as such. This is connected, as we would expect, with the remarks I have just quoted, for Eliot says, that "in French poetry, for example, the two greatest masters of diction are also the two greatest psychologists, the most curious ex-plorers of the soul." In English poetry, however, Eliot finds that two of the greatest masters of diction are Milton and Dryden and they triumph, he says, "by a dazzling disregard of the human soul." Here again there is an underlying consistency in the operation of Eliot's mind, for what he is saying of Dryden and Milton is close to what he had said in 1920 of Swinburne as being purely verbal, of using language really divorced from any reference to objects. And it should be noted that only by a very strong sense of the actual can we distinguish between poetry which explores the human soul and poetry which is largely verbal. There is an intermediate mode: poetry whose chief aim is that of incantation, of inducing a certain state of emotion. The two instances Eliot cites are Poe and Mallarmé in an essay written in French in 1926 and never translated into English.

The essence of Eliot's concern with language in itself is perhaps best formulated in the following quotation: "The poetry of a people takes its life from the people's speech and in turn gives life to it; it represents its highest point of consciousness, its greatest power, and its most delicate sensibility." If we take this concern with language in isolation it might seem that the chief purpose of poetry is to maintain and purify the language, and indeed Eliot's praise of Dryden often seems to be bestowed on that poet merely because he effected a reformation in the use of language, rather than for his intrinsic qualities. Throughout Eliot's own poetry there are references to the difficulties and trials of anyone who attempts to use language carefully. In "The Love Song of J. Alfred Prufrock," the protagonist resents the fact that he is formulated in a phrase; in "Sweeney Agonistes" one character says "I gotta use words when I talk to you." In *The Waste Land* each human being is said to be isolated from all other human beings, to be in a prison, the prison of the self, hearing only aethereal rumors of the external world. There are many other instances but perhaps a quotation from the *Four Quartets* is the most explicit of all:

> So here I am, in the middle way, having had twenty years—
> Twenty years largely wasted, the years of *l'entre deux guerres*—
> Trying to learn to use words, and every attempt
> Is a wholly new start, and a different kind of failure
> Because one has only learnt to get the better of words
> For the thing one no longer has to say, or the way in which
> One is no longer disposed to say it. . . .

Throughout Eliot's criticism the quality of the poet's language and its effect upon the future of the English language has always concerned Eliot very much. I think we can say that never before has criticism been so conscious of all that can happen to language, how easily it can be debased, and how marvelously it can be elevated and made to illuminate the most difficult and delicate areas of experience.

VI

The fourth criterion is the dramatic sense, and Eliot maintains that all great poetry is dramatic. However, there is perhaps some confusion here, since Eliot means by dramatic the attitudes and emotions of a human being in a given situation. But when he comes to apply this broad definition, he is often influenced by his own love of Elizabethan drama, where the term, dramatic, narrows itself to the specific theatrical sense of the word, a sense in which it must be distinguished from meaning any human being's attitudes in any situation. This shift in meaning makes it possible for Eliot to say that Milton is not dramatic. For if we stick to the broad definition of the term, then, obviously, what could be more dramatic than the attitudes of Lucifer in "Paradise Lost," or the attitudes of Samson in "Samson Agonistes"? Again, if we accept Eliot's broad definition, then perhaps we must say that the "Elegy in a Country Churchyard" is just as dramatic, *qua* dramatic, as *Hamlet*. I do not mean to say that Eliot's emphasis upon the dramatic in poetry is not justified and fruitful to a certain extent; for example, there is a sense in which we can say that Gray's Elegy is less dramatic than, let us say, Donne's "The Funeral," which might be taken as a kind of elegy. My point is that Eliot sometimes uses this criterion of the dramatic to enforce prejudices about poetry which he does not like for other reasons.

We come, finally, to the question of versification. It is here that Eliot has been most influenced by his own poetic practice. For at one time or another he has enunciated practically every possible theory of what the nature of versification is. In a late essay on the poetry of Yeats he says that blank verse cannot be written in the 20th century because it still retains its period quality. The period presumably is the Elizabethan one, and such a statement is belied by the fact that not only has some of Eliot's best poetry been written in blank verse, but such a statement disregards the triumphs of blank verse, the inexhaustible variety of this form of versification to be found in Milton, Wordsworth, in Keats' "Hyperion," in certain poems of Tennyson which Eliot himself has praised precisely for their technical mastery of blank verse, and in Browning. Many other instances could be mentioned. Eliot's fundamental concern has been, however, with what he calls the "auditory imagination," "the feeling for syllable and rhythm, penetrating far below the conscious levels of thought and feeling, invigorating every word; sinking to the most primitive and forgotten, returning to the origin and bringing something back; seeking the beginning and the end." This should suggest that underneath the contradictory statements about the possibilities of versification which run throughout Eliot's criticism, there is a powerful intuition of how various, unpredictable, and profound are the possibilities of language when it is versified. The quotation I have just cited should suggest certainly that Eliot has found versification a means of raising to the surface of consciousness much that is otherwise concealed. We ought to remember Goethe's remark about Wordsworth, which is quoted by Matthew Arnold in his essay on Wordsworth: that Wordsworth was deficient as a poet because he knew too well the reason he chose every word and line. This paradoxical remark is not based upon a belief that the poet ought to be irrational and spontaneous, but, I think, based upon the sense that through rhythm the poet drew upon depths of being which could not be deliberately or consciously tapped. And let us remember that Goethe and Arnold were in no sense exponents of surrealism.

If we examine Eliot's scrutiny of English versification from the time of Marlowe to the time of Hardy and Yeats, and are not seduced into glib and futile logic-chopping, we come upon a theory of the nature of versification which seems to do justice to the many different things that Eliot has said about it. Namely, the theory that the essence of metre and thus of versification is any repetitive pattern of words, and the endless arguments about versification from Campion to Amy Lowell and the Free Verse movement are caused by the curious feeling that some *one* repetitive pattern, or kind of pattern, is the only true method of versification.

It will doubtless have been obvious by now that in a summary and incomplete way I have been attempting to make systematic the work of a critic who far from proceeding in terms of system or of *a priori* conceptions or of philosophical theory as to the nature of poetry has, on the contrary, developed the body of his work in the course of writing book-reviews, and essays inspired by a particular occasion. Indeed, Eliot has deplored the fact that he often had to write criticism when he wanted to write poetry, and it is certainly true that he did not always choose the subjects of his criticism. Yet it is likely that, to proceed in this way, at the mercy of accident, editorial whim, and his own intuitive sense of what he really felt about poetry, was probably the only way in which much of Eliot's criticism could have come into being.

VII

Let me now try to place Eliot's criticism in terms of a classification which was first suggested by the late Irving Babbitt, and I believe misused by him. Babbitt speaks of impressionistic criticism, scientific criticism, neo-classic criticism, and a fourth kind to which he gives no name, except to quote Abraham Lincoln's epigram about how you can't fool all the people all the time: a kind of criticism which is sometimes called the test of time or the verdict of posterity. This fourth kind presents many difficulties, including the fact that the posterity of the past, the only posterity we know about, has changed its mind so often, at different times preferring Dryden's *All for Love* to Shakespeare's *Antony and Cleopatra*, not to dwell upon such sad and brutal facts as that most of Sophocles' ninety plays have disappeared, and thus evaded the test of time and the fickleness of posterity, or such another dismaying piece of information as the fact that the Romans thought Ennius, whose work has almost entirely disappeared, was a far better epic poet than Virgil. Or again, let us remember that when the Mohammedans burnt the great library at Alexandria, they destroyed survival in time as a literary criterion and a basis for literary criticism.

Babbitt's other three kinds of criticism are also, I think, inadequate classifications. For example, when Babbitt speaks of scientific criticism, what he really means is historical criticism, since he cites Taine as its leading exponent. What we ought to distinguish and emphasize is the purpose which each kind of critic has in mind when he takes hold of a literary work. The neo-classic critic looks in the new literary work for the specific characteristics which he has found in masterpieces of the past, and consequently he denounces Shakespeare because he did not write like Sophocles. Thus, Voltaire condemns Shakespeare as a barbarian because he does not write like Racine. The historical critic is interested in the causes, social and biographical, of the literary work rather than in the work itself. The impressionistic critic is interested in the effects of the literary work upon himself as a delicate and rare sensibility rather than in the work as an objective and social phenomenon. The historical critic goes in back of the work to its causes; the impressionistic critic is concerned with himself rather than with the work itself; to use Pater's unfortunately immortal phrase, he wants to burn with a hard gemlike flame before the work of art, usually neglecting, in his concern with being inflamed, to distinguish and discriminate carefully between the objects which excite him. Eliot's criticism fits none of these classifications, although it is to be regretted that there has not been more of the historical critic in him. He has proceeded, as I have said, by intuition and by seeking out what most interested him from time to time. Yet, at his best he has been what I would like to call the classic kind of critic, the critic who is expert precisely because he depends upon the quality of his own experience, while, at the same time being aware that the more experience of literature he has, the more expert he becomes. There are no substitutes for experience, a platitude which is ignored invariably by the neo-classic critic, whose essential effort is to deduce from classics of the past a ready-made formula for judging any new work. Eliot's classicism at its best is illustrated when he says that if a truly classic work were written in our time, it would not be recognized as such by most of us. It would seem so monstrous, so queer and horrifying. This remark was made in 1933, when a good deal of James Joyce's Finnegans Wake had appeared and had been greeted by Eliot in the following terms: "We can't have much more of this sort of thing." Eliot has since changed his mind about this work, and though I do not know whether he considers it truly classical, certainly he admires it very much, and in this shift from dismay and perplexity to admiration we can see how the truly classical critic, the true expert, depends upon experience, and permits experience to correct his errors in appreciation. Experience is thus for the expert, or classical critic, not only the great teacher but the best textbook. Eliot, in revising his initial revaluation of English poetry, has permitted experience to teach him as no theory and no authority possibly could.

Having reviewed this long and complex critical career, we come finally to the question of what conclusions we can draw and what lessons we can gain from it. It seems to me that we have reached a point in our knowledge of the history of taste, the history of literary reputation, and literary judgment, where we can clearly mark out some of the most important dangers and pitfalls involved in any kind of literary criticism. Is it not clear that the kind of action and reaction which characterizes so good a critic as Eliot may very well be the expense of spirit in a waste of false discrimination? Is it necessary, in order to praise poets A, B, and C, to condemn poets D, E, F, G, H, and the rest of the alphabet? Perhaps it is necessary, but if we think concretely of the really shocking blunders in taste which prevail throughout literary history, then perhaps the very consciousness of these blunders can help us to arrive at a point of view in which there is no mere seesaw of praise and rejection. When Dr. Johnson declared that "Lycidas" was a worthless literary production, when Turgenev said that Dostoevsky was a "morbid mediocrity" and announced that he was very bored by the first volume of *War and Peace,* when Tolstoy ridiculed Shakespeare's *King Lear,* and asserted that his own masterpieces were worthless because they could not hold the attention of peasants; or when, for that matter, Shakespeare lost his popularity with Elizabethan audiences because Beaumont and Fletcher seemed to be able to turn out the same kind of thing in a slicker style—but it is unnecessary to continue with what might be an endless catalogue. The point is that the more we know about the history of literary reputation and literary opinion, the more conscious we are of how unjust and how stupid even the greatest critics can be, the more likely we are to avoid such errors in our own experience of literature. The matter is not merely a question of the reader's welfare; the creative writer himself is crucially involved, for just as we may suppose that Shakespeare turned to romantic comedy when his popularity declined, so too it seems likely enough that the failure of *Moby Dick* and *Pierre* reduced Melville to a silence and inactivity from which he emerged now and again for thirty years with short novels which suggest how much more he might have done, given his unquestionable genius, had his greatest work received the recognition it deserved at the time it appeared instead of some thirty years after Melville's death. Thus it does not seem to me to be claiming too much for literary criticism when one declares that upon the goodness, the consciousness, and the justice of literary criticism the very existence of great works sometimes depends, not to speak of the existence of great poets, nor to dwell too much upon mighty poets in their misery dead. I should add at this point that it is only by a knowledge of the literary past that contemporary critical practice can be of much use in preventing new neglect, stupidity, unjustified admiration, and unwarranted blindness. Two of the best poets of the 19th century, Gerard Manley Hopkins and Emily Dickinson, went to their graves with hardly any external recognition; it is quite possible that they did not really know that they had written good poetry. At present Hopkins and Emily Dickinson are much admired but only at the expense of Wordsworth and Hardy. By reviewing Eliot's critical career we can envisage a point of view which will free our scrutiny of literature from many of the sins of the past, while at the same time illuminating anew all that we have inherited from the past. And we can, I think, see how it might be desirable to have no literary dictators.

From *The Partisan Review*, Volume XVI (February, 1949), pp. 119–137, where it appeared as a "shortened version of a lecture given at the English Graduate Union of Columbia University on April 6, 1947." Reprinted in this revised version by permission of the author and editors.

RICHARD CHASE
An Approach to Melville
[1947]

LET's say that Melville was in certain demonstrable ways an artist, that he succeeded in writing certain great books. This will keep us from being too preoccupied with the Heroic Failure, the Inspired but Frustrated American— the Wounded Titan who lies athwart the vision of so many writers on Melville. Finally, of course, we must consider Melville as the Wounded Titan: one part of his personality *is* like Ahab, the Hero with the wound and the harpoon, and like Pierre, the Hero with the wound and the pen-turned-into-a-pistol. But if we see Melville's works as a whole, a total concept of personality begins to emerge and of this totality Ahab and Pierre represent only one of several parts, one person in a multiple personality which also includes Pip, Ahab's cabin boy; Bartleby, in the short story called "Bartleby the Scrivener"; Benito Cereno; Bulkington in *Moby Dick,* Jack Chase in *White Jacket,* the Confidence Man, and Billy Budd.

Our assumption that Melville was an artist cannot be fully explored so long as we make up our minds about Melville's books from the facts of his life, concluding, because he failed in certain ways, that *therefore* his books are all magnificent botches. It is easy to misrepresent these American creators and culture heroes who crack up in a riptide of alcohol or in an apocalypse of chromium and splintered glass or against the battering-ram head of the White Whale. Melville had his crack-up, in his own Victorian way; and that is our strongest image of him. But we owe it to any writer whom we profess to admire to try the experiment of looking at his books objectively. To begin, nevertheless, with the wounded Hero.

THE MAIMED MAN IN THE GLEN

Typee, Melville's first novel, is not just the young author's South Sea adventure story, separate in method and meaning from the later "philosophical" novels (which in any case are not philosophical in any strict sense of the word, but, rather, symbolic and allegorical). It contains many of the themes which Melville was later to develop. The most striking is what we may call The Maimed Man in the Glen. The hero of the story, who has injured his leg, languishes on a tropical island in the deep, secluded valley of the Typees, a tribe of Polynesians. The valley is a soporific paradise, a utopia for Archaists and Doasyoulikes. Yet there is something menacing or guilty about it. The natives are friendly to the hero and even worship him, as a glamorous object from a distant land. But they are firm in their refusal to let him leave the valley. He begins to suspect them of cannibalism. But glossing over these fears, the hero allows himself to fall into a narcissistic reverie, as monotonous and opiate as the procession of the days and nights. He oscillates between sickness and health, pain and pleasure. He is "unmanned" by the "mysterious disease" in his leg, which he is unable to cure. He is, as we come gradually to realize, symbolically castrated.

In *Mardi* (a fantastic travelogue which can be loosely compared with *Gulliver's Travels*) we discover a young king named Donjalolo. An ancient taboo forces him to spend his life within the dark, narrow defile which encloses his kingdom. Like his ancestors, he must "bury himself forever in this fatal glen." He rapidly changes from a young man of great energy and promise to an effeminate exquisite who flatters his senses with incense and languid maidens and who, to escape the oppressive libidinal intensity of the sun, passes back and forth every day between the House of the Morning and the House of the Afternoon, two dark temples constructed with phallic gigantism out of stone.

Ahab is one of these Maimed Men. He is castrated by his whalebone leg, as Melville makes apparent in the chapter called "Ahab's Leg." The central figure of *Pierre* (the novel which followed *Moby Dick*, in 1852) suffers from an Oedipus complex; he is another of these heroes—in *Pierre* Melville makes use of etymology in the names of his characters, as Joyce was later to do: Pierre Glendinning means "the stone which dwells in the glen." In *The Confidence Man,* "a kind of invalid Titan" emerges from a "cavernous old gorge" and strikes down a smooth-talking peddler for selling a phony medicine called the Samaritan Pain Dissuader. All of Melville's wounded heroes have affinities with the saint and the savior—with Christ; with Adonis; with the magician; with the *shaman,* whom primitive peoples worship because of the *mana* he has acquired through his neurotic behavior. But in Melville the fate of these heroes, as we see from Ahab and Pierre, is that they rush headlong into violent action, betraying whatever is creative within them and submitting themselves to everything that is mechanical, corrupting, repressive, and death-wishing. In doing so they kill themselves and all whose fate is in their hands. They are the Tragic Suicides. But they are only a part of a larger personality.

THE DIVINE INERT

The Divine Inert, as Melville says in *Moby Dick,* are "God's true princes of the Empire . . . a choice hidden handful "who are as superior to the

Tragic Suicides as the Tragic Suicides are to "the dead level of the mass." They are figures whose withdrawal from the world has been uncompromising and complete and who have gained the spiritual illumination which comes from dying out of life without dying into death. Pip, the Negro cabin boy, has been "mystically illumined" by the terrifying ordeal of being lost overboard: he sees "God's foot upon the treadle of the loom." He is saved from the sea, but he does not emerge from the depths of his own unconscious. To Ahab, Pip now seems "holy." And Ahab banishes Pip from the deck, saying that there is something in him "which I feel too curing to my malady"; he fears that somehow, without meaning to, Pip will dissuade him from the inexorable hunt after the whale.

Bartleby is another of the Divine Inert. An industrious scrivener who works in a Wall Street law office, he gradually becomes a schizophrenic, cutting himself off from the commercial world about him, saying little whenever he is addressed except "I should prefer not to," and inspiring his philistine employer with a sense of religious awe. Bartleby regresses into the shadows of his childhood as relentlessly as Ahab drives himself into outward action against the whale. He dies curled up like a child, a prisoner in the Tombs. "Benito Cereno" is also a story about a man cut off from the world and living in the twilight of consciousness. In this story Melville dramatizes the psychic plight of the Divine Inert by showing us a Spanish sea captain who has been subjected to the will of a mutinous band of slaves aboard a ship off the coast of South America. He is terrorized into a spiritual illumination, a fact which eludes the honest but obtuse Yankee captain, Amasa Delano. The Yankee captain saves Don Benito bodily but fails to grasp the implications of his spiritual plight.

THE HANDSOME SAILOR

The aspects of personality we have noticed so far are not mutually exclusive; there is much of Pip in Ahab, for example. The Handsome Sailor encompasses and reconciles both the Suicide and the Divine Inert, a kind of synthesis which the dialectic of personality produces out of thesis and antithesis. Yet the figure of the Handsome Sailor remains so inadequately objectified in Melville's books that it cannot fully serve as a synthesis; it is a direction, a motion, as well as an objective reality. At the beginning of *Billy Budd* the Handsome Sailor is pictured as a gigantic Negro wearing a Scotch Highland bonnet with a tartan band—the symbol, as we shall see, of the Promethean Light or the humanizing Intelligence. He is attended by a retinue of fellow sailors, an "assortment of tribes and complexions." Surrounding the superior figure, they move along the Liverpool docks as the lesser light of a constellation move with the central star. The tribes and complexions, Melville seems to be saying, have chosen to live with the Handsome

Sailor rather than, as they do in *Moby Dick,* die with the master who hurls them at the White Whale.

In *Moby Dick,* the Handsome Sailor is Bulkington—the man from the Southern mountains, with "noble shoulders and a chest like a coffer-dam"— who stands at the helm of the Pequod on the Christmas night when she "thrusts her vindictive bows" into the cold Atlantic. But Bulkington disappears from the story, with only a brief farewell from the author: "Take heart, O Bulkington. . . . Up from the spray of thy ocean-perishing—straight up, leaps thy apotheosis!" He must in fact disappear from the story if the story is to go on. Otherwise he would have done what Jack Chase, the Handsome Sailor of *White Jacket,* was driven to do: countermand the orders of the captain and save the ship. Together with Billy Budd these are Melville's Handsome Sailors. We do not see much of them (with the exception of Billy Budd, but he is too complex a problem to consider here). They are direction, force, potentiality rather than completed forms. They are the stuff and energy of an heroic American personality in the act of setting forth toward fulfillment—the Titanic body of America stirring out of the uncreated Night and passing ponderously into motion and consciousness.

PROMETHEUS

"Prometheus" is the name we may give to the total personality which encompasses the Suicide, the Divine Inert, and the Handsome Sailor. The Suicide is a false Prometheus, false because of the blind violence to which he is driven by his neurosis. The Divine Inert is also a false Prometheus because his compact with death and the unconscious is irrevocable. The Promethean man is he who has attained the spiritual illumination of the Divine Inert without losing the capacity for action of the Suicide but whose action is creative—whose action, that is, takes the direction of the Handsome Sailor. To put it another way, he is a man who is able to use the rhythms of life and death toward creative ends.

WITHDRAWAL AND RETURN

Melville symbolizes the rhythms of life and death in several ways. In these pages I can hardly do more than set them down: sea *vs.* land, valley *vs.* mountain, stasis *vs.* motion, time *vs.* space, narcissism *vs.* genius, dark *vs.* light, night *vs.* day, and so on. In his *Study of History,* Toynbee has subsumed these rhythms under the general idea of "Withdrawal and Return." Briefly, Withdrawal and Return may be described as the passage of the ego from the objective world into the unconscious and back to the outer world. This spiritual transit is the highest manifestation of the basic rhythms of the universe: the alternation of night and day, of death and life, the change of the seasons, the cycle of vegetation. The transit is not automatically productive in the higher forms of life. It succeeds only when the organism emerges on the returning beat of the rhythm transfigured by the ordeal of the journey and in possession of revived potency and "illumination." Withdrawal and Return is symbolized in a great many mythical themes—for example, awakening after a deep, deathlike sleep the folk-heroes who are beheaded or otherwise injured and magically restored; the death and rebirth of the savior-gods (Christ, Attis, Adonis, Osiris); the banishment and return of heroes like Oedipus; the ordeal of the Arthurian knights in their search for the grail. Toynbee's point, and Melville seems to be making approximately the same point, is that all creativity, whether individual or social, proceeds from individuals who can uncompromisingly embark on the transit of Withdrawal and Return and who, so to speak, can ride out the rhythms without coming into conflict with them.

The Divine Inert fail because they respond only to the first beat of the rhythm.

The Tragic Suicides fail because they allow themselves to be caught and mangled between beats. Theirs is the complex personality which demands to withdraw from the world in preparation for the ordeal of heroic accomplishment on the returning beat of the rhythm. But they are unable to countermand the demonic energy generated by their conflicts which prohibits a decisive withdrawal and goads them into violence and negation. As Freud pointed out, the repetitive rhythms of human activity are either creative postponements of death or they are short-cuts to self-destruction. For Ahab and Pierre, they are the latter. The Hero who cannot "withdraw" when the economy of his personality demands that he should, must finally withdraw by committing suicide.

In the figure of the Handsome Sailor we see personality in the act of emerging from the dark night of the soul—the giant Negro with the emblem of Light on his forehead. The particular facts of his future are unknown. But his eventual apotheosis is assured, for he has been able to ally himself with the spiritual transit.

AHAB AND THE WHALE

But of course the picture is only half complete. So far we have man and we have man transfigured into Prometheus or, to put it another way, we have man a fragment and man complete. There must be an Adversary, a God and Father—a Zeus in opposition to whom Prometheus undergoes his ordeal. Melville almost always regards God as the enemy of man. Moby Dick is God incarnate in the Mechanical Brute, the huge mindless hulk which "god-bullies" the Pequod. He is the challenge which God hurls at man, hoping that in the fight with the whale, man will "unman" himself—that is, undergo transfiguration, not into the image of Prometheus, but into the image of the

Beast-Machine. This is precisely what happens to Ahab and it is what constitutes his falseness. Like the true Promethean guardian of humanity, Ahab can shout defiantly at his "fiery father" that "in the midst of the personified impersonal, a personality stands here." Yet caught in the final violence of the whale hunt, Ahab is transfigured into the "impersonal," into the mechanical monster with blood on his brain. He knows well enough what is happening and what is at stake. The idea of the false Prometheus obsesses him. In the machinelike operations of the ship's carpenter and blacksmith he sees himself, caught in the iron hand of his own death-wishing will power, which makes such ready and fatal use of the mechanical techniques of tyranny in general and the whale hunt in particular. He has an almost hallucinatory awareness of an apotheosis looming up behind the blacksmith. The blacksmith is making a new whalebone leg for Ahab, and Ahab, addressing him ironically as "Prometheus," says,

I'll order a complete man after a desirable pattern. Imprimis, fifty feet high in his socks; then, chest modeled after the Thames Tunnel; then, legs with roots to 'em, to stay in one place; then, arms three feet through at the wrist; no heart at all, brass forehead, and about a quarter of an acre of fine brains; and let me see—shall I order eyes to see outwards? No, but put a skylight on top of his head to illuminate inwards.

It is the abortive transfiguration of Ahab himself, the master of the ship and all the tribes and complexions aboard.

In Melville, then, God manifests Himself as Death, as whatever unmans man. The incarnate Adversary is at once tantalizing and murderous. Man is tempted to forsake the creative Promethean ethos and to imitate the lure of God. Ahab fails because he imitates what is bestial and godlike and thereby fails to imitate what is pre-eminently human. For the rhythm of life out of which issues the Promethean *élan,* he substitutes the mechanical, death-wishing rhythm of the three final onslaughts against the Whale.

As for the comprehensive and pervasive meaning of *Moby Dick,* D. H. Lawrence seems to me to have been right (in his *Classic American Literature*). Melville's theme is the apocalypse and doom of civilization, the whole world hustled to extinction by an American master, the spectacular spiritual-intellectual-emotional failure of the great Prometheus of the West.

PIERRE

The theme of *Pierre* is incest and parricide. Pierre Glendinning, an aristocratic and promising youth, has made a god of his dead father. In the shrine of his heart "reposes the perfect marble form of his departed father; without blemish, unclouded, snow-white, serene." With his proud, handsome, willful mother Pierre enjoys a blissful adolescence. He falls in love with Lucy

Tartan, a pure and lovely girl. But then the dark lady of the story enters: Isabel, the daughter of Pierre's father by an illicit intercourse. Overcome with feelings of guilt, Pierre forms an incestuous attachment with Isabel. They flee to New York. Pierre tries to write a great novel. His mother dies. Lucy joins Pierre and Isabel. The two central projects of Pierre's life—his novel and a happy, productive relationship with Isabel—are both impossible to accomplish, given Pierre's temperament, capabilities, and the social system which he cannot escape even in Bohemian New York. Yet he drives towards his goal with all the mad zeal of Ahab. The whole thing ends quickly when Pierre shoots his cousin, Glendinning Stanly, who has been trying to rescue Lucy. Pierre and Isabel take poison and die in a prison cell. Lucy dies of the shock.

In many ways *Pierre* is a preposterous novel, full of clumsy melodrama and downright bad prose. But there is seldom any doubt that it was written by a great man. And through the murk we can see the scaffolding of an ambitious if imperfect allegory—so ambitious that *Pierre* can be compared with *Finnegans Wake*. *Pierre* has usually been thought of as an unsatisfactory Romantic-period *Hamlet*. But the allegory, once we have spotted it, makes the book far more impressive than that. I shall have to set down the elements of this allegory very dogmatically. As in reading Joyce, we have to recognize several levels of meaning at once. Lucy Tartan, as her first name indicates, is Light or the Promethean fire (thus the symbolism of the tartan bonnet on the head of the giant Negro, mentioned above). Isabel represents Night, Darkness, or the Unconscious. Pierre oscillates between these two figures: they are the opposite poles of the rhythm of Withdrawal and Return; they are less real women than two aspects of Pierre's mother. Pierre means "stone" —that is, he is the Earth alternating between day and night; and he is the human clay to whom "Lucy" gives the creative intelligence and to whom "Isabel" gives the spiritual experience of withdrawal. Caught in a cruel dilemma between the two, Pierre drives on toward the seductive bait of the Annihilating God: the snow-white marble form of his father—Death.

The book has other levels of meaning. For example, there is a kind of aesthetic allegory in which Lucy is the visual principle, Isabel is the auditory principle, and Pierre is Experience or Matter seeking to be transfigured into Art. Again, Lucy is Space and Isabel Time.

ALLEGORY

At one point in *Pierre* the youthful hero burns a portrait of his father, making a kind of ritualistic sacrifice. This ritual symbolizes the function of allegory in Melville's novels. As Melville writes in his essay on Hawthorne, a morally profound work of art is one which "beginning with the hollow follies and affectations of the world—all vanities and empty theories and forms are, one after another, and by admirably graduated, growing comprehensiveness, thrown into the allegorical fire." Allegory is the fire which consumes the Father—that is, every hypostatization of experience which inhibits creativity and destroys personality. Allegory is itself an hypostatization; it meets the "hollow follies" on their own ground. But it does so without losing the Promethean fire and so is able to defeat the "follies," leaving the field to "the all-engendering heart of man."

THE IMAGE OF NARCISSUS

This is important in Melville. It is sometimes touched on in *Moby Dick*; it is the theme of the short story called "The Bell Tower." In *Pierre,* the hero reflects that his cousin Glendinning Stanly, whom he shoots, is "the finest part of Pierre." The shooting of Stanly is part of the hero's suicide (etymologically Pierre Glendinning and Glendinning Stanly—for "stone field"—are virtually the same name). Nearly everyone in *Pierre* is a relative of the hero; even Lucy comes to New York as his "cousin." His mother is himself "translated into another sex." Like a child, Pierre "dabbles in the vomit of his loathed identity." The deaths of Pierre's father and mother, of Lucy, of Isabel, and of his cousin are planetary catastrophes involved in Earth's general suicide. The whole Ptolemaic universe is a mocking hypostatization of the young Titan's ego.

THE CONFIDENCE MAN

No account of Melville can afford to ignore or underestimate *The Confidence Man*. To begin with, it is a great book (and almost unobtainable in America). It is not at all a chaotic cry of despair but a buoyant, energetic piece of writing, on the whole free of Melville's often clumsy rhetoric. It is even a finished work, if read in the light of Melville's over-all themes; by no means is it a fragment, broken off in a fit of neurotic nihilism, as some writers have dramatically proclaimed. *The Confidence Man* (like *Israel Potter*) is a book of folklore. It is a wonderfully perceptive study of the American character, done at the folklore level, where character is clear and vulnerable. Many of the characters can be found in Constance Rourke's *American Humor:* the Yankee peddler, the Negro, the frontiersman, and so on. Also, the confidence man, peddling phony wares to his compatriots on a Mississippi river boat, is another false Prometheus, Prometheus in a loud American suit. He is a do-gooder, a Progressive in fact, and an emotional-intellectual-spiritual cutpurse. The ironical joke about him is that among other things he sells an Omni-Balsamic Reinvigorator—the life-principle of Promethean *élan,* patented and bottled.

THE LARGER VIEW

Melville's books have enough energy, coherence, and intelligence to justify our calling the author an artist. At the present stage of Melville criticism that is the important fact. Certainly it is wrong to discuss Melville as a great progressive, an heroic democrat, a culture hero, a noble heart, or a prophet of the good society apart from Melville as an artist—as so many liberal or progressive critics have been content to do. To do this is to make Melville a lesser man than he was, and to repeat the old heresy about art not being connected with life and morals.

Melville's moral intelligence must not be underestimated either. It is wrong to allow our liberal political scruples to keep us from fully understanding Melville's idea of the Heroic American. Is this Heroic American "undemocratic?" Perhaps and perhaps not. The important point is that Melville does not discount the resources of personality. Melville's Promethean Hero is no vaporous or irresponsible extravagance of the Romantic Age. He is elementary psychology for American moralists.

From *The Partisan Review*, Vol. XIV (May–June, 1947), pp. 285–294. Reprinted by permission of the author and editors. The "approach" to Melville proposed in this essay has been developed in Mr. Chase's book *Herman Melville* (New York: The Macmillan Company, 1949).

ALFRED KAZIN

William James and Henry James: "Our Passion is Our Task"

[1943]

. . . This method of narration by interminable elaboration of suggestive reference (I don't know what to call it, but you know what I mean) goes agin the grain
of all my own impulses in writing; and yet in spite of it all, there is a brilliancy
and cleanness of effect, and in this book especially a high-toned social atmosphere
that are unique and extraordinary. . . . But why won't you, just to please Brother,
sit down and write a new book, with no twilight or mustiness in the plot, with
great vigor and decisiveness in the action, no fencing in the dialogue, no psychological commentaries, and absolute straightness in the style? . . .

I mean . . . to try to produce some uncanny form of thing, in fiction, that will
gratify you, as Brother—but let me say, dear William, that I shall greatly be humiliated, if you *do* like it, and thereby lump it, in your affection, with things of the
current age, that I have heard you express admiration for and that I would sooner
descend to a dishonored grave than have written. . . . I'm always sorry when I
hear of your reading anything of mine, and always hope you won't—you seem to
me so constitutionally unable to "enjoy" it. . . . How far apart and to what different ends we have had to work out (very naturally and properly!) our respective
intellectual lives.

THUS William James to Henry James on the publication of *The Golden
Bowl* in 1905, and the latter's unusually sharp reply to the older brother whom
he adored—and could barely read. There is always a certain irony in honoring
the Jameses together: they could never fully honor or, after a certain point,
really understand each other. This was a fact both recognized and that
William openly enjoyed. They were always seeking to gratify each other, "as
Brother," for the Jameses loved each other as frankly as they insisted on their
differences and delighted in each other's careers. Perhaps never as in the
James family was so little envy or indifference brought to so many conflicting
intellectual ambitions, and rarely has so much fraternity been conferred on

597

so little mutual understanding. How deeply the elder James delighted in his genius sons, though he could only, from his vast intimacy with God, look down on both science and art as frivolously incomplete! How ready William always was to read each of Henry's essays and novels as it came along, how quick with eager brotherly praise, how ready to define Henry's subtlest triumphs and to miss them! How much Henry stood in awe of William, showered him with adulation, professed himself a "pragmatist," and resented it when William forgot to send even a technical monograph!

Their devotion to each other was deep; their essential antipathy of spirit went deeper still. But antipathy is not the word: there was only a kind of loving non-recognition. Parallel as they were in their studies of human consciousness, in raising to an ideal end the supreme operativeness and moral certainty of an individual "center of revelation," they could only smile to each other across the grooves in which each had his temperament. Henry at least knew his failure to recognize the design unfolded in William's empiricism, where William so genially slid over the symbolic design stamped on Henry's every effort, praised him for his "high-toned social atmosphere," patronized him, and missed that need to *use* the novel as a creed of perfection that cut Henry's career off from the Anglo-American fiction of his generation. Henry was an isolated figure even in the philosophic James household, where William was its reigning heir, the versatile young naturalist who spoke in his father's hearty voice even when he revolted against his father's theology, the naturalist in a scientific era whose interests drew him everywhere. William could at least follow Henry's works and comment on them (he commented on everything)—praise the early style or deplore the later, admire a character and confer a judgment. When William's first book, the great *Psychology*, appeared in 1890, Henry could only fidget in embarrassment and complain that he was too absorbed properly to appreciate "your mighty and magnificent book, which requires a stretch of leisure and an absence of 'crisis' in one's own egotistical little existence." Or, later, say of *The Pluralistic Universe* that he had read it "with enchantment, with pride, and almost with comprehension. It may sustain and inspire you a little to know that I'm *with* you, all along the line. . . . Thank the powers—that is, thank *yours*—for a relevant and assimilable and referable philosophy . . . your present volume seems to me exquisitely and adorably cumulative. . . ."

There it was: William's thought was always "adorable," but Henry was too absorbed. Henry had always been absorbed, where William's mind opened out to all the world, from his father's notations on Swedenborg to psychical research, from Kant to William Jennings Bryan: Henry was absorbed in making novels. William tried to be an artist and a chemist, went to Brazil with Agassiz to collect fishes, took an M. D. between periods of almost suicidal depression, debated endlessly with his opponents and loved them all, learned psychology by teaching it, wrote letters to all the cranks about their manias, gravitated into philosophy, fought against imperialism; Henry went on making novels. He made novels as he had made his first critical essays; his famous "impressions" and the enduring myth of England he kept from his childhood reading in *Punch*: by storing and molding what he had, and by never taking in anything he would not use. They had tried to make a lawyer out of him, they tried to teach him some elementary facts of science; Henry went on collecting impressions—impressions of Italy and of the pictures he found in Italy (Emerson loved these), impressions of Newport, Paris, Geneva and Saratoga; impressions of the mourned cousin, Mary Temple, whose face was the face of Milly Theale, Maggie Verver and Isabel Archer. The only culture he had was literature and pictures, and the only literature he sought was the nineteenth-century novel—he did not care much even for poetry; but he had a mission and his mind and life composed a single order of desire: he made novels.

To the other Jameses Henry was always the mysterious child who sat quietly alone, dreaming pictures and studying novels, and always bewilderingly content with his own mind. He adhered to nothing but his own taste; he had no "message," no positive belief or apparent need of one. William, on the other hand, was racked until he could find an ontology as plastic as life and true of every last thing in it; and he ran excitedly through all the disciplines, rejecting, disputing, extracting, until he could square the "irreducible facts" with the highest fact of his own nature. To Henry he might have said what their father had said to Emerson: "Oh, you man without a handle! shall one never be able to help himself out of you, according to his needs, and be dependent only upon your fitful tippings-up?" William always needed a handle; and he could use one only by reacting against something. What he principally reacted against was his father. Henry drew from the elder James by enclosing himself in the independence the father preached; he did not react against his father's theology, he ignored it. William, however, was too much like his father in combativeness and vivacious curiosity to reproduce anything but his temperament. Nothing could have seemed more boring to him than his father's metaphysics, poetic as many elements in it were. The elder James had escaped the dreariness of Calvinism—its belief in a kind of haphazard criminality of human nature—by nailing the human mind and will to the dreariness of a perpetual mysticism. The world was now joy, where Calvin's had been the fear of fate; but the only release allowed man was submission; the only hope a projected drowning in God. Utopian socialist though he fancied himself, he saw the natural world only as a lens on supernatural truth. Thought was reduced to the labored ecstasy of extracting mystic "secrets"; man lived in an unremitting effort at revelation.

Nothing was more alien to William than any belief which bound man to

something not in his particular nature and experience. In his biological theory of mind the mind was not a mere faculty, as the soul was not a region; it
was an effect and transmission of consciousness, purposive by definition; the
endlessly probing antennae of the whole human organism, it was what it did.
All of a man's life was engaged in his thought or spoke or hid in it; the mind
did not "receive" ideas, it shaped them in seeking adaptability; it sought ends.
Yet what was so significant in William's psychology, often condemned as
"literary," was that it buttressed in moral terms a theory of knowledge.
Though he was almost the first American to establish psychological studies in
the laboratory, he was always impatient with laboratory psychology and a mere
corpus of data. What he was getting at, as in his pragmatism, was not only a
more elastic sense of reality, a more honest and imaginative perception that all
life and thought begin in discrete individuals and are shaped by their differences, but a need to show that what was not a real experience to an individual
had no existence that one could name and take account of.

To the merely bookish, who would rather intone their knowledge than be
shaped by it; to the merely devout, who would rather worship their God than
be transformed by Him; to the formal logicians and contented monists, for
whom the world's radical disorder and depth are so easily sacrificed, William
James has always seemed loose or even vulgar because he preached that an
idea has meaning only as it is expressed in action and experience. That he was
so misunderstood is partly James's own fault, since he *would* speak of "the
cash-value" of an idea in his characteristic attempt to reach the minds even of
those for whom cash-value was the main value. But that he continues to be
misunderstood is largely the fault of our personal culture, since the rarest
thing in it is still the *active* moral imagination. For what James was leading to
in his pragmatism—once it had served as a theory of knowledge—was moral in
the most burning sense of conduct, moral in the enduring sense of the use a
human life is put to. Tell me, he seemed always to be saying to those who were
so content with ideas rather than with thinking, with thinking rather than
realization, what is it you *experience,* what is it that is changed in you or by
you, when you have achieved your certainty or knowledge? What is it you
live by, appreciably, when you have proved that something is true? James
knew well enough, and could formulate the ends and satisfactions of his opponents better than many of them could; but that was only incidental to his
essential aim. Knowledge is for men that they may live—and men may live
for ideal ends. So is the monist happy in his all-enveloping unity, the rational-
ist in his ideal symmetry, the mystic in his visions. And all of these exist, said
James: all of these must be taken into our account of the human experience
and the demands of our nature. But do not confuse, he went on, your individual need of certainty with the illusion that some supra-human order is
ascertained by it; do not confuse your use of reason—and delight in it—with

the illusion that what cannot be named or verified by rationalism does not exist.

To say this is not to forget how treacherous James's ideal of the provisional can be, and that he is particularly dissatisfying when he leaves us at the borders of metaphysics. He triumphed by disproving all the cults and systems which ignored the shaping power of man's individuality, by threshing his way through pre-scientific myths and post-scientific arrogance. But like so many American naturalistic thinkers, he took a certain necessary definition of the good life for granted (or confused it with the Elysian fields of the Harvard Department of Philosophy?); whereas it is the unrelenting consciousness of it that is most lacking. Yet what is most important here is that the great particular for him, as for all the Jameses, was the human self, and that out of it they made all their universals (though it is always a question what Henry's universals were). For the elder James the center of existence was the self that seeks to know God and to be sublimated in Him; William's theory of knowledge began with the knowing mind that *initiates* the ideas to which the test of experience is to be applied; Henry found his technical—and moral—triumph in the central Jamesian intelligence which sifts the experiences of all the other characters and organizes them. This, had William not so clearly pined for Stevenson when he read Henry's novels, he might have recognized as Henry's "handle." For in an age when all the materials through which William was running so eagerly demanded large positive answers, wholesale reconstructions and a world view, Henry had quietly and stubbornly reproduced his father's mystical integrity in the radiance of the observing self—in a prose which was more and more attuned to the most spontaneous music of the mind. The novel for him was to be *histoire morale*, a branch of history that sought the close textures and hidden lights of painting; but the highest morality was not so much in the story as in the exercise of the creative principle behind it.

That devotion to a creative principle was the great epic of Henry's integrity, as everything he ever sought or wrote was a commentary on it. In most writers their works exemplify their ambition; Henry's were about his ambition, as they were, in one sense, only his ambition written large. Just as William's vision always came back to a loose sea of empiricism in which man could hold on only to his own plurality, so Henry's was to define and to fill out the moral history of composition. His theory of art was not preparatory to a manipulation of experience; it *was* his experience. His interest was fixed on writing about the symbolic devotion of writing, as so many of his stories were of writers (but only of depressed or unsuccessful writers: there was no "dramatic process" in the surface of success). And the central Jamesian intelligence, in all his disguises as "the foreground observer," "the center of revelation," the artist planning his effects, the critic "remounting the stream of composition," was always sifting and commenting in turn. "The private history of any sincere work," he wrote once, "looms large with its own completeness"; the artist was his symbol of man's sincerity in operation. He studied his novels endlessly as he wrote them, corrected them endlessly when they were published, wrote prefaces in which he summarized the history of their composition, defined his every intent and use of means, speculated on the general principles they illustrated, and at the end, as he hinted to Grace Norton, might have written a preface to the prefaces, commenting on *them* in turn. The figure in the carpet was woven out of honor, not secrecy: out of so self-driven an integrity, as out of the intense interior life of his characters, there could be grasped the central fact of the effort, the search, the aura of devotion, that gave meaning to the artist's life and form to his work. And always the thread remained firmly in the artist's hand, pulling it back to himself—the story of Henry James was the story of Henry James writing his novels.

Life for both always returned to the central self. Significantly, it was always the richness of their personal nature that distinguished all the Jameses, and the overflow of life in them that gave them their vascular styles. Ralph Barton Perry says of the elder James that he felt his visions so intensely, and had so many together, that he had to get them all out at once. The elder James was always running over, laughing at himself for it, and never stopped running over. Like William, he had so many possible thoughts about so many things; and he had the James exuberance (the seed *was* Irish) that always ran so high in them despite (or in protest against) the family neurosis. Superficially, of course, no two styles would seem to be so different as William's and Henry's: the one so careful to sound spontaneous, the other so spontaneously labored; the one so informal in its wisdom, flinging witticisms, philosophical jargon, homeliness and hearty German abstractions about with a seeming carelessness, protesting doubt at every point, yet probing with angelic friendliness into all the blocks around the human mind; the other so *made* a style, solemnly and deliciously musical, reverberating with all the echoes of all the books Henry had ever read, forever sliding into cozy French idioms, shyly offering the commonest spoken expressions in quotation marks—Henry always sought to be friendly. Yet both were great spoken styles, intimate and with an immense range of tone: the only difference being that William talked to friendly Harvard seniors and Henry addressed some ideally patient friend. What no one has ever said enough about Henry's style, of course, is that it was the family style at its most intense: like all the Jameses, he wrote straight out of amplitude. He gushed and he purred, but there was always the James motor power behind him, their insatiable need to seize and define everything in range. And more, there was that "blague and benignity" in his style, as Ezra Pound named it: the tricky interior changes of pace, the slow mandarin whisperings, the adjectives that opened all vistas for him like great bronze doors, the wonderful tone *soundings* he could make with words, and covering them all, always his deceiving gentleness, the ceremonial diffidence, and his sudden barbs and winks.

To think of their styles is to be aware of the great and radiant innocence that was in all the Jameses, an innocence of personal spirit if hardly of moral perception. Financially secure, encouraged by their father to be different and uncontrolled, even to be without a profession, both ranged at will in what was still the household age of modern thought—a period when the security of their society encouraged those first studies in the naturalism of the psyche, and a voracious interior life. The only revolution either could envision was in new ways of knowing; and it is significant that William led the way to "the stream of consciousness." They all had the natural outpouring that came with innocence, the innocence that trusted in all the data of their enquiry, took the social forms for granted, and based life upon the integrity of the observing self. "In self-trust are all the virtues comprehended." It was the last and the best of Emerson in their culture, in all its lovable trust in individuality. Just as the elder James's theology committed man, as it were, to be a recording angel, to seek the necessary revelation and inscribe it, so they were all recording angels, as William said of Henry that under all his "rich sea-weeds" and "rigid barnacles and things" he cared only for making novels. Life was here and now, in all that system of relations between minds in which experience immediately consists; man *studied* it. The highest aim, of course, was to be an author. But there is no very great sense of revolt in any of them (compare them with the Adamses), no sense of that deeper radicalism, or metaphysical despair, which is uncontained even by pluralism and is not mollified by the individual creatingness.

Yet in a time like our own, when men are so peculiarly lost in themselves because they are so lost from each other, the Jamesian integrity is the very rock of comfort. We can take no social form for granted; we cannot possess or be possessed by those explorations in human consciousness which only parallel —or at best reveal—our quest for security. Our enforced sense of evil has nothing so creative in it as their innocence; and their legacy is still most precious for its symbolic integrity, its trust in mind, its superiority to our "failure of nerve." Even Henry James's greatest contributions to human pleasure and self-comprehension, or his insistence on the integrity of a work of art, are less important now than the emblem his pride raises before us. Even William's full devotion to realism, his imaginative projection of complexity, are less important to us now than the respect he breeds in us for all the forms of reality and our necessary understanding of them. And it is this which is now most visible in them and most important to us: the bounteousness of their feeling for life and the intensity of their respect for it. They both worked in that period of modern history when the trust of man in his power to know was at its highest, when the revolution of modern political democracy, science and materialism carried along even those who were skeptical of the idea of progress. But if we feel at times that they are geater than their thought, more beautiful than the books that contain them, it is because they burned with that indestructible zeal which we need so badly to recover—the zeal that cries that life does have a meaning: we seek to *be*.

In "The Middle Years," one of those exquisite stories in which Henry James was always writing out the lesson of his own loneliness and neglect in the story of the celebrated writer neglected and misunderstood by those nearest him, the writer cries on his deathbed: "It *is* glory—to have been tested, to have had our little quality, and cast our spell." "You're a great success!" his young attendant assures him. And Dencombe replies, wearily, but with mounting exaltation: "We work in the dark—we do what we can—we give what we have. Our doubt is our passion, and our passion is our task."

From *The New Republic,* Vol. CVIII (February 15, 1943), pp. 216–218. Reprinted in this revised version by permission of the author and editors.

PART V

Modern Criticism: Its Problems, Methods, and Prospects

T. S. ELIOT
Experiment in Criticism

[1929]

THERE is no department of literature in which it is more difficult to establish a distinction between "traditional" and "experimental" work than literary criticism. For here both words may be taken in two senses. By traditional criticism we may mean that which follows the same methods, aims at the same ends, and expresses much the same state of mind as the criticism of the preceding generation. Or we may mean something quite different; a criticism which has a definite theory of the meaning and value of the term "tradition," and which may be experimental in reverting to masters who have been forgotten. And as for "experiment" one may mean the more original work of the present generation, or else the work of critics who are pushing into new fields of inquiry, or enlarging the scope of criticism with other kinds of knowledge. To use the word "experimental" in the first sense would be invidious, for it would cover all the critical work of our time which one considers to have merit. For it is obvious that every generation has a new point of view, and is self-conscious in the critic; his work is twofold: to interpret the past to the present, and to judge the present in the light of the past. We have to see literature through our own temperament in order to see it at all, though our vision is always partial and our judgment always prejudiced; no generation, and no individual, can appreciate every dead author and every past period; universal good taste is never realized. In this way, all criticism is experimental, just as the mode of life of every generation is an experiment. It is only in my second sense, therefore, that it is worth while to talk of experimental criticism; only by considering what critics today may be deliberately attempting some kind of critical work which has not been deliberately attempted before.

In order to make clear exactly what there is that is new in contemporary critical writing I shall have to go back a hundred years. We may say, roughly, that modern criticism begins with the work of the French critic Sainte-Beuve, that is to say about the year 1826. Before him, Coleridge had attempted a new type of criticism, a type which is in some respects more allied to what is now called esthetics than to literary criticism. But from the Renaissance through the eighteenth century literary criticism had been confined to two narrow, and closely related, types. One was a type which has always existed and I hope always will, for it can always have very great value; it may be called practical notes on the art of writing by practitioners, parallel to the treatises on painting which have been left us by Leonardo da Vinci and others. Such notes are of the greatest value to other artists, particularly when studied in conjunction with the author's own work. Two classical examples in English are the Elizabethan treatises on rhymed and unrhymed verse written by Thomas Campion and Samuel Daniel. The prefaces and essays of Dryden, the prefaces of Corneille, are of the same type but on a larger scale and engage wider issues. But at the same time there is a large body of criticism, a considerable quantity in English and still more in French, written by men who were professionally critics rather than creative writers; the most famous critic of this sort is of course Boileau. This type of critic was primarily the *arbiter of taste,* and his task was to praise and condemn the work of his contemporaries, and especially to lay down the laws of good writing. These laws were supposed to be drawn from the practice, but still more from the theory, of the ancients. Aristotle was highly respected; but in practice this type of criticism was usually far from following the profound insight of Aristotle, and confined itself to translating, imitating, and plagiarizing Horace's *Art of Poetry.* At its best, it confirmed and maintained permanent standards of good writing; at its worst, it was a mere sequence of precepts. In general, French criticism was more theoretic and, as in La Harpe, more desiccated; the normal English type was nearer to plain good sense, as in Johnson's *Lives of the Poets;* though interesting theory, usually on specific literary types such as the drama, is found in authors like Thomas Rymer and Daniel Webb in the seventeenth and eighteenth centuries.

It is worth delaying for a moment to point out one of the qualities of seventeenth- and eighteenth-century literary criticism, which gives it enduring value and at the same time marks it off from more modern criticism. We are apt to think of this older criticism as dry and formal, and as setting up classical molds in which no living literature could be shaped. But we should remember in its favor that this criticism recognized literature as literature, and not another thing. Literature was something distinct from philosophy and psychology and every other study; and its purpose was to give a refined pleasure to persons of sufficient leisure and breeding. If the older critics had not taken for granted that literature was something primarily to be enjoyed, they could not have occupied themselves so sedulously with laying down rules of what was right to enjoy. This seems a very commonplace remark, and no distinction; but if you compare the criticism of those two centuries with that of the nineteenth, you will see that the latter does not take this simple truth wholly for granted. Literature is often treated by the critic rather as a means for eliciting truth or acquiring knowledge. If the critic is of a more philosophic or religious mind, he will look for the expression of philosophic or religious intuition in the work of the author criticised; if he is of a more realistic turn, he will look to literature as material for the discovery of psychological truths, or as documents illustrating social history. Even in the mouths of Walter Pater and his disciples, the phrase "art for art's sake" means something very different from the sense in which literature was literature for literature's sake up to the latter part of the eighteenth century. If you read carefully the famous epilogue to Pater's *Studies in the Renaissance* you will see that "art for art's sake" means nothing less than art as a substitute for everything else, and as a purveyor of emotions and sensations which belong to life rather than to art. To distinguish clearly between these two attitudes, that of art for art's sake and that of the eighteenth century, does require a strong effort of imagination. But the former doctrine would have been unintelligible to the earlier age. For the earlier period, art and literature were not substitutes for religion or philosophy or morals or politics, any more than for dueling or love-making: they were special and limited adornments of life. On each side there is a profit and a loss. We have gained perhaps a deeper insight, now and then; whether we enjoy literature any more keenly than our ancestors I do not know; but I think we should return again and again to the critical writings of the seventeenth and eighteenth centuries, to remind ourselves of that simple truth that literature is primarily literature, a means of refined and intellectual pleasure.

How, we ask immediately, did human beings ever come to abandon so simple and satisfying a limitation of criticism? The change comes about incidentally to a larger change, which may be described as the growth of the historical attitude. But this change—to which I shall return in a moment—is preceded, so far as literary criticism is concerned—by a freakish phenomenon, by a book written by one of the wisest and most foolish men of his time and perhaps the most extraordinary; a book which is itself one of the wisest and silliest, the most exciting and most exasperating book of criticism ever written—the *Biographia Literaria* of Coleridge. There, if you like, was "experiment in criticism," everything in fact except the power of sticking to the point—a power noticeably absent from Coleridge's ill-regulated life. Coleridge was one of the most learned men of his time, and no man of his time had wider interests except Goethe; and one of the first things that strikes us about his book, besides its uncommon diffuseness, is the novel variety of knowledge which he brings to bear on literary criticism. Much of his knowledge, as of the romantic German philosophers, does not seem to us today particularly worth having, but it was held to be valuable then; and we owe to Coleridge as much as to anybody our enjoyment of the doubtful benefits of German Idealism. His book naturally contains specimens of several types of criticism; its impulse, of course, was a defense of the new—or as the newspapers of our time would say, "modernist"—poetry of Wordsworth; and as such belongs to the type of technical notes of a craftsman; but when Coleridge started on anything, it could lead to almost everything else. He had not the historical point of view, but by the catholicity of his literary lore, and his ability for sudden and illuminating comparisons drawn from poetry of different ages and different languages, he anticipated some of the most useful accomplishments of the historical method. But one thing that Coleridge did effect for literary criticism is this. He brought out clearly the relation of literary criticism to that branch of philosophy which has flourished amazingly under the name of esthetics; and, following German writers whom he had studied, he puts the criticism of literature in its place as merely one department of the theoretic study of the Fine Arts in general. His fine discrimination of Fancy and Imagination cannot be held as permanent, for terms and relations change; but it remains one of the important texts for all who would consider the nature of poetic imagination. And he establishes literary criticism as a part of philosophy: or, to put it more moderately, he made it necessary for the "literary critic" to acquaint himself with general philosophy and metaphysics.

Biographia Literaria appeared in 1817; the activities of Charles Augustin Sainte-Beuve may be said to begin about 1826. Coleridge and Sainte-Beuve have very little in common—as little, that is, as two men who were both great critics could have in common. And Sainte-Beuve would not have been a great critic solely on the ground of what is new and experimental in his work. He had a very French intelligence and good taste which enabled him to share the ideals and sympathies of the great French writers of every time; there was much in him of the eighteenth century, a good deal even of the seventeenth. There were many gaps, certainly, in his appreciations, both of his contemporaries and of his predecessors; but he had that essential critical quality of imagination which made it possible for him to grasp literature as a whole. Where he differed from previous French critics was in his implicit conception of literature, not only as a body of writings to be enjoyed, but as a process of change in history, and as a part of the study of history. The notion that literary values are relative to literary periods, that the literature of a period is primarily an expression and a symptom of the time, is so natural to us now that we can hardly detach our minds from it. We can hardly conceive that the degree and kind of self-consciousness which we have could ever not have been. How much criticism of contemporary literature is taken up with discussing whether, and in what degree, this book or novel or poem is expressive of our mentality, of the personality of our age; and how often our critics seemed to be interested rather in inquiring what we (including themselves) are like, than with the book, novel, or poem as a work of art! This is an extreme, but the extreme of a tendency which began, in criticism, a good hundred years ago. Sainte-Beuve was not, like Coleridge, a metaphysician; he is indeed more modern and more skeptical; but he was the first interesting historian in criticism. And it is by no means irrelevant that he began his career with the study of medicine; he is not only an historian but a biologist in criticism.

It is, I think, interesting to turn to some good recent piece of literary criticism, and underline some of the assumptions of knowledge and theory which you would not find in criticism of two hundred years ago. Mr. Herbert Read's lucid little primer, *Phases of English Poetry*, will do for our purpose. On the second page he tells us that his is an inquiry into the evolution of poetry, and speaks presently of English poetry as a "living and developing organism." Even these few words should give a hint of the extent to which the critical apparatus has changed with the general changes in scientific and historical conceptions, when a literary critic can treat his audience to terms like "evolution" and "living organism" with the assurance of their being immediately apprehended. He is taking for granted certain vague but universal biological ideas. A little later he informs us that "the beginning of this study belongs to anthropology." Now, a great deal of work has had to be done by a great many people, and already more or less popularized, before a critic of literature can talk in this way. The work of Bastian, Tylor, Mannhardt, Durkheim, Lévy-Bruhl, Frazer, Miss Harrison, and many others has gone before. And a great deal of purely literary investigation has been made too, before anyone can talk of the evolution of poetry. Mr. Read begins by studying the origins of ballad poetry. It would not have been possible for him to do so without a great deal of work done in the later nineteenth century and the early twentieth; for example, by Professor Child of Harvard, Professor Gummere of Haverford, Professor Gaston Paris of the Sorbonne, and Professor W. P. Ker of London. Such studies in ballad poetry, and in all the heretofore unexplored ages of literature, have fostered in us the sense of flux and evolution, the sense of the relation of the poetry of each period to the civilization of the period, and also have tended slightly to *level* literary values. It was W. P. Ker, who perhaps knew the whole history of European poetry better than any man of his time, who said that in literature there were no Dark Ages. And in the next paragraph to the one which I have just quoted, Mr. Read observes that in theories of the origin of poetry we "go right back to the origin of speech." Even to make so simple a remark as this requires the work of another group of scientists: the philologists. The modern critic must have some acquaintance with them too—with the work of such contemporary philologists as Professor Jespersen of Copenhagen.

There are other branches of knowledge (or at least of science) some acquaintance with which you take for granted in any applicant whom you may employ as literary critic. Especially, of course, psychology, particularly analytical psychology. All of the studies I have mentioned, and more, do themselves touch the edges, and handle some of the problems, of criticism; so conversely the critic is distinguished first by the current notions which he shares with all educated or half-educated persons, such as the notion of evolution, and by the number and variety of sciences of which he has to know a little. And he has to know them, not in order to do their work for them, but to collaborate—and also in order that he may know where to stop. We require much general knowledge in order to see the limits of our particular ignorance.

Now although Sainte-Beuve did not have the equipment which we expect of our contemporaries, he had a great deal of the method, and very typically the state of mind which results from such a method at our stage of history. The awareness of the process of time has obscured the frontiers between literature and everything else. If you read the earlier critics, such as Dryden, you find the problems of literature comparatively simple ones. For Dryden and his contemporaries there were the Greek and Latin classics, a solid block of accepted canon, and there were their contemporaries, that is to say, English literature from Shakespeare and French literature from Malherbe; and they spent a good deal of their time in discussing whether the moderns, as they called themselves, had any literary virtues not surpassed by the ancients. Their estimate of the classics was not complicated by worrying about serpent and mistletoe cults, or the finances of the Athenian government. And between the ancients and Shakespeare and Malherbe there was nothing much to think about. They had really a great deal more faith in themselves than we have. They were certainly not bothered about "the future." It often seems to me that all our concern of it, which Mr. Shaw and Mr. Wells used to enjoy, are tokens of a profound pessimism. We hardly have time to get any fun out of what is being written now, so concerned are we about the quality of what may be written fifty years hence. Even Mr. Read's chapter on "Modern Poetry" seems to be as much engrossed by the puzzle of what poetry will be as by the puzzle of what it is. This kind of doubt seems to me to continue the doubt of Sainte-Beuve and Renan. Sainte-Beuve wrote a book of seven volumes on that remarkable French religious movement of the seventeenth century known as "Port Royal," and on that remarkable group of religious people of whom the most famous is Pascal. It is the masterpiece on that subject. It comes to no conclusion. It ends with the words: "He who had it most at heart to know his object, whose ambition was most engaged in seizing it, whose pride was most alert to paint it—how powerless he feels, and how far beneath his task, on the day when, seeing it almost finished and the result obtained, he feels his exaltation sink, feels himself overcome by faintness and inevitable disgust, and perceives in his turn that he too is only a fleeting illusion in the midst of the infinite illusory flux!" Sainte-Beuve was a modern critic for this reason: he was a man of restless curiosity about life, society, civilization, and all the problems which the study of history arouses. He studied these things through literature, because that was the center of his interests; and he never lost his literary sensibility in his investigation of problems reaching far beyond literature. But he was an historian, a sociologist (in the best sense of that word) and a moralist. He is a typical modern critic in that he found himself obliged to brood over the larger and darker problems which, in the modern world, lie behind the specific problems of literature.

The criticism of literature has by no means been absorbed in something else, as alchemy into chemistry. The core of the matter is still there, though the ramifications are endless, and the task of the critic is indeed hard. But there is still a valid distinction to be drawn between those modern critics who would make literature a substitute for a definite philosophy and theology, and thus promulgate, in an inverted form, the old gospel of art for art's sake, and those who would try to keep the distinctions clear, while admitting that the study of the one leads to the other, and that the possession of clear literary standards must imply the possession of clear moral standards. The various attempts to find the fundamental axioms behind both good literature and good life are among the most interesting "experiments" of criticism in our time.

The most considerable of such attempts so far is that which is known under the name of Humanism, and which owes its origin chiefly to the work of Professor Babbitt of Harvard. Mr. Babbitt, who is one of the most learned men of our time, is to some extent a disciple of Sainte-Beuve. There is no one living who knows more intimately (among many other things) the whole history of literary criticism. In his own writings, criticism of literature has been a means of criticising every aspect of modern society. He is a scholar of classical education, and classical tastes. He is keenly aware of the fact that the weaknesses of modern literature are symptoms of the weaknesses of modern civilization, and he has set himself with immense patience and perseverance to analyze these weaknesses. His conclusions may be read in his two most recent books, *Rousseau and Romanticism,* an account and a theory of the deterioration of taste since the early eighteenth century, and a book of still wider scope, *Democracy and Leadership.* As a moralist and as an Anglo-Saxon, he has on one side more in common with Matthew Arnold than with Sainte-Beuve. The tendency of the "humanist" in France is rather to diagnose, without prescribing a remedy; witness two recent books of brilliant literary and social criticism by M. Julien Benda, *Belphégor* and *La Trahison des clercs;* the Anglo-Saxon finds it intolerable to diagnose a disease without prescribing a remedy. Mr. Babbitt, like Arnold and Sainte-Beuve, finds that the decay of religious dogma has inflicted grave injury on society; like Arnold and Sainte-Beuve, he refuses to accept the remedy of returning to religious dogma; like Arnold and unlike Sainte-Beuve, he proposes another remedy, a theory of positive ethics based on human experiment, on the needs and capacities of the human as human, without reference to revelation or to supernatural authority or aid.

I do not propose, in this brief account, to discuss Mr. Babbitt's positive contribution, or the points at which I agree or disagree. I only want to call attention to a most important movement which is primarily, or in its inception, a movement within literary criticism, and of which a great deal more will be heard. It is significant because it shows that the modern literary critic must be an "experimenter" outside of what you might at first consider his own province; and as evidence that nowadays there is no literary problem which does not lead us irresistibly to larger problems. There is one weakness, or rather danger, of literary criticism which perceives the inevitable continuation of literary questions into general questions, which I might as well point out, because otherwise you will see it for yourselves and attach too much importance to it. The danger is that when a critic has grasped these vital moral problems which rise out of literary criticism, he may lose his detachment and submerge his sensibility. He may become too much a servant of his mind and conscience; he may be too impatient with contemporary literature, having pigeonholed it under one or another of the modern social maladies; and may demand edification at once, when appreciation of genius and accomplishment should come first. When he upholds "classicism" and denounces "romanticism" he is likely to give the impression that we should write like Sophocles or Racine; that everything contemporary is "romantic" and therefore not worth talking about. He makes us suspect that if a truly great, original classical work of imagination were to be written today, no one would like it. There will always be romantic people to admire romantic work; but we wonder whether the classicists would certainly know a classical work when it came. But these qualifications should not lead us to reject the humanist's theories: they should only lead us to apply them for ourselves.

Mr. Ramon Fernandez is a younger critic who has also taken the word humanism for his device, though his humanism, arrived at independently in France, is of a rather different brand from that which has arisen in America. His humanism has this in common: that it is also a development from literary criticism, and that it is also an attempt to arrive at a positive ethics while rejecting any revealed religion or supernatural authority. His first volume of essays, *Messages,* has been translated into English. It is important I think not so much by its achievement—for indeed the author has still a great many tangled knots in his style, which is cumbered by a good deal of philosophical and psychological terminology—as by its new attempt. Mr. Fernandez is less encyclopedic, less concerned with the past. He pores steadily over contemporaries and over the nineteenth century, and is more devoted to the study of special individuals, such as Montaigne, than to the study of the general course of literary history. Like the American humanists, he ponders over "classicism" and "romanticism"; but he wishes to be flexible, and is anxious to distinguish the essentials of classicism (which he finds, for instance, in George Eliot) from its appearances at any particular time. His theory is one which I do not wholly understand, and which has not yet been fully expounded, and probably not yet fully developed: but he illustrates, as clearly as the American humanists, the new experimental method of dealing with literary problems as moral problems, and the attempt to find guidance in conduct out of statement in literature—especially from the great novelists, and particularly, for he is a close student of English literature, from George Eliot and George Meredith. (In any case, his essay on Marcel Proust, the French novelist, in the volume mentioned, is a masterpiece of his particular method.) He is, in general, less the sociologist and more the individual psychologist. And from the best of his essays on novelists one draws this conclusion: that if we should exclude from literary criticism all but purely literary considerations, there would not only be very little to talk about, but actually we should be left without even literary appreciation. This is true of our appreciation of ancient authors but still more obviously of our appreciation of modern authors. For the same expansion of interest which has been imposed upon the modern critic has been imposed, or at least has been assumed, by the modern imaginative writer. We cannot write a purely literary criticism of George Eliot, for instance, unless it is admittedly a very imperfect criticism: for as the interests of the author were wide, so must be those of the critic.

I have tried to show that the tendency throughout a whole epoch to the present moment has been to widen the scope of criticism and increase the demands made upon the critic. This development might be traced in terms of the development of human self-consciousness, but that is a general philosophical question beyond the margin of this paper. There is along with this expansion a compensating tendency. As the number of sciences multiply, of sciences that is which have a bearing upon criticism, so we ask ourselves first whether there is still any justification for literary criticism at all, or whether we should not merely allow the subject to be absorbed gently into exacter sciences which will each annex some side of criticism. Just as in the history of philosophy, we find many subjects surrendered from time to time by philosophy, now to mathematics and physics, now to biology and psychology; until there seems to be almost nothing left to philosophize about. I think that the answer is clear: that so long as literature is literature, so long will there be a place for criticism of it—for criticism, that is, on the same basis as that on which the literature itself is made. For so long as poetry and fiction and such things are written, its first purpose must always be what it always has been—to give a peculiar kind of pleasure which has something constant in it throughout the ages, however difficult and various our explanations of that pleasure may be. The task of criticism will be, accordingly, not only to expand its borders but to clarify its center, and the insistency of the latter need grows with that of the former. Two hundred years ago, when it was taken for granted that one knew well enough what literature was, and it was not the number of other things which it is always now seeming to be, terms could be used more freely and carelessly without close definition. Now, there is an urgent need for experiment in criticism of a new kind, which will consist largely in a logical and dialectical study of the terms used. My own interest in these problems has been fostered partly by dissatisfaction with the *meaning* of my own statements in criticism, and partly by dissatisfaction with the terminology of the Humanists. In literary criticism we are constantly using terms which we cannot define, and defining other things by them. We are constantly using terms which have an *in*tension and an *ex*tension which do not quite fit; theoretically they ought to be made to fit; but if they cannot, then some other way must be found of dealing with them so that we may know at every moment what we mean. I will take a very simple example with which I have been dealing myself: the possibility of defining "metaphysical poetry." Here is a term which has a whole history of meanings down to the present time, all of which must be recognized, although it cannot have all of them at once. The term means on the one hand a certain group of English poets in the seventeenth century. On the other hand it must have an intensive meaning, must stand for a peculiar whole of qualities which is exemplified by the several poets. The ordinary critical method would be to define what "metaphysical poetry" means to you in the abstract, fit as many poets to it as well as you can, and reject the rest. Or else, you take the poets who have been held to be "metaphysical," and find out what they have in common. The odd thing is that by doing the sum, so to speak, in two different ways, you get two different results. A larger problem in the same kind of definition is that of "classicism" and "romanticism." Everyone who writes about these two abstractions believes that he knows what the words mean; actually they mean something a little different for each observer, and merely mean to mean the same things. In this way you have material for endless wrangling with no conclusion, which is not satisfactory. Such problems involve, of course, both logic and the theory of knowledge and psychology; there is no one, perhaps, more concerned with them than Mr. I. A. Richards, the author of *Principles of Literary Criticism* and *Practical Criticism*.

There is good cause for believing—apart from the obvious assertion that every generation must criticize for itself—that literary criticism, far from being exhausted, has hardly begun its work. On the other hand, I am more than skeptical of the old superstition that criticism and "creative writing" never flourish in the same age: that is a generalization drawn from a superficial inspection of some past ages. "Creative writing" can look after itself; and certainly it will be none the better for suppressing the critical curiosity. And in any case, the times which we have lived in seem to me, on the false antithesis mentioned, rather "creative" than "critical." (The current superstition that our epoch is Alexandrine, decadent, or "disillusioned" is parallel; there are no "disillusioned ages," only disillusioned individuals; and our time is just as deluded as any other.) The present age has been, rather, uncritical, and partly for economic causes. The "critic" has been chiefly the reviewer, that is to say, the hurried amateur wage-slave. I am aware of the danger that the types of criticism in which I am interested may become too professional and technical. What I hope for is the collaboration of critics of various special training, and perhaps the pooling and sorting of their contributions by men who will be neither specialists nor amateurs.

From *The Bookman*, Vol. LXX (November, 1929), pp. 225–233. Reprinted by permission of the author and editor. The essay has not been collected by the author in his books. It was included in *Tradition and Experiment in Present-Day Literature* (London: Oxford University Press–Humphrey Milford, 1929), pp. 198–215.

Religion and Literature
[1935]

WHAT I have to say is largely in support of the following propositions: Literary criticism should be completed by criticism from a definite ethical and theological standpoint. In so far as in any age there is common agreement on ethical and theological matters, so far can literary criticism be substantive. In ages like our own, in which there is no such common agreement, it is the more necessary for Christian readers to scrutinize their reading, especially of works of imagination, with explicit ethical and theological standards. The "greatness" of literature cannot be determined solely by literary standards; though we must remember that whether it is literature or not can be determined only by literary standards.[1]

We have tacitly assumed, for some centuries past, that there is *no* relation between literature and theology. This is not to deny that literature—I mean, again, primarily works of imagination—has been, is, and probably always will be judged by some moral standards. But moral judgments of literary works are made only according to the moral code accepted by each generation, whether it lives according to that code or not. In any age which accepts some precise Christian theology, the common code may be fairly orthodox: though even in such periods the common code may exalt such concepts as "honour," "glory" or "revenge" to a position quite intolerable to Christianity. The dramatic ethics of the Elizabethan Age offers an interesting study. But when the common code is detached from its theological background, and is consequently

---

[1] As an example of literary criticism given greater significance by theological interests, I would call attention to Theodor Haecker: *Virgil* (Sheed and Ward).

more and more merely a matter of habit, it is exposed both to prejudice and to change. At such times morals are open to being altered *by* literature; so that we find in practice that what is "objectionable" in literature is merely what the present generation is not used to. It is a commonplace that what shocks one generation is accepted quite calmly by the next. This adaptability to change of moral standards is sometimes greeted with satisfaction as an evidence of human perfectibility: whereas it is only evidence of what unsubstantial foundations people's moral judgments have.

I am not concerned here with religious literature but with the application of our religion to the criticism of any literature. It may be as well, however, to distinguish first what I consider to be the three senses in which we can speak of "religious literature." The first is that of which we say that it is religious "literature" in the same way that we speak of "historical literature" or of "scientific literature." I mean that we can treat the Authorized translation of the Bible, or the works of Jeremy Taylor, as literature, in the same way that we treat the historical writing of Clarendon or of Gibbon—our two great English historians—as literature; or Bradley's *Logic*, or Buffon's *Natural History*. All of these writers were men who, incidentally to their religious, or historical, or philosophic purpose, had a gift of language which makes them delightful to read to all those who can enjoy language well written, even if they are unconcerned with the objects which the writers had in view. And I would add that though a scientific, or historical, or theological, or philosophic work which is also "literature," may become superannuated as anything but literature, yet it is not likely to be "literature" unless it had its scientific or other value for its own time. While I acknowledge the legitimacy of this enjoyment, I am more acutely aware of its abuse. The persons who enjoy these writings *solely* because of their literary merit are essentially parasites; and we know that parasites, when they become too numerous, are pests. I could easily fulminate for a whole hour against the men of letters who have gone into ecstasies over "the Bible as literature," the Bible as "the noblest monument of English prose." Those who talk of the Bible as a "monument of English prose" are merely admiring it as a monument over the grave of Christianity. I must try to avoid the by-paths of my discourse: it is enough to suggest that just as the work of Clarendon, or Gibbon, or Buffon, or Bradley would be of inferior literary value if it were insignificant as history, science, and philosophy respectively, so the Bible has had a *literary* influence upon English literature *not* because it has been considered as literature, but because it has been considered as the report of the Word of God. And the fact that men of letters now discuss it as "literature" probably indicates the *end* of its "literary" influence.

The second kind of relation of religion to literature is that which is found in what is called "religious" or "devotional" poetry. Now what is the usual attitude of the lover of poetry—and I mean the person who is a genuine and first-hand enjoyer and appreciator of poetry, not the person who follows the admirations of others—towards this department of poetry? I believe, all that may be implied in his calling it a *department*. He believes, not always explicitly, that when you qualify poetry as "religious" you are indicating very clear limitations. For the great majority of people who love poetry, "*religious po-etry*" is a variety of *minor* poetry: the religious poet is not a poet who is treating the whole subject matter of poetry in a religious spirit, but a poet who is dealing with a confined part of this subject matter: who is leaving out what men consider their major passions, and thereby confessing his ignorance of them. I think that this is the real attitude of most poetry lovers towards such poets as Vaughan, or Southwell, or Grashaw, or George Herbert, or Gerard Hopkins.

But what is more, I am ready to admit that up to a point these critics are right. For there is a kind of poetry, such as most of the work of the authors I have mentioned, which is the product of a special religious awareness, which may exist without the general awareness which we expect of the major poet. In some poets, or in some of their works, this general awareness may have existed; but the preliminary steps which represent it may have been suppressed, and only the end-product presented. Between these, and those in which the religious or devotional genius represents the *special* and limited awareness, it may be very difficult to discriminate. I do not pretend to offer Vaughan, or Southwell, or George Herbert, or Hopkins as major poets: I feel sure that the first three, at least, are poets of this limited awareness. They are not great religious poets in the sense in which Dante, or Corneille, or Racine, even in those of their plays which do not touch upon Christian themes, are great Christian religious poets. Or even in the sense in which Villon and Baudelaire, with all their imperfections and delinquencies, are Christian poets. Since the time of Chaucer, Christian poetry (in the sense in which I shall mean it) has been limited in England almost exclusively to minor poetry.

I repeat that when I am considering Religion and Literature, I speak of these things only to make clear that I am not concerned primarily with Religious Literature. I am concerned with what should be the relation between Religion and all Literature. Therefore the third type of "religious literature" may be more quickly passed over. I mean the literary works of men who are sincerely desirous of forwarding the cause of religion: that which may come under the heading of Propaganda. I am thinking, of course, of such delightful fiction as Mr. Chesterton's *Man Who Was Thursday,* or his *Father Brown.* No one admires and enjoys these things more than I do; I would only remark that when the same effect is aimed at by zealous persons of less talent than Mr. Chesterton the effect is negative. But my point is that such writings do not enter into any serious consideration of the relation of Religion and Literature: because they are conscious operations in a world in which it is assumed that Religion and Literature are not related. It is a conscious and limited relating. What I want is a literature which should be *un*consciously, rather than deliberately and defiantly, Christian: because the work of Mr. Chesterton has its point from appearing in a world which is definitely not Christian.

I am convinced that we fail to realize how completely, and yet how irrationally, we separate our literary from our religious judgments. If there could be a complete separation, perhaps it might not matter: but the separation is not, and never can be, complete. If we exemplify literature by the novel—for the novel is the form in which literature affects the greatest number—we may remark this gradual secularization of literature during at least the last three hundred years. Bunyan, and to some extent Defoe, had moral purposes: the former is beyond suspicion, the latter may be suspect. But since Defoe the secularization of the novel has been continuous. There have been three chief phases. In the first, the novel took the Faith, in its contemporary version, for granted, and omitted it from its picture of life. Fielding, Dickens, and Thackeray belong to this phase. In the second, it doubted, worried about, or contested the Faith. To this phase belong George Eliot, George Meredith, and Thomas Hardy. To the third phase, in which we are living, belong nearly all contemporary novelists except Mr. James Joyce. It is the phase of those who have never heard the Christian Faith spoken of as anything but an anachronism.

Now, do people in general hold a definite opinion, that is to say religious or anti-religious; and do they read novels, or poetry for that matter, with a separate compartment of their minds? The common ground between religion and fiction is behaviour. Our religion imposes our ethics, our judgment and criticism of ourselves, and our behaviour toward our fellow men. The fiction that we read affects our behaviour towards our fellow men, affects our patterns of ourselves. When we read of human beings behaving in certain ways, with the approval of the author, who gives his benediction to this behaviour by his attitude toward the result of the behaviour arranged by himself, we can be influenced towards behaving in the same way.[2] When the contemporary novelist is an individual thinking for himself in isolation, he may have something important to offer to those who are able to receive it. He who is alone may speak to the individual. But the majority of novelists are persons drifting in the stream, only a little faster. They have some sensitiveness, but little intellect.

We are expected to be broadminded about literature, to put aside prejudice or conviction, and to look at fiction as fiction and at drama as drama. With what is inaccurately called "censorship" in this country—with what is much

[2] Here and later I am indebted to Montgomery Belgion. *The Human Parrot* (chapter on "The Irresponsible Propagandist").

more difficult to cope with than an official censorship, because it represents
the opinions of individuals in an irresponsible democracy, I have very little
sympathy; partly because it so often suppresses the wrong books, and partly
because it is little more effective than Prohibition of Liquor; partly because it
is one manifestation of the desire that state control should take the place of
decent domestic influence; and wholly because it acts only from custom and
habit, not from decided theological and moral principles. Incidentally, it gives
people a false sense of security in leading them to believe that books which
are *not* suppressed are harmless. Whether there *is* such a thing as a harmless
book I am not sure: but there very likely are books so utterly unreadable as to
be incapable of injuring anybody. But it is certain that a book is not harmless
merely because no one is consciously offended by it. And if we, as readers,
keep our religious and moral convictions in one compartment, and take our
reading merely for entertainment, or on a higher plane, for aesthetic pleasure,
I would point out that the author, whatever his conscious intentions in writing, in practice recognizes no such distinctions. The author of a work of imagination is trying to affect us wholly, as human beings, whether he knows it or
not; and we are affected by it, as human beings, whether we intend to be or
not. I suppose that everything we eat has some other effect upon us than
merely the pleasure of taste and mastication; it affects us during the process of
assimilation and digestion; and I believe that exactly the same is true of anything we read.

The fact that what we read does not concern merely something called our
literary taste, but that it affects directly, though only amongst many other influences, the whole of what we are, is best elicited, I think, by a conscientious
examination of the history of our individual literary education. Consider the
adolescent reading of any person with some literary sensibility. Everyone, I
believe, who is at all sensible to the seductions of poetry, can remember some
moment in youth when he or she was completely carried away by the work of
one poet. Very likely he was carried away by several poets, one after the other.
The reason for this passing infatuation is not merely that our sensibility to
poetry is keener in adolescence than in maturity. What happens is a kind of
inundation, of invasion of the undeveloped personality, the empty (swept
and garnished) room, by the stronger personality of the poet. The same thing
may happen at a later age to persons who have not done much reading. One
author takes complete possession of us for a time; then another; and finally
they begin to affect each other in our mind. We weigh one against another;
we see that each has qualities absent from others, and qualities incompatible
with the qualities of others: we begin to be, in fact, critical; and it is our
growing critical power which protects us from excessive possession by any
one literary personality. The good critic—and we should all try to be critics,
and not leave criticism to the fellows who write reviews in the papers—is

the man who, to a keen and abiding sensibility, joins wide and increasingly discriminating reading. Wide reading is not valuable as a kind of hoarding, an accumulation of knowledge, or what sometimes is meant by the term "a well-stocked mind." It is valuable because in the process of being affected by one powerful personality after another, we cease to be dominated by any one, or by any small number. The very different views of life, cohabiting in our minds, affect each other, and our own personality asserts itself and gives each a place in some arrangement peculiar to ourself.

It is simply not true that works of fiction, prose or verse, that is to say works depicting the actions, thoughts and words and passions of imaginary human beings, *directly* extend our knowledge of life. Direct knowledge of life is knowledge directly in relation to ourselves, it is our knowledge of *how* people behave in general, of *what* they are like in general, in so far as that part of life in which we ourselves have participated gives us material for generalization. Knowledge of life obtained through fiction is only possible by another stage of self-consciousness. That is to say, it can only be a knowledge of other people's knowledge of life, not of life itself. So far as we are taken up with the happenings in any novel in the same way in which we are taken up with what happens under our eyes, we are acquiring at least as much falsehood as truth. But when we are developed enough to say: "This is the view of life of a person who was a good observer within his limits, Dickens, or Thackeray, or George Eliot, or Balzac; but he looked at it in a different way from me, because he was a different man; he even selected rather different things to look at, or the same things in a different order of importance, because he was a different man; so what I am looking at is the world as seen by a particular mind"—then we are in a position to gain something from reading fiction. We are learning *something* about life from these authors direct, just as we learn something from the reading of history direct; but these authors are only really helping us when we can see, and allow for, their differences from ourselves.

Now what we get, as we gradually grow up and read more and more, and read a greater diversity of authors, is a variety of views of life. But what people commonly assume, I suspect, is that we gain this experience of other men's views of life only by "improving reading." This, it is supposed, is a reward we get by applying ourselves to Shakespeare, and Dante, and Goethe, and Emerson, and Carlyle, and dozens of other respectable writers. The rest of our reading for amusement is merely killing time. But I incline to come to the alarming conclusion that it is just the literature that we read for "amusement," or "purely for pleasure" that may have the greatest, and least suspected influence upon us. It is the literature which we read with the least effort that can have the easiest and most insidious influence upon us. Hence it is that the influence of popular novelists, and of popular plays of contemporary life, requires to be scrutinized most closely. And it is chiefly *contemporary* literature that the majority of people ever read in this attitude of "purely for pleasure," of pure passivity.

The relation of what I have been saying to the subject announced for my discourse should now be a little more apparent. Though we may read literature merely for pleasure, of "entertainment" or of "aesthetic enjoyment," this reading never affects simply a sort of special sense: it affects us as entire human beings; it affects our moral and religious existence. And I say that while individual modern writers of eminence can be improving, contemporary literature as a whole tends to be degrading. And that even the effect of the better writers, in an age like ours, may be degrading to some readers; for we must remember that what a writer does to people is not necessarily what he intends to do. It may be only what people are capable of having done to them. People exercise an unconscious selection, in being influenced. A writer like D. H. Lawrence may be in his effect either beneficial or pernicious. I am not even sure that I have not had some pernicious influence myself.

At this point I anticipate a rejoinder from the liberal-minded, from all those who are convinced that if everybody says what he thinks, and does what he likes, things will somehow, by some automatic compensation and adjustment, come right in the end. "Let everything be tried," they say, "and if it is a mistake, then we shall learn by experience." This argument might have some value, if we were always the same generation upon earth; or if, as we know to be not the case, people ever learned much from the experience of their elders. These liberals are convinced that only by what is called unrestrained individualism, will truth ever emerge. Ideas, views of life, they think, issue distinct from independent heads, and in consequence of their knocking violently against each other, the fittest survive, and truth rises triumphant. Anyone who dissents from this view must be either a mediaevalist, wishful only to set back the clock, or else a fascist, and probably both.

If the mass of contemporary authors were really individualists, every one of them inspired Blakes, each with his separate vision, and if the mass of the contemporary public were really a mass of *individuals* there might be something to be said for this attitude. But this is not, and never has been, and never will be. It is not only that the reading individual to-day (or at any day) is not enough an individual to be able to absorb all the "views of life" of all the authors pressed upon us by the publishers' advertisements and reviewers, and to be able to arrive at wisdom by considering one against another. It is that the contemporary authors are not individuals enough either. It is not that the world of separate individuals of the liberal democrat is undesirable; it is simply that this world does not exist. For the reader of contemporary literature is not, like the reader of the established great literature of all time, exposing himself to the influence of divers and contradictory personalities; he is exposing himself to a mass movement of writers who, each of them, think that they have something individually to offer, but are really all working together in the same direction. And there never was a time, I believe, when the reading public was so large, or so helplessly exposed to the influences of its own time. There never was a time, I believe, when those who read at all, read so many more books by living authors than books by dead authors; there never was a time so completely parochial, so shut off from the past. There may be too many publishers; there are certainly too many books published; and the journals ever incite the reader to "keep up" with what is being published. Individualistic democracy has come to high tide: and it is more difficult to-day to be an individual than it ever was before.

Within itself, modern literature has perfectly valid distinctions of good and bad, better and worse; and I do not wish to suggest that I confound Mr. Bernard Shaw with Mr. Noel Coward, Mrs. Woolf with Miss Mannin. On the other hand, I should like it to be clear that I am not defending a "high"-brow against a "low"-brow literature. What I do wish to affirm is that the whole of modern literature is corrupted by what I call Secularism, that it is simply unaware of, simply cannot understand the meaning of, the primacy of the supernatural over the natural life: of something which I assume to be our primary concern.

I do not want to give the impression that I have delivered a mere fretful jeremiad against contemporary literature. Assuming a common attitude between you, or some of you, and myself, the question is not so much, what is to be done about it? as, how should we behave towards it?

I have suggested that the liberal attitude towards literature will not work. Even if the writers who make their attempt to impose their "view of life" upon us were really distinct individuals, even if we as readers were distinct individuals, what would be the result? It would be, surely, that each reader would be impressed, in his reading, merely by what he was previously prepared to be impressed by; he would follow the "line of least resistance," and there would be no assurance that he would be made a better man. For literary judgment we need to be acutely aware of two things at once: of "what we like," and of "what we *ought* to like." Few people are honest enough to know either. The first means knowing what we really feel: very few know that. The second involves understanding our shortcomings; for we do not really know what we ought to like unless we also know why we ought to like it, which involves knowing why we don't yet like it. It is not enough to understand what we ought to be, unless we know what we are; and we do not understand what we are, unless we know what we ought to be. The two forms of self-consciousness, knowing what we are and what we ought to be, must go together.

It is our business, as readers of literature, to know what we like. It is our business, as Christians, *as well as* readers of literature, to know what we ought to like. It is our business as honest men not to assume that whatever we like is what we ought to like; and it is our business as honest Christians not to assume that we do like what we ought to like. And the last thing I would wish for would be the existence of two literatures, one for Christian consumption and the other for the pagan world. What I believe to be incumbent upon all Christians is the duty of maintaining consciously certain standards and criteria of criticism over and above those applied by the rest of the world; and that by these criteria and standards everything that we read must be tested. We must remember that the greater part of our current reading matter is written for us by people who have no real belief in a supernatural order, though some of it may be written by people with individual notions of a supernatural order which are not ours. And the greater part of our reading matter is coming to be written by people who not only have no such belief, but are even ignorant of the fact that there are still people in the world so "backward" or so "eccentric" as to continue to believe. So long as we are conscious of the gulf fixed between ourselves and the greater part of contemporary literature, we are more or less protected from being harmed by it, and are in a position to extract from it what good it has to offer us.

There are a very large number of people in the world to-day who believe that all ills are fundamentally economic. Some believe that various specific economic changes alone would be enough to set the world right; others demand more or less drastic changes in the social as well, changes chiefly of two opposed types. These changes demanded, and in some places carried out, are alike in one respect, that they hold the assumptions of what I call Secularism: they concern themselves only with changes of a temporal, material, and external nature; they concern themselves with morals only of a collective nature. In an exposition of one such new faith I read the following words:

In our morality the one single test of any moral question is whether it impedes or destroys in any way the power of the individual to serve the State. [The individual] must answer the questions: "Does this action injure the nation? Does it injure other members of the nation? Does it injure my ability to serve the nation?" And if the answer is clear on all those questions, the individual has absolute liberty to do as he will.

Now I do not deny that this is a kind of morality, and that it is capable of great good within limits; but I think that we should all repudiate a morality which had no higher ideal to set before us than that. It represents, of course, one of the violent reactions we are witnessing, against the view that the community is solely for the benefit of the individual; but it is equally a gospel of this world, and of this world alone. My complaint against modern literature is of the same kind. It is not that modern literature is in the ordinary sense "immoral" or even "amoral"; and in any case to prefer that charge would not be enough. It is simply that it repudiates, or is wholly ignorant of, our most fundamental and important beliefs; and that in consequence its tendency is to encourage its readers to get what they can out of life while it lasts, to miss no "experience" that presents itself, and to sacrifice themselves, if they make any sacrifice at all, only for the sake of tangible benefits to others in this world either now or in the future. We shall certainly continue to read the best of its kind, of what our time provides; but we must tirelessly criticize it according to our own principles, and not merely according to the principles admitted by the writers and by the critics who discuss it in the public press.

From *Essays Ancient and Modern* by T. S. Eliot, pp. 93–112. Copyright, 1932, 1936, by Harcourt, Brace and Company, Inc. Reprinted by permission of the publishers. First published in *Faith that Illuminates*, ed. by V. A. Demant (London: Centenary Press, 1935), pp. 29–54.

From Poe to Valéry

[1948]

WHAT I attempt here is not a judicial estimate of Edgar Allan Poe; I am not trying to decide his rank as a poet or to isolate his essential originality. Poe is indeed a stumbling block for the judicial critic. If we examine his work in detail, we seem to find in it nothing but slipshod writing, puerile thinking unsupported by wide reading or profound scholarship, haphazard experiments in various types of writing, chiefly under pressure of financial need, without perfection in any detail. This would not be just. But if, instead of regarding his work analytically, we take a distant view of it as a whole, we see a mass of unique shape and impressive size to which the eye constantly returns. Poe's influence is equally puzzling. In France the influence of his poetry and of his poetic theories has been immense. In England and America it seems almost negligible. Can we point to any poet whose style appears to have been formed by a study of Poe? The only one whose name immediately suggests itself is— Edward Lear. And yet one cannot be sure that one's own writing has *not* been influenced by Poe. I can name positively certain poets whose work has influenced me, I can name others whose work, I am sure, has not; there may be still others of whose influence I am unaware, but whose influence I might be brought to acknowledge; but about Poe I shall never be sure. He wrote very few poems, and of those only half a dozen have had a great success: but those few are as well known to as large a number of people, are as well remembered by everybody, as any poems ever written. And some of his tales have had an important influence upon authors, and in types of writing where such influence would hardly be expected.

I shall here make no attempt to explain the enigma. At most, this is a contribution to the study of his influence; and an elucidation, partial as it may be, of one cause of Poe's importance in the light of that influence. I am trying to look at him, for a moment, as nearly as I can, through the eyes of three French poets, Baudelaire, Mallarmé and especially Paul Valéry. The sequence is itself important. These three French poets represent the beginning, the middle and the end of a particular tradition in poetry. Mallarmé once told a friend of mine that he came to Paris because he wanted to know Baudelaire; that he had once seen him at a bookstall on a quai, but had not had the courage to accost him. As for Valéry, we know from the first letter to Mallarmé, written when he was hardly more than a boy, of his discipleship of the elder poet; and we know of his devotion to Mallarmé until Mallarmé's death. Here are three literary generations, representing almost exactly a century of French poetry. Of course, these are poets very different from each other; of course, the literary progeny of Baudelaire was numerous and important, and there are other lines of descent from him. But I think we can trace the development and descent of one particular theory of the nature of poetry through these three poets and it is a theory which takes its origin in the theory, still more than in the practice, of Edgar Poe. And the impression we get of the influence of Poe is the more impressive, because of the fact that Mallarmé, and Valéry in turn, did not merely derive from Poe through Baudelaire: each of them subjected himself to that influence directly, and has left convincing evidence of the value which he attached to the theory and practice of Poe himself. Now, we all of us like to believe that we understand our own poets better than any foreigner can do; but I think we should be prepared to entertain the possibility that these Frenchmen have seen something in Poe that English-speaking readers have missed.

My subject, then, is not simply Poe but Poe's effect upon three French poets, representing three successive generations; and my purpose is also to approach an understanding of a peculiar attitude towards poetry, by the poets themselves, which is perhaps the most interesting, possibly the most characteristic, and certainly the most original development of the esthetic of verse made in that period as a whole. It is all the more worthy of examination if, as I incline to believe, this attitude towards poetry represents a phase which has come to an end with the death of Valéry. For our study of it should help towards the understanding of whatever it may be that our generation and the next will find to take its place.

Before concerning myself with Poe as he appeared in the eyes of these French poets, I think it as well to present my own impression of his status among American and English readers and critics; for, if I am wrong, you may have to criticise what I say of his influence in France with my errors in mind. It does not seem to me unfair to say that Poe has been regarded as a minor, or secondary, follower of the Romantic Movement: a successor to the so-called "Gothic" novelists in his fiction, and a follower of Byron and Shelley in his verse. This however is to place him in the English tradition; and there certainly he does not belong. English readers sometimes account for that in Poe which is outside of any English tradition, by saying that it is American; but this does not seem to me wholly true either, especially when we consider the other American writers of his own and an earlier generation. There is a certain flavour of provinciality about his work in a sense in which Whitman is not in the least provincial: it is the provinciality of the person who is not at home where he belongs, but cannot get to anywhere else. Poe is a kind of displaced European; he is attracted to Paris, to Italy and to Spain, to places which he could endow with romantic gloom and grandeur. Although his ambit of movement hardly extended beyond the limits of Richmond and Boston longitudinally, and neither east nor west of these centres, he seems a wanderer with no fixed abode. There can be few authors of such eminence who have drawn so little from their own roots, who have been so isolated from any surroundings.

I believe the view of Poe taken by the ordinary cultivated English or American reader is something like this: Poe is the author of a few, a very few short poems which enchanted him for a time when he was a boy, and which do somehow stick in the memory. I do not think that he re-reads these poems, unless he turns to them in the pages of an anthology; his enjoyment of them is rather the memory of an enjoyment which he may for a moment recapture. They seem to him to belong to a particular period when his interest in poetry had just awakened. Certain images, and still more certain rhythms, abide with him. This reader also remembers certain of the tales—not very many— and holds the opinion that "The Gold Bug" was quite good for its time, but that detective fiction has made great strides since then. And he may some-times contrast him with Whitman, having frequently re-read Whitman, but not Poe.

As for the prose, it is recognised that Poe's tales had great influence upon some types of popular fiction. So far as detective fiction is concerned, nearly everything can be traced to two authors: Poe and Wilkie Collins. The two influences sometimes concur, but are also responsible for two different types of detective. The efficient professional policeman originates with Collins, the brilliant and eccentric amateur with Poe. Conan Doyle owes much to Poe, and not merely to Monsieur Dupin of "The Murders in the Rue Morgue." Sherlock Holmes was deceiving Watson when he told him that he had bought his Stradivarius violin for a few shillings at a second-hand shop in the Tottenham Court Road. He found that violin in the ruins of the house of Usher. There is a close similarity between the musical exercises of Holmes and those of Roderick Usher: those wild and irregular improvisations which, although on one occasion they sent Watson off to sleep, must have been excruciating to any ear trained to music. It seems to me probable that the romances of improbable and incredible adventure of Rider Haggard found their inspiration in Poe—and Haggard himself had imitators enough. I think it equally likely that H. G. Wells, in his early romances of scientific exploration and invention, owed much to the stimulus of some of Poe's narratives—"Gordon Pym," or "A Descent into the Maelstrom" for example, or "The Facts in the Case of Monsieur Valdemar." The compilation of evidence I leave to those who are interested to pursue the enquiry. But I fear that nowadays too few readers open *She* or *The War of the Worlds* or *The Time Machine;* fewer still are capable of being thrilled by their predecessors.

What strikes me first, as a general difference between the way in which the French poets whom I have cited took Poe, and the way of American and English critics of equivalent authority, is the attitude of the former towards Poe's *oeuvre,* towards his work as a whole. Anglo-Saxon critics are, I think, more inclined to make separate judgments of the different parts of an author's work. We regard Poe as a man who dabbled in verse and in several kinds of prose, without settling down to make a thoroughly good job of any one *genre.* These French readers were impressed by the variety of form of expression, because they found, or thought they found, an essential unity; while admitting, if necessary, that much of the work is fragmentary or occasional, owing to circumstances of poverty, frailty and vicissitude, they nevertheless take him as an author of such seriousness that his work must be grasped as a whole. This represents partly a difference between two kinds of critical mind; but we must claim, for our own view, that it is supported by our awareness of the blemishes and imperfections of Poe's actual writing. It is worth while to illustrate these faults, as they strike an English-speaking reader.

Poe had, to an exceptional degree, the feeling for the incantatory element in poetry, of that which may, in the most nearly literal sense, be called "the magic of verse." His versification is not, like that of the greatest masters of prosody, of the kind which yields a richer melody, through study and long habituation, to the maturing sensibility of the reader returning to it at times throughout his life. Its effect is immediate and undeveloping; it is probably much the same for the sensitive schoolboy and for the ripe mind and cultivated ear. In this unchanging immediacy, it partakes perhaps more of the character of very good *verse* than of poetry—but that is to start a hare which I have no intention of following here, for it is, I am sure, "poetry" and not "verse." It has the effect of an incantation which, because of its very crudity, stirs the feelings at a deep and almost primitive level. But, in his choice of the word which has the right *sound,* Poe is by no means careful that it should have also the right *sense.* I will give one comparison of uses of the same word by Poe and by Tennyson—who, of all English poets since Milton, had probably the most accurate and fastidious appreciation of the sound of syllables. In Poe's "Ulalume"—to my mind one of his most successful, as well as typical, poems—we find the lines

> It was night in the lonesome October
> Of my most immemorial year.

Immemorial, according to the Oxford Dictionary, means: "that is beyond memory or out of mind; ancient beyond memory or record: extremely old." None of these meanings seems applicable to this use of the word by Poe. The year was not beyond memory—the speaker remembers one incident in it very well; at the conclusion he even remembers a funeral in the same place just a year earlier. The line of Tennyson, equally well known, and justly admired because the sound of the line responds so well to the sound which the poet wishes to evoke, may already have come to mind:

> The moan of doves in immemorial elms.

Here *immemorial,* besides having the most felicitous sound value, is exactly the word for trees so old that no one knows just how old they are.

Poetry, of different kinds, may be said to range from that in which the attention of the reader is directed primarily to the sound, to that in which it is directed primarily to the sense. With the former kind, the sense may be apprehended almost unconsciously; with the latter kind—at these two extremes —it is the sound, of the operation of which upon us we are unconscious. But, with either type, sound and sense must cooperate; in even the most purely incantatory poem, the dictionary meaning of words cannot be disregarded with impunity.

An irresponsibility towards the meaning of words is not infrequent with Poe. "The Raven" is, I think, far from being Poe's best poem; though, partly because of the analysis which the author gives in "The Philosophy of Composition," it is the best known.

> In there stepped a stately Raven of the saintly days of yore.

Since there is nothing particularly saintly about the raven, if indeed the ominous bird is not wholly the reverse, there can be no point in referring his origin to a period of saintliness, even if such a period can be assumed to have existed. We have just heard the raven described as *stately;* but we are told presently that he is *ungainly,* an attribute hardly to be reconciled, without a good deal of explanation, with *stateliness.* Several words in the poem seem to be inserted either merely to fill out the line to the required measure, or for the sake of a rhyme. The bird is addressed as "no craven" quite needlessly, except for the pressing need of a rhyme to "raven"—a surrender to the exigencies of rhyme with which I am sure Malherbe would have had no patience. And there is not always even such schoolboy justification as this: to say that the lamplight "gloated o'er" the sofa cushions is a freak of fancy which, even were it relevant to have a little gloating going on somewhere, would appear forced.

Imperfections in "The Raven" such as these—and one could give others— may serve to explain why "The Philosophy of Composition," the essay in which Poe professes to reveal his method in composing "The Raven"—has not been taken so seriously in England or America as in France. It is difficult for us to read that essay without reflecting, that if Poe plotted out his poem with such calculation, he might have taken a little more pains over it: the result hardly does credit to the method. Therefore we are likely to draw the conclusion that Poe in analysing his poem was practising either a hoax, or a piece of self-deception in setting down the way in which he wanted to think that he had written it. Hence the essay has not been taken so seriously as it deserves.

Poe's other essays in poetic esthetic deserve consideration also. No poet, when he writes his own *art poétique,* should hope to do much more than explain, rationalise, defend or prepare the way for his own practice: that is, for writing his own kind of poetry. He may think that he is establishing laws for all poetry; but what he has to say that is worth saying has its immediate relation to the way in which he himself writes or wants to write: though it may well be equally valid to his immediate juniors, and extremely helpful to them. We are only safe in finding, in his writing about poetry, principles valid for any poetry, so long as we check what he says by the kind of poetry he writes. Poe has a remarkable passage about the impossibility of writing a long poem— for a long poem, he holds, is at best a series of short poems strung together. What we have to bear in mind is that he himself was incapable of writing a long poem. He could conceive only a poem which was a single simple effect: for him, the whole of a poem had to be in one mood. Yet it is only in a poem of some length that a variety of moods can be expressed; for a variety of moods requires a number of different themes or subjects, related either in themselves or in the mind of the poet. These parts can form a whole which is more than the sum of the parts; a whole such that the pleasure we derive from the reading of any part is enhanced by our grasp of the whole. It follows also that in a long poem some parts may be deliberately planned to be less "poetic" than others: these passages may show no lustre when extracted, but may be intended to elicit, by contrast, the significance of other parts, and to unite them into a whole more significant than any of the parts. A long poem may gain by the widest possible variations of intensity. But Poe wanted a poem to be of the first intensity throughout: it is questionable whether he could have appreciated the more philosophical passages in Dante's *Purgatorio*. What Poe had said has proved in the past of great comfort to other poets equally incapable of the long poem; and we must recognize that the question of the possibility of writing a long poem is not simply that of the strength and staying power of the individual poet, but may have to do with the conditions of the age in which he finds himself. And what Poe has to say on the subject is illuminating, in helping us to understand the point of view of poets for whom the long poem is impossible.

The fact that for Poe a poem had to be the expression of a single mood—it would here be too long an excursus to try to demonstrate that "The Bells," as a deliberate exercise in several moods, is as much a poem of one mood as any of Poe's—this fact can better be understand as a manifestation of a more fundamental weakness. Here, what I have to say I put forward only tentatively: but it is a view which I should like to launch in order to see what becomes of it. My account may go to explain, also, why the work of Poe has for many readers appealed at a particular phase of their growth, at the period of life when they were just emerging from childhood. That Poe had a powerful intellect is undeniable: but it seems to me the intellect of a highly gifted young person before puberty. The forms which his lively curiosity takes are those in which a pre-adolescent mentality delights: wonders of nature and of mechanics and of the supernatural, cryptograms and cyphers, puzzles and labyrinths, mechanical chess-players and wild flights of speculation. The variety and ardour of his curiosity delight and dazzle; yet in the end the eccentricity and lack of coherence of his interests tire. There is just that lacking which gives dignity to the mature man: a consistent view of life. An attitude can be mature and consistent, and yet be highly sceptical: but Poe was no sceptic. He appears to yield himself completely to the idea of the moment: the effect is, that all of his ideas seem to be *entertained* rather than believed. What is lacking is not brain power, but that maturity of intellect which comes only with the maturing of the man as a whole, the development and coordination of his various emotions. I am not concerned with any possible psychological or pathological explanation: it is enough for my purpose to record that the work of Poe is such as I should expect of a man of very exceptional mind and sensibility, whose emotional development has been in some respect arrested at an early age. His most vivid imaginative realisations are the realisation of a dream: significantly, the ladies in his poems and tales are always ladies lost, or ladies vanishing before they can be embraced. Even in "The Haunted Palace," where the subject appears to be his own weakness of alcoholism, the disaster has no moral significance; it is treated impersonally as an isolated phenomenon; it has not behind it the terrific forces of such lines as those of François Villon when he speaks of his own fallen state.

Having said as much as this about Poe, I must proceed to enquire what it was that three great French poets found in his work to admire, which we have not found. We must first take account of the fact that none of these poets knew the English language very well. Baudelaire must have read a certain amount of English and American poetry: he certainly borrows from Gray, and apparently from Emerson. He was never familiar with England, and there is no reason to believe that he spoke the language at all well. As for Mallarmé, he taught English and there is convincing evidence of his imperfect knowledge, for he committed himself to writing a kind of guide to the use of the language. An examination of this curious treatise, and the strange phrases which he gives under the impression that they are familiar English proverbs, should dispel any rumour of Mallarmé's English scholarship. As for Valéry, I never heard him speak a word of English, even in England. I do not know what he had read in our language: Valéry's second language, the influence of which is perceptible in some of his verse, was Italian.

It is certainly possible, in reading something in a language imperfectly understood, for the reader to find what is not there; and when the reader is himself a man of genius, the foreign poem read may, by a happy accident, elicit something important from the depths of his own mind, which he attributes to what he reads. And it is true that in translating Poe's prose into French, Baudelaire effected a striking improvement: he transformed what is often a slipshod and a shoddy English prose into admirable French. Mallarmé, who translated a number of Poe's poems into French prose, effected a similar improvement: but on the other hand, the rhythms, in which we find so much of the originality of Poe, are lost. The evidence that the French overrated Poe because of their imperfect knowledge of English remains accordingly purely negative: we can venture no farther than saying that they were not disturbed by weaknesses of which we are very much aware. It does not account for their high opinion of Poe's *thought,* for the value which they attached to his philosophical and critical exercises. To understand that we must look elsewhere.

We must, at this point, avoid the error of assuming that Baudelaire, Mallarmé and Valéry all responded to Poe in exactly the same way. They are great poets, and they are each very different from the other; furthermore, they represent, as I have reminded you, three different generations. It is with Valéry that I am here chiefly concerned. I therefore say only that Baudelaire, to judge by his introduction to his translation of the tales and essays, was the most concerned with the personality of the man. With the accuracy of his portrait I am not concerned: the point is that in Poe, in his life, his isolation and his worldly failure, Baudelaire found the prototype of *le poète maudit,* the poet as the outcast of society—the type which was to realise itself, in different ways, in Verlaine and Rimbaud, the type of which Baudelaire saw himself as a distinguished example. This nineteenth-century archetype, *le poète maudit,* the rebel against society and against middle-class morality (a rebel who descends of course from the continental myth of the figure of Byron) corresponds to a particular social situation. But, in the course of an introduction which is primarily a sketch of the man Poe and his biography, Baudelaire lets fall one remark indicative of an esthetic that brings us to Valéry:

> He believed [says Baudelaire], true poet that he was, that the goal of poetry is of the same nature as its principle, and that it should have nothing in view but itself.

"A poem does not say something—it *is* something": that doctrine has been held in more recent times.

The interest for Mallarmé is rather in the technique of verse, though Poe's is, as Mallarmé recognises, a kind of versification which does not lend itself to use in the French language. But when we come to Valéry, it is neither the man nor the poetry, but the *theory* of poetry, that engages his attention. In a very early letter to Mallarmé, written when he was a very young man, introducing himself to the elder poet, he says: "I prize the theories of Poe, so profound and so insidiously learned; I believe in the omnipotence of rhythm, and especially in the suggestive phrase." But I base my opinion, not primarily upon this credo of a very young man, but upon Valéry's subsequent theory and practice. In the same way that Valéry's poetry, and his essays on the art of poetry, are two aspects of the same interest of his mind and complement each other, so for Valéry the poetry of Poe is inseparable from Poe's poetic theories.

This brings me to the point of considering the meaning of the term *"la poésie pure":* the French phrase has a connotation of discussion and argument which is not altogether rendered by the term "pure poetry."

All poetry may be said to start from the emotions experienced by human beings in their relations to themselves, to each other, to divine beings, and to the world about them; it is therefore concerned also with thought and action, which emotion brings about, and out of which emotion arises. But, at however primitive a stage of expression and appreciation, the function of poetry can never be simply to arouse these same emotions in the audience of the poet. You remember the account of Alexander's feast in the famous ode of Dryden. If the conqueror of Asia was actually transported with the violent emotions which the bard Timotheus, by skilfully varying his music, is said to have aroused in him, then the great Alexander was at the moment suffering from automatism induced by alcohol poisoning, and was in that state completely incapable of appreciating musical or poetic art. In the earliest poetry, or in the most rudimentary enjoyment of poetry, the attention of the listener is directed upon the subject matter; the effect of the poetic art is felt, without the listener being wholly conscious of this art. With the development of the consciousness of language, there is another stage, at which the auditor, who may by that time have become the reader, is aware of a double interest in a story for its own sake, and in the way in which it is told: that is to say, he becomes aware of style. Then we may take a delight in discrimination between the ways in which different poets will handle the same subject: an appreciation not merely of better or worse, but of differences between styles which are equally admired. At a third stage of development, the subject may recede to the background: instead of being the purpose of the poem, it becomes simply a necessary means for the realisation of the poem. At this stage the reader or listener may become as nearly indifferent to the subject matter as the primitive listener was to the style. A complete unconsciousness or indifference to the style at the beginning, or to the subject matter at the end, would however take us outside of poetry altogether: for a complete unconsciousness of anything but subject matter would mean that for that listener poetry had not yet appeared; a complete unconsciousness of anything but style would mean that poetry had vanished.

This process of increasing self-consciousness—or, we may say, of increasing consciousness of language—has as its theoretical goal what we may call *la poésie pure*. I believe it to be a goal that can never be reached, because I think that poetry is only poetry so long as it preserves some "impurity" in this sense: that is to say, so long as the subject matter is valued for its own sake. The Abbé Brémond, if I have understood him, maintains that while the element of *la poésie pure* is necessary to make a poem a poem, no poem can consist of *la poésie pure* solely. But what has happened in the case of Valéry is a change of attitude toward the subject matter. We must be careful to avoid saying that the subject matter becomes "less important." It has rather a different kind of importance: it is important as *means*: the *end* is the poem. The subject exists for the poem, not the poem for the subject. A poem may employ several subjects, combining them in a particular way; and it may be meaningless to ask "What is the subject of the poem?" From the union of several subjects there appears, not another subject, but the poem.

Here I should like to point out the difference between a theory of poetry propounded by a student of esthetics, and the same theory as held by a poet. It is one thing when it is simply an account of how the poet writes, without knowing it, and another thing when the poet himself writes consciously according to that theory. In affecting writing, the theory becomes a different thing from what it was merely as an explanation of how the poet writes. And Valéry was a poet who wrote very consciously and deliberately indeed: perhaps, at his best, not wholly under the guidance of theory; but his theorising certainly affected the kind of poetry that he wrote. He was the most self-conscious of all poets.

To the extreme self-consciousness of Valéry must be added another trait: his extreme scepticism. It might be thought that such a man, without belief in anything which could be the subject of poetry, would find refuge in a doctrine of "art for art's sake." But Valéry was much too sceptical to believe even in art. It is significant, the number of times that he describes something he has written as an *ébauche*—a rough draft. He had ceased to believe in *ends,* and was only interested in *processes.* It often seems as if he had continued to write poetry, simply because he was interested in the introspective observation of himself engaged in writing it: one has only to read the several essays—sometimes indeed more exciting than his verse, because one suspects that he was more excited in writing them—in which he records his observations. There is a revealing remark in *Variété V,* the last of his books of collected papers: "As for myself, who am, I confess, much more concerned with the formation or the fabrication of works of art than with the works themselves," and, a little later in the same volume: "In my opinion the most authentic philosophy is not in the objects of reflection, so much as in the very act of thought and its manipulation."

Here we have, brought to their culmination by Valéry, two notions which can be traced back to Poe. There is first the doctrine, elicited from Poe by Baudelaire, which I have already quoted: "A poem should have nothing in view but itself"; second the notion that the composition of a poem should be as conscious and deliberate as possible, that the poet should observe himself in the act of composition—and this, in a mind as sceptical as Valéry's, leads to the conclusion, so paradoxically inconsistent with the other, that the act of composition is more interesting than the poem which results from it.

First, there is the "purity" of Poe's poetry. In the sense in which we speak of "purity of language" Poe's poetry is very far from pure, for I have commented upon Poe's carelessness and unscrupulousness in the use of words. But in the sense of *la poésie pure,* that kind of purity came easily to Poe. The subject is little, the treatment is everything. He did not have to achieve purity by a process of purification, for his material was already tenuous. Second, there is that defect in Poe to which I alluded when I said that he did not appear to believe, but rather to entertain, theories. And here again, with Poe and Valéry, extremes meet, the immature mind playing with ideas because it had not developed to the point of convictions, and the very adult mind playing with ideas because it was too sceptical to hold convictions. It is by this contrast, I think, that we can account for Valéry's admiration for "Eureka"—that cosmological fantasy which makes no deep impression upon most of us, because we are aware of Poe's lack of qualification in philosophy, theology or natural science, but which Valéry, after Baudelaire, esteemed highly as a "prose poem." Finally, there is the astonishing result of Poe's analysis of the composition of "The Raven." It does not matter whether "The Philosophy of Composition" is a hoax, or a piece of self-deception, or a more or less accurate record of Poe's calculations in writing the poem; what matters is that it suggested to Valéry a method and an occupation—that of observing himself write. Of course, a greater than Poe had already studied the poetic process. In the *Biographia Literaria* Coleridge is concerned primarily, of course, with the poetry of Wordsworth; and he did not pursue his philosophical enquiries concurrently with the writing of his poetry; but he does anticipate the question which fascinated Valéry: "What am I doing when I write a poem?" Yet Poe's "Philosophy of Composition" is a *mise au point* of the question which gives it capital importance in relation to this process which ends with Valéry. For the penetration of the poetic by the introspective critical activity is carried to the limit by Valéry, the limit at which the latter begins to destroy the former. M. Louis Bolle, in his admirable study of this poet, observes pertinently: "This intellectual narcissism is not alien to the poet, even though he does not explain the whole of his work: 'why not conceive as a work of art the production of a work of art?'"

Now, as I think I have already hinted, I believe that the *art poétique* of which we find the germ in Poe, and which bore fruit in the work of Valéry, has gone as far as it can go. I do not believe that this esthetic can be of any help to later poets. What will take its place I do not know. An esthetic which merely contradicted it would not do. To insist on the all-importance of subject-matter, to insist that the poet should be spontaneous and irreflective, that he should depend upon inspiration and neglect technique, would be a lapse from what is in any case a highly civilised attitude to a barbarous one. We should have to have an esthetic which somehow comprehended and transcended that of Poe and Valéry. This question does not greatly exercise my mind, since I think that the poet's theories should arise out of his practice rather than his practice out of his theories. But I recognise first that within this tradition from Poe to Valéry are some of those modern poems which I most admire and enjoy; second, I think that the tradition itself represents the most interesting development of poetic consciousness anywhere in that same hundred years; and finally I value this exploration of certain poetic possibilities for its own sake, as we believe that all possibilities should be explored. And I find that by trying to look at Poe through the eyes of Baudelaire, Mallarmé and most of all Valéry, I become more thoroughly convinced of his importance, of the importance of his *work* as a whole. And, as for the future: it is a tenable hypothesis that this advance of self-consciousness, the extreme awareness of and concern for language which we find in Valéry, is something which must ultimately break down, owing to an increasing strain against which the human mind and nerves will rebel; just as, it may be maintained, the indefinite elaboration of scientific discovery and invention, and of political and social machinery, may reach a point at which there will be an irresistible revulsion of humanity and a readiness to accept the most primitive hardships rather than carry any longer the burden of modern civilisation. Upon that I hold no fixed opinion: I leave it to your consideration.

JOHN CROWE RANSOM

Criticism as Pure Speculation[1]

[1941]

A CHASM, perhaps an abyss, separates the critic and the esthetician ordinarily, if the books in the library are evidence. But the authority of criticism depends on its coming to terms with esthetics, and the authority of literary esthetics depends on its coming to terms with criticism.

When we inquire into the "intent of the critic," we mean: the intent of the generalized critic, or critic as such. We will concede that any professional critic is familiar with the technical practices of poets so long as these are conventional, and is expert in judging when they perform them badly. We expect a critical discourse to cover that much, but we know that more is required. The most famous poets of our time, for example, make wide departures from conventional practices: how are they to be judged? Innovations in poetry, or even conventions when pressed to their logical limits, cause the ordinary critic to despair. They cause the good critic to review his esthetic principles; perhaps to reformulate his esthetic principles. He tries the poem against his best philosophical conception of the peculiar character that a poem should have.

Mr. T. S. Eliot is an extraordinarily sensitive critic. But when he discusses the so-called "metaphysical" poetry, he surprises us by refusing to study the so-called "conceit" which is its reputed basis; he observes instead that the metaphysical poets of the seventeenth century are more like their immediate predecessors than the latter are like the eighteenth and nineteenth century poets, and then he goes into a very broad philosophical comparison between two whole "periods" or types of poetry. I think it has come to be understood that his comparison is unsound; it has not proved workable enough to assist critics who have otherwise borrowed liberally from his critical principles. (It contains the famous dictum about the "sensibility" of the earlier poets, it im-

---

[1] This essay was presented as a lecture at Princeton University in the winter of 1940-41 in a series of four lectures entitled *The Intent of the Critic*. The other participants were Edmund Wilson, Norman Foerster, and W. H. Auden. The first two paragraphs, referring to the local occasion of the discussion, have here been condensed into the present first paragraph by the editor, with the author's permission.

putes to them a remarkable ability to "feel their thought," and to have a kind of "experience" in which the feeling cannot be differentiated from the thinking.) Now there is scarcely another critic equal to Eliot at distinguishing the practices of two poets who are closely related. He is supreme as a comparative critic when the relation in question is delicate and subtle; that is, when it is a matter of close perception and not a radical difference in kind. But this line of criticism never goes far enough. In Eliot's own range of criticism the line does not always answer. He is forced by discontinuities in the poetic tradition into sweeping theories that have to do with esthetics, the philosophy of poetry; and his own philosophy probably seems to us insufficient, the philosophy of the literary man.

The intent of the critic may well be, then, first to read his poem sensitively, and make comparative judgments about its technical practice, or, as we might say, to emulate Eliot. Beyond that, it is to read and remark the poem knowingly; that is, with an esthetician's understanding of what a poem generically "is."

Before I venture, with inadequate argument, to describe what I take to be the correct understanding of poetry, I would like to describe two other understandings which, though widely professed, seem to me misunderstandings. First, there is a smart and belletristic theory of poetry which may be called "psychologistic." Then there is an altogether staid and commonplace theory which is moralistic. Of these in their order.

II

It could easily be argued about either of these untenable conceptions of poetry that it is an act of despair to which critics resort who cannot find for the discourse of poetry any precise differentia to remove it from the category of science. Psychologistic critics hold that poetry is addressed primarily to the feelings and motor impulses; they remind us frequently of its contrast with the coldness, the unemotionality, of science, which is supposed to address itself to the pure cognitive mind. Mr. Richards came out spectacularly for the doctrine, and furnished it with detail of the greatest ingenuity. He very nearly severed the dependence of poetic effect upon any standard of objective knowledge or belief. But the feelings and impulses which he represented as gratified by the poem were too tiny and numerous to be named. He never identified them; they seemed not so much psychological as infra-psychological. His was an esoteric poetic: it could not be disproved. But neither could it be proved, and I think it is safe at this distance to say that eventually his readers, and Richards himself, lost interest in it as being an improvisation, much too unrelated to the public sense of a poetic experience.

With other critics psychologism of some sort is an old story, and one that will probably never cease to be told. For, now that all of us know about psy-

chology, there must always be persons on hand precisely conditioned to declare that poetry is an emotional discourse indulged in resentment and compensation for science, the bleak cognitive discourse in its purity. It becomes
less a form of knowledge than a form of "expression." The critics are willing
to surrender the honor of objectivity to science if they may have the luxury
of subjectivity for poetry. Science will scarcely object. But one or two things
have to be said about that. In every experience, even in science, there is feeling. No discourse can sustain itself without interest, which is feeling. The
interest, or the feeling, is like an automatic index to the human value of the
proceeding—which would not otherwise proceed. Mr. Eliseo Vivas is an
esthetician who might be thought to reside in the camp of the enemy, for his
affiliations are positivist; yet in a recent essay he writes about the "passion"
which sustains the heroic labors of the scientist as one bigger and more intense than is given to most men.

I do not mean to differ with that judgment at all in remarking that we might
very well let the passions and the feelings take care of themselves; it is precisely what we do in our pursuit of science. The thing to attend to is the object to which they attach. As between two similar musical phrases, or between
two similar lines of poetry, we may often defy the most proficient psychologist
to distinguish the one feeling-response from the other; unless we permit him
to say at long last that one is the kind of response that would be made to the
first line, and the other is the kind of response that would be made to the
second line. But that is to do, after much wasted motion, what I have just suggested: to attend to the poetic object and let the feelings take care of themselves. It is their business to "respond." There may be a feeling correlative
with the minutest alteration in an object, and adequate to it, but we shall
hardly know. What we do know is that the feelings are grossly inarticulate
if we try to abstract them and take their testimony in their own language.
Since it is not the intent of the critic to be inarticulate, his discriminations
must be among the objects. We understand this so well intuitively that the
critic seems to us in possession of some esoteric knowledge, some magical insight, if he appears to be intelligent elsewhere and yet refers confidently to the
"tone" or "quality" or "value" of the feeling he discovers in a given line. Probably he is bluffing. The distinctness resides in the cognitive or "semantical"
objects denoted by the words. When Richards bewilders us by reporting affective and motor disturbances that are too tiny for definition, and other
critics by reporting disturbances that are too massive and gross, we cannot fail
to grow suspicious of this whole way of insight as incompetent.

Eliot has a special version of psychologistic theory which looks extremely
fertile, though it is broad and nebulous as his psychologistic terms require it
to be. He likes to regard the poem as a structure of emotion and feeling. But
the emotion is singular, there being only one emotion per poem, or at least per

passage: it is the central emotion or big emotion which attaches to the main
theme or situation. The feeling is plural. The emotion combines with many
feelings; these are our little responses to the single words and phrases, and he
does not think of them as being parts of the central emotion or even related
to it. The terminology is greatly at fault, or we should recognize at once, I
think, a principle that might prove very valuable. I would not answer for the
conduct of a technical philosopher in assessing this theory; he might throw it
away, out of patience with its jargon. But a lay philosopher who respects his
Eliot and reads with all his sympathy might salvage a good thing from it,
though I have not heard of anyone doing so. He would try to escape from the
affective terms, and translate Eliot into more intelligible language. Eliot would
be saying in effect that a poem has a central logic or situation or "paraphrasable core" to which an appropriate interest doubtless attaches, and that
in this respect the poem is like a discourse of science behind which lies the
sufficient passion. But he would be saying at the same time, and this is the
important thing, that the poem has also a context of lively local details to
which other and independent interests attach; and that in this respect it is
unlike the discourse of science. For the detail of scientific discourse intends
never to be independent of the thesis (either objectively or affectively) but
always functional, and subordinate to the realization of the thesis. To say that
is to approach to a structural understanding of poetry, and to the kind of understanding that I wish presently to urge.

III

As for the moralistic understanding of poetry, it is sometimes the specific
moralists, men with moral axes to grind, and incidentally men of unassailable
public position, who cherish that; they have a "use" for poetry. But not exclusively, for we may find it held also by critics who are more spontaneous
and innocent: apparently they fall back upon it because it attributes some
special character to poetry, which otherwise refuses to yield up to them a
character. The moral interest is so much more frequent in poetry than in science that they decide to offer its moralism as a differentia.

This conception of poetry is of the greatest antiquity—it antedates the
evolution of close esthetic philosophy, and persists beside it too. Plato sometimes spoke of poetry in this light—perhaps because it was recommended to
him in this light—but nearly always scornfully. In the *Gorgias,* and other
dialogues, he represents the poets as moralizing, and that is only what he, in
the person of Socrates, is doing at the very moment, and given to doing; but
he considers the moralizing of poets as mere "rhetoric," or popular philosophy,
and unworthy of the accomplished moralist who is the real or technical philosopher. Plato understood very well that the poet does not conduct a technical
or an original discourse like that of the scientist—and the term includes here

the moral philosopher—and that close and effective moralizing is scarcely to be had from him. It is not within the poet's power to offer that if his intention is to offer poetry; for the poetry and the morality are so far from being identical that they interfere a little with each other.

Few famous estheticians in the history of philosophy have cared to bother with the moralistic conception; many critics have, in all periods. Just now we have at least two schools of moralistic critics contending for the official possession of poetry. One is the Neo-Humanist, and Mr. Foerster has identified himself with that. The other is the Marxist, and I believe it is represented in some degree and shade by Mr. Wilson, possibly by Mr. Auden. I have myself taken profit from the discussions by both schools, but recently I have taken more—I suppose this is because I was brought up in a scholastic discipline rather like the Neo-Humanist—from the writings of the Marxist critics. One of the differences is that the Neo-Humanists believe in the "respectable" virtues, but the Marxists believe that respectability is the greatest of vices, and equate respectable with "genteel." That is a very striking difference, and I think it is also profound.

But I do not wish to be impertinent; I can respect both these moralities, and appropriate moral values from both. The thing I wish to argue is not the comparative merits of the different moralities by which poetry is judged, but their equal inadequacy to the reading of the poet's intention. The moralistic critics wish to isolate and discuss the "ideology" or theme or paraphrase of the poem and not the poem itself. But even to the practitioners themselves, if they are sophisticated, comes sometimes the apprehension that this is moral rather than literary criticism. I have not seen the papers of my colleagues in this discussion, for that was against the rules, but it is reported to me that both Mr. Wilson and Mr. Foerster concede in explicit words that criticism has both the moral and the esthetic branches; Mr. Wilson may call them the "social" and esthetic branches. And they would hold the critical profession responsible for both branches. Under these circumstances the critics cease to be mere moralists and become dualists; that is better. My feeling about such a position would be that the moral criticism we shall have with us always, and have had always, and that it is easy—comparatively speaking—and that what is hard, and needed, and indeed more and more urgent after all the failures of poetic understanding, is a better esthetic criticism. This is the branch which is all but invariably neglected by the wise but morally zealous critics; they tend to forget their dual responsibility. I think I should go so far as to think that, in strictness, the business of the literary critic is exclusively with an esthetic criticism. The business of the moralist will naturally, and properly, be with something else.

If we have the patience to read for a little while in the anthology, paying some respect to the varieties of substance actually in the poems, we cannot logically attribute ethical character by definition to poetry; for that character is not universal in the poems. And if we have any faith in a community of character among the several arts, we are stopped quickly from risking such a definition for art at large. To claim a moral content for most of sculpture, painting, music, or architecture, is to plan something dialectically very round-about and subtle, or else to be so arbitrary as to invite instant exposure. I should think the former alternative is impractical, and the latter, if it is not stupid, is masochistic.

The moralistic critics are likely to retort upon their accusers by accusing them in turn of the vapid doctrine known as Art for Art's Sake. And with frequent justice; but again we are likely to receive the impression that it is just because Art for Art's Sake, the historic doctrine, proved empty, and availed them so little esthetically, like all the other doctrines that came into default, that they have fled to their moralism. Moralism does at least impute to poetry a positive substance, as Art for Art's Sake does not. It asserts an autonomy for art, which is excellent; but autonomy to do what? Only to be itself, and to reduce its interpreters to a tautology? With its English adherents in the 'nineties the doctrine seemed to make only a negative requirement of art, that is, that it should be anti-Victorian as we should say today, a little bit naughty and immoral perhaps, otherwise at least non-moral, or carefully squeezed dry of moral substance. An excellent example of how two doctrines, inadequate equally but in opposite senses, may keep themselves alive by abhorring each other's errors.

It is highly probable that the poem considers an ethical situation, and there is no reason why it should repel this from its consideration. But, if I may say so without being accused of verbal trifling, the poetic consideration of the ethical situation is not the same as the ethical consideration of it. The straight ethical consideration would be prose; it would be an act of interested science, or an act of practical will. The poetic consideration, according to Schopenhauer, is the objectification of this act of will; that is, it is our contemplation and not our exercise of will, and therefore qualitatively a very different experience; knowledge without desire. That doctrine also seems too negative and indeterminate. I will put the point as I see it in another way. It should be a comfort to the moralist that there is ordinarily a moral composure in the poem, as if the poet had long known good and evil, and made his moral choice between them once and for all. Art is post-ethical rather than unethical. In the poem there is an increment of meaning which is neither the ethical content nor opposed to the ethical content. The poetic experience would have to stop for the poet who is developing it, or for the reader who is following it, if the situation which is being poetically treated should turn back into a situation to be morally determined; if, for example, the situation were not a familiar one, and one to which we had habituated our moral wills; for it would rouse the moral will again to action, and make the poetic treatment impossible under its heat. Art is more cool than hot, and a moral fervor is as disastrous to it as a burst of passion itself. We have seen Marxists recently so revolted by Shakespeare's addiction to royal or noble *personae* that they cannot obtain esthetic experience from the plays; all they get is moral agitation. In another art, we know, and doubtless we approve, the scruple of the college authorities in not permitting the "department of fine arts" to direct the collegians in painting in the nude. Doctor Hanns Sachs, successor to Freud, in a recent number of his *American Imago,* gives a story from a French author as follows:

He tells that one evening strolling along the streets of Paris he noticed a row of slot machines which for a small coin showed pictures of women in full or partial undress. He observed the leering interest with which men of all kind and description, well dressed and shabby, boys and old men, enjoyed the peep show. He remarked that they all avoided one of these machines, and wondering what uninteresting pictures it might show, he put his penny in the slot. To his great astonishment the generally shunned picture turned out to be the Venus of Medici. Now he begins to ponder: Why does nobody get excited about her? She is decidedly feminine and not less naked than the others which hold such strong fascination for everybody. Finally he finds a satisfactory answer: They fight shy of her because she is beautiful.

And Doctor Sachs, though in his own variety of jargon, makes a number of wise observations about the psychic conditions precedent to the difficult apprehension of beauty. The experience called beauty is beyond the powerful ethical will precisely as it is beyond the animal passion, and indeed these last two are competitive, and coordinate. Under the urgency of either we are incapable of appreciating the statue or understanding the poem.

IV

The ostensible substance of the poem may be anything at all which words may signify: an ethical situation, a passion, a train of thought, a flower or landscape, a thing. This substance receives its poetic increment. It might be safer to say it receives some subtle and mysterious alteration under poetic treatment, but I will risk the cruder formula: the ostensible substance is increased by an x, which is an increment. The poem actually continues to contain its ostensible substance, which is not fatally diminished from its prose state: that is its logical core, or paraphrase. The rest of the poem is x, which we are to find.

We feel the working of this simple formula when we approach a poetry with our strictest logic, provided we can find deliverance from certain inhibiting philosophical prepossessions into which we have been conditioned by the critics we have had to read. Here is Lady Macbeth planning a murder with her husband:

When Duncan is asleep—
Whereto the rather shall his hard day's journey
Soundly invite him—his two chamberlains
Will I with wine and wassail so convince,
That memory, the warder of the brain,
Shall be a fume, and the receipt of reason
A limbec only; when in swinish sleep
Their drenched natures lie as in a death,
What cannot you and I perform upon
The unguarded Duncan? what not put upon
His spongy officers, who shall bear the guilt
Of our great quell?

It is easy to produce the prose argument or paraphrase of this speech; it has one upon which we shall all agree. But the passage is more than its argument. Any detail, with this speaker, seems capable of being expanded in some direction which is not that of the argument. For example, Lady Macbeth says she will make the chamberlains drunk so that they will not remember their charge, nor keep their wits about them. But it is indifferent to this argument whether memory according to the old psychology is located at the gateway to the brain, whether it is to be disintegrated into fume as of alcohol, and whether the whole receptacle of the mind is to be turned into a still. These are additions to the argument both energetic and irrelevant—though they do not quite stop or obscure the argument. From the point of view of the philosopher they are excursions into particularity. They give, in spite of the argument, which would seem to be perfectly self-sufficient, a sense of the real density and contingency of the world in which arguments and plans have to be pursued. They bring out the private character which the items of an argument can really assume if we look at them. This character spreads out in planes at right angles to the course of the argument, and in effect gives to the discourse another dimension, not present in a perfectly logical prose. We are expected to have sufficient judgment not to let this local character take us too far or keep us too long from the argument.

All this would seem commonplace remark, I am convinced, but for those philosophically timid critics who are afraid to think that the poetic increment is local and irrelevant, and that poetry cannot achieve its own virtue and keep undiminished the virtues of prose at the same time. But I will go a little further in the hope of removing the sense of strangeness in the analysis. I will offer a figurative definition of a poem.

A poem is, so to speak, a democratic state, whereas a prose discourse—mathematical, scientific, ethical, or practical and vernacular—is a totalitarian state. The intention of a democratic state is to perform the work of state as effectively as it can perform it, subject to one reservation of conscience: that it will not despoil its members, the citizens, of the free exercise of their own private and independent characters. But the totalitarian state is interested solely in being effective, and regards the citizens as no citizens at all; that is, regards them as functional members whose existence is totally defined by their allotted contributions to its ends; it has no use for their private characters, and therefore no provision for them. I indicate of course the extreme or polar opposition between two polities without denying that a polity may come to us rather mixed up.

In this trope the operation of the state as a whole represents of course the logical paraphrase or argument of the poem. The private character of the citizens represents the particularity asserted by the parts in the poem. And this last is our x.

For many years I had seen—as what serious observer has not—that a poem as a discourse differentiated itself from prose by its particularity, yet not to the point of sacrificing its logical cogency or universality. But I could get no further. I could not see how real particularity could get into a universal. The object of esthetic studies became for me a kind of discourse, or a kind of natural configuration, which like any other discourse or configuration claimed universality, but which consisted actually, and notoriously, of particularity. The poem was concrete, yet universal, and in spite of Hegel I could not see how the two properties could be identified as forming in a single unit the "concrete universal." It is usual, I believe, for persons at this stage to assert that somehow the apparent diffuseness or particularity in the poem gets itself taken up or "assimilated" into the logic, to produce a marvellous kind of unity called a "higher unity," to which ordinary discourse is not eligible. The belief is that the "idea" or theme proves itself in poetry to be even more dominating than in prose by overcoming much more energetic resistance than usual on the part of the materials, and the resistance, as attested in the local development of detail, is therefore set not to the debit but to the credit of the unifying power of the poetic spirit. A unity of that kind is one which philosophers less audacious and more factual than Hegel would be loath to claim. Critics incline to call it, rather esoterically, an "imaginative" rather than a logical unity, but one supposes they mean a mystical, an ineffable, unity. I for one could neither grasp it nor deny it. I believe that is not an uncommon situation for poetic analysts to find themselves in.

It occurred to me at last that the solution might be very easy if looked for without what the positivists call "metaphysical prepossessions." Suppose the logical substance remained there all the time, and was in no way specially remarkable, while the particularity came in by accretion, so that the poem turned out partly universal, and partly particular, but with respect to different parts. I began to remark the dimensions of a poem, or other work of art. The poem was not a mere moment in time, nor a mere point in space. It was sizeable, like a house. Apparently it had a "plan," or a central frame of logic, but it had also a huge wealth of local detail, which sometimes fitted the plan functionally or served it, and sometimes only subsisted comfortably under it; in either case the house stood up. But it was the political way of thinking which gave me the first analogy which seemed valid. The poem was like a democratic state, in action, and observed both macroscopically and microscopically.

The house occurred also, and provided what seems to be a more negotiable trope under which to construe the poem. A poem is a *logical structure* having a *local texture*. These terms have been actually though not systematically employed in literary criticism. To my imagination they are architectural. The walls of my room are obviously structural; the beams and boards have a function; so does the plaster, which is the visible aspect of the final wall. The plaster might have remained naked, aspiring to no character, and purely functional. But actually it has been painted, receiving color; or it has been papered, receiving color and design, though these have no structural value; and perhaps it has been hung with tapestry, or with paintings, for "decoration." The paint, the paper, the tapestry are texture. It is logically unrelated to structure. But I indicate only a few of the textural possibilities in architecture. There are not fewer of them in poetry.

The intent of the good critic becomes therefore to examine and define the poem with respect to its structure and its texture. If he has nothing to say about its texture he has nothing to say about it specifically as a poem, but is treating it only insofar as it is prose.

I do not mean to say that the good critic will necessarily employ my terms.

V

Many critics today are writing analytically and with close intelligence, in whatever terms, about the logical substance or structure of the poem, and its increment of irrelevant local substance or texture. I believe that the understanding of the ideal critic has to go even further than that. The final desideratum is an ontological insight, nothing less. I am committed by my title to a representation of criticism as, in the last resort, a speculative exercise. But my secret committal was to speculative in the complete sense of—ontological.

There is nothing especially speculative or ontological in reciting, or even appraising, the logical substance of the poem. This is its prose core—its science perhaps, or its ethics if it seems to have an ideology. Speculative interest asserts itself principally when we ask why we want the logical substance to be compounded with the local substance, the good lean structure with a great volume of texture that does not function. It is the same thing as asking why we want the poem to be what it is.

It has been a rule, having the fewest exceptions, for estheticians and great philosophers to direct their speculations by the way of overstating and over-valuing the logical substance. They are impressed by the apparent obedience of material nature, whether in fact or in art, to definable form or "law" imposed upon it. They like to suppose that in poetry, as in chemistry, everything that figures in the discourse means to be functional, and that the poem is imperfect in the degree that it contains items, whether by accident or intention, which manifest a private independence. It is a bias with which we are entirely familiar, and reflects the extent to which our philosophy hitherto has been impressed by the successes of science in formulating laws which would "govern" their objects. Probably I am here reading the state of mind of yesterday rather than of today. Nevertheless we know it. The world-view which ultimately forms itself in the mind so biassed is that of a world which is rational and intelligible. The view is sanguine, and naïve. Hegel's world-view, I think it is agreed, was a subtle version of this, and if so, it was what determined his view of art. He seemed to make the handsomest concession to realism by offering to knowledge a kind of universal which was not restricted to the usual abstracted aspects of the material, but included all aspects, and was a concrete universal. The concreteness in Hegel's handling was not honestly, or at any rate not fairly, defended. It was always represented as being in process of pointing up and helping out the universality. He could look at a work of art and report all its substance as almost assimilated to a ruling "idea." But at least Hegel seemed to distinguish what looked like two ultimate sorts of substance there, and stated the central esthetic problem as the problem of relating them. And his writings about art are speculative in the sense that he regarded the work of art not as of great intrinsic value necessarily, but as an object-lesson or discipline in the understanding of the world-process, and as its symbol.

I think of two ways of construing poetry with respect to its ultimate purpose; of which the one is not very handsome nor speculatively interesting, and the other will appear somewhat severe.

The first construction would picture the poet as a sort of epicure, and the poem as something on the order of a Christmas pudding, stuffed with what dainties it will hold. The pastry alone, or it may be the cake, will not serve; the stuffing is wanted too. The values of the poem would be intrinsic, or immediate, and they would include not only the value of the structure but also the incidental values to be found in the texture. If we exchange the pudding for a house, they would include not only the value of the house itself but also the value of the furnishings. In saying intrinsic or immediate, I mean that the poet is fond of the precise objects denoted by the words, and writes the poem for the reason that he likes to dwell upon them. In talking about the main value and the incidental values I mean to recognize the fact that the latter engage the affections just as truly as the former. Poetic discourse therefore would be more agreeable than prose to the epicure or the literally acquisi-

tive man; for prose has but a single value, being about one thing only; its parts
have no values of their own, but only instrumental values, which might be
reckoned as fractions of the single value proportionate to their contributions to
it. The prose is one-valued and the poem is many-valued. Indeed there will
certainly be poems whose texture contains many precious objects, and aggre-
gates a greater value than the structure.

So there would be a comfortable and apparently eligible view that poetry
improves on prose because it is a richer diet. It causes five or six pleasures to
appear, five or six good things, where one had been before; an alluring consideration for robustious, full-blooded, bourgeois souls. The view will account
for much of the poem, if necessary. But it does not account for all of it, and
sometimes it accounts for less than at other times.

The most impressive reason for the bolder view of art, the speculative one,
is the existence of the "pure," or "abstractionist," or non-representational works
of art; though these will probably occur to us in other arts than poetry. There
is at least one art, music, whose works are all of this sort. Tones are not words,
they have no direct semantical function, and by themselves they mean nothing. But they combine to make brilliant phrases, harmonies, and compositions.
In these compositions it is probable that the distinction between structure or
functional content, on the one hand, and texture or local variation and departure, on the other, is even more determinate than in an impure art like
poetry. The world of tones seems perfectly inhuman and impracticable; there
is no specific field of experience "about which" music is telling us. Yet we
know that music is powerfully affective. I take my own musical feelings, and
those attested by other audients, as the sufficient index to some overwhelming
human importance which the musical object has for us. At the same time it
would be useless to ask the feelings precisely what they felt; we must ask the
critic. The safest policy is to take the simplest construction, and try to impro-
vise as little fiction as possible. Music is not music, I think, until we grasp its
effects both in structure and in texture. As we grow in musical understanding
the structures become always more elaborate and sustained, and the texture
which interrupts them and sometimes imperils them becomes more bold and
unpredictable. We can agree in saying about the works of music that these
are musical structures, and they are richly textured; we can identify these
elements, and perhaps precisely. To what then do our feelings respond? To
music as structural composition itself; to music as manifesting the structural
principles of the world; to modes of structure which we feel to be ontologically
possible, or even probable. Schopenhauer construed music very much in that
sense. Probably it will occur to us that musical compositions bear close analogy
therefore to operations in pure mathematics. The mathematicians confess that
their constructions are "non-existential"; meaning, as I take it, that the constructions testify with assurance only to the structural principles, in the light

of which they are possible but may not be actual, or if they are actual may not be useful. This would define the mathematical operations as speculative: as motivated by an interest so generalized and so elemental that no word short of ontological will describe it.

But if music and mathematics have this much in common, they differ sharply in their respective world-views or ontological biases. That of music, with its prodigious display of texture, seems the better informed about the nature of the world, the more realistic, the less naïve. Perhaps the difference is between two ontological educations. But I should be inclined to imagine it as rising back of that point: in two ontological temperaments.

There are also, operating a little less successfully so far as the indexical evidences would indicate, the abstractionist paintings, of many schools, and perhaps also works of sculpture; and there is architecture. These arts have tried to abandon direct representational intention almost as heroically as music. They exist in their own materials and indicate no other specific materials; structures of color, light, space, stone—the cheapest of materials. They too can symbolize nothing of value unless it is structure or composition itself. But that is precisely the act which denotes will and intelligence; which becomes the act of fuller intelligence if it carefully accompanies its structures with their material textures; for then it understands better the ontological nature of materials.

Returning to the poetry. It is not all poems, and not even all "powerful" poems, having high index-ratings, whose semantical meanings contain situations important in themselves or objects precious in themselves. There may be little correlation between the single value of the poem and the aggregate value of its contents—just as there is no such correlation whatever in music. The "effect" of the poem may be astonishingly disproportionate to our interest in its materials. It is true, of course, that there is no art employing materials of equal richness with poetry, and that it is beyond the capacity of poetry to employ indifferent materials. The words used in poetry are the words the race has already formed, and naturally they call attention to things and events that have been thought to be worth attending to. But I suggest that any poetry which is "technically" notable is in part a work of abstractionist art, concentrating upon the structure and the texture, and the structure-texture relation, out of a pure speculative interest.

At the end of *Love's Labour's Lost* occurs a little diversion which seems proportionately far more effective than that laborious play as a whole. The play is over, but Armado stops the principals before they disperse to offer them a show:

ARMADO. But, most esteemed greatness, will you hear the dialogue that the two learned men have compiled in praise of the owl and the cuckoo? It should have followed in the end of our show.

KING.   Call them forth quickly; we will do so.
ARMADO.   Holla! approach.
Re-enter Holofernes, etc.
    This side is Hiems, Winter, this Ver, the Spring; the one maintained
by the owl, the other by the cuckoo. Ver, begin.

THE SONG

SPRING.   When daisies pied and violets blue
     And lady-smocks all silver-white
     And cuckoo-buds of yellow hue
     Do paint the meadows with delight,
     The cuckoo then, on every tree,
     Mocks married men; for thus sings he,
          Cuckoo;
     Cuckoo, cuckoo: O word of fear,
     Unpleasing to a married ear!

     When shepherds pipe on oaten straws,
     And merry larks are ploughmen's clocks,
     When turtles tread, and rooks, and daws,
     And maidens bleach their summer smocks,
     The cuckoo then, on every tree,
     Mocks married men; for thus sings he,
          Cuckoo;
     Cuckoo, cuckoo: O word of fear,
     Unpleasing to a married ear!

WINTER.   When icicles hang by the wall,
     And Dick the shepherd blows his nail,
     And Tom bears logs into the hall,
     And milk comes frozen home in pail,
     When blood is nipp'd and ways be foul,
     Then nightly sings the staring owl,
          Tu-who;
     Tu-whit, tu-who, a merry note,
     While greasy Joan doth keel the pot.

     When all aloud the wind doth blow,
     And coughing drowns the parson's saw,
     And birds sit brooding in the snow,
     And Marian's nose looks red and raw,
     When roasted crabs hiss in the bowl,
     Then nightly sings the staring owl,
          Tu-who;
     Tu-whit, tu-who, a merry note,
     While greasy Joan doth keel the pot.

ARMADO. The words of Mercury are harsh after the songs of Apollo.
You that way,—we this way. (*Exeunt.*)

The feeling-index registers such strong approval of this episode that a critic with ambition is obliged to account for it. He can scarcely account for it in terms of the weight of its contents severally.

At first glance Shakespeare has provided only a pleasant little caricature of the old-fashioned (to us, medieval) debate between personified characters. It is easygoing, like nonsense; no labor is lost here. Each party speaks two stanzas and concludes both stanzas with the refrain about his bird, the cuckoo or the owl. There is no generalized argument, or dialectic proper. Each argues by citing his characteristic exhibits. In the first stanza Spring cites some flowers; in the second stanza, some business by country persons, with interpolation of some birds that make love. Winter in both his stanzas cites the country business of the season. In the refrain the cuckoo, Spring's symbol, is used to refer the love-making to more than the birds; and this repeats itself, though it is naughty. The owl is only a nominal symbol for Winter, an "emblem" that is not very emblematic, but the refrain manages another reference to the kitchen, and repeats itself, as if Winter's pleasure focussed in the kitchen.

In this poem texture is not very brilliant, but it eclipses structure. The argument, we would say in academic language, is concerned with "the relative advantages of Spring and Winter." The only logical determinateness this structure has is the good coordination of the items cited by Spring as being really items peculiar to Spring, and of the Winter items as peculiar to Winter. The symbolic refrains look like summary or master items, but they seem to be a little more than summary and in fact to mean a little more than they say. The argument is trifling on the whole, and the texture from the point of view of felt human importance lacks decided energy; both which observations are to be made, and most precisely, of how many famous lyrics, especially those before that earnest and self-conscious nineteenth century! The value of the poem is greater than the value of its parts: that is what the critic is up against.

Unquestionably it is possible to assemble very fine structures out of ordinary materials. The good critic will study the poet's technique, in confidence that here the structural principles will be discovered at home. In this study he will find as much range for his activities as he desires.

Especially must he study the metrics, and their implications for structural composition. In this poem I think the critic ought to make good capital of the contrast between the amateurishness of the pleasant discourse as meaning and the hard determinate form of it phonetically. The meter on the whole is out of relation to the meaning of the poem, or to anything else specifically; it is a musical material of low grade, but plastic and only slightly resistant material, and its presence in every poem is that of an abstractionist element that belongs to the art.

And here I will suggest another analogy, this one between Shakespeare's poem and some ordinary specimen of painting. It does not matter how old-fashioned or representational the painting is, we shall all, if we are instructed in the tradition of this art, require it to exhibit along with its represented object an abstract design in terms of pure physical balance or symmetry. We sense rather than measure the success of this design, but it is as if we had drawn a horizontal axis and a vertical axis through the center of the picture, and required the painted masses to balance with respect to each of these two axes. This is an over-simple statement of a structural requirement by which the same details function in two worlds that are different, and that do not correlate with each other. If the painting is of the Holy Family, we might say that this object has a drama, or an economy, of its own, but that the physical masses which compose it must enter also into another economy, that of abstract design; and that the value of any unit mass for the one economy bears no relation to its value for the other. The painting is of great ontological interest because it embodies this special dimension of abstract form. And turning to the poem, we should find that its represented "meaning" is analogous to the represented object in the painting, while its meter is analogous to the pure design.

A number of fascinating speculative considerations must follow upon this discovery. They will have to do with the most fundamental laws of this world's structure. They will be profoundly ontological, though I do not mean they must be ontological in some recondite sense; ontological in such a homely and compelling sense that perhaps a child might intuit the principles which the critic will arrive at analytically, and with much labor.

I must stop at this point, since I am desired not so much to anticipate the critic as to present him. In conclusion I will remark that the critic will doubtless work empirically, and set up his philosophy only as the drift of his findings will compel him. But ultimately he will be compelled. He will have to subscribe to an ontology. If he is a sound critic his ontology will be that of his poets; and what is that? I suggest that the poetic world-view is Aristotelian and "realistic" rather than Platonic and "idealistic." He cannot follow the poets and still conceive himself as inhabiting the rational or "tidy" universe that is supposed by the scientists.

From *The Intent of the Critic* edited, with an Introduction, by Donald A. Stauffer, pp. 91–124. Copyright, 1941, by Princeton University Press. Reprinted by permission of the author and publishers.

HARRY LEVIN

Literature as an Institution

[1946]

I. THE CONTRIBUTION OF TAINE

"LITERATURE is the expression of society, as speech is the expression of man."
In this aphorism the Vicomte de Bonald summed up one of the bitter lessons
that the French Revolution had taught the world. With the opening year of
the nineteenth century, and the return of the Emigration, coincided a two-
volume study by Madame de Staël: *De la Littérature considérée dans ses rap-
ports avec les institutions sociales.* This was not the first time, of course, that
some relationship had been glimpsed. Renaissance humanism, fighting out the
invidious quarrel between ancient and modern literatures, had concluded that
each was the unique creation of its period, and had adumbrated a historical
point of view. Romantic nationalism, seeking to undermine the prestige of the
neo-classic school and to revive the native traditions of various countries, was
now elaborating a series of geographical comparisons. It was left for Hippolyte
Taine—in the vanguard of a third intellectual movement, scientific positivism
—to formulate a sociological approach. To the historical and geographical
factors, the occasional efforts of earlier critics to discuss literature in terms of
"moment" and "race," he added a third conception, which completed and
finally eclipsed them. "Milieu," as he conceived it, is the link between literary
criticism and the social sciences. Thus Taine raised a host of new problems by
settling an old one.

When Taine's history of English literature appeared, it smelled—to a contemporary reader, Amiel—like the exhalations from a laboratory. To that sensitive Swiss idealist, it conveyed a whiff of "the literature of the future in the
American style," of "the death of poetry flayed and anatomized by science."
This "intrusion of technology into literature," as Amiel was shrewd enough to
observe, is a responsibility which Taine shares with Balzac and Stendhal. As
Taine self-consciously remarked, "From the novel to criticism and from criticism to the novel, the distance at present is not very great." Taine's critical
theory is grounded upon the practice of the realists, while their novels are
nothing if not critical. His recognition of the social forces behind literature
coincides with their resolution to embody those forces in their works. The first

to acknowledge Stendhal as a master, he welcomed Flaubert as a colleague and lived to find Zola among his disciples. "When M. Taine studies Balzac," Zola acknowledged, "he does exactly what Balzac himself does when he studies Père Grandet." There is no better way to bridge the distance between criticism and the novel, or to scrutinize the presuppositions of modern literature, than by a brief reconsideration of Taine's critical method.

A tougher-minded reader than Amiel, Flaubert, noted in 1864 that—whatever the *Histoire de la littérature anglaise* left unsettled—it got rid of the uncritical notion that books dropped like meteorites from the sky. The social basis of art might thereafter be overlooked, but it could hardly be disputed. Any lingering belief in poetic inspiration could hardly withstand the higher criticism that had disposed of spontaneous generation and was disposing of divine revelation. When Renan, proclaiming his disbelief in mysteries, depicted Jesus as the son of man and analyzed the origins of Christianity, then Taine could depict genius as the outgrowth of environment and analyze the origins of literature. On the whole, though critics have deplored the crudity of his analyses and scholars have challenged the accuracy of his facts, his working hypothesis has won acceptance. He has become the stock example of a rigorous determinist—especially for those who think determinism is a modern version of fatalism. Taine's determinism, however, is simply an intensive application of the intellectual curiosity of his age. It is no philosopher's attempt to encroach upon the freedom of the artist's will; it is simply a historian's consciousness of what the past has already determined.

As for Taine's rigor, a more thoroughgoing historical materialist, George Plekhanov, has gone so far as to accuse him of arrant idealism. A recent artist-philosopher, Jean-Paul Sartre, describes Taine's empiricism as an unsuccessful effort to set up a realistic system of metaphysics. Actually his position is that of most realists, so outrageous to their early readers and so tame to later critics. His method explained too much to satisfy his contemporaries; it has not explained enough to satisfy ours. Confronted with the provocative statement, "Vice and virtue are products like vitriol and sugar," we are not shocked by the audacity that reduces moral issues to chemical formulae; we are amused at the naïveté that undertakes to solve them both by a single equation. Taine's introduction to his history of English literature, which abounds in dogmas of this sort, is rather a manifesto than a methodology. If, reading on, we expect the history to practice what the introduction preaches, we are amiably disappointed. Each successive author is more freely individualized. How does Taine's all-determining scheme meet its severest test? With Shakespeare, he explains, after canvassing the material factors, "all comes from within—I mean from his soul and his genius; circumstances and externals have contributed but little to his development."

The loophole that enables Taine to avoid the strict consequences of his three determinants is a fourth—a loose system of psychology. Psychology takes over where sociology has given up, and the sociologist has shown surprisingly little interest in classes or institutions. He has viewed history as a parade of influential individuals, themselves the creatures of historical influences. To understand their achievements is "a problem in psychological mechanics." The psychologist must disclose their ruling passions; he must hit upon that magnificent obsession, that "master faculty" which conditions have created within the soul of every great man. Let us not be put off by the circular logic, the mechanical apparatus, and the scientific jargon: Taine, conscientious child of his temperament and time, was an ardent individualist. His theory of character owes quite as much to Balzac as his theory of environment owes to Stendhal. Had it been the other way around, had he combined Stendhal's psychological insight with Balzac's sociological outlook, he might have been a better critic. His portrait of Balzac, for better or worse, is as monomaniacal as Balzac's portrait of Grandet.

Psychology is a knife, Dostoevsky warns us, which cuts two ways. We may look for a man in his books, or we may look to the man for the explanation of his books. Taine's is the more dangerous way: to deduce the qualities of a work from a presupposition about the author. The whole *Comédie humaine* follows from the consideration that Balzac was a business man, and Livy's history is what you might expect from a writer who was really an orator. This mode of critical characterization must perforce be limited to a few broad strokes, much too exaggerated and impressionistic to be compared with the detailed nuances of Sainte-Beuve's portraiture. Most of Taine's figures bear a strong family likeness. He is most adroit at bringing out the generic traits of English literature: the response to nature, the puritan strain, the fact—in short—that it was written by Englishmen. He himself, true to his theories, remains an intransigent Frenchman, and his history—to the point where he abandons Tennyson for Musset and recrosses the channel—remains a traveler's survey of a foreign culture. Why, in spite of all temptations to interpret other cultures, should Taine have been attracted to England?

Taine's critical faculties were conditioned not by science but by romanticism, and who was Taine to repudiate his own conditioning? Madame de Staël had been drawn to Germany, and Melchior de Vogüé would soon be seeking the Russian soul, but English was for most Frenchmen the typically romantic literature. France had been the Bastille of classicism, while Britain had never been enslaved to the rules; untamed nature, in Saxon garb, resisted the shackles of Norman constraint. It took very little perception of the technique of English poetry for Taine to prefer blank verse to Alexandrines. Form, as he construed it, was a body of artificial restrictions which inhibited free expression, and which English men of letters had somehow succeeded in doing without. One might almost say that they had developed a literature of pure content. "Not in Greece, nor in Italy, nor in Spain, nor in France," said Taine, "has an art been seen which tried so boldly to express the soul and the most intimate depths of the soul, the reality and the whole reality." What seemed to him so unprecedented is, on closer scrutiny, a complex tradition. Elizabethan drama is so much more baroque than the succinct tragedies of Racine that Taine missed its pattern altogether, and believed he was facing a chaos of first-hand and unconstrained realities. His impressions were those of Fielding's barber Partridge at the play, wholly taken in by theatrical make-believe, naïvely mistaking the actors for the characters they represent, quixotically confusing literature with life.

2. SOCIOLOGICAL CRITICISM AND SOCIAL CRITICS

Remembering Lamb's essay on the artificiality of Restoration comedy, we cannot share Taine's facile assumption that the English stage received and retained "the exact imprint of the century and the nation." We cannot accept this free translation of Hamlet's impulse to give "the very age and body of the time his form and pressure." We can admit that Taine was less of a critic than a historian, but we cannot forgive him for being such an uncritical historian. His professed willingness to trade quantities of charters for the letters of Saint Paul or the memoirs of Cellini does not indicate a literary taste; it merely states a preference for human documents as against constitutional documents. In exploiting literature for purposes of historical documentation, Taine uncovered a new mine of priceless source material. But he never learned the difference between ore and craftsmanship. In his *Philosophie de l'art,* to be sure, he could no longer sidestep esthetic and technical discussion. He was forced to concede that art could be idealistic as well as realistic, and to place Greek sculpture at a farther remove from reality than Flemish painting. This concession allowed him to turn his back on the sculpture, and to reconstruct, with a freer hand than ever, the moment, the race, and the milieu of ancient Greece.

The serious objection to environmentalism is that it failed to distinguish, not between one personality and another, but between personality and art. It encouraged scholars to write literary histories which, as Ferdinand Brunetière pointed out, were nothing but chronological dictionaries of literary biography. It discouraged the realization, which Brunetière called the evolution of *genres,* that literary technique had a history of its own. It advanced a brilliant generalization, and established—as first-rate ideas will do in second-rate minds—a rule of thumb. The incidental and qualified extent to which books epitomize their epoch may vary from one example to the next. Taine's successors made no allowances for the permutations of form; rather they industrialized his process for extracting the contents of the books. The prevailing aim of literary historiography, under the sponsorship of Gustave Lanson in France and other professors elsewhere, has been a kind of illustrated supplement to history. Academic research has concentrated so heavily on the backgrounds of literature that the foreground has been almost obliterated.

Meanwhile Taine's influence has been felt in the wider areas of criticism, and here it has been subordinated to political ends. Taine himself was bitterly anti-political. He did not realize the importance of ideas until he had lost faith in his own: originally he had been a proponent of the doctrines of the *philosophes,* which he blamed in his later studies, *Les Origines de la France contemporaine,* for instigating the revolution of 1789. It was a Danish critic, closely associated with Ibsen, Nietzsche, and the controversies of the eighties, who broadened the range and narrowed the tendency of literary history. For politics, and for literature too, Georg Brandes had more feeling than Taine. A cosmopolitan liberal, deeply suspicious of the ascendancy of Prussia, he found a touchstone for the romanticists in their struggles or compromises with clerical reaction and the authority of the state. Byron and Heine were his urbane prophets, the Schlegels were renegades, and the revolution of 1848 was the anticlimax toward which his *Main Currents of Nineteenth Century Literature* moved. Where a book had been an end-product to Taine, to Brandes it was continuing force, and the critic's function was to chart its repercussions.

Both aspects have been duly stressed in the critical interpretation of American writers—their reactions to their environment and their contributions to the liberal tradition. Our foremost literary historian, V. L. Parrington, extended and modified Taine's formula to fit our problems, dramatizing New England puritanism from the standpoint of western populism, and pitting a heroic Jefferson against a sinister Hamilton. His title, *Main Currents in American Thought,* conveyed a fraternal salute to Brandes, and denoted an additional qualification. Parrington got around Taine's difficulty—the difficulty of using imaginative writers as historical sources—by drawing upon the moralists and the publicists. His chapters on Roger Williams and John Marshall are ample and rewarding; his accounts of Poe and Henry James are so trivial that they might better have been omitted. The latest period is inevitably the hardest and his last volume is posthumous and fragmentary, but it seems to mark an increasing conflict between artistic and political standards. Granville Hicks, going over the same ground, was able to resolve that conflict by the simple device of discarding artistic standards.

Mr. Hicks, if he still adheres to his somewhat elusive conception of *The Great Tradition,* is a Marxist critic in the sense that Parrington was a Jeffersonian critic. The choice between them is largely a matter of political standards. Jeffersonianism, naturally the most favorable climate in which to discuss American literature, has been taken in vain so often that it has begun to resist definition. Marxism, by redefining milieu in economic terms, has presented a more rigorous theory of historical causation than Taine's and a more ruthless canon of political allegiance than Brandes'. It has introduced criticism to a sociological system which is highly illuminating and a social doctrine which is highly controversial. It has tightened the relations between literature and life by oversimplifying them beyond recognition. In this respect Karl Marx, as he occasionally confessed, was no Marxist: he repeatedly cautioned his followers against expecting the arts to show a neat conformity with his views. Perhaps if he had written his projected study of Balzac, he would have bequeathed them a critical method. For lack of one, they took what was available. Marxist criticism superimposed its socialistic doctrine on the deterministic method, and judged according to Marx what it had interpreted according to Taine.

Extension and modification have added their corollary to Taine's method: the relations between literature and society are reciprocal. Literature is not only the effect of social causes; it is also the cause of social effects. The critic may investigate its causes, as Taine tried to do; or he may, like Brandes and others, be more interested in its effects. So long as he is correlating works of art with trends of history, his function is relatively clear. It becomes less clear as he encounters his contemporaries, and as the issues become more immediate. He is then concerned, no longer with a secure past, but with a problematic future. An insecure present may commit him to some special partisanship, Marxist or otherwise, and incline him to judge each new work by its possible effect—whether it will advance or hinder his party's program. Since art can be a weapon, among other things, it will be judged in the heat of the battle by its polemical possibilities. We need not deny the relevance or significance of such judgments; we need only recognize that they carry us beyond the limits of esthetic questions into the field of moral values. There are times when criticism cannot conveniently stop at the border. Whenever there are boundary disputes, questions involving propaganda or regulation, we may be called upon to go afield. We shall be safe while we are aware that virtue and beauty are as intimately related as beauty and truth, and as eternally distinct.

3. THE RÔLE OF CONVENTION[1]

It was as if Taine had discovered that the earth was round, without realizing that another continent lay between Europe and Asia. The distance was longer, the route more devious, than sociological criticism had anticipated. Not that the intervening territory was unexplored; but those who had explored it most thoroughly were isolationists. Those who were most familiar with the techniques and traditions of literature were least conscious of its social responsibilities. Most of them were writers themselves, lacking in critical method perhaps,

---

[1] Mr. Levin's discussion of convention is further developed in another essay, "Notes on Convention," included in *Perspectives of Criticism,* edited by Harry Levin and published by the Harvard University Press, Cambridge, 1950. (Editor's note, 1950.)

yet possessing the very skills and insights that the methodologists lacked. A few were philosophers, striving—on the high plane of idealism—toward a historical synthesis of the arts. Their concept of expressive form, inherited by the esthetic of Croce from the literary history of Francesco de Sanctis, resembles the "organic principle" that Anglo-American criticism inherits from the theory of Coleridge, the preaching of Emerson, and the practice of Thoreau. By whichever name, it is too sensitive an instrument to be used effectively, except by acute critics on acknowledged masterpieces. With cruder material, in unskilled hands, its insistence on the uniqueness of each work of art and its acceptance of the artist at his own evaluation dissolve into esthetic impressionism and romantic hero-worship.

While this school is responsible for many admirable critiques, it has never produced that "new criticism" which the late J. E. Spingarn tried vainly to define. Conceiving art as the fullest expression of individuality, it has disregarded the more analytic approaches. Taine's school, though less discriminating, has been more influential, because it conceives art as a collective expression of society. The fallacy in this conception—we have already seen—is to equate art with society, to assume a one-to-one correspondence between a book and its subject-matter, to accept the literature of an age as a complete and exact replica of the age itself. One way or another, literature is bound to tell the truth; but it has told the whole truth very seldom, and nothing but the truth hardly ever; some things are bound to be left out, and others to be exaggerated in the telling. Sins of omission can usually be traced to some restriction in the artist's freedom of speech, his range of experience, or his control of his medium. Sins of commission are inherent in the nature of his materials. The literary historian must reckon with these changing degrees of restriction and exaggeration. Literary history, if it is to be accurate, must be always correcting its aim.

To mention one conspicuous case, the relations between the sexes have received a vast—possibly a disproportionate—amount of attention from writers. From their miscellaneous and contradictory testimony it would be rash to infer very much, without allowing for the artistic taboos of one period or the exhibitionism of another. An enterprising sociologist, by measuring the exposed portions of the human figure in various paintings, has arrived at a quantitative historical index of comparative sensuality. What inference could not be drawn, by some future sciolist, from the preponderance of detective stories on the shelves of our circulating libraries? Those volumes testify, for us, to the colorless comfort of their readers' lives. We are aware, because we are not dependent on literary evidence, that ours is no unparalleled epoch of domestic crime—of utterly ineffectual police, of criminals who bear all the earmarks of innocence, and of detectives whose nonchalance is only equalled by their erudition. These, we are smugly aware, have not much more sig-

nificance than the counters of a complicated game. Nevertheless, it is disturbing to imagine what literal-minded critics may deduce when the rules of the
game have been forgotten. It suggests that we ourselves may be misreading
other books through our ignorance of the lost conventions on which they
hinge.

Convention may be described as a necessary difference between art and life.
Some differences, strictly speaking, may be quite unnecessary: deliberate
sallies of the imagination, unconscious effects of miscalculation or misunderstanding. But art must also differ from life for technical reasons: limitations of
form, difficulties of expression. The artist, powerless to overcome these obstacles by himself, must have the assistance of his audience. They must agree
to take certain formalities and assumptions for granted, to take the word for
the deed or the shading for the shadow. The result of their unspoken agreement is a compromise between the possibilities of life and the exigencies of
art. Goethe might have been speaking of convention when he said, *"In der
Beschränkung zeigt sich erst der Meister."*[2] Limitation has often been a source
of new forms, and difficulty—as the defenders of rhyme have argued, from
Samuel Daniel to Paul Valéry—has prompted poets to their most felicitous
expressions. Without some sort of conventionalization art could hardly exist. It
exists by making virtues of necessities; after the necessities disappear, we forget the conventions. After perspective is invented, we misjudge the primitives; after scenery is set up, we challenge the unities. And Taine, forgetting
that feminine roles were played by boys, is appalled at finding masculine traits
in Elizabethan heroines.

His former classmate, Francisque Sarcey, who became—through forty years
of playgoing—the most practical of critics, might have supplied the needed
correction for Taine's theories. "It is inadequate to repeat that the theater is a
representation of human life," Sarcey had learned. "It would be a more precise definition to say that dramatic art is the sum of conventions, universal or
local, eternal or temporary, which help—when human life is represented on
the stage—to give a public the illusion of truth." This illusion may be sustained in the novel more easily than on the stage; but it is still an illusion, as
Maupassant frankly admitted. Although drama may be the most conventional
of literary forms, and fiction the least, even fiction is not entirely free. Even
Proust, the most unconventional of novelists, must resort to the convention of
eavesdropping in order to sustain the needs of first-person narrative. We need
not condone such melodramatic stratagems; we can observe that the modern
novel has endeavored to get along without them; upon fuller consideration we
may even conclude that the whole modern movement of realism, technically
considered, is an endeavor to emancipate literature from the sway of conventions.

[2] "The true master first reveals himself when he works under limitations."

4. TOWARD AN INSTITUTIONAL METHOD

This provisional conclusion would explain why literary historians, under the influence of realism, have slighted literary form. In their impatience to lay bare the so-called content of a work, they have missed a more revealing characteristic: the way the artist handles the appropriate conventions. Whether it is possible, or even desirable, to eliminate artifice from art—that is one of the largest questions that criticism must face. But realistic novelists who declare their intentions of transcribing life have an obvious advantage over realistic critics who expect every book to be a literal transcript. Stendhal, when he declares that "a novel is a mirror riding along a highway," is in a position to fulfil his picaresque intention. When Taine echoes this precept, defining the novel as "a kind of portable mirror which can be conveyed everywhere, and which is most convenient for reflecting all aspects of nature and life," he puts the mirror before the horse. He is then embarrassed to discover so few reflections of the *ancien régime* in French novels of the eighteenth century. His revulsion from neo-classical generalities and his preference for descriptive details carry him back across the channel, from Marmontel and Crébillon *fils* to Fielding and Smollett. Some mirrors, Taine finally discovered, are less reliable than others.

The metaphor of the mirror held up to nature, the idea that literature reflects life, was mentioned by Plato only to be rejected. By the time of Cicero it was already a commonplace of criticism. It was applied by the ancients to comedy, the original vehicle of realism, later it became a byword for artistic didacticism, for the medieval zeal to see vice exposed and virtue emulated. When Shakespeare invoked it, he had a definite purpose which those who quote him commonly ignore. Hamlet is not merely describing a play, he is exhorting the players. His advice is a critique of bad acting as well as an apology for the theater, a protest against unnatural conventions as well as a plea for realism. Like modern critics who derive their metaphors from photography, he implies a further comparison with more conventionalized modes of art—particularly with painting. To hold up a photograph or a mirror, as it were, is to compare the "abstract and brief chronicles of the time" with the distorted journeywork that "imitated humanity so abominably." Art should be a reflection of life, we are advised, not a distortion—as it has all too frequently been. Criticism, in assuming that art invariably reflects and forgetting that it frequently distorts, wafts us through the looking-glass into a sphere of its own, where everything is clear and cool, logical and literal, and more surrealistic than real.

In questioning the attempts of scholars to utilize Shakespeare as the mirror of his time, Professor Stoll has reminded them that their business is to separate historical fact from literary illusion, to distinguish the object from its reflected image. Literature, instead of reflecting life, refracts it. Our task, in any given case, is to determine the angle of refraction. Since the angle depends upon the density of the medium, it is always shifting, and the task is never easy. We are aided today, however, by a more flexible and accurate kind of critical apparatus than Taine was able to employ. An acquaintance with artistic conventions, which can best be acquired through comparative studies in technique, should complement an awareness of social backgrounds. "Literature is complementary to life." This formula of Lanson's is broad enough to include the important proviso that there is room in the world of art for ideals and projects, fantasies and anxieties, which do not ordinarily find a habitation in the world of reality. But, in recognizing that literature adds something to life or that it subtracts something from life, we must not overlook the most important consideration of all—that literature is at all times an intrinsic part of life. It is, if we can work out the implications of Leslie Stephen's phrase, "a particular function of the whole social organism."

The organic character of this relationship has been most explicitly formulated by a statesman and historian, Prosper de Barante. Writing of the ideas behind the French revolution while they were still fresh in men's minds, his comprehension of their political interplay was broader than Taine's. "In the absence of regular institutions," wrote Barante, "literature became one." The truth, though it has long been obscured by a welter of personalities and technicalities, is that literature has always been an institution. Like other institutions, the church or the law, it cherishes a unique phase of human experience and controls a special body of precedents and devices; it tends to incorporate a self-perpetuating discipline, while responding to the main currents of each succeeding period; it is continually accessible to all the impulses of life at large, but it must translate them into its own terms and adapt them to its peculiar forms. Once we have grasped this fact, we begin to perceive how art may belong to society and yet be autonomous within its own limits, and are no longer puzzled by the apparent polarity of social and formal criticism. These, in the last analysis, are complementary frames of reference whereby we may discriminate the complexities of a work of art. In multiplying these discriminations between external impulses and internal peculiarities—in other words, between the effects of environment and convention—our ultimate justification is to understand the vital process to which they are both indispensable.

To consider the novel as an institution, then, imposes no dogma, exacts no sacrifice, and excludes none of the critical methods that have proved illuminating in the past. If it tends to subordinate the writer's personality to his achievement, it requires no further apology, for criticism has long been unduly subordinated to biography. The tendency of the romanticists to live their writings and write their lives, and the consequent success of their critics as biographers, did much to justify this subordination; but even Sainte-Beuve's "natural history of souls," though it unified and clarified an author's works by fitting them into the pattern of his career, was too ready to dismiss their purely artistic qualities as "rhetoric." More recently the doctrines of Freud, while imposing a topheavy vocabulary upon the discussion of art, have been used to corroborate and systematize the sporadic intuitions of artists; but the psychologists, like the sociologists, have been more interested in utilizing books for documentary purposes than in exploring their intrinsic nature. Meanwhile, on the popular level, the confusion between a novelist and his novels has been consciously exploited. A series of novelized biographies, calling itself *Le Roman des grandes existences,* invites the common reader to proceed from "the prodigious life of Balzac" through "the mournful life of Baudelaire" to "the wise and merry life of Montaigne."

If fiction has seldom been discussed on a plane commensurate with its achievements, it is because we are too often sidetracked by personalities. If, with Henry James, we recognize the novelist's intention as a figure in a carpet, we must recognize that he is guided by his material, his training, his commission, by the size and shape of his loom, and by his imagination to the extent that it accepts and masters those elements. Psychology—illuminating as it has been—has treated literature too often as a record of personal idiosyncrasies, too seldom as the basis of a collective consciousness. Yet it is on that basis that the greatest writers have functioned. Their originality has been an ability to "seize on the public mind," in Bagehot's opinion; conventions have changed and styles have developed as lesser writers caught "the traditional rhythm of an age." The irreducible element of individual talent would seem to play the same role in the evolution of *genres* that natural selection plays in the origin of species. Amid the mutations of modern individualism, we may very conceivably have overstressed the private aspects of writing. One convenience of the institutional method is that it gives due credit to the never-ending collaboration between writer and public. It sees no reason to ignore what is relevant in the psychological prepossessions of the craftsman, and it knows that he is ultimately to be judged by the technical resources of his craftsmanship; but it attains its clearest and most comprehensive scope by centering on his craft—on his social status and his historical function as participant in a skilled group and a living tradition.

When Edgar Quinet announced a course at the Collège de France in *La Littérature et les institutions comparées de l'Europe méridionelle,* he was requested by Guizot's ministry to omit the word "institutions" and to limit himself to purely literary discussion. When he replied that this would be impossible, his course was suspended, and his further efforts went directly into those reform agitations which culminated in the democratic revolution of the following year, 1848. Thereby proceeding from sociological to social criticism, he demonstrated anew what French critics and novelists have understood particu-

larly well—the dynamic interaction between ideas and events. In a time which
has seen that demonstration repeated on so vast a scale, the institutional forces
that impinge upon literature are self-evident. The responsibilities that literature owes to itself, and the special allegiance it exacts from us, should also become apparent when we conceive it as an institution in its own right. The
misleading dichotomy between substance and form, which permits literary
historians, like Parrington, to dismiss "belletristic philandering," and esthetic
impressionists, like Mr. R. P. Blackmur, to dispose of "separable content,"
should disappear as soon as abstract categories are dropped and concrete relations are taken up. And the jurisdictional conflict between truth and beauty
should dissolve when esthetics discovers the truth about beauty; when criticism becomes—as Bacon intended, and Renan and Sainte-Beuve remembered,
and all too many other critics have forgotten—the science of art.

From *Accent*, Vol. VI (Spring, 1946), pp. 159–
168. Reprinted by permission of the author and
editors.

KENNETH BURKE

Psychology and Form

[1925]

It is not until the fourth scene of the first act that Hamlet confronts the ghost of his father. As soon as the situation has been made clear, the audience has been, consciously or unconsciously, waiting for this ghost to appear, while in the fourth scene this moment has been definitely promised. For earlier in the play Hamlet had arranged to come to the platform at night with Horatio to meet the ghost, and it is now night, he is with Horatio and Marcellus, and they are standing on the platform. Hamlet asks Horatio the hour.

> Hor. I think it lacks of twelve.
> Mar. No, it is struck.
> Hor. Indeed? I heard it not: then it draws near the season
>   Wherein the spirit held his wont to walk.

Promptly hereafter there is a sound off-stage. "A flourish of trumpets, and ordnance shot off within." Hamlet's friends have established the hour as twelve. It is time for the ghost. Sounds off-stage, and of course it is not the ghost. It is, rather, the sound of the king's carousal, for the king "keeps wassail." A tricky and useful detail. We have been waiting for a ghost, and get, startlingly, a blare of trumpets. And, once the trumpets are silent, we feel how desolate are these three men waiting for a ghost, on a bare "platform," feel it by this sudden juxtaposition of an imagined scene of lights and merriment. But the trumpets announcing a carousal have suggested a subject of conversation. In the darkness Hamlet discusses the excessive drinking of his countrymen. He points out that it tends to harm their reputation abroad, since, he argues, this one showy vice makes their virtues "in the general censure take corruption." And for this reason, although he himself is a native of this place, he does not approve of the custom. Indeed, there in the gloom he is talking very intelligently on these matters, and Horatio answers, "Look, my Lord, it comes." All this time we had been waiting for a ghost, and it comes at the one moment which was not pointing towards it. This ghost, so assiduously prepared for, is yet a surprise. And now that the ghost has come, we are waiting

667

for something further. Program: a speech from Hamlet. Hamlet must confront
the ghost. Here again Shakespeare can feed well upon the use of contrast for
his effects. Hamlet has just been talking in a sober, rather argumentative manner—but now the flood-gates are unloosed:

> Angels and ministers of grace defend us!
> Be thou a spirit of health or goblin damn'd,
> Bring with thee airs from heaven or blasts from hell . . .

and the transition from the matter-of-fact to the grandiose, the full-throated
and full-voweled, is a second burst of trumpets, perhaps more effective than
the first, since it is the rich fulfillment of a promise. Yet this satisfaction in turn
becomes an allurement, an itch for further developments. At first desiring
solely to see Hamlet confront the ghost, we now want Hamlet to learn from
the ghost the details of the murder—which are, however, with shrewdness
and husbandry, reserved for "Scene V—Another part of the Platform."

I have gone into this scene at some length, since it illustrates so perfectly the
relationship between psychology and form, and so aptly indicates how the one
is to be defined in terms of the other. That is, the psychology here is not the
psychology of the *hero,* but the psychology of the *audience.* And by that distinction, form would be the psychology of the audience. Or, seen from another
angle, form is the creation of an appetite in the mind of the auditor, and the
adequate satisfying of that appetite. This satisfaction—so complicated is the
human mechanism—at times involves a temporary set of frustrations, but in
the end these frustrations prove to be simply a more involved kind of satisfaction, and furthermore serve to make the satisfaction of fulfillment more intense. If, in a work of art, the poet says something, let us say, about a meeting,
writes in such a way that we desire to observe that meeting, and then, if he
places that meeting before us—that is form. While obviously, that is also the
psychology of the audience, since it involves desires and their appeasements.

The seeming breach between form and subject-matter, between technique
and psychology, which has taken place in the last century is the result, it seems
to me, of scientific criteria being unconsciously introduced into matters of
purely esthetic judgment. The flourishing of science has been so vigorous that
we have not yet had time to make a spiritual readjustment adequate to the
changes in our resources of material and knowledge. There are disorders of
the social system which are caused solely by our undigested wealth (the basic
disorder being, perhaps, the phenomenon of overproduction: to remedy this,
instead of having all workers employed on half time, we have half working
full time and the other half idle, so that whereas overproduction could be the
greatest reward of applied science, it has been, up to now, the most menacing
condition our modern civilization has had to face). It would be absurd to
suppose that such social disorders would not be paralleled by disorders of cul-

ture and taste, especially since science is so pronouncedly a spiritual factor. So that we are, owing to the sudden wealth science has thrown upon us, all *nouveaux-riches* in matters of culture, and most poignantly in that field where lack of native firmness is most readily exposed, in matters of esthetic judgment.

One of the most striking derangements of taste which science has temporarily thrown upon us involves the understanding of psychology in art. Psychology has become a body of information (which is precisely what psychology in science should be, or must be). And similarly, in art, we tend to look for psychology as the purveying of information. Thus, a contemporary writer has objected to Joyce's *Ulysses* on the ground that there are more psychoanalytic data available in Freud. (How much more drastically he might, by the same system, have destroyed Homer's *Odyssey!*) To his objection it was answered that one might, similarly, denounce Cézanne's trees in favor of state forestry bulletins. Yet are not Cézanne's landscapes themselves tainted with the psychology of information? Has he not, by perception, *pointed out* how one object lies against another, *indicated* what takes place between two colors (which is the psychology of science, and is less successful in the medium of art than in that of science, since in art such processes are at best implicit, whereas in science they are so readily made explicit)? Is Cézanne not, to that extent, a state forestry bulletin, except that he tells what goes on in the eye instead of on the tree? And do not the true values of his work lie elsewhere—and precisely in what I distinguish as the psychology of form?

Thus, the great influx of information has led the artist also to lay his emphasis on the giving of information—with the result that art tends more and more to substitute the psychology of the hero (the subject) for the psychology of the audience. Under such an attitude, when form is preserved it is preserved as an annex, a luxury, or, as some feel, a downright affectation. It remains, though sluggish, like the human appendix, for occasional demands are still made upon it; but its true vigor is gone, since it is no longer organically required. Proposition: The hypertrophy of the psychology of information is accompanied by the corresponding atrophy of the psychology of form.

In information, the matter is intrinsically interesting. And by intrinsically interesting I do not necessarily mean intrinsically valuable, as witness the intrinsic interest of backyard gossip or the most casual newspaper items. In art, at least the art of the great ages (Aeschylus, Shakespeare, Racine), the matter is interesting by means of an extrinsic use, a function. Consider, for instance, the speech of Mark Antony, the "Brutus is an honourable man." Imagine in the same place a very competently developed thesis on human conduct, with statistics, intelligence tests, definitions; imagine it as the finest thing of the sort ever written, and as really being at the roots of an understanding of Brutus. Obviously, the play would simply stop until Antony had finished. For in the case of Antony's speech, the value lies in the fact that his words are shaping the future of the audience's desires, not the desires of the Roman populace, but the desires of the pit. This is the psychology of form as distinguished from the psychology of information.

The distinction is, of course, absolutely true only in its nonexistent extremes. Hamlet's advice to the players, for instance, has little of the quality which distinguishes Antony's speech. It is, rather, intrinsically interesting, although one could very easily prove how the play would benefit by some such delay at this point, and that anything which made this delay possible without violating the consistency of the subject would have, in this, its formal justification. It would, furthermore, be absurd to rule intrinsic interest out of literature. I wish simply to have it restored to its properly minor position, seen as merely one out of many possible elements of style. Goethe's prose, often poorly imagined or neutral in its line-for-line texture, especially in the treatment of romantic episode—perhaps he felt that the romantic episode in itself was enough?—is strengthened into a style possessing affirmative virtues by his rich use of aphorism. But this is, after all, but one of many possible facets of appeal. In some places, notably in *Wilhelm Meisters Lehrjahre* when Wilhelm's friends disclose the documents they have been collecting about his life unbeknown to him, the aphorisms are almost rousing in their efficacy, since they involve the story. But as a rule the appeal of aphorism is intrinsic: that is, it satisfies without being functionally related to the context.[1] Also, to return to the matter of Hamlet, it must be observed that the style in this passage is no mere "information-giving" style; in its alacrity, its development, it really makes this one fragment into a kind of miniature plot.

One reason why music can stand repetition so much more sturdily than correspondingly good prose is because music, of all the arts, is by its nature least suited to the psychology of information, and has remained closer to the psychology of form. Here form cannot atrophy. Every dissonant chord cries for its solution, and whether the musician resolves or refuses to resolve this dissonance into the chord which the body cries for, he is dealing in human appetites. Correspondingly good prose, however, more prone to the temptations of pure information, cannot so much bear repetition since the esthetic value of information is lost once that information is imparted. If one returns to such a work again it is purely because, in the chaos of modern life, he has been able to forget it. With a desire, on the other hand, its recovery is as agreeable as its discovery. One can memorize the dialogue between Hamlet and Guildenstern, where Hamlet gives Guildenstern the pipe to play

---

[1] Similarly, the epigram of Racine is "pure art," because it usually serves to formulate or clarify some situation within the play itself. In Goethe the epigram is most often of independent validity, as in *Die Wahlverwandtschaften*, where the ideas of Ottilie's diary are obviously carried over boldly from the author's notebook. In Shakespeare we have the union of extrinsic and intrinsic epigram, the epigram growing out of its context and yet valuable independent of its context.

on. For, once the speech is known, its repetition adds a new element to compensate for the loss of novelty. We cannot take a recurrent pleasure in the new (in information) but we can in the natural (in form). Already, at the moment when Hamlet is holding out the pipe to Guildenstern and asking him to play upon it, we "gloat over" Hamlet's triumphal descent upon Guildenstern, when, after Guildenstern has, under increasing embarrassment, protested three times that he cannot play the instrument, Hamlet launches the retort for which all this was preparation:

Why, look you now, how unworthy a thing you make of me. You would play upon me, you would seem to know my stops; you would pluck out the heart of my mystery; you would sound me from my lowest note to the top of my compass; and there is much music, excellent voice, in this little organ, yet cannot you make it speak. 'Sblood, do you think I am easier to be played on than a pipe? Call me what instrument you will, though you can fret me, you cannot play upon me.[2]

In the opening lines we hear the promise of the close, and thus feel the emotional curve even more keenly than at first reading. Whereas in most modern art this element is underemphasized. It gives us the gossip of a plot, a plot which too often has for its value the mere fact that we do not know its outcome.[3]

Music, then, fitted less than any other art for imparting information, deals minutely in frustrations and fulfillments of desire,[4] and for that reason more often gives us those curves of emotion which, because they are natural, can bear repetition without loss. It is for this reason that music, like folk tales, is most capable of lulling us to sleep. A lullaby is a melody which comes quickly to rest, where the obstacles are easily overcome—and this is precisely the parallel to those waking dreams of struggle and conquest which (especially during childhood) we permit ourselves when falling asleep or when trying to induce sleep. Folk tales are just such waking dreams. Thus it is right that art should be called a "waking dream." The only difficulty with this definition (indicated by Charles Baudouin in his *Psychoanalysis and Aesthetics,* a very valuable study of Verhaeren) is that today we understand it to mean art as a

[2] One might indicate still further appropriateness here. As Hamlet finishes his speech, Polonius enters, and Hamlet turns to him, "God bless you, sir!" Thus, the plot is continued (for Polonius is always the promise of action) and a full stop is avoided: the embarrassment laid upon Rosencrantz and Guildenstern is not laid upon the audience.
[3] Yet modern music has gone far in the attempt to renounce this aspect of itself. Its dissonances become static, demanding no particular resolution. And whereas an unfinished modulation by a classic musician occasions positive dissatisfaction, the refusal to resolve a dissonance in modern music does not dissatisfy us, but irritates or stimulates. Thus, "energy" takes the place of style.
[4] Suspense is the least complex kind of anticipation, as surprise is the least complex kind of fulfillment.

waking dream for the artist. Modern criticism, and psychoanalysis in particular, is too prone to define the essence of art in terms of the artist's weaknesses. It is, rather, the audience which dreams, while the artist oversees the conditions which determine this dream. He is the manipulator of blood, brains, heart, and bowels which, while we sleep, dictate the mold of our desires. This is, of course, the real meaning of artistic felicity—an exaltation at the correctness of the procedure, so that we enjoy the steady march of doom in a Racinian tragedy with exactly the same equipment as that which produces our delight with Benedick's "Peace! I'll stop your mouth. (*Kisses her*)" which terminates the imbroglio of *Much Ado About Nothing*.

The methods of maintaining interest which are most natural to the psychology of information (as it is applied to works of pure art) are surprise and suspense. The method most natural to the psychology of form is eloquence. For this reason the great ages of Aeschylus, Shakespeare, and Racine, dealing as they did with material which was more or less a matter of common knowledge so that the broad outlines of the plot were known in advance (while it is the broad outlines which are usually exploited to secure surprise and suspense), developed formal excellence, or eloquence, as the basis of appeal in their work.

Not that there is any difference in kind between the classic method and the method of the cheapest contemporary melodrama. The drama, more than any other form, must never lose sight of its audience: here the failure to satisfy the proper requirements is most disastrous. And since certain contemporary work is successful, it follows that rudimentary laws of composition are being complied with. The distinction is one of intensity rather than of kind. The contemporary audience hears the lines of a play or novel with the same equipment as it brings to reading the lines of its daily paper. It is content to have facts placed before it in some more or less adequate sequence. Eloquence is the minimizing of this interest in fact, *per se,* so that the "more or less adequate sequence" of their presentation must be relied on to a much greater extent. Thus, those elements of surprise and suspense are subtilized, carried down into the writing of a line or a sentence, until in all its smallest details the work bristles with disclosures, contrasts, restatements with a difference, ellipses, images, aphorism, volume, sound-values, in short all that complex wealth of minutiae which in their line-for-line aspect we call style and in their broader outlines we call form.

As a striking instance of a modern play with potentialities in which the intensity of eloquence is missing, I might cite a recent success, Capek's R. U. R. Here, in a melodrama which was often astonishing in the rightness of its technical procedure, when the author was finished he had written nothing but the scenario for a play by Shakespeare. It was a play in which the author produced time and again the opportunity, the demand, for eloquence, only to move on. (At other times, the most successful moments, he utilized the modern discovery of silence, writing moments wherein words could not possibly serve but to detract from the effect: this we might call the "flowering" of information.) The Adam and Eve scene of the last act, a "commission" which the Shakespeare of the comedies would have loved to fill, was in the verbal barrenness of Capek's play something shameless to the point of blushing. The Robot, turned human, prompted by the dawn of love to see his first sunrise, or hear the first bird-call, and forced merely to say, "Oh, see the sunrise," or, "Hear the pretty birds"—here one could do nothing but wring his hands at the absence of that esthetic mold which produced the overslung "speeches" of *Romeo and Juliet.*

Suspense is the concern over the possible outcome of some specific detail of plot rather than for general qualities. Thus, "Will A marry B or C?" is suspense. In *Macbeth,* the turn from the murder scene to the porter scene is a much less literal channel of development. Here the presence of one quality calls forth the demand for another, rather than one tangible incident of plot awaking an interest in some other possible tangible incident of plot. To illustrate more fully, if an author managed over a certain number of his pages to produce a feeling of sultriness, or oppression, in the reader, this would unconsciously awaken in the reader the desire for a cold, fresh north wind—and thus some aspect of a north wind would be effective if called forth by some aspect of stuffiness. A good example of this is to be found in a contemporary poem, T. S. Eliot's *The Waste Land,* where the vulgar, oppressively trivial conversation in the public house calls forth in the poet a memory of a line from Shakespeare. These slobs in a public house, after a desolately low-visioned conversation, are now forced by closing time to leave the saloon. They say good-night. And suddenly the poet, feeling his release, drops into another good-night, a good-night with *désinvolture,* a good-night out of what was, within the conditions of the poem at least, a graceful and irrecoverable past.

> "Well that Sunday Albert was home, they had a hot gammon,
>> And they asked me in to dinner, to get the beauty of it hot"—
> [at this point the bartender interrupts: it is closing time]
> "Goonight Bill. Goonight Lou. Goonight May. Goonight. Ta ta.
>> Goonight. Goonight.
> Good-night, ladies, good-night, sweet ladies, good-night, good-night."

There is much more to be said on these lines, which I have shortened somewhat in quotation to make my issue clearer. But I simply wish to point out here that this transition is a bold juxtaposition of one quality created by another, an association in ideas which, if not logical, is nevertheless emotionally natural. In the case of *Macbeth,* similarly, it would be absurd to say that the audience, after the murder scene, wants a porter scene. But the audience does want the quality which this porter particularizes. The dramatist might, conceivably, have introduced some entirely different character or event in this place, provided only that the event produced the same quality of relationship and contrast (grotesque seriousness followed by grotesque buffoonery). One of the most beautiful and satisfactory "forms" of this sort is to be found in Baudelaire's "Femmes Damnées," where the poet, after describing the business of a Lesbian seduction, turns to the full oratory of his apostrophe:

> *Descendez, descendez, lamentables victimes,*
> *Descendez le chemin de l'enfer éternel . . .*

while the stylistic efficacy of this transition contains a richness which transcends all moral (or unmoral) sophistication: the efficacy of appropriateness, of exactly the natural curve in treatment. Here is morality even for the godless, since it is a morality of art, being justified, if for no other reason, by its paralleling of that staleness, that disquieting loss of purpose, which must have followed the procedure of the two characters, the *femmes damnées* themselves, a remorse which, perhaps only physical in its origin, nevertheless becomes psychic.[5]

But to return, we have made three terms synonymous: form, psychology, and eloquence. And eloquence thereby becomes the essence of art, while pity, tragedy, sweetness, humor, in short all the emotions which we experience in life proper, as non-artists, are simply the material on which eloquence may feed. The arousing of pity, for instance, is not the central purpose of art, although it may be an adjunct of artistic effectiveness. One can feel pity much more keenly at the sight of some actual misfortune—and it would be a great mistake to see art merely as a weak representation of some actual experience.[6] That artists today are content to write under such an esthetic accounts in part for the inferior position which art holds in the community. Art, at least in the great periods when it has flowered, was the conversion, or transcendence, of emotion into eloquence, and was thus a factor added to life. I am reminded of St. Augustine's caricature of the theatre: that whereas we do not dare to wish people unhappy, we do want to feel sorry for them, and therefore turn

---

[5] As another aspect of the same subject, I could cite many examples from the fairy tale. Consider, for instance, when the hero is to spend the night in a bewitched castle. Obviously, as darkness descends, weird adventures must befall him. His bed rides him through the castle; two halves of a man challenge him to a game of nine-pins played with thigh bones and skulls. Or entirely different incidents may serve instead of these. The quality comes first, the particularization follows.

[6] Could not the Greek public's resistance to Euripides be accounted for in the fact that he, of the three great writers of Greek tragedy, betrayed his art, was guilty of esthetic impiety, in that he paid more attention to the arousing of emotion *per se* than to the sublimation of emotion into eloquence?

to plays so that we can feel sorry although no real misery is involved. One might apply the parallel interpretation to the modern delight in happy endings, and say that we turn to art to indulge our humanitarianism in a well-wishing which we do not permit ourselves towards our actual neighbors. Surely the catharsis of art is more complicated than this, and more reputable.

Eloquence itself, as I hope to have established in the instance from *Hamlet* which I have analyzed, is no mere plaster added to a framework of more stable qualities. Eloquence is simply the end of art, and is thus its essence. Even the poorest is eloquent, but in a poor way, with less intensity, until this aspect is obscured by others fattening upon its leanness. Eloquence is not showiness; it is, rather, the result of that desire in the artist to make a work perfect by adapting it in every minute detail to the racial appetites.

The distinction between the psychology of information and the psychology of form involves a definition of esthetic truth. It is here precisely, to combat the deflection which the strength of science has caused to our tastes, that we must examine the essential breach between scientific and artistic truth. Truth in art is not the discovery of facts, not an addition to human knowledge in the scientific sense of the word.[7] It is, rather, the exercise of human propriety, the formulation of symbols which rigidify our sense of poise and rhythm. Artistic truth is the externalization of taste.[8] I sometimes wonder, for instance, whether the "artificial" speech of John Lyly might perhaps be "truer" than the revelations of Dostoevsky. Certainly at its best, in its feeling for a statement which returns upon itself, which attempts the systole to a diastole, it *could* be much truer than Dostoevsky.[9] And if it is not, it fails not through a mistake of Lyly's

[7] One of the most striking examples of the encroachment of scientific truth into art is the doctrine of "truth by distortion," whereby one aspect of an object is suppressed the better to emphasize some other aspect; this is, obviously, an attempt to *indicate* by art some fact of knowledge, to make some implicit aspect of an object as explicit as one can by means of the comparatively dumb method of art (dumb, that is, as compared to the perfect ease with which science can indicate its discoveries). Yet science has already made discoveries in the realm of this "factual truth," this "truth by distortion" which must put to shame any artist who relies on such matter for his effects. Consider, for instance, the motion-picture of a man vaulting. By photographing this process very rapidly, and running the reel very slowly, one has upon the screen the most striking set of factual truths to aid in our understanding of an athlete vaulting. Here, at our leisure, we can observe the contortions of four legs, a head, and a butt. This squirming thing we saw upon the screen showed us an infinity of factual truths anent the balances of an athlete vaulting. We can, from this, observe the marvelous system of balancing which the body provides for itself in the adjustments of moving. Yet, so far as the esthetic truth is concerned, this on the screen was not an athlete, but a squirming thing, a horror, displaying every fact of vaulting except the exhilaration of the act itself.

[8] The procedure of science involves the elimination of taste, employing as a substitute the corrective norm of a pragmatic test, the empirical experiment, which is entirely intellectual. Those who oppose the "intellectualism" of critics like Matthew Arnold are involved in an hilarious blunder, for Arnold's entire approach to the appreciation of art is through delicacies of taste intensified to the extent almost of squeamishness.

[9] As for instance, the "conceit" of Endymion's awakening, when he forgets his own name, yet recalls that of his beloved.

esthetic, but because Lyly was a man poor in character whereas Dostoevsky was rich and complex. When Swift, making the women of Brobdingnag enormous, deduces from this discrepancy between their size and Gulliver's that Gulliver could sit astride their nipples, he has written something which is esthetically true, which is, if I may be pardoned, profoundly "proper," as correct in its Euclidean deduction as any corollary in geometry. Given the companions of Ulysses in the cave of Polyphemus, it is true that they would escape clinging to the bellies of the herd let out to pasture. St. Ambrose, detailing the habits of God's creatures, and drawing from them moral maxims for the good of mankind, St. Ambrose in his limping natural history rich in scientific inaccuracies that are at the very heart of emotional rightness, St. Ambrose writes "Of night-birds, especially the nightingale which hatches her eggs by song; of the owl, the bat, and the cock at cock-crow; in what these may apply to the guidance of our habits," and in the sheer rightness of that program there is the truth of art. In introducing this talk of night-birds, after many pages devoted to other of God's creatures, he says:

What now! While we have been talking, you will notice how the birds of night have already started fluttering about you, and, in this same fact of warning us to leave off with our discussion, suggest thereby a further topic—

and this seems to me to contain the best wisdom of which the human frame is capable, an address, a discourse, which can make our material life seem blatant almost to the point of despair. And when the cock crows, and the thief abandons his traps, and the sun lights up, and we are in every way called back to God by the well-meaning admonition of this bird, here the very blindnesses of religion become the deepest truths of art.

From *Counter-Statement* by Kenneth Burke, pp. 38–56. Copyright, 1931. Reprinted by permission of Harcourt, Brace and Company, Inc., and the author. Originally published in *The Dial*, Vol. LXXIX (July, 1925), pp. 34–46.

LIONEL TRILLING
Freud and Literature
[1940-1947]

THE Freudian psychology is the only systematic account of the human mind which, in point of subtlety and complexity, of interest and tragic power, deserves to stand beside the chaotic mass of psychological insights which literature has accumulated through the centuries. To pass from the reading of a great literary work to a treatise of academic psychology is to pass from one order of perception to another, but the human nature of the Freudian psychology is exactly the stuff upon which the poet has always exercised his art. It is therefore not surprising that the psychoanalytical theory has had a great effect upon literature. Yet the relationship is reciprocal, and the effect of Freud upon literature has been no greater than the effect of literature upon Freud. When, on the occasion of the celebration of his seventieth birthday, Freud was greeted as the "discoverer of the unconscious," he corrected the speaker and disclaimed the title. "The poets and philosophers before me discovered the unconscious," he said. "What I discovered was the scientific method by which the unconscious can be studied."

A lack of specific evidence prevents us from considering the particular literary "influences" upon the founder of psychoanalysis; and, besides, when we think of the men who so clearly anticipated many of Freud's own ideas— Schopenhauer and Nietzsche, for example—and then learn that he did not read their works until after he had formulated his own theories, we must see that particular influences cannot be in question here but that what we must deal with is nothing less than a whole *Zeitgeist,* a direction of thought. For psychoanalysis is one of the culminations of the Romanticist literature of the nineteenth century. If there is perhaps a contradiction in the idea of a science standing upon the shoulders of a literature which avows itself inimical to science in so many ways, the contradiction will be resolved if we remember that this literature, despite its avowals, was itself scientific in at least the sense of being passionately devoted to a research into the self.

In showing the connection between Freud and this Romanticist tradition, it is difficult to know where to begin, but there might be a certain aptness in starting even back of the tradition, as far back as 1762 with Diderot's *Ra-*

677

meau's Nephew. At any rate, certain men at the heart of nineteenth-century thought were agreed in finding a peculiar importance in this brilliant little work: Goethe translated it, Marx admired it, Hegel—as Marx reminded Engels in the letter which announced that he was sending the book as a gift— praised and expounded it at length, Shaw was impressed by it, and Freud himself, as we know from a quotation in his *Introductory Lectures,* read it with the pleasure of agreement.

The dialogue takes place between Diderot himself and a nephew of the famous composer. The protagonist, the younger Rameau, is a despised, outcast, shameless fellow; Hegel calls him the "disintegrated consciousness" and credits him with great wit, for it is he who breaks down all the normal social values and makes new combinations with the pieces. As for Diderot, the deuteragonist, he is what Hegel calls the "honest consciousness," and Hegel considers him reasonable, decent, and dull. It is quite clear that the author does not despise his Rameau and does not mean us to. Rameau is lustful and greedy, arrogant yet self-abasing, perceptive yet "wrong," like a child. Still, Diderot seems actually to be giving the fellow a kind of superiority over himself, as though Rameau represents the elements which, dangerous but wholly necessary, lie beneath the reasonable decorum of social life. It would perhaps be pressing too far to find in Rameau Freud's *id* and in Diderot Freud's *ego;* yet the connection does suggest itself; and at least we have here the perception which is to be the common characteristic of both Freud and Romanticism, the perception of the hidden element of human nature and of the opposition between the hidden and the visible. We have too the bold perception of just what lies hidden: "If the little savage [i.e., the child] were left to himself, if he preserved all his foolishness and combined the violent passions of a man of thirty with the lack of reason of a child in the cradle, he'd wring his father's neck and go to bed with his mother."

From the self-exposure of Rameau to Rousseau's account of his own childhood is no great step; society might ignore or reject the idea of the "immorality" which lies concealed in the beginning of the career of the "good" man, just as it might turn away from Blake struggling to expound a psychology which would include the forces beneath the propriety of social man in general, but the idea of the hidden thing went forward to become one of the dominant notions of the age. The hidden element takes many forms and it is not necessarily "dark" and "bad"; for Blake the "bad" was the good, while for Wordsworth and Burke what was hidden and unconscious was wisdom and power, which work in despite of the conscious intellect.

The mind has become far less simple; the devotion to the various forms of autobiography—itself an important fact in the tradition—provides abundant examples of the change that has taken place. Poets, making poetry by what seems to them almost a freshly discovered faculty, find that this new power may be conspired against by other agencies of the mind and even deprived of its freedom; the names of Wordsworth, Coleridge, and Arnold at once occur to us again, and Freud quotes Schiller on the danger to the poet that lies in the merely analytical reason. And it is not only the poets who are threatened; educated and sensitive people throughout Europe become aware of the depredations that reason might make upon the affective life, as in the classic instance of John Stuart Mill.

We must also take into account the preoccupation—it began in the eighteenth century, or even in the seventeenth—with children, women, peasants, and savages, whose mental life, it is felt, is less overlaid than that of the educated adult male by the proprieties of social habit. With this preoccupation goes a concern with education and personal development, so consonant with the historical and evolutionary bias of the time. And we must certainly note the revolution in morals which took place at the instance (we might almost say) of the *Bildungsroman,* for in the novels fathered by *Wilhelm Meister* we get the almost complete identification of author and hero and of the reader with both, and this identification almost inevitably suggests a leniency of moral judgment. The autobiographical novel has a further influence upon the moral sensibility by its exploitation of all the modulations of motive and by its hinting that we may not judge a man by any single moment in his life without taking into account the determining past and the expiating and fulfilling future.

It is difficult to know how to go on, for the further we look the more literary affinities to Freud we find, and even if we limit ourselves to bibliography we can at best be incomplete. Yet we must mention the sexual revolution that was being demanded—by Shelley, for example, by the Schlegel of *Lucinde,* by George Sand, and later and more critically by Ibsen; the belief in the sexual origin of art, baldly stated by Tieck, more subtly by Schopenhauer; the investigation of sexual maladjustment by Stendhal, whose observations on erotic feeling seem to us distinctly Freudian. Again and again we see the effective, utilitarian ego being relegated to an inferior position and a plea being made on behalf of the anarchic and self-indulgent *id.* We find the energetic exploitation of the idea of the mind as a divisible thing, one part of which can contemplate and mock the other. It is not a far remove from this to Dostoevski's brilliant instances of ambivalent feeling. Novalis brings in the preoccupation with the death wish, and this is linked on the one hand with sleep and on the other hand with the perception of the perverse, self-destroying impulses, which in turn leads us to that fascination by the horrible which we find in Shelley, Poe, and Baudelaire. And always there is the profound interest in the dream—"Our dreams," said Gérard de Nerval, "are a second life"—

and in the nature of metaphor, which reaches its climax in Rimbaud and the later Symbolists, metaphor becoming less and less communicative as it approaches the relative autonomy of the dream life.

But perhaps we must stop to ask, since these are the components of the *Zeitgeist* from which Freud himself developed, whether it can be said that Freud did indeed produce a wide literary effect. What is it that Freud added that the tendency of literature itself would not have developed without him? If we were looking for a writer who showed the Freudian influence, Proust would perhaps come to mind as readily as anyone else; the very title of his novel, in French more than in English, suggests an enterprise of psychoanalysis and scarcely less so does his method—the investigation of sleep, of sexual deviation, of the way of association, the almost obsessive interest in metaphor; at these and at many other points the "influence" might be shown. Yet I believe it is true that Proust did not read Freud. Or again, exegesis of *The Waste Land* often reads remarkably like the psychoanalytic interpretation of a dream, yet we know that Eliot's methods were prepared for him not by Freud but by other poets.

Nevertheless, it is of course true that Freud's influence on literature has been very great. Much of it is so pervasive that its extent is scarcely to be determined; in one form or another, frequently in perversions or absurd simplifications, it has been infused into our life and become a component of our culture of which it is now hard to be specifically aware. In biography its first effect was sensational but not fortunate. The early Freudian biographers were for the most part Guildensterns who seemed to know the pipes but could not pluck out the heart of the mystery, and the same condemnation applies to the early Freudian critics. But in recent years, with the acclimatization of psychoanalysis and the increased sense of its refinements and complexity, criticism has derived from the Freudian system much that is of great value, most notably the license and the injunction to read the work of literature with a lively sense of its latent and ambiguous meanings, as if it were, as indeed it is, a being no less alive and contradictory than the man who created it. And this new response to the literary work has had a corrective effect upon our conception of biography. The literary critic or biographer who makes use of the Freudian theory is no less threatened by the dangers of theoretical systematization than he was in the early days, but he is likely to be more aware of these dangers; and I think it is true to say that now the motive of his interpretation is not that of exposing the secret shame of the writer and limiting the meaning of his work, but, on the contrary, that of finding grounds for sympathy with the writer and for increasing the possible significances of the work.

The names of the creative writers who have been more or less Freudian in tone or assumption would of course be legion. Only a relatively small number, however, have made serious use of the Freudian ideas. Freud himself seems to have thought this was as it should be: he is said to have expected very little of the works that were sent to him by writers with inscriptions of gratitude for all they had learned from him. The Surrealists have, with a certain inconsistency, depended upon Freud for the "scientific" sanction of their program. Kafka, with an apparent awareness of what he was doing, has explored the Freudian conceptions of guilt and punishment, of the dream, and of the fear of the father. Thomas Mann, whose tendency, as he himself says, was always in the direction of Freud's interests, has been most susceptible to the Freudian anthropology, finding a special charm in the theories of myths and magical practices. James Joyce, with his interest in the numerous states of receding consciousness, with his use of words as things and of words which point to more than one thing, with his pervading sense of the interrelation and interpenetration of all things, and, not least important, his treatment of familial themes, has perhaps most thoroughly and consciously exploited Freud's ideas.

II

It will be clear enough how much of Freud's thought has significant affinity with the anti-rationalist element of the Romanticist tradition. But we must see with no less distinctness how much of his system is militantly rationalistic. Thomas Mann is at fault when, in his first essay on Freud, he makes it seem that the "Apollonian," the rationalistic, side of psychoanalysis is, while certainly important and wholly admirable, somehow secondary and even accidental. He gives us a Freud who is committed to the "night side" of life. Not at all: the rationalistic element of Freud is foremost; before everything else he is positivistic. If the interpreter of dreams came to medical science through Goethe, as he tells us he did, he entered not by way of the *Walpurgisnacht* but by the essay which played so important a part in the lives of so many scientists of the nineteenth century, the famous disquisition on Nature.

This correction is needed not only for accuracy but also for any understanding of Freud's attitude to art. And for that understanding we must see how intense is the passion with which Freud believes that positivistic rationalism, in its golden-age pre-Revolutionary purity, is the very form and pattern of intellectual virtue. The aim of psychoanalysis, he says, is the control of the night side of life. It is "to strengthen the ego, to make it more independent of the super-ego, to widen its field of vision, and so to extend the organization of the *id*." "Where *id* was,"—that is, where all the irrational, non-logical, pleasure-seeking dark forces were—"there shall ego be,"—that is, intelligence and control. "It is," he concludes, with a reminiscence of Faust, "reclamation work, like the draining of the Zuyder Zee." This passage is quoted by Mann when, in taking up the subject of Freud a second time, he does indeed speak of

Freud's positivistic program; but even here the bias induced by Mann's artistic interest in the "night side" prevents him from giving the other aspect of Freud its due emphasis. Freud would never have accepted the role which Mann seems to give him as the legitimizer of the myth and the dark irrational ways of the mind. If Freud discovered the darkness for science he never endorsed it. On the contrary, his rationalism supports all the ideas of the Enlightenment that deny validity to myth or religion; he holds to a simple materialism, to a simple determinism, to a rather limited sort of epistemology. No great scientist of our day has thundered so articulately and so fiercely against all those who would sophisticate with metaphysics the scientific principles that were good enough for the nineteenth century. Conceptualism or pragmatism are anathema to him through the greater part of his intellectual career, and this, when we consider the nature of his own brilliant scientific methods, has surely an element of paradox in it.

From his rationalistic positivism comes much of Freud's strength and what weakness he has. The strength is the fine, clear tenacity of his positive aims, the goal of therapy, the desire to bring to men a decent measure of earthly happiness. But upon the rationalism must also be placed the blame for the often naïve scientific principles which characterize his early thought—they are later much modified—and which consist largely of claiming for his theories a perfect correspondence with an external reality, a position which, for those who admire Freud and especially for those who take seriously his views on art, is troublesome in the extreme.

Now Freud has, I believe, much to tell us about art, but whatever is suggestive in him is not likely to be found in those of his works in which he deals expressly with art itself. Freud is not insensitive to art—on the contrary —nor does he ever intend to speak of it with contempt. Indeed, he speaks of it with a real tenderness and counts it one of the true charms of the good life. Of artists, especially of writers, he speaks with admiration and even a kind of awe, though perhaps what he most appreciates in literature are specific emotional insights and observations; as we have noted, he speaks of literary men, because they have understood the part played in life by the hidden motives, as the precursors and coadjutors of his own science.

And yet eventually Freud speaks of art with what we must indeed call contempt. Art, he tells us, is a "substitute gratification," and as such is "an illusion in contrast to reality." Unlike most illusions, however, art is "almost always harmless and beneficent" for the reason that "it does not seek to be anything but an illusion. Save in the case of a few people who are, one might say, obsessed by Art, it never dares make any attack on the realm of reality." One of its chief functions is to serve as a "narcotic." It shares the characteristics of the dream, whose element of distortion Freud calls a "sort of inner dishonesty." As for the artist, he is virtually in the same category with the neurotic. "By such separation of imagination and intellectual capacity," Freud says of the hero of a novel, "he is destined to be a poet or a neurotic, and he belongs to that race of beings whose realm is not of this world."

Now there is nothing in the logic of psychoanalytical thought which requires Freud to have these opinions. But there is a great deal in the practice of the psychoanalytical therapy which makes it understandable that Freud, unprotected by an adequate philosophy, should be tempted to take the line he does. The analytical therapy deals with illusion. The patient comes to the physician to be cured, let us say, of a fear of walking in the street. The fear is real enough, there is no illusion on that score, and it produces all the physical symptoms of a more rational fear, the sweating palms, pounding heart, and shortened breath. But the patient knows that there is no cause for the fear, or rather that there is, as he says, no "real cause": there are no machine guns, man traps, or tigers in the street. The physician knows, however, that there is indeed a "real" cause for the fear, though it has nothing at all to do with what is or is not in the street; the cause is within the patient, and the process of the therapy will be to discover, by gradual steps, what this real cause is and so free the patient from its effects.

Now the patient in coming to the physician, and the physician in accepting the patient, make a tacit compact about reality; for their purpose they agree to the limited reality by which we get our living, win our loves, catch our trains and our colds. The therapy will undertake to train the patient in proper ways of coping with this reality. The patient, of course, has been dealing with this reality all along, but in the wrong way. For Freud there are two ways of dealing with external reality. One is practical, effective, positive; this is the way of the conscious self, of the ego which must be made independent of the super-ego and extend its organization over the *id,* and it is the right way. The antithetical way may be called, for our purpose now, the "fictional" way. Instead of doing something about, or to, external reality, the individual who uses this way does something to, or about, his affective states. The most common and "normal" example of this is daydreaming, in which we give ourselves a certain pleasure by imagining our difficulties solved or our desires gratified. Then, too, as Freud discovered, sleeping dreams are, in much more complicated ways, and even though quite unpleasant, at the service of this same "fictional" activity. And in ways yet more complicated and yet more unpleasant, the actual neurosis from which our patient suffers deals with an external reality which the mind considers still more unpleasant than the painful neurosis itself.

For Freud as psychoanalytic practitioner there are, we may say, the polar extremes of reality and illusion. Reality is an honorific word, and it means what is *there*; illusion is a pejorative word, and it means a response to what is *not there*. The didactic nature of a course of psychoanalysis no doubt requires a certain firm crudeness in making the distinction; it is after all aimed not at theoretical refinement but at practical effectiveness. The polar extremes are practical reality and neurotic illusion, the latter judged by the former. This, no doubt, is as it should be; the patient is not being trained in metaphysics and epistemology.

This practical assumption is not Freud's only view of the mind in its relation to reality. Indeed what may be called the essentially Freudian view assumes that the mind, for good as well as bad, helps create its reality by selection and evaluation. In this view, reality is malleable and subject to creation; it is not static but is rather a series of situations which are dealt with in their own terms. But beside this conception of the mind stands the conception which arises from Freud's therapeutic-practical assumptions; in this view, the mind deals with a reality which is quite fixed and static, a reality that is wholly "given" and not (to use a phrase of Dewey's) "taken." In his epistemological utterances, Freud insists on this second view, although it is not easy to see why he should do so. For the reality to which he wishes to reconcile the neurotic patient is, after all, a "taken" and not a "given" reality. It is the reality of social life and of value, conceived and maintained by the human mind and will. Love, morality, honor, esteem—these are the components of a created reality. If we are to call art an illusion then we must call most of the activities and satisfactions of the ego illusions; Freud, of course, has no desire to call them that.

What, then, is the difference between, on the one hand, the dream and the neurosis, and, on the other hand, art? That they have certain common elements is of course clear; that unconscious processes are at work in both would be denied by no poet or critic; they share too, though in different degrees, the element of fantasy. But there is a vital difference between them which Charles Lamb saw so clearly in his defense of the sanity of true genius: "The . . . poet dreams being awake. He is not possessed by his subject but he has dominion over it."

That is the whole difference: the poet is in command of his fantasy, while it is exactly the mark of the neurotic that he is possessed by his fantasy. And there is a further difference which Lamb states; speaking of the poet's relation to reality (he calls it Nature), he says, "He is beautifully loyal to that sovereign directress, even when he appears most to betray her"; the illusions of art are made to serve the purpose of a closer and truer relation with reality. Jacques Barzun, in an acute and sympathetic discussion of Freud, puts the matter well: "A good analogy between art and *dreaming* has led him to a false one between art and *sleeping*. But the difference between a work of art and a dream is precisely this, that the work of art *leads us back to the outer reality by taking account of it.*" Freud's assumption of the almost exclusively hedonistic nature and purpose of art bar him from the perception of this.

Of the distinction that must be made between the artist and the neurotic Freud is of course aware; he tells us that the artist is not like the neurotic in that he knows how to find a way back from the world of imagination and "once more get a firm foothold in reality." This however seems to mean no more than that reality is to be dealt with when the artist suspends the practice of his art; and at least once when Freud speaks of art dealing with reality he actually means the rewards that a successful artist can win. He does not deny to art its function and its usefulness; it has a therapeutic effect in releasing mental tension; it serves the cultural purpose of acting as a "substitute gratification" to reconcile men to the sacrifices they have made for culture's sake; it promotes the social sharing of highly valued emotional experiences; and it recalls men to their cultural ideals. This is not everything that some of us would find that art does, yet even this is a good deal for a "narcotic" to do.

III

I started by saying that Freud's ideas could tell us something about art, but so far I have done little more than try to show that Freud's very conception of art is inadequate. Perhaps, then, the suggestiveness lies in the application of the analytic method to specific works of art or to the artist himself? I do not think so, and it is only fair to say that Freud himself was aware both of the limits and the limitations of psychoanalysis in art, even though he does not always in practice submit to the former or admit the latter.

Freud has, for example, no desire to encroach upon the artist's autonomy; he does not wish us to read his monograph on Leonardo and then say of the "Madonna of the Rocks" that it is a fine example of homosexual, autoerotic painting. If he asserts that in investigation the "psychiatrist cannot yield to the author," he immediately insists that the "author cannot yield to the psychiatrist," and he warns the latter not to "coarsen everything" by using for all human manifestations the "substantially useless and awkward terms" of clinical procedure. He admits, even while asserting that the sense of beauty probably derives from sexual feeling, that psychoanalysis "has less to say about beauty than about most other things." He confesses to a theoretical indifference to the form of art and restricts himself to its content. Tone, feeling, style, and the modification that part makes upon part he does not consider. "The layman," he says, "may expect perhaps too much from analysis . . . for it must be admitted that it throws no light upon the two problems which probably interest him the most. It can do nothing toward elucidating the nature of the artistic gift, nor can it explain the means by which the artist works—artistic technique."

What, then, does Freud believe that the analytical method can do? Two things: explain the "inner meanings" of the work of art and explain the temperament of the artist as man.

A famous example of the method is the attempt to solve the "problem" of *Hamlet* as suggested by Freud and as carried out by Dr. Ernest Jones, his early and distinguished follower. Dr. Jones's monograph is a work of painstaking scholarship and of really masterly ingenuity. The research undertakes not only the clearing up of the mystery of Hamlet's character, but also the discovery of "the clue to much of the deeper workings of Shakespeare's mind." Part of the mystery in question is of course why Hamlet, after he had so definitely resolved to do so, did not avenge upon his hated uncle his father's death. But there is another mystery to the play—what Freud calls "the mystery of its effect," its magical appeal that draws so much interest toward it. Recalling the many failures to solve the riddle of the play's charm, he wonders if we are to be driven to the conclusion "that its magical appeal rests solely upon the impressive thoughts in it and the splendor of its language." Freud believes that we can find a source of power beyond this.

We remember that Freud has told us that the meaning of a dream is its intention, and we may assume that the meaning of a drama is its intention, too. The Jones research undertakes to discover what it was that Shakespeare intended to say about Hamlet. It finds that the intention was wrapped by the author in a dreamlike obscurity because it touched so deeply both his personal life and the moral life of the world; what Shakespeare intended to say is that Hamlet cannot act because he is incapacitated by the guilt he feels at his unconscious attachment to his mother. There is, I think, nothing to be quarreled with in the statement that there is an Oedipus situation in *Hamlet;* and if psychoanalysis has indeed added a new point of interest to the play, that is to its credit.[1] And, just so, there is no reason to quarrel with Freud's conclusion when he undertakes to give us the meaning of *King Lear* by a tortuous tracing of the mythological implications of the theme of the three caskets, of the relation of the caskets to the Norns, the Fates, and the Graces, of the connection of these triadic females with Lear's daughters, of the transmogrification of the death goddess into the love goddess and the identification of Cordelia with both, all to the conclusion that the meaning of *King Lear* is to be found in the tragic refusal of an old man to "renounce love, choose death, and make friends with the necessity of dying." There is something both beautiful and suggestive in this, but it is not *the* meaning of *King Lear* any more than the Oedipus motive is *the* meaning of *Hamlet.*

It is not here a question of the validity of the evidence, though that is of

---

[1] However, A. C. Bradley, in his discussion of Hamlet (*Shakespearean Tragedy*), states clearly the intense sexual disgust which Hamlet feels and which, for Bradley, helps account for his uncertain purpose; and Bradley was anticipated in this view by Löning. It is well known, and Dover Wilson has lately emphasized the point, that to an Elizabethan audience Hamlet's mother was not merely tasteless, as to a modern audience she seems, in hurrying to marry Claudius, but actually adulterous in marrying him at all because he was, as her brother-in-law, within the forbidden degrees.

course important. We must rather object to the conclusions of Freud and Dr. Jones on the ground that their proponents do not have an adequate conception of what an artistic meaning is. There is no single meaning to any work of art; this is true not merely because it is better that it should be true, that is, because it makes art a richer thing, but because historical and personal experience show it to be true. Changes in historical context and in personal mood change the meaning of a work and indicate to us that artistic understanding is not a question of fact but of value. Even if the author's intention were, as it cannot be, precisely determinable, the meaning of a work cannot lie in the author's intention alone. It must also lie in its effect. We can say of a volcanic eruption on an inhabited island that it "means terrible suffering," but if the island is uninhabited or easily evacuated it means something else. In short, the audience partly determines the meaning of the work. But although Freud sees something of this when he says that in addition to the author's intention we must take into account the mystery of *Hamlet's* effect, he nevertheless goes on to speak as if, historically, *Hamlet's* effect had been single and brought about solely by the "magical" power of the Oedipus motive to which, unconsciously, we so violently respond. Yet there was, we know, a period when *Hamlet* was relatively in eclipse, and it has always been scandalously true of the French, a people not without filial feeling, that they have been somewhat indifferent to the "magical appeal" of *Hamlet*.

I do not think that anything I have said about the inadequacies of the Freudian method of interpretation limits the number of ways we can deal with a work of art. Bacon remarked that experiment may twist nature on the rack to wring out its secrets, and criticism may use any instruments upon a work of art to find its meanings. The elements of art are not limited to the world of art. They reach into life, and whatever extraneous knowledge of them we gain—for example, by research into the historical context of the work—may quicken our feelings for the work itself and even enter legitimately into those feelings. Then, too, anything we may learn about the artist himself may be enriching and legitimate. But one research into the mind of the artist is simply not practicable, however legitimate it may theoretically be. That is, the investigation of his unconscious intention as it exists apart from the work itself. Criticism understands that the artist's statement of his conscious intention, though it is sometimes useful, cannot finally determine meaning. How much less can we know from his unconscious intention considered as something apart from the whole work? Surely very little can be called conclusive or scientific. For, as Freud himself points out, we are not in a position to question the artist; we must apply the technique of dream analysis to his symbols, but, as Freud says with some heat, those people do not understand his theory who think that a dream may be interpreted without the dreamer's free association with the multitudinous details of his dream.

We have so far ignored the aspect of the method which finds the solution to the "mystery" of such a play as *Hamlet* in the temperament of Shakespeare himself and then illuminates the mystery of Shakespeare's temperament by means of the solved mystery of the play. Here it will be amusing to remember that by 1935 Freud had become converted to the theory that it was not Shakespeare of Stratford but the Earl of Oxford who wrote the plays, thus invalidating the important bit of evidence that Shakespeare's father died shortly before the composition of *Hamlet*. This is destructive enough to Dr. Jones's argument, but the evidence from which Dr. Jones draws conclusions about literature fails on grounds more relevant to literature itself. For when Dr. Jones, by means of his analysis of *Hamlet*, takes us into "the deeper workings of Shakespeare's mind," he does so with a perfect confidence that he knows what *Hamlet* is and what its relation to Shakespeare is. It is, he tells us, Shakespeare's "chief masterpiece," so far superior to all his other works that it may be placed on "an entirely separate level." And then, having established his ground on an entirely subjective literary judgment, Dr. Jones goes on to tell us that *Hamlet* "probably expresses the core of Shakespeare's philosophy and outlook as no other work of his does." That is, all the contradictory or complicating or modifying testimony of the other plays is dismissed on the basis of Dr. Jones's acceptance of the peculiar position which, he believes, *Hamlet* occupies in the Shakespeare canon. And it is upon this quite inadmissible judgment that Dr. Jones bases his argument: "It may be expected *therefore* that anything which will give us the key to the inner meaning of the play will *necessarily* give us the clue to much of the deeper workings of Shakespeare's mind." (The italics are mine.)

I should be sorry if it appeared that I am trying to say that psychoanalysis can have nothing to do with literature. I am sure that the opposite is so. For example, the whole notion of rich ambiguity in literature, of the interplay between the apparent meaning and the latent—not "hidden"—meaning, has been reinforced by the Freudian concepts, perhaps even received its first impetus from them. Of late years, the more perceptive psychoanalysts have surrendered the early pretensions of their teachers to deal "scientifically" with literature. That is all to the good, and when a study as modest and precise as Dr. Franz Alexander's essay on *Henry IV* comes along, an essay which pretends not to "solve" but only to illuminate the subject, we have something worth having. Dr. Alexander undertakes nothing more than to say that in the development of Prince Hal we see the classic struggle of the ego to come to normal adjustment, beginning with the rebellion against the father, going on to the conquest of the super-ego (Hotspur, with his rigid notions of honor and glory), then to the conquests of the *id* (Falstaff, with his anarchic self-indulgence), then to the identification with the father (the crown scene) and the assumption of mature responsibility. An analysis of this sort is not momentous and not exclusive of other meanings; perhaps it does no more than point up and formulate what we all have already seen. It has the tact to *accept* the play and does not, like Dr. Jones's study of *Hamlet,* search for a "hidden motive" and a "deeper working," which implies that there is a reality to which the play stands in the relation that a dream stands to the wish that generates it and from which it is separable; it is this reality, this "deeper working," which, according to Dr. Jones, produced the play. But *Hamlet* is not merely the product of Shakespeare's thought, it is the very instrument of his thought, and if meaning is intention, Shakespeare did not intend the Oedipus motive or anything less than *Hamlet;* if meaning is effect then it is *Hamlet* which affects us, not the Oedipus motive. *Coriolanus* also deals, and very terribly, with the Oedipus motive, but the effect of the one drama is very different from the effect of the other.

IV

If, then, we can accept neither Freud's conception of the place of art in life nor his application of the analytical method, what is it that he contributes to our understanding of art or to its practice? In my opinion, what he contributes outweighs his errors; it is of the greatest importance, and it lies in no specific statement that he makes about art but is, rather, implicit in his whole conception of the mind.

For, of all mental systems, the Freudian psychology is the one which makes poetry indigenous to the very constitution of the mind. Indeed, the mind, as Freud sees it, is in the greater part of its tendency exactly a poetry-making organ. This puts the case too strongly, no doubt, for it seems to make the working of the unconscious mind equivalent to poetry itself, forgetting that between the unconscious mind and the finished poem there supervene the social intention and the formal control of the conscious mind. Yet the statement has at least the virtue of counterbalancing the belief, so commonly expressed or implied, that the very opposite is true, and that poetry is a kind of beneficent aberration of the mind's right course.

Freud has not merely naturalized poetry; he has discovered its status as a pioneer settler, and he sees it as a method of thought. Often enough he tries to show how, as a method of thought, it is unreliable and ineffective for conquering reality; yet he himself is forced to use it in the very shaping of his own science, as when he speaks of the topography of the mind and tells us with a kind of defiant apology that the metaphors of space relationship which he is using are really most inexact since the mind is not a thing of space at all, but that there is no other way of conceiving the difficult idea except by metaphor. In the eighteenth century Vico spoke of the metaphorical, imagistic language of the early stages of culture; it was left to Freud to discover how, in a scientific age, we still feel and think in figurative formations, and to create, what psychoanalysis is, a science of tropes, of metaphor and its variants, synecdoche and metonymy.

Freud showed, too, how the mind, in one of its parts, could work without logic, yet not without that directing purpose, that control of intent from which, perhaps it might be said, logic springs. For the unconscious mind works without the syntactical conjunctions which are logic's essence. It recognipes no *because*, no *therefore*, no *but*; such ideas as similarity, agreement, and community are expressed in dreams imagistically by compressing the elements into a unity. The unconscious mind in its struggle with the conscious always turns from the general to the concrete and finds the tangible trifle more congenial than the large abstraction. Freud discovered in the very organization of the mind those mechanisms by which art makes its effects, such devices as the condensations of meanings and the displacement of accent.

All this is perhaps obvious enough and, though I should like to develop it in proportion both to its importance and to the space I have given to disagreement with Freud, I will not press it further. For there are two other elements in Freud's thought which, in conclusion, I should like to introduce as of great weight in their bearing on art.

Of these, one is a specific idea which, in the middle of his career (1920), Freud put forward in his essay *Beyond the Pleasure Principle*. The essay itself is a speculative attempt to solve a perplexing problem in clinical analysis, but its relevance to literature is inescapable, as Freud sees well enough, even though his perception of its critical importance is not sufficiently strong to make him revise his earlier views of the nature and function of art. The idea is one which stands besides Aristotle's notion of the catharsis, in part to supplement, in part to modify it.

Freud has come upon certain facts which are not to be reconciled with his earlier theory of the dream. According to this theory, all dreams, even the unpleasant ones, could be understood upon analysis to have the intention of fulfilling the dreamer's wishes. They are in the service of what Freud calls the pleasure principle, which is opposed to the reality principle. It is, of course, this explanation of the dream which had so largely conditioned Freud's theory of art. But now there is thrust upon him the necessity for reconsidering the theory of the dream, for it was found that in cases of war neurosis—what we once called shellshock—the patient, with the utmost anguish, recurred in his dreams to the very situation, distressing as it was, which had precipitated his neurosis. It seemed impossible to interpret these dreams by any assumption of a hedonistic intent. Nor did there seem to be the usual amount of distortion in them: the patient recurred to the terrible initiatory situation with great literalness. And the same pattern of psychic behavior could be observed in the play of children; there were some games which, far from fulfilling wishes, seemed to concentrate upon the representation of those aspects of the child's life which were most unpleasant and threatening to his happiness.

To explain such mental activities Freud evolved a theory for which he at first refused to claim much but to which, with the years, he attached an increasing importance. He first makes the assumption that there is indeed in the psychic life a repetition-compulsion which goes beyond the pleasure principle. Such a compulsion cannot be meaningless, it must have an intent. And that intent, Freud comes to believe, is exactly and literally the developing of fear. "These dreams," he says, "are attempts at restoring control of the stimuli by developing apprehension, the pretermission of which caused the traumatic neurosis." The dream, that is, is the effort to reconstruct the bad situation in order that the failure to meet it may be recouped; in these dreams there is no obscured intent to evade but only an attempt to meet the situation, to make a new effort of control. And in the play of children it seems to be that "the child repeats even the unpleasant experiences because through his own activity he gains a far more thorough mastery of the strong impression than was possible by mere passive experience."

Freud, at this point, can scarcely help being put in mind of tragic drama; nevertheless, he does not wish to believe that this effort to come to mental grips with a situation is involved in the attraction of tragedy. He is, we might say, under the influence of the Aristotelian tragic theory which emphasizes a qualified hedonism through suffering. But the pleasure involved in tragedy is perhaps an ambiguous one; and sometimes we must feel that the famous sense of cathartic resolution is perhaps the result of glossing over terror with beautiful language rather than an evacuation of it. And sometimes the terror even bursts through the language to stand stark and isolated from the play, as does Oedipus's sightless and bleeding face. At any rate, the Aristotelian theory does not deny another function for tragedy (and for comedy, too) which is suggested by Freud's theory of the traumatic neurosis—what might be called the mithridatic function, by which tragedy is used as the homeopathic administration of pain to inure ourselves to the greater pain which life will force upon us. There is in the cathartic theory of tragedy, as it is usually understood, a conception of tragedy's function which is too negative and which inadequately suggests the sense of active mastery which tragedy can give.

In the same essay in which he sets forth the conception of the mind embracing its own pain for some vital purpose, Freud also expresses a provisional assent to the idea (earlier stated, as he reminds us, by Schopenhauer) that there is perhaps a human drive which makes of death the final and desired goal. The death instinct is a conception that is rejected by many of even the most thoroughgoing Freudian theorists (as, in his last book, Freud mildly noted); the late Otto Fenichel in his authoritative work on the neurosis argues cogently against it. Yet even if we reject the theory as not fitting the facts in any operatively useful way, we still cannot miss its grandeur, its ultimate tragic courage in acquiescence to fate. The idea of the reality principle and the idea of the death instinct form the crown of Freud's broader speculation on the life of man. Their quality of grim poetry is characteristic of Freud's system and the ideas it generates for him.

And as much as anything else that Freud gives to literature, this quality of his thought is important. Although the artist is never finally determined in his work by the intellectual systems about him, he cannot avoid their influence; and it can be said of various competing systems that some hold more promise for the artist than others. When, for example, we think of the simple humanitarian optimism which, for two decades, has been so pervasive, we must see that not only has it been politically and philosophically inadequate, but also that it implies, by the smallness of its view of the varieties of human possibility, a kind of check on the creative faculties. In Freud's view of life no such limitation is implied. To be sure, certain elements of his system seem hostile to the usual notions of man's dignity. Like every great critic of human nature —and Freud is that—he finds in human pride the ultimate cause of human wretchedness, and he takes pleasure in knowing that his ideas stand with those of Copernicus and Darwin in making pride more difficult to maintain. Yet the Freudian man is, I venture to think, a creature of far more dignity and far more interest than the man which any other modern system has been able to conceive. Despite popular belief to the contrary, man, as Freud conceives him, is not to be understood by any simple formula (such as sex) but is rather an inextricable tangle of culture and biology. And not being simple, he is not simply good; he has, as Freud says somewhere, a kind of hell within him from which rise everlastingly the impulses which threaten his civilization. He has the faculty of imagining for himself more in the way of pleasure and satisfaction than he can possibly achieve. Everything that he gains he pays for in more than equal coin; compromise and the compounding with defeat constitute his best way of getting through the world. His best qualities are the result of a struggle whose outcome is tragic. Yet he is a creature of love; it is Freud's sharpest criticism of the Adlerian psychology that to aggression it gives everything and to love nothing at all.

One is always aware in reading Freud how little cynicism there is in his thought. His desire for man is only that he should be human, and to this end his science is devoted. No view of life to which the artist responds can insure the quality of his work, but the poetic qualities of Freud's own principles, which are so clearly in the line of the classic tragic realism, suggest that this is a view which does not narrow and simplify the human world for the artist but on the contrary opens and complicates it.

From *The Liberal Imagination* by Lionel Trilling. Viking Press. Copyright, 1950, by Lionel Trilling. Reprinted by permission of the author and publishers. Originally published as "The Legacy of Sigmund Freud: Literary and Aesthetic" in *The Kenyon Review*, Vol. II (Spring, 1940), pp. 152–173; and, in a revised version, as "Freud and Literature" in *Horizon* (London), Vol. XVI (September, 1947), pp. 182–200.

EDMUND WILSON

Marxism and Literature

[1937]

1. LET us begin with Marx and Engels. What was the role assigned to literature and art in the system of Dialectical Materialism? This role was much less
cut-and-dried than is nowadays often supposed. Marx and Engels conceived
the forms of human society in any given country and epoch as growing out
of the methods of production which prevailed at that place and time; and out
of the relations involved in the social forms arose a "superstructure" of higher
activities such as politics, law, religion, philosophy, literature and art. These
activities were not, as is sometimes assumed, wholly explicable in terms of
economics. They showed the mold, in ways direct or indirect, of the social
configuration below them, but each was working to get away from its roots
in the social classes and to constitute a professional group, with its own discipline and its own standards of value, which cut across class lines. These departments "all react upon one another and upon the economic base. It is not
the case that the economic situation is the sole active cause and everything
else only a passive effect. But there is a reciprocal interaction within a fundamental economic necessity, which in the last instance always asserts itself"
(Engels to Hans Starkenburg, January 25, 1894). So that the art of a great
artistic period may reach a point of vitality and vision where it can influence
the life of the period down to its very economic foundations. Simply, it must
cease to flourish with the social system which made it possible by providing
the artist with training and leisure, even though the artist himself may have
been working for the destruction of that system.

2. Marx and Engels, unlike some of their followers, never attempted to furnish social-economic formulas by which the validity of works of art might be
tested. They had grown up in the sunset of Goethe before the great age of
German literature was over, and they had both set out in their youth to be
poets; they responded to imaginative work, first of all, on its artistic merits.
They could ridicule a trashy writer like Eugène Sue for what they regarded
as his *petit bourgeois* remedies for the miseries of contemporary society (*The*

Holy Family); they could become bitter about Ferdinand Freiligrath, who had deserted the Communist League and turned nationalist in 1870 (Marx to Engels, August 22, 1870). And Marx could even make similar jibes at Heine when he thought that the latter had stooped to truckling to the authorities or when he read the expressions of piety in his will (Marx to Engels, December 21, 1866 and May 8, 1856). But Marx's daughter tells us that her father loved Heine "as much as his work and was very indulgent of his political shortcomings. He used to say that the poets were originals, who must be allowed to go their own way, and that one shouldn't apply to them the same standards as to ordinary people." It was not characteristic of Marx and Engels to judge literature—that is, literature of power and distinction—in terms of its purely political tendencies. In fact, Engels always warned the socialist novelists against the dangers of *Tendenz-Literatur* (Engels to Minna Kautsky, November 26, 1885; and to Margaret Harkness, April 1888). In writing to Minna Kautsky about one of her novels, he tells her that the personalities of her hero and heroine have been dissolved in the principles they represent. "You evidently," he says, "felt the need of publicly taking sides in this book, of proclaiming your opinions of the world. . . . But I believe that the tendency should arise from the situation and the action themselves without being explicitly formulated, and that the poet is not under the obligation to furnish the reader with a ready-made historical solution for the future of the conflict which he describes." When Ferdinand Lassalle sent Marx and Engels his poetic tragedy, *Franz von Sickingen,* and invited them to criticize it, Marx replied that, "setting aside any purely critical attitude toward the work," it had on a first reading affected him powerfully—characteristically adding that upon persons of a more emotional nature it would doubtless produce an even stronger effect; and Engels wrote that he had read it twice and had been moved by it so profoundly that he had been obliged to lay it aside in order to arrive at any critical perspective. It was only after pulling themselves together and making some purely literary observations that they were able to proceed to discuss, from their special historical point of view, the period with which the drama dealt and to show how Lassalle's own political position had led him to mistake the role of his hero. Aeschylus Marx loved for his grandeur and for the defiance of Zeus by Prometheus; Goethe they both immensely admired: Engels wrote of him as a "colossal" and "universal" genius whose career had been marred by an admixture in his character of the philistine and the courtier (*German Socialism in Verse and Prose*); Shakespeare Marx knew by heart and was extremely fond of quoting, but never—despite the long, learned and ridiculous essays which have appeared in the Soviet magazine, *International Literature*—attempted to draw from his plays any general social moral. So far, indeed, was Marx from having worked out a systematic explanation of the relation of art to social arrangements that he could assert, apropos of

Greek art, in his *Introduction to the Critique of Political Economy*, that "certain periods of highest development of art stand in no direct connection with the general development of society, nor with the material basis and the skeleton structure of its organization."

3. With Marx and Engels there is not yet any tendency to specialize art as a "weapon." They were both too much under the influence of the ideal of the many-sided man of the Renaissance, of the "complete" man, who, like Leonardo, had been painter, mathematician and engineer, or, like Machiavelli, poet, historian and strategist, before the division of labor had had the effect of splitting up human nature and limiting everyone to some single function (Engels' preface to his *Dialectic and Nature*). But with Lenin we come to a Marxist who is specialized himself as an organizer and fighter. Like most Russians, Lenin was sensitive to music; but Gorky tells us that on one occasion, after listening to Beethoven's Appassionata Sonata and exclaiming that he "would like to listen to it every day: it is marvelous superhuman music —I always think with pride . . . what marvelous things human beings can do," he screwed up his eyes and smiled sadly and added: "But I can't listen to music too often. It affects your nerves, makes you want to say stupid, nice things, and stroke the heads of people who could create such beauty while living in this vile hell. And now you mustn't stroke anyone's head—you might get your hand bitten off." Yet he was fond of fiction, poetry and the theater, and by no means doctrinaire in his tastes. Krupskaya tells how, on a visit to a Youth Commune, he asked the young people, "What do you read? Do you read Pushkin?" " 'Oh, no!' someone blurted out. 'He was a bourgeois. Mayakovsky for us.' Ilyitch smiled. 'I think Pushkin is better.' " Gorky says that one day he found Lenin with *War and Peace* lying on the table: " 'Yes, Tolstoy. I wanted to read over the scene of the hunt, then remembered that I had to write a comrade. Absolutely no time for reading.' . . . Smiling and screwing up his eyes, he stretched himself deliciously in his armchair and, lowering his voice, added quickly, 'What a colossus, eh? What a marvelously developed brain! Here's an artist for you, sir. And do you know something still more amazing? You couldn't find a genuine *muzhik* in literature till this count came upon the scene.' " In his very acute essays on Tolstoy, he deals with him much as Engels deals with Goethe—with tremendous admiration for Tolstoy's genius, but with an analysis of his non-resistance and mysticism in terms not, it is interesting to note, of the psychology of the landed nobility, but of the patriarchal peasantry with whom Tolstoy had identified himself. And Lenin's attitude toward Gorky was much like that of Marx toward Heine. He suggests in one of his letters that Gorky would be helpful as a journalist on the side of the Bolsheviks, but adds that he mustn't be bothered if he is busy writing a book.

4. Trotsky is a literary man as Lenin never was, and he published in 1924 a most remarkable little study called *Literature and Revolution*. In this book he tried to illuminate the problems which were arising for Russian writers with the new society of the Revolution. And he was obliged to come to grips with a question with which Marx and Engels had not been much concerned—the question of what Mr. James T. Farrell in his book, *A Note on Literary Criticism*, one of the few sensible recent writings on this subject, calls "the carryover value" of literature. Marx had assumed the value of Shakespeare and the Greeks and more or less left it at that. But what, the writers in Russia were now asking, was to be the value of the literature and art of the ages of barbarism and oppression in the dawn of socialist freedom? What in particular was to be the status of the culture of that bourgeois society from which socialism had just emerged and of which it still bore the unforgotten scars? Would there be a new proletarian literature, with new language, new style, new form, to give expression to the emotions and ideas of the new proletarian dictatorship? There had been in Russia a group called the Proletcult, which aimed at monopolizing the control of Soviet literature; but Lenin had discouraged and opposed it, insisting that proletarian culture was not something which could be produced synthetically and by official dictation of policy, but only by natural evolution as a "development of those reserves of knowledge which society worked for under the oppression of capitalism, of the landlords, of the officials." Now, in *Literature and Revolution*, Trotsky asserted that "such terms as 'proletarian literature' and 'proletarian culture' are dangerous, because they erroneously compress the culture of the future into the narrow limits of the present day." In a position to observe from his Marxist point of view the effects on a national literature of the dispossession of a dominant class, he was able to see the unexpected ways in which the presentments of life of the novelists, the feelings and images of the poets, the standards themselves of the critics, were turning out to be determined by their attitudes toward the social-economic crisis. But he did not believe in a proletarian culture which would displace the bourgeois one. The bourgeois literature of the French Revolution had ripened under the old regime; but the illiterate proletariat and peasantry of Russia had had no chance to produce a culture, nor would there be time for them to do so in the future, because the proletarian dictatorship was not to last: it was to be only a transition phase and to lead the way to "a culture which is above classes and which will be the first truly human culture." In the meantime, the new socialist literature would grow directly out of that which had already been produced during the domination of the bourgeoisie. Communism, Trotsky said, had as yet no artistic culture; it had only a political culture.

5. All this seems to us reasonable enough. But, reasonable and cultured as Trotsky is, ready as he is to admit that "one cannot always go by the principles of Marxism in deciding whether to accept or reject a work of art," that such a work "should be judged in the first place by its own law—that is, by the law of art," there is none the less in the whole situation something which is alien to us. We are not accustomed, in our quarter of the world, either to having the government attempt to control literature and art or to having literary and artistic movements try to identify themselves with the government. Yet Russia, since the Revolution, has had a whole series of cultural groups which have attempted to dominate literature either with or without the authority of the government; and Trotsky himself, in his official position, even in combating these tendencies, cannot avoid passing censure and pinning ribbons. Sympathizers with the Soviet regime used to assume that this state of affairs was inseparable from the realization of socialism: that its evils would be easily outgrown and that in any case it was a great thing to have the government take so lively an interest in culture. I believe that this view was mistaken. Under the Tsar, imaginative literature in Russia played a role which was probably different from any role it had ever played in the life of any other nation. Political and social criticism, pursued and driven underground by the censorship, was forced to incorporate itself in the dramatic imagery of fiction. This was certainly one of the principal reasons for the greatness during the nineteenth century of the Russian theater and novel, for the mastery by the Russian writers—from Pushkin's time to Tolstoy's—of the art of implication. In the 'fifties and 'sixties, the stories of Turgenev, which seem mild enough to us today, were capable of exciting the most passionate controversies—and even, in the case of *A Sportsman's Sketches*, causing the dismissal of the censor who had passed it—because each was regarded as a political message. Ever since the Revolution, literature and politics in Russia have remained inextricable. But after the Revolution the intelligentsia themselves were in power; and it became plain that in the altered situation the identification of literature with politics was liable to terrible abuses. Lenin and Trotsky, Lunacharsky and Gorky, worked sincerely to keep literature free; but they had at the same time, from the years of Tsardom, a keen sense of the possibility of art as an instrument of propaganda. Lenin took a special interest in the moving pictures from the propaganda point of view; and the first Soviet films, by Eisenstein and Pudovkin, were masterpieces of implication, as the old novels and plays had been. But Lenin died; Trotsky was exiled; Lunacharsky died. The administration of Stalin, unliterary and uncultivated himself, slipped into depending more and more on literature as a means of manipulating a people of whom, before the Revolution, 70 or 80 per cent had been illiterate and who could hardly be expected to be critical of what they read. Gorky seems to have exerted what influence he could in the direction of liberalism: to him was due, no doubt, the liquidation of RAPP, the latest device for the monopoly of culture, and the opening of the Soviet canon to the best contemporary foreign writing and the classics. But though this made possible more freedom of form and a wider range of reading, it could not, under the dictatorship of Stalin, either stimulate or release a living literature. Where no political opposition was possible, there was possible no political criticism; and in Russia political questions involve vitally the fate of society. What reality can there be for the Russians, the most socially-minded writers on earth, in a freedom purely "esthetic"? Even the fine melodramatic themes of the post-revolutionary cinema and theater, with their real emotion and moral conviction, have been replaced by simple trash not very far removed from Hollywood, or by dramatized exemplifications of the latest "directive" of Stalin which open the night after the speech that has announced the directive. The recent damning of the music of Shostakovich on the ground that the commissars were unable to hum it seems a withdrawal from the liberal position. And it is probable that the death of Gorky, as well as the imprisonment of Bukharin and Radek, have removed the last brakes from a precipitate descent, in the artistic as well as the political field, into a nightmare of informing and repression. The practice of deliberate falsification of social and political history which began at the time of the Stalin-Trotsky crisis and which has now attained proportions so fantastic that the government does not seem to hesitate to pass the sponge every month or so over everything that the people have previously been told and to present them with a new and contradictory version of their history, their duty, and the characters and careers of their leaders—this practice cannot fail in the end to corrupt every department of intellectual life, till the serious, the humane, the clear-seeing must simply, if they can, remain silent.

6. Thus Marxism in Russia for the moment has run itself into a blind alley —or rather, it has been put down a well. The Soviets seem hardly at the present time to have retained even the Marxist political culture, even in its cruder forms—so that we are relieved from the authority of Russia as we are deprived of her inspiration. To what conclusions shall we come, then, at this time of day about Marxism and literature—basing our views not even necessarily upon texts from the Marxist Fathers, but upon ordinary commonsense? Well, first of all, that we can go even further than Trotsky in one of the dicta I have quoted above and declare that Marxism by itself can tell us nothing whatever about the goodness or badness of a work of art. A man may be an excellent Marxist, but if he lacks imagination and taste he will be unable to make the choice between a good and an inferior book both of which are ideologically unexceptionable. What Marxism *can* do, however, is throw a great deal of light on the origins and social significance of works of art. The study of literature in its relation to society is as old as Herder—and even Vico. Coleridge had flashes of insight into the connection between literary and social phenomena, as when he saw the Greek state in the Greek sentence and the individualism of the English in the short separate statements of Chaucer's Prologue. But the

great bourgeois master of this kind of criticism was Taine, with his *race* and *moment* and *milieu;* yet Taine, for all his scientific professions, responded artistically to literary art, and responded so vividly that his summings-up of writers and re-creations of periods sometimes rival or surpass their subjects. Marx and Engels further deepened this study of literature in relation to its social background by demonstrating for the first time inescapably the importance of economic systems. But if Marx and Engels and Lenin and Trotsky are worth listening to on the subject of books, it is not merely because they created Marxism, but also because they were capable of literary appreciation.

7. Yet the man who tries to apply Marxist principles without real understanding of literature is liable to go horribly wrong. For one thing, it is usually true in works of the highest order that the purport is not a simple message, but a complex vision of things, which itself is not explicit but implicit; and the reader who does not grasp them artistically, but is merely looking for simple social morals, is certain to be hopelessly confused. Especially will he be confused if the author *does* draw an explicit moral which is the opposite of or has nothing to do with his real purport. Friedrich Engels, in the letter to Margaret Harkness already referred to above, in warning her that the more the novelist allows his political ideas to "remain hidden, the better it is for the work of art," says that Balzac, with his reactionary opinions, is worth a thousand of Zola, with all his democratic ones. (Balzac was one of the great literary admirations of both Engels and Marx, the latter of whom had planned to write a book on him.) Engels points out that Balzac himself was, or believed himself to be, a legitimist engaged in deploring the decline of high society; but that actually "his irony is never more bitter, his satire never more trenchant, than when he is showing us these aristocrats . . . for whom he felt so profound a sympathy," and that "the only men of whom he speaks with undissimulated admiration are his most determined political adversaries, the republican heroes of the Cloître-Saint-Merri, the men who at that period (1830–1836) truly represented the popular masses." Nor does it matter necessarily in a work of art whether the characters are shown engaged in a conflict which illustrates the larger conflicts of society or in one which from that point of view is trivial. In art—it is quite obvious in music, but it is also true in literature—a sort of law of moral interchangeability prevails: we may transpose the the actions and the sentiments that move us into terms of whatever we do or are ourselves. Real genius of moral insight is a motor which will start any engine. When Proust, in his wonderful chapter on the death of the novelist Bergotte, speaks of those moral obligations which impose themselves in spite of everything and which seem to come through to humanity from some source outside its wretched self (obligations "invisible only to fools—and are they really to them?"), he is describing a kind of duty which he felt only in connec-

tion with the literary work which he performed in his dark and fetid room; yet he speaks for every moral, esthetic or intellectual passion which holds the expediencies of the world in contempt. And the hero of Thornton Wilder's *Heaven's My Destination*, the traveling salesman who tries to save souls in the smoking car and writes Bible texts on hotel blotters, is something more than a symptom of Thornton Wilder's religious tendencies: he is the type of all saints who begin absurdly; and Wilder's story would be as true of the socialist Upton Sinclair as of the Christian George Brush. Nor does it necessarily matter, for the moral effect of a work of literature, whether the forces of bravery or virtue with which we identify ourselves are victorious or vanquished in the end. In Hemingway's story *The Undefeated*, the old bullfighter who figures as the hero is actually humiliated and killed, but his courage has itself been a victory. It is true, as I. Kashkin, the Soviet critic, has said, that Hemingway has written much about decadence, but in order to write tellingly about death you have to have the principle of life, and those that have it will make it felt in spite of everything.

8. The Leftist critic with no literary competence is always trying to measure works of literature by tests which have no validity in that field. And one of his favorite occupations is giving specific directions and working out diagrams for the construction of ideal Marxist books. Such formulas are of course perfectly futile. The rules observed in any given school of art become apparent, not before but after, the actual works of art have been produced. As we were reminded by Burton Rascoe at the time of the Humanist controversy, the esthetic laws involved in Greek tragedy were not formulated by Aristotle until at least half a century after Euripides and Sophocles were dead. And the behavior of the Marxist critics has been precisely like that of the Humanists. The Humanists knew down to the last comma what they wanted a work of literature to be, but they never—with the possible exception, when pressed, of *The Bridge of San Luis Rey*, about which they had, however, hesitations— were able to find any contemporary work which fitted their specifications. The Marxists did just the same thing. In an article called "The Crisis in Criticism" in the *New Masses* of February 1933, Granville Hicks drew up a list of requirements which the ideal Marxist work of literature must meet. The primary function of such a work, he asserted, must be to "lead the proletarian reader to recognize his role in the class struggle"—and it must therefore (1) "directly or indirectly show the effects of the class struggle"; (2) "the author must be able to make the reader feel that he is participating in the lives described"; and, finally, (3) the author's point of view must "be that of the vanguard of the proletariat; he should be, or should try to make himself, a member of the proletariat." This formula, he says, "gives us . . . a standard by which to recognize the perfect Marxian novel"—and adds "no novel as yet

written perfectly conforms to our demands." But the doctrine of "socialist realism" promulgated at the Soviet Writers' Congress of August 1934 was only an attempt on a larger scale to legislate masterpieces into existence—a kind of attempt which always indicates sterility on the part of those who engage in it, and which always actually works, if it has any effect at all, to legislate existing good literature *out of* existence and to discourage the production of any more. The prescribers for the literature of the future usually cherish some great figure of the past whom they regard as having fulfilled their conditions and whom they are always bringing forward to demonstrate the inferiority of the literature of the present. As there has never existed a great writer who really had anything in common with these critics' conception of literature, they are obliged to provide imaginary versions of what their ideal great writers are like. The Humanists had Sophocles and Shakespeare; the socialist realists had Tolstoy. Yet it is certain that if Tolstoy had had to live up to the objectives and prohibitions which the socialist realists proposed he could never have written a chapter; and that if Babbitt and More had been able to enforce against Shakespeare their moral and esthetic injunctions he would never have written a line. The misrepresentation of Sophocles, which has involved even a tampering with his text in the interests not merely of Humanism but of academic classicism in general, has been one of the scandalous absurdities of scholarship. The Communist critical movement in America, which had for its chief spokesman Mr. Hicks, tended to identify their ideal with the work of John Dos Passos. In order to make this possible, it was necessary to invent an imaginary Dos Passos. This ideal Dos Passos was a Communist, who wrote stories about the proletariat, at a time when the real Dos Passos was engaged in bringing out a long novel about the effects of the capitalist system on the American middle-class and had announced himself—in the *New Republic* in 1930—politically a "middle-class liberal." The ideal Dos Passos was something like Gorky without the mustache—Gorky, in the meantime, having himself undergone some transmogrification at the hands of Soviet publicity—and this myth was maintained until the Communist critics were finally compelled to repudiate it, not because they had acquired new light on Dos Passos, the novelist and dramatist, but because of his attitude toward events in Russia.

9. The object of these formulas for the future, as may be seen from the above quotations from Mr. Hicks, is to make of art an effective instrument in the class struggle. And we must deal with the dogma that "art is a weapon." It is true that art may be a weapon; but in the case of some of the greatest works of art, some of those which have the longest carry-over value, it is difficult to see that any important part of this value is due to their direct functioning as weapons. The *Divine Comedy*, in its political aspect, is a weapon for Henry of Luxemburg, whom Dante—with his medieval internationalism and his

lack of sympathy for the nationalistic instincts which were impelling the Italians of his time to get away from their Austrian emperors—was so passionately eager to impose on his countrymen. Today we may say with Carducci that we would as soon see the crown of his "good Frederick" rolling in Olona vale: "Jove perishes; the poet's hymn remains." And, though Shakespeare's *Henry IV* and *Henry V* are weapons for Elizabethan imperialism, their real center is not Prince Hal but Falstaff; and Falstaff is the father of *Hamlet* and of all Shakespeare's tragic heroes, who, if they illustrate any social moral—the moral, perhaps, that Renaissance princes, supreme in their little worlds, may go to pieces in all kinds of terrible ways for lack of a larger social organism to restrain them—do so evidently without Shakespeare's being aware of it. If these works may be spoken of as weapons at all, they are weapons in the more general struggle of modern European man emerging from the Middle Ages and striving to understand his world and himself—a function for which "weapon" is hardly the right word. The truth is that there is short-range and long-range literature. Long-range literature attempts to sum up wide areas and long periods of human experience, or to extract from them general laws; short-range literature preaches and pamphleteers with the view to an immediate effect. A good deal of the recent confusion of our writers in the Leftist camp has been due to their not understanding, or being unable to make up their minds, whether they are aiming at long-range or short-range writing.

10. This brings us to the question of what sort of periods are most favorable for works of art. One finds an assumption on the Left that revolutionary or pre-revolutionary periods are apt to produce new and vital forms of literature. This, of course, is very far from the truth in the case of periods of actual revolution. The more highly developed forms of literature require leisure and a certain amount of stability; and during a period of revolution the writer is usually deprived of both. The literature of the French Revolution consisted of the orations of Danton, the journalism of Camille Desmoulins and the few political poems that André Chenier had a chance to write before he was guillotined. The literature of the Russian Revolution was the political writing of Lenin and Trotsky, and Alexander Blok's poem, *The Twelve*, almost the last fruit of his genius before it was nipped by the wind of the storm. As for pre-revolutionary periods in which the new forces are fermenting, they *may* be great periods for literature—as the eighteenth century was in France and the nineteenth century in Russia (though here there was a decadence after 1905). But the conditions that make possible the masterpieces are apparently not produced by the impending revolutions, but by the phenomenon of literary technique, already highly developed, in the hands of a writer who has had the support of long-enduring institutions. He may reflect an age of transition, but it will not necessarily be true that his face is set squarely in the direction of

the future. The germs of the Renaissance are in Dante and the longing for a better world in Virgil, but neither Dante nor Virgil can in any real sense be described as a revolutionary writer: they sum up or write elegies for ages that are passing. The social organisms that give structure to their thought—the Roman Empire and the Catholic Church—are already showing signs of decay. It is impossible, therefore, to identify the highest creative work in art with the most active moments of creative social change. The writer who is seriously intent on producing long-range works of literature should, from the point of view of his own special personal interests, thank his stars if there is no violent revolution going on in his own country in his time. He may disapprove of the society he is writing about, but if it were disrupted by an actual upheaval he would probably not be able to write.

11. But what about "proletarian literature" as an accompaniment of the social revolution? In the earlier days of the Communist regime in Russia, one used to hear about Russian authors who, in the effort to eliminate from their writings any vestige of the bourgeois point of view, had reduced their vocabulary and syntax to what they regarded as an A B C of essentials—with the result of becoming more unintelligible to the proletarian audience at whom they were aiming than if they had been Symbolist poets. (Indeed, the futurist poet Mayakovsky has since that time become a part of the Soviet canon.) Later on, as I have said, Soviet culture followed the road that Trotsky recommended: it began building again on the classics and on the bourgeois culture of other countries and on able revolutionary Russian writers who had learned their trade before the Revolution. "Soviet publishers"—I quote from the Russian edition of *International Literature,* issue 2 of 1936—"are bringing out Hemingway and Proust not merely in order to demonstrate 'bourgeois decay.' Every genuine work of art—and such are the productions of Hemingway and Proust—enriches the writer's knowledge of life and heightens his esthetic sensibility and his emotional culture—in a word, it figures, in the broad sense, as a factor of educational value. Liberated socialist humanity inherits all that is beautiful, elevating and sustaining in the culture of previous ages." The truth is that the talk in Soviet Russia about proletarian literature and art has resulted from the persistence of the same situation which led Tolstoy under the old regime to put on the muzhik's blouse and to go in for carpentry, cobbling and plowing: the difficulty experienced by an educated minority, who were only about 20 per cent of the people, in getting in touch with the illiterate majority. In America the situation is quite different. The percentage of illiterates in this country is only something like 4 per cent; and there is relatively little difficulty of communication between different social groups. Our development away from England, and from the old world generally, in this respect—in the direction of the democratization of our idiom—is demonstrated clearly in H. L. Mencken's *The American Language;* and if it is a question of either the use for high literature of the language of the people or the expression of the dignity and importance of the ordinary man, the country which has produced *Leaves of Grass* and *Huckleberry Finn* has certainly nothing to learn from Russia. We had created during our pioneering period a literature of the common man's escape, not only from feudal Europe, but also from bourgeois society, many years before the Russian masses were beginning to write their names. There has been a section of our recent American literature of the last fifteen years or so—the period of the boom and the depression—which has dealt with our industrial and rural life from the point of view of the factory hand and the poor farmer under conditions which were forcing him to fight for his life, and this has been called proletarian literature; but it has been accompanied by books on the white-collar worker, the storekeeper, the well-to-do merchant, the scientist and the millionaire in situations equally disastrous or degrading. And this whole movement of critical and imaginative writing—though with some stimulus, certainly, from Russia— had come quite naturally out of our literature of the past. It is curious to observe that one of the best of the recent strike novels, *The Land of Plenty* by Robert Cantwell, himself a Westerner and a former mill worker, owes a good deal to Henry James.

12. Yet when all these things have been said, all the questions have not been answered. All that has been said has been said of the past; and Marxism is something new in the world: it is a philosophical system which leads directly to programs of action. Has there ever appeared before in literature such a phenomenon as M. André Malraux, who alternates between attempts, sometimes brilliant, to write long-range fiction on revolutionary themes, and exploits of aviation for the cause of revolution in Spain? Here creative political action and the more complex kind of imaginative writing have united at least to the extent that they have arisen from the same vision of history and have been included in the career of one man. The Marxist vision of Lenin— Vincent Sheean has said it first—has in its completeness and its compelling force a good deal in common with the vision of Dante; but, partly realized by Lenin during his lifetime and still potent for some years after his death, it was a creation, not of literary art, but of actual social engineering. It is society itself, says Trotsky, which under communism becomes the work of art. The first attempts at this art will be inexpert and they will have refractory material to work with; and the philosophy of the Marxist dialectic involves idealistic and mythological elements which have led too often to social religion rather than to social art. Yet the human imagination has already come to conceive the possibility of re-creating human society; and how can we doubt that, as it acquires the power, it must emerge from what will seem by comparison the

revolutionary "underground" of art as we have always known it up to now and deal with the materials of actual life in ways which we cannot now even foresee? This is to speak in terms of centuries, of ages; but, in practicing and prizing literature, we must not be unaware of the first efforts of the human spirit to transcend literature itself.

From *The Triple Thinkers* by Edmund Wilson. First published in 1938, by Harcourt, Brace and Company, Inc.; and in a revised edition by the Oxford University Press, 1948, from which the essay is here reproduced by permission of the author and publishers. First published in *The Atlantic Monthly,* Volume CLX (December, 1937), pp. 741–750.

WILLIAM PHILLIPS and
PHILIP RAHV
Private Experience and Public Philosophy
[1936]

THAT "free individual interpretation" and "private experience" are essential to poetry is one postulate that few critics have cared to question. Also, for the most part they agree that the greatness of a poem is in some way related to the outlook or public philosophy of the poet. But here the argument begins. For what is "private" to one group is "public" to another, and frequently it is claimed that a harmonious marriage of the two is impossible because ultimately they are incompatible. Thus compartmentalized, experience and philosophy are pitted against each other. T. S. Eliot, who embodies the contradictions as well as the achievements of his period, sees the necessity for both elements while contending they are incompatible. The two quotations are from "Poetry and Propaganda," written in 1930:

Yet we can hardly doubt that the "truest" philosophy is the best material for the greatest poet; so that the poet must be rated in the end both by the philosophy he realizes in his poetry and by the fullness and adequacy of the realization.

There is a gulf, and I think an impassable one, between the intuitions of the poets as such, and any particular philosophy, or even any philosophical direction rather than any other.

The position Eliot takes in this essay and his eclectic conclusions betray a rudderless philosophy of value; that is, a notion that no one philosophy is true and that any "profound" philosophy may be held and used by poets. Sharing this notion, poets during the last few decades felt relieved of responsibility for their ideas. Experience—personal, ever more unique experience— became the touchstone of poetry. Today the problem looms again: as poets pass from one intellectual climate into another public philosophy and private experience are put up as the horns of a poetic dilemma. Suspension among a variety of beliefs, with the consequent gyrations into formal experiments, is no longer acceptable to those who have taken a definite attitude toward the world we live in. How to communicate this attitude, even while maintaining the integrity of personal experience, is one of the major problems of the poet in this age.

We are convinced that behind many of the attacks on revolutionary poetry lurks the notion of the contradiction we have just discussed. What else will account for the charge that the philosophy of social revolution strait-jackets the poet's experience, leaving no room for the play of his imagination and the unique quality of his personal emotions? We are led to believe that the revolutionary poet is a mere puppet pulled by the strings of sociology and politics, and that his talent is spent on the linguistic decoration of a closed order of beliefs. Naturally, such poetry is regarded as a violent break with tradition—a noble medium reduced to the service of menial utilitarian ends.

If, however, theory is at bottom no more than history generalizing about itself, then let us check the indictment against the poetic objects involved. You could easily fit this theory to a body of anonymous poetry, inasmuch as all the poems, expressing an impersonal public philosophy, would prove to be essentially identical. But except for ideological direction, what is there in common between Fearing and Schneider, either in method, intention, or feeling? And though both Gregory and Aragon move within the Marxian orbit, in his actual verse-texture Gregory is as far away from Aragon as he is from Allen Tate. The fact is that revolutionary poetry teems with personal tonalities, and is composed of many strains and tendencies. It is true, of course, that the work of a small scattered group of "leftists," poaching on the fringes of revolutionary poetry, does illustrate in several ways the charges of impersonality and barren publicism. But it is just as dishonest to identify this group with revolutionary poetry in its representative aspects as it would be for a Marxist to identify the criticism of T. S. Eliot with that of William Lyon Phelps for the sole reason that from a strictly political point of view both are anti-communist. Caught in the wiles of literalism, the infantile "leftists" have equated the weapon of art with the art of weapons, with the result that they are not writing poetry but clichéd slogans and stale manifestoes. Yet the critics of the right hardly excel in this respect, for in their own field they too have accepted this monstrous equation. Fundamentally it involves the same faulty understanding of Marxism, though one group accepts it and the other rejects it.

If we were to explore all the corners of the creative problem implied in this controversy, we should hear its echoes in the philosophic question concerning the relation of the ego to the objective world. Or, granting that poetry is an objective body of poems, having continuity and a social status, what is the relation of poetry to the individual poet? Assume a contradiction between a public philosophy and the private experience of the poet and what you get is poetic solipsism, whereby the history and tradition of poetry are dissolved in the acid of uniqueness. A contradiction arises between the poet and the objective meanings of the poetry that has been written, and the only reality remaining to him is his own work. French poetry of post-symbolist days and the writing of the *transition* school actually approached this state. In Paul Valéry's essay, "A Foreword," we observe the process of ideas by means of which any given poetry purges itself of all else, even of other poetry:

. . . One can say that the greatest . . . of the versified works which have come down to us belong to the didactic or historical order.

Finally, toward the middle of the nineteenth century, French literature saw the birth of a remarkable ambition—that of isolating poetry from every essence other than its own.

I mean to say that our tendency . . . toward a beauty always more independent of all *subjects,* and free from sentimental vulgar interest . . . was leading to an almost inhuman state.

This inhuman state was the dead end, though much important poetry steered clear of it.

It would be almost gratuitous to recall that Shakespeare was soaked in prevailing "Elizabethan" attitudes, and that Dante did not seek poetic pastures fenced off from Catholic philosophy. It is only in times like the present, when opposing philosophies battle for power and art is compelled to choose between several public viewpoints, that the presence of social thought in poetry is questioned. The choice before him makes the writer aware of the implications of his work in other fields of discourse and action; it shows him how his private experience illustrates and confirms one public philosophy rather than another. He does not choose between freedom and bondage, but between freedom within one frame and freedom within another. Homer was not free to write from the outlook of Goethe, and many poets today reject the "freedom" to see through the eyes of Robinson Jeffers, for example. Whether a poet has consciously or unconsciously taken to a set of beliefs is irrelevant if we are concerned with objective social effects. In facing the task of creation, however, the distinction may be crucial. In this decade many of our most important poets are pitching their writing in a revolutionary key. But since this is in defiance of habitual attitudes, the poet must consciously adjust his medium to his philosophy. At this point a host of creative questions take on new meaning, because the way the adjustment is made has much to do with the quality of the poem.

Consider the question of theme. Unfortunately many misguided enthusiasts of revolution, effacing their own experience, take for their subject-matter the public philosophy as such, or attempt to adorn with rhetorical language conventionalized patterns of feeling and action. What they don't see is that these patterns are, in the final analysis, just as impersonal as the philosophy itself. Hence we get poems that are really editorial write-ups, a kind of "reality" on parade from which the deeper spiritual and emotional insights are necessarily banished. If there is to be an ever-fresh balance between the accent of the poet and the attitude he shares with other people, he must understand the connection between what is *real* to him as an individual and what is *real* to him as a partisan of some given philosophy.

Too often reality is thought of as a pictorial essence, or invoked as a platonic idea. Both the kind of poetry which is a series of snapshots and the kind which is pure generalization fail to convey the full human meaning of the subject. Experience as such, abstracted from the social situation that bore and reared it, is merely a fake short-cut to a desperate originality; and philosophy divested of the *genius loci,* no matter how nobly declaimed, is like a pedant preaching in meter. To see oneself truly is to see oneself in relation to the larger social issue, and to see the larger social issue truly is to see oneself in it.

Of course, to talk about a philosophy without considering its validity would be like talking about international diplomacy without reference to the concrete interests of nations. We have argued that there is no contradiction between philosophy and experience, but patently such a contradiction is inevitable if the philosophy is false. It was necessary for Eliot to pervert the testimony of his early poems before he could enter credibly into the sanctum of theology. On the other hand, poets like Verlaine, Rimbaud, and Crane accepted no philosophies within their reach, for their experience denied its validity. But today poets are being drawn to an interpretation of the world which is but a broader generalization of the evidence inherent in their own material. No honest and typical experience of our age can exclude a sense of the organized vulgarity and corruption of modern society. The movement of history has again made possible the much desired integration of the poet's conception with the leading ideas of his time.

This necessary integration is being achieved by those revolutionary poets who have been most aware that their revolt is esthetic as well as social, and that as such it is a revolt within the tradition of poetry rather than against it. In the work of Horace Gregory, Kenneth Fearing, and a number of younger poets—who make up the representative school of revolutionary poetry in this country—we observe the emergence of a basic symbolism of rejection and aspiration marking the development of the medium to articulate in its own terms a new hope and a valiant effort. On this ground they have come in conflict with a counter-symbolism of barricades and flag-waving lifted from the surface of events. Those following the line of least resistance grasp these precipitant and standardized emblems as substitutes for the living tissue of the thing itself. In their own right such emblems may exercise a certain appeal for naïve readers, yet they remain a means of evading poetic endeavor. No matter what color it runs to, centrally heated rhetoric stifles the spirit. It is only when the poet, sustained by an objective world-view, tempers his symbols in the fires of his own imagination, that he is able to achieve that intensity and truth which is poetry.

From *Poetry: A Magazine of Verse,* Vol. XLVIII (May, 1936), pp. 98–105. Reprinted by permission.

R. S. CRANE

I. A. Richards on the Art of Interpretation

[1949]

No ONE in our time has written more voluminously than Mr. I. A. Richards on the difficulties that confront the interpreter of philosophical and literary texts, and no one has been more widely credited with the discovery of new principles and techniques by the aid of which, once they are fully elaborated, we may attain, in his own words, to "levels of intelligence in interpretation higher than those yet reached." The books which are cited in support of these high claims, from *The Meaning of Meaning* and *Principles of Literary Criticism* through *Mencius on the Mind* to *The Philosophy of Rhetoric, Interpretation in Teaching,* and *How To Read a Page,* constitute, indeed, an impressive series of disquisitions on what were once called the Liberal Arts, which cannot be neglected by those curious about contemporary developments in intellectual criticism and exegesis. Their originality is undeniable; what is not so certain—and it is into this that I propose to inquire—is whether they have anything substantial to contribute, in the way either of general concepts or of particular methods, which would justify the confidence of Mr. Richards' admirers that he has succeeded in putting the old art of interpreting texts on not only a new but a greatly improved basis.

Although he has written a great many pages in explanation of his doctrine, the doctrine itself is comparatively simple. Let us note two facts, to begin with, concerning the manner in which, according to him, correct thought about both the meaning of texts and the meaning of the meaning of texts must be derived. The two facts are closely related, and they are—as will become evident later—at once postulates of the right method of inquiry into both these questions and necessary consequences of the application of this method to the problems it allows or compels us to pose. In the first place, as Mr. Richards constantly reminds us, there is no thinking about anything that does not proceed inevitably by sorting and analogy. "Thinking," he remarks, "is radically metaphoric. Linkage by analogy is its constituent law or principle, its causal nexus. . . . To think of anything is to take it *as* of a sort." Nor is this true only of the "fluid" discourse which, because of its relaxation of definition, is nearly related to poetry. Recognition of likes and discrimination of unlikes is the universal mode of generalization, and "Mathematics and the sciences, so often praised, and rightly, for the training in Logic they provide, are the leisurely, analyzed, explicitly recorded developments of the very same processes that, well or ill, operate in the main mode of metaphor." "To think of anything is to take it *as* of a sort." To think of the interpretation of discourse, as of discourse itself and of language in general, is, therefore, to think of it in terms of some fundamental analogy, some context or causal nexus with our past experience, by which the words we employ in the inquiry may be made to yield useful generalizations.

But—and this is the second postulate—since the end of our inquiry is knowledge, the only analogy which will serve our purpose is one that exhibits meaning and the meaning of meaning as instances of a sort of thing that in some sense can be pointed to rather than as instances merely of the theorist's attitudes or desires. We must endeavor, in other words, to rid our thinking about the subject from the fictions which have obscured it in the speculations of our predecessors, and to this end we must fashion our language in speaking of it as nearly as possible according to the pattern of natural science. And this means that we must dispense systematically with all terms which men have employed in the vain attempt to say *what* meaning or discourse is or *why* it is so and so, and confine ourselves to the terms we use to say *how* something behaves.

For science, which is simply our most elaborate way of *pointing* to things systematically, tells us and can tell us nothing about the nature of things in any *ultimate* sense. It can never answer any questions of the form: *What* is so and so? It can only tell us *how* so and so behaves. And it does not attempt to do more than this. Nor, indeed, can more than this be done. Those ancient, deeply troubling, formulations that begin with "What" and "Why" prove, when we examine them, to be not questions at all; but requests—for emotional satisfaction. They indicate our desire not for knowledge but for assurance, a point which appears clearly when we look into the "How" of questions and requests, of knowledge and desire.

The only meaningful way, then, in which we can talk about meaning is in terms of some analogy to the local motion of natural objects considered as a temporal sequence of events linked merely by efficient causes. It is a revealing fact that the terms and metaphors (in Mr. Richards' sense of the word) that recur most frequently in the key positions of his analysis are those designated by such expressions as "action," "motion," "behavior," "event." Thus thought "in the widest sense" is "any event in the mind"; "our knowledge is a reaction in us to something"; and the principles of Basic English—a language the theory of which recognizes no categories other than action and reaction— are "the oldest and most indubitable of all" (though at the same time the most modern and scientific) precisely because they represent "what we and our pre-human ancestors know most about," namely, how to perform those movements by which we maintain our vulnerable bodies in a world of "hard, moving, impenetrable and excarnificatory objects." The method of the inquiry is thus determined in a way strictly appropriate to the findings it seeks to obtain; and it will consequently occasion no surprise to the reader to learn from *The Philosophy of Rhetoric* that for Mr. Richards the true theory of interpretation—as distinguished from the superficial or erroneous theories of the past, which have been content with "bad analogies" based on unanswerable questions—not only has some affinities with physics but is "obviously a branch of biology."

It is at this point that the beautiful simplicity of Mr. Richards' scheme shines most clearly through the sophisticated diction and tortuous movement of the prose in which it is explained. Like the early Greek physicists who accounted for all things by means of one or two pairs of contrary terms such as the dense and the rare or Love and Strife, he has found a way of reducing the whole problem of reading texts, even the most elaborately organized ones, to no more than two closely related distinctions, the one primarily psychological, the other (in the broadest sense of the term) linguistic. Meaning, he argues, is a kind of event which occurs whenever these two pairs of contraries mingle in the experience of any sensible creature, whether animal or human being, and there is no variety of meaning, at whatever level of intelligence or education, that cannot be adequately understood by considering it as an instance of this sort of behavior. Pavlov's dog hearing a bell from a distant part of the mansion and thereupon rushing incontinently to the dining-room; a man expecting a flame when he hears the scratch of a match; a scientist in the laboratory observing an instrument and writing down a formula in his notebook; a scholar expounding a passage in Plato—the only principles we need to interpret any of these example of what Mr. Richards calls the universal "sign-situation" are, first, the fact that any response of an organism to a stimulus from its environment involves at once, though in varying proportions on different occasions, an appropriation of the stimulus and a reaction against it, and, second, the circumstance that any awareness the organism may have of the relation between the felt impression and its antecedents or consequences in the environment or in the organism itself is a resultant of the interaction of the immediate experience with remembered experiences of like character in the past. Whether dog or scholar, we are all merely organisms living and functioning in the midst of things, capable of responding both to stimuli from without and to motions or feelings from within; and when we do respond, whether the result is to submit ourselves to things or to assert our purposes emotively with respect to them, the process is invariably one in which something taken as a sign is referred to something, real or fictitious, taken as a thing, by means of the co-operation in our minds of the present occasion with parallel or analogous events remembered from our past.

We need not ask why this is so; it is enough that we are so constituted that whenever a sign (as the sound of the dinner-bell or the occurrence of a puzzling word or construction in a text) is presented to our mind at a particular moment and in a particular set of circumstances, it acts upon us, through a kind of metaphoric attraction of like to like, by calling up the missing parts of the "context" of things or actions with which it has been linked in our previous experience. The meaning of any sign is thus the missing parts of its contexts; it is the "delegated efficacy" which any symbol acquires through its peculiar ability to serve as a substitute "exerting the powers of what is not there." We can have no sign-situation—no act of thinking or interpretation—of which this linking, by analogy, of past and present is not the essential feature; but it is obvious, given our nature as organisms in a world of things, that the process by which signs function as meanings may vary widely from time to time according as the major pull in the experience comes from the world of external objects to which the sign is being referred or from the needs and desires of the organism demanding emotional satisfaction. We may use signs or react to them, in other words, either in terms of their reference to objects or in terms of the effects in emotion and attitude which the reference produces; in the one case the mind is subjected to things, in the other it moulds things to its own purposes and passions. No thought is possible in which the rivalry of the two functions is not to be discerned; however completely we teach our reactions to correspond with external states of affairs, the disturbing factor of the organism is always present.

The theory of discourse which Mr. Richards constructs by analogy with his account of the natural sign-situation is inevitably a theory in which the essential parts of any written composition—its meanings or our perceptions of its meanings—are treated as discrete events involving the co-operation or rivalry of "contexts." The term "context," as he points out, must here be understood in a double sense.

(1) A word, like any other sign, gets whatever meaning it has through belonging to a recurrent group of events, which may be called its context. Thus a word's context, *in this sense,* is a certain recurrent pattern of *past* groups of events, and to say that its meaning depends upon its context would be to point to the process by which it has acquired its meaning. (2) In another, though a connected sense, a word's context is *the words which surround it in the utterance,* and the other *contemporaneous signs* which govern its interpretation. . . . For clarity we may distinguish the second sort of context by calling it the *setting.*

Whenever, in short, we use words to make a statement, or what looks like a statement, about anything, we are taking part in a process of analogical interaction between the "setting" in which our words are placed and the various "contexts"—there may be an indefinite number of them—which have surrounded the words in their past careers. A meaning is always an instance of a sort, its efficacy dependent upon a perceived likeness between present and former occasions—that is what is meant by the dictum that all thinking is radically metaphoric; and when the former occasions have been particularly numerous and conflicting, it is obvious that the pull of divergent possible interpretations upon the new "setting" must be severe. In his chapter on the meanings of the word "definite" in *Interpretation in Teaching*, Mr. Richards gives some striking examples, from the "protocols" of his students, of the force of these opposing attractions, but there is every reason to suppose that they operate more or less constantly in the literary prose of more expert writers. It is only rarely, indeed—and chiefly in the vocabulary of the rigorously limited laboratory sciences—that the "contexts" determining the meanings of terms approach a state of uniformity which allows us to say that the words and sentences in a passage "mean what they mean absolutely and unconditionally." The function of definition in the sciences is precisely to effect such a control over the interaction of contexts for the specific purpose in hand, but it is seldom, outside "the relatively *simple* fields of the sciences," that an equivalent control is possible, or even desirable.

Argument is a peculiar, specialized use of language to which it has not yet accommodated itself. To put it more strictly, the logical use of words, with single constant senses that are the same for each recurrence, maintained unchanged through a series of sentence manipulations, is an extremely artificial sort of behaviour to which our minds do not lend themselves until after a long and severe training. It is no more like our usual ways of talking than the goosestep is like our strolling gait. And the fluidity, the incessant delicate variation in the meaning of our words, which is a hindrance to explicit argument, is the virtue of language for our other purposes.

It is an error, consequently, to suppose that "if a passage means one thing it cannot at the same time mean another and an incompatible thing." The different contexts or types of context which supply the meaning for a single utterance are in constant rivalry one with another, with the result that we should "expect ambiguity to the widest extent and of the subtlest kinds nearly everywhere, and of course we find it."

The problem of the interaction of contexts is inseparable, for Mr. Richards, from the larger question, arising from the double character of all organic behavior, of the differences and connections among "the various aims of discourse, the purposes for which we speak or write." It is characteristic that here again, abandoning as unfruitful the traditional attempt to differentiate kinds of writing in terms of subject-matter, method, or end, he reduces the problem to a distinction, by analogy with the facts of the universal sign-situation, among "the functions of language." The fundamental opposition thus derived

—familiar to all his readers since the *Principles of Literary Criticism*—is that between "pure scientific impersonal or neutral statement," in which words are used to point to things, and "emotive utterance which expresses and evokes states of feeling." The theory of discourse, thus, must take account of all the complicated ways in which emotional attitude may be combined with reference and reference distorted by attitude; it must be prepared to distinguish clearly the varieties of "statement, full and explicit, or condensed (by abstraction, ambiguity or implication, the hint, the aposiopesis); statement literal or direct, and indirect (by metaphor, simile, comparison, parallel, etc.); suasion, open (from cajolery) or concealed (either as mere statement or as mere ornament) and so on." And the principle which unifies the extremes is still the same principle of the interinanimation of contexts on which, as we have seen, all significances depend.

From Pavlov's dog responding meaningfully to the sound of the dinner-bell to the writer or reader of a prose masterpiece successfully contending with the divergent attractions of linguistic contexts and functions, the transition is thus perfectly clear: to understand the behavior of the one is to know by simple analogy all the truth that can be found out about the behavior of the other. The statement of that truth in words which must themselves necessarily exemplify it constitutes the scientific or theoretical aspect of the philosophy of interpretation. But interpretation, like any sort of animal response, exists only as event, so that to interpret a particular text is to function in a sign-situation in no way different in kind from those precipitated by the sound of the dinner-bell or the scratch of the match, but of course immensely more complicated in the number of co-operating and conflicting stimuli, whether contexts or settings, that are brought to bear on the mind of the interpreter. It is here, in Mr. Richards' argument, that we abandon, at least momentarily, the simplicities of theory for the paradoxes and duplicities of practice. It would seem, on the one hand, that, since interpretation is a natural process, nature herself, assisted by a kind of exercise similar to that which gives strength to the muscles, could well be trusted to make us all at least reasonably good interpreters of books. And this, indeed, is largely true. We are all born, Mr. Richards assures us, with a "natural skill in interpretation"—a skill that need not wait upon training in principles to be "inexplicably, unimaginably and all-but-triumphantly, successful already." Let us then avoid, in education, anything that will interfere with the working of the instinctive dialectic by which, as in all our thinking, we recognize likes and discriminate unlikes as a normal result of the process of contextual interaction. Yet nothing is more evident, we are also told (and the students' "protocols" quoted by Mr. Richards bear out the point), than that the natural skill in interpretation, when it is brought to bear on the words of a particular text, too often becomes confused and fails. An art of interpretation is therefore needed which will start with the "uncanny powers" we have already developed and help us develop them a little further.

For the outlines of such an art Mr. Richards reverts to the distinctions of the medieval trivium. "Less by design than from the nature, history and life of its subject," he says in the introduction to *Interpretation in Teaching*, "this treatise has grown into three parts which correspond roughly to ancient provinces of thought. Rhetoric, Grammar and Logic—the first three liberal Arts, the three ways to intelligence and a command of the mind that met in the Trivium, meet here again." What is needed is precisely the training they are fitted to give, a training now almost entirely lacking in the curriculum; but such a training can be fruitful, can lead to better interpretations, only if Rhetoric, Grammar, and Logic are taught to students not as sciences but as arts, and as arts, moreover, which have in common, for all their differences in emphasis, the basic problems of the sign-situation.

For improvement of the natural skill in interpretation, however, even the minimum of theoretical analysis to which the arts are thus reduced is of little direct importance. The difficulty is not that our students are ignorant of principles; it is rather that they do not know "how to distinguish and meet the varying modes of language *in practice.*" Our only sure reliance, therefore, must be the art of the teacher who, though he himself is an expert in the theory of meaning, takes care not to interfere with the natural growth of his pupils by imposing ideas upon them but contents himself with inventing occasions for self-discovery and with devising exercises which will bring his students to an awareness of their failures through comparison with the failures or only partial successes of others. The essential character of the method, as Mr. Richards expounds and illustrates it, is that of a free dialectic working on passages or sentences through exhibition of the contexts of their words or through construction of parallels between them and other passages or sentences. Controls are no doubt necessary, but they take the form not of explicit criteria for determining when a proper adjustment has been made between context and setting but rather of collections of the chief contexts of key words, such as "grammar" or "definite" or "is," or of translations into the vocabulary of Basic English.

The spirit of the procedure Mr. Richards recommends is well exemplified in his own "interpretation," in chapter xvii of *Interpretation in Teaching*, of a sentence from John Stuart Mill's *Inaugural Address at St. Andrews*. The problem is how we know what the pronoun 'their' refers to in the last clause of the following: "Even as mere languages, no modern European language is so valuable a discipline to the intellect as those of Greece and Rome, on account of their regular and complicated structure."

How do we know what 'their' refers to? If we wrote 'their irregular and oversimple structure' the sentence would in several minor ways not mean the same, but most of Mill's main point would be preserved—only 'their' would have been switched over then to modern European languages, not to Greek and Latin. And equally it would be the context [i.e., our knowledge of the recurrent group of past events in which 'irregular' and 'simple' have referred to the structure of modern languages] which told us how to read it. . . . With the setting he is not likely to misread, for we know that Greek and Latin will be thought to be more regular and complicated than modern languages—whatever the facts in the matter, and the assumptions, as to the sorts of regularity and complication involved may be. Moreover, 'regular,' at least, in such an occurrence as this, seems a word of praise [i.e., to have an emotive context] and so goes with 'valuable.' This joins with the setting to bar out the possibility that Mill (as others have sometimes thought) was thinking that the less regular a language the harder the task of learning it and therefore the better the discipline. There is an articulation between 'regular' and 'complicated,' which was lost by my rephrasing, 'their irregular and over-simple structure.' Mill's full point is 'though complicated yet regular.' And this articulation shows us that Mill is thinking of a certain sort of discipline which he expects from Greek and Latin.

It will no doubt have occurred to many readers that the problem of the reference of "their" in Mill's sentence—if problem it be—could have been solved much more expeditiously than it is solved here by the traditional devices of grammatical analysis. Mr. Richards seems to be aware of the objection, but he readily dismisses it as already outlawed by the original assumptions and analogies on which his system is erected:

This kind of analysis of the factors in interpretation can I believe usefully take the place of formal grammatical parsing. Parsing gave exercise in it incidentally, and had value as far as it did; but, in itself, it is an unnatural and distracting antic. This other sort of interpretative study follows closely the actual processes that take place in composition; parsing does not. No one asks, or should ask, himself in writing, 'What does this dependent phrase qualify?' We do all inquire, all the time we are writing, about the consiliences and the articulations of the meanings of the parts with one another; or, if we don't, we can very easily be made to.

It should be clear from what has gone before why he thinks this a completely cogent answer. For if the only questions that can give us the truth about things are questions concerning *how* something behaves, then obviously we are merely troubling our mind with fictions and seeking emotional assurance rather than knowledge if we permit ourselves, whether in writing something of our own or in reading the work of others, to put such queries as *"What does this dependent phrase qualify?"* The antic is indeed both unnatural and distracting—unnatural since it is an arbitrary intrusion into the process of contextual interaction, and distracting since it tends to mingle emotive with

referential words. What we can know—and to know this is precisely the end
of the art of interpretation—is *how* we have become aware, in so far as we
have been successful in our reading, of *how* the words in a particular passage
"behave."

Such, in its broad outlines, is the new art of interpreting prose, and of
teaching the interpretation of prose, which Mr. Richards would have us substitute for the pre-scientific or magic-mongering systems of the past. His success
in winning support for his proposals has been, as we all know, very considerable; and the secret is not hard to find. He has had the great advantage
of knowing how to deal with perennial issues in a thoroughly modern style.
In an age of faith in biology, he has contrived to frame the problems of literature, with rare consistency, in terms of primordial organic processes; in
an age convinced beyond any in the past that the key to all philosophic
mysteries, and to most of our practical difficulties as well, is to be found
in the study of words, he has effected a remarkable renovation of the liberal
arts by substituting for their traditional distinctions and devices a universal
theory of signs. The natural appeal of his doctrine, moreover, has been greatly
enhanced by the assured, not to say dogmatic, manner of its delivery. Nothing
is more distinctive of his exposition, in all his many books, than the "damna-
tory clauses" in which, as Macaulay said of the Benthamites, his creed
abounds "far beyond any theological symbol with which we are acquainted."
"I neither am," he has said, "nor hope to be a scholar"; but this modesty has
not prevented him from exposing, with his usual vigor of expression, the
trivialities, the confusions, the absurdities, the false problems and unnecessary
mysteries, the gross evasions of the most interesting issues, which have characterized, almost without exception, the efforts of scholars in the past to deal
with the meaning of texts. It is no wonder that, armed with such credentials,
he has succeeded in convincing a wide public that only now at last, in this
crucial matter of literary interpretation, have our eyes been opened to the
reality of things, our first principles properly established, and the one true
method of procedure clearly revealed.

It behooves us, therefore, if we are to form an independent judgment of a
system so alluring in its modernity, so imposing in its dogmatic rigor, to look a
little more closely both at the first principles upon which it is founded and at
the practical consequences which appear to flow inevitably from them.

It is obvious, first of all, that Mr. Richards' consideration of discourse is
organized about three fundamental terms—the venerable triad which has
served countless writers on logic, grammar, and rhetoric since Plato and Aristotle: the words in which texts are composed, the ideas or thoughts they symbolize, and the "real" things or events to which their words and statements

refer. This triple distinction is the basis of the famous triangle of meaning first presented in *The Meaning of Meaning* and since then employed consistently in all his linguistic or rhetorical arguments. There is nothing in this fact by itself, of course, that is in any way unique: how else, indeed, could we say anything intelligible about any human discourse save by reference to the subject-matter dealt with in its statements, the doctrines or beliefs set forth concerning this subject-matter, and the words by which these doctrines are expressed? Everything turns, therefore, on the manner in which, in any given theory of discourse or interpretation, the three indispensable factors are related to each other as organizing principles of the discussion. There are only two major possibilities: on the one hand, we may recognize that, since the three terms are in themselves, apart from any use we make of them, completely equivocal words, the literal senses we give to them and the relations constructed among these senses may legitimately vary from context to context, so that our treatment of words or of thought or of subject-matter may be quite distinct according as we are concerned, let us say, with the analysis of poems, or of rhetorical compositions, or of philosophical arguments. Or, on the other hand, we may prefer once for all to fix the relation of words, thoughts, and things in a single pattern, determined by a fundamental analogy, which will henceforth persist throughout our consideration of individual problems as a device by which the particularities of our subject-matter may be resolved into a set of simple universal laws. Now the choice as between these two primary modes of procedure is obviously one that cannot be avoided by any writer who proposes to treat of the problem of interpretation, and once made it just as obviously entails consequences which, if the resulting analysis is self-consistent, must be expected to manifest themselves even in the least details of the system. And the essential point is that the choice itself—however deplorable the fact may seem—is a choice that involves, for the theorist of discourse, simply a decision as to the way in which he intends to use his own words—whether, on the one hand, to mark off sharp distinctions of meaning, so that no one distinguishable aspect of an object is resolved into anything else, or, on the other hand, to make possible a reduction of such distinctions in the interest of a simple unified truth. The choice is therefore independent of the nature of things, except as the nature of things may be held responsible for the necessity of such a choice; and it is logically prior to any true conclusions that may be reached about characteristics of writings which can be attributed to them only through use of the particular mode of definition and argument that has been selected.

Mr. Richards, it need hardly be said, has chosen the second rather than the first of these two ways of dealing with words, thoughts, and things as basic factors in the interpretation of discourse. He has chosen to fix the meanings and relations of his three central terms prior to his use of them in any particular inquiries; and he has chosen to fix them by means of a fundamental analogy or "metaphor" (in his sense of that word) which takes various forms in his writings, but is perhaps best represented by the parallel, in *The Meaning of Meaning*, of Pavlov and his dog.

The basis of that metaphor, it will be recalled, is a situation involving two distinct elements, one of which—the dog moving toward the dining-room—is biological strictly, and the other of which—Pavlov conditioning the dog so that it will perform this action whenever the dinner-bell rings—is biological only in an indirect and unimportant sense, its essential character being that of an interference by human art with the processes of nature. From each of these elements Mr. Richards derives one of the two basic distinctions of his scheme: from the motions of the dog considered as an organism capable both of attending to things outside itself and of responding to stimuli from within, he takes the distinction which emerges on the level of human speech as the contrast of emotive and referential language or of fluid and rigid discourse; from the purposive actions of Pavlov so connecting food and the sound of the dinner-bell in the reflexes of the dog that, whenever the bell is heard, a motion is set up toward the usual place of food, he borrows the distinction, central to the art of interpretation as he conceives it, between linguistic "contexts" and "settings." The device whereby he brings the two elements of the analogy together in his system involves taking the sound of the dinner-bell as at once a sign of the previous situations, arranged by Pavlov, in which it had been connected with food, and as a stimulus to biological reactions on the part of the dog when it is again heard. When symbols are interpreted thus, the terms of the original triad of words, thoughts, and things fall into a characteristically simple pattern: the only problem we need consider is that of the function of individual words as the medium by which, in the uninterrupted flow of experience, human thought is shaped by reference either to things (considered always as "sorts") or to fictions that take the place of things. In this function words may obviously become important instruments for manipulating thoughts to one or another of the two purposes, given by the biological part of the analogy, for which symbols may be employed—to point to things or to express our own emotions; but the ways in which they work are determined by things in the sense of the contexts of past events, whether involving things or thoughts, in which they have been used. The processes of nature, of meaning, and of intention are thus separable only dialectically, as a consequence of our acquired ability to discriminate signs; no independent consideration of any of the three is possible, and hence no independent analysis, such as has been attempted by writers in the past, of words as applied to things or to ideas or to words or of ideas in relation to their objects or of objects in relation to other objects; rather all the problems tend to merge into one, which can only be examined with profit—that is, as a problem of things rather than merely of thought or words—by considering how particular words "behave" with respect to each other and to the things and thoughts they bring before our minds.

It is this radical unification of the whole traditional analysis in terms of the "behavior" of individual words that impels Mr. Richards to dismiss, with such telling effect, not only the notion that any art or methodology is involved in his firsthand dealings with language, but likewise all the various systems of grammar, logic, and rhetoric in which previous writers—more concerned, in his view, with theories than with applications—have developed principles for an analysis of the structural aspects of discourse or for a particularized consideration of its various kinds. Preoccupied as he is with inducing a heightened awareness of individual sign-situations by comparisons of words, he has nothing to offer but a universal method for the reading of texts—a method without any devices for discriminating differences in subject-matter or in method or in intention in the sense of the specific ends, peculiar to the given work, to which means have been rationally adapted by the author.

The causes of this curious dialectical asceticism will perhaps become clear if we revert to the analogy in the light of which Mr. Richards' system has been constructed. The difficulty is not, of course, that the facts upon which one half of the metaphor is based involve nothing more exalted than the natural motions of a dog; readers of Plato, at all events, will not have forgotten the excellent use which Socrates makes of this same animal in the *Republic* when it is a question of determining what virtues are appropriate to the guardians of the state. And there is surely no reason why an analysis of argument, more nearly adequate than any Mr. Richards gives us for the explanation of structural characteristics in prose, could not be developed from postulates as strictly biological as his. The proof, if proof were needed, is afforded by the recent work of John Dewey, *Logic: The Theory of Inquiry*. The condition of such a development, as Mr. Dewey shows, is simply the recognition that organic behavior is typically sequential; that, as appears plainly in such "unified and continuous" animal responses as hunting and stalking prey, it is not merely "a succession and compounding of independent discrete reflex-art units" but a kind of elementary problem-solving with direction and cumulative force. If this is granted, and if we assume a continuity of evolution from animal forms and activities to those of man, then, given the potentiality, on the human level, of a cultural environment and of reflective thought, we need no other principles whereby to justify, in purely naturalistic terms, a fairly elaborate analysis of intellectual discourse as an art of fitting logical means to consequences in the solution of problems. Mr. Richards, however, although he can insist that the theory of interpretation is obviously a branch of biology, is not free to push the biological part of his metaphor as far as this; the dog is not simply a dog, it is Pavlov's dog; and this being the case, its contribution to the explanation of language is necessarily limited to those aspects of its natural behavior which are adequately described—to borrow Mr. Dewey's phrase—as "simply a succession of isolated and independent units of excitation-reaction," or, in other words, as discrete events considered apart from any possible sequence of actions in which they function as means to an intelligible end. To the extent, therefore, that the problem of discourse and of the interpretation of discourse is determined by this part of Mr. Richard's analogy, the most we can expect in the way of principles is a simple pair of contraries applicable only to particular words.

The relation of means and consequences, however, is clearly implied in the part of the metaphor which concerns Pavlov, and the beginnings at least of an analysis of intellectual method, relevant to many kinds of prose literature, might easily have been derived by considering what is involved when a scientist selects one experiment rather than another as more directly conducive to a specific end. Needless to say, it is not this aspect of Pavlov that interests Mr. Richards, but rather two more limited aspects, one of which has to do with the results of his acts of conditioning as these appear in the subsequent operations of the dog whenever the dinner-bell rings, and the other of which relates to the processes and immediate intentions of the experiment itself. From the first comes the idea of the interaction of "contexts" and "settings" which is, for Mr. Richards, the essence of "meaning" interpreted as a natural event solely in terms of its efficient cause. But it is still necessary to account for the contexts themselves which determine materially the behavior of signs whenever these occur in a novel setting; and since, when the problem is transferred to the level of human discourse, there can be no longer a Pavlov conditioning our reflexes, some substitute, less external in a literal sense to the individual organism but still in a way external, must evidently be discovered for the function he performs as experimenter in the original situation. That substitute is, in the first place, the long history of contextual interactions, in other men and in our past lives, which we call our cultural and linguistic inheritance. By this, as represented, for example, in the vast proliferation of meanings contained in the *Oxford English Dictionary* or in Mr. Richards' lists, we are all controlled, much as Pavlov's dog was controlled, in each of our uses or interpretations of any of the words we write or read, so that ambiguity—i.e., the intrusion into a particular setting of many contexts—is an ever-present and never entirely soluble problem. But what has been conditioned may also, to a certain extent at least, be reconditioned; and if Pavlov persists in Mr. Richards' account of language and discourse as the more or less external control exercised over our words and thoughts by past associations of words with things, he also re-emerges, especially in practical treatises like *In-*

terpretation in Teaching, in the person of the teacher who sets his pupils exercises in verbal comparisons and translations to the end of heightening their awareness of how words behave in relation to other words and to things and ideas. He is the enlightened teacher, but he is also that most valuable instrument of the enlightened teacher, Basic English—a language that contributes to our understanding of both things and words by reducing the vocabulary of English to those words which are closest to things inasmuch as their primary contexts are the organic motions of putting and taking, giving and getting, pointing and feeling; a language, moreover, that enables us to cope more efficiently with the problem of ambiguity by increasing still farther that disproportion between the finiteness of words and the infiniteness of things from which ambiguity arises!

It would be unfair to say of the procedure Mr. Richards recommends for the practice and teaching of interpretation that it consists merely of a technique of lexicographical exercise without other ends than the exercise itself. The ends are there, and they are stated variously as understanding, as intelligence, as heightened awareness, as intellectual discernment, as insight, as self-discovery, as improvement of our command of all the interconnections of thought, non-verbal as well as verbal. Yet, however distinct these aims may appear in statements of them taken out of their context in Mr. Richards' system, it is evident, when we recall the basic principles of that system, that they are all ends as nearly identifiable with the means devised for their realization as was Pavlov's awareness of the behavior of his dog with the experiment he conducted for the sake of inducing that behavior. What Mr. Richards gives us, in short, in following out this aspect of his analogy, is simply a set of experimental devices for bringing about in the reader a sharpened consciousness of linguistic particulars as sorts of universal motions.

To go beyond this either by traveling the biological road taken by Mr. Dewey or by developing the implications of Pavlov as the artist in experiments would entail the elaboration of a general scheme of analysis applicable to particular texts in such a way that the particularity of their structure rather than the universality of their material constituents would become the center of attention. He is restrained, however, from adopting either of these courses by the peculiar character of the metaphor from which his whole method springs. It is a metaphor resting on what is clearly a constructed situation, partly natural and partly artificial, with the two elements so related that any full development of one of them is immediately checked or interfered with by some trait in the other. In the end, for Mr. Richards, it is nature which exerts the stronger dialectical pull, and it does so by virtue of the skeptical implications for our understanding of the terms of philosophy and the arts contained in his biological distinction between pointing and feeling, with its equivalent in the linguistic contrast of referential and emotive words. We

have seen that this distinction underlies his doubts about the scientific meaningfulness of any other questions than those which ask *how* something behaves, and so deprives him from the start of all explanatory resources except
such as are furnished by his very limited conception of the efficient cause. We
have seen how it leads him to posit, as the ideal mode of interpretation, a
procedure which, unlike the unnatural and distracting antic of parsing, follows closely the actual processes of composition as these should be if not as
they are. And we may suggest that the strong suspicion of previous theories of
criticism and interpretation which runs throughout his works, and which confirms him in his preference for a method so nearly universal that it seems to
him no method at all, gains much of its force from precisely this bias in favor
of one rather than the other of the two components, not quite perfectly fused,
of the original metaphor.

The method is a universal one, but it *is* a method, and as such it is only
fair to judge it, finally, in terms of its consequences apart from the somewhat
arbitrarily constructed first principles by which it is validated theoretically.
And first of all, as we have noted so often, there is a whole range of problems
—real problems, too, since they force themselves on us, independently of any
theories of interpretation, whenever we attempt to understand a text as a
whole or to compare two writings on the same subject—for the solution of
which his scheme provides no apparatus whatever. Thus we are constantly
tempted to ask, in reading prose works of any distinction, on what principles
the words or sentences are ordered in this or that passage, or why the parts of
the argument are arranged as they are, or how we may account for the author's insistence on certain aspects of his problem and his neglect of other
aspects which, in the writings of his predecessors or successors, have usually
been given a prominent place. In order to find answers to such questions we
obviously need devices which will enable us to discover a writer's basic terms,
not merely as so many frequently recurrent words, but rather as the fundamental scheme of concepts by means of which his problem is stated and the
parts and order of his argument determined; we need principles by which,
once the terms have been established, possible modes of working with them
may be distinguished; and we need other principles, involving still more particularized discriminations of ends and means, in the light of which the peculiar structural characteristics of individual works may be understood and
appreciated. It is evident that no such principles or devices are to be looked
for anywhere in Mr. Richards' many publications. He speaks much of purposes in writing, but what he has in mind are the universal purposes, or
linguistic "functions," common to the sophisticated author and the simplest
biological organism, not those which differentiate writers as voluntary agents.
He writes books which expound, as we have seen, a highly characteristic

system of thought; but nowhere in these books does he provide means whereby the system may be understood in its distinctive outlines or whereby we may progress, in our reading of his books, beyond what is stated in separate paragraphs and sentences.

It is to these, indeed—the significant wholes to which his method tends to reduce all literature—that he systematically endeavors to confine our attention. For the Richardian interpreter of discourse there can be only one problem, and whether that problem is stated generally as the interaction of contexts and settings or is specified as ambiguity or metaphor or confusion of statement and definition, it is clearly one which can be adequately posed and solved in terms of isolated statements considered apart from the total artistic or logical structure of the works in which they appear. For the problem is really one of the universal behavior of words as determined by events which in any strict sense are extra-literary, and a solution is possible just as soon as we have enough of the immediate setting of the word before us to permit an estimate of what various contexts have been at work. Thus—to adapt an example from *Basic Rules of Reason*—it is not necessary to read the whole of the *Preface to the "Lyrical Ballads"* in order to deal with the question of what is meant by "poetry" in Wordsworth's assertion that "poetry is the look on the face of science"; instead we have only to recognize that the problem turns essentially on the meaning of "is," that "is" may have different meanings according as the sentences in which it occurs are definitions of words or statements about the things of which the word is the name, that if we compare the saying of Wordsworth with other sayings about "poetry" (Mr. Richards gives a good many of them) we see that it is more like a statement than a definition, and that as such, separated from a definition, it may have as many senses as Wordsworth or we ourselves at any time have attached to the word.

All this, granted the way in which the problem is stated, is no doubt true, and there is clearly abundant justification in the circumstance for Mr. Richards' insistence on our need of a "better apparatus for controlling the senses of our words." A twofold difficulty, however, immediately confronts us. On the one hand, even if we allow that the question of Wordsworth's meaning in the sentence quoted can be intelligibly discussed in terms of that sentence alone plus the "contexts" of its words, there is nothing, so far as one can see, in the "better apparatus" Mr. Richards gives us—neither in his lists of the senses of "is" or of "poetry" nor in his directions for translation exercises into Basic English—that can do anything more than heighten our awareness of the problem. And, on the other hand, if we are seriously interested in discovering Wordsworth's intention rather than simply in playing a new and somewhat complicated linguistic game, and if consequently we insist on considering the question not in the vacuum of a single sentence but in the total context, highly particularized as it is, of Wordsworth's argument and method in the *Preface,* then we are already provided, in various of the devices afforded by traditional dialectic, with much of the apparatus we need. For the problem of ambiguity is not, as many of Mr. Richards' disciples suppose, a new one; and if the problem is what we have always thought it to be, the means of dealing with it available to us in (say) the first book of the *Topics* would still seem adequate to most of our uses. It is not easy, therefore, to escape the suspicion that what is at issue for Mr. Richards is not the question of ambiguity, in the usual meaning, at all; that his concern is less with solutions that make sense of difficult texts in their authors' terms than with the discovery or manufacture of problems by which linguistic wonder may be excited, and that that method is best, accordingly, which so restricts its means of solution that what emerges from any act of interpretation is not so much understanding of the author as increased insight into our own marvelous but somewhat confused minds.

There would be no objection to this were it not that the reading of a book in any sense that involves doing justice to the distinctive intentions of its author is rendered impossible thereby. For the essence of Mr. Richards' method, so far as it assumes a positive character at all, is translation; and what inevitably happens when that technique is applied to a writer of any intellectual sophistication or systematic integrity will be plain to whoever meditates on the strange fate of John Stuart Mill in chapter xvii of *Interpretation in Teaching.* But translation in the mode exhibited in this chapter is innocent enough when compared to the fundamental distortion necessarily undergone by any writer who philosophizes in other categories than action and reaction when his statements are subjected to the Procrustean dialectic of Basic English—a language whose key terms have been selected in explicit opposition to most of the varied ways of dealing with the problem of words, ideas, and things to be found in the important prose writers of the past.

It is at this point that the question of method and the practical consequences thereof rejoins the question of principles. For if it be indeed true, as has been occasionally insinuated by followers of Mr. Richards, that his is a theory that ends all theories except itself and the better thought about language we may look for in the future, then the objections we have brought against his program for the reform of interpretation are not only irrelevant but philosophically unsound—expressions of our wishes that carry over into a new age the fictions and magic-charged concepts of the past. Our examination of Mr. Richards' views will perhaps have been justified if it has revealed the essential circularity of all such retorts. For what is the force of an appeal to the nature of things against rival doctrines of language or discourse when that nature itself has been determined by a decision, prior to any inquiry, to identify reality only with what can be signified in a particular fixed relationship among three equivocal words? And what is there to compel an abandonment of the distinctions of traditional grammar or logic in an argument which derives all its negative cogency from a metaphor so admirably adapted to the end of destroying such distinctions as that upon which Mr. Richards' system is based?

From *Ethics,* Vol. LIX, No. 2, Part I, (January, 1949), pp. 112–126. Reprinted by permission of the author and editors.

CLEANTH BROOKS

Irony as a Principle of Structure

[1949]

ONE can sum up modern poetic technique by calling it the rediscovery of metaphor and the full commitment to metaphor. The poet can legitimately step out into the universal only by first going through the narrow door of the particular. The poet does not select an abstract theme and then embellish it with concrete details. On the contrary, he must establish the details, must abide by the details, and through his realization of the details attain to whatever general meaning he can attain. The meaning must issue from the particulars; it must not seem to be arbitrarily forced upon the particulars. Thus, our conventional habits of language have to be reversed when we come to deal with poetry. For here it is the tail that wags the dog. Better still, here it is the tail of the kite—the tail that makes the kite fly—the tail that renders the kite more than a frame of paper blown crazily down the wind.

The tail of the kite, it is true, seems to negate the kite's function: it weights down something made to rise; and in the same way, the concrete particulars with which the poet loads himself seem to deny the universal to which he aspires. The poet wants to "say" something. Why, then, doesn't he say it directly and forthrightly? Why is he willing to say it only through his metaphors? Through his metaphors, he risks saying it partially and obscurely, and risks not saying it at all. But the risk must be taken, for direct statement leads to abstraction and threatens to take us out of poetry altogether.

The commitment to metaphor thus implies, with respect to general theme, a principle of indirection. With respect to particular images and statements, it implies a principle of organic relationship. That is, the poem is not a collection of beautiful or "poetic" images. If there really existed objects which were somehow intrinsically "poetic," still the mere assemblage of these would not give us a poem. For in that case, one might arrange bouquets of these poetic images and thus create poems by formula. But the elements of a poem are related to each other, not as blossoms juxtaposed in a bouquet, but as the blossoms are related to the other parts of a growing plant. The beauty of the poem is the flowering of the whole plant, and needs the stalk, the leaf, and the hidden roots.

If this figure seems somewhat highflown, let us borrow an analogy from another art: the poem is like a little drama. The total effect proceeds from all the elements in the drama, and in a good poem, as in a good drama, there is no waste motion and there are no superfluous parts.

In coming to see that the parts of a poem are related to each other organically, and related to the total theme indirectly, we have come to see the importance of *context*. The memorable verses in poetry—even those which seem somehow intrinsically "poetic"—show on inspection that they derive their poetic quality from their relation to a particular context. We may, it is true, be tempted to say that Shakespeare's "Ripeness is all" is poetic because it is a sublime thought, or because it possesses simple eloquence; but that is to forget the context in which the passage appears. The proof that this is so becomes obvious when we contemplate such unpoetic lines as "vitality is all," "serenity is all," "maturity is all,"—statements whose philosophical import in the abstract is about as defensible as that of "ripeness is all." Indeed, the commonplace word "never" repeated five times becomes one of the most poignant lines in *Lear,* but it becomes so because of the supporting context. Even the "meaning" of any particular item is modified by the context. For what is said is said in a particular situation and by a particular dramatic character.

The last instances adduced can be most properly regarded as instances of "loading" from the context. The context endows the particular word or image or statement with significance. Images so charged become symbols; statements so charged become dramatic utterances. But there is another way in which to look at the impact of the context upon the part. The part is modified by the pressure of the context.

Now the *obvious* warping of a statement by the context we characterize as "ironical." To take the simplest instance, we say "this is a fine state of affairs," and in certain contexts the statement means quite the opposite of what it purports to say literally. This is sarcasm, the most obvious kind of irony. Here a complete reversal of meaning is effected: effected by the context, and pointed, probably, by the tone of voice. But the modification can be most important even though it falls far short of sarcastic reversal, and it need not be underlined by the tone of voice at all. The tone of irony can be effected by the skillful disposition of the context. Gray's *Elegy* will furnish an obvious example.

> Can storied urn or animated bust
> Back to its mansion call the fleeting breath?
> Can Honour's voice provoke the silent dust,
> Or Flatt'ry soothe the dull cold ear of death?

In its context, the question is obviously rhetorical. The answer has been implied in the characterization of the breath as fleeting and of the ear of death as dull and cold. The form is that of a question, but the manner in which the question has been asked shows that it is no true question at all.

These are obvious instances of irony, and even on this level, much more poetry is ironical than the reader may be disposed to think. Many of Hardy's poems and nearly all of Housman's, for example, reveal irony quite as definite and overt as this. Lest these examples, however, seem to specialize irony in the direction of the sardonic, the reader ought to be reminded that irony, even in its obvious and conventionally recognized forms, comprises a wide variety of modes: tragic irony, self-irony, playful, arch, mocking, or gentle irony, etc. The body of poetry which may be said to contain irony in the ordinary senses of the term stretches from *Lear*, on the one hand, to "Cupid and Campaspe Played," on the other.

What indeed would be a statement wholly devoid of an ironic potential—a statement that did not show any qualification of the context? One is forced to offer statements like "Two plus two equals four," or "The square on the hypotenuse of a right triangle is equal to the sum of the squares on the two sides." The meaning of these statements is unqualified by any context; if they are true, they are equally true in any possible context.[1] These statements are properly abstract, and their terms are pure denotations. (If "two" or "four" actually happened to have connotations for the fancifully minded, the connotations would be quite irrelevant: they do not participate in the meaningful structure of the statement.)

But connotations are important in poetry and do enter significantly into the structure of meaning which is the poem. Moreover, I should claim also—as a corollary of the foregoing proposition—that poems never contain abstract statements. That is, any "statement" made in the poem bears the pressure of the context and has its meaning modified by the context. In other words, the statements made—including those which appear to be philosophical generalizations—are to be read as if they were speeches in a drama. Their relevance, their propriety, their rhetorical force, even their meaning, cannot be divorced from the context in which they are imbedded.

The principle I state may seem a very obvious one, but I think that it is nonetheless very important. It may throw some light upon the importance of

---

[1] This is not to say, of course, that such statements are not related to a particular "universe of discourse." They are indeed, as are all statements of whatever kind. But I distinguish here between "context" and "universe of discourse." "Two plus two equals four" is not dependent on a special dramatic context in the way in which a "statement" made in a poem is. Compare "two plus two equals four" and the same "statement" as contained in Housman's poem:

> —To think that two and two are four
> And neither five nor three
> The heart of man has long been sore
> And long 'tis like to be.

the term *irony* in modern criticism. As one who has certainly tended to over-use the term *irony* and perhaps, on occasion, has abused the term, I am closely concerned here. But I want to make quite clear what that concern is: it is not to justify the term *irony* as such, but rather to indicate why modern critics are so often tempted to use it. We have doubtless stretched the term too much, but it has been almost the only term available by which to point to a general and important aspect of poetry.

Consider this example: The speaker in Matthew Arnold's "Dover Beach" states that the world, "which seems to lie before us like a land of dreams . . . hath really neither joy nor love nor light. . . ." For some readers the statement will seem an obvious truism. (The hero of a typical Hemingway short story or novel, for example, will say this, though of course in a rather different idiom.) For other readers, however, the statement will seem false, or at least highly questionable. In any case, if we try to "prove" the proposition, we shall raise some very perplexing metaphysical questions, and in doing so, we shall certainly also move away from the problems of the poem and, finally, from a justification of the poem. For the lines are to be justified in the poem in terms of the context: the speaker is standing beside his loved one, looking out of the window on the calm sea, listening to the long withdrawing roar of the ebbing tide, and aware of the beautiful delusion of moonlight which "blanches" the whole scene. The "truth" of the statement, and of the poem itself, in which it is imbedded, will be validated, not by a majority report of the association of sociologists, or a committee of physical scientists, or of a congress of meta-physicians who are willing to stamp the statement as proved. How is the statement to be validated? We shall probably not be able to do better than to apply T. S. Eliot's test: does the statement seem to be that which the mind of the reader can accept as coherent, mature, and founded on the facts of ex-perience? But when we raise such a question, we are driven to consider the poem as drama. We raise such further questions as these: Does the speaker seem carried away with his own emotions? Does he seem to oversimplify the situation? Or does he, on the other hand, seem to have won to a kind of detachment and objectivity? In other words, we are forced to raise the ques-tion as to whether the statement grows properly out of a context; whether it acknowledges the pressures of the context; whether it is "ironical"—or merely callow, glib, and sentimental.

I have suggested elsewhere that the poem which meets Eliot's test comes to the same thing as I. A. Richards' "poetry of synthesis"—that is, a poetry which does not leave out what is apparently hostile to its dominant tone, and which, because it is able to fuse the irrelevant and discordant, has come to terms with itself and is invulnerable to irony. Irony, then, in this further sense, is not only an acknowledgment of the pressures of a context. Invulnera-bility to irony is the stability of a context in which the internal pressures balance and mutually support each other. The stability is like that of the arch: the very forces which are calculated to drag the stones to the ground actually provide the principle of support—a principle in which thrust and counterthrust become the means of stability.

In many poems the pressures of the context emerge in obvious ironies. Marvell's "To His Coy Mistress" or Raleigh's "Nymph's Reply" or even Gray's "Elegy" reveal themselves as ironical, even to readers who use irony strictly in the conventional sense.

But can other poems be subsumed under this general principle, and do they show a comparable basic structure? The test case would seem to be presented by the lyric, and particularly the simple lyric. Consider, for example, one of Shakespeare's songs:

> Who is Silvia: what is she
>   That all our swains commend her?
> Holy, fair, and wise is she;
>   The heavens such grace did lend her,
> That she might admired be.
>
> Is she kind as she is fair?
>   For beauty lives with kindness.
> Love doth to her eyes repair,
>   To help him of his blindness,
> And, being help'd, inhabits there.
>
> Then to Silvia let us sing,
>   That Silvia is excelling;
> She excels each mortal thing
>   Upon the dull earth dwelling:
> To her let us garlands bring.

On one level the song attempts to answer the question "Who is Silvia?" and the answer given makes her something of an angel and something of a goddess. She excels each mortal thing "Upon the dull earth dwelling." Silvia herself, of course, dwells upon that dull earth, though it is presumably her own brightness which makes it dull by comparison. (The dull earth, for example, yields bright garlands which the swains are bringing to her.) Why does she excel each mortal thing? Because of her virtues ("Holy, fair, and wise is she"), and these are a celestial gift. She is heaven's darling ("The heavens such grace did lend her").

Grace, I suppose, refers to grace of movement, and some readers will insist that we leave it at that. But since Silvia's other virtues include holiness and wisdom, and since her grace has been lent from above, I do not think that we can quite shut out the theological overtones. Shakespeare's audience would have found it even more difficult to do so. At any rate, it is interesting to see what happens if we are aware of these overtones. We get a delightful richness, and we also get something very close to irony.

The motive for the bestowal of grace—that she might admired be—is oddly untheological. But what follows is odder still, for the love that "doth to her eyes repair" is not, as we might expect, Christian "charity" but the little pagan god Cupid ("Love doth to her eyes repair, / To help him of his blindness.") But if Cupid lives in her eyes, then the second line of the stanza takes on another layer of meaning. "For beauty lives with kindness" becomes not merely a kind of charming platitude—actually often denied in human experience. (The Petrarchan lover, for example, as Shakespeare well knew, frequently found a beautiful and *cruel* mistress.) The second line, in this context, means also that the love god lives with the kind Silvia, and indeed has taken these eyes that sparkle with kindness for his own.

Is the mixture of pagan myth and Christian theology, then, an unthinking confusion into which the poet has blundered, or is it something wittily combined? It is certainly not a confusion, and if blundered into unconsciously, it is a happy mistake. But I do not mean to press the issue of the poet's self-consciousness (and with it, the implication of a kind of playful irony). Suffice it to say that the song is charming and delightful, and that the mingling of elements is proper to a poem which is a deft and light-fingered attempt to suggest the quality of divinity with which lovers perennially endow maidens who are finally mortal. The touch is light, there is a lyric grace, but the tone is complex, nonetheless.

I shall be prepared, however, to have this last example thrown out of court since Shakespeare, for all his universality, was a contemporary of the metaphysical poets, and may have incorporated more of their ironic complexity than is necessary or normal. One can draw more innocent and therefore more convincing examples from Wordsworth's Lucy poems.

> She dwelt among the untrodden ways
>   Beside the springs of Dove,
> A maid whom there were none to praise
>   And very few to love;
>
> A violet by a mossy stone
>   Half hidden from the eye!
> Fair as a star, when only one
>   Is shining in the sky.
>
> She lived unknown, and few could know
>   When Lucy ceased to be;
> But she is in her grave, and, oh,
>   The difference to me.

Which is Lucy really like—the violet or the star? The context in general seems to support the violet comparison. The violet, beautiful but almost unnoticed, already half hidden from the eye, is now, as the poem ends, completely hidden in its grave, with none but the poet to grieve for its loss. The star comparison may seem only vaguely relevant—a conventional and here a somewhat anomalous compliment. Actually, it is not difficult to justify the star comparison: to her lover's eyes, she is the solitary star. She has no rivals, nor would the idea of rivalry, in her unselfconscious simplicity, occur to her.

The violet and the star thus balance each other and between themselves define the situation: Lucy was, from the viewpoint of the great world, unnoticed, shy, modest, and half hidden from the eye, but from the standpoint of her lover, she is the single star, completely dominating that world, not arrogantly like the sun, but sweetly and modestly, like the star. The implicit contrast is that so often developed ironically by John Donne in his poems where the lovers, who amount to nothing in the eyes of the world, become, in their own eyes, each the other's world—as in "The Good-Morrow," where their love makes "one little room an everywhere," or as in "The Canonization," where the lovers drive into the mirrors of each other's eyes the "towns, countries, courts"—which make up the great world; and thus find that world in themselves. It is easy to imagine how Donne would have exploited the contrast between the violet and the star, accentuating it, developing the irony, showing how the violet was really like its antithesis, the star, etc.

Now one does not want to enter an Act of Uniformity against the poets. Wordsworth is entitled to his method of simple juxtaposition with no underscoring of the ironical contrast. But it is worth noting that the contrast with its ironic potential is there in his poem. It is there in nearly all of Wordsworth's successful lyrics. It is certainly to be found in "A slumber did my spirit seal."

> A slumber did my spirit seal;
>   I had no human fears:
> She seemed a thing that could not feel
>   The touch of earthly years.
>
> No motion has she now, no force;
>   She neither hears nor sees,
> Rolled round in earth's diurnal course,
>   With rocks, and stones, and trees.

The lover's insensitivity to the claims of mortality is interpreted as a lethargy of spirit—a strange slumber. Thus the "human fears" that he lacked are apparently the fears normal to human beings. But the phrase has a certain pliability. It could mean fears *for* the loved one as a mortal human being; and the lines that follow tend to warp the phrase in this direction: it does not occur to the lover that he needs to fear for one who cannot be touched by "earthly years." We need not argue that Wordsworth is consciously using a witty device, a purposed ambiguity; nor need we conclude that he is confused. It is enough to see that Wordsworth has developed, quite "normally," let us say, a context calculated to pull "human fears" in opposed directions, and that the slightest pressure of attention on the part of the reader precipitates an ironical effect.

As we move into the second stanza, the potential irony almost becomes overt. If the slumber has sealed the lover's spirit, a slumber, immersed in which he thought it impossible that his loved one could perish, so too a slumber has now definitely sealed *her* spirit: "No motion has she now, no force; / She neither hears nor sees." It is evident that it is her unnatural slumber that has waked him out of his. It is curious to speculate on what Donne or Marvell would have made of this.

Wordsworth, however, still does not choose to exploit the contrast as such. Instead, he attempts to suggest something of the lover's agonized shock at the loved one's present lack of motion—of his response to her utter and horrible inertness. And how shall he suggest this? He chooses to suggest it, not by saying that she lies as quiet as marble or as a lump of clay; on the contrary, he attempts to suggest it by imagining her in violent motion—violent, but imposed motion, the same motion indeed which the very stones share, whirled about as they are in earth's diurnal course. Why does the image convey so powerfully the sense of something inert and helpless? Part of the effect, of course, resides in the fact that a dead lifelessness is suggested more sharply by an object's being whirled about by something else than by an image of the object in repose. But there are other matters which are at work here: the sense of the girl's falling back into the clutter of things, companioned by things chained like a tree to one particular spot, or by things completely inanimate, like rocks and stones. Here, of course, the concluding figure leans upon the suggestion made in the first stanza, that the girl once seemed something not subject to earthly limitations at all. But surely, the image of the whirl itself is important in its suggestion of something meaningless—motion that mechanically repeats itself. And there is one further element: the girl, who to her lover seemed a thing that could not feel the touch of earthly years, is caught up helplessly into the empty whirl of the earth which measures and makes time. She is touched by and held by earthly time in its most powerful and horrible image. The last figure thus seems to me to summarize the poem—to offer to almost every facet of meaning suggested in the earlier lines a concurring and resolving image which meets and accepts and reduces each item to its place in the total unity.

Wordsworth, as we have observed above, does not choose to point up specifically the ironical contrast between the speaker's former slumber and the loved one's present slumber. But there is one ironical contrast which he does stress: this is the contrast between the two senses in which the girl becomes insulated against the "touch of earthly years." In the first stanza, she "could not feel / The touch of earthly years" because she seemed divine and immortal. But in the second stanza, now in her grave, she still does not "feel the touch of earthly years," for, like the rocks and stones, she feels nothing at all. It is true that Wordsworth does not repeat the verb "feels"; instead he writes "She neither *hears* nor *sees*." But the contrast, though not commented upon directly by any device of verbal wit, is there nonetheless, and is bound to make itself felt in any sensitive reading of the poem. The statement of the first stanza has been literally realized in the second, but its meaning has been ironically reversed.

Ought we, then, to apply the term *ironical* to Wordsworth's poem? Not necessarily. I am trying to account for my temptation to call such a poem ironical—not to justify my yielding to the temptation—least of all to insist that others so transgress. Moreover, Wordsworth's poem seems to me admirable, and I entertain no notion that it might have been more admirable still had John Donne written it rather than William Wordsworth. I shall be content if I can make a much more modest point: namely, that since both Wordsworth and Donne are poets, their work has at basis a similar structure, and that the dynamic structure the pattern of thrust and counterthrust which we associate with Donne has its counterpart in Wordsworth. In the work of both men, the relation between part and part is organic, which means that each part modifies and is modified by the whole.

Yet to intimate that there are potential ironies in Wordsworth's lyric may seem to distort it. After all, is it not simple and spontaneous? With these terms we encounter two of the critical catchwords of the nineteenth century, even as *ironical* is in danger of becoming a catchword of our own period. Are the terms *simple* and *ironical* mutually exclusive? What after all do we mean by *simple* or by *spontaneous*? We may mean that the poem came to the poet easily and even spontaneously: very complex poems may—indeed have—come just this way. Or the poem may seem in its effect on the reader a simple and spontaneous utterance: some poems of great complexity possess this quality. What is likely to cause trouble here is the intrusion of a special theory of composition. It is fairly represented as an intrusion since a theory as to how a poem is written is being allowed to dictate to us how the poem is to be read. There is no harm in thinking of Wordsworth's poem as simple and spontaneous unless these terms deny complexities that actually exist in the poem, and unless they justify us in reading the poem with only half our minds. A slumber ought not to seal the *reader's* spirit as he reads this poem, or any other poem.

I have argued that irony, taken as the acknowledgment of the pressures of context, is to be found in poetry of every period and even in simple lyrical poetry. But in the poetry of our own time, this pressure reveals itself strikingly. A great deal of modern poetry does use irony as its special and perhaps its characteristic strategy. For this there are reasons, and compelling reasons. To cite only a few of these reasons: there is the breakdown of a common symbolism; there is the general scepticism as to universals; not least important, there is the depletion and corruption of the very language itself, by advertising and by the mass-produced arts of radio, the moving picture, and pulp fiction. The modern poet has the task of rehabilitating a tired and drained language so that it can convey meanings once more with force and with exactitude. This task of qualifying and modifying language is perennial; but it is imposed on the modern poet as a special burden. Those critics who attribute the use of ironic techniques to the poet's own bloodless sophistication and tired scepticism would be better advised to refer these vices to his potential readers, a public corrupted by Hollywood and the Book of the Month Club. For the modern poet is not addressing simple primitives but a public sophisticated by commercial art.

At any rate, to the honor of the modern poet be it said that he has frequently succeeded in using his ironic techniques to win through to clarity and passion. Randall Jarrell's "Eighth Air Force" represents a success of this sort.

> If, in an odd angle of the hutment,
> A puppy laps the water from a can
> Of flowers, and the drunk sergeant shaving
> Whistles O Paradiso!—shall I say that man
> Is not as men have said: a wolf to man?
>
> The other murderers troop in yawning;
> Three of them play Pitch, one sleeps, and one
> Lies counting missions, lies there sweating
> Till even his heart beats: One; One; One.
> O murderers! . . . Still, this is how it's done:
>
> This is a war. . . . But since these play, before they die,
> Like puppies with their puppy; since, a man,
> I did as these have done, but did not die—
> I will content the people as I can
> And give up these to them: Behold the man!
>
> I have suffered, in a dream, because of him,
> Many things; for this last saviour, man,
> I have lied as I lie now. But what is lying?

> Men wash their hands, in blood, as best they can:
> I find no fault in this just man.

There are no superfluous parts, no dead or empty details. The airmen in their hutment are casual enough and honest enough to be convincing. The raw building is domesticated: there are the flowers in water from which the mascot, a puppy, laps. There is the drunken sergeant, whistling an opera aria as he shaves. These "murderers," as the poet is casually to call the airmen in the next stanza, display a touching regard for the human values. How, then, can one say that man is a wolf to man, since these men "play before they die, like puppies with their puppy." But the casual presence of the puppy in the hutment allows us to take the stanza both ways, for the dog is a kind of tamed and domesticated wolf, and his presence may prove on the contrary that the hutment is the wolf den. After all, the timber wolf plays with its puppies.

The second stanza takes the theme to a perfectly explicit conclusion. If three of the men play pitch, and one is asleep, at least one man is awake and counts himself and his companions murderers. But his unvoiced cry "O murderers" is met, countered, and dismissed with the next two lines: ". . . Still this is how it's done: / This is a war. . . ."

The note of casuistry and cynical apology prepares for a brilliant and rich resolving image, the image of Pontius Pilate, which is announced specifically in the third stanza:

> I will content the people as I can
> And give up these to them: behold the man!

Yet if Pilate, as he is first presented, is a jesting Pilate, who asks "What is truth?" it is a bitter and grieving Pilate who concludes the poem. It is the integrity of Man himself that is at stake. Is man a cruel animal, a wolf, or is he the last savior, the Christ of our secular religion of humanity?

The Pontius Pilate metaphor, as the poet uses it, becomes a device for tremendous concentration. For the speaker (presumably the young airman who cried "O murderers") is himself the confessed murderer under judgment, and also the Pilate who judges, and, at least as a representative of man, the savior whom the mob would condemn. He is even Pilate's better nature, his wife, for the lines "I have suffered, in a dream, because of him, / Many things" is merely a rearrangement of *Matthew* 27:19, the speech of Pilate's wife to her husband. But this last item is more than a reminisence of the scriptural scene. It reinforces the speaker's present dilemma. The modern has had high hopes for man; are the hopes merely a dream? Is man incorrigible, merely a cruel beast? The speaker's present torture springs from that hope and from his reluctance to dismiss it as an empty dream. This Pilate is even harder-pressed than was the Roman magistrate. For he must convince himself of this last savior's innocence. But he has lied for him before. He will lie for him now.

> Men wash their hands in blood, as best they can:
> I find no fault in this just man.

What is the meaning of "Men wash their hands in blood, as best they can"? It can mean: Since my own hands are bloody, I have no right to condemn the rest. It can mean: I know that man can love justice, even though his hands are bloody, for there is blood on mine. It can mean: Men are essentially decent: they try to keep their hands clean even if they have only blood in which to wash them.

None of these meanings cancels out the others. All are relevant, and each meaning contributes to the total meaning. Indeed, there is not a facet of significance which does not receive illumination from the figure.

Some of Jarrell's weaker poems seem weak to me because they lean too heavily upon this concept of the goodness of man. In some of them, his approach to the theme is too direct. But in this poem, the affirmation of man's essential justness by a Pilate who contents the people as he washes his hands in blood seems to me to supply every qualification that is required. The sense of self-guilt, the yearning to believe in man's justness, the knowledge of the difficulty of so believing—all work to render accurately and dramatically the total situation.

It is easy at this point to misapprehend the function of irony. We can say that Jarrell's irony pares his theme down to acceptable dimensions. The theme of man's goodness has here been so qualified that the poet himself does not really believe in it. But this is not what I am trying to say. We do not ask a poet to bring his poem into line with our personal beliefs—still less to flatter our personal beliefs. What we do ask is that the poem dramatize the situation so accurately, so honestly, with such fidelity to the total situation that it is no longer a question of our beliefs, but of our participation in the poetic experience. At his best, Jarrell manages to bring us, by an act of imagination, to the most penetrating insight. Participating in that insight, we doubtless become better citizens. (One of the "uses" of poetry, I should agree, is to make us better citizens.) But poetry is not the eloquent rendition of the citizen's creed. It is not even the accurate rendition of his creed. Poetry must carry us beyond the abstract creed into the very matrix out of which, and from which, our creeds are abstracted. That is what "The Eighth Air Force" does. That is what, I am convinced, all good poetry does.

For the theme in a genuine poem does not confront us as abstraction—that is, as one man's generalization from the relevant particulars. Finding its proper symbol, defined and refined by the participating metaphors, the theme becomes a part of the reality in which we live—an insight, rooted in and growing out of concrete experience, many-sided, three-dimensional. Even the resistance to generalization has its part in this process—even the drag of the particulars away from the universal—even the tension of opposing themes— play their parts. The kite properly loaded, tension maintained along the kite string, rises steadily *against* the thrust of the wind.

Published in this form for the first time by permission of the author.

RANDALL JARRELL

The End of the Line

[1942]

WHAT has impressed everyone about modernist poetry is its *differentness*. The familiar and rather touching "I like poetry—but not modern poetry" is only another way of noticing what almost all criticism has emphasized: that modernist poetry is a revolutionary departure from the romantic poetry of the preceding century. Less far-reaching changes would have seemed a revolutionary disaster to "conventional" poets, critics, and readers, who were satisfied with romantic poetry; a revolutionary improvement to more "advanced" poets and critics, who disliked romanticism with the fervor of converts. *Romantic* once again, after almost two centuries, became a term of simple derogation; correspondingly, there grew up a rather blank cult of the "classical," and poets like Eliot hinted that poets like Pound might be the new classicism for which all had been waiting.

All this seems to me partially true, essentially false. The change from romantic poetry was evolutionary, not revolutionary: the modernists were a universe away from the great-grandfathers they admired; they *were* their fathers, only more so. I want to sketch this evolution. But if the reader understands me to be using *romantic* as an unfavorably weighted term, most of what I say will be distorted. Some of the tendencies of romanticism are bad; some of the better tendencies, exaggerated enough, are bad; but a great deal of the best poetry I know is romantic. Of course, one can say almost that about any of the larger movements into which critics divide English poetry; and one might say even better things about the "classical tradition" in English poetry, if there were one. (It is not strange that any real movement, compared to this wax monster, comes off nowhere; but it is strange that anyone should take the comparison for a real one.) If I pay more attention to unfortunate or exaggerated romantic tendencies, it is because these are the most characteristic: the "good" tendencies of movements are far more alike than the "bad" ones, and a proof that two movements are essentially similar needs to show that they share each other's vices.

Modernist poetry—the poetry of Pound, Eliot, Crane, Tate, Stevens, Cummings, MacLeish, et cetera—appears to be and is generally considered to be a violent break with romanticism; it is actually, I believe, an extension of romanticism, an end product in which most of the tendencies of romanticism have been carried to their limits. Romanticism—whether considered as the product of a whole culture or, in isolation, as a purely literary phenomenon—is necessarily a process of extension, a vector; it presupposes a constant experimentalism, the indefinite attainment of "originality," generation after generation, primarily by the novel extrapolation of previously exploited processes. (Neo-classicism, in theory at least, is a static system.) All these romantic tendencies are exploited to their limits; and the movement which carries out this final exploitation, apparently so different from earlier stages of the same process, is what we call modernism. Then, at last, romanticism is confronted with an impasse, a critical point, a genuinely novel situation that it can meet successfully only by contriving genuinely novel means—that is, means which are not romantic; the romantic means have already been exhausted. Until these new means are found, romanticism operates by repeating its last modernist successes or by reverting to its earlier stages; but its normal development has ended, and—the momentum that gave it most of its attraction gone—it becomes a relatively eclectic system, much closer to neo-classicism than it has hitherto been. (A few of these last romanticists resort to odd varieties of neo-classicism.) If this account seems unlikely to the reader, let me remind him that a similar course of development is extremely plain in modern music.

A good many factors combine to conceal the essentially romantic character of modernist poetry. (1) A great quantitative change looks like a qualitative one: for instance, the attenuation or breaking-up of form characteristic of romanticism will not be recognized or tolerated by the average romantic when it reaches its limit in modernist poetry. (2) The violent contrast between the modernist limits of romantic tendencies and the earlier stages of these tendencies, practiced belatedly and eclectically by "conventional" poets, is an important source of confusion. (3) Most of the best modern criticism of poetry is extremely anti-romantic—a poet's criticism is frequently not a reflection of but a compensation for his own poetry; and this change in theory has helped to hide the lack of any essential change in practice. (4) Modernist poems, while possessing some romantic tendencies in hypertrophied forms, often lack others so spectacularly that the reader disregards those they still possess; and these remaining tendencies may be too common for him to be conscious of them as specifically romantic. (Most of the romantic qualities that poetry has specialized in since 1800 seem to the average reader "normal" or "poetic," what poetry inescapably is.) (5) Romanticism holds in solution contradictory tendencies which, isolated and exaggerated in modernism, look startlingly opposed both to each other and to the earlier stages of romanticism. (6) Both modernist and conventional critics have been unable to see the fundamental similarities between modernist and romantic poetry because they were unwilling

to see anything but differences: these were to the former a final recommenda-
tion, and to the latter a final condemnation.

We can understand modernist poetry better by noticing where and how it
began. The English poetry that we call *fin de siècle*—the most important
tendency of its time—was a limit of one easily recognizable extension of romanticism. These "decadent" poets were strongle influenced by Baudelaire,
Verlaine, and similar French poets. Rimbaud, Laforgue, and Corbière—who
had already written "modern" poetry—had no influence on them. Why? Because a section of French poetry was developing a third of a century ahead of
English poetry: Rimbaud wrote typically modernist poetry in the 1870's; in
the '90's a surrealist play, Jarry's *Ubu Roi*, scared the young Yeats into crying:
"After us the Savage God!" France, without England's industrial advantages
and enormous colonial profits, had had little of the Victorian prosperity which
slowed up the economic and political rate of change in England—had still
less of that complacent mercantile Christianity the French dismissed as "English hypocrisy." And—if we stick to a part of the culture, literature—the rate
of change could be greater in France because romanticism was more of a surface phenomenon there. English poetry was not *ready* to be influenced by
French modernism for many years. Meanwhile there were two movements
particularly suited to criticism. Accompanying the triumph of prose naturalism there was a prosy, realistic, rather limited reaction against "decadent"
poetry (it included Robinson, Frost, Masters, Masefield, some of the Geor-
gians, etc.). The other movement, Imagism, carried three or four romantic
tendencies to their limits with the perfection of a mathematical demonstration.

French modernist poetry first influenced poetry in English through Americans who, lacking a determining or confining tradition of their own, were
particularly accessible and susceptible: Pound and Eliot (like Picasso, Stra-
vinsky, and Joyce) were in some sense expatriates in both space and time.
They imported modernism into English rather more deliberately and openly
than Wordsworth and Coleridge had imported romanticism; but all Pound's
early advice to poets could be summed up in a sentence half of which is pure
Wordsworth: Write like prose, like speech—and *read French poetry!* The
work of this most influential of modern poets, Ezra Pound, is a recapitulation
of the development of our poetry from late romanticism to modernism. His
early work is a sort of anthology of romantic sources: Browning, early Yeats,
the *fin de siècle* poets, Villon and the troubadours (in translations or imitations that remind one of Swinburne's and Rossetti's), Heine. *His* variety of
imagism is partly a return to the fresh beginnings of romantic practices, from
their diluted and perfunctory ends; partly an extension to their limits of some
of the most characteristic obsessions of romanticism—for instance, its passion
for "pure" poetry, for putting everything in terms of sensation and emotion,

with logic and generalizations excluded; and partly an adaptation of the exotic procedures of Chinese poetry, those silks that swathe a homely heart. When Pound first wrote poems that are modernist in every sense of the word, their general "feel" is reminiscent of what one might call a lowest common denominator of Corbière, Laforgue, and Rimbaud; but Heine had by no means disappeared; and the original Cantos I and II, gone now, were still full of Browning. But if Eliot was willing to base his form on Browning's (the dramatic monologue is primarily a departure from the norm of ordinary poetry; but in modernist poetry this departure *itself becomes the norm*), he had no interest in Browning's content and manner; in even his earliest poems one is seeing romanticism through Laforgue, and one can reconstruct this romanticism, in the pure form in which it had once existed, only from Eliot's remarks about his early feelings for Rossetti and Swinburne. . . . All during this time the Irish expatriate Joyce was making his way from late-romantic lyrics (in verse, though there is much that is similar in his early prose) to the modernist poetry (in prose) that crops up here and there in *Ulysses,* and that is everywhere in *Finnegans Wake.*

But it would take fifty or a hundred pages to write about this development in terms of specific poets. One can indicate the resemblances of romanticism and modernism more briefly, by making a list of some of the general characteristics of modernist poetry:

(1) A pronounced experimentalism: "originality" is everyone's aim, and novel techniques are as much prized as new scientific discoveries. Eliot states it with surprising naïveté: "It is exactly as wasteful for a poet to do what has been done already as for a biologist to rediscover Mendel's discoveries." (2) External formlessness, internal disorganization: these are justified either as the disorganization necessary to express a disorganized age or as new and more complex forms of organization. Language is deliberately disorganized, meter becomes irregular or disappears; the rhythmical flow of verse is broken up into a jerky half-prose *collage* or *montage*. (3) Heightened emotional intensity; violence of every sort. (4) Obscurity, inaccessibility: logic, both for structure and for texture, is neglected; without this for a ground the masses of the illogical or a-logical lose much of their effectiveness. The poet's peculiar erudition and allusiveness (compare the Alexandrian poet Lycophron) consciously restrict his audience to a small, highly specialized group; the poet is a specialist like everyone else. He intimidates or overawes the public by an attitude one may paraphrase as: "The poet's cultivation and sensibility are of a different order from those of his readers; even if he tried to talk down to them—and why should he try?—he would talk about things they have never heard of, in ways they will never understand." But he did not despair of their understanding a slap in the face. (5) A lack of restraint or proportion: all tendencies are forced to their limits, even contradictory tendencies—and not merely in the same movement but, frequently, in the same poet or the same

poem. Some modernist poetry puts an unparalleled emphasis on texture, connotation, violently "interesting" language (attained partly by an extension of romantic principles, partly by a more violent rhetoric based on sixteenth and seventeenth century practices); but there has never before been such prosaic poetry—conversational-colloquial verse without even a pretense at meter. (6) A great emphasis on details—on parts, not wholes. Poetry is essentially lyric: the rare narrative or expository poem is a half-fortuitous collocation of lyric details. Poetry exploits particulars and avoids and condemns generalizations. (7) A typically romantic preoccupation with sensation, perceptual nuances. (8) A preoccupation with the unconscious, dreams, the stream of consciousness, the irrational: this *surréaliste* emphasis might better have been called *sousréaliste*. (9) Irony of every type: Byronic, Laforguian, dryly metaphysical, or helplessly sentimental. Poetry rejects a great deal, accepts a little, and is embarrassed by that little. (10) *Fauve* or neo-primitive elements. (11) Modernist poets, though they may write about the ordinary life of the time, are removed from it, have highly specialized relations with it. The poet's naturalism is employed as indictment, as justification for his own isolation; prosaic and sordid details become important as what writers like Wallace Stevens and William Carlos Williams somewhat primitively think of as the *anti-poetic*. Contemporary life is condemned, patronized, or treated as a disgraceful aberration or special case, compared to the past; the poet hangs out the window of the Ivory Tower making severe but obscure remarks about what is happening below—he accepts the universe with several (thin) volumes of reservations. What was happening below was bad enough; the poet could characterize it, truthfully enough, with comparative forms of all those adjectives that Goethe and Arnold had applied to their ages. But its disasters, at least, were of unprecedented grandeur; it was, after all, "the very world, which is the world/ Of all of us,—the place where, in the end,/ We find our happiness or not at all"; and the poet's rejection or patronizing acceptance of it on his own terms—and, sometimes, what terms they were!—hurt his poetry more than he would have believed. (12) Individualism, isolation, alienation. The poet is not only different from society, he is as different as possible from other poets; all this differentness is exploited to the limit—is used as subject-matter, even. Each poet develops an elaborate, "personalized," bureaucratized machinery of effect; *refine your singularities* is everybody's maxim. (13) These poets, typically, dislike and condemn science, industrialism, humanitarianism, "progress," the main tendencies of Western development; they want to trade the present for a somewhat idealized past, to turn from a scientific, commercial, and political world-view to one that is literary, theological, and personal.

This complex of qualities is essentially romantic, and the poetry that exhibits it is the culminating point of romanticism.

It is the end of the line. Poets can go back and repeat the ride; they can settle in attractive, atavistic colonies along the railroad; they can repudiate the whole system, à la Yvor Winters, for some neo-classical donkey-caravan of their own. But Modernism As We Knew It—the most successful and influential body of poetry of this century—is dead. Compare a 1940 issue of *Poetry* with a 1930 issue. Who could have believed that modernism would collapse so fast? Only someone who realized that modernism is a limit which it is impossible to exceed. How can poems be written that are more violent, more disorganized, more obscure, more—supply your own adjective—than those that have already been written? But if modernism could go no further, it was equally difficult for it to stay where it was: how could a movement completely dynamic in character, as "progressive" as the science and industrialism it accompanied, manage to become static or retrogressive without going to pieces? Among modernist poets, from 1910 to 1925, there was the same feeling of confident excitement, of an individual but irregularly cooperative experimentalism, of revolutionary discoveries just around the corner, that one regularly sees at certain stages in the development of a science; they had ahead of them the same Manifest Destiny that poets have behind them today. Today, for the poet, there is an embarrassment of choices: young poets can choose—do choose—to write anything from surrealism to imitations of Robert Bridges; the only thing they have no choice about is making their own choice. The Muse, forsaking her sterner laws, says to everyone: "Do what you will." Originality can no longer be recognized by, and condemned or applauded for, its obvious experimentalism; the age offers to the poet a fairly heartless eclecticism or a fairly solitary individuality. He can avoid being swept along by the current—there is no current; he can congratulate himself on this, and see behind him, glittering in the distance of time, all those bright streams sweeping people on to the wildest of excesses, the unlikeliest of triumphs.

For a long time society and poetry have been developing in the same direction, have been carrying certain tendencies to their limits: how could anyone fail to realize that the excesses of modernist poetry are the necessary concomitants of the excesses of late-capitalist society? (An example too pure and too absurd even for allegory is Robinson Jeffers, who must prefer a hawk to a man, a stone to a hawk, because of an individualism so exaggerated that it contemptuously rejects affections, obligations, relations of any kind whatsoever, and sets up as a nostalgically-awaited goal the war of all against all. Old Rocky Face, perched on his sea crag, is the last of *laissez faire*; Free Economic Man at the end of his rope.) How much the modernist poets disliked their society, and how much they resembled it! How often they contradicted its letter and duplicated its spirit! They rushed, side by side with their society, to the limits of all tendencies. When, at the beginning of the '30's, these limits were reached, what became of these individualists? They turned toward anything collective: toward Catholicism, communism, distributism, social credit, agrarianism; they wrote neo-classical criticism or verse; they wrote political (Marxist or fellow-traveller) criticism or verse; they stopped writing; and when they read the verse of someone like E. E. Cummings, as it pushed on into the heart of that last undiscovered continent, *e. e. cummings*, they thought of this moral impossibility, this living fossil, with a sort of awed and incredulous revulsion.

I have no space to write of later developments. Auden was so influential because his poetry was the only novel and successful reaction away from modernism; and a few years later Dylan Thomas was so influential—in England—because his poetry was the only novel and successful reaction away from Auden. But his semi-surrealist experimentalism could be as good as it was, and as influential as it was, only in a country whose poets had never carried modernism to the limits of its possibilities. No one can understand these English developments if he forgets that, while we were having the modernism of Pound, Stevens, Williams, Moore, Eliot, Tate, Crane, Cummings, and all the rest, England was having the modernism of the Sitwells.

I am afraid that my hypothesis about romanticism and modernism, without the mass of evidence that can make a theory plausible, or the tangle of extensions and incidental insights that can make it charming, may seem improbable or unpleasant to some of my readers. It is intended to be partial: I have not written about the hard or dry or "classical" tendencies of some modern verse—what Empson and Marianne Moore have in common, for instance; and I have not listed the differences between modernism and romanticism that everybody has seen and stated. But I hope that nobody will dislike my article because he thinks it an attack on romanticism or modernism. This has been description, not indictment. Burke said that you can't indict a whole people, and I hope I am not such a fool as to indict a century and a half of a world. Besides, so far as its poetry is concerned, it was wonderful. Wordsworth and Blake and Heine, Baudelaire and Corbière, Hardy and Yeats and Rilke—the names crowd in; and there are dozens more. That some of these poets were, sometimes, as strange as they were wonderful; that some of their successors were, alas, rather stranger: all this is as true as it is obvious. But the "classical" prejudice which hints that these poets were somehow deceived and misguided as (say) Dryden and Valéry were not, seems every year more grotesque. One repeats to oneself, *Whom God deceives is well deceived,* and concludes that if these poets were not classical, so much the worse for classicism.

From *The Nation,* Vol. CLIV (February 21, 1942), pp. 222–228. Reprinted in this revised version by permission of the author and editors.

WILLIAM BARRETT

The End of Modern Literature: Existentialism and Crisis

[1949]

WE ARE told that this is the century when man has become for the first time fully and thoroughly problematic to himself. If so, it would only seem natural that literature too should be posed as a new and extreme kind of problem for literary men. Natural and inevitable too, that this problem should be raised particularly by the French, whose literature, whatever its rank, has always been the most programmatic of all literatures, and the most self-consciously attached to critical theory. For some time now French critics have been talking about a "crisis" in their literature. "Crisis" is a violent word, and there has possibly been some over-dramatization in its use; but there can be no doubt about the seriousness of the situation that has evoked this word: French literature suggests a countryside overrun by generations of industrious cultivators until the point of diminishing returns seems reached, where the soil continues to yield crops only after exacting very much more drastic methods of cultivation and ever more painful labor. By the turn of the century some traditional genres already looked exhausted, and recently some French writers have been declaring that the language itself (so much narrower in its range of effects than our protean English) demands new means of expression. American literature is very far from reaching this stage, and perhaps we are wrong to bother our heads at all with asking any extreme or ultimate questions of literature; we are primitives and perhaps for the time being we shall do better to remain such; but if we do choose to think about the problem of literature as a total one, then we can learn much from seeing this problem raised within the French context, which may very well represent the extreme state toward which modern literature, so long as it still remembers its ambitions, is tending everywhere in the world.

The background of Sartre's book[1] is this continuing crisis in French literature. But he is also beset by another and much more urgent crisis—the condition of French and European society after the Second World War—which penetrates so much of European life now that it places the writer in a precarious relation even to his craft. It is very useful to us to have a writer like

[1] *What Is Literature?* By Jean-Paul Sartre. Philosophical Library.

749

Sartre confront this double crisis. By this time it seems clear that he is not, nor is likely to become, a great writer: clever, enormously, furiously energetic, he does not possess the authentic gifts of a really first-rate creative talent. But in the present case this may be no disadvantage: a greater writer, for whom literature itself might never become a question, might be less sensitive to the historic forces that now push the literary man into such an odd and difficult place in the world. And what we can always count on in Sartre is the prodigious intelligence (however it may miscarry in details) with which he plunges into any problem. Sartre divides the problem of literature into three questions: *What is writing? Why write? For whom does one write?* These questions themselves breathe the air of crisis, for they are not the kinds of question that enter the writer's head during his periods of fertility and overflow; they become urgent and sometimes paralyzing for him only when he has descended into the pits of silence, anguish, artistic nihilism; when he exists on the margins of literature where language itself seems to become impossible. But since the writer cannot exist without descending from time to time into these waste places, these are questions that cannot be shirked, and it is better to raise and try to answer them whenever we can than to wait till the heavy silence descends and makes their answer seem hopeless.

Coming out of this double crisis in the French situation, Sartre's book is really a revolutionary one, though he himself gives the rather odd impression of not quite grasping the real revolution he announces. He hardly presents us any radically new theory of literature: most of Sartre's views had their antecedents in the Marxist theorizing of the 'thirties, though he gives them a new philosophical color. The revolutionary import of Sartre's message lies in his complete acceptance of the conditions under which, it appears, the writer may soon have to work, even though to accept these conditions may imply a radical break with the whole tradition of literature in France. Thus his book is revolutionary as a symptom of what is happening to literature, culture, and human society in this epoch—and not only in France.

Sartre attempts to give a historical answer to the three questions that divide his book by reviewing the conditions of author, public, and society during the major periods of French literature. This history is sketched in large rapid strokes: the seventeenth, eighteenth, nineteenth or bourgeois century; the present period (the situation of the writer in 1947) and Sartre's hope for the future. Inevitably the treatment of history shows more of the influence of Marx and Hegel than of Existentialism. Sartre has obviously profited a good deal from a sympathetic reading of Hegel, but the Hegelian apparatus often seems unnecessary and cumbrous, and his use of it an exuberant but self-indulgent practice of virtuosity. The influence of Marxism shows itself in another direction: it actually forms Sartre's judgments of taste at certain points. Thus he undervalues the literature of the seventeenth century because it was aristocratic, actually preferring the comedies of Beaumarchais, which belong to the more democratic eighteenth century, to those of Molière, and going so far as to describe Molière's *Le Misanthrope* as a comedy dealing only with the trivial subject of manners. The trouble is not that Sartre lacks taste —the whole book is evidence of his passionate addiction to literature—but that, as usual, he is driven too furiously by his ideas into the violation of perceptible fact—here the perceptible facts of taste. The result is that the brilliance of his insights on the past is often spoiled by extreme and doctrinaire judgments.

This lack of critical balance has its most serious consequences when Sartre is dealing with the bourgeois literature of the nineteenth century. Here Sartre's judgments are obviously colored by his passionate hatred of the bourgeois class itself, and in this respect he reveals the state of mind of France, and indeed of all Europe, where the bourgeoisie is so discredited that the unpleasant associations of the word reflect back on the whole century of civilization dominated by that class. We in America who have not yet had to live through the ruin of that class are still permitted another point of view: as bourgeois civilization—in France, England, and elsewhere—disappears, it is possible to regret its passing and to question very seriously the superiority of the culture that is replacing it. Though Sartre makes some telling points against bourgeois literature, they are usually directed at its weakest side and hardly do justice to its main bulk of significant work. Sartre's error is the familiar one of seeking to convert political and social sympathies too directly into literary judgment, so that he accepts much too simply and wholeheartedly the plebeian or populist taste embedded in the Marxist mind. In general, it can be said of Sartre that he has come to Marxism too late, that he has not lived through it and beyond it, so that he still sees political and cultural realities under the too drastic Marxist simplifications. The facts, however, are always more complex. Flaubert, to take one example, has always been a target for Sartre, and in this book Sartre attempts to justify his severity by citing long passages from Flaubert's letters that express an aristocratic hatred of the mob. This is all very well; but then we are suddenly reminded of the human complications of literary composition when we recall that Flaubert, despite his correspondence, has produced in the few pages of *Un Coeur Simple* a more profound and sympathetic picture of the poor than in all the thousand pages of Sartre's recent trilogy. And if we are going to insist at all on the social role of literature, we may as well remember that it was the bourgeois epoch which first produced the conception of a literature embracing the whole of society in a single understanding vision.

All this brings us now to the core of Sartre's message, which is of course his now well-known concept of *littérature engagée,* where we will also be dealing with some of the hazy notions left in the American mind by the "social-consciousness" of the 'thirties. ("Engaged literature," by the way, is a piece of linguistic nonsense that the translator might have spared us; if some of the literal force of the French is to be kept, he might have rendered it as "enlisted literature," which is the connotation to French ears; but, all told, "engagement" is probably best done into English as *commitment*.) Sartre complains that he has been misunderstood, but despite all his efforts in this book his idea of commitment still remains somewhat unclear. He has still not dealt adequately with the kinds and degrees of commitment, nor with the question of the necessary *artistic* detachment that must accompany the writer's *human* commitments. It is easy to be sympathetic to the causes that prompt Sartre's doctrine. The most eloquent pages in this book are those on the French experience under the German occupation, which make it quite clear that after such experiences the writer could no longer immure himself in an aestheticism for which neither concentration camps, executioners, nor victims would exist. We can very well accept the decisive force of such experiences for the young men of Sartre's generation. But then, can this experience be generalized for the writer everywhere and allowed to circumscribe his material, methods, and attitudes?

The point is, again, that the writer's involvement is a more complicated matter than Sartre allows. Commitment may work on various levels and in various degrees: the detached writer sometimes turns out to be the most committed at a deeper level, and the most blatantly committed writer to have only a transitory connection with the deeper issues of history, society, and literary tradition. Proust complains in one of his letters of the criticism (made after the first volumes of his novel had already appeared and been acclaimed) that his was the work of a snob, showing no recognition of social (by which was meant socialist) ideas. The criticism was in fact just, in the sense that the socialist ideology plays no role at all in the work of Proust. Yet, by some curious irony of detachment not at all unusual in works of art, *A La Recherche du Temps Perdu* is a profounder study of the breakdown of a social class than anything given us by proletarian or "social realist" literature. No modern writer seems to offer us a more fanatical example of detachment than Joyce. Certainly, during the seventeen years in which he was composing his last work, withdrawn from the ideological battles of the 'twenties and 'thirties, he seemed a curiously eccentric and private figure. Yet the appearance of *Finnegans Wake* in 1939 coincided portentously with the outbreak of a War that seemed the destruction of the whole civilization so laboriously embedded in Joyce's pages, and by some miracle of literary creation the book seemed to sum up a whole epoch. Was Joyce a committed writer? It depends, of course, on what kinds of commitment one has in mind. Joyce was committed in the deepest sense to the fact of human language, and consequently to the whole literary tradition in which he was working; he drew deeply upon the modern consciousness in matters like anthropology and psychoanalysis; and beyond all these, he had a human commitment, which became also the writer's deepest message, to the most primitive and universal emotions of familial life. In the face of such formidable commitments, the absence of a political ideology looks like a rather superficial deficiency in Joyce. The examples could be multiplied, but the point that emerges from them is already clear: we demand of the writer a commitment to his time in the sense that his work incorporate contemporary mind and feeling at their deepest levels; but to exist deeply in one's time is not the same as to exist in the spotlight, to pass oneself off as a political leader or sage, and to lose oneself in all the more violently public currents. Withdrawal and silence may open to the writer resources that reflect his time at a profounder level than those works which—in their insistence on being relevant, committed, or conscripted—are only a step beyond the daily newspaper. Some of Sartre's recent work gives the impression of a man writing with the Zeitgeist breathing hotly down his neck.

In the broad human sense, no doubt, Sartre is in the right direction. His doctrine is an insistence upon the reintegration of literature into life, against the idea of the priesthood of letters that germinated during the whole of the nineteenth century to come to full and final bloom in Flaubert and the symbolists. Mallarmé put it perfectly when he said, "Everything exists in order to get into a book," willing to countenance the inversion of existence that would subordinate the man to the writer. Our own period hardly permits this attitude: we have to insist that the writer is a man, that he never leaves humanity, and that, living in his period, he has political opinions like everybody else. But expecting the writer to be a citizen, we should not also expect that the literary profession gives him any special privileges of trespass into politics. Politics is usually considered fair game for everybody, and literary men have sometimes been the worst offenders, confusing their vaguest feelings with facts, their rhetoric with logic, and their will to belong with moral heroism. Sartre's own forays into politics show a good deal of this naïveté and confusion. It is time we recognized that there is such a thing as "literary" politics, to be taken no more seriously than "literary" philosophizing, "literary" psychology, and the rest of these adulterated products. During the 'thirties, of course, "literary" politics was the universal pastime; the mood of the period was some excuse, but that period has now passed, and literary men and fellow-travelers ought to be told that politics is a special discipline, with its own data and rules, concerning which one ought occasionally to think before one talks.

But the real revolution that Sartre announces for literature is not a matter chiefly of politics. He hardly states this revolution in so many words; we glimpse it only if we measure his theory by his practice, taking the present book along with his novels and plays, which are, after all, his deliberate attempts to realize his own projects for literature; and only too if we read a little between the lines in the present work, observing the writers to whom he makes most frequent and essential reference. Sartre once said that Dos Passos was the greatest modern novelist; in the present work his admiration for American writers is more cautious than in the past, but we notice repeated reference to Richard Wright as a great writer. This is entirely natural, for Wright's books, dealing with the Negro question in America, satisfy Sartre's demand that literature be directed at changing the fundamental conditions of social existence. The highbrow critic in America is likely to settle on altogether different names in any fundamental literary discussion: Joyce or Eliot or Proust are the names that remind us of the possible ambitions of literature. Sartre, however, is interested in a very practical program for literature, and his point would seem to be effectively this: that in the crisis of exhaustion, or threatened exhaustion, in which French literature now seems to find itself, the way out may be just to propose the second-rate as an ideal. Perhaps, being second-rate, it is something within reach, and therefore a thoroughly practicable goal for literature. In the sense that his book represents a deliberate abnegation from the great ambitions of modern literature, Sartre is in effect announcing the end of a whole literary period.

For the fact is that the one thing that distinguishes modern literature as a whole from the literature of previous periods is its extraordinary, and perhaps even overweening, ambition. We are now at the mid-point of the century, and looking back on the half-century of writers who will eventually give their names to the period, we seem to see them in retrospect as belonging almost to a vanished culture, so different were the conditions of their existence from those of the period into which we are now entering. If they inherited the nineteenth-century view of the writer as a separate and anointed being, a kind of priest, they were able to hold on to this role only with the tensions of an irony that provided it with a new human content. Proust, Joyce, Mann and the others, all exist in the full plenitude of a tradition, of which they sought to lose no part, so that their work in its richness already carries the seeds of disorder and dissolution. Probably a moment like this in literary history could not be prolonged any further. Sartre's is perhaps the first conscious announcement that the conditions of literature must return to a lower and less ambitious level; but even if the program did not become conscious, the attitude has already begun to prevail generally. We are now able to understand our surprise at the evolution of Sartre's career. The discrepancy between the very abstract and involved philosophy and the rudimentary and plodding fiction is no longer a puzzle. It was something of a shock, after the intellectual sophistication and complexity of *L'être et le néant,* to descend upon the first volume of Sartre's trilogy, not because his creative gifts were lacking but because he was willing to aim so low in the novel. But all this now turns out to have been intentional: the deliberate aiming at the second-rate is part of Sartre's program for literature. The committed writer disdains the creation of masterpieces, and even the very concept of the masterpiece, with whatever silence, exile, or cunning it may exact, no longer seems to have any connection with that act of writing that aims essentially at making an impact, just as one might strike a blow or fire a pistol.

Sartre is therefore entirely consistent with himself when he proposes that the writer neglect none of the mass media, like radio and cinema, available in this period. He notes with satisfaction that the modern writer is able to reach a much vaster audience than his predecessor of the nineteenth century: for Sartre this is the great opportunity in the present situation. It is true that he also observes the other side of the coin—that when Gide, for example, becomes known through the cinema to thousands who have not read him, the writer also becomes inseparable from the face of Michele Morgan—but he fails to consider what will happen if this process continues unchecked. The cultural process in modern society (which, whatever its form of economy, is everywhere becoming a mass society) is precisely this watering down of content as the writer reaches larger masses of people, and usually not through his own written word but through the mechanical image that an advanced technology substitutes for the printed page. Sartre accepts the process, in fact seeks to assist it; for in his view the writer should aim essentially at addressing the concrete collectivity, which is the total mass of mankind, and eventually this mass is a classless society. This is as utopian as most of Sartre's politics; but programs—and a program for literature is no exception—should deal with present possibilities, and the contemporary writer who seeks to reach this mass audience will inevitably find himself rejecting his own essential difficulties, his complications and subtleties, and indeed the very limitations of personality that have in the past defined his most authentic themes. Here again we have nothing less than a proposal to put an end to modern literature. For the qualities that define modern literature have been in great part the result of a desperate effort to preserve itself by a deliberate escape from a mass audience.

It would be a mistake, however, to discount too easily Sartre's attitudes toward literature as simply the result of his own unhappy will to have a political vocation. We would be right in part, but we would be wrong to forget the more significant question why the writer today should be so furiously haunted by the need to search for such a vocation. Sartre's position might be very different without the large and vocal presence of the Communists upon the French scene: the writer of La Nausée, in becoming the leader of a school, has had to sacrifice himself to the public figure who is drawn into competition with the Communists and has had consequently to offer a message emphasizing more and more the "positive" and social role of literature. It

is very significant, thus, that the discussion of the present situation of the
writer in 1947, with which this book concludes, should be in large part an
unequivocal attack upon communism as a moral and intellectual phenomenon
(a section which, along with his destruction of the literary theories of surrealism, represents Sartre at his polemic best); but it is even more significant
of the ambiguous situation of the French writer now that Sartre's anti-
communism on the political level has been so very much less equivocal. Communism and communist ideology do not play the same role in America; but
in this respect the French situation may not be so much different as simply
in advance of our own, and what we must be prepared for all over the world
is a literature produced under the conditions of a mass society, whatever may
be the political regime imposed upon this mass base. The end of modern literature, however, does not mean the end of literature. We may regret the
passing of a period, but lamentation cannot become the content of a critical
doctrine. In the new period which we are now entering the literary medium
may discover new forms and adventures for itself: for one thing, the social
process in which the writer is now caught up may put an end to his famous
alienation in our time, and a literature with very different possibilities may
result. Unfortunately all this is still very much in the future, while right
now I do not think there can be much doubt that these new conditions are
producing, and will probably produce for some time, a literature that is
plainly inferior to the old.

From *The Partisan Review*, Vol. XVI (September,
1949), pp. 942–950. Reprinted by permission of
the author and editors.

STANLEY EDGAR HYMAN

Attempts at an Integration

[1948]

I: THE IDEAL CRITIC

IF WE could, hypothetically, construct an ideal modern literary critic out of plastics and light metals, his method would be a synthesis of every practical technique or procedure used by his flesh-and-blood colleagues. From all the rival approaches he would borrow as much as could be used in a synthesis without distorting the whole, he would balance one bias or excess or over-specialization against another so that both canceled out, and he was left with only neutral elements adaptable to his own purposes. From Edmund Wilson he would take the function of translation or interpretation, of explaining the work's paraphrasable content, and augment it with the greater concern for poetic and formal values found, say, in the early interpretative criticism of Ezra Pound. From Yvor Winters he would borrow the emphasis on evalua-tion and comparative judgment, as well as Winters's refusal to be intimidated by conventional opinions in his judgments, rather than the judgments them-selves. He could use T. S. Eliot's passionate concern with grounding litera-ture in a tradition although his tradition would probably look more like V. F. Parrington's, and he could also use Eliot's functional relationship between poetry and criticism. From Van Wyck Brooks our ideal critic would take the biographical method of the early books, and the general concern with the cultural climate of a writer. Constance Rourke would contribute her em-phasis on the folk background of a work, as well as her insistence that this tradition tends to be one of form rather than content, and abstract rather than realistic. Maud Bodkin's psychoanalytic method would go into the synthesis, augmented by theories and procedures from Gestalt, revisionist Freudian, and other psychologies; as would Christopher Caudwell's Marxist method, modi-fied by Plekhanov's historical relativism, Alick West's detailed concern with specific texts, and many insights from other sociologies.

Our ideal critic would adopt Caroline Spurgeon's conscientious scholar-ship, going to John Livingston Lowes's lengths and extending the results with

Reprinted from *The Armed Vision* by Stanley Edgar Hyman, by permission of Alfred A. Knopf, Inc. Copyright 1947, 1948 by Alfred A. Knopf, Inc.

the imaginative rashness of G. Wilson Knight; as well as Armstrong's pre-occupation with the image cluster as a unit of special poetic significance. From R. P. Blackmur he would take the technique of hard work and re-search, the preoccupation with language and diction, and the insistence on the high importance of art and the symbolic imagination. William Empson would furnish his exploration of categories and ambiguities, his close and ingenious textual reading, and his general concern with the significance of literary forms. From I. A. Richards our ideal critic would borrow the concern with communication, techniques of interpretation, and the experimental method; from Kenneth Burke, the concern with symbolic action, techniques of integration within a framework of dramatism, and the introspective method. Other critics would furnish still other elements to the synthesis: Jane Harrison's ritual anthropology and Margaret Schlauch's linguistics; Herbert Read's sympathetic attention to every new current of thought and every youthful artist; the balanced concern with the totality of the work of the *Scrutiny* group; F. O. Matthiessen's subtle correlations between the socio-logical and the aesthetic; Francis Fergusson's use of the ritual drama and William Troy's use of the ritual myth; the focus on poetic structure of John Crowe Ransom, Allen Tate, Cleanth Brooks, and Robert Penn Warren; and much else from others. Finally, the ideal critic would be a neo-Aristotelian, scrupulously inducing from poetic practice, as well as a neo-Coleridgean, frankly deducing from philosophic concepts.

At the same time our ideal critic would discard from all these critics those features of their practice that seemed to him irrelevant, worthless, or private to them, stripping from the neutral and objective method their special obses-sions, preoccupations, and weaknesses. He would have no use for Wilson's superficiality or dealings in second-hand ideas or impatience with form. He would not want Winters's obsessive morality, nor his semantically meaning-less dogmatism with no basis for judgment given, nor his bad temper, nor his high percentage of error. In adopting Eliot's concern with tradition, he would husk it of its religious and political bias, and in adopting Eliot's or-ganic continuity between the poetic and critical function, he would maintain criticism's independence and integrity. Rejecting Brooks's *a priori* assumptions and contempt for imaginative literature, the ideal critic would not use his biographical method as a Procrustean bed for writers, or as an excuse for escaping from the work to the personality, or as a way of dispensing sweet-ness and light at a literary tea. In taking over Miss Rourke's method, he would steer clear of both the "folksy" and the "*völkisch*," and would operate from a far wider learning than hers. Miss Bodkin's mystic and religious em-phasis would be discarded (along with Jung's Nazi racialism and blood-and-soil irrationalism, which she avoided); as would Caudwell's bias against psy-choanalysis, guilt about poetry, class debunking, absolutism, and preference for generalities rather than texts. Both Freud and Marx would be used with as sharp a sense as theirs, and a sharper sense than their followers', of the limitations of their approaches applied to literature. Our ideal critic would operate from the same sharp awareness of the limits of scholarship, the area where it must shade over into criticism to be fulfilled, and he would adopt neither Miss Spurgeon's timidity about following through on conclusions nor her personal mysticism. He would probably find not very much to reject in Blackmur, Empson, Richards, and Burke, but could probably get along without the traces of preciousness in the first, the occasional overelaboration of the second, the blind alley of Basic English in the third, and the anachronistic resistance to progress in the fourth. From the other critics he drew on he would make similar scrapings, and in most cases would probably find more to scrape away than to keep. Even Aristotle and Coleridge would not be entirely to his purpose.

This ideal integration of all of modern critical method into one super-method could not be on the analogy of stew, with everything thrown at random into the pot, but would have to be on the analogy of construction, with the structure built up according to an orderly plan on some foundation or around some skeleton framework. What, then, would that foundation, framework, or basis be? The most enthusiastic candidate for the job is Marxism, whose spokesmen have regularly insisted that dialectical materialism is an integrative frame able to encompass and use the newest advances in all fields of knowledge, and in fact must do so to function. This was undoubtedly true of Marx and Engels, who drew enthusiastically on immense accumulations of knowledge in every area, and adapted to new developments so elastically that Engels remarked: "With each epoch-making discovery in the department of natural science, materialism has been obliged to change its form." It is also to a large extent true of Caudwell, who insists in the Introduction to *Illusion and Reality*: "But physics, anthropology, history, biology, philosophy and psychology are also products of society, and therefore a sound sociology would enable the art critic to employ criteria drawn from these fields without falling into eclecticism or confusing art with psychology or politics." Later Marxists, however, with the exception of a few isolated figures like Caudwell, have lacked the elasticity and scrupulousness of Marx and Engels, as well as their learning and brilliance, so that Marxism in practice has hardly made good its claim as an all-embracing integrative system. Most contemporary Marxist thinkers, in fact, would toss the greater part of our ideal critical method out the window immediately as "decadent" frippery.

Few other individual methods or disciplines are even formulated so as to embrace other approaches, and where they are sciences or near-sciences, like psychology and anthropology, or clearly demarcated fields, like scholarship or biography, they obviously could not invade other territories without automatically losing their special character. Clearly, the basis for an ideal critical integration would have to be a literary or philosophic concept (it should be obvious from the foregoing that when Marxism sets itself up as a giant integrative frame, it is not in its aspect as a sociology but in its aspect as a philosophic *Weltanschauung*). Without aspiring to solve the problem offhand, we might note a few possible bases for such a synthesis. One would be the concept of Organicism, the organic unity of the human personality, Richards's continuity of experience, in terms of which all these critical approaches could be unified as dealing with related aspects of human behavior: man as poet, man as reader, the family man, the social man, man communicating, and so on. Another, avoiding the nominalism inherent in the first, would be Social Activity, organizing the various approaches as relational aspects with different groups, inherent in the work of art. Others would include: Burke's metaphor of Dramatism, with its pentad of act, scene, agent, agency, and purpose, treating the other approaches as emphases on one term or another, conflicting and co-operating like characters in a play; Empson's concept of Ambiguity extended, with all other approaches as further ambiguities of meaning in the words of the poem; or even Blackmur's doctrine of Hard Work, equated with Burke's Use All There Is to Use, as simply the rather disorganized organizing principle of investigating every possible line of significance.

In our ideal critic we would assume not only the use of all the fruitful methods of modern criticism on some organizing base, but necessarily all the abilities and special aptitudes behind them, a fearful assumption of personal capacity, as well as the requisite learning in all these areas, and the requisite flexibility of focus. Our ideal critic would not only have to *do* more than any actual critic, he would have to *know* more, *range* farther, and *be* more (as well as *write* better, certainly). The classification of critics in this book has been largely by method; noting other possible classifications that cut across this one on the bias should suggest how much else is involved. Thus classification by focus would have: Blackmur the specialist in words, Miss Spurgeon in images, Empson in forms, Burke in the totality of a man's work, and so forth. Classification by learning would have: Eliot the man knowing literature temporarily out of fashion, Caudwell the man knowing modern science, Brooks the man knowing minor writers of the period, Miss Bodkin knowing the classics, and so on. Classification by attribute (which has been necessarily assumed as underlying the method) would have: Empson the keen reader, Burke the intelligence shooting sparks, Richards the patient teacher, Blackmur and Miss Spurgeon (in different senses) the painstaking workers. (It might be pointed out here that Blackmur's hard work, which has been treated throughout as a method, is much more definitely a personal attribute. It has been classified as a method only because it seems both essential and transmissible: any critic can and must do hard work, in the sense in which he cannot or need not at all set himself to becoming an intelligence shooting sparks.)

The last problem that our ideal critic would have to face, and the most overwhelming of all, is that each of the methods developed by modern critics is only in a first preliminary stage of exploration, and at one time or another all of their originators have had to recognize that they have only scratched the surface and will hardly be able to do more in their lifetimes. Each method is capable of almost limitless extension and ramification, and our harried ideal critic would have not only to use them all, but to proliferate each of them enormously, solving the problems and adjusting to the perspectives confronting each method in isolation. . . . He would have to do it all himself, too. Each of our modern critics needs disciples, a school to carry on, apply, and extend his work; but the difficulty is that in so far as the disciples are themselves brilliant and creative (and the problem if they are not is obvious), they inevitably tend to go off in their own directions—as in the case of Richards's star pupil, Empson—and in turn to need disciples of their own, Blackmur, Fergusson, Slochower, and Cowley are all to some extent applying Burke's method to other literary problems and texts, but at the same time they are in business for themselves, and they will be efficient disciples in inverse proportion to how original, creative, and ultimately valuable to criticism they are. Only in the world inhabited by our ideal critic do people use a method with exactly the same aims and in exactly the same fashion as its originator. In the real world of criticism there is probably nothing we would want less.

To sum up, our ideal critic would extend his whole integrated method just as far as its individual component methods are capable of extension in isolation. He would, in short, do everything possible with a work of literature. For a brief lyric, as can be imagined, this would result in a tome of several volumes; for a more elaborate work, a long poem, play, or novel, it would obviously be a life study. Our ideal critic, however, has an infinity of time, and we might take advantage of his patience to note at random some of the things he would do with a poem, without attempting to assign any temporal or hierarchical priorities. He would tell what the poem is about, that is, translate its paraphrasable content as far as possible (considering the economy inherent in the work of art, this in itself should bulk much larger than the work). He would relate it to its sources and analogues in earlier literature, place it fully in a tradition, and compare it at length with contemporary and earlier works both within and outside of the tradition. He would analyze it exhaustively in terms of any available biographical information about its author: his mind, life, and personality; his family, amatory, and marital relations; his occupation, his childhood, his social relations, his physical appearance and habits. He would find its folk sources and analogues, and investigate the author's dependence on his native folk tradition, the poem's surface texture of folk speech and characteristics, and its deeper polarization in the patterns of timeless primitive ritual. He would interpret it psychologically as an expression of the author's deepest wishes and fears, in terms of complexes, repressions, sublimations, and compensations, as an expression of the archetypal patterns of collective experience, as an expression of behavioral, neurological, and endocrinological phenomena, and as an expression of the socially conditioned patterns of the author's personality and character structure; he would relate it to comparable manifestations in primitives, psychotics, children, and even animals; he would explore its organization in terms of clusters of imagery related in unconscious associations, in terms of structure functioning as psychological ritual, and in terms of the *Gestalt* configurations of its totality and their relation to other configurations.

He would interpret the poem socially as a complex and interacting reflection of the poet's social class, status, and occupation; analyze it in terms of the productive relations of his time and nation and their related climate of ideas, and the climate of ideas transcending those productive relations and going backward or forward to others; and he would discuss the social and political attitudes the poem advocates, states, or implies. He would turn all the vast resources of literary scholarship on it, or utilize all that had already been done, and follow the conclusions through with a quite unscholarly courage and imagination. He would explore at the greatest length possible its diction and the relevant ambiguous possibilities of meaning and relations in the significant words; its images and symbols and all their relevant suggestions; its formal pattern or patterns and their function and effects; its formal or informal sound-devices, rhythmic structure, and other musical effects; and its larger patterns of movement and organization; as well as the interrelationships of all the foregoing. He would study all the things outside the poem to which it makes reference and interpret it in their light. He would explore and categorize the key attitude that arises out of the interrelationship of the poem's content and form, note the implications of that category, and discuss the poem comparatively with contemporary and earlier literary expressions of the same category in different terms. Our ideal critic would investigate the whole problem of what the poem communicates, how, and to whom, using every available source of information to find out what it was meant to communicate; and then every technique, from introspection to the most objective laboratory testing, to find out what it actually does communicate, to differing individuals and groups at different times and under different circumstances. He would investigate the whole problem of symbolic action in the poem, what it does symbolically for the poet, what it does symbolically for the reader, what the relationship is between these two actions, and how it functions within the larger symbolic structure of the total development of the author's writing, or even larger symbolic movements, like a literary age. He would discuss a vast number of other problems involved in the poem, far too many to be even listed, from ultimate philosophic and ethical questions like the beliefs and ideas reflected by the poem and the values it affirms, and their relation to beliefs and values (or their absence) in the reader and the cultural context; to such minutiae as the poem's title and any unusual features of typography, spelling, or punctuation. He would place the poem in the development of the author's writing from every angle (for which purpose, naturally, he would be familiar with everything else the author wrote), confront the problem of the circumstances under which it arose, and discuss the unique features of its style and its unique reflections of a mind and personality. Finally, on the basis of all this analysis, our ideal critic would subjectively evaluate the poem and its parts aesthetically in relation to aim, scope and validity of aim, and degree of accomplishment, place its value in terms of comparable works by the same poet and others, estimate its present and future significance and popularity, assign praise or blame, and, if he cared to, advise the reader or writer or both about it. If he were so inclined, he could go on and discuss his data and opinions in relation to the data and opinions of other critics, ideal or not. He would then wipe his brow, take a deep breath, and tackle another poem.

II: THE ACTUAL CRITIC

Our ideal critic is of course nonsense, although perhaps useful nonsense as a Platonic archetype. Let us demolish him and return to the real world and the practical human possibilities of the individual. A substantial and quite impressive amount of integration is possible in the work of one rounded man using a number of methods and disciplines. At one time or another Kenneth Burke has done almost everything in the repertoire of modern criticism, and generally a number of things in conjunction. This has been only less true of Richards, Empson, and Blackmur; they have not synthesized quite so much, and they have tended, particularly Blackmur, to do only one thing at a time, whichever the work under discussion seemed particularly to call for. These are our best critics, and their individual and shifting integrations tend to be enormously successful. Their formula for avoiding the endless labors of theoretical total integration is: pursuing none of their techniques to the end of the line, but merely far enough to suggest the further possibilities; and stressing at any given time only those approaches that seem most fruitful for the specific work under discussion, slighting or ignoring others temporarily less fruitful, which would then have their place in dealing with a different type of work. Even within these limitations our best critics never seem to have enough time or space to go as far as they would like, and the demand on their learning is formidable. In the future we can expect that the burden of having a working command of every field of man's knowledge applicable to literary criticism will grow increasingly difficult to bear, and eventually simply become impossible.[1] With the tremendous growth of the social sciences in particular, sooner or later knowing enough of any one of them to turn it fruitfully on literature will demand a life study, leaving no time for anything else except some acquaintance with the corpus of literature itself. The Baconian critic, taking all knowledge for his province, is our most impressive figure, but the days of the Baconian critic in an age of more and more complete specialization seem inevitably numbered.

We must, then, consider the specialist critic, the man using one highly developed method. The ones we have had are individually less impressive than the Baconians, and we tend to feel that their very specialization makes them lopsided, inevitably distorters of literature. For the most part, they are either extremely limited figures able to do only one thing well, like Edmund Wilson's paraphrases or Van Wyck Brooks's biographies; or else they are specialists in some extra-literary field: Miss Bodkin's psychoanalysis, Caudwell's Marxism, or Miss Rourke's folk material. These critics with a single developed method are most fruitful either when specializing in literature that their method is best equipped to handle, as the Cambridge school does in Greek literature, so close to its ritual origins; or when specializing in those aspects of any work of literature which their points of view can best elucidate, as psychoanalytic and Marxist critics do (or should do).

Both these types of critical specialization need something else to make them fruitful. That something must be some form of plural, co-operative or collective criticism—Eliot's hope, expressed as far back as "Experiment in Criticism" in the Bookman, November 1929, for "the collaboration of critics of various special training, and perhaps the pooling and sorting of their contributions by men who will be neither specialists nor amateurs." This collaborative criticism we might call the Symposium, a word that, whatever heavy-handed use it has had in the past, still carries some pleasant associations from its root meaning, a convivial drinking-party. We have had a number of published examples of the critical symposium, some of them fairly successful, some less so. They include: scholarly and reference works done by specialists, like A Companion to Shakespeare Studies; symposia on special topics, like Humanism in America and its answer, The Critique of Humanism, Books That Changed Our Minds, and The Mind in Chains; symposia on a country or a period, like American Writers on American Literature, After the Genteel Tradition, and The Great Tudors; symposia on a writer, sometimes memorial,

---

[1] Thomas Young, an English physician, optical physicist, physiologist, Egyptologist, etc., who died in 1829, is supposed to have been the last man who knew everything scientific there was to know. No one since has come forward to dispute the honor.

like *A Garland for John Donne, Herbert Read: an introduction to his work,* and *Scattering Branches: Tributes to the Memory of W. B. Yeats;* or special issues of one of the literary magazines devoted to a writer, like the *Hound & Horn* James number, the *Southern Review* Yeats number, the *Kenyon Review* Hopkins numbers, the *Quarterly Review of Literature* Valéry number, and the *Harvard Wake* Cummings number; or even periodical symposia devoted to a single work, like the *transition* series on *Finnegans Wake,* published as *Our Exagmination,* etc., or a topic, like the *Chimera* Myth and Detective Fiction numbers, or problems of varying scope, like the several issues of *Focus.* In addition, we have had a number of false symposia or anthologies compiled after the fact, assemblages of work written at different times for different purposes, like *The Question of Henry James, The Kafka Problem,* the Critics Group *Ibsen,* and others.

The chief fault with all of these, particularly the false symposia, is that they are not specialized enough: the choice of critics tends to be haphazard and overlapping, with many methods and points of view not represented at all. In some cases the fault lies in attempting to cover too much ground, so that the contributors never meet on the same subject at all, losing the chief value of the symposium, which is not in the differences of subject-matter, but in the differences of approach to the same subject-matter. A wholly successful critical symposium would have to consist in the planned and organized co-operation of specialists, with the lines of their specialties rigidly drawn on the basis of method rather than subject. (Even the *Hound & Horn* Henry James issue, one of the best of the symposia so far, assigns most of its contributors a reserve safe from poaching, "The Early Novels," "The Critical Prefaces," and so on, and in only a few cases is the specialization purely one of method, like Francis Fergusson's study of "Drama in *The Golden Bowl.*") At the same time such a symposium would of necessity encourage an increasing division of labor, men more and more clearly demarcating just what they are doing in criticism, and doing that one thing and nothing else. It would thus tend to make modern critics even more partial, limited, specialized, and fragmentary, but they would gain in depth and assurance by way of compensation, and the whole critical job would have the virtues of scope and completeness that the modern critic can rarely get except at the cost of superficiality.

What possibilities are there in practice for such a symposium criticism? First, of course, there are the literary quarterlies, in their special numbers on a man or a topic. Even granting that the planning and organization were ideal, their handicap is that they are rarely in complete control: they cannot get any critic or type of critic they want for any project and perforce have to make do with what they can get; they lack the power to impose rigid limits of subject or method on professional critics, who tend to spread out automatically, or the money to make it worth the critic's while to remain within imposed limits; their information as to just who is capable of doing what is always haphazard; they are restricted to the amount of detailed critical study their readers will put up with; and frequently they are forced to build a symposium around work already written for other purposes and fill in the cracks as best they can, sometimes in the office. A new magazine, calling itself the *Critic* or the *Symposium*, devoted to a detailed collective study of a man or a book or a poem in each issue, acquiring and training a body of specialist critics capable of doing the things it wanted done, and gaining the prestige to get independent critics to bend their work to its purposes and readers to like it, could solve some of these problems; others would still remain.[2]

Next there are the universities, which have the money and prestige for such a project and are accustomed to procedures of specialization almost identical, in scholarship of all sorts. Whether they would be likely to indulge it in so dubious an activity as criticism, either in the form of a magazine, a series of books, or even the organization of their own literature studies in such a fashion is another thing. One of the most encouraging signs is the recent publication by the press of Princeton University of several series of papers on literature and the humanities, including *The Intent of the Artist, The Intent of the Critic,* and *The Language of Poetry,* each of them a small excellent symposium by four or five specialized authorities. Another is the sponsorship, by the English Institute, of precisely such a symposium or experiment in co-operative criticism as is here described. A seminar was held at Columbia University during a week in September 1941, under the direction of Norman Holmes Pearson of Yale. Four critics spoke for an hour each on the same poem, each on a different day. The critics chosen were Horace Gregory, Lionel Trilling, Cleanth Brooks, and Frederick Pottle (a fifth critic invited, Morton Dauwen Zabel, was not able to be present). The poem chosen was Wordsworth's "Ode on Intimations of Immortality." The audience numbered almost a hundred. I was not present at the affair, but from Donald Stauffer's account of it in "Cooperative Criticism: A Letter from the Critical Front" in the *Kenyon Review,* Winter 1942, I would guess that its relative failure lay chiefly in its narrowness of range. An even more encouraging long-range sign is the existence of a few teachers in universities throughout the country (among them Professor Leonard Brown of Syracuse University, under whom I studied) whose advanced literature classes study by the symposium method, with each student tackling the work over a long period from a different viewpoint and method, and the whole organized and assembled by the teacher. Besides the quarterlies and the universities, no likely area for

[2] The closest thing to this ideal in existence is probably the English critical magazine *Scrutiny,* which certainly has both the body of co-operating talents and the requisite prestige. Its scope is too limited ever to give the complete picture, however, and its celebrated "scrutinies," or co-operative surveys, have tended to be on cultural or educational problems rather than on writers or literary works.

the critical symposium to flourish in comes to mind. A good many oral critical symposia go on over the radio and in various forums, but the nature of impromptu speaking and the demands of a mass audience tend to confine them to inevitable triviality (as a reading of the published programs of one of the best of them, Invitation to Learning, makes unhappily clear).

One of the greatest hopes for collective criticism by symposium is that it would be equipped to unravel works so complex that they have not yet been successfully dealt with by any individual critic. *Moby Dick* is the obvious example here. When Matthiessen remarked in the introduction to *American Renaissance*: "I have not yet seen in print an adequately detailed scrutiny . . . of *Moby Dick,*" he was understating badly; we have not yet had any reading that made much sense beyond the most superficial and one-dimensional. To perhaps a lesser extent this is true of every great work of literature; all readings are inadequate, and we only satisfy ourselves by an act of impromptu collective criticism, by suspending several in our mind at once. Even where we are satisfied with our reading of the work, the addition of other meanings gives it greater depth and richness. When the old-fashioned Shakespeare professor tells his class that Hamlet's line to Polonius about Ophelia: "Let her not walke i' th' Sunne," does not carry any weight unless it is seen as a complicated pun, with at least the four suggestions of the sun as a source of madness, corruption and decay, the King and his court, and the son (Hamlet), added to its explicit meaning of pregnancy by spontaneous generation, he is not suddenly enlisted in the cause of Empsonian ambiguity, but merely recognizing that no one meaning, however reasonable, quite explains the line's sense of significance and ominousness.

In so far as great works, or key spots in any work, or the bulk of serious modern literature as a special product of the divided modern mind, all have many levels of meaning, we must have a many-leveled criticism to deal with them. Essentially this means that where the work is worth the trouble, the critic going into it with any vocabulary will emerge with a meaning paraphrasable in that vocabulary. Increasingly this has been generally recognized in recent times. Charles Baudouin, in *Psychoanalysis and Aesthetics,* speaks of it as "multiple parallelism" and compares it with the polyglot Bible. Richards calls it "multiple definition" or "multiple interpretation," and it is actually . . . the subject of all his work. Burke calls it "multiple causation" and speaks of "a set of widening circles, ranging from the uniquely particularized, through placement in terms of broad cultural developments, to absolute concepts of relationship or ground." Erich Fromm is working from a similar concept in things like his palimpsest reading of Kafka in psychoanalytic, social, and religious terms, as is Harry Slochower in his psychoanalytic, social and philosophic readings of Mann and other writers. William Troy is after the same thing in his mythic, psychoanalytic, and social readings of a number of authors, as well as in his campaign to revive the medieval "four levels of meaning" or something analogous; and on a smaller scale Jack Lindsay operates similarly in his Marxist, psychoanalytic, and anthropological readings. F. C. Prescott's "multiple significance," Herbert Muller's "multiple meaning and multivalence," Donald A. Stauffer's "multiplex meanings," and Raymond Preston's "co-operative reading" all approximate it; Empson's "ambiguity" points at it, and Philip Wheelwright's "plurisignation" and Austin Warren's "concurrent multivalence" come even closer. All criticism of *Finnegans Wake* has been automatically pluralistic from the first.

Whatever this type of criticism is called, plural or multiple or many-leveled, it is clearly becoming increasingly essential. We might if we wish call it "continuum criticism" and leave a place for all possible levels of meaning on a continuum from the most completely individual, subjective, and personal (the unconscious) to the most completely social, objective, and impersonal (the historical). The addition of Jung's "racial unconscious" would bring the two ends of our continuum together in a circle. Thus we could take, say, Eliot's symbol of the Waste Land in the poem of that name, a symbol of great depth and complexity, and read it at any level we cared to insert a vocabulary: at the most intimate level, to the Freudian, it would be castration and impotence; at a more conscious level, to a post-Freudian psychology, perhaps the fear of artistic sterility; on the daily-life level, in the biographical terms of Van Wyck Brooks, the symbol of Eliot's preconversion state; on a more social level, to a critic like Parrington, the empty life of the artist or the frustration of the upper class; to Eliot himself, the irreligion of the times; in broadly historical terms, to the Marxist, the decay of capitalism; in Jungian terms, the archetypal ritual of rebirth. Similarly, the symbol of Mynheer Peeperkorn in Mann's *Magic Mountain* would range from the Oedipal father, through the forceful rival personality, to the power of agrarian capital or the Corn God; Hitler's concept of German unity in *Mein Kampf* would range from the Oedipal mother, through "in unity there is strength," to such events in history as the absorption of Austria and Czechoslovakia, and so forth. In the symbol or work of depth there are as many meanings as critics can find levels or vocabularies with which to explore; name it, in other words, and you can have it.

There is another advantage to this sort of multiple-level or plural-meaning criticism. Thinking about the fact that Italian criticism contemporary with it completely ignored the Commedia dell' Arte, and the Elizabethan criticism for a long time completely ignored Shakespeare and the Elizabethan drama, the critic sometimes gets the nightmare idea that we in our time may similarly be ignoring works and whole art forms that will ultimately prove to be of greater significance than anything with which we deal. By sampling the movies, the detective story, the radio, and the comic book, the likely fields for this great ignored art form in our time, the critic generally manages to assuage his fears. Nevertheless, the nightmare itself is significant. What is actually disturbing his peace of mind is the tremendous responsibility the individual critic carries. He is, alone and on the authority of his own knowledge, taste, and intelligence, the sole guardian of art and its magic portals. A collective or symposium criticism would have the virtue not only of establishing a multiplicity of readings and meanings, but also of giving them all a hearing, and in the last analysis of establishing some true and valid ones. It would be not only plural, but in a very real sense dialectic or dramatistic. From the interplay of many minds, even many errors, truth arises, as our wise men have known since Plato's dialogues. This synthesis of critical method is not simple multiplicity or plurality or anarchy, but a genuine dialectic contest or *agon*. From it, too, truth will arise. We may get it within the individual critic, in an integrated method, or outside the individual critic, in the group symposium, but in some form or other we must get it. And "we" here stands for the whole world, for where "truth" is at issue, we are all of necessity critics.

From *The Armed Vision: A Study in the Methods of Modern Literary Criticism* by Stanley Edgar Hyman (New York: Alfred A. Knopf, 1948), pp. 395–407, where it appears as "Conclusion: Attempts at an Integration." Reprinted by permission of the author and publisher.

R. P. BLACKMUR

A Critic's Job of Work

[1935]

CRITICISM, I take it, is the formal discourse of an amateur. When there is enough love and enough knowledge represented in the discourse it is a self-sufficient but by no means an isolated art. It witnesses constantly in its own life its interdependence with the other arts. It lays out the terms and parallels of appreciation from the outside in order to convict itself of internal intimacy; it names and arranges what it knows and loves, and searches endlessly with every fresh impulse or impression for better names and more orderly arrangements. It is only in this sense that poetry (or some other art) is a criticism of life; poetry names and arranges, and thus arrests and transfixes its subject in a form which has a life of its own forever separate but springing from the life which confronts it. Poetry is life at the remove of form and meaning; not life lived but life framed and identified. So the criticism of poetry is bound to be occupied at once with the terms and modes by which the remove was made and with the relation between—in the ambiguous stock phrase—content and form; which is to say with the establishment and appreciation of human or moral value. It will be the underlying effort of this essay to indicate approaches to criticism wherein these two problems—of form and value—will appear inextricable but not confused—like the stones in an arch or the timbers in a building.

These approaches—these we wish to eulogize—are not the only ones, nor the only good ones, nor are they complete. No approach opens on anything except from its own point of view and in terms of its own prepossessions. Let us set against each other for a time the facts of various approaches to see whether there is a residue, not of fact but of principle.

The approaches to—or the escapes from—the central work of criticism are as various as the heresies of the Christian church, and like them testify to occasional needs, fanatic emphasis, special interest, or intellectual pride, all flowing from and even the worst of them enlightening the same body of insight. Every critic like every theologian and every philosopher is a casuist in spite of himself. To escape or surmount the discontinuity of knowledge, each

770

resorts to a particular heresy and makes it predominant and even omnivorous.[1]

For most minds, once doctrine is sighted and is held to be the completion of insight, the doctrinal mode of thinking seems the only one possible. When doctrine totters it seems it can fall only into the gulf of bewilderment; few minds risk the fall; most seize the remnants and swear the edifice remains, when doctrine becomes intolerable dogma.[2] All fall notwithstanding; for as knowledge itself is a fall from the paradise of undifferentiated sensation, so equally every formula of knowledge must fall the moment too much weight is laid upon it—the moment it becomes omnivorous and pretends to be omnipotent—the moment, in short, it is taken literally. Literal knowledge is dead knowledge; and the worst bewilderment—which is always only comparative —is better than death. Yet no form, no formula, of knowledge ought to be surrendered merely because it runs the risk in bad or desperate hands of being used literally; and similarly, in our own thinking, whether it is carried to the point of formal discourse or not, we cannot only afford, we ought scrupulously to risk the use of any concept that seems propitious or helpful in getting over gaps. Only the use should be consciously provisional, speculative, and dramatic. The end-virtue of humility comes only after a long train of humiliations; and the chief labor of humbling is the constant, resourceful restoration of ignorance.

The classic contemporary example of use and misuse is attached to the name of Freud. Freud himself has constantly emphasized the provisional, dramatic character of his speculations: they are employed as imaginative illumination, to be relied on no more and no less than the sailor relies upon his buoys and beacons.[3] But the impetus of Freud was so great that a school of literalists arose with all the mad consequence of schism and heresy and fundamentalism which have no more honorable place in the scientific than the artistic imagination. Elsewhere, from one point of view, Caesarism in Rome and Berlin is only the literalist conception of the need for a positive state. So, too, the economic insights of Marxism, merely by being taken literally in their own field, are held to affect the subject and value of the arts, where actually they offer only a limited field of interest and enliven an irrelevant purpose. It is an amusing exercise—as it refreshes the terms of bewilderment and provides a common clue to the secrets of all the modes of thinking —to restore the insights of Freud and Fascism and Marxism to the terms of

[1] The rashest heresy of our day and climate is that exemplified by T. S. Eliot when he postulates an orthodoxy which exists whether anyone knows it or not.

[2] Baudelaire's sonnet "Le Gouffre" dramatizes this sentiment at once as he saw it surmounted in Pascal and as it occurred insurmountably in himself.

[3] Santayana's essay "A Long Way Round to Nirvana" (in *Some Turns of Thought in Modern Philosophy*) illustrates the poetic-philosophic character of Freud's insight into death by setting up its analogue in Indian philosophy; and by his comparison only adds to the stimulus of Freud.

the Church; when the sexual drama in Freud becomes the drama of original sin, and the politics of Hitler and Lenin becomes the politics of the City of God in the sense that theology provides both the sanctions of economics and the values of culture. Controversy is in terms absolutely held, when the problems argued are falsely conceived because necessarily abstracted from "real" experience. The vital or fatal nexus is in interest and emotion and is established when the terms can be represented dramatically, almost, as it were, for their own sakes alone and with only a pious or ritualistic regard for the doctrines in which they are clothed. The simple, and fatal, example is in the glory men attach to war; the vital, but precarious example, is in the intermittent conception of free institutions and the persistent reformulation of the myth of reason. Then the doctrines do not matter, since they are taken only for what they are worth (whatever rhetorical pretensions to the contrary) as guides and props, as aids to navigation. What does matter is experience, the life represented and the value discovered, and both dramatized or enacted under the banner of doctrine. All banners are wrong-headed, but they make rallying points, free the impulse to cry out, and give meaning to the cry itself simply by making it seem appropriate.

It is on some analogue or parallel to these remarks alone that we understand and use the thought and art of those whose doctrines differ from our own. We either discount, absorb, or dominate the doctrine for the sake of the life that goes with it, for the sake of what is *formed* in the progressive act of thinking. When we do more—when we refine or elaborate the abstracted notion of form—we play a different game, which has merit of its own like chess, but which applied to the world we live in produces false dilemmas like solipsism and infant damnation. There is, taking solipsism for example, a fundamental distinction. Because of the logical doctrine prepared to support it, technical philosophers employ years[4] to get around the impasse in which it leaves them; whereas men of poetic imagination merely use it for the dramatic insight it contains—as Eliot uses it in the last section of *The Waste Land;* or as, say, everyone uses the residual mythology of the Greek religion —which its priests nevertheless used as literal sanction for blood and power.

Fortunately, there exist archetypes of unindoctrinated thinking. Let us incline our minds like reflectors to catch the light of the early Plato and the whole Montaigne. Is not the inexhaustible stimulus and fertility of the *Dialogues* and the *Essays* due as much as anything to the absence of positive doctrine? Is it not that the early Plato always holds conflicting ideas in shifting balance, presenting them in contest and evolution, with victory only the last shift? Is it not that Montaigne is always making room for another idea, and

---

⁴ Santayana found it necessary to resort to his only sustained labor of dialectic, *Scepticism and Animal Faith,* which, though a beautiful monument of intellectual play, is ultimately valuable for its *incidental* moral wisdom.

implying always a third for provisional adjudicating irony? Are not the forms of both men themselves ironic, betraying in its most intimate recesses the duplicity of every thought, pointing out, so to speak, in the act of self-incrimination, and showing it not paled on a pin but in the buff life? . . . Such an approach, such an attempt at vivid questing, borrowed and no doubt adulterated by our own needs, is the only rational approach to the multiplication of doctrine and arrogant technologies which fills out the body of critical thinking. Anything else is a succumbing, not an approach; and it is surely the commonest of ironies to observe a man altogether out of his depth do his cause fatal harm merely because, having once succumbed to an idea, he thinks it necessary to stick to it. Thought is a beacon not a life-raft, and to confuse the functions is tragic. The tragic character of thought—as any perspective will show—is that it takes a rigid mold too soon; chooses destiny like a Calvinist, in infancy, instead of waiting slowly for old age, and hence for the most part works against the world, good sense, and its own object: as anyone may see by taking a perspective of any given idea of democracy, of justice, or the nature of the creative act.

Imaginative skepticism and dramatic irony—the modes of Montaigne and Plato—keep the mind athletic and the spirit on the stretch. Hence the juvenescence of *The Tempest* and hence, too, perhaps, the air almost of precocity in *Back to Methuselah*. Hence, at any rate, the sustaining power of such varied works as *The Brothers Karamazoff, Cousine Bette,* and *The Magic Mountain*. Dante, whom the faithful might take to the contrary, is yet "the chief imagination of Christendom"; he took his doctrine once and for all from the Church and from St. Thomas and used it as a foil (in the painter's sense) to give recessiveness, background, and contrast. Virgil and Aristotle, Beatrice and Bertrans de Born have in their way as much importance as St. Thomas and the Church. It was this security of reference that made Dante so much more a free spirit than were, say, Swift and Laurence Sterne. Dante had a habit (not a theory) of imagination which enabled him to dramatize with equal ardor and effect what his doctrine blessed, what it assailed, and what, at heart, it was indifferent to. Doctrine was the seed and structure of vision, and for his poems (at least to us) never more. *The Divine Comedy* no less than the *Dialogues* and the *Essays* is a true *Speculum Mentis*.

With lesser thinkers and lesser artists—and in the defective works of the greater—we have in reading, in criticising, to supply the skepticism and the irony, or, as may be, the imagination and the drama, to the degree, which cannot be complete since then we should have had no prompts, that they are lacking. We have to rub the looking-glass clear. With Hamlet, for example, we have to struggle and guess to bring the motive out of obscurity: a struggle which, aiming at the wrong end, the psychoanalysts have darkened with counsel. With Shelley we have to flesh out the Platonic Ideas, as with

Blake we have to cut away, since it cannot be dramatized, all the excrescence of doctrine. With Baudelaire we have sometimes to struggle with and sometimes to suppress the problem of belief, working out the irony implicit in either attitude. Similarly, with a writer like Pascal, in order to get the most out of him, in order to compose an artistic judgment, we must consider such an idea as that of the necessity of the wager, not solemnly as Pascal took it, but as a dramatized possibility, a savage, but provisional irony; and we need to show that the skepticisms of Montaigne and Pascal are not at all the same thing—that where one produced serenity the other produced excruciation.

Again, speaking of André Gide, we should remind ourselves not that he has been the apologist of homosexuality, not that he has become a communist, but that he is *par excellence* the French puritan chastened by the wisdom of the body, and that he has thus an acutely scrupulous ethical sensibility. It is by acknowledging the sensibility that we feel the impact of the apologetics and the political conversion. Another necessity in the apprehension of Gide might be put as the recognition of similarity in difference of the precocious small boys in Dostoevski and Gide, *e.g.*, Kolya in *Karamazoff* and young George in *The Counterfeiters*: they are small, cruel engines, all naked sensibility and no scruple, demoniacally possessed, and used to keep things going. And these in turn may remind us of another writer who had a predilection for presenting the *terrible* quality of the young intelligence: of Henry James, of the children in *The Turn of the Screw*, of *Maisie*, and all the rest, all beautifully efficient agents of dramatic judgment and action, in that they take all things seriously for themselves, with the least prejudice of preparation, candidly, with an intelligence life has not yet violated.

Such feats of agility and attention as these remarks illustrate seem facile and even commonplace, and from facile points of view there is no need to take them otherwise. Taken superficially they provide escape from the whole labor of specific understanding; or, worse, they provide an easy vault from casual interpretation to an omnivorous world-view. We might take solemnly and as of universal application the two notions of demonic possession and inviolate intelligence of Gide, Dostoievski, and James, and on that frail nexus build an unassailable theory of the sources of art, wisdom, and value; unassailable because affording only a stereotyped vision, like that of conservative capitalism, without reference in the real world. The maturity of Shakespeare and of Gertrude Stein would then be found on the same childish level.

But we need not go so far in order to draw back. The modes of Montaigne and Plato contain their own safety. Any single insight is good only at and up to a certain point of development and not beyond, which is to say that it is a provisional and tentative and highly selective approach to its field. Furthermore, no observation, no collection of observations, ever tells the whole story; there is always room for more, and at the hypothetical limit of attention and interest there will always remain, quite untouched, the thing itself. Thus the complex character—I say nothing of the value—of the remarks above reveals itself. They flow from a dramatic combination of all the skills and conventions of the thinking mind. They are commonplace only as a criticism—as an end-product or function. Like walking, criticism is a pretty nearly universal art; both require a constant intricate shifting and catching of balance; neither can be questioned much in process; and few perform either really well. For either a new terrain is fatiguing and awkward, and in our day most men prefer paved walks or some form of rapid transit—some easy theory or outmastering dogma. A good critic keeps his criticism from becoming either instinctive or vicarious, and the labor of his understanding is always specific, like the art which he examines; and he knows that the sum of his best work comes only to the pedagogy of elucidation and appreciation. He observes facts and he delights in discriminations. The object remains, and should remain, itself, only made more available and seen in a clearer light. The imagination of Dante is for us only equal to what we can know of it at a given time.

Which brings us to what, as T. S. Eliot would say,[5] I have been leading up to all the time, and what has indeed been said several times by the way. Any rational approach is valid to literature and may be properly called critical which fastens at any point upon the work itself. The utility of a given approach depends partly upon the strength of the mind making it and partly upon the recognition of the limits appropriate to it. Limits may be of scope, degree, or relevance, and may be either plainly laid out by the critic himself, or may be determined by his readers; and it is, by our argument, the latter case that commonly falls, since an active mind tends to overestimate the scope of its tools and to take as necessary those doctrinal considerations which habit has made seem instinctive. No critic is required to limit himself to a single approach, nor is he likely to be able to do so; facts cannot be exhibited without comment, and comment involves the generality of the mind. Furthermore, a consciously complex approach like that of Kenneth Burke or T. S. Eliot, by setting up parallels of reference, affords a more flexible, more available, more stimulating standard of judgment—though of course at a greater risk of prejudice—than a single approach. What produces the evil of stultification and the malice of controversy is the confused approach, when the limits are not seen because they tend to cancel each other out, and the driving power becomes emotional.

[5] . . . that when "morals cease to be a matter of tradition and orthodoxy—that is, of the habits of the community formulated, corrected, and elevated by the continuous thought and direction of the Church—and when each man is to elaborate his own, then *personality* becomes a thing of alarming importance." (*After Strange Gods.*) Thus Mr. Eliot becomes one of those viewers-with-alarm whose next step is the very hysteria of disorder they wish to escape. The hysteria of institutions is more dreadful than that of individuals.

The worse evil of fanatic falsification—of arrogant irrationality and barbarism in all its forms—arises when a body of criticism is governed by an *idée fixe*, a really exaggerated heresy, when a notion of genuine but small scope is taken literally as of universal application. This is the body of tendentious criticism where, since something is assumed proved before the evidence is in, distortion, vitiation, and absolute assertion become supreme virtues. I cannot help feeling that such writers as Maritain and Massis—no less than Nordau before them—are tendentious in this sense. But even here, in this worst order of criticism, there is a taint of legitimacy. Once we reduce, in a man like Irving Babbitt, the magnitude of application of such notions as the inner check and the higher will, which were for Babbitt paramount—that is, when we determine the limits within which he really worked—then the massive erudition and acute observation with which his work is packed become permanently available.

And there is no good to be got in objecting to and disallowing those orders of criticism which have an ulterior purpose. *Ulterior* is not in itself a pejorative, but only so when applied to an enemy. Since criticism is not autonomous —not a light but a process of elucidation—it cannot avoid discovering constantly within itself a purpose or purposes ulterior in the good sense. The danger is in not knowing what is ulterior and what is not, which is much the same as the cognate danger in the arts themselves. The arts serve purposes beyond themselves; the purposes of what they dramatize or represent at that remove from the flux which gives them order and meaning and value; and to deny those purposes is like asserting that the function of a handsaw is to hang above a bench and that to cut wood is to belittle it. But the purposes are varied and so bound in his subject that the artist cannot always design for them. The critic, if that is his bent, may concern himself with those purposes or with some one among them which obsess him; but he must be certain to distinguish between what is genuinely ulterior to the works he examines and what is merely irrelevant; and he must further not assume except within the realm of his special argument that other purposes either do not exist or are negligible or that the works may not be profitably discussed apart from ulterior purposes and as examples of dramatic possibility alone.

II

Three examples of contemporary criticism primarily concerned with the ulterior purposes of literature should, set side by side, exhibit both the defects and the unchastened virtues of that approach; though they must do so only tentatively and somewhat invidiously—with an exaggeration for effect. Each work is assumed to be a representative ornament of its kind, carrying within it the seeds of its own death and multiplication. Let us take then, with an eye sharpened by the dangers involved, Santayana's essay on Lucretius (in *Three*

Philosophical Poets), Van Wyck Brooks' *Pilgrimage of Henry James,* and Granville Hicks' *The Great Tradition.* Though that of the third is more obvious in our predicament, the urgency in the approach is equal in all three.

Santayana's essay represents a conversion or transvaluation of an actually poetic ordering of nature to the terms of a moral philosophy which, whatever its own responsibilities, is free of the special responsibility of poetry. So ably and so persuasively is it composed, his picture seems complete and to contain so much of what was important in Lucretius that *De Rerum Natura* itself can be left behind. The philosophical nature of the insight, its moral scope and defect, the influence upon it of the Democritan atom, once grasped intellectually as Santayana shows us how to grasp them, seem a good substitute for the poem and far more available. But, what Santayana remembers but does not here emphasize since it was beyond his immediate interest, there is no vicar for poetry on earth. Poetry is idiom, a special and fresh saying, and cannot for its life be said otherwise; and there is, finally, as much difference between words used about a poem and the poem as there is between words used about a painting and the painting. The gap is absolute. Yet I do not mean to suggest that Santayana's essay—that any philosophical criticism—is beside the point. It is true that the essay may be taken as a venture in philosophy for its own sake, but it is also true that it reveals a body of facts about an ulterior purpose in Lucretius' poem—doubtless the very purpose Lucretius himself would have chosen to see enhanced. If we return to the poem it will be warmer as the facts come alive in the verse. The re-conversion comes naturally in this instance in that, through idioms differently construed but equally imaginative, philosophy and poetry both buttress and express moral value. The one enacts or represents in the flesh what the other reduces to principle or raises to the ideal. The only precaution the critic of poetry need take is negative: that neither poetry nor philosophy can ever fully satisfy the other's purposes, though each may seem to do so if taken in an ulterior fashion. The relationship is mutual but not equivalent.

When we turn deliberately from Santayana on Lucretius to Van Wyck Brooks on Henry James, we turn from the consideration of the rational ulterior purposes of art to the consideration of the irrational underlying predicament of the artist himself, not only as it predicts his art and is reflected in it, but also, and in effect predominantly, as it represents the conditioning of nineteenth-century American culture. The consideration is sociological, the method of approach that of literary psychology, and the burden obsessive. The conversion is from literary to biographical values. Art is taken not as the objectification or mirroring of social experience but as a personal expression and escape-fantasy of the artist's personal life in dramatic extension. The point for emphasis is that the cultural situation of Henry James' America stultified the expression and made every escape ineffectual—even that of Europe.

This theme—the private tragedy of the unsuccessful artist—was one of Henry James' own; but James saw it as typical or universal—as a characteristic tragedy of the human spirit—illustrated, as it happened for him, against the Anglo-American background. Brooks, taking the same theme, raises it to an obsession, an omnivorous concept, under which all other themes can be subsumed. Applied to American cultural history, such obsessive thinking is suggestive in the very exaggeration of its terms, and applied to the private predicament of Henry James the man it dramatically emphasizes—uses for all and more than it is worth—an obvious conflict that tormented him. As history or as biography the book is a persuasive imaginative picture, although clearly not the only one to be seen. Used as a nexus between James the man and the novels themselves, the book has only possible relevance and cannot be held as material. *Hamlet,* by a similar argument, could be shown to be an unsuccessful expression of Shakespeare's personality. To remain useful in the field of literary criticism, Brooks' notions ought to be kept parallel to James' novels but never allowed to merge with them. The corrective, the proof of the gap, is perhaps in the great air of freedom and sway of mastery that pervades the "Prefaces" James wrote to his collected edition. For James art was enough because it molded and mirrored and valued all the life he knew. What Brooks' parallel strictures can do is to help us decide from another point of view whether to choose the values James dramatized. They cannot affect or elucidate but rather—if the gap is closed by will—obfuscate the values themselves.

In short, the order of criticism of which Brooks is a masterly exponent, and which we may call the psycho-sociological order, is primarily and in the end concerned less with the purposes, ulterior or not, of the arts than with some of the ulterior *uses* to which the arts can be appropriately put. Only what is said in the meantime, by the way—and does not depend upon the essence of argument but only accompanies it—can be applied to the arts themselves. There is nothing, it should be added, in Brooks' writings to show that he believes otherwise or would claim more; he is content with that scope and degree of value to which his method and the strength of his mind limit him; and his value is the greater and more urgent for that.

Such tacit humility, such implicit admission of contingency, are not immediate characteristics of Granville Hicks' *The Great Tradition,* though they may, so serious is his purpose, be merely virtues of which he deliberately, for the time being and in order to gain his point, deprives himself of the benefit. If this is so, however expedient his tactics may seem on the short view they will defeat him on the long. But let us examine the book on the ground of our present concern alone. Like Brooks, Hicks presents an interpretation of American literature since the Civil War, dealing with the whole body rather than single figures. Like Brooks he has a touchstone in an obsessive idea, but where we may say that Brooks *uses* his idea—as we think for more than it is worth—we must say that Hicks is victimized by his idea to the point where the travail of judgment is suspended and becomes the mere reiteration of formula. He judges literature as it expressed or failed to express the economic conflict of classes sharpened by the industrial revolution, and he judges individual writers as they used or did not use an ideology resembling the Marxist analysis as prime clue to the clear representation of social drama. Thus Howells comes off better than Henry James, and Frank Norris better than Mark Twain, and, in our own day, Dos Passos is stuck on a thin eminence that must alarm him.

Controversy is not here a profitable exercise, but it may be said for the sake of the record that although every period of history presents a class struggle, some far more acute than our own, the themes of great art have seldom lent themselves to propaganda for an economic insight, finding, as it happened, religious, moral or psychological—that is to say, interpretative—insights more appropriate impulses. If *Piers Plowman* dealt with the class struggle, *The Canterbury Tales* did not, and Hicks would be hard put, if he looked sharp, to make out a better case of social implication in Dostoievski than in Henry James.

What vitiates *The Great Tradition* is its tendentiousness. Nothing could be more exciting, nothing more vital, than a book by Hicks which discovered and examined the facts of a literature whose major theme hung on an honest dramatic view of the class struggle—and there is indeed such a literature now emerging from the depression. And on the other hand it would be worth while to have Hicks sharpen his teeth on all the fraudulent or pseudo-art which actually slanders the terms of the class and every other struggle.

The book with which he presents us performs a very different operation. There is an initial hortatory assumption that American literature ought to represent the class struggle from a Marxist viewpoint, and that it ought thus to be the spur and guide to political action. Proceeding, the point is either proved or the literature dismissed and its authors slandered. Hicks is not disengaging for emphasis and contemporary need an ulterior purpose; he is not writing criticism at all; he is writing a fanatic's history and a casuist's polemic, with the probable result—which is what was meant by suggesting above that he had misconceived his tactics—that he will convert no one who retains the least love of literature or the least knowledge of the themes which engage the most of life. It should be emphasized that there is no more quarrel with Hicks' economic insight as such than there was with the insights of Santayana and Van Wyck Brooks. The quarrel is deeper. While it is true and good that the arts may be used to illustrate social propaganda—though it is not a great use—you can no more use an economic insight as your chief critical tool than you can make much out of the Mass by submitting the doctrine of transubstantiation to chemical analysis.

These three writers have one great formal fact in common, which they illustrate as differently as may be. They are concerned with the separable content of literature, with what may be said without consideration of its specific setting and apparition in a form; which is why, perhaps, all three leave literature so soon behind. The quantity of what can be said directly about the content alone of a given work of art is seldom great, but the least saying may be the innervation of an infinite intellectual structure, which, however valuable in itself, has for the most part only an asserted relation with the works from which it springs. The sense of continuous relationship, of sustained contact, with the works nominally in hand is rare and when found uncommonly exhilarating; it is the fine object of criticism; as it seems to put us in direct possession of the principles whereby the works move without injuring or disintegrating the body of the works themselves. This sense of intimacy by inner contact cannot arise from methods of approach which hinge on seized separable content. We have constantly—if our interest is really in literature—to prod ourselves back, to remind ourselves that there was a poem, a play, or a novel of some initial and we hope terminal concern, or we have to falsify and set up fictions[6] to the effect that no matter what we are saying we are really talking about art after all. The question must often be whether the prodding and reminding is worth the labor, whether we might not better assign the works that require it to a different category than that of criticism.

III

Similar strictures and identical precautions are necessary in thinking of other, quite different approaches to criticism, where if there are no ulterior purposes to allow for there are other no less limiting features—there are certainly such, for example, for me in thinking of my own. The ulterior motive, or the limiting feature, whichever it is, is a variable constant. One does not always know what it is, nor what nor how much work it does; but one always knows it is there—for strength or weakness. It may be only the strength of emphasis—which is necessarily distortion; or it may be the worse strength of a simplifying formula, which skeletonizes and transforms what we want to recognize in the flesh. It may be only the weakness of what is unfinished, undeveloped, or unseen—the weakness that follows on emphasis; or it may be the weakness that shows when pertinent things are deliberately dismissed or

---

[6] Such a fiction, if not consciously so contrived, is the fiction of the organic continuity of all literature as expounded by T. S. Eliot in his essay, "Tradition and the Individual Talent." The locus is famous and represents that each new work of art slightly alters the relationships among the whole order of existing works. The notion has truth, but it is a mathematical truth and has little relevance to the arts. Used as Eliot uses it, it is an experimental conceit and pushes the mind forward. Taken seriously it is bad constitutional law, in the sense that it would provoke numberless artificial and insoluble problems.

ignored, which is the corresponding weakness of the mind strong in formula. No mind can avoid distortion and formula altogether, nor would wish to; but minds rush to the defense of qualities they think cannot be avoided, and that, in itself, is an ulterior motive, a limiting feature of the mind that rushes. I say nothing of one's personal prepossessions, of the damage of one's private experience, of the malice and false tolerance they inculcate into judgment. I know that my own essays suffer variously, but I cannot bring myself to specify the indulgences I would ask; mostly, I hope, that general indulgence which consists in the task of bringing my distortions and emphases and opinions into balance with other distortions, other emphases and better opinions.

But rather than myself, let us examine briefly, because of their differences from each other and from the three critics already handled, the modes of approach to the act of criticism and habits of critical work of I. A. Richards, Kenneth Burke, and S. Foster Damon. It is to characterize them and to judge the *character* of their work—its typical scope and value—that we want to examine them. With the objective validity of their varying theories we are not much here concerned. Objective standards of criticism, as we hope them to exist at all, must have an existence anterior and superior to the practice of particular critics. The personal element in a given critic—what he happens to know and happens to be able to understand—is strong or obstinate enough to reach into his esthetic theories; and as most critics do not have the coherence of philosophers it seems doubtful if any outsider could ever reach the same conclusions as the critic did by adopting his esthetics. Esthetics sometimes seems only as implicit in the practice of criticism as the atomic physics is present in sunlight when you feel it.

But some critics deliberately expand the theoretic phase of every practical problem. There is a tendency to urge the scientific principle and the statistical method, and in doing so to bring in the whole assorted world of thought. That Mr. Richards, who is an admirable critic and whose love and knowledge of poetry are incontestable, is a victim of the expansiveness of his mind in these directions, is what characterizes, and reduces, the scope of his work as literary criticism. It is possible that he ought not to be called a literary critic at all. If we list the titles of his books we are in a quandary: *The Foundations of Aesthetics, The Meaning of Meaning* (these with C. K. Ogden), *The Principles of Literary Criticism, Science and Poetry, Practical Criticism, Mencius on the Mind,* and *Coleridge on Imagination.* The apparatus is so vast, so labyrinthine, so inclusive—and the amount of actual literary criticism is so small that it seems almost a by-product instead of the central target. The slightest volume, physically, *Science and Poetry,* contains proportionally the most literary criticism, and contains, curiously, his one obvious failure in appreciation— since amply redressed—his misjudgment of the nature of Yeats' poetry. His work is for the most part *about* a department of the mind which includes the

pedagogy of sensibility and the practice of literary criticism. The matters he
investigates are the problems of belief, of meaning, of communication, of the
nature of controversy, and of poetic language as the supreme mode of imagination. The discussion of these problems is made to focus for the most part
on poetry because poetry provides the only great monuments of imagination
available to verbal imagination. His bottom contention might, I think, be put
as this: that words have a synergical power, in the realms of feeling, emotion,
and value, to create a reality, or the sense of it, not contained in the words
separately; and that the power and the reality as experienced in great poetry
make the chief source of meaning and value for the life we live. This contention I share; except that I should wish to put on the same level, as sources of
meaning and value, modes of imagination that have no medium in words—
though words may call on them—and are not susceptible of verbal reformulation: the modes of great acting, architecture, music and painting. Thus I can
assent to Mr. Richards' positive statement of the task of criticism, because I
can add to it positive tasks in analogous fields: "To recall that poetry is the
supreme use of language, man's chief co-ordinating instrument, in the service
of the most integral purposes of life; and to explore, with thoroughness, the
intricacies of the modes of language as working modes of the mind." But I
want this criticism, engaged in this task, constantly to be confronted with
examples of poetry, and I want it so for the very practical purpose of assisting
in pretty immediate appreciation of the use, meaning, and value of the language in that particular poetry. I want it to assist in doing for me what it actually assists Mr. Richards in doing, whatever that is, when he is reading poetry
for its own sake.

Mr. Richards wants it to do that, too, but he wants it to do a great deal else
first. Before it gets to actual poetry (from which it is said to spring) he wants
literary criticism to become something else and much more: he wants it to
become, indeed, the master department of the mind. As we become aware of
the scope of poetry, we see, according to Mr. Richards that the

> . . . study of the modes of language becomes, as it attempts to be thorough, the
> most fundamental and extensive of all inquiries. It is no preliminary or preparation
> for other profounder studies. . . . The very formation of the objects which these
> studies propose to examine takes place through the processes (of which imagina-
> tion and fancy are modes) by which the words they use acquire their meanings.
> Criticism is the science of these meanings. . . . Critics in the future must have a
> theoretical equipment which has not been felt to be necessary in the past. . . .
> But the critical equipment will not be *primarily* philosophical. It will be rather a
> command *of the methods of general linguistic analysis.*[7]

I think we may take it that *Mencius on the Mind* is an example of the kind of
excursion on which Mr. Richards would lead us. It is an excursion into multi-

[7] All quoted material is from the last four pages of *Coleridge on Imagination.*

ple definition, and it is a good one if that is where you want to go and are in no hurry to come back: you learn the enormous variety and complexity of the operations possible in the process of verbally describing and defining brief passages of imaginative language and the equal variety and complexity of the result; you learn the practical impossibility of verbally ascertaining what an author means—and you hear nothing of the other ways of apprehending meaning at all. The instance is in the translation of Mencius, because Mr. Richards happens to be interested in Mencius, and because it is easy to see the difficulties of translating Chinese; but the principles and method of application would work as well on passages from Milton or Rudyard Kipling. The real point of Mr. Richards' book is the impossibility of understanding, short of a lifetime's analysis and compensation, the mechanism of meaning in even a small body of work. There is no question of the exemplary value and stimulus of Mr. Richards' work; but there is no question either that few would care to emulate him for any purpose of literary criticism. In the first place it would take too long, and in the second he does not answer the questions literary criticism would put. The literal adoption of Mr. Richards' approach to literary criticism would stultify the very power it was aimed to enhance—the power of imaginative apprehension, of imaginative co-ordination of varied and separate elements. Mr. Richards' work is something to be aware of, but deep awareness is the limit of use. It is notable that in his admirable incidental criticism of such poets as Eliot, Lawrence, Yeats and Hopkins, Mr. Richards does not himself find it necessary to be more than aware of his own doctrines of linguistic analysis. As philosophy from Descartes to Bradley transformed itself into a study of the modes of knowing, Mr. Richards would transform literary criticism into the science of linguistics. Epistemology is a great subject, and so is linguistics; but they come neither in first nor final places; the one is only a fragment of wisdom and the other only a fraction of the means of understanding. Literary criticism is not a science—though it may be the object of one; and to try to make it one is to turn it upside down. Right side up, Mr. Richards' contribution shrinks in weight and dominion but remains intact and preserves its importance. We may conclude that it was the newness of his view that led him to exaggerate it, and we ought to add the probability that had he not exaggerated it we should never have seen either that it was new or valuable at all.

From another point of view than that of literary criticism, and as a contribution to a psychological theory of knowledge, Mr. Richards' work is not heretical, but is integral and integrating, and especially when it incorporates poetry into its procedure; but from our point of view the heresy is profound —and is far more distorting than the heresies of Santayana, Brooks, and Hicks, which carry with them obviously the impetus for their correction. Because it is possible to apply scientific methods to the language of poetry, and because sci-

entific methods engross their subject matter, Mr. Richards places the whole
burden of criticism in the application of a scientific approach, and asserts it to
be an implement for the judgment of poetry. Actually, it can handle only the
language and its words and cannot touch—except by assertion—the imaginative product of the words which is poetry: which is the object revealed or
elucidated by criticism. Criticism must be concerned, first and last—whatever
comes between—with the poem as it is read and as what it represents is felt.
As no amount of physics and physiology can explain the *feeling* of things seen
as green or even certify their existence, so no amount of linguistic analysis can
explain the *feeling* or existence of a poem. Yet the physics in the one case and
the linguistics in the other may be useful both to the poet and the reader. It
may be useful, for example, in extracting facts of meaning from a poem, to
show that, whether the poet was aware of it or not, the semantic history of a
word was so and so; but only if the semantics can be resolved into the ambiguities and precisions created by the poem. Similarly with any branch of
linguistics; and similarly with the applications of psychology—Mr. Richards'
other emphasis. No statistical description can either explain or demean a
poem unless the description is translated back to the imaginative apprehension
or feeling which must have taken place without it. The light of science is
parallel or in the background where feeling or meaning is concerned. The
Oedipus complex does not explain *Oedipus Rex;* not that Mr. Richards would
think it did. Otherwise he could not believe that "poetry is the supreme use
of language" and more, could not convey in his comments on T. S. Eliot's *Ash
Wednesday* the actuality of his belief that poetry is the supreme use.

It is the interest and fascination of Mr. Richards' work in reference to
different levels of sensibility, including the poetic, that has given him both a
wide and a penetrating influence. No literary critic can escape his influence;
an influence that stimulates the mind as much as anything by showing the
sheer excitement as well as profundity of the problems of language—many of
which he has himself made genuine problems, at least for the readers of poetry: an influence, obviously, worth deliberately incorporating by reducing it
to one's own size and needs. In T. S. Eliot the influence is conspicuous if
slight. Mr. Kenneth Burke is considerably indebted, partly directly to Mr.
Richards, partly to the influences which acted upon Mr. Richards (as Bentham's theory of Fictions) and partly to the frame of mind which helped mold
them both. But Mr. Burke is clearly a different person—and different from
anyone writing today; and the virtues, the defects, and the élan of his criticism
are his own.

Some years ago, when Mr. Burke was an animating influence on the staff of
The Dial, Miss Marianne Moore published a poem in that magazine called
"Picking and Choosing" which contained the following lines:

and Burke is a
psychologist—of acute and racoon-
like curiosity. *Summa diligentia*
to the humbug, whose name is so amusing—very young
and ve-
ry rushed, Caesar crossed the Alps on the 'top of a
diligence.' We are not daft about the meaning but this
familiarity
with wrong meanings puzzles one.

In the index of Miss Moore's *Observations,* we find under Burke that the reference is to Edmund, but it is really to Kenneth just the same. There is no acuter curiosity than Mr. Burke's engaged in associating the meanings, right and wrong, of the business of literature with the business of life and vice versa. No one has a greater awareness—not even Mr. Richards—of the important part wrong meanings play in establishing the consistency of right ones. The writer of whom he reminds us, for the buoyancy and sheer remarkableness of his speculations, is Charles Santiago Saunders Peirce; one is enlivened by them without any *necessary* reference to their truth; hence they have truth for their own purposes, that is, for their own uses. Into what these purposes or uses are it is our present business to inquire.

As Mr. Richards in fact uses literature as a springboard or source for scientific method of a philosophy of value, Mr. Burke uses literature, not only as a springboard but also as a resort or home, for philosophy or psychology of moral possibility. Literature is the hold-all and the persuasive form for the patterns of possibility. In literature we see unique possibilities enacted, actualized, and in the moral and psychological philosophies we see the types of possibility generalized, see their abstracted, convertible forms. In some literature, and in some aspects of most literature of either great magnitude or great possibility, we see, so to speak, the enactment or dramatic representation of the type or patterns. Thus Mr. Burke can make a thrilling intellectual pursuit of the subintelligent writing of Erskine Caldwell: where he shows that Caldwell gains a great effect of humanity by putting in *none himself,* appealing to the reader's common stock: *i.e.,* what is called for so desperately by the pattern of the story must needs be generously supplied. Exactly as thrilling is his demonstration of the great emotional rôle of the outsider as played in the supremely intelligent works of Thomas Mann and André Gide. His common illustrations of the pervasive spread of symbolic pattern are drawn from Shakespeare and from the type of the popular or pulp press. I think that on the whole his method could be applied with equal fruitfulness to Shakespeare, Dashiell Hammett, or Marie Corelli; as indeed he does apply it with equal force both to the field of anarchic private morals and to the outline of a secular conversion to Communism—as in, respectively, *Toward a Better Life* and *Permanence and Change*.

The real harvest that we barn from Mr. Burke's writings is his presentation of the types of ways the mind works in the written word. He is more interested in the psychological means of the meaning, and how it might mean (and often really does) something else, than in the meaning itself. Like Mr. Richards, but for another purpose, he is engaged largely in the meaning of meaning, and is therefore much bound up with considerations of language, but on the plane of emotional and intellectual patterns rather than on the emotional plane; which is why his essays deal with literature (or other writings) as it dramatizes or unfolds character (a character is a pattern of emotions and notions) rather than with lyric or meditative poetry which is Mr. Richards' field. So we find language containing felt character as well as felt co-ordination. The representation of character, and of aspiration and symbol, must always be rhetorical; and therefore we find that for Mr. Burke the rightly rhetorical is the profoundly hortatory. Thus literature may be seen as an inexhaustible reservoir of moral or character philosophies in action.

It is the technique of such philosophies that Mr. Burke explores, as he pursues it through curiosities of development and conversion and duplicity; it is the technique of the notions that may be put into or taken out of literature, but it is only a part of the technique of literature itself. The final reference is to the psychological and moral possibilities of the mind, and these certainly do not exhaust the technique or the reality of literature. The reality in literature is an object of contemplation and of feeling, like the reality of a picture or a cathedral, not a route of speculation. If we remember this and make the appropriate reductions here as elsewhere, Mr. Burke's essays become as pertinent to literary criticism as they are to the general ethical play of the mind. Otherwise they become too much a methodology for its own sake on the one hand, and too much a philosophy at one remove on the other. A man writes as he can; but those who use his writings have the further responsibility of redefining their scope, an operation (of which Mr. Burke is a master) which alone uses them to the full.

It is in relation to these examples which I have so unjustly held up of the philosophical, the sociological, or psychological approaches to criticism that I wish to examine an example of what composes, after all, the great bulk of serious writings about literature: a work of literary scholarship. Upon scholarship all other forms of literary criticism depend, so long as they are criticism, in much the same way that architecture depends on engineering. The great editors of the last century—men such as Dyce and Skeat and Gifford and Furness—performed work as valuable to the use of literature, and with far less complement of harm, as men like Hazlitt and Arnold and Pater. Scholarship, being bent on the collection, arrangement, and scrutiny of facts, has the positive advantage over other forms of criticism that it is a co-operative labor, and may be completed and corrected by subsequent scholars; and it has the negative advantage that it is not bound to investigate the mysteries of meaning or to connect literature with other departments of life—it has only to furnish the factual materials for such investigations and connections. It is not surprising to find that the great scholars are sometimes good critics, though usually in restricted fields; and it is a fact, on the other hand, that the great critics are themselves either good scholars or know how to take great advantage of scholarship. Perhaps we may put it that for the most part dead critics remain alive in us to the extent that they form part of our scholarship. It is Dr. Johnson's statements of fact that we preserve of him as a critic; his opinions have long since become a part of that imaginative structure, his personality. A last fact about scholarship is this, that so far as its conclusions are sound they are subject to use and digestion not debate by those outside the fold. And of bad scholarship as of bad criticism we have only to find means to minimize what we cannot destroy.

It is difficult to find an example of scholarship pure and simple, of high character, which can be made to seem relevant to the discussion in hand. What I want is to bring into the discussion the omnipresence of scholarship as a background and its immediate and necessary availability to every other mode of approach. What I want is almost anonymous. Failing that, I choose S. Foster Damon's *William Blake* (as I might have taken J. L. Lowes' *Road to Xanadu*) which, because of its special subject matter, brings its scholarship a little nearer the terms of discussion than a Shakespeare commentary would have done. The scholar's major problem with Blake happened to be one which many scholars could not handle, some refused to see, and some fumbled. A great part of Blake's meaning is not open to ordinarily well-instructed readers, but must be brought out by the detailed solution of something very like an enormous and enormously complicated acrostic puzzle. Not only earnest scrutiny of the poems as printed, but also a study of Blake's reading, a reconstruction of habits of thought, and an industrious piecing together into a consistent key of thousands of clues throughout the work, were necessary before many even of the simplest appearing poems could be explained. It is one thing to explain a mystical poet, like Crashaw, who was attached to a recognized church, and difficult enough; but it is a far more difficult thing to explain a mystical poet like Blake, who was so much an eclectic in his sources that his mystery as well as his apprehension of it was practically his own. All Mr. Damon had to go on besides the texts, and the small body of previous scholarship that was pertinent, were the general outlines of insight to which all mystics apparently adhere. The only explanation would be in the facts of what Blake meant to mean when he habitually said one thing in order to hide and enhance another; and in order to be convincing—poetry being what it is—the facts adduced had to be self-evident. It is not a question here whether the mystery enlightened was worth it. The result for emphasis is that Mr. Damon made Blake exactly what he seemed least to be, perhaps the most intellectually consistent of the greater poets in English. Since the chief weapons used are the extended facts of scholarship, the picture Mr. Damon produced cannot be destroyed even though later and other scholarship modifies, re-arranges, or adds to it with different or other facts. The only suspicion that might attach is that the picture is too consistent and that the facts are made to tell too much, and direct, but instructed, apprehension not enough.

My point about Mr. Damon's work is typical and double. First, that the same sort of work, the adduction of ultimately self-evident facts, can be done and must be done in other kinds of poetry than Blake's. Blake is merely an extreme and obvious example of an unusually difficult poet who hid his facts on purpose. The work must be done to the appropriate degree of digging out the facts in all orders of poetry—and especially perhaps in contemporary poetry, where we tend to let the work go either because it seems too easy or because it seems supererogatory. Self-evident facts are paradoxically the hardest to come by; they are not evident till they are seen; yet the meaning of a poem—the part of it which is intellectually formulable—must invariably depend on this order of facts, the facts about the meanings of the elements aside from their final meaning in combination. The rest of the poem, what it is, what it shows, its final value as a created emotion, its meanings, if you like, *as* a poem, cannot in the more serious orders of poetry develop itself to the full without this factual or intellectual meaning to show the way. The other point is already made, and has been made before in this essay, but it may still be emphasized. Although the scholarly account is indispensable it does not tell the whole story. It is only the basis and perhaps ultimately the residue of all the other stories. But it must be seen to first.

My own approach, such as it is, and if it can be named, does not tell the whole story either; the reader is conscientiously left with the poem, with the real work yet to do; and I wish to advance it—as indeed I have been advancing it *seriatim*—only in connection with the reduced and compensated approaches I have laid out; and I expect, too, that if my approach is used at all it will require its own reduction as well as its compensations. Which is why this essay has taken its present form, preferring for once, in the realm of theory and apologetics, the implicit to the explicit statement. It is, I suppose, an approach to literary criticism—to the discourse of an amateur—primarily through the technique, in the widest sense of that word, of the examples handled; technique on the plane of words and even of linguistics in Mr. Richards' sense, but also technique on the plane of intellectual and emotional patterns in Mr. Burke's sense, and technique, too, in that there is a technique of securing and arranging and representing a fundamental view of life. The advantage of the technical approach is I think double. It readily admits other approaches and is anxious to be complemented by them. Furthermore, in a sense, it is able to incorporate the technical aspect, which always exists, of what is secured by other approaches—as I have argued elsewhere that so un-promising a matter as T. S. Eliot's religious convictions may be profitably considered as a dominant element in his technique of revealing the actual. The second advantage of the technical approach is a consequence of the first; it treats of nothing in literature except in its capacity of reduction to literary fact, which is where it resembles scholarship, only passing beyond it in that its facts are usually further into the heart of the literature than the facts of most scholarship. Aristotle, curiously, is here the type and master; as the *Poetics* is nothing but a collection and explanation of the facts of Greek poetry, it is the factual aspect that is invariably produced. The rest of the labor is in the effort to find understandable terms to fit the composition of the facts. After all, it is only the facts about a poem, a play, a novel, that can be reduced to tractable form, talked about, and examined; the rest is the product of the facts, from the technical point of view, and not a product but the thing itself from its own point of view. The rest, whatever it is, can only be known, not talked about.

But facts are not simple or easy to come at; not all the facts will appear to one mind, and the same facts appear differently in the light of different minds. No attention is undivided, no single approach sufficient, no predilec-tion guaranteed, when facts or what their arrangements create are in question. In short, for the arts, *mere* technical scrutiny of any order is not enough with-out the direct apprehension—which may come first or last—to which all scru-tinies that show facts contribute.

It may be that there are principles that cover both the direct apprehension and the labor of providing modes for the understanding of the expressive arts. If so, they are Socratic and found within, and subject to the fundamental skepticism as in Montaigne. There must be seeds, let us say—seeds, germs, beginning forms upon which I can rely and to which I resort. When I use a word, an image, a notion, there must be in its small nodular apparent form, as in the peas I am testing on my desk, at least prophetically, the whole future growth, the whole harvested life; and not rhetorically, nor in a formula, but stubbornly, pervasively, heart-hidden, materially, in both the anterior and the eventual prospect as well as in the small handled form of the nub. What is it, what are they, these seeds of understanding? And if I know, are they logical? Do they take the processional form of the words I use? Or do they take a form like that of the silver backing a glass, a dark that enholds all brightness? Is every metaphor—and the assertion of understanding is our great metaphor—mixed by the necessity of its intention? What is the mixture of a word, an image, a notion?

The mixture, if I may start a hare so late, the mixture, even in the fresh use of an old word, is made in the pre-conscious, and is by hypothesis un-ascertainable. But let us not use hypotheses, let us not desire to ascertain. By intuition we adventure in the pre-conscious; and there, where the adventure is, there is no need or suspicion of certainty or meaning; there is the living, ex-panding, *prescient* substance without the tags and handles of conscious form. Art is the looking-glass of the pre-conscious, and when it is deepest seems to participate in it sensibly. Or, better, for purposes of criticism, our sensibility resumes the division of the senses and faculties at the same time that it preens itself into conscious form. Criticism may have as an object the establishment and evaluation (comparison and analysis) of the modes of making the pre-conscious *consciously* available.

But this emphasis upon the pre-conscious need not be insisted on; once recognized it may be tacitly assumed, and the effort of the mind will be, as it were, restored to its own plane—only a little sensitive to the tap-roots below. On its own plane—that is, the plane where almost everything is taken for granted in order to assume adequate implementation in handling what is taken for granted by others; where because you can list the items of your bewilderment and can move from one to another you assert that the achieve-ment of motion is the experience of order; where, therefore, you must adopt always an attitude of provisional skepticism; where, imperatively, you must scrutinize and scrutinize until you have revealed, if it is there, the inscrutable divination, or, if it is not, the void of personal ambition; where, finally, you must stop short only when you have, with all the facts you can muster, indi-cated, surrounded, detached, somehow found the way demonstrably to get at, in pretty conscious terms which others may use, the substance of your chosen case.

From *The Double Agent. Essays in Craft and Elu-cidation* by R. P. Blackmur, pp. 269–302. Ar-row Editions. Copyright, 1935, by R. P. Black-mur. Reprinted by permission of the author.

APPENDICES

APPENDIX I

Recent Works of American Criticism

THIS list is selective. It includes works of several varieties that relate to modern American criticism: some on the backgrounds of American literature, some of literary biography, some on general problems of aesthetics and theory, some studies in the analysis of form and style. Those of the last three groups are of special value in extending the interests of the present volume. Books of historical and linguistic scholarship are not as a rule listed except where they are relevant to critical problems and methods. Books by critics discussed in the "Foreword" and "Introduction" are included except in the case of earlier critics who preceded Henry James, but books by critics whose work appears in this volume will be found listed not here but in Appendix IV. The writers included here are of American birth or residence, though a few foreign critics who have worked, taught, or been notably influential in the United States (I. A. Richards, Jacques Maritain, Alfred Korzybski, et al.), as well as those who have adopted American citizenship, have been added.

For fuller bibliographies of American authors and critics, the reader is referred to two standard works of reference: Volume III of *Literary History of the United States* (*Bibliography*), edited by Robert E. Spiller, Willard Thorp, Thomas H. Johnson, and Henry Seidel Canby, with Howard Mumford Jones, Dixon Wecter, and Stanley T. Williams as associates (New York: The Macmillan Company, 1948); and *Contemporary Am~   ~ Authors: A Critical Survey and 219 Bio-Bibliographies*, by Fred B. Mu.   ~ York: Harcourt, Brace and Company, 1940). Further reference may be n..   ~ current annual bibliographies in *Publications of the Modern Language Ass.   n of America*, in the *Annual Bibliography of English Language and Literature* of the Modern Humanities Research Association, and in the quarterly *American Literature*, as well as in *The Reader's Guide to Periodical Literature*, *The International Index to Periodicals*, and *The Book Review Digest*.

Abbott, Charles D.   *Poets at Work* (editor, 1948).
Adler, Mortimer.   *Art and Prudence: A Study in Practical Philosophy* (1937).
    How to Read a Book (1940).
Aiken, Conrad.   *Skepticisms: Notes on Contemporary Poetry* (1919).
Ames, Van Meter.   *Aesthetics of the Novel* (1928).
    André Gide (1947).

Arvin, Newton. See Appendix IV.
Auden, W. H. See Appendix IV.

Babbitt, Irving. See Appendix IV.
Baker, Carlos. *Shelley's Major Poetry* (1948).
Baker, Howard. *Induction to Tragedy* (1937).
Barnes, Albert C. *The Art in Painting* (1928).
Barrett, William. See Appendix IV.
Barzun, Jacques. *Romanticism and the Modern Ego* (1943).
Basler, Roy P. *Sex, Symbolism, and Psychology in Literature* (1948).
Beach, Joseph Warren. *The Method of Henry James* (1918).
    The Comic Spirit of George Meredith (1920).
    The Technique of Thomas Hardy (1922).
    The Outlook for American Prose (1924).
    The Twentieth Century Novel: Studies in Technique (1932).
    American Fiction: 1920–1940 (1941).
Beer, Thomas. *Stephen Crane: A Study in American Letters* (1924).
Bennett, Joseph D. *Baudelaire* (1944).
Bentley, Eric. See Appendix IV.
Bishop, John Peale. *The Collected Essays of John Peale Bishop* (edited by Edmund Wilson, 1948).
Blackmur, R. P. See Appendix IV.
Boas, George. *Philosophy and Poetry* (1932).
    A Primer for Critics (1937).
Bogan, Louise. See Appendix IV.
Bourne, Randolph. See Appendix IV.
Boynton, Percy Holmes. *Some Contemporary Americans* (1924).
    More Contemporary Americans (1927).
    The Challenge of American Criticism (1927).
    Literature and American Life (1936).
Brooks, Cleanth. See Appendix IV.
Brooks, Van Wyck. See Appendix IV.
Brown, E. K. See Appendix IV.
Brownell, William Crary. *American Prose Masters* (1909).
    Criticism (1914).
    Standards (1917).
    The Genius of Style (1924).
    Democratic Distinction in America (1927).
    The Spirit of Society (1927).
Buchanan, Scott. *Poetry and Mathematics* (1929).
Buermeyer, Laurence. *The Aesthetic Experience* (1924).
    Art and Education (with others, 1929).
Burgum, Edwin Berry. *The Novel and the World's Dilemma* (1947).
Burke, Kenneth. See Appendix IV.
Bush, Douglas. *Mythology in the Renaissance Tradition in English Poetry* (1932, 1937).

The *Renaissance and English Humanism* (1939).
Paradise Lost in Our Time: Some Comments (1945).

Cairns, Huntington.   *The Limits of Art* (anthology with critical commentaries, 1947).
Calverton, V. F.   *The Newer Spirit: A Sociological Criticism of Literature* (1925).
   The New Grounds of Criticism (1930).
   The Liberation of American Literature (1932).
Campbell, Joseph.   *A Skeleton Key to Finnegans Wake* (with Henry Morton Robinson, 1944).
   The Hero with a Thousand Faces (1949).
Canby, Henry Seidel.   *Definitions* (first series, 1922; second series, 1924).
   American Estimates (1929).
   Classic Americans (1931).
   Thoreau (1939).
   Walt Whitman, An American: A Study in Biography (1943).
Cantwell, Robert.   See Appendix IV.
Cargill, Oscar.   *Intellectual America: Ideas on the March* (1941).
Chamberlain, John.   *Farewell to Reform* (1932).
Chapman, John Jay.   See Appendix IV.
Chase, Richard.   See Appendix IV.
Cheney, Sheldon.   *The New Movement in the Theatre* (1914).
   Expressionism in Art (1934).
Colum, Mary M.   *From These Roots* (1938; new edition, 1945).
Cowley, Malcolm.   See Appendix IV.
Crane, R. S.   See Appendix IV.

Daiches, David.   *The Place of Meaning in Poetry* (1935).
   New Literary Values: Studies in Modern Literature (1936).
   Literature and Society (1938).
   The Novel and the Modern World (1940).
   Poetry and the Modern World (1940).
   Virginia Woolf (1942).
   Robert Louis Stevenson (1947).
   A Study of Literature (1948).
Damon, S. Foster.   *William Blake: His Philosophy and Symbols* (1924).
   The Odyssey in Dublin (on Joyce: reprinted from *The Hound and Horn*, 1930).
   Amy Lowell: A Chronicle (1935).
Davidson, Donald.   *The Attack on Leviathan* (1938).
DeMille, George E.   *Literary Criticism in America: A Preliminary Survey* (1931).
Deutsch, Babette.   *This Modern Poetry* (1935).
De Voto, Bernard.   *Mark Twain's America* (1932).
   The Literary Fallacy (1944).

Dickinson, Thomas H.   *The Case of the American Drama* (1915).
   Playwrights of the New American Theatre (1925).
Drew, Elizabeth.   *The Modern Novel: Some Aspects of Contemporary Fiction*
   (1926).
   Discovering Poetry (1933).
   The Enjoyment of Literature (1935).
   Directions in Modern Poetry (with John L. Sweeney, 1940).
   T. S. Eliot: The Design of His Poetry (1949).
Ducasse, John.   *The Philosophy of Art* (1930).
   Art, The Critics, and You (1944).
Dudley, Dorothy.   *Forgotten Frontiers: Dreiser and the Land of the Free* (1932).
Dupee, F. W.   See Appendix IV.

Eastman, Max.   *The Literary Mind: Its Place in an Age of Science* (1931).
   Artists in Uniform: A Study of Literature and Bureaucratism (1934).
   Art and the Life of Action (1934).
   The Enjoyment of Poetry (1939).
Edgar, Pelham.   *The Art of the Novel* (1933).
   Henry James: Man and Author (1935).
Eliot, T. S.   See Appendix IV.
Elliott, G. R.   *The Cycle of Modern Poetry* (1939).
   Humanism and Imagination (1939).

Farrell, James T.   *A Note on Literary Criticism* (1936).
   The League of Frightened Philistines (1945).
   The Fate of Writing in America (1946).
   Literature and Morality (1947).
Fergusson, Francis.   See Appendix IV.
Flores, Angel.   *Henrik Ibsen* (editor, 1937).
   Literature and Marxism: A Controversy (1938).
   The Kafka Problem (editor, 1946).
Foerster, Norman.   *American Criticism: A Study in Literary Theory from Poe to*
   the Present (1928).
   Toward Standards: A Study of the Present Critical Movement in Ameri-
   can Letters (1930).
   Humanism and America (editor, 1930).
Follett, Wilson.   *The Modern Novel* (1933).
Fowlie, Wallace.   *Clowns and Angels* (1943).
   Rimbaud (1946).
   Jacob's Night (1947).
   The Clown's Grail (1948).
   Mallarmé (1951).
Fraenkel, Michael.   *Death is Not Enough: Essays in Active Negation* (1939).
Frank, Waldo.   *Salvos: An Informal Book about Books and Plays* (1924).
   The Re-Discovery of America (1928).
   In the American Jungle (1937).

Freeman, Joseph. *An American Testament: A Narrative of Rebels and Romantics* (1936).
  Voices of October (with Joshua Kunitz and Louis Lozowick, 1930).
Frye, Northrop. *Fearful Symmetry: A Study of Blake* (1947).
Frye, Prosser Hall. *Romance and Tragedy* (1922).
  Visions and Chimeras (1929).

Gates, Lewis E. *Studies and Appreciations* (1900).
Geismar, Maxwell. *Writers in Crisis: The American Novel Between Two Wars* (1942).
  The Last of the Provincials: The American Novel, 1915–1925 (1948).
Gilman, Margaret. *Baudelaire the Critic* (1943).
Glasgow, Ellen. *A Certain Measure: An Interpretation of Prose Fiction* (1943).
Grabo, Carl. *The Creative Critic* (1948).
Greene, Theodore M. *The Arts and the Art of Criticism* (1940).
Greenlaw, Edwin. *The Province of Literary History* (1931).
Gregory, Horace. See Appendix IV.
Grudin, Louis. *A Primer of Aesthetics: Logical Approaches to a Philosophy of Art* (1930).
  Mr. Eliot among the Nightingales (1931).
Guérard, Albert. *Literature and Society* (1935).
  Art for Art's Sake (1936).
Guérard, Albert, Jr. *Robert Bridges: A Study in Traditionalism* (1942).
  Joseph Conrad (1947).
  Thomas Hardy: The Novels and Stories (1949).

Hackett, Francis. *Horizons: A Book of Criticism* (1918).
Hatcher, Harlan. *Creating the Modern American Novel* (1935).
Hazlitt, Henry. *The Anatomy of Criticism* (1933).
Hearn, Lafcadio. *Appreciations of Poetry* (1916).
  Complete Lectures on Criticism, Literature, and Philosophy (1932).
Heilman, Robert B. *This Great Stage* (on Shakespeare and *King Lear,* 1948).
Hicks, Granville. *The Great Tradition: An Interpretation of American Literature since the Civil War* (1933; revised edition, 1935).
  John Reed: The Making of a Revolutionary (with John Stuart, 1936).
  Figures of Transition (1939).
Hoffman, Frederick J. *Freudianism and the Literary Mind* (1945).
  The Little Magazine: A History and a Bibliography (with Charles Allen and Carolyn F. Ulrich (1946; new edition, 1947).
Honig, Edwin. *Garcia Lorca* (1945).
Horton, Philip. *Hart Crane: The Life of an American Poet* (1937).
Hospers, John. *Meaning and Truth in the Arts* (1946).
Howells, William Dean. See Appendix IV.
Hughes, Glenn. *Imagism and the Imagists* (1941).
Huneker, James Gibbons. See Appendix IV.
Hyman, Stanley Edgar. See Appendix IV.

James, Henry.   See Appendix IV.
Jarrell, Randall.   See Appendix IV.
Jones, Howard Mumford.   *Hamlet: With a Psychoanalytical Study* (1948).
    The Theory of American Literature (1948).
Jones, Llewellyn.   *First Impressions* (1925).
    How to Criticize Books (1928).
Josephson, Matthew.   *Zola and His Time* (1928).
    Portrait of the Artist as an American (1930).
    Jean-Jacques Rousseau (1931).
    Victor Hugo (1942).
    Stendhal, or The Pursuit of Happiness (1946).

Kazin, Alfred.   See Appendix IV.
Korzybski, Alfred.   *Science and Sanity* (1934; third edition, 1948).
Krutch, Joseph Wood.   See Appendix IV.

Langer, Suzanne K.   *Philosophy in a New Key* (1942).
Levin, Harry.   See Appendix IV.
Lewisohn, Ludwig.   *The Drama and the Stage* (1922).
    The Creative Life (1924).
    Expression in America (1932).
    The Artist and His Message (with Adolph Gillis, 1933).
Littell, Robert.   *Read America First* (1926).
Lovejoy, Arthur O.   *The Revolt against Dualism* (1930).
    The Great Chain of Being (1936).
    A Documentary History of Primitivism (with George Boas, 1936).
Lovett, Robert Morss.   See Appendix IV.
Lowell, Amy.   *Six French Poets* (1915).
    Tendencies in Modern American Poetry (1917).
    A Critical Fable (1922).
    John Keats (1925).
    Poetry and Poets (1930).
Lowes, John Livingston.   *Convention and Revolt in Poetry* (1919; new edition,
    1922).
    The Road to Xanadu: A Study in the Ways of the Imagination (on Cole-
    ridge, 1927).
    Of Reading Books (1929).
    Geoffrey Chaucer (1934).
    Essays in Appreciation (1936).

MacLeish, Archibald.   *The Irresponsibles* (1940).
    A Time to Speak: Selected Prose (1941).
    A Time to Act (1942).
Macy, John.   *The Spirit of American Literature* (1913).
    The Critical Game (1922).
March, H. M.   *The Two Worlds of Marcel Proust* (1948).

Maritain, Jacques. *Art and Scholasticism* (translated by F. S. Flint, 1930; translated by J. F. Scanlan, 1935, 1942).
  Art and Poetry (1943).
Masters, Edgar Lee. *Vachel Lindsay: A Poet in America* (1935).
  Whitman (1937).
Matthiessen, F. O. See Appendix IV.
McMahon, Philip. *The Meaning of Art* (1930).
Mencken, H. L. See Appendix IV.
Mercier, Louis J. A. *The Challenge of Humanism: A Study in Comparative Criticism* (1933).
Miller, Perry. *Orthodoxy in Massachusetts: A Genetic Study* (1933).
  The Puritans (edited with Thomas H. Johnson, 1938).
  The New England Mind: The Seventeenth Century (1939).
  Jonathan Edwards (1949).
  The Transcendentalists (edited, 1950).
Millett, Fred B. *Contemporary British Literature* (with J. M. Manly and Edith Rickert, revised edition, 1935).
  Contemporary American Authors: A Critical Survey and 219 Bio-Bibliographies (1940).
  The Rebirth of Liberal Education (1945).
Mizener, Arthur. *The Far Side of Paradise* (on F. Scott Fitzgerald, 1951).
Monroe, Harriet. *Poets and Their Art* (1926; new edition, 1932).
  A Poet's Life: Seventy Years in a Changing World (1938).
More, Paul Elmer. See Appendix IV.
Moore, Marianne. See Appendix IV.
Muller, Herbert J. *Modern Fiction* (1937).
  Science and Criticism: The Humanist Tradition (1943).
  Thomas Wolfe (1947).
Mumford, Lewis. *The Story of Utopias* (1922).
  Sticks and Stones: A Study of American Architecture and Civilization (1924).
  The Golden Day: A Study of American Experience and Culture (1926).
  Herman Melville (1929).
  American Taste (1929).
  The Brown Decades: A Study of the Arts in America: 1865–1895 (1931).
  Technics and Civilization (1934).
  The Culture of Cities (1938).
Munson, Gorham B. *Destinations: A Canvass of American Literature since 1900* (1928).
  Style and Form in American Prose (1929).
  The Dilemma of the Liberated (1930).

Nabokov, Vladimir. *Nikolai Gogol* (1945).
Nahm, Milton C. *Aesthetic Experience and Its Presuppositions* (1946).
Nathan, George Jean. *Another Book on the Theatre* (1915).
  The Popular Theatre (1918).

The Critic and the Drama (1922).
Materia Critica (1924).
Land of the Pilgrims' Pride (1927).
Art of the Night (1928).
Testament of a Critic (1931).
The Intimate Notebooks of George Jean Nathan (1932).
Since Ibsen: A Statistical Historical Outline of the Popular Theatre Since 1900 (1933).
The Theatre of the Moment: A Journalistic Commentary (1936).
Neff, Emery. *Carlyle and Mill: Mystic and Utilitarian* (1924; 1930).
A Revolution in European Poetry: 1660–1900 (1940).
The Poetry of History (1947).
Edwin Arlington Robinson (1948).
Neider, Charles. *The Frozen Sea* (a study of Kafka, 1948).
Nuhn, Ferner. *The Wind Blew from the East: A Study in the Orientation of American Culture* (1942).

O'Brien, Justin. *The Journals of André Gide* (translator and editor, 3 vols., 1947–1949).
O'Connor, William Van. *Sense and Sensibility in Modern Poetry* (1948).
Forms of Modern Fiction (editor, 1948).
The Shaping Spirit: A Study of Wallace Stevens (1950).
Olson, Charles. *Call Me Ishmael* (a study of Herman Melville, 1947).

Parker, DeWitt. *The Principles of Aesthetics* (1920; new edition, 1946).
The Analysis of Art (1924).
The Analysis of Beauty (1926).
Parkes, Henry Bamford. *The Pragmatic Test* (1941).
Parrington, Vernon Louis. *Main Currents in American Thought: An Interpretation of American Literature from the Beginnings to 1920* (3 volumes, 1927–1930).
Pepper, S. C. *Aesthetic Quality: A Contextualist Theory* (1938).
The Basis of Criticism in the Arts (1946).
Peyre, Henri. *Writers and Their Critics* (1944).
Phillips, William. See Appendix IV.
Porter, Katherine Anne. See Appendix IV.
Pottle, Frederick. *The Idiom of Poetry* (1942; revised edition, 1946).
Pound, Ezra. See Appendix IV.
Prall, D. W. *Aesthetic Judgment* (1929).
Aesthetic Analysis (1936).
Prescott, F. C. *Poetry and Dreams* (1919).
The Poetic Mind (1922).
Poetry and Myth (1927).
Prior, Moody E. *The Language of Tragedy* (1947).

Quinn, Arthur Hobson. *A History of the American Drama from the Beginnings to the Civil War* (revised edition, 1943).

A History of the American Drama from the Civil War to the Present Day (revised edition, 1936).
American Fiction: An Historical and Critical Survey (1936).
Edgar Allan Poe: A Critical Biography (1941).

Rader, Melvin. *A Modern Book of Aesthetics* (editor, 1935).
Rahv, Philip. See Appendix IV.
Ranson, John Crowe. See Appendix IV.
Rice, Philip Blair. See Appendix IV.
Richards, I. A. *The Foundations of Aesthetics* (with C. K. Ogden and James Wood, 1922).
The Meaning of Meaning (with C. K. Ogden, 1923).
The Principles of Literary Criticism (1924).
Practical Criticism: A Study of Literary Judgment (1929).
Mencius on the Mind (1932).
Coleridge on Imagination (1934).
The Philosophy of Rhetoric (1936).
Interpretation in Teaching (1938).
How To Read a Page (1942).
Riding, Laura. *A Survey of Modernist Poetry* (with Robert Graves, 1927).
Contemporaries and Snobs (1928).
Roberts, Morris. *Henry James's Criticism* (1929).
Roditi, Edouard. *Oscar Wilde* (1947).
Rosenfeld, Paul. *Port of New York: Essays on Fourteen American Moderns* (1924).
Men Seen (1925).
Rourke, Constance. *American Humor: A Study of the National Character* (1931).
Audubon (1936).
Charles Sheeler: Artist in the American Tradition (1938).
The Roots of American Culture (edited by Van Wyck Brooks, 1942).

Santayana, George. See Appendix IV.
Schorer, Mark. *William Blake: The Politics of Vision* (1946).
Schwartz, Delmore. See Appendix IV.
Shafer, Robert M. *Paul Elmer More and American Criticism* (1935).
Shapiro, Karl. *Essay on Rime* (1945).
Sherman, Stuart Pratt. *Americans* (1922).
The Genius of America: Studies on Behalf of the Younger Generation (1923).
The Main Stream (1927).
Shipley, Joseph T. *The Quest for Literature: A Survey of Literary Criticism and the Theories of Literary Forms* (1931).
A Dictionary of World Literature (editor, 1943).
Encyclopedia of Literature (editor, 1946).
Shuster, George N. *The Catholic Spirit in Modern English Literature* (1922).
The Catholic Church and Current Literature (1929).

Sinclair, Upton.   *Mammonart* (1925).

Slochower, Harry.   *Three Ways of Modern Man* (1937).
> *Thomas Mann's Joseph Story* (1938).
> *No Voice Is Wholly Lost* (1945).

Smith, Bernard.   *Forces in American Criticism* (1939).

Smith, Chard Powers.   *Pattern and Variation in Poetry* (1932).
> *Annals of the Poets* (1935).

Smith, Logan Pearsall.   *Words and Idioms* (1925).
> *On Reading Shakespeare* (1933).
> *Reperusals and Re-Collections* (1936).
> *Milton and His Modern Critics* (1940).

Spencer, Theodore.   See Appendix IV.

Spingarn, J. E.   See Appendix IV.

Stauffer, Donald A.   *The Intent of the Critic* (editor, 1941).
> *The Nature of Poetry* (1946).
> *Shakespeare's World of Images* (1949).
> *The Golden Nightingale: Essays on Some Principles of Poetry in the Lyrics of William Butler Yeats* (1949).

Stearns, Harold E.   *America and the Young Intellectual* (1921).
> *Civilization in the United States: An Enquiry by Thirty Americans* (editor, 1922).
> *America Now: An Enquiry into Civilization in the United States by Thirty-Six Americans* (editor, 1938).

Stein, Leo.   *The A. B. C. of Aesthetics* (1927).

Stoll, E. E.   *Art and Artifice in Shakespeare* (1933).
> *From Shakespeare to Joyce* (1944).

Tate, Allen.   See Appendix IV.

Taupin, René.   *L'Influence du Symbolisme français sur la Poésie américaine de 1910 à 1920* (1929).

Thorp, Willard.   *Herman Melville: Representative Selections* (editor, 1938).
> *The Lost Tradition of American Letters* (1945).
> *Moby Dick* by Herman Melville (critical edition, 1947).

Tindall, William York.   *D. H. Lawrence and Susan His Cow* (1939).
> *Forces in Modern British Literature: 1885–1946* (1947).
> *James Joyce* (1949).

Trilling, Lionel.   See Appendix IV.

Troy, William.   See Appendix IV.

Tuve, Rosamund.   *Elizabethan and Metaphysical Imagery* (1947).

Tyler, Parker.   *Magic and Myth of the Movies* (1947).

Untermeyer, Louis.   *American Poetry since 1900* (1923).
> *Modern American Poetry* and *Modern British Poetry* (successive editions, apart or combined, since 1919; latest edition, 1950, with biographies and critical introductions).

Van Doren, Carl.   *The American Novel* (1921; revised, 1940).
   Contemporary American Novelists (1922).
   The Roving Critic (1923).
   Many Minds (1924).
   American and British Literature since 1900 (with M. van Doren, 1925).
   American Literature: An Introduction (1933; republished as *What Is American Literature?*, 1933; included in *The Portable Carl van Doren*, 1945).
   Three Worlds (autobiography, 1936).
   Benjamin Franklin (three volumes, 1938).
Van Doren, Mark.   *Henry David Thoreau: A Critical Study* (1916).
   The Poetry of John Dryden (1920; reissued 1946).
   Edwin Arlington Robinson (1927).
   Shakespeare (1939).
   The Private Reader (1942).
   The Noble Voice (1946).
   Nathaniel Hawthorne (1949).

Warren, Austin.   See Appendix IV.
Warren, Robert Penn.   See Appendix IV.
Wellek, René.   *Theory of Literature* (with Austin Warren, 1949).
Wells, Henry.   *Poetic Imagery* (1924).
   The Judgment of Literature: An Outline of Aesthetics (1928).
   New Poets from Old: A Study in Literary Genetics (1940).
   The American Way of Poetry (1943).
West, Ray B., Jr.   *Writing in the Rocky Mountains* (1947).
   The Art of Modern Fiction (editor, with R. W. Stallman, 1949).
Weston, Jessie L.   *From Ritual to Romance* (1920; reissued 1946).
Wharton, Edith.   *The Writing of Fiction* (1925).
   A Backward Glance (memoirs, 1934).
Whipple, T. K.   *Spokesmen: Modern Writers and American Life* (1928).
   Study Out the Land (1943).
Wickham, Harvey.   *The Impuritans* (1929).
Wilder, Amos.   *The Spiritual Aspects of the New Poetry* (1940).
Williamson, George.   *The Talent of T. S. Eliot* (1929).
   The Donne Tradition (1930).
Wilson, Edmund.   See Appendix IV.
Winters, Yvor.   See Appendix IV.
Woodberry, George Edward.   *The Torch* (1905).
   The Appreciation of Literature (1907).
   Two Phases of Criticism (1914).
   Collected Essays (1920–1921).
   Literary Memoirs, Studies, Heart of Man, and other Papers (1922).

Young, Stark.   See Appendix IV.

Zabel, Morton Dauwen. *Literary Opinion in America: Essays Illustrating the Status, Methods, and Problems of Criticism in the United States since the War* (editor, 1937).

The Condition of American Criticism: 1939 (reprinted from *The English Journal*, 1939).

Two Years of Poetry: 1937–1939 (reprinted from *The Southern Review*, 1939).

The Contemporary Period in *A Book of English Literature* (editor, 1943).

A Literatura dos Estados Unidos (a book on the masters of American literature, in Portuguese translation, Rio de Janeiro, 1947; in Spanish translation as *Historia de la Literatura Norte-Americana*, Buenos Aires, 1950).

The Portable Conrad (editor, 1947).

The Portable Henry James (editor, 1951).

Zukovsky, Louis. *A Test for Poetry* (1949).

APPENDIX II

Collections of Contemporary American Criticism

THE list is selective, and titles are arranged chronologically. All important collections of American criticism of the years 1919–1951 are listed. In addition, there have been included a number of the special critical symposia published in literary journals like *The Hound and Horn, The Southern Review,* and *The Kenyon Review,* which have become a feature of contemporary critical activity. Other special numbers of this kind may be traced in *The New Republic, The Nation, The Sewanee Review, Partisan Review,* etc., during the past thirty years. When a large number of essays by foreign critics are included in the books listed below, the names of these critics are not given; when such foreign contributions are few in any given volume, their authors are named. Where collections of criticism are devoted to special programs or purposes, or where they issued from special occasions, these are briefly indicated.

A Modern Book of Criticism, edited by Ludwig Lewisohn (1919).
  Essays defining and illustrating the impressionist and liberal points of view by French critics (Anatole France, Jules Lemaître, Remy de Gourmont); German (Friedrich Hebbel, Wilhelm Dilthey, Johannes Volkelt, Richard Moritz Meyer, Hugo von Hofmannsthal, Richard Mueller-Freienfels, Alfred Kerr); English and Irish (George Moore, George Bernard Shaw, Arthur Symons, John Galsworthy, Arnold Bennett, W. L. George, Thomas MacDonagh, John Cooper Powys); and American (James Gibbons Huneker, J. E. Spingarn, H. L. Mencken, Ludwig Lewisohn, Francis Hackett, Van Wyck Brooks, Randolph Bourne).
Criticism in America: Its Function and Status, edited by J. E. Spingarn (1924).
  Essays by Irving Babbitt, Van Wyck Brooks, William Crary Brownell, Ernest Boyd, T. S. Eliot, H. L. Mencken, Stuart Pratt Sherman, J. E. Spingarn, George Edward Woodberry.
Contemporary American Criticism, edited by James Cloyd Bowman (1926).
  Essays by James Russell Lowell, Walt Whitman, J. E. Spingarn, H. L. Mencken, William Crary Brownell, Irving Babbitt, Grant Showerman, Stuart Pratt Sherman, Percy H. Boynton, Van Wyck Brooks, Sherwood Anderson, Robert Morss Lovett, Carl van Doren, Irwin Edman, Llewellyn Jones, Theodore Maynard, William McFee, John Macy, Henry Seidel Canby, Amy Lowell, Conrad Aiken, Fred Lewis Pattee, George Edward Woodberry.

American Criticism: 1926, edited by William A. Drake (1926).

Essays and reviews of the year July 1925 to July 1926 by Henry Seidel Canby, Samuel C. Chew, Mary M. Colum, Robert L. Duffus, Waldo Frank, Zona Gale, Herbert S. Gorman, Alyse Gregory, Albert Guérard, Joseph Wood Krutch, Sinclair Lewis, Archibald MacLeish, Edgar Lee Masters, H. L. Mencken, W. B. Pressey, Agnes Repplier, Edith Rickert, Cameron Rogers, Anne Douglas Sedgwick, Gilbert Seldes, Stuart Pratt Sherman, Harrison Smith, Logan Pearsall Smith, C. B. Tinker, Charles K. Trueblood, Carl van Doren, Arnold Whitredge, Edmund Wilson, P. W. Wilson.

The New Criticism, edited by Edwin Berry Burgum (1930).

Essays chiefly in aesthetic theory by American critics: J. E. Spingarn, George Santayana, Laurence Buermeyer, DeWitt Parker, T. S. Eliot; and by English and European critics: Benedetto Croce, Bernard Bosanquet, E. F. Carritt, I. A. Richards, J. B. S. Haldane, J. W. N. Sullivan, Roger Fry, Ramon Fernandez, Oswald Spengler, Élie Faure.

American Critical Essays, edited by Norman Foerster (1930).

Essays illustrating the history of criticism in America by Edgar Allan Poe, Ralph Waldo Emerson, James Russell Lowell, Walt Whitman, William Dean Howells, Henry James, Lewis E. Gates, George Edward Woodberry, William Crary Brownell, Irving Babbitt, Paul Elmer More, Prosser Hall Frye, J. E. Spingarn, Stuart Pratt Sherman, Van Wyck Brooks.

Humanism and America: Essays on the Outlook of Modern Civilization, edited by Norman Foerster (1930).

Essays defending the Humanist position by Lewis Trenchard More, Irving Babbitt, Paul Elmer More, G. R. Elliott, T. S. Eliot, Frank Jewett Mather, Jr., Alan Reynolds Thompson, Robert Shafer, Harry Hayden Clark, Stanley P. Chase, Gorham B. Munson, Bernard Bandler II, Sherlock Bronson Gass, Richard Lindley Brown.

The Critique of Humanism: A Symposium, edited by C. Hartley Grattan (1930).

Essays in opposition to Humanism by C. Hartley Grattan, Edmund Wilson, Malcolm Cowley, Henry Hazlitt, Burton Rascoe, Allen Tate, Kenneth Burke, Henry-Russell Hitchcock, Jr., R. P. Blackmur, John Chamberlain, Bernard Bandler II, Yvor Winters, Lewis Mumford.

A Garland for John Donne: 1631–1931, edited by Theodore Spencer (1931).

Essays on Donne on the tercentenary of his death by T. S. Eliot, Evelyn M. Simpson, Mario Praz, John Hayward, Mary Paton Ramsay, John Sparrow, George Williamson, Theodore Spencer.

Homage to Henry James: 1843–1916. A special number of *The Hound and Horn*, Volume VII, No. 3 (April–May, 1934), pages 361–562. Edited by Lincoln Kirstein (1934).

Essays on the life and work of Henry James by Marianne Moore, Lawrence Leighton, Edmund Wilson, Francis Fergusson, Stephen Spender, Newton Arvin, R. P. Blackmur, Alice Boughton, John Wheelwright, Robert Cantwell, Edna Kenton, H. R. Hays, Glenway Wescott.

Proletarian Literature in the United States: An Anthology, edited by Granville

Hicks, Michael Gold, Isidor Schneider, Joseph North, Paul Peters, Alan Calmer (1935).

> Includes, besides verse, fiction, etc., essays defining the proletarian theory of literature by Obed Brooks, Edwin Berry Burgum, Alan Calmer, Malcolm Cowley, Michael Gold, Granville Hicks, Joshua Kunitz, William Phillips and Philip Rahv, Bernard Smith.

After the Genteel Tradition: American Writers Since 1910, edited by Malcolm Cowley (1937).

> Essays on American writers after 1910, chiefly 1918–1937, by John Chamberlain, Robert Cantwell, Lionel Trilling, Bernard Smith, Newton Arvin, Robert Morss Lovett, Louis Kronenberger, Peter Monro Jack, Hildegarde Flanner, Malcolm Cowley, John Peale Bishop, Hamilton Basso.

Literary Opinion in America: Essays Illustrating the Status, Methods, and Problems of Criticism in the United States since the War, edited by Morton Dauwen Zabel (1937).

> The first edition of the present volume, including a history of American criticism since Poe and Emerson by the editor, and essays of the years 1919–1937 by T. S. Eliot, Van Wyck Brooks, Irving Babbitt, Paul Elmer More, J. E. Spingarn, H. L. Mencken, John Crowe Ransom, George Santayana, Edmund Wilson, Allen Tate, Yvor Winters, Marianne Moore, Charles K. Trueblood, Theodore Spencer, Stark Young, Joseph Wood Krutch, Francis Fergusson, Robert Morss Lovett, William Troy, Robert Penn Warren, Louise Bogan, Morton Dauwen Zabel, George N. Shuster, Philip Blair Rice, Kenneth Burke, Malcolm Cowley, Horace Gregory, Newton Arvin, Robert Cantwell, William Phillips and Philip Rahv, R. P. Blackmur.

Books That Changed Our Minds, edited by Malcolm Cowley and Bernard Smith (1939).

> Essays on thinkers, scientists, and writers of the nineteenth and twentieth centuries by George Soule, Louis Kronenberger, Charles A. Beard, John Chamberlain, Rexford Guy Tugwell, C. E. Ayres, Paul Radin, Max Lerner, David Daiches, Bernard Smith, Lewis Mumford, Malcolm Cowley.

Thomas Hardy Centennial Number. A special number of *The Southern Review,* Volume VI, No. 1 (Summer, 1940), pages 1–224. Edited by Charles W. Pipkin, Cleanth Brooks, and Robert Penn Warren (1940).

> Essays on the prose and poetry of Hardy by John Crowe Ransom, R. P. Blackmur, Howard Baker, Delmore Schwartz, W. H. Auden, F. R. Leavis, Allen Tate, Bonamy Dobrée, Morton Dauwen Zabel, Katherine Anne Porter, Donald Davidson, Jacques Barzun, Arthur Mizener, Herbert J. Muller.

The Intent of the Artist, edited with an introduction by Augusto Centeno (1940).

> Discussions of creative process in the arts, by Sherwood Anderson, Thornton Wilder, Roger Sessions, William Lescaze. The essays were given as a series of lectures at Princeton University in 1938–1939.

The English Institute Annual: 1939 (1940).

> Essays read before the English Institute, September 1939, by Carleton Brown, Robert E. Spiller, Carl van Doren, James M. Osborn, Marjorie Nicolson, Howard F. Lowry, Townsend Scudder, MacEdward Leach.

William Butler Yeats Memorial Number. A special number of *The Southern Review,* Volume VII, No. 3 (Winter, 1941), pages 407–666. Edited by Cleanth Brooks and Robert Penn Warren (1941).

> Essays on the work of Yeats by R. P. Blackmur, L. C. Knights, T. S. Eliot, F. O. Matthiessen, Delmore Schwartz, Horace Gregory, Donald Davidson, John Crowe Ransom, Kenneth Burke, Morton Dauwen Zabel, Allen Tate, Arthur Mizener, Austin Warren, Howard Baker, Randall Jarrell.

The English Institute Annual: 1940 (1941).

> Essays read before the English Institute, September 1940, by W. H. Auden, Cleanth Brooks, William York Tindall, Norman Holmes Pearson, René Wellek, Willard Thorp, Harry Hayden Clark, Ralph Thompson, Randolph G. Adams, Walter L. Pforzheimer.

The Intent of the Critic, edited with an introduction by Donald A. Stauffer (1941).

> Four essays forming a symposium on the nature and motives of modern criticism, by Edmund Wilson, Norman Foerster, John Crowe Ransom, W. H. Auden. The essays were given as lectures at Princeton University in 1940–1941.

The Language of Poetry, edited by Allen Tate (1942).

> Essays on poetry based on lectures read for the Creative Arts Program at Princeton University, Spring 1941, by Philip Wheelwright, Cleanth Brooks, I. A. Richards, Wallace Stevens.

The English Institute Annual: 1941 (1942).

> Essays read before the English Institute, September 1941, by Lionel Trilling, René Wellek, J. Burke Severs, Madeleine Doran, Arthur Friedman, Sculley Bradley, R. C. Bald, Fredson Bowers, Charlton Hinman.

The Shock of Recognition: The Development of Literature in the United States Recorded by the Men Who Made It, edited by Edmund Wilson (1943).

> Documents by Lowell, Poe, Melville, Emerson, Whitman, Bayard Taylor, Mallarmé, Henry James, Mark Twain, John Jay Chapman, H. G. Wells, W. D. Howells, Henry Adams, T. S. Eliot, George Santayana, D. H. Lawrence, Amy Lowell, H. L. Mencken, John Dos Passos, Sherwood Anderson.

Henry James Number of *The Kenyon Review,* Volume V, No. 4 (Autumn, 1943), pp. 481–618 (1943).

> A centenary collection of essays by Katherine Anne Porter, Francis Fergusson, Jacques Barzun, John L. Sweeney, F. O. Matthiessen, Austin Warren, David Daiches, Eliseo Vivas, R. P. Blackmur, with editorial note by John Crowe Ransom; prepared under the editorship of Robert Penn Warren.

Gerard Manley Hopkins, by the Kenyon Critics (1945).

> Essays on Hopkins, most of which originally appeared in *The Kenyon Review* in 1944, by Austin Warren, Herbert Marshall McLuhan, Harold Whitehall, Josephine Miles, Robert Lowell, Arthur Mizener, F. R. Leavis.

The Question of Henry James. A Collection of Critical Essays, edited by F. W. Dupee (1945).

> Critical essays selected to describe the critical reputation of Henry James from 1879 to 1943 by the following American critics: Thomas Wentworth

Higginson, William Dean Howells, Frank Moore Colby, Herbert Croly, Stuart P. Sherman, Joseph Warren Beach, Thomas Beer, T. S. Eliot, Van Wyck Brooks, Vernon Louis Parrington, Edna Kenton, Constance Rourke, Edmund Wilson, R. P. Blackmur, Morton Dauwen Zabel, F. O. Matthiessen, W. H. Auden, Jacques Barzun, William Troy; and by the following Europeans: Max Beerbohm, Joseph Conrad, Ford Madox Ford, Percy Lubbock, André Gide.

The Kafka Problem, edited by Angel Flores (1946).

Criticism and exposition of Franz Kafka and his works by European critics and the following Americans: Max Lerner, W. H. Auden, Austin Warren, John Kelly, Frederick J. Hoffman, Edwin Berry Burgum, T. Weiss, Charles Neider, Angel Flores, Kate Flores.

Twentieth Century English, edited by William S. Knickerbocker (1946).

Includes, besides essays on language and linguistic problems, essays on the relation of language and literature by F. B. Millett, René Wellek, Louise Pound, Archibald MacLeish, Kenneth Burke, Austin Warren, Oscar Cargill, Wylie Sypher, Walter J. Ong, Cleanth Brooks, Roy T. Basler, Walter Pritchard Eaton, George Coffin Taylor.

Accent Anthology: Selections from *Accent, A Quarterly of New Literature, 1940–1945,* edited by Kerker Quinn and Charles Shattuck (1946).

Includes critical prose by Eric Bentley, R. P. Blackmur, Marjorie Brace, Cleanth Brooks, Edwin Berry Burgum, Kenneth Burke, David Daiches, Richard Eberhart, Otis Ferguson, Wallace Fowlie, Ruth Herschberger, F. O. Matthiessen, Henry Miller, Arthur Mizener, Paul Rosenfeld, Delmore Schwartz, Harry Slochower, T. Weiss.

The Partisan Reader: Ten Years of Partisan Review, 1934–1944, edited by William Phillips and Philip Rahv. Introduction by Lionel Trilling. (1946).

Includes, besides fiction and verse, critical essays and discussions printed in the *Partisan Review,* 1934–1944, by the following American writers and critics: Edmund Wilson, Meyer Schapiro, Philip Rahv, William Troy, W. H. Auden, F. W. Dupee, Clement Greenberg, Katherine Anne Porter, Morton Dauwen Zabel, Sidney Hook, Eugene Jolas, Robert Vigneron, William Phillips, T. S. Eliot, John Dewey, Ernest Nagel, Dwight Macdonald, Wylie Sypher, Randall Jarrell, Mary McCarthy, James Burnham, Harold Rosenberg, James Johnson Sweeney, George L. K. Morris, Sherwood Anderson, R. P. Blackmur, Louise Bogan, John Dos Passos, James T. Farrell, Horace Gregory, Gertrude Stein, Wallace Stevens, Allen Tate.

A Southern Vanguard, edited by Allen Tate (1947).

Being "The John Peale Bishop Memorial Volume," and containing, besides verse and fiction, critical essays by John Peale Bishop, Malcolm Cowley, Robert Wooster Stallman, Nathan L. Rothman, Eunice Glenn, William Van O'Connor, Herbert Marshall MacLuhan, Robert B. Heilman, Louis B. Wright—all dealing with Southern writers, tradition, and history.

The Stature of Thomas Mann, edited by Charles Neider (1947).

Essays on the life, personality, and work of Thomas Mann by European and English critics as well as the following Americans: G. A. Borgese, Martin Gumpert, Charles Jackson, Erika Mann, Klaus Mann, Dorothy Thompson,

Robert Morss Lovett, Ludwig Lewisohn, Vernon Venable, Joseph Warren Beach, Lewis Mumford, Hermann J. Weigand, Conrad Aiken, Henry C. Hatfield, Reinold Niebuhr, Harry Levin, Kenneth Burke, Helen Muchnic, Agnes E. Meyer, Charles Neider, Philip Blair Rice, Philo M. Buck, Jr., Albert Guérard, H. T. Lowe-Porter.

English Institute Essays: 1946 (1947).

Essays read before the English Institute, September 1946, by Gerald E. Bentley, Douglas Bush, Louis A. Landa, Carlos Baker, Marion Witt, Arthur Mizener, René Wellek, Cleanth Brooks, Alan S. Downer, E. L. MacAdam, Jr.

Forms of Modern Fiction: Essays Collected in Honor of Joseph Warren Beach, edited by William Van O'Connor (1948).

Essays on the theory and craft of fiction by American critics: Mark Schorer, Allen Tate, Joseph Warren Beach, David Daiches, Francis Fergusson, William Troy, Ray B. West, Jr., Richard Chase, T. S. Eliot, Robert Penn Warren, Lionel Trilling, E. K. Brown, Carlos Lynes, Jr., Frederick J. Hoffman, C. W. M. Johnson, Robert Bechtold Heilman, Robert Wooster Stallman, Warren Beck, Charles Child Walcutt, Eric Bentley, Morton Dauwen Zabel, C. H. Rickword.

James Joyce: Two Decades of Criticism, edited by S. Given (1948).

Essays on Joyce by American critics: Eugene Jolas, Irene Hendry, R. Levin and C. Shattuck, James T. Farrell, Hugh Kenner, T. S. Eliot, S. Foster Damon, Vivian Mercier, William Troy, Edmund Wilson, Joseph Campbell, Frederick J. Hoffman, J. F. Hendry; and European critics: Frank Budgen, Philip Toynbee, Stuart Gilbert.

T. S. Eliot: A Selected Critique, edited by Leonard Unger (1948).

Essays of the years 1919–1947 on the poetry and prose of T. S. Eliot, including discussions by the following American critics: Conrad Aiken, Ezra Pound, Mark Van Doren, Paul Elmer More, Malcolm Cowley, Granville Hicks, Delmore Schwartz, John Crowe Ransom, Yvor Winters, Van Wyck Brooks, Ferner Nuhn, Karl Shapiro, Edmund Wilson, F. O. Matthiessen, R. P. Blackmur, Allen Tate, Cleanth Brooks, Leonard Unger, James Johnson Sweeney, C. L. Barber, Louis L. Martz.

English Institute Essays: 1947 (1948).

Essays read before the English Institute, September 1947, by Richard Chase, Donald A. Stauffer, William Carlos Williams, M. M. Mathews, M. A. Shaaber, Matthew W. Black, Hereward T. Price, Giles E. Dawson.

Criticism: The Foundations of Modern Literary Judgment, edited by Mark Schorer, Josephine Miles, and Gordon McKenzie (1948).

Essays in critical theory and practice from Aristotle and Plato to the present day, including articles and essays by the following Americans: Henry James, Joseph Wood Krutch, Constance Rourke, James T. Farrell, Arthur O. Lovejoy, Edmund Wilson, W. H. Auden, Lionel Trilling, Allen Tate, T. S. Eliot, Yvor Winters, R. P. Blackmur, John Crowe Ransom, David Daiches, Cleanth Brooks, Robert Penn Warren, Joseph Frank, W. K. Wimsatt, Jr., Edgar Allan Poe, Kenneth Burke, Paul Elmer More, Harry Levin.

Critiques and Essays in Criticism: 1920–1948. Representing the Achievement of Modern British and American Critics, selected by Robert Wooster Stallman. With a Foreword by Cleanth Brooks. (1949).

Critical theory and practice since 1920, including essays by American critics: John Crowe Ransom, T. S. Eliot, Allen Tate, Cleanth Brooks, Robert Penn Warren, Robert B. Heilman, Yvor Winters, René Wellek, Kenneth Burke, Elder Olson, Joseph Frank, Delmore Schwartz, R. P. Blackmur, Eliseo Vivas, W. K. Wimsatt, Jr. and Monroe C. Beardsley, Edmund Wilson, F. W. Dupee.

Immortal Diamond: Studies in Gerard Manley Hopkins, edited by Norman Weyand, S.J., with the assistance of Raymond Schoder, S.J. (1949).

Essays by M. C. Carroll, Arthur MacGillivray, J. L. Bonn, W. J. Ong, C. A. Burns, R. V. Schoder, M. B. McNamee, W. T. Noon, Youree Watson, R. R. Boyle.

English Institute Essays: 1948 (1949).

Essays read before the English Institute, September 1948, by Wallace Stevens, Robert B. Heilman, Northrop Frye, Leslie A. Fiedler, Edward Hubler, Craig La Drière, Ruth C. Wallerstein, W. K. Wimsatt, Jr.

Lectures in Criticism, edited by Huntington Cairns (1949).

A symposium of lectures on historical and modern theory in criticism, delivered at Johns Hopkins University in April, 1948, by R. P. Blackmur, Benedetto Croce, Henri Peyre, John Crowe Ransom, Herbert Read, and Allen Tate.

The Permanence of Yeats, edited by James Hall and Martin Steinmann (1950).

Selected critical essays on William Butler Yeats by English critics (J. Middleton Murry, F. R. Leavis, Stephen Spender, D. S. Savage, A. Norman Jeffares) and the following Americans: Edmund Wilson, R. P. Blackmur, Cleanth Brooks, John Crowe Ransom, Allen Tate, David Daiches, Arthur Mizener, Joseph Warren Beach, Austin Warren, Eric Bentley, Kenneth Burke, William York Tindall, Donald Davidson, Elder Olson, Delmore Schwartz, T. S. Eliot, W. H. Auden, Morton Dauwen Zabel, Walter E. Houghton.

Perspectives of Criticism, edited by Harry Levin (1950).

Essays in criticism on various aspects of ancient and modern literature—Volume XX of the Harvard Studies in Comparative Literature—by Jean-Joseph Seznec, William C. Greene, Harry Levin, Alfred Schwartz, Perry Miller, Walter Jackson Bate, Geoffrey Tillotson, John V. Kelleher, Renato Poggioli.

English Institute Essays: 1949 (1950).

Essays read before the English Institute, September 1949, by Moody E. Prior, Arthur Mizener, Francis Fergusson, William Charvat, Roy Harvey Pearce, Benjamin Townley Spencer, Frederick J. Hoffman.

Critics and Criticism: Ancient and Modern, edited by R. S. Crane (1951).

Essays on ancient and modern theory and practice in criticism by R. S. Crane, W. R. Keast, Richard P. McKeon, Norman F. Maclean, Elder Olson, Bernard Weinberg.

APPENDIX III

American Magazines Publishing Criticism

THIS check-list includes the most important magazines that have published the work of American critics since 1900. A number of standard magazines are included, but a point has been made of including the best of the independent journals and "little magazines" that have encouraged literary experiment and critical activity. The dates and personnel of these have been described as closely as their irregular careers permit. [A more complete account of their careers will be found in *The Little Magazine: A History and a Bibliography*, by Frederick J. Hoffman, Charles Allen, and Carolyn F. Ulrich. Princeton University Press, 1946; revised edition, 1947.] Standard magazines devoted chiefly to public affairs, politics, and fiction have not been included. Magazines published in foreign countries are included when they have been edited and contributed to by American writers.

Accent: A Quarterly of New Literature. Urbana Illinois. Founded 1940. Edited by Kerker Quinn, Kenneth Andrews, Charles Shattuck, W. R. Moses, Thomas Bledsoe, Keith Huntress, W. McNeal Lowry, and others in subsequent years. Published quarterly.

The American Caravan: A Yearbook of American Literature. New York. Begun in 1927 "in the interests of a growing American literature"; established as an annual, but issued irregularly until 1936. Edited by Van Wyck Brooks (in 1927), Alfred Kreymborg, Lewis Mumford, Paul Rosenfeld (1927–1936). Discontinued in 1936.

American Literature: A Journal of Literary History, Criticism, and Bibliography. Durham, N. C. Founded in 1929. Edited by a board of American scholars. Published quarterly.

The American Mercury. New York. Founded in 1924 by H. L. Mencken and George Jean Nathan, who served as editors 1924–1925; edited by H. L. Mencken alone, 1925–1933; subsequent editors: Henry Hazlitt, Charles Angoff, Paul Palmer, Eugene Lyons, Lawrence Spivak. Published monthly.

American Prefaces: A Journal of Critical and Imaginative Writing. Iowa City, Iowa. Founded in 1935; discontinued in 1943. Edited by Wilbur Schramm, Paul Engle, Frederick Brantley, Jean Garrigue. Published quarterly.

The American Review. New York. Founded in 1933 and edited by Seward Collins. Published ten months of the year. Discontinued in 1938.

The American Spectator: A Literary Newspaper. New York. Founded in 1932; discontinued in 1937. Edited by George Jean Nathan, Ernest Boyd, James Branch Cabell, Eugene O'Neill; later by Theodore Dreiser, Sherwood Anderson, Charles Angoff, Max Lehman. Published monthly, with some periods of irregularity.

The Arizona Quarterly: A Journal of Literature, History, Folklore. University of Arizona, Tuscon, Arizona. Founded in 1945. Edited by Frederick Cromwell and Harry Behn. Published quarterly.

Blast: An Anglo-American Quarterly. A Review of the Great English Vortex. London, England. Founded in 1914 by Wyndham Lewis and Ezra Pound; edited by Wyndham Lewis. Discontinued in 1915. Two issues only.

Blues: A Magazine of New Rhythms. Columbus, Mississippi; later New York City. Founded in 1929 and edited by Charles Henri Ford. Discontinued in 1933, after irregular publication. Issued monthly, then irregularly.

The Bookman. New York City. Edited by John Farrar, 1921–1928; by Seward Collins and Burton Rascoe, 1928–1929; by Seward Collins, 1930–1933. Published monthly. Discontinued in 1933 with the founding of *The American Review* by Seward Collins.

Books Abroad: A Quarterly Publication Devoted to Comment on Foreign Books. Norman, Oklahoma. Founded in 1928 by Roy Temple House; edited by him and later by an editorial board, centering at the University of Oklahoma. Published quarterly.

Broom: An International Magazine of the Arts. Rome; Berlin; New York City. Founded in 1921. Edited by Harold A. Loeb, Alfred Kreymborg, Slater Brown, Matthew Josephson, Malcolm Cowley. Published monthly. Discontinued in 1924.

The Catholic World: A Monthly Magazine of General Literature and Science. New York City. Founded in 1865. Various successive editors. Published monthly.

The Chicago Literary Times. Chicago. Founded in 1923. Edited by Ben Hecht, with Maxwell Bodenheim as Associate. Published biweekly. Discontinued in 1924.

The Chimera: A Rough Beast. New York City. Founded in 1942 as a quarterly; later appearances irregular. Edited by Benjamin Ford, William Arrowsmith, Fearon Brown, Frederick Morgan, Barbara Howes, and others.

Commentary. Incorporating The Contemporary Jewish Record. New York City. Founded in 1945. Published by the American Jewish Committee. Editor: Elliot E. Cohen; associate editor, Clement Greenberg. Published monthly.

The Commonweal: A Weekly Review of Literature, the Arts, and Public Affairs. New York City. Founded in 1924 and edited by Michael Williams, with George Shuster as Associate Editor, and a board of consultants; later edited by Philip Wheelwright, Philip Burnham, Harry Lorin Binsse, and others. A Catholic lay journal. Published weekly.

Contact. New York City. Founded in 1921 and edited by William Carlos Williams and Robert McAlmon until 1923; revived briefly in 1933 as *Contact: An*

American Quarterly and edited by William Carlos Williams. Published irregularly. Discontinued in 1933.

The Criterion: A Quarterly Review. London, England. Founded in 1922 and edited by T. S. Eliot. Published quarterly except during 1927–1928 when it was called *The Monthly Criterion.* Discontinued in January, 1939.

Decision: A Review of Free Culture. New York City. Founded in 1941 and edited by Klaus Mann, later with Muriel Rukeyser as Associate Editor. Published monthly. Discontinued in 1942.

The Dial. Founded in New York in 1920 as a monthly devoted to literature and the arts, after an earlier career as a weekly, later a monthly, in Chicago and in New York. Edited by Scofield Thayer, 1920–1925; by Marianne Moore, 1925–1929; with John B. Watson as an advisory director, and Stewart Mitchell, Gilbert Seldes, Alyse Gregory, Kenneth Burke, and Ellen Thayer as editorial assistants. Published monthly. Discontinued in 1929.

Direction: A Quarterly of New Literature. Peoria, Illinois. Founded in 1934. Edited by Kerker Quinn, Rhody Fisher, Howard Nutt, Nelson Bittner. Published quarterly. Discontinued in 1935. Some of the editors and the general purpose of the magazine reappeared when *Accent* was founded in 1940.

The Double Dealer. New Orleans. Founded in 1921. Edited by Julius Weis Friend, Basil Thompson, John McClure. Published monthly. Discontinued in 1926.

The Drama. Chicago. Founded in 1911. Successively edited by William Norman Guthrie, Charles Hubbard Sergel, Theodore Ballou Hinckley, Albert E. Thompson, with various boards of advisory and associate editors. Titled *The Drama Magazine,* 1930–1931. Discontinued in 1931.

Dynamo: A Journal of Revolutionary Poetry. New York City. Founded in 1934. Edited by S. Funaroff, Herman Spector, Joseph Vogel, Nicholas Wirth, Stephen Foster. Published bimonthly, with some periods of irregularity. Discontinued in 1936.

The Egoist: An Individualist Review. London, England. Founded in 1914. Edited by Dora Marsden and Harriet Shaw Weaver, with Richard Aldington, H. D. (Hilda Doolittle), and T. S. Eliot as assistant editors. Published bimonthly. Discontinued in 1919.

The Exile. Founded in 1927 and edited by Ezra Pound from Paris and Rapallo, Italy, later numbers bearing a publication imprint of Chicago. Four issues only. Discontinued in 1928.

The Explicator. Fredericksburg, Virginia; now at Lynchburg, Virginia. Founded in 1942. Edited by G. W. Arms, J. P. Kirby, L. G. Locke, J. E. Whitesell. Published monthly from October to June.

The Figure in the Carpet: A Magazine of Prose. New York City. Founded in 1927. Edited by Hansell Baugh, then by John Riordan. Called *The Salient* after December, 1928. Published monthly but later irregularly. Discontinued in 1929.

The Forum and Century. New York City. *The Forum* founded in 1886; combined with *The Century* Magazine in 1931. Last editor, Henry Goddard Leach. Published monthly. Discontinued in 1939.

The Freeman. New York City. Founded in 1920. Edited by Francis Neilson and Albert Jay Nock; Associate Editor, Van Wyck Brooks. Published weekly. Discontinued in 1924. Re-established as a biweekly in 1950.

Front: A Radical Tri-Lingual Magazine. Being an International Review of Literature. The Hague, Holland. Edited by Sonja Prins, with Foreign Editors: Xavier Abril for Spain, Masaki Ikeda for Japan, Secretariat F. O. S. P. for Russia, Norman Macleod for the United States. Published bimonthly. Discontinued in 1931.

The Frontier. Missoula, Montana (University of Montana). Founded in 1920 as "a literary magazine"; later subtitled *A Regional Literary Quarterly*. Incorporated *Muse and Mirror* in 1932, and *The Midland* in 1933. Edited by H. G. Merriam and a board of editors. Three issues a year. Discontinued in 1939.

The Fugitive. Nashville, Tennessee. Founded in 1922. Edited by Walter Clyde Curry, Donald Davidson, Merrill Moore, John Crowe Ransom, James M. Frank, Sidney Mttron Hirsch, Stanley Johnson, Alec Brock Stevenson, Allen Tate, and others, including Robert Penn Warren and Laura Riding for short periods. Published bimonthly. Discontinued in 1925.

Furioso. New Haven, Conn.; later Northfield, Minnesota. Founded in 1939 as "a magazine of verse," appearing irregularly until 1942; resumed as quarterly in 1947. First editors: James Angleton and E. Reed Whittemore; later edited by James J. Angleton, Ambrose Gordon, Jr., Carmen Angleton Hauser, W. R. Johnson, Arthur Mizener, Rosemary Mizener, Howard Nemerov, John Pauker, Irwin Touster, and Reed Whittemore. Published quarterly.

The Guardian: A Monthly Journal of Life, Art, and Letters. Philadelphia. Founded in 1924. Board of Editors: Abraham N. Gerbovoy, Madelin Leof, Abe Grosner, Herman Silverman. Published monthly. Discontinued in 1925.

The Gyroscope. Palo Alto, California. Founded in 1929 and edited by Yvor Winters, Janet Lewis, Howard Baker. Issued irregularly. Discontinued in 1931.

The Harkness Hoot: A Yale Undergraduate Review. New Haven, Conn. Founded in 1930 and edited successively by William Harlan Hale, Selden Rodman, Richard M. Bissell, Richard S. Childs, and others. Published irregularly. Discontinued in 1934.

The Harvard Advocate. Cambridge, Mass. A literary review of Harvard University. Founded in 1866 and edited by successive student editors. Published biweekly.

The Harvard Monthly. Cambridge, Mass. Founded in 1885 and edited by successive student editors. Published monthly.

The Harvard Wake. Cambridge, Mass. An irregularly published journal, founded in 1944 and edited by students of Harvard University.

Hemispheres. Brooklyn, N. Y. Founded in 1943 as "a French-American quarterly of poetry," and edited by Yvan Goll. Discontinued in 1945.

The Hound and Horn. Cambridge, Mass., later New York City. Founded as "A Harvard Miscellany" in 1927 and edited by Bernard Bandler II, R. P. Blackmur, Lincoln E. Kirstein, Varian Fry, A. Hyatt Mayor. Edited after 1931 by

Lincoln Kirstein, with Allen Tate and Yvor Winters as Regional Editors. Published quarterly. Discontinued in 1934.

The Hudson Review. New York City. Founded in 1948 and edited by William Arrowsmith, Joseph D. Bennett, Frederick Morgan. Published quarterly.

The Kenyon Review. Kenyon College, Gambier, Ohio. Founded in 1939. Edited by John Crowe Ransom, with Philip Blair Rice as Associate Editor, and with advisory boards that have included R. P. Blackmur, Allen Tate, Mark Van Doren, Eliseo Vivas, Cleanth Brooks, Robert Penn Warren, Eric Bentley, Lionel Trilling, and Roger Sessions. Published quarterly.

Larus: The Celestial Visitor, with which has been combined Tempo. Lynn, Mass. Founded in 1927 and edited by Sherry Mangan, with Virgil Thomson as French editor. Issued irregularly. Discontinued in 1928.

The Laughing Horse: A Magazine of Satire from the Pacific Slope. Berkeley, California; later at Guadalajara, Mexico, Santa Fe and Taos, New Mexico. Founded in 1922. Edited by Roy E. Chanslor, James T. Van Renssalaer, Jr., and Willard Johnson. Published quarterly; later irregularly. Discontinued in 1939.

The Left: A Quarterly Review of Radical and Experimental Art. Davenport, Iowa. Founded in 1931. Edited by George Redfield, Jay du Von, Marvin Klein, R. C. Lorenz, W. K. Jordan, with various associate editors. Published quarterly. Discontinued in 1932.

The Liberator. New York City. Founded in 1918 as successor to *The Masses.* Edited by Max Eastman, Robert Minor, Floyd Dell, Chrystal Eastman, and others, with numerous editorial associates. Published monthly. Later merged with *Workers' Monthly, Labor Herald,* and *Soviet Russia Pictorial.* Published monthly. Discontinued as *The Liberator* in 1924.

Literary America. New York City. A "journal devoted to the American scene." Founded in 1934, and edited by Kenneth Houston and S. Robert Morse. Published monthly. Discontinued in 1936.

The Literary World: A Monthly Survey of International Letters. New York City. Founded in 1934 and edited by Angel Flores and Victor Robinson, with Samuel Putnam, Pierre Loving, Clifton Fadiman, and Willy Haas among the editorial advisers. Discontinued in 1935.

The Little Review: A Monthly Devoted to Literature, Drama, Music, and Art. Chicago; New York; Paris. Founded in 1914 as a monthly; later irregular in appearance. Edited by Margaret C. Anderson; later with Jane Heap (1922–1929). Ezra Pound as Foreign Editor, 1917–1921. Discontinued in 1929.

Mainstream: A Literary Quarterly. New York City. Founded in 1947 as a journal of Marxist-Communist opinion. Editor-in-chief: Samuel Sillen, assisted by an editorial board. Published monthly. In 1948 combined with *The New Masses* to form *Masses and Mainstream.*

Manuscripts. New York City. Founded in 1922 and edited coöperatively by Sherwood Anderson, Paul Rosenfeld, William Carlos Williams, Waldo Frank, and others. Issued irregularly. Discontinued in 1923.

The Maryland Quarterly, later *The Briarcliff Quarterly.* College Park, Maryland; later at Briarcliff Junior College, New York. Founded in 1944. Edited by

Norman Macleod, Jane Woodring, Pauline Howard, Arthur O'Keefe, and others. Published quarterly.

The Masses: A Monthly Devoted to the Interests of the Working People. New York City. Founded in 1911, and edited successively by Thomas Seltzer, Horatio Winslow, Piet Vlag, and Max Eastman, with Floyd Dell, John Reed, Mary Heaton Vorse, Louis Untermeyer, Arthur Bullard among the contributing editors, and Art Young, George Bellows, Boardman Robinson, and H. J. Glintenkamp as art editors. Discontinued in 1917, but continued in *The Liberator* and *The New Masses.*

Masses and Mainstream. New York City. Founded in 1948, combining *Mainstream* and *The New Masses.* Edited by Samuel Sillen, with Herbert Apotheker, Lloyd L. Brown, and Charles Humboldt as associate editors. Published monthly.

The Measure: A Journal of Poetry. New York City. Founded in 1921 and edited by a board including Maxwell Anderson, Padraic Colum, Frank E. Hill, David Morton, Louise Townsend Nicoll, George O'Neill, Genevieve Taggard, Joseph Auslander, Elinor Wylie, Louise Bogan, and others. Published monthly. Discontinued in 1926.

Measure: A Critical Journal. Chicago. Founded in 1949. Board of editors: Daniel J. Boorstin, David Grene, Robert M. Hutchins (chairman), John U. Nef, Robert Redfield, Henry Regnery, Otto G. von Simson (managing editor). Editorial advisers: Montgomery Belgion, A. P. d'Entrèves, Jacques Maritain, Franz Joseph Schöningh. Published quarterly.

The Miscellany. New York City. Founded in 1931 and edited by F. W. Dupee, Geoffrey T. Hellman, Dwight Macdonald, George L. K. Morris. Published bimonthly. Discontinued in 1931.

Modern Philology. University of Chicago. Founded in 1905 by John Matthews Manly, its first editor; present managing editor, R. S. Crane, with a board of consultants. Published quarterly.

The Modern Quarterly. Baltimore. Founded in 1923 and edited by V. F. Calverton, with assistants: Rachel North, Mortin Levin, Savington Crampton, Samuel D. Schmalhausen, Max Eastman, Edmund Wilson, Ernest Sutherland Bates, Carleton Beals, Bruno Fischer, Diego Rivera, Thomas Benton, and others. Published quarterly except 1933–1938 when it was called *The Modern Monthly.* Discontinued in 1940.

Modern Review. Winchester, Mass. Founded in 1922 and edited by Fiskwoode Tarleton. Published quarterly. Discontinued in 1924.

The Morada: A Tri-Lingual Advance Guard Quarterly. Albuquerque, New Mexico, and Cagnes-sur-Mer, France. Founded in 1929 and edited by Norman Macleod, William Flynn, C. V. Wicker, Donal McKenzie, with various contributing editors. Published quarterly. Discontinued in 1931.

The Nation. New York City. Founded in 1865 and edited by E. L. Godkin. Edited by Paul Elmer More, 1909–1914. Reorganized by Oswald Garrison Villard in 1918 and edited by him and others until 1932. Edited 1935–1938 by Joseph Wood Krutch, Max Lerner, Freda Kirchwey. After 1938 edited by Freda Kirchwey, with Margaret Marshall as Literary Editor, Joseph Wood

Krutch as Drama Critic, B. H. Haggin as Music Critic, and with Robert Bendiner, Keith Hutchison, and others as associates. Published weekly.

Nativity: An American Quarterly. Delaware and Columbus, Ohio. Founded in 1930 and edited by Boris J. Israel. Published quarterly. Discontinued in 1931.

The New Act: A Literary Review. New York City. Founded in 1933 and edited by H. R. Hays and Harold Rosenberg. Issued irregularly. Discontinued in 1934.

New Directions in Prose and Poetry. Norfolk, Conn. An annual founded in 1936 and edited by James Laughlin IV; devoted to new and experimental writing and art, and including critical essays and surveys. Published annually.

The New Freeman. New York City. Founded in 1930 and edited by Suzanne LaFollette. Published weekly. Discontinued in 1931.

The New Masses. New York City. Founded in 1926 and edited successively by Egmont Arens, Hugo Gellert, Michael Gold, Joseph Freeman, James Rorty, John Sloan, William Gropper, and numerous others. Published monthly, with intervals as a weekly. Discontinued in 1948 when it was merged with *Mainstream* as *Masses and Mainstream*.

The New Mexico Quarterly. University of New Mexico, Albuquerque, N. M. Founded in 1941; after 1941 titled as *The New Mexico Quarterly Review*. Edited successively by J. F. Zimmerman, John D. Clark, J. W. Diefendorf, with T. M. Pearce and Dudley Wynn as active editors, 1932 and following; Alan Swallow as Poetry Editor; and others. Published quarterly.

The New Republic. New York City. Founded in 1914 and edited by Herbert Croly, Walter Lippmann, Francis Hackett, Randolph Bourne, Philip Littell, and others; later by Bruce Bliven, Robert Morss Lovett, Edmund Wilson, Stark Young, George Soule, Malcolm Cowley, and others; at present by Michael Straight, Bruce Bliven, and others. Published weekly.

The New Review: An International Notebook of the Arts. Paris. Founded in 1931; edited by Samuel Putnam, with Peter Neagoe, Ezra Pound, Maxwell Bodenheim, Richard Thoma as associates. Published quarterly. Discontinued in 1932.

The Pacific Spectator. Palo Alto, California. Founded in 1947, with John W. Dodds (chairman), Frederick Hard, Wallace Stegner, George R. Stewart, Dixon Wecter as board of editors, and Edith R. Mirrielees as managing editor. Published quarterly by the Stanford University Press for the Pacific Coast Committee for the Humanities and 26 supporting colleges and universities.

Pagany: A Native Quarterly. Boston; later New York. Founded in 1930 and edited by Richard Johns. Published quarterly. Discontinued in 1933.

Partisan Review. New York City. Founded in 1934 as "A Bi-Monthly of Revolutionary Literature" under the auspices of the John Reed Club of New York, with Nathan Adler, Edward Dahlberg, Joseph Freeman, Philip Rahv, William Phillips, Alan Calmer, Jack Conroy, Ben Field, Clinton Simpson, and others on the editorial board, 1934–1937. Reorganized in 1937 with Philip Rahv, William Phillips, Dwight Macdonald, F. W. Dupee, George L. K. Morris, and Mary McCarthy as editors. Published quarterly, later bimonthly, from 1937 to 1947. As monthly beginning in 1948, but reverting to bimonthly in 1950, with William Phillips and Philip Rahv as editors, Delmore Schwartz and William Barrett as associate editors, with advisory board.

The Playboy: A Portfolio of Art and Satire. New York City. Founded in 1919 and edited by Egmont Arens. Published irregularly. Discontinued in 1924.

The Plowshare: A Magazine of the Literature, Arts, and Life Evolving in Woodstock. Woodstock, N. Y. Founded as *The Wild Hawk* in 1912, with Hervey White, Carl Eric Lindin, Allan Updegraff as editors. Published monthly; later irregularly. Discontinued in 1920. Briefly resumed in 1935.

Poetry: A Magazine of Verse. Chicago. Founded in 1912 and edited 1912–1936 by Harriet Monroe, with Alice Corbin Henderson, Ezra Pound, Eunice Tietjens, Helen Hoyt, Emanuel Carnevali, Marion Strobel, George Dillon, Jessica Nelson North, and Morton Dauwen Zabel as successive associate editors. Edited 1936–1937 by Morton Dauwen Zabel; 1937–1942 and 1946–1949 by George Dillon; 1949 by Hayden Carruth; 1950–   by Karl Shapiro.

Politics. New York City. Founded in 1942 and edited by Dwight Macdonald. Published weekly; then monthly; later irregularly. Discontinued in 1949.

The Quarterly Review of Literature. Chapel Hill, N. C., New Haven, Conn., and Annandale-on-Hudson, N. Y. Founded in 1944. Edited by Warren Carrier and T. Weiss, with T. Weiss as editor after 1946. Published quarterly.

Reedy's Mirror: A Weekly Dealing in Politics and Literature. St. Louis, Missouri. Founded in 1891 as *The Mirror;* edited as *Reedy's Mirror* from 1913 to 1920 by William Marion Reedy. Published weekly. Discontinued in 1920, and superseded by *All's Well, or The Mirror Repolished.*

The Reviewer. Richmond, Virginia. Edited by Emily Clark and Hunter Stagg as a bimonthly, 1921–1924 (with Margaret Freeman, Mary D. Street, James Branch Cabell as temporary associates). Edited by Paul Green, 1925. Absorbed by *The Southwest Review* in 1926.

S4N. Publication of the S4N Society to Promote Open-Minded Consideration of Theories and Practices of Art. Northampton, Mass., and New Haven, Conn. Founded in 1919 and edited by Norman Fitts, with Gorham B. Munson, E. E. Cummings, Thornton Wilder, Jean Toomer, Stephen Vincent Benét among the members of the editorial board. Published monthly and irregularly. Combined with *The Modern Review* in 1926 to form *The Modern S4N Review.*

The Saturday Review of Literature. New York. Founded in 1924 and edited until 1936 by Henry Seidel Canby; from 1936 to 1938 by Bernard De Voto; now edited by Norman Cousins, with Amy Loveman, John Mason Brown, and Harrison Smith as associate editors; Bennett Cerf, John T. Winterich, Mary Gould Davis, Irving Kolodin, James Thrall Soby as contributing editors; Henry Seidel Canby as chairman of Board of Directors. Published weekly.

Science and Society: A Marxian Quarterly. New York City. Founded in 1936, with Albert E. Blumberg, Edwin Berry Burgum, V. J. McGill, Margaret Schlauch, and Bernhard J. Stern as editors; now edited by Bernhard J. Stern (chairman), Samuel Bernstein, Edwin Berry Burgum, V. J. McGill, Henry F. Mins, Margaret Schlauch, Dirk J. Struik. Published quarterly.

Secession: A Quarterly. An Independent Magazine of Modern Letters. Vienna,
Berlin, Reutte (Tirol, Austria), New York. Founded in 1922 and edited
successively by Gorham B. Munson, Matthew Josephson, Kenneth Burke.
Published monthly, then irregularly. Discontinued in 1924.

The Seven Arts: A Monthly. New York. Founded in 1916. Editor: James Oppenheim; with Waldo Frank and Van Wyck Brooks as associate editors. Discontinued in 1917, to be absorbed by *The Dial.*

The Sewanee Review: A Quarterly of Life and Letters. Sewanee, Tennessee (The
University of the South). Founded in 1892 and edited successively by Telfair
Hodgson, W. P. Trent, B. W. Wells, and others; by William S. Knickerbocker, 1926–1942; by Tudor S. Long in 1943; by Andrew C. Lytle, 1943–
1944; by Allen Tate, 1944–1946; by J. E. Palmer, 1946–   . Published
quarterly.

The Smart Set: A Magazine of Cleverness. New York. Founded earlier; edited
from 1912 to 1914 by Willard Huntington Wright; from 1914–1923 by
H. L. Mencken and George Jean Nathan. Published monthly. The literary
importance of the magazine belongs to the years 1912–1923.

The Southern Review. Baton Rouge, Louisiana (Louisiana State University).
Founded in 1935, with Charles W. Pipkin as editor, Cleanth Brooks, Jr.,
and Robert Penn Warren as associate editors; Brooks and Warren as editors
1941–1942. Published quarterly. Discontinued in 1942.

The Southwest Review. University of Texas; Southern Methodist University.
Founded as *The Texas Review* in 1912 with Stark Young as editor; later
edited, 1917–1924, by Robert Adger Law; reorganized as *The Southwest
Review* in 1924 and edited by Jay B. Hubbell, George Bond, and others.
Published quarterly.

Story. Vienna; Majorca; New York. Founded in 1931 and edited by Whit Burnett,
with Martha Foley as associate, 1931–1941. Published bimonthly.

The Symposium: A Critical Review. New York. Founded in 1930. Editors: James
Burnham and Philip E. Wheelwright. Published quarterly. Discontinued in
1933.

Tambour. Paris, France. Founded in 1929 and edited by Harold Salemson. Published irregularly. Discontinued in 1930.

Theatre Arts Magazine. New York. Founded in 1916 with Sheldon Cheney as
editor 1916–1921; Edith J. R. Isaacs editor from 1919 to 1946; Marion
Tucker and Stark Young editors 1919–1921 and 1922–1924 respectively;
Ashley Dukes, John Mason Brown, Carl Carmer, Rosamond Gilder, Morton
Eustis, Stark Young, Kenneth Macgowan sometime associate editors; Charles
MacArthur, editor, 1946–   . Published quarterly, later monthly.

This Quarter: An International Quarterly Review of Arts and Letters. Milan,
Monte Carlo, Cannes, and Paris, France. Founded in 1925 and edited by
Ernest Walsh, 1925–1926, and Ethel Moorhead, 1925–1927; edited by
Edward W. Titus, 1929–1932. Published quarterly. Discontinued in 1933.

The Transatlantic Review. Paris, France. Founded in 1924 and edited by Ford
Madox Ford. Published monthly. Discontinued in 1925.

Transition: An International Magazine for Creative Experiment. Paris; The Hague;
New York. Founded in 1927. Editors: Eugene Jolas and Elliot Paul, with

Robert Sage, Harry Crosby, Matthew Josephson, and others as associates; edited by Eugene Jolas after 1929. Published monthly, later quarterly, with periods of suspension.

Twice a Year: A Journal of Literature, the Arts, and Civil Liberties. New York City. Founded in 1938 and edited by Dorothy Norman. Published semi-annually.

The University Review. University of Kansas City, Missouri. Founded in 1934; edited by Clarence Decker. Published quarterly.

Vice Versa. New York City. Founded in 1940, with Harry Brown and Dunstan Thompson as editors. Published bimonthly. Discontinued in 1942.

View. New York City. Founded in 1940, with Charles Henri Ford as editor, James Decker as managing editor, and Parker Tyler later as associate editor. Four irregular issues a year. Discontinued in 1947.

The Virginia Quarterly Review. Charlottesville, Virginia. Founded in 1925, with James Southall Wilson as editor, assisted by others. Now edited by Charlotte Kohler, with James Southall Wilson, R. K. Gooch, Thomas Perkins Abernethy, Hardy C. Dillard, and William S. Weedon as advisory editors. Published quarterly.

Voices: A Journal of Verse. Boston; later New York City. Founded in 1921 and edited by Harold Vinal. Published bimonthly.

The Wave: A Journal of Art and Letters. Chicago; later Copenhagen. Editor: Vincent Starret. Published irregularly. Discontinued in 1924.

The Western Review. Founded at Murray, Utah, in 1937 as *The Intermountain Review* by Ray B. West, Jr. In 1938 moved to Ogden, Utah, and became *The Rocky Mountain Review* with Ray B. West, Jr., as editor; George Snell and Grant H. Redford as associates; Brewster Ghiselin as poetry editor. In 1946 moved to Lawrence, Kansas, with title changed to *The Western Review,* Ray B. West, Jr., continuing as editor, R. W. Stallman and Alwyn Berland as associate editors. In 1949 moved to State University of Iowa, Iowa City, with Ray B. West, Jr., as editor; Warren Carrier and Robie Macauley as associate editors; Alwyn Berland, George Bluestone, John Hunt, Carl Hartman, E. F. McGuire, Austryn Wainhouse as assistants; Dean Cadle as business manager. Published quarterly.

The Westminster Magazine. Oglethorpe University, Georgia. Founded in 1911. Various editors. Published quarterly with periods of suspension. Absorbed *Bozart* and *Contemporary Verse* in 1935.

The Windsor Quarterly. Hartland Four Corners, Vermont. Founded in 1933 with Frederick B. Maxham and Irene Merrill as editors. Published quarterly. Discontinued in 1935.

The Yale Review: A National Quarterly. New Haven, Conn. First founded in 1879; reëstablished in 1892; reorganized in 1911 with Wilbur Cross as editor and Helen MacAfee as assistant editor, Miss MacAfee later succeeding Wilbur Cross as editor. Present editor (1950): David M. Potter, with Paul Pickrel as managing editor, Helen MacAfee as editor emeritus, and William Clyde DeVane, Edgar S. Furniss, and Arnold Wolfers as the editorial board. Published quarterly.

APPENDIX IV

Notes on Contributors

THESE notes are chiefly bibliographical in character. In addition to their books, all of the contributors to this volume have written for critical and literary journals; the titles of these are not, however, listed, except in the case of periodicals on which editorial positions have been held. Such contributions may be traced by consulting *The Reader's Guide to Periodical Literature* and *The International Index to Periodicals*. For lists of selected critical essays see Appendix V.

ARVIN, NEWTON. Born: Valparaiso, Indiana, 1900. Educated: Harvard University, B.A., 1921. Member of the English Department of Smith College since 1922: instructor, 1926–1928; assistant professor, 1928–1932; associate professor, 1932–1940; professor of English since 1940. Associate editor of *The Living Age*, 1925–1926. Editor: *The Heart of Hawthorne's Journals* (1929); *Hawthorne's Short Stories* (1946). Books of criticism and biography: *Hawthorne* (1929); *Whitman* (1938); *Herman Melville* (1950).

AUDEN, WYSTAN HUGH. Born: York, England, 1907. Educated: Gresham's School, Holt; Christ Church, Oxford University. School teacher at Malvern, 1930–1935. Worked with the G. P. O. Film Unit, 1935–1936. Traveled in France, Germany, Spain, Iceland, China, United States. Came to the United States in 1939 and presently adopted American citizenship. Has taught at University of Michigan, Haverford College, New School in New York City, and lectured in many other colleges and universities. Verse first published in *Oxford Poetry*, 1926. King's Medal for Poetry (England), 1937; Pulitzer Prize in Poetry, 1947. Books of verse: *Poems* (1930); *The Orators* (1932); *Letters from Iceland* (with Louis MacNeice, 1937); *Spain* (1937); *On This Island* (1937); *Selected Poems* (1938); *Journey to a War* (with Christopher Isherwood, 1939); *Another Time* (1940); *The Double Man* (1941); *For the Time Being* (1944); *Collected Poems* (1945); *The Age of Anxiety* (1948). Plays in verse: *The Dance of Death* (1933); *The Dog Beneath the Skin* (with Christopher Isherwood, 1935); *The Ascent of F 6* (with Christopher Isherwood, 1936); *On the Frontier* (with Christopher Isherwood, 1939). Editor of: *The Poet's Tongue* (with John Garrett, 1935); *The Oxford Book of Light Verse* (1938); *Selections from Tennyson* (1944); *The Portable Greek Reader* (1948); *Poets of the English Language* (5 volumes, with N. H. Pearson, 1950). Book of critical prose: *The Enchafèd Flood: or, The Romantic Iconography of the Sea* (1950).

BABBITT, IRVING. Born: Dayton, Ohio, 1865. Died in 1932. Educated: Harvard University, B.A., 1889; M.A., 1893; Sorbonne, Paris, 1891–1892. Instructor of French, Williams College, 1893–1894; instructor of French, Harvard, 1894–1902; assistant professor, 1902–1912; professor of French, 1912–1932. Lecturer at the Sorbonne, 1923. Editor of: Taine's *Introduction à l'Histoire de la Littérature anglaise* (1898); Renan's *Souvenirs de l'Enfance* (1902); Voltaire's *Zadig* (1905); Racine's *Phèdre* (1910), etc. Translator and editor of *The Dhammapada* (1936). Books of critical and philosophical prose: *Literature and the American College* (1908); *The New Laokoön* (1910); *The Masters of Modern French Criticism* (1912); *Rousseau and Romanticism* (1919); *Democracy and Leadership* (1924); *On Being Creative and Other Essays* (1932).

BARRETT, WILLIAM. Born: New York City, 1915. Educated: New York City schools; College of the City of New York; Columbia University, B.A., M.A., Ph. D. Taught philosophy at the University of Illinois and Brown University, 1938–1942; and English composition at College of the City of New York. Instructor for the Navy, 1942–1945; served with State Department in Italy, 1945–1946. Associate Editor of *Partisan Review*, 1946–   . Works of criticism: *Aristotle's Theory of Nature; What is Existentialism?* (1947).

BENTLEY, ERIC (RUSSELL). Born: England, 1916. Educated: Oxford University, B.A.; Yale University, Ph.D. While at Oxford acted in Shakespeare and studied production under John Gielgud and Esme Church. Has taught literature at Oxford, The University of California, Black Mountain College, The Kenyon School of English, and the University of Minnesota (Associate Professor of English since 1946). Guggenheim Fellowship, 1948. Guest director, Hedgerow Theatre, 1948; at the Abbey Theatre, Dublin, 1950. European correspondent, *Theatre Arts Magazine*, 1948–1950. Editor: *The Importance of Scrutiny* (1948); *From the Modern Repertoire* (1949). Translator: *The Private Life of the Master Race* by Bert Brecht (1944), and other works of Brecht. Books of critical prose: *A Century of Hero Worship* (1944); *The Playwright as Thinker* (in England published as *The Modern Theatre*) (1946); *Bernard Shaw* (1947).

BLACKMUR, RICHARD P. Born: Springfield, Massachusetts, 1904. Member of the editorial board of *The Hound and Horn*, 1928–1929. Assistant in Creative Arts Program, Princeton University, 1940–1943; member of the Institute of Advanced Study, Princeton, 1943–1946; Resident Fellow in Creative Writing, Princeton University, 1946–   . Books of verse: *From Jordan's Delight* (1937); *The Second World* (1942); *The Good European and Other Poems* (1947). Books of criticism: *The Double Agent: Essays in Craft and Elucidation* (1935); *The Expense of Greatness* (1940).

BOGAN, LOUISE. Born: Livermore Falls, Maine, 1897. Educated: Mount St. Mary's Academy, Manchester, N.H., 1907–1909; Girls' Latin School, Boston,

1910–1915; Boston University, 1915–1916. Visiting lecturer on poetry at University of Washington, 1948; University of Chicago, 1949; has lectured at University of Utah, University of Indiana, University of Iowa, and other colleges. John Reed Memorial Prize (*Poetry*), 1930; Helen Haire Levinson Prize (*Poetry*), 1937; Guggenheim Fellowship, 1933 and 1937; Fellow in American Letters, Library of Congress, 1944, and incumbent of the Chair of Poetry, 1945–1946; Harriet Monroe Poetry Award (University of Chicago), 1948. Poetry critic of *The New Yorker* since 1929. Books of verse: *Body of This Death* (1923); *Dark Summer* (1929); *The Sleeping Fury* (1937); *Poems and New Poems* (1941).

BOURNE, RANDOLPH SILLIMAN. Born: Bloomfield, New Jersey, 1886. Died in 1918. Educated: public schools, Bloomfield, N.J., Columbia University, B.A., 1912; M.A., 1913. Gilder Fellowship for travel and study in Europe, 1913–1914. Member of the first editorial board of *The New Republic*, 1914–1918. Contributing editor of *The Dial*, 1917–1918; of *The Seven Arts*, 1917. Editor of a symposium *Towards a Lasting Peace* (1916). Books of prose and criticism: *Youth and Life* (1913); *Arbitration and International Politics* (1913); *The Gary Schools* (1916); *Education and Living* (1917); *Untimely Papers* (edited by James Oppenheim, 1919); *The History of a Literary Radical and Other Essays* (edited by Van Wyck Brooks, 1920).

BROOKS, CLEANTH. Born: Murray, Kentucky, 1906. Educated: McTeire School, 1920–1924; Vanderbilt University, B.A., 1928; Tulane University, M.A., 1929; Exeter College, Oxford University (Rhodes Scholar), B.A., 1931 (Honors); B. Litt., 1932. A founder and editor of *The Southern Review*, 1935–1942. Assistant professor of English, Vanderbilt University, 1932–1934; assistant professor, associate professor, professor of English, Louisiana State University, 1934–1947; professor of English, Yale University, 1947–   . Visiting professor of English, universities of Texas, Michigan, Chicago. Fellow, Kenyon School of English, 1948. Books of criticism: *Modern Poetry and the Tradition* (1939); *The Well Wrought Urn: Studies in the Structure of Poetry* (1947). Books for literary study: *An Approach to Literature* (with Robert Penn Warren and Jack Purser, 1936, 1938, 1943); *Understanding Poetry* (with Robert Penn Warren, 1938, 1950); *Understanding Fiction* (with Robert Penn Warren, 1943); *Understanding Drama* (with Robert B. Heilman, 1945). Coauthor: *The Language of Poetry* (1942); *Twentieth Century English* (1946); *T. S. Eliot: A Study of His Writings by Several Hands* (1947). Editor: *The Percy Letters* (with David Nichol Smith, 1944–   ). Linguistic study: *The Relation of the Alabama-Georgia Dialect to the Provincial Dialects of Great Britain* (1935).

BROOKS, VAN WYCK. Born: Plainfield, New Jersey, 1886. Educated: Harvard University, A.B., 1908. On the editorial staff of Doubleday, Page and Co., 1907–1909; editor for The Century Company, 1915–1918. Lecturer at Leland Stanford University, 1911–1913. Assistant editor of *The Seven Arts*, 1917; associate editor of *The Freeman*, 1920–1924; founder and editor of *The American Caravan* in 1927 (with Alfred Kreymborg, Paul Rosenfeld, Lewis Mumford). Translator of works by Amiel, André Chamson, Georges Duhamel, Paul Gauguin, Léon Bazalgette, Romain Rolland. Editor of *The History of a Literary Radical* by Randolph Bourne (1920), *Journal of the First Voyage to America* by Christopher Columbus (1924), etc. Litt. D. of Columbia, Tufts, Bowdoin, Boston, Dartmouth; L.H.D., Northwestern University. Member of American Academy of Arts and Letters; National Institute of Arts and Letters; American Philosophical Society; Phi Beta Kappa. Granted the Dial Award, 1923; Pulitzer Prize in History, 1937. Books of prose and criticism: *The Wine of the Puritans* (1909); *The Malady of the Ideal* (1913); *John Addington Symonds* (1914); *The World of H. G. Wells* (1915); *America's Coming-of-Age* (1915); *Letters and Leadership* (1918); *The Ordeal of Mark Twain* (1920; revised 1932); *The Pilgrimage of Henry James* (1925); *Emerson and Others* (1927); *Sketches in Criticism* (1932); *Life of Emerson* (1932); *Three Essays on America* (1934); *The Flowering of New England* (1936); *New England: Indian Summer* (1940); *On Literature Today* (1941); *The Opinions of Oliver Allston* (1941); *The World of Washington Irving* (1944); *The Times of Melville and Whitman* (1947); *A Chilmark Miscellany* (1947).

BROWN, EDWARD KILLORAN. Born: Toronto, Canada, 1905. Educated: University of Toronto, B.A., 1926; Docteur ès Lettres, University of Paris, 1935. Lecturer, later assistant professor of English, University of Toronto, 1929–1935; professor and chairman of English, University of Manitoba, 1935–1937; professor of English, University of Toronto, 1938–1941; professor and chairman of English, Cornell University, 1941–1944; professor of English, University of Chicago, 1944–   . Alexander lecturer, University of Toronto, 1949. Translations: *Carlyle* by Louis Cazamian (1932); *Le Père Goriot* by Balzac (1946). Editor: *Representative Essays of Matthew Arnold* (1936); *Victorian Poetry* (1942); *At the Long Sault* by Archibald Lampman (with D. C. Scott, 1943). Books of criticism: *Edith Wharton: Étude critique* (Paris, 1935); *Studies in the Text of Matthew Arnold's Prose Works* (1935); *On Canadian Poetry* (1943); *Matthew Arnold: A Study in Conflict* (1948). In preparation: a biography of Willa Cather.

BURKE, KENNETH. Born: Pittsburgh, Pennsylvania, 1897. Educated: Ohio State University; Columbia University. Research worker, Laura Spellman Rockefeller Foundation, 1926–1927. Editor for the Bureau of Social Hygiene, 1928–1929. On the staff of *The Dial*, 1922–1929; music critic, 1927–1929. Visiting lecturer, University of Chicago, 1939 and 1949–1950; member of the staff of Bennington College, 1943–   . Received the Dial Award, 1928; Guggenheim Fellowship, 1935; grant of the American Academy of Arts and Letters, 1946. Has lectured at the New School for Social Research and other institutions. Fellow of the Institute of Advanced Study, 1948–1949. Translator of books by Thomas Mann, Emil Ludwig, Emile Baumann, and others. Books of narrative: *The White Oxen* (1924); *Toward a Better Life* (1932). Books of criticism and philosophical enquiry: *Counter-Statement* (1931); *Permanence and Change: Anatomy of Purpose* (1935); *Attitudes Toward History* (1937); *The Philosophy of Literary Form* (1941); *A Grammar of Motives* (1945); *A Rhetoric of Motives* (1950).

CANTWELL, ROBERT EMMETT. Born: Little Falls, Washington, 1908. Educated: Weatherwax High School, Aberdeen, Wash., 1921–1924; University of Washington, 1924–1925. Worked as factory hand, section hand, common laborer, welder's assistant. On the editorial staff of *Time*, 1935–1936; of *Fortune*, 1937; associate editor of *Time*, 1938–1945. Novels: *Laugh and Lie Down* (1931); *The Land of Plenty* (1934). Critical biography: *Nathaniel Hawthorne: The American Years* (1948).

CHAPMAN, JOHN JAY. Born: New York City, 1862. Died in 1933. Educated: St. Paul's School, Concord, N.H.; Harvard College, B.A., 1885; Harvard Law School. Admitted to Bar in 1888. Practised law briefly in New York; traveled in the West, in Europe and Russia. Edited *The Nursery*, later *The Political Nursery*, 1897. Active in New York politics, 1896–1910, in "Third Ticket" Movement, Good Government Club, etc. L.H.D., Hobart College; Phi Beta Kappa poet, Harvard, 1912; Litt. D., Yale University, 1916. Books of plays: *Four Plays for Children* (1908); *The Maid's Forgiveness* (1908); *A Sausage from Bologna* (1909); *The Treason and Death of Benedict Arnold* (1910); *Neptune's Isle and Other Plays for Children* (1916); *Cupid and Psyche* (1916); *Two Greek Plays: The Philoctetes of Sophocles and the Medea of Euripides* (1928); *The Antigone of Sophocles* (1929). Books of verse: *Homeric Scenes* (1914); *Songs and Poems* (1919). Books of political and social discussion: *Causes and Consequences* (1898); *Practical Agitation* (1900); *William Lloyd Garrison* (1913); *Memories and Milestones* (1915); *Notes on Religion* (1915); *New Horizons in American Life* (1932). Books of criticism: *Emerson and Other Essays* (1898); *Learning and Other Essays* (1910); *Greek Genius and Other Essays* (1915); *A Glance Toward Shakespeare* (1922); *Letters and Religion* (1924); *Dante* (1927); *Lucian, Plato, and Greek Morals* (1931).

CHASE, RICHARD. Born: Lakeport, New Hampshire, 1914. Educated: Dartmouth College, B.A., 1937; Columbia University, Ph. D., 1946. Instructor in English, Connecticut College, 1946–1949; assistant professor of English, Columbia University, 1949–   . Books of criticism and literary history: *Quest for Myth* (1949); *Herman Melville: A Critical Study* (1949).

COWLEY, MALCOLM. Born: Belsano, Pennsylvania, 1898. Educated: Harvard University, B.A., 1920; University of Montpellier, France, on American Field Service Fellowship, 1921–1922. Free-lance writer in New York, 1923–1929. Translator of books by Paul Valéry, Maurice Barrès, Raymond Radiguet, Pierre Mac Orlan, Princess Bibesco, André Gide, and others. Guarantors Prize, *Poetry*, 1928. Associate Editor of *The New Republic*, 1929–1944; contributing editor, 1944–   . Editor: *After the Genteel Tradition* (1937); *Books That Changed Our Minds* (1939); *The Portable Hemingway* (1944); *The Portable Faulkner* (1948). Books of verse: *Blue Juniata* (1929); *The Dry Season* (1941). Book of prose: *Exile's Return: A Narrative of Ideas* (1934).

CRANE, RONALD SALMON. Born: Tecumseh, Michigan, 1886. Educated: University of Michigan, B.A., 1908; University of Pennsylvania, Ph. D., 1911. Instructor of English, Northwestern University, 1911–1915; assistant professor, 1915–1920; associate professor, 1920–1924; associate professor, University of Chicago, 1924–1925; professor of English, 1925–   ; chairman, Department of English, 1935–1947. Member: American Association of Arts and Letters; Phi Beta Kappa. Managing Editor of *Modern Philology*, 1930–   . Studies of literary history: *The Vogue of Guy of Warwick from the Close of the Middle Ages to the Romantic Revival* (1915); *The Vogue of Medieval Chivalric Romance during the English Renaissance* (1919). Compiler: *A Census of British Newspapers and Periodicals, 1620–1800* (with F. B. Kaye and M. E. Prior, 1927). Editor: *The English Familiar Essay* (with W. F. Bryan, 1916); *New Essays by Oliver Goldsmith* (1927); *A Collection of English Poems: 1660–1800* (1932); *Critics and Criticism: Ancient and Modern* (1951).

DUPEE, FREDERICK W. Born: Chicago, Illinois, 1904. Educated: Yale University, Ph. B., 1927; Columbia University Graduate School. Teacher of English, Bowdoin College, 1927–1929; Bard College, 1944–1948; instructor of English, Columbia University, 1941–1944; assistant professor of English, 1948–   . An associate editor of *Partisan Review*, 1937–1940. Editor: *The Question of Henry James* (1945). Critical biography: *Henry James* (1951).

ELIOT, THOMAS STEARNS. Born: St. Louis, Missouri, 1888. Educated: Smith Academy, St. Louis, 1898–1905; Milton Academy, Mass., 1905–1906; Harvard University, B.A., 1909, M.A., 1910; The Sorbonne, 1910–1911; Merton College, Oxford, 1914–1915. Worked in London as teacher, editor, bank clerk. Assistant editor of *The Egoist*, 1917–1919. Founder and editor of *The Criterion*, 1922–1939. A director of Faber and Faber, Ltd., publishers, London, since 1923. Became a British subject in 1927. Held the Charles Eliot Norton professorship of poetry at Harvard, 1932–1933; delivered Page-Barbour Lectures, University of Virginia, 1933. Granted the Dial Award, 1922; Nobel Prize for Literature, 1948. LL.D., Edinburgh; Litt. D., Columbia, Cambridge, Bristol, Leeds, Harvard, Yale, Princeton, Oxford; Ph. D., Munich; D. ès Lettres, Aix-Marseilles. Honorary Fellow, Magdalene College, Cambridge. Fellow in American Letters, Library of Congress. Books of verse: *Prufrock and Other Observations* (1917); *Poems* (1919); *Ara Vos Prec* (1919); *Poems* (1920); *The Waste Land* (1922); *Poems: 1909–1925* (1925); *The Journey of the Magi* (1927); *A Song for Simeon* (1928); *Animula* (1929); *Ash-Wednesday* (1930); *Marina* (1930); *Triumphal March* (1931); *Poems: 1909–1935* (1936); *Old Possum's Book of Practical Cats* (1939); *Four Quartets* (1943). Books of criticism and speculation: *The Sacred Wood* (1920); *Homage to John Dryden* (1924); *For Launcelot Andrewes* (1928); *Shakespeare and the Stoicism of Seneca* (1928); *Dante* (1929); *Thoughts after Lambeth* (1931); *Charles Whibley: A Memoir* (1931); *Selected Essays: 1917–1932* (1932; new edition with additional essays, 1950); *John Dryden* (1932); *The Use of Poetry and the Use of Criticism* (1933); *After Strange Gods* (1934); *Elizabethan Essays* (1935); *Essays Ancient and Modern* (1936); *The Idea of a Christian Society* (1939); *Points of View* (edited by John Hayward, 1941); *The Music of Poetry* (1942); *The Classics and the Man of Letters* (1942); *What is a Classic?* (1945); *From Poe to Valéry* (1948). Plays in verse: *Sweeney Agonistes* (1932); *The Rock* (coauthor, 1934); *Murder in the Cathedral* (1935); *The Family Reunion* (1939); *The Cocktail Party* (1950). Translations: *Anabase* by St. John Perse (1930; new edition, 1949). Editor: *Seneca: His Tenne Tragedies* (1927); John Dryden's *Of Dramatick Poesie* (1928); *Selected Poems* by Ezra Pound (1928); Samuel Johnson's *London: A Poem, and The Vanity of Human Wishes* (1930); Baudelaire's *Intimate Journals* (1930); *Selected Poems* by Marianne Moore (1935); *Nightwood* by Djuna Barnes (1937); *Introducing James Joyce* (1941), etc. Enquiry: *Notes Towards the Definition of Culture* (1948).

FERGUSSON, FRANCIS. Born: Albuquerque, New Mexico, 1904. Educated: Harvard University, 1921–1923; Oxford University (Rhodes Scholar), B.A., 1926. Associate director of the American Laboratory Theatre, New York, 1926–1930; drama critic of *The Bookman*, 1930–1932. Lecturer and executive secretary, New School for Social Research, 1932–1934; professor of Humanities and Drama, Bennington College, 1934–1947; member of the Institute for Advanced Study, Princeton, 1948–1949; associate professor of literature, Princeton University, 1949–   . Translator: *The Electra of Sophocles* (1937). Editor: *Exiles* by James Joyce (1946). Book of criticism: *The Idea of a Theatre* (1949).

GREGORY, HORACE. Born: Milwaukee, Wisconsin, 1898. Educated: German-English Academy, Milwaukee, 1914–1919; Milwaukee School of Fine Arts, 1913–1916; University of Wisconsin, B.A., 1923. Lecturer in English, Sarah Lawrence College, 1934–   . Awarded Lyric Prize by *Poetry*, 1928; Helen Haire Levinson Prize, 1934; Russell Loines Award for poetry, American Institute of Arts and Letters, 1942. Books of verse: *Chelsea Rooming House* (1930); *No Retreat* (1933); *Chorus for Survival* (1935); *Poems: 1930–1940* (1941). Editor: *New Letters in America* (1937); *The Portable Sherwood Anderson* (1948). Translation: *The Poems of Catullus* (1931). Books of criticism: *Pilgrim of the Apocalypse: A Critical Study of D. H. Lawrence* (1933); *The Shield of Achilles: Essays on Poetry and Beliefs* (1944); *A History of American Poetry: 1900–1940* (with Marya Zaturenska, 1946).

HOWELLS, WILLIAM DEAN. Born: Martin's Ferry, Belmont Co., Ohio, 1837. Died, 1920. Common schooling in Ohio; studied Latin, German, Spanish, and literature alone. Reporter and editorial writer, *Ohio State Journal*, 1856–1861. Went to Boston, 1860. Campaign biography of Lincoln, 1860. U.S. consul in Venice, Italy, 1861–1865. Assistant on *The Nation* under E. L. Godkin, 1865; subeditor, *The Atlantic Monthly*, under James T. Fields, 1866–1871; editor-in-chief, 1871–1881; associated with Harper & Brothers, 1885–1916; wrote "Editor's Study," *Harper's Monthly*, 1886–1891; moved to New York, 1891; editor, *Cosmopolitan Magazine*, 1891–1892; wrote "Easy Chair," *Harper's Monthly Magazine*, 1900–1920. Novelist, essayist, critic, dramatist, editor, diplomat. Refused professorships at Yale, Harvard, Johns Hopkins universities. Honorary degrees from Oxford, Yale, Harvard, Columbia, etc. Author of *Their Wedding Journey, A Foregone Conclusion, The Lady of Aroostook, A Modern Instance, The Rise of Silas Lapham, In-*

dian Summer, A Hazard of New Fortunes, A Traveler from Altruria, The Kentons, The Leatherwood God, and other novels. Books of criticism and literary reminiscence: *Modern Italian Poets* (1887); *Criticism and Fiction* (1891); *My Literary Passions* (1895); *Impressions and Experiences* (1896); *Literary Friends and Acquaintances* (1900); *Heroines of Fiction* (1901); *Literature and Life* (1902); *My Mark Twain* (1910); *Imaginary Interviews* (1910). Books of travel, verse, autobiography.

HUNEKER, JAMES GIBBONS. Born: Philadelphia, 1860. Died in 1921. Educated: Roth's Military Academy, Philadelphia; Philadelphia Law Academy; the Sorbonne, Paris; music under Michael Cross, Georges Matthias, Rafael Joseffy. Assistant to Rafael Joseffy in piano department of the National Conservatory of Music, New York, 1881–1891. Wrote a column on music for the *Musical Courier,* New York, 1887–1902. Music critic for the *New York Evening Recorder,* 1891–1895; for the *Morning Advertiser,* 1895–1897; for the *New York Sun,* 1900–1902; drama critic, *New York Sun,* 1902–1917; music critic, *Philadelphia Press,* 1917; *New York Times,* 1918; *New York World,* 1919–1921. Member of the National Institute of Arts and Letters; officer of Legion of Honor. Books of literary and musical criticism: *Mezzotints in Modern Music* (1899); *Chopin: The Man and His Music* (1900); *Melomaniacs* (1902); *Overtones* (1904); *Iconoclasts: A Book of Dramatists* (1905); *Visionaries* (1905); *Egoists: A Book of Supermen* (1909); *Promenades of an Impressionist* (1910); *Franz Liszt* (1911); *The Pathos of Distance* (1913); *Old Fogy* (1913); *Ivory, Apes, and Peacocks* (1915); *The New Cosmopolis* (1915); *Unicorns* (1917); *Bedouins* (1920); *Variations* (1921); *Essays* (edited by H. L. Mencken, 1929). Fiction: *Painted Veils* (1920). Autobiography: *Steeplejack* (1920).

HYMAN, STANLEY EDGAR. Born: New York City, 1919. Educated: Syracuse University, B.A., 1940. Editorial assistant, *The New Republic,* 1940; staff writer, *The New Yorker,* 1940–   . Teacher of literary criticism and folk literature, Bennington College, 1945–1946. Book of criticism: *The Armed Vision: A Study in the Methods of Modern Literary Criticism* (1948).

JAMES, HENRY. Born: New York City, 1843. Died in London in 1916. Educated in schools in New York, France, Switzerland, Germany; Harvard Law School, 1862–1863. Began adult travels to Europe, 1869; began residence in Europe and England, 1876; settled in England, 1883; adopted British citizenship, 1915. Novelist, writer of tales, critic, dramatist, writer of books of travel, autobiography, biography. Author of *Roderick Hudson, The American, The Portrait of a Lady, The Bostonians, The Princess Casamassima, The Tragic Muse, What Maisie Knew, The Awkward Age, The Spoils of Poynton, The Sacred Fount, The Ambassadors, The Wings of the Dove, The Golden Bowl,* etc. Books of literary criticism: *French Poets and Novelists* (1878); *Hawthorne* (1879); *Partial Portraits* (1888); *Essays in London and Elsewhere* (1893); *Notes on Novelists with Some Other Notes* (1914); *Views and Reviews* (collection of early essays and reviews, edited by LeRoy Phillips, 1908); *Notes and Reviews* (collection of early reviews, edited by Pierre de Chaignon la Rose, 1921); *The Art of the Novel* (collection of prefaces for his works in the New York Edition of 1907–1909; 1934); *The Scenic Art: Notes on Acting and the Drama: 1872–1901* (edited by Allan Wade, 1948). Critical biography: *William Wetmore Story and His Friends* (1903). Art criticism: *Picture and Text* (1893). Literary journal: *The Notebooks of Henry James* (edited by F. O. Matthiessen and Kenneth B. Murdock, 1947).

JARRELL, RANDALL. Born: Nashville, Tennessee, 1914. Educated: Vanderbilt University, B.S., 1936; M.A., 1939. Instructor in English, University of Texas, 1938–1942; at Kenyon College; at Sarah Lawrence College, 1946–1947; at Salzburg Seminar in American Civilization, 1949; associate professor, Woman's College of University of North Carolina, 1947– . Acting literary editor, *The Nation*, 1946–1947. Books of verse: *Blood for a Stranger* (1942); *Little Friend, Little Friend* (1945); *Losses* (1948). Editor: *Selected Poems of William Carlos Williams* (1949).

KAZIN, ALFRED. Born: Brooklyn, New York, 1915. Educated: College of the City of New York, B.S., 1935; Columbia University, M.A., 1938. Tutor in English, College of the City of New York, 1937–1939 (summers); member of the Department of English, 1939–1942; tutor in English, Queen's College, New York, 1940; lecturer, New School for Social Research, 1941–1942, 1948–1949; lecturer, Black Mountain College, 1944. Literary editor of *The New Republic*, 1942–1943; contributing editor, 1943–1945; contributing editor, *Fortune*, 1943–1944. Visiting lecturer, Quinzaine Anglo-Américaine, Paris, 1945; visiting professor, University of Minnesota, summer 1946; lecturer, John L. Elliott Institute, 1946; Salzburg Seminar in American Studies, summer 1947. Guggenheim Fellowships, 1940, 1947. Rockefeller Foundation Fellowship for study of trade-union and army popular education movements in Great Britain, 1945. Award from National Institute of Arts and Letters, 1947. Editor: *The Portable William Blake* (1946), *Crime and Punishment by Dostoevsky* (1946), *A Raw Youth* by Dostoevsky (1946). Book of criticism: *On Native Grounds: An Interpretation of Modern American Prose Literature* (1942).

KRUTCH, JOSEPH WOOD. Born: Knoxville, Tennessee, 1893. Educated: University of Tennessee, B.A., 1915; Columbia University, M.A., 1916; Ph. D., 1923. Assistant professor of English, Brooklyn Polytechnic Institute, 1920–1923; professor of English, Vassar College, 1924–1925; assistant professor, School of Journalism, Columbia University, 1925–1931; associate professor, 1931–1937; professor, 1937–1943; lecturer, New School for Social Research, 1932–1935; Brander Matthews Professor of dramatic literature, at Columbia University, 1943– . Dramatic critic of *The Nation* since 1924; associate editor, 1924–1932; member of board of editors, 1932–1937. Member of the editorial board of the Literary Guild, 1925–1935. Guggenheim Fellowship, 1930. Books of criticism and literary history: *Comedy and Conscience after the Restoration* (1924); *Edgar Allan Poe: A Study in Genius* (1926); *Five Masters* (1930); *Experience and Art*

(1932); *The American Drama since 1918* (1939); *Samuel Johnson* (1944); *Henry David Thoreau* (1948). Other books: *The Modern Temper* (1929); *Was Europe a Success?* (1934); *The Twelve Seasons* (1949).

LEVIN, HARRY TUCHMAN. Born: Minneapolis, Minnesota, 1912. Educated: Harvard University, B.A., 1933; University of Paris, 1934. Faculty instructor and tutor in English, Harvard University, 1939–1944; associate professor of English, 1944–1948; professor of English, 1948–   ; chairman of the Department of Comparative Literature, 1947–   . Junior fellow, Society of Fellows, Harvard University, 1934–1939; senior fellow, 1947–   . Guggenheim Fellowship, 1943. Editor: *Selected Works of Ben Jonson* (1938); *A Satire against Mankind, and Other Poems* by the Earl of Rochester (1942); *Three Tales* by Flaubert (1944); *The Portable James Joyce* (1945). Books: *The Broken Column: A Study in Romantic Hellenism* (1931); *James Joyce: A Critical Introduction* (1941); *Toward Stendhal* (1945); *Toward Balzac* (1947). In preparation: *The Gates of Horn*, a study of the classic French novel.

LOVETT, ROBERT MORSS. Born: Boston, Massachusetts, 1870. Educated: Boston Latin School; Harvard University, B.A., 1892. Assistant and instructor in English, Harvard University, 1892–1893; instructor of English, University of Chicago, 1893–1896; assistant professor, 1896–1904; associate professor, 1904–1909; professor of English, 1909–1936. Dean in junior colleges, University of Chicago, 1903–1907; dean of junior colleges, 1907–1920. Associate Editor, *The Dial*, 1918–1919; Associate editor, *The New Republic*, 1921–1940. Government Secretary, Virgin Islands, 1939–1943. Visiting professor of English, University of Puerto Rico, 1944; visiting professor at universities of Colorado, Fisk, Kansas City, etc. Editor: *Selected Poems of William Vaughn Moody* (1930); *The College Reader* (with Howard Mumford Jones, 1937), etc. Novels: *Richard Gresham* (1904); *A Winged Victory* (1907). Play: *Cowards* (1914). Books of criticism and literary history: *A History of English Literature* (with William Vaughn Moody, 1902); *A First View of English Literature* (with W. V. Moody, 1905); *Edith Wharton* (1925); *A Preface to Fiction* (1930); *A History of the Novel in English* (with Helen Sard Hughes, 1932). Autobiography: *All Our Years* (1948).

MATTHIESSEN, FRANCIS OTTO. Born: Pasadena, California, 1902. Died in 1950. Educated: Hackley School, Tarrytown, N.Y., 1914–1918; Yale University, B.A., 1923; Oxford University (Rhodes Scholar, New College), B. Litt., 1925; Harvard, M.A., 1926; Ph. D., 1927. D. Litt., Princeton University, 1947. Instructor of English, Yale University, 1927–1929; instructor and tutor, Harvard University, 1929–1930; assistant professor, 1930–1934; associate professor, 1934–1942; professor of English and American Literature, 1942–1950. Chairman, Board of Tutors, Harvard, 1931–1949; senior tutor, Eliot House, 1931–1933. Alexander Lecturer, University of Toronto, 1944; visiting professor, Charles University, Prague, 1947; Salzburg Seminar in American Studies, 1947; senior fellow, Kenyon School of English, 1948–1950. Member of editorial board, *The New England Quarterly*, 1937–1940. Member, Massachusetts Civil Liberties Union (president, 1940–1942); of the Harvard Teachers Union, 1935–1950. Editor: *Stories of Writers and Artists* by Henry James (1944); *Selected Poems of Herman Melville* (1944); *The American Novels and Stories of Henry James* (1947); *The Notebooks of Henry James* (with Kenneth B. Murdock, 1947); *The Oxford Book of American Verse* (1950). Books of criticism and literary history: *Sarah Orne Jewett* (1929); *Translation: An Elizabethan Art* (1931); *The Achievement of T. S. Eliot* (1935; new edition, 1947); *American Renaissance: Art and Expression in the Age of Emerson and Whitman* (1941); *Henry James: The Major Phase* (1944); *Russell Cheney: A Record of his Work* (1947); *The James Family* (1947); *Theodore Dreiser* (to be published posthumously). Book of social and political observation: *From the Heart of Europe* (1948).

MENCKEN, HENRY LOUIS. Born: Baltimore, Maryland, 1880. Educated: private schools in Baltimore; Baltimore Polytechnic, graduated, 1896. Reporter, *Baltimore Morning Herald*, 1899; city editor, 1903–1905; editor, *Baltimore Evening Herald*, 1905–1906; on staff of the *Baltimore Sun*, 1906–1910; of *Evening Sun*, 1910–1917, 1920–1935; of both *Sunpapers*, 1936–1941. Literary critic of *The Smart Set*, 1908–1923; coeditor, 1914–1923. Editor of *The American Mercury*, 1924–1933. Books of criticism: *George Bernard Shaw* (1905); *The Philosophy of Friedrich Nietzsche* (1908); *A Book of Burlesques* (1916); *A Book of Prefaces* (1917); *Damn: A Book of Calumny* (1918); *In Defense of Women* (1918); *Prejudices* (six series, 1919–1927); *Selected Prejudices* (1927); *James Branch Cabell* (1927); *A Mencken Chrestomathy* (1949). Books of speculative prose: *Notes on Democracy* (1926); *Treatise on the Gods* (1930); *Treatise on Right and Wrong* (1934). Verse: *Ventures into Verse* (1903). Plays: *The Artist* (1912); *Heliogabalus* (with George Jean Nathan, 1920). Coauthor of *Men vs. the Man* (1910); *Europe after 8:15* (1914); *A Little Book in C Major* (1916); *The American Credo* (1920); *Americana* (1925–26). Linguistic history: *The American Language* (1918; fourth revised edition, 1936); *Supplement I* (1945); *Supplement II* (1948). Dictionary: *A New Dictionary of Quotations* (1942). Autobiographies: *Happy Days* (1940); *Newspaper Days* (1941); *Heathen Days* (1943); *The Days of H. L. Mencken* (1947). Fiction: *Christmas Story* (1946). Editor: *We Moderns* by Edwin Muir (1920); *Essays* by James Gibbons Huneker (1929); *The American Democrat* by James Fenimore Cooper (1931).

MOORE, MARIANNE CRAIG. Born: St. Louis, Missouri, 1887. Educated: Metzger Institute, Carlisle, Penn., 1896–1905; Bryn Mawr College, B.A., 1909; Carlisle Commercial College, 1910. Teacher, United States Indian School, Carlisle, 1911–1915; assistant, Hudson Park Branch, New York Public Library, 1919–1925. Editor of *The Dial*, 1925–1929. Granted the Dial Award, 1924; Levinson Prize (*Poetry*), 1933; Ernest Hartsock Memorial Prize, 1935; Shelley Memorial Award, 1940; *Contemporary Poetry's* Poetry Prize, 1944; Harriet Monroe Award in Poetry (University of Chicago), 1944; Guggenheim Fellowship, 1945; National Institute of Arts and Letters Award, 1946. Books of verse: *Poems* (1921); *Observations* (1924); *Selected Poems* (1935); *The Pangolin and Other Verse* (1936); *What Are Years?* (1941); *Nevertheless* (1944); *Collected Poems* (1951).

MORE, PAUL ELMER. Born: St. Louis, Missouri, 1864. Died in 1937. Educated: Washington University, B.A., 1887; M.A., 1892; Harvard University, M.A., 1893. Taught Sanscrit at Harvard, 1894–1895; assistant professor of Sanscrit, Bryn Mawr College, 1895–1897. Literary editor of *The Independent*, 1901; literary editor of *The New York Evening Post*, 1903; editor of *The Nation*, 1909–14. Retired to Princeton in 1914; sometime lecturer on Plato in the Department of Classics, Princeton University. Books of critical and literary essays: *Shelburne Essays* (eleven volumes, 1904–1921, of which the last four carried individual titles: *The Drift of Romanticism* [1913]; *Aristocracy and Justice* [1915]; *With the Wits* [1919]; *A New England Group and Others* [1921]); *The New Shelburne Essays: The Demon of the Absolute* (1928); *The Skeptical Approach to Religion* (1934); *On Being Human* (1936); *Selected Shelburne Essays* (1935). Poems: *Helena* (1890). Novel: *The Jessica Letters* (with Corra May Harris, 1904). Biography: *Benjamin Franklin* (1900). Books of philosophical and religious enquiry: *Nietzsche* (1912); *Platonism* (1917); *The Religion of Plato* (1921); *Hellenistic Philosophies* (1923); *The Christ of the New Testament* (1924); *Christ the Word* (1927); *The Catholic Faith* (1931).

PHILLIPS, WILLIAM. Born: New York City, 1907. Educated: College of the City of New York, B.A., 1928; New York University, M.A., 1930. Taught English at New York University, 1929–1932. An editor of *Partisan Review* since its founding in 1934. Editor: *Great American Short Novels* (1946); *The Partisan Reader: Ten Years of Partisan Review: 1934–1944* (with Philip Rahv, 1946).

PORTER, KATHERINE ANNE. Born: Indian Creek, Texas, 1894. Educated: private schools in Texas and New Orleans. Lecturer and consultant, Olivet College Writers' Conference, 1937; Fellow in Regional American Literature, Library of Congress, 1944; Fellow in American Letters, Library of Congress; writer-in-residence and lecturer on literature, Stanford University, 1948–1949; lecturer in English, University of Chicago, 1951; lecturer at numerous colleges and universities. Has lived and traveled in Mexico, Germany, France. Guggenheim Fellowships, 1931, 1938; Book of the Month Club Award, 1937; first annual gold medal for literature, Society for Libraries of New York University, 1940. Books of fiction: *Flowering Judas* (1930; new edition, 1935); *Hacienda* (1934); *Noon Wine* (1937); *Pale Horse, Pale Rider* (1939); *The Leaning Tower* (1944). Translation: *The Itching Parrot* (from the Spanish, 1942). Editor: *Katherine Anne Porter's French Song Book* (1933); *Fiesta in November* (1942).

POUND, EZRA. Born: Hailey, Idaho, 1885. Educated: University of Pennsylvania, 1901–1903; Hamilton College, Ph. B., 1905; University of Pennsylvania, M.A., 1906. "Instructor with professorial functions," University of Pennsylvania, 1905–1907; instructor at Wabash College, Crawfordsville, Indiana, for four months, 1907–1908. To Europe in 1908, traveling and living in Spain, Italy, France, England, France, Italy, 1908–1945. Returned to America, 1938, and again in 1945. Associate editor (European correspondent) of *Poetry*, 1912–1918; London editor of *The Little Review*, 1917–1919; editor of *The Exile*, 1927–1928.

Books of verse: *A Lume Spento* (1908); *Personae* (1909); *Exultations* (1909); *Provenca* (1910); *Canzoni* (1911); *Ripostes* (1912); *Cathay* (1915); *Lustra* (1916); *Lustra and Other Poems* (1917); *Quia Pauper Amavi* (1919); *Umbra* (1920); *Hugh Selwyn Mauberley* (1920); *Cantos I–XVI* (1925); *Personae: Collected Poems* (1926); *Cantos XVII–XXVII* (1928); *A Draft of XXX Cantos* (1930); *Eleven New Cantos XXXI–LXI* (1934); *The Fifth Decad of Cantos* (1937); *Cantos LII–LXXI* (1940); *The Pisan Cantos* (1948); *The Cantos* (complete edition, 1948). Translations: *Sonnets and Ballate of Guido Cavalcanti* (1912, 1913, complete edition 1932); *Certain Noble Plays of Japan* (1916); *Noh, or Accomplishment* (1917); *Twelve Dialogues of Fontenelle* (1917); *Physique de l'Amour* by Remy de Gourmont (1921); *The Ta Hio* (1920); *The Analects of Confucius* (1949–1950). Operas: *Le Testament* (1919–1921; partial performance, Paris, 1926); *Guido Cavalcanti* (1931–1932). Books of criticism and literary enquiry: *The Spirit of Romance* (1910); *Gaudier Brzeska* (1916); *Pavannes and Divisions* (1918); *Instigations* (1920); *Indiscretions* (1923); *Antheil and the Treatise on Harmony* (1924); *Imaginary Letters* (1930); *How To Read* (1931); *Prolegomena* (1932); *The ABC of Reading* (1934); *Make It New* (1934); *Polite Essays* (1937); *Digest of the Analects* (1937); *Guide to Kulchur* (1938; in American edition: *Culture*, 1939); *Patria Mia* (1950). Books on economics and politics: *The ABC of Economics* (1933); *Social Credit and Impact* (1935); *Jefferson and/or Mussolini* (1935); *What is Money For?* (1938). Editor: *Des Imagistes* (1914); *Catholic Anthology* (1915); *Letters of John Butler Yeats* (1917); *Profile* (1932); *Active Anthology* (1933); *The Chinese Written Character* by Ernest Fenollosa (1936), etc; *The Letters of Ezra Pound* (1950).

RAHV, PHILIP. Born: Kupin, Ukraine, 1908. Came to America, 1922. Educated: elementary and high school, Providence, R.I. An editor of *Partisan Review* since 1934. Editor: *The Great Short Novels of Henry James* (1944); *The Bostonians* by Henry James (1945); *The Short Novels of Tolstoy* (1946); *The Partisan Reader: Ten Years of Partisan Review: 1934–44* (with William Phillips, 1946); *Discovery of Europe: The Story of American Experience in the Old World* (1947). Book of criticism: *Image and Idea: Fourteen Essays on Literary Themes* (1949).

RANSOM, JOHN CROWE. Born: Pulaski, Tennessee, 1888. Educated: Vanderbilt University, B.A., 1909; Christ Church, Oxford University (Rhodes Scholar), B.A., 1913. Member of the faculty, Department of English, Vanderbilt University, 1914–1937; professor of English 1927–1937; Carnegie Professor of English, Kenyon College, 1937–   . Senior Fellow, at Kenyon School of English, 1948–   . Lecturer and visiting professor, summers, at University of New Mexico, University of Florida, University of Kentucky, University of Texas, Women's College of University of North Carolina. Bread Loaf School of English, Colorado State Teachers' College, Peabody College for Teachers. A founder and editor of *The Fugitive*, 1922–1925; editor of *The Kenyon Review*, 1939–   . Guggenheim Fellowship, 1931. Verse: *Poems About God* (1919); *Grace After Meat* (1924); *Chills and Fever* (1924); *Two Gentlemen in Bonds* (1926); *Selected*

Poems (1945). Book of speculative prose: *God Without Thunder* (1930). Books of literary criticism: *The World's Body* (1938); *The New Criticism* (1941). Co-author: *I'll Take My Stand* (1930); *Who Owns America?* (1936); *The Intent of the Critic* (1941).

RICE, PHILIP BLAIR. Born: Martinsville, Indiana, 1904. Educated: University of Illinois; University of Indiana, B.A., 1925; Oxford University (Rhodes Scholar), B.A., 1928. Newspaper work in Paris and Cincinnati, 1928–1930. Instructor in philosophy, University of Cincinnati, 1930–1937; assistant professor, 1937–1938; Guy Despard Gaff associate professor of philosophy and chairman of department, Kenyon College, 1938–1948; now professor of philosophy. Associate editor, *The Kenyon Review,* 1939–　.

SANTAYANA, GEORGE. Born: Madrid, Spain, 1863. Came to the United States in 1872. Educated: Latin School, Boston; Harvard University, B.A., 1886; University of Berlin, 1886–1888; King's College, Cambridge University, 1896–1897. Member and professor of Philosophy, Harvard University, 1889–1912. Hyde Lecturer at the Sorbonne, 1905–1906. Returned to Europe to live in 1914—England, France, Italy. Books of philosophic and critical enquiry: *The Sense of Beauty* (1896); *Interpretations of Poetry and Religion* (1900); *The Life of Reason: Reason and Common Sense* (1905); *Reason in Society* (1905); *Reason in Religion* (1905); *Reason in Art* (1905); *Reason in Science* (1906); *Three Philosophical Poets: Lucretius, Dante, Goethe* (1910); *Winds of Doctrine* (1913); *Egoism in German Philosophy* (1916); *Philosophical Opinion in America* (1918); *Character and Opinion in the United States* (1920); *Soliloquies in England, and Later Soliloquies* (1922); *Skepticism and Animal Faith* (1923); *Dialogues in Limbo* (1925); *Platonism and the Spiritual Life* (1927); *The Realm of Essence* (1927); *The Realm of Matter* (1930); *The Genteel Tradition at Bay* (1931); *Some Turns of Thought in Modern Philosophy* (1933); *Obiter Dicta: Lectures, Essays, and Reviews* (1936); *The Realm of Truth* (1937); *The Realm of Spirit* (1940); *The Realms of Being* (1942); *The Idea of Christ in the Gospels, or God in Man* (1946); *Atoms of Thought* (1950). Verse: *Sonnets and Other Verse* (1894); *Lucifer, or The Heavenly Truce* (1898; new edition, 1924); *Poems* (1922). Novel: *The Last Puritan* (1935). Memoirs: *Persons and Places* (1944); *The Middle Span* (1945). *The Works of George Santayana* (Triton Edition, 14 volumes, 1936–37).

SCHWARTZ, DELMORE. Born: Brooklyn, N.Y., 1913. Educated: New York University, B.A., 1935; studied at Columbia, Wisconsin, and Harvard universities. Instructor in English, Harvard University, 1940–1945; assistant professor of English Composition, 1946–1947. Associate editor of *Partisan Review,* 1943–　. Guggenheim Fellowship, 1939. Books of verse and narrative: *In Dreams Begin Responsibilities* (1938); *Shenandoah* (1941); *Genesis: Book One* (1943); *The World Is a Wedding* (1948); *Vaudeville for a Princess* (1950). In preparation: books on T. S. Eliot and F. Scott Fitzgerald.

SPENCER, THEODORE. Born: Villa Nova, Pennsylvania, 1902. Died in 1949. Educated: Princeton University, B.A., 1923; Cambridge University, B.A., 1925; Harvard University, Ph. D., 1928. Instructor and tutor, in English, Harvard, 1927–1933; assistant professor of English, 1933–1939; appointed lecturer, Cambridge University, 1939–1940; associate professor of English, Harvard University, 1940–1946; Boylston professor of Rhetoric and Oratory, 1946–1949. Lowell lecturer, Boston, 1942. Phi Beta Kappa poet, William and Mary College, 1942; Tufts College, 1943; Harvard, 1943. Editor: *A Garland for John Donne* (1931); *Stephen Hero* by James Joyce (1944). Books of verse: *The Paradox in the Circle* (1941); *The World in Your Hand* (1943); *An Act of Life* (1944); *Poems: 1940–1947* (1948). Books of criticism and literary history: *Death and Elizabethan Tragedy* (1936); *Studies in Metaphysical Poetry* (with Mark Van Doren, 1939); *Shakespeare and the Nature of Man* (1942).

SPINGARN, JOEL ELIAS. Born: New York City, 1875. Died in 1939. Educated: Columbia University, B.A., 1895; Ph. D., 1899; Harvard University, 1895–1896. Assistant and tutor in Comparative Literature, Columbia University, 1899–1909; adjunct professor, 1904; professor, 1909–1911. Engaged in political, military, and journalistic activities, 1911–1923; a founder and adviser of Harcourt, Brace and Co., 1919–1932; chairman of directors, Association for the Advancement of Colored Peoples, 1913–1919, treasurer until 1930, president until 1939. Editor: *Critical Essays of the Seventeenth Century* (1908–1909); *Essays of Sir William Temple* (1909); *A Renaissance Courtesy Book: The Galateo of Della Casa* (1914); *Goethe's Literary Essays* (1921); *Civilization in the United States* (1923); *Criticism in America* (1924); *Troutbeck Leaflets* (1924–1926); *The European Library* (1920–1925). Books of criticism and literary history: *A History of Literary Criticism in the Renaissance* (1899; revised edition, 1908); *The New Criticism* (1911); *Creative Criticism and Other Essays* (1917; revised edition, 1931). Verse: *The New Hesperides* (1911); *Poems* (1924). Controversy: *A Question of Academic Freedom* (1911); *A Spingarn Enchiridion* (1929).

TATE, (JOHN ORLEY) ALLEN. Born: Winchester, Clark County, Kentucky, 1899. Educated: schools in Louisville and Nashville; Georgetown University; University of Virginia; Vanderbilt University, B.A., 1922. A founder and editor of *The Fugitive*, 1922–1925. Guggenheim Fellowship, 1928–1930. Lecturer on English Literature, Southwestern University, 1934–1936; professor of English, Woman's College of the University of North Carolina, 1938–1939; resident fellow, Creative Arts Program, Princeton University, 1939–1942; fellow in American Letters, Library of Congress, 1943–   ; Chair of Poetry, Library of Congress, 1943–1944; editor, Henry Holt and Co., 1946–1948; lecturer in English, New York University, 1947–   ; visiting professor of Humanities, University of Chicago, 1949; fellow, Kenyon School of English, 1949; lecturer at writers' conferences, universities of Colorado, Utah, Indiana, Kansas, Olivet College, etc. Southern editor, *The Hound and Horn*, 1932–1934; editor, *The Sewanee Review*, 1944–1946. Caroline Sinkler Prize of the Poetry Society of South Carolina, 1928; Midland Authors' Prize (*Poetry*), 1933; award of American Institute of Arts and

Letters, 1948. Books of verse: Mr. *Pope and Other Poems* (1928); *Three Poems* (1930); *Poems: 1928–31* (1932); *The Mediterranean and Other Poems* (1936); *Selected Poems* (1937); *The Winter Sea* (1944); *Poems: 1922–47* (1948). Translator: *The Vigil of Venus* (1943). Novel: *The Fathers* (1938). Editor: *I'll Take My Stand* (with others, 1930); *Who Owns America?* (with Herbert Agar, 1936); *Invitation to Learning* (with Huntington Cairns and Mark Van Doren, 1941); *Princeton Verse Between Two Wars* (1942); *The Language of Poetry* (1942); *American Harvest* (with J. P. Bishop, 1942); *A Southern Vanguard* (1947); *The House of Fiction* (with Caroline Gordon, 1950). Books of criticism: *Reactionary Essays on Poetry and Ideas* (1936); *Reason in Madness: Critical Essays* (1941); *On the Limits of Poetry: Selected Essays 1928–48* (1948); *The Hovering Fly* (1949).

TRILLING, LIONEL. Born: New York City, 1905. Educated: Columbia University, B.A., 1925; M.A., 1926; Ph. D., 1938. Instructor in English, University of Wisconsin, 1926–1927; instructor in English, Hunter College, 1927–1930; instructor in English, Columbia University, 1931–1938; assistant professor, 1938–1943; associate professor, 1943–1948; professor since 1948. Advisory editor, *The Kenyon Review*, 1942– ; advisory editor, *Partisan Review*, 1946– ; member of board of editors, American Men of Letters Series. Editor: *The Great Gatsby* by F. Scott Fitzgerald (1945); *The Princess Casamassima* by Henry James (1948); *The Portable Matthew Arnold* (1949), etc. Books of criticism: *Matthew Arnold* (1939); *E. M. Forster* (1943); *The Liberal Imagination: Essays on Literature and Society* (1950). Novel: *The Middle of the Journey* (1947).

TROY, WILLIAM. Born: Chicago, Illinois, 1903. Educated: Yale University, B.A., 1925; Columbia University; University of Grenoble, France (American Field Service Fellowship, 1929–1930); the Sorbonne. Taught English at the University of New Hampshire and New York University, 1932–1935; a member of the faculty of the Department of English, Bennington College, 1935–1937, 1938–1946; lecturer on literature, New School for Social Research, 1946– . Film critic, *The Nation*, 1933–1935.

WARREN, AUSTIN. Born: Waltham, Massachusetts, 1899. Educated: Wesleyan University, Conn., B.A., 1920; Harvard University, M.A., 1922; Princeton University, Ph. D., 1926. Instructor in English, University of Kentucky, 1920–1921; instructor in English, University of Minnesota, 1922–1924; dean of St. Peter's School of Liberal and Humane Studies (summers), Hebron, Conn., 1922–1930; instructor in English, Boston University, 1926–1929; assistant and associate professor, 1929–1934; professor of English, 1934–1939; professor of English, University of Iowa, 1939–1948; professor of English, University of Michigan, 1948– . Fellow, American Council of Learned Societies. Guggenheim Fellowship, 1949. Associate editor of *The New England Quarterly*, 1937–1940, 1942–1946; associate editor of *American Literature*, 1940–1942. Books of criticism and literary history: *Alexander Pope as Critic and Humanist* (1929); *The Elder Henry James* (1934); *Richard Crashaw* (1939); *Rage for Order* (1948). Editor:

Hawthorne (American Writers Series, 1934). Coauthor: *Literary Scholarship* (1941); *Theory of Literature* (with René Wellek, 1948). In preparation: a study of John Donne.

WARREN, ROBERT PENN. Born: Guthrie, Kentucky, 1905. Educated: Vanderbilt University, B.A., 1925; University of California, M.A., 1927; Yale University, 1927–1928; Oxford University (Rhodes Scholar), B. Litt., 1930. Assistant professor, Southwestern University, 1930–1931; acting assistant professor of English, Vanderbilt University, 1931–1934; assistant professor of English, Louisiana State University, 1934–1936; associate professor, 1936–1942; professor of English, University of Minnesota, 1942. Chair of Poetry, Library of Congress, 1944–1945; Fellow in American Letters, Library of Congress, 1944. Visiting professor and consultant at writers' conferences at University of Iowa, Kenyon College, University of Colorado, etc. A founder and editor of *The Southern Review*, 1935–1942. Houghton, Mifflin Fellowship, 1936; Levinson Prize (*Poetry*), 1936; Caroline Sinkler Prize, Poetry Society of South Carolina, 1936; Guggenheim Fellowships, 1939 and 1947; Shelley Memorial Award, 1942; Pulitzer Prize in fiction, 1947. Books of verse: *Eleven Poems on the Same Theme* (1942); *Selected Poems* (1944). Novels and books of fiction: *Night Rider* (1939); *At Heaven's Gate* (1943); *All the King's Men* (1946); *Blackberry Winter* (1946); *The Circus in the Attic and Other Stories* (1947); *World Enough and Time* (1950). Books for literary study: *An Approach to Literature* (with Cleanth Brooks and Jack Purser, 1936 and 1938); *Understanding Poetry* (with Cleanth Brooks, 1938 and 1950); *Understanding Fiction* (with Cleanth Brooks, 1943). Editor: *A Southern Harvest* (1937); *The Rime of the Ancient Mariner* by S. T. Coleridge (1946).

WILSON, EDMUND. Born: Red Bank, New Jersey, 1895. Educated: Hill School, Pottstown, Pa.; Princeton University, B.A., 1916. On staff of *The New York Sun*, 1919–1920; managing editor of *Vanity Fair*, 1920–1921; associate and literary editor of *The New Republic*, 1926–1931; book reviewer of *The New Yorker*, 1944–1948, etc. Guggenheim Fellowship, 1935. Novels: *I Thought of Daisy* (1929); *Memoirs of Hecate County* (1946). Imaginative verse and prose: *The Undertaker's Garland* (with John Peale Bishop, 1922). Verse: *Poets, Farewell!* (1929). Plays: *This Room and This Gin and These Sandwiches* (1937); *The Little Blue Light* (1950). Miscellany: *Notebooks of Night* (1942). Books of travel and social reporting: *The American Jitters* (1932); *Travels in Two Democracies* (1936); *Europe without Baedeker* (1947). Political-cultural history: *To the Finland Station* (1940). Criticism and literary studies: *Discordant Encounters* (1927); *Axel's Castle: A Study of the Imaginative Literature of 1870–1930* (1931); *The Triple Thinkers* (1938; revised edition, 1948); *The Boys in the Back Room* (1941); *The Wound and the Bow* (1941); *The Shock of Recognition* (1943); *Classics and Commercials: A Literary Chronicle of the Forties* (1950).

WINTERS, (ARTHUR) YVOR. Born: Chicago, Illinois, 1900. Educated: high schools in Evanston and Chicago; University of Chicago, 1917–1919; University of Colorado, B.A., M.A., both 1925; Stanford University, Ph. D., 1934. Teacher of Spanish and French, University of Idaho, 1925–1927; instructor, assistant professor, and associate professor of English, Stanford University, 1927–1948; professor of English, 1948–   . A founder and editor of *The Gyroscope* (with Janet Lewis and Howard Baker), 1928–1929; regional editor (Western) of *The Hound and Horn*, 1932–1934. Fellow, Kenyon School of English, 1949. Editor: *Twelve Poets of the Pacific* (1937); *Poets of the Pacific: Second Series* (1949). Books of verse: *The Immobile Wind* (1921); *The Magpie's Shadow* (1922); *The Bare Hills* (1927); *The Proof* (1930); *The Journey and Other Poems* (1931); *Before Disaster* (1934); *Poems* (1940); *The Giant Weapon* (1943). Criticism: *Notes on the Mechanics of the Poetic Image: The Testament of a Stone* (1925); *Primitivism and Decadence: A Study of American Experimental Poetry* (1937); *Maule's Curse: Seven Studies in the History of American Obscurantism* (1938); *The Anatomy of Nonsense* (1943); *In Defense of Reason* (1947).

YOUNG, STARK. Born: Como, Mississippi, 1881. Educated: University of Mississippi, B.A., 1901; Columbia University, M.A., 1902. Instructor in English, University of Mississippi, 1904–1907; instructor in English, University of Texas, 1907–1910; professor of General Literature, 1910–1915; professor of English, Amherst College, 1915–1921. An associate editor and drama critic of *The New Republic*, 1921–1924, 1925–1947; associate editor of *Theatre Arts Monthly*, 1921–1940; drama critic of *The New York Times*, 1924–1925. Plays: *The Blind Man at the Window* (1906); *Guenevere* (1906); *Madretta Addio, The Twilight Saint, and other One-Act Plays* (1911); *Three Plays* (1919); *The Saint* (1924); *The Colonnade* (1926); *Rose Windows* (1926). Novels and fiction: *Heaven Trees* (1926); *The Torches Flare* (1927); *River House* (1929); *The Street of the Islands* (1930); *So Red the Rose* (1934); *Feliciana* (1935). Books of dramatic criticism: *The Flower in Drama* (1923); *The Three Fountains* (1924); *Glamour* (1925); *The Theatre* (1927); *Immortal Shadows* (1948).

APPENDIX V

A Supplementary List of Essays in Criticism: 1900–1950

THE following index of essays, articles, and reviews dates from about 1900 to the present day, and is designed both to supplement the essays printed in this book and to provide a program for the further study of modern American criticism. The list, though drastically selective, includes a wide variety of writing, ranging from popular literary journalism to historical and aesthetic scholarship. Both these types of material are shown, however, in a small number of selections, the largest part of the space being given to work of critical motivation and method. The writers listed are usually those who have shown some persistence and continuity of critical performance, though a few exceptions have been made in the case of articles of individual or special interest.

Included are discussions of the writer's and critic's roles in American life, of the function and problems of modern criticism, of its connections with political, social, scientific, and educational developments, and of its bearing on the modern cultural situation generally, as well as many discussions of specific authors and texts. Work in historical and philosophical scholarship has not as a rule been included except where it bears closely on the interests of criticism. From the work of each critic a small number of typical or relevant writings have been chosen. The reader will soon find his way to others, as well as to other critics who could not be included here. The articles listed are usually in American literary and critical journals, though a number written by Americans for foreign magazines have been admitted. Reference has also been made, in the case of critics of large output, to essays or revised versions of essays which have appeared more accessibly in book form.

The books listed in Appendices I, II, and IV take precedence over the writings in the present list as representing the work of their authors, and the reader should refer to those books in all cases. The student wishing seriously to trace the development of modern criticism in the United States will investigate the files of the magazines listed in Appendix III. Among these journals, the following will be found especially important in shaping the growth of contemporary American literature and criticism: *Accent, The American Mercury, The American Review, Broom, The Dial, The Freeman, The Fugitive, The Hound and Horn, The Hudson Review, The Kenyon Review, The Little Review, The Nation, The New Republic, New Directions, Partisan Review, Poetry: A Magazine of Verse, The Seven Arts, The Sewanee Review, The Smart Set, The Southern Review, The Symposium, Transition, The Western Review.*

The indexes and bibliographies named at the beginning of Appendix I will again be found useful in tracing further work by the critics listed below, and by others.

The titles of certain magazines in the following list have been abbreviated as follows (all others being printed in full):

A:	Accent	N:	The Nation
Am Merc:	The American Mercury	No Am:	The North American
Ant R:	The Antioch Review		Review
AR:	The American Review	NR:	The New Republic
AS:	The American Scholar	P:	Poetry: A Magazine of
At Mon:	The Atlantic Monthly		Verse
B:	The Bookman	PR:	Partisan Review
CE:	College English	RMR:	The Rocky Mountain
Century:	The Century Magazine		Review
D:	The Dial	Scribner's:	Scribner's Magazine
EHL:	English Literary History	Sew R:	The Sewanee Review
EJ:	The English Journal	Sou R:	The Southern Review
F:	The Forum	SRL:	The Saturday Review of
Harper's:	Harper's Monthly Maga-		Literature
	zine or Harper's Magazine	Sym:	The Symposium
HH:	The Hound and Horn	VQR:	The Virginia Quarterly
HR:	The Hudson Review		Review
KR:	The Kenyon Review	WR:	The Western Review
MP:	Modern Philology	YR:	The Yale Review (new
			series)

Aiken, Conrad, "John Keats," D, 78: 475–490 (June, 1925).

Aiken, Conrad, "The Novel as a Work of Art," D, 83: 41–44 (July, 1927).

Aiken, Conrad, "A Plea for Anonymity," NR, 84: 155–157 (September 18, 1935).

Aiken, Conrad, "A. E. Housman," NR, 89: 51 (November 11, 1936).

Aiken, Conrad, "William Faulkner," At Mon, 164: 650–654 (November, 1939).

Aiken, Conrad, "Back to Poetry," At Mon, 166: 217–223 (August, 1940).

Aiken, Conrad, "Poetry: What Direction?" NR, 104: 670–677 (May 12, 1941).

Aiken, Conrad, "American Writers Come of Age," At Mon, 169: 476–481 (April, 1942).

Anderson, Quentin, "Henry James and the New Jerusalem," KR, 8: 515–566 (Autumn, 1946).

Arendt, Hannah, "Franz Kafka: A Revaluation," PR, 11: 412–422 (Fall, 1944).

Arendt, Hannah, "What is Existenz Philosophy?" PR, 13: 34–56 (Winter, 1946).

Arendt, Hannah, "Beyond Personal Frustration: The Poetry of Bert Brecht," KR, 10: 304–312 (Spring, 1948).

Arvin, Newton, "Stuart Sherman," HH, 3: 304–313 (April–June, 1930).

Arvin, Newton, "Whitman's Individualism," NR, 71: 212–213 (July 6, 1932).

Arvin, Newton, "Society and Solitude," NR, 76: 284 (October 18, 1933).

Arvin, Newton, "Henry James and the Almighty Dollar," HH, 7: 434–443 (April–May, 1934).

Arvin, Newton, "Homage to Robert Herrick," NR, 82: 93–95 (March 6, 1935).

Arvin, Newton, "The Usableness of Howells," NR, 91: 227–228 (June 30, 1937).

Arvin, Newton, "Counterfeit Presentments," PR, 15: 673–680 (June, 1948).

Arvin, Newton, "Melville's Shorter Poems," PR, 16: 1034–1046 (October, 1949).

Auden, W. H., "Psychology and Art Today," in The Arts Today (edited by Geoffrey Grigson, London, 1935).

Auden, W. H., "Rilke in English," NR, 100: 135 (September 6, 1939).

Auden, W. H., "A Literary Transference" (on Hardy), Sou R, 6: 78–86 (Summer, 1940).

Auden, W. H., "Yeats: Master of Diction," SRL, 22: 14 (June 8, 1940).

Auden, W. H., "The Fabian Figaro" (on Shaw), Commonweal, 37: 12–13 (October 23, 1942).

Auden, W. H., "Preface to Kierkegaard," NR, 110: 683–684 plus (May 15, 1944).

Auden, W. H., "Some Notes on D. H. Lawrence," N, 164: 482–484 (April 26, 1947).

Auden, W. H., "Yeats as an Example," KR, 10: 163–181 (Spring, 1948).

Auden, W. H., "Henry James and the Artist in America," Harper's, 197: 36–40 (July, 1948).

Auden, W. H., "Criticism in a Mass Society," in The Intent of the Critic (edited by Donald A. Stauffer, Princeton, 1941).

Babbitt, Irving, "Are the English Critical?" N, 94: 282–284, 309–311 (March 21, 28, 1912).

Babbitt, Irving, "Bergson and Rousseau," N, 95: 452–455 (November 14, 1912).

Babbitt, Irving, "Humanists and Humanitarians," N, 10: 288–289 (September 2, 1915).

Babbitt, Irving, "Matthew Arnold," N, 105: 117–121 (August 2, 1917).

Babbitt, Irving, "Genius and Taste," N, 106: 138–141 (February 7, 1918).

Babbitt, Irving, "Croce and the Philosophy of Flux," YR, 14: 377–381 (January, 1925).

Babbitt, Irving, "Coleridge and Imagination," B, 70: 113–124 (October, 1929).

Babbitt, Irving, "What I Believe," F, 83: 80–87 (February, 1930).

Babbitt, Irving, "On Being Creative," B, 73: 113–122 (April, 1931).

Babbitt, Irving, "Style in a Democracy," SRL, 9: 325–326 (December 17, 1932). "The Primitivism of Wordsworth," "The Problem of the Imagination: Dr. Johnson," "Schiller as Aesthetic Theorist," "Julien Benda," and "The Critic and American Life" in On Being Creative and Other Essays (1932).

Baker, Howard, "Wallace Stevens and Other Poets," Sou R, 1: 373–396 (Autumn, 1935).

Baker, Howard, "The Contemporary Short Story," Sou R, 3: 576–596 (Winter, 1938).

Baker, Howard, "Hardy's Poetic Certitude," Sou R, 6: 49–63 (Summer, 1940).

Baker, Howard, "An Essay on Fiction with Examples," Sou R, 7: 385–406 (Autumn, 1941).

Baker, Howard, "Domes of Byzantium" (on Yeats), Sou R, 7: 639–652 (Winter, 1942).

Barrett, William, "The Talent of Jean-Paul Sartre," PR, 13: 237–246 (Spring, 1946).

Barrett, William, "The Resistance" (on the little magazine), PR, 13: 479–488 (September–October, 1946).

Barrett, William, "Writers and Madness," PR, 14: 5–22 (January–February, 1947).

Barrett, William, "Dialogue on Anxiety," PR, 14: 151–159 (March–April, 1947).

Barrett, William, "Temptations of St. Yvor" (on Yvor Winters), KR, 9: 532–551 (Autumn, 1947).

Barrett, William, "A Prize for Ezra Pound," PR, 16: 344–347 (April, 1949).

Barrett, William, "The Liberal Mind" (an exchange with Lionel Trilling and Richard Chase), PR, 16: 649–665 (June, 1949).

Barzun, Jacques, "To the Rescue of Romanticism," AS, 9: 147–158 (Spring, 1940).

Barzun, Jacques, "Truth and Poetry in Thomas Hardy," Sou R, 6: 179–192 (Summer, 1940).

Barzun, Jacques, "The American as Critic," SRL, 23: 30 plus (December 7, 1940).

Barzun, Jacques, "William James as Artist," NR, 108: 218–220 (February 15, 1943).

Barzun, Jacques, "Bernard Shaw in Twilight," KR, 5: 321–345 (Summer, 1943).

Barzun, Jacques, "James the Melodramatist," KR, 5: 508–521 (Autumn, 1943).

Barzun, Jacques, "The Critic as Statesman," At Mon, 178: 128–132 (August, 1946).

Barzun, Jacques, "Twenty-five Years of American Sensuality," N, 166: 355–357 (March 27, 1948).

Barzun, Jacques, "The Fetish of Form: An Example from Music," KR, 12: 86–98 (Winter, 1950).

Beach, Joseph Warren, "Decade of the Doomed," N, 131: 622 (December 3, 1930).

Beach, Joseph Warren, "The Novel from James to Joyce," N, 132: 634–636 (June 10, 1931).

Beach, Joseph Warren, "Thackeray Full Length," VQR, 22: 280–295 (Spring, 1946).

Beach, Joseph Warren, "The Sacred and Solitary Refuge" (on Henry James), Furioso, 3: 23–37 (Winter, 1947).

Beach, Joseph Warren, "Dos Passos: 1947," Sew R, 55: 406–418 (Summer, 1947).

Beach, Joseph Warren, "Sartre's Roads to Freedom," WR, 12: 180–191 (Spring, 1948).

Beach, Joseph Warren, "The Poems of Auden and the Prose Diathesis," VQR, 25: 365–383 (Summer, 1949).
> For Mr. Beach's more extended essays on modern English, European, and American novelists, see his books *The Twentieth Century Novel* (1932) and *American Fiction: 1920–40* (1941).

Bentley, Eric, "The Story of Stefan George," PR, 9: 321–330 (July–August, 1942).

Bentley, Eric, "The Theatres of Wagner and Ibsen," KR, 6: 542–569 (Autumn, 1944).

Bentley, Eric, "Romanticism: A Re-Evaluation," Ant R, 4: 6–20 (Spring, 1944).

Bentley, Eric, "The Drama at Ebb," KR, 7: 169–184 (Spring, 1945).

Bentley, Eric, "Jean-Paul Sartre, Dramatist," KR, 8: 66–79 (Winter, 1946).

Bentley, Eric, "Bernard Shaw's Politics," KR, 8: 347–371 (Summer, 1946).

Bentley, Eric, "Yeats as a Playwright," KR, 10: 196–208 (Spring, 1948).

Bentley, Eric, "The Meaning of Robert Penn Warren's Novels," KR, 10: 407–424 (Summer, 1948).

Bentley, Eric, "Chekhov as Playwright," KR, 11: 226–250 (Spring, 1949).

Bentley, Eric, "Jean-Louis Barrault," KR, 12: 222–242 (Spring, 1950).

Berryman, John, "F. Scott Fitzgerald," KR, 8: 103–112 (Winter, 1946).

Berryman, John, "The Poetry of Ezra Pound," PR, 16: 377–394 (April, 1949).

Bewley, Marius, "Kenneth Burke as Literary Critic," *Scrutiny* (Cambridge, England), 15: 254–277 (December, 1948).

Bewley, Marius, "The Poetry of Wallace Stevens," PR, 16: 895–916 (September, 1949).

Bewley, Marius, "James's Debt to Hawthorne," *Scrutiny*, 16: 178–195 (September, 1949), 16: 301–317 (Winter, 1949), 17: 14–31 (Spring, 1950).

Bishop, John Peale, "Homage to Hemingway," NR, 89: 39–42 (November 11, 1936).

Bishop, John Peale, "The Poems of Ford Madox Ford," P, 50: 336–341 (September, 1937).

Bishop, John Peale, "The Discipline of Poetry," VQR, 14: 343–356 (Summer, 1938).

Bishop, John Peale, "The Poems and Prose of E. E. Cummings," Sou R, 4: 173–186 (Summer, 1938).

Bishop, John Peale, "Myth and Modern Literature," SRL, 20: 3–4 plus (July 22, 1939).

Bishop, John Peale, "Finnegans Wake," Sou R, 5: 439–452 (Winter, 1940).

Bishop, John Peale, "The Poetry of A. E. Housman," P, 56: 144–153 (June, 1940).

Bishop, John Peale, "Poetry and Painting," Sew R, 53: 247–258 (Spring, 1945).
> For further essays and reviews see *The Collected Essays of John Peale Bishop* (edited by Edmund Wilson, 1948).

Blackmur, R. P., "Wallace Stevens," HH, 5: 223–256 (January–March, 1932).

Blackmur, R. P., "Masks of Ezra Pound," HH, 7: 177–212 (January–March, 1934).

Blackmur, R. P., "The Later Poetry of W. B. Yeats," Sou R, 2: 339–362 (Autumn, 1936).

Blackmur, R. P., "Emily Dickinson: Notes on Prejudice and Fact," Sou R, 3: 323–347 (Autumn, 1937).

Blackmur, R. P., "Henry Adams: Three Late Moments," KR, 2: 7–29 (Winter, 1940).

Blackmur, R. P., "The Shorter Poems of Thomas Hardy," Sou R, 6: 20–48 (Summer, 1940).

Blackmur, R. P., "The Enabling Act of Criticism," in *American Issues* (edited by Willard Thorp, 1941).

Blackmur, R. P., "The Sacred Fount" (on Henry James), KR, 4: 328–352 (Autumn, 1942).

Blackmur, R. P., "In the Country of the Blue" (on Henry James), KR, 5: 595–617 (Autumn, 1943).

Blackmur, R. P., "The Economy of the American Writer," Sew R, 53: 175–185 (Spring, 1945).

Blackmur, R. P., "Notes on Four Categories of Criticism," Sew R, 54: 576–589 (Autumn, 1946).

Blackmur, R. P., "In the Birdcage" (on Dostoevsky), HR, 1: 7–28 (Spring, 1948).

Blackmur, R. P., "A Burden for Critics," HR, 1: 170–185 (Summer, 1948).

Blackmur, R. P., "*Anna Karenina*: The Dialectic of Incarnation," KR, 12: 433–456 (Summer, 1950).

"D. H. Lawrence and Expressive Form," "New Thresholds, New Anatomies: Notes on a Text by Hart Crane," "The Method of Marianne Moore," "The Dangers of Authorship," "T. S. Eliot: From *Ash-Wednesday* to *Murder in the Cathedral*," and "The Critical Prefaces of Henry James" in *The Double Agent* (1935); and "A Featherbed for Critics" in *The Expense of Greatness* (1940).

Bogan, Louise, "Rilke in his Age," P, 50: 34–42 (April, 1937).

Bogan, Louise, "William Butler Yeats," At Mon, 161: 637–644 (May, 1938).

Bogan, Louise, "The Cutting of an Agate," N, 148: 234–235 (February 25, 1939).

Bogan, Louise, "The Poetry of Paul Eluard," PR, 6: 76–84 (Fall, 1939).

Bogan, Louise, "The Brontë Fantasies," NR, 105: 285–286 (September 1, 1941).

Bogan, Louise, "*Sentimental Education* Today," N, 155: 301–302 (October 3, 1942).

Bogan, Louise, "Some Notes on Popular and Unpopular Art," PR, 10: 391–401 (September–October, 1943).

Bogan, Louise, "The Time of the Assassins," N, 158: 475–476 plus (April 22, 1944).

Bogan, Louise, "The Mystic Experience," N, 161: 15 (July 7, 1945).

Bogan, Louise, "The Portrait of New England" (on James's *The Bostonians*), N, 161: 582–583 plus (December 1, 1945).

See *The New Yorker*, 1929–1950, *passim*, for reviews of current poetry.

Bourne, Randolph, "Two Generations," At Mon, 107: 591–598 (May, 1911).

Bourne, Randolph, "Theodore Dreiser," NR, 2: supp 7–8 (April 17, 1915).

Bourne, Randolph, "John Dewey's Philosophy," NR, 2: 154–156 (May 13, 1915).

Bourne, Randolph, "The Cult of the Best," NR, 5: 275–277 (January 15, 1916).

Bourne, Randolph, "The Art of Theodore Dreiser," D, 62: 507–509 (June 14, 1917).

Bourne, Randolph, "The History of a Literary Radical," YR, 8: 468–484 (April, 1919).

   For other essays by Bourne see *Untimely Papers* (edited by James Oppenheim, 1919), and *The History of a Literary Radical and Other Essays* (edited by Van Wyck Brooks, 1920).

Brooks, Cleanth, "Three Revolutions in Poetry," Sou R, 1: 151–163 (Summer, 1935), 1: 328–338 (Autumn, 1935), 1: 568–583 (Winter, 1936).

Brooks, Cleanth, "The Reading of Modern Poetry," AR, 8: 435–449 (February, 1937).

Brooks, Cleanth, "*The Waste Land*: An Analysis," Sou R, 3: 106–136 (Summer, 1937). For a revised version see *T. S. Eliot: A Study of his Writings by Several Hands* (edited by B. Rajan, 1947).

Brooks, Cleanth, "Literary History versus Criticism," KR, 2: 403–412 (Autumn, 1940).

Brooks, Cleanth, "The Poem as Organism," in *English Institute Annual: 1940* (1941).

Brooks, Cleanth, "The Language of Paradox," in *The Language of Poetry* (edited by Allen Tate, 1942).

Brooks, Cleanth, "The New Criticism: A Brief for the Defense," AS, 13: 435–449 (Summer, 1944).

Brooks, Cleanth, "The Intimations of the Ode" (on Wordsworth), KR, 8: 80–102 (Winter, 1946).

Brooks, Cleanth, "Criticism and Literary History: Marvell's Horatian Ode," Sew R, 55: 199–222 (Spring, 1947).

   See also "Metaphor and the Tradition," "Metaphysical Poetry and Propaganda Art," "The Modern Poet and the Tradition," "Yeats: The Poet as Myth-Maker," and "Notes for a Revised History of English Poetry," in *Modern Poetry and the Tradition* (1939); and "The Heresy of Paraphrase," "Criticism, History, and Critical Relativism," and "The Problem of Belief and the Problem of Cognition," in *The Well Wrought Urn* (1947).

Brooks, Van Wyck, "Highbrow and Lowbrow," F, 53: 481–492 (April, 1915).

Brooks, Van Wyck, "On Creating a Usable Past," D, 64: 337–341 (April 11, 1918).

Brooks, Van Wyck, "Mark Twain's Humor," D, 68: 275–291 (March, 1920).

Brooks, Van Wyck, "Mark Twain's Satire," D, 68: 424–443 (April, 1920).

Brooks, Van Wyck, "Henry James: The First Phase," D, 74: 433–450 (May, 1923).

Brooks, Van Wyck, "Henry James: The American Scene," D, 75: 29–42 (July, 1923).

Brooks, Van Wyck, "Henry James: An International Episode," D, 75: 225–238 (September, 1923).

Brooks, Van Wyck, "Emerson and the Reformers," *Harper's,* 154: 114–119 (December, 1926).

Brooks, Van Wyck, "What is Primary Literature?" YR, 31: 25–37 (Summer, 1941).

Van Wyck Brooks's three most important essays, "America's Coming-of-Age" of 1915, "Letters and Leadership" of 1918, and "The Literary Life in America," are now collected in *Three Essays on America* (1934).

Brown, E. K., "The Revival of E. M. Forster," YR, 33: 668–681 (June, 1944).

Brown, E. K., "James and Conrad," YR, 35: 265–285 (December, 1945).

Brown, E. K., "David Copperfield," YR, 37: 651–666 (June, 1948).

Brownell, William Crary, "Criticism," At Mon, 107: 548–567 (April, 1911).

Brownell, William Crary, "Standards," *Scribner's,* 61: 277–284 March, 1917), 61: 435–444 (April, 1917), 61: 619–626 (May, 1917).

See also the books listed in Appendix I.

Burgum, Edwin Berry, "Romanticism," KR, 3: 479–490 (Autumn, 1941).

Burke, Kenneth, "Symbolic War," Sou R, 2: 134–147 (Summer, 1936).

Burke, Kenneth, "Acceptance and Rejection," Sou R, 2: 600–632 (Winter, 1937).

Burke, Kenneth, "Semantic and Poetic Meaning," Sou R, 3: 501–523 (Winter, 1939).

Burke, Kenneth, "The Calling of the Tune," KR, 1: 272–282 (Summer, 1939).

Burke, Kenneth, "Four Master Tropes," KR, 3: 421–438 (Autumn, 1941).

Burke, Kenneth, "On Motivation in Yeats," Sou R, 7: 547–561 (Winter, 1942).

Burke, Kenneth, "The Tactics of Motivation," *Chimera,* 1: 21–33, 2: 37–53 (Spring, Summer, 1943).

Burke, Kenneth, "Container and Thing Contained," Sew R, 53: 56–78 (Winter, 1945).

Burke, Kenneth, "The Temporizing of Essence," KR, 7: 616–627 (Autumn, 1945).

Burke, Kenneth, "The Imagery of Killing," HR, 1: 151–167 (Summer, 1948).

See also "The Poetic Process," "The Status of Art," "Program," "Lexicon Rhetoricae," and "Applications of the Terminology," in *Counter-Statement* (1931); and "Freud—And the Analysis of Poetry," "Twelve Propositions," "On Musicality in Verse," "Antony on Behalf of the Play," and "The Rhetoric of Hitler's *Battle,*" in *The Philosophy of Literary Form* (1941); as well as the other books listed in Appendix IV.

Burnham, James, "Marxism and Esthetics," Sym, 4: 3–30 (January, 1933).

Calverton, V. F., "The American Revolutionary Tradition," *Scribner's,* 95: 352–357 (May, 1934).

Calverton, V. F., "Literature as a Revolutionary Force," *Canadian Forum,* 15: 221–227 (March, 1935).

Canby, Henry Seidel, "Sex in Fiction," *Century,* 105: 98–105 (November, 1922).

Canby, Henry Seidel, "The Age of Experiment," *Century,* 107: 571–578 (February, 1924).

Canby, Henry Seidel, "Anon is Dead," Am Merc, 8: 79–84 (May, 1926).

Canby, Henry Seidel, "Interpreting our Literature," SRL, 5: 721–722 (March 2, 1929).

Cantwell, Robert, "No Landmarks," Sym, 4: 70–84 (January, 1933).

Cantwell, Robert, "The Influence of James Joyce," NR, 77: 200–201 (December 27, 1933).

Cantwell, Robert, "The Return of Henry James," NR, 81: 119–121 (December 12, 1934).

Cantwell, Robert, "Upton Sinclair," NR, 90: 69–71 (February 24, 1937).

Cantwell, Robert, "A Warning to Pre-War Novelists," NR, 91: 177–180 (June 23, 1937).

Cantwell, Robert, "America and the Writers' Project," NR, 98: 323–325 (April 26, 1939).

Cantwell, Robert, "The Future of American Journalism," NR, 101: 39–41 (November 8, 1939).

Cather, Willa, "The Novel Démeublé," NR, 30: supp 5–6 (April 12, 1922).

Chapman, John Jay, "Emerson Sixty Years After," At Mon, 79: 27–41 (January, 1897), 79: 222–240 (February, 1897).

Chapman, John Jay, "Literature," The Critic, 36: 53–60 (January, 1900).

Chapman, John Jay, "Learning," At Mon, 106: 125–136 (July, 1910).

Chapman, John Jay, "The Greek Genius," At Mon, 114: 70–82 (July, 1914).

Chapman, John Jay, "Lincoln and Hamlet," No Am, 209: 371–379 (March, 1919).

Chapman, John Jay, "Dante and Modern Criticism," NR, 51: 71–72 (June 8, 1927).

   Of the books by Chapman listed in Appendix IV, see especially Emerson and Other Essays (1898); Learning and Other Essays (1910); The Greek Genius and Other Essays (1915); and Letters and Religion (1924).

Chase, Richard, "History vs. the City of God" (on Arnold Toynbee), PR, 11: 45–55 (Winter, 1944).

Chase, Richard, "The Sense of the Present," KR, 7: 218–231 (Spring, 1945).

Chase, Richard, "Notes on the Study of Myth," PR, 13: 338–346 (Summer, 1946).

Chase, Richard, "The Brontës," KR, 9: 487–506 (Autumn, 1947).

Chase, Richard, "The Stone and the Crucifixion: Faulkner's Light in August," KR, 10: 538–551 (Autumn, 1948).

Chase, Richard, "Dissent on Billy Budd," PR, 15: 1212–1218 (November, 1948).

Chase, Richard, "The Progressive Hawthorne," PR, 16: 96–100 (January, 1949).

Chase, Richard, "Melville's Confidence Man," KR, 11: 122–140 (Winter, 1949).

   For Mr. Chase's fuller discussion of myth, see his Quest for Myth (1949); for his fuller study of Melville, see his Herman Melville: A Critical Study (1949).

Clark, Eleanor, "Death of a Thinker: A Note on the French Novel 1925–40," KR, 3: 322–335 (Summer, 1941).

Chevalier, Haakon M., "André Malraux: The Return of the Hero," KR, 2: 35–47 (Winter, 1940).

Collins, Seward, "Criticism in America," B, 71: 241–256 (June, 1930), 71: 400–415 (July, 1930), 72: 145–164, 209–228 (October, 1930).

Colum, Mary M., "A Critical Credo," Scribner's, 79: 387–392 (April, 1926).

Colum, Mary M., "The Changing Novel," SRL, 5: 1070–1071 (June 1, 1929).

Colum, Mary M., "Self-Critical America," Scribner's, 87: 197–206 (February, 1930).

Colum, Mary M., "Debating Humanism," SRL, 6: 1063–1064 (May 24, 1930).

Colum, Mary M., "The American Mind in Literature," F, 90: 330–334 (December, 1933).

Colum, Mary M., "On Thinking Critically," F, 91: 76–82 (February, 1934).

Colum, Mary M., "Marxism and Literature," F, 91: 145–149 (March, 1934).

Cowley, Malcolm, "A Farewell to Spain" (on Hemingway), NR, 73: 76–77 (November 30, 1932).

Cowley, Malcolm, "Farewell to the 1930's," NR, 101: 42–44 (November 8, 1939).

Cowley, Malcolm, "Remembering Hart Crane," NR, 104: 504–506 (April 14, 1941).

Cowley, Malcolm, "Robert Frost: A Dissenting Opinion," NR, 111: 312–313 (September 11, 1944).

Cowley, Malcolm, "The Case against Mr. Frost: II," NR, 111: 345–347 (September 18, 1944).

Cowley, Malcolm, "William Faulkner's Legend of the South," Sew R, 53: 343–361 (Summer, 1945).

Cowley, Malcolm, "William Faulkner Revisited," SRL, 28: 13–16 (April 14, 1945).

Cowley, Malcolm, "Walt Whitman: The Miracle," NR, 114: 385–388 (March 18, 1946).

Cowley, Malcolm, "Walt Whitman: The Secret," NR, 114: 481–484 (April 8, 1946).

Cowley, Malcolm, " 'Not Men': A Natural History of American Naturalism," KR, 9: 414–435 (Summer, 1947).

Cowley, Malcolm, "Hawthorne in the Looking Glass," Sew R, 56: 545–563 (Autumn, 1948).

See also the "Introduction" to The Portable Faulkner (edited by Malcolm Cowley, 1946).

Crane, Hart, "A Discussion with Hart Crane" (by Harriet Monroe), P, 29: 34–41 (October, 1926).

Crane, Hart, "Two Letters on The Bridge," HH, 7: 677–682 (July, 1934).

Crane, Hart, "Modern Poetry," in Collected Poems of Hart Crane (1933).

Crane, R. S., "History versus Criticism in the University Study of Literature," EJ (College Edition), 24: 645–667 (October, 1935).

Crane, R. S., Foreword to "Two Essays in Practical Criticism" by Norman F. Maclean and Elder Olson, University Review (Kansas City), 8: 199–219 (Spring, 1942).

Crane, R. S., "Cleanth Brooks; or, The Bankruptcy of Critical Monism," MP, 45: 226–245 (May, 1948).

Crane, R. S., "The Plot of *Tom Jones*," *Journal of General Education*, 4: 112–130 (January, 1950).

Cunningham, J. V., "The Ancient Quarrel between History and Poetry," P, 74: 336–342 (September, 1949).

Cunningham, J. V., "The Poetry of Wallace Stevens," P, 75: 149–165 (December, 1949).

Daiches, David, "The Principles of Literary Criticism" (on I. A. Richards), NR, 98: 95–98 (March 1, 1939).

Daiches, David, "The Novels of Aldous Huxley," NR, 100: 362–365 (November 1, 1939).

Daiches, David, "Sensibility and Technique: Preface to a Critique" (on Henry James), KR, 5: 569–579 (Autumn, 1943).

Daiches, David, "Jane Austen, Karl Marx, and the Aristocratic Dance," AS, 17: 289–296 (July, 1948).

Daiches, David, "T. S. Eliot," YR, 38: 460–470 (March, 1949).

Daiches, David, "The Novels of Elizabeth Bowen," EJ, 38: 305–313 (June, 1949).

Daiches, David, "The New Criticism: Some Qualifications," CE, 39: 64–72 (February, 1950).

See also the books listed in Appendix I.

Damon, S. Foster, "The Odyssey in Dublin" (on James Joyce), HH, 3: 7–44 (October–December, 1929).

Davidson, Donald, "Sectionalism in the United States," HH, 6: 561–589 (July–September, 1933).

Davidson, Donald, "The Traditional Basis of Thomas Hardy's Fiction," Sou R, 6: 162–178 (Summer, 1940).

Davidson, Donald, "Yeats and the Centaur," Sou R, 7: 510–516 (Winter, 1942). For further essays, especially on Southern tradition and literature, see *The Attack on Leviathan* (1938).

Davis, Robert Gorham, "Art and Anxiety," PR, 12: 310–320 (Summer, 1945).

Davis, Robert Gorham, "History, Tragedy, and Sentimentality," SRL, 32: 13 (December 24, 1949).

Davis, Robert Gorham, "The New Criticism and the Democratic Tradition," AS, 19: 9–19 (Winter, 1949).

Deutsch, Babette, "The Future of Poetry," NR, 60: 12–15 (August 21, 1929).

Deutsch, Babette, "Understanding Poetry," AS, 10: 67–71 (January, 1941).

Deutsch, Babette, "War Poetry Then and Now," NR, 104: 565–567 (April 21, 1941).

De Voto, Bernard, "My dear Edmund Wilson," (a reply to Edmund Wilson's criticism in NR, 89: 405–408, February 3, 1937), SRL, 15: 8 plus (February 13, 1937).

De Voto, Bernard, "The Critics and Robert Frost," SRL, 17: 3–4 plus (January 1, 1938).

De Voto, Bernard, "Freud's Influence on Literature," SRL, 20: 10–11 (October 7, 1939).

De Voto, Bernard, "American Novels," At Mon, 165: 66–74 (January, 1940).

Dupee, F. W., "André Malraux," PR, 4: 24–35 (March, 1938).

Dupee, F. W., "The English Literary Left," PR, 5: 11–21 (August–September, 1938).

Dupee, F. W., "Frost and Tate," N, 160: 464 plus (April 21, 1945).

Dupee, F. W., "Difficulty as Style," AS, 14: 355–357 (July, 1945).

Dupee, F. W., "Cecil Day Lewis and Louis MacNeice," N, 161: 380 (October 13, 1945).

Dupee, F. W., "Henry James and the Play," N, 171: 40–42 (July 8, 1950).

Eastman, Max, "American Ideals in Poetry," NR, 16: 190–192 (September 14, 1918, 16: 222–225 (September 21, 1918).

Eastman, Max, "Humor and America," Scribner's, 100: 9–13 (July, 1936).

Eastman, Max, "Wit and Nonsense: Freud's Mistake," YR, 26: 71–87 (September, 1936).

Eastman, Max, "Pushkin and his English Translators," NR, 89: 187–188 (December 9, 1936).

Eastman, Max, "The End of Socialism in Russia," Harper's, 174: 302–314 (February, 1937).

Eastman, Max, "Russia and the Socialist Ideal," Harper's, 176: 374–385 (March, 1938).

Edel, Leon, "Introduction" and Notes to The Ghostly Tales of Henry James (edited by Leon Edel, 1948).

Edel, Leon, "Foreword," Introduction: "Henry James: The Dramatic Years," and Notes to The Complete Plays of Henry James (edited by Leon Edel, 1949).

Eliot, T. S., "In Memory" and "The Hawthorne Aspect" (both on Henry James), The Little Review, 5: 44–53 (August, 1918).

Eliot, T. S., "Studies in Contemporary Criticism," The Egoist (London), 5: 113–114 (October, 1918) and 5: 131–133 (November–December, 1918).

Eliot, T. S., "American Literature," The Athenaeum (London), No. 4643: 236–237 (April 25, 1919).

Eliot, T. S., "A Brief Treatise on the Criticism of Poetry," The Chapbook (London), 2: 1–10 (March, 1920).

Eliot, T. S., "The Perfect Critic," The Athenaeum (London), No. 4706: 40–41 (July 9, 1920) and No. 4708: 102–104 (July 23, 1920).

Eliot, T. S., "The Possibility of a Poetic Drama," D, 69: 441–447 (November, 1920).

Eliot, T. S., "The Function of Criticism," The Criterion (London), 2: 31–42 (October, 1923).

Eliot, T. S., "Ulysses, Order, and Myth" (on Joyce's Ulysses), D, 75: 480–483 (November, 1923).

Eliot, T. S., "A Note on Poetry and Belief," The Enemy (London), 1: 15–17 (January, 1927).

Eliot, T. S., "Literature, Science, and Dogma," D, 82: 239–243 (March, 1927).

Eliot, T. S., "Isolated Superiority" (on Ezra Pound), D, 84: 4–7 (January, 1928).

Eliot, T. S., "Literature and the Modern World," American Prefaces, 1: 19–22 (November, 1935).

Eliot, T. S., "A Note on the Verse of John Milton," *Essays and Studies of the English Association* (1936), 21: 32–40.

Eliot, T. S., "The Poetry of William Butler Yeats," Sou R, 7: 442–454 (Winter, 1942).

Eliot, T. S., "The Music of Poetry," PR, 9: 450–465 (November–December, 1942).

Eliot, T. S., "Notes Towards a Definition of Culture," PR, 11: 145–157 (Spring, 1944).

Eliot, T. S., "The Man of Letters and the Future of Europe," Sew R, 53: 333–342 (Summer, 1945).

Eliot, T. S., "The Social Function of Poetry," *The Adelphi* (London), 21: 152–161 (July, 1945).

Eliot, T. S., "What Is Minor Poetry?" Sew R, 54: 1–18 (Winter, 1946).

Eliot, T. S., "Ezra Pound," P, 68: 326–338 (September, 1946).

Eliot, T. S., "Milton," Sew R, 56: 185–209 (Spring, 1948).

See *The Criterion* (London), 1922–1939, *passim*, for editorials, essays, and reviews by T. S. Eliot during the years of his editorship.

See also the books of criticism listed in Appendix IV, especially *The Sacred Wood: Essays on Poetry and Criticism* (1920), in which appear "The Perfect Critic," "Imperfect Critics," "Tradition and the Individual Talent," "The Possibility of a Poetic Drama," "Rhetoric and Poetic Drama"; *For Lancelot Andrewes* (1928), in which appear "Baudelaire in our Time" and "The Humanism of Irving Babbitt"; *Selected Essays* (1932; new edition, 1950), in which appear most of the above-named essays as well as "Dante," "Shakespeare and the Stoicism of Seneca," the three influential essays on "John Dryden," "The Metaphysical Poets," and "Andrew Marvell" which were first collected as *Homage to John Dryden* in 1924, the series on the Elizabethan dramatists, "Arnold and Pater," and, now added in 1950 from *Essays Ancient and Modern* of 1935, the papers on "Religion and Literature," "Modern Education and the Classics," and essays on Pascal and Tennyson; and for a compilation of critical passages by Eliot, *Points of View* (1941).

For a list of Eliot's writings in books and magazines, see *A Bibliographical Check-List of the Writings of T. S. Eliot,* compiled by Donald Gallup (1947).

Ellmann, Richard, "Robartes and Aherne: Two Sides of a Penny" (on Yeats), KR, 10: 177–186 (Spring, 1948).

See also the book-length study of Yeats by Richard Ellmann—*Yeats: The Man and the Masks* (1948).

Farrell, James T., "A Note on Literary Criticism," N, 142: 276–277 (March 4, 1936), 142: 314–315 (March 11, 1936).

Farrell, James T., "Ignazio Silone," Sou R, 4: 771–783 (Spring, 1939).

Farrell, James T., "The End of a Literary Decade," Am Merc, 48: 408–414 (December, 1939).

Farrell, James T., "The Faith of Lewis Mumford," Sou R, 6: 417–438 (Spring, 1941).

Farrell, James T., "The Frightened Philistines," NR, 111: 764 plus (December 4, 1944).

Farrell, James T., "Tolstoy: Husband and Writer," NR, 113: 290–292 (September 3, 1945).

See also "The Duality of Literature," "Marx on the Relative Validity of Literature," "Individualism and the Class Struggle," "Literature and Propaganda," and "Growth and Decay in Literature," in A Note on Literary Criticism (1936); the title essay, "Literature and Ideology," and "The Language of Hollywood," in The League of Frightened Philistines and Other Papers (1945); and the title essay, "Social Themes in American Realism," "Theodore Dreiser: In Memoriam," and "The Fate of Writing in America," in Literature and Morality (1947).

Fergusson, Francis, "Joyce's Exiles and Ibsen," HH, 5: 345–353 (April–June, 1932).

Fergusson, Francis, "D. H. Lawrence's Sensibility," HH, 6: 447–463 (April–June, 1933).

Fergusson, Francis, "James's Idea of Dramatic Form," KR, 5: 495–507 (Autumn, 1943).

Fergusson, Francis, "Action as Passion: Tristan and Murder in the Cathedral," KR, 9: 201–221 (Spring, 1947).

Fergusson, Francis, "The Theatricality of Shaw and Pirandello," PR, 16: 589–604 (June, 1949).

See also The Idea of a Theatre by Francis Fergusson (1949).

Fiedler, Leslie J., "The Sufferings and Greatness of Self-Love" (on Thomas Mann), PR, 14: 524–526 (September–October, 1947).

Fiedler, Leslie J., "Come Back to the Raft Ag'in, Huck Honey!" PR, 15: 664–672 (June, 1948).

Fiedler, Leslie J., "The Impotence of Scrutiny," N, 168: 252–253 (February 26, 1949).

Fiedler, Leslie J., "Out of the Whale" (on Melville), N, 169: 494–496 (November 19, 1949).

Fiedler, Leslie J., "The Third Thomas Hardy," N, 171: 210–211 (September 2, 1950).

Flint, F. Cudworth, "Metaphor in Contemporary Poetry," Sym, 1: 310–335 (July, 1930).

Flint, F. Cudworth, "Five Poets," Sou R, 1: 650–674 (Winter, 1936).

Flint, F. Cudworth, "Contemporary Criticism," Sou R, 2: 208–224 (Summer, 1936).

Flint, F. Cudworth, "New Leaders in English Poetry," VQR, 14: 502–518 (Summer, 1938).

Foerster, Norman, "Humanism and Religion," F, 82: 146–150 (September, 1929).

Foerster, Norman, "The Impressionists," B, 70: 337–347 (December, 1929).

Foerster, Norman, "Literary Historians," B, 71: 365–374 (July, 1930).

Foerster, Norman, "Literary Prophets," B, 72: 35–44 (September, 1930).

Foerster, Norman, "Toward a New Scholarship," SRL, 8: 1–3 (July 25, 1931).

Foerster, Norman, "The Study of Letters," in *Literary Scholarship* (1941).

Foerster, Norman, "The Esthetic Judgment and the Ethical Judgment," in *The Intent of the Critic* (edited by Donald A. Stauffer, 1941).

  Consult also the books listed in Appendix I.

Fowlie, Wallace, "Swann and Hamlet: A Note on the Contemporary Hero," PR, 9: 195–202 (May–June, 1942).

Fowlie, Wallace, "The Novel of Jules Romains," Sou R, 7: 880–892 (Spring, 1942).

Fowlie, Wallace, "François Mauriac," KR, 5: 189–200 (Spring, 1943).

Fowlie, Wallace, "Homage to Valéry," Sew R, 54: 250–257 (April–June, 1946).

Fowlie, Wallace, "Andre Bréton in the Age of Surrealism," WR, 14: 5–17 (Autumn, 1949).

Fowlie, Wallace, "Mallarmé's Island Voyage," MP, 47: 178–190 (February, 1950).

Frank, Joseph, "Spatial Form in Modern Literature," Sew R, 53: 221–240 (Summer, 1945), 53: 433–456 (Autumn, 1945), 53: 643–653 (Winter, 1945).

Frank, Joseph, "Force and Form: A Study of John Peale Bishop," Sew R, 55: 71–107 (Winter, 1947).

Frye, Northrop, "Levels of Meaning in Literature," KR, 12: 246–262 (Spring, 1950).

Gates, Lewis E., "English Literature in the Nineteenth Century," *The Critic*, 36: 69–80 (January, 1900), 36: 172–180 (February, 1900), 36: 268–275 (March, 1900).

Gates, Lewis E., "Tennyson's Relation to Common Life," *The Critic*, 36: 530–537 (June, 1900).

Gates, Lewis E., "Impressionism and Appreciation," At Mon, 86: 73–84 (July, 1900).

  See *Studies and Appreciations*, by Lewis E. Gates (1900).

Ghiselin, Brewster, "D. H. Lawrence and a New World," WR, 11: 150–159 (Spring, 1947).

Ghiselin, Brewster, "Bridge into the Sea" (on Hart Crane), PR, 16: 679–686 (July, 1949).

Gold, Michael, "Thornton Wilder: Prophet of the Genteel Christ," NR, 64: 266–267 (October 22, 1930).

Gold, Michael, "Out of the Fascist Unconscious" (on Archibald MacLeish), NR, 75: 295–296 (July 26, 1933).

Goodman, Paul, "Neo-Classicism, Platonism, and Romanticism," *Journal of Philosophy*, 31: 148–163 (1934).

Goodman, Paul, "The Shape of the Screen and the Darkness of the Theatre," PR, 9: 141–152 (March–April, 1942).

Gordon, Caroline, "Notes on Faulkner and Flaubert," HR, 1: 222–231 (Summer, 1948).

Gordon, Caroline, "Notes on Hemingway and Kafka," Sew R, 57: 215–226 (Spring, 1949).

Gordon, Caroline, "Notes on Chekhov and Maugham," Sew R, 57: 401–410 (Summer, 1949).

See *The House of Fiction,* edited by Caroline Gordon and Allen Tate (1950).

Greenberg, Clement, "Avant-Garde and Kitsch," PR, 6: 34–49 (Fall, 1939).

Greenberg, Clement, "Towards a Newer Laocoön, PR, 7: 296–310 (July–August, 1940).

Greenberg, Clement, "The Renaissance of the Little Mag," PR, 8: 72–75 (January–February, 1941).

Greenberg, Clement, "Bertolt Brecht's Poetry," PR, 8: 114–127 (March–April, 1941).

Gregory, Horace, "Wordsworth: An Evaluation," NR, 67: 25–26 (May 20, 1931).

Gregory, Horace, "Rugged Skelton," NR, 72: 333–334 (November 2, 1932).

Gregory, Horace, "The Search for a Frontier" (on Ezra Pound), NR, 75: 292–294 (July 25, 1933).

Gregory, Horace, "Two Critics in Search of an Absolute," N, 138: 189–191 (February 14, 1934).

Gregory, Horace, "The Man of Feeling" (on T. S. Eliot), NR, 79: 23–24 (May 16, 1934).

Gregory, Horace, "A Defense of Poetry," NR, 76: 237–238 (October 11, 1933).

Gregory, Horace, "The Proletarian Poet" (on Cecil Day Lewis), PR, 3: 27–28 (May, 1936).

Gregory, Horace, "W. B. Yeats and the Mask of Jonathan Swift," Sou R, 7: 492–509 (Winter, 1941).

Gregory, Horace. "Within the Private View: A Note on Rereading the Poetry of Edgar Allan Poe," PR, 10: 263–274 (May, 1943).

Gregory, Horace, "On Paul Elmer More and his *Shelburne Essays,* A, 4: 140–149 (Spring, 1944).

For the selected essays of Horace Gregory see *The Shield of Achilles: Essays on Poetry and Beliefs* (1944).

Guérard, Albert J., "Prometheus and the Aeolian Lyre," YR, 33: 482–497 (March, 1944).

Guérard, Albert J., "French and American Pessimism," *Harper's,* 191: 267–272 (September, 1945).

Guérard, Albert J., "Montherlant and the Collaborators," YR, 35: 93–98 (September, 1945).

Guérard, Albert J., "Literature and the Western Colleges," NR, 116: 27–28 (May 19, 1947).

Heilman, Robert B., "The Freudian Reading of *The Turn of the Screw,*" MLN, 62: 433–445 (November, 1947).

Heilman, Robert B., "*The Turn of the Screw* as Poem," *University Review* (Kansas City), 14: 277–289 (Summer, 1948).

Heilman, Robert B., "The Unity of *King Lear,*" Sew R, 56: 58–68 (Winter, 1948).

Hicks, Granville, "Conrad After Five Years," NR, 61: 192–194 (January 8, 1930).

Hicks, Granville, "The Twenties in American Literature," N, 130: 183–185 (February 12, 1930).

Hicks, Granville, "Ford Madox Ford: A Neglected Contemporary," B, 72: 364–370 (December, 1930).

Hicks, Granville, "Robert Herrick, Liberal," NR, 67: 129–130 (June 17, 1931).

Hicks, Granville, "The Past and Future of William Faulkner," B, 70: 17–24 (September, 1931).

Hicks, Granville, "John Dos Passos," B, 75: 32–42 (April, 1932).

Hicks, Granville, "The Failure of 'Left' Criticism," NR, 103: 345–347 (September 9, 1940).

Hicks, Granville, "Arthur Koestler and the Future of the Left," Antioch Review, 5: 212–223 (June, 1945).

Hicks, Granville, "The Intransigence of Edmund Wilson," Antioch Review, 6: 550–562 (December, 1946).

Hoffman, Frederick W., "From Surrealism to 'The Apocalpyse,'" ELH, 15: 147–165 (June, 1948).

Hook, Sidney, "Some Social Uses and Abuses of Semantics," PR, 4: 14–25 (April, 1938).

Hook, Sidney, "The Integral Humanism of Jacques Maritain," PR, 7: 204–229 (May–June, 1940).

Hook, Sidney, "The Future of Socialism," PR, 14: 23–36 (January–February, 1947).

Howe, Irving, "James T. Farrell: The Critic Calcified," PR, 14: 545–552 (September–October, 1947).

Howe, Irving, "The Critic as Stuffed Head" (on Stanley Edgar Hyman), N, 167: 22–24 (July 3, 1948).

Howe, Irving, "Edmund Wilson: A Revaluation," N, 167: 430–431 (October 16, 1948).

Howells, William Dean, "Mr. James's Masterpiece," Harper's Bazar, 36: 9–14 (January, 1902).

Howells, William Dean, "George Eliot," Harper's, 105: 963–967 (November, 1902).

Howells, William Dean, "Emile Zola," No Am, 175: 587–596 (November, 1902).

Howells, William Dean, "Frank Norris," No Am, 175: 769–778 (December, 1902).

Howells, William Dean, "Henry James's Later Work," No Am, 176: 125, 177–179 (January, 1903).

Howells, William Dean, "Certain of the Chicago School of Fiction," No Am, 176: 734–746 (May, 1903).

Howells, William Dean, "Shaw and Shakespeare," Harper's, 111: 633–635 (September, 1905).

Howells, William Dean, "Henrik Ibsen," No Am, 183: 1–14 (July, 1906).

Howells, William Dean, "The Novels of Robert Herrick," No Am, 189: 812–820 (June, 1909).

Howells, William Dean, "Mark Twain: An Enquiry," No Am, 191: 836–850 (June, 1910).

Howells, William Dean, "Mr. Henry James's Later Work," No Am, 203: 572–584 (April, 1916).

Howells, William Dean, "The Conjecture of Intensive Fiction," No Am, 204: 869–880 (December, 1916).

> The above represents a small portion of Howells' output as critic and reviewer during the last twenty years of his life. His best critical work in book form is in two small volumes, *Criticism and Fiction* (1891) and *My Mark Twain* (1910). A good collection of his practical criticism is needed. His critical papers and journalism will be found listed and collated in the *Bibliography of William Dean Howells* by W. M. Gibson and George Arms.

Humphries, Rolfe, "Poet or Prophet?" (on Robinson Jeffers), NR, 61: 228–229 (January 15, 1930).

Humphries, Rolfe, "Archibald MacLeish," *Modern Monthly*, 8: 264–270, 274 (June, 1934).

Humphries, Rolfe, "Foreword, with Poems" (on Yvor Winters), P, 45: 288–291 (February, 1935).

Humphries, Rolfe, "Miss Millay as Artist," N, 153: 644–645 (December 30, 1941).

Humphries, Rolfe, "A Disciple of Aristippus" (on A. E. Housman), N, 154: 550–552 (May 9, 1942).

Humphries, Rolfe, "On the Creative Imagination," N, 157: 411–412 (October 9, 1943).

Humphries, Rolfe, "On Writers and their Critics," N, 159: 691–692 (December 2, 1944).

Huneker, James Gibbons, "Arthur Symons and his New Book," *The Lamp*, 28: 374–378 (June, 1904).

Huneker, James Gibbons, "Gerhardt Hauptmann," *The Lamp*, 29: 91–104 (September, 1904).

Huneker, James Gibbons, "August Strindberg," *The Lamp*, 29: 573–582 (January, 1905).

Huneker, James Gibbons, "Henrik Ibsen," *Scribner's*, 40: 351–361 (September, 1906).

Huneker, James Gibbons, "Anatole France," No Am, 184: 59–72 (January, 1907).

Huneker, James Gibbons, "The Baudelaire Legend," *Scribner's*, 45: 240–249 (February, 1909).

Huneker, James Gibbons, "The Genius of Joseph Conrad," No Am, 200: 270–279 (August, 1914).

Huneker, James Gibbons, "Jules Laforgue," No Am, 202: 80–91 (July, 1915).

Huneker, James Gibbons, "Dostoevsky and Tolstoy," F, 54: 201–216 (August, 1915).

Huneker, James Gibbons, "Remy de Gourmont," No Am, 205: 935–42 (June, 1917).

>The above is a small selection of Huneker's critical journalism during the last twenty years of his life. His writings on literature, music, and the other arts will be found listed in Appendix IV. A convenient selection is the volume of *Essays* edited by H. L. Mencken (1929), in which see especially "The Quintessence of Shaw," "Villiers de l'Isle-Adam," "The Real Flaubert," "A Study of De Maupassant," "George Sand," and "Ibsen."

Hyman, Stanley Edgar, "Henry Thoreau in Our Time," At Mon, 178: 137–138 plus (November, 1946).

Hyman, Stanley Edgar, "The Psychoanalytic Criticism of Literature," WR, 12: 106–115 (Winter, 1948).

Hyman, Stanley Edgar, "The Critic as Narcissus," A, 8: 187–191 (Spring, 1948).

Hyman, Stanley Edgar, "Some Bankrupt Treasuries," KR, 10: 484–500 (Summer, 1948).

Hyman, Stanley Edgar, "Notes on the Organic Unity of John Peale Bishop," A, 9: 102–113 (Winter, 1949).

Hyman, Stanley Edgar, "Five Books in Search of an Author," HR, 2: 139–151 (Spring, 1949).

Hyman, Stanley Edgar, "Myth, Ritual, and Nonsense," KR, 11: 454–475 (Summer, 1949).

Hyman, Stanley Edgar, "The Deflowering of New England," HR, 2: 600–612 (Winter, 1950).

>*The Armed Vision* by Stanley Edgar Hyman (1948) contains essays on Edmund Wilson, Yvor Winters, T. S. Eliot, Van Wyck Brooks, Constance Rourke, Maud Bodkin, Christopher Caudwell, Caroline Spurgeon, R. P. Blackmur, William Empson, I. A. Richards, and Kenneth Burke.

James, Henry, "James Russell Lowell," At Mon, 69: 35–50 (January, 1892).

James, Henry, "The Present Literary Situation in France," No Am, 169: 488–500 (October, 1899).

James, Henry, "Letters of Robert Louis Stevenson," No Am, 170: 61–77 (January, 1900).

James, Henry, "George Sand," No Am, 174: 546–554 (April, 1902).

James, Henry, "The Lesson of Balzac," At Mon, 96: 166–180 (August, 1905).

James, Henry, "The Novel in *The Ring and the Book*," Quarterly Review, 217: 68–87 (July, 1912).

James, Henry, "The Founding of *The Nation*," N, 101: 44–45 (July 8, 1915).

>The above are a few of James's essays after 1890; his work as critic, journalist, and essayist will be found comprehensively indexed in LeRoy Phillips' *Bibliography of the Writings of Henry James* (new edition, 1930). James's books of criticism are listed in Appendix IV of the present volume. Of special importance are the book on *Hawthorne* (1879); the essays "The Art of Fiction," "Emerson," "Guy de Maupassant," and "Ivan Turgénieff" in *Partial Portraits* (1888); "Gustave Flaubert," "James Russell Lowell," and "Criticism" in *Essays in London and Elsewhere* (1893); "Matthew Arnold's Es-

says," "Mr. Walt Whitman," and "The Limitations of Dickens" in the collection of early writings called *Views and Reviews* (edited by LeRoy Phillips (1908); and the essays on Stevenson, Zola, Flaubert, Balzac, George Sand, Gabriele D'Annunzio, and "The New Novel, 1914" in *Notes on Novelists* (1914).

Jarrell, Randall, "Contemporary Poetry Criticisms," NR, 105: 88–90 (August 21, 1941).

Jarrell, Randall, "Changes of Attitude and Rhetoric in Auden's Poetry," Sou R, 7: 326–349 (Autumn, 1941).

Jarrell, Randall, "Freud to Paul: Stages in Auden's Ideology," PR, 12: 437–457 (Autumn, 1945).

Jarrell, Randall, "From the Kingdom of Necessity" (on Robert Lowell), N, 164: 74–75 (January 18, 1947).

Jarrell, Randall, "The Other Robert Frost," N, 165: 588, 590–601 (November 29, 1947).

Jarrell, Randall, "John Ransom's Poetry," Sew R, 56: 378–390 (Summer, 1948).

Jarrell, Randall, "The Profession of Poetry," PR, 17: 724–731 (September–October, 1950).

Jones, Howard Mumford, "Literary Scholarship and Contemporary Criticism," EJ, 23: 740–758 (November, 1934).

Jones, Howard Mumford, "The Limits of Contemporary Criticism," SRL, 24: 3–4, 17 (September 6, 1941).

[Cf. "Editorial," SR, 7: iv-xii (Autumn, 1941.)]

Josephson, Matthew, "The Literary Life in Russia," NR, 79: 90–93 (June 6, 1934).

Kazin, Alfred, "Mr. Brooks's New England," PR, 7: 402–405 (September–October, 1940).

Kazin, Alfred, "Faulkner: The Rhetoric and the Agony," VQR, 18: 389–402 (July, 1942).

Kazin, Alfred, "The Irreducible Element," NR, 107: 259–260 (August 31, 1942).

Kazin, Alfred, "Criticism at the Poles," NR, 107: 492–495 (October 19, 1942).

Kazin, Alfred, "But What Is an American?" NR, 110: 218–220 (February 14, 1944).

Kazin, Alfred, "The Inmost Leaf" (on Melville), NR, 111: 840–841 (December 18, 1944).

Kazin, Alfred, "Introduction" to *The Portable Blake* (1947).

Kazin, Alfred, "The Indignant Flesh" (on Hemingway), *The New Yorker,* September 9, 1950, pp. 101–103.

See *On Native Grounds: An Interpretation of Modern American Prose Literature* (1942).

Kelly, John, "Franz Kafka's *Trial* and the Theology of Crisis," SR, 5: 748–766 (Spring, 1940).

Kronenberger, Louis, "T. S. Eliot as Critic," N, 140: 452–453 (April 17, 1935).

Kronenberger, Louis, "H. L. Mencken," NR, 88: 243–245 (October 7, 1936).

Kronenberger, Louis, "The Education of Henry Adams," NR, 18: 155–158 (March 15, 1939).
Kronenberger, Louis, "Virginia Woolf as Critic," N, 155; 382 plus (October 17, 1942).
Kronenberger, Louis, "Peacock," N, 155: 134–135 (August 15, 1942).
Kronenberger, Louis, "Lytton Strachey," N, 159: 158–159 (August 5, 1944).
Kronenberger, Louis, "The Perfect Trifler" (on Max Beerbohm), SRL, 30: 9–10 (June 21, 1947).
Krutch, Joseph Wood, "Realism and Drama," N, 133: 440–441 (October 21, 1931).
Krutch, Joseph Wood, "Lytton Strachey," N, 134: 199–200 (February 17, 1932).
Krutch, Joseph Wood. "Philosophical Criticism," N, 134: 407–408 (April 6, 1932).
Krutch, Joseph Wood, "The Comic Wisdom of S. N. Behrman," N, 137: 74–76 (July 19, 1933).
Krutch, Joseph Wood, "A Poem is a Poem" (on Eliot), N, 137: 679–680 (December 13, 1933).
Krutch, Joseph Wood, "The Meaning of Modern Drama," N, 141: 269–270 (September 4, 1935), 141: 291–293 (September 11, 1935), 141: 320–323 (September 18, 1935), 141: 351–353 (September 25, 1935).
Krutch, Joseph Wood, "On the Difficulty of Modern Poetry," N, 142: 283–284 (March 4, 1936).
Krutch, Joseph Wood, "What Is a Good Review?" N, 144: 438 (April 17, 1937).
Krutch, Joseph Wood, "New, Newer, Newest" (vogues in criticism), N, 171: 62–63 (July 15, 1950).
See also reviews of drama in The Nation since 1924 and his book The American Drama since 1918 (1939).

Langer, Suzanne, "The Principles of Creation in Art," HR, 2: 515–534 (Winter, 1950).
Langer, Suzanne, "The Primary Illusions and the Great Orders of Art," HR, 3: 219–233 (Summer, 1950).
Levin, Harry, "Literature and the Lively Sciences," At Mon, 155: 303–311 (March, 1935).
Levin, Harry, "Everybody's Earwicker," NR, 111: 106–107 (July 24, 1944).
Levin, Harry, "The Self-Condemned Playboy" (on Cyril Connolly), NR, 115: 49–50 (July 15, 1946).
Levin, Harry, "Stendhal in Technicolor," NR, 115: 595–597 (November 4, 1946).
Levin, Harry, "James Joyce," At Mon, 178: 125–129 (December, 1946).
Levin, Harry, "America Discovers Bohemia," At Mon, 180: 68–75 (September, 1947).
Levin, Harry, "Flaubert: Portrait of the Artist as a Saint," KR, 10: 28–43 (Winter, 1948).

Levin, Harry, "Flaubert and the Spirit of '48," YR, 38: 96–108 (September, 1948).

Levin, Harry, "Marcel Proust," At Mon, 182: 85–89 (October, 1948).

Lewis, Sinclair, "Fools, Liars, and Mr. De Voto," SRL, 17: 9, 12 (April 15, 1944).

Lovett, Robert Morss, "The Betrayal of Henry Adams," D, 65: 468–472 (November 30, 1918).

Lovett, Robert Morss, "The Function of Criticism," NR, 28: 247–249 (October 26, 1921).

Lovett, Robert Morss, "The World of Havelock Ellis," B, 67: 573–575 (July, 1928).

Lovett, Robert Morss, "Tolstoy: The Lesson of the Artist," NR, 56: 63–66 (September 5, 1928).

Lovett, Robert Morss, "William Crary Brownell," NR, 56: 204–206 (October 19, 1928).

Lovett, Robert Morss, "The Legend of Charles Dickens," NR, 56: 252–253 (October 17, 1928).

Lovett, Robert Morss, "Fuller of Chicago," NR, 60: 16–18 (August 21, 1929).

Lovett, Robert Morss, "The Centenary of Scott," NR, 72: 360–361 (November 9, 1932).

McCarthy, Mary, "Theatre Chronicle," serially in PR from 1937 to 1949.

McKeon, Richard P., "Literary Criticism and the Concept of Imitation in Antiquity," MP, 34: 1–35 (August, 1936).

McKeon, Richard P., "Education and the Disciplines," International Journal of Ethics, 47: 370–381 (April, 1937).

McKeon, Richard P., "Rhetoric in the Middle Ages," Speculum, 17: 1–32 (January, 1942).

McKeon, Richard P., "The Philosophic Bases of Art and Criticism," MP, 41: 65–87, 129–147 (November, 1943 and February, 1944).

McKeon, Richard P., "Aristotle's Conception of Language and the Arts of Language," Classical Philology, 41: 193–206 (October, 1946), 42: 21–50 (January, 1947).

McKeon, Richard P., "The Nature and Teaching of the Humanities," Journal of General Education, 3: 290–303 (July, 1949).

MacLeish, Archibald, "The Social Cant," NR, 73: 156–158 (December 21, 1932).

MacLeish, Archibald, "Public Speech and Private Speech in Poetry," YR, 27: 536–547 (Spring, 1938).

MacLeish, Archibald, "Poetry and the Public World," At Mon, 163: 823–831 (June, 1939).

MacLeish, Archibald, "The Irresponsibles," N, 150: 618–623 (May 18, 1940).

MacLeish, Archibald, "Post-War Writers and Pre-War Readers," NR, 102: 789–790 (June 10, 1940).

McLuhan, Herbert Marshall, "Poetic versus Rhetorical Exegesis," Sew R, 52: 266–276 (Spring, 1944).

McLuhan, Herbert Marshall, "The Analogical Mirrors" (on Hopkins), KR, 6: 322–332 (Summer, 1944).

McLuhan, Herbert Marshall, "The Southern Quality," Sew R, 55: 357–383 (Summer, 1947).

Macauley, Robie, "The Good Ford" (on Ford Madox Ford), KR, 11: 269–288 (Spring, 1949).

Macdonald, Dwight, "Reading from Left to Right," PR, 8: 24–33 (January–February, 1941).

Macdonald, Dwight, "Kulturbolschiwismus is Here," PR, 8: 442–459 (November–December, 1941).

Macdonald, Dwight, "The Future of Undemocratic Values," PR, 10: 321–344 (July–August, 1943).

Marshall, Margaret, "Our Critics, Right or Wrong" (with Mary McCarthy), N, 141: 468–469 (October 23, 1935), 542–544 (November 6, 1935), 595–598 (November 20, 1935), 653–655 (December 4, 1935), 717–719 (December 18, 1935).

Marshall, Margaret, "The Artist in America," N, 147: 270–271 (September 17, 1938).

Marshall, Margaret, "Writers in the Wilderness," N, 149: 576–579 (November 25, 1939), 150: 15–18 (January 6, 1940), 150: 473–475 (April 13, 1940).

Marshall, Margaret, "Katherine Anne Porter," N, 150: 473–475 (April 13, 1940).

Marshall, Margaret, "Constance Rourke: Artist and Citizen," N, 152: 726–728 (June 21, 1941).

Marshall, Margaret, "Socialism, Communism, and the West," N, 150: 473–475 (September 13, 1947).

Matthiessen, F. O., "The Crooked Road" (on Yeats), Sou R, 7: 455–470 (Winter, 1942).

Matthiessen, F. O., "James and the Plastic Arts," KR, 5: 533–550 (Autumn, 1943).

Matthiessen, F. O., "Henry James's Portrait of the Artist," PR, 11: 71–87 (Winter, 1944).

Matthiessen, F. O., "The Problem of the Private Poet" (on Emily Dickinson), KR, 7: 584–597 (Autumn, 1945).

Matthiessen, F. O., "Poe," Sew R, 54: 175–205 (Spring, 1946).

Matthiessen, F. O., "American Poetry 1920–1940," Sew R, 55: 25–55 (Winter, 1947).

Matthiessen, F. O., "Phelps Putnam," KR, 11: 61–82 (Winter, 1949).

Matthiessen, F. O., "The Responsibilities of the Critic," Michigan Alumnus Quarterly Review, 55: 283–292 (July 30, 1949).
    See also the books listed in Appendix IV, notably American Renaissance: Art and Expression in the Age of Emerson and Whitman (1941), Henry James: The Major Phase (1944), and The Achievement of T. S. Eliot (new edition, 1947).

Mencken, H. L., "James Huneker," Century, 102: 191–197 (June, 1921).

Mencken, H. L., "The Motive of the Critic," NR, 28: 249–251 (October 26, 1921).

Mencken, H. L., "The Future of English," Harper's, 170: 541–548 (April, 1935).

Mencken, H. L., "The American Future," Am Merc, 40: 129–136 (February, 1937).

Mencken's writings, published widely in magazines and newspapers over a space of more than forty years, and especially in *The Smart Set* and *The American Mercury* during his years of editorship and literary influence, are most conveniently consulted in the volumes listed in Appendix IV. Among his critical writings the following may be noted:

"Theodore Dreiser," "Joseph Conrad," "James Huneker," and "Puritanism as a Literary Force" in *A Book of Prefaces* (1917).

"Criticism of Criticism of Criticism," "The Late Mr. Wells," "Arnold Bennett," "The New Poetry Movement," "Six Members of the Institute," "The American Magazine," "Jack London," and "Three American Immortals" in *Prejudices: First Series* (1919).

"The National Letters," "The Sahara of the Bozart," and "The Allied Arts" in *Prejudices: Second Series* (1920).

"Huneker: A Memory," "Footnote on Criticism," "The Poet and his Art," "The Novel," and "Reflections on the Drama" in *Prejudices: Third Series* (1922).

"The American Tradition," "From a Critic's Notebook," "Toward a Realistic Aesthetic," and "The American Novel" in *Prejudices: Fourth Series* (1924).

"Journalism in America," "Souvenirs of a Book Reviewer," and "Ambrose Bierce" in *Prejudices: Sixth Series* (1927).

Selected critical essays will be found in *Selected Prejudices* (1927) and in *A Mencken Chrestomathy* (1949).

Miles, Josephine, "The Sweet and Lovely Language," KR, 6: 355–368 (Summer, 1944).

Mizener, Arthur, "The Structure of Figurative Language in Shakespeare's Sonnets," Sou R, 5: 730–747 (Spring, 1940).

Mizener, Arthur, "*Jude the Obscure* as a Tragedy," Sou R, 6: 193–213 (Summer, 1940).

Mizener, Arthur, "The Romanticism of W. B. Yeats," Sou R, 7: 601–623 (Winter, 1942).

Mizener, Arthur, "The Elizabethan Art of our Movies," KR, 4: 181–194 (Spring, 1942).

Mizener, Arthur, "Victorian Hopkins," KR, 6: 590–606 (Autumn, 1944).

Mizener, Arthur, "Scott Fitzgerald and the Imaginative Possession of American Life," Sew R, 54: 66–86 (January–March, 1946).

Mizener, Arthur, "The Novel of Manners in America," KR, 12: 1–19 (Winter, 1950).

Moore, Marianne, "The Cantos" (on Ezra Pound), P, 39: 37–50 (October, 1931).

Moore, Marianne, "If a Man Die" (on Conrad Aiken), HH, 5: 312–320 (January–March, 1932).
Moore, Marianne, "Emily Dickinson," P, 41: 219–226 (January, 1933).
Moore, Marianne, "Words for Music Perhaps" (on Yeats), P, 42: 40–44 (April, 1933).
Moore, Marianne, " 'It is Not Forbidden to Think' " (on Eliot), N, 142: 680–681 (May 27, 1935).
Moore, Marianne, *The Dial:* A Retrospect," PR, 9: 52–58 (January–February, 1942).
Moore, Marianne, "Feeling and Precision," Sew R, 52: 499–507 (Autumn, 1944).
More, Paul Elmer, "Taste and Tradition," *Unpopular Review,"* 8: 112–132 (July, 1917).
More, Paul Elmer, "Henry Adams," *Unpopular Review,* 10: 255–272 (October, 1918).
More, Paul Elmer, "The Modern Current in American Literature," F, 79: 127–136 (January, 1928).
More, Paul Elmer, "The Revival of Humanism," B, 71: 1–11 (March, 1930).
More, Paul Elmer, "The Cleft Eliot," SRL, 9: 233 plus (November 12, 1932).
More, Paul Elmer, "Proust: The Two Ways," AR, 1: 50–75 (April, 1933).
More, Paul Elmer, "Irving Babbitt," AR, 3: 23–40 (April, 1934).
More, Paul Elmer, "James Joyce," AR, 5: 129–157 (May, 1935).
More, Paul Elmer, "The Modernism of French Poetry," AR, 5: 329–348 (June, 1935).

Paul Elmer More's most representative writings on literature will be found in the series of volumes called *Shelburne Essays,* from 1904 to 1936, with the following essays especially notable:

In the *First Series* (1904): "The Solitude of Nathaniel Hawthorne," "The Origins of Hawthorne and Poe," and "Arthur Symons: The Two Illusions."

In the *Second Series* (1905): "Lafcadio Hearn," "Kipling and Fitzgerald," and "The Novels of George Meredith."

In the *Third Series* (1905): "The Centenary of Sainte-Beuve," "Swinburne," "Christina Rossetti," and "The Quest of a Century."

In the *Fourth Series* (1906): "John Keats" and "Walt Whitman."

In the *Fifth Series* (1908): "The Praise of Gissing," "Mrs. Gaskell," "The Centenary of Longfellow," and "James Thomson."

In the *Seventh Series* (1910): "Tennyson," "Criticism," "Victorian Literature," and "The Pragmatism of William James."

In the *Eighth Series,* titled *The Drift of Romanticism* (1913): "Cardinal Newman" and "Walter Pater."

In the *Ninth Series,* titled *Aristocracy and Justice* (1915): "The New Morality" and "Natural Aristocracy."

In the *Eleventh Series,* titled *A New England Group and Others* (1921): "Henry Adams," "Samuel Butler of Erewhon," and "Charles Eliot Norton."

In *New Shelburne Essays: Volume I*, titled *The Demon of the Absolute* (1928): the title essay, and "Modern Currents in American Literature," "A Note on Poe's Method," and "Henry Vaughan."

In *New Shelburne Essays: Volume III*, titled *On Being Human* (1936): the essays on Humanism, Irving Babbitt, Proust, Joyce, French Poetry listed above, and "A Scholar-Saint," "Religion and Social Discontent," and "How to Read *Lycidas*" (included in the present volume).

Muller, Herbert J., "The Worlds of Henry Miller," KR, 2: 312–318 (Summer, 1940).

Muller, Herbert J., "Pathways in Recent Criticism," Sou R, 4: 187–208 (Summer, 1939).

Muller, Herbert J., "The New Criticism in Poetry," Sou R, 6: 811–839 (Spring, 1941).

Muller, Herbert J., "The Relative and the Absolute" (an exchange with Cleanth Brooks), Sew R, 57: 357–377 (Summer, 1949).

Mumford, Lewis, "Aesthetics: A Palaver," AM, 3: 360–365 (November, 1924).

Mumford, Lewis, "The Emergence of a Past," NR, 45: 18–19 (November 25, 1925).

Mumford, Lewis, "The Writing of *Moby Dick*," AM, 15: 482–490 (December, 1928).

Mumford, Lewis, "American Condescension and European Superiority," *Scribner's*, 87: 518–527 (May, 1930).

Mumford, Lewis, "The Image of Randolph Bourne," NR, 64: 151–152 (September 24, 1930).

Mumford, Lewis, "Thorstein Veblen," NR, 67: 314 316 (August 5, 1931).

Mumford, Lewis, "What Has 1932 Done for Literature?" At Mon, 150: 761–767 (December, 1932).

Of the books listed in Appendix I, see *The Golden Day* (1926) and *The Brown Decades* (1931).

Munson, Gorham B., "Van Wyck Brooks, his Sphere and his Encroachments," D, 78: 28–42 (January, 1925).

Munson, Gorham B., "The Dandyism of Wallace Stevens," D, 79: 413–417 (November, 1925).

Munson, Gorham B., "Embattled Humanists," B, 68: 404–410 (December, 1928).

Munson, Gorham B., "Criticism for Black Sheep," Sew R, 37: 459–477 (October, 1929).

Munson, Gorham B., "Young Critics of the Nineteen-Twenties," B, 70: 369–373 (December, 1929).

Munson, Gorham B., "American Criticism and the Fighting Hope," YR, 20: 568–582 (March, 1931).

Munson, Gorham B., "The Impracticality of the Contemporary American Writer," Sew R, 39: 257–261 (July, 1931).

Munson, Gorham B., "The Literary Profession in America," Sew R, 39: 398–406 (October, 1931).

Munson, Gorham B., "The Fledgling Years, 1916–24," Sew R, 40: 24–54 (January, 1932).

Nathan, George Jean: for his reviews and criticisms of drama since 1906 in many newspapers as well as in magazines like *The Smart Set, The American Mercury, The New Freeman,* and *Esquire,* see his published volumes, of which a selection is listed in Appendix I, as well as his recent annual on the New York theatre titled *The Theatre Book of the Year,* issued yearly since 1943.

O'Brien, Justin, "French Literature and the War," SRL, 22: 3–4 plus (June 15, 1940).

O'Brien, Justin, "On Re-reading the Modern Classics," N, 155: 579–580 (November 28, 1942).

O'Brien, Justin, "Poet on Horseback" (on Roy Campbell), KR, 4: 75–86 (Winter, 1942).

O'Brien, Justin, "Marcel Proust as a *Moraliste,*" Romantic Review, 39: 50–57 (February, 1948).

O'Connor, William Van, "André Gide and the Poet in Wartime," P, 63: 276–278 (February, 1944).

O'Connor, William Van, "This Alexandrian Criticism," AS, 14: 357–361 (July, 1945).

O'Connor, William Van, "The Direction of the Little Mag," P, 71: 281–284 (February, 1948).

O'Connor, William Van, "Wallace Stevens and Imagined Reality," WR, 12: 156–163 (Spring, 1948).

O'Connor, William Van, "The Little Magazine as a Cultural Journal," P, 72: 339–342 (September, 1948).

Olson, Elder, "Rhetoric and the Appreciation of Pope," MP, 37: 13–35 (August, 1939).

Olson, Elder, "The Argument of Longinus' *On the Sublime,*" MP, 39: 225–258 (February, 1942).

Olson, Elder, "Recent Literary Criticism," MP, 40, 275–283 (February, 1943).

Olson, Elder, "An Outline of Poetic Theory," in *Critiques and Essays in Criticism* (edited by R. W. Stallman, 1949).

Olson, Elder, "William Empson, Contemporary Criticism and Poetic Diction," MP, 47: 222–252 (May, 1950).

Parkes, Henry Bamford, "The Puritan Heresy," HH, 5: 165–190 (January–March, 1932).

Parkes, Henry Bamford, "William James," HH, 7: 6–28 (October–December, 1933).

Parkes, Henry Bamford, "The Limitations of Marxism," HH, 7: 565–581 (July–September, 1934).

Parkes, Henry Bamford, "Attitudes toward History" (on Kenneth Burke), Sou R, 3: 693–706 (Spring, 1938).

Parkes, Henry Bamford, "Some Marxist Fallacies," Sou R, 4: 474–488 (Winter, 1939).

Parkes, Henry Bamford, "Poe, Hawthorne, Melville: An Essay in Sociological Criticism," PR, 16: 157–165 (February, 1949).

Pepper, Stephen C., "The Outlook for Aesthetics," KR, 8: 179–187 (Spring, 1946).

Phillips, William, "Categories for Criticism," Sym, 4: 31–47 (January, 1933).

Phillips, William, "The Esthetic of the Founding Fathers," PR, 4: 11–21 (March, 1938).

Phillips, William, "The Devil Theory of the Dialectic," PR, 6: 82–90 (Fall, 1938).

Phillips, William, "The Intellectualists' Tradition," PR, 8: 481–490 (November–December, 1941).

Phillips, William, "Dostoevsky's Underground Man," PR, 13: 551–561 (November–December, 1946).

Porter, Katherine Anne, "A Bright Particular Faith, A.D. 1700" (on Cotton Mather), HH, 7: 246–257 (January–March, 1934).

Porter, Katherine Anne, "The Art of Katherine Mansfield," N, 145: 435–436 (October 23, 1937).

Porter, Katherine Anne, "Notes on a Criticism of Thomas Hardy," Sou R, 6: 150–161 (Summer, 1940).

Porter, Katherine Anne, "The Days Before" (on Henry James), KR, 5: 481–494 (Autumn, 1943).

Pound, Ezra, "A Few Don'ts by an Imagist," P, 1: 200–206 (March, 1913).

Pound, Ezra, "Irony, Laforgue, and Some Satire," P, 11: 93–98 (November, 1917).

Pound, Ezra, "In Explanation," "Brief Note," "A Shake Down," and "The Middle Years" (all on Henry James), *Little Review*, 5: 5–41 (August, 1918).

Pound, Ezra, "On Criticism in General," *Criterion* (London), 1: 143–156 (January, 1923).

Pound, Ezra, "Where Is American Culture?" N, 126: 443–444 (April 18, 1928).

Pound, Ezra, "Dr. Williams' Position," D, 85: 395–404 (November, 1928).

Pound, Ezra, "Small Magazines," EJ, 19: 689–704 (November, 1930).

Pound, Ezra, "Ford Madox Ford," Nineteenth Century (London), 126: 178–181 (August, 1939).

Ezra Pound's innumerable contributions to magazines and literary journals, American, English, French, and Italian, extend from 1907 to the present day. The most representative have been collected in the prose volumes listed under his name in Appendix IV, especially in *The Spirit of Romance* (1910), *Pavannes and Divisions* (1918), *Instigations* (1920), *How to Read* (1931), *The ABC of Reading* (1934), *Make It New* (1934), *Polite Essays* (1937), *Guide to Kulchur* (1938), the last-named published in America as *Culture* (1939). See also the early essay of 1913 on the possibilities of a Renaissance in American arts and literature, *Patria Mia* (published in 1950).

For representative essays, see *Make It New* (1934): "Troubadours: Their Sorts and Conditions," "Arnaut Daniel," "Notes on Elizabethan Classicists,"

"French Poets," "Henry James and Remy de Gourmont," and "Cavalcanti"; and *Polite Essays* (1937): "Mr. Housman in Little Bethel," "Hell," "The Prose Tradition in Verse," "James Joyce and Pécuchet," "Mr. Eliot's Solid Merit," "The Teacher's Mission," "How to Read," "Civilization," and "Note on Dante."

Rahv, Philip, "Franz Kafka: The Hero as Lonely Man," KR, 1: 60–74 (Winter, 1939).
Rahv, Philip, "Proletarian Literature: A Political Autopsy," Sou R, 4: 616–628 (Winter, 1939).
Rahv, Philip, "Paleface and Redskin," KR, 1: 251–256 (Summer, 1939).
Rahv, Philip, "The Dark Lady of Salem," PR, 8: 362–381 (September–October, 1941).
Rahv, Philip, "The Heiress of all the Ages" (on Henry James), PR, 10: 227–247 (May–June, 1943).
Rahv, Philip, "Concerning Tolstoy," PR, 13: 420–432 (September–October, 1946).
Rahv, Philip, "The Unfuture of Utopia," PR, 16: 743–749 (July, 1949).
Rahv, Philip, "Melville and his Critics," PR, 17: 732–735 (September–October, 1950).
    See *Image and Idea* by Philip Rahv (1949) for fourteen selected essays, including some of the above, usually in revised form.
Ransom, John Crowe, "The Tense of Poetry," Sou R, 1: 221–238 (Autumn, 1935).
Ransom, John Crowe, "Yeats and his Symbols," KR, 1: 309–322 (Summer, 1939).
Ransom, John Crowe, "The Pragmatics of Art," KR, 2: 76–87 (Winter, 1940).
Ransom, John Crowe, "Yvor Winters: The Logical Critic," Sou R, 6: 558–583 (Winter, 1941).
Ransom, John Crowe, "An Address to Kenneth Burke," KR, 4: 219–237 (Spring, 1942).
Ransom, John Crowe, "The Bases of Criticism," Sew R, 52: 556–571 (Autumn, 1944).
    [Cf. "Aristotle and the 'New Criticism,'" by Hoyt Trowbridge, in Sew R, 52: 537–555 (Autumn, 1944).]
Ransom, John Crowe, "On Shakespeare's Language," Sew R, 55: 181–198 (Spring, 1947).
Ransom, John Crowe, "Poetry: The Formal Analysis," KR, 9: 436–456 (Summer, 1947).
Ransom, John Crowe, "Poetry: The Final Cause," KR, 9: 640–658 (Autumn, 1947).
Ransom, John Crowe, "The Literary Criticism of Aristotle," KR, 10: 382–402 (Summer, 1948).
Ransom, John Crowe, "The Understanding of Fiction," KR, 12: 189–218 (Spring, 1950).
    See also *The Kenyon Review* from 1939, *passim;* also Ransom's volumes of

collected essays: in *The World's Body* (1938) especially "A Poem nearly Anonymous," "Poetry: A Note in Ontology," "The Cathartic Principle," "The Mimetic Principle," "Art and Mr. Santayana," and "Criticism, Inc."; and in *The New Criticism* (1941) "I. A. Richards: The Psychological Critic; and William Empson, his Pupil," "T. S. Eliot: The Historical Critic," "Yvor Winters: The Logical Critic," and "Wanted: An Ontological Critic."

Rice, Philip Blair, "A Modern Poet's Technique: Guillaume Apollinaire," Sym, 2: 468–483 (October, 1931).

Rice, Philip Blair, "Jeffers and the Tragic Sense," N, 141: 480–482 (October 23, 1935).

Rice, Philip Blair, "George Santayana: The Philosopher as Poet," KR, 2: 460–475 (Autumn, 1940).

Rice, Philip Blair, "Thomas Mann and the Religious Revival," KR, 7: 361–377 (Summer, 1945).

Rice, Philip Blair, "The Merging Parallels: Mann's *Doctor Faustus*," KR, 11: 199–217 (Spring, 1949).

Rice, Philip Blair, "Existentialism and the Self," KR, 12: 304–330 (Spring, 1950).

Roditi, Edouard, "Paul Valéry: Poetics as an Exact Science," KR, 6: 398–408 (Summer, 1944).

Rosenberg, Harold, "Myth and Poem," Sym, 2: 179–191 (April, 1931).

Rosenberg, Harold, "Myth and History" (on Thomas Mann), PR, 6: 19–39 (Winter, 1939).

Rosenberg, Harold, "The Profession of Poetry, or Trails through the Night for M. Maritain," PR, 9: 392–413 (September–October, 1942).

Rosenberg, Harold, "The Case of the Baffled Radical" (on Arthur Koestler), PR, 11: 100–103 (Winter, 1944).

Rosenfeld, Paul, "Carl Sandburg," B, 53: 389–396 (July, 1921).

Rosenfeld, Paul, "Sherwood Anderson," D, 72: 29–42 (January, 1922).

Rosenfeld, Paul, "Randolph Bourne," D, 75: 545–560 (December, 1923).

Rosenfeld, Paul, "D. H. Lawrence," NR, 62: 155–156 (March 26, 1930).

Rosenfeld, Paul, "An Affirmative Romantic: Phelps Putnam," B, 74: 607–613 (March, 1932).

Rosenfeld, Paul, "Authors and Politics," *Scribner's*, 93: 318–320 (May, 1933).

Rosenfeld, Paul, "Resistances to Rilke," Sou R, 4: 784–794 (Spring, 1939).

Rosenzweig, Saul, "The Ghost of Henry James," PR, 11: 436–455 (Fall, 1944). Reprinted from *Character and Personality*, XII, No. 2 (December, 1943), where it appeared as "The Ghost of Henry James: A Study in Thematic Apperception."

Rourke, Constance, "Dorothy M. Richardson," NR, 20: sup 14–15 (November 26, 1919).

Rourke, Constance, "The Genius of the Novel," NR, 29: 149–151 (January 4, 1922).

Rourke, Constance, "Our Comic Heritage," SRL, 7: 678–679 (March 21, 1931).

Rourke, Constance, "American Art: A Possible Future," *American Magazine of Art*, 28: 390–405 (July, 1935).

See the books by Constance Rourke listed in Appendix I, notably *American Humor: A Study of the National Character* (1931), and the chapters of an unfinished work which appeared as *The Roots of American Culture* (edited by Van Wyck Brooks, 1942).

Santayana, George, "Liberalism and Culture," NR, 4: 123–125 (September 4, 1915).

Santayana, George, "Materialism and Idealism in America," Living Age, 300: 583–595 (March 8, 1919).

Santayana, George, "Dickens," D, 71: 537–549 (November, 1921).

Santayana, George, "America's Young Radicals," F, 67: 371–375 (May, 1922).

Santayana, George, "An Aesthetic Soviet," D, 82: 361–370 (May, 1927).

Santayana, George, "The Genteel Tradition at Bay," SRL, 7: 502–503 (January 3, 1931), 7: 518–519 (January 10, 1931), 7: 534–535 (January 17, 1931).

Santayana, George, "Alternatives to Liberalism," SRL, 10: 761–762 (June 23, 1934).

Santayana's most important writings on aesthetics and literature appear in the following books listed in Appendix IV: *The Sense of Beauty* (1896); *Interpretations of Poetry and Religion* (1900), in which see especially the essays "Understanding, Imagination, and Mysticism," "The Absence of Religion in Shakespeare," "The Poetry of Barbarism," "Emerson," and "The Elements and Function of Poetry"; *Three Philosophical Poets: Lucretius, Dante, Goethe* (1910); *Character and Opinion in the United States* (1920); and *Obiter Scripta* (1936), in which see "The Two Idealisms," "What Is Aesthetics?" "Hamlet," "Literal and Symbolic Knowledge," and "Proust on Essences."

Schappes, Morris U., "Notes on the Concrete as Method in Criticism," Sym, 2: 315–324 (July, 1931).

Schorer, Mark, "Mythology (For the Study of William Blake)," KR, 4: 366–380 (Autumn, 1942).

Schorer, Mark, "Blake as a Religious Poet," Sew R, 54: 241–249 (April–June, 1946).

Schorer, Mark, "Technique as Discovery," HR, 1: 67–87 (Spring, 1948).

Schorer, Mark, "Fiction and the Matrix of Analogy," KR, 11: 539–560 (Autumn, 1949).

Schwartz, Delmore, "Ernest Hemingway's Literary Situation," Sou R, 3: 769–789 (Spring, 1938).

Schwartz, Delmore, "John Dos Passos and the Whole Truth," Sou R, 4: 351–367 (Autumn, 1938).

Schwartz, Delmore, "The Critical Method of R. P. Blackmur," P, 53: 28–39 (October, 1938).

Schwartz, Delmore, "The Two Audens," KR, 1: 34–45 (Winter, 1939).

Schwartz, Delmore, "*The Criterion*: 1922–1939," KR, 1: 437–450 (Autumn, 1939).

Schwartz, Delmore, "The Poetry of Allen Tate," Sou R, 5: 419–438 (Winter, 1940).

Schwartz, Delmore, "Poetry and Belief in Thomas Hardy," Sou R, 6: 64–77 (Summer, 1940).

Schwartz, Delmore, "The Fiction of William Faulkner," Sou R, 7: 145–160 (Summer, 1941).

Schwartz, Delmore, "The Isolation of Modern Poetry," KR, 3: 209–220 (Spring, 1941).

Schwartz, Delmore, "The Writings of Edmund Wilson," A, 3: 177–186 (Summer, 1942).

Schwartz, Delmore, "T. S. Eliot as the International Hero," PR, 12: 199–206 (Spring, 1945).

Shafer, Robert, "The Definition of Humanism," HH, 3: 533–557 (July–September, 1930).

Shapiro, Karl, "English Prosody and Modern Poetry," English Literary History, 14: 77–92 (June, 1947).

Shapiro, Karl, "A Farewell to Criticism," P, 71: 196–217 (January, 1948).

Shapiro, Karl, "The Meaning of the Discarded Poem," in Poets at Work (edited by Charles D. Abbott, 1948).

Shuster, George, "Thomas Hardy," Catholic World, 126: 721–729 (March, 1928).

Shuster, George, "Jacques Maritain, Revivalist," B, 70: 1–10 (September, 1929).

Shuster, George, "François Mauriac," B, 72: 466–475 (January, 1931).

Shuster, George, "Paul Bourget and Reality," B, 73: 273–283 (May, 1931).

Slochower, Harry, "Thomas Mann and Universal Culture," Sou R, 4: 726–744 (Spring, 1939).

Slochower, Harry, "John Dewey: Philosopher of the Possible," Sew R, 52: 151–168 (Winter, 1944).

Spencer, Theodore, "The Critic's Function," Sew R, 47: 552–558 (October, 1939).

Spencer, Theodore, "The Central Problem in Literary Criticism," College English, 4: 159–163 (1942).

Spencer, Theodore, "How to Criticize a Poem" (a parody), NR, 109: 816–818 (December 6, 1943).

Spingarn, J. E., "Grocer-shop Critic and Real Critic," D, 57: 96–99 (August 16, 1914).

Spingarn, J. E., "The Growth of a Literary Myth," Freeman, 7: 181–183 (May 2, 1923).

 Spingarn's important work as critic will be found in Creative Criticism and Other Essays (new and enlarged edition, 1931), in which see especially "The New Criticism," "Prose and Verse," "Dramatic Criticism and the Theatre," "Creative Connoisseurship," "The Younger Generation," "The American Critic," "The American Scholar," and "The Seven Arts and the Seven Confusions."

Stallman, Robert W., "Hardy's Hour-Glass Novel," Sew R, 55: 283–296 (April, 1947).

Stallman, Robert W., "The New Criticism and the Southern Critics," in A Southern Vanguard (edited by Allen Tate, 1947).

Stallman, Robert W., "The New Critics," in *Critiques and Essays in Criticism* (edited by Stallman, 1949).

Stauffer, Donald A., "Cooperative Criticism: A Letter from the Critical Front," KR, 4: 133–144 (Winter, 1942).

Stauffer, Donald A., "Critical Principles and a Sonnet," AS, 12: 52–62 (Winter, 1942).

Stauffer, Donald A., "Which Side Am I Supposed to Be On?: The Search for Beliefs in Auden's Poetry," VQR, 22: 570–580 (Autumn, 1946).

Stauffer, Donald A., "Poetry as Symbolic Thinking," SRL, 30: 9–10 (March 22, 1947).

Stauffer, Donald A., "W. B. Yeats and the Medium of Poetry," *English Literary History*, 15: 227–246 (September, 1948).

Stauffer, Donald A., "The Reading of a Lyric," KR, 11: 426–440 (Summer, 1949).

Stevens, Wallace, "The Noble Rider and the Sound of Words," in *The Language of Poetry* (edited by Allen Tate, 1942).

Stevens, Wallace, "The Figure of the Youth as Virile Poet," Sew R, 52: 508–529 (October, 1944).

Swallow, Alan, "An Examination of Modern Critics. 6: Yvor Winters," RMR, 9: 31–37 (Fall, 1944).

Sypher, Wylie, "The Metaphysicals and the Baroque," PR, 9: 3–17 (Winter, 1944).

Sypher, Wylie, "Connoisseur in Chaos: Wallace Stevens," PR, 13: 83–95 (Winter, 1946).

Sypher, Wylie, "Aesthetic of Revolution: The Marxist Melodrama," KR, 10: 431–444 (Summer, 1948).

Sypher, Wylie, "Gide's Cubist Novel," KR, 11: 291–309 (Spring, 1949).

Tate, Allen, "The Fallacy of Humanism," HH, 3: 234–258 (January–March, 1930).

Tate, Allen, "Irony and Humility" (on Eliot's *Ash-Wednesday*), HH, 4: 298–300 (January–March, 1931).

Tate, Allen, "New England Culture and Emily Dickinson," Sym, 3: 206–226 (April, 1932).

Tate, Allen, "The Function of the Critical Quarterly," Sou R, 1: 551–559 (Winter, 1936).

Tate, Allen, "Tension in Poetry," Sou R, 4: 101–115 (Summer, 1938).

Tate, Allen, "Hardy's Philosophic Metaphors," Sou R, 6: 99–108 (Summer, 1940).

Tate, Allen, "Literature as Knowledge: Comment and Comparison," Sou R, 6: 629–657 (Spring, 1941).

Tate, Allen, "Dostoevsky's Hovering Fly," Sew R, 51: 353–369 (Summer, 1943).

Tate, Allen, "Techniques of Fiction," Sew R, 52: 210–225 (Spring, 1944).

Tate, Allen, "A Reading of Keats," AS, 15: 55–63 (January, 1946), 15: 189–197 (April, 1946).

Tate, Allen, "Longinus," HR, 1: 344–361 (Autumn, 1948).

Tate, Allen, "Johnson on the Metaphysicals," KR, 11: 377–394 (Summer, 1949).

Tate, Allen, "Our Cousin, Mr. Poe," PR, 16: 1207–1219 (December, 1949).

See also in *Reactionary Essays* by Allen Tate (1936) the essays "Three Types of Poetry," "Humanism and Naturalism," "The Profession of Letters in the South," and the essays on E. A. Robinson, MacLeish's *Conquistador*, Edna St. Vincent Millay, and E. E. Cummings; and in *Reason in Madness* (1941) the essays "The Present Function of Criticism," "Literature as Knowledge," "Understanding Modern Poetry," "Narcissus as Narcissus," and "Liberalism and Tradition."

Further essays will be found in *The Hovering Fly* (1949); and a collection of essays from these three volumes, including most of those listed above, appears in *On the Limits of Poetry: Selected Essays 1928–1948* (1948).

Taupin, René, "The Classicism of T. S. Eliot," Sym, 2: 64–82 (January, 1932).

Thorp, Willard, "The Present State of American Literary Scholarship," Sew R, 53: 325–331 (Spring, 1945).

Trilling, Diana, "Men, Women, and Sex," PR, 17: 365–378 (April, 1950).

Trilling, Diana, "A Memorandum on the Hiss Case," PR, 17: 484–500 (May–June, 1950).

For reviews and essays on current fiction, see *The Nation, passim*, 1943–1949.

Trilling, Lionel, "The America of John Dos Passos," PR, 4: 26–32 (April, 1938).

Trilling, Lionel, " 'Elements that Are Wanting,' " (on Eliot's *Idea of a Christian Society*), PR, 7: 367–379 (September–October, 1940).

Trilling, Lionel, "Sherwood Anderson," KR, 3: 293–302 (Summer, 1941).

Trilling, Lionel, "The Sense of the Past," PR, 9: 229–241 (May–June, 1942).

Trilling, Lionel, "A Note on Art and Neurosis," PR, 12: 41–48 (Winter, 1945).

Trilling, Lionel, "Sermon on a Text from Whitman," N, 160: 215–216, 218–220 (February 24, 1945).

Trilling, Lionel, "The Life of the Novel," KR, 8: 658–667 (Autumn, 1946).

Trilling, Lionel, "Manners, Morals and the Novel," KR, 12: 477–497 (Winter, 1948).

Trilling, Lionel, "Sex and Science: The Kinsey Report," PR, 15: 460–476 (April, 1948).

Trilling, Lionel, "Art and Fortune," PR, 15: 1271–1292 (December, 1948).

See also *Matthew Arnold* by Lionel Trilling (1939) and *E. M. Forster* (1943), as well as the collection of critical papers *The Liberal Imagination* (1950), in which see especially the essays (in addition to those listed above, most of which appear here in a revised form) "The Princess Casamassima," "The Function of the Little Magazine," "Huckleberry Finn," "Kipling," "The Immortality Ode," "F. Scott Fitzgerald," and "The Meaning of a Literary Idea."

Troy, William, "Proust in Retrospect," Sym, 2: 385–392 (July, 1931).

Troy, William, "The Letters of D. H. Lawrence," Sym, 4: 85–94 (January, 1933).

Troy, William, "The D. H. Lawrence Myth," PR, 4: 3–13 (January, 1937).

Troy, William, "Thomas Mann: Myth and Reason," PR, 5: 24–32 (June, 1938).

Troy, William, "On Re-reading Balzac: The Artist as Scapegoat," KR, 2: 333–344 (Summer, 1940).

Troy, William, "Stendhal: In Quest of Henri Beyle," PR, 9: 3–22 (January–February, 1942).

Troy, William, "Paul Valéry and the Poetic Universe," QRL, 3: 232–239 (1946).

Tyler, Parker, "The Impressionism of Marcel Proust," KR, 8: 46–54 (Winter, 1946).

Unger, Leonard, "T. S. Eliot's Rose Garden: A Persistent Theme," Sou R, 7: 667–689 (Spring, 1942).

Unger, Leonard, "Keats and the Music of Autumn," WR, 14: 275–284 (Summer, 1950).

Van Doren, Carl, "Literature and a New Heroic Age," N, 107: 644–645 (November 30, 1918).

Van Doren, Carl, "On Studying Biography," N, 109: 244–245 (August 23, 1919).

Van Doren, Carl, "The Flower of Puritanism," N, 111: 649–650 (December 8, 1920).

Van Doren, Carl, "The Soil of the Puritans," Century, 105: 629–636 (February, 1923).

Van Doren, Carl, "American Realism," NR, 34: 107–109 (March 21, 1923).

Van Doren, Carl, "The American Rhythm," Century, 107: 150–156 (November, 1923).

Van Doren, Carl, "Stephen Crane," Am Merc, 1: 11–14 (January, 1924).

Van Doren, Carl, "Lucifer in Nantucket" (on Melville), Century, 110: 494–501 (August, 1925).

Van Doren, Carl, "Toward a New Canon," N, 134: 429–430 (April 13, 1932). See also "What Is American Literature?" (included in The Portable Carl Van Doren, 1945) and The American Novel (revised edition, 1940), and for collected essays The Roving Critic (1923) and Many Minds (1924).

Van Doren, Mark, "The Progress of Poetry," N, 112: 883–885 (June 23, 1921).

Van Doren, Mark, "W. H. Hudson," N, 115: 373–374 (October 11, 1922).

Van Doren, Mark, "Thomas Hardy, Poet," N, 126: 151–152 (February 8, 1928).

Van Doren, Mark, "What Is a Poet?" N, 134: 624–625 (June 1, 1932).

Van Doren, Mark, "The Art of American Fiction," N, 138: 471–473 (April 25, 1934).

Van Doren, Mark, "The Unity of Shakespeare," N, 138: 595–596 (May 23, 1934).

Van Doren, Mark, "Walt Whitman, Stranger," Am Merc, 35: 277–285 (July, 1935).

Van Doren, Mark, "The Achievements of Intellectualist Poetry," AR, 8: 449–456 (February, 1937).

Van Doren, Mark, "Good Critics Rare and Common," N, 154: 94–95 (January 24, 1942).

Van Doren, Mark, "Poets and Trimmers," Sew R, 53: 52–55 (January–March, 1945).

Van Doren, Mark, "The Divine Comedy," Sew R, 54: 349–395 (July–September, 1946).

Van Doren, Mark, "The Teaching of Literature: The Riches and the Terrors," Sew R, 55: 569–571 (October–December, 1947).

Van Doren, Mark, "The Happy Critic," N, 168: 663 (June 11, 1949).
    See also the books listed in Appendix I, notably *Henry David Thoreau* (1916), *The Poetry of John Dryden* (new edition, 1946), *Shakespeare* (1939), and for essays and studies *The Private Reader* (1942) and *The Noble Voice* (1946).

Vigneron, Pierre Robert, "Genesis of *Swann*," PR, 8: 460–475 (November–December, 1941).

Vivas, Eliseo, "The Legacy of Sigmund Freud: Philosophical," KR, 2: 173–185 (Spring, 1940).

Vivas, Eliseo, "Lawrence's Problems," KR, 3: 83–94 (Winter, 1941).

Vivas, Eliseo, "The New Naturalism," KR, 3: 445–459 (Autumn, 1941).

Vivas, Eliseo, "Henry and William" (on the Jameses), KR, 5: 580–594 (Autumn, 1943).

Vivas, Eliseo, "The Objective Correlative of T. S. Eliot," *American Bookman*, 1: 7–18 (Winter, 1944).

Vivas, Eliseo, "Kafka's Distorted Mask," KR, 10: 51–69 (Winter, 1948).

Vivas, Eliseo, "The Objective Basis of Criticism," WR, 12: 197–210 (Summer, 1948).

Warren, Austin, "The Mysticism of Richard Crashaw," Sym, 4: 135–155 (April, 1933).

Warren, Austin, "The Novels of E. M. Forster," AR, 9: 226–251 (Summer, 1937).

Warren, Austin, "Edward Taylor's Poetry: Colonial Baroque," KR, 3: 355–371 (Summer, 1941).

Warren, Austin, "Religio Poetae" (on Yeats), Sou R, 7: 624–638 (Winter, 1942).

Warren, Austin, "Myth and Dialectic in the Later Novels" (on Henry James), KR, 5: 551–568 (Autumn, 1943).

Warren, Austin, "Instress of Inscape" (on G. M. Hopkins), KR, 6: 369–382 (Summer, 1944).

Warren, Austin, "The Case of Vachel Lindsay," A, 6: 320–339 (August, 1946).
    See also *Richard Crashaw: A Study in Baroque Sensibility* (1939) and *Theory of Literature* (written with René Wellek, 1948), and for selected essays, including some of the above in revised form, *Rage for Order* (1947), especially those on George Herbert, Hopkins, Yeats, Hawthorne, Kafka, E. M. Forster, and Henry James.

Warren, Robert Penn, "T. S. Stribling: A Paragraph in the History of Critical Realism," AR, 2: 463–486 (February, 1934).

Warren, Robert Penn, "The Hamlet of Thomas Wolfe," AR, 5: 191–208 (September, 1935).

Warren, Robert Penn, "The Reading of Modern Poetry" (with Cleanth Brooks), AR, 8: 435–449 (February, 1937).

Warren, Robert Penn, "Katherine Anne Porter," KR, 4: 29–42 (Winter, 1942).

Warren, Robert Penn, "Pure and Impure Poetry," KR, 5: 228–254 (Spring, 1943).

Warren, Robert Penn, "The Love and the Separateness in Miss Welty," KR, 6: 246–259 (Spring, 1944).

Warren, Robert Penn, "Melville the Poet," KR, 8: 208–223 (Spring, 1946).

Warren, Robert Penn, "A Poem of Pure Imagination" (on Coleridge's "Ancient Mariner"), KR, 8: 391–427 (Summer, 1946).

Warren, Robert Penn, "Hemingway," KR, 9: 1–28 (Winter, 1947).

Weiss, T., "T. S. Eliot and the Courtyard Revolution," Sew R, 54: 289–307 (April–June, 1946).

Wellek, René, "Literary Criticism and Philosophy," Scrutiny (Cambridge, England), 5: 375–383 (March, 1937).

Wellek, René, "Literary History," in Literary Scholarship (1941).

Wellek, René, "Periods and Movements in Literary History," in English Institute Annual: 1940 (1941).

Wellek, René, "The Parallelism between Literature and the Arts," in English Institute Annual: 1941 (1942).

Wellek, René, "The Mode of Existence of a Literary Work of Art," Sou R, 7: 735–754 (Spring, 1942).

Wellek, René, "Six Types of Literary History," in English Institute Essays: 1946 (1947).

    See also Theory of Literature (written with Austin Warren, 1948).

West, Ray B., Jr., "R. P. Blackmur," RMR, 8: 139–145 (Summer, 1944).

West, Ray B., Jr., "Ernest Hemingway," Sew R, 53: 120–135 (January–March, 1945).

West, Ray B., Jr., "Portrait of the Artist as American" (on Hart Crane), WR, 12: 247–251 (Summer, 1948).

Wheelwright, Philip, "Poetry and Logic," Sym, 1: 440–457 (Autumn, 1930).

Wheelwright, Philip, "On the Semantics of Poetry," KR, 2: 263–283 (Summer, 1940).

Wheelwright, Philip, "The Failure of Naturalism," KR, 3: 460–472 (Autumn, 1941).

Wheelwright, Philip, "The Burnt Norton Trilogy" (on T. S. Eliot), Chimera, 1: 7–18 (1942).

Wheelwright, Philip, "Poetry, Myth, and Reality," in The Language of Poetry (edited by Allen Tate, 1942).

Whipple, T. K., "Willa Cather," The Literary Review, 4: 331–332 (December 8, 1923).

Whipple, T. K., "Robert Frost," The Literary Review, 4: 605–606 (March 22, 1924).

    See Spokesmen: Modern Writers and American Life (1928) for essays on

Henry Adams, E. A. Robinson, Theodore Dreiser, Robert Frost, Sherwood Anderson, Willa Cather, Carl Sandburg, Vachel Lindsay, Sinclair Lewis, Eugene O'Neill, "The Poetic Temper," and "The American Situation"; and *Study Out the Land* (1943), especially the essays "Machinery, Magic, and Art," "American Sagas," "The American Predicament," "The American Land," "The Myth of the Old West," "Dos Passos and the U.S.A.," "Jack London—Wonder Boy," "Steinbeck," "The American Way," "Poetry and Morals," and "Literature as Action."

Williams, William Carlos, "Marianne Moore," D, 78: 393–401 (May, 1925).

Williams, William Carlos, "Federico Garcia Lorca," KR, 1: 148–158 (Spring, 1939).

Williams, William Carlos, "An Approach to the Poem," in *English Institute Essays: 1947* (1948).

Williamson, George, "Libertine Donne," *Philological Quarterly*, 13: 276–291 (July, 1934).

Williamson, George, "Textual Difficulties in the Interpretation of Donne's Poetry," MP, 38: 37–72 (August, 1940).

Williamson, George, "The Structure of *The Waste Land*," MP, 47: 191–206 (February, 1950).

Wilson, Edmund, "A. E. Housman," NR, 92: 206–210 (September 29, 1937).

Wilson, Edmund, "Flaubert's Politics," PR, 4: 13–24 (December, 1937).

Wilson, Edmund, "The Myth of the Marxist Dialectic," PR, 6: 66–81 (Fall, 1938).

Wilson, Edmund, "Ernest Hemingway," At Mon, 164: 36–46 (July, 1939).

Wilson, Edmund, "H. C. Earwicker and Family" (on James Joyce), NR, 99: 203–206 (June 28, 1939) and 99: 270–274 (July 12, 1939).

Wilson, Edmund, "Dickens and the Marshalsea Prison," At Mon, 165: 473–483 (April, 1940) and 165: 681–691 (May, 1940).

Wilson, Edmund, "Archibald MacLeish and 'The Word,' " NR, 103: 30–32 (July 1, 1940).

Wilson, Edmund, "The Kipling That Nobody Read," At Mon, 167: 201–214 (February, 1941) and 167: 340–354 (March, 1941).

See *The Dial*, 1921–1929 *passim, The New Republic*, 1926–1941, *passim,* and *The New Yorker*, 1944–1950, *passim,* for contributions to those magazines.

See *Axel's Castle* (1931) for essays on "Symbolism," W. B. Yeats, Paul Valéry, Marcel Proust, Gertrude Stein, and "Axel and Rimbaud," as well as those on James Joyce and T. S. Eliot included in the present volume.

See *The Triple Thinkers* (revised edition, 1948) for essays on "Mr. More and the Mithraic Bull," "Is Verse a Dying Technique?" "In Honor of Pushkin," "A. E. Housman," "The Politics of Flaubert," "The Ambiguity of Henry James," "John Jay Chapman," "Bernard Shaw at Eighty," "Morose Ben Jonson," and "The Historical Interpretation of Literature," as well as "Marxism and Literature" included in the present volume.

See *The Wound and the Bow* (1941, 1947) for the essays "Dickens: The Two Scrooges," "The Kipling That Nobody Read," "Justice to Edith Wharton," "Hemingway: Gauge of Morale," "The Dream of H. C. Earwicker," "Philoctetes: The Wound and the Bow."

See *Classics and Commercials: A Literary Chronicle of the Forties* (1950) for essays and reviews on the books of the decade 1940–1950.

Wimsatt, William Kurtz, Jr., "The Intentional Fallacy" (with M. C. Beardsley), Sew R, 54: 468–488 (July–September, 1946).

Wimsatt, William Kurtz, Jr., "The Structure of the 'Concrete Universal,'" PMLA, 62: 262–280 (March, 1947).

Wimsatt, William Kurtz, Jr., "Poetry and Morals," *Thought,* 23: 281–299 (June, 1948).

Wimsatt, William Kurtz, Jr., "The Affective Fallacy" (with M. C. Beardsley), Sew R, 57: 31–55 (January–March, 1949).

Winters, Yvor, "Holiday and Day of Wrath" (on Marianne Moore), P, 26: 39–44 (April, 1925).

Winters, Yvor, "The Extension and Reintegration of the Human Spirit Through the Poetry Mainly French and American since Poe and Baudelaire," in *The American Caravan* (No. 3, 1929).

Winters, Yvor, "The Symbolist Influence" (on the French Influence on American Poetry), HH, 4: 607–618 (July–September, 1931).

Winters, Yvor, "Traditional Mastery" (on Robert Bridges), HH, 5: 321–327 (January–March, 1932).

Winters, Yvor, "Poets and Others," HH, 4: 675–686 (July–September, 1932).

Winters, Yvor, "T. Sturge Moore," HH, 6: 534–545 (April–June, 1933).

Winters, Yvor, "The Sixteenth Century Lyric in England," P, 53: 258–272 (February, 1939), 53: 320–335 (March, 1939), 54: 35–51 (April, 1939).

Winters, Yvor, "T. S. Eliot: The Illusion of Reaction," KR, 3: 7–30 (Winter, 1941), 3: 221–239 (Spring, 1941).

Winters, Yvor, "The Poetry of Gerard Manley Hopkins," HR, 1: 455–476 (Winter, 1949) and 2: 61–93 (Spring, 1949).

See *Primitivism and Decadence: A Study of American Experimental Poetry* (1937); *Maule's Curse: Seven Studies in the History of American Obscurantism* (1938) for essays on Hawthorne, Cooper, Melville, Poe, Jones Very and Emerson, Emily Dickinson, and Henry James; *The Anatomy of Nonsense* (1943) for essays on Henry Adams, Wallace Stevens, T. S. Eliot, and John Crowe Ransom; and *In Defense of Reason* (1947) for a collection of the foregoing three volumes with the addition of an essay on Hart Crane and *The Bridge.*

Young, Stark, "Ideas in Art," *Theatre Arts Monthly,* 7: 275–283 (October, 1923).

Young, Stark, "Duse," No Am, 218: 776–784 (December, 1923).

Young, Stark, "Isadora Duncan," NR, 57: 43–44 (November 28, 1928).

See *The New Republic,* 1921–47, *passim,* for reviews and articles on the drama forming a critical chronicle of the New York theatre during those twenty-six years. Some of these writings were collected in *The Flower in Drama* (1923), *The Three Fountains* (1924), *Glamour* (1925), *The Theatre* (1927), and *Immortal Shadows* (1949).

Zabel, Morton Dauwen, "Hardy in Defense of his Art: The Aesthetic of Incongruity," Sou R, 6: 125–149 (Summer, 1940).

Zabel, Morton Dauwen, "Two Years of Poetry: 1937–39," Sou R, 5: 568–608 (Winter, 1940).

Zabel, Morton Dauwen, "Rimbaud: Life and Legend," PR, 7: 268–282 (July–August, 1940).

Zabel, Morton Dauwen, "The Whole of Housman," N, 150: 684–686 (June 1, 1940).

Zabel, Morton Dauwen, "The Poet on Capitol Hill" (Archibald MacLeish), PR, 8: 1–17 (January–February, 1941) and 8: 128–158 (March–April, 1941).

Zabel, Morton Dauwen, "Conrad: The Secret Sharer," NR, 104: 567–584 (April 21, 1941).

Zabel, Morton Dauwen, "The Thinking of the Body: Yeats in the Autobiographies," Sou R, 7: 562–590 (Winter, 1942).

Zabel, Morton Dauwen, "Yeats: The Image and the Book," N, 156: 348–350 (March 6, 1943).

Zabel, Morton Dauwen, "Joseph Conrad: Chance and Recognition," Sew R, 53: 1–22 (Winter, 1945).

Zabel, Morton Dauwen, "Willa Cather," N, 164: 713–716 (July 14, 1947).

Zabel, Morton Dauwen, "Dickens: The Reputation Revised," N, 169: 279–281 (September 17, 1949).

Zukovsky, Louis, "Henry Adams: A Criticism in Autobiography," HH, 3: 333–354 (April–June, 1930), 3: 518–530 (July–September, 1930), 4: 46–72 (October–December, 1930).

Zukovsky, Louis, "American Poetry: 1920–30," Sym, 2: 60–84 (January–March, 1931).

APPENDIX VI

A Note on Contemporary English Criticism

THOUGH contemporary criticism in England lies outside the scope of the present volume, its relations with American criticism are close and some of its relevant activities must be noted.

English criticism at the end of the Nineteenth Century fell into several fairly distinct categories. There was a continuation of the line that had been sponsored in the Romantic and Victorian periods by Wordsworth, Coleridge, Hazlitt, Carlyle, Ruskin, Mill, and most influentially by Matthew Arnold: it now appeared in an attenuated or popular form in the work of men like R. H. Hutton, Walter Bagehot, Walter Besant, Robert Louis Stevenson, George Saintsbury, Edmund Gosse, and a new age of literary journalism. There was also the activity, usually resisting this tradition, of the newer aesthetic critics under the leadership of Walter Pater, whose disciples numbered John Addington Symonds, Arthur Symons, Vernon Lee, Lionel Johnson, George Moore, Oscar Wilde, the youthful William Butler Yeats, and the men of the 'nineties. These asserted an alliance with the aesthetic and impressionist criticism of France and came to exert a marked influence on Americans of similar tastes—James Huneker, Lafcadio Hearn, Lewis E. Gates, Edgar Saltus, Percival Pollard. There was also the work in England of Henry James, with its marked effect on the criticism and techniques of fiction. There was likewise the special case of Bernard Shaw, who brought his social and political purposes into combination with criticism by producing the most brilliant musical and dramatic journalism of modern times and who, more than anyone else, fathered the work in America of such men as Huneker, Mencken, Nathan, and their followers. These several critical activities in England continued well into the first and second decades of the Twentieth Century.

Around 1908 or 1910 a new phase asserted itself. It derived on one side from the French and English aesthetic developments of the 'nineties and now found spokesmen in Ford Madox Hueffer (Ford), in T. E. Hulme, in the American Ezra Pound, and the men who made Hueffer's magazine *The English Review* (in 1908–1909), the Imagist movement, Wyndham Lewis' *Blast*, Vorticism, A. R. Orage's journal *The New Age*, and the new poetry of 1910–1920 their centers of activity. The emphasis here was on a new discipline in the form and style of poetry and fiction, on a reassertion of classical principles and models (particularly as advocated by Hulme and Pound), on an antiprovincial alliance with French and European

880

standards, and on a renewed interest in both classical and experimental forms of writing. Against this activity stood a revival of traditionalism among the "Georgian" poets and critics, whose spokesmen were Robert Bridges, Lascelles Abercrombie, Laurence Binyon, G. K. Chesterton, Edward Thomas, Harold Monro, and J. C. Squire. The combat between these factions showed the basic issues and positions in English criticism in the decade 1910–1920.

A fresh stimulus to the historical and textual study of literature also came, after 1900, from academic quarters. Here the name to be emphasized is that of A. C. Bradley, whose famous book on *Shakespearean Tragedy* appeared in 1904 and initiated a new age in the interpretation of Shakespeare and classical English literature in the work of such university men as Gilbert Murray, W. P. Ker, Herbert J. C. Grierson, H. W. Garrod, W. W. Greg, John Dover Wilson, G. Wilson Knight, and C. M. Bowra.

By 1920 the work and influence of T. S. Eliot had asserted itself, notably with the publication of his first book of critical essays, *The Sacred Wood* in 1920, and presently, after 1922, through his editorship of *The Criterion*. In the course of the next thirty years his role in English poetry and criticism became dominant. The work of John Middleton Murry in his earlier years, particularly during his brief editorship of *The Athenaeum* (1919–1920) and his later editorship of *The Adelphi*, also counted in this decade, as did the art criticism of Clive Bell and Roger Fry, with their resistance to the Ruskinian tradition of critical moralism and their insistence on the formal and structural properties of the plastic arts. Another important factor made its appearance in the new semantic, analytical, and interpretational investigation of literature and the related arts that was carried on by I. A. Richards, C. K. Ogden, and their disciples following the publication of a series of influential volumes by these men—*The Foundations of Aesthetics* (1922), *The Meaning of Meaning* (1923), *Principles of Literary Criticism* (1924), and *Practical Criticism* (1929). Contrasting with these experimental and revisionist programs was a continuing activity in criticism of a more personal, belletristic order in the hands of writers like Lytton Strachey, Virginia Woolf, E. M. Forster, Percy Lubbock, Katherine Mansfield, Aldous Huxley, Desmond MacCarthy, Peter Quennell, Harold Nicolson, and the Sitwells. But the serious critical activity of the 1920's was dominated by T. S. Eliot and by I. A. Richards, whose differing but in some respects complementary ideas found issue in the work of followers (or dissenters) like Herbert Read, Edwin Muir, Edgell Rickword and Bertram Higgins during their editorship of *The Calendar of Modern Letters* (1925–1927), and the Cambridge group that included Richards' pupil William Empson, and F. R. Leavis at Downing College.

In the 1930's the work of Eliot, Richards, Empson, Muir, and Read continued, but perhaps the most important single activity was that which centered at Cambridge in the work of F. R. Leavis and his magazine *Scrutiny*, founded in 1932. This journal, originating in the programs laid down by Eliot and Richards, soon developed a purpose and standard of its own, emphasizing the formal and stylistic analysis of literature but also insisting on the relevance of critical standards to culture and education in arguments that descend from the tradition of Bentham, Coleridge, Arnold, and Mill. The books of Leavis and his collaborators—Q. D.

Leavis, L. C. Knights, Denys Thompson, D. W. Harding, and Martin Turnell among them—as well as the quarterly issues of *Scrutiny*, form the outstanding critical program in England during the past two decades. Psychological and psychoanalytical method in criticism has also had its sponsors, in Herbert Read and Ernest Jones notably; so has the Marxist theory of literature, especially in books by Christopher Caudwell, John Strachey, Ralph Fox, R. D. Charques, and Alick West.

The literary monthly *Horizon* (1940–1949), under the editorship of Cyril Connolly, formed a center of original work in writing and criticism during the 1940's, with the younger generation of English talents—W. H. Auden, Stephen Spender, George Orwell, Louis MacNeice—contributing to its pages. That activity is still in progress in 1950; and while the work of Eliot, Richards, and Leavis remains paramount in the critical developments of the past quarter-century, a generation of younger critical talents, usually recognizable as continuators of the ideas or methods of these men, has become evident in the years since 1945.

The following is a short selective bibliography of books of English criticism in the Twentieth Century, with emphasis on those of the period from 1920 to the present day:

Abercrombie, Lascelles. *Thomas Hardy: A Critical Study* (1912).
　　Principles of English Prosody (1923).
　　The Idea of Great Poetry (1925).
　　Romanticism (1926).
　　Poetry: Its Music and Meaning (1932).
　　Principles of Literary Criticism (1932).
Aldington, Richard. *Literary Studies and Reviews* (1924).
Auden, W. H. See Appendix IV.
Barfield, Owen. *Poetic Diction: A Study in Meaning* (1928).
Bates, H. E. *The Modern Short Story: A Survey* (1942).
Bell, Clive. *Art* (1914).
Bennett, Joan. *Four Metaphysical Poets* (1944).
　　Virginia Woolf (1943).
Bentley, Eric. See Appendix IV.
Blunden, Edmund. *Nature in English Literature* (1929).
　　Votive Tablets: Studies chiefly Appreciative of English Authors and Books (1931).
　　The Mind's Eye: Essays (1934).
　　Shelley (1946).
Bodkin, Maud. *Archetypal Patterns in Poetry* (1934).
Bowen, Elizabeth. *Collected Impressions* (1950).
Bowra, C. M. *The Heritage of Symbolism* (1943).
　　The Creative Experiment (1949).
Bradbrook, M. C. *Joseph Conrad: Poland's English Genius* (1942).
　　Ibsen, the Norwegian: A Revaluation (1946).

Bradley, Andrew C. *Shakespearean Tragedy* (1904).
Oxford Lectures on Poetry (1909, 1926).
Bridges, Robert. *Milton's Prosody, with a Chapter on Accentual Verse* (revised, 1921).
Collected Essays and Papers (1927–1930).
Bronowski, J. *The Poet's Defense* (1939).
A Man without a Mask (on Blake, 1947).
Burdett, Osbert. *The Beardsley Period* (1925).
Critical Essays (1927).
Caudwell, Christopher. *Illusion and Reality* (1937).
Studies in a Dying Culture (1939).
Cecil, David. *Hardy the Novelist* (1946).
Charques, R. D. *Contemporary Literature and Social Revolution* (1933).
Collingwood, R. G. *The Principles of Art* (1938).
Connolly, Cyril. *Enemies of Promise* (1939).
The Unquiet Grave (by "Palinurus," 1945).
The Condemned Playground: Essays 1927–1944 (1946).
Conrad, Joseph. *Notes on Life and Letters* (1921).
Prefaces to his Works (edited by Edward Garnett, 1937).
Crankshaw, Edward. *Joseph Conrad: Some Aspects of the Art of the Novel* (1936).
Day Lewis, Cecil. *A Hope for Poetry* (1934).
The Poetic Image (1947).
Dobrée, Bonamy. *The Lamp and the Lute* (1929). *Modern Prose Style* (1934).
Eliot, T. S. See Appendix IV.
Empson, William. *Seven Types of Ambiguity* (1930).
Some Versions of Pastoral (1935; American edition: *English Pastoral Poetry*, 1938).
Ford, Ford Madox (Hueffer). *The Critical Attitude* (1911).
Henry James: A Critical Study (1913).
Joseph Conrad: A Personal Remembrance (1924).
The March of Literature (1938).
Forster, E. M. *Aspects of the Novel* (1927).
Abinger Harvest (collected essays, 1936).
Fox, Ralph. *The Novel and the People* (1937).
Frazer, James M. *The Golden Bough: A Study in Magic and Religion* (shorter version, 1922).
Fry, Roger. *The Artist and Psychoanalysis* (1924).
Garrod, H. W. *The Profession of Poetry* (1929).
Poetry and the Criticism of Life (1931).
The Study of Poetry (1936).
Gaunt, William. *The Aesthetic Adventure* (1945).
Gilby, Thomas. *Poetic Experience: An Introduction to the Thomist Aesthetic* (1934).
Gosse, Edmund. *Books on the Table* (1921).

Aspects and Impressions (1922).

Selected Essays (1928).

Granville-Barker, Harley.   *Prefaces to Shakespeare* (2 volumes, 1947).

Graves, Robert.   *On English Poetry* (1922).

> *Poetic Unreason and Other Studies* (1925).

> *A Survey of Modernist Poetry* (with Laura Riding, 1927).

> *The Reader Over Your Shoulder* (with Alan Hodge, 1943).

Grierson, H. J. C.   *Metaphysical Lyrics and Poems of the Seventeenth Century* (edited, 1921).

> *The Background of English Literature* (1925).

Hopkins, Gerard Manley.   *The Letters of Gerard Manley Hopkins to Robert Bridges and The Correspondence of Gerard Manley Hopkins and Richard Watson Dixon* (edited by Claude Colleer Abbott, 2 volumes, 1935).

> *The Notebooks and Papers of Gerard Manley Hopkins* (edited by Humphry House, 1937).

> *Further Letters of Gerard Manley Hopkins* (edited by Abbott, 1938).

Housman, A. E.   *The Name and Nature of Poetry* (1933).

Hulme, T. E.   *Speculations* (edited by Herbert Read, 1924).

Ker, W. P.   *The Art of Poetry* (1920).

> *Collected Essays* (edited by Charles Whibley, 2 volumes, 1925).

> *Form and Style in Poetry* (1928).

Knight, G. Wilson.   *The Wheel of Fire* (1930).

> *The Imperial Theme* (1931).

> *The Shakespearean Tempest* (1932).

> *The Burning Oracle* (1939).

> *The Starlit Dome* (1941).

> *The Olive and the Sword* (1941).

Knights, L. C.   *How Many Children Had Lady Macbeth?* (1933).

> *Explorations: Essays in Criticism* (1946).

Lawrence, D. H.   *Psychoanalysis and the Unconscious* (1921).

> *Fantasia of the Unconscious* (1922).

> *Studies in Classic American Literature* (1923).

> *Pornography and Obscenity* (1929).

> *Assorted Articles* (1930).

Leavis, F. R.   *Mass Civilization and Minority Culture* (1930).

> *New Bearings in English Poetry* (1932).

> *How to Teach Reading: A Primer for Ezra Pound* (1933).

> *For Continuity* (1933).

> *Culture and Environment* (with Denys Thompson, 1933).

> *Towards Standards of Criticism: Selections from "The Calendar of Modern Letters,"* 1925–1927 (edited, 1933).

> *Determinations: Critical Essays* (edited, 1934).

> *Revaluation: Tradition and Development in English Poetry* (1936).

> *Education and the University* (1943).

> *The Great Tradition* (1948).

See also *The Importance of Scrutiny* (essays collected from *Scrutiny,* 1932– 1948, edited by Eric Bentley, 1948).

Leavis, Q. D.   *Fiction and the Reading Public* (1932).

Lewis, C. S.   *The Personal Heresy* (with E. M. W. Tillyard, 1939).

Liddell, Robert.   *A Treatise on the Novel* (1947).

Listowell, W. F.   *A Critical History of Modern Aesthetics* (1933).

Lubbock, Percy.   *The Craft of Fiction* (1921).

Lucas, F. L.   *Authors Dead and Living* (1926).
   The Decline and Fall of the Romantic Ideal (1936).

MacCarthy, Desmond.   *Portraits* (1931).
   Criticism: Collected Essays (1932).

MacNeice, Louis.   *Modern Poetry: A Personal Essay* (1938).
   The Poetry of W. B. Yeats (1941).

Mansfield, Katherine.   *Novels and Novelists* (1930).

Maugham, W. Somerset.   *The Summing Up* (1938).

Mégroz, R. L.   *Joseph Conrad's Mind and Method* (1931).
   Modern English Poetry: 1882–1932 (1933).

Meynell, Alice.   *Hearts of Controversy* (1917).
   The Second Person Singular and Other Essays (1921).

Moore, George.   *Avowals* (1919).
   Conversations in Ebury Street (1924).

Moore, T. Sturge.   *Art and Life* (1910).
   Armour for Aphrodite (1929).

Mortimer, Raymond.   *Channel Packet* (1942)

Muir, Edwin.   *We Moderns* (1918).
   Latitudes (1924).
   Transition: Essays on Contemporary Literature (1926).
   The Structure of the Novel (1928).
   The Present Age from 1914 (1939).
   Essays on Literature and Society (1948).

Murry, J. Middleton.   *Aspects of Literature* (1920).
   Countries of the Mind: Essays in Literary Criticism (1922).
   The Problem of Style (1922).
   Keats and Shakespeare (1925).
   D. H. Lawrence: Two Essays (1932).
   Shakespeare (1936).

Orage, A. R.   *Readers and Writers* (1922).
   The Art of Reading (1930).
   Selected Essays and Critical Writings (edited by Herbert Read and Denis Saurat, 1935).

Orwell, George.   *Inside the Whale* (1940).
   Dickens, Dali, and Others (1946; in England as *Critical Essays,* 1946).

Peacock, Ronald.   *The Poet in the Theatre* (1946).

Potter, Stephen.   *The Muse in Chains* (1937).

Pritchett, V. S.   *In My Good Books* (1942).
   The Living Novel (1946).

Why Do I Write? (an exchange with Elizabeth Bowen and Graham
    Greene, 1948).
Quennell, Peter. *Baudelaire and the Symbolists* (1929).
Rajan, B., ed. *Focus* (No. 3: *T. S. Eliot: A Study of his Writings by Several
    Hands,* 1947).
    Focus (No. 4: *The Novelist as Thinker,* 1948).
Read, Herbert. *Reason and Romanticism: Essays in Literary Criticism* (1926).
    English Prose Style (1928).
    Phases of English Poetry (1928).
    The Sense of Glory: Essays in Criticism (1929).
    Julien Benda and the New Humanism (1930).
    Wordsworth (1930).
    Form in Modern Poetry (1932).
    In Defense of Shelley and Other Essays (1936).
    Art and Society (1937).
    Collected Essays in Literary Criticism (1938).
    Poetry and Anarchism (1938).
Richards, I. A.   See Appendix I.
Rickword, Edgell.   *Rimbaud: The Boy and the Poet* (1924).
    Scrutinies (essays by various critics, two series, edited, 1928 and 1931).
Roberts, Michael.   *New Signatures* (edited, 1932).
    New Country: Prose and Poetry by Various Authors (edited, 1933).
    A Critique of Poetry (1934).
    The Modern Mind (1937).
    T. E. Hulme (1938).
Rylands, George.   *Words and Poetry* (1928).
Saintsbury, George.   *Collected Essays: 1875–1920* (4 volumes, 1923–1924).
    Prefaces and Essays (1933).
Sassoon, Siegfried.   *George Meredith* (1948).
Saurat, Denis.   *Blake and Modern Thought* (1929).
Savage, D. S.   *The Personal Principle: Studies in Modern Poetry* (1944).
    The Withered Branch (1950).
Scarfe, Francis.   *Auden and After: The Liberation of Poetry: 1930–1941* (1942).
Scott-James, R.   *The Making of Literature: Some Principles of Criticism* (1938).
Shaw, George Bernard.   *The Quintessence of Ibsenism* (1891).
    The Perfect Wagnerite (1898).
    Dramatic Opinions and Essays (1906).
    The Sanity of Art (1908).
    Music in London: 1890–94 (three volumes, 1932).
    Our Theatres in the Nineties (three volumes, 1932).
    Pen Portraits and Reviews (1932).
Sitwell, Edith.   *Aspects of Poetry* (1934).
    A Poet's Notebook (1943).
Smith, Logan Pearsall.   See Appendix I.
Sparrow, John.   *Sense and Poetry* (1934).

Spender, Stephen. *The Destructive Element: A Study of Modern Writers and Beliefs* (1935).
    Life and the Poet (1942).
Spurgeon, Caroline. *Leading Motives in the Imagery of Shakespeare's Tragedies* (1930).
    Shakespeare's Imagery and What It Tells Us (1935).
Starkie, Enid. *Baudelaire* (1933).
    Arthur Rimbaud (1938; revised, 1947).
Stonier, G. W. *Gog Magog, and Other Critical Essays* (1933).
Strachey, John. *Literature and Dialectical Materialism* (1934).
Strachey, Lytton. *Landmarks in French Literature* (1912).
    Books and Characters (1922).
    Portraits in Miniature (1931).
    Characters and Commentaries (1933).
Strong, L. A. G. *Common Sense about Poetry* (1931).
    The Sacred River: An Approach to James Joyce (1949).
Swinnerton, Frank. *The Georgian Scene: A Literary Panorama* (1934).
Symons, Arthur. *The Symbolist Movement in Literature* (1899).
    Studies in Seven Arts (1906).
    The Romantic Movement in English Poetry (1909).
    Charles Baudelaire: A Study (1920).
    Collected Works (16 volumes, 1924).
Thompson, Denys. *Reading and Discrimination* (1936).
Tillotson, Geoffrey. *Essays in Criticism and Research* (1942).
Tillyard, E. M. W. *Poetry Direct and Oblique* (1934).
Traversi, D. A. *Approach to Shakespeare* (1939).
Turnell, Martin. *The Poetry of Crisis* (1938).
    The Classical Moment: Studies of Corneille, Molière, Racine (1947).
    The Novel in France (1950).
Vines, Sherard. *Movements in Modern English Poetry and Prose* (1927).
West, Alick. *Crisis and Criticism* (1937).
West, Rebecca. *The Strange Necessity: Essays and Reviews* (1928).
Whitehead, Alfred North. *Science and the Modern World* (1925).
    Symbolism: Its Meaning and Effect (1927).
Wilde, Oscar. *Intentions* (1891).
    A Critic in Pall Mall (edited by E. V. Lucas, 1922).
Williams, Charles. *The English Poetic Mind* (1932).
Wilson, John Dover. *What Happens in Hamlet* (1935).
    The Fortunes of Falstaff (1944).
Woolf, Virginia. *The Common Reader* (1925).
    The Second Common Reader (1932).
    The Death of the Moth and Other Essays (1942).
    The Moment and Other Essays (1948).
    The Captain's Death-Bed and Other Essays (1950).
Yeats, William Butler. *Ideas of Good and Evil* (1903).
    Discoveries: A Volume of Essays (1907).

The Cutting of an Agate (1912).
Per Amica Silentiae Lunae (1918).
Essays (1924).
A Vision (1925; revised edition, 1938).
Autobiographies: Reveries over Childhood and Youth and The Trembling of the Veil (1926).
The Oxford Book of Modern Verse (edited, 1936).
Letters on Poetry from W. B. Yeats to Dorothy Wellesley (1940).

Several anthologies will be found useful in the study of English criticism in the Twentieth Century:

English Critical Essays: Twentieth Century, edited by Phyllis M. Jones (1933).
Contains essays by Robert Bridges, George Saintsbury, Alice Meynell, A. C. Bradley, George Moore, W. P. Ker, A. C. Benson, E. K. Chambers, Max Beerbohm, J. A. Chapman, H. W. Garrod, Desmond MacCarthy, E. M. Forster, Lytton Strachey, Lascelles Abercrombie, R. W. Chapman, G. M. Young, Charles Williams, T. S. Eliot, J. Middleton Murry, Bonamy Dobree, Herbert Read, F. L. Lucas, Virginia Woolf.
Scrutinies I, edited by Edgell Rickword (1928).
Essays on writers of the earlier Twentieth Century by Edgell Rickword, Edwin Muir, Dorothy Edwards, Douglas Garman, D. H. Lawrence, Robert Graves, Bertram Higgins, Thomas McGreevy, W. J. Turner, John Holms, Roy Campbell.
Scrutinies II, edited by Edgell Rickword (1931).
Essays on English writers of the 1920's by Alec Brown, Bertram Higgins, Mary Butts, Jack Lindsay, Peter Quennell, Edgell Rickword, Sherard Vines, Christopher Saltmarshe, William Empson, Gilbert Armitage, Brian Penton, Montagu Slater, Constant Lambert.
Towards Standards of Criticism, edited by F. R. Leavis (1933).
Selections from *The Calendar of Modern Letters*, 1925–1927, by Douglas Garman, Bertram Higgins, Samuel Hoare, J. F. Holms, Edwin Muir, Peter Quennell, C. H. Rickword, Edgell Rickword, and other contributors to that magazine.
Determinations: Critical Essays, edited by F. R. Leavis (1934).
Essays from *Scrutiny* on earlier and modern English literature by James Smith, William Empson, D. W. Harding, F. R. Leavis, L. C. Knights, John Spiers, W. A. Edwards, Ronald Bottrall, Denys Thompson, Michael Oakeshott, J. L. Russell.
Turnstile One, edited by V. S. Pritchett (1948).
A Literary Miscellany from *The New Statesman and Nation* that includes critical articles by Rebecca West, James Joyce, Raymond Mortimer, H. N. Brailsford, David Garnett, Leonard Woolf, Arthur Marshall, Desmond MacCarthy, Desmond Shawe-Taylor, Lytton Strachey, Cyril Connolly, R. H. S. Crossman, Robert Lynd, D. H. Lawrence, Derek Verschoyle, C. E. M. Joad.

Virginia Woolf, Harold Laski, E. M. Forster, Harold Nicolson, Stella Benson, Peter Quennell, G. W. Stonier, Logan Pearsall Smith.

Focus, edited by B. Rajan (1945 and following).

A series of volumes of critical studies: *One* is devoted to articles on Kafka and Rex Warner by D. S. Savage, G. W. Stonier, Tom Harrisson, Julian Symons, Kathleen Raine, and others. *Two* contains articles on the realistic novel of the 1930's by D. S. Savage, George Orwell, George Woodcock, Walter Allen, and Arthur Barea, as well as essays on Auden and Eliot. *Three* is entitled *T. S. Eliot: A Study of his Writings by Several Hands,* with essays by Cleanth Brooks, E. E. Duncan Jones, Helen L. Gardner, B. Rajan, Philip Wheelwright, Anne Ridler, M. C. Bradbrook, and Wolf Mankowitz. *Four* is entitled *The Novelist as Thinker,* with essays on Aldous Huxley, Evelyn Waugh, Christopher Isherwood, L. H. Myers, Sartre, and Mauriac by various critics. *Five* is devoted to *Modern American Poetry.* Future titles in the series will be *The Yeats Companion, The Critic and Psychoanalysis,* and *The Writer and Politics.*

The Importance of Scrutiny, edited by Eric Bentley (1948).

Selections from *Scrutiny* during the years 1932–1948 by F. R. Leavis, James Smith, D. A. Traversi, L. C. Knights, R. G. Cox, Marius Bewley, D. W. Harding, R. C. Churchill, W. H. Mellers, R. G. Leinhardt, Edgell Rickword, R. O. C. Winkler, H. A. Mason, Boris Ford, Martin Turnell, Q. D. Leavis, and other contributors.

There remains the question of the influence that European criticism—French, Italian, German, Russian—has had on American criticism in the Twentieth Century. The matter cannot be surveyed here, but it must be noted that this influence has been in some cases strong and fairly continuous. It began, so far as modern developments are concerned, with the interest of Henry James, William Dean Howells, and their contemporaries in the French masters of the Nineteenth Century—Sainte-Beuve, Taine, Renan, Schérer, Lemaître, Brunetière; continued through the influence of Baudelaire, Gautier, Mallarmé, Anatole France, and the aesthetic critics on Francis Grierson, Lafcadio Hearn, James Huneker, and the American impressionists of 1890–1920; became marked in the influence exerted by Remy de Gourmont on Ezra Pound and T. S. Eliot; and has persisted to the present day through the work of such Frenchmen as Paul Valéry, André Gide, Henri Brémond, Ramon Fernandez, Jacques Maritain, Etienne Gilson, Charles Péguy, and their contemporaries of the past thirty years.

The Italian influence has been chiefly that of Benedetto Croce and his theory of creative expressionism, which acted chiefly in America in the work of J. E. Spingarn and his program for a "new criticism" around 1910. Mario Praz has been the most important link between Italian and English and American criticism since 1930.

The influence of Germany and Austria has been strongest in the case of the psychological and psychoanalytical theory and methods of Freud and Jung during the past forty years. The Russian influence—Plekhanov, Trotsky, and other literary spokesmen of the Soviet regime—has been a paramount factor in the growth of a Marxist interpretation of literature in the United States since 1910, with Marx, Engels, and the founding fathers of communist theory behind it.

The tracing of these affiliations and connections is a task which the student of modern American criticism will inevitably encounter, and for whose furtherance abundant evidence exists in the books and journals of the past fifty years.